Dec. 25 - 1966

To Dr. Peter G. Kenner
To increase your appreciation
of the Bible.
Doc. + Cov. 88 : 76, 78 - 79, 86, 124, 125

Peloubet's
BIBLE DICTIONARY

Based Upon the Foundation Laid by
William Smith; Edited by

F. N. PELOUBET, D. D.

Former Editor of "Select Notes on the
International Sunday School Lessons"

Assisted by

ALICE D. ADAMS, M.A.

Assistant Editor
Peloubet's "Select Notes on the
International Sunday School Lessons"

❧

Self-pronouncing
500 illustrations
and maps

❧

Holt, Rinehart and Winston

NEW YORK / CHICAGO / SAN FRANCISCO

86980–0110

PREFACE.

The purpose of this New Bible Dictionary is to bring to the great body of our Sunday School teachers, and intelligent Christian households, a Bible Dictionary fully abreast of the latest modern scholarship, giving them the things which will most aid them in their work but omitting long discussions and theories, and questions which are still in the melting pot, both for want of room, and because they can be discussed intelligently only by trained scholars.

About four decades ago, the Editor supervised the revision of the smaller one-volume Bible Dictionary of that great scholar Dr. William Smith, which he had himself condensed from his large four-volume work.

But since even that time there has been an immense increase in our knowledge concerning the Bible, from almost every direction. Investigations and discoveries in Egypt, Palestine and Babylonia; new inscriptions and monuments; new light from scholarship in textual and higher criticism and from literature, science, exploration and travel,—these and other sources of knowledge demand a new revision of the older work, bringing the book up to date.

Every article has been tested by the best and most modern authority and there is scarcely an article which has not been changed in some respect, while in many cases the changes have been great and important, or the articles wholly rewritten.

Proper names used in the Revised Version have been added wherever they have differed from the Authorized Version.

The signification of proper names has been given in all instances where there was any good authority.

The pronunciation of proper names is in a chaotic state, on account of the frequent transliteration of Hebrew names into Greek and Latin, the English coming sometimes through one language, and at other times through another. But the accent is marked according to the best authorities available, while the syllables are pronounced according to the English mode, except that *g* and *ch* (*k*) are hard except in Bethphage, Rachel and cherub.

PREFACE.

The tables of money, weights, and measures are new, and in the best known form, and as accurately worked out as is possible from the latest and best authorities and special articles by experts. It is necessary to read the notes appended to the tables, because the values depend on the date, the country where they are used, and various influences; just as we have in this country four different sizes of quarts, two different weights for a ton, two or three different pounds.

The chronological tables, the dates of events, are also in new tables and forms. Archbishop Ussher's dates have been retained by the side of other dates, because they are given in the margin of most of our Bibles, and are necessary for comparison with the Revised dates, and in the early history give at least the order of events. Besides these the dates of the Assyrian Eponym Canon are given; the generally accepted dates of the New Testament, and for Old Testament the dates given in Professor Willis J. Beecher's "Dated Events of the Old Testament," which is the most carefully and wisely worked out scheme yet devised.

The maps are new, and in accord with the very latest authorities, such as Professors William M. Ramsay and George Adam Smith.

Many **new pictures** have been added, and several plans which will make the descriptions both more accurate and more vivid.

This Dictionary has no room for detailed speculations and debatable theories, but devotes itself to the facts of the Bible itself, illuminated from every possible source that can aid the ordinary reader to know and love and understand the Word of God for his knowledge and education and daily life.

A large part of this work has been done under my direction by Miss Alice Dana Adams, B.A., M.A. (Wellesley), an historical student (author of Radcliffe Monograph, No. 14), and an expert in this kind of work.

F. N. P.

Auburndale, Mass.

INDEX OF ILLUSTRATIONS.

BIBLE DICTIONARY

A

A. See ALPHA.

Aa'ron (âr'on) (*bright* or *shining*), the son of Amram and Jochebed, and the elder brother of Moses and Miriam. Num. 26:59; 33:39. (B.C. 1573.) He was a Levite, and is first mentioned in Ex. 4:14. He was appointed by Jehovah to be the interpreter, Ex. 4:16, of his brother Moses, who was "slow of speech;" and accordingly he was not only the organ of communication with the Israelites and with Pharaoh, Ex. 4:30; 7:2, but also the actual instrument of working most of the miracles of the Exodus. Ex. 7:19, etc. On the way to Mount Sinai, during the battle with Amalek, Aaron with Hur stayed up the weary hands of Moses, when they were lifted up for the victory of Israel. Ex. 17:10. He is mentioned as dependent upon his brother and deriving all his authority from him. Left, on Moses' departure into Sinai, to guide the people, Aaron is tried for a moment on his own responsibility, and he fails from a weak inability to withstand the demand of the people for visible "gods to go before them," by making an image of Jehovah, in the well-known form of Egyptian idolatry (Apis or Mnevis). He repented of his sin, and Moses gained forgiveness for him. Deut. 9:20. Aaron was now consecrated by Moses to the new office of the high priesthood. Ex. 29:9. From this time the history of Aaron is almost entirely that of the priesthood, and its chief feature is the great rebellion of Korah and the Levites. Leaning, as he seems to have done, wholly on Moses, it is not strange that he should have shared his sin at Meribah and its punishment. See story in Num. 20:10–12. Aaron's death seems to have followed very speedily. It took place on Mount Hor, after the transference of his robes and office to Eleazar. Num. 20:28. This mount is still called the "Mountain of Aaron." See HOR. The wife of Aaron was Elisheba, Ex. 6:23; and the two sons who survived him, Eleazar and Ithamar. The high priesthood descended to the former, and to his descendants until the time of Eli, who, although of the house of Ithamar, received the high priesthood and transmitted it to his children; with them it continued till the accession of Solomon, who took it from Abiathar and restored it to Zadok (of the house of Eleazar). See ABIATHAR.

Aar'onites (âr'on-ītes), 1 Chron. 12:27, priests of the family of Aaron.

Ab (ăb) (*father*), an element in the composition of many proper names, of which Abba is the Aramaic form, meaning "father" or "my father."

Ab. See MONTH.

Abad'don (à-băd'don). See APOLLYON.

Abag'tha (ā-băg'thà) (*given by fortune*), one of the seven eunuchs in the Persian court of Ahasuerus. Esther 1:10.

Ab'ana (probably *stony*), one of the "rivers of Damascus." 2 Kings 5:12. The *Barada* and the *Awaj* are now the chief streams of Damascus, the former representing the Abana and the latter the Pharpar of the text. The *Barada* (Abana) rises in the Anti-Lebanon, at about 23 miles from the city, after flowing through which it runs across the plain, of whose fertility it is the chief source, till it loses itself in the lake or marsh *Bahret-el-Kibliyeh*.

Ab'arim (*part beyond*), a mountain or range of highlands on the east of the Jordan, in the land of Moab, facing Jer-

ABB 2 ABI

icho, and forming the eastern wall of the Jordan valley at that part. Its most elevated spot was "the Mount Nebo, 'head' of 'the' Pisgah," from which Moses viewed the Promised Land before his death. These mountains are mentioned in Num. 27:12; 33:47, 48, and Deut. 32:49.

Ab'ba (ăb'bȧ). See AB.

Ab'da (ăb'dȧ). 1. Father of Adoniram. 1 Kings 4:6.

2. Son of Shammua, Neh. 11:17, a Levite.

Ab'de-el (ăb'dē-ĕl), father of Shelemiah. Jer. 36:26.

Ab'di (ăb'dī) (*servant of* (God)). 1. A Merarite, and ancestor of Ethan the singer. 1 Chron. 6:44.

2. The father of Kishi, a Merarite in the reign of Hezekiah. 2 Chron. 29:12.

3. One of the Bene-Elam in the time of Ezra, who had married a foreign wife. Ezra 10:26. (B.C. 458.)

Ab'diel (ăb'dĭ-el) (*servant of God*), son of Guni and father of Ahi, one of the Gadites who were settled in the land of Bashan, 1 Chron. 5:15.

Ab'don (ăb'don) (*servile*). 1. A judge of Israel, Judges 12:13, 15; perhaps the same person as Bedan, in 1 Sam. 12:11.

2. Son of Shashak. 1 Chron. 8:23.

3. First-born son of Jehiel, father of Gibeon. 1 Chron. 8:30; 9:35, 36.

4. Son of Micah, a contemporary of Josiah, 2 Chron. 34:20, called Achbor in 2 Kings 22:12. (B.C. 628.)

5. A city in the tribe of Asher, given to the Gershonites, Josh. 21:30; 1 Chron. 6:74; the modern *Abdeh*, 10 miles northeast of Accho.

Abed'-nego (ȧ-bĕd'ne-gō) (*servant of Nego,* probably the same as *Nebo*), the Chaldæan name given to Azariah, one of the three friends of Daniel, miraculously saved from the fiery furnace. Dan. 3.

A'bel (ā'bĕl) (*breath, vapor, transitoriness,* probably so called from the shortness of his life), the second son of Adam, murdered by his brother Cain, Gen. 4:1–16; he was a keeper or feeder of sheep. Our Lord spoke of Abel as the first martyr, Matt. 23:35; so did the early Church subsequently. The traditional site of his murder and his grave are pointed out near Damascus.

A'bel (ā'bĕl), the name of several places in Palestine, probably signifies a *meadow.*

A'bel-beth=ma'achah (ā'bel-bĕth-mā'-a-kah) (*meadow of the house of Maachah*), a town of some importance, 2 Sam. 20:15, in the extreme north of Palestine, which fell an early prey to the invading kings of Syria, 1 Kings 15:20, and Assyria. 2 Kings 15:29.

A'bel-ma'im (ā'bel-mā'im) (*Abel of waters*), also called simply Abel, 2 Sam. 20:14, 18, another name for Abel-beth-maachah. 2 Chron. 16:4.

A'bel-meho'lah (ā'bel-mė-hō'lah) (*meadow of the dance*), in the northern part of the Jordan valley, 1 Kings 4:12, to which the routed Bedouin host fled from Gideon. Judges 7:22. Here Elisha was found at his plough by Elijah returning up the valley from Horeb. 1 Kings 19:16–19.

A'bel-miz'raim (ā'bel-mĭz'ra-ĭm) (*meadow of Egypt*), the name given by the Canaanites to the floor of Atad, at which Joseph, his brothers and the Egyptians made their mourning for Jacob. Gen. 50:11. It was "beyond Jordan," which generally means to the east of Jordan. See ATAD. Schaff and others say it was on the *west* bank, for the writer was on the east of Jordan. It was between Egypt and Hebron.

A'bel-shit'tim (ā'bel-shĭt'tim) (*meadow of acacias*), in the "plains" of Moab, on the low level of the Jordan valley, opposite Jericho. The last resting-place of Israel before crossing the Jordan. Num. 33:49. The place is most frequently mentioned by its shorter name of Shittim. See SHITTIM.

A'bel (ā'bĕl), **Stone of** ("the great stone"), the place where the ark rested in the field of Joshua at Beth-shemesh. 1 Sam. 6:18. Abel should be Eben = stone.

A'bez (ā'bĕz) (*white*), a town in the possession of Issachar, named between Kishion and Remeth in Josh. 19:20 only.

A'bi (ā'bī), mother of King Hezekiah, 2 Kings 18:2; written ABIJAH in 2 Chron. 29:1.

Abi'a, Abi'ah (ȧ-bī'ȧ). 1. Son of Becher, the son of Benjamin. 1 Chron. 7:8.

2. Wife of Hezron. 1 Chron. 2:24.

3. Second son of Samuel. 1 Sam. 8:2; 1 Chron. 6:28.

4. The son of Rehoboam. 1 Chron. 3:10; Matt. 1:7. See ABIJAH, 1.

5. A son of Jeroboam, 1 Kings 14:1.

Abi'a (ȧ-bī'ȧ), **Course of,** the eighth of the 24 courses or classes into which the priests were divided for serving at the altar. 1 Chron. 24 : 10; Luke 1 : 5. See ABIJAH, 4.

A'bi=al'bon (à'bĭ-ăl'bŏn) (*father of strength*). See ABIEL.

Abi'asaph (à-bī'ă-săf) (*father has gathered*), Ex. 6 : 24, otherwise written **Ebi'asaph.** 1 Chron. 6 : 23, 37; 9 : 19. One of the descendants of Korah, and head of the Korhites. Among the remarkable descendants of Abiasaph were Samuel the prophet, 1 Chron. 6 : 33, and Heman the singer.

Abi'athar (à-bī'a-thär) (*father of abundance*), high priest and fourth in descent from Eli. (B.C. 1060–1012.) Abiathar was the only one of all the sons of Ahimelech the high priest who escaped the slaughter inflicted upon his father's house by Saul, in revenge for his having inquired of the Lord for David and given him the shew-bread to eat. 1 Sam. 22. Abiathar having become high priest fled to David, and was thus enabled to inquire of the Lord for him. 1 Sam. 23 : 9; 30 : 7; 2 Sam. 2 : 1; 5 : 19, etc. He adhered to David in his wanderings while pursued by Saul; he was with him while he reigned in Hebron, and afterwards in Jerusalem. 2 Sam. 2 : 1-3. He continued faithful to him in Absalom's rebellion. 2 Sam. 15 : 24, 29, 35, 36; 17 : 15-17; 19 : 11. When, however, Adonijah set himself up for David's successor on the throne, in opposition to Solomon, Abiathar sided with him, while Zadok was on Solomon's side. For this Abiathar was deprived of the high priesthood. Zadok had joined David at Hebron, 1 Chron. 12 : 28, so that there were henceforth two high priests in the reign of David, and till the deposition of Abiathar by Solomon, when Zadok became the sole high priest.

A'bib (ā'bĭb). [MONTH.]

Abi'da, or **Abi'dah** (à-bī'dah) (*father of knowledge*), a son of Midian. Gen. 25 : 4; 1 Chron. 1 : 33.

Abi'dan (à-bī'dăn) (*father of the judge*), chief of the tribe of Benjamin at the time of the Exodus. (B.C. 1491.) Num. 1 : 11; 2 : 22; 7 : 60, 65; 10 : 24.

A'biel (ā'bĭ-ĕl), or **Abi'el** (à-bī'ĕl), (*father of strength*, i. e. *strong*). 1. Father of Kish, and consequently grandfather of Saul, 1 Sam. 9 : 1, as well as of Abner, Saul's commander-in-chief. 1 Sam 14 : 51.

2. One of David's mighty men. 1 Chron. 11 : 32. In 2 Sam. 23 : 31 he is called ABI-ALBON.

Abi-e'zer (ā-bĭ-ē'zēr) (*father is help*). 1. Eldest son of Gilead, and descendant of Manasseh. Josh. 17 : 2; 1 Chron. 7 : 18; Judges 6 : 11. He was the ancestor of the great judge Gideon. [GIDEON.]

2. One of David's mighty men. 2 Sam. 23 : 27; 1 Chron. 11 : 28; 27 : 12.

Ab'igail (ăb'ĭ-găl) (*father is joy*). 1. The beautiful wife of Nabal, a wealthy owner of goats and sheep in Carmel. (B.C. 1060.) When David's messengers were slighted by Nabal, Abigail supplied David and his followers with provisions, and succeeded in appeasing his anger. Ten days after this Nabal died, and David sent for Abigail and made her his wife. 1 Sam. 25 : 14, etc. By her he had a son, called Chileab in 2 Sam. 3 : 3, but Daniel in 1 Chron. 3 : 1.

2. A sister of David, married to Jether the *Ishmaelite*, and mother, by him, of Amasa. 1 Chron. 2 : 17. In 2 Sam. 17 : 25, for *Israelite* read *Ishmaelite*.

Abiha'il (ăb-i-hā'il) (*father is might*). 1. Father of Zuriel, chief of the Levitical family of Merari, a contemporary of Moses. Num. 3 : 35. (B.C. 1490.)

2. Wife of Abishur. 1 Chron. 2 : 29.

3. Son of Huri, of the tribe of Gad. 1 Chron. 5 : 14.

4. Wife of Rehoboam. She is called the daughter, i. e. descendant, of Eliab, the elder brother of David. 2 Chron. 11 : 18.

5. Father of Esther and uncle of Mordecai. Esther 2 : 15; 9 : 29.

Abi'hu (à-bī'hū) (*he [God] is father*), the second son, Num. 3 : 2, of Aaron by Elisheba. Ex. 6 : 23. Being, together with his elder brother Nadab, guilty of offering strange fire to the Lord, he was consumed by fire from heaven. Lev. 10 : 1, 2. (B.C. 1490.)

Abi'hud (à-bī'hud), son of Bela and descendant of Benjamin. 1 Chron. 8 : 3.

Abi'jah (à-bī'jah), or **Abi'jam** (*my father is Jehovah*). 1. Son and successor of Rehoboam on the throne of Judah. 1 Kings 14 : 31; 2 Chron. 12 : 16. He is called ABIJAH in Chronicles, ABIJAM in Kings. He began to reign B.C. 920, and reigned three years. He endeavored to recover the kingdom of the Ten Tribes, and made war on Jeroboam. He was successful in battle, and took several of the cities of Israel. We are told that he walked in all the sins of Rehoboam. 1 Kings 14:23, 24.

2. The second son of Samuel, called ABIAH in our version. [ABIA, ABIAH, No. 3.]

3. Son of Jeroboam I., king of Israel; died in his childhood. 1 Kings 14.

4. A descendant of Eleazar, who gave his name to the eighth of the 24 courses into which the priests were divided by David. 1 Chron. 24:10; 2 Chron. 8:14; Neh. 12:4, 17. Perhaps the same as

5. One of the priests who entered into a covenant with Nehemiah to walk in God's law, Neh. 10:7.

6. The mother of king Hezekiah, 2 Chron. 29:1. [ABI.]

Abi'jam (à-bī'jăm). [ABIJAH, 1.]

Ab'ila (ăb'ĭ-là). [ABILENE.]

Abile'ne (ăb-ĭ-lē'nė), Luke 3:1, a district situated on the eastern slope of Anti-Lebanon, fertilized by the river Barada (Abana). The capital, Abila, was 18 miles from Damascus, and stood in a remarkable gorge called *Sûk Wady Barada*.

Abim'ael (à-bĭm'a-el), a descendant of Joktan, Gen. 10:28; 1 Chron. 1:22, and probably the progenitor of an Arab tribe.

Abim'elech (à-bĭm'e-lĕk) (*Melech is father*), the name of several Philistine kings, was probably a common title of these kings, like that of Pharaoh among the Egyptians and that of Cæsar and Augustus among the Romans. Hence in the title of Ps. 34 the name of Abimelech is given to the king, who is called Achish in 1 Sam. 21:11. 1. A Philistine, king of Gerar, Gen. 20, 21, who, exercising the right claimed by Eastern princes of collecting all the beautiful women of their dominions into their harem, Gen. 12:15; Esther 2:3, sent for and took Sarah. A similar account is given of Abraham's conduct on this occasion to that of his behavior towards Pharaoh. [ABRAHAM.]

2. Another king of Gerar in the time of Isaac, of whom a similar narrative is recorded in relation to Rebekah. Gen. 26:1, etc.

3. Son of the judge Gideon by his Shechemite concubine. Judges 8:31. After his father's death he murdered all his brethren, 70 in number, with the exception of Jotham, the youngest, who concealed himself; and he then per-suaded the Shechemites to elect him king. Shechem now became an independent state. After Abimelech had reigned three years, the citizens of Shechem rebelled. He was absent at the time, but he returned and quelled the insurrection. Shortly after he stormed and took Thebez, but was struck on the head by a woman with the fragment of a millstone, comp. 2 Sam. 11:21; and lest he should be said to have died by a woman, he bade his armor-bearer slay him.

4. A son of Abiathar. 1 Chron. 18:16. Properly AHIMELECH.

Abin'adab (à-bĭn'a-dăb). 1. A Levite, a native of Kirjath-jearim, in whose house the ark remained 20 years. 1 Sam. 7:1, 2; 1 Chron. 13:7. (B.C. 1042.)

2. Second son of Jesse, who followed Saul to his war against the Philistines. 1 Sam. 16:8; 17:13.

3. A son of Saul, who was slain with his brothers at the fatal battle on Mount Gilboa. 1 Sam. 31:2. (B.C. 1055.)

4. Father of one of the twelve chief officers of Solomon. 1 Kings 4:11.

Ab'iner (ăb'nēr). Same as ABNER. 1 Sam. 14:50, margin.

Abin'oam (à-bĭn'o-ăm), the father of Barak. Judges 4:6, 12; 5:1, 12.

Abi'ram (à-bī'ram). 1. A Reubenite, son of Eliab, who with Korah, a Levite, organized a conspiracy against Moses and Aaron. Num. 16. [For details, see KORAH.] (B.C. 1490.)

2. Eldest son of Hiel the Bethelite, who died when his father laid the foundations of Jericho, 1 Kings 16:34, and thus accomplished the first part of the curse of Joshua. Josh. 6:26. (B.C. about 905.)

Abish'ag (à-bĭsh'ăg), a beautiful Shunammite (from Shunem, in the tribe of Issachar), taken into David's harem to comfort him in his extreme old age. 1 Kings 1:1-4.

Abisha'i, or **Abish'ai** (à-bĭsh'ă-ī) (*my father is Jesse*), the eldest of the three sons of Zeruiah, David's sister, and brother to Joab and Asahel. 1 Chron. 2:16. Like his two brothers he was the devoted follower of David. He was his companion in the desperate night expedition to the camp of Saul. 1 Sam. 26:6-9. (B.C. 1060.) On the outbreak of Absalom's rebellion he remained true to the king, and commanded a third part of the army in the decisive battle against Absalom. He rescued David from the hands of a gigantic Philistine, Ishbi-benob. 2 Sam. 21:17. His personal prowess on this, as on another occasion, when he fought single-handed against three hundred, won for him a place as captain of the second three of David's mighty men. 2 Sam. 23:18; 1 Chron. 11:20.

Abish'alom (à-bĭsh'a-lŏm) (*father is peace*), father or grandfather of Maachah, who was the wife of Rehoboam and mother of Abijah. 1 Kings 15:2, 10. He is called Absalom in 2 Chron. 11:20, 21. This person must be David's son. Absalom's daughter Tamar, 2 Sam. 14:27 is with much probability identified with Maachah.

Abishu'a, or **Abish'ua** (à-bĭsh'u-à) (*father of salvation*). 1. Son of Bela, of the tribe of Benjamin. 1 Chron. 8: 4.

2. Son of Phinehas, the son of Eleazar, and father of Bukki, in the genealogy of the high priests. 1 Chron. 6: 4, 5, 50, 51; Ezra 7: 4, 5.

Ab'ishur (ăb'ĭ-shur) (*father is a wall*), son of Shammai. 1 Chron. 2:28.

Ab'ital (ăb'ĭ-tăl) (*father is dew*), one of David's wives. 2 Sam. 3:4; 1 Chron. 3:3.

Ab'itub (ăb'ĭ-tŭb) (*father of goodness*), son of Shaharaim by Hushim. 1 Chron. 8:11.

Abi'ud (à-bī'ŭd), descendant of Zorobabel in the genealogy of Jesus Christ. Matt. 1:13.

Ablution. [PURIFICATION.]

Ab'ner (ăb'nẽr) (*father is light or my father is Ner*). 1. Son of Ner, who was the brother of Kish, 1 Chron. 9:36, the father of Saul. (B.C. 1063.) Abner, therefore, was Saul's first cousin, and was made by him commander-in-chief of his army. 1 Sam. 14:50; 17:55; 26:5–14. After the death of Saul David was proclaimed king of Judah; and some time subsequently Abner proclaimed Ish-bosheth, Saul's son, king of Israel. War soon broke out between the two rival kings, and a "very sore battle" was fought at Gibeon between the men of Israel under Abner and the men of Judah under Joab. 2 Sam. 2: 16. Abner had married Rizpah, Saul's concubine, and this, according to the views of Oriental courts. might be so

interpreted as to imply a design upon the throne. Rightly or wrongly, Ish-bosheth so understood it, and he even ventured to reproach Abner with it. Abner, incensed at his ingratitude, opened negotiations with David, by whom he was most favorably received at Hebron. He then undertook to procure his recognition throughout Israel; but after leaving his presence for the purpose was enticed back by Joab, and treacherously murdered by him and his brother Abishai, at the gate of the city, partly, no doubt, from fear lest so distinguished a convert to their cause should gain too high a place in David's favor, but ostensibly in retaliation for the death of Asahel. David, in sorrow and indignation, poured forth a simple dirge over the slain hero. 2 Sam. 3: 33, 34.

2. The father of Jaasiel, chief of the Benjamites in David's reign, 1 Chron. 27:21; probably the same as the preceding.

Abomination of Desolation, mentioned by our Saviour, Matt. 24:15, as a sign of the approaching destruction of Jerusalem, with reference to Dan. 9: 27; 11:31; 12:11. The prophecy referred ultimately to the destruction of Jerusalem by the Romans, and consequently the "abomination" must describe some occurrence connected with that event. It appears most probable that the profanities of the Zealots constituted the abomination, which was the sign of impending ruin; but most people refer it to the standards or banners of the Roman army. They were abomination because there were idolatrous images upon them.

A'braham (ā'brà-hăm), originally **Abram** (ā'brăm) (*exalted father*), changed to Abraham (*father of a multitude*), was the founder of the Hebrew nation. He was born in Ur of the Chaldees, the ruins of which have been identified as Mugheir on the lower Euphrates, where lately successful excavations have been made.

Ussher's date (B.C. 1996–1822), cannot be far from right, for Abraham rescued Lot from Amraphel (Gen. 14), who has been identified with Hammurabi, about B.C. 2100. (Prof. Clay.) Terah, Abraham's father, with their families migrated to Haran in Mesopotamia. On the death of his father, Abram, then in the 75th year of his age, with Sarai and

Lot, pursued his course to the land of Canaan, by divine command. Gen. 12: 5. He passed through the heart of the country by the great highway to Shechem, and pitched his tent beneath the terebinth of Moreh. Gen. 12 : 6. Here he received in vision from Jehovah the further revelation that this was the land which his descendants should inherit. Gen. 12: 7. The next halting-place of the wanderer was on a mountain between Bethel and Ai, Gen. 12 : 8; but the country was suffering from famine, and Abram journeyed still southward to the rich corn-lands of Egypt. There, fearing that the great beauty of Sarai might tempt the pow-

THE TRADITIONAL OAK OF ABRAHAM.
(Near Hebron.)

erful monarch of Egypt and expose his own life to peril, he arranged that Sarai should represent herself as his sister, which her actual relationship to him, as probably the daughter of his father Terah, allowed her to do with some semblance of truth. But her beauty was reported to the king, and she was taken into the royal harem. The deception was discovered, and Pharaoh with some indignation dismissed Abram from the country. Gen. 12 : 10–20. He left Egypt with great possessions, and, accompanied by Lot, returned by the south of Palestine to his former encampment between Bethel and Ai. The increased wealth of the two kinsmen was the ulti-

mate cause of their separation. Lot chose the fertile plain of the Jordan near Sodom, while Abram pitched his tent among the oak groves of Mamre, close to Hebron. Gen. 13. Lot with his family and possessions having been carried away captive by Chedorlaomer king of Elam, who had invaded Sodom, Abram pursued the conquerors and utterly routed them not far from Damascus. The captives and plunder were all recovered, and Abram was greeted on his return by the king of Sodom, and by Melchizedek king of Salem, priest of the most high God, who mysteriously appears upon the scene to bless the patriarch and receive from him a tenth of the spoil. Gen. 14. After this the thrice-repeated promise that his descendants should become a mighty nation and possess the land in which he was a stranger was confirmed with all the solemnity of a religious ceremony. Gen. 15. Ten years had passed since he had left his father's house, and the fulfilment of the promise was apparently more distant than at first. At the suggestion of Sarai, who despaired of having children of her own, he took as his concubine Hagar, her Egyptian maid, who bore him Ishmael in the 86th year of his age. Gen. 16. [HAGAR; ISHMAEL.] But this was not the accomplishment of the promise. Thirteen years elapsed, during which Abram still dwelt in Hebron, when the covenant was renewed, and the rite of circumcision established as its sign. This most important crisis in Abram's life, when he was 99 years old, is marked by the significant change of his name to Abraham, "father of a multitude;" while his wife's from Sarai became Sarah. The promise that Sarah should have a son was repeated in the remarkable scene described in ch. 18. Three men stood before Abraham as he sat in his tent door in the heat of the day. The patriarch, with true Eastern hospitality, welcomed the strangers, and bade them rest and refresh themselves. The meal ended, they foretold the birth of Isaac, and went on their way to Sodom. Abraham accompanied them, and is represented as an interlocutor in a dialogue with Jehovah, in which he pleaded in vain to avert the vengeance threatened to the devoted cities of the plain. Gen. 18 : 17–33. In remarkable contrast with Abraham's firm faith with regard to the magnificent fortunes of his posterity stands the incident which occurred during his temporary residence among the Philistines in Gerar, whither he had for some cause removed after the destruction of Sodom. It was almost a repetition of what took place in Egypt a few years before. At length Isaac, the long-looked-for child, was born. Sarah's jealousy, aroused by the mockery of Ishmael at the "great banquet" which Abraham made to celebrate the weaning of her son, Gen. 21:9, demanded that, with his mother Hagar, he should be driven out. Gen. 21:10. But the severest trial of his faith was yet to come. For a long period the history is almost silent. At length he receives the strange command to take Isaac, his only son, and offer him for a burnt offering at an appointed place. Abraham hesitated not to obey. His faith, hitherto unshaken, supported him in this final trial, "accounting that God was able to raise up his son, even from the dead, from whence also he received

Sarah died, Gen. 23:2, and was buried in the cave of Machpelah. The remaining years of Abraham's life are marked by but few incidents. After Isaac's marriage with Rebekah and his removal to Lahai-roi, Abraham took to wife Keturah, by whom he had six children, Zimran, Jokshan, Medan, Midian, Ishbak and Shuah, who became the ancestors of nomadic tribes inhabiting the countries south and southeast of Palestine. Abraham lived to see the gradual accomplishment of the promise in the birth of his grandchildren Jacob and Esau, and witnessed their growth to manhood. Gen. 25:26. At the goodly age of 175 he was "gathered to his people," and laid beside Sarah in the tomb of Machpelah by his sons Isaac and Ishmael. Gen. 25:7–10.

A'bram (ā'brăm) (*a high father*), the earlier name of Abraham.

Ab'salom (ăb'sa-lŏm) (*father is peace*), third son of David by Maachah, daughter of Talmai king of Geshur, a Syrian district adjoining the northeast

THE "PILLAR OF ABSALOM."

him in a figure." Heb. 11:19. The sacrifice was stayed by the angel of Jehovah, the promise of spiritual blessing made for the first time, and Abraham with his son returned to Beersheba, and for a time dwelt there. Gen. 22. But we find him after a few years in his original residence at Hebron, for there

frontier of the Holy Land. Absalom had a sister, Tamar, who was violated by her half-brother Amnon. The natural avenger of such an outrage would be Tamar's full brother Absalom. He brooded over the wrong for two years, and then invited all the princes to a sheep-shearing feast at his estate in

Baal-hazor, on the borders of Ephraim and Benjamin. Here he ordered his servants to murder Amnon, and then fled for safety to his grandfather's court at Geshur, where he remained for three years. At the end of that time he was brought back by an artifice of Joab. David, however, would not see Absalom for two more years; but at length Joab brought about a reconciliation. Absalom now began at once to prepare for rebellion. He tried to supplant his father by courting popularity, standing in the gate, conversing with every suitor, and lamenting the difficulty which he would find in getting a hearing. He also maintained a splendid retinue, 2 Sam. 15 : 1, and was admired for his personal beauty. It is probable too that the great tribe of Judah had taken some offence at David's government. Absalom raised the standard of revolt at Hebron, the old capital of Judah, now supplanted by Jerusalem. The revolt was at first completely successful; David fled from his capital over the Jordan to Manhanaim in Gilead, and Absalom occupied Jerusalem. At last, after being s o l e m n l y anointed king of Jerusalem, 2 Sam. 19 : 10, Absalom crossed the Jordan to attack his father, who by this time had rallied around him a considerable force. A decisive battle was fought in Gilead, in the wood of Ephraim. Here Absalom's forces were totally defeated, and as he himself was escaping his head was caught in the branches of a terebinth, where he was left hanging while the mule on which he was riding ran away from under him. He was dispatched by Joab in spite of the prohibition of David, who, loving him to the last, had desired that his life might be spared. He was buried in a great pit in the forest, and the conquerors threw stones over his grave, an old proof of bitter hostility. Josh. 7 : 26.

Absalom's Pillar, or Place, a mon-

ument or tomb which Absalom had built during his lifetime in the king's dale, *i. e.*, the valley of the Kidron, at the foot of Mount Olivet, near Jerusalem, 2 Sam. 18 : 18, comp. with 14 : 27, for his three sons, and where he probably expected to be buried. The tomb there now, and called by Absalom's name, was probably built at a later date. The decorations are Græco-Roman.

PANORAMA OF BAY OF ACRE AND THE MODERN TOWN HAIFA.

Ac'cad (ăc'căd), one of the cities in the land of Shinar. Gen. 10 : 10. It is probably the same as *Agade*, named as being in northern Babylonia, but no further clue to its position is known.

Ac'cho (ăc'chō) (the PTOLEMAIS of the Maccabees and New Testament), now called *Acca*, or more usually by Europeans *St. Jean d'Acre*, the most important seaport town on the Syrian coast, about 30 miles south of Tyre. It was situated on a slightly projecting headland, at the northern extremity of that spacious bay which is formed by the bold promontory of Carmel on the opposite side. In the 2nd or 3rd century B.C. it was named Ptolemais, after one of the Ptolemies. Later it reverted to its original name. It is named in Judges 1 : 31, as a Canaanite city in the tribe of Asher. The only notice of it in the New Testament is in Acts 21 : 7, where it is called *Ptolemais*.

Acel'dama (acĕl'dăma) (*the field of blood*) (*Akeldama* in the Revised Version), the name given by the Jews of Jerusalem to a field near Jerusalem pur-

hence Achaia and Macedonia are frequently mentioned together in the New Testament to indicate all Greece. Acts 18 : 12; 19 : 21; Rom. 15 : 26; 16 : 5; 1 Cor. 16 : 15; 2 Cor. 7 : 5; 9 : 2; 11 : 10; 1 Thess. 1 : 7, 8. In the time of the emperor Claudius it was governed by a proconsul, translated in the Authorized Version " deputy," of Achaia. Acts 18 : 12.

Acha'icus (ăchā'ĭcŭs) (*belonging to Achaia*), a name of a Christian. 1 Cor. 16 : 17.

A'chan (ā'chăn) (*trouble*), an Is-

TRADITIONAL " FIELD OF BLOOD." (*See Aceldama.*)

chased with the money which Judas received for the betrayal of Christ, and so called from his violent death therein. Acts 1 : 19. The " field of blood " is now shown on the steep face of the so-called " valley of Hinnom," south of the pool of Siloam.

Acha'ia (ăchā'ĭä) (*Greece*) signifies in the New Testament a Roman province which included the whole of the Peloponnesus and the greater part of Hellas proper, with the adjacent islands. This province, with that of Macedonia, comprehended the whole of Greece :

raelite of the tribe of Judah, who, when Jericho and all that it contained were accursed and devoted to destruction, secreted a portion of the spoil in his tent. For this sin he was stoned to death with his whole family by the people, in a valley situated between Ai and Jericho, and their remains, together with his property, were burnt. Josh. 7 : 19-26. From this event the valley received the name of Achor (i. e., *trouble*). [ACHOR.] (B.C. 1451.)

A'char (a'chăr). **1 Chron. 2 : 7.** [ACHAN.]

A'chaz (ā'chăz), king of Judah. Matt. 1 : 9. [AHAZ.]

Ach'bor (ăch'bor) (*mouse*). 1. Father of Baal-hanan king of Edom. Gen. 36 : 38, 39 ; 1 Chron. 1 : 49. 2. Son of Michaiah, a contemporary of Josiah, 2 Kings 22 : 12, 14 ; Jer. 26 : 22 ; 36 : 12, called ABDON in 2 Chron. 34 : 20. (B.C. 623.)

A'chim (ā'kim), son of Sadoc and father of Eliud in our Lord's genealogy. Matt. 1 : 14. The Hebrew form of the name would be *Jachin,* which is a short form of Jehoiachim, *Jehovah will establish.*

A'chish (ā'kish), a Philistine king of Gath, who in the title to the 34th Psalm is called Abimelech. David twice found a refuge with him when he fled from Saul. (B.C. 1061.) On the first occasion he was alarmed for his safety, feigned madness, and escaped. The second time he barely avoided accompanying the army against Saul. 1 Sam. 21 : 10 ; 27 : 1 ; 28 : 1 ; 29 : 1–11.

A'chor (ā'kôr), **Valley of** (*valley of trouble*), the spot at which Achan was stoned. Josh. 7 : 24, 26. On the northern boundary of Judah, Josh. 15 : 7, near Jericho.

Ach'sa. 1 Chron. 2 : 49. [ACHSAH.]

Ach'sah (ăk'sah) (*ankle-chain, anklet*), daughter of Caleb. Her father promised her in marriage to whoever should take Debir. Othniel, her father's younger brother, took that city, and accordingly received the hand of Achsah as his reward. Caleb added to her dowry the upper and lower springs. Josh. 15 : 15–19 ; Judges 1 : 11–15.

Ach'shaph (ăk'shaf) (*fascination*), a city within the territory of Asher, named between Beten and Alammelech, Josh. 19 : 25 ; originally the seat of a Canaanite king. Josh. 11 : 1 ; 12 : 20.

Ach'zib (ăk'zib) (*lying, false*). 1. A city in the lowlands of Judah, named with Keilah and Mareshah. Josh. 15 : 44 ; Micah 1 : 14. It is probably the same with CHEZIB and CHOZEBA, which see.

2. A town belonging to Asher, Josh. 19 : 29, from which the Canaanites were not expelled, Judges 1 : 31 ; afterwards Ecdippa. It is now *es-Zib,* on the seashore, 8½ miles north of Acre.

Acrab'bim. See MAALEH-ACRABBIM, Josh. 15 : 3, in the margin.

Acts of the Apostles.—*Characteristics.* It is the history of the founding of the Christian Church and its early development. The Gospels record what Jesus *began* to do and to teach, the Acts records what he *continued* to do, as the ever-living leader in heaven, with a personal presence on earth through the Holy Spirit. The Acts is "the Church of God in action."

It is a book of missionary activity. It is a book of victories, the greatest victories recorded in history.

The author was Luke, according to most of the leading English scholars.

Date of writing must have been after the publication of Luke's Gospel. The arguments are almost conclusive for a date somewhere between A.D. 62 and 70. The date is not far from A.D. 63, for the narrative breaks off abruptly at the end of Paul's two years' residence at Rome. Evidently because there is no more to tell at the time.

The extent of the history in time covers about thirty-three years, or one generation, from the Resurrection of Jesus to the close of the first imprisonment of Paul.

The extent of the history as to subject is limited chiefly to—

1. The records of the church at Jerusalem (chaps. 1–12).

2. The record of Paul's missionary work in so far as it describes the development of the Jewish type of Christianity into a world-wide Christianity.

The geographical extent of the history carries us over nearly the whole Roman world. It begins at Jerusalem and ends at Rome.

Ad'adah (ăd'a-dah) (*festival* or *holiday*), one of the cities in the extreme south of Judah, named with Dimonah and Kedesh. Josh. 15 : 22.

A'dah (ā'dah) (*adornment, beauty*). 1. The first of the two wives of Lamech, by whom were borne to him Jabal and Jubal. Gen. 4 : 19.

2. A Hittitess, one of the three wives of Esau, mother of Eliphaz. Gen. 36 : 2, 10, 12, 16. In Gen. 26 : 34 she is called BASHEMATH. (B.C. 1797.)

Ada'iah (ăd-ā'-yah) (*Jehovah has adorned*). 1. Maternal grandfather of King Josiah, and native of Boscath in the lowlands of Judah. 2 Kings 22 : 1.

2. A Levite of the Gershonite branch, and ancestor of Asaph. 1 Chron. 6 : 41. In v. 21 he is called IDDO.

3. A Benjamite, son of Shimhi. 1

Chron. 8:21, who is apparently the same as Shema in v. 13.

4. A priest, son of Jeroham. 1 Chron. 9:12; Neh. 11:12.

5. Ancestor of Maaseiah, one of the captains who supported Jehoiada. 2 Chron. 23:1.

6. One of the descendants of Bani, who had married a foreign wife after the return from Babylon. Ezra 10:29. (B.C. 459.)

7. The descendant of another Bani, who had also taken a foreign wife. Ezra 10:39.

8. A man of Judah, of the line of Pharez. Neh. 11:5.

Ada'lia (ăd-ā'lĭ-à), the fifth son of Haman. Esther 9:8.

Ad'am (ăd'ăm) (*ruddy* or *one made or produced*), the name of the first man, and of mankind collectively. Man was created of the dust of the earth, the last of all things on the same (sixth) day as the beasts, but by a separate act of creation and in the image of God; he received a special blessing, according to which he was given dominion over the earth and its inhabitants, and the vegetable creation was assigned to him, to provide him with food. While it is expressly said of the light, the heavens, the earth, and seas, the vegetable world, the heavenly bodies, the birds, the fish, and the other animals, that God saw that they were good, this is not separately stated concerning man, but is left to be inferred from the general statement that God saw that everything that He had made was very good. Adam was created (not born) a perfect man in body and spirit. The man Adam was placed in a garden which the Lord God had planted "eastward in Eden," for the purpose of dressing it and keeping it. [EDEN.] He was permitted to eat of the fruit of every tree in the garden but one, which was called "the tree of the knowledge of good and evil," because it was the test of Adam's obedience. By it Adam could know good and evil in the divine way, through obedience; thus knowing good by experience in resisting temptation and forming a strong and holy character, while he knew evil only by observation and inference. Or he could "know good and evil," in Satan's way, by experiencing the evil and knowing good only by contrast. By the subtlety of the serpent the woman who was given to be with Adam was beguiled into a vio-

lation of the one command which had been imposed upon them. She took of the fruit of the forbidden tree and gave it to her husband. The propriety of its name was immediately shown in the results which followed: self-consciousness was the first result of sin; their eyes were opened and they knew that they were naked. Though the curse of Adam's rebellion of necessity fell upon him, yet the very prohibition to eat of the tree of life after his transgression was probably a manifestation of divine mercy, because the greatest malediction of all would have been to have the gift of indestructible life superadded to a state of wretchedness and sin. The divine mercy was also shown in the promise of a deliverer given at the very time the curse was imposed, Gen. 3:15, and opening a door of hope to Paradise regained for him and his descendants. Adam is stated to have lived 930 years. His sons mentioned in Scripture are Cain, Abel and Seth; it is implied, however, that he had others.

Ad'am (ăd'ăm). *Man*, generically, for the name Adam was not confined to the father of the human race, but like *homo* was applicable to *woman* as well as to *man*. Gen. 5:2.

Ad'am (ăd'ăm), a city on the Jordan, "beside Zaretan," in the time of Joshua. Josh. 3:16. It is often identified with *ed-Damieh* on the western bank of the river, 18 miles above Jericho; but this is by no means certain.

Ad'amah(ăd'a-mah) (*red lands*), one of the "fenced cities" of Naphtali, named between Chinnereth and Ramah. Josh. 19:36.

Adamant, the translation of the Hebrew word *Shamir* in Ezek. 3:9 and Zech. 7:12. In Jer. 17:1 it is translated "diamond," a word which is derived from "Adamant." In these three passages the word is the representative of some stone of excessive hardness, and is used metaphorically. It is very probable that by *Shamir* is intended *emery*, a variety of *corundum*, a mineral inferior only to the diamond in hardness.

Ad'ami (ăd'a-mĭ) (*red lands*), a place on the border of Naphtali. Josh. 19:33.

A'dar (a'där), a place on the south boundary of Judah. Josh. 15:3.

A'dar (a'där). [MONTH.]

Ad'beel (ăd'bė-el) (*a miracle of God*), a son of Ishmael, Gen. 25:13; 1

Chron. 1: 29, and probably the progenitor of an Arab tribe.

Ad'dan (ăd'dăn), one of the places from which some of the captivity returned with Zerubbabel to Judea who could not show their pedigree as Israelites. Ezra 2: 59. Called ADDON in Neh. 7: 61.

Ad'dar, son of Bela, 1 Chron. 8: 3; called ARD in Num. 26: 40.

Ad'der. This word is used for any poisonous snake, and is applied in this general sense by the translators of the Authorized Version. The word adder occurs five times in the text of the Authorized Version (see below), and three times in the margin as synonymous with *cockatrice,* viz., Isa. 11: 8; 14: 29; 59: 5. It represents four Hebrew words:

HORNED CERASTES (ADDER).

1. *Acshub* is found only in Ps. 140: 3, and may be represented by the *Toxicoa* of Egypt and North Africa.

2. *Pethen.* [ASP.]

3. *Tsepha,* or *Tsiphoni,* occurs five times in the Hebrew Bible. In Prov. 23: 32 it is translated *adder,* and in Isa. 11: 8, 14: 29, 59: 5, Jer. 8: 17, it is rendered *cockatrice.* From Jeremiah we learn that it was of a hostile nature, and from the parallelism of Isa. 11: 8 it appears that the *Tsiphoni* was considered even more dreadful than the *Pethen.*

4. *Shephiphon* occurs only in Gen. 49: 17, where it is used to characterize the tribe of Dan. The habit of lurking in the sand and biting at the horse's heels here alluded to suits the character of a well-known species of venomous snake, and helps to identify it with the celebrated horned viper, the asp of Cleopatra (*Cerastes*), which is found abundantly in the dry sandy deserts of Egypt, Syria and Arabia. The cer-

astes is extremely venomous, a foot to eighteen inches long, of grey color, with brown or blackish spots, and a horn above each eye. At Thebes it was regarded as sacred.

Ad'di (ăd'di). Luke 3: 28. Son of Cosam, and father of Melchi in our Lord's genealogy; the third above Salathiel.

Ad'don. [ADDAN.]

A'der (ā'-dĕr) (*flock*), a Benjamite, son of Beriah, chief of the inhabitants of Aijalon. 1 Chron. 8: 15. The name is more correctly Eder.

Ad'ida (ăd'-ĭ-dă), a fortified town near Jerusalem, probably the HADID of Ezra 2: 33, and perhaps the same as ADITHAIM.

A'diel (ā'dĭ-el) (*ornament of God*). 1. A prince of the tribe of Simeon, descended from the prosperous family of Shimei. 1 Chron. 4: 36. He took part in the murderous raid made by his tribe upon the peaceable Hamite shepherds of the valley of Gedor in the reign of Hezekiah.

2. A priest, ancestor of Maasiai. 1 Chron. 9: 12.

3. Father of Azmaveth, David's treasurer. 1 Chron. 27: 25.

A'din (ā'dĭn) (*delicate*), ancestor of a family who returned from Babylon with Zerubbabel, to the number of 454, Ezra 2: 15, or 655 according to the parallel list in Neh. 7: 20. (B.C. 536.) They joined with Nehemiah in a covenant to separate themselves from the heathen. Neh. 10: 16.

Ad'ina (ăd'ĭ-nà) (*delicate*), one of David's captains beyond the Jordan, and a chief of the Reubenites. 1 Chron. 11: 42.

Adi'no, or Ad'ino, the Eznite. 2 Sam. 23: 8. See JASHOBEAM.

Aditha'im (ăd-i-thā'im), a town belonging to Judah, lying in the low country, and named, between Sharaim and Gederah, in Josh. 15: 36 only.

Adla'i (ad-lā'ĭ) or **Ad'la-i,** father of Shaphat, the overseer of David's herds that fed in the broad valleys. 1 Chron. 27: 29.

Ad'mah (ăd'mah) (*red lands*), one of the "cities of the plain," always coupled with Zeboim. Gen. 10: 19; 14: 2, 8; Deut. 29: 23; Hos. 11: 8.

Ad'matha (ăd'ma-thà) (*unrestrained*), one of the seven princes of Persia. Esther 1: 14.

Ad'na (ăd'nà) (*pleasure*). 1. One of the family of Pahath-moab, who returned with Ezra and married a foreign wife. Ezra 10:30. (B.C. 459.)

2. A priest, descendant of Harim in the days of Joiakim, the son of Jeshua. Neh. 12:15. (B.C. 500.)

Ad'nah (ăd'nà) (*pleasure*). 1. A Manassite who deserted from Saul and joined the fortunes of David on his road to Ziklag from the camp of the Philistines. He was captain of a thousand of his tribe, and fought at David's side in the pursuit of the Amalekites. 1 Chron. 12:20. (B.C. 1055.)

2. The captain of over 300,000 men of Judah who were in Jehoshaphat's army. 2 Chron. 17:14. (B.C. 908.)

Ado'ni-be'zek (à-dō'nī-bē'zĕk) (*lord of Bezek*), king of Bezek, a city of the Canaanites. [BEZEK.] This chieftain was vanquished by the tribe of Judah, Judges 1:4–7, who cut off his thumbs and great toes, and brought him prisoner to Jerusalem, where he died. He confessed that he had inflicted the same cruelty upon 70 petty kings whom he had conquered.

Adoni'jah (ăd-o-nī'jah) (*my Lord is Jehovah*). 1. The fourth son of David by Haggith, born at Hebron while his father was king of Judah. 2 Sam. 3:4. After the death of his three brothers, Amnon, Chileab and Absalom, he became eldest son; and when his father's strength was visibly declining, put forward his pretensions to the crown. Adonijah's cause was espoused by Abiathar and by Joab the famous commander of David's army. [JOAB.] His name and influence secured a large number of followers among the captains of the royal army belonging to the tribe of Judah, comp. 1 Kings 1:9; and these, together with all the princes except Solomon, were entertained by Adonijah at a great sacrificial feast held "by the stone of Zoheleth, which is by En-rogel." [EN-ROGEL.] Apprised of these proceedings, David immediately caused Solomon to be proclaimed king, 1 Kings 1:33, 34, at Gihon. [GIHON.] This decisive measure struck terror into the opposite party, and Adonijah fled to the sanctuary, but was pardoned by Solomon on condition that he should "show himself a worthy man." 1 Kings 1:52. The death of David quickly followed on these events; and Adonijah begged Bath-sheba to procure Solomon's consent to his marriage with Abishag, who had been the wife of David in his old age. 1 Kings 1:3. This was regarded as equivalent to a fresh attempt on the throne, and therefore Solomon ordered him to be put to death by Benaiah. 1 Kings 2:25.

2. A Levite in the reign of Jehoshaphat. 2 Chron. 17:8.

3. The same as Adonikam. Neh. 10:16. [ADONIKAM.]

Adoni'kam (à-don-ī'kam) or **Adon'ikam.** The sons of Adonikam, 666 in number, were among those who returned from Babylon with Zerubbabel. Ezra 2:13; 8:13; Neh. 7:18; 8:39. The name is given as ADONIJAH in Neh. 10:16.

Adoni'ram (ăd-o-nī'ram) (*the Lord is exalted*), 1 Kings 4:6. By an unusual contraction ADORAM, 2 Sam. 20:24 and 1 Kings 12:18; also HADORAM, 2 Chron. 10:18, chief receiver of the tribute during the reigns of David, 2 Sam. 20:24, Solomon, 1 Kings 4:6, and Rehoboam, 1 Kings 12:18. This last monarch sent him to collect the tribute from the rebellious Israelites, by whom he was stoned to death. (B.C. 937.)

Adoni-ze'dek (à-dō'nī-zē'dĕk) (*lord of righteousness*), the king of Jerusalem who organized a league with four other Amorite princes against Joshua. The confederate kings having laid siege to Gibeon, Joshua marched to the relief of his new allies and put the besiegers to flight. The five kings took refuge in a cave at Makkedah, whence they were taken and slain, their bodies hung on trees, and then buried in the place of their concealment. Josh. 10:1–27.

Adoption, an expression used by St. Paul in reference to the present and prospective privileges of Christians. Rom. 8:15, 23; Gal. 4:5; Eph. 1:5. He probably alludes to the Roman custom by which a person not having children of his own might adopt as his son one born of other parents. The relationship was to all intents and purposes the same as existed between a natural father and son. The term is used figuratively to show the close relationship to God of the Christian. Gal. 4:4, 5; Rom. 8:14–17. He is received into God's family from the world, and becomes a child and heir of God, with all which that implies.

Adora'im (ăd-o-rā'im), a city fortified by Rehoboam, 2 Chron. 11: 9, in Judah. Robinson identifies it with *Dura*, a "large village" on a rising ground west of Hebron.

Ado'ram (à-dō'ram). [ADONIRAM; HADORAM.]

Adoration. The acts and postures by which the Hebrews expressed adoration bear a great similarity to those still in use among Oriental nations. To rise up and suddenly prostrate the body was the most simple method; but, generally speaking, the prostration was conducted in a more formal manner, the person falling upon the knee and then gradually inclining the body until the forehead touched the ground. Such prostration was usual in the worship of Jehovah, Gen. 17: 3; Ps. 95: 6; it was the formal mode of receiving visitors, Gen. 18: 2, of doing obeisance to one of superior station, 2 Sam. 14: 4, and of showing respect to equals, 1 Kings 2: 19. It was accompanied by such acts as a kiss, Ex. 18: 7, laying hold of the knees or feet of the person to whom the adoration was paid, Matt. 28: 9, and kissing the ground on which he stood, Ps. 72: 9; Micah 7: 17. Similar adoration was paid to idols, 1 Kings 19: 18; sometimes, however, the act consisted simply in kissing the hand to the object of reverence, Job 31: 27, and in kissing the statue itself, Hos. 13: 2.

Adram'melech (à-drăm'me-lek) (i. e. *Adar-prince* or *Adar-Molech*). 1. The name of an idol introduced into Samaria by the colonists from Sepharvaim. 2 Kings 17: 31. He was worshipped with rites resembling those of Molech, children being burnt in his honor. Adrammelech was probably the male power of the sun, and ANAMMELECH, who is mentioned with Adrammelech as a companion god, the female power of the sun.

2. Son of the Assyrian king Sennacherib, who, with his brother Sharezer, murdered their father in the temple of Nisroch at Nineveh, after the failure of the Assyrian attack on Jerusalem. The parricides escaped into Armenia. 2 Kin. 19: 37; 2 Chr. 32: 21; Isa. 37: 38.

Adramyt'tium (ăd-ra-mỹt'tĭ-um), named from *Adramys*, brother of Crœsus king of Lydia. A seaport in the province of Asia [ASIA], situated on a bay of the Ægean Sea, about 70 miles north of Smyrna, in the district anciently called Æolis, and also Mysia. See Acts 16: 7. [MITYLENE.] Acts 27: 2. The modern *Adramyti* is a poor village.

A'dria (a'drĭ-à), more properly **A'drias**, the Adriatic Sea. Acts 27: 27. The word seems to have been derived from the town of Adria, near the Po. In Paul's time it included the whole sea between Greece and Italy, reaching south as far as Crete and Sicily, although in the narrowest sense it included only that portion near the city from which it was named.

A'driel (*flock of God*), son of Barzillai, to whom Saul gave his daughter Merab, although he had previously promised her to David, 1 Sam. 18: 19. (B.C. about 1062.) His five sons were amongst the seven descendants of Saul whom David surrendered to the Gibeonites. 2 Sam. 21: 8.

Adul'lam (à-dŭl'lăm) (*Feast of water*), in the valley of Elah, near where David fought Goliath. It was the seat of a Canaanite king, Josh. 12: 15, and evidently a place of great antiquity. Gen. 38: 1, 12, 20. Fortified by Rehoboam, 2 Chron. 11: 7, it was one of the towns reoccupied by the Jews after their return from Babylon, Neh. 11: 30, and still a city in the time of the Maccabees, 2 Macc. 12: 38. David's cave of Adullam was probably in that vicinity, 10 miles N. W. of Hebron. The limestone cliffs of the whole of that locality are pierced with extensive excavations, which suit all we are told about David's stronghold. 1 Sam. 22: 1; 2 Sam. 23: 13; 1 Chron. 11: 15.

Adultery. Ex. 20: 14. The parties to this crime, according to Jewish law, were a married woman and a man who was not her husband. The Mosaic penalty was that both the guilty parties should be stoned, and it applied as well to the betrothed as to the married woman, provided she were free. Deut. 22: 22-24. A bondwoman so offending was to be scourged, and the man was to make a trespass offering. Lev. 19: 20-22. At a later time, and when, owing to Gentile example, the marriage tie became a looser bond of union, public feeling in regard to adultery changed, and the penalty of death was seldom or never inflicted. The famous trial by the waters of jealousy, Num. 5: 11-29, was probably an ancient custom, which

Moses found deeply seated. But this ordeal was wholly in favor of the innocent, and exactly opposite to most ordeals. For the water which the accused drank was perfectly harmless, and only by a miracle could it produce a bad effect; while in most ordeals the accused must suffer what naturally produces death, and be proved innocent only by a miracle. Symbolically adultery is used to express unfaithfulness to covenant vows to God, who is represented as the husband of his people.

Adum'mim (*red objects*), a rising ground or pass "over against Gilgal," and "on the south side of the 'torrent,'" Josh. 15 : 7; 18 : 17, which is the position still occupied by the road leading up from Jericho and the Jordan valley to Jerusalem, on the south face of the gorge of the *Wady Kelt.* Luke 10 : 30-36.

Advocate, or *Paraclete,* one that pleads the cause of another. 1 John 2 : 1. Used by Christ, John 14 : 16; 15 : 26; 16 : 7, to describe the office and work of the Holy Spirit, and translated *Comforter,* i. e. (see margin of Revised Version) Advocate, Helper, Intercessor. This use of the word is derived from the fact that the Jews, being largely ignorant of the Roman law and the Roman language, had to employ Roman *advocates* in their trials before Roman courts. Applied to Christ, 1 John 2 : 1.

Æ'gypt. [EGYPT.]

Æ'neas (ē'ne-ăs), a paralytic at Lydda healed by St. Peter. Acts 9 : 33, 34.

Æ'non (ē'nŏn) (*springs*), a place "near to Salim," at which John baptized. John 3 : 23. It was evidently west of the Jordan, comp. 3 : 22 with 26, and with 1 : 28, and abounded in water. It is given in the *Onomasticon* as eight miles south of Scythopolis, "near Salem and the Jordan."

Æra. [CHRONOLOGY.]

Æthio'pia. [ETHIOPIA.]

Affinity. [MARRIAGE.]

Ag'abus (ăg'a-bŭs), a Christian prophet in the apostolic age, mentioned in Acts 11 : 28 and 21 : 10. He predicted, Acts 11 : 28, that a famine would take place in the reign of Claudius. Josephus mentions a famine which prevailed in Judea in the reign of Claudius, and swept away many of the inhabitants. In Acts 21 : 10 we learn that Agabus and

Paul met at Cæsarea some time after this.

A'gag (ā'găg), possibly the title of the kings of Amalek, like Pharaoh of Egypt. One king of this name is mentioned in Num. 24 : 7, and another in 1 Sam. 15 : 8, 9, 20, 32. The latter was the king of the Amalekites, whom Saul spared contrary to Jehovah's well-known will. Ex. 17 : 14; Deut. 25 : 17. For this act of disobedience Samuel was commissioned to declare to Saul his rejection, and he himself sent for Agag and cut him in pieces. (B.C. about 1079.) 1 Sam. 15 : 33. Haman is called the AGAGITE in Esther 3 : 1, 10; 8 : 3, 5. The Jews consider him a descendant of Agag the Amalekite, but the connection is doubtful.

A'gagite (ā'gag-īte). [AGAG.]

A'gar (ā'gär). [HAGAR.]

Agate, a beautifully-veined semi-transparent precious stone, a variety of quartz. Its colors are delicately arranged in stripes or bands or blended in clouds. It is mentioned four times in the text of the Authorized Version, viz., in Ex. 28 : 19; 39 : 12; Isa. 54 : 12; Ezek. 27 : 16. In the two former passages, where it is represented by the Hebrew word *shebo,* it is spoken of as forming the second stone in the third row of the high priest's breastplate; in each of the two latter places the original word is *cadcod,* by which, no doubt, is intended a different stone. [RUBY.] Our English *agate* derives its name from the Achates, on the banks of which it was first found.

Age, Old. The aged occupied a prominent place in the social and political system of the Jews. In *private* life they were looked up to as the depositaries of knowledge, Job 15 : 10; the young were ordered to rise up in their presence, Lev. 19 : 32; they allowed them to give their opinion first, Job 32 : 4; they were taught to regard grey hairs as a "crown of glory," Prov. 16 : 31; 20 : 29. The attainment of old age was regarded as a special blessing. Job 5 : 26. In *public* affairs age formed under Moses the main qualification of those who acted as the representatives of the people in all matters of difficulty and deliberation. [ELDERS.]

Ag'ee, or **A'gee,** a Hararite, father of Shammah, one of David's three mightiest heroes. 2 Sam. 23 : 11.

Agriculture. This was little cared

for by the patriarchs. The pastoral life, however, was the means of keeping the sacred race, whilst yet a family, distinct from mixture and locally unattached, especially whilst in Egypt. When grown into a nation it supplied a similar check on the foreign intercourse, and became the basis of the Mosaic commonwealth. "The land is mine," Lev. 25:23, was a dictum which made agriculture likewise the basis of the theocratic relation. Thus every family felt its own life with intense keenness, and had its divine tenure which it was to guard from alienation. The prohibition of culture in the sabbatical year formed a kind of rent reserved by the divine Owner. Land-

10. Two kinds of cummin (the black variety called "fitches," Isa. 28:27), and such podded plants as beans and lentils, may be named among the staple produce.

Ploughing and Sowing.—The plough was probably very light, one yoke of oxen usually sufficing to draw it. Mountains and steep places were hoed. Isa. 7:25. New ground and fallows, Jer. 4:3; Hos. 10:12, were cleared of stones and of thorns, Isa. 5:2, early in the year, sowing or gathering from "among thorns" being a proverb for slovenly husbandry. Job 5:5; Prov. 24:30, 31. Sowing also took place without previous ploughing, the seed being scattered

SOWING AND PLOUGHING IN THE GRAIN.

marks were deemed sacred, Deut. 19:14, and the inalienability of the heritage was insured by its reversion to the owner in the year of jubilee; so that only so many years of occupancy could be sold. Lev. 25:8–16, 23–34.

Rain.—Water was abundant in Palestine from natural sources. Deut. 8:7; 11:8–12. Rain was commonly expected soon after the autumnal equinox. The period denoted by the common scriptural expressions of the "early" and the "latter rain," Deut. 11:14; Jer. 5:24; Hos. 6:3; Zech. 10:1; James 5:7, generally reaching from November to April, constituted the "rainy season," and the remainder of the year the "dry season."

Crops.—The cereal crops of constant mention are wheat and barley, and more rarely rye and millet (?). Of the two former, together with the vine, olive and fig, the use of irrigation, the plough and the harrow, mention is made in the book of Job, 31:40; 15:33; 24:6; 39:

broadcast and ploughed in afterwards. The soil was then brushed over with a light harrow, often of thorn bushes. In highly-irrigated spots the seed was trampled in by cattle. Isa. 32:20. Seventy days before the passover was the time prescribed for sowing. The oxen were urged on by a goad like a spear. Judges 3:31. The proportion of harvest gathered to seed sown was often vast; a hundred fold is mentioned, but in such a way as to signify that it was a limit rarely attained. Gen. 26:12; Matt. 13:8. Sowing a field with divers seed was forbidden. Deut. 22:9.

Reaping and Threshing.—The wheat, etc., was reaped by the sickle or pulled up by the roots. It was bound in sheaves. The sheaves or heaps were carted, Amos 2:13, to the floor—a circular spot of hard ground probably as now, from 50 to 80 or 100 feet in diameter. 2 Sam. 24:16, 18. On these the oxen. etc., forbidden to be muzzled,

Deut. 25:4, trampled out the grain. At a later time the Jews used a threshing sledge called *morag*, Isa. 41:15;

THRESHING IMPLEMENTS OF ASIA MINOR.

2 Sam. 24:22; 1 Chron. 21:23, probably resembling the *noreg*, still employed in Egypt—a stage with three rollers ridged with iron, which, aided by the driver's weight, crushed out, often injuring, the grain, as well as cut or tore the straw, which thus became fit for fodder. Lighter grains were beaten out with a stick. Isa. 28:

THRESHING INSTRUMENT (SIDE VIEW).

THRESHING INSTRUMENT (UPPER VIEW).

27. The use of animal manure was frequent. Ps. 83:10; 2 Kings 9:37; Jer. 8:2, etc.

Winnowing.—The shovel and fan, Isa. 30:24, indicate the process of winnowing—a conspicuous part of ancient husbandry. Ps. 35:5; Job 21:18; Isa. 17:13. Evening was the favorite time, Ruth 3:2, when there was mostly a breeze. The fan, Matt. 3:12, was perhaps a broad shovel which threw the grain up against the wind. The last process was the shaking in a sieve to separate dirt and refuse. Amos 9:9. Fields and floors were not commonly enclosed; vineyards mostly were, with a tower and other buildings. Num. 22:24; Ps. 80:12; Isa. 5:5; Matt. 21:33; comp. Judges 6:11. The gardens also and orchards were enclosed, frequently by banks of mud from ditches.

With regard to occupancy, a tenant might pay a fixed money rent, Cant. 8:11, or a stipulated share of the fruits. 2 Sam. 9:10; Matt. 21:34. A passer-by might eat any quantity of corn or grapes, but not reap or carry off fruit. Deut. 23:24, 25; Matt. 12:1. The rights of the corner to be left, and of gleaning [CORNER; GLEANING], formed the poor man's claim on the soil for support. For his benefit, too, a sheaf forgotten in carrying to the floor was to be left; so also with regard to the vineyard and the olive grove. Lev. 19:9, 10; Deut. 24:19.

THRESHING FLOOR (EASTERN)

Agrip'pa (á-grĭp'pá). [HEROD.]

BRONZE COIN OF HEROD AGRIPPA I.

LARGE BRONZE COIN OF AGRIPPA II.

A'gur (á'gûr) (*a gatherer*, i. e. *collector of wise words*), the son of Jakeh, an unknown Hebrew sage, who uttered or collected the sayings of wisdom recorded in Prov. 30.

A'hab (ā'hăb) (*father's brother*), probably with the signification of "one who closely resembles his father." 1. Son of Omri, seventh king of Israel, reigned B.C. 876–854. He married Jezebel, daughter of Ethbaal king of Tyre; and in obedience to her wishes, caused a temple to be built to Baal in Samaria itself, and an *Asherah-pole* to be consecrated to Astarte. See 1 Kings 18: 19. One of Ahab's chief tastes was for splendid architecture, which he showed by building an ivory house and several cities. Desiring to add to his pleasuregrounds at Jezreel the vineyard of his neighbor Naboth, he proposed to buy it or give land in exchange for it; and when this was refused by Naboth in accordance with the Levitical law, Lev. 25 : 23, a false accusation of blasphemy was brought against him, and he was murdered, and Ahab took possession of the coveted fields. 1 Kings 21: 16. Thereupon Elijah declared that the entire extirpation of Ahab's house was the penalty appointed for his long course of wickedness. [ELIJAH.] The execution, however, of the sentence was delayed in consequence of Ahab's deep repentance. 1 Kings 21: 29.

Ahab undertook three campaigns against Ben-hadad II. king of Damascus, two defensive and one offensive. In the first Ben-hadad laid siege to Sa-maria, but was repulsed with great loss. 1 Kings 20: 1–21. Next year Ben-hadad again invaded Israel by way of Aphek, on the east of Jordan; yet Ahab's victory was so complete that Ben-hadad himself fell into his hands, but was released contrary to God's will, 1 Kings 20: 22–34, on condition of restoring the cities of Israel, and admitting Hebrew commissioners into Damascus. After this great success Ahab enjoyed peace for three years, when he attacked Ramoth in Gilead, on the east of Jordan, in conjunction with Jehoshaphat king of Judah, which town he claimed as belonging to Israel. Being told by the prophet Micaiah that he would fall, he disguised himself, but was slain by "a certain man who drew a bow at a venture." When buried in Samaria, the dogs licked up his blood as a servant was washing his chariot; a partial fulfilment of Elijah's prediction, 1 Kings 21: 19, which was more literally accomplished in the case of his son. 2 Kings 9: 26.

2. A lying prophet, who deceived the captive Israelites in Babylon, and was burnt to death by Nebuchadnezzar. Jer. 29: 21.

Ahar'ah (á-här'āh), third son of Benjamin. 1 Chron. 8: 1. [AHER; AHIRAM.]

Ahar'hel (ă-här'hĕl), a name occurring in an obscure fragment of the genealogies of Judah. 1 Chron. 4: 8.

A'hasai (ā'hă-sāi), a priest, ancestor of Amashai, Neh. 11 : 13; called JAHZE-RAH in 1 Chron. 9 : 12.

Ahas'bai (a-hăs'bā-ī), father of Eliphelet, one of David's thirty-seven captains. 2 Sam. 23: 34. In the corrupt list in 1 Chron. 11: 35, Eliphelet appears as "Eliphal the son of Ur."

Ahashve'rosh. Another (the Hebrew) form of AHASUERUS. Ezra 4: 6, in margin.

Ahasue'rus (á-hăs-ū-ē'rŭs), the name of one Median and two Persian kings mentioned in the Old Testament.

1. In Dan. 9: 1 Ahasuerus is said to be the father of Darius the Mede. It is difficult to place this Ahasuerus, because no Darius the Mede has been found in the records. [DARIUS, 1.]

2. The Ahasuerus king of Persia, referred to in Ezra 4 : 6, is placed by Cheyne between Cyrus and Artaxerxes Longimanus. Others identify him with Xerxes. [See below.]

3. The third is the Ahasuerus of the book of Esther, who is recognized by most as the Xerxes of history, Esther 1 : 1 (B.C. 485), and this conclusion is fortified by the resemblance of character, the accounts of his life and character agreeing with the book of Esther. In the third year of Ahasuerus was held a great feast and assembly in Shushan the palace, Esther 1 : 3, following a council held to consider the invasion of Greece. He divorced his queen Vashti for refusing to appear in public at this banquet, and married, four years afterwards, the Jewess Esther, cousin and ward of Mordecai. Five years after this, Haman, one of his counsellors, having been slighted by Mordecai, prevailed upon the king to order the destruction of all the Jews in the empire. But before the day appointed for the massacre, Esther and Mordecai induced the king to put Haman to death, and to give the Jews the right of self-defence. [ESTHER.]

Aha′va (ā-hā′vah), a place, Ezra 8 : 15, or a river, 8 : 21, on the banks of which Ezra collected the second expedition which returned with him from Babylon to Jerusalem. Perhaps it is the modern *Hit*, on the Euphrates due east of Damascus.

A′haz (ā′hăz) (*he hath grasped*), 1. twelfth king of Judah, son of Jotham, reigned 742–726 (exact dates unsettled). At the time of his accession, Rezin king of Damascus and Pekah king of Israel had recently formed a league against Judah, and they proceeded to lay siege to Jerusalem. Upon this Isaiah hastened to give advice and encouragement to Ahaz, and the allies failed in their attack on Jerusalem. Isa. 7 : 1–9. But the allies inflicted a most severe injury on Judah by the capture of Elath, a flourishing port on the Red Sea, while the Philistines invaded the west and south. 2 Kings 16 ; 2 Chron. 28. Ahaz having forfeited God's favor by his wickedness, sought deliverance from these numerous troubles by appealing to Tiglath-pileser king of Assyria, who freed him from his most formidable enemies. But Ahaz had to purchase this help at a costly price; he became tributary to Tiglath-pileser. He was weak, a gross idolater, and sought safety in heathen ceremonies, making his son pass through the fire to Molech, consulting wizards and necromancers, Isa. 8 : 19, and other idol-

atrous practices. 2 Kings 23 : 12. His only service of permanent value was the introduction of the sun-dial. On account of his character he was refused a burial with the kings his ancestors. 2 Chron. 28 : 27.

2. Son of Micah. 1 Chron. 8 : 35, 36; 9 : 41, 42.

Ahazi′ah (ā-ha-zī′ah) (*Jehovah hath grasped*). 1. Son of Ahab and Jezebel, eighth king of Israel, reigned B.C. 854–853. After the battle of Ramoth in Gilead, in which Ahab perished [AHAB], the vassal king of Moab refused his yearly tribute; comp. Isa. 16 : 1. Before Ahaziah could take measures for enforcing his claim, he was seriously injured by a fall through a lattice in his palace at Samaria. Being an idolater, he sent to inquire of the oracle of Baalzebub in the Philistine city of Ekron whether he should recover his health. But Elijah, who now for the last time exercised the prophetic office, rebuked him for this impiety, and announced to him his approaching death. The only other recorded transaction of his reign is his endeavor to join the king of Judah in trading to Ophir or Tarshish. [See TARSHISH.] 1 Kings 22 : 48–53; 2 Kings 1 ; 2 Chron. 20 : 35–37.

2. Sixth king of Judah, son of Jehoram and Athaliah (daughter of Ahab), and therefore nephew of the preceding Ahaziah, reigned one year, B.C. 843. He is called AZARIAH, 2 Chron. 22 : 6, probably by a copyist's error, and JEHOAHAZ. 2 Chron. 21 : 17. He was 22 years old at his accession. 2 Kings 8 : 26 (his age 42, in 2 Chron. 22 : 2, is a copyist's error). Ahaziah was an idolater, and he allied himself with his uncle Jehoram king of Israel against Hazael, the new king of Syria. The two kings were, however, defeated at Ramoth, where Jehoram was severely wounded. The revolution carried out in Israel by Jehu under the guidance of Elisha broke out while Ahaziah was visiting his uncle at Jezreel. As Jehu approached the town, Jehoram and Ahaziah went out to meet him; the former was shot through the heart by Jehu, and Ahaziah was pursued and mortally wounded. He died when he reached Megiddo.

Ah′ban (*brother of an intelligent one*), son of Abishur by his wife Abihail. 1 Chron. 2 : 29. He was of the tribe of Judah.

A′her (*another*), ancestor of Hushim

a Benjamite. The name occurs in the genealogy of Benjamin. 1 Chron. 7:12. It is not improbable that Aher and Ahiram, Num. 26:38, are the same.

A'hi (ā'hī) (*a brother*). 1. A Gadite, chief of a family who lived in Gilead in Bashan, 1 Chron. 5:15. Probably an abbreviation of Ahijah.

2. A descendant of Shamer, of the tribe of Asher. 1 Chron. 7:34.

Ahi'ah (à-hī'ah) or **Ahi'jah** (*Jehovah is brother*). 1. Son of Ahitub, grandson of Phinehas and great-grandson of Eli, succeeded his father as high priest in the reign of Saul. 1 Sam. 14:3, 18. Ahiah is probably the same person as Ahimelech the son of Ahitub.

2. One of Solomon's princes. 1 Kings 4:3.

3. A prophet of Shiloh, 1 Kings 14:2, hence called the Shilonite, 11:29, of whom we have two remarkable prophecies extant, the one in 1 Kings 11:30–39, addressed to Jeroboam, announcing the rending of the ten tribes from Solomon; the other in 1 Kings 14:6–16, in which he foretold the death of Abijah, the king's son, who was sick, and the destruction of Jeroboam's house on account of the images which he had set up. 1 Kings 14:2, 3.

4. Father of Baasha king of Israel. 1 Kings 15:27, 33.

5. Son of Jerahmeel. 1 Chron. 2:25.

6. A Benjamite, apparently. 1 Chron. 8:7. [AHOAH.]

7. One of David's mighty men. 1 Chron. 11:36.

8. A Levite in David's reign. 1 Chron. 26:20.

9. One of the "heads of the people" who joined in the covenant with Nehemiah. Neh. 10:26.

Ahi'am, son of Sharar the Hararite (or of Sacar, 1 Chron. 11:35), one of David's thirty mighty men. 2 Sam. 23:33.

Ahi'an, a Manassite of the family of Shemidah. 1 Chron. 7:19.

Ahie'zer (à-hī-ē'zēr) (*brother is help*). 1. Son of Ammishaddai, hereditary chieftain of the tribe of Dan. Num. 1:12; 2:25; 7:66. (B.C. 1490.)

2. The Benjamite chief of a body of archers in the time of David. 1 Chron. 12:3.

Ahi'hud (ā-hī'hud) (*brother is majesty*). 1. The son of Shelomi and prince of the tribe of Asher. Num. 34:27.

2. Chieftain of the tribe of Benjamin. 1 Chron. 8:7.

Ahi'jah (à-hī'jah). [AHIAH.]

Ahi'kam (à-hī'kam) (*the brother riseth up*), son of Shaphan the scribe, an influential officer at the court of Josiah, was one of the delegates sent by Hilkiah to consult Huldah. 2 Kings 22:12–14. In the reign of Jehoiakim he successfully used his influence to protect the prophet Jeremiah. Jer. 26:24. He was the father of Gedaliah. [GEDALIAH.] (B.C. 623.)

Ahi'lud (à-hī'lud) (*child's brother*), 1. Father of Jehoshaphat, the recorder or chronicler of the kingdom in the reigns of David and Solomon. 2 Sam. 8:16; 20:24; 1 Kings 4:3; 1 Chron. 18:15.

2. The father of Baana, one of Solomon's twelve commissariat officers. 1 Kings 4:12.

Ahim'aaz (à-hĭm'a-ăz) (*my brother is anger*). 1. Son of Zadok, the high priest in David's reign, and celebrated for his swiftness of foot. During Absalom's rebellion he carried to David the important intelligence that Ahithophel had counselled an immediate attack upon David and his followers. 2 Sam. 15:24–37; 17:15–22. Shortly afterwards he was the first to bring to the king the good news of Absalom's defeat. 2 Sam. 18:19–33. (B.C. 1023.)

2. Saul's wife's father. 1 Sam. 14:50.

3. One of Solomon's commissariat officers, who became his son-in-law. 1 Kings 4:15.

Ahi'man (à-hī'măn). 1. One of the three giant Anakim who inhabited Mount Hebron, Num. 13:22, 23, seen by Caleb and the spies. (B.C. 1490.) The whole race was cut off by Joshua, Josh. 11:21, and the three brothers were slain by the tribe of Judah. Judges 1:10.

2. A Levite porter. 1 Chron. 9:17.

Ahim'elech (à-hĭm'e-lĕk) (*brother of Melech*). 1. Son of Ahitub, 1 Sam. 22:11, 12, and high priest at Nob in the days of Saul. He gave David the shewbread to eat, and the sword of Goliath; and for so doing was put to death, with his whole house, by Saul's order. Abiathar alone escaped. [ABIATHAR.] (B.C. 1085–1060.)

2. A Hittite. 1 Sam. 26:6.

Ahi'moth (à-hī'mŏth) (*brother is death*), a Levite apparently in the time of David. 1 Chron. 6:25.

Ahin'adab (à-hĭn'a-dăb) (*brother is generous*), son of Iddo, one of Solomon's twelve commissaries who supplied provisions for the royal household. 1 Kings 4 : 14.

Ahin'oam (à-hĭn'o-ăm) (*brother is pleasantness*). 1. The daughter of Ahimaaz and wife of Saul. 1 Sam. 14 : 50. 2. A native of Jezreel who was married to David during his wandering life. 1 Sam. 25 : 43. (B.C. 1060.) She lived with him and his other wife Abigail at the court of Achish, 27 : 3; was taken prisoner with her by the Amalekites when they plundered Ziklag, 30 : 5, but was rescued by David. 30 : 18. She was the mother of Amnon. 2 Sam. 3 : 2.

Ahi'o (à-hĭ'ó) (*brotherly*). 1. Son of Abinadab, who accompanied the ark when it was brought out of his father's house. 2 Sam. 6 : 3, 4; 1 Chron. 13 : 7. (B.C. 1042.) 2. A Benjamite, one of the sons of Beriah. 1 Chron. 8 : 14. 3. A Benjamite, son of Jehiel. 1 Chron. 8 : 31; 9 : 37.

Ahi'ra (à-hĭ'rà) (*Ra is brother*, i. e. *protector*). Chief of the tribe of Naphtali. Num. 1 : 15; 2 : 29; 7 : 78, 83; 10 : 27.

Ahi'ram (à-hĭ'ram) (*brother is exalted*), one of the sons of Benjamin, and ancestor of the Ahiramites. Num. 26 : 38. In Gen. 46 : 21 the name appears as "Ehi and Rosh." It is uncertain whether Ahiram is the same as AHER, 1 Chron. 7 : 12, or AHARAH, 1 Chron. 8 : 1.

Ahis'amach (à-hĭs'a-măk) (*brother has supported*), a Danite, father of Aholiab, one of the architects of the tabernacle. Ex. 31 : 6; 35 : 34; 38 : 23.

Ahish'ahar (à-hĭsh'a-här) (*brother of the dawn*), one of the sons of Bilhan, the grandson of Benjamin. 1 Chron. 7 : 10.

Ahi'shar (à-hĭ'shär), the controller of Solomon's household. 1 Kings 4 : 6.

Ahith'ophel (à-hĭth'o-fĕl) (*my brother is folly*), a native of Giloh, was a privy councillor of David, whose wisdom was highly esteemed, though his name had an exactly opposite signification. 2 Sam. 16 : 23. (B.C. 1055–1023.) He was, according to the opinion of many, the grandfather of Bath-sheba. Comp. 2 Sam. 11 : 3 with 23 : 34. Ahithophel joined the conspiracy of Absalom against David, and persuaded him to take possession of the royal harem, 2

Sam. 16 : 21, and recommended an immediate pursuit of David. His advice was wise; but Hushai advised otherwise. When Ahithophel saw that Hushai's advice prevailed, he despaired of success, and returning to his own home "put his household in order and hanged himself." 2 Sam. 17 : 1–23.

Ahi'tub (à-hĭ'tub) (*brother is goodness*). 1. The son of Phinehas and grandson of Eli, and therefore of the family of Ithamar. 1 Sam. 14 : 3; 22 : 9, 11. He was succeeded by his son Ahijah or Ahimelech. 2. Son of Amariah, and father of Zadok the high priest, 1 Chron. 6 : 7, 8; 2 Sam. 8 : 17, of the house of Eleazar.

Ah'lab (äh'lăb) (*fertile*), a city of Asher from which the Canaanites were not driven out. Judges 1 : 31.

Ah'lai (äh'lai) or **Ah'la=i** (*O that!*) 1. Daughter of Sheshan, whom, having no sons, he gave in marriage to his Egyptian slave Jarha. 1 Chron. 2 : 31, 35. She was the granddaughter of Isha, a Jerahmeelite. 2. Father (or mother?) of Zabad of Judah, one of David's mighty men, 1 Chron. 11 : 41.

Aho'ah, son of Bela, the son of Benjamin. 1 Chron. 8 : 4. In 1 Chron. 8 : 7 he is called AHIAH. The patronymic, AHOHITE, is found in 2 Sam. 23 : 9, 28; 1 Chron. 11 : 12, 29; 27 : 4.

Aho'hite. [AHOAH.]

Aho'lah (à-hō'lah) and **Aho'libah** (à-hŏ'li-bà), two symbolical names, described as harlots, the former representing Samaria and the latter Judah. Ezek. 23. R. V. Oholah and Oholibah.

Aho'liab (à-hō'li-ăb), a Danite of great skill as a weaver and embroiderer, whom Moses appointed with Bezaleel to erect the tabernacle. Ex. 35 : 30–35. (B.C. 1490.) R. V. Oholiab.

Aholiba'mah (à-hŏl-i-bà'mah) or **Aholib'amah** (*tent of the high place*), one of the three wives of Esau. (B.C. 1797.) She was the daughter of Anah. Gen. 36 : 2, 25. R. V. Oholibamah. In the earlier narrative, Gen. 26 : 34, Aholibamah is called Judith, which may have been her original name.

Ahu'mai (à-hū'ma-ĭ), son of Jahath, a descendant of Judah, and head of one of the families of the Zorathites. 1 Chron. 4 : 2. Probably of the house of Caleb. Comp. 1 Chron. 2 : 18, 19, 50.

Ahu'zam (à-hū'zam) (*possessor*), properly Ahuzzam, son of Ashur, the father or founder of Tekoa, by his wife Naarah. 1 Chron. 4 : 6.

Ahuz'zath (à-hŭz'zath) (*possession*), one of the friends of the Philistine king Abimelech, who accompanied him at his interview with Isaac. Gen. 26 : 26. (B.C. about 1804.)

A'i (ā'ī) (*heap*). 1. A city lying east of Bethel and "beside Beth-aven." Josh. 7 : 2; 8 : 9. It was the second city taken by Israel after the passage of the Jordan, and was "utterly destroyed." Its site is found at *Haiyan* about two miles S. E. of Bethel. Josh. 7 : 3–5; 8; 9 : 3; 10 : 1, 2; 12 : 9.

2. A city of the Ammonites, apparently attached to Heshbon. Jer. 49 : 3.

Ai'ah (à-ī'ah) (*falcon*). 1. Son of Zibeon, a descendant of Seir and ancestor of one of the wives of Esau, 1 Chron. 1 : 40, called in Gen. 36 : 24, AJAH. He probably died before his father, as the succession fell to his brother Anah.

2. Father of Rizpah, the concubine of Saul. 2 Sam. 3 : 7; 21 : 8, 10, 11. (B.C. before 1055.)

Ai'ath (à-ī'ath) (feminine of *Ai*), a place named by Isaiah, Isa. 10 : 28, in connection with Migron and Michmash, probably the same as Ai.

Ai'ja (à-ī'jà), like Aiath probably a variation of the name Ai, mentioned with Michmash and Bethel. Neh. 11 : 31.

Aij'alon (āj'a-lŏn) or **Aj'alon** (āj'-a-lŏn) (*place of gazelles*). 1. A city of the Kohathites. Josh. 21 : 24; 1 Chron. 6 : 69. It was a Levitical city and a city of refuge. It was originally allotted to the tribe of Dan, Josh. 19 : 42, (Authorized Version, AJALON), which tribe, however, was unable to dispossess the Amorites of the place. Judges 1 : 35. Aijalon was one of the towns fortified by Rehoboam, 2 Chron. 11 : 10, and the last we hear of it is as being in the hands of the Philistines. 2 Chron. 28 : 18. Being on the very frontier of the two kingdoms, we can understand how Aijalon should be spoken of sometimes, 1 Chron. 6 : 69, comp. with 66, as in Ephraim, and sometimes, 2 Chron. 11 : 10; 1 Sam. 14 : 31, as in Judah and Benjamin. It is represented by the modern *Yalo*, a little to the north of the Jaffa road, about 14 miles out of Jerusalem.

2. A broad and beautiful valley near the city of Aijalon over which Joshua commanded the moon to stand still during the pursuit after the battle of Gibeon. Josh. 10 : 12.

3. A place in Zebulun, mentioned as the burial-place of Elon, one of the Judges. Judges 12 : 12.

Aij'eleth Sha'har (āj'e-leth shā'-här) (*the hind of the dawn*), to be found once only in the Bible, in the title of Ps. 22. It probably is the name of the melody to which the psalm was to be sung.

A'in (ā'in) (*eye*, or *spring*). 1. One of the landmarks on the eastern boundary of Palestine. Num. 34 : 11. It is probably *'Ain el-'Azy*, the main source of the Orontes.

2. One of the southernmost cities of Judah, Josh. 15 : 32; afterwards allotted to Simeon, Josh. 19 : 7; 1 Chron. 4 : 32, and given to the priests, Josh. 21 : 16.

A'jah = Ai'ah, 1. Gen. 36 : 24.

Aj'alon (āj'a-lŏn). [AIJALON.]

A'kan (ā'kăn), son of Ezer, one of the "dukes" or chieftains of the Horites, and descendant of Seir. Gen. 36 : 27. He is called JAKAN in 1 Chron. 1 : 42.

Akel'dama. R. V. of Acts 1 : 19 for ACELDAMA.

Ak'kub (ăk'kŭb) (*insidious*). 1. A descendant of Zerubbabel and son of Elioenai. 1 Chron. 3 : 24.

2. One of the porters or doorkeepers at the east gate of the temple. 1 Chron. 9 : 17; Ezra 2 : 42; Neh. 7 : 45.

3. One of the Nethinim, whose family returned with Zerubbabel. Ezra 2 : 45. (B.C. 536.)

4. A Levite who assisted Ezra in expounding the law to the people. Neh. 8 : 7. Perhaps the same as 2.

Akrab'bim (à-krăb'bim) (*Scorpions*). The full form is MAALEH-ACRABBIM (*the scorpion pass*), a pass between the south end of the Dead Sea and Zin, forming one of the landmarks on the south boundary at once of Judah, Josh. 15 : 3, and of the Holy Land. Num. 34 : 4. Also the boundary of the Amorites. Judges 1 : 36. As to the name, scorpions abound in the whole of this district.

Alabaster, from the Arabic *al bastraton*, a whitish stone, or from *Albastron*, the place in Egypt where it is found. It occurs only in Matt. 26 : 7; Mark 14 : 3; Luke 7 : 37. The ancients considered alabaster to be the best material in which to preserve their ointments. The Oriental alabaster (referred to in the Bible) is a translucent carbonate of lime, formed on the floors of limestone caves by the percolation of water. It is of the same material as our marbles, but differently formed. It is usually clouded or banded like agate, hence sometimes called onyx marble.

ALABASTER VASES

Inscription on the center vessel denotes the quantity it holds.

Our common alabaster is different from this, being a variety of gypsum or sulphate of lime, used in its finer forms for vases, etc.; in the coarser it is ground up for plaster of Paris. The noted sculptured slabs from Nineveh are made of this material.

Al′ameth (ăl′a-mĕth), properly **Al′ =emeth** (*covering*), one of the sons of Becher, the son of Benjamin. 1 Chron. 7: 8.

Alam′melech (à-lăm′mē-lĕk) (*king's oak*), a place within the limits of Asher, named between Achshaph and Amad. Josh. 19: 26 only.

Al′amoth (ăl′a-mŏth) (*virgins*). Ps. 46, title; 1 Chron. 15: 20. Some interpret it to mean a musical instrument, and others a melody for treble voices.

Al′emeth (ăl′e-mĕth) (*covering*). 1. A Benjamite, son of Jehoadah or Jarah. 1 Chron. 8: 36; 9: 42, and descended from Jonathan the son of Saul.

2. A Levitical city of Benjamin. 1 Chron. 6: 60. Given as Almon in Joshua 21: 18. Now *Almit* on the hills north of Anathoth.

Alexan′der III. (*defender of men*), king of Macedon, surnamed the Great, the son of Philip and Olympias, was born at Pella B.C. 356, and succeeded his father B.C. 336. Two years afterwards he crossed the Hellespont (B.C. 334) to carry out the plans of his father, and execute the mission of Greece to the civilized world. He subjugated Syria and Palestine B.C. 334–332. Egypt next submitted to him B.C. 331, and in this year he founded Alexandria. In the same year he finally defeated Darius at Gaugamela, who in B.C. 330 was murdered. The next two years were occupied by Alexander in the consolidation of his Persian conquests and the reduction of Bactria. In B.C. 327 he crossed the Indus; turning westward he reached Susa B.C. 325, and proceeded to Babylon B.C. 324, which he chose as the capital of his empire. In the next year (B.C. 323) he died there of intemperance, at the early age of 32, in the midst of his gigantic plans; and those who inherited his conquests left his designs unachieved and unattempted. Alexander is generally supposed to be intended in Dan. 2 : 39 and also Dan. 7 : 6; 8 : 5–7; 11 : 3, 4, the latter indicating the rapidity of his conquests and his power. He ruled with great dominion, and did according to his will, Dan. 11 : 3; "and there was none that could deliver . . . out of his hand." Dan. 8 : 7.

Alexan′der (ăl-ĕx-ăn′dẽr). 1. Son of Simon the Cyrenian, who was compelled to bear the cross for our Lord. Mark 15 : 21.

2. One of the kindred of Annas the high priest. Acts 4 : 6.

3. A Jew at Ephesus whom his countrymen put forward during the tumult raised by Demetrius the silversmith, Acts 19 : 33, to plead their cause with the mob.

4. An Ephesian Christian reprobated by St. Paul in 1 Tim. 1 : 20 as having, together with one Hymenæus, put from him faith and a good conscience, and so made shipwreck concerning the faith. This may be the same with

5. Alexander the coppersmith, mentioned by the same apostle, 2 Tim. 4 : 14, as having done him many mischiefs.

Alexan′dria (ăl-ĕx-ăn′drĭ-à) (from *Alexander*, by whom it was founded), Acts 18 : 24; 6 : 9, the Hellenic, Roman and Christian capital of Egypt.

Situation.—Alexandria was situated on the Mediterranean Sea, directly opposite the island of Pharos, 12 miles west of the Canopic branch of the Nile and 120 miles from the present city of Cairo.

It was founded by Alexander the Great, B.C. 331, who himself traced the ground plan of the city. The work thus begun was continued after the death of Alexander by the Ptolemies.

Description.—Under the despotism of the later Ptolemies the trade of Alex-

POMPEY'S PILLAR, ALEXANDRIA.

andria declined, but its population and wealth were enormous. Its importance as one of the chief grain ports of Rome secured for it the general favor of the first emperors. Its population was mixed from the first. According to Josephus, Alexander himself assigned to the Jews a place in his new city. Philo estimates the number of the Alexandrine Jews in his time at a little less than 1,000,000; and adds that two of the five districts of Alexandria were called "Jewish districts," and that many Jews lived scattered in the remaining three. "For a long period Alexandria was the greatest of known cities." After Rome became the chief city of the world, Alexandria ranked second to Rome in wealth and importance, and second to Athens only in literature and science. Its collection of books grew to be the greatest library of ancient times, and contained at one time 700,000 rolls or volumes. Here was made the Septuagint translation of the Old Testament into Greek, begun about B.C. 285. The commerce of Alexandria, especially in grain, was very great. According to the common legend, St. Mark first "preached the gospel in Egypt, and founded the first church in Alexandria." At the beginning of the second century the number of Christians at Alexandria

must have been very large, and the great leaders of Gnosticism who arose there (Basilides, Valentinus) exhibit an exaggeration of the tendency of the Church. "Cleopatra's Needle," now set up in New York, was taken from this city.

Present Condition.—The city still bears the same name and is a thriving metropolis, with inhabitants from nearly every European and Oriental nation.

Alexan′drians, the Jewish colonists of Alexandria, who were admitted to the privileges of citizenship and had had a synagogue at Jerusalem. Acts 6 : 9.

Algum or **Almug Trees,** the former

THE ALMUG.

occurring in 2 Chron. 2 : 8; 9 : 10, 11, the latter in 1 Kings 10 : 11, 12. These words are identical. From 1 Kings 10 : 11, 12; 2 Chron. 9 : 10, 11, we learn that the almug was brought in great plenty from Ophir for Solomon's temple and house, and for the construction of musical instruments. It is probable that this tree is the red sandal wood, which is a native of India and Ceylon. The wood is very heavy, hard and fine grained, and of a beautiful garnet color.

Ali′ah (à-lī′ah). [ALVAH.]

Ali′an (à-lī′an). [ALVAN.]

Allegory, a figure of speech, which has been defined by Bishop Marsh, in accordance with its etymology, as "a representation of one thing which is intended to excite the representation of another thing." "A figurative representation containing a meaning other than and in addition to the literal." "A fable or parable is a short allegory with one definite moral."—*Encyc. Brit.* In every allegory there is a twofold sense—the immediate or historic, which is understood from the words, and the ultimate, which is concerned with the things signified by the words. The allegorical interpretation is not of the words, but of the things signified by them, and not only may, but actually does, coexist with the literal interpretation in every allegory, whether the narrative in which it is conveyed be of things possible or real. An illustration of this may be seen in Gal. 4:24, where the apostle gives an allegorical interpretation to the historical narrative of Hagar and Sarah, not treating that narrative as an allegory in itself, as our Authorized Version would lead us to suppose, but drawing from it a deeper sense than is conveyed by the immediate representation. (Addison's *Vision of Mirza* and Bunyan's *Pilgrim's Progress* are among the best allegories in all literature.)

Alleluia, so written in Rev. 19:1, foll., or more properly HALLELUJAH, *praise ye Jehovah,* as it is found in the margin of Ps. 104:35; 105:45; 106:1; 111:1; 112:1; 113:1; comp. Ps. 113:9; 115:18; 116:19; 117:2. The literal meaning of "hallelujah" sufficiently indicates the character of the Psalms in which it occurs as hymns of praise and thanksgiving.

Alliances. On the first establishment of the Hebrews in Palestine no connections were formed between them and the surrounding nations. But with the extension of their power under the kings alliances became essential to the security of their commerce. Solomon concluded two important treaties exclusively for commercial purposes; the first with Hiram king of Tyre, 1 Kings 5: 2-12; 9:27, the second with a Pharaoh, king of Egypt, 1 Kings 10:28, 29. When war broke out between Amaziah and Jeroboam II. a coalition was formed between Rezin, king of Syria, and Pekah on the one side, and Ahaz and Tiglath-pileser, king of Assyria, on the other, 2 Kings 16:5-9.

The formation of an alliance was attended with various religious rites. A victim was slain and divided into two parts, between which the contracting parties passed. Gen. 15:10. Generally

speaking, the oath alone is mentioned in the contracting of alliances, either between nations, Josh. 9:15, or individuals. Gen. 26:28; 31:53; 1 Sam. 20; 17; 2 Kings 11:4. The event was celebrated by a feast. Gen. 26:30; Ex. 24: 11; 2 Sam. 3:12, 20. Salt, as symbolical of fidelity, was used on these occasions. Occasionally a pillar or a heap of stones was set up as a memorial of the alliance. Gen. 31:52. Presents were also sent by the parties soliciting the alliance. 1 Kings 15:18; Isa. 30:6; 1 Macc. 15:18. The fidelity of the Jews to their engagements was conspicuous at all periods of their history, Josh. 9: 18, and any breach of covenant was visited with very severe punishment. 2 Sam. 21:1; Ezek. 17:16.

Al'lon (ăl'lŏn) (*an oak*), a Simeonite, ancestor of Ziza, a prince of his tribe in the reign of Hezekiah. 1 Chron. 4:37.

Allon (ăl'lŏn), a large strong tree of some description, probably an oak.

1. ALLON, more accurately ELON, a place named among the cities of Naphtali. Josh. 19:33. Probably the more correct construction is to take it with the following word, *i. e.,* "the oak by Zaanannim."

2. ALLON-BACHUTH (ăl'lŏn-băk'uth) (*oak of weeping*), the tree under which Rebekah's nurse, Deborah, was buried. Gen. 35:8.

Almo'dad (ăl-mō'dăd), the first in order of the descendants of Joktan. Gen. 10:26; 1 Chron. 1:20.

Al'mon (ăl'mŏn) (*concealed*), a city within the tribe of Benjamin, with "suburbs" given to the priests. Josh. 21:18. [ALEMETH.]

Al'mon-diblatha'im (ăl'mŏn-dĭb-la-thā'ĭm) (*concealing the two cakes*), one of the latest stations of the Israelites, between Dibon-gad and the mountains of Abarim. Num. 33:46, 47. It is probably identical with Beth-diblathaim.

Almond Tree; Almond. This word is found in Gen. 43:11; Ex. 25:33, 34; 37:19, 20; Num. 17:8; Eccles. 12:5; Jer. 1:11, in the text of the Authorized Version. The Hebrew means *to wake* or *watch,* because it is the first to awake from the sleep of winter. The tree is a native of Asia and North Africa, but it is cultivated in the milder parts of Europe. "It resembles the peach tree in form, blossom and fruit. It is in fact only another species of the same genus." The height of the tree is about 15 to 30 feet; the flowers are pink, and arranged for the most part in pairs; the leaves are long ovate, with a serrated margin and an acute point. The covering of the fruit is downy and succulent, enclosing the hard shell which contains the kernel. It is this nut for

ALMOND.

which the tree is chiefly valued. It is curious to observe, in connection with the almond-bowls of the golden candlestick, that, in the language of lapidaries, almonds are pieces of rock crystal, even now used in adorning branch candlesticks.

Alms. The duty of alms-giving, especially in kind, consisting chiefly in portions to be left designedly from produce of the field, the vineyard and the oliveyard, Lev. 19:9, 10; 23:22; Deut. 15:11; 24:19; 26:2-13; Ruth 2:2, is strictly enjoined by the law. Every third year also, Deut. 14:28, 29, each proprietor was directed to share the tithe of his produce with "the Levite, the stranger, the fatherless and the widow." The theological estimate of alms-giving among the Jews is indicated in the following passages: Job 31:17; Prov. 10:2; 11:4; Esther 9:22; Ps. 112:9; Acts 9:36, the case of Dorcas; 10:2, of Cornelius; to which may be added Tobit 4:10, 11; 14:10, 11, and Ecclus. 3:30; 40:24. The Pharisees were zealous in alms-giving, but too ostentatious in their mode of performance, for which our Lord finds fault with them. Matt. 6:2. The duty of relieving the poor was not neglected by the Christians. Matt. 6:1-4. Luke 14:13; Acts 20:

35; Gal. 2:10. Regular proportionate giving was expected. Acts 11:29; Rom. 15:25-27; 1 Cor. 16:1-4.

Almug Trees. [ALGUM TREES.]

Aloes, Lign Aloes (in Heb. *Ahalim, Ahaloth*), the name of a costly and sweet-smelling wood which is mentioned in Num. 24:6; Ps. 45:8; Prov.

LIGN ALOES.

7:17; Cant. 4:14; John 19:39. It is usually identified with the *Aquilaria agallocha,* an aromatic wood much valued in India. This tree sometimes grows to the height of 120 feet, being 12 feet in girth.

A'loth (ā'lŏth), a place or district, forming with Asher the jurisdiction of the ninth of Solomon's commissariat officers. 1 Kings 4:16.

Alpha (ăl'fä) (A), the first letter of the Greek alphabet. With *Omega* (Ω), the last letter, it is used in the Old Testament and in the New to express the eternity of God, as including both the beginning and the end. Rev. 1:8, 11; 21:6; 22:13; Isa. 41:4; 44:6; hence these letters became a favorite symbol of the eternal divinity of our

Lord, and were used for this purpose in connection with the cross, or the monogram of Christ (*i. e.,* the first two letters, *ch* and *r,* of Christ's name in Greek). Both Greeks and Hebrews employed the letters of the alphabet as numerals.

Alphabet. [WRITING.]

Alphæ'us (ăl-fē'ŭs) (*changing*). 1. The father of the apostle James the

Less. Matt. 10 : 3 ; Mark 3 : 18 ; Luke 6 : 15 ; Acts 1 : 13. He has been identified with Cleophas, R. V. Clopas, the husband of Mary, John 19 : 25, but the identification is very doubtful. But comp. Mark 15 : 40. For a fuller discussion see JAMES.

2. Father of the Apostle Matthew. Mark 2 : 14, comp. Matt. 9 : 9.

Altar. The first altar of which we have any account is that built by Noah when he left the ark. Gen. 8 : 20. In the early times altars were usually built in certain spots hallowed by religious

ANCIENT ROCK ALTAR AT MEGIDDO.
(With cavities for receiving fluid offerings.)

associations, *e. g.*, where God appeared. Gen. 12 : 7 ; 13 : 18 ; 26 : 25 ; 35 : 1. Though generally erected for the offering of sacrifice, in some instances they appear to have been only memorials. Gen. 12 : 7 ; Ex. 17 : 15, 16. Altars were most probably originally made of earth. The law of Moses allowed them to be made of either earth or unhewn stones. Ex. 20 : 24, 25.

I. *The Altar of Burnt Offering.* It differed in construction at different times. (1) In the tabernacle, Ex. 27 : 1 ff.; 38 : 1 ff., it was comparatively small and portable. In shape it was square. It was five cubits in length, the same in breadth, and three cubits high. It was made of planks of shittim (or acacia) wood overlaid with brass. The interior was hollow. Ex. 27 : 8. At the four corners were four projections called horns, made, like the altar itself, of shittim wood overlaid with brass, Ex. 27 : 2. and to them the victim was

bound when about to be sacrificed. Ps. 118 : 27. Round the altar, midway between the top and bottom, ran a projecting ledge, on which perhaps the priest stood when officiating. To the outer edge of this, again, a grating or net work of brass was affixed, and

EGYPTIAN ALTAR FIGURE.

reached to the bottom of the altar. At the four corners of the network were four brazen rings, into which were inserted the staves by which the altar was carried. These staves were of the same materials as the altar itself. As the priests were forbidden to ascend the altar by steps, Ex. 20 : 26, it has been conjectured that a slope of earth led gradually up to the ledge from which they officiated. The place of the altar was at "the door of the tabernacle of the congregation." Ex. 40 : 29. (2) In Solomon's temple the altar was considerably larger in its dimensions. It differed too in the material of which it was made, being entirely of brass. 1 Kings 8 : 64 ; 2 Chron. 7 : 7. It had no grating, and instead of a single gradual slope, the ascent to it was probably made by three successive platforms, to each of which it has been supposed that steps led. The altar erected by Herod in front of the temple was 15 cubits in height and 50 cubits in length and breadth. According to Lev. 6 : 12, 13, a perpetual fire was to be kept burning on the altar.

II. *The Altar of Incense,* called also the *golden* altar to distinguish it from the altar of burnt offering, which was called the *brazen altar.* Ex. 38 : 30. (*a*) That in the tabernacle was made of acacia wood, overlaid with pure gold. In shape it was square, being a cubit in length and breadth and two cubits in height. Like the altar of burnt offering it had horns at the four corners, which were of one piece with the rest of the altar. This altar stood in the holy place, "before the vail that is by the ark of the testimony." Ex. 30 : 6 ; 40 : 5. (*b*) The altar of Solomon's temple was similar, 1 Kings 7 : 48 ; 1 Chron. 28 : 18, but was made of cedar overlaid with gold.

III. *Other Altars.* In Acts 17 : 23 reference is made to an altar to an unknown god. There were several altars in Athens with this inscription, erected during the time of a plague, since they knew not what god was offended and required to be propitiated.

Al-taschith (ăl-tăs'chĭth) (*destroy not*), found in the introductory verse to Psalms 57, 58, 59, 75. It was probably the beginning of some song or poem to the tune of which those psalms were to be chanted.

A'lush (ā'lŭsh) (*tumult of men*), one of the stations of the Israelites on their journey to Sinai, the last before Rephidim. Num. 33 : 13, 14.

Al'vah (*tall*), a duke of Edom, Gen. 36 : 40 ; written ALIAH in 1 Chron. 1 : 51.

Al'van (*tall*), a Horite, son of Shobal, Gen. 36 : 23 ; written ALIAN in 1 Chron. 1 : 40.

A'mad (ā'măd) (*domicile*), an unknown place in Asher, between Alammelech and Misheal. Josh. 19 : 26 only.

A'mal (ā'măl) (*labor*), an Asherite, son of Helem. 1 Chron. 7 : 35.

Am'alek (ăm'a-lĕk), a son of Eliphaz by his concubine Timnah, grandson of Esau, and chieftain ("duke," Authorized Version) of Edom. Gen. 36 : 12, 16 ; 1 Chron. 1 : 36.

Am'alekites (ăm'a-lĕk-ītes), a nomadic tribe descended from Esau, which occupied the peninsula of Sinai and the wilderness intervening between the southern hill-ranges of Palestine and the border of Egypt. Num. 13 : 29 ; 1 Sam. 15 : 7 ; 27 : 8. Their wealth consisted in flocks and herds. Mention is made of a "city," 1 Sam. 15 : 5, but their towns could have been little more than stations or nomadic enclosures. The Amalekites first came in contact with the Israelites at Rephidim, but were signally defeated. Ex. 17 : 8-16. In union with the Canaanites they again attacked the Israelites on the borders of Palestine, and defeated them near Hormah, Num. 14 : 45. Saul undertook an expedition against them. 1 Sam. 14 : 48. Their power was thenceforth broken, and they degenerated into a horde of banditti. Their destruction was completed by David. 1 Sam. 30 : 1-17.

Am'alekites, Mount of, a mountain in Ephraim, Judges 12 : 15, probably so named because the Amalekites once held possession of it.

A'mam (ā'mam), a city in the south of Judah, named with Shema and Moladah in Josh. 15 : 26 only.

Am'ana (ăm'a-nà) (*a covenant*), apparently a mountain in or near Lebanon. Cant. 4 : 8. It is commonly assumed that this is the mountain in which the river Abana, 2 Kings 5 : 12, has its source.

Amari'ah (ăm-a-rī'ah) (*Jehovah hath promised*). 1. Father of Ahitub, according to 1 Chron. 6 : 7, 52, and son of Meraioth, in the line of the high priests.

2. The high priest in the reign of Jehoshaphat. 2 Chron. 19 : 11.

3. The head of a Levitical house of the Kohathites. 1 Chron. 23 : 19 ; 24 : 23.

4. The head of one of the twenty-four courses of priests. 2 Chron. 31 : 15.

5. One of the sons of Bani in the time of Ezra. Ezra 10 : 42.

6. A priest who returned with Zerubbabel. Neh. 10 : 3 ; 12 : 2, 13.

7. A descendant of Pharez. Neh. 11 : 4.

8. An ancestor of Zephaniah the prophet. Zeph. 1 : 1.

9. Another in the high-priestly line. 1 Chron. 6 : 11 ; Ezra 7 : 3.

Am'asa (ăm'a-sà) (*a burden*). 1

Son of Ithra or Jether, by Abigail, David's sister. 2 Sam. 17:25. He joined in Absalom's rebellion, B.C. 1023, was appointed commander-in-chief, and suffered defeat by Joab. 2 Sam. 18:6–8. David, incensed against Joab for killing Absalom, forgave Amasa and appointed him Joab's successor. 2 Sam. 19:13. Joab afterwards, when they were both in pursuit of the rebel Sheba, pretending to salute Amasa, stabbed him with his sword. 2 Sam. 20:10.

2. A prince of Ephraim, son of Hadlai, in the reign of Ahaz. 2 Chron. 28:12.

Amas'ai (à-mas'a-ī), or **Amasa'i** (*burdensome*). 1. A Kohathite, father of Mahath and ancestor of Samuel. 1 Chron. 6:25, 35.

2. Chief of the captains of Judah and Benjamin, who deserted to David while an outlaw at Ziklag. 1 Chron. 12:18. (B.C. 1057.)

3. One of the priests who blew trumpets before the ark. 1 Chron. 15:24.

4. Another Kohathite, in the reign of Hezekiah. 2 Chron. 29:12.

Amash'ai (à-măsh'a-ī), or **Amasha'i** (*burdensome*), son of Azareel, a priest in the time of Nehemiah, Neh. 11:13.

Amasi'ah (ăm-a-sī'ah) (*Jehovah hath borne*), son of Zichri and captain of 200,000 warriors of Judah in the reign of Jehoshaphat. 2 Chron. 17:16. (B.C. 910.)

A'math. [HAMATH.]

Amazi'ah (ăm-a-zī'ah) (*Jehovah is strong*). 1. Son of Joash, and ninth king of Judah, reigned B.C. 796–767. He succeeded to the throne at the age of 25, on the murder of his father, and punished the murderers. In order to restore his kingdom to the greatness of Jehoshaphat's days, he made war on the Edomites, defeated them in the Valley of Salt, south of the Dead Sea, and took their capital, Selah or Petra, to which he gave the name of Jokteel, *i. e.* "God-subdued." Flushed with his success, he challenged Joash king of Israel to battle, but was completely defeated, and himself was taken prisoner and conveyed by Joash to Jerusalem, which opened its gates to the conqueror. Amaziah lived 15 years after the death of Joash; and in the 29th year of his reign was murdered by conspirators at Lachish, whither he had retired from Jerusalem for safety. 2 Kings 14:1–20; 2 Chron. 25:1–27.

2. A descendant of Simeon. 1 Chron. 4:34.

3. A Levite who is mentioned in 1 Chron. 6:45.

4. Priest of the golden calf at Bethel, who endeavored to drive the prophet Amos from Israel into Judah. Amos 7:10, 12, 14.

Ambassador, a person of high rank employed by a government to represent it and transact its business at the seat of government of some other power. The earliest examples of ambassadors employed occur in Num. 20:14; 21:21; afterwards in that of the fraudulent Gibeonites, Josh. 9:4, etc., and in the instances of civic strife mentioned in Judges 11:12 and 20:12. Ambassadors are found to have been employed not only on occasions of hostile challenge or insolent menace, 1 Kings 20:2, 6; 2 Kings 14:8, but of friendly compliment, of request for alliance or other aid, of submissive deprecation and of curious inquiry. 2 Kings 16:7; 18:14; 2 Chron. 32:31. Ministers are called ambassadors of Christ.

Ambassage, embassy, a message of a public nature brought by ambassadors. The word also sometimes includes the ambassadors themselves. Luke 14:32.

Amber (Heb. *chasmal*) occurs only in Ezek. 1:4, 27; 8:2. It is usually supposed that the Hebrew word *chasmal* denotes a metal. But Cheyne's "Encyclopædia Biblica" decides in favor of the yellow amber.

Amen, literally "true;" and, used as a substantive, "that which is true," "truth," Rev. 3:14; a word used in strong asseverations, fixing, as it were, the stamp of truth upon the assertion which it accompanied, and making it binding as an oath. Comp. Num. 5:22. In the synagogues and private houses it was customary for the people or members of the family who were present to say "amen" to the prayers which were offered. Matt. 6:13; 1 Cor. 14:16. And not only public prayers, but those offered in private, and doxologies, were appropriately concluded with "amen." Rom. 9:5; 11:36; 15:33; 16:27; 2 Cor. 13:14, etc.

Amethyst (Heb. *achlamah*), a subspecies of quartz of a bluish-violet color. Mention is made of this precious stone, which formed the third in the third row of the high priest's breastplate, in Ex.

28:19; 39:12. It occurs also in Rev. 21:20.

A'mi (ā'mī), one of the descendants of Solomon's servants, Ezra 2:57; called AMON in Neh. 7:59.

Amin'adab (à-mĭn'a-dăb). Matt. 1:4; Luke 3:33. [AMMINADAB 1.]

Amit'tai (à-mĭt'ta-ī) (*true*), father of the prophet Jonah. 2 Kings 14:25; Jonah 1:1.

Am'mah (ăm'mah) (*head*), **The hill of,** a hill facing Giah by the way of the wilderness of Gibeon, named as the point to which Joab pursued Abner. 2 Sam. 2:24.

Am'mi (ăm'mī), *i. e.,* as explained in the margin of the Authorized Version, *my people.* Hos. 2:1.

Am'miel (ăm'mĭ-el) (*God is my kinsman*). 1. The spy from the tribe of Dan. Num. 13:12. (B.C. 1490.) He perished by the plague for his evil report.

2. Father of Machir of Lo-debar. 2 Sam. 9:4, 5; 17:27.

3. Father of Bath-sheba, 1 Chron. 3:5, called ELIAM in 2 Sam. 11:3.

4. The sixth son of Obed-edom, 1 Chron. 26:5, and one of the doorkeepers of the temple.

Am'mihud (ăm'mĭ-hŭd) (*my kinsman is glory*). 1. An Ephraimite, father of Elishama, the chief of the tribe at the time of the Exodus. Num. 1:10; 2:18; 7:48, 53; 10:22; 1 Chron. 7:26, and, through him, ancestor of Joshua.

2. A Simeonite, father of Shemuel. Num. 34:20.

3. The father of Pedahel, prince of the tribe of Naphtali. Num. 34:28.

4. The father of Talmai king of Geshur. 2 Sam. 13:37.

5. A descendant of Pharez, son of Judah. 1 Chron. 9:4.

Ammin'adab (ăm-mĭn'a-dăb) (*my kinsman is generous*). 1. Son of Ram or Aram, and father of Nahshon, or NAASSON (as it is written Matt. 1:4; Luke 3:33); Num. 1:7; 2:3; Ruth 4:19, 20; 1 Chron. 2:10. One of the ancestors of Jesus Christ.

2. The chief of the 112 sons of Uzziel, a junior Levitical house of the family of the Kohathites. Ex. 6:23; 1 Chron. 15:10, 11.

3. In 1 Chron. 6:22, Izhar, the son of Kohath, is called AMMINADAB; probably a clerical error.

Ammin'adib (ăm-mĭn'a-dĭb). Probably another form of Amminadab. He was noted for the swiftness of his chariots. Cant. 6:12. It is uncertain whether we ought to read here AMMINADIB, with the Authorized Version, or *my willing people,* as in the margin.

Ammishad'dai (ăm'mi-shăd'da-ī) (*kinsman is the Almighty*), the father of Ahiezer, prince of the tribe of Dan at the time of the Exodus. Num. 1:12; 2:25; 7:66, 71; 10:25.

Ammiz'abad (ăm-mĭz'a-băd) (*kinsman has made a present*), the son of Benaiah, who commanded the third division of David's army. 1 Chron. 27:6.

Am'mon (ăm'mŏn), **Am'monites** (ăm'mon-ītes), **Children of Ammon,** a people descended from Ben-ammi, the son of Lot by his younger daughter. Gen. 19:38; comp. Ps. 83:7, 8. The Ammonites are frequently mentioned with the Moabites (descendants of Ben-ammi's half-brother), and sometimes under the same name. Comp. Judges 10:6; 2 Chron. 20:1; Zeph. 2:8, etc. The precise position of the territory of the Ammonites is not ascertainable. In the earliest mention of them, they seem to have a settled place won by conquest of "giants" called Zamzummim. Num. 21:24; Deut. 2:19–21, 37; 3:16. Land or country is, however, but rarely ascribed to them. Their capital city was Rabbath, called also Rabbath Ammon, on the Jabbok. We find everywhere traces of the fierce habits of marauders in their incursions, 1 Sam. 11:2; Amos 1:13, and a very high degree of crafty cruelty to their foes. Jer. 49:1–6; Judges 11:12. Moab was the settled and civilized half of the nation of Lot, and Ammon formed its predatory and Bedouin section. On the west of Jordan they never obtained a footing. The hatred in which the Ammonites were held by Israel is stated to have arisen partly from their denial of assistance, Deut. 23:4, to the Israelites on their approach to Canaan. But whatever its origin the animosity continued in force to the latest date. The tribe was governed by a king, Judges 11:12, etc.; 1 Sam. 12:12; 2 Sam. 10:1; Jer. 40:14, and by "princes." 2 Sam. 10:3; 1 Chron. 19:3. The divinity of the tribe was Molech [MOLECH], and they were gross idolaters.

Ammoni'tess, a woman of Ammonite race. 1 Kings 14:21, 31; 2 Chron. 12:13.

Am′mon=no. See No-AMON.

Am′non (ăm′nŏn) (*faithful*). 1. Eldest son of David. He dishonored his half-sister Tamar, and was in consequence murdered by her brother. 2 Sam. 13 : 1–29.

2. Son of Shimon. 1 Chron. 4 : 20.

A′mok (ā′mok), a priest who returned with Zerubbabel. Neh. 12 : 7, 20. (B.C. 536.)

A′mon (ā′mon) or **A′men** (*the hidden one*), an Egyptian divinity, whose name occurs in that of No-amon. Nah. 3 : 8. Amen was one of the eight gods of the first order, and chief of the triad of Thebes. He was worshiped at that city as Amen Ra, or "Amen the Sun."

A′mon (ā′mon) (*a master workman*). 1. One of Ahab's governors. 1 Kings 22 : 26; 2 Chron. 18 : 25.

2. Same as AMI. Neh. 7 : 59.

3. King of Judah, son and successor of Manasseh, reigned two years, from B.C. 641–639. Amon devoted himself wholly to the service of false gods, but was killed in a conspiracy, and was succeeded by his son Josiah. 2 Kings 21.

Am′orite, the Am′orites (ăm′ŏr-ītes) (commonly explained as *mountaineer*, but the explanation is doubtful). One of the chief nations who possessed the land of Canaan before its conquest by the Israelites. As dwelling on the elevated portions of the country, they are contrasted with the Canaanites, who were the dwellers in the lowlands; and the two thus formed the main broad divisions of the Holy Land, Num. 13 : 29; and see Gen. 14 : 7; Deut. 1 : 7, 20, "mountain of the Amorites," 44; Josh. 5 : 1; 10 : 6; 11 : 3. They first occupied the barren heights west of the Dead Sea, at the place called afterwards Engedi. From this point they stretched west to Hebron. At the date of the invasion of the country, Sihon, their then king, had taken the rich pasture land south of the Jabbok. This rich tract, bounded by the Jabbok on the north, the Arnon on the south, the Jordan on the west and "the wilderness" on the east, Judges 11 : 21, 22, was, perhaps, in the most special sense the "land of the Amorites," Num. 21 : 31; Josh. 12 : 2, 3; 13 : 10; Judges 11 : 21, 22; but their possessions are distinctly stated to have extended to the very foot of Hermon, Deut. 3 : 8; 4 : 48, embracing "Gilead and all Bashan," 3 :

10, with the Jordan valley on the east of the river. 4 : 49. After the conquest

AMON.

or Canaan nothing of importance is heard of the Amorites in the Bible.

A′mos (*burden*), native of Tekoa in Judah, about six miles south of Bethlehem, originally a shepherd and dresser of sycomore trees, who was called by God's Spirit to be a prophet, although not trained in any of the regular prophetic schools. Amos 1 : 1; 7 : 14, 15. He travelled from Judah into the northern kingdom of Israel or Ephraim, and there exercised his ministry, apparently not for any long time. His date cannot be later than B.C. 741, for he lived in the reigns of Uzziah king of Judah and Jeroboam II. king of Israel; but his ministry probably took place at an earlier date, perhaps about the middle of Jeroboam's reign. Nothing is known of the time or manner of his death.

A′mos, Book of. The book of the prophecies of Amos seems to be divided into four principal portions closely connected together. (1) From 1 : 1 to 2 : 3 he denounces the sins of the nations bordering on Israel and Judah. (2) From 2 : 4 to 6 : 14 he describes the state of those two kingdoms, especially the former. (3) From 7 : 1 to 9 : 10 he relates his visit to Bethel, and sketches the impending punishment of Israel. At last he promises blessings. The chief peculiarity of the style consists in the number of allusions to natural objects and agricultural occupations, as might be expected from the early life of the author.

A'moz (ā'mŏz) (*strong*), father of the prophet Isaiah, and, according to rabbinical tradition, brother of Amaziah king of Judah. 2 Kings 19:2, 20; 20: 1; Isa. 1:1.

Amphip'olis (ăm-fĭp'o-lĭs) (*a city surrounded* by water), a city of Macedonia, through which Paul and Silas passed on their way from Philippi to Thessalonica. Acts 17:1. It was distant 33 Roman miles from Philippi, to the southwest, and about three miles from the sea. Its site is now occupied by a village called *Neokhorio;* in Turkish *Jeni-Keui,* or " New Town."

Am'plias (ăm'plĭ-ăs) (*large*), a Christian at Rome. Rom. 16:8.

Amplia'tus (R. V., Rom. 16:8) the full name of which AMPLIAS, above, is the contraction. The name in this form is " common in the sepulchral inscriptions of persons connected with Cæsar's household."

Am'ram (ăm'răm) (*an exalted people*). 1. A Levite of the family of the Kohathites, and father of Moses. Ex. 3:18, 20; Num. 26:59.

2. A son of Dishon and descendant of Seir, 1 Chron. 1:41; properly " Hamram "= HEMDAN in Gen. 36:26.

3. One of the sons of Bani in the time of Ezra, who had married a foreign wife. Ezra 10:34. (B.C. 459.)

Am'ramites. A branch of the great Kohathite family of the tribe of Levi, Num. 3:27; 1 Chron. 26:23; descended from Amram, the father of Moses.

Am'raphel (ăm'ra-fĕl), generally identified with Hammurabi the first to make a united kingdom of Babylonia. He joined in the incursion of the Elamite Chedorlaomer against the kings of Sodom and Gomorrah and the cities of the plain. Gen. 14. (B.C. 2100 or 2200.)

Amulets were ornaments, gems, scrolls, etc., worn as preservatives against the power of enchantments, and generally inscribed with mystic forms or characters. The " earrings " in the Bible (in some cases nose-rings) were often ornamented with some talis-manic symbol, and served as amulets. Those in Gen. 35:4 are often supposed to be of this sort. They are subsequently mentioned among the spoils of Midian. Judges 8:24. The " earrings " in Isa. 3:20 were also amulets, as in R. V.

Am'zi (ăm'zī) (*strong*). 1. A Levite of the family of Merari. 1 Chron. 6: 46.

2. A priest. Neh. 11:12.

A'nab (ā'năb) (*grape*), a town in the mountains of Judah, Josh. 15:50, named with Debir and Hebron as once belonging to the Anakim. Josh. 11:21.

A'nah (ā'nah) (*hearkening to*), the son of Zibeon and father of Aholibamah, one of Esau's wives. Gen. 36: 2, 14, 25. He is supposed to have discovered the " hot springs " (not " mules," as in the Authorized Version) in the desert as he fed the asses of Zibeon his father.

Ana'harath (ăn-a'hā-rath) (*gorge* or *pass*), a place within the border of Issachar, named with Shihon and Rabbith. Josh. 19:19.

Anai'ah (ăn-a-i'ah) (*Jehovah has answered*). 1. Probably a priest. Neh. 8:4.

2. One of the "heads of the people" who signed the covenant with Nehemiah. Neh. 10:22.

An'akim (ăn'a-kĭm) (*long-necked*), a race of giants, descendants of Arba, Josh. 15:13; 21:11, dwelling in the southern part of Canaan, and particularly at Hebron, which from their progenitor received the name of " city of Arba." Anak was the name of the race rather than that of an individual. Josh. 14:15. The race appears to have been divided into three tribes or families, bearing the names Sheshai, Ahiman and Talmai. Though the warlike appearance of the Anakim had struck the Israelites with terror in the time of Moses, Num. 13:28; Deut. 9:2, they were nevertheless dispossessed by Joshua, Josh. 11:21, 22, and their chief city, Hebron became the possession of Caleb. Josh. 15:14; Judges 1:20. After this time they vanish from history.

An'amim, a Mizraite people or tribe. Gen. 10:13; 1 Chron. 1:11.

Anam'melech (à-năm'me-lĕk) (*god Anu is king*), one of the idols worshiped by the colonists introduced into Samaria from Sepharvaim. 2 Kings 17:31. He was worshiped with rites resembling those of Molech, and is the companion-god to Adrammelech.

A'nan (ā'nan) (*a cloud*), one of the "heads of the people" who signed the covenant with Nehemiah. Neh. 10 : 26.

Ana'ni (ăn-ā'nī) ([God] *hath covered*), the seventh son of Elioenai, descended from the royal line of Judah. 1 Chron. 3 : 24.

Anani'ah (ăna-nī'ă) (*Jehovah hath covered*), probably a priest, and ancestor of Azariah, who assisted in rebuilding the city wall in the days of Nehemiah. Neh. 3 : 23.

Anani'ah, a place, named between Nob and Hazor, in which the Benjamites lived after their return from captivity. Neh. 11 : 32.

Anani'as (ăn-a-nī'as) (*Jehovah hath been gracious*). 1. A high priest in Acts 23 : 2–5 ; 24 : 1. He was the son of Nedebæus. He was nominated to the office by Herod king of Chalcis, in A. D. 47 ; was deposed shortly before Felix left the province, and assassinated by the Sicarii at the beginning of the last Jewish war.

2. A disciple at Jerusalem, husband of Sapphira. Acts 5 : 1–11. Having sold his goods for the benefit of the church, he kept back a part of the price, bringing to the apostles the remainder as if it was the whole, his wife being privy to the scheme. St. Peter denounced the fraud, and Ananias fell down and expired.

3. A Jewish disciple at Damascus, Acts 9 : 10–17, of high repute, Acts 22 : 12, who sought out Saul during the period of blindness which followed his conversion, and announced to him his future commission as a preacher of the gospel. Tradition makes him to have been afterwards bishop of Damascus, and to have died by martyrdom.

A'nath (ā'năth) (*answer*), father of Shamgar. Judges 3 : 31; 5 : 6.

Anathema (à-năth'e-mà), which literally means a thing suspended, is the equivalent of the Hebrew word signifying a thing or person *devoted*. Any object so devoted to Jehovah was irredeemable. If an inanimate object, it was to be given to the priests, Num. 18 : 14; if a living creature or even a man, it was to be slain. Lev. 27 : 28, 29. The word anathema frequently occurs in St. Paul's writings, and is generally translated *accursed*. An examination of the passages in which it

occurs shows that it had acquired a more general sense as expressive either of strong feeling, Rom. 9 : 3, or of dislike and condemnation. 1 Cor. 12 : 3, 16 : 22; Gal. 1 : 9.

An'athoth (ăn'a-thŏth) (*answered prayer*). 1. Son of Becher, a son of Benjamin. 1 Chron. 7 : 8.

2. One of the "heads of the people" who signed the covenant in the time of Nehemiah. Neh. 10 : 19.

An'athoth (ăn'a-thŏth), a priests' city belonging to the tribe of Benjamin, with "suburbs." Josh. 21 : 18; 1 Chron. 6 : 60. Anathoth lay two or three miles from Jerusalem. Isa. 10 : 30. It was the home of Abiathar the high priest (1 Kings 2 : 26), and the birthplace of Jeremiah, and the prophet's life was also endangered here (Jer. 1 : 1; 11: 21). The town was repeopled after the exile. Ezra 2 : 23. It is the modern *Anata*. The cultivation of the priests survives in tilled fields of grain, with figs and olives. There are the remains of walls and strong foundations, and the quarries still supply Jerusalem with building stones.

Anchor. Acts 27 : 29.

An'drew (ăn'drụ) (*manly*), one of the apostles of our Lord, John 1 : 40; Matt. 4 : 18, brother of Simon Peter. He was of Bethsaida, and had been a disciple of John the Baptist, leaving him to follow our Lord. By his means his brother Simon was brought to Jesus. John 1 : 41. His place among the apostles seems to have been fourth, next after the three Peter, James and John, and in company with Philip. Mark 3 : 18; Acts 1 : 13. The traditions about him are various. He is said to have preached in Scythia, in Greece, in Asia Minor and Thrace, and to have been crucified at Patræ in Achaia.

Androni'cus (ăn-dro-nī'kus) (*man-conqueror*). A Christian at Rome, saluted by St. Paul, Rom. 16 : 7, together with Junia, or Junias.

A'nem (ā'nem) (*two springs*), a city of Issachar, with "suburbs," belonging to the Gershonites. 1 Chron. 6 : 73. Perhaps EN-GANNIM.

A'ner (ā'nēr), a city of Manasseh, west of Jordan, with "suburbs," given to the Kohathites. 1 Chron. 6 : 70.

A'ner (ā'nēr), one of the three Amorite chiefs of Hebron who aided Abraham in the pursuit after the four invading kings. Gen. 14 : 13, 24.

Aneth'othite, 2 Sam. 23:27, **Anet'-othite,** 1 Chron. 27:12, and **An'toth-ite** (ăn'toth-īte), 1 Chron. 11:28; 12:3, an inhabitant of Anathoth, of the tribe of Benjamin.

Angel of the Lord. Gen. 16:7, etc. The special form in which God manifested himself to man, and hence Christ's visible form before the incarnation. Compare Acts 7:30–38 with the corresponding Old Testament history; and Gen. 18:1, 13, 14, 33 and 19:1.

Angels. By the word "angels" (*i. e.,* "messengers" of God) we ordinarily understand a race of spiritual beings of a nature exalted far above that of man, although infinitely removed from that of God—whose office is "to do him service in heaven, and by his appointment to succor and defend men on earth." I. *Scriptural use of the word.* —There are many passages in which the expression "angel of God" is certainly used for a manifestation of God himself. Gen. 22:11 with 12, and Ex. 3:2 with 6 and 14. It is to be observed, also, that side by side with these expressions we read of God's being manifested in the form of *man*—as to Abraham at Mamre, Gen. 18:2, 22, comp. 19:1; to Jacob at Penuel, Gen. 32:24, 30; to Joshua at Gilgal, Josh. 5:13, 15, etc. Besides this, which is the highest application of the word angel, we find the phrase used of any messengers of God, such as the prophets, Isa. 42:19; Hag. 1:13; Mal. 3:1, the priests, Mal. 2:7, and the rulers of the Christian churches. Rev. 1:20.

II. *Nature of angels.*—Angels are termed "spirits," as in Heb. 1:14; but were able to appear in bodily form as repeatedly in O. T. history and expressly implied in Luke 20:36; Philip. 3:21. The angels are revealed to us as beings such as man might be, and will be when the power of sin and death is removed, because always beholding his face, Matt. 18:10, and therefore being "made like him." 1 John 3:2. Their *number* must be very large, 1 Kings 22:19; Matt. 26:53; Heb. 12:22; their *strength* is great, Ps. 103:20; Rev. 5:2; 18:21; their *activity* marvelous, Isa. 6:2–6; Matt. 26:53; Rev. 8:13; their *appearance* varied according to circumstances, but was often brilliant and dazzling. Matt. 28:2–7; Rev. 10:1, 2. Of the nature of "fallen angels," the circumstances and nature of the tempta-

tion by which they fell, we know absolutely nothing. All that is certain is that they "left their first estate," and that they are now "angels of the devil." Matt. 25:41; Rev. 12:7, 9. On the other hand, the title specially assigned to the angels of God—that of the "holy ones," see Dan. 4:13, 23; 8:13; Matt. 25:31—is precisely the one which is given to those men who are renewed in Christ's image. Comp. Heb. 2:10; 5:9; 12:23.

III. *Office of the angels.*—Of their office in heaven we have only vague prophetic glimpses, as in 1 Kings 22:19; Isa. 6:1–3; Dan. 7:9, 10; Rev. 5:11, etc., which show us nothing but a never-ceasing adoration. They are represented as being, in the widest sense, agents of God's providence, *natural* and *supernatural,* to the body and to the soul. In one word, they are Christ's ministers of grace now, as they shall be of judgment hereafter. Matt. 13:39, 41, 49; 16:27; 24:31, etc. That there are degrees of the angelic nature, both fallen and unfallen, and special titles and agencies belonging to each, is clearly declared by St. Paul, Eph. 1:21; Rom. 8:38; but what their general nature is it is useless to speculate.

A'niam (ā'ni-am) (*sighing of the people*), a Manassite, son of Shemidah. 1 Chron. 7:19.

A'nim (ā'nĭm) (*fountains*), a city in the mountains of Judah, named in connection with Eshtemoh and Goshen. Josh. 15:50.

Anise (ăn'ĭs). This word occurs only in Matt. 23:23. Dill (*Anethum graveolens*) is intended here rather than the similar plant now called Anise. There is direct evidence for this in the statement by Rabbi Eliezer (Tract. Maaseroth, c. iv, 5) that the seeds, leaves and the stem of dill are "subject to tithe." "Dill is an annual or a biennial herb, of the order Umbelliferæ, with a stem one to three feet high, much dissected leaves, small yellow flowers, and flattened oval fruits about one-fifth of an inch long, of a brownish color, with a lighter-colored wing-like border, and a pungent aromatic odor and taste. It is found wild in corn fields in central and southern Europe and Egypt, perhaps escaped from cultivation. It has been cultivated from remote antiquity." Its seeds are used in cookery as a condiment, their flavor being greatly liked by the people of the East generally. It is also used in medicine, as a carminative; it diminishes swellings and its infusion is useful as a wash for indolent ulcers. Its oil is useful in neuralgia and joint affections.

Anklet. This word does not occur in the Authorized Version; but anklets are referred to in Isa. 3 : 16, 18, 20. They were as common as bracelets and armlets, and made of much the same materials. The pleasant jingling and tinkling which they made as they knocked against each other was no doubt one of the reasons why they were admired. They are still worn in the East.

An'na (ăn'nà) (*grace*), a "prophetess" in Jerusalem at the time of our Lord's presentation in the temple. Luke 2 : 36. She was of the tribe of Asher.

An'nas (ăn'nas) (*merciful*), son of one Sethi, was appointed high priest A.D. 7 by Quirinius, the imperial governor of Syria, but was obliged by Valerius Gratus, procurator of Judea, to give way to Ismael, son of Phabi, at the beginning of the reign of Tiberius, A.D. 15. About A.D. 18 Joseph Caiaphas, son-in-law of Annas, became high priest, John 18 : 13; but in Luke 3 : 2 Annas and Caiaphas are both called high priests. Our Lord's first hearing, John 18 : 13, was before Annas, who then sent him bound to Caiaphas. Some maintain that the two, Annas and Caiaphas, were together at the head of the Jewish people,—Caiaphas as actual high priest, Annas as president of the Sanhedrin. Acts 4 : 6. Others again suppose that Annas held the office of *sagan*, or substitute of the high priest; others still that Annas held the title and was really the ruling power. He lived to old age, having had five sons high priests.

Anointing, in Holy Scripture, is either, I. Material—with oil—or II. Spiritual—with the Holy Ghost. I. MATERIAL.—(1) *Ordinary.* Anointing the body or head with oil was a common practice with the Jews, as with other Oriental nations. Deut. 28 : 40; Ruth 3 : 3; Micah 6 : 15. Anointing the head with oil or ointment seems also to have been a mark of respect sometimes paid by a host to his guests. Luke 7 : 46 and Ps. 23 : 5. (2) *Official.* It was a rite of inauguration into each of the three typical offices of the Jewish commonwealth. *a.* Prophets were occasionally anointed to their office, 1 Kings 19 : 16, and were called messiahs, or anointed. 1 Chron. 16 : 22; Ps. 105 : 15. *b.* Priests, at the first institution of the Levitical priesthood, were all anointed to their offices, Ex. 40 : 15; Num. 3 : 3; but afterwards anointing seems to have been specially reserved for the high priest, Ex. 29 : 29; Lev. 16 : 32; so that "the priest that is anointed," Lev. 4 : 3, is generally thought to mean the high priest. *c.* Kings. Anointing was the principal and divinely-appointed ceremony in the inauguration of the Jewish kings. 1 Sam. 9 : 16; 10 : 1; 1 Kings 1 : 34, 39. The rite was sometimes performed more than once. David was thrice anointed. *d.* Inanimate objects also were anointed with oil, in token of their being set apart for religious service. Thus Jacob anointed a pillar at Bethel. Gen. 31 : 13; Ex. 30 : 26–28. (3) *Ecclesiastical.* Anointing with oil is prescribed by St. James to be used for the recovery of the sick. James 5 : 14. Analogous to this is the anointing with oil practiced by the twelve. Mark 6 : 13. II. SPIRITUAL.—(1) In the Old Testament a Deliverer is promised under the title of Messiah, or Anointed, Ps. 2 : 2; Dan. 9 : 25, 26; and the nature of his anointing is described to be spiritual, with the Holy Ghost. Isa. 61 : 1; see Luke 4 : 18. In the New Testament Jesus of Nazareth is shown to be the Messiah, or Christ, or Anointed, of the Old Testament, John 1 : 41; Acts 9 : 22; 17 : 2, 3; 18 : 4, 28; and the historical fact of his being anointed with the Holy Ghost is asserted and recorded. John 1 : 32, 33; Acts 4 : 27; 10 : 38. Christ was anointed as prophet, priest and king. (2) Spiritual anointing with the Holy Ghost is conferred also upon Christians by God. 2 Cor. 1 : 21. "Anointing" expresses the sanctifying influences of the Holy Spirit upon Christians, who are priests and kings unto God.

Ant (Heb. *nemâlâh*). This insect is mentioned twice in the Old Testament: in Prov. 6 : 6; 30 : 25. In the former of these passages the diligence of this insect is instanced by the wise man as an example worthy of imitation; in the second passage the ant's wisdom is especially alluded to; for these insects, "though they be little on the earth, are exceeding wise." For a long time European commentators and naturalists denied that ants stored up grain for future use, as was asserted in Proverbs; but while this is true of most of the 104 European species, two of those species do lay up food, and are called *harvesting ants*. Like species have been found in Texas and South America, and are known to exist in Palestine. They show many other proofs of their skill. Some of them build wonderful houses; these are often several stories high, sometimes five hundred times the height of the builders, with rooms, corridors, and vaulted roofs supported by pillars. Some species keep a kind of cows; others have a regular army of soldiers; some keep slaves. "No closer imitation of the ways of man could be found in the entire animal economy." (See *Encyc. Brit.*) McCook's "The Honey Ants" gives many curious facts about the habits of this peculiar kind of ant, and of the harvesting ants of the American plains.

An'tichrist (ăn'tĭ-chrīst). This term is employed by the apostle John alone, and is defined by him in a manner which leaves no doubt as to its intrinsic meaning. With regard to its application there is less certainty. In the first passage—1 John 2:18—in which it occurs, the apostle makes direct reference to the false Christs whose coming, it had been foretold, should mark the last days. In v. 22 we find, "he is antichrist, that denieth the Father and the Son;" and still more positively, "every spirit that confesseth not that Jesus Christ is come in the flesh is of antichrist." Comp. 2 John 7. Antichrist is the embodiment of the spirit which stands in opposition to the true nature and spirit of Christ whether this moral antagonism is embodied in individuals or in institutions. At the time Revelation was written the Roman Emperors and the priestly cult were antichrist. But the same spirit has existed ever since.

The coming of Antichrist was believed to be foretold in the "vile person" of Daniel's prophecy, Dan. 11:21, which received its first accomplishment in Antiochus Epiphanes, but of which the complete fulfillment was reserved for the last times. He is identified with "the man of sin, the son of perdition." 2 Thess. 2:3. This interpretation brings Antichrist into close connection with the gigantic power of evil, symbolized by the "beast," Rev. 13, who received his power from the dragon (*i. e.,* the devil, the serpent of Genesis), continued for forty and two months, and was invested with the kingdom of the ten kings who destroyed the harlot Babylon, Rev. 17:12, 17, the city of seven hills. The destruction of Babylon is to be followed by the rule of Antichrist for a short period, Rev. 17:10, to be in his turn overthrown in "the battle of that great day of God Almighty," Rev. 16: 14, with the false prophet and all his followers. Rev. 19. The personality of Antichrist is to be inferred as well from the personality of his historical precursor as from that of him to whom he stands opposed. For all that Antichrist stands for, the persecutions of Christians, the inquisitions, the spirit of political ambitions that would crush true reforms, is ever embodied in some personality, the interpreter and servant of Satan, the great Antichrist.

An'tioch (ăn'tĭ-ŏk) (from *Antiochus*). 1. IN SYRIA. The capital of the Greek kings of Syria, and afterwards the residence of the Roman governors of the province which bore the same name.

Situation.— This metropolis was situated where the chain of Lebanon, running northward, and the chain of Taurus, running eastward, are brought to an abrupt meeting. Here the Orontes breaks through the mountains; and Antioch was placed at a bend of the river, 16½ miles from the Mediterranean, partly on an island, partly on the levee which forms the left bank, and partly on the steep and craggy ascent of Mount Silpius, which rose abruptly on the south. It is about 300 miles north of Jerusalem. In the immediate neighborhood was Daphne, the celebrated sanctuary of Apollo, 2 Macc. 4:33; whence the city was sometimes called *Antioch by Daphne*, to distinguish it from other cities of the same name.

Description.— The city was founded about 300 B.C. by Seleucus Nicator. It grew under the successive Seleucid kings till it became a city of great extent and of remarkable beauty. One feature, which seems to have been characteristic of the great Syrian cities,— a vast street with colonnades, intersecting the whole from end to end,—was added by Antiochus Epiphanes. By Pompey it was made a free city, and such it continued till the time of Antoninus Pius. The early emperors raised there some large and important structures, such as aqueducts, amphitheatres and baths. Antioch, in Paul's time, was the third city of the Roman em-

TETRADRACHM OF ANTIOCH.

pire, and contained over 200,000 inhabitants. Its population in 1923 was, in round numbers, 24,000 (Rand, McNally).

Bible History.— No city, after Jerusalem, is so intimately connected with the history of the apostolic church. Jews were settled there from the first in large numbers, were governed by their own ethnarch, and allowed to have the same political privileges with the Greeks. The chief interest of Antioch, however, is connected with the progress of Christianity among the heathen. Here the first Gentile church was founded, Acts 11:20, 21; here the disciples of Jesus Christ were first called Christians. 11:26. It was from Antioch that St. Paul started on his three missionary journeys.

2. IN PISIDIA, Acts 13:14; 14:19, 21; 2 Tim. 3:11, on the borders of Phrygia, corresponds to *Yalobatch,* which is distant from *Ak-sher* six hours over the mountains. This city, like the Syrian Antioch, was founded by Seleucus Nicator. Under the Romans it became the centre of administration in southern Galatia.

Anti'ochus (ăn-tī'-ō-kŭs) (*an opponent*), the name of a number of kings of Syria who lived during the interval between the Old and New Testaments, and had frequent connection with the Jews during that period. They are referred to in the Apocrypha, especially in the books of the Maccabees.

An'tipas (ăn'tĭ-păs) (*like the father*), martyr at Pergamos, Rev. 2:13, and according to tradition the bishop of that place.

An'tipas (ăn'tĭ-păs). [HEROD.]

Antip'atris (*belonging to Antipater*),

a town to which the soldiers conveyed St. Paul by night on their march. Acts 23:31. It was about 28 miles south of Cæsarea. Herod, when he rebuilt the city, changed it to Antipatris, in honor of his father, Antipater. The site is now called *Ras el 'Ain,* "the Springhead."

Anto'nia (ăn-tō'nĭ-à) (from *Marc Antony*), a square stone fortress or castle adjoining the northwest corner of the temple area at Jerusalem. There was a tower at each corner. It was rebuilt by Herod the Great, and named by him from Marc Antony. From the stairs of this castle Paul addressed the multitude who had assaulted him. Acts 21:31-40.

Antothi'jah (ăn-to-thī'jah) (*answers of Jehovah*), a Benjamite, one of the sons of Jeroham. 1 Chron. 8:24.

An'tothite (ăn'-toth-īte), a dweller at Anathoth. 1 Chron. 11:28; 12:3. [ANATHOTH.]

A'nub (à'nub) (*confederate*), son of Coz and descendant of Judah, through Ashur the father of Tekoa. 1 Chron. 4:8.

Apel'les (à-pěl'lēs), a Christian saluted by St. Paul in Rom. 16:10. Tradition makes him bishop of Smyrna or Heraclea.

Apes (Heb. *kôphîm*) are mentioned in 1 Kings 10:22 and 2 Chron. 9:21. There can be little doubt that the apes were brought from the same country which supplied ivory and peacocks, both of which are common in Ceylon; and Sir E. Tennent has drawn attention to the fact that the Tamil names for apes, ivory and peacocks are identical with the Hebrew.

Aphar'sathchites (à-fär'sath-kītes), **Aphar'sites** (à-fär'sītes), **Aphar'sacites,** the names of certain tribes colonies from which had been planted in Samaria by the Assyrian leader Asnapper. Ezra 4:9; 5:6. The first and last are regarded as the same. Whence these tribes came is entirely a matter of conjecture.

A'phek (à'fek) (*fortress*), the name of several places in Palestine. 1. A royal city of the Canaanites, the king of which was killed by Joshua, Josh. 12:18; probably the same as APHEKAH in Josh. 15:53.

2. A city, apparently in the extreme north of Asher, Josh. 19:30, from which the Canaanites were not ejected, Judges

1:31; though here it is APHIK. This is probably the same place as APHEK, Josh. 13:4, on the extreme north "border of the Amorites," identified with the Aphaca of classical times, the modern *Afka.*

3. A place at which the Philistines encamped while the Israelites pitched in Eben-ezer, before the fatal battle in which the sons of Eli were killed and the ark was taken. 1 Sam. 4:1. This would be somewhere to the northwest of and at no great distance from Jerusalem. Perhaps the same as 1.

4. The scene of another encampment of the Philistines, before an encounter not less disastrous than that just named, —the defeat and death of Saul. 1 Sam. 29:1. It is possible that it may be the same place as the preceding.

5. A city on the military road from Syria to Israel. 1 Kings 20:26. It is now found in *Fîk,* at the head of the *Wady Fîk,* 3 miles east of the Sea of Galilee. G. A. Smith says, in Sharon.

Aphe′kah (à-fē′kah) (*strong place*), a city of Judah, in the mountains, Josh. 15:53; probably the same as APHEK, 1.

Aphi′ah (à-fī′ah) (*refreshed*), one of the forefathers of King Saul. 1 Sam. 9:1.

A′phik (à′fĭk), a city of Asher from which the Canaanites were not driven out. Judges 1:31. Probably the same place as APHEK, 2.

Aph′rah (ăf′rah) (*dust*), **The house of,** a place mentioned in Micah 1:10. Its site is uncertain.

Aph′ses (*the dispersion*), chief of the 18th of the 24 courses in the service of the temple. 1 Chron. 24:15.

Apoc′alypse. A Greek word meaning *revelation,* applied chiefly to the book of Revelation by John. [REVELATION.]

Apoc′rypha (*concealed, hidden*). 1. *Old Testament Apocrypha.*— The collection of books to which this term is popularly applied includes the following (the order given is that in which they stand in the English version): I. 1 Esdras; II. 2 Esdras; III. Tobit; IV. Judith; V. The rest of the chapters of the book of Esther, which are found neither in the Hebrew nor in the Chaldee; VI. The Wisdom of Solomon; VII. The Wisdom of Jesus the Son of Sirach, or Ecclesiasticus; VIII. Baruch; IX. The

Song of the Three Holy Children; X. The History of Susanna; XI. The History of the destruction of Bel and the Dragon; XII. The Prayer of Manasses king of Judah; XIII. 1 Maccabees; XIV. 2 Maccabees. The primary meaning of *apocrypha,* "hidden, secret," seems, toward the close of the second century, to have been associated with the signification "spurious," and ultimately to have settled down into the latter. The separate books of this collection are treated of in distinct articles.

2. *New Testament Apocrypha.*— A collection of legendary and spurious Gospels, Acts of the Apostles, and Epistles. They are so entirely inferior to the genuine books, so full of nonsensical and unworthy stories of Christ and the apostles, that they have never been regarded as divine, or bound up in our Bibles. It is said that Mohammed obtained his ideas of Christ entirely from these spurious gospels.

Apollo′nia (ăp-ŏl-lō′nĭ-à) (*belonging to Apollo*), a city of Macedonia, through which Paul and Silas passed on their way from Philippi and Amphipolis to Thessalonica. Acts 17:1. According to the *Antonine Itinerary* it was distant 30 Roman miles from Amphipolis and 37 Roman miles from Thessalonica.

Apol′los (à-pŏl′lŏs), a Jew from Alexandria, eloquent (which may also mean *learned*) and mighty in the Scriptures; one instructed in the way of the Lord, according to the imperfect view of the disciples of John the Baptist, Acts 18:24, but on his coming to Ephesus during a temporary absence of St. Paul, A.D. 53, more perfectly taught by Aquila and Priscilla. After this he became a preacher of the gospel, first in Achaia and then in Corinth. Acts 18:27; 19:1. When the apostle wrote his First Epistle to the Corinthians, Apollos was with or near him, 1 Cor. 16:12; probably at Ephesus in A.D. 57. He is mentioned but once more in the New Testament, in Titus 3:13. After this nothing is known of him. Tradition makes him bishop of Cæsarea.

Apol′lyon (à-pŏl′lĭ-ŏn), or, as it is literally in the margin of the Authorized Version of Rev. 9:11, "*a destroyer,*" is the rendering of the Hebrew word ABADDON, "the angel of the bottomless pit." From the occurrence of the word in Ps. 88:11, the rabbins have made Abaddon the nethermost of the two regions into which they divide the lower world; but that in Rev. 9:11 Abaddon is the angel and not the abyss is perfectly evident in the Greek.

Apostle (*one sent forth*), in the New Testament originally the official name of those twelve of the disciples whom Jesus chose to send forth first to preach the gospel and to be with him during the course of his ministry on earth. The word also appears to have been used in a non-official sense to designate a much wider circle of Christian messengers and teachers. See 2 Cor. 8:23; Philip. 2:25. It is only of those who were officially designated apostles that we treat in this article. Their names are given in Matt. 10:2–4. A summary of their history will be found in the APPENDIX.

Their office.—(1) The original qualification of an apostle, as stated by St. Peter on the occasion of electing a successor to the traitor Judas, was that he should have been personally acquainted with the whole ministerial course of our Lord, from his baptism by John till the day when he was taken up into heaven. (2) They were chosen by Christ himself. (3) They had the power of working miracles. (4) They were inspired. John 16:13. (5) Their work seems to have been pre-eminently that of founding the churches and upholding them by supernatural power specially bestowed for that purpose. (6) The office ceased, as a matter of course, with its first holders; all continuation of it, from the very conditions of its existence (cf. 1 Cor. 9:1), being impossible.

Early history and training.— The apostles were from the lower ranks of life, simple and uneducated; some of them were related to Jesus according to the flesh; some had previously been disciples of John the Baptist. Our Lord chose them early in his public career. They seem to have been all on an equality, both during and after the ministry of Christ on earth. Early in our Lord's ministry he sent them out two and two to preach repentance and to perform miracles in his name. Matt. 10; Luke 9. They accompanied him in his journeys, saw his wonderful works, heard his discourses addressed to the people, and made inquiries of him on religious matters. They recognized him as the Christ of God, Matt. 16:16; Luke 9:20, and ascribed to him supernatural power, Luke 9:54; but in the recognition of the spiritual teaching and mission of Christ they made very slow progress, held back as they were by weakness of apprehension and by national prejudices. Even at the removal of our Lord from the earth they were yet weak in their knowledge, Luke 24:11; John 16:12, though he had for so long been carefully preparing and instructing them. On the feast of Pentecost, ten days after our Lord's ascension, the Holy Spirit came down on the assembled church, Acts 2; and from that time the apostles became altogether different men, giving witness with power of the life and death and resurrection of Jesus, as he had declared they should. Luke 24:48; Acts 1:8, 22; 2:32; 3:15; 5:32; 13:31.

Later labors and history.— First of all the mother-church at Jerusalem grew up under their hands, Acts 3–7, and their superior dignity and power were universally acknowledged by the rulers and the people. Acts 5:12 ff. Their first mission out of Jerusalem was to Samaria, Acts 8:5–25, where the Lord himself had, during his ministry, sown the seed of the gospel. Here ends the first period of the apostles' agency, during which its centre is Jerusalem and the prominent figure is that of St. Peter. The centre of the second period of the apostolic agency is Antioch, where a church soon was built up, consisting of Jews and Gentiles; and the central figure of this and of the subsequent period is St. Paul. The third apostolic period is marked by the almost entire disappearance of the twelve from the sacred narrative, and the exclusive agency of St. Paul, the great apostle of the Gentiles. Of the missionary work of the rest of the twelve we know absolutely nothing from the sacred narrative.

Ap′paim (ăp′pa-im), or **Appa′im** (*the nostrils*), son of Nadab, and descended from Jerahmeel, the founder of an important family of the tribe of Judah. 1 Chron. 2:30, 31.

Appeal. The principle of appeal was recognized by the Mosaic law in the establishment of a central court under the presidency of the judge or ruler for the time being, before which all cases too difficult for the local courts were to be tried. Deut. 17:8, 9. According to the above regulation, the appeal lay in the time of the Judges to the judge, Judges 4: 5, and under the monarchy to the king. Jehoshaphat delegated his judicial authority to a court permanently established for the purpose. 2 Chron. 19: 8. These courts were re-established by Ezra. Ezra 7: 25. After the institution of the Sanhedrin the final appeal lay to them. St. Paul, as a Roman citizen, exercised a right of appeal from the jurisdiction of the local court at Jerusalem to the emperor. Acts 25: 11.

Ap'phia (ăf'fĭ-à), a Christian woman addressed jointly with Philemon and Archippus in Phil. 2; apparently a member of Philemon's household, and not improbably his wife.

Ap'pii Fo'rum (ăp'pĭ-ĭ-fō'rum (*market of Appius*), a well-known station on the Appian Way, the great road which led from Rome to the neighborhood of the Bay of Naples. Acts 28: 15. There is no difficulty in identifying the site with some ruins near *Treponti,* 43 miles from Rome.

Ap'pius, Market of. Revised Version for **Appii Forum.** Acts 28: 15.

Apple Tree, Apple (Heb. *tappûach*). Mention of the apple tree occurs in the Authorized Version in Cant. 2: 3; 8: 5, and Joel 1: 12. The fruit of this tree is alluded to in Prov. 25: 11 and Cant. 2: 5; 7: 8. It is a difficult matter to say what is the specific tree denoted by the Hebrew word *tappûach.* "The apple proper is rare in Syria, and its fruit inferior." Most modern writers maintain that it is either the quince or the citron; others speak of the apricot, which is abundant and deliciously perfumed. The quince has some plausible arguments in its favor. Its fragrance was held in high esteem by the ancients. The quince was sacred to Venus. On the other hand, Dr. Royle says, "The rich color, fragrant odor and handsome appearance of the citron, whether in flower or in fruit, are particularly suited to the passages of Scripture mentioned above." Dr. G. E. Post, who lived many years in Palestine, tells us that the apple fulfills all the conditions perfectly. The tree often grows to a large size, is planted in orchards, and is a special favorite of the people of Palestine and Syria. The fruit is indeed inferior to the apples of Europe and America; but the better kinds have a delicious aroma, and it is for this that they are chiefly prized.—*Hastings' Bib. Dic.*

Aq'uila (ăk'wĭ-là) (*an eagle*), a Jew whom St. Paul found at Corinth on his arrival from Athens. Acts 18: 2. (A.D. 52.) He was a native of Pontus, but had fled, with his wife Priscilla, from Rome, in consequence of an order of Claudius commanding all Jews to leave the city. He became acquainted with St. Paul, and they abode together, and wrought at their common trade of making the Cilician tent or haircloth. On the departure of the apostle from Corinth, a year and six months after, Priscilla and Aquila accompanied him to Ephesus. There they remained, and there they taught Apollos. At what time they became Christians is uncertain.

Ar (*a city*), or **Ar of Moab,** one of the chief places of Moab. Num. 21: 28; Isa. 15: 1. In later times the place was known as Areopolis and Rabbath-Moab. After its destruction by an earthquake the city was rebuilt about 10 miles south of the old site. The ruins of this later city, still called Rabbah, lie about halfway between *Kerak* and the *Wady Mojeb,* the Roman road passing through it.

A'ra, one of the sons of Jether, the head of a family of Asherites. 1 Chron. 7: 38.

A'rab (à'rab) (*ambush*), a city of Judah in the mountainous district, probably in the neighborhood of Hebron; mentioned only in Josh. 15: 52.

Ar'abah (ăr'a-bah) (*burnt up*). Although this word appears in the Authorized Version in its original shape only in Josh. 18: 18, yet in the Hebrew text it is of frequent occurrence. It indicates more particularly the deep-sunken valley or trench which forms the most striking among the many striking natural features of Palestine, and which extends with great uniformity of formation from the slopes of Hermon to the Elanitic Gulf (*Gulf of Akabah*) of the Red Sea; the most remarkable depression known to exist on the surface of the globe. Through the northern portion of this extraordinary fissure the Jordan rushes through the lakes of Huleh and Gennesaret down its tortuous course to the deep chasm of the Dead Sea. This portion, about 150 miles in length, is known amongst the Arabs by the name of *el-Ghor*. The southern boundary of the Ghor is the wall of cliffs which crosses the valley about 10 miles south of the Dead Sea. From their summits, southward to the Gulf of Akabah, the valley changes its name, or, it would be more accurate to say, retains its old name of *Wady el-Arabah*.

Ara'bia (à-rā'bĭ-à) (*desert, barren*), a country known in the Old Testament under two designations: (1) *The East Country*, Gen. 25:6, or perhaps the *East,* Gen. 10:30; Num. 23:7; Isa. 2: 6; and *Land of the Sons of the East,*

A BEDOUIN SHEIKH.

Gen. 29:1; Gentile name, *Sons of the East.* Judges 6:3; 7:12; 1 Kings 4:30; Job 1:3; Isa. 11:14; Jer. 49:28; Ezek. 25:4. From these passages it appears that *Land of the East* and *Sons of the East* indicate, primarily, the country east of Palestine, and the tribes descended from Ishmael and from Keturah; and that this original signification may have become gradually extended to Arabia and its inhabitants generally, though without any strict limitation. (2) *'Arâb* and *'Arab,* whence Arabia. 2 Chron. 9:14; Isa. 21:13; Jer. 25:24; Ezek. 27:21. "Arabia is a triangular peninsula, included between the Mediterranean and Red seas,

the Indian Ocean and the Persian Gulf. Its extreme length, north and south, is about 1300 miles, and its greatest breadth 1500 miles."—*Encyc. Brit.*

Divisions.—Arabia may be divided into *Arabia Proper,* containing the whole peninsula as far as the limits of the northern deserts; *Northern Arabia* (*Arabia Deserta*), constituting the great desert of Arabia; and *Western Arabia,* the desert of Petra and the peninsula of Sinai, or the country that has been called *Arabia Petræa.* I. *Arabia Proper,* or the *Arabian peninsula,* consists of high table-land, declining towards the north. Most of it is well peopled, watered by wells and streams, and enjoys periodical rains. The most fertile tracts are those on the southwest and south. II. *Northern Arabia,* or the Arabian Desert, is a high, undulating, parched plain, of which the Euphrates forms the natural boundary from the Persian Gulf to the frontier of Syria, whence it is bounded by the latter country and the desert of Petra on the northwest and west, the peninsula of Arabia forming its southern limit. It has few oases, the water of the wells is generally either brackish or unpotable, and it is visited by the sand-wind called *Samoom.* The inhabitants, principally descended from Ishmael and from Keturah, have always led a wandering and pastoral life. They conducted a considerable trade of merchandise of Arabia and India from the shores of the Persian Gulf. Ezek. 27:20–24. III. *Western Arabia* includes the peninsula of Sinai [SINAI] and the desert of Petra, corresponding generally with the limits of Arabia Petræa. The latter name is probably derived from that of its chief city, not from its stony character. It was mostly peopled by descendants of Esau, and was generally known as the land of Edom or Idumæa [EDOM], as well as by its older appellation, the desert of Seir or Mount Seir. [SEIR.]

Inhabitants.—"Arabia, which once ruled from India to the Atlantic, now has eight or nine millions of inhabitants, about one-fifth of whom are Bedouin or wandering tribes, and the other four-fifths settled Arabs."—*Encyc. Brit.* The latest accounts, since the changes produced by the World War, give the country about 5,000,000 inhabitants. (1) The descendants of JOKTAN occupied the principal portions of the south and southwest of the peninsula, with colonies in the interior. The principal Joktanite kingdom, and the chief state of ancient Arabia, was that of the Yemen. (2) The ISHMAELITES appear to have entered the peninsula from the northwest. That they have spread over the whole of it (with the exception of one or two districts on the south coast), and that the modern nation is predominantly Ishmaelite, is asserted by the Arabs. (3) Of the descendants of KETURAH the Arabs say little. They appear to have settled chiefly north of the peninsula in Desert Arabia, from Palestine to the Persian Gulf. (4) In northern and western Arabia are other peoples which, from their geographical position and mode of life, are sometimes classed with the Arabs. Of these are AMALEK, the descendants of ESAU, etc.

Productions.—"The productions are varied. The most noted animal is the horse. Camels, sheep, cattle, asses, mules and cats are common. Agricultural products are coffee, wheat, barley, millet, beans, pulse, dates and the common garden plants. In pasture lands Arabia is peculiarly fortunate. In mineral products it is singularly poor, lead being most abundant. —*Encyc. Brit.*

Religion.—The most ancient idolatry of the Arabs we must conclude to have been fetishism. Magianism, an importation from Chaldæa and Persia, must be reckoned among the religions of the pagan Arabs; but it never had very numerous followers. Christianity was introduced into southern Arabia toward the close of the second century, and about a century later it had made great progress. It flourished chiefly in the Yemen, where many churches were built. Judaism was propagated in Arabia, principally by Karasites, at the captivity. They are now nominally Mohammedans.

Language.—Arabic, the language of Arabia, is the most developed and the richest of Shemitic languages, and the only one of which we have an extensive literature; it is, therefore, of great importance to the study of Hebrew.

Government.—In modern times Arabia has been under the sway of the Ottoman empire, as was nearly all of Asia. At the time of the World War a large number took the part of the Allies and independence was secured. The latest authorities give it as divided into several kingdoms with native rulers but under British advisers.

Ara'bians, the nomadic tribes inhabiting the country to the east and south of Palestine, who in the early times of Hebrew history were known as Ishmaelites and descendants of Keturah.

A'rad (a'răd) (*a wild ass*), a Benjamite, son of Beriah, who drove out the inhabitants of Gath. 1 Chron. 8 : 15.

A'rad (a'răd), a royal city of the Canaanites, named with Hormah and Libnah. Josh. 12 : 14. The wilderness of Judah was to "the south of Arad." Judges 1 : 16. It may be identified with a hill, *Tel 'Arâd*, northeast by east from *Milh* (Moladah), and sixteen miles from Hebron.

A'rah (*wayfarer*). 1. An Asherite, of the sons of Ulla. 1 Chron. 7 : 39.

2. The sons of Arah returned with Zerubbabel in number 775 according to Ezra 2 : 5, but 652 according to Neh. 7 : 10. One of his descendants, Shechaniah, was the father-in-law of Tobiah the Ammonite. Neh. 6 : 18.

A'ram (a'ram). 1. The name by which the Hebrews designated, generally, the country lying to the northeast of Palestine; the great mass of that high table-land which, rising with sudden abruptness from the Jordan and the very margin of the lake of Gennesaret, stretches, at an elevation of no less than 2000 feet above the level of the sea, to the banks of the Euphrates itself. Throughout the Authorized Version the word is, with only a few exceptions, rendered, as in the Vulgate and LXX., SYRIA. Its earliest occurrence in the book of Genesis is in the form of *Aram-naharaim, i. e.* "Aram of or between the two rivers." Gen. 24 : 10, Authorized Version "Mesopotamia." In the later history we meet with a number of small nations or kingdoms forming parts of the general land of Aram; but as Damascus increased in importance it gradually absorbed the smaller powers, 1 Kings 20 : 1, and the name of Aram was at last applied to it alone. Isa. 7 : 8; also 1 Kings 11 : 24, 25; 15 : 18, etc.

2. Another Aram is named in Gen. 22 : 21, as a son of Kemuel and descendant of Nahor.

3. An Asherite, one of the sons of Shamer. 1 Chron. 7 : 34.

4. Son of Esrom or Hezron, and the Greek form of the Hebrew RAM. Matt. 1 : 3, 4; Luke 3 : 33.

A'ram=nahara'im (ā'ram-nā-hā-rā'-im) (*Aram of two rivers*). Ps. 60, title. [ARAM, 1.]

A'ram-zo'bah (ā'ram-zō'-bah). Ps. 60, title. [ARAM, 1.]

Arami'tess, a female inhabitant of Aram. 1 Chron. 7 : 14.

A'ran (ā'răn) (*wild goat*), a Horite, son of Dishan and brother of Uz. Gen. 36 : 28; 1 Chron. 1 : 42.

Ar'arat (âr'a-răt) (*high ground*), a mountainous district of Asia mentioned in the Bible in connection with the following events:—(1) As the resting-place of the ark after the deluge. Gen. 8 : 4. (2) As the asylum of the sons of Sennacherib. 2 Kings 19 : 37; Isa. 37 : 38; Authorized Version has "the land of Armenia." (3) As the ally, and probably the neighbor, of Minni and Ashchenaz. Jer. 51 : 27. [ARMENIA.] The name Ararat was unknown to the geographers of Greece and Rome, as it still is to the Armenians of the present day; but it was an ancient name for a portion of Armenia. In its Biblical sense it is descriptive generally of the Armenian highlands—the lofty plateau which overlooks the plain of the Araxes on the north and of Mesopotamia on the south. Various opinions have been put forth as to the spot where the ark rested, as described in Gen. 8 : 4; but it is probable that it rested on some of the lower portions of the range rather than on the lofty peak to which exclusively Europeans have given the name Ararat, the mountain which is called *Massis* by the Armenians, *Agri-Dagh*, i. e. *Painful Mountain*, by the Turks, and *Kuh-i-Nuh*, i. e. *Noah's Mountain*, by the Persians. It rises immediately out of the plain of the Araxes, and terminates in two conical peaks, named the Great and Less Ararat, about seven miles distant from each other; the former of which attains an elevation of 17,-260 feet above the level of the sea and about 14,000 above the plain of the Araxes, while the latter is lower by 4000 feet. The summit of the higher is covered with eternal snow for about 3000 feet. *Arguri*, the only village known to have been built on its slopes, was the spot where, according to tradi-

tion, Noah planted his vineyard. "The mountains of Ararat" are co-extensive with the Armenian plateau from the base of *Ararat* in the north to the range of *Kurdistan* in the south. The plains as well as the mountains supply evidence of volcanic agency.

Winter lasts from October to May, and is succeeded by a brief spring and a summer of intense heat. Grass grows luxuriantly on the plateau, and furnishes abundant pasture during the summer months to the flocks of the nomad Kurds. Wheat, barley and vines ripen at far higher altitudes than on the Alps and the Pyrenees.

Arau'nah (a-rau'nah), a Jebusite who sold his threshing-floor on Mount Moriah to David as a site for an altar to Jehovah, together with his oxen. 2 Sam. 24 : 18–24; 1 Chron. 21 : 25. The place was later the site of the temple built by Solomon.

Ar'ba (är'bà), the progenitor of the Anakim, or sons of Anak, from whom their chief city, HEBRON, received its name of Kirjath-Arba. Josh. 14 : 15; 15 : 13; 21 : 11.

Ar'bah (är'bä). Hebron, or Kirjath-Arba, as "the city of Arbah" is always rendered elsewhere. Gen. 35 : 27.

Ar'bathite (är'băth-ïte). Perhaps a native of Beth-arabah. Abi-albon the Arbathite was one of David's mighty men. 2 Sam. 23 : 31; 1 Chron. 11 : 32.

Ar'bite (är'bïte), a native of Arba. Paarai the Arbite was one of David's guard. 2 Sam. 23 : 35.

Arch of Titus. A triumphal arch erected at Rome, and still remaining there, to commemorate the conquest of Judea and the destruction of Jerusalem by the emperor Titus. It was erected after his death, A.D. 91, by the senate and people of Rome. It was a magnificent structure, decorated with bas-reliefs and inscriptions, and is of especial interest because its historic bas-reliefs represent the captors carrying in triumph to Rome the golden candlestick and sacred utensils from the Jewish temple at Jerusalem. From these we obtain our best idea of their shape and appearance.

Archela'us (är-kě-là'ŭs) (*prince of the people*), son of Herod the Great by a Samaritan woman, Malthaké, and, with his brother Antipas, brought up at Rome. At the death of Herod (B.C. 4) his kingdom was divided between his three sons: Herod Antipas, Archelaus and Philip. Archelaus never properly bore the title of king, Matt. 2:22, but

COINS OF ARCHELAUS.

only that of ethnarch. In the tenth year of his reign, or the ninth according to Dion Cassius, i. e. A.D. 6, a complaint was preferred against him by his brothers and his subjects on the ground of his tyranny, in consequence of which he was banished to Vienne in Gaul, where he is generally said to have died.

Archery. [ARMS.]

Ar'chevites (är'ke-vītes), perhaps the inhabitants of Erech, some of whom had been placed as colonists in Samaria. Ezra 4:9.

Ar'chi (är'kī). Josh. 16:2. A clan in the neighborhood of Bethel, on the boundary between Ephraim and Benjamin. It designates a clan perhaps originally from Erech in Babylonia, of which Hushai was one. [ARCHITE.]

Archip'pus (är-kip'pus) (*master of the horse*), a Christian teacher in Colossæ, Col. 4:17, called by St. Paul his "fellow soldier," Phil. 2. He was probably a member of Philemon's family. (A.D. 62.)

Ar'chite (är'kite), **The** (as if from a place named Erech, on the frontiers of Ephraim), the usual designation of David's friend Hushai. 2 Sam. 15:32; 17:5, 14; 1 Chron. 27:33.

Architecture. The book of Genesis, 4:17, 20, appears to divide mankind into two great characteristic sections, viz., the "dwellers in tents" and the "dwellers in cities." To the race of Shem is attributed, Gen. 10:11, 12, 22; 11:2-9, the foundation of those cities in the plain of Shinar, Babylon, Nineveh and others. The Israelites were by occupation shepherds, and by habit dwellers in tents. Gen. 47:3. They had therefore originally, speaking

properly, no architecture. From the time of the occupation of Canaan they became dwellers in towns and in houses of stone. Lev. 14:34, 45; 1 Kings 7:10. The peaceful reign and vast wealth of Solomon gave great impulse to architecture; for besides the temple and his other great works, he built fortresses and cities in various places, among which Baalath and Tadmor are in all probability represented by Baalbec and Palmyra. But the reigns of Herod and his successors were especially remarkable for their great architectural works. Not only was the temple restored, but the fortifications and other public buildings of Jerusalem were enlarged and embellished. Luke 21:5. The town of Cæsarea was built on the site of Strato's Tower; Samaria was enlarged, and received the name of Sebaste. Of the original splendor of these great works no doubt can be entertained; but of their style and appearance we can only conjecture that they were formed on Greek and Roman models. The enormous stones employed in the Assyrian, Persepolitan and Egyptian buildings find a parallel in the substructions of Baalbec and in the huge blocks which still remain at Jerusalem, relics of the buildings either of Solomon or of Herod.

Arctu'rus (ärk-tū'rus) (*bear-keeper*). The Hebrew words *'Ash* and *'Aish,* rendered "Arcturus" in the Authorized Version of Job 9:9; 38:32, in conformity with the Vulgate of the former passage, are now generally believed to be identical, and to represent the constellation Ursa Major, known commonly as the Great Bear or Charles' Wain.

Ard, the son of Bela and grandson of Benjamin. Gen. 46:21; Num. 26:40. In 1 Chron. 8:3 he is called AD-DAR.

Ard'ites, the descendants of Ard or Addar, the grandson of Benjamin. Num. 26:40.

Ar'don (är'don), a son of Caleb, the son of Hezron, by his wife Azubah. 1 Chron. 2:18.

Are'li (à-rē'lī), a son of Gad. Gen. 46:16; Num. 26:17. His descendants are called Arelites. Num. 26:17.

Areop'agite (är-e-ŏp'a-gite), a member of the court of Areopagus. Acts 17:34.

Areop'agus (ăr-e-ŏp'a-gus). [MARS' HILL.]

Ar'etas (är'e-tas), or **Are'tas** (*graver*). Father-in-law of Herod Antipas. When Herod prepared to divorce his wife in order to marry Herodias, Aretas declared war against Herod, and totally defeated his army in A.D. 36. St. Paul refers to him in 2 Cor. 11 : 32.

Ar'gob (är'gŏb) (*stony*), a tract of country on the east of the Jordan, in Bashan, the kingdom of Og, containing 60 great and fortified cities. In later times it was called Trachonitis, and it is now apparently identified with the *Lejah*, a very remarkable district south of Damascus and east of the Sea of Galilee. Deut. 3 : 4, 13, 14.

Ar'gob (är'gŏb), perhaps a Gileadite officer who was governor of Argob. He was either an accomplice of Pekah in the murder of Pekahiah or was slain by Pekah. 2 Kings 15 : 25.

Arid'ai (à-rid'a-i), ninth son of Haman. Esther 9 : 9.

Arid'atha (à-rĭd'a-thà), sixth son of Haman. Esther 9 : 8.

Ari'eh (à-ri'eh) (*the lion*). Either one of the accomplices of Pekah in his conspiracy against Pekahiah, or one of the princes of Pekahiah who was put to death with him. 2 Kings 15 : 25. (B.C. 737.)

A'riel (a'rĭ-el) (*lion of God*). **1.** One of the "chief men" who under Ezra directed the caravan which he led back from Babylon to Jerusalem. Ezra 8 : 16.

2. The word occurs also in reference to two Moabites slain by Benaiah. 2 Sam. 23 : 20; 1 Chron. 11 : 22. Many regard the word as an epithet, "lionlike;" but it seems better to look upon it as a proper name, and translate "two [sons] of Ariel," as in R. V.

3. A designation given by Isaiah to the city of Jerusalem. Isa. 29 : 1, 2, **7.** We must understand by it either "lion of God," as the chief city, or "hearth of God," a synonym for the altar of burnt offerings. On the whole, it seems most probable that, as a name given to Jerusalem, Ariel means "lion of God," whilst the word used by Ezekiel, Ezek. 43 : 15, 16, means "hearth of God."

Arimathæ'a (ăr-ĭ-mă-thē'à) (*height*). Matt. 27 : 57; Luke 23 : 51; John 19 : 38. St. Luke calls it "a city of Judea." It is situated near Lydda.

A'rioch (à'rĭ-ŏk). **1.** The king of

Larsa, probably Ellasar, one of the allies of Chedorlaomer in his expedition against his rebellious tributaries, in the time of Abraham. Gen. 14 : 1. Probably Ellasar is represented by the mounds of *Senkerah*, a little east of Erech. **2.** The captain of Nebuchadnezzar's body-guard. Dan. 2 : 14, etc. It was his duty to execute sentences of death.

Aris'ai (à-rĭs'a-ī), eighth son of Haman. Esther 9 : 9.

Aristar'chus (ăr-ĭs-tär'kus) (*the best ruling*), a Thessalonian, Acts 20 : 4; 27 : 2, who accompanied St. Paul on his third missionary journey. Acts 19 : 29. He was with the apostle on his return to Asia, Acts 20 : 4; and again, 27 : 2, on his voyage to Rome. We trace him afterwards as St. Paul's fellow prisoner in Col. 4 : 10 and Phil. 24. Tradition makes him bishop of Apamea.

Aristobu'lus (ăr-ĭs-tŏ-bū'lus) (*the best counsellor*), a resident at Rome, some of whose household are greeted in Rom. 16 : 10. Tradition makes him one of the 70 disciples, and reports that he preached the gospel in Britain.

Ark, Noah's. [NOAH.]

Ark of the Covenant. The first piece of the tabernacle's furniture, for which precise directions were delivered. Ex. 25. I. *Description.*—It appears to have been an oblong chest of shittim (acacia) wood, 2½ cubits long by 1½ broad and deep. Within and without gold was overlaid on the wood, and on the upper side or lid, which was edged round about with gold, the mercy-seat was placed. The ark was fitted with rings, one at each of the four corners, and through these were passed staves of the same wood similarly overlaid, by which it was carried by the Kohathites. Num. 7 : 9; 10 : 21. The ends of the staves were visible without the veil in the holy place of the temple of Solomon. 1 Kings 8 : 8. The Ark, when transported, was enveloped in the "veil" of the dismantled tabernacle, in the curtain of badgers' skins, and in a blue cloth over all, and was therefore not seen. Num. 4 : 5. 20.

II. Its purpose was to contain inviolate the divine autograph of the two tables, that "covenant" from which it derived its title. It was also probably a reliquary for the pot of manna and the rod of Aaron.

III. *History.*—Before David's time its abode was frequently shifted. It sojourned among several, probably Levitical, families, 1 Sam. 7:1; 2 Sam. 6:3, 11; 1 Chron. 13:13; 15:24, 25, in the border villages of eastern Judah, and did not take its place in the tabernacle, but dwelt in curtains, *i. e.* in a separate tent pitched for it in Jerusalem by David. Subsequently the temple, when completed, received, in the installation of the ark in its shrine, the signal of its inauguration by the effulgence of divine glory instantly manifested. It was probably taken captive or destroyed by Nebuchadnezzar, 2 Esdr. 10:22, so that there was no ark in the second temple.

Ark of Moses. A small boat or basket made of the papyrus, _ reed which grows in the marshes ot Egypt. It was covered with bitumen to make it water-tight.

Ar'kite (är'kīte), **The,** from *Arka,* one of the families of the Canaanites, Gen. 10:17; 1 Chron. 1:15, and from the context evidently located in the north of Phœnicia. The site which now bears the name of *'Arka* lies on the coast, about 12 miles north of Tripoli and 5 south of the *Nahr el-Kebir.*

Armaged'don (är-ma-gĕd'don) (*the hill* or *city of Megiddo*). Rev. 16:16. The scene of the struggle of good and evil is suggested by that battle-field, the plain of Esdraelon, which was famous for two great victories, of Barak over the Canaanites and of Gideon over the Midianites; and for two great disasters, the deaths of Saul and Josiah. Hence it signifies in Revelation a place of great slaughter, the scene of a terrible retribution upon the wicked. The Revised Version gives the name as *Har-Magedon, i. e.* the *hill* (as *Ar* is the *city*) of *Megiddo.*

Arme'nia (är-mē'nĭ-à) (*land of Aram*) is nowhere mentioned under that name in the original Hebrew, though it occurs in the English version, 2 Kings 19:37, for ARARAT, which see. Three districts are mentioned in the Bible. (1) ARARAT, Isa. 37:38; (2) MINNI, Jer. 51:27; (3) TOGARMAH, Ezekiel, 27:14; 38:6.

Modern History.—Armenia has for centuries been divided among its neighbors, Russia, Turkey, and Persia, the greater part belonging to Turkey. The people have from the earliest times been Christians (Gregorians). For many reasons, religious and political, there

has always been hatred between Turks and Armenians, resulting in the terrible massacres of recent times which threatened to annihilate the Armenian race. The World War, resulting as it did in the defeat of Turkey, won the independence of Armenia, although with a sadly reduced population, and the loss of some of its land. "Armenia, first winning recognition of independence from Turkey and Germany, joined with the Georgians and the Tartars, to form a federal republic in 1918. It was overthrown in five weeks, Georgia and Armenia declaring their independence. Armenian independence was recognized by the Allies in 1920. On April 1, 1921 Armenia became a Soviet Republic." (World Almanac.) They number about 1,200,000.

Armlet, an ornament universal in the East, especially among women; used by

PERSIAN ARMLETS.

princes as one of the insignia of royalty, and by distinguished persons in general. The word is not used in the Authorized Version, as even in 2 Sam. 1:10 it is rendered by "the bracelet on his arm."

Armo'ni (är-mō'nī), son of Saul by Rizpah. 2 Sam. 21:8.

Arms, Armor. The subject naturally divides itself into—I. Offensive weapons: Arms. II. Defensive weapons: Armor.

I. *Offensive weapons.*—(1) Apparently the earliest known and most widely used was the *Chereb* or SWORD. Very little can be gathered as to its shape, size, material or mode of use. Perhaps if anything is to be inferred it is that the *Chereb* is both a lighter and a shorter weapon than the modern sword. It was carried in a sheath, 1 Sam. 17:51; 2 Sam. 20:8; 1 Chron. 21:27, slung by a girdle, 1 Sam. 25:13, and resting upon the thigh, Ps. 45:3; Judges 3:16, or upon the hips, 2 Sam. 20:8. (2) Next we have the SPEAR, and of this weapon we meet with at least three distinct kinds. *a. The Chanîth,* a "spear," and that of the largest kind. It was the weapon of Goliath, 1 Sam. 17:7, 45; 2 Sam. 21:19; 1 Chron. 20:5, and also of other giants, 2 Sam. 23:21; 1 Chron. 11:23, and mighty warriors, 2 Sam. 2:23; 23:18; 1 Chron. 11:11, 20.

ROMAN SOLDIER IN FULL ARMOR.

b. Apparently lighter than the preceding was the *Cîdôn* or "javelin." When not in action the *Cîdôn* was carried on the back of the warrior, 1 Sam. 17:6,

EGYPTIAN ARCHER.

Authorized Version "target." *c*. Another kind of spear was the *Rômach*. In the historical books it occurs in Num. 25:7 and 1 Kings 18:28, and frequently in the later books, as in 1

Chron. 12:8 ("buckler"); 2 Chron. 11:12. It varied much in length, weight and size. *d*. The *Shelach* was probably a lighter missile or "dart." See 2 Chron. 23:10; 32:5 ("darts");

EGYPTIAN BATTLE-AXES.

Neh. 4:17, 23 (see margin); Job 33:18; 36:12; Joel 2:8. *e*. *Shebet*, a rod or staff, is used once only to denote a weapon. 2 Sam. 18:14. (3) Of missile weapons of offence the chief was undoubtedly the Bow, *Kesheth*. The ARROWS were carried in a quiver. Gen. 27:3; Isa. 22:6; 49:2; Ps. 127:5.

A LEATHER CUIRASS.

From an allusion in Job 6:4 they would seem to have been sometimes poisoned; and Ps. 120:4 may point to a practice of using arrows with some burning material attached to them. (4) The SLING is first mentioned in Judges

20:16. This simple weapon, with which David killed the giant Philistine, was the natural attendant of a shepherd. Later in the monarchy, slingers formed part of the regular army. 2 Kings 3:25. (5) The BATTLE-AXE, Jer. 51:20, a powerful weapon, of whose exact form we have no knowledge.

II. *Armor.*—(1) The BREASTPLATE, enumerated in the description of the arms of Goliath, a "*coat* of mail," literally a "*breastplate* of scales." 1 Sam. 17:5; Rev. 9:9. It was made of leather, quilted cloth, brass, iron, or even gold. There were joints between

ASSYRIAN HELMETS.

it and the other armor. 1 Kings 22:34. (2) The HABERGEON was a coat of mail for the breast, 2 Chron. 26:14. (3) The HELMET is referred to in 1 Sam. 17:5; 2 Chron. 26:14; Ezek. 27:10. (4) GREAVES or defences for the legs made of brass, are named in 1 Sam. 17:6 only. (5) Two kinds of SHIELD are distinguishable. *a.* The large shield, encompassing, Ps. 5:13, the whole person. When not in actual conflict it was carried before the warrior. 1 Sam. 17: 7, 41. *b.* Of smaller dimensions was the *buckler* or *target*, probably for use in hand-to-hand fight. 1 Kings 10:16; 2 Chron. 9:15, 16.

Army. I. JEWISH ARMY.—Every man above 20 years of age was a soldier, Num. 1:3; each tribe formed a regiment, with its own banner and its own leader, Num. 2:2; 10:14; their positions in the camp or on the march were accurately fixed, Num. 2; the whole army started and stopped at a given signal, Num. 10:5, 6; thus they came up out of Egypt ready for the fight. Ex. 13:18. On the approach of an enemy a conscription was made from the general body, under the direction of a muster-master, Deut. 20:5; 2 Kings 25:19, by whom also the officers were appointed, Deut. 20:9. The army

was then divided into thousands and hundreds under their respective captains, Num. 31:14, and still further into families, Num. 2:34; 2 Chron. 25:5; 26:12. With the kings arose the custom of maintaining a body-guard, which formed the nucleus of a standing army, and David's band of 600, 1 Sam. 23:13; 25:13, he retained after he became king, and added the CHERETHITES and PELETHITES. 2 Sam. 15:18; 20:7. David further organized a national militia, divided into twelve regiments under their respective officers, each of which was called out for one month in

ARCHERS IN LINE OF BATTLE.

the year. 1 Chron. 27. It does not appear that the system established by David was maintained by the kings of Judah; but in Israel the proximity of the hostile kingdom of Syria necessitated the maintenance of a standing army. The maintenance and equipment of the soldiers at the public expense dates from the establishment of a standing army. It is doubtful whether the soldier ever received pay even under the kings. The numbers of soldiers at various times as given in the Biblical accounts seem almost incredible. It may be that they signify the numbers of "thousands," as in our day the numbers of "regiments," without any indication that the nominal number is actually full.

II. ROMAN ARMY.—The Roman Army was divided into legions, the number of which varied considerably (from 3000 to 6000), each under six tribuni ("chief captains," Acts 21:31), who commanded by turns. The legion was subdivided into ten cohorts ("band," Acts 10:1), the cohort into three maniples, and the maniple into two centuries, containing originally 100 men, as the name implies, but subsequently from 50 to 100 men, according to the strength of the legion. There were thus 60 centuries in a legion, each under the command of a centurion. Acts 10:1, 22; Matt. 8:5; 27:54. In addition to the legionary cohorts, independent cohorts of volunteers served under the Roman standards. One of these cohorts was named the Italian, Acts 10:1, as consisting of volunteers from Italy. The headquarters of the Roman forces in Judea were at Cæsarea.

Ar'nan (är'nan). In the received Hebrew text "the sons of Arnan" are mentioned in the genealogy of Zerubbabel. 1 Chron. 3:21.

Ar'ni. Used in the Revised Version for Aram in Luke 3:33, and is probably another name or form of the name of Aram. [ARAM, 4.]

Ar'non (är'nŏn) (*noisy*), the river or torrent which formed the boundary between Moab and the Amorites, on the north of Moab, Num. 21:13, 14, 24, 26; Judges 11:22; and afterwards between Moab and Israel (Reuben). Deut. 2:24, 36; 3:8, 12, 16; 4:48; Josh. 12:1, 2; 13:9, 16; Judges 11:13, 26. There can be no doubt that the *Wady el-Mojib* of the present day is the Arnon. Its principal source is near *Katrane*, on the Haj route.

A'rod (ā'rŏd), a son of Gad, Num. 26:17, called ARODI in Gen. 46:16.

Ar'odi. [AROD.]

Ar'odites. [AROD.]

Ar'oer (är'ŏ-ēr) (*juniper thicket*). 1. A city on the Arnon, the southern point of the territory of Sihon king of the Amorites, and afterwards of the tribe of Reuben, Deut. 2:36; 3:12; 4:48; Josh. 12:2; 13:9, 16; Judges 11:26; 2 Kings 10:33; 1 Chron. 5:8, but later again in possession of Moab. Jer. 48:19. It is the modern *Arâ'ir*, upon the very edge of the precipitous north bank of the *Wady el-Mojib*.

2. Aroer, "that is 'facing' Rabbah" (Rabbah of Ammon), a town built by and belonging to Gad. Num. 32:34; Josh. 13:25; 2 Sam. 24:5. This is

probably the place mentioned in Judges 11:33, which was shown in Jerome's time.

3. Aroer, in Isa. 17:2, if a place at all, must be still farther north than either of the two already named. It is considered by many commentators to be a noun meaning nakedness or ruin.

4. A town in Judah, named only in 1 Sam. 30:28, perhaps *Wady Ar'ârah*, on the road from Petra to Gaza. David sent spoil there from his victory over the Amalekites.

Ar'oerite (är'ŏ-ēr-ite). Hotnan the Aroerite was the father of two of David's captains. 1 Chron. 11:44.

Ar'pad (är'pad), or **Ar'phad**, Isa. 36:19; 37:13, a city or district in Syria, apparently dependent on Damascus. Jer. 49:23. Arpad is now Tell-Erfud, 13 miles from Aleppo to N. W. 2 Kings 18:34; 19:13; Isa. 10:9.

Arphax'ad (är-făx'ad). R. V. better ARPACHSHAD. The son of Shem and ancestor of Eber. Gen. 10:22, 24; 11:10.

Arrows. [ARMS.]

Artaxerx'es (är-tăx-ĕrx'ēs). Artaxerxes is first mentioned in Ezra 4:7, and was supposed identical with Smerdis, the Magian impostor and pretended brother of Cambyses, who usurped the throne B.C. 522, and reigned eight months. It is now proved, however, that he is identical with the king of Neh. 2:1.

We may safely identify him with Artaxerxes Macrocheir or Longimanus, the son of Xerxes, who reigned B.C. 464-425. It was this king who allowed the rebuilding of the wall of Jerusalem.

Ar'temas (är'te-mas) (*gift of Artemis*), a companion of St. Paul. Titus 3:12 According to tradition he was bishop of Lystra.

Ar'uboth (*windows*), the third of Solomon's commissariat districts. 1 Kings 4:10. It included Sochoh, and was therefore probably a name for the rich corn-growing lowland country.

Aru'mah (à-ru'mah) (*height*), a place apparently in the neighborhood of Shechem, at which Abimelech resided. Judges 9:41.

Ar'vad (är'văd) (*wandering*). Ezek. 27:8, 11. The island of *Ruad*, which lies off Tortosa (*Tartus*), two or three miles from the Phœnician coast. In agreement with this is the mention of "the Arvadite," in Gen. 10:18 and 1

Chron. 1:16, as a son of Canaan, with Zidon, Hamath and other northern localities.

Ar'vadite (är'vad-ītes). [ARVAD.]

Ar'za (är'zà), prefect of the palace at Tirzah to Elah king of Israel, who was assassinated at a banquet in his house by Zimri. 1 Kings 16:9.

A'sa (ā'sà) (*physician, healer*). 1. Son of Abijah and third king of Judah. (B.C. 917–875.) His long reign of 40 years was peaceful in its earlier portion, and he undertook the reformation of all abuses, especially of idolatry. He burnt the symbol of his grandmother Maachah's religion and deposed her from the dignity of "king's mother," and renewed the great altar which the idolatrous priests apparently had desecrated. 2 Chron. 15:8. Besides this he fortified cities on his frontiers, and raised an army, amounting, according to 2 Chron. 14:8, to 580,000 men, a number perhaps exaggerated by an error of the copyist, but see under ARMY. During Asa's reign, Zerah, at the head of an enormous host, 2 Chron. 14:9, attacked Mareshah. There he was utterly defeated, and driven back with immense loss to Gerar. The peace which followed this victory was broken by the attempt of Baasha of Israel to fortify Ramah. To stop this Asa purchased the help of Ben-hadad I. king of Damascus, by a large payment of treasure, forced Baasha to abandon his purpose, and destroyed the works which he had begun at Ramah. In his old age Asa suffered from gout. He died, greatly loved and honored, in the 41st year of his reign.

2. Ancestor of Berechiah, a Levite who resided in one of the villages of the Netophathites after the return from Babylon. 1 Chron. 9:16.

As'ahel (ăs'-ă-hĕl) (*made by God*). 1. Nephew of David, being the youngest son of his sister Zeruiah. He was celebrated for his swiftness of foot. When fighting under his brother Joab at Gibeon, he pursued Abner, who was obliged to kill him in self-defence. 2 Sam. 2:18 ff. (B.C. 1050.)

2. One of the Levites in the reign of Jehoshaphat, who went throughout the cities of Judah to instruct the people in the knowledge of the law. 2 Chron. 17:8. (B.C. 873.)

3. A Levite in the reign of Hezekiah, who had charge of the tithes and ded-icated things in the temple. 2 Chron. 31:13. (B.C. 726.)

4. A priest, father of Jonathan, in the time of Ezra, Ezra 10:15.

Asahi'ah (à-sa-hī'ah) (*Jehovah hath made*), a servant of King Josiah, sent by him to seek information of Jehovah respecting the book of the law which Hilkiah found in the temple, 2 Kings 22:12, 14; also called ASAIAH. 2 Chron 34:20. (B.C. 623.)

Asa'iah (a-sā'yà) (*Jehovah hath made*). 1. A prince of one of the families of the Simeonites in the reign of Hezekiah. 1 Chron. 4:36.

2. A Levite in the reign of David, chief of the family of Merari. 1 Chron. 6:30. With 120 of his brethren he took part in bringing the ark from the house of Obed-edom to the city of David. 1 Chron. 15:6, 11.

3. The first-born of "the Shilonite," from Shiloni, 1 Chron. 9:5, who with his family dwelt in Jerusalem after the return from Babylon. (B.C. 536.) In Neh. 11:5 he is called MAASEIAH.

4. An officer of Josiah. 2 Chron. 34:20. [ASAHIAH.]

A'saph (ā'saf) (*collector, or gatherer*). 1. A Levite, son of Berechiah, one of the leaders of David's choir. 1 Chron. 6:39. Psalms 50 and 73–83 are attributed to him; and he was in after times celebrated as a seer as well as a musical composer, 2 Chron. 29:30; Neh. 12:46.

2. The father or ancestor of Joah, the chronicler to the kingdom of Judah in the reign of Hezekiah, 2 Kings 18:18, 37; Isa. 36:3, 22; possibly the same as the preceding.

3. The keeper of the royal forest or "paradise" of Artaxerxes, Neh. 2:8; a Jew, in high office of the court of Persia. (B.C. 536.)

4. Ancestor of Mattaniah, the conductor of the temple-choir after the return from Babylon. 1 Chron. 9:15; Neh. 11:17. Most probably the same as 1.

A'saph (ā'saf), **Sons of.** A guild of poets and musical composers founded by Asaph.

Asa'reel (à-sā'rė-el) (*God hath bound*), a son of Jehaleleel, in the genealogies of Judah. 1 Chron. 4:16.

Asare'lah (ăs-a-rē'lah) (*upright toward God*), one of the sons of Asaph, a musician, 1 Chron. 25:2: called JESHARELAH in ver. 14.

As'enath (ăs'e-năth) *(belonging to Neith)*, daughter of Potipherah, priest, or possibly prince, of On [POTIPHERAH], wife of Joseph, Gen. 41 : 45, and mother of Manasseh and Ephraim. Gen. 41 : 50; 46 : 20. (B.C. 1715.)

A'ser (ā'sĕr). Luke 2 : 36; Rev. 7 : 6. [ASHER.]

Ash (Heb. *ôren*), only in Isa. 44 : 14. As the true ash is not a native of Palestine, some understand this to be a species of pine tree. Cheyne thinks that the cedar or fir is intended.

A'shan (ā'shan) *(smoke)*, a city in the low country of Judah. Josh. 15 : 42. In Josh. 19 : 7 and 1 Chron. 4 : 32 it is mentioned again as belonging to Simeon. It has not yet been identified, though it must have been on the slopes east of Gaza.

Ash'bea (ăsh'bē-a) *(I adjure)*, a proper name, but whether of a person or place is uncertain. 1 Chron. 4 : 21.

Ash'bel (ăsh'bel), second son of Benjamin and ancestor of the Ashbelites. Gen. 46 : 21; Num. 26 : 38.

Ash'chenaz (ăsh'ke-năz). 1 Chron. 1 : 6; Jer. 51 : 27. [ASHKENAZ.]

Ash'dod (ăsh'dŏd), or **Azo'tus** (*a stronghold*), Acts 8 : 40; one of the five confederate cities of the Philistines, situated about 30 miles from the southern frontier of Palestine, three from the Mediterranean Sea, and nearly midway between Gaza and Joppa. It was assigned to the tribe of Judah, Josh. 15 : 47, but was never subdued by the Israelites. The ark of God was carried to Ashdod by the Philistines after they captured it, and was placed in the temple of Dagon. The city was taken by Uzziah of Judah. Josh. 13 : 3; 1 Sam. 5 : 1; 16 : 17; 2 Chron. 26 : 6. Its chief importance arose from its position on the high road from Palestine to Egypt. It is now an insignificant village, with no memorials of its ancient importance, but is still called *Esdud*.

Ash'dodites, the inhabitants of Ashdod, Neh. 4 : 7; called Ashdothites in Josh. 13 : 3.

Ash'doth=pis'gah (ăsh'dŏth-pĭṣ'gah), Deut. 3 : 17; Josh. 12 : 3; 13 : 20; and in Deut. 4 : 49, Authorized Version, translated *springs of Pisgah, i. e.*, a valley or fountain near Mount Pisgah.

Ash'er (ăsh'ĕr), Apocrypha and New Testament, **A'ser** (*happy*). 1. The eighth son of Jaccb, by Zilpah, Leah's handmaid. Gen. 30 : 13. The general position of his tribe was on the seashore from Carmel northward, with Manasseh on the south, Zebulun and Issachar on the northeast, and Napthali on the northeast. Josh. 19 : 24–31; 17 : 10, 11 and Judges 1 : 31, 32. They possessed the maritime portion of the rich plain of Esdraelon, probably for a distance of 8 or 10 miles from the shore. This territory contained some of the richest soil in all Palestine.

2. A town east of Shechem. Josh. 17 : 7. Perhaps it is the modern *Teyâsîr.*

Ashe'rah (ăsh-ē'rah) *(upright)*, the name of a Phœnician goddess, or rather of the idol itself (Authorized Version "grove"). Asherah is closely connected with ASHTORETH and her worship, Judges 3 : 7, comp. 2 : 3; Judges 6 : 25; 1 Kings 18 : 19; Ashtoreth being, perhaps, the proper name of the goddess, whilst Asherah is the name of her image or symbol, which was of wood. See Judges 6 : 25–30; 2 Kings 23 : 14.

Ash'erites (ăsh'er-ītes), descendants of Asher, and members of his tribe. Judges 1 : 32.

Ashes. The ashes on the altar of burnt offering were gathered into a cavity in its surface. The ashes of a red heifer burnt entire, according to regulations prescribed in Num. 19, had the ceremonial efficacy of purifying the unclean, Heb. 9 : 13, but of polluting the clean. [UNCLEANNESS.] Ashes about the person, especially on the head, were used as a sign of sorrow. [MOURNING.]

Ash'ima (ăsh'ĭ-mà), a god of the Hamathite colonists in Samaria. 2 Kings 17 : 30. It has been regarded as identical with the Pan of the Greeks. Cheyne says *Ishtar.*

Ash'kelon (ăsh'ke-lŏn), **As'kelon,** (*migration*), one of the five leading cities of the Philistines, Josh. 13 : 3; 1 Sam. 6 : 17; Jer. 47 : 5, 7; a seaport on the Mediterranean, 10 miles north of Gaza. Samson went down from Timnath to Ashkelon. Judges 14 : 19. In the post-Biblical times Ashkelon rose to considerable importance. Near the town were the temple and sacred lake of Derceto, the fish-goddess. The soil around was remarkable for its fertility. Ashkelon played a memorable part in the struggles of the Crusades for the recovery of the Holy Land.

Ash'kenaz (ăsh'ke-năz) *(spreading fire)*, one of the three sons of Gomer, son of Japheth. Gen. 10 : 3. Cheyne says that Ashkenaz must have been one of the migratory peoples which in the time of Esar-haddon burst upon the northern provinces of Asia Minor and upon Armenia. A horde from the north, perhaps of Indo-Germanic origin.

Ash'nah (ăsh'nah), the name of two cities, both in the lowlands of Judah: (1) named between Zoreah and Zanoah, and therefore probably northwest of Jerusalem, Josh. 15:33; and (2) between Jiptah and Nezib, and therefore to the southwest of Jerusalem. Josh. 15:43. Their site is unknown, though tradition places them about 16 miles from Jerusalem.

Ash'penaz (ăsh'pe-năz), the master of the eunuchs of Nebuchadnezzar. Dan. 1:3.

Ash'riel, properly **As'riel** (ăs'rĭ-el) (*vow of God*). 1 Chron. 7:14.

Ash'taroth (ăsh'ta-rŏth), and once **As'taroth** (the plural of the word *Ashtoreth*), a city on the east of Jordan, in Bashan, in the kingdom of Og, doubtless so called from being a seat of the worship of the goddess of the same name. Deut. 1:4; Josh. 9:10; 12:4; 13:12.

Ash'terathite (ăsh'tĕ-răth-īte), a native or inhabitant of Ashtaroth, 1 Chron. 11:44, beyond Jordan.

Ash'teroth Karna'im (ăsh'tĕ-rŏth kär-nā'im) (*Ashteroth of the two horns* or *peaks*), a place of very great antiquity, the abode of the Rephaim. It was smitten by Chedorlaomer on his expedition against the cities of the plain. Gen. 14:5. Its name suggests that its inhabitants worshiped the horned moon. Ewing in Hastings' *Bible Dictionary* says the common identification with the modern *Es-Sanamein*, on the Haj route, about 25 miles south of Damascus, is wrong, but no other is more decisive.

Ash'toreth (ăsh'tŏ-rĕth), the principal female divinity of the Phœnicians, called Ishtar by the Assyrians and Astarte by the Greeks and Romans. She was by some ancient writers identified with the moon. But on the other hand the Assyrian Ishtar was not the moongoddess, but the planet Venus; and Astarte was by many identified with the goddess Venus (or Aphrodite), as well as with the planet of that name. It is certain that the worship of Astarte became identified with that of Venus, and that this worship was connected with the most impure rites is apparent

from the close connection of this goddess with Asherah. 1 Kings 11:5, 33; 2 Kings 23:13.

Ash'ur (ăsh'ŭr) (*black*), the posthumous son of Hezron by his wife Abiah. 1 Chron. 2:24; 4:5. He became "father" or founder of the town of Tekoa.

Ash'urites (ăsh'ŭr-ītes), **The.** Only in 2 Sam. 2:9. By some of the old interpreters the name is taken as meaning the Geshurites; but if we follow the Targum of Jonathan, "the Asherites" will denote the inhabitants of the whole of the country west of the Jordan above Jezreel.

Ash'vath (ăsh'văth), one of the sons of Japhlet, of the tribe of Asher. 1 Chron. 7:33.

A'sia (ā'sià). The passages in the New Testament where this word occurs are the following: Acts 2:9; 6:9; 16:6; 19:10, 22, 26, 27, 31; 20:4, 16, 18; 21:27; 24:18; 27:2; 1 Cor. 16:19; 2 Cor. 1:8; 2 Tim. 1:15; 1 Pet. 1:1; Rev. 1:4, 11. In all these it may be confidently stated that the word is used for a Roman province which embraced the western part of the peninsula of Asia Minor, and of which Ephesus was the capital.

Asiar'chæ (ā-shi-är'kē) (*chief of Asia:* Authorized Version; Acts 19:31), officers chosen annually by the cities of that part of the province of Asia of which Ephesus was, under Roman government, the metropolis. They had charge of the public games and religious theatrical spectacles, the expenses of which they bore. While chosen each year they formed in time influential bodies and often were able to secure reëlection. The Asiarchs of Ephesus seem to have been friends of St. Paul.

A'siel (ā'sĭ-el) (*God hath made*). A Simeonite whose descendant Jehu lived in the reign of Hezekiah. 1 Chron. 4:35.

As'nah (ăs'nah) (*thorn-bush*). The children of Asnah were among the Nethinim who returned with Zerubbabel. Ezra 2:50.

Asnap'per (ăs-năp'pēr), mentioned in Ezra 4:10 as the person who settled the Cuthæans in the cities of Samaria. The identification of Asnapper R. V. Osnapper, with Assurbanipal is conceded by most authorities.

Asp (Heb. *pethen*), translated *adder* in Ps. 58:4; 91:13. Probably the Egyp-

tian cobra, a small and very poisonous serpent, a dweller in the holes of walls, Isa. 11 : 8, and a snake upon which the serpent-charmers of the East practiced their art.

As'patha (ăs'pa-thà), third son of Haman. Esth. 9 : 7.

As'riel (ăs'rĭ-el), the son of Gilead and great-grandson of Manasseh. Num. 26 : 31; Josh. 17 : 2. He was the founder of the family of the Asrielites.

Ass. Five Hebrew names of the genus *Asinus* occur in the Old Testament. (1) *Chamôr* and (2) *Athôn* denote the common domestic ass, male and female, respectively. Gen. 12 : 16; 32 : 3; 49 : 14. (3) *Aîr*, the young ass or colt, which occurs Gen. 32 : 15; 49 : 11. (4) *Pere*, a species of wild ass mentioned in Job 24 : 5; Ps. 104 : 11; Isa. 32 : 14. This is the species represented on the Ninevite sculptures. (5) *Arôd* occurs Dan. 5 : 21; Job 39 : 5; but in what respect it differs from the *Pere* is uncertain. It is very possibly the *Asinus onagu*, which was once common, but is now rare. It is the progenitor of the domestic ass.

The ass as found in eastern countries is a very different animal from what he is in western Europe. The most noble and honorable amongst the Jews were wont to be mounted on asses. "With us the ass is a symbol of stubbornness and stupidity, while in the East it is especially remarkable for its patience, gentleness, intelligence, meek submission and great power of endurance." —*L. Abbott.* The color is usually a

EASTERN ASS.

reddish brown, but there are white asses, which are much prized. The ass was the animal of peace, as the horse was the animal of war; hence the appropriateness of Christ in his triumphal entry riding on an ass. The wild ass is

a beautiful animal. Mr. Layard remarks that in fleetness the wild ass (*Asinus hemippus*) equals the gazelle, and to overtake it is a feat which only one or two of the most celebrated mares have been known to accomplish.

Assh'ur (ăsh'ur), second son of Shem, Gen. 10 : 22; also the Hebrew form for Assyria. [ASSYRIA.]

Asshu'rim, a tribe descended from Dedan, the grandson of Abraham. Gen. 25 : 3. Knobel considers them the same as the Asshur of Ezek. 27 : 23, and connected with southern Arabia.

As'sir (ăs'sĭr) (*captive*). 1. Son of Korah. Ex. 6 : 24; 1 Chron. 6 : 22.

2. Son of Ebiasaph, and a forefather of Samuel. 1 Chron. 6 : 23, 37.

3. Son of Jeconiah, 1 Chron. 3 : 17, unless "Jeconiah the captive" be the true rendering. Jeconiah was 18 years old at the time of his captivity and Assir may have been his son, born in Babylon. He did not succeed to the royal title, however.

As'sos (ăs'sŏs), or **As'sus,** a seaport of the Roman province of Asia, in the district anciently called Mysia, on the northern shore of the Gulf of Adramyttium, and about seven miles from Lesbos. Acts 20 : 13, 14.

As'sur (ăs'sur). Ezra 4 : 2; Ps. 83 : 8. [ASSHUR; ASSYRIA.]

Assyr'ia (ăs-sўr'ĭ-à), **Assh'ur,** was a great and powerful country lying on

AN ASSYRIAN PALACE GENIUS.

the Tigris, Gen. 2 : 14, the capital of which was Nineveh. Gen. 10 : 11, etc. It derived its name apparently from Asshur, the son of Shem, Gen. 10 : 22, who in later times was worshiped by the Assyrians as their chief god.

1. *Extent.*—The boundaries of Assyria differed greatly at different periods. Probably in the earliest times it was confined to a small tract of low country lying chiefly on the left bank of the Tigris. Gradually its limits were extended, until it came to be regarded as comprising the whole region between the Armenian mountains (lat. 37° 30') upon the north, and upon the south the country about Baghdad (lat. 33° 30'). Eastward its boundary was the high range of Zagros, or mountains of *Kurdistán;* westward it was, according to the views of some, bounded by the Mesopotamian desert, while according to others it reached the Euphrates.

2. *General character of the country.*— On the north and east the high mountain-chains of Armenia and Kurdistán are succeeded by low ranges of limestone hills of a somewhat arid aspect. To these ridges there succeeds at first an undulating zone of country, well watered and fairly productive, which ex-

AN ASSYRIAN SIEGE.

Siege of a city by Tiglath-pileser III., king of Assyria, about B.C. 745–727. (From a bas-relief on the walls of the palace of Tiglath-pileser III., discovered at Calah (Nimrud), now in the British Museum.)

A battering-ram is making a breach in the wall, under protection of archers, who are shooting from behind screens. In the background are impaled captives.

tends in length for 250 miles, and is interrupted only by a single limestone range. Above and below this barrier is an immense level tract, now for the most part a wilderness, which bears marks of having been in early times well cultivated and thickly peopled throughout.

3. *Original peopling.*—Scripture informs us that Assyria was peopled from Babylon, Gen. 10:11, and both classical tradition and the monuments of the country agree in this representation.

4. *Date of the foundation of the kingdom.*—As a country, Assyria was evidently known to Moses. Gen. 2:14; 25:18; Num. 24:22, 24. The earliest beginnings of Assyria are veiled in darkness, but there are stone records from about B.C. 2000.

5. *History.*—The excavations, referred to later, have brought to light the story of Assyria, written with great detail and exactness on clay tablets, cylinders and slabs. The most remarkable monarch of the earlier kings was called Tiglath-pileser. He appears to have been king towards the close of the twelfth century, and thus to have been contemporary with Samuel. Afterwards followed Pul, who invaded Israel in the reign of Menahem, 2 Kings 15:19, about B.C. 738, and Shalmaneser, who besieged Samaria three years, and destroyed the kingdom of Israel B.C. 721, himself or by his successor Sargon, who usurped the throne at that time. Under Sargon the empire was as great as at any former era, and Nineveh became a most beautiful city. Sargon's son Sennacherib became the most famous of the Assyrian kings. He began to reign 704 B.C. He invaded the kingdom of Judea in the reign of Hezekiah. He was followed by Esarhaddon, and he by a noted warrior and builder, Sardanapalus. In Scripture it is remarkable that we hear nothing of Assyria after the reign of Esarhaddon, and profane history is equally silent until the attacks began which brought about her downfall. The fall of Assyria, long previously prophesied by Isaiah, Isa. 10:5–19, was effected by the growing strength and boldness of the Medes, about 607 B.C. The prophecies of Nahum and Zephaniah (2:13–15) against Assyria were probably delivered shortly before the catastrophe.

6. *General character of the empire.*— The Assyrian monarchs bore sway over a number of petty kings through the entire extent of their dominions. These native princes were feudatories of the great monarch, of whom they held their crown by the double tenure of homage and tribute. It is not quite certain how far Assyria required a religious conformity from the subject people. Her religion was a gross and complex polytheism, comprising the worship of thirteen principal and numerous minor divinities, at the head of all of whom stood the chief god, Asshur, who seems to be the deified patriarch of the nation. Gen. 10:22.

7. *Civilization of the Assyrians.*—The civilization of the Assyrians was derived originally from the Babylonians. They were a Shemitic race, originally resident in Babylonia (which at that time was Cushite), and thus acquainted with the Babylonian inventions and discoveries, who ascended the valley of the Tigris and established in the tract immediately below the Armenian mountains a separate and distinct nationality. Still, as their civilization developed it became in many respects peculiar. Their art is of home growth. But they were still in the most important points barbarians. Their government was rude and inartificial, their religion coarse and sensual, and their conduct of war cruel.

8. *Modern discoveries.*—When Alexander the Great fought a battle near the site of ancient Nineveh, no one knew of its existence. But in 1843 excavations were begun in that vicinity, which have continued to the present time by various learned men. They found great numbers of inscriptions, and an immense library of stone tablets and slabs written in cuneiform or wedge-shaped letters. On one cylinder was recorded Sennacherib's own account of his war with Hezekiah. On tablets were written the Babylonian stories of creation and the Deluge in the time of Noah.

Great light has been thrown upon the Bible history, in various directions.

As'taroth. Deut. 1:4. [ASHTA-ROTH.]

Astar'te. [ASHTORETH.]

Asup'pim (à-sŭp'pim), and **House of,** 1 Chron. 26:15, 17, literally *house of the gatherings.* Some understand it as the proper name of chambers on the south of the temple; others of certain store-rooms, or of the council chambers in the outer court of the temple in which the elders held their deliberations. The Revised Version renders it by "storehouse."

Asyn'critus (à-sўn'krĭ-tus) (*incomparable*), a Christian at Rome, saluted by St. Paul. Rom. 16:14.

A'tad (ā'tad) (*thorn*), **The threshing-floor of,** called also Abel-mizraim, Gen. 50:10, 11, afterwards called Beth-nogla, and known to have lain between the Jordan and Jericho, therefore on the west side of Jordan.

At'arah (ăt'a-rah) (*a crown*), a wife of Jerahmeel, and mother of Onam. 1 Chron. 2:26.

At'aroth (ăt'a-rŏth) (*crowns*). 1. One of the towns in the "land of Jazer and land of Gilead," Num. 32:3, east of the Jordan, taken and built by the tribe of Gad. Num. 32:34. Probably *Attarus,* 3 or 4 miles from Macherus.

2. A place on the boundary of Ephraim and Benjamin. Josh. 16:2. Conder identifies it with the modern *Ed-Darieh* just south of the nether Beth-horon. Apparently the same place as

3. ATAROTH-ADAR, or -ADDAR, on the west border of Benjamin, "near the 'mountain' that is on the south side of the nether Beth-horon." Josh. 16:5; 18:13.

4. A town on the same boundary of Ephraim and Manasseh, but towards the east. Josh. 16:7. Several identifications are given, but none with certainty.

5. "ATAROTH, THE HOUSE OF JOAB," a place (?) occurring in the list of the descendants of Judah. 1 Chron. 2:54.

A'ter (ā'tẽr). 1. The children of Ater were among the porters or gate-keepers of the temple who returned with Zerubbabel. Ezra 2:42; Neh. 7:45.

2. The children of ATER OF HEZE-KIAH to the number of 98 returned with Zerubbabel, Ezra 2:16; Neh. 7:21, and were among the heads of the people who signed the covenant with Nehemiah. Neh. 10:17.

A'thach (ā'thăk) (*lodging place*), 1 Sam. 30:30. As the name does not occur elsewhere, it has been suggested that it is an error of the transcriber for Ether, a town in the low country of Judah. Josh. 15:42.

Athai'ah (ăth-a-ī'ah), a descendant of Pharez, the son of Judah, who dwelt at Jerusalem after the return from Babylon, Neh. 11:4.

Athali'ah (ăth-a-lī'ah), daughter of Ahab and Jezebel, married Jehoram, the son of Jehoshaphat king of Judah, and introduced into that kingdom the worship of Baal. (B.C. 891.) After the great revolution by which Jehu seated himself on the throne of Samaria, she killed all the members of the royal family of Judah who had escaped his sword. 2 Kings 11:1. From the slaughter one infant, named Joash, the youngest son of Ahaziah, was rescued by his aunt Jehosheba, wife of Jehoiada, 2 Chron. 22:11, the high priest. 2 Chron. 24:6. The child was brought up under Jehoiada's care, and concealed in the temple for six years, during which period Athaliah reigned over Judah. At length Jehoiada thought it time to produce the lawful king to the people, trusting to their zeal for the worship of God and their loyalty to the house of David. His plan was successful, and Athaliah was put to death.

Athe'nians (ạ-thē'nĭ-ạns), natives of Athens. Acts 17:21.

Ath'ens (ăth'ĕns) (*city of Athene*), the capital of Attica, and the chief seat of Grecian learning and civilization during the golden period of the history of Greece.

Description.—Athens is situated about five miles from the seacoast, in the central plain of Attica. In this plain rise several eminences. Of these the most prominent is a lofty insulated mountain, with a conical peaked summit, now called the Hill of St. George, and which bore in ancient times the name of *Lycabettus.* This mountain, which was not included within the ancient walls, lies to the northeast of Athens, and forms the most striking feature in the environs of the city. It is to Athens what Vesuvius is to Naples or Arthur's Seat to Edinburgh. Southwest of Lycabettus there are four hills of moderate height, all of which formed part of the city. Of these the nearest to Lycabettus, and at the distance of a mile from the latter, was the *Acropolis,* or citadel of Athens, a square, craggy rock rising abruptly about 512 feet, with a flat summit of about 1000 feet long from east to west, by 500 feet broad from north to south. Immediately west of the Acropolis is a second hill of irregular form, the *Areopagus* (Mars' Hill). To the southwest there rises a third hill, the *Pnyx,* on which the assemblies of the citizens were held. South of the city was seen the Saronic Gulf, with the harbors of Athens.

History.—Athens is said to have derived its name from the prominence given to the worship of the goddess Athena (Minerva) by its king, Erechtheus. The inhabitants were previously called Cecropidæ, from Cecrops, who, according to tradition, was the original founder of the city. This at first occupied only the hill or rock which afterwards became the Acropolis; but gradually the buildings spread over the ground at the southern foot of this hill. It was not till the time of Pisistratus and his sons (B.C. 560–514) that the city began to assume any degree of splendor. The most remarkable building of these despots was the gigantic temple of the Olympian Zeus or Jupiter. Under Themistocles the Acropolis began to form the centre of the city, round which the new walls described an irregular circle of about 60 stadia or 7½ miles in circumference. Themistocles transferred the naval station of the Athenians to the peninsula of Piræus, which is distant about 4½ miles from Athens, and contains three natural harbors. It was not till the administration of Pericles that the walls were built which connected Athens with her ports.

Buildings.—Under the administration of Pericles, Athens was adorned with numerous public buildings, which existed in all their glory when St. Paul visited the city. The Acropolis was the centre of the architectural splendor of Athens. It was covered with the temples of gods and heroes; and thus its platform presented not only a sanctuary, but a museum containing the finest productions of the architect and the sculptor, in which the whiteness of the marble was relieved by brilliant colors, and rendered still more dazzling by the transparent clearness of the Athenian atmosphere. The chief building was the *Parthenon* (*i. e.* House of the Virgin), the most perfect production of Grecian architecture. It derived its name from its being the temple of Athena Parthenos, or Athena the Virgin, the invincible goddess of war. It stood on the highest part of the Acropolis, near its centre. It was entirely of Pentelic marble, on a rustic basement of ordinary limestone, and its architecture, which was of the Doric order, was of the purest kind. It was adorned with the most exquisite sculptures, executed by various artists under the direction of Phidias. But the chief wonder of the Parthenon was the colos-

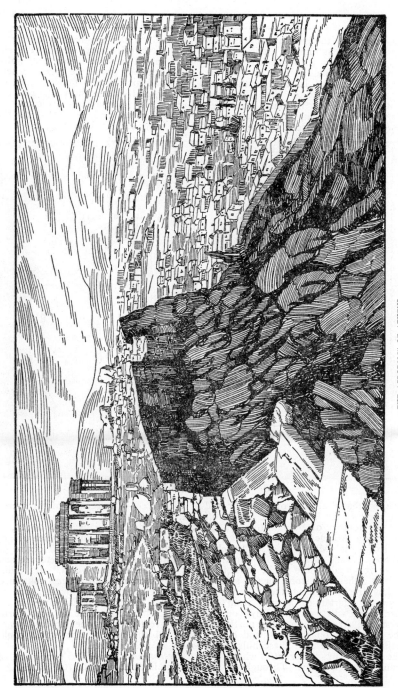

THE ACROPOLIS OF ATHENS.

sal statue of the virgin goddess executed by Phidias himself. The Acropolis was adorned with another colossal figure of Athena, in bronze, also the work of Phidias. It stood in the open air, nearly opposite the Propylæa. With its pedestal it must have been about 70 feet high, and consequently towered above the roof of the Parthe-

the road to the gymnasium and gardens of the *Academy,* which were situated about a mile from the walls. The Academy was the place where Plato and his disciples taught. East of the city, and outside the walls, was the *Lyceum,* a gymnasium dedicated to Apollo Lyceus, and celebrated as the place in which Aristotle taught.

NORTH COLONNADE OF THE PARTHENON.

non, so that the point of its spear and the crest of its helmet were visible off the promontory of Sunium to ships approaching Athens. The *Areopagus,* or Hill of Ares (Mars), is described elsewhere. [MARS' HILL.] The Pnyx, or place for holding the public assemblies of the Athenians, stood on the side of a low, rocky hill, at the distance of about a quarter of a mile from the Areopagus. Between the Pnyx on the west, the Areopagus on the north and the Acropolis on the east, and closely adjoining the base of these hills, stood the *Agora* or *"Market,"* where St. Paul disputed daily. Through it ran

Character.—The remark of the sacred historian respecting the inquisitive character of the Athenians, Acts 17: 21, is attested by the unanimous voice of antiquity. Athens "became the centre of enlightenment in science, literature and art for the ancient world." Its influence in literature and art has continued down the ages, and has made it one of the three most influential cities in all history. "In its prime it sent forth more great men in one hundred years than all the rest of the world could show in five hundred."

Present condition.—The population of Athens in 1922 was 300,701. (World Almanac). Educational institutions are very numerous. There are two universities in Athens. Education is compulsory between the ages of 6 and 12, but the law is not well enforced. A railway connects the Piræus or port with the city, and its terminus stands in the midst of what was once the Agora.

Ath'lai (ăth'lāi), one of the sons of Bebai, who put away his foreign wife. Ezra 10 : 28.

Atonement, The day of. I. The

THE WILDERNESS OF THE SCAPEGOAT, EAST OF JERUSALEM.
(According to Jewish tradition, the scapegoat was led out to a precipice and hurled down.)

great day of national humiliation, and the only one commanded in the Mosaic law. [FASTS.] The mode of its observance is described in Lev. 16, and the conduct of the people is emphatically enjoined in Lev. 23 : 26–32.

II. *Time.*—It was kept on the tenth day of Tisri, that is, from the evening of the ninth to the evening of the tenth of that month, five days before the feast of tabernacles. Tisri corresponds to our September–October, so that the 10th of Tisri would be about the first of October. See MONTHS in Appendix.

III. *How observed.*—It was kept by the people as a high solemn sabbath.

On this occasion only the high priest was permitted to enter into the holy of holies. Having bathed his person and dressed himself entirely in the holy white linen garments, he brought forward a young bullock for a sin offering, purchased at his own cost, on account of himself and his family, and two young goats for a sin offering, with a ram for a burnt offering, which were paid for out of the public treasury, on account of the people. He then presented the two goats before the Lord at the door of the tabernacle and cast lots upon them. On one lot *"For Jehovah"* was inscribed, and on the other *"For Azazel,"* —a phrase of unusual difficulty. Many modern scholars agree that it designates the *personal being* to whom the goat was sent, probably Satan. This goat was called the *scapegoat.* After various sacrifices and ceremonies the goat upon which the lot *"For Jehovah"* had fallen was slain and the high priest sprinkled its blood before the mercy-seat in the same manner as he had done that of the bullock. Going out from the holy of holies he purified the holy place, sprinkling some of the blood of both the victims on the altar of incense At this time no one besides the high priest was suffered to be present in the holy place. The purification of the holy of holies and of the holy place being thus completed, the high priest laid his hands upon the head of the goat on which the lot *"For Azazel"* had fallen, and confessed over it all the sins of the people. The goat was then led, by a man chosen for the purpose, into the wilderness, into "a land not inhabited," and was there let loose. The high priest after this returned into the holy place, bathed himself again, put on his usual garments of office, and offered the two rams as burnt offerings, one for himself and one for the people.

IV. *Significance.*—In considering the meaning of the particular rites of the day, three points appear to be of a very distinctive character. (1) The white garments of the high priest. (2) His entrance into the holy of holies. (3) The scapegoat. The writer of the Epistle to the Hebrews, Heb. 9:7-25, teaches us to apply the first two particulars. The high priest himself, with his person cleansed and dressed in white garments, was the best outward type which a living man could present in his own person of that pure and Holy One who was to purify his people and to cleanse them from their sins. But respecting the meaning of the scapegoat we have no such light to guide us, and the subject is one of great doubt and difficulty. It has been generally considered that it was dismissed to signify the carrying away of the sins of the people, as it were, out of the sight of Jehovah. If we keep in view that the two goats are spoken of as parts of one and the same sin offering, we shall not have much difficulty in seeing that they form together but one symbolical expression; the slain goat setting forth the act of sacrifice, in giving up its own life for others "to Jehovah;" and the goat which carried off its load of sin "for complete removal" signifying the cleansing influence of faith in that sacrifice.

At'roth (ăt'rŏth) (*crowns*), a city of Gad. Num. 32:35. Properly, as in R.V., Atroth-Shophan.

At'tai (ăt'tāi) (*opportune*). 1. Grandson of Sheshan the Jerahmeelite through his daughter Ahlai, whom he gave in marriage to Jarha, his Egyptian slave. 1 Chron. 2:35, 36. His grandson Zabad is by some identified with the Zabad of 1 Chron. 11:41.
2. One of the lion-faced warriors of Gad, captains of the host, who forded the Jordan at the time of its overflow, and joined David in the wilderness. 1 Chron. 12:11.
3. Second son of King Rehoboam by Maachah the daughter of Absalom. 2 Chron. 11:20.

Attali'a (ăt-tă-lī'à) (from *Attalus*), a coast-town of Pamphylia, mentioned Acts 14:25. It was built by Attalus Philadelphus, king of Pergamos, and named after the monarch. All its remains are characteristic of the date of its foundation. It is without doubt the present *Adalia,* on the south coast of Asia Minor, north of the *Duden Su,* the ancient Catarrhactes.

Augus'tus (ạu-gŭs'tus) (*venerable*) **Cæ'sar,** the first Roman emperor. He was born A.U.C. 691, B.C. 63. His father

THE EMPEROR AUGUSTUS.
The founder of the empire. Born B.C. 63; died A.D. 14. (From a marble head in the Vatican Museum.)

was Caius Octavius; his mother Atia, daughter of Julia the sister of C. Julius Cæsar. He was principally educated by his great-uncle Julius Cæsar, and was made his heir. After his murder, the young Octavius, then Caius Julius Cæsar Octavianus, was taken into the triumvirate with Antony and Lepidus, and, after the removal of the latter, divided the

Silver Stater of Augustus, or Tetradrachm of Antioch, equals 4 denarii, equals 65 cents (Matt. 17:27).

empire with Antony. The struggle for the supreme power was terminated in favor of Octavianus by the battle of Actium, B.C. 31. On this victory he was saluted imperator by the senate, who conferred on him the title Augustus, B.C. 27. The first link binding him to New Testament history is his treatment of Herod after the battle of Actium. That prince, who had espoused Antony's side, found himself pardoned, taken into favor and confirmed, nay even increased, in his power. After Herod's death, in 4 B.C., Augustus divided his dominions, almost exactly according to his dying directions, among his sons. Augustus died in Nola in Campania, Aug. 19, A.U.C. 767, A.D. 14, in his 76th year; but long before his death he had associated Tiberius with him in the empire. **Augus'tus' Band** (au-gŭs'tus). Acts 27 : 1. [ARMY.]

A'va (ā'và), a place in the empire of Assyria, apparently the same as Ivah. In R. V. Avvah. 2 Kings 17 : 24.

A'ven (ā'ven) (*idolatry*). 1. The "plain of Aven" is mentioned by Amos (1 : 5) in his denunciation of Syria and the country to the north of Palestine. This Aven is by some supposed to be the once magnificent Heliopolis, "city of the sun," now Baalbec (Bäl'bĕk) of Cœle-Syria, whose ruins are one of the wonders of the ages. It was situated in a plain near the foot of the Anti-Libanus range of mountains, 42 miles northwest of Damascus. It is famous for the colossal ruins of its temples, one of which, with its courts and porticos, extended over 1000 feet in length. The temples were built of marble or limestone and granite. Some of the columns were 7 feet in diameter and 62 feet high, or, including capital and pedestal, 89 feet. Some of the building-stones were 64 feet long and 12 feet thick. The temples are of Roman origin.

2. In Hos. 10 : 8 the word is clearly an abbreviation of Beth-aven, that is, Bethel. Comp. 4 : 15, etc.

3. The sacred city of Heliopolis or On, in Egypt. Ezek. 30 : 17.

A'vim (ā'vĭm) (*ruins*), **A'vims** or **A'vites.** 1. A people among the early inhabitants of Palestine, whom we meet with in the southwest corner of the sea-coast, whither they may have made their way northward from the desert, Deut. 2 : 23. Bedouin who had adopted a settled life.

2. The people of Ava, among the colonists who were sent by the king of Assyria to reinhabit the depopulated cities of Israel. 2 Kings 17 : 31.

A'vith (ā'vĭth) (*ruins*), the city of Hadad ben-Bedad, one of the kings of Edom before there were kings in Israel. Gen. 36 : 35; 1 Chron. 1 : 46.

Awl, a tool of which we do not know the ancient form. The only notice of it is in connection with the custom of boring the ear of the slave. Ex. 21 : 6; Deut. 15 : 17.

A'zal (ā'zăl), a name only occurring in Zech. 14 : 5. It is mentioned as the limit to which the ravine of the Mount of Olives will extend when "Jehovah shall go forth to fight." R. V. Azel.

Azali'ah (ăz-a-lī'ah) (*whom Jehovah hath set apart*), the father of Shaphan the scribe in the reign of Josiah. 2 Kings 22 : 3; 2 Chron. 34 : 8.

Azani'ah (ăz-a-nī'ah) (*Jehovah hath heard*), the father or immediate ancestor of Jeshua the Levite, in the time of Nehemiah. Neh. 10 : 9.

Azar'ael (à-zăr'e-el), a Levite musician. Neh. 12 : 36.

Aza'reel (aza're-el), or **Azar'eel** (*God has helped*). 1. A Korhite who joined David in his retreat at Ziklag. 1 Chron. 12 : 6. (B.C. 1057.)

2. A Levite musician of the family of Heman in the time of David, 1 Chron. 25 : 18; called UZZIEL in 25 : 4.

3. Son of Jeroham, and prince of the tribe of Dan when David numbered the people. 1 Chron. 27 : 22.

4. One of the sons of Bani, who put away his foreign wife on the remonstrance of Ezra. Ezra 10 : 41. (B.C. 459.)

5. Father or ancestor of Maasiai, or Amashai, a priest who dwelt in Jerusalem after the return from Babylon. Neh. 11 : 13.

Azari'ah (ăz-a-rī'ah) (*whom Jehovah helps*), a common name in Hebrew, and especially in the families of the priests of the line of Eleazar, whose name has precisely the same meaning as Azariah. It is nearly identical, and is often confounded, with Ezra as well as with Zerahiah and Seraiah. The principal persons who bore this name were—

1. Son of Ahimaaz. 1 Chron. 6 : 9. He appears from 1 Kings 4 : 2 to have succeeded Zadok, his grandfather, in the high priesthood, in the reign of Solomon, Ahimaaz having died before Zadok. [AHIMAAZ.]

2. A chief officer of Solomon's, the son of Nathan, perhaps David's nephew. 1 Kings 4 : 5.

3. Tenth king of Judah, more frequently called Uzziah. 2 Kings 14 : 21; 15 : 1, 6, 7, 8, 17, 23, 27; 1 Chron. 3 : 12. (B.C. 767.)

4. Son of Ethan, of the sons of Zerah, where, perhaps, Zerahiah is the more probable reading. 1 Chron. 2 : 8.

5. Son of Jehu of the family of the Jerahmeelites, and descended from Jarha the Egyptian slave of Sheshan. 1 Chron. 2 : 38, 39. He was probably one of the captains of hundreds in the time of Athaliah mentioned in 2 Chron. 23 : 1. (B.C. 840.)

6. The son of Johanan. 1 Chron. 6 : 10. He must have been high priest in the reigns of Abijah and Asa. (B.C. 920.)

7. Another Azariah is inserted between Hilkiah, in Josiah's reign, and Seraiah, who was put to death by Nebuchadnezzar, in 1 Chron. 6 : 13, 14.

8. Son of Zephaniah, a Kohathite, and ancestor of Samuel the prophet. 1 Chron. 6 : 36. Apparently the same as Uzziah in ver. 24.

9. Azariah, the son of Oded, 2 Chron. 15 : 1, called simply Oded in ver. 8, was a remarkable prophet in the days of King Asa, and a contemporary of Azariah the son of Johanan the high priest, and of Hanani the seer. (B.C. 920.)

10. Son of Jehoshaphat king of Judah. 2 Chron. 21 : 2. (B.C. 880.)

11. Another son of Jehoshaphat, and brother of the preceding. 2 Chron. 21 : 2.

12. In 2 Chron. 22 : 6 Azariah is a clerical error for Ahaziah.

13. Son of Jeroham, one of the captains of Judah in the time of Athaliah. 2 Chron. 23 : 1. Perhaps 5.

14. The high priest in the reign of Uzziah king of Judah. The most memorable event of his life is that which is recorded in 2 Chron. 26 : 17-20. (B.C. 789.) Azariah was contemporary with Isaiah the prophet and with Amos and Joel. Perhaps 6.

15. Son of Johanan, one of the captains of Ephraim in the reign of Ahaz. 2 Chron. 28 : 12.

16. A Kohathite, father of Joel, in the reign of Hezekiah. 2 Chron. 29 : 12.

17. A Merarite, son of Jehalelel, in the time of Hezekiah. 2 Chron. 29 : 12.

18. The high priest in the days of Hezekiah. 2 Chron. 31 : 10, 13. He appears to have co-operated zealously with the king in that thorough purification of the temple and restoration of the temple services which was so

conspicuous a feature in his reign. He succeeded Urijah, who was high priest in the reign of Ahaz.

19. Son of Maaseiah, who repaired part of the wall of Jerusalem in the time of Nehemiah. Neh. 3 : 23, 24.

20. One of the leaders of the children of the province who went up from Babylon with Zerubbabel. Neh. 7 : 7.

21. One of the Levites who assisted Ezra in instructing the people in the knowledge of the law. Neh. 8 : 7.

22. One of the priests who sealed the covenant with Nehemiah, Neh. 10 : 2, and probably the same with the Azariah who assisted in the dedication of the city wall. Neh. 12 : 33.

23. Jer. 43 : 2 (Jezaniah).

24. The original name of Abed-nego. Dan. 1 : 6, 7, 11, 19. He appears to have been of the seed-royal of Judah.

A'zaz (ā'zăz) (*strong*), a Reubenite, father of Bela. 1 Chron. 5 : 8.

Azazi'ah (ăz-a-zī'ah) (*Jehovah strengthens*, or *is strong*). 1. A Levite musician in the reign of David, appointed to play the harp in the service which attended the procession by which the ark was brought up from the house of Obed-edom. 1 Chron. 15 : 21. (B.C. 1042.)

2. The father of Hoshea, prince of the tribe of Ephraim when David numbered the people. 1 Chron. 27 : 20.

3. One of the Levites in the reign of Hezekiah, who had charge of the tithes and dedicated things in the temple. 2 Chron. 31 : 13.

Az'buk (ăz'bŭk), father or ancestor of Nehemiah, the prince of part of Bethzur. Neh. 3 : 16.

Aze'kah (à-zē'kah) (*dug over*), a town of Judah, with dependent villages, lying in the Shefelah or rich agricultural plain. It is most clearly defined as being near Shochoh, 1 Sam. 17 : 1; but its position has not yet been recognized. Josh. 10 : 10, 11; 15 : 35; 2 Chron. 11 : 9; Jer. 34 : 7; Neh. 11 : 30.

A'zel (ā'zel) (*noble*), a descendant of Saul. 1 Chron. 8 : 37, 38; 9 : 43, 44.

A'zem (ā'zem) (*bone*), a city in the extreme south of Judah, Josh. 15 : 29, afterwards allotted to Simeon. Josh. 19 : 3. Also given as Ezem.

Az'gad (ăz'găd) (*strength of fortune*). The children of Azgad, to the number of 1222 (2322 according to Neh. 7 : 17), were among the laymen who returned with Zerubbabel. Ezra 2 : 12;

8:12. With the other heads of the people they joined in the covenant with Nehemiah. Neh. 10:15.

A'ziel (ā'zĭ-el) (*God comforts*), a Levite. 1 Chron. 15:20. The name is a shortened form of Jaaziel in ver. 18.

Azi'za (à-zī'zà) (*strong*), a layman of the family of Zattu, who had married a foreign wife after the return from Babylon. Ezra 10:27.

Az'maveth (ăz'ma-vĕth) (*strong unto death*). 1. One of David's mighty men, a native of Bahurim, 2 Sam. 23:31; 1 Chron. 11:33, and therefore probably a Benjamite.

2. A descendant of Mephibosheth, or Merib-baal. 1 Chron. 8:36; 9:42.

3. The father of Jeziel and Pelet, two of the skilled Benjamite slingers and archers who joined David at Ziklag, 1 Chron. 12:3; perhaps identical with No. 1.

4. Overseer of the royal treasures in the reign of David. 1 Chron. 27:25.

Az'maveth (ăz'ma-vĕth), a place to all appearance in Benjamin, being named with other towns belonging to that tribe. Ezra 2:24. The name elsewhere occurs as BETH-AZMAVETH. Now *Hizmeh* near Gibeah.

Az'mon (ăz'mŏn) (*strong*), a place named as being on the southern boundary of the Holy Land, apparently near the torrent of Egypt (*Wadi el-Arish*). Num. 34:4, 5; Josh. 15:4. It has not yet been identified.

Az'noth-ta'bor (ăz'nŏth-tā'bôr) (*the ears* [i. e. the slopes or summits] *of Tabor*), one of the landmarks of the boundary of Naphtali. Josh. 19:34. The town, if town it be, has hitherto escaped recognition.

A'zor (ā'zôr) (*a helper*), son of Eliakim, in the line of our Lord. Matt. 1:13, 14.

Azo'tus (à-zō'tus). [ASHDOD.]

Az'riel (ăz'rĭ-el) (*help of God*). 1. The head of a house of the half-tribe of Manasseh beyond Jordan, a man of renown. 1 Chron. 5:24.

2. A Naphtalite, ancestor of Jerimoth, the head of the tribe at the time of David's census. 1 Chron. 27:19.

3. The father of Seraiah, an officer of Jehoiakim. Jer. 36:26.

Az'rikam (ăz'ri-kam) (*help against the enemy*). 1. A descendant of Zerubbabel, and son of Neariah of the royal line of Judah. 1 Chron. 3:23.

2. Eldest son of Azel, and descendant of Saul, 1 Chron. 8:38; 9:44.

3. A Levite, ancestor of Shemaiah, who lived in the time of Nehemiah. 1 Chron. 9:14; Neh. 11:15.

4. Governor of the house, or prefect of the palace, to King Ahaz, who was slain by Zichri, an Ephraimite hero, in the successful invasion of the southern kingdom by Pekah king of Israel. 2 Chron. 28:7. (B.C. 735.)

Azu'bah (à-zū'bah) (*forsaken*). 1. Wife of Caleb, son of Hezron. 1 Chron. 2:18; 19.

2. Mother of King Jehoshaphat. 1 Kings 22:42; 2 Chron. 20:31. (B.C. 910.)

A'zur (ā'zur), properly **Az'zur** (*helper*). 1. A Benjamite of Gibeon, and father of Hananiah the false prophet. Jer. 28:1.

2. Father of Jaazaniah, one of the princes of the people against whom Ezekiel was commanded to prophesy. Ezek. 11:1.

Az'zah (ăz'zah) (*strong*). Another rendering of the name of the well-known Philistine city Gaza. Deut. 2:23; 1 Kings 4:24; Jer. 25:20.

Az'zan (ăz'zan) (*strong*), the father of Paltiel, prince of the tribe of Issachar, who represented his tribe in the division of the promised land. Num. 34:26.

Az'zur (ăz'zur) (*one who helps*), one of the heads of the people who signed the covenant with Nehemiah. Neh. 10:17. The name is probably that of a family, and in Hebrew is the same as is elsewhere represented by AZUR.

B

Ba'al (bā'al). The word means *owner* or *lord* and is used of both men and gods. When used of men it implies possession, and comes to mean *husband*. As applied to gods it means rather possessor of lands than ruler of men. In its original meaning it is a part of the names of many true worshipers of Jehovah. It is commonly held that there was a supreme deity known as Baal who was the supreme male divinity of the Phœnician and Canaanitish nations, as Ashtoreth was their supreme female divinity. Some suppose Baal to correspond to the sun and Ashtoreth to the moon; others that Baal was Jupiter and Ashtoreth Venus. But evidence seems to warrant the statement that there was no supreme Baal, but many Baals, the gods of particular places. The word *Baalim*, the plural of Baal, occurs frequently. There can be no doubt of the very high antiquity of the worship of Baalim. It prevailed in the time of Moses among the Moabites and Midianites, Num. 22:41, and through them spread to the Israelites. Num. 25:3-18; Deut. 4:3. In the times of the kings it became the religion of the court and people of the ten tribes, 1 Kings 16:31-33; 18:19, 22, and appears never to have been permanently abolished among them. 2 Kings 17:16. Temples were erected to Baal in Samaria, 1 Kings 16:32, and he was worshiped with much ceremony. 1 Kings 18:19, 26-28; 2 Kings 10:22. This Baal was Melkart the chief deity of Tyre. The attractiveness of this worship to the Jews undoubtedly grew out of its licentious character. We find this worship also in Phœnician colonies. The religion of the ancient British islands much resembled this ancient worship of Baal, and may have been derived from it. Nor need we hestitate to regard the Babylonian Bel, Isa. 46:1, or Belus, as essentially identical with Baal, though perhaps under some modified form. The Baals of different places were sometimes worshiped under different compounds, among which appear—

1. BAAL-BERITH (bā'al-bē'rith) (*the covenant Baal*), Judges 8:33; 9:4, the god who comes into covenant with the worshipers.

2. BAAL-ZEBUB (bā'al-zē'bŭb) (*lord of the fly*), and worshiped at Ekron. 2 Kings 1:2, 3, 16.

3. BAAL-PEOR (bā'al-pē'or) (*lord of Peor*). The narrative (Num. 25) seems clearly to show that this form of Baal worship was connected with licentious rites.

Ba'al (bā'al) (*lord*). 1. A Reubenite. 1 Chron. 5:5.

2. The son of Jehiel, and grandfather of Saul. 1 Chron. 8:30; 9:36.

Ba'al (bā'al), *geographical*. This word occurs as the prefix or suffix to the names of several places in Palestine, some of which are as follows:

1. BAAL (bā'al), a town of Simeon, named only in 1 Chron. 4:33, which from the parallel list in Josh. 19:8 seems to have been identical with BAAL-ATH-BEER.

2. BAALAH (bā'al-ah) (*mistress*), *a.* Another name for KIRJATH-JEARIM, or KIRJATH-BAAL, the well-known town, also called Baale-Judah. Josh. 15:9, 10; 1 Chron. 13:6. *b.* A town in the south of Judah, Josh. 15:29, which in 19:3 is called BALAH, in the parallel list, 1 Chron. 4:29, BILHAH.

3. BAALATH (bā'al-äth) (*mistress*), a town of Dan named with Gibbethon, Gath-rimmon and other Philistine places. Josh. 19:44.

4. BAALATH-BEER (bā'al-äth-bē'ĕr) (*lord of the well*). BAAL 1, a town among those in the south part of Judah, given to Simeon, which also bore the name of RAMATH-NEGEB, or "the height of the south." Josh. 19:8.

5. BAAL-GAD (bā-al-găd) (*lord of fortune*), used to denote the most northern Josh. 11:17; 12:7, or perhaps northwestern, 13:5, point to which Joshua's victories extended. It was in all probability a sanctuary where Gad, or For-

RUINS OF THE TEMPLE OF BAAL. BAALBEC SYRIA.

tune, was worshiped. Probably its site is *Ain Jedeideh* on the northwest slopes of Hermon.

6. BAAL-HAMON (bā'al-hā'mon) (*lord of a multitude*), a place at which Solomon had a vineyard, evidently of great extent. Cant 8 : 11.

7. BAAL-HAZOR (bā'al-hā'zôr) (*lord of a village*), a place where Absalom appears to have had a sheep-farm, and where Amnon was murdered. 2 Sam. 13 : 23. It is probably *Tell Asur,* near Ephraim.

8. MOUNT BAAL-HERMON (bā'al-hĕr'-mon) (*lord of Hermon*), Judges 3 : 3, and simply Baal-hermon. 1 Chron. 5 : 23. This is usually considered as a distinct place from Mount Hermon; but we know that this mountain had at least three names (Deut. 3 : 9) and Baal-hermon may have been a fourth.

9. BAAL-MEON (bā'al-mē'on) (*lord of the house*), one of the towns which were rebuilt by the Reubenites. Num. 32 : 38. It also occurs in 1 Chron. 5 : 8, and on each occasion with Nebo. In the time of Ezekiel it was Moabite, one of the cities which were the "glory of the country." Ezek. 25 : 9. It is named on the Moabite Stone as built by Mesha. The present ruin, Ma'in, is four miles from Medeba, but the ruins are largely Roman.

10. BAAL-PERAZIM (bā'al-pĕr'a-zim) (*lord of breaking forth*), the scene of a victory of David over the Philistines, and of a great destruction of their images. 2 Sam. 5 : 20; 1 Chron. 14 : 11. See Isa. 28 : 21, where it is called MOUNT PERAZIM.

11. BAAL-SHALISHA (bā'al-shăl'ĭ-shà) (*lord of Shalisha*), a place named only in 2 Kings 4 : 42; apparently not far from Gilgal; comp. 4 : 38. Conder locates it at Kefr Thilth, 16 miles northeast of Lydda and 13½ miles northwest of Gilgal

12. BAAL-TAMAR (bā'al-tā'mär) (*lord of the palm tree*), a place named only in Judges 20 : 33, as near Gibeah of Benjamin. The palm tree (*tâmâr*) of Deborah, Judges 4 : 5, was situated somewhere in the locality, and is possibly alluded to.

13. BAAL-ZEPHON (bā'al-zē'fon) (*lord of the north*). a place in Egypt near where the Israelites crossed the Red Sea. Num. 33 : 7; Exod. 14 : 2, 9. Both the meaning and situation are extremely

uncertain. It may have been a little below the head of the Gulf of Suez.

Ba'alah (bā'al-ah). [BAAL, No. 2.]
Ba'alath (bā'al-ăth). [BAAL, 3, 4.]
Baal'bec. See AVEN.
Ba'ale of Judah. [BAAL, No. 2, *a.*]
Ba'al=ha'nan (bā'al-hā'nan). **1.** The name of one of the early kings of Edom. Gen. 36 : 38, 39; 1 Chron. 1 : 49, 50.

2. The name of one of David's officers, who had the superintendence of his olive and sycomore plantations. 1 Chron. 27 : 28.

Ba'ali. Hos. 2 : 16. [BAAL.]
Ba'alim. [BAAL.]
Ba'alis (bā'al-is), king of the Ammonites at the time of the destruction of Jerusalem by Nebuchadnezzar. Jer. 40 : 14. (B.C. 586.)

Ba'ana (bā'a-nà). **1.** The son of Ahilud, Solomon's commissariat officer in Jezreel and the north of the Jordan valley. 1 Kings 4 : 12.

2. Father of Zadok, who assisted in rebuilding the wall of Jerusalem under Nehemiah. Neh. 3 : 4.

Ba'anah (bā'a-nà). **1.** Son of Rimmon, a Benjamite, who with his brother Rechab murdered Ish-bosheth. For this they were killed by David, and their mutilated bodies hung up over the pool at Hebron. 2 Sam. 4 : 2, 5, 6, 9. (B.C. 1048.)

2. A Netophathite, father of Heleb or Heled, one of David's mighty men. 2 Sam. 23 : 29; 1 Chron. 11 : 30.

3. Accurately Baana, son of Hushai, Solomon's commissariat officer in Asher. 1 Kings 4 : 16.

4. A man who accompanied Zerubbabel on his return from the captivity. Ezra 2 : 2; Neh. 7 : 7. Possibly the same person is intended in Neh. 10 : 27. (B.C. 536.)

Ba'ara, one of the wives of Shaharaim, a descendant of Benjamin. 1 Chron. 8 : 8.

Baase'iah (bā'a-sē'iah), or **Bassei'-ah** (*work of Jehovah*), a Gershonite Levite, one of the forefathers of Asaph the singer. 1 Chron. 6 : 40.

Ba'asha (bā'a-shà), B.C. 914–891, third sovereign of the separate kingdom of Israel, and the founder of its second dynasty. He was son of Ahijah of the tribe of Issachar, and conspired against King Nadab, 1 Kings 15 : 27, and killed him with his whole family.

He appears to have been of humble origin. 1 Kings 16 : 2. It was probably in the 13th year of his reign that he made war on Asa, and began to fortify Ramah. He was defeated by the unexpected alliance of Asa with Ben-hadad I, of Damascus. Baasha died in the 24th year of his reign, and was buried in Tirzah, Cant. 6 : 4, which he had made his capital. 1 Kings 16 : 6; 2 Chron. 16 : 1–6.

Ba'bel (bā'bel) (*confusion*), **Bab'-ylon** (Greek form of *Babel*), is properly the capital city of the country which is called in Genesis *Shinar,* and in the later books *Chaldea,* or the land of the Chaldeans. The first rise of the Chaldean power was in the region close upon the Persian Gulf; thence the nation spread northward up the course of the rivers, and the seat of government moved in the same direction, being finally fixed at Babylon, perhaps not earlier than B.C. 1700.

I. *Topography of Babylon—Ancient descriptions of the city.*—All the ancient writers appear to agree in the fact of a district of vast size, more or less inhab-

THE SO-CALLED BABYLONIAN SCENE
OF THE FALL OF MAN.
An impression of a seal cylinder, with Sacred Tree, Fruit and Serpent

ited, having been enclosed within lofty walls, and included under the name of Babylon. With respect to the exact extent of the circuit they differ. The estimate of Herodotus and of Pliny is 480 stades (60 Roman miles, 53 of our

EXCAVATED TEMPLE AT NIPPUR — OF THIRD MILLENNIUM B. C.

EXCAVATIONS IN THE TEMPLE AT NIPPUR, BABYLONIA.
(Showing the structure of an ancient Babylonian temple such as that described as the Tower of Babel.)

miles), of Strabo 385, of Q. Curtius 368, of Clitarchus 365 and of Ctesias 360 stades (40 miles). George Smith, in his "Assyrian Discoveries," differs entirely from all these estimates, making the circuit of the city but *eight* miles. Perhaps Herodotus spoke of the *outer* wall, which could be traced in his time. Taking the lowest estimate of the extent of the circuit, we shall have for the space within the rampart an area of above 100 square miles—nearly the present size of London. This area was not entirely covered with houses, but large spaces were reserved for gardens and fields, which enabled it to endure a siege. Around all four sides between the two walls was a space where houses were not allowed to be built. The city was situated on both sides of the river Euphrates, and the two parts were connected together by a stone bridge five stades (above 1000 yards) long and 30 feet broad. At either extremity of the bridge was a royal palace, that in the eastern city being the more magnificent of the two. The two palaces were joined not only by the bridge, but by a tunnel under the river. The houses, which were frequently three or four stories high, were laid out in straight streets crossing each other at right angles.

II. *Present state of the ruins.*—A portion of the ruins is occupied by the modern town of *Hillah*. About five miles above Hillah, on the opposite or left bank of the Euphrates, occurs a series of artificial mounds of enormous size. Scattered over the country on both sides of the Euphrates are a number of remarkable mounds, usually standing single, which are plainly of the same date with the great mass of ruins upon the river bank. Of these by far the most striking is the vast ruin called the *Birs-Nimrûd*, about six miles to the southwest of Hillah.

For many years these mounds have been excavated by learned men from Germany, France, England and America, who have found ancient cylinders, bricks, seals used by kings and business men, and inscriptions, which have thrown a great deal of light upon the ancient Babylonians, and the Scripture references to them.

III. *Identification of sites.*—The great mound of *Babil* is probably the ancient temple of Belus. The mound

of the *Kasr* marks the site of the great palace of Nebuchadnezzar. The mound of *Amrám* is thought to represent the "hanging gardens" of Nebuchadnezzar; but most probably it represents the ancient palace, coeval with Babylon itself, of which Nebuchadnezzar speaks in his inscriptions as adjoining his own more magnificent residence.

IV. *History of Babylon.*—Scripture represents the "beginning of the kingdom" as belonging to the time of Nimrod. Gen. 10: 6-10. The early annals of Babylon are filled by Berosus, the native historian, with three dynasties: one of 49 Chaldean kings, who reigned 458 years; another of 9 Arab kings, who reigned 245 years; and a third of 49 Assyrian monarchs, who held dominion for 526 years. The line of Babylonian kings becomes exactly known to us from B.C. 747. The "Canon of Ptolemy" gives us the succession of Babylonian monarchs from B.C. 747 to B.C. 331, when the last Persian king was dethroned by Alexander. On the fall of Nineveh, B.C. 607, Babylon became not only an independent kingdom, but an empire. The city was taken by surprise B.C. 539, as Jeremiah had prophesied, Jer. 51: 31, 39,—and as intimated 170 years earlier by Isaiah, Isa. 21: 1-9,—by Cyrus and his general Gobryas, who is probably the Darius of Dan. 5. With the conquest of Cyrus commenced the decay of Babylon, which has since been a quarry from which all the tribes in the vicinity have derived the bricks with which they have built their cities. The "great city" has thus emphatically "become heaps." Jer. 51: 37.

Ba'bel (bā'bel), **Tower of.** The "tower of Babel" is only mentioned once in Scripture, Gen. 11: 4, 5, 9, and then as incomplete. It was built of bricks, and the "slime" used for mortar was probably bitumen. Such authorities as we possess represent the building as destroyed soon after its erection. When the Jews, however, were carried captive into Babylonia, they thought they recognized it in the famous temple of Belus, the modern *Birs-Nimrûd*. But the *Birs-Nimrûd*, though it cannot be the tower of Babel itself, may well be taken to show the probable shape and character of the edifice. This building appears to have been a sort of oblique pyramid built in seven receding stages, each successive one being nearer to the southwestern end, which constituted the back of the building. The first, second and third stories were each 26 feet high, the remaining four being 15 feet high. On the seventh stage there was probably placed the ark or tabernacle, which seems to have been again 15 feet high, and must have nearly, if not entirely, covered the top of the seventh story. The entire original height, allowing three feet for the platform, would thus have been 156 feet, or without the platform 153 feet.

Bab'ylon (băb'ў-lon), in the Apocalypse, is the symbolical name by which Rome is denoted. Rev. 14:8; 17:18. The power of Rome was regarded by the later Jews as was that of Babylon

PLAN OF ANCIENT BABYLON.

by their forefathers. Comp. Jer. 51:7 with Rev. 14:8. The occurrence of this name in 1 Pet. 5:13 has given rise to a variety of conjectures, many giving it the same meaning as in the Apocalypse; others refer it to Babylon in Asia, and others still to Babylon in Egypt. The most natural supposition of all is that by Babylon is intended the old Babylon of Assyria, which was largely inhabited by Jews at the time in question.

Babylo'nians, the inhabitants of Babylon, a race of Shemitic origin, who were among the colonists planted in the cities of Samaria by the conquering Assyrians. Ezra 4:9.

Babylonish (băb-ў-lō'nish) **garment,** literally "robe of Shinar," Josh. 7:21; an ample robe, naturally coveted by Achan, for it was such as kings wore, and was ornamented with embroidery, or perhaps a variegated garment with figures inwoven in the fashion for which the Babylonians were celebrated.

Ba'ca (bā'ká) (*weeping*), **The Valley of,** a valley in Palestine, through which the exiled Psalmist sees in vision the pilgrims passing in their march towards the sanctuary of Jehovah at Zion. Ps. 84:6. That it was a real locality is most probable from the use of the definite article before the name. But the expression "passing through the valley of Baca (*i. e.* of weeping) make it a well," R. V. a place of springs, is used metaphorically of religion transforming sorrow into joy.

Bach'rites, The, the family of BECHER, son of Ephraim. Num. 26:35.

Badger Skins. There is much obscurity as to the meaning of the word *tachash*, rendered "badger" in the Authorized Version, Ex. 25:5; 35:7, etc. The ancient versions seem nearly all agreed that it denotes not an animal but a color. But modern scholars favor the view that it is an animal. The Arabic *duchash* or *tuchash* denotes a dolphin, including seals and cetaceans. The skins referred to are probably those of these marine animals, some of which are found in the Red Sea. The skin of the *Halicore,* one of these, from its hardness would be well suited for making soles for shoes. Ezek. 16 : 10.

Bag is the rendering of several words in the Old and New Testaments. (1) *Chărîtim,* the "bags" in which Naaman bound up the two talents of silver for Gehazi. 2 Kings 5 : 23. In Isa. 3 : 22 it is mentioned in the list of women's adornments, and is probably some kind of ornamentally woven pouch or satchel. (See R. V.) (2) *Kîs,* a bag for carrying weights, Deut. 25 : 13; also used as a purse. Prov. 1 : 14. (3) *Kĕlî,* in Gen. 42 : 25, is the "sack" in which Jacob's sons carried the corn which they brought from Egypt. (4) The shepherd's "bag" used by David was for the purpose of carrying the lambs unable to walk. 1 Sam. 17 : 40; Isa. 40 : 11. (5) *Tseror,* properly a "bundle," Gen. 42 : 35, appears to have been used by travelers for carrying money during a long journey. Prov. 7 : 20. (6) The "bag" which Judas carried was probably a small box or chest. John 12 : 6; 13 : 29.

Baha'rumite, The. [BAHURIM.]

Bahu'rim (bà-hū'rim) (*young men*), a village, 2 Sam. 16 : 5, apparently on or close to the road leading up from the Jordan valley to Jerusalem, and near the south boundary of Benjamin. 2 Sam. 3 : 16; 17 : 18; 19 : 16; 1 Kings 2 : 8.

Ba'jith (bā'jith) (*the house*), referring to the "temple" of the false gods of Moab, as opposed to the "high places" in the same sentence. Isa. 15 : 2, and comp. 16 : 12.

Bakbak'kar a Levite, apparently a descendant of Asaph. 1 Chron. 9 : 15.

Bak'buk (*pitcher*). "Children of Bakbuk" were among the Nethinim who returned from captivity with Zerubbabel. Ezra 2 : 51; Neh. 7 : 53.

Bakbuki'ah (băk-bu-kî'ah) (*pitcher of Jehovah*), a Levite in the time of Nehemiah. Neh. 12 : 9.

Bake. Reference to baking is found in Gen. 40; Lev. 26 : 26; 1 Sam. 8 : 13; 2 Sam. 13 : 8; Jer. 37 : 21; Hos. 7 : 4–7.

Ba'laam (bā'lam) (B.C. 1452), the son of Beor, a man endowed with the gift of prophecy. Num. 22 : 5. He is mentioned in conjunction with the five kings of Midian, apparently as a person of the same rank. Num. 31 : 8; cf. 31 : 16. He seems to have lived at Pethor, Deut.

23 : 4; Num. 22 : 5, on the river Euphrates, in Mesopotamia. Such was his reputation that when the Israelites were encamped in the plains of Moab, Balak, the king of Moab, sent for Balaam to curse them. Balaam at first was prohibited by God from going. He was again sent for by the king and again refused, but was at length allowed to go. He yielded to the temptations of riches and honor which Balak set before him; but God's anger was kindled at this manifestation of determined self-will, and the angel of the Lord stood in the way for an adversary against him. See 2 Pet. 2 : 15, 16. Balaam predicted a magnificent career for the people whom he was called to curse, but he nevertheless suggested to the Moabites the expedient of seducing them to commit fornication. The effect of this is recorded in Num. 25. A battle was afterwards fought against the Midianites, in which Balaam sided with them, and was slain by the sword of the people whom he had endeavored to curse. Num. 31 : 8.

Ba'lac Rev. 2 : 14. [BALAK.]

Bal'adan (băl'a-dăn). [MERODACH-BALADAN.]

Ba'lah. Josh. 19 : 3. [BAAL, *Geogr.* No. 2, *b.*]

Ba'lak (bā'lăk) (*making waste*), son of Zippor, king of the Moabites, who hired Balaam to curse the Israelites; but his designs were frustrated in the manner recorded in Num. 22–24. (B.C. 1452.)

Balances. Reference to balances is

EGYPTIAN BALANCER WEIGHING RINGS OF GOLD.

found in Lev. 19 : 36. They were in common use, gold and silver being paid out and received by weight. Reference is also made in Micah 6 : 11; Hosea 12 : 7, to the dishonest practice of buying by heavier and selling by lighter weights.

Baldness. Natural baldness seems to have been uncommon, since it exposed people to public derision. Lev. 13 : 29; 2 Kings 2 : 23; Isa. 3 : 24; 15 : 2; Jer. 47 : 5; Ezek. 7 : 18. Artificial baldness marked the conclusion of a Nazirite's vow, and was a sign of mourning. Num. 6 : 9; Acts 18 : 18.

Balm (from *balsam*, Heb. *tzôrî, tzerî*) occurs in Gen. 37 : 25; 43 : 11; Jer. 8 : 22; 46 : 11; 51 : 8; Ezek. 27 : 17. It is an aromatic plant, or the resinous odoriferous sap or gum which exudes from such

BALM OF GILEAD.

plants. It is impossible to identify it with any certainty. It may represent the gum of the *Pistacia lentiscus*, or more probably that of the *Balsamodendron opobalsamum*, allied to the *balm of Gilead*, which abounded in Gilead east of the Jordan. The trees resembled fig trees (or grape vines), but were lower, being but 12 to 15 feet high. It is now called the BALM OF GILEAD, or *Meccabalsam*, the tree or shrub being indigenous in the mountains around Mecca. [INCENSE; SPICES.] Hasselquist says that the exudation from the plant "is of a yellow color, and pellucid. It has a most fragrant smell, which is resinous, balsamic and very agreeable. It is very tenacious or glutinous, sticking to the fingers, and may be drawn into long threads." It was supposed to have healing as well as aromatic qualities.

Ba'mah (bā'mah) (*high place*). Found only in Ezek. 20 : 29, applied to places of idolatrous worship.

Ba'moth=ba'al (bā'mŏth-bā'al) (*high places of Baal*), a sanctuary of Baal in the country of Moab, Josh. 13 : 17, which is probably mentioned in Num. 21 : 19 under the shorter form of Bamoth, or Bamoth-in-the-ravine (20), and possibly again in Isa. 15 : 2.

Band. The "band of Roman soldiers" referred to in Matt. 27 : 27 and elsewhere was the tenth part of a legion. It was called a "cohort," and numbered, nominally, 600 men under the command of six centurions. Usually it numbered from 400 to 600. [See ARMY.]

Ba'ni (bā'nī) (*built*). 1. A Gadite, one of David's mighty men. 2 Sam. 23 : 36. There is some uncertainty as to this verse. See 1 Chron. 11 : 38.

2. A Levite of the line of Merari, and forefather to Ethan. 1 Chron. 6 : 46.

3. A man of Judah of the line of Pharez. 1 Chron. 9 : 4.

4. "Children of Bani" returned from captivity with Zerubbabel. Ezra 2 : 10; 10 : 29, 34; Neh. 10 : 14. [BINNUI.]

5. An Israelite "of the sons of Bani." Ezra 10 : 38.

6. A Levite. Neh. 3 : 17.

7. A Levite. Neh. 8 : 7; 9 : 4, 5; 10 : 13.

8. Another Levite, of the sons of Asaph. Neh. 11 : 22.

Banner. [See ENSIGN.]

Banquets, among the Hebrews, were not only a means of social enjoyment, but were a part of the observance of religious festivity. At the three solemn festivals the family also had its domestic feast. Deut. 16 : 11. Sacrifices, both ordinary and extraordinary, Ex. 34 : 15; Judges 16 : 23, included a banquet. Birthday banquets are only mentioned Gen. 40 : 20; Matt. 14 : 6. The usual time of the banquet was the evening, and to begin early was a mark of excess. Eccles. 10 : 16; Isa. 5 : 11. The most essential materials of the banqueting-room, next to the viands and wine, which last was often drugged with spices, Prov. 9 : 2, were perfumed unguents, garlands or loose flowers, white or brilliant robes; after these, exhibitions of music, singers and dancers, riddles, jesting and merriment. Judges 14 : 12; 2 Sam. 19 : 35; Neh. 8 : 10; Eccles. 10 : 19; Isa. 5 : 12; 25 : 6; 28 : 1;

Matt. 22:11; Luke 15:25. The posture at table in early times was sitting, 1 Sam. 16:11; 20:5, 18, and the guests were ranged in order of dignity. Gen. 43:33; 1 Sam. 9:22. Words which imply the recumbent posture belong to the New Testament.

Baptism. It is well known that ablution or bathing was common in most ancient nations as a preparation for prayers and sacrifice or as expiatory of sin. In warm countries this connection is probably even closer than in colder climates; and hence the frequency of ablution in the religious rites throughout the East. Baptism in the name of the Father, Son and Holy Ghost is the rite or ordinance by which persons are admitted into the Church of Christ. It is the public profession of faith and discipleship. Baptism signifies—(1) A confession of faith in Christ; (2) A cleansing or washing of the soul from sin; (3) A death to sin and a new life in righteousness. The *mode* and *subjects* of baptism being much-controverted subjects, each one can best study them in the works devoted to those questions. The command to baptize was co-extensive with the command to preach the gospel. All nations were to be evangelized; and they were to be made disciples, admitted into the fellowship of Christ's religion, by baptism. Matt. 28:19. It appears to have been a kind of transition from the Jewish baptism to the Christian. The distinction between John's baptism and Christian baptism appears in the case of Apollos, Acts 18:25, 27, and of the disciples at Ephesus mentioned Acts 19:1-6. We cannot but draw from this history the inference that in Christian baptism there was a deeper spiritual significance.

Barab'bas (bà-răb'bas) (*son of Abba*), a robber, John 18:40, who had committed murder in an insurrection, Mark 15:7; Luke 23:18, in Jerusalem, and was lying in prison at the time of the trial of Jesus before Pilate.

Bar'achel (băr'a-kel) (*God has blessed*), father of Elihu. Job 32:2, 6. [BUZ.]

Barachi'as (băr-a-kī'as). Matt. 23:35. [ZACHARIAS.]

Ba'rak (bā'răk) (*lightning*), son of Abinoam of Kedesh, a refuge city in Mount Naphtali, was incited by Deborah, a prophetess of Ephraim, to deliver Israel from the yoke of Jabin.

Judges 4. He utterly routed the Canaanites in the plain of Jezreel (Esdraelon).

Barbarian. "Every one not a Greek is a barbarian" is the common Greek definition, and in this strict sense the word is used in Rom. 1:14. It often retains this primitive meaning, as in 1 Cor. 14:11; Acts 28:4.

Barhu'mite (bär-hū'mite), **The.** [BAHURIM.]

Bari'ah (bà-rī'ah) (*fugitive*), a descendant of the royal family of Judah. 1 Chron. 3:22.

Bar=je'sus (*son of Jesus*). [ELYMAS.]

Bar=jo'na (*son of Jonah*). [PETER.]

Bar'kos (bär'kos) (*painter*). "Children of Barkos" were among the Nethinim who returned from the captivity with Zerubbabel. Ezra 2:53; Neh. 7:55.

Barley is one of the most important of the cereal grains, and the most hardy of them all. It was grown by the Hebrews, Lev. 27:16; Deut. 8:8; Ruth 2:17, etc., who used it for baking into bread, chiefly among the poor, Judges 7:13; 2 Kings 4:42; John 6:9, 13, and as fodder for horses. 1 Kings 4:28. The barley harvest, Ruth 1:22; 2:23; 2 Sam. 21:9, 10, takes place in Palestine in March and April, and in the hilly districts as late as June. It always precedes the wheat harvest, in some places by a week, in others by fully three weeks. In Egypt the barley is about a month earlier than the wheat; whence its total destruction by the hail storm. Ex. 9:31.

Bar'nabas (bär'na-bas) (*son of consolation* or *exhortation*), name given by the apostles, Acts 4:36, to Joseph (or Joses), a Levite of the island of Cyprus, who was early a disciple of Christ. In Acts 9:27 we find him introducing the newly-converted Saul to the apostles at Jerusalem. Barnabas was sent to Antioch, Acts 11:19-26, and went to Tarsus to seek Saul, as one specially raised up to preach to the Gentiles. Acts 26:17. He brought him to Antioch, and was sent with him to Jerusalem. Acts 11:30. On their return, they were ordained by the church for the missionary work, Acts 13:2, and sent forth (A.D. 45). From this time Barnabas and Paul enjoy the title and dignity of apostles. Their first missionary journey is related in Acts 13,

14. Returning to Antioch (A.D. 48 or 49), they were sent (A.D. 50), with some others, to Jerusalem. Acts 15:1, 36. Afterwards they parted, and Barnabas took Mark and sailed to Cyprus, his native island. Here the Scripture notices of him cease. The epistle attributed to Barnabas is believed to have been written early in the second century.

Bar'sabas (bär'sa-băs) (*son of Sabas* or *rest*). [JOSEPH BARSABAS; JUDAS BARSABAS.]

Barsab'bas (bär-sab'bäs). R. V. of Acts 1:23 for BAR'SABAS.

Barthol'omew (bär-thŏl'o-mew) (*son of Tolmai*), one of the twelve apostles of Christ. Matt. 10:3; Mark 3:18; Luke 6:14; Acts 1:13. It has been not improperly conjectured that he is identical with Nathanael. John 1:45 ff. He is said to have preached the gospel in India, that is, probably, Arabia Felix, and according to some in Armenia.

Bartimæ'us (bär-ti-mē'us) (*son of Timæus*), a blind beggar of Jericho who, Mark 10:46 ff., sat by the wayside begging as our Lord passed out of Jericho on his last journey to Jerusalem.

Ba'ruch (bä'ruk) (*blessed*). 1. Son of Neriah, the friend, Jer. 32:12, amanuensis, Jer. 36:4–32, and faithful attendant of Jeremiah. Jer. 36:10 ff. (B.C. 603.) He was probably of a noble family, comp. Jer. 51:59, and of distinguished acquirements. After the capture of Jerusalem, B.C. 586, his enemies accused him of influencing Jeremiah in favor of the Chaldæans, Jer. 43:3; compare 27:13; and although by the permission of Nebuchadnezzar he remained with Jeremiah at Mizpeh, Jos. *Ant.* x. 9, § 1, he was afterwards forced to go down to Egypt. Jer. 43:6. Nothing is known certainly of the close of his life.

2. The son of Zabbai, who assisted Nehemiah in rebuilding the walls of Jerusalem. Neh. 3:20. (B.C. 446.)

3. A priest, or family of priests, who signed the covenant with Nehemiah. Neh. 10:6.

4. The son of Col-hozeh, a descendant of Perez or Pharez, the son of Judah. Neh. 11:5. (B.C. 536.)

Ba'ruch (bä'ruk), **Book of.** One of the apocryphal books of the Old Testament. The book was held in little esteem by the Jews, and both its date and authorship are very uncertain.

Barzil'lai (bär-zĭl'la-ī) (*made of iron*). 1. A wealthy Gileadite who showed hospitality to David when he fled from Absalom. 2 Sam. 17:27. (B.C. 1023.) He declined the king's offer of ending his days at court. 2 Sam. 19:32–39.

2. A Meholathite, whose son Adriel married Michal, Saul's daughter. 2 Sam. 21:8.

3. Son-in-law to Barzillai the Gileadite. Ezra 2:61; Neh. 7:63, 64, who took his father-in-law's name, and founded a family.

Ba'shan (bä'shăn) (*soft, rich soil*), a district on the east of Jordan. It is sometimes spoken of as the "land of Bashan," 1 Chron. 5:11, and comp. Num. 21:33; 32:33, and sometimes as "all Bashan." Deut. 3:10, 13; Josh. 12:5; 13:12, 30. It was taken by the children of Israel after their conquest of the land of Sihon from Arnon to Jabbok. The limits of Bashan are very strictly defined. It extended from the "border of Gilead" on the south to Mount Hermon on the north, Deut. 3:3, 10, 14; Josh. 12:5; 1 Chron. 5:23, and from the Arabah or Jordan valley on the west to Salchah (*Sulkhad*) and the border of the Geshurites and the Maachthites on the east. Josh. 12:3–5; Deut. 3:10. This important district was bestowed on the half-tribe of Manasseh, Josh. 13:29–31, together with "half Gilead." This country is now full of interesting ruins, which have lately been explored and from which much light has been thrown upon Bible times.

Ba'shan-ha'voth-ja'ir (bä'shăn-hä'-voth-jä'ïr), according to the Authorized Version, a name given to Argob after its conquest by Jair. Deut. 3:14. In R. V. it is rightly separated —"he called them, even Bashan, after his own name, Havvoth-Jair."

Bash'emath (băsh'e-măth) (*fragrant*), daughter of Ishmael, the last married of the three wives of Esau. Gen. 36:3, 4, 13. In Gen. 28:9 she is called Mahalath. In Gen. 26:34 the name is evidently given to the Hittite ADAH.

Basin. Among the smaller vessels for the tabernacle or temple service, many must have been required to receive from the sacrificial victims the blood to be sprinkled for purification. The "basin" from which our Lord washed the disciples' feet was probably deeper and larger than the hand-basin for sprinkling.

ORIENTAL BASIN, EWER, ETC.

Basket. The Hebrew terms used in the description of this article are as fol-

EGYPTIAN BASKETS.

lows: (1) *Sal,* so called from the *twigs* of which it was originally made, specially used for holding bread. Gen. 40: 16 ff.; Ex. 29: 3, 23; Lev. 8: 2, 26, 31; Num. 6: 15, 17, 19. (2) *Salsillôth,* a word of kindred origin, applied to the basket used in gathering grapes. Jer. 6: 9. (3) *Tene,* in which the first-fruits of the harvest were presented. Deut.

BASKET FOR BOTTLES.

26: 2, 4. (4) *Celub,* so called from its similarity to a bird-cage. (5) *Dûd,* used for carrying fruit, Jer. 24: 1, 2, as well as on a larger scale for carrying clay to the brick-yard, Ps. 81: 6 (*pots,* Authorized Version), or for holding bulky articles. 2 Kings 10: 7. In the New Testament baskets are described under three different terms.

Bas'math (*fragrant*), a daughter of Solomon, married to Ahimaaz, one of his commissariat officers. 1 Kings 4: 15. R. V. Basemath.

Bastard. Among those who were excluded from entering the congregation, even to the tenth generation, was the bastard. Deut. 23: 2. The term is not, however, applied to any illegitimate offspring, born out of wedlock, but is restricted by the rabbins to the issue of any connection within the degrees prohibited by the law.

Bat. Lev. 11: 19; Deut. 14: 18. Many travelers have noticed the immense numbers of bats that are found in caverns in the East, and Mr. Layard says that on the occasion of a visit to a cavern these noisome beasts compelled him to retreat.

Bath, Bathing. This was a prescribed part of the Jewish ritual of purification in cases of accident, or of leprous or ordinary uncleanness, Lev. 15; 16: 28; 22: 6; Num. 19: 7, 19; 2 Sam. 11: 2, 4; 2 Kings 5: 10; as also after mourning, which always implied defilement. Ruth 3: 3; 2 Sam. 12: 20. The eastern climate made bathing essential alike to health and pleasure, to which luxury added the use of perfumes. Ex. 2: 5; 2 Sam. 11: 2; Esther 2: 12. The "pools," such as that of Siloam and Hezekiah, 2 Kings 20: 20; Neh. 3: 15, 16; Isa. 22: 11; John 9: 7, often sheltered by porticos, John 5: 2, are the first indications we have of public bathing accommodation.

Bath. [WEIGHTS AND MEASURES.]

Bath=rab'bim (bath-răb'bim) (*daughter of many*), **The gate of,** one of the gates of the ancient city of Heshbon. Cant. 7: 4.

Bath'=sheba (băth'shĕ-bà), or **Bath-she'ba** (*daughter of the oath*), 2 Sam. 11: 3, etc., also called Bath-shua in 1 Chron. 3: 5, the daughter of Eliam, 2 Sam. 11: 3, or Ammiel, 1 Chron. 3: 5, the son of Ahithophel, 2 Sam. 23: 34, and wife of Uriah the Hittite. The child which was the fruit of her adulterous intercourse with David died; but after marriage she became the mother of four sons, Solomon, Matt. 1:6; Shimea, Shobab and Nathan. When Adonijah attempted to set aside the succession promised to Solomon, Bathsheba informed the king of the conspiracy. 1 Kings 1:11, 15, 23. After the accession of Solomon, she, as queen-mother, requested permission of her son for Adonijah to take in marriage Abishag the Shunammite. 1 Kings 2: 21-25.

Bath'=shua. [BATH-SHEBA.]

Battering=ram, Ezek. 4:2; 21:22, a large beam with a head of iron which was sometimes made to resemble the head of a ram. It was suspended by ropes to a beam supported by posts, and balanced so as to swing backward and forward, and was impelled by men against the wall. In attacking the walls of a fort or city, the first step appears to have been to form an inclined plane or bank of earth, comp. Ezek. 4:2, "cast a mount against it," by which the besiegers could bring their battering-rams and other engines to the foot of the walls. "The battering-rams," says Mr. Layard, "were of several kinds. Some were joined to movable towers which held warriors and armed men. The whole then formed one great temporary building, the top of which is represented in sculptures as on a level with the walls, and even turrets, of the besieged city. In some bas-reliefs the battering-ram is without wheels; it was then perhaps constructed upon the spot and was not intended to be moved."

Battle=axe. Jer. 51:20. [MAUL.]

Battlement. Among the Jews a battlement was required by law to be built upon every house. It consisted of a low wall built around the roofs of the houses to prevent persons from falling off, and sometimes serving as a partition from another building. Deut. 22:8; Jer. 5: 10.

Bav'a=i, son of Henadad, ruler of a district of Keilah in the time of Nehemiah. Neh. 3:18. (B.C. 446.)

Bay tree. A species of laurel, *Laurus nobilis.* An evergreen, with leaves like our mountain laurel. In the only passage where this word occurs, Ps. 37: 35, the R. V. renders it a "tree in its native soil," a much more natural translation.

Baz'lith (băz'lith) (*stripping*).

"Children of Bazlith" were among the Nethinim who returned with Zerubbabel. Neh. 7:54. In Ezra 2:52 the name is given as BAZLUTH.

Baz'luth. [BAZLITH.]

Bdellium (*bedôlach*). Gen. 2:12; Num. 11:7. It is quite impossible to say whether *bedôlach* denotes a mineral or an animal production or a vegetable exudation. Bdellium is an odoriferous exudation from a tree which is perhaps the *Borassus flabelliformis,* Lin., of Arabia Felix. Hastings' *Bible Dictionary* argues for the pearl.

Beacon. A signal or conspicuous mark erected on an eminence for direction. Isa. 30:17.

Beali'ah (bē'a-lī'ah) (*Jehovah is lord*), a Benjamite who went over to David at Ziklag. 1 Chron. 12:5. (B.C. 1057.)

Be'aloth (bē'a-lŏth) (*mistresses*), a town in the extreme south of Judah. Josh. 15:24.

Beans. 2 Sam. 17:28; Ezek. 4:9. Beans are cultivated in Palestine, which produces many of the leguminous order of plants, such as lentils, kidney-beans, vetches, etc.

Bear. 1 Sam. 17:34; 2 Sam. 17:8 The Syrian bear, *Ursus syriacus,* which is without doubt the animal mentioned in the Bible, is still found on the higher mountains of Palestine. During the summer months these bears keep to the

SYRIAN BEAR.

snowy parts of Lebanon, but descend in winter to the villages and gardens. It is probable also that at this period in former days they extended their visits to other parts of Palestine.

Beard. Western Asiatics have always cherished the beard as the badge of the dignity of manhood, and attached to it the importance of a feature. The Egyptians, on the contrary, for the most part shaved the hair of the face and head, though we find some instances to the contrary. The beard is the object of an oath, and that on which blessing or shame is spoken of as resting. The custom was and is to shave or pluck it and the hair out in mourning, Ezra 9 : 3; Isa. 15 : 2; 50 : 6; Jer. 41 : 5; 48 : 37; to neglect it in seasons of permanent affliction, 1 Sam. 21 : 13; 2 Sam. 19 : 24, and to regard any insult to it as the last outrage which enmity can inflict. 2 Sam. 10 : 4. The beard was the object of salutation. 2 Sam. 20 : 9. The dressing, trimming, anointing, etc., of the beard was performed with much ceremony by persons of wealth and rank. Ps. 133 : 2. The removal of the beard was a part of the ceremonial treatment proper to a leper. Lev. 14 : 9.

Beb'ai (bĕb'-a-ī). 1. "Sons of Bebai," 623 (Neh. 628) in number, returned from Babylon with Zerubbabel, Ezra 2 : 11; Neh. 7 : 16. Four of this family had taken foreign wives. Ezra 10 : 28. The name occurs also among those who sealed the covenant. Neh. 10 : 15.

2. Father of Zechariah, who was the leader of the twenty-eight men of the tribe who returned with Ezra. Ezra 8 : 11.

Be'cher (bē'kēr) (*young camel*). 1. The second son of Benjamin, according to the list in both Gen. 46 : 21 and 1 Chron. 7 : 6, but omitted in 1 Chron. 8 : 1.

2. Son of Ephraim, Num. 26 : 35, and founder of the family of the BACHRITES; called BERED in 1 Chron. 7 : 20.

Becho'rath (bē-kō'răth) (*first-born*), son of Aphiah, an ancestor of Saul. 1 Sam. 9 : 1. It is the name of Saul's clan.

Bed. The Jewish bed consisted of the mattress, a mere mat, or one or more quilts; the covering, a finer quilt, 1 Sam. 19 : 13, or sometimes the outer garment worn by day, which the law provided should not be kept in pledge after sunset, that the poor man might not lack his needful covering, Deut. 24 : 13; the pillow, 1 Sam. 19 : 13, probably formed of sheep's fleece or goat's skin, with a stuffing of cotton, etc.; the bedstead, a divan or bench along the side

or end of the room, sufficing as a support for the bedding. Besides we have bedsteads made of ivory, wood, etc., re-

EGYPTIAN BEDS, OR COUCHES.— SEE BED.

ferred to in Deut. 3 : 11; Amos 6 : 4. The ornamental portions were pillars and a canopy, Prov. 7 : 16, ivory carvings, gold and silver, and probably mosaic work, purple and fine linen. Esth. 1 : 6; Cant. 3 : 9, 10. The ordinary furniture of a bed-chamber in private life is given in 2 Kings 4 : 10.

Be'dad (bē'dăd) (*separation*), the father of Hadad king of Edom. Gen. 36 : 35; 1 Chron. 1 : 46.

Be'dan (bē'dăn). 1. Mentioned in 1 Sam. 12 : 11 as a judge of Israel between Jerubbaal (Gideon) and Jephthah. The Chaldee Paraphrast reads Samson for Bedan; the LXX., Syriac and Arabic all have Barak. Ewald suggests that it may be a false reading for Abdon.

2. The son of Gilead. 1 Chron. 7 : 17.

Bede'iah (bē-dē'iah), one of the sons of Bani, in the time of Ezra, who had taken a foreign wife. Ezra 10 : 35. (B.C. 458.)

Bee (*debôrâh*). Deut. 1 : 44; Judges 14 : 8; Ps. 118 : 12; Isa. 7 : 18. Bees abounded in Palestine, honey being a common article of food, Ps. 81 : 16, and was often found in the clefts of rocks and in hollow trees. 1 Sam. 14 : 25, 27. English naturalists know little of the species of bees that are found in Palestine, but are inclined to believe that the honey-bee of Palestine is distinct from the honey-bee (*Apis mellifica*) of this country. The passage in Isa. 7:18 refers "to the custom of the people in the East of calling attention to any one by a significant *hiss* or rather *hist*."

We read, Judges 14:8, that "after a time," probably many days, Samson returned to the carcass of the lion he had slain, and saw bees and honey therein. "If any one here represents to himself a corrupt and putrid carcass, the occurrence ceases to have any true similitude, for it is well known that in these countries, at certain seasons of the year, the heat will in the course of twenty-four hours completely dry up the moisture of dead camels, and that, without their undergoing decomposition, their bodies long remain like mummies, unaltered and entirely free from offensive odor."

Beeli'ada (bē-ĕl-ī'a-dà) (*Baal knows* i. e. the master), one of David's sons, born in Jerusalem. 1 Chron. 14:7. In the lists in Samuel the name is ELIADA.

Beel'zebub (bē-ĕl'ze-bŭb). [See BAAL-ZEBUB; BAAL, 2.]

Beel'zebul (*lord of the house*), the title of a heathen deity, to whom the Jews ascribed the sovereignty of the evil spirits; Satan, the prince of the devils. Matt. 10: 25; 12:24; Mark 3: 22; Luke 11:15 ff. The Greek form is *Beelzebul* but R. V. as well as A. V. translate Beelzebub.

Be'er (bē'er) (*a well*). 1. One of the latest halting-places of the Israelites, lying beyond the Arnon. Num. 21:16-18. This is possibly the BEER-ELIM of Isa. 15:8.

2. A place to which Jotham, the son of Gideon, fled for fear of his brother Abimelech. Judges 9:21.

Bee'ra (*a well*), son of Zophah, of the tribe of Asher. 1 Chron. 7:37.

Bee'rah, prince of the Reubenites, carried away by Tiglath-pileser. 1 Chron. 5:6. (B.C. 738.)

Beer=e'lim (bē'er-ē'lim) (*well of heroes*), a spot named in Isa. 15:8 as on the "border of Moab." Num. 21:16; comp. 13.

Bee'ri (bè-ē'rī). 1. The father of Judith, one of the wives of Esau. Gen. 26:34.

2. Father of the prophet Hosea. Hos. 1:1.

Beer-lahai'roi (bē'er-la-hā'roi) (*a well of the living one who sees me*), so named because here the angel appeared to Hagar (Gen. 16:7-14), in the wilderness of Shur, between Kadesh and Bered.

Bee'roth (bè-ē'rŏth) (*wells*), one of the four cities of the Hivites who deluded Joshua into a treaty of peace with them. Josh. 9:17. It is now *el-Bireh*, which stands about 8 miles north of Jerusalem.

Bee'roth of the children of Jaakan, the wells of the tribe of Bene-Jaakan, which formed one of the halting-places of the Israelites in the desert. Deut. 10:26. In Num. 33:31 the name is given as BENE-JAAKAN only.

Beer'=sheba, or Be=er=she'ba (bē'er-shē'bà) (*well of the oath*), the name of one of the old places in Palestine

BEERSHEBA. (The Main Street.)

which formed the southern limit of the country. There are two accounts of the origin of the name. According to the first, the well was dug by Abraham, and the name given, Gen. 21: 31; the other narrative ascribes the origin of the name to Isaac instead of Abraham. Gen. 26: 31–33.

become a populous and important center.

The photograph shows one of these wells operated by a *sâkiyeh,* an Egyptian device consisting of buckets or earthen jars attached to ropes and made to revolve over a wheel; the entire machinery being usually worked

BEERSHEBA. (The East Well.)

In 1907 there were eleven wells, eight of which were open and furnished a copious supply of good sweet water. They vary in depth to the surface of the water from 38 to 126 feet, the deepest of which is to be sunk 30 feet deeper. In diameter they vary from 6 feet 9 inches to 12 feet 6 inches. In 1900 Beersheba, Bir es-Seba, was a mere watering place in the desert. Now it is become a large village of several hundred inhabitants, and is becoming the chief watering place of the Negeb (the south land). Many shops and flour mills have been built. During the rainy season from December to April the country all about is carpeted with herbage and flowers. From May till November it has the appearance of a desert. With more wells and modern modes of irrigation there is reason to believe that Beersheba will

at Beersheba by a blinded camel.— From *The Biblical World,* May, 1908, article by Professor George L. Robinson, D.D.

Beesh'=terah (bē-ĕsh'tē-rah) (*house of Ashterah*), one of the two cities allotted to the sons of Gershon out of the tribe of Manasseh beyond Jordan. Josh. 21: 27. Probably identical with Ashtaroth. 1 Chron. 6: 71.

Beetle. [LOCUST.]

Beeves. Same as cattle. Lev. 22: 19. [See BULL.]

Beggar, Begging. The poor among the Hebrews were much favored. They were allowed to glean in the fields, and to gather whatever the land produced in the year in which it was not tilled. Lev. 19: 10; 25: 5, 6; Deut. 24: 19. They were also invited to feasts. Deut. 14:

29. In O. T. times the Israelite could not be an absolute pauper. His land was inalienable, except for a certain term, when it reverted to him or his posterity. And if this resource were insufficient, he could pledge the services of himself and family for a valuable sum. Those who were indigent through bodily infirmities were usually taken care of by their kindred. A beggar was sometimes seen, however, and was regarded and abhorred as a vagabond. Ps. 109:10. In later times beggars were accustomed, it would seem, to have a fixed place at the corners of the streets, Mark 10:46, or at the gates of the temple, Acts 3:2, or of private houses. Luke 16:20.

Be'hemoth (bē'hē-mŏth) (*great beast*). There can be little or no doubt that by this word, Job 40:15–24, the hippopotamus is intended, since all the details descriptive of the *behemoth* accord entirely with the ascertained habits of that animal. The hippopotamus is an immense creature having a thick and square head, a large mouth often two feet broad, small eyes and ears, thick and heavy body, short legs terminated by four toes, a short tail, skin without hair except at the extremity of the tail. It inhabits nearly the whole of Africa, and has been found of the length of 14 feet. It delights in the water, but feeds on herbage on land. It is not found in Palestine, but may at one time have been a native of western Asia.

Be'kah (bē'kah). [WEIGHTS AND MEASURES.]

Bel (bĕl). The chief god of Babylon, Isa. 46:1; Jer. 50:2; 51:44. [BAAL.]

Be'la (bē'là) (*destruction*). 1. One of the five cities of the plain which was spared at the intercession of Lot, and received the name of Zoar. Gen. 14:2; 19:22. [ZOAR.]

2. Son of Beor, who reigned over Edom in the city of Dinhabah, five generations before Shaul. Gen. 36:31–33; 1 Chron. 1:43, 44.

3. Eldest son of Benjamin, according to Gen. 46:21 (Authorized Version "Belah"); Num. 26:38, 40; 1 Chron. 7:6; 8:1, and head of the family of the Belaites.

4. Son of Azaz, a Reubenite. 1 Chron. 5:8.

Be'lah. [BELA, 3.]

Be'laites (bē'là-ītes), **The.** Num. 26:38. [BELA, 3.]

Be'lial (bē'lĭ-al). The meaning of this word as found in the Scriptures is *worthlessness,* and hence *recklessness, lawlessness.* The expression *son* or *man of Belial* must be understood as meaning simply a worthless, lawless fellow. The term as used in 2 Cor. 6:15 is generally understood as an appellative of Satan, as the personification of all that was bad.

Bellows. The word occurs only in Jer. 6:29, where it denotes an instrument to heat a smelting furnace. Wilkinson in "Ancient Egypt," ii, 312, says, "They consisted of a leather bag secured and fitted into a frame, from which a long pipe extended for carrying the wind to the fire. They were worked by the feet, the operator standing upon them, with one under each foot, and pressing them alternately, while he pulled up each exhausted skin with a string he held in his hand."

Bells. In Ex. 28:33 the bells alluded to were the golden ones, 72 in number, round the hem of the high priest's ephod. The object of them was "that his sound might be heard." Ex. 28:35. In the East to this day bells are frequently attached, for the sake of their pleasant sound, to the anklets of women. The little girls of Cairo wear strings of them around their feet. In Zech. 14:20 "bells of the horses" were concave or flat pieces of brass, which were sometimes attached to horses for the sake of ornament.

Belshaz'zar (Bĕl-shăz'zar.) (*May Bel protect the king*), the last king of Babylon. According to Dan. 5:2 Nebuchadnezzar is called the father of Belshazzar. This, of course, need only mean grandfather or ancestor. According to the well-known narrative, Belshazzar gave a splendid feast in his palace during the siege of Babylon (B.C. 538), using the sacred vessels of the temple, which Nebuchadnezzar had brought from Jerusalem. The miraculous appearance of the handwriting on the wall, the calling in of Daniel to interpret its meaning, the prophecy of the overthrow of the kingdom, and Belshazzar's death, are recorded in Dan. 5. By the cuneiform inscriptions we find that Nabonidus was the last king of Babylon, but that his eldest son, Belshazzar, was regent during his absence.

Belteshaz′zar (bĕl-te-shăz′zar) (*Bel protect his life*). [DANIEL.]

Ben (*son*), a Levite, one of the porters appointed by David for the ark. 1 Chron. 15:18.

Bena′iah (Bē-nā′iah) (*Jehovah hath built up*). 1. The son of Jehoiada the chief priest, 1 Chron. 27:5, of the tribe of Levi, though a native of Kabzeel, 2 Sam. 23:20; set by David, 1 Chron. 11:25, over his body-guard, 2 Sam. 8:18; 20:23; 1 Kings 1:38; 1 Chron. 18:17. One of the mighty men. 2 Sam. 23:22, 23; 1 Chron. 11:25; 27:6. The exploits which gave him this rank are narrated in 2 Sam. 23:20, 21; 1 Chron. 11:22. He was captain of the host for the third month. 1 Chron. 27:5. Benaiah remained faithful to Solomon during Adonijah's attempt on the crown, 1 Kings 1:8, 10, 32, 38, 44, and was raised into the place of Joab as commander-in-chief of the whole army. 1 Kings 2:35; 4:4.

2. Benaiah the Pirathonite, an Ephraimite, one of David's thirty mighty men, 2 Sam. 23:30; 1 Chron. 11:31, and the captain of the eleventh monthly course. 1 Chron. 27:14.

3. A Levite in the time of David, who "played with a psaltery on Alamoth." 1 Chron. 15:18, 20; 16:5.

4. A priest in the time of David, appointed to blow the trumpet before the ark. 1 Chron. 15:24; 16:6.

5. A Levite of the sons of Asaph. 2 Chron. 20:14.

6. A Levite in the time of Hezekiah. 2 Chron. 31:13.

7. One of the "princes" of the families of Simeon. 1 Chron. 4:36.

8. Four laymen in the time of Ezra who had taken strange wives. Ezra 10:25, 30, 35, 43.

9. The father of Pelatiah. Ezek. 11:1, 13.

Ben=am′mi (bĕn-ăm′mī) (*son of my people*), the son of the younger daughter of Lot, and progenitor of the Ammonites. Gen. 19:38.

Ben′e-be′rak (bĕn-e-bē′răk) (*sons of Berak*), one of the cities of the tribe of Dan, mentioned only in Josh. 19:45.

Bene-ja′akan (bĕn-e-jā′a-kăn) (*sons of Jaakan*), a tribe who gave their name to certain wells in the desert which formed one of the halting-places of the Israelites on their journey to Canaan. [BEEROTH BENE-JAAKAN.] Also given in Gen. 36:27 as AKAN.

Ben=ha′dad (bĕn-hā′dăd) (*son of Hadad*), the name of three kings of Damascus. BENHADAD I., king of Damascus, which in his time was supreme in Syria. He made an alliance with Asa, and conquered a great part of the north of Israel. 1 Kings 15:18.

BEN-HADAD II., son of the preceding, and also king of Damascus. Long wars with Israel characterized his reign. Some time after the death of Ahab, Benhadad renewed the war with Israel, attacked Samaria a second time, and pressed the siege so closely that there was a terrible famine in the city. But the Syrians broke up in the night in consequence of a sudden panic. Soon after Ben-hadad fell sick, and sent Hazael to consult Elisha as to the issue of his malady. On the day after Hazael's return Ben-hadad was murdered, probably by some of his own servants. 2 Kings 8:7-15. Ben-hadad's death was about B.C. 842, and he must have reigned some 30 years.

BEN-HADAD III., son of Hazael, and his successor on the throne of Syria. When he succeeded to the throne, Jehoash recovered the cities which Jehoahaz had lost to the Syrians, and beat him in Aphek. 2 Kings 13:17, 25. The date of Ben-hadad III. is about B.C. 792.

Ben=ha′il (bĕn-hā′il) (*son of might*), one of the princes whom King Jehoshaphat sent to teach in the cities of Judah. 2 Chron. 17:7.

Ben=ha′nan (bĕn-hā′nan) (*son of the gracious*), son of Shimon, in the line of Judah. 1 Chron. 4:20.

Beni′nu (bĕn-ĭ′-nū) (*our son*), a Levite; one of those who sealed the covenant with Nehemiah. Neh. 10:13.

Ben′jamin (*son of the right hand, fortunate*). 1. The youngest of the children of Jacob. His birth took place on the road between Bethel and Bethlehem, near the latter, B.C. 1729. His mother, Rachel, died in the act of giving him birth, naming him with her last breath Ben-oni (*son of my sorrow*). This was by Jacob changed into Benjamin. Gen. 35:16, 18. Until the journeys of Jacob's sons and of Jacob himself into Egypt we hear nothing of Benjamin. Nothing personal is known of him. Henceforward the history of Benjamin is the history of the tribe.

2. A man of the tribe of Benjamin, son of Bilhan, and the head of a family of warriors. 1 Chron. 7:10.

3. One of the "sons of Harim," an Israelite in the time of Ezra who had married a foreign wife. Ezra 10:32.

Ben'jamin, The tribe of. The contrast between the warlike character of the tribe and the peaceful image of its progenitor comes out in many scattered notices. Benjamin was the only tribe which seems to have pursued archery to any purpose, and their skill in the bow, 1 Sam. 20:20, 36; 2 Sam. 1:22; 1 Chron. 8:40; 12:2; 2 Chron. 17:17, and the sling, Judges 20:16, is celebrated. The dreadful deed recorded in Judges 19 was defended by Benjamin. Later the tribe seems, however, to assume another position, as Ramah, 1 Sam. 8:4, etc., Mizpeh, 1 Sam. 7:5, Bethel and Gibeon, 1 Kings 3:4, were all in the land of Benjamin. After the struggles and contests which followed the death of Saul, the history of Benjamin becomes merged in that of the southern kingdom.

Ben'jamin, The land of. The proximity of Benjamin to Ephraim during the march to the promised land was maintained in the territory allotted to each. That given to Benjamin formed almost a parallelogram, of about 26 miles in length by 12 in breadth, lying between Ephraim, the Jordan, Judah and Dan. The general level of this part of Palestine is not less than 2000 feet above the Mediterranean or than 3000 feet above the valley of the Jordan, the surrounding country including a large number of eminences—almost every one of which has borne some part in the history of the tribe—and many torrent beds and deep ravines.

Ben'jamin, High gate or **gate of.** Jer. 20:2; 37:13; 38:7; Zech. 14:10. [JERUSALEM.]

Be'no (bē'nō) (*his son*), a Levite of the sons of Merari. 1 Chron. 24:26, 27.

Ben-o'ni (bĕn-ō'nī) (*son of my sorrow*). Gen. 35:18. [BENJAMIN.]

Ben-zo'heth (bĕn-zō'heth) (*son of Zoheth*), a descendant of Judah. 1 Chron. 4:20.

Be'on (bē'ŏn). Num. 32:3. [BETH-BAAL-MEON.] Comp. ver. 38.

Be'or (bē'or) (*burning*). 1. The father of Bela, one of the early Edomite kings. Gen. 36:32; 1 Chron. 1:43.
2. Father of Balaam. Num. 22:5; 24:3, 15; 31:8; Deut. 23:4; Josh. 13:22; 24:9; Micah 6:5. He is called BOSOR in the New Testament.

Be'ra (bē'ra) (*excellence*), king of Sodom. Gen. 14:2; also 17, 21.

Ber'achah (bĕr'a-kah) (*blessing*), a Benjamite who attached himself to David at Ziklag. 1 Chron. 12:3. (B.C. 1057.)

Ber'achah, Valley of, a valley in which Jehoshaphat and his people assembled to "bless" Jehovah after the overthrow of the hosts of Moabites. 2 Chron. 20:26. It is now called *Bereikût,* and lies between Tekoa and the main road from Bethlehem to Hebron.

Berachi'ah (bĕr-a-kī'ah) (*blessed of Jehovah*), a Gershonite Levite, father of Asaph. 1 Chron. 6:39. [BERECHIAH.]

Berai'ah (bĕr-a-ī'ah) (*created by Jehovah*), son of Shimhi, a chief man of Benjamin. 1 Chron. 8:21.

Bere'a (bē-rē'à) (*well watered*). 1. A city of Macedonia, mentioned in Acts 17:10, 13. It is now called *Verria* or *Kara-Verria,* and is situated on the eastern slope of the Olympian mountain range. From the fact of their searching the Scriptures, the name is now often applied to classes for Bible study.
2. A place in Judea near Jerusalem, near which Judas Maccabeus was slain.

Berechi'ah (bĕr-e-kī'ah) (*blessed of Jehovah*). 1. A descendant of the royal family of Judah. 1 Chron. 3:20.
2. A man mentioned as the father of Meshullam, who assisted in rebuilding the walls of Jerusalem. Neh. 3:4, 30; 6:18.
3. A Levite. 1 Chron. 9:16.
4. A doorkeeper for the ark. 1 Chron. 15:23.
5. One of the tribe of Ephraim in the time of Ahaz. 2 Chron. 28:12.
6. Father of Asaph the singer. 1 Chron. 15:17. [BERACHIAH.]
7. Father of Zechariah. Zech. 1:1, 7.

Be'red (bē'red) (*hail*). 1. A place in the south of Palestine, near the well Lahai-roi. Gen. 16:14.
2. A son or descendant of Ephraim, 1 Chron. 7:20, possibly identical with Becher in Num. 26:35.

Bereni'ce (bĕr-ĕ-nī'cĕ). [BERNICE.]

Be'ri (bē'ri), son of Zophah, of the tribe of Asher. 1 Chron. 7:36.

Beri'ah (bē-rī'ah). 1. A son of Asher. Gen. 46:17; Num. 26:44, 45.
2. A son of Ephraim. 1 Chron. 7:20, 23.
3. A Benjamite. 1 Chron. 8:13, 16.
4. A Levite. 1 Chron. 23:10, 11.

Beri'ites (bē-rī'ītes). [BERIAH, 1.]

Be'rites, The, a tribe of people who are named with Abel and Beth-maachah, and who were therefore doubtless situated in the north of Palestine. 2 Sam. 20 : 14.

Be'rith (bē'rith). Judges 9 : 46. [BAAL-BERITH ; BAAL, 1.]

Berni'ce (bẽr-nī'cĕ), or **Bereni'ce** (*bringing victory*), the eldest daughter of Herod Agrippa I. Acts 12 : 1, etc. She was first married to her uncle Herod, king of Chalcis, and after his death (A.D. 48) she lived under circumstances of great suspicion with her own brother, Agrippa II., in connection with whom she is mentioned, Acts 25 : 13, 23; 26 : 30, as having visited Festus on his appointment as procurator of Judea.

Ber'odach=bal'adan (ber'ō-dăk-băl'a-dăn). 2 Kings 20 : 12. [MERODACH-BALADAN.]

Bero'thah (bĕ-rō'thah) (*toward the wells*), **Bero'thai** (ber-ō'-thāi) (*my wells*). The first of these two names is given by Ezekiel, 47 : 16, in connection with Hamath and Damascus as forming part of the northern boundary of the promised land. The second is mentioned, 2 Sam. 8 : 8, in the same connection. The well-known city *Beirût* (Berytus) naturally suggests itself as identical with one at least of the names; but in each instance the circumstances of the case seem to require a position farther east.

Bero'thite, The. 1 Chron. 11 : 39. [BEEROTH.]

Beryl (*tarshîsh*) occurs in Ex. 28 : 20. It is generally supposed that the *tarshîsh* derives its name from the place so called, in Spain. Beryl is a mineral of great hardness, and, when transparent, of much beauty. By *tarshîsh* the modern yellow topaz is probably intended, while in Rev. 21 : 20 a different stone is perhaps referred to, probably the mineral now called beryl, which is identical with the emerald except in color, being a light green or bluish green.

Be'sai (bĕ'sāi). "Children of Besai" were among the Nethinim who returned to Judea with Zerubbabel. Ezra 2 : 49; Neh. 7 : 52.

Besode'iah (bĕs-o-dē'iah) (*in the secret of Jehovah*), father of one of the repairers of the wall of Jerusalem. Neh. 3 : 6.

Be'som, a brush or broom of twigs for sweeping. Isa. 14 : 23.

Be'sor (bĕ'sôr), **The brook** (*cool*), a torrent-bed or wady in the extreme south of Judah. 1 Sam. 30 : 9, 10, 21.

Be'tah (bē'tah) (*confidence*), a city belonging to Hadadezer king of Zobah, mentioned with Berothai. 2 Sam. 8 : 8. In the parallel account, 1 Chron. 18 : 8, the name is called Tibhath.

Be'ten (bē'ten) (*valley*), one of the cities on the border of the tribe of Asher. Josh. 19 : 25.

Beth, the most general word for a house or habitation. It has the special meaning of a temple or house of worship. Beth is more frequently employed in compound names of places than any other word.

Bethab'ara (bĕth-ăb'a-rà) (*house of the ford*), a place beyond Jordan, in which, according to the Authorized Version of the New Testament, John was baptizing. John 1 : 28. If this reading be correct, Bethabara may be identical with Beth-barah (*fords of Abârah*), the ancient ford of Jordan on the road to Gilead; or, as some think, with Beth-nimrah, on the east of the river, nearly opposite Jericho. The Revised Version reads BETHANY, which see below.

Beth-a'nath (bĕth-ā'nath) (*house of goddess Anath*), one of the "fenced cities" of Naphtali, named with Beth-shemesh, Josh. 19 : 38; from neither of them were the Canaanites expelled. Judges 1 : 33.

Beth-a'noth (bĕth-ā'noth) (*house of Anath*), a town in the mountainous district of Judah, named with Halhul, Bethzur and others in Josh. 15 : 59 only.

Beth'any (bĕth'a-nỹ) (*house of dates, or house of misery*), a village which, scanty as are the notices of it contained in Scripture, is more intimately associated in our minds than perhaps any other place with the most familiar acts and scenes of the last days of the life of Christ. It was situated "at" the Mount of Olives, Mark 11 : 1; Luke 19 : 29, about fifteen stadia (furlongs, *i. e.* 1½ or 2 miles) from Jerusalem, John 11 : 18, on or near the usual road from Jericho to the city, Luke 19 : 29, comp. 1; Mark 11 : 1, comp. 10 : 46, and close by the west (?) of another village called *Bethphage,* the two being several times mentioned together. Bethany was the home of Mary and Martha and Lazarus, and is now known by a name derived from Lazarus—*el-'Azarîyeh* or *Lazarieh*. It lies on the eastern slope of the Mount of Olives, fully a mile beyond the summit, and not very far from the point at which the road to

BETHANY.

Jericho begins its more sudden descent towards the Jordan valley. *El-' Azariyeh* is a ruinous and wretched village, a wild mountain hamlet of some twenty families. Bethany has been commonly explained "house of dates," but it more probably signifies "house of misery." H. Dixon, "Holy Land," ii. 214, foll.

Beth'any. In the Revised Version

God's Court), named only in Hosea 10: 14, as the scene of a sack and massacre by Shalman.

Beth=a'ven (bĕth-ā'ven) (*house of idolatry*), a place on the mountains of Benjamin, east of Bethel, Josh. 7:2; 18:12, and lying between that place and Michmash. 1 Sam. 13:5; 14:23. In Hosea 4:15; 5:8; 10:5, the name is

VIEW OF BETHANY.

for BETHABARA, John 1:28, where Jesus was baptized by John. It was probably an obscure village near Bethabara, and in time its name faded out and was replaced by the larger and more important Bethabara.

Beth=ar'abah (bĕth-är'a-bah) (*house of the desert*), one of the six cities of Judah which were situated down in the Arabah, the sunken valley of the Jordan and Dead Sea, Josh. 15:61, on the north border of the tribe. It is also included in the list of the towns of Benjamin. Josh. 18:22.

Beth=a'ram (bĕth-ā'răm) (*house of the height*), accurately BETH-HARAM, one of the towns of Gad on the east of Jordan, described as in "the valley," Josh. 13:27, and no doubt the same place as that named BETH-HARAN in Num. 32:36.

Beth=ar'bel (bĕth-är'bel) (*house of*

transferred to the neighboring Bethel,— once the "house of God," but then the house of idols, of "naught."

Beth=az'maveth (bĕth-ăz'ma-veth (*house of Azmaveth*). Under this name is mentioned, in Neh. 7:28 only, the town of Benjamin which is elsewhere called AZMAVETH.

Beth=baal=me'on (*house of Baal-meon*), a place in the possessions of Reuben, on the downs (Authorized Version "plain") east of Jordan. Josh. 13: 17. At the Israelites' first approach its name was BAAL-MEON, Num. 32:38, or, in its contracted form, BEON, 32:3, to which the Beth was possibly a Hebrew addition. Later it would seem to have come into possession of Moab, and to be known either as Beth-meon, Jer. 48:23, or Baal-meon. Ezek. 25:9. The name is still attached to a ruined place of considerable size a short distance to the

THE SITE OF ANCIENT BETHEL.

Beth-gil'gal (bĕth-gĭl'gal). Same as Gilgal. Neh. 12:29.

Beth-hac'cerem (bĕth-hăk'çe-rĕm) (*house of the vineyard*), Neh. 3:14; Jer. 6:1. A beacon station near Tekoa, supposed to be the *Frank Mountain*, a few miles southeast of Bethlehem. Cheyne and Conder consider it as *'Ain Karim*, west of Jerusalem, where there are vineyards.

Beth-ha'ran (bĕth-hā'ran). Num. 32:36. It is no doubt the same place as BETH-ARAM. Josh. 13:27.

Beth-hog'la (bĕth-hŏg'là) (*partridge-house*), and **Hog'lah**, a place on the border of Judah, Josh. 15:6, and of Benjamin. Josh. 18:19, 21. A magnificent spring and a ruin between Jericho and the Jordan still bear the names of *Ain Hajala*.

Beth-ho'ron (bĕth-hō'rŏn) (*house of caverns*), the name of two towns or villages, an "upper" and a "nether," Josh. 16:3, 5; 1 Chron. 7:24, on the road from Gibeon to Azekah, Josh. 10:10, 11, and the Philistine plain. 1 Sam. 13:18. Beth-horon lay on the boundary line between Benjamin and Ephraim, Josh. 16:3, 5, and, Josh. 18:13, 14, was counted to Ephraim, Josh. 21:22; 1 Chron. 7:24, and given to the Kohathites. Josh. 21:22; 1 Chron. 6:66–68. The two Beth-horons still survive in the modern villages of *Beit-ur*, *et-Tahta* and *el-Foka*.

Beth-jesh'imoth (bĕth-jĕsh'ĭ-mŏth) (*house of deserts*), or **Jes'imoth**, a town or place east of Jordan, on the lower level at the south end of the Jordan valley, Num. 33:49, and named with Ashdod-pisgah and Beth-peor. It was one of the limits of the encampment of Israel before crossing the Jordan. Later it was allotted to Reuben, Josh. 12:3; 13:20, but came at last into the hands of Moab, and formed one of the cities which were "the glory of the country." Ezek. 25:9.

Beth-leb'aoth (bĕth-lĕb'a-ŏth) (*house of lionesses*), a town in the lot of Simeon, Josh. 19:6, in the extreme south of Judah. [Josh. 15:32, LEBAOTH.] In 1 Chron. 4:31 the name is given BETH-BIREI.

Beth'lehem (bĕth'lĕ-hĕm) (*house of bread*). 1. One of the oldest towns in Palestine, already in existence at the time of Jacob's return to the country.

CHURCH OF THE NATIVITY, BETHLEHEM.
Enclosing, according to legend, the birthplace of the Saviour.

Photo by Jan Wilga

VIEW OF BETHLEHEM.

Its earliest name was EPHRATH or EPHRATAH. See Gen. 35:16, 19; 48:7. After the conquest Bethlehem appears under its own name, BETHLEHEM-JUDAH. Judges 17:7; 1 Sam. 17:12; Ruth 1:1, 2. The book of Ruth is a page from the domestic history of Bethlehem. It was the home of Ruth, Ruth 1:19, and of David. 1 Sam. 17:12. It was fortified by Rehoboam. 2 Chron. 11:6. It was here that our Lord was born, Matt. 2:1, and here that he was visited by the shepherds, Luke 2:15-17, and the Magi. Matt. 2. The modern town of *Beit-lahm* lies to the east of the main road from Jerusalem to Hebron, six miles from the former. It covers the east and northeast parts of the ridge of a long gray hill of Jura limestone, which stands nearly due east and west, and is about a mile in length. The hill has a deep valley on the north and another on the south. On the top lies the village in a kind of irregular triangle. The population is given as 6,658, entirely Christians. The Church of the Nativity, built by the empress Helena A.D. 330, is the oldest Christian church in existence. It is built over the grotto where Christ is supposed to have been born.

2. A town in the portion of Zebulun, named only in Josh. 19:15. Now known as *Beit-lahm*, near Nazareth. It was apparently from this town that the judge Ibzan came. Judges 11:8-10.

Beth-ma′achah (bĕth-mā′a-kah) (*house of Maachah*), a place named only in 2 Sam. 20:14, 15. Used also in composition with Abel, a town in Dan. Others identify it with Maachah or Aram-maachah, one of the petty Syrian kingdoms in the north of Palestine. Comp. 2 Kings 15:29.

Beth=mar′caboth (bĕth-mär′ka-bŏth) (*house of the chariots*), one of the towns of Simeon, situated to the extreme south of Judah. Josh. 19:5; 1 Chron. 4:31. In the parallel list, Josh. 15:31, MADMANNAH occurs in place of Beth-marcaboth.

Beth=me′on (bĕth-mē′on). Jer. 48:23. A contracted form of Beth-baal-meon.

Beth=nim′rah (bĕth-nĭm′rah) (*house of leopards*), one of the fenced cities on the east of Jordan, taken and built by the tribe of Gad, Num. 32:36, and described as lying in the valley beside Beth-haran. Josh. 13:27. In Num. 32:3 it is called simply NIMRAH. The

name still survives in the modern *Nahr Nimrim*, above Jericho on the Jordan.

Beth=pa′let (*house of flight*), a town among those in the extreme south of Judah, named in Josh. 15:27.

Beth=paz′zez (*house of the dispersion*), a town of Issachar named with En-haddah, Josh. 19:21, and of which nothing is known.

Beth=pe′or (bĕth-pē′ôr) (*house of Peor*), a place on the east of Jordan, opposite Jericho, and six miles above Libias or Beth-haran. Josh. 13:20; Deut. 3:29; 4:46.

Beth′phage (bĕth′fa-gē) (g hard) (*house of figs*), the name of a place on the Mount of Olives, on the road between Jericho and Jerusalem. It was apparently close to Bethany. Matt. 21:1; Mark 11:1; Luke 19:29.

Beth-phe′let. Neh. 11:26. [BETH-PALET.]

Beth=ra′pha (bĕth-rā′fà), a name which occurs in the genealogy of Judah as the son of Eshton. 1 Chron. 4:12.

Beth=re′hob (bĕth-rē′hŏb) (*house of Rehob*), a place mentioned as having near it the valley in which lay the town of Laish or Dan. Judges 18:28. It was one of the little kingdoms of Aram or Syria. 2 Sam. 10:6. Robinson conjectures that this ancient place is represented by the modern *Hûnin*. Thomson says, *Banias*.

Bethsa′ida (bĕth-sā′ĭ-dà) (*house of fish*) **of Galilee,** John 12:21, a city which was the native place of Andrew, Peter and Philip, John 1:44; 12:21, in the land of Gennesareth, Mark 6:45, comp. 53, and therefore on the west side of the lake. By comparing the narratives in Mark 6:31-53 and Luke 9:10-17 it appears certain that the Bethsaida at which the five thousand were fed must have been a second place of the same name on the east of the lake. But in reality—as not unfrequently occurs in adjoining states or countries, Bethsaida of Galilee and Bethsaida Julias, although in two provinces, were separated by only a narrow stream and were practically one town, situated on both sides of the Jordan as it enters the Sea of Galilee on the north, so that the western part of the village was in Galilee and the eastern portion in Gaulonitis, part of the tetrarchy of Philip. This eastern portion was built up into a beautiful city by Herod Philip, and named by him *Bethsaida Julias*, after Julia the daughter of the Roman em-

THE TRADITIONAL BETHPHAGE.

peror Tiberius Cæsar. On the plain of Butaiha, a mile or two to the east, the five thousand were fed. The western part of the town remained a small village.

Beth=she'an (bĕth-shē'an) (*house of rest*), or in Samuel, BETHSHAN, a city which belonged to Manasseh, 1 Chron. 7: 29, though within the limits of Issachar, Josh. 17: 11, and therefore on the

THE CITADEL OF ANCIENT BETHSHEAN.

west of Jordan. 1 Sam. 31 : 10–13; 2 Sam. 21 : 12–14. In later times it was called Scythopolis. The place is still known as *Beisân*. It lies in the Ghôr or Jordan valley, about twelve miles south of the Sea of Galilee and four miles west of the Jordan.

Beth-she'mesh (bĕth-shē'mesh) (*house of the sun*). 1. One of the towns which marked the north boundary of Judah. Josh. 15:10. It is now *Ain Shems,* about two miles from the great Philistine plain, and seven from Ekron. 2. A city on the border of Issachar. Josh. 19:22. 3. One of the "fenced cities" of Naphtali. Josh. 19:38; Judges 1:33. 4. An idolatrous temple or place in Egypt. Jer. 43:13. In the middle ages Heliopolis was still called by the Arabs *Ain Shems.*

Beth-shit'tah (bĕth-shĭt'tah) (*home of the acacia*), one of the spots to which the flight of the host of the Midianites extended after their discomfiture by Gideon. Judges 7:22.

Beth-tap'puah (bĕth-tăp'pu-ah) (*home of apples*), one of the towns of Judah, in the mountainous district, and near Hebron. Josh. 15:53; comp. 1 Chron. 2:43. Here it has actually been discovered by Robinson under the modern name of *Teffûh,* five miles west of Hebron, on a ridge of high table-land.

Bethu'el (bĕth-ụ'el) (*abode of God*), 1. the son of Nahor by Milcah; nephew of Abraham, and father of Rebekah, Gen. 22 : 22, 23; 24 : 15, 24, 47; 28 : 2. He is also called "Bethuel the Syrian." 2. A town in Simeon. BETHUL.

Be'thul (*abode of God*), a town of Simeon in the south, named with Eltolad and Hormah, Josh. 19:4; called also Chesil and Bethuel. Josh. 15:30; 1 Chron. 4:30.

Beth'=zur (bĕth'zûr) (*house of rock*), a town in the mountains of Judah, built by Rehoboam, Josh. 15:58; 2 Chron. 11:7, now *Beit-zûr.* It commands the road from Beersheba and Hebron, which has always been the main approach to Jerusalem from the south.

Bet'onim (bĕt'o-nĭm), a town of Gad, apparently on the northern boundary. Josh. 13:26.

Betrothing. [MARRIAGE.]

Beu'lah (bū'lah) (*married*), the name which the land of Israel is to bear when "the land shall be married." Isa. 62:4.

Be'zai (bē'zāi), **Be'za.** "Children of Bezai," to the number of 323, returned from captivity with Zerubbabel. Ezra 2:17; Neh. 7:23; 10:18.

Bezal'eel (bĕ-zăl'e-el) (*in the shadow of God*). 1. The son of Uri, the son of Hur, of the tribe of Judah, and one of the architects of the tabernacle. Ex. 31:1–6. His charge was chiefly in all works of metal, wood and stone. (B.C. 1490.)

2. One of the sons of Pahath-moab who had taken a foreign wife. Ezra 10:30. (B.C. 458.)

Be'zek (bē'zek) (*plantation*). 1. The residence of Adoni-bezek, Judges 1 : 5, in the lot of Judah, ver. 3.

2. Where Saul numbered the forces of Israel and Judah before going to the relief of Jabesh-gilead. 1 Sam. 11:8. This was doubtless somewhere in the centre of the country. Condor places it at Ibzik, 17 miles northeast of Shechem, on the road to Scythopolis.

Be'zer (bē'zêr) (*fortress*), son of Zophah, one of the heads of the houses of Asher. 1 Chron. 7:37.

Be'zer in the wilderness, a city of refuge in the downs on the east of the Jordan. Deut. 4:43; Josh. 20:8; 21:36; 1 Chron. 6:78.

Bi'ble. The Bible is the name given to the revelation of God to man contained in sixty-six books or pamphlets, bound together and forming one book and only one, for it has in reality one author and one purpose and plan, and is the development of one scheme of the redemption of man.

I. ITS NAMES.—(1) *The Bible,* i. e. *The Book,* from the Greek "ta biblia," the books. The word is derived from a root designating the inner bark of the linden tree, on which the ancients wrote their books. It is *the* book, as being superior to all other books. But the application of the word BIBLE to the collected books of the Old and New Testaments is not to be traced farther back than the fifth century of our era. (2) *The Scriptures,* i. e. the writings, as recording what was spoken by God. (3) *The Oracles,* i. e. the things spoken, because the Bible is what God spoke to man, and hence also called (4) *The Word.* (5) *The Testaments* or *Covenants,* because it is the testimony of God to man, the truths to which God bears witness; and is also the *covenant* or agreement of God with man for his salvation. (6) *The Law,* to express that it contains God's commands to men.

II. COMPOSITION.—The Bible consists of two great parts, called the Old and New Testaments, separated by an interval of nearly four hundred years. These Testaments are further divided into sixty-six books, thirty-nine in the Old Testament and twenty-seven in the New. These books are a library in themselves, being written in every known form of literature. Twenty-two of them are historical, five are poetical, eighteen are prophetical, twenty-one are epistolary. They contain logical arguments, poetry, songs and hymns, history, biography, stories, parables, fables, eloquence, law, letters and philosophy.

There are at least thirty-six different authors, who wrote in three continents, in many countries, in three languages, and from every possible human standpoint. Among these authors were kings, farmers, mechanics, scientific men, lawyers, generals, fishermen, ministers and priests, a tax-collector, a doctor, some rich, some poor, some city bred, some country born—thus touching all the experiences of men—extending over 1500 years.

III. DEVELOPMENT.—There is a law of progress or evolution running through the Bible from beginning to end, from Eden to the city of God. It describes the progress of man under God's training through a perfect moral law as the ideal. But its special applications are adapted to the circumstances of untrained and imperfect men, as a wise father deals with his children differently as they grow in understanding and character. This explains most of the moral difficulties in the O. T.

IV. ORIGINAL LANGUAGES.—The Old Testament was written in Hebrew, a Shemitic language, except that parts of the books of Ezra (5:8; 6:12; 7:12–26) and of Daniel (2:4–7:28), and one verse in Jeremiah (Jer. 10:11), were written in the Chaldee language. The New Testament is written wholly in Greek.

V. ANCIENT MANUSCRIPTS OF THE ORIGINAL.—There are no ancient Hebrew manuscripts older than the tenth century, but we know that these are in the main correct, because we have a translation of the Hebrew into Greek, called the Septuagint, made nearly three hundred years before Christ. Our He-brew Bibles are a reprint from what is called the Masoretic text. The ancient Hebrew had only the consonants printed, and the vowels were vocalized in pronunciation, but were not written. Some Jewish scholars living at Tiberias, and at Sora by the Euphrates, from the sixth to the twelfth century, punctuated the Hebrew text, and wrote in the vowel points and other tone-marks to aid in the reading of the Hebrew; and these, together with notes of various kinds, they called *Masora* (tradition), hence the name Masoretic text.

Of the Greek of the New Testament there are a number of ancient manuscripts. They are divided into two kinds, the *Uncials,* written wholly in *capitals,* and the *Cursives,* written in a *running hand.* The chief of these are—(1) *the Alexandrian (codex Alexandrinus,* marked A), so named because it was found in Alexandria in Egypt, in 1628. It dates back to A.D. 350, and is now in the British Museum. (2) The *Vatican (codex Vaticanus,* B), named from the Vatican library at Rome, where it is kept. Its date is A.D. 300 to 325. (3) The *Sinaitic (codex Sinaiticus),* so called from the convent of St. Catherine on Mount Sinai, where it was discovered by Dr. Tischendorf in 1844. It is now at St. Petersburg, Russia. This is one of the earliest and best of all the manuscripts.

VI. TRANSLATIONS.—The Old Testament was translated into Greek by a company of learned Jews at Alexandria, who began their labor about the year B.C. 286. It is called the *Septuagint,* i. e. the Seventy, from the tradition that it was translated by seventy (more exactly seventy-two) translators. The *Vulgate,* or translation of the Bible into Latin by Jerome, A.D. 385–405, is the authorized version of the Roman Catholic Church.

The first complete translation of the whole Bible into English was made by John Wycliffe (1380–1382).

The first book ever printed was the Bible. The first Bible was printed between the years 1450 and 1455, at Mentz, by Guttenberg, the reputed inventor of printing.

First New Testament printed in English was that of William Tyndale (1525–1526).

First Bible printed in English was Miles Coverdale's (1535).

As the sum and fruit of all these appeared our present *Authorized Version*, or *King James Version*, in 1611, made by forty-seven learned men.

A REVISED VERSION of this authorized edition was made by a committee consisting of eighty American and English scholars, of various denominations, the English committee having been appointed in 1870 and the American in 1871. This revision was necessary because of the changes in the English language during the nearly 300 years, and because much light has been thrown upon the original Scriptures, and upon all matters pertaining to biblical studies. The *Revised New Testament* was published simultaneously in this country and in England in May, 1881, and the *Revised Old Testament* in May, 1885. The *American Revision* of the Bible was published in 1901, and contained the changes preferred by the American Revisers.

Modern-speech translations have been made from time to time between 1898–1945. Among these were Moulton's *Modern Reader's Bible*, Weymouth's, Moffatt's, and Goodspeed's.

As a result of the modern-speech translations that have appeared and been widely received, the American Revision Committee set to work again, and in 1946 the Revised Standard Version of the New Testament was published.

VII. DIVISIONS INTO CHAPTERS AND VERSES.—The present division of the whole Bible into chapters was made by Cardinal Hugo de St. Cher about 1250. These chapters were divided into verses as we now have them by Rabbi Nathan, and adopted by Robert Stephens in his Greek Testament, published in 1551, in his edition of the Vulgate, in 1555. The first English Bible printed with these chapters and verses was the Geneva Bible, in 1560.

VIII. CIRCULATION OF THE BIBLE.—The first book ever printed was the Bible; and more Bibles have been printed than any other book. It has been translated, in its entirety or in part, into more than a thousand languages and dialects and various systems for the blind. The American Bible Society alone has published over 356 million volumes of Scripture.

Bich′ri (bĭk′rĭ) (*youthful*), 2 Sam. 20 : 1, an ancestor of Sheba.

Bid′kar (bĭd′kär), Jehu's "captain," originally his fellow officer, 2 Kings 9 :

25, who completed the sentence on Jehoram, son of Ahab.

Bier. [BURIAL.]

Big′tha (bĭg′thä) (*gift of God*), one of the seven chamberlains or eunuchs of the harem of King Ahasuerus. Esther 1 : 10. (B.C. 483.)

Big′than (bĭg′than), or **Big′thana** (*gift of fortune*), a eunuch (chamberlain, Authorized Version) in the court of Ahasuerus, one of those "who kept the door," and conspired with Teresh against the king's life. Esther 2 : 21.

Big′vai (bĭg′va-ī) (*happy*). 1. "Children of Bigvai," 2056 (Neh. 2067) in number, returned from the captivity with Zerubbabel, Ezra 2 : 14; Neh. 7 : 19, and 72 of them at a later date with Ezra. Ezra 8 : 14.

2. Apparently one of the chiefs of Zerubbabel's expedition, Ezra 2 : 2; Neh. 7 : 7, whose family afterwards signed the covenant. Neh. 10 : 16.

Bil′dad (bĭl′dăd) (*Bel hath loved*), the second of Job's three friends. He is called "the Shuhite," which implies both his family and nation. Job 2 : 11. There is no clue to his date.

Bil′eam (*destruction*), a town in the western half of the tribe of Manasseh, named only in 1 Chron. 6 : 70; same as Ibleam and Gath-rimmon. Josh. 17 : 11 and 21 : 25.

Bil′gah (bĭl′gah) (*cheerfulness*). 1. A priest in the time of David; the head of the fifteenth course for the temple service. 1 Chron. 24 : 14.

2. A priest or priestly family who returned from Babylon with Zerubbabel and Jeshua. Neh. 12 : 5, 18. (B.C. 536.)

Bil′gai. Neh. 10 : 8. [BILGAH, 2.]

Bil′hah (bĭl′hah) (*timid, bashful*), handmaid of Rachel, Gen. 29 : 29, and concubine of Jacob, to whom she bore Dan and Naphtali. Gen. 30 : 3–8; 35 : 25; 46 : 25; 1 Chron. 7 : 13.

Bil′han. 1. A Horite chief dwelling in Mount Seir. Gen. 36 : 27; 1 Chron. 1 : 42.

2. A Benjamite, son of Jediael. 1 Chron. 7 : 10.

Bil′shan (bĭl′shăn) (*inquirer*), one of Zerubbabel's companions on his expedition from Babylon. Ezra 2 : 2; Neh. 7 : 7. (B.C. 536.)

Bim′hal (bĭm′hăl) (*circumcised*), one of the sons of Japhlet in the line of Asher. 1 Chron. 7 : 33.

Bin′ea, one of the descendants of Saul. 1 Chron. 8 : 37; 9 : 43.

Bin'nui (bǐn'nu-ī) (*building up*). 1. A Levite, father of Noadiah. Ezra 8:33.
2. One who had taken a foreign wife. Ezra 10:30.
3. Another Israelite who had also taken a foreign wife. Ezra 10:38.
4. Altered from BANI in the corresponding list in Ezra. Neh. 7:15.
5. A Levite, son of Henadad, who assisted at the reparation of the wall of Jerusalem, under Nehemiah. Neh. 3:24; 10:9.

Birds. [SPARROW.]

Bir'sha (bīr'shà), a king of Gomorrah. Gen. 14:2.

Birthdays. The custom of observing birthdays is very ancient, Gen. 40:20; Jer. 20:15; and in Job 1:4, etc., we read that Job's sons "feasted every one his day." In Persia birthdays were celebrated with peculiar honors and banquets, and in Egypt those of the king were kept with great pomp. It is very probable that in Matt. 14:6 the feast to commemorate Herod's accession is intended, for we know that such feasts were common, and were called "the day of the king." Hos. 7:5.

Birthright, the advantages accruing to the *eldest son*. These were not definitely fixed in patriarchal times. Great respect was paid to him in the household, and, as the family widened into a tribe, this grew into a sustained authority, undefined save by custom, in all matters of common interest. Thus the "princes" of the congregation had probably rights of primogeniture. Num. 7:2; 21:18; 25:14. Gradually the rights of the eldest son came to be more definite: (1) The functions of the priesthood in the family, with the paternal blessing. (2) A "double portion" of the paternal property was allotted by the Mosaic law. Deut. 21:15–17. (3) The eldest son succeeded to the official authority of the father. The first-born of the king was his successor by law. 2 Chron. 21:3. In all these Jesus was the *first-born* of the Father.

Bir'zavith (bīr'za-vǐth), a name occurring in the genealogies of Asher. 1 Chron. 7:31.

Bishop. The word originally signified an "overseer" or spiritual superintendent. The titles bishop and elder, or presbyter, were essentially equivalent. Bishop is from the Greek, and denotes one who exercises the *function* of overseeing. Presbyter was derived from the office in the synagogue. Presbyter is a transliteration of the Greek word meaning "elder," "older"; and expresses the authority of age and experience. Hence the rulers of the Jews were called elders, as those of Rome were senators, *i. e.* old men. The duties of the bishop-elders appear to have been as follows: (1) General superintendence over the spiritual well-being of the flock. 1 Pet. 5:2. (2) The work of teaching, both publicly and privately. 1 Thess. 5:12; Titus 1:9; 1 Tim. 5:17. (3) The work of visiting the sick. James 5:14. (4) Among other acts of charity, that of receiving strangers occupied a conspicuous place. 1 Tim. 3:2; Titus 1:8. Peter calls Christ "the shepherd and bishop of your souls." 1 Pet. 2:25.

Bishopric, the district over which the jurisdiction of a bishop extended. Acts 1:20; 1 Tim. 3:1.

Bithi'ah (bǐth-ī'ah) (*daughter i. e. worshiper of Jehovah*), daughter of a Pharaoh, and wife of Mered. 1 Chron. 4:18.

Bith'ron (bǐth'rŏn), more accurately **the Bithron** (*a gorge* or *ravine*), a place, doubtless a district, in the Jordan valley on the east side of the river. 2 Sam. 2:29.

Bithyn'ia (bi-thy̆n'ĭ-à), a Roman province of Asia Minor. Mentioned only in Acts 16:7 and in 1 Pet. 1:1. The chief town of Bithynia was Nicæa, celebrated for the general Council of the Church held there in A.D. 325 against the Arian heresy.

Bitter herbs. The Israelites were commanded to eat the paschal lamb "with unleavened bread and with bitter herbs." Ex. 12:8. These "bitter herbs" consisted of such plants as chicory, bitter cresses, hawkweeds, sowthistles and wild lettuces, which grow abundantly in the peninsula of Sinai, in Palestine and in Egypt. The purpose of this observance was to recall to the minds of the Israelites their deliverance from the bitter bondage of the Egyptians.

Bittern. The word occurs in Isa. 14:23; 34:11; Zeph. 2:14. The Revised Version translates "porcupine," but authorities vary. The bittern (*Botaurus stellaris*) belongs to the *Ardeidæ*, the heron family of birds, and is famous for the peculiar nocturnal booming sound which it emits.

Bizjoth'jah (bĭz-jŏth'jah) (*contempt*

of Jehovah), a town in the south of Judah. Josh. 15:28. Probably a corruption for "her villages."

Biz'tha (*eunuch*), the second of the seven eunuchs of King Ahasuerus' harem. Esther 1:10. (B.C. 483.)

Blains, violent ulcerous inflammations, the sixth plague of Egypt, Ex. 9:9, 10, and hence called in Deut. 28:27, 35 "the botch of Egypt." It seems to have been the bubo plague (Cheyne). It was Job's disease, perhaps ulcers.

Blasphemy, in its technical English sense, signifies the speaking evil of God, and in this sense it is found Ps. 74:18; Isa. 52:5; Rom. 2:24, etc. But according to its derivation it may mean any species of calumny and abuse: see 1 Kings 21:10; Acts 18:6; Jude 9, etc. Blasphemy was punished by stoning, which was inflicted on the son of Shelomith. Lev. 24:11, 23. On this charge both our Lord and St. Stephen were condemned to death by the Jews.

The blasphemy against the Holy Ghost, Matt. 12:32; Mark 3:28, consisted in attributing to the power of Satan those unquestionable miracles which Jesus performed by "the finger of God" and the power of the Holy Spirit. It is plainly such a state of willful, determined opposition to God and the Holy Spirit that no efforts will avail to lead to repentance. Among the Jews it was a sin against God answering to treason in our times.

Blas'tus (*blas'tus*) (*sprout*), the chamberlain of Herod Agrippa I. Acts 12:20.

Blindness is extremely common in the East from many causes. Blind beggars figure repeatedly in the New Testament (Matt. 12:22), and "opening the eyes of the blind" is mentioned in prophecy as a peculiar attribute of the Messiah. Isa. 29:18; 42:7, etc. The Jews were specially charged to treat the blind with compassion and care. Lev. 19:14; Deut. 27:18. Blindness willfully inflicted for political or other purposes is alluded to in Scripture. 1 Sam. 11:2; Jer. 39:7.

Blood. To blood is ascribed in Scripture the mysterious sacredness which belongs to life, and God reserves it to himself when allowing man the dominion over and the use of the lower animals for food. Thus reserved, it acquires a double power: (1) that of sacrificial atonement; and (2) that of becoming a curse when wantonly shed,

unless duly expiated. Gen. 9:4, 5; Lev. 7:26; 17:11–13.

Blood, Avenger of. He who avenged the blood of one who had been killed. The nearest relative of the deceased became the authorized avenger of blood. Num. 35:19. The law of retaliation was not to extend beyond the immediate offender. Deut. 24:16; 2 Kings 14:6; 2 Chron. 25:4; Jer. 31:29, 30. It was the early method of punishing murder.

Boaner'ges (bō-a-nĕr'gĕs), a name signifying *sons of thunder,* given by our Lord to the two sons of Zebedee, James and John, probably on account of their fiery earnestness. Mark 3:17. See Luke 9:54; Mark 9:38; comp. Matt. 20:20, etc.

Boar. [SWINE.]

Bo'az (bō'ăz) (*fleetness*). 1. A wealthy Bethlehemite, kinsman to Elimelech the husband of Naomi. He married Ruth, and redeemed the estates of her deceased husband Mahlon. Ruth 4:1 ff. Boaz is mentioned in the genealogy of Christ, Matt. 1:5. There is great difficulty in assigning his date. According to some chronologies it was about B.C. 1200.

2. The name of one of Solomon's brazen pillars erected in the temple porch. [JACHIN.] It stood on the left, and was eighteen cubits high. 1 Kings 7:15, 21; 2 Chron. 3:15; Jer. 52:21.

Boch'eru (bŏk'e-ru̇) (*first-born*), son of Azel, according to the present Hebrew text of 1 Chron. 8:38.

Bo'chim (bō'kim) (*the weepers*), a place on the west of Jordan, above Gilgal; so named from the weeping of Israel. Judg. 2:1, 5.

Bo'han (bō'hăn) (*thumb*), a Reubenite. Josh. 15:6; 18:17.

Bo'han, Stone of, a stone erected in honor of Bohan, on the boundary between Judah and Benjamin, in the valley of Achor, a well-known landmark so named on account of its resemblance to a thumb. Josh. 15:6; 18:17.

Boil. [MEDICINE.]

Bondage. [SLAVE.]

Book. [WRITING.]

Booths. [SUCCOTH; TABERNACLES, FEAST OF.]

Booty consisted of captives of both sexes, cattle, and whatever a captured city might contain, especially metallic treasures. Within the limits of Canaan no captives were to be made, Deut. 20:14, 16; beyond these limits, in case of

7

THE SO-CALLED FIELD OF BOAZ, NEAR BETHLEHEM.

warlike resistance, all the women and children were to be made captives, and the men put to death. The law of booty is given in Num. 31:26–47. As regarded the army, David added a regulation that the baggage guard should share equally with the troops engaged. 1 Sam. 30:24, 25.

Bo'oz. Matt. 1:5; Luke 3:32. [BOAZ.]

Bos'cath. 2 Kings 22:1. [BOZKATH.]

Bo'sor (bō'sôr), same as BEOR. 2 Pet. 2:15.

Bottle. The Arabs keep their water, milk and other liquids in leathern bottles. These are made of goatskins. When the animal is killed they cut off its feet and its head, and draw it in this manner out of the skin without opening its belly. The great leathern bottles are made of the skin of a he-goat, and the small ones, that serve instead of a bottle of water on the road, are made of a kid's skin. The effect of external heat upon a skin bottle is indicated in Ps. 119:83, "a bottle in the smoke," and of expansion produced by fermentation in Matt. 9:17, "new wine in old bottles." Vessels of metal, earthen or glassware for liquids were in use among the Greeks, Egyptians, Etruscans and Assyrians, and also no doubt among the Jews, especially in later times. Thus Jer. 19:1, "a potter's earthen bottle." Bottles

ANCIENT GREEK GLASS BOTTLE.

SKIN BOTTLES.

were made by the ancient Egyptians of alabaster, gold, ivory and stone. They were of most exquisite workmanship and elegant forms. Tear-bottles were small urns of glass or pottery, made to contain the tears of mourners at funerals, and placed in the sepulchres at Rome and in Palestine. In some ancient tombs they are found in great numbers. Ps. 56:8 refers to this custom.

Bow. Gen. 37:10. The eastern mode of salutation, by kneeling upon one knee and bending the head forward till it touched the ground.

Box tree. Isa. 41:19; 60:13. A beautiful evergreen growing in many parts of Europe and Asia. Its hard wood is much prized by engravers. The reference in Isa. 60:13 is supposed by some to mean a species of cedar.

Bo'zez (bō'zez) (*shining*), one of the two sharp rocks between the passages by which Jonathan entered the Philistine garrison. It seems to have been that on the north. 1 Sam. 14:4, 5.

Boz'kath (bŏs'kath) (*rocky height*), a city of Judah in the lowlands. Josh. 15:39; 2 Kings 22:1.

Boz'rah (bŏz'rah) (*fortification*). 1. In Edom, the city of Jobab the son of Zerah, one of the early kings of that nation. Gen. 36:33; 1 Chron. 1:44. Mentioned by Isaiah, 34:6; 63:1, in connection with Edom, and by Jeremiah, 49:13, 22; Amos, 1:12, and Micah, 2:12. Its modern representative is *el-Busaireh*, which lies on the mountain district to the southeast of the Dead Sea. (Cheyne.)

2. In his catalogue of the cities of the land of Moab, Jeremiah, 48:24, mentions a Bozrah as in "the plain country" (ver. 21), *i. e.* the high level downs on the east of the Dead Sea.

Bracelet. [See ARMLET.] Bracelets

BRACELETS.

of fine twisted Venetian gold are still common in Egypt. In Gen. 38:18, 25 the word rendered "bracelet" means probably a string by which a seal-ring was suspended. Men as well as women wore bracelets, as we see from 2 Sam. 1:10. Layard says of the Assyrian kings, "The arms were encircled by armlets, and the wrists by bracelets."

Bramble. [THORNS.]

Brass. The word *nechôsheth* is improperly translated by "brass." In most places of the Old Testament the correct translation would be copper, although it may sometimes possibly mean bronze, a compound of copper and tin. Indeed a simple metal was obviously intended, as we see from Deut. 8:9; 33:25; Job 28:2. Copper was known at a very early period. Gen. 4:22.

Brazen serpent. [SERPENT.]

Bread. The preparation of bread as an article of food dates from a very early period. Gen. 18:6. The corn or grain employed was of various sorts. The best bread was made of wheat, but "barley" and spelt were also used. John 6:9, 13; Isa. 28:25. The process of making bread was as follows: the flour was first mixed with water or milk; it was then kneaded with the hands (in Egypt with the feet also) in a small wooden bowl or "kneading-trough" until it became dough. Ex. 12:34, 39; 2 Sam. 13:8; Jer. 7:18. When the kneading was completed, leaven was generally added [LEAVEN]; but when the time for preparation was short, it was omitted, and unleavened cakes, hastily baked, were eaten, as is still the prevalent custom among the Bedouins. Gen. 18:6; 19:3; Ex. 12:39; Judges 6:19; 1 Sam. 28:24. The leavened mass was allowed to stand for some time, Matt. 13:33; Luke 13:21; the dough was then divided into round cakes, Ex. 29:23; Judges 7:13; 8:5; 1 Sam. 10:3; Prov. 6:26, not unlike flat stones in shape and appearance, Matt. 7:9, comp. 4:3, about a span in diameter and a finger's breadth in thickness. In the towns where professional bakers resided, there were no doubt fixed ovens, in shape and size resembling those in use among ourselves: but more usually each household possessed a portable oven, consisting of a stone or metal jar, about three feet high, which was heated inwardly with wood, 1 Kings 17:12; Isa. 44:15; Jer. 7:18, or dried grass and flower-stalks. Matt. 6:30. Lev. 2 names several kinds of bread.

Breastplate. [ARMS.]

Brethren of Jesus. [JAMES.]

Brick. Gen. 11:3. The bricks in use among the Jews were much larger than with us, being usually from 12 to 13 inches square and 3½ inches thick; they thus possess more of the character of tiles. Ezek. 4:1. The Israelites, in common with other captives, were employed

ASSYRIAN BRICK FROM NIMROUD.
Inscribed with Shalmaneser's Name and Title.

by the Egyptian monarchs in making bricks and in building. Ex. 1:14; 5:7. Egyptian bricks were not generally dried in kilns, but in the sun. That brick-kilns were known is evident from 2 Sam. 12:31; Jer. 43:9. When made of the Nile mud they required straw to prevent cracking. [See STRAW.]

JEWS AND CAPTIVES MAKING BRICKS IN EGYPT.

Bride, Bridegroom. [MARRIAGE.]

Brigandine. Jer. 46:4; elsewhere "habergeon," or "coat of mail," R. V.

Brimstone. Brimstone, or sulphur, is found in considerable quantities on the shores of the Dead Sea. Gen. 19:24. It is a well-known simple mineral substance, crystalline, easily melted, very inflammable, and when burning emits a peculiar suffocating odor. It is found in great abundance near volcanoes. The soil around Sodom and Gomorrah abounded in sulphur and bitumen.

Brother. The Hebrew word is used in various senses in the Old Testament, as (1) Any kinsman, and not a mere brother; *e. g.* nephew, Gen. 13:8; 14:16; husband, Cant. 4:9. (2) One of the same tribe. 2 Sam. 19:12. (3) Of the same people, Ex. 2:11, or even of a cognate people. Num. 20:14. (4) An ally. Amos 1:9. (5) Any friend. Job 6:15. (6) One of the same office. 1 Kings 9:13. (7) A fellow man. Lev. 19:17. (8) Metaphorically of any similarity, as in Job 30:29. The word ἀδελφός has a similar range of meanings in the New Testament.

Buk'ki (bŭk'kī). 1. Son of Abishua and father of Uzzi, fifth from Aaron in the line of the high priests in 1 Chron. 6:5, 51 (Authorized Version), and in the genealogy of Ezra. Ezra 7:4.

2. Son of Jogli, prince of the tribe of Dan, one of the ten men chosen to apportion the land of Canaan between the tribes. Num. 34:22.

Bukki'ah (bŭk-kī'ah), a Kohathite Levite, of the sons of Heman, one of the musicians in the temple. 1 Chron. 25:4, 13.

Bul. [MONTH.]

Bull, Bullock, terms used synonymously with ox, oxen, and properly a generic name for horned cattle when of full age and fit for the plough. It is variously rendered "bullock," Isa. 65:25, "cow," Ezek. 4:15, "oxen," Gen. 12:16. *Kine* is used in the Bible as the plural of cow. In Isaiah 51:20, the "wild bull" ("wild ox" in Deut. 14:5) was possibly one of the larger species of antelope, and took its name from its swiftness. Dr. Robinson mentions large herds of black and almost hairless buffaloes as still existing in Palestine, and these may be the animal indicated.

Bulrush (or papyrus), a reed growing in the shallow water on the banks of the Nile. It grows to the height of 12 or 15 feet, with a stalk two or three inches in diameter. The stalks are very pliable and can be very closely interwoven, as is evident from their having been used in the construction of arks. Ex. 2:3, 5. Paper was made from this plant, from which it derives its name.

BULRUSH.

Bu'nah (bū'nah) (*understanding*), a son of Jerahmeel, of the family of Pharez in Judah. 1 Chron. 2:25.

Bun'ni (bŭn'nī) (*built*). 1. One of the Levites in the time of Nehemiah. Neh. 9:4.

2. Another Levite, but of earlier date than the preceding. Neh. 11:15.

Burial, Sepulchres. [TOMBS.] On this subject we have to notice—1. The place of burial, its site and shape; 2. The mode of burial; 3. The prevalent notions regarding this duty.

1. A natural cave enlarged and adapted by excavation, or an artificial imitation of one, was the standard type of sepulchre. Sepulchres, when the owner's means permitted it, were commonly prepared beforehand, and stood often in gardens, by roadsides, or even adjoining houses. Kings and prophets alone were probably buried within towns. 1 Kings 2:10; 16:6, 28. Cities soon became populous and demanded cemeteries, Ezek. 39:15, which were placed without the walls. Sepulchres were marked sometimes by pillars or by pyramids. Such as were not otherwise noticeable were scrupulously "whited," Matt. 23:27, once a year, after the rains before the passover, to warn passers-by of defilement.

BURIAL JAR WITH SKELETON OF A CHILD. (from Megiddo.)

2. "The manner of the Jews" included the use of spices, where they could command the means. 2 Chron. 16:14. A portion of these was burnt in honor of the deceased, and to this use was probably destined part of the

one hundred pounds weight of "myrrh and aloes" in our Lord's case. In no instance, save that of Saul and his sons, were the bodies burned; and even then the bones were interred, and re-exhumed for solemn entombment. It was the office of the next of kin to perform and preside over the whole funeral office; though public buriers were not unknown in New Testament times. Acts 5 : 6, 10. The body was borne by the nearest

POTTERY COFFINS, FOUND AT NIPPUR, BABYLONIA.

relatives. The grave-clothes were probably of the fashion worn in life, but swathed and fastened with bandages, and the head covered separately.

3. The precedent of Jacob's and Joseph's remains being returned to the land of Canaan was followed, in wish at least, by every pious Jew.

Burnt offering. The word is applied to the offering which was wholly consumed by fire on the altar, and the whole of which, except the refuse ashes, "ascended" in the smoke to God. The meaning of the whole burnt offering was that which is the original idea of all sacrifice, the offering by the sacrificer of himself, soul and body, to God—the submission of his will to the will of the Lord. The ceremonies of the burnt offering are given in detail in the book of Leviticus. [SACRIFICE.]

Bush. The Hebrew word *sĕneh* occurs only in those passages which refer to Jehovah's appearance to Moses "in the flame of fire in the bush." Ex. 3 : 2, 3, 4; Deut. 33 : 16. It is quite impossible to say what kind of thorn bush is intended; but it was possibly the acacia, a small variety of the shittim tree found in the Sinai region.

Bushel. [WEIGHTS AND MEASURES.]

Butler. One of the officers of the king's household, Neh. 1 : 11, who had charge of the wine and poured it out for the king. The chief butler, as the title signifies, was in charge of the butlers. Gen. 40 : 1–13.

Butter. Curdled milk. Gen. 18 : 8; Deut. 32 : 14; Judges 5 : 25; Job 20 : 17. Milk is generally offered to travelers in Palestine in a curdled or sour state, *lebben,* thick, almost like butter. Hasselquist describes the method of making butter employed by the Arab women as follows:

"They made butter in a leather bag, hung on three poles erected for the purpose, in the form of a cone, and drawn to and fro by two women."

Buz (bŭz) (*contempt*). 1. The second son of Milcah and Nahor. Gen. 22 : 21. Elihu "the Buzite" was probably a descendant of Buz. Job 32 : 2.

2. A name occurring in the genealogies of the tribe of Gad. 1 Chron. 5 : 14.

Bu′zi (bū′zī) (*contempt*), father of Ezekiel the prophet. Ezek. 1 : 3.

C

Cab. [WEIGHTS AND MEASURES.]

Cab'bon (kăb'bon), a town in the low country of Judah. Josh. 15:40.

Ca'bul (kā'bŭl). 1. One of the landmarks on the boundary of Asher, Josh. 19:27; now *Kabûl*, 9 or 10 miles east of *Accho*.

2. Name of the land given to Hiram by Solomon. 1 Kings 9:10–13.

Cæ'sar, always in the New Testament the Roman emperor, the sovereign of Judea. John 19:12, 15; Acts 17:7, etc.

Cæsare'a (Acts 8:40; 9:30; 10:1, 24; 11:11; 12:19; 18:22; 21:8, 16; 23:23, 33; 25:1, 4, 6, 13) was situated on the coast of Palestine, on the line of the great road from Tyre to Egypt, and about halfway between Joppa and Dora. The distance from Jerusalem was about 70 miles; Josephus states it in round numbers as 600 stadia. In Strabo's time there was on this point of the coast merely a town called "Strato's Tower," with a landing-place, whereas in the time of Tacitus Cæsarea is spoken of as being the head of Judea. It was in this interval that the city was built by Herod the Great. It was the official residence of the Herodian kings, and of Festus, Felix and the other Roman procurators of Judea. Here also lived Philip the deacon and his four prophesying daughters. Cæsarea continued to be a city of some importance even in the time of the Crusades, and the name still lingers on the site (*Kaisariyeh*), which is a complete desolation, many of the building-stones having been carried to other towns.

Cæsare'a Philip'pi is mentioned only in the first two Gospels, Matt. 16:13; Mark 8:27, and in accounts of the same transactions. It was at the easternmost and most important of the two recognized sources of the Jordan, the other being at *Tel-el-Kadi*. The spring rises from and the city was built on a lime-stone terrace in a valley at the base of Mount Hermon, 20 miles north of the Sea of Galilee. It was enlarged by Herod Philip, and named after Cæsar, with his own name added to distinguish it from Cæsarea. Its present name is *Banias,* a village of some 50 houses, with many interesting ruins. Cæsarea Philippi has no Old Testament history, though it has been not unreasonably identified with *Baal-gad*. It was visited by Christ shortly before his transfiguration, Matt. 16:13–28, and was the northern limit of his journeys. Mark 8:27.

Cage. The term so rendered in Jer. 5:27 is more properly a *trap*, in which decoy birds were placed. In Rev. 18:2 the Greek term means a prison.

Ca'iaphas (kā'ia-fas) (*depression*), in full JOSEPH CAIAPHAS, high priest of the Jews under Tiberius. Matt. 26:3, 57; John 11:49; 18:13, 14, 24, 28; Acts 4:6. The procurator Valerius Gratus appointed him to the dignity. He was son-in-law of Annas. [ANNAS.]

Cain (kān) (*possession*). Gen. 4. He was the eldest son of Adam and Eve; he followed the business of agriculture. In a fit of jealousy, roused by the rejection of his own sacrifice and the acceptance of Abel's, he committed the crime of murder, for which he was expelled from Eden, and led the life of an exile. He settled in the land of Nod, and built a city, which he named after his son Enoch. His descendants are enumerated, together with the inventions for which they were remarkable.

Cain (kān), one of the cities in the low country of Judah, named with Zanoah and Gibeah. Josh. 15:57.

Cai'nan (kā'-nan). 1. Son of Enos, aged 70 years when he begat Mahalaleel his son. He lived 840 years afterwards, and died aged 910. Gen. 5:9–14.

2. Son of Arphaxad, and father of Sala, according to Luke 3:36, 37, and usually called the second Cainan. He is nowhere named in the Hebrew MSS. The name, however, is found in the LXX from which Luke quotes, both in

104

EXCAVATIONS IN THE TEMPLE AT NIPPUR, PERHAPS THE BIBLICAL CALNEH.
Excavations made by the University of Pennsylvania.

Gen. 10:24 and 11:12, and for this reason is found in the genealogy of Christ in St. Luke's Gospel.

Ca'lah (kā'lah) (*completion, old age*), one of the most ancient cities of Assyria. Gen. 10:11. The site of Calah is probably marked by the *Nimrûd* ruins. It was built and made the capital by Shalmaneser I. ab. 1300 B.C. Rebuilt and adorned during 885–735 B.C. It was a part of Nineveh and fell with it. It was in Calah that the Black Obelisk was found.

Calamus. [REED.]

Cal'col (kăl'kŏl) (*sustenance*), a man of Judah, son or descendant of Zerah. 1 Chron. 2:6. Probably identical with CHALCOL.

Caldron, a vessel for boiling flesh, for either ceremonial or domestic use. 1 Sam. 2:14; 2 Chron. 35:13; Job 41:20; Micah 3:3.

Ca'leb (kā'leb) (*capable*). 1. According to 1 Chron. 2:9, 18, 19, 42, 50, the son of Hezron the son of Pharez the son of Judah, and the father of Hur and consequently an ancestor of the skilled artificer Bezaleel.

2. Son of Jephunneh, one of the twelve spies sent by Moses to Canaan. Num. 13:6. (B.C. 1490.) He and Oshea or Joshua the son of Nun were the only two of the whole number who encouraged the people to enter in boldly to the land and take possession of it. Forty-five years afterwards Caleb came to Joshua and claimed possession of the land of the Anakim, Kirjath-arba or Hebron, and the neighboring hill country. Josh. 14. This was immediately granted to him, and the following chapter relates how he took possession of Hebron, driving out the three sons of Anak; and how he offered Achsah his daughter in marriage to whoever would take Kirjath-sepher, *i. e.* Debir; and how when Othniel, his younger brother, had performed the feat, he not only gave him his daughter to wife, but with her the upper and nether springs of water which she asked for. It is probable that Caleb was a foreigner by birth,—a proselyte, incorporated into the tribe of Judah.

Calf. The calf was held in high esteem by the Jews as food. 1 Sam. 28:24; Luke 15:23. The molten calf prepared by Aaron for the people to worship, Ex. 32:4, was probably a wooden figure overlaid with gold, a process

which is known to have existed in Egypt. [AARON.]

Cal'neh (kăl'neh), or **Cal'no,** appears in Gen. 10:10 among the cities of Nimrod. There is no way to identify its site. In the eighth century B.C. Calneh was taken by one of the Assyrian kings, and never recovered its prosperity. Isa. 10:9; Amos 6:2.

Cal'vary. [See GOLGOTHA.]

Camel. The species of camel which was in common use among the Jews and the heathen nations of Palestine was the Arabian or one-humped camel,

A SADDLED CAMEL.

Camelus arabicus. The dromedary is a swifter animal than the baggage-camel, and is used chiefly for riding purposes; it is merely a finer breed than the other. The Arabs call it the *heirie.* The speed of the dromedary has been greatly exaggerated, the Arabs asserting that it is swifter than the horse. Eight or nine miles an hour is the utmost it is able to perform; this pace, however, it is able to keep up for hours together. The Arabian camel carries about 500 pounds. "The hump on the camel's back is chiefly a store of fat, from which the animal draws as the wants of his system require; and the Arab is careful to see that the hump is in good condition before a long journey. Another interesting adaptation is the thick sole which protects the foot of the camel from the burning sand. The nostrils may be closed by valves against blasts of sand. Most interesting is the provision for drought made by providing the second stomach with great cells in which water is long retained. Sight and smell are exceedingly acute in the camel."—*Johnson's Encyc.* It is clear from Gen. 12: 16 that camels were early known to the Egyptians. The importance of the camel is shown by Gen. 24:64; 37:25; Judges 7:12; 1 Sam. 27:9; 1 Kings 10:2; 2 Chron. 14:15; Job 1:3; Jer. 49:29, 32, and many other texts. John the Baptist wore a garment made of camel's hair, Matt. 3:4; Mark 1:6, the coarser hairs of the camel; and some have supposed that Elijah was clad in a dress of the same stuff.

Ca'mon (kā'mŏn), the place in which Jair the judge was buried. Judges 10:5.

Camp. [ENCAMPMENT.]

Camphire. There can be no doubt that "camphire" is the *Lawsonia alba* of botanists, the *henna* of Arabian natu-

CAMPHIRE.

ralists. The henna plant grows in Egypt, Syria, Arabia and northern India. The flowers are white and grow in clusters, and are very fragrant. The whole shrub is from four to six feet high. S. of Sol. 4:13.

Ca'na (kā'nà) (*place of reeds*) of Galilee, once **Cana in Galilee**, a village or town not far from Capernaum, memorable as the scene of Christ's first miracle, John 2:1, 11; 4:46, as well as of a subsequent one, John 4:46, 54, and also as the native place of the apostle Nathanael. John 21:2. The traditional site is at *Kefr-Kenna*, a small village about 3¾ miles northwest of Nazareth.

The rival site is a village situated farther north, called Kana-el-Jelil, or more often, Khirbet Kana, 8 miles north of Nazareth.

Ca'naan (kā'nän) (*low, flat*). 1. The fourth son of Ham, Gen. 10:6; 1 Chron. 1:8, the progenitor of the Phœnicians [ZIDON], and of the various nations who before the Israelite conquest peopled the seacoast of Palestine, and generally the whole of the country westward of the Jordan. Gen. 10:15; 1 Chron. 1:13. The name is on the Tel-el-Amarna tablets.

2. The name "Canaan" is sometimes employed for the country itself.

Ca'naan, The land of (lit. *lowland*), a name denoting the country west of the Jordan and the Dead Sea, and between those waters and the Mediterranean; given by God to Abraham's posterity, the children of Israel. Ex. 6:4; Lev. 25:38. [PALESTINE.]

Cananæ'an (kā-nän-ē'an). Matt. 10:4. Used in the Revised Version in place of "Canaanite." [See CANAANITE.]

Ca'naanite, The (kā'nän-īte), the designation of the apostle Simon, otherwise known as "Simon Zelotes." It occurs in Matt. 10:4; Mark 3:18, and is derived from a Chaldee or Syriac word by which the Jewish sect or faction of the "Zealots" was designated—a turbulent and seditious sect, especially conspicuous at the siege of Jerusalem. They taught that all foreign rule over Jews was unscriptural, and opposed that rule in every way.

Ca'naanites, The, a word used in two senses: 1. A tribe which inhabited a particular locality of the land west of the Jordan before the conquest; and 2. The people who inhabited generally the whole of that country. (1) In Gen. 10:18–20 the seats of the Canaanite tribe are given as on the seashore and in the Jordan valley; comp. Josh. 11:3. (2) Applied as a general name to the non-Israelite inhabitants of the land, as we have already seen was the case with "Canaan." Instances of this are, Gen. 12:6; Num. 21:3. The Canaanites were descendants of Canaan. Their language was very similar to the Hebrew. The Canaanites were probably given to commerce; and thus the name became probably in later times an occasional synonym for a merchant.

Can'da-ce (kăn'da-çē) or **Canda'ce**, a queen of Ethiopia (Meroë), mentioned

Acts 8:27. (A.D. 36.) The name was not a proper name of an individual, but that of a dynasty of Ethiopian queens.

Candlestick, which Moses was commanded to make for the tabernacle, is described Ex. 25:31–37; 37:17–24. It was not strictly a "candlestick," as it held seven richly-adorned lamps. With its various appurtenances it required a talent of "pure gold;" and it was not moulded, but "of beaten work," and has been estimated to have been worth in our money over $25,000. From the Arch of Titus, where are sculptured the spoils taken from Jerusalem, we learn that it consisted of a central stem, with six branches, three on each side. It was several feet high. [See ARCH OF TITUS.] The candlestick was placed on the south side of the first apartment of the tabernacle, opposite the table of shewbread, Ex. 40:24, and was lighted every evening and dressed every morning. Ex. 27:20, 21; 30:8; comp. 1 Sam. 3:3. Each lamp was supplied with cotton and about two wineglasses of the purest olive oil, which was sufficient to keep it burning during a long night. In Solomon's temple, instead of or in addition to this candlestick there were ten golden candlesticks similarly embossed, five on the right and five on the left. 1 Kings 7:49; 2 Chron. 4:7.

GOLDEN CANDLESTICK.
(From the Arch of Titus.)

They were taken to Babylon. Jer. 52:19. In the temple of Zerubbabel there was again a single candlestick. 1 Macc. 1:21; 4:49.

Candlestick, in Matt. 5:15; Mark 4:21, is merely a lamp-stand, made in various forms, to hold up the simple Oriental hand-lamps.

Cane. [REED.]

Cankerworm. [LOCUST.]

Can'neh (kän'neh). Ezek. 27:23. [See CALNEH.]

Canon of Scripture, The, may be generally described as the "collection of books which form the original and authoritative written rule of the faith and practice of the Christian Church," i. e. the Old and New Testaments. The word *canon,* in classical Greek, is properly a *straight rod,* "a rule" in the widest sense, and especially in the phrases "the rule of the Church," "the rule of faith," "the rule of truth." The first direct application of the term *canon* to the Scriptures seems to be in the verses of Amphilochius (cir. 380 A.D.), where the word indicates the rule by which the contents of the Bible must be determined, and thus secondarily an index of the constituent books. The uncanonical books were described simply as "those without" or "those uncanonized." The canonical books were also called "books of the testament," and Jerome styled the whole collection by the striking name of "the holy library," which happily expresses the unity and variety of the Bible. After the Maccabean persecution the history of the formation of the Canon is merged in the history of its contents. The Old Testament appears from that time as a whole. The complete Canon of the New Testament, as commonly received at present, was ratified at the third Council of Carthage (A.D. 397), and from that time was accepted throughout the Latin Church. Respecting the books of which the Canon is composed, see the article BIBLE. The books of Scripture were not *made* canonical by act of any council, but the council gave its sanction to the results of long and careful investigations as to what books were really of divine authority and expressed the universally-accepted decisions of the church. The Old Testament Canon is ratified by the fact that the present Old Testament books were those accepted in the time of Christ and endorsed by him, and that of the 275 quotations of the Old Testament in the New, no book out of the Canon is quoted from except perhaps the words of Enoch in Jude. It has been stated that most of the New Testament is similarly quoted in writings of the Church Fathers before A.D. 300.

Canticles or **The Song of Songs.** This poem is a wedding song, and is more probably a song about Solomon, than by Solomon. It is a poem, and should be so printed, as it is in the Revised Versions. It has been called a drama, or melodrama, because various persons speak, in varied situations, and dialogue and songs are frequent, with monologues as in a Greek chorus. But the most accurate characterization is that by Professor Moulton, in the Modern Reader's Bible, who calls it a lyric idyl, "sufficiently elaborate in its structure to exhibit dramatic, epic and lyric in combination." The idyl treats not of wars and heroism, but of pure and simple domestic life, while the lyric has a wide range of forms.

There are three leading schools of interpretation:—1. The Literal, which regards the poem as a historical tale, founded on fact. As a song of the home, of pure family love, of marriage the highest manifestation of sweet un-

2. The allegorical interpretation which makes the poem an allegory, like Pilgrim's Progress, setting forth the love of Christ for his people who are his bride, who also love him with the most unselfish love.

3. The third interpretation is the typical, uniting the other two, a real human love, typifying union of God with his people. This is doubtless the true interpretation.

Caper′naum (kȧ-pĕr′na-ŭm) (*village of Nahum*) was on the western shore of the Sea of Galilee. Matt. 4:13; comp. John 6:24. It was in the "land of Gennesaret," Matt. 14:34; comp. John 6:17, 21, 24. It was of sufficient size to be always called a "city," Matt. 9:1; Mark 1:33; had its own synagogue, in which our Lord frequently taught, Mark 1:21; Luke 4:33, 38; John 6:59; and there was also a customs station, where the dues were gathered both by stationary and by itinerant officers. Matt. 9:9; 17:24; Mark 2:14; Luke 5:27. The only interest attaching to Capernaum is as the residence of our Lord and his apostles, the

SITE OF CAPERNAUM (TELL HUM).

selfish love and devotion, honored in the Bible, this song is worthy of a place in the Canon of Scripture. The symbols have been called too material, but they are given as supreme types of excellence, "symbols hallowed by associations of holy writ, and they seem material only to those who read with a defective sense of the symbolic."

scene of so many miracles and "gracious words." It was when he returned thither that he is said to have been "in the house." Mark 2:1. The spots which lay claim to its site, are (1) *Khan Minyeh*, a mound of ruins which takes its name from an old khan hard by. This mound is situated close upon the seashore at the northwestern extremity of the plain (now *El Ghuweir*). (2) Three miles north of *Khan Minyeh* is the other claimant, *Tell Hûm*—ruins of walls and foundations covering a space of half a mile long by a quarter wide, on a point of the shore projecting into the lake and backed by a very gently-rising ground. It is impossible to locate it with certainty, but the probability is in favor of *Tell Hûm.*

Caphar, one of the numerous words employed in the Bible to denote a village or collection of dwellings smaller than a city (*Ir*). Mr. Stanley proposes to render it by "hamlet." In names of places it occurs in Chephar-ha-Ammonai, Chephirah, Caphar-salama. To us its chief interest arises from its forming a part of the name of Capernaum, *i. e.* Capharnahum.

Caph'tor (kăf'tôr), **Caph'torim** (kăf'tŏ-rĭm), thrice mentioned as the primitive seat of the Philistines, Deut. 2:23; Jer. 47:4; Amos 9:7, who are once called **Caphtorim**. Deut. 2:23. Now generally identified with Crete.

Cappado'cia (kăp'pa-dō'shĭ-à), **Cappado'cians**, Acts 2:9; 1 Pet. 1:1, the largest province in ancient Asia Minor. Cappadocia is an elevated table-land intersected by mountain chains. It seems always to have been deficient in wood; but it was a good grain country, and particularly famous for grazing. Its Roman metropolis was Cæsarea. The native Cappadocians seem to have originally belonged to the Syrian stock.

Captain. (1) As a purely military title, "captain" answers to *sar* in the Hebrew army and *tribune* in the Roman. The "captain of the guard" in Acts 28: 16 was probably the *præfectus prætorio*. (2) *Kâtsin,* occasionally rendered captain, applies sometimes to a military, Josh. 10:24; Judges 11:6, 11; Isa. 22: 3; Dan. 11:18, sometimes to a civil command, *e. g.* Isa. 1:10; 3:6. (3) The "captain of the temple," mentioned Luke 22:4; Acts 4:1; 5:24, superintended the guard of priests and Levites who kept watch by night in the temple.

Captive. A prisoner of war. Such were usually treated with great cruelty by the heathen nations. They were kept for slaves, and often sold; but this was a modification of the ancient cruelty, and a substitute for putting them to death. Although the treatment of captives by the Jews seems sometimes to be cruel, it was very much milder than that of the heathen, and was mitigated, as far as possible in the circumstances, by their civil code.

Captivities of the Jews. The present article is confined to the forcible deportation of the Jews from their native land, and their forcible detention, under the Assyrian or Babylonian kings.

Captivities of Israel.—The kingdom of Israel was invaded by four successive kings of Assyria. Pul or Sardanapalus, according to Rawlinson, imposed a tribute (B.C. 738 Assyr. Canon) upon Menahem. 2 Kings 15: 19 and 1 Chron. 5:26. Tiglath-pileser carried away (B.C. 735) the trans-Jordanic tribes, 1 Chron. 5:26, and the inhabitants of Galilee, 2 Kings 15:29, comp. Isa. 9:1, to Assyria. Shalmaneser twice invaded, 2 Kings 17:3, 5, the kingdom which remained to Hoshea, took Samaria (B.C. 721) after a siege of three years, and carried Israel away into Assyria. This was the end of the kingdom of the ten tribes of Israel.

Captivities of Judah.—Sennacherib (B.C. 701) is stated to have carried into Assyria 200,000 captives from the Jewish cities which he took. 2 Kings 18: 13. Nebuchadnezzar, in the first half of his reign (B.C. 605-562), repeatedly invaded Judea, besieged Jerusalem, carried away the inhabitants to Babylon, and destroyed the temple. The 70 years of captivity predicted by Jeremiah, Jer. 25:12, are dated by Prideaux from B.C. 606. The captivity of Ezekiel dates from B.C. 597, when that prophet, like Mordecai the uncle of Esther, Esther 2:6, accompanied Jehoiachin. The captives were treated not as slaves but as colonists. The Babylonian captivity was brought to a close by the decree, Ezra 1:2, of Cyrus (B.C. 537), and the return of a portion of the nation under Sheshbazzar or Zerubbabel (B.C. 536), Ezra (B.C. 458) and Nehemiah (B.C. 446). Those who were left in Assyria, Esther 8:9, 11, and kept up their national distinctions, were known as The Dispersion. John 7:35; 1 Pet. 1:1; James 1:1.

The lost tribes.—Many attempts have been made to discover the ten tribes existing as a distinct community; but though history bears no witness of their present distinct existence, it enables us to track the footsteps of the departing race in four directions after the time of the Captivity. (1) Some returned and mixed with the Jews. Luke 2 : 36; Acts 26 : 7, etc. (2) Some were left in Samaria, mingled with the Samaritans, Ezra 6 : 21; John 4 : 12, and became bitter enemies of the Jews. (3) Many remained in Assyria, and were recognized as an integral part of the Dispersion; see Acts 2 : 9; 26 : 7. (4) Most, probably, apostatized in Assyria, adopted the usages and idolatry of the nations among whom they were planted, and became wholly swallowed up in them.

Carbuncle. This word represents two Hebrew words. The first may be a general term to denote crystal or any *sparkling gem,* Isa. 54 : 12; the second, Ex. 28 : 17; 39 : 10; Ezek. 28 : 13, is supposed to be the garnet.

Car′cas (kär′kas) (*possibly vulture*), the seventh of the seven "chamberlains," *i. e.* eunuchs, of King Ahasuerus. Esther 1 : 10. (B.C. 483.)

Car′chemish (kär′ke-mĭsh), the eastern capital of the Hittites, at a ford of the Euphrates. Its probable site is Jerabis on the west bank between Birejik and the river Sajur. Carchemish appears to have been taken by Pharaoh Necho shortly after the battle of Megiddo (cir. B.C. 608), and retaken by Nebuchadnezzar after a battle three years later, B.C. 605. Jer. 46 : 2.

Care′ah (kā-rē′ah) (*bald*), father of Johanan, 2 Kings 25 : 23; elsewhere spelt KAREAH.

Ca′ria (kā′rĭ-à), the southern part of the region which in the New Testament is called ASIA, and the southwestern part of the peninsula of Asia Minor. Acts 20 : 15; 27 : 7.

Car′mel (kär′mel) (*garden* or *park*). 1. A mountain which forms one of the most striking and characteristic features of the country of Palestine. It is a noble ridge, the only headland of lower and central Palestine, and forms its southern boundary, running out with a bold bluff promontory, nearly 600 feet high, almost into the very waves of the Mediterranean, then extending southeast for a little more than twelve miles, when it terminates suddenly in a bluff somewhat corresponding to its western end. In form Carmel is a tolerably continuous ridge, its highest point, about four miles from the eastern end, being 1740 feet above the sea. That which has made the name of Carmel most familiar to the modern world is its intimate connection with the history of the two great prophets of Israel, Elijah and Elisha. 2 Kings 2 : 25; 4 : 25; 1 Kings 18 : 20–42. It is now commonly called *Mar Elyas; Kürmel* being occasionally, but only seldom, heard.

2. A town in the mountainous country of Judah, Josh. 15 : 55, familiar to us as the residence of Nabal. 1 Sam. 25 : 2, 5, 7, 40.

Car′mi (kär′mī) (*vine dresser*). 1. The fourth son of Reuben, the progenitor of the family of the Carmites. Gen. 46 : 9; Ex. 6 : 14; Num. 26 : 6; 1 Chron. 5 : 3.

2. A man of the tribe of Judah, father of Achan, the "troubler of Israel." Josh. 7 : 1, 18; 1 Chron. 2 : 7.

Carpenter. [HANDICRAFT.]

Car′pus (kär′pus), a Christian at Troas. 2 Tim. 4 : 13.

Carriage. This word signifies what we now call "baggage." In the margin of 1 Sam. 17 : 20 and 26 : 5–7, "carriage" is employed in the sense of a wagon or cart.

Carshe′na (kär-shē′nà), one of the seven princes of Persia and Media. Esther 1 : 14.

ETHIOPIAN OX-CART.

Cart, Gen. 45 : 19, 27; Num. 7 : 3, 7, 8, a vehicle drawn by cattle, 2 Sam. 6 : 6; to be distinguished from the chariot drawn by horses. Carts and wagons were either open or covered, Num. 7:3, and were used for conveyance of persons, Gen. 45:19, burdens, 1 Sam. 6:7, 8, or produce. Amos 2:13. The only cart used in western Asia has two wheels of solid wood.

Carving. The arts of carving and engraving were much in request in the construction of both the tabernacle and the temple, Ex. 31:5; 35:33; 1 Kings 6:18, 35; Ps. 74:6, as well as in the ornamentation of the priestly dresses. Ex. 28:9-36; 2 Chron. 2:7, 14; Zech. 3:9.

Casiph′ia (kà-sĭf′ĭ-à), a place of uncertain site on the road between Babylon and Jerusalem. Ezra 8:17.

Cas′luhim (kăs′lu-hĭm), a Mizraite people or tribe. Gen. 10:14; 1 Chron. 1:12.

Cassia. Ex. 30:24; Ezek. 27:19. The cassia bark of commerce is yielded by various kinds of *Cinnamomum*, which grow in different parts of India. The Hebrew word in Ps. 45:8 is generally supposed to be another term for cassia.

Castle. [FENCED CITIES.]

Cas′tor and Pol′lux, Acts 28:11, the twin sons of Jupiter and Leda, were regarded as the tutelary divinities of sailors; hence their image was often used as a figure-head for ships. They appeared in heaven as the constellation *Gemini*. In art they were sometimes represented simply as stars hovering over a ship.

Caterpillar. The representative in the Authorized Version of the Hebrew word *châsîl* and *yelek*. (1) *Châsîl* occurs in 1 Kings 8:37; 2 Chron. 6:28; Ps. 78:46; Isa. 33:4; Joel 1:4, and seems to be applied to a locust, perhaps in its larva state. (2) *Yelek*. [LOCUST.]

Cattle. [BULL.]

Cau′da. Acts 27:16. The form given in the Revised Version to *Clauda*, an island south of Crete. It bears a closer relation to the modern name *Gaudonesi* of the Greek, the *Gaudus* of P. Mela. [CLAUDA.]

Caul, a sort of ornamental head-dress, Isa. 3:18, with a net for its base. The name is derived from the caul, the fatty envelope around the liver, always burnt in the sacrifices. It is in popular use often applied to the membrane that surrounds the heart, the pericardium.

Cave. The most remarkable caves noticed in Scripture are, that in which Lot dwelt after the destruction of Sodom, Gen. 19:30; the cave of Machpelah, Gen. 23:17; cave of Makkedah, Josh. 10:10; cave of Adullam, 1 Sam. 22:1; cave of Engedi, 1 Sam. 24:3; Obadiah's cave, 1 Kings 18:4; Elijah's cave in Horeb, 1 Kings 19:9; the rock sepulchres of Lazarus and of our Lord. Matt. 27:60; John 11:38. Caves were used for temporary dwelling-places and for tombs.

Cedar. The Hebrew word *erez*, invariably rendered "cedar" by the Authorized Version, stands for that tree in most of the passages where the word occurs. While the word is sometimes used in a wider sense, Lev. 14:6, for evergreen cone-bearing trees, generally the cedar of Lebanon (*Cedrus libani*) is intended. 1 Kings 7:2; 10:27; Ps. 92: 12; S. of Sol. 5:15; Isa. 2:13; Ezek. 31:3-6. The wood is of a reddish color, of bitter taste and aromatic odor, offensive to insects, and very durable. The cedar is a type of the Christian, being evergreen, beautiful, aromatic, wide spreading, slow growing, long lived, and having many uses. As far as is at present known, the cedar of Lebanon is confined in Syria to one valley of the Lebanon range, viz., that of the Kedisha river, which flows from near the highest point of the range westward to the Mediterranean, and enters the sea at the port of Tripoli. The grove is at the very upper part of the valley, about 15 miles from the sea, 6500 feet above that level, and its position is moreover above that of all other arboreous vegetation. Dr. Leo Anderlind speaks of three groups which he visited in 1884. The famous B'Sherreh grove is three-quarters of a mile in circumference, and contains about 400 trees, young and old. Perhaps a dozen of these are very old. The greatest height of any of the trees, he says, is about 82 feet; the majority are between 46 and 72 feet. Some exceed 50 feet in girth.

Ce′dron (cĕ′dron). John 18:1. [See KIDRON.]

Ceiling. The descriptions of Scripture, 1 Kings 6:9, 15; 7:3; 2 Chron. 3: 5, 9; Jer. 22:14; Hag. 1:4, and of Josephus, show that the ceilings of the temple and the palaces of the Jewish kings were formed of cedar planks applied to the beams or joists crossing from wall to wall. "Oriental houses seem to have been the reverse of ours, the ceiling being of wood, richly ornamented, and the floor of plaster or tiles."

Celosyria. [CŒLESYRIA.]

Cen'chrea or **Cenchre'a** (cĕn-krē'à) (accurately **Cenchre'æ**) (*millet*), the eastern harbor of Corinth (*i. e.* its harbor on the Saronic Gulf) and the emporium of its trade with the Asiatic shores of the Mediterranean, as Lechæum on the Corinthian Gulf connected it with Italy and the west. St. Paul sailed from Cenchreæ, Acts 18 : 18, on his return to Syria from his second missionary journey. An organized church seems to have been formed here, Rom. 16 : 1, of which Phebe was "servant" or deaconess. The village of *Kikries* is probably Cenchrea.

Censer, a small portable vessel of metal fitted to receive burning coals from the altar, and on which the incense for burning was sprinkled. 2 Chron. 26 : 19; Luke 1 : 9. The only distinct precepts regarding the use of the censer are found in Lev. 16 : 12 and in Num. 4 : 14. Solomon prepared "censers of pure gold" as part of the temple furniture. 1 Kings 7 : 50; 2 Chron. 4 : 22. The word rendered "censer" in

EGYPTIAN CENSERS.

Heb. 9 : 4 probably means the "altar of incense."

Census. [TAXING.]

Centurion. [ARMY.]

Ce'phas (cĕ'fas). [PETER.]

Chaff, the husk of corn or wheat which was separated from the grain by being thrown into the air, the wind blowing away the chaff, while the grain was saved. The carrying away of chaff by the wind is an ordinary scriptural image of the destruction of the wicked and of their powerlessness to resist God's judgments. Ps. 1 : 4; Isa. 17 : 13; Hos. 13 : 3; Zeph. 2 : 2.

Chain. Chains were used, 1. As badges of office; 2. For ornament; 3. For confining prisoners. (1) The gold chain placed about Joseph's neck, Gen. 41 : 42, and that promised to Daniel, Dan. 5 : 7, are instances of the first use. (2) Chains for ornamental purposes were worn by men as well as women. Prov. 1 : 9; Ezek. 16 : 11. The Midianites adorned the necks of their camels with chains. Judges 8 : 21, 26. Step-chains were attached to the ankle-rings. Isa. 3 : 16, 18. (3) The means adopted for confining prisoners among the Jews were fetters similar to our handcuffs. Judges 16 : 21; 2 Sam. 3 : 34; 2 Kings 25 : 7; Jer. 39 : 7. Among the Romans the prisoner was handcuffed to his guard, and occasionally to two guards. Acts 12 : 6, 7; 21 : 33.

Chalcedony, only in Rev. 21 : 19. The name is applied in modern mineralogy to one of the varieties of agate. It is generally translucent and exhibits a great variety of colors. So named because it was found near the ancient Chalcedon, near Constantinople.

Chal'col (kăl'kŏl). 1 Kings 4 : 31. [CALCOL.]

Chalde'a (kăl-dē'à), more correctly **Chaldæ'a,** the ancient name of a country of Asia bordering on the Persian Gulf. Chaldea proper was the southern part of Babylonia, and is used in Scripture to signify that vast alluvial plain which has been formed by the deposits of the Euphrates and the Tigris. This extraordinary flat, unbroken except by the works of man, extends a distance of 400 miles along the course of the rivers, and is on an average about 100 miles in width. In addition to natural advantages these plains were nourished by a complicated system of canals, and vegetation flourished bountifully. It is said to be the only country in the world where wheat grows wild. Herodotus declared (i. 193) that grain commonly returned two hundred fold to the sower, and occasionally three hundred fold.

Cities.—Babylonia has long been celebrated for the number and antiquity of its cities. The most important of those which have been identified are Borsippa (*Birs-Nimrûd*), Sippara or Sepharvaim (*Mosaib*), Cutha (*Ibrahim*), Calneh (*Nippur?*), Erech (*Warka*), Ur (*Mugheir*), Chilmad (*Kalwadha*), Larancha (*Senkereh*), Is (*Hit*), Duraba (*Akkerkuf*); but besides these there were a multitude of others, the sites of which have not been determined.

Present condition.—This land, once so rich in corn and wine, is to-day but a mass of mounds, "an arid waste; the dense population of former times is vanished, and no man dwells there."

Chalde'ans, or Chaldees'. The Hebrew prophets applied the term "land of the Chaldeans" to all Babylonia and "Chaldeans" to all the subjects of the Babylonian empire. The Ancient Chaldeans (*Kaldai* or *Kaldi*) were in the earliest times merely one out of the many Cushite tribes inhabiting the great alluvial plain known afterwards as Chaldea or Babylonia. Their special seat was probably that southern portion of the country which is found to have so late retained the name of Chaldea. In process of time, as the *Kaldi* grew in power, their name gradually prevailed over those of the other tribes inhabiting the country; and by the era of the Jewish captivity it had begun to be used generally for all the inhabitants of Babylonia. The language of the Chaldeans was almost identical with the Assyrian. The term "Chaldee," to denote the language in which certain chapters of Daniel and Ezra were written, is incorrect. It was the Aramaic. We find the term Chaldeans used as the name for a caste of wise men, learned in literature and science, a member of which Daniel became. Daniel 1:4. They were priests, magicians or astronomers, and in the last of the three capacities they probably effected discoveries of great importance. In later times they seem to have degenerated into mere fortune-tellers.

Chaldees', or Chal'dees. [CHALDEANS.]

Chalk stones. [LIME.]

Chamber. Gen. 43:30; 2 Sam. 18:33; Ps. 19:5; Dan. 6:10. The word chamber in these passages has much the same significance as with us, meaning the private rooms of the house—the guest chamber, as with us, meaning a room set apart for the accommodation of the visiting friend. Mark 14:14, 15; Luke 22:11. The upper chamber was used more particularly for the lodgment of strangers. Acts 9:37.

Chamberlain, an officer attached to the court of a king, who formerly had charge of the private apartments or chambers of the palace. He kept the accounts of the public revenues. Blastus, in Acts 12:20, was a court officer in charge of Herod's bed-chamber. It was in all times a post of honor which involved great intimacy and influence with the king. For chamberlain as used in the Old Testament, see EUNUCH.

Chameleon, a species of lizard. The reference in Lev. 11:30 is to some kind of an unclean animal, supposed to be the lizard, known by the name of the "monitor of the Nile," a large, strong reptile common in Egypt and other parts of Africa.

Chamois (pronounced often shăm'ĕ), the translation of the Hebrew *zemer* in Deut. 14:5. But the translation is incorrect; for there is no evidence that the chamois has ever been seen in Palestine or the Lebanon. It is probable that some mountain sheep is intended.

Cha'naan. [CANAAN.]

Chapiter, the capital of a pillar; *i. e.* the upper part, as the term is used in modern architecture. 1 Kings 7:17.

Chapman (*i.e.* trade man), merchant. 2 Chron. 9:14. Used also in R. V. of 1 Kings 10:15, where the A. V. gives "merchantmen." It comes from an Anglo-Saxon word meaning trade.

Char'ashim (kăr'a-shĭm), **The valley of** (*ravine of craftsmen*), a place near Lydda, a few miles east of Joppa. 1 Chron. 4:14.

Char'chemish. 2 Chron. 35:20. [CARCHEMISH.]

Charger, a shallow vessel for receiving water or blood, also for presenting offerings of fine flour with oil. Num. 7:79. The daughter of Herodias brought the head of St. John the Baptist in a charger, Matt. 14:8; probably a trencher or platter. [BASIN.]

Chariot, a vehicle used either for warlike or peaceful purposes, but most commonly the former. The Jewish chariots were patterned after the Egyptian, and consisted of a single pair of wheels on an axle, upon which was a

8

car with high front and sides, but open at the back. The earliest mention of chariots in Scripture is in Egypt, where Joseph, as a mark of distinction, was placed in Pharaoh's second chariot. Gen. 41:43. Later on we find mention of Egyptian chariots for a warlike purpose. Ex. 14:7. In this point of view chariots were regarded as among the most important arms of war. 1 Kings 22:34; 2 Kings 9:16, 21; 13:7, 14; 18:24; 23:30; Isa. 31:1. Most commonly two persons, and sometimes three, rode in the chariot, of whom the third was employed to carry the state umbrella. 1 Kings 22:34; 2 Chron. 9:25; Acts 8:

BAS-RELIEF OF A ROMAN CHARIOTEER.

chariots among some nations of antiquity, as elephants among others, may be regarded as filling the place of heavy artillery in modern times, so that the military power of a nation might be estimated by the number of its chariots. Thus Pharaoh in pursuing Israel took with him 600 chariots. The Philistines in Saul's time had 30,000. 1 Sam. 13:5. David took from Hadadezer, king of Zobah, 1000 chariots, 2 Sam. 8:4, and from the Syrians a little later 700, 2 Sam. 10:18, who, in order to recover their ground, collected 32,000 chariots. 1 Chron. 19:7. Up to this time the Israelites possessed few or no chariots. They were first introduced by David, 2 Sam. 8:4; and Solomon maintained a force of 1400 chariots, 1 Kings 10:26, by taxation on certain cities agreeably to eastern custom in such matters. 1 Kings 9:19; 10:25. From this time

38. The prophets allude frequently to chariots as typical of power. Ps. 20:7; 104:3; Jer. 51:21; Zech. 6:1.

Char′ran. Acts 7:2, 4. [HARAN.]

Chase. [HUNTING.]

Che′bar (kē′bär), a river in the "land of the Chaldeans." Ezek. 1:3; 3:15, 23, etc. It was commonly regarded as identical with the Habor, 2 Kings 17:6; but Hilprecht has finally proved it to be "a large, navigable canal a little to the east of Nippur 'in the land of the Chaldeans.'"

Chedorlao′mer or **Chedorla′omer** (kĕd-or-lā′o-mēr) (*servant of Lagamar*, one of the principal Elamite gods), a king of Elam, beyond Babylonia, in the time of Abraham. He with Amraphel (Hammurabi) and other chiefs, in war with Sodom, took Lot captive. Abraham by a night attack rescued Lot. Gen. 14.

Cheese is mentioned only three times in the Bible, and on each occasion under a different name in the Hebrew. 1 Sam. 17:18; 2 Sam. 17:29; Job 10:10. It is difficult to decide how far these terms correspond with our notion of cheese, for they simply express various degrees of coagulation. Cheese is not at the present day common among the Bedouin Arabs, butter being decidedly preferred; but there is a substance closely corresponding to those mentioned in 1 Sam. 17, 2 Sam. 17, consisting of coagulated buttermilk, which is dried until it becomes quite hard, and is then ground; the Arabs eat it mixed with butter.

Che'lal (kē'lăl) (*perfection*), Ezra 10:30, one who had a strange wife.

Chel'luh (kĕl'luh), Ezra 10:35, another like the above.

Che'lub (kē'lŭb). 1. A man among the descendants of Judah. 1 Chr. 4:11.

2. Ezri the son of Chelub, one of David's officers. 1 Chron. 27:26.

Chelu'bai (kĕ-lū'bai) (*capable*), the son of Hezron. Same as Caleb 1. 1 Chron. 2:9, 18, 42.

THE TRADITIONAL BROOK CHERITH.

Chem'arim (kĕm'a-rĭm), **The** (*those who go about in black*, i. e. *ascetics*). In the Hebrew applied to the priests of the worship of false gods. 2 Kings 23:5; Hos. 10:5, in margin; Zeph. 1:4.

Che'mosh (kē'mŏsh) (*subduer*), the national deity of the Moabites. Num. 21:29; Jer. 48:7, 13, 46. In Judges 11:24 he also appears as the god of the Ammonites. Solomon introduced, and Josiah abolished, the worship of Chemosh at Jerusalem. 1 Kings 11:7; 2 Kings 23:13. Also identified with Baal-peor, Baal-zebub, Mars and Saturn.

Chena'anah (kĕ-nā'a-nah) (feminine of Canaan). 1. Son of Bilhan, son of Jediael, son of Benjamin, head of a Benjamite house, 1 Chron. 7:10, probably of the family of the Belaites. [BELA.]

2. Father or ancestor of Zedekiah the false prophet. 1 Kings 22:11, 24; 2 Chron. 18:10, 23.

Chen'ani (a contraction of Chenaniah), one of the Levites who assisted at the solemn purification of the people under Ezra. Neh. 9:4.

Chenani'ah (kĕn-a-nī'ah) (*Jehovah is firm*), chief of the Levites when David carried the ark to Jerusalem. 1 Chron. 15:22; 26:29.

Che'phar-Haam'monai (kē'făr-hà-ăm'mo-nāi (*hamlet of the Ammonites*), a place mentioned among the towns of Benjamin. Josh. 18:24.

Chephi'rah (kĕ-fī'rah) (*the hamlet*), one of the four cities of the Gibeonites, Josh. 9:17, named afterwards among the towns of Benjamin. Ezra 2:25; Neh. 7:29.

Che'ran (kē'ran), one of the sons of Dishon the Horite "duke." Gen. 36:26; 1 Chron. 1:41.

Cher'ethim (kĕr'e-thĭm) (*axe men*), Ezek. 25:16, same as CHERETHITES.

Cher'ethites (kĕr'ĭth-ites) (Carians or Cretans), and **Pel'ethites**, the foreign lifeguards of King David. 2 Sam. 8:18; 15:18; 20:7, 23; 1 Kings 1:38, 44; 1 Chron. 18:17. It is plain that these royal guards were employed as executioners, 2 Kings 11:4, and as couriers, 1 Kings 14:27. These with the Gittites, 2 Sam. 15:18, were doubtless foreign mercenaries.

and therefore probably Philistines, of which name Pelethites may be only another form.

Che'rith (kē'rĭth), **The brook** (*cutting, ravine*), the torrent-bed or *wady* in which Elijah hid himself during the early part of the three-years' drought. 1 Kings 17:3, 5. The position of the Cherith has been much disputed. The argument from probability is in favor of the Cherith being on the east of Jordan, and the name may possibly be discovered there.

Che'rub (kē'rub), apparently a place in Babylonia from which some persons of doubtful extraction returned to Judea with Zerubbabel. Ezra 2:59; Neh. 7:61.

Cher'ub, Cher'ubim. The symbolical figure so called was a composite creature-form which finds a parallel in the religious insignia of Assyria, Egypt and Persia, *e. g.* the sphinx, the winged bulls and lions of Nineveh, etc. A cherub guarded paradise. Gen. 3:24. Figures of cherubim were placed on the mercy-seat of the ark. Ex. 25:18. A pair of colossal size overshadowed it in Solomon's temple with the canopy of their contiguously extended wings. 1 Kings 6:27. Those on the ark were to be placed with wings stretched forth, one at each end of the mercy-seat, and to be made "of the mercy-seat." Their wings were to be stretched upwards, and their faces "towards each other and towards the mercy-seat." It is remarkable that with such precise directions as to their position, attitude and material, nothing, save that they were winged, is said concerning their shape. On the whole it seems likely that the word "cherub" meant not only the composite creature-form, of which the man, lion, ox and eagle were the elements, but, further, some peculiar and mystical form. Eze. 1:6. Some suppose that they represented *God's providence* among men, the four faces expressing the characters of that providence: its wisdom and intelligence (man), its strength (ox), its kingly authority (lion), its swiftness, farsighted (eagle). Others, combining all the other references with the description of the living creatures in Revelation, making the cherubim to represent *God's redeemed people.* The qualities of the four faces are those which belong to God's people. Their facing four ways, towards

all quarters of the globe, represents their duty of extending the truth. The wings show swiftness of obedience; and only the redeemed can sing the song put in their mouths in Rev. 5:8–14.

Ches'alon (kĕs'a-lŏn) (*hopes*), a place named as one of the landmarks on the west part of the north boundary of Judah, Josh. 15:10, probably *Kesla,* about ten miles west of Jerusalem.

Che'sed (kē'sed) (perhaps the word from which the name Chaldeans is derived), fourth son of Nahor. Gen. 22:22.

Che'sil (kē'sil) (*a fool*), a town in the extreme south of Palestine, Josh. 15:30, 15 miles southwest of Beersheba. In Josh. 19:4 the name is BETHUL.

Chest. By this word are translated in the Authorized Version two distinct Hebrew terms: (1) *Arôn;* this is invariably used for the ark of the covenant, and, with two exceptions, for that only. The two exceptions alluded to are (*a*) the "coffin" in which the bones of Joseph were carried from Egypt, Gen. 50:26, and (*b*) the "chest" in which Jehoiada the priest collected the alms for the repairs of the temple. 2 Kings 12:9, 10; 2 Chron. 24:8–11. (2) *Gĕnazîm,* "chests." Ezek. 27:24 only. According to Hastings' *Bible Dictionary* this probably means garments, and the passage should be translated "cloths of cords twined and durable."

Chestnut tree (Heb. *'armôn.* Gen. 30:37; Ezek. 31:8). Probably the "plane tree" (*Platanus orientalis*) is intended. This tree thrives best in low and rather moist situations in the north of Palestine, and resembles our sycamore or buttonwood (*Platanus occidentalis*).

Chesul'loth (kĕ-sŭl'lŏth) (*the loins*), one of the towns of Issachar. Josh. 19:18. From its position in the lists it appears to be between Jezreel and Shunem (*Salam*). Now the ruin of *Iksal* at the foot of the Nazareth hills.

Che'zib (kē'zĭb) (*lying*), a name which occurs but once, Gen. 38:5; probably the same as ACHZIB.

Chi'don (kī'don) (*a javelin*), the name which in 1 Chron. 13:9 is given to the threshing-floor at which the accident to the ark took place. In the parallel account in 2 Sam. 6 the name is given as NACHON.

Children. The blessing of offspring, but especially of the male sex, is highly valued among all eastern nations, while the absence is regarded as one of the severest punishments. Gen. 16:2; Deut. 7:14; 1 Sam. 1:6; 2 Sam. 6:23; 2 Kings 4:14; Isa. 47:9; Jer. 20:15; Ps. 127:3, 5. As soon as the child was born it was washed in a bath, rubbed with salt and wrapped in swaddling clothes. Ezek. 16:4; Job 38:9; Luke 2:7. On the 8th day the rite of circumcision, in the case of a boy, was performed and a name given. At the end of a certain time (forty days if a son and twice as long if a daughter) the mother offered sacrifice for her cleansing. Lev. 12:1-8; Luke 2:22. The period of nursing appears to have been sometimes prolonged to three years. Comp. 1 Sam. 1:11, 22, 24. The time of weaning was an occasion of rejoicing. Gen. 21:8. Both boys and girls in their early years were under the care of the women. Prov. 31:1. Afterwards the boys were taken by the father under his charge. Daughters usually remained in the women's apartments till marriage. Lev. 21:9; Num. 12:14; 1 Sam. 9:11. The authority of parents, especially of the father, over children was very great, as was also the reverence enjoined by the law to be paid to parents. The inheritance was divided equally between all the sons except the eldest, who received a double portion. Gen. 25:31; 49:3; Deut. 21:17; Judges 11:2, 7; 1 Chron. 5:1, 2. Daughters had by right no portion in the inheritance; but if a man had no son, his inheritance passed to his daughters, who were forbidden to marry out of the father's tribe. Num. 27:1, 8; 36:2, 8.

Chil'eab (kĭl'e-ăb), a son of David by Abigail. 2 Sam. 2:3. [ABIGAIL.]

Chil'ion (kĭl'ĭ-on) (*wasting away*), the son of Naomi and husband of Orpah. Ruth 1:2-5; 4:9.

Chil'mad (kĭl'măd), a place or country mentioned in conjunction with Sheba and Asshur. Ezek. 27:23.

Chim'ham (kĭm'hăm) (*longing*), a follower, and probably a son, of Barzillai the Gileadite, who returned from beyond Jordan with David. 2 Sam. 19: 37, 38, 40. (B.C. 1023.) David appears to have bestowed on him a possession at Bethlehem, on which, in later times, an inn or *khan* was standing. Jer. 41: 17.

Chin'nereth (kĭn'ne-rĕth) (*lute, harp*), sometimes Chinneroth, a fortified city in the tribe of Naphtali, Josh.

19:35 only, of which no trace is found in later writers, and no remains by travelers.

Chin'nereth, Sea of. Num. 34:11; Josh. 13:27, the inland sea, which is most familiarly known to us as the "Lake of Gennesareth" or "Sea of Galilee."

Chin'neroth. [CHINNERETH.]

Chi'os (kī'os), an island of the Ægean Sea, 12 miles from Smyrna. It is separated from the mainland by a strait of only 5 miles. Its length is about 32 miles, and in breadth it varies from 8 to 18. Paul passed it on his return voyage from Troas to Cæsarea. Acts 20:15. It is now called Scio.

Chis'leu (kĭs'leū). [MONTH.]

Chis'lon (kĭs'lon) (*strength*), father of Elidad, the prince of the tribe of Benjamin, chosen to assist in the division of the land of Canaan among the tribes. Num. 34:21.

Chis'loth=ta'bor (kĭs'lŏth-tā'bôr) (*loins of Tabor*), a place to the border of which reached the border of Zebulun. Josh. 19:12. It is now the village *Iksâl*, which is now standing about 2½ miles to the west of Mount Tabor.

Chit'tim, Kit'tim (kĭt'tim), a family or race descended from Javan. Gen. 10:4; 1 Chron. 1:7. Authorized Version KITTIM. Chittim is frequently noticed in Scripture. Num. 24:24; Isa. 23:1, 12; Jer. 2:10; Ezek. 27:6; Dan. 11:30. In the above passages, the "isles of Chittim," the "ships of Chittim," the "coasts of Chittim," are supposed to refer to the island of Cyprus. Josephus considered Cyprus the original seat of the Chittim. The name Chittim is variously regarded as applying to Phœnicians, to the Greeks in the island of Cyprus, or to the western power which for the time being held the front place. It may be derived from Kition.

Chi'un (kī'un) (*apparently*), an idol made by the Israelites in the wilderness. Am. 5:26. It is generally supposed to represent the planet Saturn. [REMPHAN.]

Chlo'e (klō'ē) (*green herb*), a woman mentioned in 1 Cor. 1:11.

Chora'=shan (kôr-ā'shan). 1 Sam. 30:30. It may, perhaps, be identified with ASHAN of Simeon.

Chora'zin (kō-rā'zin), one of the cities in which our Lord's mighty works were done, but named only in his denunciation. Matt. 11:21; Luke 10:13.

St. Jerome describes it as on the shore of the lake, two miles from Capernaum, but its modern site is uncertain.

Choze'ba (kŏ-zē'bȧ). 1 Chron. 4: 22. Perhaps the same as ACHZIB.

Christ. [JESUS.]

Chris'tian. The disciples, we are told, Acts 11 : 26, were first called Christians at Antioch on the Orontes, somewhere about A.D. 43. They were known to each other as, and were among themselves called, *brethren,* Acts 15 : 1, 23 ; 1 Cor. 7 : 12 ; *disciples,* Acts 9 : 26 ; 11 : 29 ; *believers,* Acts 5 : 14 ; *saints,* Rom. 8 : 27 ; 15 : 25. The name "Christian," which, in the only other cases where it appears in the New Testament, Acts 26 : 28, 1 Pet. 4 : 16, is used contemptuously, could not have been applied by the early disciples to themselves, but was imposed upon them by the Gentile world. There is no reason to suppose that the name "Christian" of itself was intended as a term of scurrility or abuse, though it would naturally be used with contempt.

Chron'icles, First and Second Books of. These books cover nearly the same period as Kings, from David to the exile, but written from a different point of view, the author selecting those facts which could best produce spiritual and moral education. The constant tradition of the Jews is that they were for the most part compiled by Ezra. But most modern scholars place them later. The first nine chapters are genealogical; for one of the greatest difficulties connected with the captivity and return must have been the maintenance of that genealogical distribution of the lands which yet was a vital point of the Jewish economy. To supply this want and that each tribe might secure the inheritance of its fathers on its return was one object of the author of these books. Another difficulty intimately connected with the former was the maintenance of the temple services at Jerusalem. Zerubbabel, and after him Ezra and Nehemiah, labored most earnestly to restore the worship of God among the people, and to reinfuse something of national life and spirit into their hearts. Nothing could more effectually aid these designs than setting before the people a compendious history of the kingdom of David, its prosperity under God; the sins that led to its overthrow; the captivity and return. These considerations explain the plan and scope of that historical work which consists of the two books of Chronicles. The first book contains the sacred history by genealogies from the Creation to David, including an account of David's reign. In the second book he continues the story, giving the history of the kings of Judah, without those of Israel, down to the return from the captivity. As regards the *materials* used by Ezra, they are not difficult to discover. The genealogies are obviously transcribed from some register, in which were preserved the genealogies of the tribes and families drawn up at different times; while the history is mainly drawn from the same documents as those used in the books of Kings. [KINGS, BOOKS OF.]

Chronology. The details of the Chronology of the Bible, according to the latest authorities, are given in APPENDIX. But some general remarks may help us to understand better the different eras of the history.

There is more or less uncertainty about all dates earlier than David and Solomon.

Ussher's dates in the margins of most of our Bible, are not authoritative, but are convenient for keeping the order and succession of events.

He finds the date of Adam, the first man by a computation from the list of ages of the patriarchs given in Gen. 5, and they would be correct, if he has interpreted the record rightly.

But it may be, as even conservative scholars think, that many links have been omitted, and only the more marked ones enumerated, as for instance a descendant of even the third or fourth generation is called a son. In Matt. 1 : 8, R. V., Joram is said to have begotten Uzziah his great-great-grandson. So it may be that when it is said that Seth at the age of 105 begat Enos, Enos was his descendant, the famous man worth noting in his line.

Or, again, Adam, Seth, Enos and the others represent families, and that Adam's family directed affairs for 930 years, when Seth and his family held the headship for 912 years.

By either of these interpretations the first man may have lived many centuries or thousands of years before Ussher's date for Adam.

The chronology of the United Kingdom has been tested and modified by the Assyrian Eponym canon found on slabs discovered in the ruins of Nineveh.

The peculiarity of the date of the birth of Christ being four years earlier than his actual birth, Dec. B.C. 5, is puzzling to some. The reason is that the dating of events from his birth began centuries later; and the monk Dīŏnys'ĭŭs Exĭg'ūŭs, who first published the calculations in A.D. 526, made a mistake of about four years.

Chrysolite, one of the precious stones in the foundation of the heavenly Jerusalem. Rev. 21:20. This may have been, not improbably, a particular shade of *Beryl,* or perhaps identical with the modern Oriental topaz, the *tarshish* of the Hebrew Bible.

Chrysoprase occurs only in Rev. 21:20. The true chrysoprase is sometimes found in antique Egyptian jewelry set alternately with bits of lapis-lazuli. It may be that the green chalcedony is the stone named as the tenth in the walls of the heavenly Jerusalem.

Chrysoprasus, Latin form of CHRYSOPRASE.

Chub (kŭb), the name of a people in alliance with Egypt in the time of Nebuchadnezzar, Ezek. 30:5, and probably of northern Africa.

Chun (kŭn), 1 Chron. 18:8, called Berothai in 2 Sam. 8:8.

Church. (1) The derivation of the word is generally said to be from the Greek *kuriakon* (κυριακόν), "belonging to the Lord." But the derivation has been too hastily assumed. It is probably connected with *kirk,* the Latin *circus, circulus,* the Greek *kuklos* (κύκλος), because the congregations were gathered in circles. (2) *Ecclesia* (ἐκκλησία), the Greek word for church, originally meant an assembly called out by the magistrate, or by legitimate authority. It was in this last sense that the word was adopted and applied by the writers of the New Testament to the Christian congregation. In the one Gospel of St. Matthew the church is spoken of no less than thirty-six times as "the kingdom." Other descriptions or titles are hardly found in the evangelists. It is Christ's household, Matt. 10:25; the salt and light of the world, Matt. 5:13, 14; Christ's flock, Matt. 26:31; John 10:1; its members are the branches growing on Christ the Vine, John 15; but the general description of it, not metaphorical but direct, is that

it is a kingdom. Matt. 16:19. From the Gospel then we learn that Christ was about to establish his heavenly kingdom on earth, which was to be the substitute for the Jewish Church and kingdom, now doomed to destruction. Matt. 21:43.

The day of Pentecost is the birthday of the Christian Church. Before they had been individual followers of Jesus; now they became his mystical body, animated by his spirit. On the evening of the day of Pentecost, the 3140 members of which the Church consisted were— (1) Apostles; (2) previous Disciples; (3) Converts. In Acts 2:41 we have indirectly exhibited the essential conditions of church communion. They are (1) Baptism; baptism implying on the part of the recipient repentance and faith; (2) Apostolic Doctrine; (3) Fellowship with the Apostles; (4) the Lord's Supper; (5) Public Worship. The *real* Church consists of all who belong to the Lord Jesus Christ as his disciples, and are one in love, in character, in hope, in Christ as the head of all, though as the body of Christ it consists of many parts.

Chu'shan-rishatha'im (kū'shan-rĭsh'-a-thā'-im) (*Cushan of double wickedness*), king of Mesopotamia who oppressed Israel during eight years in the generation immediately following Joshua. Judges 3:8. His yoke was broken from the neck of the people of Israel by Othniel, Caleb's younger brother. Judges 3:10.

Chu'za (chū'zà), properly **Chu'zas,** the house-steward of Herod Antipas. Luke 8:3. His wife Joanna was one of the "ministering women."

Cilic'ia (ci-lĭsh'ià) (*the land of Celix*), a maritime province in the southeast of Asia Minor, bordering on Pamphylia in the west, Lycaonia and Cappadocia in the north, and Syria in the east. Acts 6:9. Cilicia was from its geographical position the high road between Syria and the west; it was also the native country of St. Paul, hence it was visited by him, firstly, soon after his conversion, Acts 9:30; Gal. 1:21, and again in his second apostolical journey. Acts 15:41.

Cinnamon, a well-known aromatic substance, the inner bark of the *Cinnamomum zeylanicum,* a native of Ceylon. It is mentioned in Ex. 30:23 as one of the component parts of the holy anointing oil. In Rev. 18:13 it is enumerated among the merchandise of the great Babylon.

CINNAMON.

Cin'neroth. 1 Kings 15:20. This was possibly the small enclosed district north of Tiberias, and by the side of the lake, afterwards known as "the plain of Gennesareth."

Circumcision was peculiarly, though not exclusively, a *Jewish* rite. It was enjoined upon Abraham, the father of the nation, by God, at the institution and as the token of the covenant, which assured to him and his descendants the promise of the Messiah. Gen. 17. It was thus made a necessary condition of Jewish nationality. Every male child was to be circumcised when eight days old, Lev. 12:3, on pain of death. The biblical notice of the rite describes it as distinctively Jewish; so that in the New Testament "the circumcision" and "the uncircumcision" are frequently used as synonyms for the Jews and the Gentiles, because most of the "nationalities with whom the Jews were in contact were uncircumcised; so the term 'uncircumcised' as a term of reproach, meant almost practically (not etymologically) the same as heathen (Gen. 34:14; Jud. 14:3; 15:18; 1 Sam. 17:26, 36; 31:4; 2 Sam. 1:20; 1 Chr. 10:4; Ezek. 28:

10; 31:18; 32:19–32)." "Circumcision was an act of religious purification (Herod. ii. 37), and in its full significance betokened the putting away of carnal lust (Col. 2:11). To circumcise the heart is so to regenerate it that its irreligious obstinacy shall disappear. (Deut. 10:16), and it will be able and willing to love God with all its powers (30:6)." Dr. John D. Davis.

Cis (cĭs), the father of Saul, Acts 13:21, usually called KISH.

Cistern, a receptacle for water, either conducted from an external spring or proceeding from rain-fall. The dryness of the summer months and the scarcity of springs in Judea made cisterns a necessity, and they are frequent throughout the whole of Syria and Palestine. On the long-forgotten way from Jericho to Bethel, "broken cisterns" of high antiquity are found at regular intervals. Jerusalem depends mainly for water upon its cisterns, of which almost every private house possesses one or more, excavated in the rock on which the city is built. The cisterns have usually a round opening at the top, sometimes built up with stonework above and furnished with a curb and a wheel for the bucket. Eccles. 12:6. Empty cisterns were sometimes used as prisons and places of confinement. Joseph was cast into a "pit," Gen. 37:22, as was Jeremiah. Jer. 38:6.

Cities. The earliest notice in Scripture of city-building is of Enoch by Cain, in the land of his exile. Gen. 4:17. After the confusion of tongues the descendants of Nimrod founded Babel, Erech, Accad and Calneh, in the land of Shinar, and Asshur, a branch from the same stock, built Nineveh, Rehoboth-by-the-river, Calah and Resen, the last being "a great city." The earliest description of a city, properly so called, is that of Sodom. Gen. 19:1–22. Even before the time of Abraham there were cities in Egypt, Gen. 12:14, 15; Num. 13:22, and the Israelites, during their sojourn there, were employed in building or fortifying the "treasure cities" of Pithon and Raamses. Ex. 1:11.

Fenced cities, fortified with high walls, Deut. 3:5, were occupied and perhaps partly rebuilt after the conquest, by the settled inhabitants of Syria on both sides of the Jordan.

Cities of refuge, six Levitical cities specially chosen for refuge to the involuntary homicide until released from banishment by the death of the high priest. Num. 35:6, 13, 15; Josh. 20:2, 7, 9. There were three on each side of Jordan. (1) KEDESH, in Naphta.i. 1 Chron. 6:76. (2) SHECHEM, in Mount Ephraim. Josh. 21:21; 1 Chron. 6:67; 2 Chron. 10:1. (3) HEBRON, in Judah. Josh. 21:13; 2 Sam. 5:5; 1 Chron. 6: 55; 29:27; 2 Chron. 11:10. (4) On the east side of Jordan—BEZER, in the tribe of Reuben, in the plains of Moab. Deut. 4:43; Josh. 20:8; 21:36; 1 Chron. 6:78. (5) RAMOTH-GILEAD, in the tribe of Gad. Deut. 4:43; Josh. 21:38; 1 Kings 22:3. (6) GOLAN, in Bashan, in the half-tribe of Manasseh. Deut. 4: 43; Josh. 21:27; 1 Chron. 6:71.

Citizenship. The use of this term in Scripture has exclusive reference to the usages of the Roman empire. The privilege of Roman citizenship was originally acquired in various ways, as by purchase, Acts 22:28, by military services, by favor or by manumission. The right once obtained descended to a man's children. Acts 22:28. Among the privileges attached to citizenship we may note that a man could not be bound or imprisoned without a formal trial, Acts 22:29, still less be scourged. Acts 16: 37; Cic. *in Verr.* v. 63, 66. Another privilege attaching to citizenship was the appeal from a provincial tribunal to the emperor at Rome. Acts 25:11.

Citron. [APPLE TREE.]

Clau'da (klạu'dȧ), Acts 27:16, a small island nearly due west of Cape Matala on the south coast of Crete; now *Gozzo*, corruption of *Gaudonesi*.

Clau'dia (klạu'dĭ-à) (*lame*), a Christian woman mentioned in 2 Tim. 4:21, as saluting Timotheus.

Clau'dius (klau'dĭ-ŭs) (*lame*), fourth

COIN OF CLAUDIUS.

Roman emperor, reigned from 41 to 54 A.D. He was nominated to the supreme power mainly through the influence of Herod Agrippa the First. In the reign

of Claudius there were several famines, arising from unfavorable harvests, and one such occurred in Palestine and Syria. Acts 11:28–30. Claudius was induced by a tumult of the Jews in Rome to expel them from the city. Cf. Acts 18:2. The date of this event is uncertain. After a weak and foolish reign he was poisoned by his fourth wife, Agrippina, the mother of Nero, October 13, A.D. 54.

Clau'dius Lys'ias. [LYSIAS.]

Clay. As the sediment of water remaining in pits or in streets (mire), the word is used frequently in the Old Testament, Ps. 18:42; Isa. 57:20; Jer. 38: 6; and in the New Testament, John 9:6, a mixture of sand or dust with spittle. It is also found in the sense of potter's clay. Isa. 41:25. The great seat of the pottery of the present day in Palestine is Gaza, where are made the vessels in dark-blue clay so frequently met with. Another use of clay was for sealing. Job 38:14. Our Lord's tomb may have been thus sealed, Matt. 27:66, as also the earthen vessel containing the evidences of Jeremiah's purchase. Jer. 32: 14. The seal used for public documents was rolled on the moist clay, and the tablet was then placed in the fire and baked.

Clem'ent (*mild, merciful*), Philip. 4: 3, a fellow laborer of St. Paul when he was at Philippi. (A.D. 51.) It was generally believed in the ancient Church that this Clement was identical with the bishop of Rome who afterwards became so celebrated.

Cle'opas (klē'o-păs), one of the two disciples who were going to Emmaus on the day of the resurrection. Luke 24: 18. Some think the same as Cleophas in John 19:25. But they are probably two different persons. Cleopas is a Greek name, contracted from Cleopater.

Cle'ophas (klē'o-făs), in R. V. **Clo'pas,** a man named only in John 19:25 as the husband of one of the Marys who stood at the cross at the time of the crucifixion. He should not be confused with the CLEOPAS of Luke 24:18. As to his identification with Alphæus see JAMES.

Clothing. [DRESS.]

Cloud. The shelter given, and refreshment of rain promised, by clouds give them their peculiar prominence in Oriental imagery. Prov. 16:15; Isa. 18: 4; 25:5. When a cloud appears rain is ordinarily apprehended, and thus the "cloud without rain" becomes a proverb for the man of promise without performance. Jude 12; comp. Prov. 25: 14. The cloud is a figure of transitoriness, Job 30:15; Hos. 6:4, and of whatever intercepts divine favor or human supplication. Lam. 2:1; 3:44. A bright cloud at times visited and rested on the mercy-seat. Ex. 29:42, 43; 40: 34–38; 1 Kings 8:10, 11; 2 Chron. 5: 14; Ezek. 43:4, and was by later writers named Shechinah.

Cloud, Pillar of. The pillar of cloud by day and of fire by night that God caused to pass before the camp of the children of Israel when in the wilderness. The cloud, which became a pillar when the host moved, seems to have rested at other times on the tabernacle, whence God is said to have "come down *in* the pillar." Num. 12:5; so Ex. 33:9, 10. It preceded the host, apparently resting on the ark which led the way. Ex. 13:21; 40:36, etc.; Num. 9:15–23; 10:34.

Clouted, patched. Josh. 9:5.

Cni'dus (nī'dus), a city of great consequence, situated at the extreme southwest of the peninsula of Asia Minor, on a promontory now called *Cape Crio,* which projects between the islands of Cos and Rhodes. See Acts 21:1. It is now in ruins. Acts 27:7.

Coal. The first and most frequent use of the word rendered coal is a live ember, burning fuel. Prov. 26:21. In 2 Sam. 22:9, 13, "coals of fire" are put metaphorically for the lightnings proceeding from God. Ps. 18:8, 12, 13; 140:10. In Prov. 26:21, fuel not yet lighted is clearly signified. The fuel meant in the above passage is probably charcoal, and not coal in our sense of the word.

Coast, border, with no more reference to lands bordering on the sea than to any other bordering lands.

Coat. [DRESS.]

Cock. Matt. 26:34; Mark 13:35; 14: 30, etc. The domestic cock and hen had their home in India, coming thence to Babylonia and Persia, and then to Palestine and, probably, Egypt. The cock is thought by some to be referred to in 1 Kings 4:23, and also in Prov. 30:31, where the translation is "greyhound," the word in the Talmud certainly meaning some kind of bird, ac-

cording to Cheyne. They were prized by both Romans and Greeks.

Cockatrice. [ADDER.]

Cockle probably signifies bad weeds or fruit. Job 31:40.

Cœle=Syr'ia (sěl'ē) (*hollow Syria*), the remarkable valley or hollow which intervenes between Lebanon and Anti-Lebanon, stretching a distance of nearly a hundred miles. The only mention of the region as a separate tract of country which the Jewish Scriptures contain is probably that in Amos 1:5, where "the inhabitants of the plain of Aven" are threatened in conjunction with those of Damascus. The word is given in the Authorized Version as CELO-SYRIA.

Coffer (*argaz*), a movable box hanging from the side of a cart. 1 Sam. 6: 8, 11, 15. The word is found nowhere else.

Coffin. [BURIAL.]

Col=ho'zeh (kŏl-hō'zeh) (*all-seeing*), a man of the tribe of Judah in the time of Nehemiah. Neh. 3:15; 11:5. (B.C. 536.)

Collar. For the proper sense of this term, as it occurs in Judges 8:26, see Revisions, where the word is "pendants."

College, The. In 2 Kings 22:14, it is probable that the word translated "college" represents here not an institution of learning, but that part of Jerusalem known as the "lower city" or suburb, built on the hill Akra, including t.e Bezetha or new city.

Colony, a designation of Philippi, in Acts 16:12. After the battle of Actium, Augustus assigned to his veterans those parts of Italy which had espoused the cause of Antony, and transported many of the expelled inl bitants to Philippi, Dyrrhachium and other cities. In this way Philippi was made a Roman colony with the "Jus Italicum." At first the colonists were all i.oman citizens, and entitled to vote at Rome.

Colors. The terms relative to color, occurring in the Bible, may be arranged in two classes, the first including those applied to the description of natural objects, the second those artificial mixtures which were employed in dyeing or painting. The *purple* and the *blue* were derived from a small shellfish found in the Mediterranean, and were very costly, and hence they were the royal colors. *Red,* both scarlet and crimson, was derived from an insect resembling the cochineal. The natural colors noticed in the Bible are white, black, red, yellow and green. The only fundamental color of which the Hebrews appear to have had a clear conception was *red;* and even this is not very often noticed.

Colos'se (kȯ-lŏs'sė), more properly **Colos'sæ**, was a city of Phrygia in Asia Minor, in the upper part of the basin of the Mæander, on the Lycus. Hierapolis and Laodicea were in its immediate neighborhood. Col. 4 : 13. A church was formed here probably by Christians from Ephesus; of which Epaphras was pastor (Col. 1 : 7), and Philemon and Onesimus were members (Col. 4 : 9; Phile. 2.). Col. 1 : 2; Rev. 1 : 11; 3 : 14.

Colos'sians, The Epistle to the, was written by the apostle St. Paul during his first captivity at Rome. Acts 28 : 16. (A.D. 62.) The epistle was addressed to the Christians of the city of Colosse, and was delivered to them by Tychicus, whom the apostle had sent both to them, Col. 4 : 7, 8, and to the church of Ephesus, Eph. 6 : 21, to inquire into their state and to administer exhortation and comfort. The main object of the epistle is to warn the Colossians against a spirit of semi-Judaistic and semi-Oriental philosophy which was corrupting the simplicity of their belief, and was noticeably tending to obscure the eternal glory and dignity of Christ. The similarity between this epistle and that to the Ephesians is striking, although there are equally noteworthy differences.

Comforter. John 14 : 16. The name given by Christ to the Holy Spirit. The original word is *Paraclete*, and means first *Advocate*, a defender, helper, strengthener, as well as comforter.

Commerce. From the time that men began to live in cities, trade, in some shape, must have been carried on to supply the town-dwellers with necessaries from foreign as well as native sources, for we find that Abraham was rich, not only in cattle, but in silver, gold and silver plate and ornaments. Gen. 13 : 2; 24 : 22, 53. Among trading nations mentioned in Scripture, Egypt holds in very early times a prominent position. The internal trade of the Jews, as well as the external, was much promoted by the festivals, which brought large numbers of persons to Jerusalem. 1 Kings 8 : 63. The places of public market were chiefly the open spaces near the gates, to which goods were brought for sale by those who came from the

outside. Neh. 13 : 15, 16; Zeph. 1 : 10. The traders in later times were allowed to intrude into the temple, in the outer courts of which victims were publicly sold for the sacrifice. Zech. 14 : 21; Matt. 21 : 12; John 2 : 14.

Conani'ah (kŏn-a-nī'ah) (*Jehovah hath established*), a chief of the Levites in the time of Josiah. 2 Chron. 35 : 9. (B.C. 628.)

Concubine. The difference between wife and concubine was less marked among the Hebrews than among us, owing to the absence of moral stigma. The difference probably lay in the absence of the right of the bill of divorce, without which the wife could not be repudiated. With regard to the children of wife and of concubine, there was no such difference as our illegitimacy implies. The latter were a supplementary family to the former; their names occur in the patriarchal genealogies, Gen. 22 : 24; 1 Chron. 1 : 32, and their position and provision would depend on the father's will. Gen. 25 : 6. The state of concubinage is assumed and provided for by the law of Moses. A concubine would generally be either (1) a Hebrew girl bought of her father; (2) a Gentile captive taken in war; (3) a foreign slave bought; or (4) a Canaanitish woman, bond or free. The rights of the first two were protected by the law, Ex. 21 : 7; Deut. 21 : 10–14; but the third was unrecognized and the fourth prohibited. Free Hebrew women also might become concubines. To seize on royal concubines for his use was often a usurper's first act. Such was perhaps the intent of Abner's act, 2 Sam. 3 : 7, and similarly the request on behalf of Adonijah was construed. 1 Kings 2 : 21–24.

Conduit, meaning an aqueduct or trench through which water was carried. Tradition, both oral and as represented by Talmudical writers, ascribes to Solomon the formation of the original aqueduct by which water was brought to Jerusalem. 2 Kings 18 : 17; 20 : 20; Isa. 7 : 3; 36 : 2.

Coney (*shâphân*), a gregarious animal of the class Pachydermata, which is found in Palestine, living in the caves and clefts of the rocks, and has been erroneously identified with the rabbit or coney. Its scientific name is *Hyrax syriacus.* The hyrax satisfies exactly the expressions in Ps. 104 : 18; Prov.

30:26. Its color is gray or brown on the back, white on the belly; it is like the alpine marmot, scarcely of the size of the domestic cat, having long hair, a very short tail and round ears. It is found on Lebanon and in the Jordan and Dead Sea valleys.

selection was made by Moses of 70, who formed a species of standing committee. Num. 11:16. Occasionally indeed the whole body of the people was assembled at the door of the tabernacle, hence usually called the tabernacle of the congregation. Num. 10:3. The people

THE CONEY. (*Hyrax Syriacus.*)

Congregation. This describes the Hebrew people in its collective capacity under its peculiar aspect as a holy community, held together by religious rather than political bonds. Sometimes it is used in a broad sense as inclusive of foreign settlers, Ex. 12:19, but more properly as exclusively appropriate to the Hebrew element of the population. Num. 15:15. The congregation was governed by the father or head of each family and tribe. The number of these representatives being inconveniently large for ordinary business, a further

were strictly bound by the acts of their representatives, even in cases where they disapproved of them. Josh. 9:18.

Coni'ah (kō-nī'ah). [JEHOIACHIN.]

Cononi'ah (*Jehovah hath established*), a Levite, ruler of the offerings and tithes in the time of Hezekiah. 2 Chron. 31:12, 13. (B.C. 726.)

Consecration. [PRIEST.]

Convocation. This term is applied to meetings of a *religious* character, such as those on the Sabbaths, and on the first and seventh days of the great fasts or feasts.

Cooking. As meat did not form an article of ordinary diet among the Jews, the art of cooking was not carried to any perfection. Few animals were slaughtered except for purposes of hospitality or festivity. The proceedings on such occasions appear to have been as follows:—On the arrival of a guest, the animal, either a kid, lamb or calf, was killed, Gen. 18:7; Luke 15:23, its throat being cut so that the blood might be poured out, Lev. 7:26; it was then flayed, and was ready for either roasting or boiling. In roasting, a small animal was preserved entire, Ex. 12:46, and roasted either over a fire, Ex. 12:8, of wood, Isa. 44:16, or perhaps in an oven, consisting simply of a hole dug in the earth, well heated, and covered up. Boiling, however, was the more usual method of cooking.

Co'os (kō'ŏs). Acts 21:1. [Cos.]

Copper. Heb. *nĕchôsheth*, in the Authorized Version always rendered "brass," except in Ezra 8:27 and Jer. 15:12. It was almost exclusively used by the ancients for common purposes, and for every kind of instrument, as chains, pillars, lavers and the other temple vessels. We read also of copper mirrors, Ex. 38:8, and even of copper arms, as helmets, spears, etc. 1 Sam. 17:5, 6.

Cor. See Measures.

Coral. Ezek. 27:16. A production of the sea, formed by minute animals called zoophytes. It is their shell or

COMMON CORAL OF THE MEDITERRANEAN.

house. It takes various forms, as of trees, shrubs, hemispheres. The principal colors are red and white. It was used for beads and ornaments. With regard to the estimation in which coral

was held by the Jews and other Orientals, it must be remembered that coral varies in price with us. Pliny says that the Indians valued coral as the Romans valued pearls. Job 28:18.

Corban, an offering to God of any sort, bloody or bloodless, but particularly in fulfilment of a vow. The law laid down rules for vows, (1) affirmative; (2) negative. Lev. 27; Num. 30. Upon these rules the traditionists enlarged, and laid down that a man might interdict himself by vow, not only from using for himself, but from giving to another or receiving from him, some particular object, whether of food or any other kind whatsoever. The thing thus interdicted was considered as *corban*. A person might thus exempt himself from any inconvenient obligation under plea of corban. It was practices of this sort that our Lord reprehended, Matt. 15:5; Mark 7:11, as annulling the spirit of the law.

Cord. The materials of which cord was made varied according to the strength required; the strongest rope was probably made of strips of camel hide, as still used by the Bedouins. The finer sorts were made of flax, Isa. 19:9, and probably of reeds and rushes. In the New Testament the term is applied to the whip which our Saviour made, John 2:15, and to the ropes of a ship. Acts 27:32.

Co're (kō'rė). Jude 11. [Korah, 4.]

Coriander. The plant called *Cori-*

THE CORIANDER.

andrum sativum is found in Egypt, Persia and India, and has a round tall stalk; it bears umbelliferous white or reddish flowers, from which arise globular, grayish, spicy seed-corns, marked with fine striæ. It is mentioned twice in the Bible. Ex. 16:31; Num. 11:7.

Cor'inth, an ancient and celebrated city of Greece, on the Isthmus of Corinth, and about 40 miles west of Athens. In consequence of its geographical position it formed the most direct communication between the Ionian and Ægean seas. A remarkable feature was the *Acrocorinthus,* a vast citadel of rock, which rises abruptly to the height of 2000 feet above the level of the sea, and the summit of which is so extensive that it once contained a whole town. The situation of Corinth, and the possession of its eastern and western harbors, Cenchreæ and Lechæum, are the secrets of its history. Corinth was a place of great mental activity, as well as of commercial and manufacturing enterprise. Its wealth was so celebrated as to be proverbial; so were the vice and profligacy of its inhabitants. The worship of Venus here was attended with shameful licentiousness. Corinth is still an episcopal see. The modern town 3½ miles N. E. of the ancient site, on the gulf of Corinth, is a strongly fortified seaport of 4800 population. St. Paul preached here, Acts 18:11, and founded a church, to which his Epistles to the Corinthians are addressed. [EPISTLES TO THE CORINTHIANS.]

Corinth'ians, First Epistle to the, was written by the apostle St. Paul toward the close of his nearly three-years stay at Ephesus, Acts 19:10; 20:31, which, we learn from 1 Cor. 16:8, probably terminated with the Pentecost of A.D. 57 (or 56.) The bearers were probably (according to the common subscription) Stephanas, Fortunatus and Achaicus. It appears to have been called forth by the information the apostle had received of dissension in the Corinthian church, which may be thus explained:—The Corinthian church was planted by the apostle himself, 1 Cor. 3:6, in his second missionary journey. Acts 18:1, *seq.* He abode in the city a year and a half. Acts 18:11. A short time after the apostle had left the city the eloquent Jew of Alexandria, Apollos, went to Corinth, Acts 19:1,

and gained many followers, dividing the church into two parties, the followers of Paul and the followers of Apollos. Later on Judaizing teachers from Jerusalem preached the gospel in a spirit of direct antagonism to St. Paul *personally.* To this third party we may perhaps add a fourth, that, under the name of "the followers of Christ," 1 Cor. 1:12, sought at first to separate themselves from the factious adherence to particular teachers, but eventually were driven by antagonism into positions equally sectarian and inimical to the unity of the church. At this momentous period, before parties had become consolidated and had distinctly withdrawn from communion with one another, the apostle writes; and in the outset of the epistle, 1 Cor. 1–4:21, we have his noble and impassioned protest against this fourfold rending of the robe of Christ.

Corinth'ians, Second Epistle to the, was written a few months subsequent to the first, in the same year—about the autumn of A.D. 57 (or 56)—at Macedonia. The epistle was occasioned by the information which the apostle had received from Titus, and also, as it would certainly seem probable, from Timothy, of the reception of the first epistle. This information, as it would seem from our present epistle, was mainly favorable; the better part of the church were returning to their spiritual allegiance to their founder, 2 Cor. 1:13, 14; 7:9, 15, 16; but there was still a faction who strenuously denied Paul's claim to apostleship. The contents of this epistle comprise, (1) the apostle's account of the character of his spiritual labors, chs. 1–7; (2) directions about the collections, chs. 8, 9; (3) defence of his own apostolical character, chs. 10–13:10. The words in 1 Cor. 5: 9 seem to point to further epistles to this church by Paul, but we have no positive evidence of any.

Cormorant, the representative in the Authorized Version of the Hebrew words *kâath* and *shâlâc.* As to the former, see PELICAN. *Shâlâc* occurs only as the name of an unclean bird in Lev. 11:17; Deut. 14:17. The word has been variously rendered. The etymology points to some plunging bird. The common cormorant (*Phalacrocorax carbo*), which many writers have identified with the *shâlâc,* is common along the coast, coming up the Kishon and visiting the Sea of Galilee. It is likewise abundant along the Jordan.

Corn = grain. Our Indian corn was unknown in Bible times. The most common kinds were wheat, barley, spelt, Auth. Ver., Ex. 9 : 32 and Isa. 28 : 25, "rye;" Ezek. 4 : 9 "fitches" and millet; oats are mentioned only by rabbinical writers. The grain-crops are still reckoned at twenty-fold what was sown, and were anciently much more. Gen. 41 : 22. The Jewish law permitted any one in passing through a field of standing corn to pluck and eat. Deut. 23 : 25; see also Matt. 12 : 1. From Solomon's time, 2 Chron. 2 : 10, 15, as agriculture became developed under a settled government, Palestine was a grain-exporting country, and her grain was largely taken by her commercial neighbor Tyre. Ezek. 27 : 17; comp. Amos 8 : 5.

Corne'lius (kôr-nē'lĭ-ŭs), a Roman centurion of the Italian cohort stationed in Cæsarea, Acts 10 : 1, etc., a man full of good works and alms-deeds. With his household he was baptized by St. Peter, and thus Cornelius became the first-fruits of the Gentile world to Christ.

Corner. The "corner" of the field was not allowed, Lev. 19 : 9, to be wholly reaped. It formed a right of the poor to carry off what was so left, and this was a part of the maintenance from the soil to which that class were entitled. Under the scribes, minute legislation fixed one-sixtieth as the portion of a field which was to be left for the legal "corner." The proportion being thus fixed, all the grain might be reaped, and enough to satisfy the regulation subsequently separated from the whole crop. This "corner" was, like the gleaning, tithe-free.

Corner-stone, a quoin or corner-stone, of great importance in binding together the sides of a building. The phrase "corner-stone" is sometimes used to denote any principal person, as the princes of Egypt, Isa. 19 : 13, and is thus applied to our Lord. Isa. 28 : 16; Matt. 21 : 42; 1 Pet. 2 : 6, 7.

Cornet (Heb. *shôphâr*), a loud-sounding instrument, made of the horn of a ram or of a chamois (sometimes of an ox), and used by the ancient Hebrews for signals, Lev. 25 : 9, and much used by the priests. 1 Chron. 15 : 28.

Cos (kŏs), or **Co'os** (now *Stanchio*

or *Stanko*). This small island of the Grecian Archipelago has several interesting points of connection with the Jews. Herod the Great conferred many favors on the island. St. Paul, on the return from his third missionary journey, passed the night here, after sailing from Miletus. Probably referred to in Acts 21 : 1.

Co'sam (kō'sam), son of Elmodam, in the line of Joseph the husband of Mary. Luke 3 : 28.

Cotton. Cotton is now both grown and manufactured in various parts of Syria and Palestine; but there is no proof that, till they came in contact with Persia, the Hebrews generally knew of it as a distinct fabric from linen. [LINEN.]

Couch. [BED.]

Council. 1. The great council of the Sanhedrin, which sat at Jerusalem. [SANHEDRIN.]

2. The lesser courts, Matt. 10 : 17; Mark 13 : 9, of which there were two at Jerusalem and one in each town of Palestine. The constitution of these courts is a doubtful point. The existence of local courts, however constituted, is clearly implied in the passages quoted from the New Testament; and perhaps the "judgment," Matt. 5 : 21, applies to them.

3. A kind of jury or privy council, Acts 25 : 12, consisting of a certain number of assessors, who assisted Roman governors in the administration of justice and in other public matters.

Court (Heb. *châtsêr*), an open enclosure surrounded by buildings, applied in the Authorized Version most commonly to the enclosures of the tabernacle and the temple. Ex. 27 : 9; 40 : 33; Lev. 6 : 16; 1 Kings 6 : 36; 7 : 8; 2 Kings 23 : 12; 2 Chron. 33 : 5, etc.

Covenant. The Heb. *bĕrîth* is by modern scholars derived from the Babylonian *biritu,* "binding." It was formerly explained as "cutting," referring to the custom of cutting or dividing animals in two and passing between the parts in ratifying a covenant. Gen. 15; Jer. 34 : 18, 19. In the New Testament the corresponding word is *diathécē* (διαθήκη), which is frequently translated *testament* in the Authorized Version. In its biblical meaning of a compact or agreement between two parties the word is used—1. Of a covenant between God and man; *e. g.* God covenanted with Noah, after the flood, that a like judgment should not be repeated. It is not precisely like a covenant between men, but was a promise or agreement by God. The principal covenants are the *covenant of works*—God promising to save and bless men on condition of perfect obedience—and the *covenant of grace*, or God's promise to save men on condition of their believing in Christ and receiving him as their Master and Saviour. The first is called the Old Covenant, from which we name the first part of the Bible the Old Testament, the Latin rendering of the word covenant. The second is called the New Covenant, or New Testament. 2. Covenant between man and man, *i. e.* a solemn compact or agreement, either between tribes or nations, Josh. 9 : 6, 15; 1 Sam. 11 : 1, or between individuals, Gen. 31 : 44, by which each party bound himself to fulfill certain conditions and was assured of receiving certain advantages. In making such a covenant God was solemnly invoked as witness, Gen. 31 : 50, and an oath was sworn. Gen. 21 : 31. A sign or witness of the covenant was sometimes framed, such as a gift, Gen. 21 : 30, or a pillar or heap of stones erected. Gen. 31 : 52.

Cow. [BULL.]

Coz (kŏz) (*thorn*), a man among the descendants of Judah. 1 Chron. 4 : 8.

Coz'bi (kŏz'bī) (*deceitful*), daughter of Zur, a chief of the Midianites. Num. 25 : 15, 18.

Crane. The crane (*Grus cinerea*) is a native of Europe and Asia. It stands about four feet high. Its color is ashen gray, with face and neck nearly black. It feeds on seeds, roots, insects and small quadrupeds. It retires in winter to the warmer climates. Jer. 8 : 7.

Create. To create is to cause something to exist which did not exist before, as distinguished from *make*, to reform something already in existence.

Creation. The creation of all things is ascribed in the Bible to God, and is the only reasonable account of the origin of the world. The *method* of creation is not stated and may have been largely by evolution. The word *create* (bârâ) is used but three times in the first chapter of Genesis—(1) as to the origin of matter; (2) as to the origin of life; (3) as to the origin of man's soul; and science has always

THE CRANE.

failed here. All other things are said to be *made*. The order of creation as given in Genesis expresses in the simplest possible form the actual facts of the great eras of the world's history as revealed by geology in this twentieth century. One of the chief difficulties has been removed very recently by Professor Lowell who has shown the true connection between the third and fourth days. Plants grew on the earth in the third day by its internal heat, before the thick clouds allowed the sun to mark day from night or summer from winter. The sun was *made* to do this on the fourth day.

Cres'cens (krĕs'çenş) (*growing*), 2 Tim. 4 : 10, an assistant of St. Paul, said to have been one of the seventy disciples.

Crete (krēte), the modern *Candia*.

COIN OF CRETE.

This large island, which closes in the Greek Archipelago on the south, extends through a distance of 140 miles between its extreme points. Though exceedingly bold and mountainous, this island has very fruitful valleys, and in early times it was celebrated for its hundred cities. It seems likely that a very early acquaintance existed between the Cretans and the Jews. Cretans, Acts 2:11, were among those who were at Jerusalem at the great Pentecost. In Acts 27:7-12 we have an account of Paul's shipwreck near this island; and it is evident from Titus 1:5 that the apostle himself was here at no long interval of time before he wrote the letter. The Cretans were proverbial liars. Titus 1:12.

Cretes. Acts 2:11. Cretans, inhabitants of Crete.

Crisping pins. Isa. 3:22. The original word means some kind of female ornament, probably a reticule or richly-ornamented purse, often made of silk inwrought with gold or silver.

Cris'pus (kris'pus) (*curled*), ruler of the Jewish synagogue at Corinth, Acts 18:8; baptized with his family by St. Paul. 1 Cor. 1:14. (A.D. 50.)

Cross. As the emblem of a slave's

THE CROSS.
1. Latin Cross. 2. Patriarchal Cross. 3. Papal Cross. 4. St. Andrew's Cross. 5. Maltese Cross. 6. St. Anthony's Cross. 7. Eastern Cross, "Susa." 8. Cross Patté. 9. Pectoral Cross, or Cross Fleury. 10. Altar-cloth Cross. 11. Double Greek Cross.

death and a murderer's punishment, the cross was naturally looked upon with the profoundest horror. But after the celebrated vision of Constantine, he ordered his friends to make a cross of

gold and gems, such as he had seen, and "the towering eagles resigned the flags unto the cross," and "the tree of cursing and shame" "sat upon the sceptres and was engraved and signed on the foreheads of kings." (Jer. Taylor, "Life of Christ," iii., xv. 1.) The new standards were called by the name Labarum, and may be seen on the coins of Constantine the Great and his nearer successors. The Latin cross, on which our Lord suffered, was in the form of the letter T, and had an upright above the cross-bar, on which the "title" was placed. There was a projection from the central stem, on which the body of the sufferer rested. This was to prevent the weight of the body from tearing away the hands. Whether there was also a support to the feet (as we see in pictures) is doubtful. An inscription was generally placed above the criminal's head, briefly expressing his guilt, and generally was carried before him. It was covered with white gypsum, and the letters were black.

THREE FORMS OF THE CROSS.

Crown. This ornament, which is both ancient and universal, probably originated from the fillets used to prevent the hair from being dishevelled by the wind. Such fillets are still common; they gradually developed into turbans, which by the addition of ornamental or precious materials assumed the dignity of mitres or crowns. Both the ordinary priests and the high priest wore them. The crown was a symbol of royalty, and was worn by kings, 2 Chron. 23:11, and also by queens. Esther 1:11; 2:17; 6:8. The head-dress of bridegrooms, Ezek. 24:17; Isa. 61:10; and of women, Isa. 3:20; a head-dress of great splendor, Isa. 28:5; a wreath of flowers, Prov. 1:9; 4:9, denote crowns. In general we must attach to it the notion of a costly *turban* irradiated with pearls and gems of priceless value, which often form aigrettes for feathers, as in the crowns of modern Asiatic sovereigns. Such was probably the crown which weighed (or rather "was worth") a talent, mentioned in 2 Sam. 12:30, taken by

CROWNS.

1. Crown of Upper Egypt. **2.** Crown of Upper and Lower Egypt United. **3.** Assyrian Crown, from Nineveh Marbles. **4.** Laurel Crown. **5.** Crown of Herod the Great. **6.** Crown of Aretas, King of Arabia.

David from the king of Ammon at Rabbah, and used as the state crown of Judah. In Rev. 12:3; 19:12, allusion is made to "*many* crowns" worn in token of extended dominion. The laurel, pine or parsley crowns given to victors in the great games of Greece are finely alluded to by St. Paul. 1 Cor. 9:25; 2 Tim. 2:5, etc.

Crown of thorns, Matt. 27:29. Our Lord was crowned with thorns in mockery by the Roman soldiers. Obviously some small flexile thorny shrub is meant; perhaps *Capparis spinosa.* "Hasselquist, a Swedish naturalist, supposes a very common plant, *naba* or *nubka* of the Arabs, with many small and sharp spines; soft, round and pliant branches; leaves much resembling ivy, of a very deep green, as if in designed mockery of a victor's wreath."—*Alford.*

Crucifixion was in use among the Egyptians, Gen. 40:19, the Carthaginians, the Persians, Esther 7:10, the Assyrians, Scythians, Indians, Germans, and from the earliest times among the Greeks and Romans. Whether this mode of execution was known to the ancient Jews is a matter of dispute. Probably the Jews borrowed it from the Romans. It was unanimously con-

sidered the most horrible form of death. Among the Romans the degradation was also a part of the infliction, and the punishment if applied to freemen was only used in the case of the vilest criminals. The one to be crucified was stripped naked of all his clothes, and then followed the most awful moment of all. He was laid down upon the implement of torture. His arms were stretched along the cross-beams, and at the centre of the open palms the point of a huge iron nail was placed, which, by the blow of a mallet, was driven home into the wood. Then through either foot separately, or possibly through both together, as they were placed one over the other, another huge nail tore its way through the quivering flesh. Whether the sufferer was also bound to the cross we do not know; but, to prevent the hands and feet being torn away by the weight of the body, which could not "rest upon nothing but four great wounds," there was, about the centre of the cross, a wooden projection strong enough to support, at least in part, a human body, which soon became a weight of agony. Then the "accursed tree" with its living human burden was slowly heaved up and the end fixed firmly in a hole in the ground. The feet were but a little raised above the earth. The victim was in full reach of every hand that might choose to strike. A death by crucifixion seems to include all that pain and death can have of the horrible and ghastly,—dizziness, cramp, thirst, starvation, sleeplessness, traumatic fever, tetanus, publicity of shame, long continuance of torment, horror of anticipation, mortification of untended wounds, all intensified just up to the point at which they can be endured at all, but all stopping just short of the point which would give to the sufferer the relief of unconsciousness. The unnatural position made every movement painful; the lacerated veins and crushed tendons throbbed with incessant anguish; the wounds, inflamed by exposure, gradually gangrened; the arteries, especially of the head and stomach, became swollen and oppressed with surcharged blood; and, while each variety of misery went on gradually increasing, there was added to them the intolerable pang of a burning and raging thirst. Such was the death to which Christ was doomed.—*Farrar's "Life of Christ."* The crucified was watched, according to custom, by a party of four soldiers, John 19:23, with their centurion, Matt. 27:54, whose express office was to prevent the stealing of the body. This was necessary from the lingering character of the death, which sometimes did not supervene even for three days, and was at last the result of gradual benumbing and starvation. But for this guard, the persons might have been taken down and recovered, as was actually done in the case of a friend of Josephus. Fracture of the legs was especially adopted by the Jews to hasten death. John 19:31. In most cases the body was suffered to rot on the cross by the action of sun and rain, or to be devoured by birds and beasts. Sepulture was generally therefore forbidden; but in consequence of Deut. 21:22, 23, an express national exception was made in favor of the Jews. Matt. 27:58. This accursed and awful mode of punishment was happily abolished by Constantine.

Cruse, a small vessel for holding water, such as was carried by Saul when on his night expedition after David, 1 Sam. 26:11, 12, 16, and by Elijah. 1 Kings 19:6.

Crystal, the representative in the Authorized Version of two Hebrew words. 1. *Zecûcîth* occurs only in Job 28:17, where "glass" probably is intended. 2. *Kerach* occurs in numerous passages in the Old Testament to denote "ice," "frost," etc.; but once only, Ezek. 1:22, as is generally understood, to signify "crystal." The ancients supposed rock-crystal to be merely ice congealed by intense cold. The similarity of appearance between ice and crystal caused no doubt the identity of the terms to express these substances. The Greek word occurs in Rev. 4:6; 21:1. It may mean either "ice" or "crystal."

Cubit. [WEIGHTS AND MEASURES.]

Cuckoo, Lev. 11:16; Deut. 14:15, the name of some unclean bird, and probably of some of the larger petrels which abound in the east of the Mediterranean.

Cucumbers (Heb. *kishshuîm*). This word occurs in Num. 11:5 as one of the good things of Egypt for which the Israelites longed. Egypt produces excellent cucumbers, melons, etc., the *Cucumis chate* being the best of its

THE CUCKOO OF PALESTINE.

tribe yet known. Besides the *Cucumis chate*, the common cucumber (*C. sativus*), of which the Arabs distinguish a number of varieties, is common in Egypt. "Both *Cucumis chate* and *C. sativus*," says Mr. Tristram, "are now grown in great quantities in Palestine. On visiting the Arab school in Jerusalem (1858) I observed that the dinner which the children brought with them to school consisted, without exception, of a piece of barley-cake and a raw cucumber, which they ate rind and all." The "lodge in a garden of cucumbers," Isa. 1:8, is a rude temporary shelter erected in the open grounds where vines, cucumbers, gourds, etc., are grown, in which some lonely man or boy is set to watch, either to guard the plants from robbers or to scare away the foxes and jackals from the vines.

Cummin, one of the cultivated plants of Palestine. Isa. 28:25, 27; Matt. 23:23. It is an umbelliferous plant something like fennel. The seeds have a bitterish warm taste and an aromatic flavor. The Maltese are said to grow it at the present day, and to thresh it in the manner described by Isaiah.

Cup. The cups of the Jews, whether of metal or earthenware, were possibly borrowed, in point of shape and design, from Egypt and from the Phœnicians, who were celebrated in that branch of workmanship. Egyptian cups were of various shapes, either with handles or without them. In Solomon's time all his drinking vessels were of gold, none of silver. 1 Kings 10:21. Babylon is compared to a golden cup. Jer. 51:7. The great laver, or "sea," was made w￪th a rim like the rim of a cup (*côs*), "with flowers of lilies," 1 Kings 7:26, a form which the Persepolitan cups resemble. The cups of the New Testament were often no doubt formed on Greek and Roman models. They were sometimes of gold. Rev. 17:4.

Cupbearer, an officer of high rank with Egyptian, Persian and Assyrian as well as Jewish monarchs. 1 Kings 10:5. It was his duty to fill the king's cup and present it to him personally. Neh. 1:11. The chief cupbearer, or butler, to the king of Egypt was the means of raising Joseph to his high position. Gen. 40:1, 21; 41:9.

Cush (kŭsh). 1. A Benjamite mentioned only in the title to Ps. 7. He was probably a follower of Saul, the head of his tribe.

2. The name of a son of Ham, apparently the eldest, and of a territory or territories occupied by his descendants. The Cushites appear to have spread along tracts extending from the higher Nile to the Euphrates and Tigris. History affords many traces of this relation of Babylonia, Arabia and Ethiopia. Gen. 10:6–8; 1 Chron. 1:8–10.

Cu'shan (kṳ'shan), Hab. 3:7, possibly the same as Chushan-rishathaim, king of Mesopotamia. Judges 3:8, 10.

Cu'shi (kṳ'shī). Properly "the Cushite," "the Ethiopian," a man apparently attached to Joab's person. 2 Sam. 18:21–25, 31, 32.

Cuth, or **Cu'thah** (kū'thah), one of the countries whence Shalmaneser introduced colonists into Samaria. 2 Kings 17:24, 30. Now identified with *Tell-Ibrahim,* N. E. of Babylon, but opinions still differ.

Cuttings [in the flesh]. Cuttings in the flesh, or the laceration of one's body for the "propitiation of their gods," 1 Kings 18:28, constituted a prominent feature of idolatrous worship, especially among the Syrians. The Israelites were prohibited from indulging in such practices. Lev. 19:28; 21:5; Deut. 14:1; Jer. 16:6.

Cymbal, Cymbals, a percussive musical instrument. Two kinds of cymbals are mentioned in Ps. 150:5, "loud cymbals" perhaps castanets, and "highsounding cymbals." The former consisted of four small plates of brass or of some other hard metal; two plates were attached to each hand of the performer, and were struck together to produce a great noise. The latter consisted of two larger plates, one held in each hand and struck together as an accompaniment to other instruments. Cymbals were used not only in the temple but for military purposes, and also by Hebrew women as a musical accompaniment to their national dances. Both kinds of cymbals are still common in the East.

Cypress (Heb. *tirzâh*). The Hebrew word is found only in Isa. 44:14. We are quite unable to assign any definite rendering to it. The true cypress is a native of the Taurus. The Hebrew word points to some tree with a hard grain, and this is all that can be positively said of it.

Cy'prus (çȳ'prus), an island of Asia in the Mediterranean. It is about 140 miles long and 69 miles wide at the widest part. Its two chief cities were Salamis, at the east end of the island, and Paphos, at the west end. "Cyprus occupies a distinguished place in both sacred and profane history. It early belonged to the Phœnicians of the neighboring coast; was afterwards colonized by Greeks; passed successively under the power of the Pharaohs, Persians, Ptolemies and Romans, excepting a short period of independence in the fourth century B.C. It was one of the chief seats of the worship of Venus, hence called Cypria." It was the native place of Barnabas, Acts 4:36, and was visited by Paul. Acts 13:4–13. See also Acts 15:39; 21:3; 27:4. Since 1571 it has been a part of the Turkish empire, though since 1878 administered by Great Britain. After the World War the island was made a British possession.

Cyre'ne (çȳ-rē'nè), the principal city of that part of northern Africa which was anciently called Cyrenaica, lying between Carthage and Egypt, and corresponding with the modern Tripoli. It was a Greek city, and many Jews were settled there. The Greek colonization of this part of Africa under Battus began as early as B.C. 631. After the death of Alexander the Great it became a dependency of Egypt, and a Roman province B.C. 75. Simon, who bore our Saviour's cross,

COIN OF CYRENE.

Matt. 27:32, was a native of Cyrene. Jewish dwellers in Cyrenaica were in Jerusalem at Pentecost, Acts 2:10, and gave their name to one of the synagogues in Jerusalem. Acts 6:9. Christian converts from Cyrene were among those who contributed actively to the formation of the first Gentile church at Antioch. Acts 11:20.

Cyre'nius (*warrior*), the Greek form of the Roman name of Quirinius. The full name is Publius Sulpicius Quirinius. He was consul B.C. 12, and after the banishment of Archelaus in A.D. 6, was made governor of Syria including Judea, and carried out an assessment or enrolment for taxation.

A difficulty arises in connection with the statement of Luke (2:1-3) that the enrolment ordered by Augustus Cæsar caused Mary and Joseph to go from Nazareth to Bethlehem so that Jesus was born in Bethlehem, as foretold, in the latter part of B.C. 5, and that this decree was carried out by Cyrenius governor of Syria; who did not become governor until A.D. 6, nine or ten years later than the date of Jesus' birth.

There are two solutions of the difficulty, either one of which shows that Luke is correct in his statements.

Dr. Horner shows that the first uni-versal enrolment by Augustus was *decreed* B.C. 5, but was *put in effect* A.D. 6, by Cyrenius when he became governor. (*Gospels of Matthew and Luke,* "Cyrenius," 1907.)

On the other hand Canon E. R. Bernard (in an English Bib. Dic. 1908), shows that while there was no governorship of Cyrenius in Syria previous to A.D. 6, yet it is probable that Cyrenius was in the province during the government of Varus (B.C. 5) with a military command; and the vague word translated governor (not the usual word) might well describe such a command as distinct from the civil governorship held by Varus. In this case both the decree and the putting it into effect were in B.C. 5-6, just before the death of Herod.

Cy'rus (çy'rus) (*the sun*), the founder of the Persian empire—see 2 Chron. 36:22, 23; Dan. 6:28; 10:1, 13—was, according to the common legend, the son of Cambyses, a Persian of the royal family of the Achæmenidæ. When he grew up to manhood his courage and genius placed him at the head of the Persians. His conquests were numerous and brilliant. He defeated and captured the Median king B.C. 559. In B.C. 546 (?) he defeated Crœsus, and the kingdom of Lydia was the prize of his success. Babylon fell before his army, and the ancient dominions of Assyria were added to his empire B.C. 538. The prophet Daniel's home for a time was at his court. Dan. 6:28. The edict of Cyrus for the rebuilding of the temple, 2 Chron. 36:22, 23; Ezra 1:1-4; 3:7; 4:3; 5:13, 17; 6:3, was in fact the beginning of Judaism; and the great changes by which the nation was transformed into a church are clearly marked. His tomb is still shown at Pasargadæ, the scene of his first decisive victory.

D

Dab′areh (dăb′a-reh) (*pasture*),
Josh. 21:28, or DABERATH, a town on
the boundary of Zebulun. Josh. 19:12.
Under the name of *Deburieh* it still lies
at the western foot of Tabor.

Dab′basheth (dăb′ba-shĕth) (*hump
of a camel*), a town on the boundary
of Zebulun. Josh. 19:11.

Dab′erath (dăb′e-răth). [See DAB-
AREH.]

Da′gon (dā′gŏn), commonly held to
be a diminutive or term of endearment
from *dag,* "fish," was the national god
of the Philistines. The most famous
temples of Dagon were at Gaza, Judges
16:21–30, and Ashdod. 1 Sam. 5:5, 6;
1 Chron. 10:10. The latter temple was
destroyed by Jonathan in the Maccabæan wars. Traces of the worship of
Dagon likewise appear in the names
Caphar-dagon (near Jamnia) and Beth-
dagon in Judah, Josh. 15:41, and Asher,
Josh. 19:27. Dagon is represented with
the face and hands of a man and the
tail of a fish. There is, however, great
uncertainty as to the correctness both
of this representation and the derivation of the name. Cheyne considers its

SCENE IN DAMASCUS.
Showing houses on the walls.

PANORAMA OF DAMASCUS.
Showing the River Abana.

foundation very doubtful, derived from a confusion with the fish-goddess Derceta.

Dalai'ah (*freed by Jehovah*), a descendant of the royal family of Judah. 1 Chron. 3 : 24.

Dalmanu'tha (dăl-ma-nū'thà), a town on the west side of the Sea of Galilee, near Magdala. Matt. 15 : 39 and Mark 8 : 10. [MAGDALA.] The site is very uncertain and widely differing identifications have been proposed.

Dalma'tia (dăl-mā'shĭ-à), a mountainous district on the eastern coast of the Adriatic Sea. St. Paul sent Titus there. 2 Tim. 4 : 10.

Dal'phon (dăl'fon), the second of the ten sons of Haman. Esther 9 : 7. (B.C. 473.)

Dam'aris (dăm'a-rĭs) (*a heifer*), an Athenian woman converted to Christianity by St. Paul's preaching. Acts 17 : 34. (A.D. 51.) Chrysostom and others held her to have been the wife of Dionysius the Areopagite.

Damas'cus (dà-màs'kus), one of the most ancient and most important of the cities of Syria. It is situated 145 miles northeast of Jerusalem, in a plain of vast size and of extreme fertility, which lies east of the great chain of Anti-Lebanon, on the edge of the desert. This fertile plain, which is nearly circular and about 30 miles in diameter, is due to the river *Barada,* which is probably the "Abana" of Scripture. Two other streams, the *Wady Helbon* upon the north and the *Awaj,* which flows direct from Hermon, upon the south, increase the fertility of the Dam-

THE GREAT MOSQUE AT DAMASCUS.

DAMASCUS — THE GRAND MOSQUE.

ascene plain, and contend for the honor of representing the "Pharpar" of Scripture. According to Josephus, Damascus was founded by Uz, grandson of Shem. It is first mentioned in Scripture in connection with Abraham, Gen. 14:15, whose steward was a native of the place. Gen. 15:2. At one time David became complete master of the whole territory, which he garrisoned with Israelites. 2 Sam. 8:5, 6. It was in league with Baasha, king of Israel, against Asa, 1 Kings 15:19; 2 Chron. 16:3, and afterwards in league with Asa against Baasha. 1 Kings 15:20. About 735 it was taken by Tiglathpileser, 2 Kings 16:7, 8, 9, the kingdom of Damascus brought to an end, and the city itself destroyed, the inhabitants being carried captive into Assyria. 2 Kings 16:9; comp. Isa. 7:8 and Amos 1:5. Afterwards it passed successively under the dominion of the Assyrians, Babylonians, Persians, Macedonians, Romans and Saracens, and was at last captured by the Turks in 1516 A.D. Here the apostle Paul was converted and preached the gospel. Acts 9:1–25.

Damascus has always been a great centre for trade. Its present population (1924) is estimated at 300,000. It has a delightful climate. Certain localities are shown as the site of those scriptural events which specially interest us in its history. Queen's Street, which runs straight through the city from east to west, may be the street called Straight. Acts 9:11. The house of Judas and that of Ananias are shown, but little confidence can be placed in any of these traditions.

Dan (*a judge*). 1. The fifth son of Jacob, and the first of Bilhah, Rachel's maid. Gen. 30:6 (B.C. after 1753.) The origin of the name is given in the exclamation of Rachel. The records of Dan are unusually meagre. Only one son is attributed to him, Gen. 46:23. The portion received by Dan in the allotment of the land of Palestine, Josh. 19:40–48, was almost, if not quite, the smallest of the twelve. It might be said to consist of two parts: the hill country, a very small section, entirely surrounded by other and more powerful tribes,— Ephraim, Benjamin and Judah, and the country of the Philistines,—and the lowlands along the coast south of the tribe of Manasseh, Joppa being about midway. This last section they never

occupied, as the Philistines were too strong for them, and drove them back to the hills. Small as their tribe had grown to be this was too small for them. An expedition went to the extreme north of Palestine, took Laish, and rebuilt it under the name of Dan. In the "security" and "quiet," Judges 18:7, 10, of their rich northern possession the Danites enjoyed the leisure and repose which had been denied them in their original seat. In the time of David Dan still kept its place among the tribes. 1 Chron. 12:35. Asher is omitted, but the "prince of the tribe of Dan" is mentioned in the list of 1 Chron. 27:22. But from this time forward the name as applied to the tribe vanishes; it is kept alive only by the northern city. In the genealogies of 1 Chron. 2–12, Dan is omitted entirely. Lastly, Dan is omitted from the list of those who were sealed by the angel in the vision of St. John. Rev. 7:5–7.

2. The well-known city, so familiar as the most northern landmark of Palestine, in the common expression "from Dan even to Beersheba." The name of the place was originally LAISH or LESHEM. Josh. 19:47. After the establishment of the Danites at Dan it became the acknowledged extremity of the country. It is now *Tell el-Kadi,* a mound, three miles from Banias, from the foot of which gushes out one of the largest fountains in the world, the main source of the Jordan.

Dance. The dance is spoken of in Holy Scripture universally as symbolical of some rejoicing, and is often coupled for the sake of contrast with mourning, as in Eccles. 3:4; comp. Ps. 30:11; Matt. 11:17. In the earlier period it is found combined with some song or refrain, Ex. 15:20; 32:18, 19; 1 Sam. 21:11, and with the tambourine (Authorized Version "timbrel"), more especially in those impulsive outbursts of popular feeling which cannot find sufficient vent in voice or in gesture singly. Dancing formed a part of the religious ceremonies of the Egyptians, and was also common in private entertainments. For the most part dancing was carried on by the women, the two sexes seldom and not customarily intermingling. The one who happened to be near of kin to the champion of the hour led the dance. In the earlier period of the Judges the dances of the virgins of Shiloh, Judges 21:19-23, were certainly part of a religious festivity. Dancing also had its place among merely festive amusements, apart from any religious character. Jer. 31: 4, 13; Mark 6:22.

But the dancing of Salome before Herod was due to the introduction of Greek fashions and was not approved by the better classes among the Jews.

Dan'iel (dăn'iel) (*God is my judge*). 1. The second son of David, by Abigail the Carmelitess. 1 Chron. 3:1. In 2 Sam. 3:3 he is called Chileab.

2. The fourth of "the greater prophets." Nothing is known of his parentage or family. He appears, however, to have been of royal or noble descent, Dan. 1:3, and to have possessed considerable personal endowments. Dan. 1:4. He was taken to Babylon in "the third year of Jehoiakim" (B.C. 604), and trained for the king's service. He was divinely supported in his resolve to abstain from the "king's meat" for fear of defilement. Dan. 1:8-16. At the close of his three-years' discipline, Dan. 1:5, 18, Daniel had an opportunity of exercising his peculiar gift, Dan. 1:17, of interpreting dreams, on the occasion of Nebuchadnezzar's decree against the Magi. Dan. 2:14 ff. In consequence of his success he was made "ruler over the whole province of Babylon." Dan. 2:48. He afterwards interpreted the second dream of Nebuchadnezzar, Dan. 4:8-27, and the handwriting on the wall which disturbed the feast of Belshazzar. Dan. 5:10-28. At the accession of Darius he was made first of the "three presidents" of the empire, Dan. 6:2, and was delivered from the lions' den, into which he had been cast for his faithfulness to the rites of his faith. Dan. 6:10-23. He was reinstated and at the accession of Cyrus still retained his prosperity, Dan. 6:28, cf. 1:21, though he does not appear to have remained at Babylon, cf. Dan. 1: 21; and in "the third year of Cyrus" (B.C. 534) he saw his last recorded vision, on the banks of the Tigris. Dan. 10:1, 4. In the prophecies of Ezekiel mention is made of Daniel as a pattern of righteousness, Ezek. 14:14, 20, and wisdom. Ezek. 28:3. The narrative in Dan. 1:11-16 implies that Daniel was conspicuously distinguished for purity and knowledge at a very early age.

3. A descendant of Ithamar, who returned with Ezra. Ezra 8:2.

4. A priest who sealed the covenant drawn up by Nehemiah. Neh. 10:6. He is perhaps the same as No. 3.

Dan'iel, The book of, stands at the head of a series of writings in which the deepest thoughts of the Jewish people found expression after the close of the prophetic era. Daniel is composed partly in the vernacular Aramaic (Chaldee) and partly in the sacred Hebrew.

The book of Daniel is divided into two parts. The first six chapters are written in the third person, and give an account of the wonderful deliverances of Daniel. The remaining chapters relate the visions of Daniel told in apocalyptic, that is a peculiar form of symbolic, language. All are intended to sustain the faith of the people for whom he wrote, by means of the great and precious promises and truths they reveal.

There are three views by modern scholars as to the interpretation of this book. The first treats the book as a real history of the captive Daniel, and his visions as prophetic outlooks upon the future giving to the exiles an assured hope of deliverance and final victory for their nation and the religion for which they stood. In this case the book belongs to the century beginning about 600 B.C., but it is unknown when it was finally edited. The second view, adopted by a large number of modern scholars, is that the first six chapters are hero-tales, fictions founded on fact, and told to the Jews in their terrible sufferings and conflicts in the days of the Maccabees in the second century B.C. to encourage and strengthen them, while the visions are chiefly history rather than prophecy. The third view is that the book of Daniel is an apocalypse, like to the book of Revelation; truths and facts told by means of symbols, as Paul's trials in Ephesus are expressed as fighting with the beasts of Ephesus, or Bunyan's real conflicts with the opposition of his times are pictured by means of Apollyon. While the visions are real prophecy, told by apocalyptic symbols. There are unsolved difficulties in each view, perhaps not more in one view than in the others. The power of the teaching and inspiration to trust in God is in proportion to the real truth of the narrative.

Dan'iel, Apocryphal additions to.
The Greek translations of Daniel contain several pieces which are not found in the original text. The most important are contained in the Apocrypha of the English Bible under the titles of *The Song of the Three Holy Children, The History of Susannah,* and *The History of . . . Bel and the Dragon.* The first of these is supposed to be the triumphal song of the three confessors in the furnace, Dan. 3:23, praising God for their deliverance, of which a chief part (35–66) has been used as a hymn in the Christian Church since the fourth century. The second, called also *The Judgment of Daniel,* relates the story of the clearing of Susannah from a charge of adultery; and the third gives an exaggerated account of Daniel's deliverance.

Dan'ites (dăn'ītes), **The.** The descendants of Dan and the members of his tribe. Judges 13:2; 18:1, 11; 1 Chron. 12:35.

Dan-ja'an (dăn-jā'an) (*Danian,* i. e. *belonging to Dan*). 2 Sam. 24:6. Probably the same as DAN.

Dan'nah (dăn'nah), a city in the mountains of Judah, Josh. 15:49, and probably south or southwest of Hebron. Conder considers that it probably is the modern *Idnah.*

Da'ra (dā'rà). 1 Chron. 2:6. [DARDA.]

Dar'da (där'dà) (*pearl of wisdom*), a son of Mahol, one of four men of great fame for their wisdom, but surpassed by Solomon. 1 Kings 4:31.

Daric (from *dara,* a *king*), Authorized Version "dram," 1 Chron. 29:7; Ezra 2:69; 8:27; Neh. 7:70, 71, 72, a gold coin current in Palestine in the period after the return from Babylon. It weighed 128 grains, and was worth about five dollars. At these times there was no large issue of gold money except by the Persian kings. The darics which have been discovered are thick pieces of pure gold, of archaic style, bearing on the obverse the figure of a king with bow and javelin or bow and dagger, and on the reverse an irregular incuse square. The silver daric was worth about fifty cents.

Dari'us (dä-rī'us) (*lord*), the name of several kings of Media and Persia. 1. DARIUS THE MEDE, Dan. 6:1; 11:1, "the son of Ahasuerus," Dan. 9:1, who succeeded to the Babylonian kingdom on the death of Belshazzar, being then sixty-two years old. Dan. 5:31; 9:1. (B.C. 538.) Only one year of his reign is mentioned, Dan. 9:1; 11:1, but that was of great importance for the Jews. Daniel was advanced by the king to the highest dignity, Dan. 6:1 ff., and in his reign was cast into the lions' den. Dan.

THE IMPRESSION OF THE CYLINDER SEAL OF DARIUS.
The trilingual inscription, in Old Persian, Median, and Babylonian, reads: "I am Darius, the Great King."

6. The identification of this Darius is a subject of dispute among modern scholars. Perhaps the most satisfactory explanation is that he was governor of the city of Babylon during the interim between the conquest and the coming of Cyrus, and perhaps known to secular history by another name.

2. DARIUS, the son of Hystaspes the founder of the Perso-Arian dynasty. Upon the usurpation of the magian Smerdis, he conspired with six other Persian chiefs to overthrow the impostor, and on the success of the plot was placed upon the throne, B.C. 521. With regard to the Jews, Darius Hystaspes pursued the same policy as Cyrus, and restored to them the privileges which they had lost. Ezra 4:24; 6:1, etc.

3. DARIUS THE PERSIAN, Neh. 12:22, may be identified with Darius II. Nothus (Ochus), king of Persia B.C. 424–3 to 405–4; but it is not improbable that it points to Darius III. Codomannus, the antagonist of Alexander and the last king of Persia, B.C. 336–330.

Darkness is spoken of as encompassing the actual presence of God, as that out of which he speaks,—the envelope, as it were, of divine glory. Ex. 20:21; 1 Kings 8:12. The plague of darkness in Egypt was miraculous. The darkness "over all the land," Matt. 27:45, attending the crucifixion has been attributed to an eclipse, but was undoubtedly miraculous, as no eclipse of the sun could have taken place at that time, the moon being at the full at the time of the passover. Darkness is also, as in the expression "land of darkness," used for the state of the dead, Job 10:21, 22; and frequently, figuratively, for ignorance and unbelief, as the privation of spiritual light. John 1:5; 3:19.

Dar'kon (där'kon) (*scattering*). Children of Darkon were among the "servants of Solomon" who returned from Babylon with Zerubbabel. Ezra 2:56; Neh. 7:58.

Dates. 2 Chron. 31:5, marg. [PALM TREE.]

Da'than (dā'than), a Reubenite chieftain, son of Eliab, who joined the conspiracy of Korah the Levite. Num. 16:1; 26:9; Deut. 11:6; Ps. 106:17. (B.C. about 1471.)

Daughter. The word is used in Scripture not only for daughter, but for granddaughter or other female descendant. Gen. 24:48. It is used of the female inhabitants of a place or country, Gen. 6:2; Luke 23:28, and of cities in general, Isa. 10:32; 23:12, but more specifically of dependent towns or hamlets, while to the principal city the correlative "mother" is applied. Num. 21:25. "Daughters of music," *i. e.* singing birds, Eccles. 12:4, refers to the power of making and enjoying music.

Da'vid (*well-beloved*), the son of Jesse. His life may be divided into three portions: 1. His youth before his introduction to the court of Saul; 2. His relations with Saul; 3. His reign.

1. *The early life of David* contains in many important respects the antecedents of his future career. It appears that David was the youngest son, probably the youngest child, of a family of ten, and was born in Bethlehem B.C. 1085. The first time that David appears in history at once admits us to the whole family circle. The annual sacrificial feast is being held when Samuel appears, sent by God to anoint one of Jesse's sons as king of Israel in place of Saul. 1 Sam. 16:1. Rejecting the elder sons as they pass before him, 16:6–10, Samuel sends for the youngest, David, who was "keeping the sheep," and anoints him. 1 Sam. 16:11–13. As David stood before Samuel we are enabled to fix his appearance at once in our minds. He was of short stature, with red or auburn hair, such as is not unfrequently seen in his countrymen of the East at the present day. In later life he wore a beard. His bright eyes are specially mentioned, 1 Sam. 16:12, and generally he was remarkable for the grace of his figure and countenance, "fair of eyes," "comely," "goodly," 1 Sam. 16:12, 18; 17:42, well made, and of immense strength and agility. His swiftness and activity made him like a wild gazelle, his feet like hart's feet, and his arms strong enough to break a bow of steel. Ps. 18:33, 34. After the anointing David resumes his accustomed duties, and the next we know of him he is summoned to the court to chase away the king's madness by music, 1 Sam. 16:14–19, and in the successful effort of David's harp we have the first glimpse into that genius for music and poetry which was afterwards consecrated in the Psalms. After this he returned to the old shepherd life again. One incident alone of his solitary shepherd life has come down to us—his conflict with the lion and the bear in defence of his father's flocks. 1 Sam. 17:34, 35. It was some years after this that David suddenly appears before his brothers in the camp of the army, and hears the defiant challenge of the Philistine giant Goliath. With his shepherd's sling and five small pebbles he goes forth and defeats the giant. 1 Sam. 17:40–51.

2. *Relations with Saul.*—We now enter on a new aspect of David's life. The victory over Goliath had been a turning-point of his career. Saul inquired his parentage, and took him finally to his court. Jonathan was inspired by the romantic friendship which bound the two youths together to the end of their lives. Unfortunately David's fame proved the foundation of that unhappy jealousy of Saul towards him which, mingling with the king's constitutional malady, poisoned his whole future relations to David. His position in Saul's court seems to have been first armor-bearer, 1 Sam. 16:21; 18:2, then captain over a thousand, 18:13, and finally, on his marriage with Michal, the king's second daughter, he was raised to the high office of captain of the king's body-guard, second only, if not equal, to Abner, the captain of the host, and Jonathan, the heir apparent. David was now chiefly known for his successful exploits against the Philis-

tines, by one of which he won his wife, and drove back the Philistine power with a blow from which it only rallied at the disastrous close of Saul's reign. He also still performed from time to time the office of minstrel; but the successive attempts of Saul upon his life convinced him that he was in constant danger. He had two faithful allies, however, in the court—the son of Saul, his friend Jonathan, and the daughter of Saul, his wife Michal. Warned by the one and assisted by the other, he escaped by night, and was from thenceforward a fugitive. He at first found a home at the court of Achish, among the Philistines; but his stay was short. Discovered possibly by "the sword of Goliath," his presence revived the national enmity of the Philistines against their former conqueror, and he only escaped by feigning madness. 1 Sam. 21: 13. His first retreat was the cave of Adullam. In this vicinity he was joined by his whole family, 1 Sam. 22: 1, and by a motley crowd of debtors and discontented men, 22: 2, which formed the nucleus of his army. David's life for the next few years was made up of a succession of startling incidents. He secures an important ally in Abiathar, 1 Sam. 23: 6; his band of 400 at Adullam soon increased to 600, 23: 13; he is hunted by Saul from place to place like a partridge. 1 Sam. 23: 14, 22, 25–29; 24: 1–22; 26. He marries Abigail and Ahinoam. 1 Sam. 25: 42, 43. Finally comes the news of the battle of Gilboa and the death of Saul and Jonathan. 1 Sam. 31. The reception of the tidings of the death of his rival and of his friend, the solemn mourning, the vent of his indignation against the bearer of the message, the pathetic lamentation that followed, well close the second period of David's life. 2 Sam. 1: 1–27.

3. *David's reign.*—1. As king of Judah at Hebron, 7½ years. 2 Sam. 2: 1–5: 5. Here David was first formally anointed king. 2 Sam. 2: 4. To Judah his dominion was nominally confined. Gradually his power increased, and during the two years which followed the elevation of Ish-bosheth a series of skirmishes took place between the two kingdoms. Then rapidly followed the successive murders of Abner and of Ish-bosheth. 2 Sam. 3: 30; 4: 5. The throne, so long waiting for him, was

now vacant, and the united voice of the whole people at once called him to occupy it. For the third time David was anointed king, and a festival of three days celebrated the joyful event. 1 Chron. 12: 39. One of David's first acts after becoming king was to secure Jerusalem, which he seized from the Jebusites and fixed the royal residence there. Fortifications were added by the king and by Joab, and it was known by the special name of the "city of David." 2 Sam. 5: 9; 1 Chron. 11: 7. The ark was now removed from its obscurity at Kirjath-jearim with marked solemnity, and conveyed to Jerusalem.

2. The erection of the new capital at Jerusalem introduces us to a new era in David's life and in the history of the monarchy. He became a king on the scale of the great Oriental sovereigns of Egypt and Persia, with a regular administration and organization of court and camp; and he also founded an imperial dominion which for the first time realized the prophetic description of the bounds of the chosen people. Gen. 15: 18–21. During the succeeding ten years the nations bordering on his kingdom caused David more or less trouble, but during this time he reduced to a state of permanent subjection the Philistines on the west, 2 Sam. 8: 1; the Moabites on the east, 2 Sam. 8: 2, by the exploits of Benaiah, 2 Sam. 23: 20; the Syrians on the northeast as far as the Euphrates, 2 Sam. 8: 3; the Edomites, 2 Sam. 8: 14, on the south; and finally the Ammonites, who had broken their ancient alliance, and made one grand resistance to the advance of his empire. 2 Sam. 10: 1–19; 12: 26–31.

Three great calamities may be selected as marking the beginning, middle and close of David's otherwise prosperous reign, which appear to be intimated in the question of Gad, 1 Chron. 21 : 12, "a three-years famine, a three-months flight or a three-days pestilence." *a.* Of these the first (the three-years famine) introduces us to the last notices of David's relations with the house of Saul, already referred to. *b.* The second group of incidents contains the tragedy of David's life, which grew in all its parts out of the polygamy, with its evil consequences, into which he had plunged on becoming king. Underneath the splendor of his last glorious campaign against the Ammonites was a dark story, known probably at that time only to a very few—the double crime of adultery with Bathsheba and the virtual murder of Uriah. The clouds from this time gathered over David's fortunes, and henceforward "the sword never departed from his house." 2 Sam. 12 : 10. The outrage on his daughter Tamar, the murder of his eldest son Amnon, and then the revolt of his best-beloved, Absalom, brought on the crisis which once more sent him forth a wanderer, as in the days when he fled from Saul. 2 Sam. 15 : 18. The final battle of Absalom's rebellion was fought in the " forest of Ephraim," and terminated in the accident which led to the young man's death; and, though nearly heart-broken at the loss of his son, David again reigned in undisturbed peace at Jerusalem. 2 Sam. 20 : 1–22. *c.* The closing period of David's life, with the exception of one great calamity, may be considered as a gradual preparation for the reign of his successor. This calamity was the three-days pestilence which visited Jerusalem at the warning of the prophet Gad. The occasion which led to this warning was the census of the people taken by Joab at the king's orders, 2 Sam. 24 : 1–9 ; 1 Chron. 21 : 1–7 ; 27 : 23, 24, which was for some reason sinful in God's sight. 2 Sam. 24. A formidable conspiracy to interrupt the succession broke out in the last days of David's reign; but the plot was stifled, and Solomon's inauguration took place under his father's auspices. 1 Kings 1 : 1–53. By this time David's infirmities had grown upon him. His last song is preserved—a striking union of the ideal of a just ruler which he had placed before him and of the difficulties which he had felt in realizing it. 2 Sam. 23 : 1–7. His last words to his successor are general exhortations to his duty. 1 Kings 2 : 1–9. He died, according to Josephus, at the age of 70, and " was buried in the city of David." After the return from the captivity, " the sepulchres of David " were still pointed out " between Siloah and the house of the mighty men," or " the guard-house." Neh. 3 : 16. His tomb, which became the general sepulchre of the kings of Judah, was pointed out in the latest times of the Jewish people. The edifice shown as such from the Crusades to the present day is on the southern hill of modern Jerusalem,

Genealogical Chart Showing the Ancestry of David.

commonly called Mount Zion, under the so-called "Cœnaculum;" but it cannot be identified with the tomb of David, which was emphatically *within* the walls.

Da'vid, City of. [JERUSALEM.]

Day. The variable length of the natural day at different seasons led in the very earliest times to the adoption of the civil day (or one revolution of the sun) as a standard of time. The Hebrews reckoned the day from evening to evening, Lev. 23 : 32, deriving it from Gen. 1 : 5, "the *evening* and the *morning* were the first day." The Jews are supposed, like the modern Arabs, to have adopted from an early period minute specifications of the parts of the natural day. Roughly, indeed, they were content to divide it into "morning, evening and noonday," Ps. 55 : 17; but when they wished for greater accuracy they pointed to six unequal parts, each of which was again subdivided. These are held to have been—1. "The dawn." 2. ' Sunrise." 3. "Heat of the day," about 9 o'clock. 4. "The two noons," Gen. 43 : 16; Deut. 28 : 29. 5. "The cool (lit. *wind*) of the day," before sunset, Gen. 3 : 8,—so called by the Persians to this day. 6. "Evening." Before the captivity the Jews divided the night into three watches, Ps. 63 : 6; 90 : 4, viz. the first watch, lasting till midnight, Lam. 2 : 19; the "middle watch," lasting till cockcrow, Judges 7 : 19; and the "morning watch," lasting till sunrise, Ex. 14 : 24. In the New Testament we have allusions to four watches, a division borrowed from the Greeks and Romans. These were—1. From twilight till 9 o'clock, Mark 11 : 11; John 20 : 19. 2. Midnight, from 9 till 12 o'clock, Mark 13 : 35. 3. Till 3 in the morning, Mark 13 : 35; 3 Macc. 5 : 23. 4. Till daybreak. John 18 : 28. The word held to mean "hour" is first found in Dan. 3 : 6, 15; 5 : 5. Perhaps the Jews, like the Greeks, learned from the Babylonians the division of the day into twelve parts. In our Lord's time the division was common. John 11 : 9.

Daysman, an old English term, meaning *umpire* or *arbitrator.* Job 9 : 33.

Deacon. The office described by this title appears in the New Testament as the correlative of bishop. [BISHOP.] The two are mentioned together in Philip. 1 : 1; 1 Tim. 3 : 2, 8. Its original meaning implied a helper, an assistant.

The bishops were the "elders," the deacons the young active men, of the church. The narrative of Acts 6 is commonly referred to as giving an account of the institution of this office. The apostles, in order to meet the complaints of the Hellenistic Jews that their widows were neglected in the daily ministration, call on the body of believers to choose seven men "full of the Holy Ghost and of wisdom," whom they "may appoint over this business." It may be questioned, however, whether the seven were not appointed to higher functions than those of the deacons of the New Testament. *Qualifications and duties.*—Special directions as to the qualifications for and the duties of deacons will be found in Acts 6 : 1–6 and 1 Tim. 3 : 8–12. From the analogy of the synagogue, and from the scanty notices in the New Testament, we may think of the deacons or "young men" at Jerusalem as preparing the rooms for meetings, distributing alms, maintaining order at the meetings, baptizing new converts, distributing the elements at the Lord's Supper.

Deaconess. The word διάκονος is found in Rom. 16 : 1 (Authorized Version "servant") associated with a female name, and this has led to the conclusion that there existed in the apostolic age, as there undoubtedly did a little later, an order of women bearing that title, and exercising in relation to their own sex functions which were analogous to those of the deacons. On this hypothesis it has been inferred that the women mentioned in Rom. 16 : 6, 12 belonged to such an order. The rules given as to the conduct of women in 1 Tim. 3 : 11, Titus 2 : 3, have in like manner been referred to them, and they have been identified even with the "widows" of 1 Tim. 5 : 3–10.

Dead Sea. This name nowhere occurs in the Bible, and appears not to have existed until the second century after Christ. [See SEA, THE SALT.]

Dearth. [FAMINE.]

De'bir (dē'bĭr) (*a sanctuary*), the name of three places of Palestine. 1. A town in the mountains of Judah, Josh. 15 : 49, one of a group of eleven cities to the west of Hebron. The earlier name of Debir was Kirjath-sepher, "city of book," Josh. 15 : 15; Judges 1 : 11, and Kirjath-sannah, "city of palm." Josh. 15 : 49. It was one of the cities given with their "suburbs" to the priests. Josh. 21:15; 1 Chron. 6:58. Debir has not been discovered with certainty in modern times; but about three miles to the West of Hebron is a deep and secluded valley called the *Wady Nunkûr*, enclosed on the north by hills, of which one bears a name certainly suggestive of Debir—*Dewîrban*.

2. A place on the north boundary of Judah; near the "valley of Achor." Josh. 15:7. Some identify it with the present *Throghret ed Debir* near Adummim on the way from Jerusalem to Jericho.

3. The "border of Debir" is named as forming part of the boundary of Gad, Josh. 13:26, and as apparently not far from Mahanaim.

De'bir, king of Eglon; one of the five kings hanged by Joshua. Josh. 10: 3, 23.

Deb'orah (dĕb'o-rah) (*a bee*). (B.C. 1857.) 1. The nurse of Rebekah. Gen. 35:8. Deborah accompanied Rebekah from the house of Bethuel, Gen. 24:59, and is only mentioned by name on the occasion of her burial under the oak tree of Bethel, which was called in her honor Allon-bachuth.

2. A prophetess who judged Israel. Judges 4, 5. She lived under the palm tree of Deborah, between Ramah and Bethel in Mount Ephraim, Judges 4:5, which, as palm trees were rare in Palestine, "is mentioned as a well-known and solitary landmark." She was probably a woman of Ephraim. Lapidoth was probably her husband, and not Barak, as some say. She was not so much a judge as one gifted with prophetic command, Judges 4:6, 14; 5:7, and by virtue of her inspiration "a mother in Israel." The tyranny of Jabin, a Canaanitish king, was peculiarly felt in the northern tribes, who were near his capital and under her jurisdiction. Under her direction Barak encamped on the broad summit of Tabor. Deborah's prophecy was fulfilled, Judges 4:9, and the enemy's general perished among the "oaks of the wanderers" (Zaanaim), in the tent of the Bedouin Kenite's wife, Judges 4:21, in the northern mountains.

Decap'olis (dē-kăp'o-lĭs). A district beginning where the plain of Esdraelon opens into the Jordan valley, and expanding eastward, which was dominated

by ten associated Greek cities. It included Gadara. Matt. 4:25.

De'dan (dē'dan). 1. The name of a son of Raamah, son of Cush. Gen. 10: 7; 1 Chron. 1:9.

2. A son of Jokshan, son of Abraham by his second wife Keturah. Gen. 25: 3; 1 Chron. 1:32.

Ded'anim (dĕd'a-nĭm), descendants of Dedan 1. Isa. 21:13. [DEDAN.]

Dedication, Feast of the, the festival instituted to commemorate the purging of the temple and the rebuilding of the altar after Judas Maccabæus had driven out the Syrians, B.C. 164. 1 Macc. 4:52–59. It is named only once in the canonical Scriptures. John 10:22. It commenced on the 25th of Chisleu (early in December), the anniversary of the pollution of the temple by Antiochus Epiphanes, B.C. 167. Like the great Mosaic feasts, it lasted eight days, but it did not require attendance at Jerusalem. It was an occasion of much festivity, and was celebrated in nearly the same manner as the feast of tabernacles, with the carrying of branches of trees and with much singing. In the temple at Jerusalem the "Hallel" was sung every day of the feast.

Deer. [FALLOW-DEER.]

Degrees, Songs of, a title given to fifteen Psalms, from 120 to 134 inclusive. Four of them are attributed to David, one is ascribed to the pen of Solomon, and the other ten give no indication of their author. With respect to the term rendered in the Authorized Version "degrees" a great diversity of views prevails, but the most probable opinion is that they were pilgrim songs, sung by the people as they went up to Jerusalem.

Deha'vites (dė-hā'vītes), mentioned only once in Scripture, Ezra 4:9, among the colonists planted in Samaria after the completion of the captivity of Israel. They are possibly the Daï or Dahi, mentioned by Herodotus (i. 125) among the nomadic tribes of Persia.

De'kar (dē'kär) (*perforation*). The son of Dekar, *i. e.* Ben Dekar, was Solomon's commissariat officer in the western part of the hill-country of Judah and Benjamin, Shaalbim and Bethshemesh. 1 Kings 4:9. R. V. Deker.

Delai'ah (dĕl-a-ī'ah) (*freed by Jehovah*). 1 A priest in the time of

David, leader of the twenty-third course of priests. 1 Chron. 24 : 18.

2. "Children of Delaiah" were among the people of uncertain pedigree who returned from Babylon with Zerubbabel. Ezra 2 : 60; Neh. 7 : 62.

3. Son of Mehetabeel and father of Shemaiah. Neh. 6 : 10.

4. Son of Shemaiah, one of the "princes" about the court of Jehoiakim. Jer. 36 : 12, 25. (B.C. 604.)

Deli'lah (dḗ-lī'lah) or **Del'ilah** (*languishing*), a woman who dwelt in the valley of Sorek, beloved by Samson. Judges 16 : 4–18. There seems to be little doubt that she was a Philistine courtesan. [SAMSON.]

Deluge. [NOAH.]

De'mas (dḗ'mas) (*governor of the people*), most probably a contraction from Demetrius, or perhaps from Demarchus, a companion of St. Paul, Phil. 24; Col. 4 : 14, during his first imprisonment at Rome. (A.D. 62.) At a later period, 2 Tim. 4 : 10, we find him mentioned as having deserted the apostle through love of this present world, and gone to Thessalonica.

Deme'trius (dḗ-mē'trĭ-ŭs) (*belonging to Demeter*). 1. A maker of silver shrines of Artemis at Ephesus. Acts 19 : 24 (about A.D. 57). These were small models of the great temple of the Ephesian Artemis, with her statue, which it was customary to carry on journeys, and place on houses as charms.

2. A disciple, 3 John 12, mentioned with commendation (about A.D. 90). Possibly the first Demetrius, converted; but this is very doubtful.

Demon. In the Gospels generally, in James 2 : 19 and in Rev. 16 : 14 the demons are spoken of as spiritual beings, at enmity with God, and having power to afflict man not only with disease, but, as is marked by the frequent epithet "unclean," with spiritual pollution also. They "believe" the power of God "and tremble," James 2 : 19; they recognized the Lord as the Son of God, Matt. 8 : 29; Luke 4 : 41, and acknowledged the power of his name, used in exorcism, in the place of the name of Jehovah, by his appointed messengers, Acts 19 : 15; and looked forward in terror to the judgment to come. Matt. 8 : 29. The description is precisely that of a nature akin to the angelic in knowledge and powers, but

with the emphatic addition of the idea of positive and active wickedness.

Demoniacs. This word is frequently used in the New Testament, and applied to persons suffering under the possession of a demon or evil spirit, such possession generally showing itself visibly in bodily disease or mental derangement. It has been maintained by many persons that our Lord and the evangelists, in referring to demoniacal possession, spoke only in accommodation to the general belief of the Jews, without any assertion as to its truth or its falsity. It is concluded that, since the symptoms of the affliction were frequently those of bodily disease (as dumbness, Matt. 9 : 32; blindness, Matt. 12 : 22; epilepsy, Mark 9 : 17–27), or those seen in cases of ordinary insanity (as in Matt. 8 : 28; Mark 5 : 1–5), the demoniacs were merely persons suffering under unusual diseases of body and mind. But demoniacs are frequently distinguished from those afflicted with bodily sickness, see Mark 1 : 32; 16 : 17, 18; Luke 6 : 17, 18; the same outward signs are sometimes referred to possession, sometimes merely to disease, comp. Matt. 4 : 24 with 17 : 15; Matt. 12 : 22 with Mark 7 : 32, etc.; the demons are represented as speaking in their own persons with superhuman knowledge. Matt. 8 : 29; Mark 1 : 24; 5 : 7; Luke 4 : 41, etc. All these things speak of a personal power of evil. Twice our Lord distinctly connects demoniacal possession with the power of the evil one. Luke 10 : 18. Lastly, the single fact recorded of the entrance of the demons at Gadara, Mark 5 : 10–14, into the herd of swine, and the effect which that entrance caused, is sufficient to overthrow the notion that our Lord and the evangelists do not assert or imply any objective reality of possession. We are led, therefore, to the ordinary and literal interpretation of these passages, that there are evil spirits, subjects of the evil one, who, in the days of the Lord himself and his apostles especially, were permitted by God to exercise a direct influence over the souls and bodies of certain men.

Denarius (*containing ten*), Authorized Version "penny," Matt. 18 : 28; 20 : 2, 9, 13, a Roman silver coin in the time of our Saviour and the apostles, worth about 16 cents. It took its name from its being first equal to ten "asses," a number afterwards increased to sixteen. It was the principal silver coin of the Roman commonwealth. From the parable of the laborers in the vineyard it would seem that a denarius was then the ordinary pay for a day's labor. Matt. 20: 2, 4, 7, 9, 10, 13.

Deputy. Acts 13: 7, 8, 12; 19: 38. The Greek word signifies proconsul, the title of the Roman governors who were appointed by the senate.

Der'be (dēr'bè). Acts 14: 20, 21; 16: 1; 20: 4. The exact position of this town has not yet been ascertained, but its general situation is undoubted. It was in the eastern part of the great upland plain of Lycaonia, which stretches from Iconium eastward along the north side of the chain of Taurus. Professor Sterrett places it at *Zosta* or *Losta* about 45 miles south of *Konia* (Iconium); but the identification is still uncertain, though it seems probable, and doubtless is in that region.

Desert. Not a stretch of sand, an utterly barren waste, but a wild, uninhabited region. The words rendered in the At .orized Version by "desert," when used in the historical books denote definite localities.

1. ARABAH. This word means that very depressed and enclosed region—the deepest and the hottest chasm in the world—the sunken valley north and south of the Dead Sea, but more particularly the former. [ARABAH.] Arabah in the sense of the Jordan valley is translated by the word "desert" only in Ezek. 47: 8.

2. MIDBAR. This word, which our translators have most frequently rendered by "desert," is accurately "the pasture ground." It is most frequently used for those tracts of waste land which lie beyond the cultivated ground in the immediate neighborhood of the towns and villages of Palestine, and which are a very familiar feature to the traveller in that country. Ex. 3: 1; 5: 3; 19: 2.

3. CHARBAH appears to have the force of dryness, and thence of desolation. It is rendered "desert" in Ps. 102: 6; Isa. 48: 21; Ezek. 13: 4. The term commonly employed for it in the Authorized Version is "waste places" or "desolation."

4. JESHIMON, with the definite article, apparently denotes the waste tracts on both sides of the Dead Sea. In all these cases it is treated as a proper name in the Authorized Version. Without the article it occurs in a few passages of poetry, in the following of which it is rendered "desert:" Ps. 78: 40; 106: 14; Isa. 43: 19, 20.

De'uel, or **Deu'el** (deū'el) (*knowledge of God*), father of Eliasaph, the "captain" of the tribe of Gad at the time of the numbering of the people at Sinai. Num. 1: 14; 7: 42, 47; 10: 20. (B.C. 1491.) The same man is mentioned again in Num. 2: 14, but here the name appears as Reuel.

Deuteron'omy—which means "the repetition of the law"—is the reformulation of the legislation of the previous books for a special purpose, with such changes and revisions as are fitting to a people about to leave the wilderness and enter upon their permanent home. This book is one of the chief storm centres around which the critical discussions of our day are raging. In our brief space there is not room for any adequate statement of the critical position, for which the larger dictionaries must be consulted.

"Deuteronomy as a literary work is a collection of Orations and Songs of Moses, constituting his Farewell to the people of Israel."

Professor Moulton regards the orations as masterpieces of oratory to the level of which even Demosthenes did not rise,—orations "culminating in song which no other oratory has ever surpassed;" and "no work of literature has produced a greater sensation."

Deuteronomy or some part of it is generally regarded by scholars as the "Book of the Law" discovered by Hilkiah in the eighteenth year of the reign of Josiah (B.C. 621) which produced "the most sudden reformation movement in all history." It would be an anomaly in literary history, if a book of such power and influence had been written by an unknown author in the reigns immediately preceding Josiah. Even if the book has had additions and revisions by later authors, the portions that produced this effect must have been old, and included the chapters which proclaimed so vividly the terrible denunciations against disobedience, and the one only way of making a prosperous nation. "We must emphasize," says George Adam Smith, in his latest book *Jerusalem* (1908), "that what these reformers did, was not to create a body of fresh and novel laws. . . . Deuteronomy is a living and divine Book, because, like every other religious reformation in which God's spirit may be felt, it is at once loyal to the essential truth revealed in the past . . . while receptive of the fresh directions of the living God."

There are three addresses by Moses, containing a recapitulation of the law; "the Song of Moses;" "The Blessing of Moses" upon the twelve tribes; and the story of the death of Moses.

The great lessons of the spirituality and unity of God, the love of God and of man as the sum of the commandments, are most impressively taught.

But the part which had the greatest influence was the setting forth of the two ways that lay before individuals and the nation, on the choice of which their destiny depended, in terms of material prosperity, as a visible illustration of moral and spiritual reality.

Devil (*slanderer*). The name describes Satan as slandering God to man and man to God. The former work is, of course, a part of his great work of temptation to evil; and is not only exemplified but illustrated as to its general nature and tendency by the narrative of Gen. 3. The other work, the slandering or accusing man before God, is the imputation of selfish motives, Job 1:9, 10, and its refutation is placed in the self-sacrifice of those "who loved not their own lives unto death." [SATAN; DEMON.]

Dew. This in the summer is so copious in Palestine that it supplies to some extent the absence of rain and becomes important to the agriculturist. Thus it is coupled in the divine blessing with rain, or mentioned as a prime source of fertility, Gen. 27:28; Deut. 33:13; Zech. 8:12, and its withdrawal is attributed to a curse. 2 Sam. 1:21; 1 Kings 17:1; Hag. 1:10. It becomes a leading object in prophetic imagery by reason of its penetrating moisture without the apparent effort of rain, Deut. 32:2; Job 29:19; Ps. 133:3; Hos. 14:5; while its speedy evanescence typifies the transient goodness of the hypocrite. Hos. 6:4; 13:3.

Diadem. What the "diadem" of the Jews was we know not.

That of other nations of antiquity was a fillet of silk, two inches broad, bound round the head and tied behind. Its invention is attributed to Liber. Its color was generally white; sometimes, however, it was of blue, like that of Darius; and it was sown with pearls or other gems, Zech. 9:16, and enriched with gold. Rev. 9:7. It was peculiarly the mark of Oriental sovereigns. In Esther 1:11; 2:17, we have *cether* for the turban worn by the Persian king, queen or other eminent persons to whom it was conceded as a special favor. The diadem of the king

A DIADEM.

differed from that of others in having an *erect* triangular peak. The words in Ezek. 23:15 mean long and flowing head-dresses or turbans of gorgeous colors. [CROWN.]

Dial. "An instrument for showing the time of day from the shadow of a style or gnomon on a graduated arc or surface;" rendered "steps" in Author-

ANCIENT DIALS.

ized Version, Ex. 20:26; 1 Kings 10: 19, and "degrees," 2 Kings 20:9, 10, 11; Isa. 38:8, where to give a consistent rendering we should read with the margin the "degrees" rather than the "dial" of Ahaz. It is probable that the dial of Ahaz was really a series of steps or stairs, and that the shadow (perhaps of some column cr obelisk on the top) fell on a greater or smaller number of them according ; s the sun was low or high. The terrace of a palace might easily be thus ornamented.

Diamond (Heb. *yahălôm*), a gem, crystallized carbon, the most valued and brilliant of precious stones, remarkable for its hardness, the third precious stone in the second row on the breastplate of the high priest, Ex. 28:18; 39:11, and mentioned by Ezekiel, 28:13, among the precious stones of the king of Tyre. Some suppose *yahălôm* to be the "emerald." Respecting *shâmîr,* which is translated "diamond" in Jer. 17:1, see under ADAMANT.

Dian'a (dī-ăn'à). This Latin word, properly denoting a Roman divinity, is the representative of the Greek *Arte-*

DIANA OF THE EPHESIANS.

mis, the tutelary goddess of the Ephesians, who plays so important a part in the narrative of Acts 19. The Ephesian Diana was, however, regarded as invested with very different attributes, and is rather to be identified with Astarte and other female divinities of the East. The head wore a mural crown, each hand held a bar of metal, and the

TEMPLE OF DIANA OF THE EPHESIANS.

lower part ended in a rude block covered with figures of animals and mystic inscriptions. This idol was regarded as an object of peculiar sanctity, and was believed to have fallen down from heaven. Acts 19:35.

Dibla'im (dĭb-lā'ĭm) (*double cake*), mother or father of Hosea's wife Gomer. Hos. 1:3.

Dib'lath (dĭb'lăth) (accurately Diblah), a place named only in Ezek. 6:14. Probably another form of RIBLAH.

Di'bon (dī'bŏn) (*wasting*). 1. A town on the east side of Jordan, in the rich pastoral country, which was taken possession of and rebuilt by the children of Gad. Num. 32:3, 34. From this circumstance it possibly received the name of DIBON-GAD. Num. 33:45, 46. Its first mention is in Num. 21:30, and from this it appears to have belonged originally to the Moabites. We find Dibon counted to Reuben in the lists of Joshua. Josh. 13:9, 17. In the time of Isaiah and Jeremiah, however, it was again in possession of Moab. Isa. 15:2; Jer. 48:18, 22, comp. 24. In modern times the name *Dhiban* has been discovered as attached to extensive ruins on the Roman road, about three miles north of the Arnon (*Wady Modjib*). It has acquired especial interest since the discovery there of the Moabite Stone in 1868.

2. One of the towns which were reinhabited by the men of Judah after the return from captivity, Neh. 11:25; identified by some with DIMONAH.

Di'bon-gad (dī'bŏn-găd). [DIBON, **1.**]

Dib'ri (dĭb'rī), a Danite, father of Shelomith. Lev. 24:11.

Didrachmon. [MONEY; SHEKEL.]

Did'ymus (dĭd'ў-mŭs) (*the twin*), a surname of the apostle Thomas. John 11:16; 20:24; 21:2. [THOMAS.]

Dik'lah (dĭk'lah) (*palm grove*). Gen. 10:27; 1 Chron. 1:21, a son of Joktan, whose settlements, in common with those of the other sons of Joktan, must be looked for in Arabia. It is thought that Diklah is a part of Arabia containing many palm trees.

Dil'ean (dĭl'e-ăn), or **Dilan**, one of the cities in the lowlands of Judah. Josh. 15:38. It has not been identified with certainty.

Dim'nah (dĭm'nah) (*dung*), a city in the tribe of Zebulun, given to the Merarite Levites. Josh. 21:35.

Di'mon (dĭ'mon), **The waters of,** some streams on the east of the Dead Sea, in the land of Moab, against which Isaiah uttered denunciation. Isa. 15:9. Gesenius conjectures that the two names Dimon and Dibon are the same.

Dimo'nah (dĭ-mō'nah), a city in the south of Judah, Josh. 15:22, perhaps the same as DIBON in Neh. 11:25.

Di'nah (dĭ'nah) (*judged, acquitted*), the daughter of Jacob by Leah. Gen. 30:21. She accompanied her father from Mesopotamia to Canaan, and, having ventured among the inhabitants, was violated by Shechem the son of Hamor, the chieftain of the territory in which her father had settled. Gen. 34. Shechem proposed to make the usual reparation by paying a sum to the father and marrying her. Gen. 34:12. This proposal was accepted, the sons of Jacob demanding, as a condition of the proposed union, the circumcision of the Shechemites. They therefore assented; and on the third day, when the pain and fever resulting from the operation were at the highest, Simeon and Levi, own brothers of Dinah, attacked them unexpectedly, slew all the males, and plundered their city. Both at the time and on his death-bed their father Jacob spoke with indignation and abhorrence of this act.

Di'naites (dĭ'na-ītes), Ezra 4:9, the name of some of the Cuthæan colonists who were placed in the cities of Samaria after the captivity of the ten tribes.

Din'habah (dĭn'ha-bah), Gen. 36:32; 1 Chron. 1:43, the capital city, and probably the birthplace, of Bela, son of Beor king of Edom.

Dionys'ius (dī-ŏ-nĭs'ĭ-us) (*devoted to Dionysus*, i. e. *Bacchus*) **the Areop'= agite,** Acts 17:34, an eminent Athenian, converted to Christianity by the preaching of St. Paul. (A.D. 52.) He is said to have been first bishop of Athens. The writings which were once attributed to him are now confessed to be the production of some neo-Platonists circulated in the fifth century.

Diot'rephes (di-ŏt're-fēs) (*nourished by Zeus*), a Christian mentioned in 3 John 9, but of whom nothing is known.

Disciple. [APOSTLES.]

Diseases. [MEDICINE.]

Di'shan (dī'shan) (*antelope*), the youngest son of Seir the Horite. Gen. 36:21, 28, 30; 1 Chron. 1:38, 42.

Di'shon (dī'shon) (*antelope*). 1. The fifth son of Seir. Gen. 36:21, 26, 30; 1 Chron. 1:38. Perhaps same as 2. The son of Anah, and grandson of Seir. Gen. 36:25; 1 Chron. 1:41.

Dispersion, The Jews of the, or simply THE DISPERSION, was the general title applied to those Jews who remained settled in foreign countries after the return from the Babylonian exile, and during the period of the second temple. At the beginning of the Christian era the Dispersion was divided into three great sections, the Babylonian, the Syrian, the Egyptian. From Babylon the Jews spread throughout Persia, Media and Parthia. Large settlements of Jews were established in Cyprus, in the islands of the Ægean, and on the western coast of Asia Minor. Jewish settlements were also established at Alexandria by Alexander and Ptolemy I. The Jewish settlements in Rome were consequent upon the occupation of Jerusalem by Pompey, B.C. 63. The influence of the Dispersion on the rapid promulgation of Christianity can scarcely be overrated. The course of the apostolic preaching followed in a regular progress the line of Jewish settlements. The mixed assembly from which the first converts were gathered on the day of Pentecost represented each division of the Dispersion. Acts 2:9–11. (1) Parthians . . . Mesopotamia; (2) Judea (*i. e. Syria*) . . . Pamphylia; (3) Egypt . . . Greece; (4) Romans . . . , and these converts naturally prepared the way for the apostles in the interval which preceded the beginning of the separate apostolic missions. St. James and St. Peter wrote to the Jews of the Dispersion. James 1:1; 1 Pet. 1:1.

Divination is a "foretelling future events, or discovering things secret by the aid of superior beings, or other than human means." It is used in Scripture of *false* systems of ascertaining the divine will. It has been universal in all ages, and all nations alike civilized and savage. Numerous forms of divination are mentioned, such as divination by rods, Hos. 4:12; divination by arrows, Ezek. 21:21; divination by cups, Gen. 44:5; consultation of teraphim, 1 Sam. 15:23; Ezek. 21:21; Zech. 10:2 [TERAPHIM]; divination by the liver, Ezek. 21:21; divination by dreams, Deut. 13: 2, 3; Judges 7:13; Jer. 23:32; consultation of oracles, Isa. 41:21-24; 44: 7. Moses forbade every species of divination, because a prying into the future clouds the mind with superstition, and because it would have been an incentive to idolatry. But God supplied his people with substitutes for divination which would have rendered it superfluous, and left them in no doubt as to his will in circumstances of danger, had they continued faithful. It was only when they were unfaithful that the revelation was withdrawn. 1 Sam. 28:6; 2 Sam. 2:1; 5:23, etc. Superstition not unfrequently goes hand in hand with skepticism, and hence, amid the general infidelity prevalent throughout the Roman empire at our Lord's coming, imposture was rampant. Hence the lucrative trade of such men as Simon Magus, Acts 8:9, Bar-jesus, Acts 13:6, the slave with the spirit of Python, Acts 16:16, the vagabond Jews, exorcists, Luke 11:19; Acts 19:13, and others, 2 Tim. 3:13; Rev. 19:20, etc., as well as the notorious dealers in magical books at Ephesus. Acts 19:19.

Divorce, "a legal dissolution of the marriage relation." The law regulating this subject is found, Deut. 24:1-4, and the cases in which the right of a husband to divorce his wife was lost are stated *ibid.,* 22:19, 29. The ground of divorce is a point on which the Jewish doctors of the period of the New Testament differed widely; the school of Shammai seeming to limit it to a moral delinquency in the woman, whilst that of Hillel extended it to trifling causes, *e.g.,* if the wife burnt the food she was cooking for her husband. The Pharisees wished perhaps to embroil our Saviour with these rival schools by their question, Matt. 19:3; by his answer to which, as well as by his previous maxim, Matt. 5:31, he declares that he regarded all the lesser causes than "fornication" as standing on too weak ground, and declined the question of how to interpret the words of Moses.

Diz′ahab (dĭz′a-hăb) (*region of gold*), a place in the Arabian desert, mentioned Deut. 1:1. The situation is unknown, all proposed sites being very doubtful.

Do′dai (dō′dă-ī) (*loving, amorous*), an Ahohite who commanded the course of the second month. 1 Chron. 27:4. It is probable that he is the same as DODO, 2.

Do′danim (dō′dă-nĭm) (*leaders*), a race descended from Javan, the son of Japhet. Gen. 10:4; 1 Chron. 1:7. Dodanim was regarded as identical with the Dardani, who were found in historical times in Illyricum and Troy. Modern scholars, however, consider this impossible, and many are inclined to identify them with the Rhodians and the neighboring islands, especially as some versions have *Rodanim.*

Do′davah (dō′dă-vah) (*beloved of Jehovah*), a man of Mareshah in Judah, father of Eliezer, who denounced Jehoshaphat's alliance with Ahaziah. 2 Chron. 20:37.

Do′do (dō′dŏ) (*loving*). 1. A man of Bethlehem, father of Elhanan, who was one of David's thirty captains. 2 Sam. 23:24; 1 Chron. 11:26. He is a different person from

2. DODO THE AHOHITE, father of Eleazar, the second of the three mighty men who were over the thirty. 2 Sam. 23:9; 1 Chron. 11:12.

Do′eg (dō′eg) (*fearful*), an Idumean, chief of Saul's herdmen. (B.C. 1062.) He was at Nob when Ahimelech gave David the sword of Goliath, and not only gave information to Saul, but when others declined the office, himself executed the king's order to destroy the priests of Nob, with their families, to the number of 85 persons, together with all their property. 1 Sam. 21:7; 22:9, 18, 22; Ps. 52.

Dog, an animal frequently mentioned in Scripture. It was used by the Hebrews as a watch for their houses, Isa. 56:10, and for guarding their flocks.

Job 30 : 1. Then also, as now, troops of hungry and semi-wild dogs used to wander about the fields and the streets of the cities, devouring dead bodies and other offal, 1 Kings 14 : 11; 21 : 19, 23; 22 : 38; Ps. 59 : 6, and thus became so savage and

SYRIAN DOG.

fierce and such objects of dislike that fierce and cruel enemies are poetically styled dogs in Ps. 22 : 16, 20. Moreover, the dog being an unclean animal, Isa. 66 : 3, the epithets dog, dead dog, dog's head, were used as terms of reproach or of humility in speaking of one's self. 1 Sam. 24 : 14; 2 Sam. 3 : 8; 9 : 8; 16 : 9; 2 Kings 8 : 13.

Doors. [GATE.]

Doph'kah (dŏf'kah), a place mentioned, Num. 33 : 12, as a station in the desert where the Israelites encamped. [WILDERNESS OF THE WANDERING.]

Dor (dôr) (*dwelling*), Josh. 17 : 11; 1 Kings 4 : 11, an ancient royal city of the Canaanites, Josh. 12 : 23, whose ruler was an ally of Jabin king of Hazor against Joshua. Josh. 11 : 1, 2. It appears to have been within the territory of the tribe of Asher, though allotted to Manasseh. Josh. 17 : 11; Judges 1 : 27. Solomon stationed at Dor one of his twelve purveyors. 1 Kings 4 : 11. Jerome places it on the coast, " in the ninth mile from Cæsarea, on the way to Ptolemais." Just at the point indicated is the small village of *Tantûra,* probably an Arab corruption of *Dora,* consisting of about thirty houses, wholly constructed of ancient materials; but Conder does not think that this answers the conditions.

Dor'cas (dôr'kas) (*gazelle*). The Greek equivalent of the Hebrew TABITHA, which see. This name is used for "Dorcas Societies" organized to sew for the poor. Acts 9 : 36.

Do'than (dō'than) (*two wells*), a place first mentioned, Gen. 37 : 17, in connection with the history of Joseph, and apparently as in the neighborhood of Shechem. It next appears as the residence of Elisha. 2 Kings 6 : 13. It was known to Eusebius, who places it 12 miles to the north of Sebaste (Samaria); and here it has been discovered in our own times, still bearing its ancient name unimpaired.

Dove. The first mention of this bird occurs in Gen. 8. The dove's rapidity of flight is alluded to in Ps. 55 : 6; the beauty of its plumage in Ps. 68 : 13; its dwelling in the rocks and valleys in Jer. 48 : 28 and Ezek. 7 : 16; its mournful voice in Isa. 38 : 14; 59 : 11; Nah. 2 : 7; its harmlessness in Matt. 10 : 16; its simplicity in Hos. 7 : 11, and its amativeness in Cant. 1 : 15; 2 : 14. Doves are kept in a domesticated state in many parts of the East. In Persia pigeon-houses are erected at a distance from the dwellings, for the purpose of collecting the dung as manure. There is probably an allusion to such a custom in Isa. 60 : 8.

Dove's dung. Various explanations have been given of the passage in 2 Kings 6 : 25. Bochart has labored to show that it denotes a species of *cicer,*

STAR OF BETHLEHEM.

" chick-pea," which he says the Arabs call *usnân,* and sometimes improperly " dove's " or " sparrow's dung." Great quantities of these are sold in Cairo to the pilgrims going to Mecca. Later authorities incline to think it the bulbous root of the *Star of Bethlehem* (*ornithogalum*, i. e. bird-milk), a common root in Palestine, and sometimes eaten. It can scarcely be believed that even in the worst horrors of a siege a substance so vile as is implied by the literal rendering should have been used for food. In this connection it is interesting to note that "the Arabs call a species of soap plant sparrow's dung."

Dowry. [MARRIAGE.]

Drachm, a Greek silver coin, varying in weight on account of the use of different talents. In Luke 15 : 8, 9 denarii (Authorized Version "piece of silver") seem to be intended. [MONEY; SILVER.]

Dragon. The translators of the Authorized Version, apparently following the Vulgate, have rendered by the same word "dragon" the two Hebrew words *tan* and *tannin*, which appear to be quite distinct in meaning. (1) The former is used, always in the plural, in Job 30 : 29 ; Ps. 44 : 19 ; Isa. 34 : 13 ; 43 : 20 ; Jer. 9 : 11. It is always applied to some creatures inhabiting the desert, and we should conclude from this that it refers rather to some wild beast than to a serpent. The Syriac renders it by a word meaning "jackal." The R. V. so translates it also. (2) The word *tannin* seems to refer to any great monster, whether of the land or the sea, being indeed more usually applied to some kind of serpent or reptile, but not exclusively restricted to that sense. Ex. 7: 9, 10, 12; Deut. 32 : 33; Ps. 91: 13. In the New Testament it is found only in the Apocalypse, Rev. 12:3, etc., as applied metaphorically to "the old serpent, called the devil, and Satan."

Dreams. The Scripture declares that the influence of the Spirit of God upon the soul extends to its sleeping as well as its waking thoughts. But, in accordance with the principle enunciated by St. Paul in 1 Cor. 14: 15, dreams, in which the understanding is asleep, are placed below the visions of prophecy, in which the understanding plays its part. Under the Christian dispensation, while we read frequently of trances and visions, dreams are never referred to as vehicles of divine revelation. In exact accordance with this principle are the actual records of the dreams sent by God. The greater number of such dreams were granted, for prediction or for warning, to those who were aliens to the Jewish covenant. And where dreams are recorded as means of God's revelation to his chosen servants, they are almost always referred to the periods of their earliest and most imperfect knowledge of him. Among the Jews, " if any person dreamed a dream which was peculiarly striking and significant, he was permitted to go to the high priest in a peculiar way, and see if it had any special import. But the observance of ordinary dreams and the consulting of those who pretend to skill in their interpretation are repeatedly forbidden. Deut. 13: 1–5; 18 : 9–14."—*Schaff.*

Dress. This subject includes the following particulars: 1. Materials; 2. Color and decoration; 3. Name, form, and mode of wearing the various articles; 4. Special usages relating thereto.

1. *Materials.*—After the first "apron" of fig leaves, Gen. 3 : 7, the skins of animals were used for clothing. Gen. 3 : 21. Such was the 'mantle" worn by Elijah. Pelisses of sheepskin still form an ordinary article of dress in the East. The art of weaving hair was known to the Hebrews at an early period, Ex. 25 : 4; 26 : 7; and wool was known earlier still. Gen. 31: 19. Their acquaintance with linen and perhaps cotton dates from the captivity in Egypt, 1 Chron. 4 : 21; silk was introduced much later. Rev. 18 : 12. The use of mixed material, such as wool and flax, was forbidden. Lev. 19 : 19; Deut. 22 : 11.

2. *Color and decoration.*—The prevailing color of the Hebrew dress was the natural white of the materials employed, which might be brought to a high state of brilliancy by the art of the fuller. Mark 9 : 3. The notice of scarlet thread, Gen. 38 : 28, implies some acquaintance with dyeing. The elements of ornamentation were—(1) weaving with threads previously dyed, Ex. 35 : 25; (2) the introduction of gold thread or wire, Ex. 28 : 6 ff.; (3) the addition of figures. Robes decorated with gold, Ps. 45 : 13, and with silver thread, cf. Acts 12 : 21, were worn by royal personages; other kinds of embroidered robes were worn by the wealthy, Judges 5 : 30; Ps. 45 : 14; Ezek. 16 : 13; as well as purple, Prov. 31 : 22; Luke 16 : 19, and scarlet. 2 Sam. 1 : 24.

3. *The names, forms, and modes of wearing the robes.*—The general characteristics of Oriental dress have pre-

served a remarkable uniformity in all ages: the modern Arab dresses much as the ancient Hebrew did. The costume of the men and women was very similar; there was sufficient difference, however, to mark the sex, and it was strictly forbidden to a woman to wear the appendages, such as the staff, signet-ring, and other ornaments, of a man; as well as to a man to wear the outer robe of a woman. Deut. 22:5. We shall first describe the robes which were common to the two sexes, and then those which were peculiar to women. (1) *The inner garment* was the most essential article of dress. It was a closely-fitting garment, resembling in form and use our shirt, though unfortunately translated "coat" in the Authorized Version. The material of which it was made was either wool, cotton or linen. It was without sleeves, and reached only to the knee. Another kind reached to the wrists and ankles. It was in either case kept close to the body by a girdle, and the fold formed by the overlapping of the robe served as an inner pocket. A person wearing the inner garment alone was described as *naked*. (2) There was an *upper* or *second* tunic, the difference being that it was longer than the first. (3) The *linen cloth* appears to have been a wrapper of fine linen, which might be used in various ways, but especially as a night-shirt. Mark 14:51. (4) *The outer garment* consisted of a quadrangular piece of woollen cloth, probably resembling in shape a Scotch plaid. The size and texture would vary with the means of the wearer. It might be worn in various ways, either wrapped round the body or thrown over the shoulders like a shawl, with the ends or "skirts" hanging down in front; or it might be thrown over the head, so as to conceal the face. 2 Sam. 15:30; Esther 6:12. The ends were skirted with a fringe and bound with a dark purple ribbon, Num. 15:38; it was confined at the waist by a girdle. The outer garment was the poor man's bed clothing. Ex. 22:26, 27. The dress of the women differed from that of the men in regard to the outer garment, the inner garment being worn equally by both sexes. Cant. 5:3. Among their distinctive robes we find a kind of shawl, Ruth 3:15; Isa. 3:22, light summer dresses of handsome appearance and ample dimensions, and gay holiday dresses. Isa. 3:24. The garments of females were terminated by an ample border of fringe (*skirts*, Authorized Version), which concealed the feet. Isa. 47:2; Jer. 13:22. The travelling *cloak* referred to by St. Paul, 2 Tim. 4:13, is generally identified with the Roman *pænula*. It is, however, otherwise explained as a travelling-case for carrying clothes or books. The *coat of many colors* worn by Joseph, Gen. 37:3, 23, is variously taken to be either a "coat of divers colors" or a tunic furnished with sleeves and reaching down to the ankles. The latter is probably the correct sense.

4. *Special usages relating to dress.—* The length of the dress rendered it inconvenient for active exercise; hence the outer garments were either left in the house by a person working close by, Matt. 24:18, or were thrown off when the occasion arose, Mark 10:50; or, if this were not possible, as in the case of a person traveling, they were girded up. 1 Kings 18:46; 1 Pet. 1:13. On entering a house the upper garment was probably laid aside, and resumed on going out. Acts 12:8. In a sitting posture, the garments concealed the feet; this was held to be an act of reverence. Isa. 6:2. The number of suits possessed by the Hebrews was considerable: a single suit consisted of an under and an upper garment. The presentation of a robe in many instances amounted to installation or investiture, Gen. 41:42; Esther 8:15; Isa. 22:21; on the other hand, taking it away amounted to dismissal from office. 2 Macc. 4:38. The production of the best robe was a mark of special honor in a household. Luke 15:22. The number of robes thus received or kept in store for presents was very large, and formed one of the main elements of wealth in the East, Job 22:6; Matt. 6:19; James 5:2, so that *to have clothing* implied the possession of wealth and power. Isa. 3:6, 7. On grand occasions the entertainer offered becoming robes to his guests. The business of making clothes devolved upon women in a family. Prov. 31:22; Acts 9:39. Little art was required in what we may term the tailoring department; the garments came forth for the most part ready made from the loom, so that the weaver supplanted the tailor.

Drink, Strong. The Hebrew term

shêcar, in its etymological sense, applies to any beverage that had *intoxicating* qualities. With regard to the application of the term in later times we have the explicit statement of Jerome, as well as other sources of information, from which we may state that the following beverages were known to the Jews:—1. *Beer,* which was largely consumed in Egypt under the name of "hek," and was thence introduced into Palestine. It was made of barley; certain herbs, such as lupine and skirret, were used as substitutes for hops. 2. *Cider,* which is noticed in the Mishna as *apple wine.* 3. *Honey wine,* of which there were two sorts, one consisting of a mixture of wine, honey and pepper; the other a decoction of the juice of the grape, termed *dĕbash* (honey) by the Hebrews, and *dibs* by the modern Syrians. 4. *Date wine,* which was also manufactured in Egypt. It was made by mashing the fruit in water in certain proportions. 5. Various other fruits and vegetables are enumerated by Pliny as supplying materials for *factitious* or home-made wine, such as figs, millet, the carob fruit, etc. They probably put raisins in jars of water and buried them in the ground until fermentation took place.

The Jews, however, rarely used strong drink, usually drinking water or milk. There are many passages describing the evils of strong drink.

Dromedary. [CAMEL.]

Drusil'la (dru-sĭl'là), daughter of Herod Agrippa I., Acts 24:24 ff., and Cypros. Born A.D. 38. She was at first betrothed to Antiochus Epiphanes, prince of Commagene, but was married to Azizus, king of Emesa. Soon after, Felix, procurator of Judea, brought about her seduction by means of the Cyprian sorcerer Simon, and took her as his wife. In Acts 24:24 we find her in company with Felix at Cæsarea. Felix had by Drusilla a son named Agrippa, who, together with his mother, perished in the eruption of Vesuvius.

Dulcimer (Heb. *sumphoniah*), a musical instrument, mentioned in Dan. 3: 5, 15, probably the bagpipe. The same instrument is still in use amongst peasants in the northwest of Asia and in southern Europe, where it is known by the similar name *sampogna* or *zampogna.*

Du'mah (du'mah) (*silence*). 1. A son of Ishmael, most probably the founder of the Ishmaelite tribe of Arabia, and thence the name of the principal place or district inhabited by that tribe. Gen. 25:14; 1 Chron. 1:30; Isa. 21:11.

2. A city in the mountainous district of Judah, near Hebron, Josh. 15:52, represented by the ruins of a village called *ed-Daumeh,* six miles southwest of Hebron.

Dung. The uses of dung were twofold—as manure and as fuel. The manure consisted either of straw steeped in liquid manure, Isa. 25:10, or the sweepings, Isa. 5:25, of the streets and roads, which were carefully removed from about the houses, and collected in heaps outside the walls of the towns at fixed spots—hence the dung-gate at Jerusalem —and thence removed in due course to the fields. The difficulty of procuring fuel in Syria, Arabia and Egypt has made dung in all ages valuable as *z* substitute. It was probably used for heating ovens and for baking cakes Ezek. 4:12, 15, the equable heat which it produced adapting it peculiarly for the latter operation. Cow's and camel's dung is still used for a similar purpose by the Bedouins.

Dungeon. [PRISON.]

Du'ra (dü'rà) (*a wall*), the plain where Nebuchadnezzar set up the golden image, Dan. 3:1, has been sometimes identified with a tract a little below *Tekrit,* on the left bank of the Tigris, where the name *Dur* is still found. M. Oppert places the plain (or, as he calls it, the "valley") of Dura to the southeast of Babylon, in the vicinity of the mound of *Dowair* or *Dùair,* where was found the pedestal of a huge statue. This is now considered the most probable locality. (Hastings.)

Dust. [MOURNING.]

E

Eagle (Heb. *nesher,* i. e. *a tearer with the beak*). At least eight distinct kinds of eagles have been observed in Palestine, *e.g.,* the golden eagle, *Aquila chrysaëtos,* the spotted eagle, *Aquila*

perhaps more particular **reference to** the golden and imperial eagles and the *griffon vulture* may be intended. The passage in Micah, 1:16, "enlarge thy baldness as the eagle," may refer to the griffon vulture, *Vultur fulvus,* in which case the simile is peculiarly appropriate, f o r t h e whole head and neck of this bird are destitute of true feathers. The "eagles" of Matt. 24:28, Luke 17:37, may include the *Vultur fulvus* and *Neophron percnopterus;* though, as eagles frequently prey upon dead bodies, there is no necessity to restrict the Greek word t o t h e *Vulturidæ.* The figure of an eagle is now and has long been a favorite military e n s i g n. The Persians so employed it; a fact which illustrates the passage i n Isa. 46:11. T h e same bird was similarly employed by t h e Assyrians and the Romans.

Earing. Gen. 45:6; E x. 34:21. Derived from the Latin *arare,* to plough; hence i t means ploughing.

Earnest. 2 Cor. 1: 22; 5:5; Eph. 1:14. The Hebrew word was u s e d generally f o r *pledge,* Gen. 38:17, and i n its cognate forms

IMPERIAL EAGLE.

clanga, the imperial eagle, *Aquila heliaca,* and the very common *Circaëtos gallicus.* The Hebrew *nesher* may stand for any of these different species, though

for *surety,* Prov. 17:18, and *hostage.* 2 Kings 14:14. The Greek derivative, however, acquired a more technical sense as signifying the *deposit* paid by

GIER EAGLES.

42:11, or offering to the service of God. Num. 31:50.

Earth. The term is used in two widely-different senses: (1) for the material of which the earth's surface is composed; (2) as the name of the planet on which man dwells. The Hebrew language discriminates between these two by the use of separate terms, *adamah* for the former, *erets* for the latter. 1. *Adamah* is the *earth* in the sense of soil or ground, particularly as being susceptible of cultivation. Gen. 2:7. 2. *Erets* is applied in a more or less extended sense—(1) to the whole world, Gen. 1:1; (2) to land as opposed to sea, Gen. 1:10; (3) to a country, Gen. 21: 32; (4) to a plot of ground, Gen. 23:15; and (5) to the ground on which a man stands. Gen. 33:3. The two former senses alone concern us, the first involving an inquiry into the opinions of the Hebrews on cosmogony, the second on geography. 1. *Cosmogony.*—(1) The Hebrew cosmogony is based upon the leading principle that the universe exists, not independently of God, nor yet co-existent with God, nor yet in opposition to him as a hostile element, but dependently upon him, subsequently to him and in subjection to him. (2) Creation was regarded as a progressive work—a gradual development from the inferior to the superior orders of things. 2. *Geography.*—There seem to be traces of the same ideas as prevailed among the Greeks, that the world was a disk, Isa. 40:22, bordered by the ocean, with Jerusalem as its centre, like Delphi as the navel, or, according to another view, the highest point of the world. As to the size of the earth, the Hebrews had but a very indefinite notion.

Earthenware. [POTTERY.]

Earthquake. Earthquakes, more or

the purchaser on entering into an agreement for the purchase of anything. In the New Testament the word is used to signify the pledge or earnest of the superior blessings of the future life.

Earrings. The material of which earrings were made was generally gold, Ex. 32:2, and their form circular. They were worn by women and by youth of both sexes. These ornaments appear to have been regarded with superstitious reverence as an amulet. On this account they were surrendered along with the idols by Jacob's household. Gen. 35:4. Chardin describes earrings with talismanic figures and characters on them as still existing in the East. Jewels were sometimes attached to the rings. The size of the earrings still worn in eastern countries far exceeds what has been usual among ourselves; hence they formed a handsome present, Job less violent, are of frequent occurrence in Palestine. The most remarkable occurred in the reign of Uzziah. Zech. 14:5. From Zech. 14:4 we are led to infer that a great convulsion took place at this time in the Mount of Olives, the mountain being split so as to leave a valley between its summit. An earthquake occurred at the time of our Saviour's crucifixion. Matt. 27:51-54. Earthquakes are not unfrequently accompanied by fissures of the earth's surface; instances of this are recorded in connection with the destruction of Korah and his company, Num. 16:32, and at the time of our Lord's death, Matt. 27:51; the former may be paralleled by a similar occurrence at Oppido in Calabria A.D. 1783, where the earth opened to the extent of five hundred and a depth of more than two hundred feet.

East. The Hebrew term *kedem* properly means that which is *before* or *in front* of a person, and was applied to the east from the custom of turning in that direction when describing the points of the compass, *before, behind*, the *right* and the *left* representing respectively east, west, south and north. Job 23:8, 9. The term as generally used refers to the lands lying immediately eastward of Palestine, viz., Arabia, Mesopotamia and Babylonia; on the other hand *mizrach* is used of the *far* east with a less definite signification. Isa. 41:2, 25; 43:5; 46:11.

Easter. Acts 12:4. In the earlier English versions Easter has been frequently used as the translation of *pascha* (*passover*). In the Authorized Version Passover was substituted in all passages but this; and in the new Revision Passover is used here. [PASSOVER.]

E'bal (ē'bal) (*stone, bare mountain*). 1. One of the sons of Shobal the son of Seir. Gen. 36:23; 1 Chron. 1:40.

2. Obal the son of Joktan. 1 Chron. 1:22; comp. Gen. 10:28.

E'bal, Mount, a mount in the promised land, on which the Israelites were to "put" the curse which should fall upon them if they disobeyed the commandments of Jehovah. The blessing consequent on obedience was to be similarly localized on Mount Gerizim. Deut. 11:26-29. Ebal and Gerizim are the mounts which form the sides of

the fertile valley in which lies *Nablûs*, the ancient Shechem—Ebal on the north and Gerizim on the south. They are nearly in the centre of the country of Samaria, about eight hundred feet above the Nablûs in the valley; and they are so near that all the vast body of the people could hear the words read from either mountain. The experiment has repeatedly been tried in modern times. The modern name of Ebal is *Jebel Salamiyah*, from a Mohammedan female saint, whose tomb is standing on the eastern part of the ridge, a little before the highest point is reached.

E'bed (ē'bed) (*a servant*). (Many MSS. have EBER.) 1. Father of Gaal, who with his brethren assisted the men of Shechem in their revolt against Abimelech. Judges 9:26, 28, 30, 31, 35.

2. Son of Jonathan; one of the Bene-Adin who returned from Babylon with Ezra. Ezra 8:6.

E'bed-me'lech (ē'bed-mē'lek) (*a king's servant*), an Ethiopian eunuch in the service of King Zedekiah, through whose interference Jeremiah was released from prison. Jer. 38:7 ff.; 39:15 ff. (B.C. 589.) The name may have been an official title.

Eben=e'zer (ĕb-en-ē'zẽr) (*stone of help*), a stone set up by Samuel after a signal defeat of the Philistines, as a memorial of the "help" received on the occasion from Jehovah. 1 Sam. 7:12. Its position is carefully defined as between Mizpeh and Shen.

E'ber (ē'bẽr) (*the region beyond*). 1. Son of Salah, and great-grandson of Shem. Gen. 10:24; 1 Chron. 1:19. The name is written Heber in Luke 3.

2. Son of Elpaal and descendant of Sharahaim of the tribe of Benjamin. 1 Chron. 8:12.

3. A priest in the days of Joiakim the son of Jeshua. Neh. 12:20.

Ebi'asaph (ė-bī'a-săf). 1 Chron. 6:23, 37. [See ABIASAPH.]

Ebony, Ezek. 27:15, one of the valuable commodities imported into Tyre by the men of Dedan; a hard, heavy and durable wood, which admits of a fine polish or gloss. The most usual color is black, but it also occurs red or green. The black is the heart of a tree called *Diospyros ebenum*. It was imported from India or Ceylon by Phœnician traders.

Ebro'nah (ē-brō'nah) (*passage*), one

of the halting-places of the Israelites in the desert, immediately preceding Ezion-geber. Num. 33 : 34, 35.

Ecbat'ana. Ezra 6 : 2, margin. In the apocryphal books Ecbatana is frequently mentioned. Two cities named Ecbatana seem to have existed in ancient times, one the capital of northern Media—the Media Atropatêné of Strabo —the other the metropolis of the larger and more important province known as Media Magna. The site of the former appears to be marked by the very curious ruins at *Takht-i-Suleïman* (lat. 36° 25', long. 47° 10') ; while that of the latter is occupied by *Hamadan,* which is one of the most important cities of modern Persia.

Ecclesias'tes (*the preacher* or *convener of an assembly*). It is probable that Solomon is not the author of the book, but the hero; and that it was written by a post-exilic writer who uses Solomon's experience to enforce great moral lessons, as Plato uses Socrates in his Dialogues—the confession of a man of wide experience looking back upon his past life and looking out upon the disorders and calamities which surround him. The hero is a man who has sinned in giving way to selfishness and sensuality, who has paid the penalty of that sin in satiety and weariness of life, but who has through all this been under the discipline of a divine education, and has learned from it the lesson which God meant to teach him.

Ecclesias'ticus (ĕk-klē-ṣĭ-ăs'ti-kŭs), one of the books of the Apocrypha. This title is given in the Latin version to the book which is called in the Septuagint THE WISDOM OF JESUS THE SON OF SIRACH. The word designates the character of the writing, as publicly used in the services of the Church.

Eclipse of the sun. No historical notice of an eclipse occurs in the Bible, but there are passages in the prophets which contain manifest allusion to this phenomenon. Joel 2 : 10, 31; 3 : 15; Amos 8 : 9; Micah 3 : 6; Zech. 14 : 6. The notice in Amos 8 : 9 very likely refers to the eclipse of June 15, B.C. 763; but in the others no historical eclipse is possible. The language is conventional, and may refer to the phenomenon as a figure. A reference in Jer. 15 : 9 may possibly have been suggested by an eclipse occurring B.C. 585 (Herod. i, 54). Some scholars consider

that Job 3 : 4, 5 has reference to this phenomenon. No other historical eclipse is referred to. The darkness that overspread the world at the crucifixion cannot with reason be attributed to an eclipse, as the moon was at the full at the time of the passover.

Ed (ĕd) (*witness*), a word inserted in the Authorized Version of Josh. 22 : 34, apparently on the authority of a few MSS., and also of the Syriac and Arabic versions, but not existing in the generally-received Hebrew text.

E'dar (ē'där), **Tower of** (accur. EDER, *a flock*), a place named only in Gen. 35 : 21. According to Jerome it was one thousand paces from Bethlehem.

E'den (*pleasure*). 1. The first residence of man, called in the Septuagint *Paradise.* The latter is a word of Persian origin, and describes an extensive tract of pleasure land, somewhat like an English park; and the use of it suggests a wider view of man's first abode than a garden. The description of Eden is found in Gen. 2 : 8–14. In the eastern portion of the region of Eden was the garden planted. The Hiddekel, one of its rivers, is the modern Tigris; the Euphrates is the same as the modern Euphrates. With regard to the Pison and Gihon a great variety of opinion exists. The location of the district of Eden is unknown beyond the fact that it included parts of the Euphrates and Tigris; nor do we know its extent. Sayce finds Eden at the head of the Persian Gulf, which was held by the Babylonians to be a river. This site is vigorously combated. Others place it in Armenia, where there is still a mountain known by the name of Mt. Ararat. 2. One of the marts which supplied the luxury of Tyre with richly-embroidered stuffs. In 2 Kings 19 : 12 and Isa. 37 : 12 "the sons of Eden" are mentioned with Gozan, Haran and Rezeph as victims of the Assyrian greed of conquest. Probability seems to point to the northwest of Mesopotamia as the locality of Eden. 3. BETH-EDEN, "house of pleasure:" probably the name of a country residence of the kings of Damascus. Amos 1 : 5.

E'den. 1. A Gershonite Levite, son of Joah, in the days of Hezekiah. 2 Chron. 29 : 12. 2. Also a Levite, probably identical with the preceding. 2 Chron. 31 : 15.

FACADE OF A ROCK-HEWN TOMB AT PETRA IN EDOM.

E'der (ē'dẽr) (*a flock*). 1. One of the towns of Judah, in the extreme south, and on the borders of Edom. Josh. 15 : 21.

2. A Levite of the family of Merari, in the time of David. 1 Chron. 23 : 23; 24 : 30.

3. [ADAR.]

E'dom (ē'dom), **Idumæ'a** or **Idume'a** (*red*). The name Edom was given to Esau, the first-born son of Isaac and twin brother of Jacob, when he sold his birthright to the latter for a meal of lentil pottage. Gen. 25 : 30. The country which the Lord subsequently gave to Esau was hence called "the country of Edom," Gen. 32 : 3, and his descendants were called Edomites. Gen. 36 : 43; Deut. 23 : 7. Edom was called

Arabah from the northern end of the Gulf of Elath to near the southern end of the Dead Sea. The ancient capital of Edom was Bozrah (*Buseireh*). Sela (Petra) appears to have been the principal stronghold in the days of Amaziah (B.C. 794). 2 Kings 14 : 7. Elath and Ezion-geber were the seaports. 2 Sam. 8 : 14; 1 Kings 9 : 26.

History.—Esau's bitter hatred of his brother Jacob for fraudulently obtaining his blessing appears to have been inherited by his latest posterity. The Edomites peremptorily refused to permit the Israelites to pass through their land. Num. 20 : 18–21. For a long period we hear no more of the Edomites. They were then attacked and defeated by Saul, 1 Sam. 14 : 47, and some forty years later by David. 2 Sam. 8 : 13, 14. In the reign of Jehoshaphat (B.C. 872) the Edomites attempted to invade Israel, but failed. 2 Chron. 20 : 22. They joined Nebuchadnezzar when that king besieged Jerusalem. For their cruelty this time they were fearfully denounced by the later prophets. Isa. 34 : 5–8; 63 : 1–4; Jer. 49 : 17. After this they settled in southern Palestine, and for more than four centuries continued to prosper. But during the warlike rule of the Maccabees they were again completely subdued, and even forced to conform to Jewish laws and rites, and submit to the government of Jewish prefects. The Edomites were now incorporated with the Jewish nation. They were idolaters. 2 Chron. 25 : 14, 15, 20. Their habits were singular. The Horites, their predecessors in Mount Seir, were supposed to have been *troglodytes,* or dwellers in caves, but they did not remain so, and

GORGE OF WADY SIK, IN EDOM.

Mount Seir and Idumea also. Edom was wholly a mountainous country. It embraced the narrow mountainous tract (about 100 miles long by 20 broad) extending along the eastern side of the

it may have been only the tradition of later generations. They were conquered by the Edomites, but intermarried with them.

E'domites (ē'dom-ītes). [EDOM.]

11

Ed'rei (ĕd're-i) (*strong*). 1. One of the two capital cities of Bashan, in the territory of Manasseh east of the Jordan. Num. 21:33; Deut. 1:4; 3:10; Josh. 12:4. In Scripture it is only mentioned in connection with the victory gained by the Israelites over the Amorites under Og their king, and the territory thus acquired. The ruins of this ancient city, still bearing the name *Edr'a*, stand on a rocky promontory which projects from the southwest corner of the Lejah. The ruins are nearly three miles in circumference, and have a strange, wild look, rising up in dark, shattered masses from the midst of a wilderness of black rocks. 2. A town of northern Palestine, allotted to the tribe of Naphtali, and situated near Kedesh. Josh. 19:37. The site is unknown, although Conder suggests *Ya'tir*. There is a rocky hill about two miles south of Kedesh which some think may be the site.

Education. There is little trace among the Hebrews in earlier times of education in any other subjects than the law. The wisdom therefore and instruction, of which so much is said in the book of Proverbs, are to be understood chiefly of moral and religious discipline, imparted, according to the direction of the law, by the teaching and under the example of parents. But Solomon himself wrote treatises on several scientific subjects, which must have been studied in those days. In later times the prophecies and comments on them, as well as on the earlier Scriptures, together with other subjects, were studied. Parents were required to teach their children some trade. Girls also were educated, and women generally among the Jews were treated with greater equality to men than in any other ancient nation. Previous to the captivity, there were no regular schools, the prophetical brotherhoods in nearly all cases providing that succession of public teachers who at various times endeavored to reform the moral and religious conduct of both rulers and people. Adults could always obtain instruction from the Levites and priests in the temple and elsewhere. [See SCHOOLS.]

Eg'lah (ĕg'lah) (*a heifer*), one of David's wives during his reign in Hebron. 2 Sam. 3:5; 1 Chron. 3:3.

Eg'laim (ĕg'la-im) (*two ponds*), a

place named only in Isa. 15:8. Its traditional site is 8 miles south of Areopolis.

Eg'lon (ĕg'lon) (*calf-like*). 1. A king of the Moabites, Judges 3:12 ff., who, aided by the Ammonites and the Amalekites, crossed the Jordan and took "the city of palm trees." Here, according to Josephus, he built himself a palace, and continued for eighteen years to oppress the children of Israel, who paid him tribute. He was slain by Ehud. [EHUD.] 2. A town of Judah in the low country. Josh. 15:39. The name survives in the modern *Ajlan*, 15 miles from Gaza. Petrie, however, declares this site unlikely and points out *Tell Nejileh* as probably the true site.

E'gypt (ē'gўpt) (*land of the Copts*), the country occupying the northeast angle of Africa. It is probably the oldest country in the world still existing, China alone being able to rival it in antiquity. Egypt proper is bounded on the north by the Mediterranean Sea, on the east by Palestine and the Red Sea, on the south by Nubia, and on the west by the Great Desert. It is divided into upper Egypt—the valley of the Nile—and lower Egypt, the plain of the Delta, from the Greek letter Δ; it is formed by the branching mouths of the Nile, and the Mediterranean Sea. The portion made fertile by the Nile under ordinary conditions is about 13,000 square miles; very nearly the area of the Netherlands. The extent of land really under cultivation changes continually. Egypt proper is about 660 miles long from north to south, and about 250 miles broad in the widest part.

NAMES.—The common name of Egypt in the Bible is "Mizraim." It is generally considered a dual form, indicating the two divisions of the country. The Arabic name of Egypt—*Mizr*—signifies "red mud." Egypt is also called in the Bible "the land of Ham," Ps. 105:23, 27, comp. 78:51—a name most probably referring to Ham the son of Noah —and "Rahab," the proud or insolent, Ps. 87:4, probably poetical appellations. The common ancient Egyptian name of the country is written in hieroglyphics Kem, which was perhaps pronounced Chem. This name signifies, in the ancient language and in Coptic, "black," on account of the blackness of its alluvial soil.

THE GREAT PYRAMIDS.

GENERAL APPEARANCE, CLIMATE, ETC. —The general appearance of the country cannot have greatly changed since the days of Moses. The whole country is remarkable for its extreme fertility, which especially strikes the beholder when the rich green of the fields is contrasted with the utterly bare, yellow atmosphere, except on the seacoast, is remarkably dry and clear, which accounts for the so perfect preservation of the monuments, with their pictures and inscriptions. The heat is extreme during a large part of the year, but owing to the dryness there is little discomfort and the nights are cool. The

SPHINX AND PYRAMIDS.

mountains or the sand-strewn rocky desert on either side. The climate is equable and healthy. Rain is not very unfrequent on the northern coast, but inland is very rare. Cultivation nowhere depends upon it. The inundation of the Nile fertilizes and sustains the country, and makes the river its chief blessing. The Nile was on this account anciently worshiped. A slight rise is discernible at the first cataract early in June. From that time it increases till the end of September, and the maximum level is held till the end of October or into November. The rise is 50 feet at Assouan and 25 at Cairo. The winters average 56° in the Delta, and 66° in upper Egypt.

CULTIVATION, AGRICULTURE, ETC.—The ancient prosperity of Egypt is attested by the Bible as well as by the numerous monuments of the country. As early as the age of the great pyramid it must have been densely populated. Egypt has naturally been an agricultural country. Vines were extensively cultivated. Of fruit trees, the date palm was the most common and valuable. The gardens resembled the fields, being watered in the same manner by irrigation. Egypt has neither woods nor forests. The commonest large trees are the sycomore fig, the acacia and the mulberry, the date palm and the banana. The best-known fruits are dates, grapes, figs, pomegranates, peaches, oranges, lemons, bananas, melons, olives and mulberries. All kinds of grain are abundant. The of wealth often had a harem whose inmates had no legal claim on him. There were no castes, although great classes were very distinct. The funeral ceremonies were far more important than any events of the Egyptian life,

PROCESS OF EMBALMING.   (From an Egyptian painting.)

gardens produce peas, beans, lentils, celery, radishes, carrots, lettuce, tomatoes, cucumbers, etc. Tobacco, sugar cane, cotton, hemp and flax are raised. The ancient reed, the papyrus, is nearly extinct.—*Encyc. Brit.*

RELIGION.—The basis of the religion was Nigritian fetichism, the lowest kind of nature worship, differing in different parts of the country, and hence obviously indigenous. Of the every-day religion of the people, we know practically nothing. We know the names of many deities, but not the way they were worshiped. The names too differed in different periods. Osiris was one of the earliest. The great doctrines of the immortality of the soul, man's responsibility, and future rewards and punishments, were taught. Among the rites, circumcision is the most remarkable: it is as old as the time of the fourth dynasty.

DOMESTIC LIFE.—The sculptures and paintings of the tombs give us a very full insight into the domestic life of the ancient Egyptians. What most strikes us in their manners is the high position occupied by women. There was but one legal wife, the mother of his heirs, who was her husband's equal in every respect. Besides this the man

as the tomb was regarded as the only true home.

INDUSTRIAL ARTS.—The industrial arts held an important place in the occupations of the Egyptians. The workers in fine flax and the weavers of white linen are mentioned in a manner that shows they were among the chief contributors to the riches of the country. Isa. 19:9. The fine linen of Egypt found its way to Palestine. Prov. 7:16. Pottery was a great branch of the native manufactures, and appears to have furnished employment to the Hebrews during the bondage. Ps. 68:13; 81:6; comp. Ex. 1:14.

HISTORY.—The history of Egypt is beset with difficulties. Chronology is very uncertain, there being many different theories. The connection with the Jews while perhaps the most important is no less a cause of much discussion. [EXODUS.] The ancient history of Egypt may be divided into four portions: the old monarchy, extending from the foundation of the kingdom till the middle of the 25th century B.C.; the middle kingdom till the close of the 18th century, the Hyksos period; and the new empire, from the re-establishment of the native monarchy by Amasis to the Persian conquest. 1. *The old monarchy.*—Memphis was the most ancient capital, the foundation of which is ascribed to Menes, the first mortal king of Egypt. The names of the kings, divided into thirty dynasties, are handed lords. After a period of conflict, during the reigns of Manetho's 7th to 10th dynasties, the true Middle Kingdom was founded, and lasted nearly 400 years. These were the 11th and 12th

OBELISKS.

down in the lists of Manetho,[1] and are also known from the works which they executed. The most memorable epoch in the history of the old monarchy is that of the Pyramid kings, placed in Manetho's fourth dynasty. Their names are found upon these monuments: *Khufu* or "Cheops" the builder of the great pyramid; *Khafra* of the second, and perhaps the Sphinx; and *Menkura* of the third.

2. *The middle kingdom.*—The old monarchy was ended about 2475 B.C. by the rise in power of the great feudal

dynasties of Manetho and included the kings known to us by the names of Amenemhet and Sesostris. To this second period is assigned the construction of the Lake of Moeris and the Labyrinth.

3. *The Hyksos period.*—The length of this period is variously estimated. Breasted thinks 200 years an ample allowance. It began by a period of confusion after which a foreign, nomadic power called the Hyksos,[2] controlled the country. Their capital was Memphis; and in the Sethroite nome they constructed an immense earth-camp, which they called Abaris. This is all that is known with any certainty of this period.

[1] Manetho was an Egyptian priest who lived under the Ptolemies in the third century B.C., and wrote in Greek a history of Egypt, in which he divided the kings into thirty dynasties. The work itself is lost, but the lists of dynasties have been preserved by the Christian writers.

[2] This, their Egyptian name, is derived by Manetho from *hyk*, a king, and *sos*, a shepherd, but this is discredited by some.

Finally, the Egyptians regained their independence and expelled the Hyksos. The three dynasties attributed to the Hyksos have no confirmation from the monuments, but it may be true. Manetho says they were Arabs, but he calls the six kings of the fifteenth dynasty Phœnicians. 4. *The new monarchy* extends from the commencement of the eighteenth to the end of the thirtieth dynasty. The kingdom was consolidated by Amasis, who succeeded in expelling the Hyksos, and thus prepared the way for the foreign expeditions which his successors carried on in Asia and Africa, extending from Mesopotamia in the former to Ethiopia in the latter continent. The glorious era of Egyptian history was under the nineteenth dynasty, when Sethi I., B.C. 1322, and his grandson, Rameses the Great, B.C. 1311, both of whom represent the Sesostris of the Greek historians, carried their arms over the whole of western Asia and southward into Soudân, and amassed vast treasures, which were expended on public works. Under the later kings of the nineteenth dynasty the power of Egypt faded: the twentieth and twenty-first dynasties achieved nothing worthy of record; but with the twenty-second we enter upon a period that is interesting from its associations with biblical history, the first of this dynasty, Sheshonk I. (Seconchis), B.C. 937, being the Shishak who invaded Judea in Rehoboam's reign and pillaged the temple. 1 Kings 14:25. Egypt makes no figure in Asiatic history during the twenty-third and twenty-fourth dynasties; under the twenty-fifth it regained, in part at least, its ancient importance. This was an Ethiopian line, the warlike sovereigns of which strove to the utmost to repel the onward stride of Assyria. So, whom we are disposed to identify with Shebek II. or Sebichus, the second Ethiopian, made an alliance with Hoshea, the last king of Israel. Tehrak or Tirhakah, the third of this house, advanced against Sennacherib in support of Hezekiah. After this a native dynasty—the twenty-sixth—of Saite kings again occupied the throne. Psametek I. or Psammetichus I. (B.C. 664), who may be regarded as the head of this dynasty, warred in Palestine, and took Ashdod (Azotus) after a siege of twenty-nine years. Neku or Necho, the son of Psammetichus. continued the

war in the east, and marched along the coast of Palestine to attack the king of Assyria. At Megiddo Josiah encountered him (B.C. 608), notwithstanding the remonstrance of the Egyptian king, which is very illustrative of the policy of the Pharaohs in the East, 2 Chron. 35:21, no less than is his lenient conduct after the defeat and death of the king of Judah. The army of Necho was after a short space routed at Carchemish by Nebuchadnezzar, B.C. 605–4. Jer. 46:2. The second successor of Necho, Apries, or Pharaoh-hophra, sent his army into Palestine to the aid of Zedekiah, Jer. 37:5, 7, 11—so that the siege of Jerusalem was raised for a time —and kindly received the fugitives from the captured city. He seems to have been afterwards attacked by Nebuchadnezzar in his own country. There is, however, no certain account of a complete subjugation of Egypt by the king of Babylon. Amasis, the successor of Apries, had a long and prosperous reign, and somewhat restored the weight of Egypt in the East. But the new power of Persia was to prove even more terrible to this house than Babylon had been to the house of Psammetichus, and the son of Amasis had reigned but six months when Cambyses reduced the country to a province of his empire, B.C. 525.

PRESENT CONDITIONS.—During modern times Egypt has been nominally a viceroyalty under the suzerainty of Turkey. Practically, however, Turkey has for years had no influence, the country having been controlled and administered by Great Britain. The Khedive, an hereditary ruler since 1866, governed through ministers subject to the approval of England. There was an English army of 3500 men, and the higher officers in the police and the native army were British. On March 16, 1922, the independence of Egypt with their hereditary native ruler as *king*, was acknowledged, and Great Britain withdrew. The actual size of Egypt is about the same as Arizona, New Mexico and Colorado; but its fertile land is only equal to the area of Massachusetts and Connecticut. The population of Egypt proper is about 17,000,000. The capital, Cairo, had in 1943 a population of 1,312,-096. Four-fifths of the people are of ancient Egyptian stock, whose forebears by their labor built the Pyramids for their kings. The bulk of the population is Moslem. Moslems form 91.4 per cent of the population, Christians 8.19 per cent, and Jews, 0.4 per cent. Public works greatly increased under British control. There is a fine system of irrigation, beginning with a large dam at Assouan, which was finished in 1903. It dams the water during the floods to a height of 65 ft. and regulates its flow during the rest of the year. Other dams at Assiout and Cairo, and a vast number of smaller dams and canals complete the system. The first railway was opened in 1855. The Suez canal was opened in 1869. Illiteracy, which was high until some years ago, is being eradicated by the Government. For children between the ages of 7 and 12, education is now compulsory, and is under the control of the state even when not state supported. The University of Alyhar, in Cairo, founded in A.D. 972, is the famous seat of Moslem learning. In addition, there is a modern and up-to-date university at Giya. There are also good teacher-training and technical schools. A new university, Faruk I University, has been established at Alexandria.

E'hi (ē'hī), head of one of the Benjamite houses according to the list in Gen. 46 : 21. He seems to be the same as Ahiram in the list in Num. 26 : 38. In 1 Chron. 8 : 1 he is called Aharah.

E'hud (ē'hŭd) (*union*). 1. Ehud son of Bilhan, and great-grandson of Benjamin the patriarch. 1 Chron. 7 : 10; 8 : 6.

2. Ehud son of Gera, of the tribe of Benjamin, Judges 3 : 15, the second judge of the Israelites. In the Bible he is not called a judge, but a deliverer : so Othniel, Judges 3 : 9, and all the Judges. Neh. 9 : 27. As a Benjamite he was specially chosen to destroy Eglon, who had established himself in Jericho, which was included in the boundaries of that tribe. He was very strong, and left-handed. [EGLON.]

E'ker (ē'kẽr) (*a rooting up*), a descendant of Judah, of the house of Jerahmeel. 1 Chron. 2 : 27.

Ek'ron (ĕk'rŏn) (*torn up by the roots; emigration*), one of the five towns belonging to the lords of the Philistines, and the most northerly of the five. Josh. 13 : 3. Like the other Philistine cities its situation was in the lowlands. It fell to the lot of Judah. Josh. 15 : 45, 46; Judges 1 : 18. Afterwards we find it mentioned among the cities of Dan. Josh. 19 : 43. Before the monarchy it was again in full posses-

sion of the Philistines. 1 Sam. 5 : 10. *Akir*, the modern Ekron, lies about five miles southwest of *Ramleh*.

El'adah (ĕl'a-dah) (*God hath adorned*), a descendant of Ephraim through Shuthelah. 1 Chron. 7 : 20.

E'lah (ē'lah) (*a terebinth*). 1. The son and successor of Baasha king of Israel. 1 Kings 16 : 8–10. His reign lasted for little more than a year; comp. ver. 8 with 10. (B.C. 891–89.) He was killed while drunk, by Zimri, in the house of his steward Arza, who was probably a confederate in the plot.

2. Father of Hoshea, the last king of Israel. 2 Kings 15 : 30; 17 : 1.

E'lah. 1. One of the dukes of Edom. Gen. 36 : 41; 1 Chron. 1 : 52.

2. Shimei ben-Elah was Solomon's commissariat officer in Benjamin. 1 Kings 4 : 18.

3. A son of Caleb the son of Jephunneh. 1 Chron. 4 : 15.

4. Son of Uzzi, a Benjamite, 1 Chron. 9 : 8, and one of the chiefs of the tribe at the time of the return to Judea. (B.C. 536.)

E'lah, The valley of (*valley of the terebinth*), the valley in which David killed Goliath. 1 Sam. 17 : 2, 19. It lay somewhere near Socoh of Judah and Azekah, and was nearer Ekron than any other Philistine town. 1 Sam. 17.

E'lam (ē'lam) (*highlands*). 1. This seems to have been originally the name of a man, the son of Shem. Gen. 10 : 22; 1 Chron. 1 : 17. Commonly, however, it is used as the appellation of a country. Gen. 14 : 1, 9; Isa. 11 : 11; 21 : 2. The Elam of Scripture appears to be the province lying south of Assyria and east of Persia proper, to which Herodotus gives the name of Cissia (iii. 91, *v.* 49, etc.), and which is termed Susis or Susiana by the geographers. Its capital was Susa. This country was originally peopled by descendants of Shem. By the time of Abraham a very important power had been built up in the same region. It is plain that at this early time the predominant power in lower Mesopotamia was Elam, which for a while held the place possessed earlier by Babylon, Gen. 10 : 10, and later by either Babylon or Assyria.

2. A Korhite Levite in the time of King David. 1 Chron. 26 : 3.

3. A chief man of the tribe of Benjamin. 1 Chron. 8 : 24.

4. "Children of Elam," to the number of 1254, returned with Zerubbabel from Babylon. Ezra 2 : 7; Neh. 7 : 12; and 75 more with Ezra. Ezra 8 : 7. Elam occurs amongst the names of the chief of the people who signed the covenant with Nehemiah. Neh. 10 : 14.

5. In the same lists is a second Elam, whose sons, to the same number as in the former case, returned with Zerubbabel, Ezra 2 : 31; Neh. 7 : 34, and which for the sake of distinction is called "the other Elam."

6. One of the priests who accompanied Nehemiah at the dedication of the new wall of Jerusalem. Neh. 12 : 42.

E'lamites. This word is mentioned in Ezra 4 : 9. The Elamites were the original inhabitants of the country called Elam; they were descendants of Shem, and perhaps drew their name from an actual man Elam. Gen. 10 : 22.

El'asah (ĕl'a-sah) (*God hath made*). 1. A priest in the time of Ezra who had married a Gentile wife. Ezra 10 : 22. (B.C. 458.)

2. Son of Shaphan, one of the two men who were sent on a mission by King Zedekiah to Nebuchadnezzar at Babylon. Jer. 29 : 3. (B.C. 594.)

E'lath (ē'lăth), **E'loth** (*a grove*), the name of a town of the land of Edom, commonly mentioned with Eziongeber, and situate at the head of the Arabian Gulf, which was thence called the Elanitic Gulf. It first occurs in the account of the wanderings, Deut. 2 : 8, and in later times must have come under the rule of David. 2 Sam. 8 : 14. We find the place named again in connection with Solomon's navy. 1 Kings 9 : 26; comp. 2 Chron. 8 : 17. In the Roman period it became a frontier town of the south and the residence of a Christian bishop. It is the modern *Akabah* or *Ailah*, which are mere heaps of rubbish.

El=beth'el (ĕl-bĕth'el) (*the God of Bethel*), the name which Jacob is said to have bestowed on the place at which God appeared to him when he was flying from Esau. Gen. 35 : 7. Compare EL-ELOHE-ISRAEL.

El'daah (ĕl'da-ah), Gen. 25 : 4; 1 Chron. 1 : 33, the last in order of the sons of Midian.

El'dad (ĕl'dăd) (*favored of God*) and **Me'dad** (*love*), two of the seventy elders to whom was communicated the prophetic power of Moses. Num. 11 : 16, 26. (B.C. 1490.) Although their names were upon the list which Moses had drawn up, Num. 11 : 26, they did not repair with the rest of their brethren to the tabernacle, but continued to prophesy in the camp. Moses, being requested by Joshua to forbid this, refused to do so, and expressed a wish that the gift of prophecy might be diffused throughout the people.

Elder. The term *elder,* or *old man* as the Hebrew literally imports, was one of extensive use, as an official title, among the Hebrews and the surrounding nations, because the heads of tribes and the leading people who had acquired influence were naturally the older people of the nation. It had reference to various offices. Gen. 24 : 2; 50 : 7; 2 Sam. 12 : 17; Ezek. 27 : 9. As betokening a political office, it applied not only to the Hebrews, but also to the Egyptians, Gen. 50 : 7, the Moabites and the Midianites. Num. 22 : 7. The earliest notice of the elders acting in concert as a political body is at the time of the Exodus. They were the representatives of the people, so much so that *elders* and *people* are occasionally used as equivalent terms; comp. Josh. 24 : 1 with 2, 19, 21; 1 Sam. 8 : 4 with 7, 10, 19. Their authority was undefined, and extended to all matters concerning the public weal. Their number and influence may be inferred from 1 Sam. 30 : 26 ff. They retained their position under all the political changes which the Jews underwent. The seventy elders mentioned in Exodus and Numbers were a sort of governing body, a parliament, and the origin of the tribunal of seventy elders called the Sanhedrin or Council. In the New Testament Church the elders or presbyters were the same as the bishops. It was an office derived from the Jewish usage of elders or rulers of the synagogues. [BISHOP.]

E'lead (ē'le-ăd) (*God hath testified*), a descendant perhaps son of Ephraim killed by the Gathites while plundering that town. 1 Chron. 7 : 21.

Elea'leh (ē-le-ā'leh) (*the ascending of God*), a place on the east of Jordan, taken possession of and rebuilt by the tribe of Reuben. Num. 32 : 3, 37. By Isaiah and Jeremiah it is mentioned as a Moabite town. Isa. 15 : 4; 16 : 9; Jer. 48 : 34.

Ele'asah (e-lē'a-sah) (*God hath made*). 1. Son of Helez, one of the descendants of Judah, of the family of Hezron. 1 Chron. 2 : 39.

2. Son of Rapha or Rephaiah; a descendant of Saul through Jonathan and Merib-baal or Mephibosheth. 1 Chron. 8 : 37; 9 : 43.

Elea'zar (ē-le-ā'zar) (*God has helped*). 1. Third son of Aaron. After the death of Nadab and Abihu without children, Lev. 10 : 6; Num. 3 : 4, Eleazar was appointed chief over the principal Levites. Num. 3 : 32. With his brother Ithamar he ministered as a priest during their father's lifetime, and immediately before his death was invested on Mount Hor with the sacred garments, as the successor of Aaron in the office of high priest. Num. 20 : 28. (B.C. 1452.) One of his first duties was in conjunction with Moses to superintend the census of the people. Num. 26 : 3. After the conquest of Canaan by Joshua he took part in the distribution of the land. Josh. 14 : 1. The time of his death is not mentioned in Scripture.

2. The son of Abinadab, of the Hill of Kirjath-jearim. 1 Sam. 7 : 1.

3. One of the three principal mighty men of David's army. 2 Sam. 23 : 9; 1 Chron. 11 : 12.

4. A Merarite Levite, son of Mahli and grandson of Merari. 1 Chron. 23 : 21, 22; 24 : 28.

5. A priest who took part in the feast of dedication under Nehemiah. Neh. 12 : 42. (B.C. 446.)

6. One of the sons of Parosh, an Israelite (*i. e.* a layman) who had married a foreign wife. Ezra 10 : 25.

7. Son of Phinehas, a Levite. Ezra 8 : 33.

8. The son of Eliud, in the genealogy of Jesus Christ. Matt. 1 : 15.

El-Elo'he-Is'rael (ĕl-e-lō'hė-is'ra-el) (*God, the God of Israel*), the name bestowed by Jacob on the altar which he erected facing the city of Shechem. Gen. 33 : 19, 20.

E'leph (ē'lef) (*the ox*), one of the towns allotted to Benjamin, and named next to Jerusalem. Josh. 18 : 28.

Elha'nan (ĕl-hā'nan) (*the grace of God*). 1. A distinguished warrior in the time of King David, who performed a memorable exploit against the Philistines. 2 Sam. 21 : 19; 1 Chron. 20 : 5.

2. One of "the thirty" of David's guard, and named first on the list. 2 Sam. 23 : 24; 1 Chron. 11 : 26.

E'li (ē'lī) (*ascension*), a descendant of Aaron through Ithamar, the younger of his two surviving sons. Lev. 10 : 1, 2, 12; comp. 1 Kings 2 : 27 with 2 Sam. 8 : 17; 1 Chron. 24 : 3. He was the first of the line of Ithamar who held the office of high priest. The office remained in his family till Abiathar was thrust out by Solomon, 1 Kings 1 : 7; 2 : 26, 27, when it passed back again to the family of Eleazar in the person of Zadok. 1 Kings 2 : 35. Its return to the elder branch was one part of the punishment which had been denounced against Eli during his lifetime, for his culpable negligence, 1 Sam. 2 : 22-25, when his sons profaned the priesthood; comp. 1 Sam. 2 : 27-36 with 1 Kings 2 : 27. Notwithstanding this one great blemish, the character of Eli is marked by eminent piety, as shown by his meek submission to the divine judgment, 1 Sam. 3 : 18, and his supreme regard for the ark of God. 1 Sam. 4 : 18. In addition to the office of high priest he held that of judge. He died at the advanced age of 98 years, 1 Sam. 4 : 15, overcome by the disastrous intelligence that the ark of God had been taken in battle by the Philistines, who had also slain his sons Hophni and Phinehas.

E'li, E'li, lama sabachthani. The Hebrew form, as Eloi, Eloi, etc., is the Syro-Chaldaic (the common language in use by the Jews in the time of Christ) of the first words of the twenty-second Psalm; they mean "*My God, my God, why hast thou forsaken me?*"

Eli'ab (ė-lī'ab) (*God is father*). 1. Son of Helon and leader of the tribe of Zebulun at the time of the census in the wilderness of Sinai. Num. 1 : 9; 2 : 7; 7 : 24, 29; 10 : 16. (B.C. 1490.)

2. A Reubenite, father of Dathan and Abiram. Num. 16 : 1, 12; 26 : 8, 9; Deut. 11 : 6.

3. One of David's brothers, the eldest of the family. 1 Sam. 16 : 6; 17 : 13, 28; 1 Chron. 2 : 13. His daughter ABIHAIL married Rehoboam. 2 Chron. 11 : 18.

4. A Levite in the time of David, who was both a "porter" and a musician on the "psaltery." 1 Chron. 15 : 18, 20; 16 : 5.

5. One of the warlike Gadite leaders who came over to David when he was in the wilderness taking refuge from Saul. 1 Chron. 12 : 9.

6. An ancestor of Samuel the prophet; a Kohathite Levite, son of Nahath. 1 Chron. 6 : 27.

Eli'ada (e-lī'a-da) (*known by God*). 1. One of David's sons; according to the lists, the youngest but one of the family born to him after his establishment in Jerusalem. 2 Sam. 5 : 16; 1 Chron. 3 : 8. Probably the same as BEELIADA.

2. A mighty man of war, a Benjamite, who led 200,000 of his tribe to the army of Jehoshaphat. 2 Chron. 17 : 17. (B.C. 875.)

Eli'adah (e-lī'a-da), father of Rezon, the captain of a marauding band that annoyed Solomon. 1 Kings 11 : 23.

Eli'ah (e-lī'ah) (*my God is Jehovah*). 1. A Benjamite, a chief man of the tribe. 1 Chron. 8 : 27.

2. One of the Bene-Elam, an Israelite (*i.e.* a layman) who had married a foreign wife. Ezra 10 : 26.

Eli'ahba (e-lī'ah-bà) (*whom God hides*), one of the thirty of David's guard. 2 Sam. 23 : 32; 1 Chron. 11 : 33.

Eli'akim (e-li'a-kĭm) (*raised up by God*). 1. Son of Hilkiah, master of Hezekiah's household ("over the house," as Isa. 36 : 3). 2 Kings 18 : 18, 26, 37. (B.C. 701.) Eliakim was a good man, as appears by the title emphatically applied to him by God, "my servant Eliakim," Isa. 22 : 20, and also in the discharge of the duties of his high station, in which he acted as a "father to the inhabitants of Jerusalem, and to the house of Judah." Isa. 22 : 21. He was one of three representatives of Hezekiah sent to confer with the Rabshakeh of Sennacherib, when the Assyrians were besieging Jerusalem. 2 Kings 18 : 18; 19 : 2.

2. The original name of Jehoiakim king of Judah. 2 Kings 23 : 34; 2 Chron. 36 : 4.

3. A priest in the days of Nehemiah, who assisted at the dedication of the new wall of Jerusalem. Neh. 12 : 41.

4. Eldest son of Abiud and father of Azor. Matt. 1 : 13.

5. Son of Melea, and father of Jonan. Luke 3 : 30, 31.

Eli'am (e-lī'am) (*God is kinsman*). 1. Father of Bath-sheba, the wife of David. 2 Sam. 11 : 3.

2. One of David's "thirty" warriors. 2 Sam. 23 : 34.

Eli'as (e-lī'as), the Greek form of Elijah.

Eli'asaph (e-lī'a-săf). 1. Head of the tribe of Gad at the time of the census in the wilderness of Sinai. Num.

1 : 14; 2 : 14; 7 : 42, 47; 10 : 20. (B.C. 1490.)

2. A Levite, and "chief of the Gershonites" at the same time. Num. 3 : 24.

Eli'ashib (e-lī'a-shĭb) (*God hath restored*). 1. A priest in the time of King David, eleventh in the order of the "governors" of the sanctuary. 1 Chron. 24 : 12.

2. One of the latest descendants of the royal family of Judah. 1 Chron. 3 : 24.

3. High priest at Jerusalem at the time of the rebuilding of the walls under Nehemiah. Neh. 3 : 1, 20, 21. (B.C. 446.)

4. A singer in the time of Ezra who had married a foreign wife. Ezra 10 : 24.

5. A son of Zattu, Ezra 10 : 27, and 6. A son of Bani, Ezra 10 : 36, both of whom had transgressed in the same manner. (B.C. 458.)

Eli'athah (e-lī'a-thath) (*God hath come*), a musician in the temple in the time of King David. 1 Chron. 25 : 4, 27.

Eli'dad (e-lī'dăd) (*whom God loves*), the man chosen to represent the tribe of Benjamin in the division of the land of Canaan. Num. 34 : 21. (B.C. 1452.)

Eli'el (e-lī'el) (*El is God*). 1. One of the heads of the tribe of Manasseh on the east of Jordan. 1 Chron. 5 : 24.

2. A forefather of Samuel the prophet. 1 Chron. 6 : 34.

3. A chief man in the tribe of Benjamin. 1 Chron. 8 : 20.

4. Also a Benjamite chief. 1 Chron. 8 : 22.

5. One of the heroes of David's guard. 1 Chron. 11 : 46.

6. Another of the same guard. 1 Chron. 11 : 47.

7. One of the Gadite heroes who came across Jordan to David when he was in the wilderness of Judah hiding from Saul. 1 Chron. 12 : 11.

8. A Kohathite Levite, at the time of transportation of the ark from the house of Obed-edom to Jerusalem. 1 Chron. 15 : 9, 11. (B.C. 1042.)

9. A Levite in the time of Hezekiah; one of the overseers of the offerings made in the temple. 2 Chron. 31 : 13.

Elie'nai (e-lī-ē'nā-ī) (*my eyes are toward Jehovah*), a descendant of Benjamin, and a chief man in the tribe. 1 Chron. 8 : 20.

Elie′zer (ė-li-ē′zēr) (*God is help*). 1. Abraham's chief servant, called by him "Eliezer of Damascus." Gen. 15 : 2. (B.C. 1857.)

2. Second son of Moses and Zipporah, to whom his father gave this name because "the God of my father was mine help, and delivered me from the sword of Pharaoh." Ex. 18 : 4; 1 Chron. 23 : 15, 17; 26 : 25.

3. One of the sons of Becher, the son of Benjamin. 1 Chron. 7 : 8.

4. A priest in the reign of David. 1 Chron. 15 : 24.

5. Son of Zichri, ruler of the Reubenites in the reign of David. 1 Chron. 27 : 16.

6. Son of Dodavah, of Mareshah in Judah, 2 Chron. 20 : 37, a prophet, who rebuked Jehoshaphat for joining himself with Ahaziah king of Israel. (B.C. 895.)

7. A chief Israelite whom Ezra sent with others from Ahava to Casiphia, to induce some Levites and Nethinim to accompany him to Jerusalem. Ezra 8 : 16. (B.C. 459.)

8, 9, 10. A priest, a Levite and an Israelite of the sons of Harim, who had married foreign wives. Ezra 10 : 18, 23, 31.

11. Son of Jorim, in the genealogy of Christ. Luke 3 : 29.

Elihoe′nai (*my eyes are toward Jehovah*), son of Zerahiah, who with 200 men returned from the captivity with Ezra. Ezra 8 : 4. (B.C. 459.)

Eliho′reph (ĕl-ĭ-hō′ref), one of Solomon's scribes. 1 Kings 4 : 3.

Eli′hu (ė-lī′hū) (*my God is he*). 1, One of the interlocutors in the book of Job. [JOB.] He is described as the "son of Barachel the Buzite."

2. A forefather of Samuel the prophet. 1 Sam. 1 : 1.

3. In 1 Chron. 27 : 18 Elihu "of the brethren of David" is mentioned as the chief of the tribe of Judah.

4. One of the captains of the thousands of Manasseh, 1 Chron. 12 : 20, who followed David to Ziklag after he had left the Philistine army on the eve of the battle of Gilboa.

5. A Korhite Levite in the time of David. 1 Chron. 26 : 7.

Eli′jah (ė-lī′jah) (*my God is Jehovah*) has been well entitled "the grandest and the most romantic char-

acter that Israel ever produced." "Elijah the Tishbite, . . . of the inhabitants of Gilead" is literally all that is given us to know of his parentage and locality. Of his appearance as he "stood before" Ahab (B.C. 868) with the suddenness of motion to this day characteristic of the Bedouins from his native hills, we can perhaps realize something from the touches, few but strong, of the narrative. His chief characteristic was his hair, long and thick, and hanging down his back. His ordinary clothing consisted of a girdle of skin round his loins, which he tightened when about to move quickly. 1 Kings 18 : 46. But in addition to this he occasionally wore the "mantle" or cape of sheepskin which has supplied us with one of our most familiar figures of speech. His introduction, in what we may call the first act of his life, is of the most startling description. He suddenly appears before Ahab, prophesies a three-years drought in Israel, and proclaims the vengeance of Jehovah for the apostasy of the king. Obliged to flee from the vengeance of the king, or more probably of the queen (comp. 1 Kings 19 : 2), he was directed to the brook Cherith. There in the hollow of the torrent bed he remained, supported in the miraculous manner with which we are all familiar, till the failing of the brook obliged him to forsake it. His next refuge was at Zarephath. Here in the house of the widow woman Elijah performed the miracles of prolonging the oil and the meal, and restored the son of the widow to life after his apparent death. 1 Kings 17. In this or some other retreat an interval of more than two years must have elapsed. The drought continued, and at last the full horrors of famine, caused by the failure of the crops, descended on Samaria. Again Elijah suddenly appears before Ahab. There are few more sublime stories in history than the account of the succeeding events—with the servant of Jehovah and his single attendant on the one hand, and the 850 prophets of Baal on the other; the altars, the descending fire of Jehovah consuming both sacrifice and altar; the rising storm, and the ride across the plain to Jezreel. 1 Kings 18. Jezebel vows vengeance, and again Elijah takes refuge in flight into the wilderness, where he is again miraculously fed, and goes forward, in the strength of that food, a journey of forty days to the mount of God, even to Horeb, where he takes refuge in a cave, and witnesses a remarkable vision of Jehovah. 1 Kings 19:9–18. He receives the divine communication, and sets forth in search of Elisha, whom he finds ploughing in the field, and anoints him prophet in his place, 19:19. For a time little is heard of Elijah, and Ahab and Jezebel probably believed they had seen the last of him. But after the murder of Naboth, Elijah, who had received an intimation from Jehovah of what was taking place, again suddenly appears before the king, and then follows Elijah's fearful denunciation of Ahab and Jezebel, which may possibly be recovered by putting together the words recalled by Jehu, 2 Kings 9:26, 36, 37, and those given in 1 Kings 21:19–25. A space of three or four years now elapses (comp. 1 Kings 22:1, 51; 2 Kings 1:17) before we again catch a glimpse of Elijah. Ahaziah is on his death-bed, 1 Kings 22:51; 2 Kings 1:1, 2, and sends to an oracle or shrine of Baal to ascertain the issue of his illness; but Elijah suddenly appears on the path of the messengers, without preface or inquiry utters his message of death, and as rapidly disappears. The wrathful king sends two bands of soldiers to seize Elijah, and they are consumed with fire; but finally the prophet goes down and delivers to Ahaziah's face the message of death. Not long after Elijah sent a message to Jehoram denouncing his evil doings, and predicting his death. 2 Chron. 21:12–15. It was at Gilgal—probably on the western edge of the hills of Ephraim—that the prophet received the divine intimation that his departure was at hand. He was at the time with Elisha, who seems now to have become his constant companion, and who would not consent to leave him. "And it came to pass as they still went on and talked, that, behold, a chariot of fire and horses of fire, and parted them both asunder; and Elijah went up by a whirlwind into heaven." (B.C. 853.) Fifty men of the sons of the prophets ascended the abrupt heights behind the town, and witnessed the scene. How deep was the impression which he made on the mind of the nation may be judged of from the fixed belief which many centuries after pre-

vailed that Elijah would again appear for the relief and restoration of his country, as Malachi prophesied. Mal. 4:5. He spoke, but left no written words, save the letter to Jehoram king of Judah. 2 Chron. 21:12–15.

Eli′ka (ĕl-ī′-kà), a Harodite, one of David's guard. 2 Sam. 23:25.

E′lim (ē′lim) (*strong trees*), Ex. 15:27; Num. 33:9, the second station where the Israelites encamped after crossing the Red Sea. It is distinguished as having had "twelve wells (rather 'fountains') of water, and three-score and ten palm trees." It is generally identified with *Wady Garundel,* about halfway down the shore of the Gulf of Suez. A few palm trees still remain, and the water is excellent.

Elim′elech (ĕ-lim′e-lĕk) (*God is king*), a man of the tribe of Judah and of the family of the Hezronites, who dwelt in Bethlehem-Ephratah in the days of the Judges, supposedly in the time of Gideon. In consequence of a great dearth in the land he went with his wife, Naomi, and his two sons, Mahlon and Chilion, to dwell in Moab, where he and his sons died without posterity. Ruth 1:2, 3, etc.

Elioe′nai (ĕ-lī-o-ē′na-ī) (*my eyes are toward Jehovah*). 1. Eldest son of Neariah, the son of Shemaiah. 1 Chron. 3:23, 24.

2. Head of a family of the Simeonites. 1 Chron. 4:36.

3. Head of one of the families of the sons of Becher, the son of Benjamin. 1 Chron. 7:8.

4. A Korhite Levite, and one of the doorkeepers of the "house of Jehovah." 1 Chron. 26:3.

5. A priest in the days of Ezra, one of those who had married foreign wives. Ezra 10:22. (B.C. 458.)

6. An Israelite of the sons of Zattu, who had also married a foreign wife. Ezra 10:27. (B.C. 458.)

Eli′phal (ĕl-ī′făl) (*God hath judged*), son of Ur, one of David's guard. 1 Chron. 11:35. [ELIPHELET, 3.]

Eliph′alet (ĕ-lĭf′a-lĕt) (*the God of deliverance*), the last of the thirteen sons born to David after his establishment in Jerusalem. 2 Sam. 5:16; 1 Chron. 14:7. [ELIPHELET, 2.]

El′iphaz (ĕl′ī-făz) (*God is his strength*). 1. The son of Esau and Adah, and the father of Teman. Gen. 36:4; 1 Chron. 1:35, 36.

2. The oldest and wisest of the three friends of Job. An Abraham-like saint, of a dignified and noble character, rather than brilliant or learned; "with a considerable likeness to Job himself in the general cast of his character and his tone of thought." Firm in his opinions; of plain common sense. He gives by far the noblest, gentlest, and most artistic expressions of the convictions and sentiments common to all. He was a chief from the land of Teman near the southern part of the Dead Sea. Probably a descendant of 1, who had a son Teman. Gen. 36 : 11.

Eliph'eleh (è-lĭf'e-leh) (*may God distinguish him*), a Merarite Levite, one of the gate-keepers appointed by David to play on the harp "on the Sheminith" on the occasion of bringing up the ark to the city of David. 1 Chron. 15 : 18, 21.

Eliph'elet (è-lĭf'e-lĕt) (*the God of deliverance*). 1. The name of a son of David, one of those born in Jerusalem. 1 Chron. 3 : 6. Also given ELPALET. 1 Chron. 14 : 7.

2. Another son of David, one of the Jerusalem family, and apparently the last of his sons. 1 Chron. 3 : 8.

3. One of the thirty warriors of David's guard. 2 Sam. 23 : 34.

4. Son of Eshek, a descendant of King Saul through Jonathan. 1 Chron. 8 : 39.

5. One of the leaders of the Bene-Adonikam who returned from Babylon with Ezra. Ezra 8 : 13. (B.C. 459.)

6. A man of the Bene-Hashum in the time of Ezra who had married a foreign wife. Ezra 10 : 33.

Elis'abeth (è-lĭs'a-bĕth) (*God is an oath*), the wife of Zacharias and mother of John the Baptist. She was herself of the priestly family, and a relation, Luke 1 : 36, of the mother of our Lord.

Elise'us (ĕl-ĭ-sē'us), the Greek form of the name Elisha. Luke 4 : 27.

Eli'sha (è-lī'shà) (*God is salvation*), son of Shaphat of Abel-meholah; the attendant and disciple of Elijah, and subsequently his successor as prophet of the kingdom of Israel. The earliest mention of his name is in the command to Elijah in the cave at Horeb. 1 Kings 19 : 16, 17. (B.C. about 840.) Elijah sets forth to obey the command, and comes upon his successor engaged in ploughing. He crosses to him and throws over his shoulders the rough mantle—a token at once of investiture with the prophet's office and of adoption as a son. Elisha delayed merely to give the farewell kiss to his father and mother and preside at a parting feast with his people, and then followed the great prophet on his northward road. We hear nothing more of Elisha for 6 or 8 years, until the translation of his master, when he reappears, to become the most prominent figure in the history of his country during the rest of his long life.

In almost every respect Elisha presents the most complete contrast to Elijah. Elijah was a true Bedouin child of the desert. If he enters a city it is only to deliver his message of fire and be gone. Elisha, on the other hand, is a civilized man, an inhabitant of cities. His dress was the ordinary garment of an Israelite, the *beged,* probably similar in form to the long *abbeyeh* of the modern Syrians. 2 Kings 2 : 12. His hair was worn trimmed behind, in contrast to the disordered locks of Elijah, and he used a walking-staff, 2 Kings 4 : 29, of the kind ordinarily carried by grave or aged citizens. Zech. 8 : 4. After the departure of his master, Elisha returned to dwell at Jericho, 2 Kings 2 : 18, where he miraculously purified the springs. We next meet with Elisha at Bethel, in the heart of the country, on his way from Jericho to Mount Carmel. 2 Kings 2 : 23. The mocking children, Elisha's curse and the catastrophe which followed are familiar to all. Later he extricates Jehoram king of Israel, and the kings of Judah and Edom, from their difficulty in the campaign against Moab arising from want of water. 2 Kings 3 : 4–27. Then he multiplies the widow's oil. 2 Kings 4 : 5–7. The next occurrence is at Shunem, where he is hospitably entertained by a woman of substance, whose son dies, and is brought to life again by Elisha. 2 Kings 4 : 8–37. Then at Gilgal he purifies the deadly pottage, 2 Kings 4 : 38–41, and multiplies the loaves. 2 Kings 4 : 42–44.

The simple records of these domestic incidents amongst the sons of the prophets are now interrupted by an occurrence of a more important character. 2 Kings 5 : 1–27. The chief captain of the army of Syria, Naaman, is attacked with leprosy, and is sent by an Israelite maid to the prophet Elisha, who directs him to dip seven times in the Jordan, which he does and is healed, 2 Kings 5 : 1–14; while Elisha's servant, Gehazi, is stricken with leprosy for his unfaithfulness, ch. 5 : 20–27. Again the scene changes. It is perhaps at Jericho that Elisha causes the iron axe to swim. 2 Kings 6 : 1–7. A band of Syrian marauders are sent to seize him, but are struck blind, and he misleads them to Samaria, where they find themselves in the presence of the Israelite king and his troops. 2 Kings 6 : 8–23. During the famine in Samaria, 2 Kings 6 : 24–33, he prophesied incredible plenty, ch. 7 : 1–2, which was soon fulfilled, ch. 7 : 3–20. We next find the prophet at Damascus. Benhadad the king is sick, and sends to Elisha by Hazael to know the result. Elisha prophesies the king's death, and announces to Hazael that he is to succeed to the throne. 2 Kings 8 : 7–15. Finally this prophet of God, after having filled the position for sixty years, is found on his death-bed in his own house. 2 Kings 13 : 14–19. The power of the prophet, however, does not terminate with his death. Even in the tomb he restores the dead to life, ch. 13 : 21.

Eli'shah (è-lī'shah) (*God is salvation*), the eldest son of Javan. Gen. 10 : 4. The residence of his descendants is described in Ezek. 27 : 7 as the isles of Elishah, whence the Phœnicians obtained their purple and blue dyes. The two most plausible identifications are that with southern Italy and Sicily, where were Greek colonies; and that with Carthage or the north African coast.

Elish'ama (è-lĭsh'a-mà) (*God has heard*). 1. The "prince" or "captain" of the tribe of Ephraim in the wilderness of Sinai. Num. 1 : 10; 2 : 18; 7 : 48; 10 : 22. (B.C. 1491.) From 1 Chron. 7 : 26 we find that he was grandfather to the great Joshua.

2. A son of King David. 2 Sam. 5 : 16; 1 Chron. 3 : 8; 14 : 7.

3. Another son of David, 1 Chron. 3 : 6, who in the other lists is called Elishua, which is probably correct.

4. A descendant of Judah. 1 Chron. 2 : 41.

5. The father of Nethaniah and grandfather of Ishmael. 2 Kings 25 : 25; Jer. 41 : 1. Probably same as

6. Scribe to King Jehoiakim. Jer. 36 : 12, 20, 21. (B.C. 605.)

7. A priest in the time of Jehoshaphat. 2 Chron. 17 : 8. (B.C. 870.)

Elish'aphat (è-lĭsh'a-făt) (*God hath judged*), son of Zichri; one of the captains of hundreds in the time of Jehoiada. 2 Chron. 23 : 1. (B.C. 836.)

Elish'eba (è-lĭsh'e-bà) (*God is an oath*), the wife of Aaron. Ex. 6 : 23. She was the daughter of Amminadab, and sister of Nahshon the captain of the host of Judah. Num. 2 : 3.

Elish'ua (è-lĭsh'-u-ạ) (*God is salvation*), one of David's sons, born after his settlement in Jerusalem. 2 Sam. 5 : 15; 1 Chron. 14 : 5.

Eli'ud (è-lī'ŭd) (perhaps *God of Judah*), son of Achim in the genealogy of Christ. Matt. 1 : 15.

Eliz'aphan (è-lĭz'a-fan) (*God has protected*). 1. A Levite, son of Uzziel, chief of the house of the Kohathites at the time of the census in the wilderness of Sinai. Num. 3 : 30. (B.C. 1491.)

2. Prince of the tribe of Zebulun. Num. 34 : 25.

Eli'zur (è-lī'zur), prince of the tribe and over the host of Reuben. Num. 1 : 5; 2 : 10; 7 : 30, 35; 10 : 18.

El'kanah (ĕl'kă-nah), or **El'konah** (*God has possessed*). 1. Son, or grandson (see 1 Chron. 6 : 22, 23), of Korah, according to Ex. 6 : 24.

2. A descendant of the above in the line of Ahimoth, otherwise Mahath, 1 Chron. 6 : 26, 35.

3. Another Kohathite Levite, father of Samuel the illustrious judge and prophet. 1 Chron. 6 : 27, 34. All that is known of him is contained in the above notices and in 1 Sam. 1 : 1, 4, 8, 19, 21, 23 and 2 : 11, 20.

4. A Levite. 1 Chron. 9 : 16.

5. A Korhite who joined David while he was at Ziklag. 1 Chron. 12 : 6. (B.C. 1057.)

6. An officer in the household of Ahaz king of Judah, who was slain by Zichri the Ephraimite when Pekah invaded Judah. 2 Chron. 28 : 7. (B.C. 735.)

El'kosh (ĕl'kosh) (*God my bow*), the birthplace of the prophet Nahum, hence called "the Elkoshite." Nah. 1 : 1. The tradition placing it at Alkush on the Tigris is late. Jerome located it in Galilee; and perhaps the most credible site is *Beit Jibrin* in Simeon.

El'lasar (ĕl'la-sär) (*oak*), the city of Arioch, Gen. 14 : 1, seems to be the Hebrew representative of the old Chaldean town called in the native dialect *Larsa*. *Larsa* was a town of lower Babylonia or Chaldea, situated nearly halfway between Ur (*Mugheir*) and Erech

(*Warka*), on the left bank of the Euphrates. It is now *Senkereh*.

Elm. Hos. 4 : 13. [See OAK.]

Elmo'dam (ĕl-mō'dăm), son of Er, in the genealogy of Joseph. Luke 3 : 28. R. V. Elmadam.

El'naam (ĕl'nā-am) (*God is pleasantness*), the father of Jeribai and Joshaviah, two of David's guard, according to 1 Chron. 11 : 46.

El'nathan (ĕl'na-thăn), or **Elna'than** (*God hath given*). 1. The maternal grandfather of Jehoiachin, 2 Kings 24 : 8; the same with Elnathan the son of Achbor. Jer. 26 : 22; 36 : 12, 25.

2. The name of three persons, apparently Levites, in the time of Ezra. Ezra 8 : 16.

El'loi. [ELI.]

E'lon (ē'lŏn) (*a terebinth*). 1. A Hittite, whose daughter was one of Esau's wives. Gen. 26 : 34; 36 : 2. (B.C. 1797.)

2. The second of the three sons attributed to Zebulun, Gen. 46 : 14; Num. 26 : 26, and the founder of the family of the Elonites. (B.C. 1706.)

3. Elon the Zebulonite, who judged Israel for ten years, and was buried in Aijalon in Zebulun. Judges 12 : 11, 12.

4. One of the towns in the border of the tribe of Dan. Josh. 19 : 43. It is not identified.

E'lon=beth=ha'nan (*terebinth of the house of grace*) is named with two Danite towns as forming one of Solomon's commissariat districts. 1 Kings 4 : 9.

E'lonites (ē'lon-ītes), **The.** Num. 26 : 26. [ELON, 2.]

E'loth (ē'lŏth). 1 Kings 9 : 26. [ELATH.]

Elpa'al (*God of doing?*), a Benjamite, son of Shaharaim by his wife Hushim, and brother of Abitub. 1 Chron. 8 : 11. He was the founder of a numerous family.

El'palet (ĕl'pa-lĕt) (*God his deliverance*), one of David's sons born in Jerusalem. 1 Chron. 14 : 5. Also called Eliphelet.

El-pa'ran (ĕl-pā'ran) (*the tree*, i. e. the palm-tree or "the terebinth" of *Paran*). Gen. 14 : 6. [PARAN.]

El'tekeh (ĕl'tē-keh) (*God its fear*), one of the cities in the border of Dan, Josh. 19 : 44, which with its suburbs was allotted to the Kohathite Levites. Josh. 21 : 23. It is mentioned in the records of Sennacherib with Ekron.

El'tekon (ĕl'te-kŏn) (*God is firmness*), one of the towns of the tribe of Judah in the mountains. Josh. 15 : 59. It has not yet been identified.

El'tolad (ĕl'to-lăd) (*birth*, *race*), one of the cities in the south of Judah, Josh. 15 : 30, allotted to Simeon, Josh. 19 : 4, and in possession of that tribe until the time of David. 1 Chron. 4 : 29.

E'lul (ē'lŭl). Neh. 6 : 15. [MONTH.]

Elu'zai (e-lū'za-i) (*God is my strength*), one of the warriors of Benjamin who joined David at Ziklag. 1 Chron. 12 : 5. (B.C. 1057.)

El'ymas (ĕl'-ȳ-măs) (*a wise man*), the Arabic name of the Jewish magus or sorcerer Bar-jesus. Acts 13 : 6 ff. (A.D. 49.)

El'zabad (ĕl'za-băd) (*God hath given*). 1. One of the Gadite heroes who came across the Jordan to David. 1 Chron. 12 : 12.

2. A Korhite Levite. 1 Chron. 26 : 7.

El'zaphan (ĕl'za-făn) (*God has protected*), second son of Uzziel, who was the son of Kohath son of Levi. Ex. 6 : 22. [ELIZAPHAN, 1.]

Embalming, the process by which dead bodies are preserved from putrefaction and decay. It was most general among the Egyptians, and it is in connection with this people that the two instances which we meet with in the Old Testament are mentioned. Gen. 50 : 2, 26. The embalmers first removed part of the brain through the nostrils, by means of a crooked iron, and destroyed the rest by injecting caustic drugs. An incision was then made along the flank with a sharp Ethiopian stone, and the whole of the intestines removed. The cavity was rinsed out with palm wine, and afterwards scoured with pounded perfumes. It was then filled with pure myrrh pounded, cassia and other aromatics, except frankincense. This done, the body was sewn up and steeped in natron (saltpeter) for seventy days. When the seventy days were accomplished, the embalmers washed the corpse and swathed it in bandages of linen, cut in strips and smeared with gum. They then gave it up to the relatives of the deceased, who provided for it a wooden case, made in the shape of a man, in which the dead was placed, and deposited in an erect position against the wall of the sepulchral chamber. Sometimes no incision was made in the body, nor were the intestines removed, but cedar-oil was injected into the stomach by the rectum. At others the oil was prevented from escaping until the end of the steeping process, when it was withdrawn, and carried off with it the stomach and intestines in a state of solution, while the flesh was consumed by the natron, and nothing was left but the skin and bones. The body in this state was returned to the relatives of the deceased. The third mode, which was adopted by the poorer classes, and cost but little, consisted in rinsing out the intestines with syrmæa, an infusion of senna and cassia, and steeping the body for several days in natron. It does not appear that embalming was practiced by the Hebrews. The cost of embalming was sometimes nearly $2000, varying from this amount down to $200 or $300.

Embroiderer. Various explanations have been offered as to the distinction between "*needle-work*" and "*cunning work.*" Probably neither term expresses just what is to-day understood by embroidery, though the latter may come nearest to it. The art of embroidery by the loom was extensively practiced among the nations of antiquity. In addition to the Egyptians, the Babylonians were celebrated for it.

Emerald, the rendering of two different words, the meaning of either being doubtful. This gem was the first in the second row on the breastplate of the high priest. Ex. 28:18; 39:11. It was imported to Tyre from Syria. Ezek. 27 : 16; was used as an ornament of clothing and bedding, Ezek. 28 : 13, and is spoken of as one of the foundations of Jerusalem. Rev. 21 : 19. The rainbow around the throne is compared to an emerald in Rev. 4 : 3.

Emerods. Deut. 28 : 27; 1 Sam. 5 : 6, 9, 12; 6 : 4, 5, 11. The word means hemorrhoids, which are very common in Syria at present, owing to Oriental habits of want of exercise and improper food. There is, however, some question as to what is intended in the Bible by the word. The R. V. margin in Deut., and the R. V. text in 1 Sam. has "tumors."

E'mims (ē'mimş) (*terrors*), correctly Emim, which is the plural form of the Hebrew. Gen. 14 : 5; Deut. 2 : 10. A tribe or family of gigantic stature which

originally inhabited the region along the eastern side of the Dead Sea. They were related to the Anakim.

Emman'uel (ĕm-măn'u-el). Matt. 1 : 23. [IMMANUEL.]

Em'maus (em'mā-us), or **Emma'us** (em-mā'us) (*warm baths*), the village to which the two disciples were going when our Lord appeared to them on the way, on the day of his resurrection. Luke 24 : 13. Luke makes its distance from Jerusalem *sixty stadia* (Authorized Version "threescore furlongs"), or about 7½ miles; and Josephus mentions "a village called Emmaus" at the same distance. The site of Emmaus is uncertain.

Em'mor (ĕm'môr) (*an ass*), the father of Shechem. Acts 7 : 16. [HAMOR.]

En, at the beginning of many Hebrew words, signifies a spring or fountain.

E'nam (ē'nam) (*the two springs*), one of the cities of Judah in the *Shefe-lah* or lowland. Josh. 15 : 34.

E'nan (ē'nan) (*having eyes*). Ahira ben-Enan was "prince" of the tribe of Naphtali at the time of the numbering of Israel in the wilderness of Sinai. Num. 1 : 15.

Encampment primarily denoted the resting-place of an army or company of travelers at night, Gen. 32 : 21; Ex. 16 : 13, and was hence applied to the army or caravan when on its march. Gen. 32 : 8, 13; Ex. 14 : 19; Josh. 10 : 5; 11 : 5. The description of the camp of the Israelites, on their march from Egypt, Num. 2, 3, supplies the greatest amount of information on the subject. The tabernacle, corresponding to the chieftain's tent of an ordinary encampment, was placed in the centre, and around and facing it, Num. 2 : 2, arranged in four grand divisions, corresponding to the four points of the compass, lay the host of Israel, according to their standards. Num. 1 : 52; 2 : 2. In the centre, round the tabernacle, and with no standard but the cloudy or fiery pillar which rested over it, were the tents of the priests and Levites. The former, with Moses and Aaron at their head, were encamped on the eastern side. The order of encampment was preserved on the march. Num. 2 : 17.

Enchantments. The words so translated have several significations: the practice of secret arts. Ex. 7:11, 22;

12

8:7; "muttered spells," 2 Kings 9:22; Micah 5:12; the charming of serpents, Eccles. 10:11; the enchantments sought by Balaam, Num. 24:1; the use of magic, Isa. 47:9, 12. Any resort to these methods of imposture was strictly forbidden in Scripture, Lev. 19:26; Isa. 47:9, etc.; but to eradicate the tendency is almost impossible, 2 Kings 17:17, and we find it still flourishing at the Christian era. Acts 13:6, 8.

En'=dor (ĕn'dôr) (*fountain of Dor*), a place in the territory of Issachar, and yet possessed by Manasseh. Josh. 17:11. Endor was the scene of the great victory over Sisera and Jabin. It was here that the witch dwelt whom Saul consulted. 1 S a m. 28:7. It was known to Eusebius, who describes it as a large village four miles south of Tabor. Here to the north of *Jebel Duhy* the n a m e still lingers. The distance from the slopes of Gilboa to Endor is seven or eight miles, over difficult ground.

En=eg'laim (ĕn-ĕg'la-ĭm) (*fountain of two calves*), a place named only by Ezekiel, 47:10, apparently a s o n t h e D e a d S e a; b u t whether near t o o r f a r from Engedi, on the east or the west side of the sea, it is impossible to ascertain.

En-gan'nim (ĕn-găn'nim) (*fountain of gardens*). 1. A city in the low country o f Judah, named between Zanoah a n d T a p p u a h. Josh. 15:34.

2. A city o n t h e border of Issachar, Josh. 19:21, allotted with its "suburbs" to the Gershonite Levites, Josh. 21:29; p r o b a b l y *Jenîn,* the first village encountered o n t h e ascent from the great plain of Esdraelon into the hills of the central country.

En-ge'di (ĕn-gē'dī) or **En'=gedi** (*fount of the kid*), a town in the wilderness of Judah, Josh. 15:62, on the western shore of the Dead Sea. Ezek. 47:10. Its original name was Hazazontamar, on account of the palm groves which surrounded it. 2 Chron. 20:2. Its site is about the middle o f the western shore of the lake, at the fountain of

Ain Jidy, from which the place gets its name. It was immediately after an assault upon the "Amorites that dwelt in Hazezon-tamar," that the five Mesopotamian kings were attacked by the rulers of the plain of Sodom. Gen. 14:7; comp. 2 Chron. 20:2. Saul was told that David was in the "wilderness of Engedi;" and he took "three thousand men, and went to seek David and his men upon the rocks of the *wild goats.*" 1 Sam. 24:1-4. The vineyards of Engedi were celebrated in Palestine. Cant. 1:14.

Engine, a term applied exclusively to military affairs in the Bible. The engines to which the term is applied in 2

BATTERING RAM.

Chron. 26:15 were designed to propel various missiles from the walls of a besieged town. One, with which the Hebrews were acquainted, was the battering ram, described in Ezek. 26:9, and still more precisely in Ezek. 4:2; 21:22.

Engraver. His chief business was cutting names or devices on rings and seals; the only notices of engraving are in connection with the high priest's dress—the two onyx stones, the twelve jewels and the mitreplate having inscriptions on them. Ex. 28 : 11, 21, 36.

En=had′dah (ĕn-hăd′dah) (*swift fountain*), one of the cities on the border of Issachar named next to Engannim. Josh. 19 : 21.

En=hak′ko=re (ĕn-hăk′kò-re) (*fount of the caller*), the spring which burst out in answer to the cry of Samson after his exploit with the jawbone. Judges 15 : 19. It was long pointed out, but modern investigation makes its identification doubtful.

En=ha′zor (ĕn-hā′zôr) (*fount of Hazor*), one of the fenced cities in the inheritance of Naphtali, distinct from Hazor. Josh. 19 : 37. It has not yet been identified with certainty.

En=mish′pat (ĕn-mĭsh′pat) (*fount of judgment*). Gen. 14 : 7. [KADESH.]

E′noch (ē′nŏk) (*dedicated*). 1. The eldest son of Cain, Gen. 4 : 17, who called after his name the city which he built. Gen. 4 : 18.

2. The son of Jared and father of Methuselah. Gen. 5 : 21 ff.; Luke 3 : 37. (B.C. 3382–3017.) In the Epistle of Jude, 14, he is described as " the *seventh* from Adam;" and the number is probably noticed as conveying the idea of divine completion and rest, while Enoch was himself a type of perfected humanity. After the birth of Methuselah it is said, Gen. 5 : 22–24, that Enoch " walked with God three hundred years . . . and he was not; for God took him." The phrase " walked with God " is elsewhere only used of Noah, Gen. 6 : 9; cf. Gen. 17 : 1, etc., and is to be explained of a prophetic life spent in immediate converse with the spiritual world. Like Elijah, he was translated without seeing death. In the Epistle to the Hebrews the spring and issue of Enoch's life are clearly marked. Both the Latin and Greek fathers commonly coupled Enoch and Elijah as historic witnesses of the possibility of a resurrection of the body and of a true human existence in glory.

E′noch, The Book of. The first trace of the existence of this work is found in the Epistle of Jude, 14, 15. An apocryphal book called Enoch was known at a very early date, but was lost sight of until 1773, when Bruce brought with him on his return from Egypt three MSS. containing the complete Ethiopic translation. In its present shape the book consists of a series of revelations supposed to have been given to Enoch and Noah, which extend to the most varied aspects of nature and life, and are designed to offer a comprehensive vindication of the action of Providence. Notwithstanding the quotation in Jude, and the wide circulation of the book itself, the apocalypse of Enoch was uniformly and distinctly separated from the canonical Scriptures. Its authorship and date are unknown.

E′non, see ÆNON.

E′nos (ē′nos) (*mortal man*), the son of Seth, Gen. 4 : 26; 5 : 6, 7, 9, 10, 11; Luke 3 : 38; properly ENOSH, as in 1 Chron. 1 : 1.

E′nosh. Same as ENOS. 1 Chron. 1 : 1.

En=rim′mon (ĕn-rĭm′mon) (*fount of the pomegranate*), one of the places which the men of Judah reinhabited after their return from the captivity. Neh. 11 : 29. Perhaps the same as " Ain and Rimmon," Josh. 15 : 32, and " Ain, Remmon," Josh. 19 : 7; and see 1 Chron. 4 : 32.

En=ro′gel (ĕn-rō′gel) (*fount of the fuller*), a spring which formed one of the landmarks on the boundary line between Judah, Josh. 15 : 7, and Benjamin. Josh. 18 : 16. It may be identified with the present " Fountain of the Virgin," '*Ain Umm ed-Daraj*, the perennial source from which the pool of Siloam is supplied. 2 Sam. 17 : 17.

En=she′mesh (ĕn-shĕ′mesh) (*fountain of the sun*), a spring which formed one of the landmarks on the north boundary of Judah, Josh. 15 : 7, and the south boundary of Benjamin, Josh. 18 : 17; perhaps *Ain-Haud* or *Ain-Chôt* —the " well of the apostles "—about a mile below Bethany.

Ensign (*nês;* in the Authorized Version generally " ensign," sometimes " standard;" *degel,* " standard," with the exception of Cant. 2 : 4, " banner;" *ôth,* " ensign "). The distinction between these three Hebrew terms is sufficiently marked by their respective uses. *Nês* is a *signal,* and not a military standard. It is an occasional signal, which was exhibited on the top of a pole from a bare mountain-top, Isa. 13 : 2; 18 : 3; *degel* a military *standard* for a large division of an army; and *ôth* the same for a small one. Neither of them, however, expresses the idea which " standard " conveys to our minds, viz. a flag. The standards in use among the Hebrews probably resembled those of the Egyptians and Assyrians—a figure or device of some kind elevated on a pole; usually a sacred emblem, such as an animal, a boat, or the king's name.

En=tap'puah. Josh. 17 : 7. [See TAPPUAH.]

Epaen'etus (ė-pĕn'e-tus) (*praiseworthy*), a Christian at Rome, greeted by St. Paul in Rom. 16 : 5, and designated as his beloved and the first-fruit of Achaia unto Christ.

Ep'aphras (ĕp'a-frăs) (*lovely*), a fellow laborer with the apostle Paul, mentioned Col. 1 : 7 as having taught the Colossian church the grace of God in truth, and designated a faithful minister of Christ on their behalf. He was at that time with St. Paul at Rome. (A.D. 62.) For Paul's estimate of him see Col. 1 : 7, 8; 4 : 12.

Epaphrodi'tus (ė-păf-ro-dī'tus) (*lovely*), the full name of which Epaphras is a contraction. Philip. 2 : 25; 4 : 18.

E'phah (ē'fah) (*darkness*), the first, in order, of the sons of Midian, Gen. 25 : 4; 1 Chron. 1 : 33, afterwards mentioned by Isaiah. Isa. 60 : 6.

E'phah. 1. Concubine of Caleb, in the line of Judah. 1 Chron. 2 : 46.

2. Son of Jahdai; also in the line of Judah. 1 Chron. 2 : 47.

Ephah. [WEIGHTS AND MEASURES.]

E'phai (ē'fā-i) (*fatigued*), a Netophathite, whose sons were among the "captains of the forces" left in Judah after the deportation to Babylon. Jer. 40 : 8; 41 : 3, comp. 40 : 13. (B.C. 586.)

E'pher (ē'fẽr) (*a calf*). 1. The second, in order, of the sons of Midian. Gen. 25 : 4; 1 Chron. 1 : 33.

2. A son of Ezra, among the descendants of Judah. 1 Chron. 4 : 17.

3. One of the heads of the families of Manasseh on the east of Jordan. 1 Chron. 5 : 24.

E'phes=dam'mim (ē'fes-dam'mim), a place between Socoh and Azekah, at which the Philistines were encamped before the affray in which Goliath was killed. 1 Sam. 17 : 1. Under the shorter form of PAS-DAMMIN it occurs once again in a similar connection. 1 Chron. 11 : 13.

Ephe'sians, The Epistle to the, was written by the apostle St. Paul during his first captivity at Rome, Acts 28 : 16, apparently immediately after he had written the Epistle to the Colossians [COLOSSIANS, EPISTLE TO], very

probably about A.D. 62, though there is a difference of opinion (See Hastings' *Bible Dictionary*). The Epistle was very likely intended as a "circular letter" to the church at Ephesus and those near in Asia. [EPHESUS.] Its contents may be divided into two portions, the first mainly *doctrinal,* ch. 1–3, the second *hortatory* and *practical.*

Eph'esus (ĕf'e-sus) (*permission*), the capital of the Roman province of Asia, and an illustrious city in the district of Ionia, nearly opposite the island of Samos.

Buildings.—Conspicuous at the head of the harbor of Ephesus was the great *temple of Diana* or Artemis, the tutelary divinity of the city. This building was raised on immense substructions, in con-

COIN OF EPHESUS.

sequence of the swampy nature of the ground. The earlier temple, which had been begun before the Persian war, was burnt down in the night when Alexander the Great was born; and another structure, raised by the enthusiastic cooperation of all the inhabitants of "Asia," had taken its place. The magnificence of this sanctuary was a proverb throughout the civilized world. In consequence of this devotion the city of Ephesus was called νεώκορος, Acts 19 : 35, or "warden" of Diana. Another consequence of the celebrity of Diana's worship at Ephesus was that a large manufactory grew up there of portable shrines, which strangers purchased, and devotees carried with them on journeys or set up in their houses. The *theatre,* into which the mob who had seized on Paul, Acts 19 : 29, rushed, was capable of holding 21,000 or over, and is claimed to be the largest ever built by the Greeks. The *stadium* or circus, 850 feet long by 200 wide, where the Ephesians held their shows, is ascribed to the time of Augustus. Paul's expression "fought with beasts at Ephesus." 1 Cor. 15 : 32, is probably figurative.

RUINS OF TEMPLE OF DIANA, EPHESUS, REAR VIEW.

Connection with Christianity.—The Jews were established at Ephesus in considerable numbers. Acts 2:9; 6:9. It is here and here only that we find disciples of John the Baptist explicitly mentioned after the ascension of Christ. Acts 18:25; 19:3. The first seeds of Christian truth were possibly sown here immediately after the great Pentecost. Acts 2. St. Paul remained in the place more than two years, Acts 19:8, 10;

originally appropriate to the high priest. Ex. 28:4.

E'phraim (ē'frȧ-ĭm) (*double fruitfulness*), the second son of Joseph by his wife Asenath, born during the seven years of plenty which preceded the famine which brought Jacob and his family to Egypt. The first indication we have of that ascendency over his elder brother Manasseh which at a later period the tribe of Ephraim so unmis-

SITE OF THE THEATRE, EPHESUS.

20:31, during which he wrote the First Epistle to the Corinthians. At a later period Timothy was set over the disciples, as we learn from the two epistles addressed to him. Among St. Paul's other companions, two, Trophimus and Tychicus, were natives of Asia, Acts 20:4, and the latter was probably, 2 Tim. 4:12, the former certainly, Acts 21:29, a native of Ephesus.

Present condition.—The whole place is now utterly desolate, with the exception of the small Turkish village at *Ayasaluk.* The ruins are of vast extent.

Eph'lal (ĕf'lăl) (*judicious*), a descendant of Judah, of the family of Hezron and of Jerahmeel. 1 Chron. 2:37.

E'phod, father of Hanniel of the tribe of Manasseh. Num. 34:23.

Ephod (ĕf'od), a sacred vestment

takably possessed is in the blessing of the children by Jacob. Gen. 48.

E'phraim (ē'frȧ-im), that portion of Canaan named after Joseph's second son. Gen. 41:50-52. The boundaries of the portion of Ephraim are given in Josh. 16:1-10. The south boundary was coincident for part of its length with the north boundary of Benjamin. It extended from the Jordan on the east, at the reach opposite Jericho, to the Mediterranean on the west, probably about Joppa. On the north of Ephraim and Manasseh were the tribes of Asher, Zebulun and Issachar. The territory thus allotted to the "house of Joseph" may be roughly estimated at 55 miles from east to west by 70 from north to south. It was one at once of great richness and great security. Its fertile plains and well-watered valleys could only be reached by a laborious ascent through steep and narrow ravines, all but impassable for an army. Under Joshua the tribe must have taken a high position in the nation, to judge from the tone which the Ephraimites assumed on occasions shortly subsequent to the conquest. After the revolt of Jeroboam the history of Ephraim is the history of the kingdom of Israel, since not only did the tribe become a kingdom, but the kingdom embraced little besides the tribe.

E'phraim. 1. In "Baal-hazor which is by Ephraim" was Absalom's sheepfarm, at which took place the murder of Amnon, one of the earliest events to be included in the revolt of Absalom. 2 Sam. 13:23. The site is extremely uncertain; some considering it identical with the EPHRAIN of 2 Chron. 13:19, Ophrah of Benjamin (1 Sam. 13:17).

2. A city "in the district near the wilderness" to which our Lord retired with his disciples when threatened with violence by the priests. John 11:54. See EPHRAIN.

E'phraim, Gate of, one of the gates of the city of Jerusalem, 2 Kings 14:13; 2 Chron. 25:23; Neh. 8:16; 12:39, probably at or near the position of the present "Damascus gate."

E'phraim, Mount, is a district which seems to extend as far south as Ramah and Bethel, 1 Sam. 1:1; 7:17; 2 Chron. 13:4, 19, compared with 15:8, places but a few miles north of Jerusalem, and within the limits of Benjamin.

E'phraim, The wood of, a wood, or rather a forest, on the east of Jordan, in which the fatal battle was fought between the armies of David and of Absalom. 2 Sam. 18:6.

E'phraimite (ē'frăm-īte). Of the tribe of Ephraim; elsewhere called "Ephrathite." Judges 12:5.

E'phrain (ē'fra-in), a city of Israel, which Judah captured from Jeroboam. 2 Chron. 13:19. This place is thought by many to be the same as EPHRAIM 2, where our Lord lived for some time, and as Ophrah a city of Benjamin, mentioned in 1 Sam. 13:17. They identify the village with the modern *et-Taiyibeh,* on a hill 4 miles northeast of Bethel, and 14 miles from Jerusalem. Hastings' *Bible Dictionary* considers this a very probable site. Another identification of Ephrain with EPHRAIM 1, near which Amnon was murdered, is thought

by the same authority extremely improbable.

Eph'ratah (ĕf'ra-tah), or **Eph'rath** (*fruitful*). 1. Second wife of Caleb the son of Hezron, mother of Hur and great grandmother of Bezaleel the architect of the tabernacle, according to 1 Chron. 2:19, 50, and probably 24, and 4:4.

2. The ancient name of Bethlehem-judah. Gen. 35:16, 19; 48:7.

Eph'rathite (ĕf'răth-īte). 1. An inhabitant of Bethlehem. Ruth 1:2.

2. An Ephraimite. 1 Sam. 1:1; 1 Kings 11:26.

Eph'ron (ĕph'ron) (*fawn-like*), the son of Zohar, a Hittite, from whom Abraham bought the field and cave of Machpelah. Gen. 23:8–17; 25:9; 49:29, 30; 50:13. (B.C. 1860.)

Eph'ron, Mount. The "cities of Mount Ephron" formed one of the landmarks on the northern boundary of the tribe of Judah. Josh. 15:9.

Epicure'ans (ĕp-i-kū-rē'ănş), **The,** derived their name from Epicurus (342–270 B.C.), a philosopher of Attic descent, whose "Garden" at Athens rivalled in popularity the "Porch" and the "Academy." The doctrines of Epicurus found wide acceptance in Asia Minor and Alexandria. (95–50 B.C.) The object of Epicurus was to find in philosophy a practical guide to happiness. True pleasure and not absolute truth was the end at which he aimed; experience and not reason the test on which he relied. It is obvious that a system thus framed would degenerate by a natural descent into mere materialism; and in this form Epicurism was the popular philosophy at the beginning of the Christian era. When St. Paul addressed "Epicureans and Stoics," Acts 17:18, at Athens, philosophy of life was practically reduced to the teaching of these two antagonistic schools.

Epistles, letters; personal correspondence by writing. The twenty-one epistles of the New Testament took the place of tracts among us. In their outward form they are such as might be expected from men who were brought into contact with Greek and Roman customs, themselves belonging to a different race, and so reproducing the imported style with only partial accuracy. They begin (the Epistle to the Hebrews and 1 John excepted) with the names of the writer and of those to whom the epistle is addressed. Then follows the formula of salutation. Then the letter itself commences in the first person, the singular and plural being used indiscriminately. When the substance of the letter has been completed, come the individual messages. The conclusion in this case was probably modified by the fact that the letters were dictated to an amanuensis. When he had done his work, the apostle took up the pen or reed, and added in his own large characters, Gal. 6 : 11, the authenticating autograph. In one instance, Rom. 16 : 22, the amanuensis in his own name adds his salutation. An allusion in 2 Cor. 3 : 1 brings before us another class of letters which must have been in frequent use in the early ages of the Christian Church, by which travelers or teachers were commended by one church to the good offices of others.

Er (ĕr) (*watchful*). 1. First-born of Judah. Er "was wicked in the sight of the Lord; and the Lord slew him." Gen. 38 : 3–7; Num. 26 : 19.

2. Descendant of Shelah the son of Judah. 1 Chron. 4 : 21.

3. Son of Jose and father of Elmodam. Luke 3 : 28.

E'ran (ē'răn) (*watchful*), the grandson of Ephraim. Num. 26 : 36.

E'ranites (ē'răn-ītes), **The**. Num. 26 : 36.

Eras'tus (ė-răs'tŭs) (*beloved*). 1. One of the attendants of St. Paul at Ephesus, who with Timothy was sent forward into Macedonia. Acts 19 : 22. (A.D. 57.) He is probably the same with Erastus who is again mentioned in the salutations to Timothy, 2 Tim. 4 : 20. 2. Erastus the chamberlain, or rather the public treasurer, of Corinth, who was one of the early converts to Christianity. Rom. 16 : 23. According to the traditions of the Greek Church, he was first treasurer to the church at Jerusalem, and afterwards bishop of Paneas.

E'rech (ē'rĕk), one of the cities of Nimrod's kingdom in the land of Shinar, Gen. 10 : 10, doubtless the same as Orchoë, 82 miles south and 43 east of Babylon, the modern designations of the site—*Warka, Irka* and *Irak*—bearing a considerable affinity to the original name.

E'ri (ē'rī) (*watcher*), son of Gad, Gen. 46 : 16, and ancestor of the Erites. Num. 26 : 16.

Esa'ias (ė-sā'ias), the Greek form of Isaiah. [ISAIAH.]

E'sar-had'don (ē'sar-hăd'don) (*Assur has given a brother*), the favorite but not the eldest son of Sennacherib, 2 Kings 19 : 37, and the grandson of Sargon, who succeeded Shalmaneser. He appears by his monuments to have been one of the most powerful, if not *the* most powerful, of all the Assyrian monarchs. He was equally eminent as a military general and political ruler. He rebuilt Babylon which had been destroyed. Bricks from a palace have been recovered bearing his name. His reign lasted very nearly thirteen years, from B.C. 680 to B.C. 668; and it was doubtless within this space of time that Manasseh king of Judah, having been seized by his captains at Jerusalem on a charge of rebellion, was brought before him at Babylon, 2 Chron. 33 : 11. and detained for a time as prisoner there. As a builder of great works Esar-haddon is particularly distinguished. Besides his palace at Babylon, he built at least three others in different parts of his dominions, either for himself or his sons, and thirty temples.

E'sau (ē'saw) (*hairy*), the eldest son of Isaac, and twin-brother of Jacob. The singular appearance of the child at his birth originated the name. Gen. 25 : 25. Esau's robust frame and "rough" aspect were the types of a wild and daring nature. He was a thorough Bedouin, a "son of the desert." He was much loved by his father, and was of course his heir, but was induced to sell his birthright to Jacob. Mention of his unhappy marriages may be found in Gen. 26 : 34. The next episode in the life of Esau is the loss of his father's covenant blessing, which Jacob secured through the craft of his mother, and the anger of Esau, who vows vengeance. Gen. 27. Later he marries a daughter of Ishmael, Gen. 28 : 8, 9, and soon after establishes himself in Mount Seir, where he was living when Jacob returned from Padan-aram rich and powerful, and the two brothers were reconciled. Gen. 33 : 4. Twenty years thereafter they united in burying Isaac's body in the cave of Machpelah. Of Esau's subsequent history nothing is known; for that of his descendants see EDOM.

Esdrae'lon (ĕs-dra-ē'lŏn). This name is merely the Greek form of the

Hebrew word *Jezreel.* "The great plain of Esdraelon" extends across central Palestine from the Mediterranean to the Jordan, separating the mountain ranges of Carmel and Samaria from those of Galilee. The western section of it is properly the plain of Accho or *'Akka.* The main body of the plain is a triangle. Its base on the east extends from *Jenin* (the ancient Engannim) to the foot of the hills below Nazareth, and is about 15 miles long; the north side, formed by the hills of Galilee, is about 12 miles long; and the south side, formed by the Samaria range, is about 18 miles. The apex on the west is a narrow pass opening into the plain of *'Akka.* From the base of this triangular plain three branches stretch out eastward, like fingers from a hand, divided by two bleak, gray ridges—one bearing the familiar name of Mount Gilboa, the other called by Franks Little Hermon, but by natives *Jebel ed-Duhy.* The central branch is the richest as well as the most celebrated. This is the "valley of Jezreel" proper—the battlefield on which Gideon triumphed, and Saul and Jonathan were overthrown. Judges 7:1, *seq.;* 1 Sam. 29 and 31. Two things are worthy of special notice in the plain of Esdraelon: (1) Its wonderful richness; (2) Its present desolation. If we except the eastern branches, there is not a single inhabited village on its whole surface, and not more than one-sixth of its soil is cultivated. It is the home of the wild wandering Bedouin.

Es'dras (*Greek form of Ezra*), **The First Book of,** the first in order of the apocryphal books in the English Bible. The first chapter is a transcript of the last two chapters of 2 Chron., for the most part *verbatim,* and only in one or two parts slightly abridged and paraphrased. Chapters 3, 4, and 5 to the end of ver. 6, are the *original* portions of the book, and the rest is a transcript more or less exact of the book of Ezra, with one transposition and one interpolation, and a portion of Nehemiah. Hence a twofold design in the compiler is discernible—one to introduce and give scriptural sanction to the legend about Zerubbabel; the other to explain the great obscurities of the book of Ezra, in which, however, he has signally failed. Its author is unknown; some peculiarities indicate that it may have

been written for the Alexandrian Jews. It has no historical value.

Esdras, The Second Book of. This exists in a Latin translation, the Greek being lost. Chapters 3–14 consist of a series of angelic revelations and visions in which Ezra is instructed in some of the great mysteries of the moral world, and assured of the final triumph of the righteous. The date is uncertain.

E'sek (ē'sek) (*contention*), a well which the herdsmen of Isaac dug in the valley of Gerar. Gen. 26:20.

Esh=ba'al (ĕsh-bā'al) (*Baal's man*), 1 Chron. 8:33; 9:39, the same as Ish-bosheth.

Esh'ban (ĕsh'ban) (*wise man*), a Horite; one of the four sons of Dishon. Gen. 36:26; 1 Chron. 1:41.

Esh'col (ĕsh'kŏl) (*cluster of grapes*), brother of Mamre the Amorite and of Aner, and one of Abraham's companions in his pursuit of the four kings who had carried off Lot. Gen. 14:13, 24. (B.C. 1913.)

Esh'col, The valley or **The brook of,** a *wady* in the neighborhood of Hebron (Mamre), explored by the spies who were sent by Moses from Kadesh-barnea. Num. 13:23, 24; Deut. 1:24. There is a spring of fine water called *'Ain Eshkali,* in a valley about two miles north of Hebron, but according to Conder there is no connection between this name and the Hebrew.

Esh'ean (ĕsh'e-ăn) (*support*), one of the cities of Judah. Josh. 15:52. The Septuagint has *Soma.* It may be a ruin *es-Simia,* 8 miles from Hebron.

E'shek (ē'shĕk) (*oppression*), one of the late descendants of Saul. 1 Chron. 8:39.

Esh'kalonites (ĕsh'ka-lŏn-ītes), **The.** Josh. 13:3. [ASHKELON.]

Esh'taol (ĕsh'ta-ŏl), a town in the low country—the *Shefelah*—of Judah, afterwards allotted to Dan. Josh. 15:33; 19:41. Here Samson spent his boyhood, and hither after his last exploit his body was brought. Judges 13:25; 16:31; 18:2, 8, 11, 12.

Esh'taulites (ĕsh'taul-ītes), **The,** inhabitants of Eshtaol. 1 Chron. 2:53. R. V. "Eshtaolites."

Eshtemo'a (ĕsh-te-mō'à), and in shorter form **Eshtemoh** (*obedience*), a town of Judah, in the mountains, Josh. 15:50, allotted to the priests. Josh. 21:14; 1 Chron. 6:57. It was one of the places frequented by David and his followers during the long period of their wanderings. 1 Sam. 30 : 28; comp. 31. Its site is at *Semu'a*, south of Hebron.

Esh'ton (ĕsh'ton) (*perhaps uxorious*), a name which occurs in the genealogies of Judah. 1 Chron. 4 : 11, 12.

Es'li (ĕs'lī), son of Nagge or Naggai, in the genealogy of Christ. Luke 3 : 25.

Es'rom (ĕs'rom). Matt. 1 : 3; Luke 3 : 33. [HEZRON.]

Essenes', a Jewish sect, who, according to the description of Josephus, combined the ascetic virtues of the Pythagoreans and Stoics with a spiritual knowledge of the divine law. The derivation of the name is obscure. It probably means *pious* or *saintly*. As a sect the Essenes were distinguished by an aspiration after ideal purity rather than by any special code of doctrines. There were isolated communities of Essenes which were regulated by strict rules, analogous to those of the monastic institutions of a later date. All things were held in common, without distinction of property; and special provision was made for the relief of the poor. Self-denial, temperance and labor—especially agriculture—were the marks of the outward life of the Essenes; purity and divine communion the objects of their aspiration. Slavery, war and commerce were alike forbidden. Their best-known settlements were on the northwest shore of the Dead Sea. They were like monasteries, and the monks numbered about 4000.

Es'ther (ĕs'thēr) (*a star*), the Persian name of HADASSAH (*myrtle*), daughter of Abihail, the son of Shimei, the son of Kish, a Benjamite. Esther was a beautiful Jewish maiden. She was an orphan, and had been brought up by her cousin Mordecai, who had an office in the household of Ahasuerus king of Persia—recognized as the Xerxes of history—and dwelt at "Shushan the palace." When Vashti was dismissed from being queen, the king chose Esther to the place on account of her beauty, not knowing her race or parentage; and on the representation of Haman the Agagite that the Jews scattered through his empire were a pernicious race, he gave her full power and authority to kill them all. The means taken by Esther to avert this great calamity from her people and her kindred are fully related in the book of Esther. The Jews still commemorate this deliverance in the yearly festival Purim, on the 14th and 15th of Adar (February-March). History is wholly silent about both Vashti and Esther.

Es'ther, Book of, one of the latest of the canonical books of Scripture, having been written late in the reign of Xerxes, or early in that of his son Artaxerxes Longimanus (B.C. 465–425). This story belongs to the times of the return. It opens about half a century after the first caravan left Babylon amid great rejoicing and with high hopes and entered Jerusalem nearly fifty thousand strong.

The author is unknown, but must have been some one "living in the heart of Persia, a man who was intimately acquainted with the scenery he describes."—*Professor Adeney*.

The date of writing is also unknown Professor Sayce places it at B.C. 425. He says that the minuteness of detail shows that the author lived before the overthrow of the Persian power, B.C. 331 Some writers place the date still later.

HISTORICAL ACCURACY. There are two principal theories concerning the historical nature of this book: one, that it is a reliable history; the other, that it is a historical romance founded on fact, or substantially true; like Shakespeare's *Julius Cæsar* and *Henry VIII*, like Scott's historical romances, or Xenophon's *Cyropedeia*. "The fact that the action of the book culminates in the establishment of the popular national feast of Purim, and that it is a standing memorial of that feast, argues for its general historicity."—*Prof. Frank K. Sanders*.

It has often been remarked as a peculiarity of this book that the name of God does not once occur in it. But the reality of God is there.

E'tam (ē'tam) (*lair of wild beasts*). 1. A village of the tribe of Simeon, specified only in the list in 1 Chron. 4 : 32; comp. Josh. 19 : 7.

2. A place in Judah, fortified and garrisoned by Rehoboam. 2 Chron. 11 : 6. Here, according to the statements of Josephus and the Talmudists, were the sources of the water from which Solomon's gardens and pleasure-grounds were fed, and Bethlehem and the temple supplied.

E'tam, The rock, a cliff or lofty rock, into a cleft or chasm of which

Samson retired after his slaughter of the Philistines. Judges 15 : 8, 11. This natural stronghold was in the tribe of Judah; and near it, probably at its foot, were Lehi or Ramath-lehi and Enhakkore. Judges 15 : 9, 14, 17, 19. The site is still undefined. Conder considers as a possible site a rocky hill to the east of Samson's home at Zorah, on which the village of *Beit Atab* now stands, under which is a curious cavern in the rock.

E′tham (ē′tham), one of the early resting-places of the Israelites when they quitted Egypt; described as "in the edge of the wilderness." Ex. 13 : 20; Num. 33 : 6, 7. Etham was to all appearances the last city on properly Egyptian ground. Its site is much disputed, partly because of the uncertainty as to the route taken.

E′than (ē′than) (*enduring*). 1. Ethan the Ezrahite, one of the four sons of Mahol, whose wisdom was excelled by Solomon. 1 Kings 4 : 31; 1 Chron. 2 : 6. His name is in the title of Ps. 89.

2. Son of Kishi or Kushaiah; a Merarite Levite, head of that family in the time of King David, 1 Chron. 6 : 44, and spoken of as a "singer." With Heman and Asaph, the heads of the other two families of Levites, Ethan was appointed to sound with cymbals. 1 Chron. 15 : 17, 19. [JEDUTHAN.]

3. A Gershonite Levite, one of the ancestors of Asaph the singer. 1 Chron. 6 : 42.

Eth′anim (ĕth′a-nĭm). [MONTH.]

Ethba′al (ĕth-bā′-al) (*with Baal*), king of Sidon and father of Jezebel. 1 Kings 16 : 31. Josephus represents him as king of the Tyrians as well as of the Sidonians. We may thus identify him with Eithobalus, who, after having assassinated Pheles, usurped the throne of Tyre for thirty-two years. The date of Ethbaal's reign was probably about 875 B.C.

E′ther (ē′thĕr) (*abundance*), one of the cities of Judah in the low country, the *Shefelah*, Josh. 15 : 42, allotted to Simeon. Josh. 19 : 7.

Ethio′pia (ē-thĭ-ō′pĭ-à) (*burnt faces*). The country which the Greeks and Romans described as "Æthiopia" and the Hebrews as "Cush" lay to the south of Egypt, and embraced, in its most extended sense, the modern *Nubia, Sennaar, Kordofan* and northern *Abys-*

sinia, and in its more definite sense the kingdom of Meroë. Ezek. 29 : 10. The Hebrews do not appear to have had much practical acquaintance with Ethiopia itself, though the Ethiopians were well known to them through their intercourse with Egypt. The inhabitants of Ethiopia were a Hamitic race. Gen. 10 : 6. They were divided into various tribes, of which the Nubians were the most powerful. The history of Ethiopia is closely interwoven with that of Egypt. The two countries were not unfrequently united under the rule of the same sovereign. Shortly before our Saviour's birth a native dynasty of females, holding the official title of Candace (Plin. vi. 35), held sway in Ethiopia, and even resisted the advance of the Roman arms. One of these is the queen noticed in Acts 8 : 27. [CUSH, 2.]

Ethio′pian (ē-thĭ-ō′pĭ-an), properly "Cushite," Jer. 13 : 23; used of Zerah, 2 Chron. 14 : 9, and Ebed-melech. Jer. 38 : 7, 10, 12; 39 : 16.

Ethio′pian eunuch, The, a Jewish proselyte, Acts 8 : 26, etc., who was treasurer of Candace queen of Ethiopia, but who was converted to Christianity on a visit to Jerusalem, through Philip the evangelist. Nothing is known of him after his return to Ethiopia.

Ethio′pian woman. The wife of Moses is so described in Num. 12 : 1. She is elsewhere said to have been the daughter of a Midianite, and in consequence of this some have supposed that the allusion is to another wife whom Moses married after the death of Zipporah.

Eth′nan (ĕth′nan) (*hire*), one of the sons of Helah the wife of Ashur. 1 Chron. 4 : 7.

Eth′ni (ĕth′nī) (*munificent*), a Gershonite Levite. 1 Chron. 6 : 41.

Eubu′lus (ū-bū′lus) (*prudent*), a Christian at Rome mentioned by St. Paul. 2 Tim. 4 : 21. (A.D. 66.)

Euni′ce (ū-nī′cē) (*good victory*), mother of Timotheus. 2 Tim. 1 : 5.

Eunuch. "The English form of the Greek word which means *bed-keeper.* In the strict and proper sense they were the persons who had charge of the bed-chambers in palaces and larger houses. But as the jealous and dissolute temperament of the East required this charge to be in the hands of persons who had been deprived of their virility, the word eunuch came naturally to denote persons in that condition. But as some of these rose to be confidential advisers of their royal masters or mistresses, the word was occasionally employed to denote persons in such a position, without indicating anything of their proper manhood."—*Abbott.*

Euo'dias (ū-ō'dĭ-as) (*fragrance*), a Christian woman at Philippi, "blemished by bickering with Syntyche." Philip. 4 : 2. (A.D. 57.) The name is correctly EUODIA, as given in the Revised Version.

Euphra'tes (ū-frā'teş) is the Greek modification of the Hebrew *Perath* which is variously explained. It is most frequently denoted in the Bible by the term "the river." The Euphrates is the largest, the longest and by far the most important of the rivers of western Asia. It rises from two chief sources in the Armenian mountains, and flows into the Persian Gulf. The entire course is 1780 miles, and of this distance more than two-thirds (1200 miles) is navigable for boats. The width of the river is greatest at the distance of about 700 miles from its mouth—that is to say, from its junction with the Khabour to the village of *Werai.* It there averages 400 yards. The annual inundation of the Euphrates is caused by the melting of the snows in the Armenian highlands. It occurs in the month of May. The great hydraulic works ascribed to Nebuchadnezzar had for their chief object to control the inundation. The Euphrates is first mentioned in Scripture as one of the four rivers of Eden. Gen. 2 : 14. We next hear of it in the covenant made with Abraham. Gen. 15 : 18. During the reigns of David and Solomon it formed the boundary of the promised land to the northeast. Deut. 11 : 24; Josh. 1 : 4. Prophetical reference to the Euphrates is found in Jer. 13 : 4–7; 46 : 2–10; 51 : 63; Rev. 9 : 14; 16 : 12. "The Euphrates is linked with the most important events in ancient history. On its banks stood the city of Babylon; the army of Necho was defeated on its banks by Nebuchadnezzar; Cyrus the Younger and Crassus perished after crossing it; Alexander crossed it, and Trajan and Severus descended it."—*Appleton's Cyc.*

Euroc'lydon (ū-rŏk'lў-dŏn), a tempestuous wind or hurricane, cyclone, on the Mediterranean, and very dangerous; now called a "levanter." This wind seized the ship in which St. Paul was ultimately wrecked on the coast of Malta. It came down from the island, and therefore must have blown more or less from the northward. Acts 27 : 14. In the Revised Version the word used is *Eura'quilo,* compounded of two words meaning *east* and *north,* and means a northeast gale.

Eu'tychus (ū'tў̄-kus) (*fortunate*), a youth at Troas, Acts 20 : 9, who sitting in a window, and having fallen asleep while St. Paul was discoursing, fell from the third story, and being taken up dead, was miraculously restored to life by the apostle.

Evangelist (*publisher of glad tidings*). In the New Testament the "evangelists" appear on the one hand after the "apostles" and "prophets;" on the other before the "pastors" and "teachers." They probably stood between the two. Acts 21 : 8; Eph. 4 : 11. The work of the evangelist is the proclamation of the glad tidings to those who have not known them, rather than the instruction and pastoral care of those who have believed and been baptized. It follows also that the name denotes a *work* rather than an *order.* Its use is nearly like our word *missionary.* The evangelist might or might not be a bishop-elder or a deacon. The apostles, so far as they evangelized, Acts 8 : 25; 14 : 7; 1 Cor. 1 : 17, might claim the title, though there were many evangelists who were not apostles. If the gospel were a written book, and the office of the evangelists was to read or distribute it, then the writers of such books were preeminently THE evangelists. In later liturgical language the word was always applied to the reader of the gospel for the day.

Eve (*life*), the name given in Scripture to the first woman. The account of Eve's creation is found in Gen. 2 : 21, 22. Perhaps that which we are chiefly intended to learn from the narrative is the foundation upon which the union between man and wife is built, viz., identity of nature and oneness of origin. Through the subtlety of the serpent Eve was beguiled into a violation of the one commandment which had been imposed upon her and Adam. The Scripture account of Eve closes with the record of the birth of Seth, her third son.

E'vi (ē'vī) (*desire*), one of the five

kings or princes of Midian slain by the Israelites. Num. 31 : 8; Josh. 13 : 21.

E'vil=mer'odach (ē'vĭl-mēr'ō-dak) (*the man of Merodach*), 2 Kings 25 : 27, the son and successor of Nebuchadnez-zar. He reigned but a short time, hav-ing ascended the throne on the death of Nebuchadnezzar in B.C. 562, and being himself succeeded by Neriglissar in B.C. 560. He was murdered by Neriglissar.

Excommunication (*expulsion from communion*). 1. *Jewish excommunica-tion.*— The word excommunication does not occur in the Bible and the practice itself is quite late. The Jews in early times excluded those ceremonially un-clean from the camp, and devoted whole cities and tribes, even of Israel itself, to destruction, but these are hardly parallel cases, though giving us the root of the later, milder practice. In the time of Ezra we find the first real example, when those who retained their foreign wives were to be separated completely from the congregation of Israel. Ezr. 10 : 8. But this was to in-clude loss of property. The Talmud speaks of 24 offences as punishable by excommunication. Two degrees are recognized, the milder being a temporary exclusion from the synagogue together with a restriction upon social inter-course, while the more severe amounted to a ban of indefinite or permanent duration. This latter could not be in-flicted by less than 10 persons. The only references to the custom in the gos-pels are Luke 6 : 22; John 9 : 22; 12 : 42; 16 : 2. The Talmud does not take us back to Christ's time and we have no source of knowledge as to methods in use. The idea that there was a third and more awful excommunication re-ferred to in the Talmud—making three forms with a reference to the three in Luke 6 : 22—is now generally acknowl-edged to be a mistake. (See Hastings' *Dictionary of Christ and the Gospels.*)

2. *Christian excommunication.*—Ex-communication, as exercised by the Christian Church, was instituted by our Lord, Matt. 18 : 15–17, and it was prac-ticed and commanded by St. Paul. 1 Cor. 5 : 11; 1 Tim. 1 : 20; Titus 3 : 10. In the epistles we find St. Paul fre-quently claiming the right to exercise discipline over his converts; comp. 2 Cor. 1 : 23; 13 : 10.

Exodus, The Book of. Exodus means "a going out," and is so named from the era which it describes. The period to which it belongs is that from the death of Joseph to the erection of the tabernacle in the wilderness.

The author and the date of its com-position are unknown. Modern scholars regard it as a composite work, as are most of the histories of to-day.

Divisions. Two great subjects are treated. Chapters 1–15 : 21, are called "The Epic of the Great Deliverance," and the remainder of the book, "The Solemn Institution of the Theocracy at Sinai." The first part contains an ac-count of the following particulars: The great increase of Jacob's posterity in the land of Egypt, and their oppression under a new dynasty, which occupied the throne after the death of Joseph; the birth, education, flight and return of Moses; the ineffectual attempts to prevail upon Pharaoh to let the Israelites go; the successive signs and wonders, ending in the death of the first-born, by means of which the deliverance of Israel from the land of bondage is at length accomplished, and the institution of the Passover; finally the departure out of Egypt and the arrival of the Israelites at Mount Sinai.

2. This part gives a sketch of the early history of Israel as a nation; and the history has three clearly-marked stages. First we see a nation en-slaved; next a nation redeemed; lastly a nation set apart, and through the blending of its religious and political life consecrated to the service of God.

Exodus, The, of the Israelites.

DATE. The common chronology places the date at 1491 B.C.

The tendency for the last few years has been to bring the date down to between 1300 and 1200 B.C., just after the death of Rameses II., the Pharaoh of the oppression. Professor Orr and others regard a previous Pharaoh, Thothmes, as the oppressor, and bring the date back to the common date.

Professor Willis J. Beecher in his *Dated Events of the Old Testament,* which is one of the most thorough studies of Bible Chronology yet issued, dated the Exodus 1498 B.C., soon after the death of Rameses II in 1501 B.C. Thus he is close to Ussher's date in the margin of our Bibles. He considered Rameses II as the Pharaoh of the oppression, but altered the date of his reign.

LENGTH OF THE SOJOURN IN EGYPT.—

In the Bible account in 1 Kings 6:1 it is stated that the building of the temple, in the fourth year of Solomon, was in the 480th year after the Exodus. The fourth year of Solomon was about B.C. 1012. Add the 480 years (leaving off one year because neither the fourth nor or 215 years, being spent in Egypt. Others make it to cover only the period of bondage spent in Egypt. St. Paul says in Gal. 3:17 that from the covenant with (or call of) Abraham to the giving of the law (less than a year after the Exodus) was 430 years. But

Abraham's call | Jacob comes into Egypt | Exodus | Temple

<——— 215 years ——> <——— 215 years ——> <——— 480 years ——>

B.C. 1921   1706   1491   1012

<——————— 430 years ———————>

the 480th was a full year), and we have B.C. 1491 as the date of the Exodus. This is probably very nearly correct; but many Egyptologists place it at 215 years later,—about B.C. 1300. Which date is right depends chiefly on the interpretation of the Scripture period of 430 years, as denoting the duration of the bondage of the Israelites. The period of bondage given in Gen. 15:13, 14, Ex. 12:40, 41 and Gal. 3:17 as 430 years has been interpreted to cover different periods. The common chronology makes it extend from the call of Abraham to the Exodus, one-half of it, in Gen. 15:13, 14 it is said that they should be strangers in a strange land, and be afflicted 400 years, and nearly the same is said in Ex. 12:40. But, in very truth, the children of Israel were strangers in a strange land from the time that Abraham left his home for the promised land, and during that whole period of 430 years to the Exodus they were nowhere rulers in the land. So in Ex. 12:40 it is said that the sojourning of the children of Israel who dwelt in Egypt was 430 years. But it does not say that the sojourning was all in Egypt, but this people who lived in Egypt had

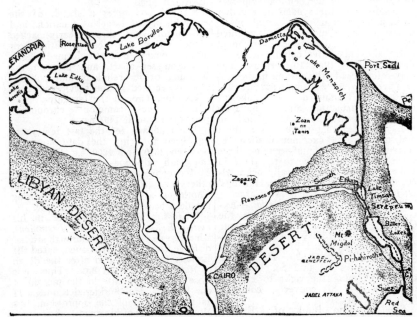

THE MODERN REGION OF EGYPT AS IT WAS WHEN THE ISRAELITES BEGAN THE EXODUS.

been sojourners for 430 years. This is the simplest way of making the various statements harmonize. The chief difficulty in the way of accepting the shorter period for the sojourn in Egypt lies in the great increase of the children of Israel from 70 to 2,000,000 in 215 years. Known facts render this possible. But probably Professor Beecher is correct in his interpretation of the numbers, that the enumeration is of even hundreds and thousands, that is of companies and regiments, as in an army. The regiments are seldom full, so that 600 thousands are 600 regiments, and the total men may have been only 200,000, or 300,000, and the total population less than a million. "In illustration of the event, a sudden retreat is recorded of a whole nomadic people—400,000 Tartars—under cover of a single night, from the confines of Russia into their native deserts as late as the close of the last century."—*Stanley.*

THE ROUTE OF THE MARCH. There has always been something strange in the movement of the Israelites from Rameses, in going northward at first, and then returning into the borders of Egypt and going south to the Red Sea. Dr. Trumbull's Kadesh-barnea throws the most light upon this movement which makes all plain and simple. There were three great routes from Egypt to Palestine,—the *Philistia Road,* the *Wall Road,* and the *Red Sea Road.* 1. The *Philistia Road,* or "the way of the land of the Philistines," was the northern road, which runs along the coast of the Mediterranean, and is the shortest, easiest and best watered route. 2. The *Wall Road,* "the Way of Shur," *i. e.,* wall (Gen. 16 : 7), is the central road, starting from the northern end of Lake Timsah, near the modern town Ismailia. It goes straight into the desert, and leads to Palestine by way of Beersheba and Hebron, and it would require a continuous miracle to sustain the people and their flocks. 3. The *Red Sea Road,* "the Way of the Wilderness of the Red Sea" was the road "which swept across the wilderness, between the two arms of the Red Sea, from the head of the Gulf of Suez to the head of the Gulf of Akabah." It is to-day the great route of the pilgrim caravans to Mecca.

THE GREAT WALL. The next important fact in understanding this story was the great wall, like the immense Chinese wall, nearly 1500 miles long, built to defend China from the invasions of the Tartars on the north. There is evidence that, at the time of the Exodus, *a great wall* extended from Pelusium on the Mediterranean across the whole isthmus to the Gulf of Suez. It was east of, and nearly parallel with, the present Suez Canal. It was dotted with special fortifications, and was the defence of Egypt against invasion from the east, and must have been specially guarded at the entrances to the three great roads. This, of course, could be made a great barrier to the Exodus.

The Israelites first moved towards the northern or the Philistia route. This seemed the nearest and safest way, and it was natural that they should choose it in their haste to get away from Egypt. The Israelites came to the edge of the desert to the northeast of Succoth and were confronted by this great wall with its garrisons and the desert. They realized, too, that without weapons or training it would be impossible to conquer the Philistine trained armies, if they continued on that route. The best route for many reasons was the southern or Red Sea route. Therefore, from Etham they made a sharp turn, by the command of God, and were led southward by the pillar of cloud and of fire, which here first appears to be their guide. They returned to the western or Egyptian side of the lakes, and marched along their shores toward the Red Sea. This seems strange at first, but we are to remember that on the Egyptian side were pastures and water and roads, but on the other side was the great wall and the deserts. They had permission to go, and hence their being in Egypt was no objection. Moreover, God had plans of his own which were necessary to the best success of their plan. This gave time for Pharaoh to recover from his fright and change his mind, close the gates in the wall, and entrap the Israelites. See RED SEA, PASSAGE OF.

Exorcist, one who pretends to expel evil spirits by conjuration, prayers and ceremonies. Exorcism was frequently practiced among the Jews. Matt. 12 : 27; Luke 11 : 19; Acts 19 : 13. The power of casting out devils was bestowed by Christ while on earth upon the apostles, Matt. 10 : 8, and the seventy disciples, Luke 10 : 17–19, and was, according to his promise, Mark 16 : 17, exercised by believers after his ascension. Acts 16 : 18.

Expiation. [SACRIFICE.]

Eye. The practice of painting the eyelids to make the eyes look large, lustrous and languishing is often alluded to in the Old Testament, and still extensively prevails among the women of the East, and especially among the Mohammedans. Jezebel, in 2 Kings 9 : 30, is said to have prepared for her meeting with Jehu by painting her face, or, as it reads in the margin, " put her eyes in paint." See also Ezek. 23 : 40. A small probe of wood, ivory or silver is wet with rose-water and dipped into paste of black antimony powder, and is then drawn between the lids of the eye nearly closed, and leaves a narrow black border, which is thought a great ornament.

Ez'bai (ĕz'ba-ī), father of Naarai, who was one of David's thirty mighty men. 1 Chron. 11 : 37.

Ez'bon (ĕz'bŏn). 1. Son of Gad, and founder of one of the Gadite families. Gen. 46 : 16 ; Num. 26 : 16. (OZNI.)

2. Son of Bela, the son of Benjamin according to 1 Chron. 7 : 7.

Ezeki'as (ĕz-e-kī'as). Matt. 1 : 9, 10. [HEZEKIAH.]

Eze'kiel (e-zē'kĭ-el) (*God is strong* or *God doth strengthen*), one of the four greater prophets, was the son of a priest named Buzi, and was taken captive in the captivity of Jehoiachin, eleven years before the destruction of Jerusalem. He was a member of a community of Jewish exiles who settled on the banks of the Chebar, a " river " or canal of Babylonia. He began prophesying B.C. 592, and continued until B.C. 570, a period of more than twenty-two years. We learn from an incidental allusion, Ezek. 24 : 18, that he was married, and had a house, Ezek. 8 : 1, in his place of exile, and lost his wife by a sudden and unforeseen stroke. He lived in the highest consideration among his companions in exile, and their elders consulted him on all occasions, though they did not always follow his advice (Ezek. 2 : 3, 4 ; 3 : 5–7). The time and manner of his death are unknown. The late tradition that he was murdered because he denounced idolatry is worthless.

Ezekiel was distinguished by his stern and inflexible energy of will and character and his devoted adherence to the rites and ceremonies of his national religion. The depth of his *matter* and the marvellous nature of his visions make him occasionally obscure.

Ezekiel, The Book of, was written at Tel-Abib on the river Chebar not far from Babylon, about the middle of the 70 years' Exile.

The book falls into three divisions. 1. Prophecies delivered during the early part of the captivity during the troublous times before the destruction of Jerusalem, warning the Jews that unless they repented, their city and temple would be destroyed on account of their sins.

2. Prophecies of judgment against seven surrounding nations. Sin would be punished in the heathen nations as well as in God's people.

3. Prophecies of restoration and return, full of hope and encouragement, written after the destruction of Jerusalem. God through the captivity would lead the people to the true God, to righteousness, and to their return from exile. He pictured by the symbol of the temple the new life, and worship and final success of the people of God.

E'zel (ē'zĕl) (*departure*), **The stone,** a well-known stone in the neighborhood of Saul's residence, the scene of the parting of David and Jonathan. 1 Sam. 20 : 19.

E'zem (ē'zĕm) (*bone*), one of the towns of Simeon. 1 Chron. 4 : 29. [AZEM.]

E'zer (ē'zēr) (*treasure*). 1. A son of Ephraim, who was slain by the aboriginal inhabitants of Gath while engaged in a foray on their cattle. 1 Chron. 7 : 21.

2. A priest who assisted in the dedication of the walls of Jerusalem under Nehemiah. Neh. 12 : 42. (B.C. 446.)

3. Father of Hushah of the sons of Hur. 1 Chron. 4 : 4.

4. One of the Gadite chiefs who fought with David. 1 Chron. 12 : 8, 9.

5. One who aided in repairing the wall at Jerusalem ; a Levite. Neh. 3 : 19.

E'zion=ga'ber, or **E'zion=ge'ber** (ē'-zĭ-on-ḡē'bēr) (*giant's backbone*), Num. 33 : 35 ; Deut. 2 : 8 ; 1 Kings 9 : 26 ; 22 : 48 ; 2 Chron. 8 : 17, the last station named for the encampment of the Israelites before they came to the wilderness of Zin. It probably stood at *Ain el-Ghudyân*, about ten miles up what is now the dry bed of the Arabah, but which was probably then the northern end of the gulf of Akaba. [ELATH.]

Ez'nite (ĕz'nīte), **The.** 2 Sam. 23 : 8. Adino the Eznite was another name for Jashobeam, a Tachmonite, or Hachmonite. 1 Chron. 11 : 11. Probably the words are a corruption for the Hebrew "he lifted up his spear."

Ez'ra (ĕz'rȧ) (*help*). 1. Called ESDRAS in the Apocrypha, the famous scribe and priest. He was a learned and pious priest residing at Babylon in the time of Artaxerxes Longimanus. The origin of his influence with the king does not appear, but in the seventh year of his reign he obtained leave to go to Jerusalem, and to take with him a company of Israelites. (B.C. 458.) The journey from Babylon to Jerusalem took just four months; and the company brought with them a large free-will offering of gold and silver, and silver vessels. It appears that Ezra's great design was to effect a religious reformation among the Palestine Jews. His first step was to enforce separation upon all who had married foreign wives. Ezra 10. This was effected in little more than six months after his arrival at Jerusalem. With the detailed account of this important transaction Ezra's autobiography ends abruptly, and we hear nothing more of him till, thirteen years afterwards, in the twentieth year of Artaxerxes, we find him again at Jerusalem with Nehemiah. It seems possible that after effecting the above reformations he returned to the king of Persia. The functions he executed under Nehemiah's government were purely ʾ of a priestly and ecclesiastical character. The date of his death is uncertain. There was a Jewish tradition that he was buried in Persia.

Ezra's work was that of a scribe, a student and interpreter of the law; not a mere copyist, nor author, but one who wrote upon it, and promulgated it among the people. He brought the law to Jerusalem for the purpose of re-instating it as the code of the community. "In particular the activity of Ezra and his successors, the scribes, guided the development of the religious life in a direction which was bound to lead to the rise of synagogues all over the country." 2. Two less prominent persons. 1 Chron. 4 : 17; Neh. 12 : 1.

Ez'ra, Book of, is a continuation of the books of Chronicles. The period covered by the book is eighty years, from the first of Cyrus, B.C. 536, to the beginning of the eighth of Artaxerxes, B.C. 457. It consists of the contemporary historical journals kept from time to time, containing, chs. 1–6, an account of the return of the captives under Zerubbabel, and the rebuilding of the temple in the reign of Cyrus and Cambyses. Most of the book is written in Hebrew, but from chs. 4 : 8 to 6 : 19 it is written in Chaldee, or, more correctly, Aramaic, being copies of provincial documents. Chapters 7–10 continue the history after a gap of fifty-eight years—from the sixth of Darius to the seventh of Artaxerxes—narrating Ezra's visit to Jerusalem, and giving an account of the reforms there accomplished, referred to under EZRA. Parts of the book seem to have been written by Ezra himself, and he may have compiled other portions. The narrative in the last chapter appears to have been by another scribe.

Ez'rahite (ĕz'ra-hīte), **The** (*son of Zerah*), a title attached to two persons —Ethan, 1 Kings 4 : 31; Ps. 89, title, and Heman, Ps. 88, title.

Ez'ri (ĕz'rī) (*help of Jehovah*), son of Chelub, superintendent of King David's farm-laborers. 1 Chron. 27 : 26.

F

Fable. A fable is a narrative in which beings irrational, and sometimes inanimate, are, for the purpose of moral instruction, feigned to act and speak with human interests and passions.—*Encyc. Brit.* The fable differs from the parable in that—(1) The parable always relates what actually takes place, and is true to fact, which the fable is not; and (2) The parable teaches the higher heavenly and spiritual truths, but the fable only earthly moralities. Of the fable, as distinguished from the parable [PARABLE], we have but two examples in the Bible: (1) That of the trees choosing their king, addressed by Jotham to the men of Shechem, Judges 9: 8–15. (2) That of the cedar of Lebanon and the thistle, as the answer of Jehoash to the challenge of Amaziah. 2 Kings 14: 9. The fables of false teachers claiming to belong to the Christian Church, alluded to by writers of the New Testament, 1 Tim. 1: 4; 4: 7; Titus 1: 14; 2 Pet. 1: 16, do not appear to have had the character of fables, properly so called.

Fair Ha'vens, a harbor in the island of Crete, Acts 27: 8, though not mentioned in any other ancient writing, is still known by its own Greek name, and appears to have been the harbor of Lasæa.

Fairs, a word which occurs only in Ezek. 27, and there no less than seven times, vs. 12, 14, 16, 19, 22, 27, 33; in the last of these verses it is rendered "wares," and this is without doubt the true meaning of the word throughout.

Fallow deer (called fallow from its reddish-brown color) (Heb. *yachmûr*). The Hebrew word, which is mentioned only in Deut. 14: 5 and 1 Kings 4: 23, possibly denotes the *Alcelaphus bubalis* (the bubale or wild cow), of Barbary and North Africa. It is about the size of a stag, and lives in herds. It is al-most exactly like the European roebuck, and is valued for its venison.

THE FALLOW DEER.

Famine. In the whole of Syria and Arabia, the fruits of the earth must ever be dependent on rain; the watersheds having few large springs, and the small rivers not being sufficient for the irrigation of even the level lands. If therefore the heavy rains of November and December fail, the sustenance of the people is cut off in the parching drought of harvest-time, when the country is almost devoid of moisture. Egypt, again, owes all its fertility to its mighty river, whose annual rise inundates nearly the whole land. The causes of dearth and famine in Egypt are defective inundation, preceded, accompanied and followed by prevalent easterly and southerly winds. Famine is likewise a natural result in the East when caterpillars, locusts or other insects destroy the products of the earth. The first famine

194

recorded in the Bible is that of Abraham after he had pitched his tent on the east of Bethel, Gen. 12 : 10; the second in the days of Isaac, Gen. 26 : 1, *seq.* We hear no more of times of scarcity until the great famine of Egypt, which "was over all the face of the earth." Gen. 41 : 53–57. The modern history of Egypt throws some curious light on these ancient records of famines; and instances of their recurrence may be cited to assist us in understanding their course and extent. The most remarkable famine was that of the reign of the Fátimee Khaleefeh, El-Mustansir billáh, which is the only instance on record of one of seven years duration in Egypt since the time of Joseph (A.H. 457–464, A.D. 1064–1071). Vehement drought and pestilence continued for seven consecutive years, so that the people ate corpses, and animals that died of themselves. The famine of Samaria resembled it in many particulars; and that very briefly recorded in 2 Kings 8 : 1, 2, affords another instance. In Arabia famines are of frequent occurrence.

Fan, *a winnowing-shovel,* with which grain was thrown up against the wind to be cleansed from the chaff and straw. Isa. 30 : 24; Matt. 3 : 12. A large wooden fork is used at the present day.

Farming. [AGRICULTURE.]

Farthing. Two names of coins in the New Testament are rendered in the Authorized Version by this word: (1) *Quadrans,* Matt. 5 : 26; Mark 12 : 42, a coin current in the time of our Lord, equivalent to one quarter of a cent; (2) The *assarion,* equal to one cent in our day. Matt. 10 : 29; Luke 12 : 6. [MONEY.]

Fasts. 1. One fast only was appointed by the Mosaic law, that on the day of atonement. There is no mention of any other periodical fast in the Old Testament except in Zech. 7 : 1–7; 8 : 19. From these passages it appears that the Jews, during their captivity, observed four annual fasts,—in the fourth, fifth, seventh and tenth months.

2. Public fasts were occasionally proclaimed to express national humiliation and to supplicate divine favor. In the case of public danger the proclamation appears to have been accompanied with the blowing of trumpets. Joel 2 : 1–15. (See 1 Sam. 7 : 6; 2 Chron. 20 : 3; Jer. 36 : 6–10). Three days after the feast of tabernacles, when the second temple

was completed, "the children of Israel assembled with fasting, and with sackclothes and earth upon them," to hear the law read and to confess their sins. Neh. 9 : 1.

3. Private occasional fasts are recognized in one passage of the law—Num. 30 : 13. The instances given of individuals fasting under the influence of grief, vexation or anxiety are numerous.

4. In the New Testament the only references to the Jewish fasts are the mention of "the fast" in Acts 27 : 9 (generally understood to denote the day of atonement) and the allusions to the weekly fasts. Matt. 9 : 14; Mark 2 : 18; Luke 5 : 33; 18 : 12; Acts 10 : 30. These fasts originated some time after the captivity.

5. The Jewish fasts were observed with various degrees of strictness. Sometimes there was entire abstinence from food. Esther 4 : 16, etc. On other occasions there appears to have been only a restriction to a very plain diet. Dan. 10 : 3. Those who fasted frequently dressed in sackcloth or rent their clothes, put ashes on their head and went barefoot. 1 Kings 21 : 27; Neh. 9 : 1; Ps. 35 : 13.

6. The sacrifice of the personal will, which gives to fasting all its value, is expressed in the old term used in the law, *afflicting the soul.*

Fat. The Hebrews distinguished between the suet or pure fat of an animal and the fat which was intermixed with the lean. Neh. 8 : 10. Certain restrictions were imposed upon them in reference to the former; some parts of the suet, viz., about the stomach, the entrails, the kidneys, and the tail of a sheep, which grows to an excessive size in many eastern countries, and produces a large quantity of rich fat, were forbidden to be eaten in the case of animals offered to Jehovah in sacrifice. Lev. 3 : 3, 9, 17; 7 : 3, 23. The ground of the prohibition was that the fat was the richest part of the animal, and therefore belonged to him. Lev. 3 : 16. The burning of the fat of sacrifices was particularly specified in each kind of offering.

Fat, *i. e.* VAT, the word employed in the Authorized Version to translate the Hebrew term *yekeb,* in Joel 2 : 24; 3 : 13. The word commonly used for *yekeb* is "winepress" or "winefat," and once "pressfat." Hag. 2 : 16. The "vats" appear to have been excavated out of the native rock of the hills on which the vineyards lay.

Father. The position and authority of the father as the head of the family are expressly assumed and sanctioned in Scripture, as a likeness of that of the Almighty over his creatures. It lies of course at the root of that so-called patriarchal government, Gen. 3:16; 1 Cor. 11:3, which was introductory to the more definite systems which followed, and which in part, but not wholly, superseded it. The father's blessing was regarded as conferring special benefit, but his malediction special injury, on those on whom it fell, Gen. 9:25, 27; 27:27–40; 48:15, 20; 49; and so also the sin of a parent was held to affect, in certain cases, the welfare of his descendants. 2 Kings 5:27. The command to honor parents is noticed by St. Paul as the only one of the Decalogue which bore a distinct promise, Ex. 20: 12; Eph. 6:2; and disrespect towards them was condemned by the law as one of the worst of crimes. Ex. 21:15, 17; 1 Tim. 1:9. It is to this well-recognized theory of parental authority and supremacy that the very various uses of the term "father" in Scripture are due. "Fathers" is used in the sense of seniors, Acts 7:2; 22:1, and of parents in general, or ancestors. Dan. 5:2; Jer. 27:7; Matt. 23:30, 32.

Fathom. [WEIGHTS AND MEASURES.]

Feasts. [FESTIVALS; MEALS.]

Fe'lix (fē'lĭx) (*happy*), a Roman procurator of Judea appointed by the emperor Claudius in A.D. 53. He ruled the province in a mean, cruel and profligate manner. His period of office was full of troubles and seditions. St. Paul was brought before Felix in Cæsarea. He was remanded to prison, and kept there two years in hopes of extorting money from him. Acts 24:26, 27. At the end of that time Porcius Festus [FESTUS] was appointed to supersede Felix, who, on his return to Rome, was accused by the Jews in Cæsarea, and would have suffered the penalty due to his atrocities had not his brother Pallas prevailed with the emperor Nero to spare him. This was probably about A.D. 60. The wife of Felix was Drusilla, daughter of Herod Agrippa I., who was his third wife and whom he persuaded to leave her husband and marry him.

Fenced cities, *i. e.* cities fortified or defended. The fortifications of the cities of Palestine, thus regularly "fenced," consisted of one or more walls (sometimes of thick stones, sometimes of combustible material), crowned with battlemented parapets, having towers at regular intervals, 2 Chron. 32: 5; Jer. 31:38, on which in later times engines of war were placed, and watch was kept by day and night in time of war. 2 Kings 9:17; 2 Chron. 26:9, 15; Ezek. 33:2.

Ferret, one of the unclean creeping things mentioned in Lev. 11:30. The animal referred to was probably a reptile of the lizard tribe (the *gecko*). The rabbinical writers seem to have identified this animal with the hedgehog.

Festivals. I. The religious times ordained in the law fall under three heads: 1. Those formally connected with the institution of the Sabbath; 2. The historical or great festivals; 3. The day of atonement. 1. Immediately connected with the institution of the Sabbath are—*a.* The Sabbath itself. *b.* The New Moon. *c.* The seventh new moon, or feast of trumpets. *d.* The sabbatical year. *e.* The year of jubilee. 2. The great feasts are—*a.* The passover. *b.* The feast of pentecost, of weeks, of wheat-harvest or of the first-fruits. *c.* The feast of tabernacles or of ingathering. On each of these occasions every male Israelite was commanded to "appear before the Lord," that is, to attend in the court of the tabernacle or the temple, and to make his offering with a joyful heart. Deut. 27:7; Neh. 8:9–12. The attendance of women was voluntary, but the zealous often went up to the passover. On all the days of holy convocation there was to be an entire suspension of ordinary labor of all kinds, Ex. 12:16; Lev. 16: 29; 23:21, 24, 25, 35; but on the intervening days of the longer festivals work might be carried on. The agricultural significance of the three great festivals is clearly set forth in the account of the Jewish sacred year contained in Lev. 23. The times of the festivals were evidently ordained in wisdom, so as to interfere as little as possible with the industry of the people. The value of these great religious festivals was threefold. (1) *Religious effects.*—They preserved the religious faith of the nation and religious unity among the people. They constantly reminded the people of the divinely-wrought deliverances of the past; promoted gratitude and trust; and testified the reverence of the people for the temple and its sacred contents. Besides this was the influence of well-conducted temple services upon the synagogues through the land. (2) *Political effects.*—The unity of the nation would be insured by this fusion of the tribes; otherwise they would be likely to constitute separate tribal states. They would carry back to the provinces glowing accounts of the wealth, power and resources of the country. (3) *Social effects.*—They promoted friendly intercourse between travelling companions; distributed information through the country at a time when the transmission of news was slow and imperfect; and imported into remote provincial districts a practical knowledge of all improvements in arts and sciences. 3. For the day of atonement see that article. II. After the captivity, the feast of Purim, Esther 9:20, *seq.*, and that of the dedication, 1 Macc. 4:56, were instituted.

Fes'tus (fĕs'tŭs), **Por'cius** (Festus means *festival*), successor of Felix as procurator of Judea, Acts 24:27, sent by Nero probably in the autumn of A.D. 60. A few weeks after Festus reached his province he heard the cause of St. Paul, who had been left a prisoner by Felix, in the presence of Herod Agrippa II. and Bernice his sister, Acts 25:11, 12. Judea was in the same disturbed state during the procuratorship of Festus which had prevailed through that of his predecessor. He died probably in the summer of A.D. 62, having ruled the province less than two years.

Fetters. Fetters were for the feet only, while chains were for any part of the body. They were usually made of brass or copper. "It is still the custom in Syria to attach a chain to each of the rings put round a prisoner's ankles, the middle of the chain being fastened to his girdle. He is thus, according to the Arabic way of speaking, bound with two chains." Iron was occasionally employed for the purpose. Ps. 105:18; 149:8.

Field. The Hebrew *sadeh* is applied to any cultivated ground, and in some instances in marked opposition to the neighboring wilderness. On the other hand the *sadeh* is frequently contrasted with what is enclosed, whether a vineyard, a garden or a walled town. In many passages the term implies what is remote from a house, Gen. 4:8; 24:63; Deut. 22:25, or settled habitation, as in the case of Esau. Gen. 25:27. The separate plots of ground were marked off by stones, which might easily be removed, Deut. 19:14; 27:17; cf. Job 24:2; Prov. 22:28; 23:10; the absence of fences rendered the fields liable to damage from straying cattle, Ex. 22:5, or fire, Ex. 22:6; 2 Sam. 14:30; hence the necessity of constantly watching flocks and herds. From the absence of enclosures, cultivated land of any size might be termed a field.

Fig, Fig tree. The fig tree (*Ficus carica*) is very common in Palestine. Deut. 8:8. Mount Olivet was famous for its fig trees in ancient times, and they are still found there. To "sit under one's own vine and one's own fig tree" became a proverbial expression among the Jews to denote peace and prosperity. 1 Kings 4:25; Micah 4:4; Zech. 3:10. The fig is a pear-shaped fruit, and is much used by the Orientals for food. The young figs are especially prized for their sweetness and flavor. The fruit always appears before the leaves; so that when Christ saw leaves on the fig tree by the wayside, Mark 11:13, he had a right to expect fruit. The usual summer crop of fruits is not gathered till May or June; but in the sunny ravines of Olivet fig trees could have ripe fruit some weeks earlier (*Dr. Thomson*), and it was not strange that so early as Easter Christ might find the young eatable figs, although it was not the usual season for gathering the fruit.

Fir. Isaiah 14:8; Ezek. 27:5, etc. The rendering of the Hebrew *Berosh*. Several trees have been named as the true meaning of the Hebrew, among them the pine, the tall juniper and the cypress. The last two would meet all the requirements, but the weight of evidence is for the cypress which is still found in the Lebanon. The wood of the fir was used for ship-building, Ezek. 27:5; for musical instruments, 2 Sam. 6:5; for beams and rafters of houses, 1 Kings 5:8, 10; 2 Chron. 2:8.

Finger's breadth, Digit. [WEIGHTS AND MEASURES.]

Fire is represented as the symbol of Jehovah's presence and the instrument of his power, in the way either of ap-

FIG TREE.

dish," Ex. 25:38; 37:23; Num. 4:9, and "censer." Lev. 10:1; 16:12; Num. 16:6 ff. There appear, therefore, to have been two articles so called: one, like a chafing-dish, to carry live coals for the purpose of burning incense; another, like a snuffer-dish, to be used in trimming the lamps, in order to carry the snuffers and convey away the snuff.

Firkin. [WEIGHTS AND MEASURES.]

Firmament. Hebrew *rakia,* which denotes an expanse beaten or hammered out. Firmament, from the Latin, means support. Numerous passages may be cited to prove that the Hebrews regarded the sky as a solid vault or arched dome, thus sharing the belief of almost all primitive peoples. See Job 37:18; Gen. 7:11; 2 Kings 7:2; Ps. 78:23; 104:2. The belief lingered late as poetic imagery but is not taught as a fact in the Bible.

proval or of destruction. Ex. 3:2; 14:19, etc. There could not be a better symbol for Jehovah than this of fire, it being immaterial, mysterious, but visible, warming, cheering, comforting, but also terrible and consuming. Parallel with this application of fire and with its symbolical meaning are to be noted the similar use for sacrificial purposes and the respect paid to it, or to the heavenly bodies as symbols of deity, which prevailed among so many nations of antiquity, and of which the traces are not even now extinct; *e.g.* the Sabean and Magian systems of worship. Isa. 27:9. Fire for sacred purposes obtained elsewhere than from the altar was called "strange fire," and for the use of such Nadab and Abihu were punished with death by fire from God. Lev. 10:1, 2; Num. 3:4; 26:61.

Firepan, one of the vessels of the temple service. Ex. 27:3; 38:3; 2 Kings 25:15; Jer. 52:19. The same word is elsewhere rendered "snuff-

First=born. Under the law, in memory of the Exodus (when the first-born of the Egyptians were slain), the eldest son was regarded as devoted to God, and was in every case to be redeemed by an offering not exceeding five shekels, within one month from birth. If he died before the expiration of thirty days, the Jewish doctors held the father excused, but liable to the payment if he outlived that time. Ex. 13:12-15; 22:29; Num. 8:17; 18:15, 16; Lev. 27:6. The eldest son received a double portion of the father's inheritance, Deut. 21:17, but not of the mother's. Under the monarchy the eldest son usually, but not always, as appears in the case of Solomon, succeeded his father in the kingdom. 1 Kings 1:30; 2:22. The male first-born of animals was also devoted to God. Ex. 13:2, 12, 13; 22:29, 30; 34:19, 20. Unclean animals were to be redeemed with the addition of one-fifth of the value, or else put to death; or, if not redeemed, to be sold, and the price given to the priests. Lev. 27 : 13, 27, 28.

First=fruits. (1) The law ordered in general that the first of all ripe fruits and of liquors, or, as it is twice expressed, the first of first-fruits, should be offered in God's house. Ex. 22 : 29; 23 : 19; 34 : 26. It was an act of allegiance to God as the giver of all. No exact quantity was commanded, but it was left to the spiritual and moral sense of each individual. (2) On the morrow after the passover sabbath, *i. e.* on the 16th of Nisan, a sheaf of new corn was to be brought to the priest and waved before the altar, in acknowledgment of the gift of fruitfulness. Lev. 2 : 12; 23 : 5, 6, 10–12. (3) At the expiration of seven weeks from this time, *i. e.* at the feast of pentecost, an oblation was to be made of two loaves of leavened bread made from the new flour, which were to be waved in like manner with the passover sheaf. Ex. 34 : 22; Lev. 23 : 15, 17; Num. 28 : 26. (4) The feast of ingathering, *i. e.* the feast of tabernacles, in the seventh month, was itself an acknowledgment of the fruits of the harvest. Ex. 23 : 16; 34 : 22; Lev. 23 : 39. These four sorts of offerings were national. Besides them, the two following were of an individual kind. (5) A cake of the first dough that was baked was to be offered as a heave offering. Num. 15 : 19, 21. (6) The first-fruits of the land were to be brought in a basket to the holy place of God's choice, and there presented to the priest, who was to set the basket down before the altar. Deut. 26 : 2–11. The offerings were the perquisite of the priests. Num. 18 : 11; Deut. 18 : 4. Nehemiah, at the return from captivity, took pains to reorganize the offerings of first-fruits of both kinds, and to appoint places to receive them. Neh. 10 : 35, 37; 12 : 44. An offering of first-fruits is mentioned as an acceptable one to the prophet Elisha. 2 Kings 4 : 42.

Fish. The Hebrews recognized fish as one of the great divisions of the animal kingdom, and as such gave them a place in the account of the creation, Gen. 1 : 21, 28, as well as in other passages where an exhaustive description of living creatures is intended. Gen. 9 : 2; Ex. 20 : 4; Deut. 4 : 18; 1 Kings 4 : 33. The Mosaic law, Lev. 11 : 9, 10, pro-

nounced unclean such fish as were devoid of fins and scales; these were and are regarded as unwholesome in Egypt. There are several idols representing the god by a figure half man and half fish. 1 Sam. 5 : 4. On this account the worship of fish is expressly prohibited. Deut. 4 : 18. In Palestine, the Sea of Galilee was and still is remarkably well stored with fish. Tristram speaks of fourteen species found there, and thinks the number inhabiting it at least three times as great. Jerusalem derived its supply chiefly from the Mediterranean. Comp. Ezek. 47 : 10. The existence of a regular fish-market is implied in the notice of the fish-gate, which was probably contiguous to it. 2 Chron. 33 : 14; Neh. 3 : 3; 12 : 39; Zeph. 1 : 10. The Orientals are exceedingly fond of fish as an article of diet. Numerous allusions to the art of fishing occur in the Bible. Fish-hooks and lines were used. Hab. 1 : 15; Am. 4 : 2. But the most usual method of catching fish was by the use of the net, either the *casting* net, Ezek. 26 : 5, 14; 47 : 10; Hab. 1 : 15, probably resembling the one used in Egypt, or the *draw* or *drag* net, Isa. 19 : 8; Hab. 1 : 15, which was larger, and required the use of a boat. The latter was probably most used on the Sea of Galilee, as the number of boats kept on it was very considerable.

Fitches (*i. e.* VETCHES), without doubt the *Nigella sativa,* an herbaceous annual plant belonging to the natural order *Ranunculaceæ* (the buttercup family), which grows in the south of Europe and in the north of Africa. Its black seeds are used like pepper, and have almost as pungent a taste. The Syrians sprinkle these seeds over their flat cakes before they are baked. [See RYE.]

Flag. There are two Hebrew words rendered "flag" in our Bible: (1) A word of Egyptian origin, and denoting "any green and coarse herbage, such as rushes and reeds, which grow in marshy places." Gen. 41 : 2, 18 (here translated meadow). It is perhaps the *Cyperus esculentus.* (2) A word which appears to be used in a very wide sense to denote "weeds of any kind," Ex. 2 : 3, 5; Isa. 19 : 6, meaning marine growths.

Flagon, a word employed in the Authorized Version to render two distinct Hebrew terms: (1) *Ashîshah,* 2 Sam.

6:19; 1 Chron. 16:3; Cant. 2:5; Hos. 3:1. It really means a cake of pressed raisins. Such cakes were considered as delicacies; they were also offered to

FENNEL FLOWER OR VETCHES (Nigella sativa).

ĭdols. (2) *Nebel*, Isa. 22:24, is commonly used for a bottle or vessel, originally probably a skin, but in later times a piece of pottery. Isa. 30:14.

Flax, a well-known plant with yellowish stem and bright-blue flowers. Its fibres are employed in the manufacture of linen. The seed contains an oil, and after the oil is expressed is used as a food for cattle. Egypt was celebrated for the culture of flax and the manufacture of linen. The spinning was anciently done by women of noble birth. It seems probable that the cultivation of flax for the purpose of the manufacture of linen was by no means confined to Egypt, but that, originating in India, it spread over Asia at a very early period of antiquity. That it was grown in Palestine even before the conquest of that country by the Israelites appears from Josh. 2:6. The various processes employed in preparing the flax for manufacture into cloth are indicated: (1) The drying process. (2) The peeling of the stalks and separation of the fibres. (3) The hackling. Isa. 19:9. That flax was one of the

FLAX.

most important crops in Palestine appears from Hos. 2:5, 9.

Flea, an insect but twice mentioned in Scripture, viz., in 1 Sam. 24:14; 26:20. Fleas are abundant in the East, and afford the subject of many proverbial expressions.

Flesh. [FOOD.]

Flint, a well-known stone, a variety of quartz. It is extremely hard, and strikes fire. It was very abundant in and about Palestine. Deut. 8:15; 32:13; Ps. 114:8; Isa. 5:28; 50:7; Ezek. 3:9.

Flood. [NOAH.]

Flute. The word so translated in Dan. 3 was probably not the modern flute. There were four Heb. words representing flute-like instruments: (1) *Halil*, "Pipe," 1 Kings 1:40; Isa. 30:29; etc. This bore a close resemblance to the modern flute and was made of reeds, of copper, and other material. It was the principal wind-instrument. (2) *Ugab*, a word of uncertain meaning, in the A. V. "organ." Gen. 4:21; Job 21:12; Ps. 150:4, etc. (3) *Mashrokitha*, the one used at the worship of Nebuchadnezzar's golden image, Dan. 3:5, 7, 15, probably the "syrinx." (4) *Symphonia*, in Dan. 3:5, 15. Traditionally a bagpipe. Perhaps it was developed from the double flute.

Flux, Bloody, Acts 28:8, the same as our dysentery, which in the East is, though sometimes sporadic, generally epidemic and infectious, and then assumes its worst form.

Fly, Flies. The two following Hebrew terms denote flies of some kind: (1) *Zĕbûb*, which occurs only in Eccles. 10:1 and in Isa. 7:18, and is probably a generic name for an insect. (2) *'Arôb* ("swarms of *flies*," "divers sorts of *flies*," Authorized Version), the name of the insect or insects which God sent to punish Pharaoh; see Ex. 8:21-31; Ps. 78:45; 105:31. The question as to what particular species is denoted, or whether any one species is to be understood, has long been a matter of dispute. As the *ârôb* are said to have filled the houses of the Egyptians, it seems not improbable that common flies (*Muscidæ*) are more especially intended. The *ârôb* may include various species of *Culicidæ* (gnats), such as the mosquito; but the common flies are to this day in Egypt regarded as a "plague," and are the great instrument of spreading the well-known ophthalmia, which is conveyed from one individual to another by these dreadful pests. According to the Septuagint "the *dog-fly* is meant," which at certain seasons is described as a far worse plague than mosquitoes. The bite is exceedingly sharp and painful, causing severe inflammation, especially in the eyelids. Coming in immense swarms, they cover all objects in black and loathsome masses, and attack every exposed part of a traveller's person with incredible pertinacity."—*Cook*.

Food. The diet of eastern nations has been in all ages light and simple. Vegetable food was more used than animal. Bread was the principal food; preparations of grain were, however, common. The Hebrews used a great variety of articles, John 6:5, 9, to give a relish to bread. Milk and its preparations hold a conspicuous place in eastern diet, as affording substantial nourishment; generally in the form of the modern *leben, i. e.* sour milk. Authorized Version "butter;" Gen. 18:8; Judges 5:25; 2 Sam. 17:29. Fruit was another source of subsistence: figs stood first in point of importance; they were generally dried and pressed into cakes.

Grapes were generally eaten in a dried state as raisins. Of vegetables we have most frequent notice of lentils, beans, leeks, onions and garlic, which were and still are of a superior quality in Egypt. Num. 11:5. Honey is extensively used, as is also olive oil.

The Orientals have been at all times sparing in the use of animal food; not only does the excessive heat of the climate render it both unwholesome to eat much meat and expensive from the necessity of immediately consuming a whole animal, but beyond this the ritual regulations of the Mosaic law in ancient, as of the Koran in modern, times have tended to the same result. The prohibition expressed against consuming the blood of any animal, Gen. 9:4, was more fully developed in the Levitical law, and enforced by the penalty of death. Lev. 3:17; 7:26; 19:26; Deut. 12:16. Certain portions of the fat of sacrifices were also forbidden, Lev. 3:9, 10, as being set apart for the altar. Lev. 3:16; 7:25.

In addition to the above, the Jews were forbidden to eat the flesh of animals portions of which had been offered to idols. All beasts and birds classed as unclean, Lev. 11:1 ff.; Deut. 14:4 ff.; were also prohibited. Under these restrictions the Hebrews were permitted the free use of animal food: generally speaking they only availed themselves of it in the exercise of hospitality or at festivals of a religious, public or private character. It was only in royal households that there was a daily consumption of meat. The animals killed for meat were—calves, lambs, oxen not above three years of age, harts, roebucks and fallow deer; birds of various kinds; fish, with the exception of such as were without scales and fins. Locusts, of which certain species only were esteemed clean, were occasionally eaten, Matt. 3:4, but were regarded as poor fare.

Footman, a word employed in the English Bible in two senses: (1) Generally, to distinguish those of the fighting men who went on foot from those who were on horseback or in chariots. (2) In a more special sense, in 1 Sam. 22:17 only, and as the translation of a different term from the above—a body of swift runners in attendance on the king. This body appears to have been afterwards kept up, and to have been distinct from the body-guard—the six hundred and the thirty—who were originated by David. See 1 Kings 14:27, 28; 2 Kings 11:4, 6, 11, 13, 19; 2 Chron. 12:10, 11. In each of these cases the word is the same as the above, and is rendered "guard," with "runners" in the margin in one instance—1 Kings 14:27.

Forehead. The practice of veiling the face (forehead) in public for women of the higher classes, especially married women, in the East, sufficiently stigmatizes with reproach the unveiled face of women of bad character. Gen. 24:65; Jer. 3:3. The custom among many Oriental nations both of coloring the face and forehead and of impressing on the body marks indicative of devotion to some special deity or religious sect is mentioned elsewhere. The "jewels for the forehead," mentioned by Ezekiel, 16:12, and in margin of Authorized Version, Gen. 24:22, were in all probability nose-rings. Isa. 3:21.

Forest. Although Palestine has never been in historical times a woodland country, yet there can be no doubt that there was much more wood formerly than there is at present, and that the destruction of the forests was one of the chief causes of the present desolation.

Fortifications. [FENCED CITIES.]

Fortuna'tus (fôr-tū-nā'tus) (*fortunate*), 1 Cor. 16:17, one of three Corinthians, the others being Stephanas and Achaïcus, who were at Ephesus when St. Paul wrote his first epistle. There is a Fortunatus mentioned in the end of Clement's first epistle to the Corinthians, who was possibly the same person.

Fountain (a spring, in distinction from a well). The springs of Palestine, though short-lived, are remarkable for their abundance and beauty, especially those which fall into the Jordan and into its lakes, of which there are hundreds throughout its whole course. The spring or fountain of living water, the "eye" of the landscape, is distinguished in all Oriental languages from the artificially-sunk and enclosed well. Jerusalem appears to have possessed either more than one perennial spring or one issuing by more than one outlet. In Oriental cities generally public fountains are frequent. Traces of such fountains at Jerusalem may perhaps be found in the names of Enrogel, 2 Sam. 17:17, the "Dragon well" or fountain,

and the "gate of the fountain." Neh. 2: 13, 14.

Fowl. Several distinct Hebrew and Greek words are thus rendered in the English Bible. Of these the most common is *'ôph*, which is usually a collective term for all kinds of birds. In 1 Kings 4:23, among the daily provisions for Solomon's table "fatted fowl" are included. In the New Testament the word translated "fowls" is most frequently that which comprehends all kinds of birds (including *ravens*, Luke 12:24). [SPARROW.]

Fox (Heb. *shû'âl*). Probably the jackal is the animal signified in almost all the passages in the Old Testament where the Hebrew term occurs. Though both foxes and jackals abound in Palestine, the *shû'âlim* (foxes) of Judges 15:

SYRIAN FOX.

4 are evidently jackals and not foxes, for the former animal is gregarious, whereas the latter is solitary in its habits; Samson could not, for that reason, have easily caught three hundred foxes, but it was easy to catch that number of jackals, which are concealed by hundreds in the caves and ruins of Syria. It is not probable, however, that Samson sent out the whole three hundred at once. With respect to the jackals and foxes of Palestine, there is no doubt that the common jackal of the country is the *Canis aureus*, which may be heard every night in the villages. It is like a medium-sized dog, with a head like a wolf, and is of a bright-yellow color. These beasts de-

vour the bodies of the dead, and even dig them up from their graves.

Frankincense, a vegetable resin, brittle, glittering, and of a bitter taste, used for the purpose of sacrificial fumigation. Ex. 30:34–36. It was called *frank* because of the freeness with which, when burned, it gives forth its odor. It burns for a long time, with a steady flame. It is obtained by successive incisions in the bark of a tree of the genus Boswellia. The first incision yields the purest and whitest resin, while the product of the after incisions is spotted with yellow, and loses its whiteness altogether as it becomes old.

FRANKINCENSE.

The Hebrews imported their frankincense from Arabia, Isa. 60:6; Jer. 6:20, and more particularly from Sheba, but it is remarkable that at present the Arabian libanum or olibanum is of a very inferior kind, and that the finest frankincense imported into Turkey comes through Arabia from the islands of the Indian Archipelago. There can be little doubt that the tree which produces the Indian frankincense is the *Boswellia serrata* of Roxburgh, or *Boswellia thurifera* of Colebrooke, and bears some resemblance when young to the mountain ash. It grows to be forty feet high.

Frog, a well-known amphibious animal of the genus *Rana.* The mention of this reptile in the Old Testament is confined to the passage in Ex. 8:2–7, etc., in which the plague of frogs is described, and to Ps. 78:45; 105:30. In the New Testament the word occurs once only, in Rev. 16:13. There is no question as to the animal meant. The only known species of frog which occurs at present in Egypt is the *Rana esculenta,* the edible frog of the continent.

Frontlets, or **Phylacteries.** Ex. 13:16; Deut. 6:8; 11:18; Matt. 23:5. These "frontlets" or "phylacteries" were strips of parchment, on which were written four passages of Scripture, Ex. 13:2–10, 11–17; Deut. 6:4–9, 13–23, in an ink prepared for the purpose. They were then rolled up in a case of black calfskin, which was at-

ARM PHYLACTERY.

tached to a stiffer piece of leather, having a thong one finger broad and one and a half cubits long. They were placed at the bend of the left arm. Those worn on the forehead were written on four strips of parchment, and put into four little cells within a square case on which the letter ש was written. The square had two thongs, on which Hebrew letters were inscribed. That phylacteries were used as amulets is certain, and was very natural. The expression "they make broad their phylacteries," Matt. 23:5, refers not so much to the phylactery itself, which seems to have been of a prescribed breadth, as to the case in which the parchment was kept, which the Pharisees, among their other pretentious customs, Mark 7:3, 4; Luke 5:33, etc., made as conspicuous as they could. It is said that the Pharisees wore them always, whereas the common people only used them at prayers.

Fuller. The trade of the fullers, so far as it is mentioned in Scripture, appears to have consisted chiefly in cleansing garments and whitening them. The process of fulling or cleansing clothes consisted in treading or stamping on the garments with the feet or with bats in tubs of water, in which some alkaline substance answering the purpose of soap had been dissolved. The substances used for this purpose which are mentioned in Scripture are natron, Prov. 25 : 20; Jer. 2 : 22, and soap. Mal. 3 : 2. Other substances also are mentioned as being employed in cleansing, which, together with alkali, seem to identify the Jewish with the Roman process, as urine and chalk. The process of whitening garments was performed by rubbing into them chalk or earth of some kind. *Creta cimolia* (cimolite) was probably the earth most frequently used. The trade of the fullers, as causing offensive smells, and also as requiring space for drying clothes, appears to have been carried on at Jerusalem outside the city.

Fuller's field, The, a spot near Jerusalem, 2 Kings 18 : 17; Isa. 7 : 3; 36 : 2, so close to the walls that a person speaking from there could be heard on them. 2 Kings 18 : 17, 26. One resort of the fullers of Jerusalem would seem to have been below the city on the southeast side. But the Rabshakeh and his "great host" must have come from the north; and the fuller's field was therefore, to judge from this circumstance, on the table-land on the northern side of the city.

Funerals. [BURIAL.]

Furlong. [WEIGHTS AND MEASURES.]

Furnace. Various kinds of furnaces are noticed in the Bible, such as a smelting or calcining furnace, Gen. 19 : 28; Ex. 9 : 8, 10; 19 : 18, especially a lime-kiln, Isa. 33 : 12; Amos 2 : 1; a refining furnace, Prov. 17 : 3; Nebuchadnezzar's furnace, a large furnace built like a brick-kiln, Dan. 3 : 22, 23, with two openings, one at the top for putting in the materials, and another below for removing them. The Persians were in the habit of using the furnace as a means of inflicting punishment. Dan. 3 : 22, 23; Jer. 29 : 22.

G

Ga'al (gā'al), son of Ebed, aided the Shechemites in their rebellion against Abimelech. Judges 9.

Ga'ash (gā'ash) (*earthquake*), a hill of Ephraim, where Joshua was buried. The brooks or valley of Gaash, 2 Sam. 23:30; 1 Chron. 11:32, were probably at the foot of the hill.

Ga'ba (gā'bà). [GEBA.]

Gab'bai (găb'bā-ī) (*tax-gatherer*), apparently the head of an important family of Benjamin resident at Jerusalem. Neh. 11:8. Perhaps the Ibneiah of 1 Chron. 9:8.

Gab'batha (găb'ba-thà) (*a platform*), the Hebrew or Chaldee appellation of a place, also called "Pavement," where the judgment-seat or bema was planted, from his place on which Pilate delivered our Lord to death. John 19:13. None of the attempted identifications of the spot have proved quite satisfactory. Possibly it was connected in some way with Herod's Palace. No such place was mentioned by Josephus.

Ga'briel (gā'brĭ-el) (*man of God*), an angel of high rank sent by God to announce to Zacharias the birth of John the Baptist, and to Mary the birth of Christ. Luke 1:11–22, 26–31. He was also sent to Daniel to explain his visions. Dan. 8:16; 9:21.

Gad (găd) (*fortune*). 1. Jacob's seventh son, the first-born of Zilpah, Leah's maid, and whole-brother to Asher. Gen. 30:11–13; 46:16, 18.

2. "The seer," or "the king's seer," *i. e.* David's, a "prophet" who appears to have joined David when in the hold. 1 Sam. 22:5. (B.C. 1061.) He reappears in connection with the punishment inflicted for the numbering of the people. 2 Sam. 24:11–19; 1 Chron. 21:9–19. He wrote a book of the Acts of David, 1 Chron. 29:29, and also assisted in the arrangements for the musical service of the "house of God." 2 Chron. 29:25.

Gad, The tribe of. The country allotted to the tribe of Gad appears, speaking roughly, to have lain chiefly about the centre of the land east of Jordan. The south of that district—from the Arnon (*Wady Mojib*), about halfway down the Dead Sea, to Heshbon, nearly due east of Jerusalem—was occupied by Reuben, and at or about Heshbon the possessions of Gad commenced. They embraced half Gilead, Deut. 3:12, or half the land of the children of Ammon, Josh. 13:25, probably the mountainous district which is intersected by the torrent Jabbok, including, as its most northern town, the ancient sanctuary of Mahanaim. The character of the tribe is throughout strongly marked—fierce and warlike.

Gadarenes' (găd-a-rēnes'), **Gerge= senes'** (gēr-ge-sēnes'), **Gerasenes'** (gēr-a-sēnes'). These three names are used indiscriminately to designate the place where Jesus healed two demoniacs. The first two are in the Authorized Version. Matt. 8:28; Mark 5:1; Luke 8:26. In Mark and Luke the Revised Version uses Gerasenes in place of Gadarenes. There has been much discussion as to the correct form of the word,—whether derived from Gadara, Gergesa or Gerasa. *Gadara* was a Greek city called by Josephus the metropolis of Perea on the east of Jordan. The miracle could not have taken place literally in the neighborhood of Gadara, as it is a three hours' ride from the Sea of Galilee, and separated from it by a steep gorge. The name *Gergesa* found in the A. V. seems to have few advocates; its site may have been several miles north. *Gerasa,* the capital of the district of the Gerasenes, was one of the cities of the Decapolis, and a well-known city of Palestine. It was about 30 miles southeast of Gadara, 37 miles south of the Dead Sea, on the borders of Perea, and a little north of the river Jabbok. It is now called

205

Jerash, and is a deserted ruin. This town is out of the question as the site of the miracle. The region may have been called by popular usage " the country of the Gadarenes," although not officially a part of the district, but as being near enough to distinguish it among those familiar with the places. The derivation of the reading from the name Gerasa is, however, advocated by many, *e. g.* Cheyne, and the R. V. translators.

For the actual identification of the site, however, there is no dispute, as the modern *Khersa* is admitted by all to be the place where the miracle took place. Indeed it seems to be the one place on the eastern side of the Lake where all the conditions are fulfilled. For one of the latest discussions of the question see Hastings' "Dictionary of Christ and the Gospels."

Gad'di (găd'dĭ) (*fortunate*), son of Susi; the Manassite spy sent by Moses to explore Canaan. Num. 13 : 11. (B.C. 1490.)

Gad'diel (găd'dĭ-el) (*God is my fortune*), a Zebulunite, one of the twelve spies. Num. 13 : 10. (B.C. 1490.)

Ga'di (gā'dĭ), a Gadite, father of Menahem, a king of Israel. 2 Kings 15 : 14, 17.

Gad'ites, The, the descendants of Gad, and the members of his tribe.

Ga'ham (gā'hăm) (*sunburnt*), son of Nahor, Abraham's brother, by his concubine Reumah. Gen. 22 : 24.

Ga'har (gā'här) (*hiding-place*). The Bene-Gahar were among the families of Nethinim who returned from the captivity with Zerubbabel. Ezra 2 : 47; Neh. 7 : 49.

Gai'us (gā'ius), or **Cai'us.** 1. A Macedonian who accompanied Paul in his travels, and whose life was in danger from the mob at Ephesus. Acts 19 : 29. (A.D. 57.)

2. Of Derbe. He went with Paul from Corinth in his last journey to Jerusalem. Acts 20 : 4. (A.D. 57.)

3. Of Corinth, whom Paul baptized, and who was his host in his second sojourn in that city. 1 Cor. 1 : 14; Rom. 16 : 23.

4. John's third epistle is addressed to a Christian of this name. Attempts have been made in vain to identify him with any other named.

Gal'aad (găl'a-ăd), the Greek form of the word Gilead.

Ga'lal (gā'lăl) (*a rolling*). 1. A Levite, one of the sons of Asaph. 1 Chron. 9 : 15.

2. Another Levite, of the family of Elkanah. 1 Chron. 9 : 16.

3. A third Levite, son of Jeduthun. Neh. 11 : 17. Probably the same as (2).

Galatia (gă-lā'shià) (*land of the Galli, Gauls*), is the central district of Asia Minor. The chief interest of Bible students with regard to this province is connected with Paul's Epistle to the Galatians. It has generally been supposed that the cities in which were " the churches of Galatia " are unknown, and that the record of Paul's missionary journeys contains no notice of his preaching in them by name. Professor Ramsay has, however, convinced most modern scholars that the Roman province of Galatia extended much farther to the southwest, and included Pisidia and Lycaonia, so that Antioch, Iconium, Lystra and Derbe were among the churches of Galatia to whom the epistle was written. These churches were founded by Paul during his first missionary journey (A.D. 45–47), and visited by him during his second journey (A.D. 49 or 50), and again on his third journey (A.D. 54).

Gala'tians (gă-lā'shŭns), **The Epistle to the,** was written by the apostle St. Paul not long after his journey through Galatia and Phrygia, Acts 18 : 23, and probably either during his long sojourn of nearly three years in Ephesus (A.D. 54–57), or soon after, at Corinth in A.D. 58. The epistle appears to have been called forth by the machinations of Judaizing teachers, who, shortly before the date of its composition, had endeavored to seduce the churches of this province into a recognition of circumcision, Gal. 5 : 2, 11, 12; 6 : 12, *seq.,* and had openly sought to depreciate the apostolic claims of St. Paul. Comp. 1 : 1, 11. " Since the days of Luther the Epistle to the Galatians has always been held in high esteem as the gospel's banner of freedom. To it and the Epistle to the Romans we owe most directly the springing up and development of the ideas and energies of the Reformation." " It gives in briefer outline, and with special application, the same scheme of salvation . . . which is . . . presented in the Epistle to the Romans. All men being under the law, and condemned as sinners by the law, salvation is impossible by the works of the law. Christ alone can save." "The declaration of these truths made Christianity a world religion, instead of a Jewish sect."—*Purves.*

Gal'banum, one of the perfumes employed in the preparation of the sacred incense. Ex. 30:34. The galbanum of commerce is brought chiefly from India and the Levant. It is a resinous gum of a brownish-yellow color and strong disagreeable smell, usually met with in masses, but sometimes found in yellowish tear-like drops. But, though galbanum itself is well known, the plant which yields it has not been exactly determined.

Gal'eed (găl'e-ed) (*cairn of witness*), the name given by Jacob to the heap which he and Laban made on Mount Gilead in witness of the covenant then entered into between them. Gen. 31:47, 48; comp. 23, 25.

Galile'ans (găl-ĭ-lē'anṣ), the inhabitants of Galilee, the northern province of Palestine. The apostles were all Galileans by either birth or residence. Acts 1:11. It appears also that the pronunciation of those Jews who resided in Galilee had become peculiar, probably from their contact with their Gentile neighbors. Matt. 26:73. In ancient times a large part of the population of Galilee was non-Jewish, and after the fall of the northern kingdom many of the people were carried away, and in some cases their places were filled by foreigners. Soon after the time of the Maccabees, however, they became a thoroughly Jewish people, and remained so during the remainder of their history. With few exceptions they were wealthy and in general an influential class, "healthy, brave and industrious." The Galileans had many manufactures, fisheries, some commerce, but were chiefly an agricultural people. They were eminent for patriotism and courage, as were their ancestors, with great respect for law and order. They were less bigoted than the Jews of Judea; partly, it is likely, because of their diverse origin, and partly it is certain because they were "too industrious to be strictly orthodox from a Pharisaic point of view."—*Cheyne.*

Gal'ilee (*circuit*). This name, which in the Roman age was applied to a large province, seems to have been originally confined to a little "circuit" of

country round Kedesh-Naphtali, in which were situated the twenty towns given by Solomon to Hiram king of Tyre as payment for his work in conveying timber from Lebanon to Jerusalem. Josh. 20:7; 1 Kings 9:11. In the time of our Lord all Palestine was divided into three provinces, Judea, Samaria and Galilee. Luke 17:11; Acts 9:31; Joseph. *B. J.* iii. 3. The latter included the whole northern section of the country, including the ancient territories of Issachar, Zebulun, Asher and Naphtali. On the west it was bounded by the whole plain of Akka to the foot of Carmel. The southern border ran along the base of Carmel and of the hills of Samaria to Mount Gilboa, and then descended the valley of Jezreel by Scythopolis to the Jordan. The river Jordan, the Sea of Galilee, and the upper Jordan to the fountain at Dan, formed the eastern border; and the northern ran from Dan westward across the mountain ridge till it touched the territory of the Phœnicians. Galilee was divided into two sections, "Lower" and "Upper." *Lower Galilee* included the great plain of Esdraelon with its offshoots, which run down to the Jordan and the Lake of Tiberias, and the whole of the hill country adjoining it on the north to the foot of the mountain range. It was thus one of the richest and most beautiful sections of Palestine. *Upper Galilee* embraced the whole mountain range lying between the upper Jordan and Phœnicia. To this region the name "Galilee of the Gentiles" is given in the Old and New Testaments. Isa. 9:1; Matt. 4:15. Galilee was the scene of the greater part of our Lord's private life and public acts. It is a remarkable fact that the first three Gospels are chiefly taken up with our Lord's ministrations in this province, while the Gospel of John dwells more upon those in Judea.

Character of the country.—Galilee was a region of great natural fertility. Such is the fertility of the soil that it rejects no plant, for the air is so genial that it suits every variety. The walnut, which delights above other trees in a wintry climate, grows here luxuriantly, together with the palm tree, which is nourished by heat. It not only possesses the extraordinary virtue of nourishing fruits of opposite climes, but also maintains a continual supply of them. Here were found all the productions which made Italy rich and beautiful. Forests covered its mountains and hills, while its uplands, gentle slopes and broader valleys were rich in pasture, meadows, cultivated fields, vineyards, olive groves and fruit trees of every kind.

The population of Galilee is variously estimated. Josephus states that there were 204 cities and villages in Galilee, the smallest of which numbered 15,000 inhabitants. Dr. Selah Merrill argues for the general correctness of Josephus' estimates.

There was a perfect network of roads covering the whole territory. "Judea was on the road to nowhere; Galilee is covered with roads to everywhere." It was the great highroad between the Mediterranean and the countries of the far East, with which there was a considerable traffic. The common idea of Nazareth, the home of Jesus, as a quiet country village, is quite erroneous. For descriptions of Galilee and its people see Hastings' "Dictionary of Christ and the Gospels."

Gal'ilee, Sea of. So called from the province of Galilee, which bordered on its western side. Matt. 4 : 18. It was also called the "Sea of Tiberias," from the celebrated city of that name. John 6 : 1. At its northwestern angle was a beautiful and fertile plain called "Gennesaret," and from that it derived the name of "Lake of Gennesaret." Luke 5 : 1. It was called in the Old Testament "the Sea of Chinnereth" or "Cinneroth," Num. 34 : 11; Josh. 12 : 3; 1 Kings 15 : 20, from a town of that name which stood on or near its shore. Josh. 19 : 35. Its modern name is *Bahr Tubariyeh*. Most of our Lord's public life was spent in the environs of this sea. The surrounding region was then the most densely peopled in all Palestine. About the Lake there were ten or twelve flourishing towns. The Sea of Galilee is of an oval or pear-shape, about thirteen geographical miles long and six broad. The river Jordan enters it at its northern end and passes out at its southern end. In fact the bed of the lake is just a lower section of the great Jordan valley. Its most remarkable feature is its deep depression, being no less than 700 feet below the level of the ocean. It is exposed to frequent sudden and violent storms, owing to the great number of hills.

On the east and west the hills rise abruptly, almost forming a mountain wall. To the north and south also are hills, though the slopes are much more gradual. Not only Jews but people of many races have praised the beauty of the Sea of Galilee. Now it is bleak and barren, and the shores lined with ruins. The great depression makes the climate of the shores almost tropical. This is very sensibly felt by the traveler in going down from the plains of Galilee. In summer the heat is intense, and even in early spring the air has something of an Egyptian balminess. The water of the lake is sweet, cool and transparent; and as the beach is everywhere pebbly it has a beautiful sparkling look. It abounds in fish now as in ancient times. There were large fisheries on the lake, and much commerce was carried on upon it.

Gall. (1) *Mereerah*, denoting "that which is bitter;" hence the term is applied to the "bile" or "gall" (the fluid secreted by the liver), from its intense bitterness, Job 16 : 13; 20 : 25; it is also used of the "poison" of serpents, Job 20 : 14, which the ancients erroneously believed was their gall. (2) *Rôsh*, generally translated "gall" in the English Bible, is in Hos. 10 : 4 rendered "hemlock:" in Deut. 32 : 33 and Job 20 : 16, *rôsh* denotes the "poison" or "venom" of serpents. From Deut. 29 : 18 and Lam. 3 : 19, compared with Hos. 10 : 4, it is evident that the Hebrew term denotes some bitter and perhaps poisonous plant. Other writers have supposed, and with some reason, from Deut. 32 : 32, that some berry-bearing plant must be intended. Gesenius understands poppies; in which case the gall mingled with the wine offered to our Lord at his crucifixion, and refused by him, would be an anæsthetic, and tend to diminish the sense of suffering.

Gallery, an architectural term describing the porticos or verandas which are not uncommon in eastern houses. It is doubtful, however, whether the Hebrew words so translated have any reference to such an object. In S. of Sol. 7 : 5, it means, as in R. V. "tresses." Elsewhere it probably means "colonnade" or "panelling."

Galley. [Ship.]

JEWISH FISHERMEN BY THE SEA OF GALILEE.

Gal'lim (găl'lim) (*heaps*). This is given as the native place of the man to whom Michal, David's wife, was given. 1 Sam. 25:44. Its site is unknown but not far from Jerusalem. The name occurs again in the catalogue of places terrified at the approach of Sennacherib. Isa. 10:30.

Gal'lio (găl'lĭ-ō), Junius Annæus Gallio, the Roman proconsul of Achaia when St. Paul was at Corinth, A.D. 52, under the emperor Claudius. Acts 18:12. He was brother to Lucius Annæus Seneca, the philosopher. Seneca was forced by Nero to commit suicide in A.D. 65. Gallio appealed for mercy but was put to death the following year. Gallio has been the type of the man who is supremely indifferent to all religious questions. This is, however, not warranted by the text, which merely intends to state that as the Roman governor he let questions of Jewish religion alone.

Gallows. [PUNISHMENTS.]

Gama'liel (gȧ-mā'lĭ-el) (*recompense of God*). 1. Son of Pedahzur; prince or captain of the tribe of Manasseh at the census at Sinai, Num. 1:10; 2:20; 7:54, 59, and at starting on the march through the wilderness. Num. 10:23. (B.C. 1490.)

2. A Pharisee and celebrated doctor of the law, who gave prudent worldly advice in the Sanhedrin respecting the treatment of the followers of Jesus of Nazareth. Acts 5:34 ff. (A.D. 34.) We learn from Acts 22:3 that he was the preceptor of St. Paul. He is generally identified with the very celebrated Jewish doctor Gamaliel, grandson of Hillel, and who is referred to as authority in the Jewish Mishna.

Games. Among the Greeks the rage for theatrical exhibitions was such that every city of any size possessed its theatre and stadium. At Ephesus an annual contest was held in honor of Diana. It is probable that St. Paul was present when these games were proceeding. A direct reference to the exhibitions that took place on such occasions is made in 1 Cor. 15:32. St. Paul's epistles abound with allusions to the Greek contests, borrowed probably from the Isthmian games, at which he may well have been present during his first visit to Corinth. These contests, 1 Tim. 6:12; 2 Tim. 4:7, were divided into two classes, the *pancratium*, consisting of boxing and wrestling, and the *pentathlon*, consisting of leaping, running, quoiting, hurling the spear and wrestling. The competitors, 1 Cor. 9:25; 2 Tim. 2:5, required a long and severe course of previous training, 1 Tim. 4, 8, during which a particular diet was enforced. 1 Cor. 9:25, 27. In the Olympic contests these preparatory exercises extended over a period of ten months, during the last of which they were conducted under the supervision of appointed officers. The contests took place in the presence of a vast multitude of spectators, Heb. 12:1, the competitors being the spectacle. 1 Cor. 4:9; Heb. 10:33.

The games were opened by the proclamation of a herald, whose office it was to give out the name and country of each candidate, and especially to announce the name of the victor before the assembled multitude. The judge was selected for his spotless integrity, 2 Tim. 4:8; he was to decide disputes, and to give the prize, 1 Cor. 9:24; Phil. 3:14, consisting of a crown, 2 Tim. 2:5; 4:8, of leaves of wild olive at the Olympic games, and of pine, or at one period ivy, at the Isthmian games. St. Paul alludes to two only out of the five contests, boxing and running, more frequently to the latter. The Jews had no public games, the great feasts of religion supplying them with anniversary occasions of national gatherings.

Gam'madim (găm'ma-dĭm). This word occurs only in Ezek. 27:11 as people in the towers of Tyre. A variety of explanations of the term have been offered, nearly all of which are based on the supposition of a slight error of the copyist, and upon none of which do modern scholars agree.

Ga'mul (gā'mŭl) (*weaned*), a priest, the leader of the twenty-second course in the service of the sanctuary. 1 Chron. 24:17.

Garden. Gardens in the East, as the Hebrew word indicates, are enclosures on the outskirts of towns, planted with various trees and shrubs. From the allusions in the Bible we learn that they were surrounded by hedges of thorn, Isa. 5:5, or walls of stone. Prov. 24:31. For further protection lodges, Isa. 1:8; Lam. 2:6, or watchtowers, Mark 12:1, were built in them, in which sat the keeper, Job 27:18, to drive away the wild beasts and robbers, as is the case to this day. The gardens of the Hebrews were planted with flowers and aromatic shrubs, Cant. 6:2; 4:16, besides olives, fig trees, nuts or walnuts, Cant. 6:11, pomegranates, and others for domestic use. Ex. 23:11; Jer. 29:5; Amos 9:14. Gardens of herbs, or kitchen gardens, are mentioned in Deut. 11:10 and 1 Kings 21:2. The rose garden in Jerusalem, said to have been situated westward of the temple mount, is remarkable as having been one of the few gardens which, from the time of the prophets, existed within the city walls. The retirement of gardens rendered them favorite places for devotion.

Ga′reb (gā′rĕb) (*scabby*), one of the heroes of David's army. 2 Sam. 23:38.

Ga′reb, The hill, in the neighborhood of Jerusalem, named only in Jer. 31:39.

Garlic, Num. 11:5, is the *Allium sativum* of Linnæus, which abounds in Egypt.

Garment. [DRESS.]

Gar′mite (gär′mīte), **The.** Keilah the Garmite is mentioned in the obscure genealogical lists of the families of Judah. 1 Chron. 4:19. The meaning of the word is unknown.

Garrison. The Hebrew words so rendered in the Authorized Version are derivatives from the root *nâtsab,* to "place, erect," which may be applied to a variety of objects. (1) *Mattsab* and *mattsabah* undoubtedly mean a "garrison" or fortified post. 1 Sam. 13:23; 14:1, 4, 12, 15; 2 Sam. 23:14. (2) *Netsib* is also used for a "garrison" in 1 Chron. 11:16, but elsewhere for a "column" erected in an enemy's country as a token of conquest. 1 Sam. 10:5. (3) The same word elsewhere means "officers" placed over a vanquished people. 2 Sam. 8:6, 14; 1 Chron. 18:13; 2 Chron. 17:2. (4) *Mattsebah* in Ezek. 26:11 means a "pillar."

Gash′mu, a variation of the name GESHEM. Neh. 6:6.

Ga′tam (*puny*), the fourth son of Eliphaz the son of Esau, Gen. 36:11; 1 Chron. 1:36, and one of the "dukes" of Eliphaz; Gen. 36:16.

Gate. The gates and gateways of eastern cities anciently held and still hold an important part, not only in the defence but in the public economy of the place. They are thus sometimes taken as representing the city itself.

Gen. 22:17; 24:60; Deut. 12:12; Judges 5:8; Ruth 4:10; Ps. 87:2; 122:2. Among the special purposes for which they were used may be mentioned—(1) As places of public resort. Gen. 19:1; 23:10; 34:20, 24; 1 Sam. 4:18, etc. (2) Places for public deliberation, administration of justice, or of audience for kings and rulers or ambassadors. Deut. 16:18; 21:19; 25:7; Josh. 20:4; Judges 9:35, etc. (3) Public markets. 2

THE GOLDEN GATE, on east of the Temple Area, Jerusalem (now closed).

Kings 7:1. In heathen towns the open spaces near the gates appear to have been sometimes used as places for sacrifice. Acts 14:13; comp. 2 Kings 23:8. Regarded therefore as positions of great importance, the gates of cities were carefully guarded, and closed at nightfall. Deut. 3:5; Josh. 2:5, 7; Judges 9:40, 44. They contained chambers over the gateway. 2 Sam. 18:24. The doors themselves of the larger gates mentioned in Scripture were two-leaved, plated with metal, closed with locks and fastened with metal bars. Deut. 3:5; Ps. 107:16; Isa. 45:1, 2. Gates not defended by metal were of course liable to be set on fire by an enemy. Judges 9:52. The gateways of royal palaces and even of private houses were often richly ornamented. Sentences from the law were inscribed on and above the gates. Deut. 6:9; Isa. 54:12; Rev. 21:21. The gates of Solomon's temple were very massive and costly, being overlaid with gold and carvings. 1 Kings 6:34, 35; 2 Kings 18:16. Those of the holy place were of olive wood, two-leaved and overlaid with gold; those of the temple of cypress. 1 Kings 6:31, 32, 34; Ezek. 41:23, 24.

Gath (gäth) (*a wine-press*), one of the five royal cities of the Philistines, Josh. 13:3; 1 Sam. 6:17, and the native place of the giant Goliath, 1 Sam. 17:4, 23. It probably stood upon the conspicuous hill now called *Tell-es-Sâfieh*, upon the side of the plain of Philistia, at the foot of the mountains of Judah; 10 miles east of Ashdod, and about the same distance south by east of Ekron. It is irregular in form, and about 300 feet high. Gath occupied a strong position, 2 Chron. 11:8, on the border of Judah and Philistia, 1 Sam. 21:10; 1 Chron. 18:1; and from its strength and resources forming the key of both countries, it was the scene of frequent struggles, and was often captured and recaptured. 2 Kings 12:17; 2 Chron. 11:8; 26:6; Amos 6:2. The ravages of war to which Gath was exposed appear to have destroyed it at a comparatively early period, as it is not mentioned among the other royal cities by the later prophets. Zeph. 2:4; Zech. 9:5, 6. It is familiar to the Bible student as the scene of one of the most romantic incidents in the life of King David. 1 Sam. 21:10–15.

Gath-he′pher (gath-hē′fẽr), or **Git′-tah-he′pher** (*wine-press of digging*), a town on the border of the territory of Zebulun, not far from Japhia, now *Yâfa,* Josh. 19:12, 13, celebrated as the native place of the prophet Jonah. 2 Kings 14:25. *El-Mesh-had,* a village two miles east of *Sefûrieh,* is the ancient Gath-hepher.

Gath-rim′mon (gäth-rĭm′mon) (*press of the pomegranate*). 1. A city given out of the tribe of Dan to the Levites. Josh. 21:24; 1 Chron. 6:69, situated on the plain of Philistia, apparently not far from Joppa. Josh. 19:45.

2. A town of the half tribe of Manasseh west of the Jordan, assigned to the Levites. Josh. 21:25. The reading Gathrimmon is probably an error of the transcribers for Ibleam.

Ga′za (gā′zà) (*the fortified; the strong*) (Hebrew *Azzah*), one of the five chief cities of the Philistines. It is remarkable for its continuous existence and importance from the very earliest times. The secret of this unbroken history is to be found in the situation of Gaza. It is the last town in the southwest of Palestine, on the frontier towards Egypt. The same peculiarity of situation has made Gaza important in a military sense. Its name means "the strong;" and this was well elucidated in its siege by Alexander Great, which lasted five months. In the conquest of Joshua the territory of Gaza is mentioned as one which he was not able to subdue. Josh. 10:41; 11:22; 13:3. It was assigned to the tribe of Judah, Josh. 15:47, and that tribe did obtain possession of it, Judges 1:18, but did not hold it long, Judges 3:3; 13:1, and apparently it continued through the times of Samuel, Saul and David to be a Philistine city. 1 Sam. 6:17; 14:52; 31:1; 2 Sam. 21:15. Solomon became master of "Azzah," 1 Kings 4:24; but in after times the same trouble with the Philistines recurred. 2 Chron. 21:16; 26:6; 28:18. The passage where Gaza is mentioned in the New Testament (Acts 8:26) is full of interest. It is the account of the baptism of the Ethiopian eunuch on his return from Jerusalem to Egypt. Gaza is the modern *Ghuzzeh,* a Mohammedan town of about 16,000 inhabitants, situated partly on an oblong hill of moderate height and partly on the lower ground. The climate of the place is almost tropical, but it has deep wells of excellent water. The terrible battles of the World War between the Turks and the Allied forces under General Allenby, made Gaza and its surroundings almost a ruin. It will probably be rebuilt, however.

Ga′zathites (gā′zăth-ītes), **The,** Josh. 13:3, the inhabitants of Gaza.

Ga′zer (gā′zẽr). 2 Sam. 5:25; 1 Chron. 14:16. [GEZER.]

Ga′zez (gā′zez) (*shearer*), a name which occurs twice in 1 Chron. 2:46—first as son of Caleb by Ephah his concubine, and second as son of Haran, the son of the same woman. The second is possibly only a repetition of the first.

Ga′zites (gā′zītes), **The,** inhabitants of Gaza. Judges 16:2.

Gaz′zam (găz′zam) (*devour*). The Bene-Gazzam were among the families of the Nethinim who returned from the captivity with Zerubbabel. Ezra 2:48; Neh. 7:51.

Ge′ba (gē′bà) (*a hill*), a city of Benjamin, with "suburbs," allotted to the priests. Josh. 21:17; 1 Chron. 6:60. It is named amongst the first group of the Benjamite towns—apparently those lying near to and along the north boundary. Josh. 18:24. Here the name is given as GABA. During the wars of the earlier part of the reign of Saul, Geba was held as a garrison by the Philistines, 1 Sam. 13:3, but they were ejected by Jonathan. It is now the modern village of *Jeba,* which stands picturesquely on the top of its steep terraced hill, six miles north of Jerusalem, on the very edge of the great *Wady Suweinit,* looking northward to the opposite village of ancient Michmash, which also retains its old name of *Mŭkhmas.*

Ge'bal (gē'bal) (*mountain*), a maritime town of Phœnicia, near Tyre, Ezek. 27:9; known by the Greeks as Byblus. It is called *Jebail* by the Arabs, thus reviving the old biblical name.

Ge'ber (gē'ber) (*man*). 1. The son of Geber resided in the fortress of Ramoth-gilead, and had charge of Havoth-jair and the district of Argob. 1 Kings 4:13.

2. Geber the son of Uri had a district south of the former—the "land of Gilead." 1 Kings 4:19.

Ge'bim (gē'bim) (*the trenches*), a village north of Jerusalem, Isa. 10:31. Its exact site is unknown, but it may possibly be the modern Jebia.

Gedali'ah (gĕd-à-lī'ah) (*Jehovah is great*), son of Ahikam (Jeremiah's protector, Jer. 26:24) and grandson of Shaphan the secretary of King Josiah. After the destruction of the temple, B.C. 586, Nebuchadnezzar departed from Judea, leaving Gedaliah with a Chaldean guard, Jer. 40:5, at Mizpah to govern the vine-dressers and husbandmen, Jer. 52:16, who were exempted from captivity. Jeremiah joined Gedaliah; and Mizpah became the resort of Jews from various quarters. Jer. 40:6, 11. He was murdered by Ishmael two months after his appointment.

Ged'eon (gĕd'e-on). The Greek form of the Hebrew name GIDEON. Heb. 11:32.

Ge'der (gē'dĕr) (*a wall*). The king of Geder was one of the thirty-one kings who were overcome by Joshua on the west of the Jordan. Josh. 12:13. (B.C. 1451.) It is possible that it may be the same place as the Gedor named in 1 Chron 4:39, or Gerar.

Gede'rah (ge-dē'rah) (*a sheepfold*), a town of Judah in the lowland country, Josh. 15:36, apparently in its eastern part. It is the modern *Jedireh* in the Shefaleh.

Ged'erathite (gĕd'e-rath-īte), **The,** the native of a place called Gederah, apparently in Benjamin. 1 Chron. 12:4.

Ged'erite (gĕd'e-rīte), **The,** the native of some place named Geder or Gederah. 1 Chron. 27:28.

Gede'roth (ge-dē'rŏth) (*sheepfolds*), a town in the low country of Judah. Josh. 15:41; 2 Chron. 28:18. Probably the modern *Katrah.*

Gederotha'im (gĕd-e-rŏth-ā'im) (*two sheepfolds*), a town in the low country of Judah. Josh. 15:36.

Ge'dor (gē'dôr) (*a wall*), 1. a town in the mountainous part of Judah, Josh. 15:58, a few miles north of Hebron. Robinson discovered a *Jedûr* halfway between Bethlehem and Hebron, about two miles west of the road.

2. A town in Simeon named in 1 Chron. 4:39.

Geha'zi (gè-hā'zī) (*valley of vision*), 1. the servant or boy of Elisha. He was sent as the prophet's messenger on two occasions to the good Shunammite, 2 Kings 4 (B.C. about 850); obtained fraudulently money and garments from Naaman, was miraculously smitten with incurable leprosy, and was dismissed from the prophet's service. 2 Kings 5.

2. A man by the same name is mentioned as being engaged in relating to King Joram all the great things which Elisha had done. 2 Kings 8:4, 5. Most probably it is not the same man.

Gehen'na (gè-hĕn'nà). [HINNOM.]

Gel'iloth (gĕl'ĭ-lŏth) (*circuits*), a place named among the marks of the south boundary line of the tribe of Benjamin. Josh. 18:17. The name Geliloth never occurs again in this locality, and it therefore seems possible that Gilgal is the right reading.

Gemal'li (gĕ-măl'lī) (*camel-owner*), the father of Ammiel, the Danite spy. Num. 13:12.

Gemari'ah (gĕm-a-rī'ah) (*Jehovah hath accomplished*). 1. Son of Shaphan the scribe, and father of Michaiah. He was one of the nobles of Judah, and had a chamber in the house of the Lord, from which Baruch read Jeremiah's alarming prophecy in the ears of all the people, B.C. 606. Jer. 36.

2. Son of Hilkiah, was made the

THE TRADITIONAL GEHENNA, to the east of Jerusalem.

'bearer of Jeremiah's letter to the captive Jews. Jer. 29:3. (B.C. 594.)

Gems. [STONES, PRECIOUS.]

Genealogy. In Hebrew the term for genealogy or pedigree is "the book of the generations;" and because the oldest histories were usually drawn up on a genealogical basis, the expression often extended to the whole history, as is the case with the Gospel of St. Matthew, where "the book of the generation of Jesus Christ" includes the whole history contained in that Gospel. The promise of the land of Canaan to the seed of Abraham, Isaac and Jacob successively, and the separation of the Israelites from the Gentile world; the expectation of Messiah as to spring from the tribe of Judah; the exclusively hereditary priesthood of Aaron with its dignity and emoluments; the long succession of kings in the line of David; and the whole division and occupation of the land upon genealogical principles by the tribes, families and houses of fathers, gave a deeper importance to the science of genealogy among the Jews than perhaps any other nation. When Zerubbabel brought back the captivity from Babylon, one of his first cares seems to have been to take a census of those that returned, and to settle them according to their genealogies. Passing on to the time of the birth of Christ, we have a striking incidental proof of the continuance of the Jewish genealogical economy in the fact that when Augustus ordered the census of the empire to be taken, the Jews in the province of Syria immediately went each one to his own city. The Jewish genealogical records continued to be kept till near the destruction of Jerusalem. But there can be little doubt that the registers of the Jewish tribes and families perished at the destruction of Jerusalem, and not before. It remains to be said that just notions of the nature of the Jewish genealogical records are of great importance with a view to the right interpretation of Scripture. Let it only be remembered that these records have respect to political and territorial divisions as much as to strictly genealogical descent, and it will at once be seen how erroneous a conclusion it may be that all who are called "sons" of such or such a patriarch or chief father must necessarily be his very children. If any one family or house became extinct, some other would succeed to its place, called after its own chief father. Hence of course a census of any tribe drawn up at a later period would exhibit different divisions from one drawn up at an earlier. The same principle must be borne in mind in interpreting any particular genealogy. Again, when a pedigree was abbreviated, it would naturally specify such generations as would indicate from what chief houses the person descended. Females are named in genealogies when there is anything remarkable about them, or when any right or property is transmitted through them. See Gen. 11:29; 22:23; 25:1–4; 35:22–26; Ex. 6:23; Num. 26:33.

Genealogy of Jesus Christ. The New Testament gives us the genealogy of but one person, that of our Saviour. This is given because it was important to prove that Jesus fulfilled the prophecies spoken of him. Only as the son and heir of David could he be the Messiah. The following propositions will explain the true construction of these genealogies:—(1) They are both the genealogies of Joseph, *i. e.* of Jesus Christ as the reputed and legal son of Joseph and Mary. (2) The genealogy of St. Matthew is Joseph's genealogy as legal successor to the throne of David. St. Luke's is Joseph's private genealogy, exhibiting his real birth as David's son, and thus showing why he was heir to Solomon's crown. The simple principle that one evangelist exhibits that genealogy which contained the successive heirs to David's and Solomon's throne, while the other exhibits the paternal stem of him who was the heir, explains all the anomalies of the two pedigrees, their agreements as well as their discrepancies, and the circumstance of there being two at all. (3) Mary, the mother of Jesus, was in all probability the daughter of Jacob, and first cousin to Joseph her husband. Thus:

| *Matt.* | Matthan or Matthat | *Luke.* |

Jacob ——— Heli
Matt. and Luke.

Mary=Jacob's heir was Joseph

JESUS, called Christ

Godet, Lange and many others take the ground that Luke gives the genealogy of Mary, rendering Luke 3:23 thus: Jesus "being the son (*as was*

supposed) of Joseph, the son of Heli," "son" being used in its very common sense of "descendant." In this case Mary, as declared in the Targums, was the daughter of Heli, and Heli was the grandfather of Jesus. Mary's name was omitted because "ancient sentiment did not comport with the mention of the mother as the genealogical link." So we often find in the Old Testament the grandson called the son. This view has this greatly in its favor, that it shows that Jesus was not merely the legal but the actual descendant of David; and it would be very strange that in the gospel accounts, where so much is made of Jesus being the son and heir of David, his *real* descent from David should not be given.

Generation. In the long-lived patriarchal age a generation seems to have been computed at 100 years, Gen. 15:16, comp. 13, and Ex. 12:40; but subsequently the reckoning was the same which has been adopted by modern civilized nations, viz. from thirty to forty years. Job 42:16. Generation is also used to signify the men of an age or time, as *contemporaries,* Gen. 6:9; Isa. 53:8; *posterity,* especially in legal formulæ, Lev. 3:17, etc.; *fathers,* or *ancestors.* Ps. 49:19.

Gen'esis (*origin*), the first book of the law or Pentateuch, so called from its title in the Septuagint, that is, *Creation.*

Professor Moulton, with true literary intuition, sees that "the portion of the Bible devoted to history seems to present a singularly clear historic whole; clear, not through a unity of plan laid down by a single writer, but through the sheer force of national consciousness animating each annalist or editor. History was to them the Chosen Nation exercising its commission to represent God to the nations."

Of the five great stages of the Bible history, Genesis is the first and describes the Formation of the Chosen Nation, "making a sketch map of general history into which the story of the coming nation can be fitted. Within this part two lesser divisions, or books, may be distinguished.

The first might be entitled The Beginnings of Things: essentials of world history viewed from their bearing upon the Chosen Nation, previous to the call of Abraham.

The second book presents the Chosen

People as a Patriarchal Family; following the fortunes of Abraham and his descendants in Canaan, the land promised to their seed, until the strange incidents which bring them, in the third generation, into Egypt. Both books may in their general character be called Primitive History. The greater part of them is made up of incidents related with an epic simplicity suited to recollections of the world's infancy." Many of the stories bring out the careful sifting of the seed that is to inherit the promises.

The early part of Genesis has the air of being made up of selections from very ancient documents, written by different authors at different periods. The variety which is observable in the names and titles of the Supreme Being is appealed to among the most striking proofs of this fact. This is obvious in the English translation, but still more so in the Hebrew original. In Gen. 1:1 to 2:3, which is really one piece of composition, as the title, 2:4, "These are the generations," shows, the name of the Most High is uniformly *Elohim*, God. In ch. 2:4 to ch. 3, which may be considered the second document, the title is uniformly *Yehovah Elohim, Lord God;* and in the third, including ch. 4, it is *Yehovah, Lord,* only; while in ch. 5 it is *Elohim, God,* only, except in v. 29, where a quotation is made, and *Yehovah* used. It is hardly conceivable that all this should be the result of mere accident.

Late discoveries have shown that writing was practised long before the time of Moses. We have laws of Hammurabi before Abraham's time, and the Amarna letters as early as 1500 B.C.

Modern critics distinguish at least four documents interwoven in Genesis, documents of different dates from 900 B.C. to the time of the Exile. Space forbids any discussion of these theories, which would make Genesis a book chiefly of myths and legends.

It is noteworthy that there are no unanswerable arguments against the traditional early date of Genesis. That most of the contradictions found by the critics are made by the separation of the narrative into parts and assuming that each interwoven part is the whole of a story and not a selected portion.

Most moral difficulties are avoided by realizing that divine revelation of truth is one thing, and the record of how people lived up to it in their gradual development is another.

Many of the narratives are traced by many critics to Babylonian legends, while other equally learned scholars think that is quite possible, even probable, that these pure and beautiful stories were the original facts; and the Babylonian and other legends are their degenerate children.

Gennes'aret (gĕn-nĕṣ'a-ret) (*garden of the princes*), **Land of.** It is generally believed that this term was applied to the fertile crescent-shaped plain on the western shore of the lake, extending from Khan Minyeh two or three miles south of Capernaum (*Tel-Hum*) on the north to the steep hill behind Mejdel (*Magdala*) on the south, and called by the Arabs *el-Ghuweir,* "the little Ghor." Its length is about 2½ miles, and its breadth one mile. Josephus speaks of its wonderful fertility and its genial air. Additional interest is given to the land of Gennesaret, or el-Ghuweir, by the probability that its scenery suggested the parable of the sower. It is mentioned only twice in Scripture—Matt. 14:34; Mark 6:53. Compare Luke 5:1.

Gennes'aret, Sea of. [See GALILEE, SEA OF.]

Gennes'areth (gĕn-nĕṣ'a-reth). Inaccurately written for GENNESARET.

Gen'tiles (*nations*). All the people who were not Jews were so called by them, being aliens from the worship, rites and privileges of Israel. The word was used contemptuously by them. In the New Testament *Greek* is used as its synonym. This use of the word seems to have arisen from the almost universal adoption of the Greek language.

Genu'bath (gĕ-nū'bath), the son of Hadad, an Edomite of the royal family, by an Egyptian princess, the sister of Tahpenes, the queen of the Pharaoh who governed Egypt in the latter part of the reign of David. 1 Kings 11: 20; comp. 16.

Ge'ra (gē'rà) (*a grain*), one of the sons, or descendants, of Benjamin. Gen. 46:21. Gera, who is named, Judges 3:15, as the ancestor of Ehud, and in 2 Sam. 16:5 as the ancestor of Shimei who cursed David, is probably also the same person (though some consider them different persons).

Gerah (gē'rah). [WEIGHTS AND MEASURES.]

Ge'rar (gē'rär), a very ancient city south of Gaza. It is named in Genesis, 10:19; 20:1; 26:17; also incidentally in 2 Chron. 14:13, 14. Its territory must have trenched on the "south" or "south country" of later Palestine. From a comparison of Gen. 21:32 with 26:23, 26, Beersheba would seem to be just on the verge of this territory, and perhaps to be its limit towards the northeast.

Gerasenes'. Mark 5:1; Luke 8:26, Revised Version. [See GADARENES.]

Gergesenes'. [See GADARENES.]

Ger'izim (gĕr'ĭ-zĭm) (cutters), a limestone mountain, 2849 feet high (800 feet above the valley at its foot), in Ephraim, near Shechem (Sychar), from which the blessings were read to the Israelites on entering Canaan. [See EBAL.] According to the traditions of the Samaritans it was here that Abraham sacrificed Isaac, that Melchizedek met the patriarch, that Jacob built an altar, and at its base dug a well, the ruins of which are still seen. There are enough grounds for the first belief to make it plausible, according to many scholars, e. g. Stanley. Still general opinion is against it. [See MORIAH.] Gerizim was the site of the Samaritan temple, which was built there after the captivity, in rivalry with the temple at Jerusalem. [See SAMARITANS.] Gerizim is still to the Samaritans what Jerusalem is to the Jews and Mecca to the Mohammedans. The ruins of the old temple are still visible. "From the days of Benjamin of Tudela, a Jewish rabbi who traveled in Palestine about A.D. 1160, on to quite recent times, the view was held that Gerizim, the mountain of blessings, was fertile, and Ebal, that of curses, barren, till Robinson pointed out that, with the exception of a small ravine coming down from Gerizim opposite the west of Nablus, both mountains are equally barren."—Davis' Bible Dictionary.

Ger'shom (gĕr'shŏm) (a stranger or exile). 1. The first-born son of Moses and Zipporah. Ex. 2:22; 18:3. (B.C. about 1530.)

2. The form under which the name GERSHON—the eldest son of Levi—is given in several passages of Chronicles, viz., 1 Chron. 6:16, 17, 20, 43, 62, 71; 15:7.

3. The representative of the priestly family of Phinehas, among those who accompanied Ezra from Babylon. Ezra 8:2. (B.C. 458.)

Ger'shon (gēr'shŏn) (exile), the eldest of three sons of Levi, born before the descent of Jacob's family into Egypt. Gen. 46:11; Ex. 6:16. (B.C. before 1706.) But, though the eldest born, the families of Gershon were outstripped in fame by their younger brethren of Kohath, from whom sprang Moses and the priestly line of Aaron.

Ger'shonites (gēr'shŏn-ītes), **The,** the family descended from Gershon or Gershom, the son of Levi. "The Gershonite," as applied to individuals, occurs in 1 Chron. 26:21. The sons of Gershon (the Gershonites) had charge of the fabrics of the tabernacle—the coverings, curtains, hangings and cords. Num. 3:25, 26; 4:25, 26.

Ge'sham (gē'shăm) (correctly written **Geshan**), one of the sons of Jahdai, in the genealogy of Judah and family of Caleb. 1 Chron. 2:47.

Ge'shem (gē'shem) and **Gash'mu** (găsh'mū) (rain), an Arabian, mentioned in Neh. 2:19 and 6:1, 2, 6. (B.C. 446.) We may conclude that he was an inhabitant of Arabia Petræa, or of the Arabian Desert, and probably the chief of a tribe. "Gashmu saith it" made him a type of those who create a common report.

Ge'shur (gē'shŭr) (a bridge), a little principality of Syria, northeast of Bashan. Deut. 3:14; 2 Sam. 15:8. David married the daughter of its ruler, and Absalom, a son of the marriage, took refuge there after the murder of Amnon. Its exact site is extremely doubtful, several being proposed by scholars.

Gesh'uri (gĕsh'u-rī) and **Gesh'urites** (gĕsh'u-rītes). 1. The inhabitants of Geshur. Deut. 3:14; Josh. 12:5; 13:11.

2. An ancient tribe which dwelt in the desert between Arabia and Philistia. Josh. 13:2; 1 Sam. 27:8. This is considered by some scholars as the same as 1.

Ge'ther (gē'thĕr), the third in order of the sons of Aram. Gen. 10:23. No satisfactory trace of the people sprung from this stock has been found.

Gethsem'ane (gĕth-sĕm'a-nè) (an oil-press), a small "place," Matt. 26:36; Mark 14:32, situated across the brook Kedron, John 18:1, probably at the foot of Mount Olivet, Luke 22:39, east of Jerusalem. What is meant by the term translated "place" is a piece of ground enclosed by a fence of some sort. There is no doubt that there was a "garden," or rather orchard, attached to it, to which the olive, fig and pomegranate doubtless invited resort by their hospitable shade. And we know from the evangelists Luke, 22:39, and John, 18: 2, that our Lord ofttimes resorted thither with his disciples. But Gethsemane has not come down to us as a

ANCIENT OLIVE TREE, in the garden of Gethsemane.

scene of mirth; its inexhaustible associations are the offspring of a single event—the agony of the Son of God on the evening preceding his passion. A garden, with eight venerable olive trees, and a grotto to the north, detached from it, and transformed into a Latin Sanctuary—the Grotto of the Agony,—is pointed out as *the* Gethsemane. Against the contemporary antiquity of the olive trees it has been urged that Titus cut down all the trees about Jerusalem. The probability would seem to be that they were planted by Christian hands to mark the spot; unless, like the sacred olive of the Ac-

ropolis, they may have reproduced themselves.

Geu'el (gĕ-ū'el) (*majesty of God*), the Gadite spy. Num. 13:15. (B.C. 1490.)

Ge'zer (gē'zẽr) (*a place cut off*), an ancient city of Canaan, whose king, Horam or Elam, coming to the assistance of Lachish, was killed with all his people by Joshua. Josh. 10:33; 12:12. It formed one of the landmarks on the south boundary of Ephraim, between the lower Beth-horon and the Mediterranean, Josh. 16:3, the western limit of the tribe. 1 Chron. 7:28. It was allotted with its suburbs to the Kohathite Levites, Josh. 21:21; 1 Chron. 6:67; but the original inhabitants were not dispossessed, Judges 1:29, and even down to the reign of Solomon the Canaanites were still dwelling there, and seem to have been entirely independent. It was burned by Pharaoh in Solomon's time, 1 Kings 9:15–17, and given to Solomon's Egyptian wife, and rebuilt by him. Now *Tell Jezer*, 4 miles from the ancient Nicopolis, near the road from Jaffa to Jerusalem.

Gez'rites (gĕz'rites), R. V. Girzites. A name given in connection with Geshurites and Amalekites in 1 Sam. 27:8. It is thought by some to denote "inhabitants of Gezer." Others connect the name with Gerizim.

Gi'ah (gī'ah) (*gushing forth*), a place named only in 2 Sam. 2:24 to designate the position of the hill Ammah.

Giants, men of extraordinary size or height. 1. They are first spoken of in Gen. 6:4, under the name *Nephilim*. We are told in Gen. 6:1–4 that "there *were* Nephilim in the earth," and that afterwards the "sons of God" mingling with the beautiful "daughters of men" produced a race of violent and insolent *Gibborim* (Authorized Version "mighty men").

2. The *Rephaim*, a name which fre-

quently occurs. The earliest mention of them is the record of their defeat by Chedorlaomer and some allied kings at Ashteroth Karnaim. The "valley of Rephaim," 2 Sam. 5:18; 1 Chron. 11: 15; Isa. 17:5, a rich valley southwest of Jerusalem, derived its name from them. They were probably an aboriginal people of which the EMIM, ANAKIM and ZUZIM were branches. [See also Go-LIATH.]

Gib'bar (gĭb'bar) (*a hero*), the father of some who returned with Zerubbabel from Babylon. Ezra 2:20.

Gib'bethon (gĭb'be-thŏn) (*height*), a town allotted to the tribe of Dan, Josh. 19:44, and afterwards given with its "suburbs" to the Kohathite Levites, Josh. 21:23.

Gib'ea (gĭb'e-à) (*a hill*). Sheva "the father of Macbenah" and "father of Gibea" is mentioned with other names, unmistakably those of places and not persons, among the descendants of Judah. 1 Chron. 2 : 49, comp. 42. Probably a variation of the familiar Gibeah.

Gib'eah (gĭb'e-ah), a word employed in the Bible to denote a *hill*. Like most words of this kind it gave its name to several towns and places in Palestine, which would doubtless be generally on or near a hill. They are—1. Gibeah, a city in the mountain district of Judah, named with Maon and the southern Carmel, Josh. 15:57; and comp. 1 Chron. 2 : 49, etc.

2. Gibeah of Benjamin first appears in the tragical story of the Levite and his concubine. Judges 19, 20. It was then a "city," with the usual open street or square, Judges 19:15, 17, 20, and containing 700 "chosen men," ch. 20: 15, probably the same whose skill as slingers is preserved in the next verse. In many particulars Gibeah agrees very closely with *Tuleil-el-Fûl*, a conspicuous eminence just four miles north of Jerusalem, to the right of the road. We next meet with Gibeah of Benjamin during the Philistine wars of Saul and Jonathan. 1 Sam. 13:15, 16. It now bears its full title. As "Gibeah of Benjamin" this place is referred to in 2 Sam. 23:29 (comp. 1 Chron. 11:31), and as "Gibeah" it is mentioned by Hosea, 5:8; 9:9; 10:9, but it does not again appear in the history. It is, however, almost without doubt identical with

3. Gibeah of Saul. This is not men-

tioned as Saul's city till after his anointing, 1 Sam. 10:26, when he is said to have gone "home" to Gibeah. In the subsequent narrative the town bears its full name, ch. 11:4.

4. Gibeah in Kirjath-jearim was no doubt a hill in that city, and the place in which the ark remained from the time of its return by the Philistines till its removal by David. 2 Sam. 6:3, 4; comp. 1 Sam. 7:1. 2. R. V. translates "the hill."

Gib'eath (gĭb'e-ath), probably the same as GIBEAH OF BENJAMIN. Josh. 18:28.

Gib'eon (gĭb'e-on) (*hill city*), one of the four cities of the Hivites, the inhabitants of which made a league with Joshua, Josh. 9:3–15, and thus escaped the fate of Jericho and Ai. Comp. ch. 11:19. Gibeon lay within the territory of Benjamin, ch. 18:25, and with its "suburbs" was allotted to the priests, ch. 21:17, of whom it became afterwards a principal station. It retains its ancient name almost intact, *el-Jib*. Its distance from Jerusalem by the main road is about 6½ miles; but there is a more direct road reducing it to 5 miles.

Gib'eonites (gĭb'e-on-ītes), **The**, the people of Gibeon, and perhaps also of the three cities associated with Gibeon, Josh. 9:17—Hivites; and who, on the discovery of the stratagem by which they had obtained the protection of the Israelites, were condemned to be perpetual bondmen, hewers of wood and drawers of water for the congregation, and for the house of God and altar of Jehovah. Josh. 9:23, 27. Saul appears to have broken this covenant, and in a fit of enthusiasm or patriotism to have devised a general massacre. 2 Sam. 21: 1, 2, 5. This was expiated many years after by giving up seven men of Saul's descendants to the Gibeonites, who hung them "before Jehovah" in Gibeah, Saul's own town, ch. 21:4, 6, 9.

Gib'lites (gĭb'lītes), **The**. [GEBAL.]

Giddal'ti (gĭd-dăl'tī) (*I magnified*), one of the sons of Heman, the king's seer. 1 Chron. 25:4.

Gid'del (gĭd'del) (*very great*). **1.** Children of Giddel were among the Nethinim who returned from the captivity with Zerubbabel. Ezra 2:47; Neh. 7:49.

2. Bene-Giddel were also among the "children of Solomon's servants" who

returned to Judea in the same caravan. Ezra 2 : 56; Neh. 7 : 58.

Gid'eon (gĭd'e-on) (*he that cuts down*), youngest son of Joash of the Abi-ezrites, an undistinguished family who lived at Ophrah, a town probably on the west of Jordan, Judges 6 : 15, in the territory of Manasseh, near Shechem. He was the fifth recorded judge of Israel, and for many reasons the greatest of them all. When we first hear of him he was grown up and had sons, Judges 6 : 11; 8 : 20; and from the apostrophe of the angel, ch. 6 : 12, we may conclude that he had already distinguished himself in war against the roving bands of nomadic robbers who had oppressed Israel for seven years. When the angel appeared, Gideon was threshing wheat with a flail in the wine-press, to conceal it from the predatory tyrants. His call to be a deliverer, and his destruction of Baal's altar, are related in Judges 6. After this begins the second act of Gideon's life. Clothed by the Spirit of God, Judges 6 : 34; comp. 1 Chron. 12 : 18; Luke 24 : 49, he blew a trumpet, and was joined by Zebulun, Naphtali and even the reluctant Asher. Strengthened by a double sign from God, he reduced his army of 32,000 by the usual proclamation at the command of God. Deut. 20 : 8. By a second test at "the spring of trembling" he further reduced the number of his followers to 300. Judges 7 : 5, *seq.* The midnight attack upon the Midianites, their panic, and the rout and slaughter that followed, are told in Judges 7. The memory of this splendid deliverance took deep root in the national traditions. 1 Sam. 12 : 11; Ps. 83 : 11; Isa. 9 : 4; 10 : 26; Heb. 11 : 32. After this there was a peace of forty years, and we see Gideon in peaceful possession of his well-earned honors, and surrounded by the dignity of a numerous household. Judges 8 : 29–31. It is not improbable that, like Saul, he owed a part of his popularity to his princely appearance. Judges 8 : 18. In this third stage of his life occur alike his most noble and his most questionable acts, viz., the refusal of the monarchy on theocratic grounds, and the irregular consecration of a jewelled ephod formed out of the rich spoils of Midian, which proved to the Israelites a temptation to idolatry, although it was doubtless intended for use in the worship of Jehovah.

Gideo'ni (gĭd-e-ō'nī) (*my cutter down*), a Benjamite, father of Abidan. Num. 1 : 11; 7 : 60, 65; 10 : 24.

Gi'dom (gĭ'dom) (*cutting off*), a place named only in Judges 20 : 45. It would appear to have been situated between Gibeah (*Tuleil-el-Fûl*) and the cliff Rimmon.

Gier=eagle, an unclean bird mentioned in Lev. 11 : 18 and Deut. 14 : 17; identical in reality as in name with the *rakham* of the Arabs, viz., the Egyptian vulture.

Gift. The giving and receiving of presents has in all ages been not only a more frequent but also a more formal and significant proceeding in the East than among ourselves. We cannot adduce a more remarkable proof of the important part which presents play in the social life of the East than the fact that the Hebrew language possesses no less than fifteen different expressions for the one idea. The mode of presentation was with as much parade as possible. The refusal of a present was regarded as a high indignity. No less an insult was it not to bring a present when the position of the parties demanded it. 1 Sam. 10 : 27. "This practice may throw light upon the asking by the Israelites of jewels of gold and silver, etc., from the Egyptians."

Gi'hon (gī'hon) (*a stream*). 1. The second river of Paradise. Gen. 2 : 13. [EDEN.]

2. A place near Jerusalem, memorable as the scene of the anointing and proclamation of Solomon as king. 1 Kings 1 : 33, 38, 45.

Gil'alai (gĭl'a-lâi), one of the priests' sons at the consecration of the wall of Jerusalem. Neh. 12 : 36. (B.C. 446.)

Gilbo'a (gĭl-bō'à) (*a bubbling spring*), a mountain range on the eastern side of the plain of Esdraelon, rising over the city of Jezreel. Comp. 1 Sam. 28 : 4 with 29 : 1. It is mentioned in Scripture only in connection with one event in Israelitish history, the defeat and death of Saul and Jonathan by the Philistines. 1 Sam. 31 : 1; 2 Sam. 1 : 6; 21 : 12; 1 Chron. 10 : 1, 8. Of the identity of Gilboa with the ridge which stretches eastward from the ruins of Jezreel no doubt can be entertained. The range of hills is known locally as

Jebel Fukua. One of the villages on its slopes is called *Jelbun.*

Gil'ead (gĭl'e-ăd) (*rocky region*). 1. A mountainous region bounded on the west by the Jordan, on the north by Bashan, on the east by the Arabian plateau, and on the south by Moab and Ammon. Gen. 31:21; Deut. 3:12–17. It is sometimes called "Mount Gilead," Gen. 31:25, sometimes "the land of Gilead," Num. 32:1, and sometimes simply "Gilead." Ps. 60:7; Gen. 37:25. In the main it is a fertile and beautiful country, though in some parts and from some points of view rocky and rugged. The mountains of Gilead, including Pisgah, Abarim and Peor, have a real elevation of from 2000 to 3000 feet; but their apparent elevation on the western side is much greater, owing to the depression of the Jordan valley, which averages about 1000 feet. Their outline is singularly uniform, resembling a massive wall running along the horizon. Gilead was specially noted for its balm collected from "balm of Gilead" trees, which it is impossible to identify with any certainty.

2. Possibly the name of a mountain west of the Jordan, near Jezreel. Judges 7:3. We are inclined, however, to think that the true reading in this place should be GILBOA.

3. Son of Machir, grandson of Manasseh. Num. 26:29, 30.

4. The father of Jephthah. Judges 11:1, 2.

Gil'eadites (gĭl'e-ad-ītes), **The,** Num. 26:29; Judges 10:3; 12:4, 5, a branch of the tribe Manasseh, descended from Gilead.

Gil'gal (gĭl'găl) (*a circle of stones; a cromlech*). 1. The site of the first camp of the Israelites on the west of the Jordan, the place at which they passed the first night after crossing the river, and where the twelve stones were set up which had been taken from the bed of the stream, Josh. 4:19, 20, comp. 3; where also they kept their first passover in the land of Canaan, ch. 5:10. It was "in the east border of Jericho," apparently on a hillock or rising ground, Josh. 5:3, comp. 9, in the plains of Jericho, that is, the hot depressed district of the Ghor which lay between the town and the Jordan, ch. 5:10. Here Samuel was judge, and Saul was made king. We again have a glimpse of it, some sixty years later, in the history of

David's return to Jerusalem. 2 Sam. 19:40. A Gilgal is spoken of in Josh. 15:7, in describing the north border of Judah. In Josh. 18:17 it is given as Geliloth. Gilgal near Jericho is doubtless intended.

2. In 2 Kings 2:1, 2; 4:38 is named a Gilgal visited by Elijah and Elisha. This could not be the Gilgal of the low plain of the Jordan, for the prophets are said to have gone *down* to Bethel, which is 3000 feet above the plain. It has been identified with *Jiljilia,* about eight miles from Bethel.

3. The "king of the nations of Gilgal," or rather perhaps the "king of Goim at Gilgal," is mentioned in the catalogue of the chiefs overthrown by Joshua. Josh. 12:23. Possibly the site of this place is marked by the modern village *Jiljûlieh,* about five miles northeast of Antipatris, which lies 16 miles northeast of Joppa.

Gi'loh (gī'loh) (*exile*), a town in the mountainous part of Judah, named in the first group with Debir and Eshtemoh, Josh. 15:51; it was the native place of the famous Ahithophel. 2 Sam. 15:12.

Gi'lonite (gī'lon-īte), **The,** native of Giloh. 2 Sam. 15:12; 23:34.

Gim'zo (gĭm'zo) (*fertile in sycomores*), a town which with its dependent villages was taken possession of by the Philistines in the reign of Ahaz. 2 Chron. 28:18. The name (*Jimzu*) still remains attached to a large village between two and three miles southeast of Lydda, south of the road between Jerusalem and Jaffa.

Gin, a trap for birds or beasts; it consisted of a net, Isa. 8:14, and a stick to act as a spring. Amos 3:5.

Gi'nath (gī'nath), father of Tibni, the rival of Omri. 1 Kings 16:21, 22.

Gin'netho (gĭn'ne-thō) (*gardener*). one of the chief of the priests and Levites who returned to Judea with Zerubbabel. Neh. 12:4.

Gin'nethon (gĭn'-ne-thon) (*gardener*), a priest who sealed the covenant with Nehemiah. Neh. 10:6.

Girdle, an essential article of dress in the East, and worn by both men and women. The common girdle was made of leather, 2 Kings 1:8; Matt. 3:4, like that worn by the Bedouins of the present day. A finer girdle was made of linen, Jer. 13:1; Ezek. 16:10, embroidered with silk, and sometimes with gold and silver thread, Dan. 10:5; Rev. 1:13; 15:6, and frequently studded with gold and precious stones or pearls. The military girdle was worn about the waist; the sword or dagger was suspended from it. Judges 3:16; 2 Sam. 20:8; Ps. 45:3. Hence girding up the loins denotes preparation for battle or for active exertion. Girdles were used as pockets, as they still are among the Arabs, and as purses, one end of the girdle being folded back for the purpose. Matt. 10:9; Mark 6:8.

Gir'gasite (gĭr'gas-īte), **The,** Gen. 10:16, or

Gir'gashites (gĭr'ga-shītes) (*dwelling on a clayey soil*), **The,** one of the nations who were in possession of Canaan east of the Sea of Galilee before the entrance thither of the children of Israel. Gen. 10:16; 15:21; Deut. 7:1.

Gis'pa (gĭs'pà) (*caress*), one of the overseers of the Nethinim, in "the Ophel," after the return from captivity. Neh. 11:21.

Git'tah-he'pher. (gĭt'tah-hē'fẽr). Josh. 19:13. [GATH-HEPHER.]

Gitta'im (gĭt-tā'ĭm). [GITTITES.]

Git'tites (gĭt'tītes) (*belonging to Gath*), the 600 men who followed David from Gath, under Ittai the Gittite, 2 Sam. 15:18, 19, and who probably acted as a kind of body-guard. Obed-edom "the Gittite" may have been so named from the town of Gittaim in Benjamin, 2 Sam. 4:3; Neh. 11:33, or from Gath-rimmon.

Gittith, a musical instrument, by some supposed to have been used by the people of Gath, and by others to have been employed at the festivities of the vintage. Ps. 8, 81, 84.

Gi'zonite (gī'zo-nīte), **The** (*inhabitant of Gizoh*). "The sons of Hashem the Gizonite" are named amongst the warriors of David's guard. 1 Chron. 11:34. As neither man nor place by the name of Gizoh has been found in the Bible scholars are inclined to think the word should be "Gunite."

Glass. The Hebrew word occurs only in Job 28:17, where in the Authorized Version it is rendered "crystal." In spite of the absence of specific allusion to glass in the sacred writings, the Hebrews must have been aware of the invention. From paintings representing the process of glass-blowing which have been discovered at Beni-hassan, and in tombs at other places, we know that the invention was known at least 3500 years ago. Fragments too of wine-vases as old as the Exodus have been discovered in Egypt. The art was also known to the ancient Assyrians. In the New Testament glass is alluded to as an emblem of brightness. Rev. 4: 6; 15:2; 21:18.

Gleaning. The gleaning of fruit trees, as well as of corn-fields, was reserved for the poor. [CORNER.]

Glede, the old name for the common kite (*Milvus ater*), occurs only in Deut. 14:13, among the unclean birds of prey.

Gnat, a species of mosquito mentioned only in the proverbial expression used by our Saviour in Matt. 23:24.

Goad. Judges 3:31; 1 Sam. 13:21. The Hebrew word in the latter passage perhaps means the point of the *plough-share*. The former word does probably refer to the goad, the long handle of which might be used as a formidable weapon. The instrument, as still used in countries of southern Europe and western Asia, consists of a rod about eight feet long, brought to a sharp point and sometimes cased with iron at the head.

Goat. There appear to be two or three varieties of the common goat, *Capra hircus,* at present bred in Palestine and Syria, but whether they are identical with those which were reared by the ancient Hebrews it is not possible to say. The most marked varieties are the Syrian goat (*Capra mambrica,* Linn.) and the Angora goat (*Capra angorensis,* Linn.), with fine long hair. Goats seem always to be herded with sheep, and kids were a choice food. As to the "wild goats," 1 Sam. 24:2; Job. 39:1; Ps. 104:18, it is not at all improbable that some species of *ibex* is denoted.

Goat, Scape. [ATONEMENT, DAY OF.]

Go'ath (gō'ăth) (*lowing*), a place apparently in the neighborhood of Jerusalem and, named, in connection with the hill Gareb, only in Jer. 31:39.

Gob (gŏb) (*cistern*), a place mentioned only in 2 Sam. 21:18, 19, as the scene of two encounters between David's warriors and the Philistines. In the parallel account in 1 Chron. 20:4 the name is given as GEZER.

God. Throughout the Old Testament Scriptures two chief names are used for the one true divine Being—

SYRIAN IBEX, OR WILD GOAT OF THE BIBLE.
(Capra beden.)

ELOHIM, commonly translated *God* in our version, and JEHOVAH, translated *Lord*. Elohim is the plural of Eloah (in Arabic *Allah*); it is often used in the short form EL (a word signifying *strength*), as in EL-SHADDAI, *God Almighty*, the name by which God was specially known to the patriarchs. Gen. 17:1; 28:3; Ex. 6:3. The etymology is uncertain, but it is generally agreed that the primary idea is that of *strength, power of effect*, and that it properly describes God in that character in which he is exhibited to all men in his works, as the creator, sustainer and supreme governor of the world. The plural form of Elohim has given rise to much discussion. The fanciful idea that it referred to the *trinity of persons* in the Godhead hardly finds now a supporter among scholars. It is either what grammarians call *the plural of majesty*, or it denotes the *fullness* of divine strength, the *sum of the powers* displayed by God.

Jehovah denotes specifically the one true God, whose people the Jews were, and who made them the guardians of his truth. The name is never applied to a false god. *Jehovah* probably means "He who in the absolute sense exists and who manifests his existence and his character."

While *Elohim* signifies the Creator, governor and upholder of the Universe, *Jehovah* is "the God of revelation and grace dwelling with his people, guiding and delivering him." It is the personal name of God.

In the Authorized Version the name is translated LORD and printed in Capitals. So in the Revision of 1884. The new American Revision retains the name *Jehovah*. Probably the best statement of what God is is the summing up of the scripture definitions and descriptions as given in the Westminster Shorter Catechism with the addition of one word,—"God is a Spirit, infinite, eternal, and unchangeable in his being, wisdom, power, justice, goodness, truth and love."

The Fatherhood of God is most clearly revealed by Jesus Christ his Son, not only by his teachings but by his character, his actions, all he was and did; by means of which we realize the character and goodness and love of our Heavenly Father.

The anthropomorphisms in which the Old Testament abounds are used in order that men may realize that God is not merely a force, or "bright spirit increate" but is a real person with mind, will, heart, feelings like his children, but in an infinite degree. They do not imply that even the earliest men thought of God as an infinite human body. We use the same expression to-day. When the Bible speaks, says Sanday, "of the hand, arm, mouth, lips and eyes of God, when he makes 'bare his mighty arm,' and musters his hosts with a shout,—all this is but a vivid conception of his being, his intelligence, his activity, and universal power; and testifies to the warmth and intensity of the religious feelings of the writers."

Gog (gŏg). 1. A Reubenite, 1 Chron. 5:4, son of Shemaiah.

2. Gog and Magog. [See MAGOG.]

Go'lan (gō'lan), a city of Bashan, Deut. 4:43, allotted out of the half tribe of Manasseh to the Levites, Josh. 21:27, and one of the three cities of refuge east of the Jordan, Josh. 20:8. Its very site is now unknown. It gave its name to the province of Gaulanitis which lay east of Galilee and north of Gadaritis, and corresponds to the modern province of *Jaulân*.

Gold. Gold was known from the very earliest times. Gen. 2:11. It was at first used chiefly for ornaments, etc. Gen. 24:22. Coined money was not known to the ancients till a comparatively late period; and on the Egyptian tombs gold is represented as being weighed in rings for commercial purposes. Comp. Gen. 43:21. Gold was extremely abundant in ancient times, 1 Chron. 22:14; 2 Chron. 1:15; 9:9; Dan. 3:1; Nah. 2:9; but this did not depreciate its value, because of the enormous quantities consumed by the wealthy in furniture, etc. 1 Kings 6:22; 10 *passim;* Esther 1:6; Cant. 3:9, 10; Jer. 10:9. The chief countries mentioned as producing gold are Havilah, Sheba and Ophir. 1 Kings 9:28; 10:1; Job 28:16.

Gol'gotha (gŏl'gȯ-thȧ) (*skull*), the Hebrew name of the spot at which our Lord was crucified. Matt. 27:33; Mark 15:22; John 19:17. By these three evangelists it is interpreted to mean the "place of a skull." Golgotha is from the Hebrew for skull, of which Calvary is the Greek and Latin equivalent. The place is so called either from the form of the hill, or from the skulls there as the place of execution. The site may have been near the Church of the Holy Sepulchre, within the present walls,— but the theory that it is outside the Damascus gate north of the city is at present in the ascendant. From certain points of view this hill has a very close resemblance to a skull.

Goli'ath (gọ-lī'ath) (*an exile*), a famous giant of Gath, who "morning and evening for forty days" defied the armies of Israel. 1 Sam. 17. (B.C. 1063.) He was possibly descended from the old Rephaim [GIANTS], of whom a scattered remnant took refuge with the Philistines after their dispersion by the Ammonites. Deut. 2:20, 21; 2 Sam. 21:22. His height was "six cubits and a span," which, taking the cubit at 18 inches, would make him 9¾ feet high. The scene of his combat with David, by whom he was slain, was the "valley of the terebinth," between Shochoh and Arekah, probably among the western passes of Benjamin. Either a brother of this Goliath, or another giant of the same name and residence, was slain by Elhanan. 2 Sam. 21:19.

Go'mer (gō'mēr) (*perfect*). 1. The eldest son of Japheth, Gen. 10:2, 3, the progenitor of the early Cimmerians, of the later Cimbri and the other branches of the Celtic family, and of the modern Gael and Cymri. 2. The wife of Hosea. Hos. 1:3.

Gomor'rah (gọ-mŏr'rah) (*submersion*), one of the five "cities of the plain" or "vale of Siddim" that under their respective kings joined battle there with Chedorlaomer, Gen. 14:2–8, and his allies, by whom they were discomfited till Abraham came to the rescue. Four out of the five were afterwards destroyed by the Lord with fire from heaven. Gen. 19:23–29. One of them only, Zoar (or Bela, which was its original name), was spared at the request of Lot, in order that he might take refuge there. The geographical position of these cities is discussed under SODOM.

Gopher wood. Only once mentioned —Gen. 6:14. Two principal conjectures have been proposed:—1. That the "trees of gopher" are any trees of the resinous kind, such as pine, fir, etc. 2. That gopher is cypress. Cheyne suggests that some variety of cedar was intended.

Go'shen (gō'shen). 1. The name of a part of Egypt where the Israelites

15

dwelt during the whole period of their sojourn in that country. It was probably situated on the eastern border of the Nile, extending from the Mediterranean to the Red Sea. It contained the treasure-cities of Rameses and Pithom. It was a pasture land, especially suited to a shepherd people, and sufficient for the Israelites, who there prospered, and were separate from the main body of the Egyptians. Gen. 47:6. 2. A district in southern Palestine conquered by Joshua. Josh. 10:41. It lay between Gaza and Gibeon. 3. A town in the mountains of Judah, probably in a part of the district of Goshen. Josh. 15:51.

Gos'pels. The name Gospel (from *god* and *spell*, Ang. Sax. *good message* or *news*, which is a translation of the Greek *euangelion*) is applied to the four inspired histories of the life and teaching of Christ contained in the New Testament, of which separate accounts are given in their place. They were all composed during the latter half of the first century: those of St. Matthew and St. Mark some years before the destruction of Jerusalem; that of St. Luke probably about A.D. 64; and that of St. John towards the close of the century. Before the end of the second century, there is abundant evidence that the four Gospels, as one collection, were generally used and accepted. As a matter of literary history, nothing can be better established than the genuineness of the Gospels. On comparing these four books one with another, a peculiar difficulty claims attention, which has had much to do with the controversy as to their genuineness. In the fourth Gospel the narrative coincides with that of the other three in a few passages only. The received explanation is the only satisfactory one, namely, that John, writing last, at the close of the first century, had seen the other Gospels, and purposely abstained from writing anew what they had sufficiently recorded. In the other three Gospels there is a great amount of agreement. If we suppose the history that they contain to be divided into 89 sections, in 42 of these all the three narratives coincide, 12 more are given by Matthew and Mark only, 5 by Mark and Luke only, and 14 by Matthew and Luke. To these must be added 5 peculiar to Matthew, 2 to Mark and 9 to Luke, and the enumeration is complete. But this applies only to general coincidence as to the facts narrated: the amount of verbal coincidence, that is, the passages either verbally the same or coinciding in the use of many of the same words, is much smaller. It has been ascertained by Stroud that "if the total contents of the several Gospels be represented by 100, the following table is obtained:

Matt. has 42 *peculiarities* and 58 *coincidences.*
Mark has 7 *peculiarities* and 93 *coincidences.*
Luke has 59 *peculiarities* and 41 *coincidences.*
John has 92 *peculiarities* and 8 *coincidences."*

Why four Gospels.—(1) To bring four separate independent witnesses to the truth. (2) It is to give the Lord's life from every point of view, four living portraits of one person. There were *four* Gospels because Jesus was to be commended to four races or classes of men, or to four phases of human thought,—the Jewish, Roman, Greek and Christian. Had not these exhausted the classes to be reached, there would doubtless have been more Gospels. In all ages, the Jewish, Roman and Greek natures reappear among men, and, in fact, make up the world of natural men, while the Christian nature and wants likewise remain essentially the same. The FIRST GOSPEL was prepared by Matthew for the Jew. He gives us the Gospel of Jesus, the Messiah of the Jews, the Messianic royalty of Jesus. He places the life and character of Jesus, as lived on earth, alongside the life and character of the Messiah, as sketched in the prophets, showing Christianity as the fulfilment of Judaism. Mark wrote the SECOND GOSPEL. It was substantially the preaching of Peter to the Romans. The Gospel for him must represent the character and career of Jesus from the Roman point of view, as answering to the idea of divine power, work, law, conquest and universal sway; must retain its old significance and ever-potent inspiration as the battle-call of the almighty Conqueror. Luke wrote the THIRD GOSPEL in Greece for the Greek. It has its basis in the gospel which Paul and Luke, by long preaching to the Greeks, had already thrown into the form best suited to commend to their acceptance Jesus as the perfect divine man. It is the gospel of the future, of progressive Christianity, of reason and culture

seeking the perfection of manhood. John, "the beloved disciple," wrote the FOURTH GOSPEL for the Christian, to cherish and train those who have entered the new kingdom of Christ, into the highest spiritual life. See Harmony of the Gospels in the APPENDIX.

THE FOURFOLD GOSPEL.—"The existence," says Farrar, "of four separate and mainly, if not absolutely, independent Gospels is a great blessing to the church of Christ." (1) "It furnishes us with such a weight of contemporaneous testimony as is wanting to the vast majority of events in ancient history. A fourfold cord is not easily broken." (2) Jesus is presented to us from several different points of view, "each different, yet each the same; each a separate mirror to take in the side presented to it, but all disclosing in life-like harmony the one grand Person." Even a man cannot be understood when seen from one point of view: how much less the Son of God! (3) It is this fourfold view that presents Jesus as the Saviour of all men, of all races, of all tendencies of thought. "When," in the words of Professor Gregory, "one has clearly grasped the characteristics of each of the Gospels, the attempt to mass them all in one, while preserving the glory of each, will appear as absurd as would the attempt of an architect to construct, from the materials of Solomon's Temple, of the Parthenon, of the Colosseum, and of Westminster Abbey a new temple, which should preserve and harmoniously combine the peculiar features of them all, and be neither Jewish, Greek, Roman, nor Gothic."

From Canon Farrar's *Message of the Books* we take the following descriptions:

A common symbol of the evangelists was derived from Ezekiel's cherubim, the "fourfold visaged four." "Like them, the Gospels are four in number; like them, they are the chariot of God who sitteth between the cherubim; like them, they bear him on a winged throne into all lands; like them, they move wherever the Spirit guides them; like them, they are marvelously joined together, intertwined with coincidences and differences, wing interwoven with wing, and wheel interwoven with wheel; like them, they are full of eyes, and sparkle with heavenly light."

"To sum up these large generalizations in a form which has been recognized by all thoughtful students as giving us a true, though not an exclusive or exhaustive, aspect of the differences of the four Gospels, we may say that

"St. Matthew's is the Gospel for the Jews, the Gospel of the past, the Gospel which sees in Christianity a *fulfilment* of Judaism, the Gospel of discourses, the didactic Gospel, the Gospel which represents Christ as the Messiah of the Jew."

His emblem is the man: expressing the kingly and human characteristics of Christ.

"St. Mark's is the Gospel for the Romans, the Gospel of the present, the Gospel of incident, the anecdotal Gospel, the Gospel which represents Christ as the Son of God and Lord of the world."

His emblem is the lion: expressing courage, dignity, and energy.

"St. Luke's is the Gospel for the Greeks, the Gospel of the future, the Gospel of progressive Christianity, of the universality and gratuitousness of the Gospel, the historic Gospel, the Gospel of Jesus as the Good Physician and the Saviour of Mankind."

His emblem is the ox: expressing power and sacrifice, Christ's priestly and mediatorial office.

"St. John's is preëminently the Gospel for the church, the Gospel of eternity, the spiritual Gospel, the Gospel of Christ as the Eternal Son, and the Incarnate Word."

His emblem is the eagle: because "he soars to heaven above the clouds of human infirmity, and reveals to us the mysteries of the God-head, and the felicities of eternal life, gazing on the light of immutable truth with a keen and steady ken."

Gourd. 1. *Kikayon* only in Jonah 4: 6–10. There are differences of opinion as regards the plant intended here. It seems identical with the Egyptian name for the *Ricinus communis,* or castor-oil plant, which, a native of Asia, is now naturalized in America, Africa and the south of Europe. This plant varies considerably in size, being in India a tree, but in England seldom attaining a greater height than three or four feet. The leaves are large and palmate, with serrated lobes, and would form an excellent shelter for the sun-stricken prophet. On the other hand many believe that the plant meant is a vine of the cucumber family, a genuine gourd, which is much used for shade in the East.

2. The wild gourd of 2 Kings 4: 39, which one of "the sons of the prophets" gathered ignorantly, supposing them to be good for food, is a poisonous gourd, supposed to be the colocynth, which bears a fruit of the color and size of an orange, with a hard, woody shell. It would be recognized by any one familiar with the region, but those coming from other parts might mistake it for the wholesome globe cucumber.

Governor. In the Authorized Version this one English word is the representative of a large number of Hebrew and Greek words. (1) The chief of a tribe or family. (2) A ruler in his capacity of *lawgiver* and dispenser of justice. (3) A ruler considered especially as having *power* over the property and persons of his subjects. "The governors of the people," in 2 Chron. 23:

20, appear to have been the king's body-guard; cf. 2 Kings 11:19. (4) A *prominent* personage, whatever his ca-pacity. It is applied to a king as the

COLOCYNTHUS OR WILD GOURD.

military and civil chief of his people, 1 Chron. 29:22. It denotes an officer of high rank in the palace, the lord high chamberlain. 2 Chron. 28:7 It is ap-plied in 1 Kings 10:15 to the petty chief-tains who were tributary to Solomon, 2 Chron. 9:14. In the O. T. it is used most frequently for *Pechah*, a district ruler administering under a sovereign. The title is employed both for Persian satraps and for their subordinate mag-istrates. It seems to be the term used in 1 Kings 10:5; 2 Chron. 9:14 for Solomon's "governors of the land;" for Benhadad's "governors" as distinguish-ed from kings, 1 Kings 20:24. In the latter case it is a military officer. In Jeremiah, Ezekiel, Daniel and Esther the civil head of the government is in-tended. The title was borne by Zerub-babel, Hag. 1:1, 14, and by Nehemiah. It appears from Ezra 6:8 that these governors were intrusted with the col-lection of the king's taxes; and from Neh. 5:18; 12:26 that they were sup-ported by a contribution levied upon the people, which was technically termed "the bread of the governor;" comp. Ezra. 4:14. They were probably assisted in discharging their official duties by a council. Ezra 4:7; 6:6.

The "governor" beyond the river had a judgment-seat beyond Jerusalem, from which probably he administered justice when making a progress through his province. Neh. 3:7. In the New Testament it is most used for Procurator — or the Roman governor of Palestine in the time of Christ and later. It is also used for Ethnarch. 2 Cor. 11:32.

Go'zan (gō'zan) seems in the Author-ized Version of 1 Chron. 5:26 to be the name of a river; but in 2 Kings 17:6 and 18:11 it is evidently applied not to a river but a country. Gozan was the tract to which the Israelites were car-ried away captive by Pul, Tiglath-pileser and Shalmaneser, or possi-bly Sargon. It is probably identical with the *Gauzanitis* of Ptolemy, and may be regarded as represented by the Myg-donia of other writers. It was the tract watered by the Habor, the modern *Khabour*, the great Mesopotamian afflu-ent of the Euphrates.

Grape. [VINE.]

Grasshopper. [LOCUST.]

Grave. [BURIAL.]

Greaves, a piece of defensive armor which reached from the foot to the knee, and thus protected the shin of the wearer. It was made of leather or brass. 1 Sam. 17:6.

Greece, Greeks, Gre'cians. The histories of Greece and Palestine are little connected with each other. In Gen. 10:2–5 Moses mentions the de-scendants of Javan as peopling the isles of the Gentiles; and when the Hebrews came into contact with the Ionians of Asia Minor, and recognized them as the long-lost islanders of the western migration, it was natural that they should mark the similarity of sound between *Javan* and Iones. Accordingly the Old Testament word which is *Gre-cia*, in Authorized Version *Greece, Greeks*, etc., is in Hebrew *Javan*, Dan. 8:21; Joel 3:6; the Hebrew, however, is sometimes retained. Isa. 66 : 19; Ezek. 27 : 13. The Greeks and Hebrews met for the first time in the slave-market. The medium of communication seems to have been the Tyrian slave-merchants. Joel speaks of the Tyrians as selling the children of Judah to the Grecians, Joel 3 : 6; and in Ezek. 27 : 13 the Greeks are mentioned as trading in brazen vessels and slaves. Prophetical notice of Greece occurs in Dan. 8 : 21, etc., where the history of Alexander and his successors is rapidly sketched. Zechariah, Zech. 9 : 13, foretells the triumphs of the Maccabees against the Græco-Syrian empire, while Isaiah looks forward to the conversion of the Greeks, amongst other Gentiles, through the instrumentality of Jewish missionaries. Isa. 66 : 19. The name of the country, Greece, occurs once in the New Testament, Acts 20 : 2, as opposed to Macedonia. [GENTILES.]

Gre'cian. The term Grecian, or Hellenist, denotes a Jew by birth or religion who spoke Greek. It is used chiefly of foreign Jews and proselytes in contrast with the Hebrews speaking the vernacular Hebrew or Aramæan. *Greeks* was the term used for non-Jewish peoples.

Greyhound, the translation in the text of the Authorized Version, Prov. 30 : 31, of the Hebrew word *zarzir mothnayin,* i. e. "one girt about the loins." Various are the opinions as to what animal "comely in going" is here intended. Some think "a leopard," others "an eagle," or "a man girt with armor," or "a zebra," or "a war-horse girt with trappings." But perhaps the word means "a wrestler," when girt about the loins for a contest. Some authorities, including the Septuagint, have "a cock walking proudly among the hens."

Grinding. [MILL.]

Grove. 1. A word used in the Authorized Version, with two exceptions, to translate the mysterious Hebrew term *Asherah,* which is not a grove, but probably an idol or image of some kind. [ASHERAH.] It is also probable that there was a connection between this symbol or image, whatever it was, and the sacred symbolic tree, the representation of which occurs so frequently on Assyrian sculptures.

2. The two exceptions noticed above are Gen. 21 : 33 and 1 Sam. 22 : 6 (margin) in which verses the Revised Version translates the word "tamarisk tree."

Guard. In Oriental countries, especially, great attention is paid to the bodyguard of the king, which must be of approved fidelity. The captain of the king's bodyguard was a high officer. Gen. 37 : 36; 2 Sam. 23 : 22; 2 Kings 25 : 8; Dan. 2 : 14, etc. They were often employed as executioners.

Gud'godah (gŭd'go-dah). Deut. 10 : 7. [See HOR-HAGIDGAD.]

Guest. [HOSPITALITY.]

Gu'ni (gū'nī) (*painted*). 1. A son of Naphtali, Gen. 46 : 24; 1 Chron. 7 : 13, the founder of the family of the Gunites. Num. 26 : 48.

2. A descendant of Gad. 1 Chron. 5 : 15.

Gu'nites (gū'nītes), **The,** descendants of Guni, son of Naphtali. Num. 26 : 48.

Gur (gûr) (*abode*), **The going up to,** an ascent or rising ground, at which Ahaziah received his death-blow while flying from Jehu after the slaughter of Joram. 2 Kings 9 : 27.

Gur=ba'al (gûr-bā'al) (*abode of Baal*), a place or district in which dwelt Arabians, as recorded in 2 Chron. 26 : 7. It appears from the context to have been in the country lying between Palestine and the Arabian peninsula, perhaps Petra; but this, although probable, cannot not be proved.

H

Haahash'tari (hā-a-hăsh'-ta-rī), a man or a family immediately descended from Ashur, "father of Tekoa," by his second wife Naarah. 1 Chron. 4:6.

Haba'iah (hà-bā'iah), or **Haba'jah** (*Jehovah hides*). Bene-Habaiah were among the sons of the priests who returned from Babylon with Zerubbabel but were unable to prove their pedigree. Ezra 2:61; Neh. 7:63.

Hab'akkuk, or **Habak'kuk** (*embrace*), the eighth in order of the minor prophets. Of the facts of the prophet's life we have no certain information. He probably lived during the reigns of Josiah, Jehoahaz and Jehoiakim.

Hab'akkuk, Prophecy of, consists of three chapters, in the first of which he foreshadows the invasion of Judea by the Chaldeans, and in the second he foretells the doom of the Chaldeans. The whole concludes with the magnificent psalm in ch. 3, a composition unrivalled for boldness of conception, sublimity of thought and majesty of diction.

Habazini'ah (hăb-a-zĭ-nī'-ah), apparently the head of one of the families of the Rechabites. Jer. 35:3.

Habergeon, a coat of mail covering the neck and breast. [ARMS.]

Ha'bor (hā'bôr), the "river of Gozan," 2 Kings 17:6 and 18:11, is identified beyond all reasonable doubt with the famous affluent of the Euphrates, which is called Aborrhas and Chaboras by ancient writers, and now *Khabour.*

Hachali'ah (hăk-a-lī'ah), the father of Nehemiah. Neh. 1:1; 10:1.

Hach'ilah (hăk'i-lah), **The hill,** a hill apparently situated in a wood in the wilderness or waste land in the neighborhood of Ziph, in Judah, in the fastnesses or passes of which David and his six hundred followers were lurking when the Ziphites informed Saul of his whereabouts. 1 Sam. 23:19; comp. 14, 15, 18.

Hach'moni (hăk'mò-nī) (*wise*), **Son of,** and **The Hach'monite** (hăk'mò-nīte). 1 Chron. 11:11; 27:32. Hachmon or Hachmoni was no doubt the founder of a family to which these men belonged: the actual father of Jashobeam was Zabdiel, 1 Chron. 27:2, and he is also said to have belonged to the Korhites. 1 Chron. 12:6.

Ha'dad (hā'dăd). 1. The name of the supreme deity of Syria. He is variously explained as the sun-god, or the god of the atmosphere. The name is used in the compounding of proper names. See also RIMMON.

2. Son of Ishmael. Gen. 25:15; 1 Chron. 1:30. Also miswritten Hadar.

3. A king of Edom who gained an important victory over the Midianites on the field of Moab. Gen. 36:35; 1 Chron. 1:46.

4. Also a king of Edom, with Pau for his capital. 1 Chron. 1:50.

5. A member of the royal house of Edom. 1 Kings 11:14 ff. In his childhood he escaped the massacre under Joab, and fled with a band of followers into Egypt. Pharaoh, the predecessor of Solomon's father-in-law, treated him kindly, and gave him his sister-in-law in marriage. After David's death Hadad resolved to attempt the recovery of his dominion. He left Egypt and returned to his own country. See 2 Kings 3:9; 8:20.

Hadade'zer (hăd-ăd-e'zēr) (*Hadad is a help*), son of Rehob, 2 Sam. 8:3, the king of the Aramite state of Zobah, who was pursued by David and defeated with great loss. 1 Chron. 18:3, 4. After the first repulse of the Ammonites and their Syrian allies by Joab, Hadadezer sent his army to the assistance of his kindred the people of Maachah, Rehob and Ishtob. 1 Chron. 19:16; 2 Sam. 10:15, comp. 8. Under the command of Shophach or Shobach, the captain of the host, they crossed the Euphrates, joined the other Syrians, and encamped at a place called Helam. David himself came from Jerusalem to take the command of the Israelite army. As on the former occasion, the rout was complete.

Ha'dadrim'mon (hā'dăd-rĭm'mon) is, according to the ordinary interpretation of Zech. 12 : 11, a place in the valley of Megiddo (a part of the plain of Esdraelon, six miles from Mount Carmel and eleven from Nazareth), where a national lamentation was held for the death of King Josiah. It was named after two Syrian idols. It is now called RUMMANEH.

Ha'dar (hā'där). [HADAD.]

Hadare'zer (hăd-ar-ē'zĕr). 2 Sam. 10: 16, 19; 1 Chron. 18: 3 ff; 19: 16, 19. An incorrect form for HADADEZER.

Had'ashah (hăd'a-shah) (*new*), one of the towns of Judah, in the maritime low country, Josh. 15: 37 only. It has not been identified.

Hadas'sah (hà-dăs'sah) (*myrtle*), the Jewish name of Esther. Esther 2: 7.

Hadat'tah (hà-dat'tah) (*new*). According to the Authorized Version, one of the towns of Judah in the extreme south. Josh. 15: 25. [HAZOR.]

Ha'des, in Revised Version. [See HELL.]

Ha'did (hā'dĭd) (*sharp*), a place named, with Lod (Lydda) and Ono, only in the later books of the history. Ezra 2: 33; Neh. 7: 37; 11: 34. Its site is located at the modern *Haditheh* in the low hills about 3¼ miles N. E. of Lydda. Probably the ADIDA of 1 Mac. 12: 38.

Had'lai (hăd'la-i), a man of Ephraim. 2 Chron. 28: 12.

Hado'ram (hà-dō'ram). 1. The fifth son of Joktan. Gen. 10: 27; 1 Chron. 1: 21. His settlements, unlike those of many of Joktan's sons, have not been identified.

2. Son of Tou or Toi king of Hamath; his father's ambassador to congratulate David on his victory over Hadadezer king of Zobah. 1 Chron. 18: 10.

3. The form assumed in Chronicles by the name of the intendant of taxes under David, Solomon and Rehoboam. 2 Chron. 10: 18. In 1 Kings 4: 6; 5: 14, the name is given in the longer form of ADONIRAM, but in Samuel, 2 Sam. 20: 24, as ADORAM.

Ha'drach (hā'drak), a country of Syria, mentioned once only, by the pro-

phet Zechariah. Zech. 9 : 1. The position of the district, with its borders, is here generally stated; but the name itself seems to have wholly disappeared. The name *Hatarikka* has been recently found in Assyrian inscriptions in connection with Damascus, and beyond doubt refers to this place.

Ha'gab (hā'găb) (*locust*). Bene-Hagab were among the Nethinim who returned from Babylon with Zerubbabel. Ezra 2: 46.

Hag'aba (hăg'a-bà) (*locust*). Bene-Hagaba were among the Nethinim who came back from captivity with Zerubbabel. Neh. 7: 48. The name is slightly different in form from

Hag'abah (hăg'a-bah), under which it is found in the parallel list of Ezra 2: 45.

Ha'gar (hā'gar) (*flight*), an Egyptian woman, the handmaid or slave of Sarah, Gen. 16: 1, whom the latter gave as a concubine to Abraham, after he had dwelt ten years in the land of Canaan and had no children by Sarah, ch. 16: 2, 3. (B.C. 1911.) When Hagar saw that she had conceived, "her mistress was despised in her eyes," v. 4, and Sarah, with the anger, we may suppose, of a free woman rather than of a wife, reproached Abraham for the results of her own act. Hagar fled, turning her steps toward her native land through the great wilderness traversed by the Egyptian road. By the fountain in the way to Shur the angel of the Lord found her, charged her to return and submit herself under the hands of her mistress, and delivered the remarkable prophecy respecting her unborn child recorded in vs. 10–12. On her return she gave birth to Ishmael, and Abraham was then eighty-six years old. When Ishmael was about sixteen years old, he was caught by Sarah making sport of her young son Isaac at the festival of his weaning, and Sarah demanded the expulsion of Hagar and her son. She again fled toward Egypt, and when in despair at the want of water, an angel again appeared to her, pointed out a fountain close by, and renewed the former promises to her. Gen. 21: 9–21. St. Paul, Gal. 4: 25, refers to her as the type of the old covenant of the law.

Hagarenes' (hā-gar-ēnĕṣ'), **Ha'garites**, a people dwelling to the east of Palestine, with whom the tribes of Reuben made war in the time of Saul. 1 Chron. 5 : 10, 18–20. The same people, as confederate against Israel, are mentioned in Ps. 83 : 6. It is generally believed that they were named after Hagar, and some think that the important town and district of *Hejer*, on the borders of the Persian Gulf, represent them.

Ha'gerite (hā'ger-īte), **The.** Jaziz the Hagerite, had the charge of David's sheep. 1 Chron. 27 : 31.

Hag'gai (hăg'ga-ī) (*festal*), a prophet of the Return, who prophesied B.C. 520 in Jerusalem. He is generally regarded as an old man at the time of his prophecy, because it is inferred from Hag. 2 : 3 that he had seen the old temple which had been destroyed 66 years before. This would make him nearly 80 years old when he prophesied. Haggai uttered four prophecies in the year B.C. 520, in a time of coldness and neglect. Fifteen years before this 50,000 Israelites returned from captivity and began to build the city and the Temple. But soon the people began to attend to their own affairs. The city was still largely in ruins. The foundations of the temple were laid but the temple was not built. Blight and drought had come upon the land, and there was general discouragement. At this time two prophets appeared on the scene, the aged Haggai and the young Zechariah. Haggai uttered four prophecies in one year. He urged every argument in an appeal to the citizens to build the Temple. He was successful, and by the end of four years the Temple was completed.

Hag'geri (hăg'ḡe-ri), was the father of one of the mighty men of David's guard, according to 1 Chron. 11 : 38. The parallel passage—2 Sam. 23 : 36—has "Bani the Gadite," which is probably the correct reading.

Hag'gi (hăg'ḡī) (*born on a festival*), second son of Gad. Gen. 46 : 16; Num. 26 : 15.

Haggi'ah (hăg-ḡī'ah) (*festival of Jehovah*), a Merarite Levite. 1 Chron. 6 : 30.

Hag'gites, The, a Gadite family sprung from Haggi. Num. 26 : 15.

Hag'gith (hăg'ḡith) (*festal*), one of David's wives, the mother of Adonijah. 2 Sam. 3 : 4; 1 Kings 1 : 5.

Ha'i (hā'ī). Same as AI.

Hair. The Hebrews were fully alive to the importance of the hair as an ele-

ment of personal beauty. Long hair was admired in the case of young men. 2 Sam. 14 : 26. Men dreaded baldness as suggesting a suspicion of leprosy. Lev. 13 : 40; 2 Kings 2 : 23; 2 Sam. 10 : 4. Tearing the hair, Ezra 9 : 3, and letting it go dishevelled were similar tokens of grief. The usual and favorite color of the hair was black, Cant. 5 : 11, as is indicated in the comparisons in Cant. 1 : 5; 4 : 1; a similar hue is probably intended by the *purple* of Cant. 7 : 5. Pure white hair was deemed characteristic of the divine Majesty. Dan. 7 : 9; Rev. 1 : 14. The chief beauty of the hair consisted in curls, whether of a natural or an artificial character. With regard to the mode of dressing the hair, we have no very precise information; the terms used are of a general character, as of Jezebel, 2 Kings 9 : 30; Cant. 7 : 5; and in the New Testament, 1 Tim. 2 : 9; 1 Pet. 3 : 3; Rev. 9 : 8. The arrangement of Samson's hair into seven locks, or more properly *braids,* Judges 16 : 13, 19, involves the practice of plaiting, which was also familiar to the Egyptians and Greeks. The locks were probably kept in their place by a fillet, as in Egypt. The Hebrews, like other nations of antiquity, anointed the hair profusely with ointments, which were generally compounded of various aromatic ingredients, Ruth 3 : 3; 2 Sam. 14 : 2; Ps. 23 : 5; 92 : 10; Eccles. 9 : 8, more especially on occasions of festivity or hospitality. Luke

BEARDS.
Egyptian, from Wilkinson (top row). Of other nations, from Rosellini and Layard.

7 : 46. It appears to have been the custom of the Jews in our Saviour's time to swear by the hair, Matt. 5 : 36, much as the Egyptian women still swear by the side-lock, and the men by their beards.

Hak'katan (hăk'ka-tăn) (*the smallest*). Johanan, son of Hakkatan, was the chief of the Bene-Azgad who returned from Babylon with Ezra. Ezra 8 : 12.

Hak'koz (hăk'kŏz) (*thorn*), a priest, the chief of the seventh course in the service of the sanctuary, as appointed by David. 1 Chron. 24 : 10. In Ezra 2 : 61 and Neh. 3 : 4, 21 the name occurs again as Koz in the Authorized Version.

Haku'pha (há-kū'fà) (*bent*). Bene-Hakupha were among the Nethinim who returned from Babylon with Zerubbabel. Ezra 2 : 51; Neh. 7 : 53.

Ha'lah (hā'làh). 2 Kings 17 : 6; 18 : 11; 1 Chron. 5 : 26. A district of Assyria to which Israelite captives were carried.

Ha'lak (hā'lăk) (*smooth*), **The mount**, a mountain twice, and twice only, named as the southern limit of Joshua's conquests, Josh. 11 : 17; 12 : 7, but which has not yet been identified with certainty.

Hal'hul (hăl'hŭl), a town of Judah in the mountain district. Josh. 15 : 58. The name still remains unaltered, attached to a village on a hill a mile to the east of the road from Jerusalem to Hebron, between three and four miles from the latter.

Ha'li (hā'lĭ) (*necklace*), a town on the boundary of Asher, named between Helkath and Beten. Josh. 19 : 25.

Hall, used of the court of the high priest's house. Luke 22 : 55. In Matt. 27 : 27 and Mark 15 : 16 "hall" is synonymous with "prætorium," which in John 18 : 28 is in Authorized Version "judgment hall."

Hallelujah (hăl-le-lū'iah) (*praise ye Jehovah*). [ALLELUIA.]

Hallo'hesh (*the speaker of charms*), one of the chief of the people who sealed the covenant with Nehemiah. Neh. 10 : 24.

Halo'hesh (há-lō'hesh). Shallum, son of Halohesh, was "ruler of the half part of Jerusalem" at the time of the repair of the wall by Nehemiah. Neh. 3 : 12. B.C. 446. R. V. Hallohesh.

Ham (*black*). 1. The name of one of the three sons of Noah, apparently the second in age. (B.C. 2348.) Of the history of Ham nothing is related except his irreverence to his father and the curse which that patriarch pronounced. The sons of Ham are stated to have been "Cush and Mizraim and Phut and Canaan." Gen. 10 : 6; comp. 1 Chron. 1 : 8. Egypt is recognized as the "land of Ham" in the Bible. Ps. 78 : 51; 105 : 23; 106 : 22. The other settlements of the sons of Ham are discussed under their respective names. The three most illustrious Hamite nations—the Cushites, the Phœnicians and the Egyptians—were greatly mixed with foreign peoples.

2. According to the present text, Gen. 14 : 5, Chedorlaomer and his allies smote the Zuzim in a place called Ham, probably in the territory of the Ammonites (Gilead), east of the Jordan.

Ha'man (hā'man), the chief minister or vizier of King Ahasuerus. Esther 3 : 1. (B.C. 473.) After the failure of his attempt to cut off all the Jews in the Persian empire, he was hanged on the gallows which he had erected for Mordecai. The Targum and Josephus interpret the description of him—the Agagite—as signifying that he was of Amalekitish descent, but this is very doubtful. The Jews hiss whenever his name is mentioned on the day of Purim.

Ha'math (hā'math) (*fortress*), the principal city of upper Syria, was situated in the valley of the Orontes, which it commanded from the low screen of hills which forms the water-shed between the source of the Orontes and Antioch. The Hamathites were a Hamitic race, and are included among the descendants of Canaan. Gen. 10 : 18. Nothing appears of the power of Hamath until the time of David. 2 Sam. 8 : 9. Hamath seems clearly to have been included in the dominions of Solomon. 1 Kings 4 : 21–24. The "store-cities" which Solomon "built in Hamath," 2 Chron. 8 : 4, were perhaps centers for trade. In the Assyrian inscriptions of the time of Ahab (B.C. 875) Hamath appears as a separate power, in alliance with the Syrians of Damascus, the Hittites and the Phœnicians. About three-quarters of a century later Jeroboam the Second "recovered Hamath." 2 Kings 14 : 28. Soon afterwards the Assyrians took it, 2 Kings 18 : 34; 19 : 13, etc., and from this time it ceased to be a place of much importance. Antiochus Epiphanes changed its name to Epiphaneia. The natives, however, called it Hamath even in St. Jerome's time, and its present name, *Hamah*, is but slightly altered from the ancient form.

THE HAMMURABI MONUMENT.

Inscribed in Archaic Babylonian, with the text of the " Code of Laws," which was drawn up by Hammurabi, King of the first dynasty of Babylonia. On the upper part the King is seen in an attitude of worship, receiving the laws from the Sun-God. The lower portion is inscribed with twenty-eight columns in which the King enumerates the benefits of his reign and sets forth in 282 clauses the laws by which the country shall be governed. This stele was originally set up in the temple of E-sagili, in Babylon, and was carried off by an Elamite to Susa, in the ruins of which city it was discovered.

Ha'mathite (hā'math-īte), **The,** one of the families descended from Canaan, named last in the list. Gen. 10:18; 1 Chron. 1:16.

Ha'math=zo'bah (hā'math-zō'bah) (*fortress of Zobah*), 2 Chron. 8:3, has been conjectured to be the same as Hamath. But the name *Hamath-zobah* would seem rather suited to another Hamath which was distinguished from the "Great Hamath" by the suffix "Zobah."

Ham'math (hăm'math) (*warm spring*), one of the fortified cities in the territory allotted to Naphtali. Josh. 19:35. It was near Tiberias, one mile distant, and had its name Chammath, "hot baths," because it contained those of Tiberias. In the list of Levitical cities given out of Naphtali, Josh. 21:32, the name of this place seems to be given as HAMMOTH-DOR.

Hammed'atha (ham-mĕd'a-thà), father of the infamous Haman. Esther 3:1, 10; 8:5; 9:24.

Ham'melech (hăm'me-lĕk), lit. "*the king*," unnecessarily rendered in the Authorized Version as a proper name. Jer. 36:26; 38:6.

Hammol'eketh (hăm-mŏl'e-kĕth) (*the queen*), a daughter of Machir and sister of Gilead. 1 Chron. 7:17, 18.

Ham'mon (hăm'mŏn) (*warm springs*). 1. A city in Asher, Josh. 19:28, apparently not far from Zidon-rabbah.

2. A city allotted out of the tribe of Naphtali to the Levites, 1 Chron. 6:76, probably identical with the similar names HAMMATH and HAMMOTH-DOR in Joshua.

Ham'moth=dor (hăm'moth-dôr), (see HAMMATH.)

Hammura'bi, see AMRAPHEL.

Hamo'nah (*multitude*), the name of a city mentioned in Ezekiel. Ezek. 39:16.

Ha'mon=gog (hā'mon-gŏg) (*the multitude of Gog*), **The valley of,** the name to be bestowed on a ravine or glen, previously known as "the ravine of the passengers on the east of the sea," after the burial there of "Gog and all his multitude." Ezek. 39:11, 15.

Ha'mor (hā'mor) (*he-ass*), a Hivite who at the time of the entrance of Jacob on Palestine was prince of the land and city of Shechem. Gen. 33:19; 34:2, 4, 6, 8, 13, 18, 20, 24, 26. (B.C. 1739.) [DINAH.]

Hamu'el (hà-mū'el) (*heat,* i. e. *wrath, of God*), a man of Simeon, of the family of Shaul. 1 Chron. 4:26.

Ha'mul (hā'mŭl) (*spared*), the younger son of Pharez, Judah's son by Tamar. Gen. 46:12; 1 Chron. 2:5.

Ha'mulites (hā'mŭl-ītes), **The,** the family of the preceding. Num. 26:21.

Hamu'tal (hà-mū'tal) (*akin to the dew*), daughter of Jeremiah of Libnah; one of the wives of King Josiah, and mother of the kings Jehoahaz and Zedekiah. 2 Kings 23:31; 24:18; Jer. 52:1.

Hanam'eel (hà-năm'e-el) (perhaps *God is gracious*), son of Shallum and cousin of Jeremiah. Jer. 32:7, 8, 9, 12.

Ha'nan (hā'nan) (*merciful*). 1. One of the chief people of the tribe of Benjamin. 1 Chron. 8:23.

2. The last of the six sons of Azel, a descendant of Saul. 1 Chron. 8:38; 9:44.

3. "Son of Maachah," *i. e.* possibly a Syrian of Aram-maachah, one of the heroes of David's guard. 1 Chron. 11:43.

4. The sons of Hanan were among the Nethinim who returned from Babylon with Zerubbabel. Ezra 2:46; Neh. 7:49.

5. One of the Levites who assisted Ezra in his public exposition of the law. Neh. 8:7. (B.C. 446.) The same person is probably mentioned in ch. 10:10.

6. One of the "heads" of "the people," who also sealed the covenant. Neh. 10:22.

7. Another of the chief laymen on the same occasion. Neh. 10:26.

8. Son of Zaccur, son of Mattaniah, whom Nehemiah made one of the storekeepers of the provisions collected as tithes. Neh. 13:13.

9. Son of Igdaliah. Jer. 35:4.

Hanan'eel (hà-năn'e-el) (*El is gracious*), **The tower of,** a tower which formed part of the wall of Jerusalem. Neh. 3:1; 12:39. From these two passages, particularly from the former, it might almost be inferred that Hananeel was but another name for the tower of Hammeah; at any rate they were close together, and stood between the sheep-gate and the fish-gate. This tower is further mentioned in Jer. 31:38. The remaining passage in which it is named, Zech. 14:10, also connects this tower with the "corner-gate," which lay on the other side of the sheep-gate.

Hana'ni (hà-nā'nī) (*gracious*). 1.

One of the sons of Heman, and head of the eighteenth course of the service. 1 Chron. 25 : 4, 25.

2. A seer who rebuked (B.C. 902) Asa king of Judah. 2 Chron. 16 : 7. For this he was imprisoned. ver. 10. He was the father of Jehu the seer, who testified against Baasha, 1 Kings 16 : 1, 7, and Jehoshaphat, 2 Chron. 19 : 2; 20 : 34.

3. One of the priests who in the time of Ezra had taken strange wives. Ezra 10 : 20.

4. A brother or near kinsman of Nehemiah, Neh. 1 : 2, who was made governor of Jerusalem under Nehemiah. ch. 7 : 2.

5. A Levite mentioned in Neh. 12 : 36.

Hanani'ah (hăn-a-nī'ah) (*Jehovah hath been gracious*). 1. A son of Heman, and chief of the sixteenth course of singers. 1 Chron. 25 : 4, 5, 23.

2. A general in the army of King Uzziah. 2 Chron. 26 : 11.

3. Father of Zedekiah, who was a prince of Judah in the reign of Jehoiakim. Jer. 36 : 12.

4. Son of Azur, a Benjamite of Gibeon and a false prophet in the reign of Zedekiah king of Judah. In the fourth year of his reign, B.C. 593, Hananiah withstood Jeremiah the prophet, and publicly prophesied in the temple that within two years Jeconiah and all his fellow captives, with the vessels of the Lord's house, should be brought back to Jerusalem. Jer. 28. Hananiah corroborated his prophecy by taking from off the neck of Jeremiah the yoke which he wore by divine command, Jer. 27, and breaking it. But Jeremiah was bidden to go and tell Hananiah that for the wooden yokes which he had broken he should make yokes of iron, so firm was the dominion of Babylon destined to be for seventy years. The prophet Jeremiah added to this rebuke the prediction of Hananiah's death, the fulfilment of which closes the history of this false prophet.

5. Grandfather of Irijah, the captain of the ward at the gate of Benjamin who arrested Jeremiah on the charge of deserting to the Chaldeans. Jer. 37 : 13.

6. Head of a Benjamite house. 1 Chron. 8 : 24.

7. The Hebrew name of Shadrach. Dan. 1 : 3, 6, 7, 11, 19 ; 2 : 17.

8. Son of Zerubbabel, 1 Chron. 3 : 19, from whom Christ derived his de-

scent. He is very possibly the same person who is by St. Luke called Joanna. R. V. Joanan. (B.C. after 536.)

9. One of the sons of Bebai who had "married strange women." Ezra 10 : 28. (B.C. 458.)

10. A priest, one of the makers of the sacred ointments and incense, who built a portion of the wall of Jerusalem in the days of Nehemiah. Neh. 3 : 8.

11. Head of the priestly course of Jeremiah in the days of the high priest Joiakim. Neh. 12 : 12.

12. Ruler of the palace at Jerusalem under Nehemiah. The arrangements for guarding the gates of Jerusalem were intrusted to him with Hanani, the Tirshatha's brother. Neh. 7 : 2, 3. (B.C. 446.)

13. An Israelite. Neh. 10 : 23.

Handicraft. Acts 18 : 3 ; 19 : 25 ; Rev. 18 : 22. A trade was taught to all the Jewish boys, as a necessary part of their education. Even the greatest rabbis maintained themselves by trades (*Delitzsch*). Says Rabbi Jehuda, "He who does not teach his son a trade is much the same as if he taught him to be a thief." In the present article brief notices only can be given of such handicraft trades as are mentioned in Scripture.

1. *Smiths or metal-workers.*—The preparation of iron for use either in war, in agriculture or for domestic purposes was doubtless one of the earliest applications of labor ; and together with iron, working in brass, or rather copper alloyed with tin (bronze), is mentioned as practised in antediluvian times. Gen. 4 : 22. After the establishment of the Jews in Canaan, the occupation of a smith became recognized as a distinct employment. 1 Sam. 13 : 19. The smith's work and its results are often mentioned in Scripture. 2 Sam. 12 : 31; 1 Kings 6 : 7; 2 Chron. 26 : 14; Isa. 44 : 12; 54 : 16. The worker in gold and silver must have found employment among both the Hebrews and the neighboring nations in very early times. Gen. 24 : 22, 53; 35 : 4; 38 : 18. Various processes of the goldsmith's work are illustrated by Egyptian monuments. After the conquest frequent notices are found of both moulded and wrought metal, including soldering.

2. *Carpenters* are often mentioned in Scripture. Gen. 6 : 14; Ex. 37; Isa. 44 : 13. In the palace built by David for

himself the workmen employed were chiefly foreigners. 2 Sam. 5 : 11. So also were those who executed the timber work in Solomon's temple. 1 Kings 5 : 6. In the time of Joash there is no mention of the carpenters being foreigners, 2 Kings 12 : 11; while those under Josiah seem to have been Jews. 2 Kings 22 : 6. In Isa. 44 : 13 there is a picture of a carpenter carving a wooden idol—but this is supposed to refer to a Babylonian rather than a Jew. In the New Testament the occupation of a carpenter is mentioned in connection with Joseph the husband of the Virgin Mary, and ascribed to our Lord himself. Matt. 13 : 55; Mark 6 : 3.

3. The *masons* employed by David and Solomon, at least the chief of them, were Phœnicians. 2 Sam. 5 : 11; 1 Kings 5 : 18. The large stones used in Solomon's temple are said by Josephus to have been fitted together exactly without either mortar or clamps, but the foundation stones to have been fastened with lead. The most common material in use now is clay, which must be prepared properly by treading and mixing with water, for if too dry it will crack and fall. The wall "daubed with untempered mortar" of Ezekiel 13 : 10 may have been of "dry clay" as it is given in the Arabic versions. The use of whitewash on tombs is remarked by our Lord. Matt. 23 : 27.

4. *Ship-building* must have been exercised to some extent for the fishing-vessels on the Lake of Gennesaret. Matt. 8 : 23; 9 : 1; John 21 : 3, 8. Solomon built ships for his foreign trade. 1 Kings 9 : 26, 27; 22 : 48; 2 Chron. 20 : 36, 37. See also Ezek. 27 : 5–9.

5. *Apothecaries* or perfumers appear to have formed a guild or association. Ex. 30 : 25, 35; 2 Chron. 16 : 14; Neh. 3 : 8; Eccles. 7 : 1; 10 : 1.

6. *Weavers.*—The arts of spinning and weaving both wool and linen are very ancient, and were carried to great proficiency. Weaving was generally carried on by men in Egypt, but women sometimes engaged in it and the spinning was largely the work of the women. Ex. 35 : 25, 26; Lev. 19 : 19; Deut. 22 : 11; 2 Kings 23 : 7; Ezek. 16 : 16; Prov. 31 : 13, 24. The loom with its beam, 1 Sam. 17 : 7, pin, Judges 16 : 14, and shuttle, Job 7 : 6, was perhaps introduced later, but as early as David's time. 1 Sam. 17 : 7.

7. *Dyeing* and *dressing cloth* were practised in Palestine, as were also *tanning* and *dressing* leather. Ex. 25 : 5; Num. 31 : 20; 2 Kings 1 : 8; Matt. 3 : 4; Acts 9 : 43.

8. *Barbers.* Num. 6 : 5, 19; Ezek. 5 : 1.

9. *Tent-makers* are noticed in Acts 18 : 3.

10. *Potters* are frequently alluded to. Jer. 18 : 2–6.

11. *Bakers* are noticed in Scripture, Jer. 37 : 21; Hos. 7 : 4; and the well-known valley Tyropœon is commonly regarded as deriving its name from the occupation of the cheese-makers, its inhabitants.

12. *Butchers*, not Jewish, are spoken of, 1 Cor. 10 : 25.

Shoemakers, tailors, glaziers and glass vessels, *painters* and *gold-workers* are mentioned in the Mishna.

Handkerchief, Napkin, Apron. Luke 19 : 20; John 11 : 44; 20 : 7; Acts 19 : 12. The first two terms are used for a small cloth used by the Romans for wiping the hands and face, and adopted by the Jews during the Roman period.

Ha'nes (hā'nĕṣ), a place in Egypt mentioned only in Isa. 30 : 4. The identification with Tahpanhes, a fortified town on the eastern frontier, is very possible.

Hanging, Hangings. (1) The "hanging" was a curtain or "covering" to close an entrance; one was placed before the door of the tabernacle. Ex. 26 : 36; 37; 39 : 38. The R. V. translates "screen." (2) The "hangings" were suspended from pillars, and fenced off the court of the tabernacle from the outer world. Ex. 27 : 9; 35 : 17; 38 : 9; Num. 3 : 26; 4 : 26.

Han'iel (hăn'ĭ-ĕl) (*grace of God*), one of the sons of Ulla of the tribe of Asher. 1 Chron. 7 : 39.

Han'nah (*grace*), one of the wives of Elkanah, and mother of Samuel. 1 Sam. 1, 2. A hymn of thanksgiving for the birth of her son is highly poetic; so much so that modern criticism pronounces it unsuited to Hannah's time and circumstances, and ascribes it to a later date. Its resemblance to that of the Virgin Mary, comp. 1 Sam. 2 : 1–10 with Luke 1 : 46–55, see also Ps. 113, has been noticed by Bible students.

Han'nathon (hăn'na-thŏn), one of the cities of Zebulun. Josh. 19 : 14.

Han'niel (hăn'nĭ-el) (*the favor of*

God), son of Ephod and prince of Manasseh. Num. 34:23.

Ha'noch (hā'nok). 1. The third in order of the children of Midian. Gen. 25:4.

2. Eldest son of Reuben, Gen. 46:9; Ex. 6:14; Num. 26:5; 1 Chron. 5:3, and founder of the family of the Hanochites. Num. 26:5.

Ha'nun (hā'nŭn) (*favored*). 1. Son of Nahash, 2 Sam. 10:1, 2; 1 Chron. 19:1, 2, king of Ammon, who dishonored the ambassadors of David, 2 Sam. 10:4, and involved the Ammonites in a disastrous war. 2 Sam. 12:31; 1 Chron. 19:6.

2. A man who, with the people of Zanoah, repaired the ravine gate in the wall of Jerusalem. Neh. 3:13. (B.C. 446.)

3. The sixth son of Zalaph, who also assisted in the repair of the wall, apparently on the east side. Neh. 3:30. (B.C. 446.)

Haphra'im (hăf-rā'im) (*two pits*), a city of Issachar, mentioned next to Shunem. Josh. 19:19. Jerome identified it with Affarea, 6 miles from Legio (*Lejjun*). This site is now called *El-Ferriyeh*. Another identification is with *el-Afuleh*, 2 miles west of *Solam* (the ancient Shunem), about 7 miles from Lejjun.

Ha'ra (hā'rà), 1 Chron. 5:26 only, is mentioned as a place where Israelitish exiles were settled by Tiglath Pileser. Its situation is unknown.

Har'adah (hăr'a-dah) (*fear*), a desert station of the Israelites, Num. 33:24, 25; its position is uncertain.

Ha'ran (hā'ran) (*a mountaineer*). 1. The third son of Terah, and therefore youngest brother of Abram. Gen. 11:26. Three children are ascribed to him —Lot, vs. 27, 31, and two daughters, viz., Milcah, who married her uncle Nahor, ver. 29, and Iscah, ver. 29. Haran was born in Ur of the Chaldees, and he died there while his father was still living, ver. 28. B.C. 1926 (Ussher).

2. A Gershonite Levite, one of the family of Shimei. 1 Chron. 23:9.

3. A son of Caleb the son of Hezron by his concubine Ephah. 1 Chron. 2:46.

4. HARAN or CHARRAN, Acts 7:2, 4, name of the place whither Abraham migrated with his family from Ur of the Chaldees, and where the descendants of his brother Nahor established themselves. Comp. Gen. 24:10 with 27:43.

It is said to be in Mesopotamia, Gen. 24:10, or more definitely in Padan-aram, ch. 25:20, the cultivated district at the foot of the hills, a name well applying to the beautiful stretch of country which lies below Mount Masius between the Khabour and the Euphrates. Here, about midway in this district, is a small village still called *Harrán*. It was celebrated among the Romans, under the name of Charræ, as the scene of the defeat of Crassus.

Ha'rarite (hā'ra-rīte), **The.** The designation of two of David's guard. 1. Shammah, the son of Agee, a Hararite. 2 Sam. 23:11, 33.

2. Sharar, 2 Sam. 23:33, or Sacar, 1 Chron. 11:35, the Hararite, was the father of Ahiam, another member of the guard.

Harbo'na (här-bō'na) (*ass-driver*), the third of the seven chamberlains or eunuchs who served King Ahasuerus. Esther 1:10. (B.C. 483–475.)

Harbo'nah (här-bō'nah), Esther 7:9, the same as the preceding.

Hare (Heb. *arnebeth*) occurs only in Lev. 11:6 and Deut. 14:7 amongst the animals disallowed as food by the Mosaic law. The hare is at this day called *Arnabeh* by the Arabs in Palestine and Syria. It was erroneously thought by the ancient Jews to have chewed the cud. They were no doubt misled, by the habit these animals have of moving the jaw about. Although some regard the statement as merely according to appearance, not scientific.

Harem. [HOUSE.]

Ha'reph (hā'ref) (*a plucking off*), a name occurring in the genealogies of Judah as a son of Caleb and as "father of Beth-gader." 1 Chron. 2:51 only.

Ha'reth (hā'reth), **The forest of,** in which David took refuge, after, at the instigation of the prophet Gad, he had quitted the "hold" or fastness of the cave of Adullam. 1 Sam. 22:5.

Harhai'ah (här-hà-ī'ah), father of Uzziel. Neh. 3:8.

Har'has (här'has), an ancestor of Shallum the husband of Huldah. 2 Kings 22:14.

Har'hur (här'hûr) (*fever* or *free-born*). The sons of Harhur were among the Nethinim who returned from Babylon with Zerubbabel. Ezra 2:51; Neh. 7:53.

Ha'rim (hā'rim) (*consecrated*). 1. A priest who had charge of the third division in the house of God. 1 Chron. 24: 8.

2. Bene-Harim, probably descendants of the above, to the number of 1017, came from Babylon with Zerubbabel. Ezra 2: 39; Neh. 7: 42.

3. It further occurs in a list of the families of priests "who went up with Zerubbabel and Jeshua," and of those who were their descendants in the next generation. Neh. 12: 15.

4. Another family of Bene-Harim, 320 in number, came from the captivity in the same caravan. Ezra 2: 32; Neh. 7: 35. The same names also appear among those who had married foreign wives, Ezra 10: 31, as well as those who sealed the covenant. Neh. 10: 27.

Ha'riph (hā'rif) (*autumn*). A hundred and twelve of the Bene-Hariph returned from the captivity with Zerubbabel. Neh. 7: 24. The name occurs again among the "heads of the people" who sealed the covenant, ch. 10: 19.

Harlot. That this class of persons existed in the earliest states of society is clear from Gen. 38: 15. They were legalized in many cases as consecrated to the worship of the heathen gods, and formed both one of the attractions of idolatry and one of its chief dangers. After the exile legitimized harlotry was made an end of with idolatry. The "harlots" are classed with "publicans," as those who lay under the ban of society, in the New Testament. Matt. 21: 32.

Har-mag'edon (här-măg'e-don) (*hill of Megiddo*), Rev. 16: 16 in the Revised Version for **Armageddon.** The change is chiefly *Har*, hill, in place of *Ar*, city.

Har'nepher (här'ne-fĕr) (*panting*), one of the sons of Zophah, of the tribe of Asher. 1 Chron. 7: 36.

Ha'rod (hā'rod) (*trembling*), **The well of,** a spring by which Gideon and his great army encamped on the morning of the day which ended in the rout of the Midianites, Judges 7: 1, and where the trial of the people by their mode of drinking apparently took place. The site is not certain but the *Ain Jalûd* is very suitable to the circumstances, as being at present the largest spring in the neighborhood.

Ha'rodite (hā'rod-īte), **The,** the designation of two of the thirty-seven warriors of David's guard, Shammah and Elika, 2 Sam. 23: 25, doubtless derived from a place named Harod.

Har'oeh (hăr'o-ē), a name occurring in the genealogical lists of Judah. 1 Chron. 2: 52.

Ha'rorite (hā'ro-rīte) (the same as Harodite), **The,** the title given to Shammoth, one of the warriors of David's guard. 1 Chron. 11: 27.

Haro'sheth (hä-rō'sheth) (*carving*) **of the Gentiles** was formerly thought near the waters of Merom. It is now generally identified with *el-Harathiyeh* a small village on the northern bank of the Kishon at the point where the stream enters the plain of Acre. It was the residence of Sisera, captain of Jabin king of Canaan, Judges 4: 2, and it was the point to which the victorious Israelites under Barak pursued the discomfited host and chariots of the second potentate of that name. Judges 4: 16.

Harp. The harp was the national instrument of the Hebrews, and was well known throughout Asia. In Genesis its invention is assigned to Jubal during the antediluvian period. Gen. 4: 21.

EGYPTIAN HARP.

Josephus records that the harp had ten strings, and that it was played on with the plectrum. Sometimes it was smaller, having only eight strings, and was usually played with the fingers.

Harrow. The word so rendered, 2 Sam. 12: 31; 1 Chron. 20: 3, is probably a threshing-machine. The verb rendered "to harrow," Job 39: 10; Isa. 28: 24; Hos. 10: 11, expresses apparently the breaking of the clods, and is so far analogous to our harrowing; but whether done by any such machine as we call a "harrow" is very doubtful.

Har'sha (här'shä). Bene-Harsha

were among the families of Nethinim who came back from Babylon with Zerubbabel. Ezra 2:52; Neh. 7:54.

Hart, the male deer. The word denotes some member of the deer tribe, either the true fallow deer or the roebuck. The hart is reckoned among the clean animals, Deut. 12:15; 14:5; 15:22, and seems from the passages quoted, as well as from 1 Kings 4:23, to have been commonly killed for food.

Ha'rum (hā'rum) (*lofty*), father of Aharhel, in one of the most obscure genealogies of Judah. 1 Chron. 4:8.

Haru'maph (hà-ru̧'maf) (*slit-nosed*), father or ancestor of Jedaiah. Neh. 3:10.

Har'uphite (hăr'u-fīte) (*native of Hariph*), **The,** the designation of Shephatiah, one of the Korhites who repaired to David at Ziklag. 1 Chron. 12:5. (B.C. 1057.)

Ha'ruz (hā'ruz) (*diligent*), a man of Jotbah, father of Meshullemeth queen of Manasseh. 2 Kings 21:19.

Harvest. [AGRICULTURE.]

Hasadi'ah (hăs-a-dī'ah) (*Jehovah is kind*). One of the sons of Zerubbabel. 1 Chron. 3:20.

Hasenu'ah (hăs-e-nū'ah), a Benjamite, named twice, unless there were two of the same name. 1 Chron. 9:7; Neh. 11:9.

Hashabi'ah (hăsh-a-bī'ah). 1. A Merarite Levite. 1 Chron. 6:45.

2. Another Merarite Levite. 1 Chron. 9:14.

3. The fourth of the six sons of Jeduthun, 1 Chron. 25:3, who had charge of the twelfth course, ver. 19.

4. One of the descendants of Hebron the son of Kohath. 1 Chron. 26:30.

5. The son of Kemuel, who was prince of the tribe of Levi in the time of David. 1 Chron. 27:17.

6. A Levite, one of the "chiefs" of his tribe, who officiated for King Josiah at his great passover feast. 2 Chron. 35:9. (B.C. 621.)

7. A Merarite Levite who accompanied Ezra from Babylon. Ezra 8:19.

8. One of the chiefs of the priests who formed part of the same caravan. Ezra 8:24.

9. Ruler of half the circuit or environs of Keilah; he repaired a portion of the wall of Jerusalem under Nehemiah. Neh. 3:17. (B.C. 446.)

10. One of the Levites who sealed the covenant of reformation after the return from the captivity. Neh. 10:11; 12:24; comp. 26.

11. Another Levite, son of Bunni. Neh. 11:15.

12. A Levite, son of Mattaniah. Neh. 11:22.

13. A priest of the family of Hilkiah in the days of Joiakim son of Jeshua. Neh. 12:21.

Hashab'nah (hă-shăb'nah), one of the chief of the "people" who sealed the covenant with Nehemiah. Neh. 10:25.

Hashabni'ah (hăsh-ab-nī'ah). 1. Father of Hattush. Neh. 3:10.

2. A Levite who was among those who officiated at the great fast under Ezra and Nehemiah when the covenant was sealed. Neh. 9:5.

Hashbad'ana (hăsh-băd'a-nà), one of the men (probably Levites) who stood on Ezra's left hand while he read the law to the people in Jerusalem. Neh. 8:4.

Ha'shem (hā'shem). The sons of Hashem the Gizonite are named amongst the members of David's guard in 1 Chron. 11:34. See JASHEN and GIZONITE.

Hashmo'nah (hăsh-mō'nah), a station of the Israelites, mentioned Num. 33:29 as next before Moseroth.

Ha'shub (hā'shub) (*considerate*). 1. A son of Pahath-moab, who assisted in the repair of the wall of Jerusalem. Neh. 3:11. (B.C. 446.)

2. Another who assisted in the same work. Neh. 3:23.

3. One of the heads of the people who sealed the covenant with Nehemiah. Neh. 10:23.

4. A Merarite Levite. Neh. 11:15.

Hashu'bah (hà-shu̧'bah) (*consideration*). One of the sons of Zerubbabel. 1 Chron. 3:20.

Ha'shum (hā'shum) (*rich*). 1. Bene-Hashum, 223 in number, came back from Babylon with Zerubbabel. Ezra 2:19; 10:33; Neh. 7:22. The chief man of the family was among those who sealed the covenant with Nehemiah. Neh. 10:18.

2. One of the priests or Levites who stood on Ezra's left hand while he read the law to the congregation. Neh. 8:4.

Hashu'pha (hà-shu̧'fà) (*stripped*), one of the families of Nethinim who returned from captivity in the first caravan. Neh. 7:46. Called HASUPHA in

Ezra 2:43, which is doubtless the correct form.

Has'rah (hăs'rah), the form in which the name Harhas is given in 2 Chron. 34:22; comp. 2 Kings 22:14.

Hassena'ah (hăs-se-nā'ah). The Bene-Hassenaah rebuilt the fish-gate in the repair of the wall of Jerusalem. Neh. 3:3.

Has'shub (hăs'shub). [See HASHUB.]

Hasu'pha (hà-sū'fà). [See HASHUPHA.]

Ha'tach (hā'tak), one of the eunuchs in the court of Ahasuerus. Esther 4: 5, 6, 9, 10. (B.C. 473.)

Ha'thath (hā'thath) (*terror*), one of the sons of Othniel the Kenazite. 1 Chron. 4:13.

Hat'ipha (hăt'ĭ-fà) (*captive*). Bene-Hatipha (*i. e.* sons of Hatipha) were among the Nethinim who returned from Babylon with Zerubbabel. Ezra 2:54; Neh. 7:56.

Hat'ita (hăt'ĭ-tà). Bene-Hatita were among the "porters" (*i. e.* the gate-keepers) who returned from the captivity with Zerubbabel. Ezra 2:42; Neh. 7:45.

Hat'til (hăt'til). Bene-Hattil were among the "children of Solomon's servants" who came back from captivity with Zerubbabel. Ezra 2:57; Neh. 7: 59.

Hat'tush (hăt'tush) (*assembled*). 1. A chief of the priests, who returned with Zerubbabel from Babylon. Neh. 12:2.

2. A descendant of the kings of Judah, apparently one of the sons of Shechaniah, 1 Chron. 3:22. A person of the same name accompanied Ezra from Babylon to Jerusalem. Ezra 8:2.

3. Son of Hashabniah; one of those who assisted Nehemiah in the repair of the wall of Jerusalem. Neh. 3:10. (B.C. 446.)

Hau'ran (hâu'ran) (*caverns*), a province of Palestine mentioned by Ezekiel. Ezek. 47:16, 18. There can be little doubt that it is identical with the well-known Greek province of Auranitis and the modern *Haurân*, east of the Sea of Galilee, on the borders of the desert, in the tetrarchy of Philip.

Hav'ilah (hăv'ĭ-lah) (*sandy*). 1. A son of Cush. Gen. 10:7.

2. A son of Joktan. Gen. 10:29.

Hav'ilah (hăv'ĭ-lah). Gen. 2:11. A part of Eden around which flowed the

16

river Pison. Its position is variously determined, some contesting that there were several districts of the name, others that the apparent differences are because different parts of a large territory are mentioned. A very similar name was found in Africa, and also widely spread in Arabia.

Havoth=ja'ir (hā'voth-jā'ir) (*villages of Jair*), certain villages on the east of Jordan, in Gilead or Bashan, which were taken by Jair the son of Manasseh, and called after his name. Num. 32:41; Deut. 3:14. In the records of Manasseh in Josh. 13:30 and 1 Chron. 2:23, the Havoth-jair are reckoned with other districts as making up sixty "cities." Comp. 1 Kings 4:13. There is apparently some confusion in these different statements as to what the sixty cities really consisted of. No less doubtful is the number of the Havoth-jair. In 1 Chron. 2:22 they are specified as twenty-three, but in Judges 10: 4 as thirty.

Hawk. Lev. 11:16; Deut. 14:15; Job 39:26. Probably a general term for

KESTREL OR HAWK.

birds of prey. With respect to the passage in Job (*l. c.*) which appears to allude to the migratory habits of hawks, it is curious to observe that of the ten or twelve lesser raptors (hawk tribe) of Palestine, nearly all are summer migrants. The kestrel remains all the year, but the others are all migrants from the south.

Hay (Heb. *châtsîr*), the rendering of the Authorized Version in Prov. 27:25 and Isa. 15:6 of the Hebrew term, which occurs frequently in the Old Testament, and denotes "grass" of any kind. There is another Hebrew word meaning "dry grass" or perhaps better "cut grass," viz. *chashash*, which, in the only two places where the word occurs, Isa. 5:24, 33:11, is rendered "chaff" in the Authorized Version. In the latter place the R. V. translates it "dry grass." The people of Palestine do not cut and dry grass for hay as do western peoples, and there is no evidence that it was done in Bible times. They do now, and probably did then, cut and pull grass and other fodder plants and give them to live stock, especially during the spring and early summer. Hay would not be necessary, since there is always either the green grass, or the stubble remaining in the fields.

Haz′ael (hăz′a-el) (*whom God sees*), a king of Damascus who reigned from about B.C. 842 to B.C. 796. He appears to have been previously a person in a high position at the court of Ben-hadad, and was sent by his master to Elisha to inquire if he would recover from the malady under which he was suffering. Elisha's answer led to the murder of Ben-hadad by his ambitious servant, who forthwith mounted the throne. 2 Kings 8:7–15. He was soon engaged in war with the kings of Judah and Israel, for the possession of the city of Ramoth-gilead, 8:28. Towards the close of the reign of Jehu, Hazael led the Syrians against the Israelites (about B.C. 819), whom he "smote in all their coasts," 2 Kings 10:32, thus accomplishing the prophecy of Elisha. 8:12. At the close of his life, having taken Gath, 12:17; comp. Amos 6:2, he proceeded to attack Jerusalem, 2 Chron. 24:24, and was about to assault the city when Joash bribed him to retire. 2 Kings 12:18. Hazael appears to have died about the year B.C. 796, 2 Kings 13:24, having reigned forty-six years.

Haza′iah (hà-zā′iah) (*Jehovah hath seen*), a man of Judah of the family of the Shilonites, or descendants of Shelah. Neh. 11:5.

Hazar=ad′dar (hā′zar-ăd′dar) (*village of Addar*), a place named as one of the landmarks on the southern boundary of the land promised to Israel. Num. 34:4; ADAR, Josh. 15:3.

Hazar=e′nan (hā′zar-ē′nan) (*village of fountains*), the place at which the northern boundary of the land promised to the children of Israel was to terminate. Num. 34:9, 10; comp. Ezek. 47:17; 48:1.

Hazar=gad′dah (hā′zar-găd′dah) (*village of fortune*), one of the towns in the southern district of Judah, Josh. 15:27, named between Moladah and Heshmon.

Hazar=ma′veth (hā′zar-mā′veth) (*village of death*), one of the sons of Joktan. Gen. 10:26. The name is preserved in the Arabic *Hadramaut*, the modern name of a province of southern Arabia, where his descendants formed one of the chief tribes in ancient times. They have left inscriptions which have recently been deciphered by Glaser. The country bordered the Indian Ocean, and its capital, Sabata, is still in existence. They were celebrated for their traffic in frankincense.

Hazar=shu′al (hā′zar-shụ′al) (*village of jackals*), a town in the southern district of Judah, lying between Hazar-gaddah and Beer-sheba. Josh. 15:28; 19:3; 1 Chron. 4:28.

Hazar=su′sah (hā′zar-sū′sah) (*village of horses*), one of the "cities" allotted to Simeon in the extreme south of the territory of Judah. Josh. 19:5.

Hazel. The Hebrew term *lûz* occurs only in Gen. 30:37. Without doubt it should be translated as in R. V. "almond." The hazel does not grow in Mesopotamia, where Laban lived, while the almond is common.

Hazelelpo′ni (hăz-e-lĕl-pō′nī), the sister of the sons of Etam in the genealogies of Judah. 1 Chron. 4:3.

Haze′rim (hà-zē′rĭm) (*villages*). The Avim, or more accurately the Avvim, are said to have lived "in Hazerim (Revised Version 'in the villages') as far as Gaza," Deut. 2:23, before their expulsion by the Caphtorim.

Haze′roth (hà-zē′roth) (*villages*), Num. 11:35; 12:16; 33:17; Deut. 1:1, a station of the Israelites in the desert, and perhaps recognizable in the Arabic

Ain el-Hudhera, forty miles northeast of Sinai.

Haz'ezon=ta'mar (hăz'e-zon-tā'mar) and **Haz'azon=ta'mar** (*Hazezon of the palm tree*), the ancient name of Engedi. Gen. 14 : 7. The name occurs in the records of the reign of Hezekiah. 2 Chron. 20 : 2.

Ha'ziel (hā'zĭ-el) (*vision of God*), a Levite in the time of David, of the family of Shimei or Shimi, the younger branch of the Gershonites. 1 Chron. 23 : 9.

Ha'zo (hā'zō) (*vision*), a son of Nahor, by Milcah his wife. Gen. 22 : 22.

Ha'zor (hā'zôr) (*castle*). 1. A fortified city, which on the occupation of the country was allotted to Naphtali. Josh. 19 : 36. Its position was apparently between Ramah and Kedesh, *ibid.* 12 : 19, on the high ground overlooking the Lake of Merom. There is no reason for supposing it a different place from that of which Jabin was king. Josh. 11 : 1; Judges 4 : 2, 17; 1 Sam. 12 : 9. It was the principal city of the whole of north Palestine. Josh. 11 : 10. It was fortified by Solomon, 1 Kings 9 : 15, and its inhabitants were carried captive by Tiglath-pileser. 2 Kings 15 : 29. The most probable site of Hazor is *Tell Khuraibeh.*

2. One of the "cities" of Judah in the extreme south, named next in order to Kedesh. Josh. 15 : 23.

3. Hazor-Hadattah = "new Hazor," another of the southern towns of Judah. Josh. 15 : 25.

4. A place in which the Benjamites resided after their return from the captivity. Neh. 11 : 33.

Head=dress. The earliest notice we have of a head covering is in connection with the sacerdotal vestments. Ex. 28 : 40. The *tsânîph* (something like a turban) is noticed as being worn by nobles, Job 29 : 14, ladies, Isa. 3 : 23, and kings, Isa. 62 : 3; while the *peêr* was an article of holiday dress, Isa. 61 : 3, Authorized Version " beauty;" Ezek. 24 : 17, 23, and was worn at weddings. Isa. 61 : 10. The ordinary head-dress of the Bedouin consists of the *keffieh,* a square handkerchief, generally of red and yellow cotton or cotton and silk, folded so that three of the corners hang down over the back and shoulders, leaving the face exposed, and bound round the head by a cord.

It is not improbable that a similar covering was used by the Hebrews on certain occasions. The Assyrian head-dress is described in Ezek. 23 : 15 under the terms " exceeding in dyed attire." The word rendered " hats " in Dan. 3 : 21 may mean a tunic or a Persian " fez."

Hearth. One way of baking much practised in the East is to place the dough on an iron plate, either laid on or supported on legs above the vessel sunk in the ground, which forms the oven. The cakes baked " on the hearth," Gen. 18 : 6, were probably baked in the existing Bedouin manner, on hot stones covered with ashes. The " hearth " of King Jehoiakim's winter palace, Jer. 36 : 23, was possibly a pan or brazier of charcoal. From this we see that the significance of the Hebrew words translated hearth is not the same as with us.

Heath, Jer. 17 : 6, was some species of juniper, probably the savin, a dwarf, stunted juniper which grows in the most sterile parts of the desert.

Hea'then. [GENTILES.]

Heaven. There are four Hebrew words thus rendered in the Old Testament which we may briefly notice. (1) *Râkî'a,* Authorized Version, firmament. [FIRMAMENT.] (2) *Shâmayim.* This is the word used in the expression " the heaven and the earth," or " the upper and lower regions." Gen. 1 : 1. (3) *Mârôm,* used for heaven in Ps. 18 : 16; Isa. 24 : 18; Jer. 25 : 30. Properly speaking it means a mountain, as in Ps. 102 : 19; Ezek. 17 : 23. (4) *Shechâkim,* " expanses," with reference to the *extent* of heaven. Deut. 33 : 26; Job 35 : 5. St. Paul's expression " third heaven," 2 Cor. 12 : 2, has led to much conjecture. Grotius said that the Jews divided the heaven into three parts, viz., 1. The air or atmosphere, where clouds gather; 2. The firmament, in which the sun, moon and stars are fixed; 3. The upper heaven, the abode of God and his angels, the invisible realm of holiness and happiness, the home of the children of God. The later Jews were fond of dividing into seven different strata, the highest of all being regarded as God's dwelling place.

He'ber (hē'bẽr) (*alliance*). 1. Grandson of the patriarch Asher, Gen. 46 : 17; Num. 26 : 45; 1 Chron. 7 : 31, from whom came the Heberites. Num. 26 : 45.

HEBRON.

2. The patriarch Eber. Luke 3:35. [EBER.]

3. The father of Socho; a Judahite. 1 Chron. 4:18.

4. A Benjamite. 1 Chron. 8:17.

5. A Benjamite. 1 Chron. 8:22. "Eber" in R. V.

6. A Gadite. 1 Chron. 5:13. "Eber" in R. V.

7. The husband of Jael, who slew Sisera by driving a nail into his temple. Judges 4:21, 22.

He'brew (hĕ'brŭ). There is a considerable difference of opinion as to the original meaning of this word. It first appears as applied to Abram, Gen. 14:13. The most common derivations are from *'êber*, "beyond, on the other side," Abraham and his posterity being called Hebrews in order to express a distinction between the races east and west of the Euphrates; and (2) from Heber or Eber, one of the ancestors of Abraham. Gen. 10:24. The term Israelite was used by the Jews of themselves among themselves; the term Hebrew was the name by which they were known to foreigners. The latter was accepted by the Jews in their external relations; and after the general substitution of the word *Jew*, it still found a place in that marked and special feature of national contradistinction, the language.

He'brew language. The books of the Old Testament are written almost entirely in the Hebrew language. It is a branch of the Shemitic language, one of the three great divisions into which all languages have been reduced. It is one of the earliest of known languages, and some suppose that it was the original language of man.

Hebrews, Epistle to. *The Author* remains unknown, and no surmise as to who wrote the book has brought us near the answer.

The Date can be inferred from the contents. The Epistle is "a supreme effort to avert an apostasy at a time of extreme peril," such as the destruction of Jerusalem.

"There is therefore a high degree of probability in the suggestion that the Epistle was written when the war which issued so disastrously for the Jewish people, was raging and drawing near to its awful crisis." (Bruce in Hastings' *Bible Dictionary*.) This would be during the years just previous to A.D. 70.

The Persons to whom written. "He-brews" means Jews speaking Hebrew. They may have lived in Judea, or, perhaps more likely, Jews in Syria speaking Greek as well as Hebrew, for the Epis- tle is written in Greek. *Contents.—* With respect to the scope of the epistle, it should be recollected that while the numerous Christian churches scattered throughout Judea, Acts 9:31; Gal. 1:22, were continually exposed to persecution from the Jews, 1 Thess. 2:14, there was in Jerusalem one additional weapon in the hands of the predominant oppressors of the Christians. The magnificent national temple might be shut against the Hebrew Christian; and even if this affliction were not often laid upon him, yet there was a secret burden which he bore within him, the knowledge that the end of all the beauty and awfulness of Zion was rapidly approaching. The writer of this epistle meets the Hebrew Christians on their own ground, showing that the new faith gave them Christ the Son of God, more prevailing than the high priest as an intercessor; that his Sabbath awaited them, his covenant, his atonement, his city heavenly not made with hands. The letter it may truthfully be said in the words of G. Campbell Morgan, "is intended for those who felt as though under the new dispensation they had lost all that was most dear to them. Judaism, with its splendid ritual and elaborate priesthood, was stricken root and branch, and was passing away. The writer of this letter teaches the fact that it is only the external elements of Judaism that are going, and that something infinitely better is taking its place,—something that contains all that was essential and eternal in the old system."

He'bron (hĕ'bron) (*alliance*). 1. The third son of Kohath, who was the second son of Levi. Ex. 6:18; Num. 3:19; 1 Chron. 6:2, 18; 23:12. He was the founder of a family of Hebronites, Num. 3:27; 26:58; 1 Chron. 26:23, 30, 31, or Bene-Hebron. 1 Chron. 15:9; 23:19.

2. A city of Judah, Josh. 15:54, situated among the mountains, Josh. 20:7, about 20 miles south of Jerusalem, and the same distance north of Beersheba. Hebron is one of the most ancient cities in the world still existing; and in this respect it is the rival of Damascus. It was a well-known town when Abraham entered Canaan. See Gen. 13:18:

Num. 13 : 22. Its original name was Kirjath-arba, Judges 1 : 10, "the city of Arba;" so called from Arba the father of Anak. Josh. 15 : 13, 14 ; 21 : 13. Sarah died at Hebron; and Abraham then bought from Ephron the Hittite the field and cave of Machpelah, to serve as a family tomb. Gen. 23 : 2–20. The cave is still there; and the massive walls of the *Haram* or mosque, within which it lies, form the most remarkable object in the whole city. Abraham is called by Mohammedans *el-Khulil*, "the Friend," *i. e.* of God, and this is the modern name of Hebron. Hebron now contains about 18,000 inhabitants, of whom less than 1000 are Jews. It is picturesquely situated in a narrow valley, surrounded by rocky hills. The valley runs from north to south; and the main quarter of the town, surmounted by the lofty walls of the venerable *Haram*, lies partly on the eastern slope. Gen. 37 : 14; comp. 23 : 19. About two miles from the town, up the valley, is one of the largest oak trees in Palestine. This, say some, is the very tree beneath which Abraham pitched his tent, and it still bears the name of the patriarch.

3. One of the towns in the territory of Asher, Josh. 19 : 28; probably Ebdon or Abdon. Not same name as 2. R. V. Ebron

He'bronites, The. A family of Kohathite Levites, descendants of Hebron the son of Kohath Num. 3 : 27; 26 : 58; 1 Chron. 26 : 23.

Hedge. In the New Testament a fence of any kind. In the Old Testament two Hebrew words are used,—one, a stone wall, *gader;* the other, *sakak,* a thorn hedge. Prov. 24 : 31; Ezek. 42 : 10. The stone walls which surround the sheepfolds of modern Palestine are frequently crowned with sharp thorns.

Heg'ai (hĕ'ga-ī), one of the Persian eunuchs of the court of Ahasuerus. Esther 2 : 8, 15. (B.C. 473.)

He'ge (hē'gē), another form of the preceding. Esther 2 : 3.

Heifer. 1 Sam. 6 : 7–12; Job 21 : 10; Isa. 7 : 21. The heifer or young cow was customarily used for ploughing, according to Jud. 14 : 18. Ploughing and harrowing are both mentioned in Hos. 10 : 11, where we find it used also in treading out the corn. See also Jer. 50 : 11. Israel is sometimes compared to a stubborn (A. V. backsliding) heifer, that will not learn the yoke; and in

Hos. 10 : 11 to one hitherto used only for threshing, but now to have the harder work of ploughing and harrowing.

Heir. The Hebrew institutions relative to inheritance were of a very simple character. Under the patriarchal system the property was divided among the sons of the legitimate wives, Gen. 21 : 10; 24 : 36; 25 : 5, a larger portion being assigned to one, generally the eldest, on whom devolved the duty of maintaining the females of the family. The sons of concubines were portioned off with presents. Gen. 25 : 6. At a later period the exclusion of the sons of concubines was rigidly enforced. Judges 11 : 1 ff. Daughters had no share in the patrimony, Gen. 31 : 14, but received a marriage portion. The Mosaic law regulated the succession to real property thus: it was to be divided among the sons, the eldest receiving a double portion, Deut. 21 : 17, the others equal shares; if there were no sons, it went to the daughters, Num. 27 : 8, on the condition that they did not marry out of their own tribe, Num. 36 : 6 ff.; otherwise the patrimony was forfeited. If there were no daughters, it went to the brother of the deceased; if no brother, to the paternal uncle; and, failing these, to the next of kin. Num. 27 : 9–11.

He'lah (hē'lah) (*rust*), one of the two wives of Ashur, father of Tekoa. 1 Chron. 4 : 5.

He'lam (hē'lam), a place east of the Jordan, but west of the Euphrates, at which the Syrians were collected by Hadarezer, and where David met and defeated them. 2 Sam. 10 : 16, 17.

Hel'bah (hĕl'bah) (*fertile*), a town of Asher. Its site is entirely unknown. Judges 1 : 31.

Hel'bon (hĕl'bon) (*fertile*), a place mentioned only in Ezek. 27 : 18. Geographers have sometimes represented Helbon as identical with the city of Aleppo, called *Haleb* by the Arabs; but there are strong reasons against this, and the ancient city must be identified with a village within a few miles of Damascus, still bearing the ancient name *Helbun,* and still celebrated as producing the finest grapes in the country.

Hel'dai (hĕl'da-ī) (*durable*). 1. The twelfth captain of the monthly courses for the temple service. 1 Chron. 27 : 15. Probably the same as HELEB.

2. An Israelite who seems to have re-

turned from the captivity, bringing gifts from Babylon. Zech. 6:10.

He'leb (hē'lĕb) or **He'led** (hē'lĕd), son of Baanah the Netophathite, one of the heroes of King David's guard. 2 Sam. 23:29; 1 Chron. 11:30. [HELDAI.]

He'lek (hē'lĕk) (*portion*), one of the descendants of Manasseh, and second son of Gilead, Num. 26:30, and founder of the Helekites.

He'lem (hē'lĕm). 1. A descendant of Asher. 1 Chron. 7:35.

2. A man mentioned only in Zech. 6:14. Apparently the same as HELDAI, 2.

He'leph (hē'lĕf), the place from which the boundary of the tribe of Naphtali started. Josh. 19:33.

He'lez (hē'lĕz) (*vigor*). 1. One of "the thirty" of David's guard, 2 Sam. 23:26; 1 Chron. 11:27; an Ephraimite, and captain of the seventh monthly course. 1 Chron. 27:10.

2. A man of Judah, son of Azariah. 1 Chron. 2:39.

He'li (hē'lī), the father of Joseph the husband of the Virgin Mary, Luke 3:23. [See GENEALOGY OF JESUS CHRIST.]

Heliop'olis (hē-lĭ-ŏp'ō-lĭs). [See ON.]

Hel'kath (hĕl'kăth) (*portion*), the town named as the starting-point for the boundary of the tribe of Asher, Josh. 19:25, and allotted with its "suburbs" to the Gershonite Levites, ch. 21:31. Some identify, doubtfully, with *Yerka*, seven miles from Acre.

Hel'kath=haz'zurim (hĕl'kăth-hăz'zu-rim) (*field of sword edges*), a piece of ground, apparently close to the pool of Gibeon, where the combat took place between the two parties of Joab's men and Abner's men which ended in the death of the whole of the combatants, and brought on a general battle. 2 Sam. 2:16.

Hell. In the Old Testament this is the word generally and unfortunately used by our translators to render the Hebrew *Sheol*. It really means the place of the dead, the unseen world, without deciding whether it be the place of misery or of happiness. It is clear that in many passages of the Old Testament *Sheol* can only mean "the grave," and is so rendered in the Authorized Version; see, for example, Gen. 37:35; 42:38; 1 Sam. 2:6; Job 14:13. In other passages, however, it seems to involve a notion of punishment, and is therefore rendered in the

Authorized Version by the word "hell." But in many cases this translation misleads the reader. The English Revisers sometimes use the word "Sheol" in the text, in other places hold to the translation hell, grave, pit, as in the A. V. and put Sheol in the margin. The American Revision discards all translations and consistently places Sheol throughout in the text. In the New Testament "hell" is the translation of two words, *Hades* and *Gehenna*. The word *Hades*, like *Sheol*, sometimes means merely "the grave," Acts 2:31; 1 Cor. 15:55; Rev. 20:13, or in general "the unseen world." It is in this sense that the creeds say of our Lord, "He went down into hell," meaning the state of the dead in general, without any restriction of happiness or misery. In cases where hell is the translation of "Hades," the revisers have put simply "Hades."

Hell is used more properly as the translation of Gehenna, as the place or state of the just retribution for the finally impenitent. The term Gehenna is the Hebrew for the "valley of Hinnom," south of Jerusalem where the unusable refuse of the city was burned. Here also was the scene of gross and cruel rites of heathenism, including the burning of children to Molech (2 Chron. 28:3; 33:6; Jer. 7:31; 2 Kings 23:5, 10).

"The terrible associations of the place, the fires said to have been kept burning in it in order to consume the foul and corrupt objects thrown into it, make it a natural and unmistakable symbol of wasting penalty" for being the polluted, sin-breeding incurable moral refuse of the world.

Hel'lenist (*Grecian*), the term applied in the New Testament to Greek-speaking or "Grecian" Jews. The Hellenists as a body included not only the proselytes of Greek (or foreign) parentage, but also those Jews who, by settling in foreign countries, had adopted the prevalent form of the current Greek civilization, and with it the use of the common Greek dialect. Acts 6:1; 9:29.

Helmet. [ARMS.]

He'lon (hē'lon) (*valorous*), father of Eliab, of the tribe of Zebulun. Num. 1:9; 2:7; 7:24, 29; 10:16.

Hem of garment. The importance which the later Jews, especially the Pharisees, Matt. 23:5, attached to the hem or fringe of their garments was founded upon the regulation in Num. 15: 38, 39, which gave a symbolical meaning to it. [See DRESS.]

He'mam (hē'mam). Hori and Hemam were sons of Lotan, the eldest son of Seir. Gen. 36:22.

He'man (hē'man) (*faithful*). 1. Son of Zerah. 1 Chron. 2:6; 1 Kings 4:31.

2. Son of Joel and grandson of Samuel the prophet, a Kohathite He is called "the singer," rather the *musician*, 1 Chron. 6:33, and was the first of the three Levites to whom was committed the vocal and instrumental music of the temple service in the reign of David. 1 Chron. 15:16–22. The 88th Psalm is ascribed to him. There is some confusion as to his descent, and later critics are inclined to doubt it.

He'math (hē'măth), a person named in the genealogical lists of Judah, as the origin of the Kenites, and the "father" of the house of Rechab. 1 Chron. 2:55. R. V. Hammath.

Hem'dan (hĕm'dan) (*pleasant*), the eldest son of Dishon, son of Anah the Horite. Gen. 36:26. [AMRAM, 2.]

Hemlock, the common ground or dwarf hemlock, a bitter, poisonous plant. The Hebrew *rôsh* is rendered "hemlock" in two passages, Hos. 10:4; Amos 6:12, but elsewhere "gall." [GALL.] It is probable that the plant is rather the poppy than an hemlock.

Hen (*kindness*). Apparently a son of Zephaniah, Zech. 6:14. But very probably not a proper name.

Hen. The hen is nowhere noticed in the Bible except in Matt. 23:37; Luke 13:34. That a bird so common in Palestine should receive such slight notice is certainly singular.

He'na (hē'nà), a city the Assyrian kings had reduced shortly before the time of Sennacherib. 2 Kings 19:13; Isa. 37:13. There are several conjectures as to its site which Hommel and Cheyne consider wasted time. The former considers it a divine name—the latter a mistake.

Hen'adad (hĕn'a-dăd) (*favor of Hadad*), the head of a family of the Levites who took a prominent part in the rebuilding of the temple. Ezra 3:9.

He'noch (hē'nŏk). 1. Enoch, 2. 1 Chron. 1:3.

2. Hanoch, 1. 1 Chron. 1:33.

He'pher (hē'fĕr) (*digging*). 1. The youngest of the sons of Gilead, Num.

26:32, and head of the family of the Hepherites.

2. Son of Ashur, the "father of Tekoa." 1 Chron. 4:6.

3. The Mecherathite, one of the heroes of David's guard. 1 Chron. 11:36.

He'pher (hē'fĕr), a place in ancient Canaan, which occurs in the list of conquered kings. Josh. 12:17. It was on the west of Jordan. Comp. 7 and 1 Kings 4:10.

He'pherites, The, the family of Hepher the son of Gilead. Num. 26:32.

Heph'zi-bah (hĕf'zĭ-bah). 1. A name signifying "*my delight in her,*" which is to be borne by the restored Jerusalem. Isa. 62:4.

2. The queen of King Hezekiah and the mother of Manasseh. 2 Kings 21:1. (B.C. 709.)

Herald, one who makes public proclamation. The only notice of this officer in the Old Testament occurs in Dan. 3:4. The term "herald" might be substituted for "preacher" in 1 Tim. 2:7; 2 Tim. 1:11; 2 Pet. 2:5.

Herd (a collection of cattle), **Herdsman.** The herd was greatly regarded in both the patriarchal and the Mosaic period. The ox was the most precious stock next to horse and mule. The herd yielded the most esteemed sacrifice. Num. 7:3; Ps. 69:31; Isa. 66:3; also flesh meat, and milk, chiefly converted, probably, into butter and cheese. Deut. 32:14; 2 Sam. 17:29. The agricultural and general usefulness of the ox in ploughing, threshing, and as a beast of burden, 1 Chron. 12:40; Isa. 46:1, made a slaughtering of him seem wasteful. Herdsmen, etc., in Egypt were a low, perhaps the lowest, caste; but of the abundance of cattle in Egypt, and of the care there bestowed on them, there is no doubt. Gen. 47:6, 17; Ex. 9:4, 20. So the plague of hail was sent to smite especially the cattle, Ps. 78:48, the firstborn of which also were smitten. Ex. 12:29. The Israelites departing stipulated for, Ex. 10:26, and took "much cattle" with them, ch. 12:38. Cattle formed thus one of the traditions of the Israelitish nation in its greatest period, and became almost a part of that greatness. The occupation of herdsman was honorable in early times. Gen. 47:6; 1 Sam. 11:5; 1 Chron. 27:29; 28:1. Saul himself resumed it in the interval of his cares as king; also Doeg was

MOUNT HERMON.

certainly high in his confidence. 1 Sam. 21:7. Pharaoh made some of Joseph's brethren "rulers over his cattle." David's herdmasters were among his chief officers of state. The prophet Amos at first followed this occupation.

He'res (hē'rēz) (*the sun*), Judges 1: 35, a city of Dan, in Mount Ephraim, near Ajalon; possibly identical with Mount Jearim (Ir-shemesh, city of the sun).

He'resh (hē'resh) (*artificer*), a Levite attached to the temple. 1 Chron. 9:15.

Heresy. In N. T. a synonym for *sect.* In its modern meaning it never appears—it being merely indicative of the sectarian spirit.

Her'mas (hēr'mas), the name of a Christian resident at Rome to whom St. Paul sends greetings in his Epistle to the Romans. Rom. 16:14. (A.D. 57.) Irenæus, Tertullian and Origen agree in attributing to him the work called *The Shepherd.* It was never received into the canon, but yet was generally cited with respect only second to that which was paid to the authoritative books of the New Testament.

Her'mes (hēr'mez) (*Mercury*), a Christian mentioned in Rom. 16:14. According to tradition he was one of the seventy disciples, and afterward bishop of Dalmatia. (A.D. 57.)

Hermog'enes (hēr-mŏg'-enēs), a person mentioned by St Paul in the latest of all his epistles, 2 Tim. 1:15, when all in Asia had turned away from him. (A.D. 64.)

Her'mon (hēr'mon) (*belonging to a sanctuary*), a mountain on the northeastern border of Palestine, Deut. 3:8; Josh. 12:1, over against Lebanon, Josh. 11:17, adjoining the plateau of Bashan. 1 Chron. 5:23. It stands at the southern end, and is the culminating point of the Anti-Lebanon range; it towers high above the ancient border city of Dan and the fountains of the Jordan, and is the most conspicuous and beautiful mountain in Palestine or Syria. At the present day it is called *Jebel esh-Sheikh,* "the mountain of the chief," because it is the residence of the religious head of the Druses. It also has the name of *Jebel eth-Thelj,* "the snow mountain" because when the whole country is parched with the summer sun, white lines of snow streak the head of Hermon. This mountain was the great landmark of the Israelites. It was as-

sociated with their northern border almost as intimately as the sea was with the western. Hermon has three summits, situated like the angles of a triangle, and about a quarter of a mile from each other. In two passages of Scripture this mountain is called *Baal-hermon,* Judges 3:3; 1 Chron. 5:23, because of its sacred character. It is more than probable that some part of Hermon was the scene of the transfiguration, as it stands near Cæsarea Philippi, where we know Christ was just before that event. Hermon rises 9166 feet above the level of the Mediterranean.

Her'monites, The. Properly "*the Hermons,*" with reference to the three summits of Mount Hermon. Ps. 42:6. R. V. "the Hermons."

Her'od (hĕr'od) (*hero-like*). This family, though of Idumean origin and thus alien by race, was Jewish in faith. I. HEROD THE GREAT was the second son of Antipater, an Idumean, who was appointed procurator of Judea by Julius

COIN OF HEROD AGRIPPA I.

Cæsar, B.C. 47. He was physically magnificent and no less conspicuous for skill in war. He was clever, able, but unscrupulous and ambitious. He grew more cruel and suspicious as he grew older until the reputation for cruelty has in popular thought almost or quite eclipsed his real ability as a ruler. At his father's elevation he was made governor of Galilee, being about 25 years old. In B.C. 41 he was appointed by Antony tetrarch of Judea. Forced to abandon Judea the following year, he fled to Rome, and received the appointment of king of Judea. In the course of a few years, by the help of the Romans he took Jerusalem (B.C. 37), and completely established his authority throughout his dominions. The terrible acts of bloodshed which Herod perpetrated in his own family were accompanied by others among his subjects equally terrible, from the number who fell victims to them. According to the well-known story, he ordered the nobles

A Genealogical Table of the Herodian Family, Including Those Members who are Mentioned in the New Testament.

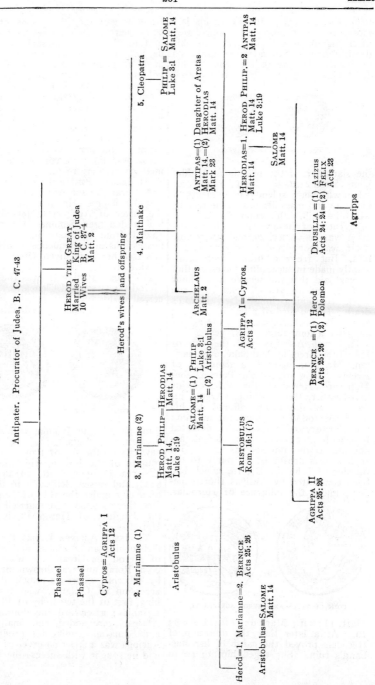

Antipater. Procurator of Judea, B. C. 47-43

Phasael

Phasael

Cypros=Agrippa I
Acts 12

Herod the Great
Married King of Judea
10 Wives B. C. 37-4
Matt. 2

Herod's wives || and offspring

2. Mariamne (1)

Aristobulus

Herod=1. Mariamne=2. Bernice
Acts 25:26

Aristobulus=Salome
Matt. 14

3. Mariamne (2)

Herod Philip=Herodias
Matt. 14, Matt. 14
Luke 3:19

Salome=(1) Philip
Matt. 14 Luke 3:1
=(2) Aristobulus

Aristobulus
Rom. 16:1 (?)

Agrippa I=Cypros.
Acts 12

Agrippa II
Acts 25:26

Bernice =(1) Herod
Acts 25:26 Polemon
(2)

Drusilla =(1) Azizus
Acts 24:24 =(2) Felix
Acts 23

Agrippa

4. Malthake

Archelaus
Matt. 2

Antipas=(1) Daughter of Aretas
Matt. 14, =(2) Herodias
Mark 23 Matt. 14

Herodias=1. Herod Philip.=2 Antipas
Matt. 14 Matt. 14 Matt. 14
Luke 3:19

Salome
Matt. 14

5. Cleopatra

Philip = Salome
Luke 3:1 Matt. 14

whom he had called to him in his last moments to be executed immediately after his decease, that so at least his death might be attended by universal mourning. It was at the time of his fatal illness that he must have caused

COIN OF HEROD ANTIPAS.

the slaughter of the infants at Bethlehem. Matt. 2:16–18. He adorned Jerusalem with many splendid monuments of his taste and magnificence. The temple, which he built with scrupulous care, was the greatest of these works. The restoration was begun B.C. 20, and the temple itself was completed in a year and a half. But fresh additions were constantly made in succeeding years, so that it was said that the temple was "built in forty and six years," John 2:20, the work continuing long after Herod's death. Herod died of a terrible disease, at Jericho, in April, B.C. 4, at the age of 69, after a long reign of 37 years.

II. Herod Antipas was the son of Herod the Great by Malthaké, a Samaritan. He first married a daughter of Aretas, "king of Arabia Petræa," but afterward Herodias, the wife of his half-brother, Herod Philip. Aretas, indignant at the insult offered to his daughter, found a pretext for invading the territory of Herod, and defeated him with great loss. This defeat, according to the famous passage in Josephus, was attributed by many to the murder of John the Baptist, which had been committed by Antipas shortly before, under the influence of Herodias.

COIN OF TITUS AND HEROD AGRIPPA II.

Matt. 14 : 3 ff.; Mark 6 : 17 ff.; Luke 3 : 19. At a later time the ambition of Herodias proved the cause of her husband's ruin. She urged him to go to Rome to gain the title of king, cf. Mark 6 : 14; but he was opposed at the court of Caligula by the emissaries of Agrippa, and condemned to perpetual banishment at Lugdunum, A.D. 39. Herodias voluntarily shared his punishment, and he died in exile. Pilate took occasion from our Lord's residence in Galilee to send him for examination, Luke 23 : 6 ff., to Herod Antipas, who came up to Jerusalem to celebrate the Passover. The city of Tiberias, which Antipas founded and named in honor of the emperor, was the most conspicuous monument of his long reign.

III. Herod Philip I. (Philip, Mark 6 : 17) was the son of Herod the Great and Mariamne. He married Herodias, the sister of Agrippa I., by whom he had a daughter, Salome. He was excluded from all share in his father's possessions in consequence of his mother's treachery, and lived afterward in a private station.

IV. Herod Philip II. was the son of Herod the Great and Cleopatra. He received as his own government Batanea, Trachonitis, Auranitis, Gaulanitis, and

COIN OF PHILIP THE TETRARCH.

some parts about Jamnia, with the title of tetrarch. Luke 3 : 1. He built a new city on the site of Paneas, near the sources of the Jordan, which he called Cæsarea Philippi, Matt. 16 : 13; Mark 8 : 27, and raised Bethsaida to the rank of a city under the title of Julias, and died there A.D. 34. He married Salome, the daughter of Herod Philip I. and Herodias.

V. Herod Agrippa I. was the son of Aristobulus and Bernice, and grandson of Herod the Great. He was brought up at Rome, and was thrown into prison by Tiberius, where he remained till the accession of Caligula, who made him king, first of the tetrarchy of Philip and Lysanias; afterward the dominions of Antipas were added, and finally Judea and Samaria. Unlike his predecessors, Agrippa was a strict observer of the law, and he sought with success the favor of the Jews. It is probable that it was with this view he put to death James the son of Zebedee, and further imprisoned Peter. Acts 12:1 ff. But his sudden death interrupted his ambitious projects. Acts 12:21, 23.

VI. HEROD AGRIPPA II. was the son of Herod Agrippa I. In A.D. 53 the emperor gave him the tetrarchies formerly held by Philip and Lysanias, with the title of king. Acts 25:13. The relation in which he stood to his sister Bernice, Acts 25:13, was the cause of grave suspicion. It was before him that Paul was tried. Acts 26:28.

Hero'dians (from Herod). Matt. 22:15 ff.; Mark 12:13 ff. Canon Cook describes these persons as "that party among the Jews who were supporters of the Herodian family as the last hope of retaining for the Jews a fragment of national government, as distinguished from absolute dependence upon Rome as a province of the empire. Supporters of the family of Herod, who held their dominions by the grant of the Roman emperor, would be in favor of paying tribute to the supreme power." Matt. 22:16.

Hero'dias (hē-rō'dĭ-as), daughter of Aristobulus, one of the sons of Mariamne and Herod the Great, and consequently sister of Agrippa I. She first married Herod Philip I.; then she eloped from him to marry Herod Antipas, her step-uncle. The head of John the Baptist was granted at the request of Herodias. Matt. 14:8–11; Mark 6:24–28. (A.D. 29.) She accompanied Antipas into exile to Lugdunum.

Hero'dion (hè-rō'dĭ-ŏn), a relative of St. Paul, to whom he sends his salutation amongst the Christians of the Roman church. Rom. 16:11. (A.D. 57.)

Heron, Lev. 11:19; Deut. 14:18, a common large, wading, unclean bird. Nearly all of the species known in English ornithology are found in the vicinity of Palestine. The family contains the Herons, Egrets, Bitterns and the White Ibis. The use of the words "after her kind" shows that the *family* was intended. It is very probable that heron is the correct rendering.

He'sed (hē'sed) (*mercy*). The son of Hesed or Ben-Hesed, was commissary for Solomon. 1 Kings 4:10.

Hesh'bon (hĕsh'bŏn) (*device*), the capital city of Sihon king of the Amorites. Num. 21:26. It stood on the western border of the high plain on the boundary line between the tribes of Reuben and Gad. The ruins of *Hesbân*, 20 miles east of the Jordan, on the parallel of the northern end of the Dead Sea, mark the site, as they bear the name, of the ancient Heshbon. There are many cisterns among the ruins. Comp. Cant. 7:4.

Hesh'mon (hĕsh'mŏn) (*fatness*), a place named, with others, as lying in the extreme south of Judah. Josh. 15:27.

Hes'ron (hĕs'ron), Hez'ron (hĕz'ron) (*enclosed*), the son of Reuben, Num. 26:6, and ancestor of the Hezronites.

Heth, probably the forefather of the nation of the Hittites. In the genealogical tables of Gen. 10:15 and 1 Chron. 1:13 Heth is a son of Canaan. Gen. 23:3, 5; 27:46; 28:1, 2.

Heth'lon (hĕth'lŏn), the name of a place on the northern border of Palestine. Ezek. 47:15; 48:1. In this reference "the way of Hethlon" seems to be the pass at the northern end of Lebanon, and thus identical with "the entrance of Hamath" in Num. 34:8, etc.

Hez'eki (hĕz'e-ki), a Benjamite, one of the Bene-Elpaal, a descendant of Shaaraim. 1 Chron. 8:17. R. V. "Hizki."

Hezeki'ah (hĕz-e-kī'ah) (*Jehovah strengtheneth*). 1. Thirteenth king of Judah, son of the apostate Ahaz and Abi or Abijah, ascended the throne at the age of 25, B.C. 726. Hezekiah was one of the three most perfect kings of Judah. 2 Kings 18:5; 23:25. His first act was to purge and repair and reopen with splendid sacrifices and perfect ceremonial the temple. He also destroyed a brazen serpent, said to have been the one used by Moses in the miraculous healing of the Israelites, Num. 21:9, which had become an object of adoration. When the kingdom of Israel had fallen, Hezekiah invited the scattered inhabitants to a peculiar passover, which was continued for the unprecedented period of fourteen days. 2 Chron. 29, 30, 31. At the head of a repentant and united people, Hezekiah ventured to assume the aggressive against the Philistines; and in a series of victories not only rewon the cities which his father had lost, 2 Chron. 28:18, but even dispossessed them of their own cities, except Gaza, 2 Kings 18:8, and Gath. He refused to acknowledge the supremacy of Assyria. 2 Kings 18:

7. Instant war was imminent, and Hezekiah used every available means to strengthen himself. 2 Kings 20:20. It was probably at this dangerous crisis in his kingdom that we find him sick and sending for Isaiah, who prophesies death as the result. 2 Kings 20:1. Hezekiah's prayer for longer life is heard. The prophet had hardly left the palace when he was ordered to return and promise the king immediate recovery and fifteen years more of life. 2 Kings 20:4–6. An embassy coming from Babylon ostensibly to compliment Hezekiah on his convalescence, but really to form an alliance between the two powers, is favorably received by the king, who shows them the treasures which he had accumulated. For this Isaiah foretells the punishment that shall befall his house. 2 Kings 20:17. The two invasions of Sennacherib occupy the greater part of the Scripture records concerning the reign of Hezekiah. The first of these took place in the third year of Sennacherib, B.C. 702, and occupies only three verses. 2 Kings 18:13–16. Respecting the commencement of the second invasion we have full details in 2 Kings 18:17, seq.; 2 Chron. 32:9, seq.; Isa. 36. Sennacherib sent against Jerusalem an army under the Tartan, the Rab-saris and the Rabshekah, officers of his court, with a blasphemous and insulting summons to surrender; but Isaiah assures the king he need not fear, promising to disperse the enemy. 2 Kings 19:6, 7. Accordingly that night "the angel of the Lord went out, and smote in the camp of the Assyrians a hundred fourscore and five thousand." Hezekiah slept with his fathers after a reign of twenty-nine years, in the 56th year of his age, B.C. 697. In 1830 there was found among the ruins of Nineveh a cylinder on which Sennacherib inscribed an account of his victories over Hezekiah. It is noticeable that Sennacherib does not refer to the destruction of his army in any of his records. But this is both natural and common. For a modern instance, any one who has visited Napoleon's tomb at Paris can notice that while the sides are full of names of places where his battles were fought, Waterloo, the scene of his great defeat, is not recorded there. See cut, page 602.

2. Son of Neariah, one of the descendants of the royal family of Judah. 1 Chron. 3:23. R. V. Hizkiah.

3. The same name, though rendered in the Authorized Version HIZKIAH, is found in Zeph. 1:1. Perhaps the same as 1.

4. Ater of Hezekiah. [ATER.]

He′zion (hē′zĭ-on) (*vision*), a king of Aram (Syria), father of Tabrimon and grandfather of Ben-hadad I. 1 Kings 15:18. He is probably identical with REZON, the contemporary of Solomon, in 1 Kings 11:23.

He′zir (hē′zir) (*swine*). 1. A priest in the time of David, leader of the seventeenth monthly course in the service. 1 Chron. 24:15.

2. One of the heads of the people (laymen) who sealed the solemn covenant with Nehemiah. Neh. 10:20.

Hez′rai (hĕz′ra-ī) (*enclosed*), one of the thirty heroes of David's guard. 2 Sam. 23:35. In the parallel list, 1 Chron. 11:37, the name appears as HEZRO.

Hez′ron (hĕz′rŏn). 1. A son of Reuben. Gen. 46:9; Ex. 6:14.

2. A son of Pharez. Gen. 46:12; Ruth 4:18.

Hez′ronites (hĕz′rŏn-ītes) (*descendants of Hezron*), The. 1. Descendants of Hezron the son of Reuben. Num. 26:6.

2. A branch of the tribe of Judah, descendants of Hezron the son of Pharez. Num. 26:21.

Hid′dai (hĭd′da-ī), one of the thirty-seven heroes of David's guard. 2 Sam. 23:30.

Hid′dekel (hĭd′de-kĕl), one of the rivers of Eden, the river which "goeth eastward to Assyria," Gen. 2:14, and which Daniel calls "the great river," Dan. 10:4, seems to have been rightly identified by the LXX. with the Tigris. Dekel is clearly an equivalent of Digla or Diglath, a name borne by the Tigris in all ages. The name now in use among the inhabitants of Mesopotamia is *Dijleh.*

Hi′el (hī′el) (*brother of God*), a native of Bethel, who rebuilt Jericho in the reign of Ahab, 1 Kings 16:34, and in whom was fulfilled the curse pronounced by Joshua, Josh. 6:26, five hundred years before.

Hierap′olis (hī-e-răp′o-lĭs) (*holy city*), a city of Phrygia, situated above the junction of the rivers Lycus and Mæander, near Colossæ and Laodicea.

Mentioned only in Col. 4 : 13 as the seat of a church probably founded during Paul's stay at Ephesus.

Higga'ion (hĭg-gā'ion) (*meditation*), a word which occurs three times in the book of Psalms—Ps. 9 : 16; 19 : 14; 92 : 3 (margin). The word has two meanings, one of a general character, implying *thought, reflection*, Ps. 19 : 14; 92 : 3 and Lam. 3 : 63. Another, Ps. 9 : 16, a musical term, the precise meaning of which cannot at this distance of time be determined. Canon Cook says that it probably means an *interlude*, giving musical expression to the feelings suggested by the preceding words.

High places. From the earliest times it was the custom among all nations to erect altars and places of worship on lofty and conspicuous spots. To this general custom we find constant allusion in the Bible, Isa. 65 : 7; Ezek. 6 : 13, and it is especially attributed to the Moabites. Isa. 15 : 2; 16 : 12. Even Abraham built an altar to the Lord on a mountain near Bethel. Gen. 12 : 7, 8; cf. 22 : 2–4; 31 : 54. Notwithstanding this we find that it was implicitly forbidden by the law of Moses, Deut. 12 : 11–14, which also gave the strictest injunction to destroy these monuments of Canaanitish idolatry. 12 : 2, 3. The command was a prospective one, and was not to come into force until such time as the tribes were settled in the promised land, and a central place of worship had been erected. Thus we find that both Gideon and Manoah built altars on high places by divine command. Judges 6 : 25, 26; 13 : 16–23. Other altars also are mentioned, those erected by Samuel at Mizpeh, 1 Sam. 7 : 10, and at Bethlehem, ch. 16 : 5; by Saul at Gilgal, ch. 13 : 9, and at Ajalon, (?) ch. 14 : 35; by David, 1 Chron. 21 : 26; by Elijah on Mount Carmel, 1 Kings 18 : 30, and by other prophets. 1 Sam. 10 : 5. The worship in high places was organized and all but universal throughout Judea, not only during, 1 Kings 3 : 2–4, but even after the time of Solomon. In most cases it was the worship of Jehovah, but gradually idolatry became more common, and even where the worship was nominally that of Jehovah it became contaminated with the corruption of the idol worship. At last Hezekiah set himself in good earnest to the suppression of this prevalent corruption, 2 Kings 18 : 4, 22, both in Judah and Israel, 2 Chron. 31 : 1; although so rapid was the growth of the evil that even his sweeping reformation required to be finally consummated by Josiah, 2 Kings 23, and that too in Jerusalem and its immediate neighborhood. 2 Chron. 34 : 3. After the time of Josiah we find no further mention of these Jehovistic high places.

High priest. The first indication that Aaron and his sons were to care for the tabernacle is found in Ex. 24 : 1; and their first distinct separation to the office of the priesthood is recorded in Ex. 28. After that the legal head of the house of Aaron became high priest, on the death of his predecessor; preferably the oldest son. The high priest alone was anointed, Lev. 8 : 12, whence one of his distinctive epithets was "the anointed priest." Lev. 4 : 3, 5, 16; 21 : 10; see Num. 35 : 25. The anointing of the sons of Aaron, *i. e.* the common priests, seems to have been confined to sprinkling their garments with the anointing oil. Ex. 29 : 21; 28 : 41, etc. The high priest had a peculiar dress, which passed to his successor at his death. This dress consisted of eight parts: (*a*) The *breastplate*, or, as it is further named, 28 : 15, 29, 30, the breastplate of judgment. The breastplate was originally two spans long and one span broad, but when doubled it was square, the shape in which it was worn. On it were the twelve precious stones, set in four rows, three in a row, thus corresponding to the twelve tribes—each stone having the name of one of the children of Israel engraved upon it. (*b*) The *ephod*. This consisted of two parts, of which one covered the back and the other the front, *i. e.* the breast and upper part of the body. These parts were clasped together on the shoulder with two large onyx stones, each having engraved on it six of the names of the tribes of Israel. They were further united by a "curious girdle" of gold, blue, purple, scarlet and fine twined linen round the waist. [EPHOD; GIRDLE.] (*c*) The *robe of the ephod*. This was of inferior material to the ephod itself, being all of blue, ver. 31, which implied its being only of "woven work." ch. 39 : 22. It was worn immediately under the ephod, and was longer than it. The skirt of this robe had a remarkable trimming of pomegranates in blue, red and crimson, with a bell of gold between the pomegranates alternately. The bells were to give a sound when the high priest went in and came out of the holy place. (*d*) The *mitre* or *upper turban*, with its gold plate, engraved with "Holiness to the Lord," fastened to it by a ribbon of blue. (*e*) The broidered *coat* was a tunic or long skirt of linen with a tessellated or diaper pattern, like the setting of a stone. (*f*) The *girdle*, also of linen, was wound round the body several times from the breast downward, and the ends hung down to the ankles. (*g*) The breeches or drawers, of linen, covered the loins and thighs; and (*h*) The bonnet was a turban of linen, partially covering the head, but not in the form of a cone like that of the high priest when the mitre was added to it. These last four were common to all priests. The high priest alone was permitted to enter the holy of holies, which he did once a year, on the great day of atonement, when he sprinkled the blood of the sin offering on the mercy seat, and burnt incense within the veil. Lev. 16. The manslayer might not leave the city of refuge during the lifetime of the existing high priest. It was also forbidden to the high priest to follow a funeral, or rend his clothes for the dead. It does not appear by whose authority the high priests were appointed to their office before there were kings of Israel. After this the office seems to have been used for political rather than religious purposes. Though at first chosen for life, we find that Solomon deposed Abiathar, 1 Kings 2 : 35, and that Herod appointed a number of high priests, which may account for there being at least two living in Christ's time, Annas and Caiaphas. Luke 3 : 2. The usual age for entering upon the functions of the priesthood, according to 2 Chron. 31 : 17, is considered to have been 20 years, though a priest or high priest was not actually incapacitated if he had attained to puberty. Again, according to Lev. 21 : 17–21, no one that had a blemish could officiate at the altar.

The theological view of the high priesthood does not fall within the scope of this work. It must suffice therefore to indicate that such a view would embrace the consideration of the office, dress, functions and ministrations of the high priest, considered as typical of the priesthood of our Lord Jesus Christ, and as setting forth under shadows the truths which are openly taught under the gospel. This has been done in the Epistle to the Hebrews.

Highways. Though during the sway of the Romans over Palestine they made a few substantial roads for their carts and chariots, yet for most of the time the Jews had nothing such as we call roads, but only footpaths through which animals walked in single file. These were never cared for, no repairs made or obstacles removed. This fact brings into striking prominence the figure of preparing a highway for the return of the captives, or the coming of the great King. On special occasions kings had roads prepared for the progress of their armies, or their own going from place to place. Of recent times roads possible for carriages have connected the principal cities, and now even automobiles are in use.

Hi'len (hī'len), the name of a city of Judah allotted with its suburbs to the priests. 1 Chron. 6 : 58.

Hilki'ah (hĭl-kī'ah) (*Jehovah is my portion*). 1. Father of Eliakim. 2 Kings 18 : 37; Isa. 22 : 20; 36 : 22. [ELIAKIM.]

2. High priest in the reign of Josiah. 2 Kings 22 : 4, *seq.*; 2 Chron. 34 : 9, *seq.*; 1 Chron. 6 : 13. (B.C. 623.) His high priesthood was rendered particularly illustrious by the great reformation effected under it by King Josiah, by the solemn Passover kept at Jerusalem in the 18th year of that king's reign, and above all by the discovery which he made of the book of the law of Moses in the temple.

3. A Merarite Levite, son of Amzi. 1 Chron. 6 : 45.

4. Another Merarite Levite, second son of Hosah. 1 Chron. 26 : 11.

5. One of those who stood on the right hand of Ezra when he read the law to the people; doubtless a Levite, and probably a priest. Neh. 8 : 4.

6. A priest of Anathoth, father of the prophet Jeremiah. Jer. 1 : 1.

7. Father of Gemariah, who was one of Zedekiah's envoys to Babylon. Jer. 29 : 3.

Hil'lel (hĭl'lel) (*he hath praised*), a native of Pirathon in Mount Ephraim, father of Abdon, one of the judges of Israel. Judges 12 : 13, 15.

Hills. From the Hebrew *gibeah*, meaning a curved round hill. But our

THE REPUTED VALLEY OF HINNOM.

translators have also employed the same English word for the very different term *har*, which has a much more extended sense than *gibeah*, meaning a whole district. For instance, in Ex. 24:4 the "hill" is the same which is elsewhere consistently and accurately rendered "mount" and "mountain." The "country of the hills," in Josh. 10:40; 11:16, is the elevated district of Judah, Benjamin and Ephraim, which is correctly called "the mountain" in the earliest descriptions of Palestine, Num. 13:29, and in many subsequent passages. Probably the terms hill and mountain are relative, what is called a mountain in one place being called a hill elsewhere.

Hin. [WEIGHTS AND MEASURES.]

Hind, the female of the common stag, in Hebrew *Ayyalah*. It is frequently noticed in the poetical parts of Scripture as emblematic of activity, Gen. 49:21; Ps. 18:33, gentleness, Prov. 5:19, modesty, Cant. 2:7; 3:5, and maternal affection. Jer. 14:5. Its shyness and remoteness from the haunts of men are also alluded to, Job 39:1, and its timidity, causing it to cast its young at the sound of thunder. Ps. 29:9.

Hinge. Both ancient Egyptian and modern Oriental doors were and are hung by means of pivots turning in sockets on both the upper and lower sides. 1 Kings 7:50. In Syria, and especially

HINGES.

the Haurân, there are many ancient doors consisting of stone slabs with pivots carved out of the same piece, inserted in sockets above and below, and fixed during the building of the house. The allusion in Prov. 26:14 is thus clearly explained.

Hin'nom (hĭn'nom), **Valley of,** otherwise called "the valley of the son" or "children of Hinnom." The earliest mention of the valley of Hinnom is in Josh. 15:8; 18:16, where the boundary line between the tribes of Judah and Benjamin is described as passing along the bed of the ravine. Otherwise it is mentioned principally with reference to the abominable rites and ceremonies of the Ammonites. Solomon erected high places for Molech, 1 Kings 11:7, whose horrid rites were revived from time to time in the same vicinity by the later idolatrous kings. Ahaz and Manasseh made their children "pass through the fire" in this valley, 2 Kings 16:3; 2 Chron. 28:3; 33:6, and the fiendish custom of infant sacrifice to the fire-gods seems to have been kept up in Tophet, which was in this valley. To put an end to these abominations the place was polluted by Josiah, who rendered it ceremonially unclean by spreading over it human bones and other corruptions, 2 Kings 23:10, 13, 14; 2 Chron. 34:4, 5. In it was probably burned all the refuse of the city, including the dead bodies of men and animals. From its ceremonial defilement, and from the detested and abominable fire of Molech, if not from the supposed ever-burning funeral piles, the later Jews applied the name of this valley—*Ge Hinnom, Gehenna* (land of Hinnom)—to denote the place of eternal torment. In this sense the word is used by our Lord. Matt. 5:29; 10:28; 23:15; Mark 9:43; Luke 12:5. The exact position of the Valley is uncertain. It was surely one of the three valleys encompassing Jerusalem, but modern scholars are undecided which one, though the name is very generally applied to the one on the south or southwest.

Hippopotamus. [BEHEMOTH.]

Hi'rah (hī'rah) (*nobility*), an Adullamite, the friend of Judah. Gen. 38:1, 12; and see 20.

Hi'ram (hī'ram), or **Hu'ram** (hū'ram). 1. The king of Tyre who sent workmen and materials to Jerusalem, first, 2 Sam. 5:11; 1 Chron. 14:1, to build a palace for David, whom he ever loved, 1 Kings 5:1, and again, 1 Kings

5 : 10 ; 7 : 13 ; 2 Chron. 2 : 16, to build the temple for Solomon, with whom he had a treaty of peace and commerce. 1 Kings 5 : 11, 12. He admitted Solomon's

REPRESENTATION OF A HITTITE GOD (excavated at Babylon).

ships, issuing from Joppa, to a share in the profitable trade of the Mediterranean, 1 Kings 10 : 22; and the Jewish sailors, under the guidance of Tyrians, were taught to bring the gold of India, 1 Kings 9 : 26, to Solomon's two harbors on the Red Sea.

2. Hiram was the name of a man of mixed race, 1 Kings 7 : 13, 40, the prin-cipal architect and engineer sent by King Hiram to Solomon.

Hit'tites (*descendants of Heth*), **The,** the nation descended from Cheth (Authorized Version HETH), the second son of Canaan. Abraham bought from the "children of Heth" the field and the cave of Machpelah, belonging to Ephron the Hittite. They were then settled at the town which was afterwards, under its new name of Hebron, to become one of the most famous cities of Palestine, and which then bore the name of Kirjath-arba. Gen. 23 : 19; 25 : 9. When the Israelites entered the promised land, we find the Hittites taking part against the invader, in equal alliance with the other Canaanite tribes. Josh. 9 : 1; 11 : 3, etc. Henceforward the notices of the Hittites are very few and faint. Beyond the notices in the Old Testament the Hittites were a forgotten people till the middle of the nineteenth century, insomuch that scholars denied the existence of any such people. But since then Egyptian and Assyrian monuments have been found describing them as a great people of the North (see 1 Kings 10 : 29; 2 Kings 7 : 6), whose armies were feared for their valor and numbers, able to cope with Egypt or any world power. Tablets and carvings have been found in great numbers on the sides of mountain passes, and in ruins of buildings in Asia Minor, Northern Syria and Boghaz-Keni in Cappadocia, Asia Minor, which is now regarded as the capital of a Hittite empire in the days of the nineteenth Egyptian dynasty. They were a sturdy race of men, usually represented as beardless. They wore shoes of the same type as those worn by the peasantry of Asia Minor, and long gloves much like our "mittens," for protection from the snow, which was plentiful in their original mountain home.

Hi'vites (hī'vītes), **The,** descendants—the sixth in order—of Canaan the son of Ham. Gen. 10 : 17; 1 Chron. 1 : 15. We first encounter the actual people of the Hivites at the time of Jacob's return to Canaan. Gen. 34 : 2. We next meet with the Hivites during the conquest of Canaan. Josh. 9 : 7; 11 : 19. The main body of the Hivites were at this time living on the northern confines of western Palestine—"under Hermon, in the land of Mizpeh," Josh. 11 : 3—"in Mount Lebanon, from Mount Baal-Hermon to the entering in of

Hamath." Judges 3:3; comp. 2 Sam. 24:7.

Hizki'ah (hĭz-kī'ah), an ancestor of Zephaniah the prophet. Zeph. 1:1. [HEZEKIAH, 3.]

Hizki'jah (hĭz-kī'jah), one of those who sealed the covenant with Nehemiah. Neh. 10:17. R. V. Hezekiah.

Ho'bab (hō'băb) (*beloved*). This name is found in two places only—Num. 10:29; Judges 4:11. Hobab was brother-in-law to Moses.

Ho'bah (hō'bah), the place to which Abraham pursued the kings who had pillaged Sodom. Gen. 14:15. It was situated "to the north of Damascus."

Hod (hŏd) (*majesty*), one of the sons of Zophah, among the descendants of Asher. 1 Chron. 7:37.

Hoda'iah (hŏd-ā'-iah), son of the royal line of Judah. 1 Chron. 3:24. R. V. Hodaviah.

Hodavi'ah (hŏd-a-vī'ah) (*Jehovah is his praise*). 1. A man of Manasseh, one of the heads of the half tribe on the east of Jordan. 1 Chron. 5:24.

2. A man of Benjamin, son of Hassenuah. 1 Chron. 9:7

3. A Levite, who seems to have given his name to an important family in the tribe. Ezra 2:40. [HODEVAH.]

Ho'desh (hō'desh) (*new moon*), a woman named in the genealogies of Benjamin, 1 Chron. 8:9, as the wife of Shaharaim.

Hode'vah (hò-dē'vah). Neh. 7:43. [HODAVIAH, 3.]

Hodi'ah (hò-dī'ah) (*my majesty is Jehovah*), a man of Judah who married a sister of Naham. 1 Chron. 4:19. The A. V. translates wrongly and makes this the name of the wife.

Hodi'jah (*my majesty is Jehovah*). 1. A Levite in the time of Ezra and Nehemiah. Neh. 8:7; and probably also 9:5; 10:10.

2. Another Levite at the same time. Neh. 10:13.

3. A layman; one of the "heads" of the people at the same time. Neh. 10:18.

Hog'lah (hŏg'lah) (*partridge*), the third of the five daughters of Zelophehad. Num. 26:33; 27:1; 36:11; Josh. 17:3. (B.C. 1450.)

Ho'ham (hō'ham), king of Hebron at the time of the conquest of Canaan. Josh. 10:3.

Holofer'nes, or more correctly *Olofernes,* was, according to the book of Judith, a general of Nebuchadnezzar

king of the Assyrians, Judith 2:4, who was slain by the Jewish heroine Judith during the siege of Bethulia (probably Jerusalem).

Ho'lon (hō'lŏn) (*sandy*). 1. A town in the mountains of Judah; mentioned with Debir. Josh. 15:51; 21:15. [HILEN.]

2. A city of Moab. Jer. 48:21 only. No identification of it has yet taken place.

Ho'mam (hō'mam), the form under which, in 1 Chron. 1:39, an Edomite name appears, which in Gen. 36:22 is given HEMAM.

Homer. [WEIGHTS AND MEASURES.]

Honey. The Hebrew *dĕbash* in the first place applies to the product of the bee, to which exclusively we give the name of honey. All travellers agree in describing Palestine as a land "flowing with milk and honey," Ex. 3:8; bees being abundant even in the remote parts of the wilderness, where they deposit their honey in the crevices of rocks or in hollow trees. In some parts of northern Arabia the hills are so well stocked with bees that no sooner are hives placed than they are occupied. In the second place the term *dĕbash* applies to a decoction of the juice of the grape, which is still called *dibs,* and which forms an article of commerce in the East; it was this, and not ordinary beehoney, which Jacob sent to Joseph, Gen. 43:11, and which the Tyrians purchased from Palestine. Ezek. 27:17. A third

kind has been described by some writers as "vegetable" honey, by which is meant the exudations of certain trees and shrubs, such as the *Tamarix mannifera,* found in the peninsula of Sinai, or the stunted oaks of Luristan and Mesopotamia. The honey which Jonathan ate in the wood, 1 Sam. 14:25, and the "wild honey" which supported John the Baptist, Matt. 3 : 4, have been referred to this species. But it was probably the honey of wild bees.

Hook, Hooks. Various kinds of hooks are noticed in the Bible, of which the following are the most important: (1) Fishing hooks. Job 41 : 2; Isa. 19 : 8; Hab. 1 : 15. (2) A *ring,* such as in our country is placed through the nose of a bull, and similarly used in the East for leading about lions—Ezek. 19 : 4, where the Authorized Version has "with chains"—camels and other animals. Called "thorn" in Job 41 : 2. A similar method was adopted for leading prisoners. 2 Chron. 33 : 11. (3) The hooks of the pillars of the tabernacle. Ex. 26 : 32, 37; 27 : 10 ff.; 38 : 10 ff. (4) A vine-dresser's pruning-hook. Isa. 2 : 4; 18 : 5; Micah 4 : 3; Joel 3 : 10. (5) A flesh-hook for getting up the joints of meat out of the boiling-pot. Ex. 27 : 3; 1 Sam. 2 : 13, 14. (6) Probably

2 : 12–17, 22, filled the people with disgust and indignation, and provoked the curse which was denounced against their father's house, first by an unknown prophet, 1 Sam. 2 : 27–36, and then by Samuel, ch. 3 : 11–14. They were both cut off in one day in the flower of their age, and the ark which they had accompanied to battle against the Philistines was lost on the same occasion. 1 Sam. 4 : 10, 11.

Hor (hòr), **Mount.** 1. The mountain on which Aaron died. Num. 20 : 25–28. It was "on the boundary line," Num. 20 : 23, or "in the edge," ch. 33 : 37, of the land of Edom. It was the halting-place of the people next after Kadesh, ch. 20 : 22; 33 : 37, and they quitted it for Zalmonah, ch. 33 : 41, in the road to the Red Sea, ch. 21 : 4. It was during the encampment at Kadesh that Aaron was gathered to his fathers. Mount Hor is situated on the eastern

THE TRADITIONAL MOUNT HOR.

"hooks" used for the purpose of hanging up animals to flay them. Ezek. 40 : 43.

Hoph'ni (hŏf'nĭ) and PHINEHAS, the two sons of Eli, who fulfilled their hereditary sacerdotal duties at Shiloh. Their brutal rapacity and lust, 1 Sam.

side of the great valley of the *Arabah,* the highest and most conspicuous of the whole range of the sandstone mountains of Edom, having close beneath it on its eastern side the mysterious city of Petra. It is now the *Jebel Nebi-Harûn,* "the mountain of the prophet Aaron." Its height is 4800 feet above the Mediterranean; that is to say, about 1700 feet above the town of Petra, 4000 above the level of the Arabah, and more than 6000 above the Dead Sea. The mountain is marked far and near by its double top, which rises like a huge castellated building from a lower base, and is surmounted by a circular dome of the tomb of Aaron, a distinct white spot on the dark red surface of the mountain. The chief interest of Mount Hor consists in the prospect from its summit, the last view of Aaron—that view which was to him what Pisgah was to his brother.

2. A mountain, entirely distinct from the preceding, named in Num. 34:7, 8 only, as one of the marks of the northern boundary of the land which the children of Israel were about to conquer. This Mount Hor is the great chain of Lebanon itself.

Ho'ram (hō'ram), king of Gezer at the time of the conquest of the southwestern part of Palestine. Josh. 10:33.

Ho'reb (hō'reb) (*desert*). [SINAI.]

Ho'rem (hō'rem) (*sacred*), one of the fortified places in the territory of Naphtali; named with Iron and Migdal-el. Josh. 19:38. Conder identifies with Hurah near Kedesh-Naphtali, but the site is disputed.

Hor-hagid'gad (hôr'hâ-gĭd'găd) (*cavern of Gidgad*), the name of the desert station where the Israelites encamped, Num. 33:32; probably the same as Gudgodah. Deut. 10:7.

Ho'ri (hō'rī) (*cave-dweller*). 1. A Horite, son of Lotan the son of Seir. Gen. 36:22; 1 Chron. 1:39; Gen. 36:30. 2. A man of Simeon, father of Shaphat. Num. 13:5.

Ho'rim (hō'rim) and **Ho'rites** (hō'rītes), the aboriginal inhabitants of Mount Seir, Gen. 14:6, and probably allied to the Emim and Rephaim. The name *Horite* appears to have been derived from their habits as "cave-dwellers." They were destroyed as a people by the descendants of Esau, Deut. 2:12, though partially preserved by intermarriage with their conquerors.

Hor'mah (hôr'mah) (*a devoted place*), or ZEPHATH, Judges 1:17, was the chief town of a king of a Canaanitish tribe on the south of Palestine, which was reduced by Joshua, and became a city of the territory of Judah, Josh. 15:30; 1 Sam. 30:30, but apparently belonged to Simeon. 1 Chron. 4:30.

Horn. The word "horn" is often used metaphorically to signify strength and honor, because horns are the chief weapons and ornaments of the animals which possess them; hence they are also used as a type of victory. Of *strength* the horns of the unicorn (probably the wild ox) were the most frequent representative, Deut. 33:17, etc., but not always; comp. 1 Kings 22:11, where probably horns of iron, worn defiantly and symbolically on the head, are intended. Among the Druses upon Mount

HORNS.
Worn as head-ornaments by modern Orientals.

Lebanon the married women wear silver horns on their heads. In the sense of *honor*, the word horn stands for the *abstract*—"my horn," Job 16:15; "all the horn of Israel," Lam. 2:3—and so for the supreme authority. It also stands for the *concrete*, whence it comes to mean king, kingdom. Dan. 7:8, 8:3, etc.; Zech. 1:18. Out of either or both of these last two metaphors sprang the idea of representing gods with horns.

Hornet. The hornet bears a general resemblance to the common wasp, only it is larger. It is exceedingly fierce and voracious, especially in hot climates, and its sting is frequently dangerous. In Scripture the hornet is referred to only as the means which Jehovah employed for the extirpation of the Canaanites. Ex. 23:28; Deut. 7:20; Josh. 24:12. It is said that the Phaselitæ, a Phœnician people, were driven from their locality by hornets; and other examples are given in Paxton's "Illustrations of Scripture," 1. 303.

Horona'im (hŏr-o-nā'im) (*two caverns*), a town of Moab, possibly a sanctuary, named with Zoar and Luhith. Isa. 15:5; Jer. 48:3, 5, 34.

Hor'onite (hŏr'o-nīte) (*native of Bethhoron*), **The**, the designation of Sanballat. Neh. 2:10, 19; 13:28. It is derived by Gesenius from Horonaim.

Horse. The most striking feature in the biblical notices of the horse is the exclusive application of it to warlike operations; in no instance is that useful animal employed for the purposes of ordinary locomotion or agriculture, if we except Isa. 28:28. The animated description of the horse in Job 39:19–25 applies solely to the war-horse. The Hebrews in the patriarchal age, as a pastoral race, did not stand in need of the services of the horse, and for a long period after their settlement in Canaan they dispensed with it, partly in consequence of the hilly nature of the country, which only admitted of the use of chariots in certain localities, Judges 1:19, and partly in consequence of the prohibition in Deut. 17:16, which would be held to apply at all periods. David first established a force of cavalry and chariots, 2 Sam. 8:4; but the great supply of horses was subsequently effected by Solomon through his connection with Egypt. 1 Kings 4:26. Solomon also established a very active trade in horses, which were brought by dealers out of Egypt and resold, at a profit, to the Hittites. With regard to the trappings and management of the horse we have little information. They had halters (Isa. 30:28) and bridles (Ps. 32:9). The bridles were decorated with bells. Zech. 14:20. The bit is mentioned Ps. 32:9 and Jas. 3:3. Saddles were not used until a late period. The horses were not shod, and therefore hoofs as hard "as flint," Isa. 5:28, were regarded as a great merit. The chariot-horses were covered with embroidered trappings. Ezek. 27:20. Horses and chariots were used also in idolatrous processions, as noticed in regard to the sun. 2 Kings 23:11.

Horse=leech, Heb. *'ălûkâh,* occurs once only, viz. Prov. 30:15. There is little doubt that *'ălûkâh* denotes some species of leech, or rather is the generic term for any blood-sucking annelid.

Ho'sah (hō'sah) (*refuge*), a city of Asher, Josh. 19:29, the next landmark on the boundary to Tyre.

Ho'sah, a Merarite Levite, 1 Chron.

26:10, chosen by David to be one of the first doorkeepers to the ark after its arrival in Jerusalem. 1 Chron. 16:38. (B.C. 1042.)

Hosanna (*save, pray*). "Save, we pray!" the cry of the multitudes as they thronged in our Lord's triumphal procession into Jerusalem. Matt. 21:9, 15; Mark 11:9, 10; John 12:13. The Psalm from which it was taken, the 118th, was one with which they were familiar from being accustomed to recite the 25th and 26th verses at the feast of tabernacles, forming a part of the great hallel. Ps. 113–118.

Hose'a (hô-ṣē'à) (*salvation*), son of Beeri, and first of the minor prophets. Probably the prophetic career of Hosea extended from some time in the reign of Jeroboam II., and on into the brief and troublous reigns that followed. He was a contemporary in part with Amos and Isaiah. The prophecies of Hosea were delivered in the kingdom of Israel. Jeroboam II. was on the throne, and Israel was at the height of its earthly splendor. Nothing is known of the prophet's life excepting what may be gained from his book.

Hose'a, Prophecies of. Hosea's message came in very evil times, when luxury and vice, oppression, drunkenness, idolatry, debauchery prevailed and every law of God was habitually broken.

Just before him Amos had tried to stem the tide. His message was one of denunciation of sin, of "Woe unto you," of punishment, of warning. It was of divine justice. He enforced his message by pointing out the disasters that had come upon the people for their sins, -—famine, blasting, locusts, pestilence, war.

Hosea follows him with a new motive, the mightiest that can be brought to bear upon the heart of man,—the love of God, the deepest, tenderest, strongest love possible. "To Amos's proposition 'God is Justice,' Hosea adds, 'God is Love.' Not as if Hosea were any less severe in his judgment of the evils of his people; on the contrary, he shows himself even more deeply affected by them. . . . But God is a kind Father, who punishes his child with a bleeding heart, for its own good, so that afterward he may enfold it all the more warmly in his arms."

Probably Part 1, chs. 1–3, record a

prophetic appeal growing out of the prophet's own experience with a beloved wife, who had been unfaithful to him, as the Israelites had been unfaithful to their God. But Hosea appeals to her, and receives her back into his home, a perfect picture of God's forgiving love.

Part 2, chs. 4–14 were probably written at a later period of the prophet's life; and appear to be a summary of his preaching at various times.

Hoshai'ah (hŏsh-a-ī'ah) (*Jehovah hath saved*). 1. A man who assisted in the dedication of the wall of Jerusalem after it had been rebuilt by Nehemiah. Neh. 12:32. (B.C. 446.)

2. The father of a certain Jezaniah or Azariah, who was a man of note after the destruction of Jerusalem by Nebuchadnezzar. Jer. 42:1; 43:2.

Hosh'ama (hŏsh'a-mà) (*Jehovah has heard*), one of the sons or descendants of Jeconiah or Jehoiachin the last king but one of Judah. 1 Chron. 3:18.

Hoshe'a (hò-shē'à) (*salvation*). 1. The nineteenth, last and best king of Israel. He succeeded Pekah, whom he slew in a successful conspiracy, thereby fulfilling a prophecy of Isaiah. Isa. 7:16. In the third year of his reign (B.C. 726), Shalmaneser cruelly stormed the strong caves of Beth-arbel, Hos. 8:14, and made Israel tributary, 2 Kings 17:3, for three years. At the end of this period Hoshea entered into a secret alliance with the king of Egypt, to throw off the Assyrian yoke. The alliance did him no good; it was revealed to the court of Nineveh by the Assyrian party in Ephraim, and Hoshea was immediately seized as a rebellious vassal, shut up in prison, and apparently treated with the utmost indignity. Micah 5:1. Of the subsequent fortunes of Hoshea nothing is known.

2. The son of Nun, *i. e.* Joshua, Deut. 32:44; and also in Num. 13:8, though there the Authorized Version has OSHEA.

3. Son of Azaziah, 1 Chron. 27:20; like his great namesake, a man of Ephraim, ruler of his tribe in the time of King David.

4. One of the heads of the people who sealed the covenant with Nehemiah. Neh. 10:23.

Hospitality. Hospitality was regarded by most nations of the ancient world as one of the chief virtues. The Jewish laws respecting strangers, Lev. 19:33, 34, and the poor, Lev. 25:14, *seq.;* Deut. 15:7, and concerning redemption, Lev. 25:23, *seq.,* etc., are framed in accordance with the spirit of hospitality. In the law compassion to strangers is constantly enforced by the words "for ye were strangers in the land of Egypt." Lev. 19:34. And before the law, Abraham's entertainment of the angels, Gen. 18:1, *seq.,* and Lot's, Gen. 19:1, are in exact agreement with its precepts, and with modern usage. Comp. Ex. 2:20; Judges 13:15; 19:17, 20, 21. In the New Testament hospitality is yet more markedly enjoined; and in the more civilized state of society which then prevailed, its exercise became more a social virtue than a necessity of patriarchal life. The good Samaritan stands for all ages as an example of Christian hospitality. The neglect of Christ is symbolized by inhospitality to our neighbors. Matt. 25:43. The apostles urged the Church to "follow after hospitality," Rom. 12:13; cf. 1 Tim. 5:10; to remember Abraham's example, Heb. 13:2; to "use hospitality one to another without grudging," 1 Pet. 4:9; while a bishop must be a "lover of hospitality." Titus 1:8, cf. 1 Tim. 3:2. The practice of the early Christians was in accord with these precepts. They had all things in common, and their hospitality was a characteristic of their belief. In the patriarchal ages we may take Abraham's example as the most fitting, as we have of it the fullest account. "The account," says Mr. Lane, "of Abraham's entertaining the three angels, related in the Bible, presents a perfect picture of the manner in which a modern Bedawee sheikh receives travelers arriving at his encampment." The Oriental respect for the covenant of bread and salt, or salt alone, certainly sprang from the high regard in which hospitality was held.

Ho'tham (hō'tham) (*seal*), a man of Asher, son of Heber, of the family of Beriah. 1 Chron. 7:32.

Ho'than (hō'than), a man of Aroer, father of Shama and Jehiel. 1 Chron. 11:44. R. V. correctly Hotham.

Ho'thir (hō'thĭr), the thirteenth son of Heman, "the king's seer," 1 Chron. 25:4, 28, and therefore a Kohathite Levite.

Hour. The ancient Hebrews were

probably unacquainted with the division of the natural day into twenty-four parts; but they afterwards parcelled out the period between sunrise and sunset into a series of divisions distinguished by the sun's course. The natural divisions of morning, noon-day, and evening were distinguished, and other expressions were used to denote more definite portions. But there seems to be no sign of any definite division until after the Exile. The division of the night into three watches was much earlier recognized, the middle watch being named in Judges 7:19. At what period the Jews first became acquainted with the division of the day into twelve hours is unknown, but it is generally supposed they learned it from the Babylonians during the captivity. It was known to the Egyptians at a very early period. They had twelve hours of the day and of the night. There are two kinds of hours, viz. (1) the astronomical or equinoctial hour, *i. e.* the 24th part of a civil day, and (2) the natural hour, *i. e.* the 12th part of the natural day, or of the time between sunrise and sunset. These are the hours meant in the New Testament, John 11:9, etc., and it must be remembered that they perpetually vary in length, so as to be very different at different times of the year.

House. The houses of the rural poor in Egypt, as well as in most parts of Syria, Arabia and Persia, are generally mere huts of mud or sunburnt bricks. In some parts of Palestine and Arabia stone is used, and in certain districts caves in the rocks are used as dwellings. Amos 5:11. The houses are usually of one story only, viz., the ground floor, and often contain only one apartment. Sometimes a small court for the cattle is attached; and in some cases the cattle are housed in the same building, or the people live on a raised platform, and the cattle round them on the ground. 1 Sam. 28:24. The windows are small apertures high up in the walls, sometimes grated with wood. The roofs are commonly but not always flat, and are usually formed of a plaster of mud and straw laid upon boughs or rafters; and upon the flat roofs, tents or "booths" of boughs or rushes are often raised to be used as sleeping-places in summer. The difference between the poorest houses and those of the class next above them is greater than between these and

the houses of the first rank. The prevailing plan of eastern houses of this class presents, as was the case in ancient Egypt, a front wall, whose blank and mean appearance is usually relieved only by the door and a few latticed and projecting windows. Within this is a court or courts with apartments opening into them. Over the door is a projecting window with a lattice more or less elaborately wrought, which, except in times

UPPER ROOM.

of public celebrations, is usually closed, 2 Kings 9:30. An awning is sometimes drawn over the court, and the floor strewed with carpets on festive occasions. The stairs to the upper apartments are in Syria usually in a corner of the court. Around part, if not the whole, of the court is a veranda, often nine or ten feet deep, over which, when there is more than one floor, runs a second gallery of like depth, with a balustrade. When there is no second floor, but more than one court, the women's apartments—*hareem, harem* or *haram*—are usually in the second court; otherwise they form a separate building within the general enclosure, or are above on the first floor. When there is an upper story, the *ka'ah* forms the most important apartment, and thus probably answers to the "upper room," which was often the guest-chamber. Luke 22:12; Acts 1:13; 9:37; 20:8. The windows of the upper rooms often project one or two feet, and form a kiosk or latticed chamber. Such may have been "the chamber in the wall." 2 Kings 4:10, 11. The "lattice," through which Ahaziah fell, perhaps belonged to an upper chamber of this kind, 2 Kings 1:2, as also the "third loft," from which Eutychus fell. Acts 20:9;

comp. Jer. 22:13. Paul preached in such a room on account of its superior size and retired position. The outer circle of an audience in such a room sat upon a dais, or upon cushions elevated so as to be as high as the window-sill. From such a position Eutychus could easily fall.

There are usually no special bedrooms in eastern houses. The outer doors are closed with a wooden lock, but in some cases the apartments are divided from each other by curtains only. There are no chimneys, but fire is made when required with charcoal in a chafing-dish; or a fire of wood might be kindled in the open court of the house. Luke 22:55. Some houses in Cairo have an apartment open in front to the court, with two or more arches and a railing, and a pillar to support the wall above. It was probably in a chamber of this kind, that our Lord was being arraigned before the high priest at the time when the denial of him by St. Peter took place. He "turned and looked" on Peter as he stood by the fire in the court, Luke 22:56, 61; John 18:28, whilst he himself was in the "hall of judgment."

In no point do Oriental domestic habits differ more from European than in the use of the roof. Its flat surface is made useful for various household purposes, as drying corn, hanging up

EASTERN BATTLEMENTED HOUSE.

linen, and preparing figs and raisins. The roofs are used as places of recreation in the evening, and often as sleeping-places at night. 1 Sam. 9:25, 26; 2 Sam. 11:2; 16:22; Job 27:18; Prov.

21:9; Dan. 4:29. They were also used as places for devotion and even idolatrous worship. 2 Kings 23:12; Jer. 19:13; 32:29; Zeph. 1:5; Acts 10:9. At the time of the feast of tabernacles booths were erected by the Jews on the tops of their houses. Protection of the roof by parapets was enjoined by the law. Deut. 22:8. Special apartments were devoted in larger houses to winter and summer uses. Jer. 36:22; Amos 3:15. The ivory house of Ahab was probably a palace largely ornamented with inlaid ivory.

Huk'kok (hŭk'kok), a place on the boundary of Naphtali. Josh. 19:34. It is probably *Yakuk,* a village in the mountains of Naphtali, west of the upper end of the Sea of Galilee, though some dispute it.

Hu'kok (hū'kok), a name which in 1 Chron. 6:75 is erroneously used for Helkath, which see.

Hul (hŭl) (*circle*), the second son of Aram, and grandson of Shem. Gen. 10:23. The strongest evidence for the location of his descendants is in favor of the district about the roots of Lebanon, but no real identification has been made.

Hul'dah (hŭl'dah) (*weasel*), a prophetess, whose husband, Shallum, was keeper of the wardrobe in the time of King Josiah. It was to her that Josiah had recourse, when Hilkiah found a book of the law, to procure an authoritative opinion on it. 2 Kings 22:14; 2 Chron. 34:22. (B.C. 623.)

Hum'tah (hŭm'tah) (*place of lizards*), a city of Judah, one of those in the mountain district, the next to Hebron. Josh. 15:54.

Hunting. Hunting, as a matter of necessity, whether for the extermination of dangerous beasts or for procuring sustenance, betokens a rude and semi-civilized state; as an amusement, it betokens an advanced state. The Hebrews, as a pastoral and agricultural people, were not given to the sports of the field; the density of the population, the earnestness of their character, and the tendency of their ritual regulations, particularly those affecting food, all combined to discourage the practice of hunting. The manner of catching animals was, first, either by digging a pitfall, or, secondly, by a trap which was set under ground, Job 18:10, in the run of the animal, Prov. 22:5, and caught it by the leg, Job 18:9; or lastly by the use of the net, of which there were various kinds, as for the gazelle, Isa. 51: 20, Authorized Version, " wild bull," and other animals of that class.

Hu'pham (hū'fam), a son of Benjamin, founder of the family of the Huphamites. Num. 26: 39. [HUPPIM.]

Hu'phamites (hū'fam-ītes), The, descendants of Hupham, of the tribe of Benjamin. Num. 26: 39.

Hup'pah (hŭp'pah) (*canopy*), a priest in the time of David. 1 Chron. 24: 13.

Hup'pim (hŭp'pim) (*coverings*), head of a Benjamite family. Gen. 46: 21; 1 Chron. 7: 12. Given as Hupham in Num. 26: 39.

Hur (hûr). 1. A man mentioned with Moses and Aaron on the occasion of the battle with Amalek at Rephidim. Ex. 17: 10, when with Aaron he stayed up the hands of Moses. ver. 12. (B.C. 1491.) He is mentioned again in ch. 24: 14 as being, with Aaron, left in charge of the people by Moses during his ascent of Sinai. The Jewish tradition is that he was the husband of Miriam, and that he was identical with

2. The grandfather of Bezaleel, the chief artificer of the tabernacle. Ex. 31: 2; 35: 30; 38: 22.

3. The fourth of the five kings of Midian who were slain with Balaam after the " matter of Peor." Num. 31: 8. (B.C. 1451.) In a later mention of them, Josh. 13: 21, they are called princes of Midian and dukes.

4. Father of Rephaiah, who was ruler of half of the environs of Jerusalem, and assisted Nehemiah in the repair of the wall. Neh. 3: 9.

5. The " son of Hur "—Ben-Hur—was commissariat officer for Solomon in Mount Ephraim. 1 Kings 4: 8.

Hu'rai (hū'rāi), or **Hura'i**, one of David's guard—Hurai of the torrents of Gaash, according to the list of 1 Chron. 11: 32. [HIDDAI.]

Hu'ram (hū'ram) (*noble*). 1. A Benjamite; son of Bela, the first-born of the patriarch. 1 Chron. 8: 5.

2. The form in which the name of the king of Tyre in alliance with David and Solomon—and elsewhere given as HIRAM—appears in Second Chronicles. 2 Chron. 2: 3, 11, 12; 8: 2, 18; 9: 10, 21.

3. The same change occurs in Chronicles in the name of Hiram the artificer, which is given as HURAM in 2 Chron. 4: 11, 16. [HIRAM.]

Hu'ri (hū'rī) (*linen weaver*), a Gadite; father of Abihail. 1 Chron. 5: 14.

Husband. [MARRIAGE.]

Hu'shah (hū'shah) (*haste*), a name which occurs in the genealogies of the tribe of Judah. 1 Chron. 4: 4.

Hu'shai (hū'shāi), or **Husha'i** (*hasting*), an Archite, *i. e.* possibly an inhabitant of a place called Erec. 2 Sam. 15: 32 ff.; 16: 16 ff. He is called the " friend " of David. 2 Sam. 15: 37; comp. 1 Chron. 27: 33. To him David confided the delicate and dangerous part of a pretended adherence to the cause of Absalom. (B.C. about 1023.) He was probably the father of Baana. 1 Kings 4: 16.

Hu'sham (hū'sham) (*haste*), one of the early kings of Edom. Gen. 36: 34, 35; 1 Chron. 1: 45, 46.

Hu'shathite (hū'shath-īte) (*inhabitant of Hushah*), The, the designation of two of the heroes of David's guard. 1. SIBBECHAI. 2 Sam. 21: 18; 1 Chron. 11: 29; 20: 4; 27: 11. Josephus, however, calls him a Hittite.

2. MEBUNNAI, 2 Sam. 23: 27, a mere corruption of SIBBECHAI.

Hu'shim (hū'shĭm). 1. In Gen. 46: 23 " the children of Dan " are said to have been Hushim. The name is plural, as if of a tribe rather than an individual. In Num. 26: 42 the name is changed to Shuham.

2. A Benjamite, 1 Chron. 7: 12; and here again apparently the plural nature of the name is recognized, and Hushim are stated to be " the sons of Aher."

3. One of the two wives of Shaharaim. 1 Chron. 8: 8.

Husks. The word in Luke 15: 16 describes really the fruit of a particular kind of tree, viz. the carob or *Ceratonia siliqua* of botanists. It belongs to the locust family. This tree is very commonly met with in Syria and Egypt; it produces pods, shaped like a horn, varying in length from six to ten inches, and about a finger's breadth, or rather more; it is dark-brown, glossy, filled with seeds, and has a sweetish taste. It is used much for food by the poor, and for the feeding of swine (page 268).

Huz (hŭz), the eldest son of Nahor and Milcah. Gen. 22: 21. The same as Uz.

Huz'zab (hŭz'zab), according to the general opinion of the Jews, was the queen of Nineveh at the time when Nahum delivered his prophecy. Nah. 2: 7. Many modern scholars regard it as a verb, translating it as in R. V. in

HUSKS OF SWINE — Carob Beans.

"it is decreed." There is no means as yet of deciding whether it is a proper noun, or what its meaning is in any case, and opinions exactly opposite are found in equally good authorities.

Hyacinth, used in the Revised Version for *jacinth* in Rev. 9:17. It is simply another English spelling of the same Greek word.

Hyæna. Authorities differ as to whether the term *tzâbû'a* in Jer. 12:9 means a "hyæna" or a "speckled bird." The only other instance in which it occurs is as a proper name, Zeboim, 1 Sam. 13:18, "the valley of hyænas," Neh. 11:34. The striped hyæna (*Hyæna striata*) is found in Africa, Asia Minor, Arabia and Persia, and is more common in Palestine than any other carnivorous animal, except perhaps the jackal. The hyæna is among the mammals what the vulture is among birds, —the scavenger of the wilderness, the woods and the shore. It often attacks animals, and sometimes digs up the dead bodies of men and beasts. From this last habit the hyæna has been regarded as a horrible and mysterious creature. Its teeth are so powerful that they can crack the bones of an ox with ease.— *Appleton's Encyc.* The hyæna was common in ancient as in modern Egypt, and is constantly depicted upon monuments; it must therefore have been well known to the Jews.

Hymenæ'us (hī-me-nē'us) (*belonging to Hymen,* the god of marriage), the name of a person occurring twice in the correspondence between St. Paul and Timothy; the first time classed with Alexander, 1 Tim. 1:20, and the second time classed with Philetus. 2 Tim. 2:17, 18. (A.D. 65–7.) He denied the true doctrine of the resurrection.

Hymn, a religious song or psalm. Eph. 5:19; Col. 3:16. Our Lord and his apostles sung a hymn after the last supper. In the jail at Philippi, Paul and Silas "sang hymns" (Authorized Version "praises") unto God, and so loud was their song that their fellow prisoners heard them.

Hyssop. (Heb. *êzôb.*) The *êzôb* was used for sprinkling in some of the sacrifices and purifications of the Jews. In consequence of its detergent qualities, or from its being associated with the purificatory services, the Psalmist makes use of the expression, "Purge me with *êzôb.*" Ps. 51:7. It is described in 1 Kings 4:33 as growing on or near walls. It is impossible to precisely identify the plant, probably because the name was given not to a particular plant but to a *family* of plants associated together by qualities easily noticed rather than by close botanical affinities. Different species of the family may have been used at different times. The plant now known by this name is "a shrub with low, bushy stalk 1½ feet high, small pear-shaped, close-setting opposite leaves, all the stalks and branches terminated by erect whorled spikes of flowers of different colors in the varieties. It is a hardy plant, with an aromatic smell and a warm, pungent taste; a native of the south of Europe and the East."

There is a considerable difference of opinion as to the identity of the hyssop mentioned in Scripture. The principal plants which are supposed to be intended

HYSSOP.

are:—1. The *Origanum maru,* the *z'atar* of the Arabs. The French consul at Sidon exhibited to Dr. Thomson ("The Land and the Book," i. 161) a specimen of this "having the fragrance of thyme, with a hot, pungent taste, and long slender stems." Dr. Post of Beirut, in Hastings' *Bible Dictionary,* argues that in John 19 : 29 the hyssop was added as a powder to the wine, to cool the mouth, the whole being lifted on a "reed" as in the parallel passages.

2. Cheyne, in the "Encyclopædia Biblica," following Tristram and others considers it the caper-plant, or *Capparis spinosa* of Linnæus. The Arabic name of this plant, *asuf,* by which it is some-times, though not commonly, described, bears considerable resemblance to the Hebrew. "It is a bright-green creeper, which climbs from the fissures of the rocks, is supposed to possess cleansing properties, and is capable of yielding a stick to which a sponge might be attached."—Stanley, "Sinai and Palestine," 23. It produces a fruit the size of a walnut, called the mountain pepper.

3. Hastings' "Dictionary of Christ and the Gospels," gives the balance of probability in favor of the view that the name is "applied to various plants of the genera Thymus, Origanus, and others nearly allied in form and habit."

I

Ib'har (ĭb'här) ([*God*] *chooses*), one of the sons of David, 2 Sam. 5 : 15; 1 Chron. 3 : 6; 14 : 5, born in Jerusalem.

Ib'leam (ĭb'le-ăm) (*the people faileth*), a city of Manasseh, with villages or towns dependent on it. Judges 1 : 27. It appears to have been situated in the territory of either Issachar or Asher. Josh. 17 : 11. The ascent of Gur was "at Ibleam," 2 Kings 9 : 27. It is generally identified with Bileam. It is probably the modern ruin *Bel'ame*.

Ibne'iah (ĭb-nē'iah) (*Jehovah buildeth up*), son of Jeroham, a Benjamite. 1 Chron. 9 : 8.

Ibni'jah (ĭb-nī'jah) (*Jehovah doth build*), a Benjamite. 1 Chron. 9 : 8.

Ib'ri (ĭb'rī) (*Hebrew*), a Merarite Levite of the family of Jaaziah, 1 Chron. 24 : 27.

Ib'zan (ĭb'zan), a native of Bethlehem of Zebulun, who judged Israel for seven years after Jephthah. Judges 12 : 8, 10.

Ich'abod (ĭk'a-bŏd) (*inglorious*), the son of Phinehas and grandson of Eli. 1 Sam. 4 : 21.

Ico'nium (i-kō'nĭ-um), the modern *Konia*, was the capital of Lycaonia, in Asia Minor. It was a large and rich city, 120 miles north from the Mediterranean Sea, at the foot of the Taurus mountains, and on the great line of communication between Ephesus and the western coast of the peninsula on one side, and Tarsus, Antioch and the Euphrates on the other. Iconium was a well-chosen place for missionary operations. Acts 14 : 1, 3, 21, 22; 16 : 1, 2. Paul's first visit here was on his first circuit, in company with Barnabas; and on this occasion he approached it from Antioch in Pisidia, which lay to the west. The modern *Konia* is between two and three miles in circumference, and contains about 45,000 (Rand, McNally, 1924) inhabitants. It contains manufactories of carpets and leather.

Id'alah (ĭd'a-lah), one of the cities of the tribe of Zebulun, named between Shimron and Bethlehem. Josh. 19 : 15.

Id'bash (ĭd'băsh) (*honey-sweet*), one of the three sons of Abi-Etam, among the families of Judah. 1 Chron. 4 : 3.

Iddo (ĭd'dŏ). The rendering of several Hebrew words with different meanings, not all of which are definitely agreed on by commentators.

1. Father of Ahinadab. 1 Kings 4 : 14.

2. A descendant of Gershom, son of Levi. 1 Chron. 6 : 21.

3. Son of Zechariah, ruler of the tribe of Manasseh east of Jordan in the time of David. 1 Chron. 27 : 21.

4. A seer whose "visions" against Jeroboam incidentally contained some of the acts of Solomon. 2 Chron. 9 : 29. He appears to have written a chronicle or story relating to the life and reign of Abijah. 2 Chron. 13 : 22.

5. The grandfather of the prophet Zechariah. Zech. 1 : 1, 7.

6. The chief of those who assembled at Casiphia at the time of the second caravan from Babylon. He was one of the Nethinim. Ezra 8 : 17; comp. 20.

Idol. An image or anything used as an object of worship in place of the true God. Among the earliest objects of worship, regarded as symbols of deity, were the meteoric stones, which the ancients believed to have been images of the gods sent down from heaven. From these they transferred their regard to rough unhewn blocks, to stone columns or pillars of wood, in which the divinity worshiped was supposed to dwell, and which were

AN ASSYRIAN DEITY.

consecrated, like the sacred stone at Delphi, by being anointed with oil and crowned with wool on solemn days. Of the forms assumed by the idolatrous images we have not many traces in the Bible. Derceto, the Philistine fish-goddess, was a human figure terminating in a fish; and that the Syrian deities were represented in later times in a symbolical human shape we know for certainty. When the process

IMAGE OF THE GOD SETUSH, from Thebes, Egypt.

of adorning the image was completed, it was placed in a temple or shrine appointed for it. Judg. 16 : 23, 27; 1 Sam.

5 : 25; 1 Cor. 8 : 10. From these temples the idols were sometimes carried in procession on festival days. The apocryphal book of Bel and the Dragon shows that their priests were maintained from the idol treasury, and feasted upon the meats which were appointed for the idols' use.

Idolatry, strictly speaking, denotes the worship of deity in a visible form, whether the images to which homage is paid are symbolical representations of the true God or of the false divinities which have been made the objects of worship in his stead.

I. *History of idolatry among the Jews.* —The first undoubted allusion to idolatry or idolatrous customs in the Bible is in the account of Rachel's stealing her father's teraphim. Gen. 31: 19. During their long residence in Egypt the Israelites defiled themselves with the idols of the land, and it was long before the taint was removed. Josh. 24: 14; Ezek. 20: 7. In the wilderness they clamored for some visible shape in which they might worship the God who had brought them out of Egypt, Ex. 32, until Aaron made the calf, the embodiment of Apis or Mnevis, and emblem of the productive power of nature. During the lives of Joshua and the elders who outlived him they kept true to their allegiance; but the generation following, who knew not Jehovah nor the works he had done for Israel, swerved from the plain path of their fathers, and were caught in the toils of the foreigner. Judges 2. From this time forth their history becomes little more than a chronicle of the inevitable sequence of offence and punishment. Judges 2: 12, 14. By turns each conquering nation strove to establish the worship of its national god. In later times the practice of secret idolatry was carried to greater lengths. Images were set up on the corn-floors, in the wine-vats, and behind the doors of private houses, Isa. 57: 8; Hos. 9: 1, 2; and to check this tendency the statute in Deut. 27: 15 was originally promulgated. Under Samuel's administration idolatry was publicly renounced, 1 Sam. 7: 3–6; but in the reign of Solomon all this was forgotten, even Solomon's own heart being turned after other gods. 1 Kings 11: 4. Rehoboam perpetuated the worst features of Solomon's idolatry, 1ᵛ Kings 14: 22–24. Jeroboam erected golden calves at Bethel and at Dan, and by this crafty state policy severed forever the kingdoms of Judah and Israel. 1 Kings 12:26-33. There is, however, no reason to charge him with actual apostasy from the worship of Jehovah. The successors of Jeroboam followed in his steps, till Ahab, who, through the influence of his wife Jezebel introduced the actual worship of the God of the Zidonians, the Zidonian Baal. The conquest of the ten tribes by Shalmaneser was for them the last scene of the drama of abominations which had been enacted uninterruptedly for upwards of 250 years. Under Hezekiah a great reform was inaugurated, that was not confined to Judah and Benjamin, but spread throughout Ephraim and Manasseh, 2 Chron. 31:1, and to all external appearance idolatry was extirpated. But the reform extended little below the surface. Isa. 29:13. With the death of Josiah ended the last effort to revive among the people a purer ritual, if not a purer faith. The lamp of David, which had long shed but a struggling ray, flickered for a while and then went out in the darkness of Babylonian captivity. Though the conquests of Alexander caused Greek influence to be felt, yet after the captivity a better condition of things prevailed, and the Jews never again fell into idolatry. The erection of synagogues has been assigned as a reason for the comparative purity of the Jewish worship after the captivity, while another cause has been discovered in the hatred for images acquired by the Jews in their intercourse with the Persians.

II. *Objects of idolatry.*—The sun and moon were early selected as outward symbols of all-pervading power, and the worship of the heavenly bodies was not only the most ancient but the most prevalent system of idolatry. Taking its rise in the plains of Chaldea, it spread through Egypt, Greece, Scythia, and even Mexico and Ceylon. Comp. Deut. 4:19; 17:3; Job 31:26-28. In the later times of the monarchy, the planets or the zodiacal signs received, next to the sun and moon, their share of popular adoration. 2 Kings 23:5. Beast-worship, as exemplified in the calves of Jeroboam, has already been alluded to. Of pure hero-worship among the Semitic races we find no trace. The singular reverence with which trees have been honored is not without example in

the history of the Hebrews. The terebinth (oak) at Mamre, beneath which Abraham built an altar, Gen. 12:7; 13:18, and the memorial grove planted by him at Beersheba, Gen. 21:33, were intimately connected with patriarchal worship. Mountains and high places were chosen spots for offering sacrifice and incense to idols, 1 Kings 11:7; 14:23; and the retirement of gardens and the thick shade of woods offered great attractions to their worshipers. 2 Kings 16:4; Isa. 1:29; Hos. 4:13. The host of heaven was worshiped on the housetop. 2 Kings 23:12; Jer. 19:13; 32:29; Zeph. 1:5. The modern objects of idolatry are less gross than the ancient, but are none the less idols. Whatever of wealth or honor or pleasure is loved and sought before God and righteousness becomes an object of idolatry.

III. *Punishment of idolatry.*—Idolatry to an Israelite was a state offence, 1 Sam. 15:23, a political crime of the greatest character, high treason against the majesty of his king. The first and second commandments are directed against idolatry of every form. Individuals and communities were equally amenable to the rigorous code. The individual offender was devoted to destruction, Ex. 22:20; his nearest relatives were not only bound to denounce him and deliver him up to punishment, Deut. 13:2-10, but their hands were to strike the first blow, when, on the evidence of two witnesses at least, he was stoned. Deut. 17:2-7. To attempt to seduce others to false worship was a crime of equal enormity. Deut. 13:6-10.

IV. *Attractions of idolatry.*—Many have wondered why the Israelites were so easily led away from the true God, into the worship of idols. (1) Visible, outward signs, with shows, pageants, parades, have an attraction to the natural heart, which often fails to perceive the unseen spiritual realities. (2) But the greatest attraction seems to have been in licentious revelries and obscene orgies with which the worship of the Oriental idols was observed. This worship, appealing to every sensual passion, joined with the attractions of wealth and fashion and luxury, naturally was a great temptation to a simple, restrained, agricultural people, whose worship and laws demanded the greatest purity of heart and of life.

Idume'a (ĭ-dụ-mē'ȧ). [EDOM.]

I'gal (ī'gal) (*God redeems*). 1. One of the spies, son of Joseph, of the tribe of Issachar. Num. 13:7. (B.C. 1490.)

2. One of the heroes of David's guard, son of Nathan of Zobah. 2 Sam. 23:36.

Igdali'ah (ĭg-da-lī'ah) (*great is Jehovah*), a prophet or holy man—"the man of God"—named once only, Jer. 35:4, as the father of Hanan.

I'geal (ī'ge-ăl), a son of Shemaiah, a descendant of the royal house of Judah. 1 Chron. 3:22. R. V. Igal.

I'im (ī'ĭm) (*ruins*). 1. The partial or contracted form of the name IJE-ABARIM. Num. 33:45.

2. A town in the extreme south of Judah. Josh. 15:29.

I'je=ab'arim (ī'je-ăb'a-rĭm), one of the later halting-places of the children of Israel. Num. 21:11; 33:44. It was on the boundary—the southeast boundary—of the territory of Moab; in the waste uncultivated "wilderness" on its skirts. ch. 21:11.

I'jon (ī'jon) (*a ruin*), a town in the north of Palestine, belonging to the tribe of Naphtali. It was taken and plundered by the captains of Ben-hadad, 1 Kings 15:20; 2 Chron. 16:4, and a second time by Tiglath-pileser. 2 Kings 15:29. Its probable site is a few miles northwest of the site of Dan, in a fertile and beautiful little plain called *Merj 'Ayûn.*

Ik'kesh (ĭk'kesh) (*perverse*), the father of Ira the Tekoite. 2 Sam. 23:26; 1 Chron. 11:28; 27:9.

I'lai (ī'lāi) (*supreme*), an Ahohite, one of the heroes of David's guard. 1 Chron. 11:29.

Illyr'icum (ĭl-lĭr'i-kŭm), an extensive district lying along the eastern coast of the Adriatic, from the boundary of Italy on the north to Epirus on the south, and contiguous to Mœsia and Macedonia on the east. Rom. 15:19.

Image. [IDOL.]

Im'la (ĭm'lȧ), father or progenitor of Micaiah the prophet. 2 Chron. 18:7, 8. The form IMLAH is employed in the parallel narrative. 1 Kings 22:8, 9.

Imman'uel (*God with us*), a child whose birth is prophesied in Isa. 7:14 as a sign from God. In its final fulfilment it has always been held to refer to the Messiah (Matt. 1:23), and the name is often applied to Christ in the

18

Bible, by early Christian writers and by modern writers to our own day.

Im'mer (*talkative*). 1. The founder of an important family of priests. 1 Chron. 9:12; Neh. 11:13. This family had charge of, and gave its name to, the sixteenth course of the service. 1 Chron. 24:14.

2. Apparently the name of a place in Babylonia. Ezra 2:59; Neh. 7:61.

Im'na (ĭm'nȧ) (*he [God] keeps back*), a descendant of Asher, son of Helem. 1 Chron. 7:35; comp. 40.

Im'nah (ĭm'nah) (*he allotteth*). 1. The first-born of Asher. 1 Chron. 7:30.

2. Kore ben-Imnah, the Levite, assisted in the reforms of Hezekiah. 2 Chron. 31:14.

Im'rah (ĭm'rah) (*stubborn*), a descendant of Asher, of the family of Zophah. 1 Chron. 7:36.

Im'ri (ĭm'rī) (*eloquent*). 1. A man of Judah, of the great family of Pharez. 1 Chron. 9:4.

2. Father or progenitor of Zaccur. Neh. 3:2.

Incense, from the Latin "to burn," "a mixture of gums or spices and the like, used for the purpose of producing a perfume when burned;" or the perfume itself of the spices, etc., burned in worship. The incense employed in the service of the tabernacle was compounded of the perfumes stacte, onycha, galbanum and pure frankincense. All incense which was not made of these ingredients was forbidden to be offered. Ex. 30:9. Aaron, as high priest, was originally appointed to offer incense each morning and evening. The times of offering incense were specified in the instructions first given to Moses. Ex. 30:7, 8. When the priest entered the holy place with the incense, all the people were removed from the temple, and from between the porch and the altar. Cf. Luke 1:10. Profound silence was observed among the congregation who were praying without, cf. Rev. 8:1, and at a signal from the prefect the priest cast the incense on the fire, and, bowing reverently toward the holy of holies, retired slowly backward. The offering of incense has formed a part of the religious ceremonies of most ancient nations. It was an element in the idolatrous worship of the Israelites. 2 Chron. 34:25; Jer. 11:12, 17; 48:35. It would seem to be symbolical, not of

ALTAR OF INCENSE.

prayer itself, but of that which makes prayer acceptable, the intercession of Christ. In Rev. 8:3, 4 the incense is spoken of as something distinct from, though offered with the prayers of, all the saints. In Rev. 5:8 it is the golden vials, and not the odors or incense, which are said to be the prayers of saints.

In'dia (ĭn'dĭ-à). The name of India does not occur in the Bible before the book of Esther, where it is noticed as the limit of the territories of Ahasuerus in the east, as Ethiopia was in the west. Esther 1:1; 8:9. The India of the book of Esther is not the peninsula of Hindostan, but the country surrounding the Indus, the *Punjâb* and perhaps *Scinde*. The people and productions of that country must have been tolerably well known to the Jews. An active trade was carried on between India and western Asia. The trade opened by Solomon with Ophir through the Red Sea consisted chiefly of Indian articles.

Inheritance. [HEIR.]

Ink, Inkhorn. [WRITING.]

Inn. The Hebrew word (*mâlôn*) thus rendered literally signifies "a lodging-place for the night." Inns, in our sense of the term, were, as they still are, unknown in the East, where hospitality is religiously practised. The khans or caravanserais are the representatives of European inns, and these were established but gradually. The halting-place of a caravan was selected originally on account of its proximity to water or pasture, by which the travelers pitched their tents and passed the night. Such was undoubtedly the "inn" at which occurred the incident in the life of Moses narrated in Ex. 4:24; comp. Gen. 42:27. On the more frequented routes, remote from towns, Jer. 9:2, caravanserais were in course of time erected, often at the expense of the wealthy. "A caravanserai is a large and substantial square building. . . . Passing through a strong gateway, the guest enters a large court, in the centre of which is a spacious raised platform, used for sleeping upon at night or for the devotions of the faithful during the day. Around this court are arranged the rooms of the building."

Inspiration. "That actuating energy of the Holy Spirit . . . guided by which the human agents chosen by God have *officially* proclaimed His will by word of mouth, or have committed to writing the several portions of the Bible." (Lee—quoted in Hastings' "Dictionary of Christ and the Gospels," 1906.) Without deciding on any of the various theories of inspiration, the general doctrine of Christians is that the Bible is so inspired by God that it is the infallible guide of men, and is perfectly trustworthy in all its parts, as given by God.

Instant, Instantly, in the Authorized Version, means urgent, urgently or fervently, as will be seen from the following passages: Luke 7:4; 23:23; Acts 26:7; Rom. 12:12.

Iphede'iah (ĭf-e-dē'iah) (*Jehovah redeems*), a descendant of Benjamin, one of the Bene-Shashak. 1 Chron. 8:25.

Ir (ĭr) (*city*). 1 Chron. 7:12. [IRI.]

I'ra (ī'rà) (*watchful of a city*). 1. "The Jairite," named in the catalogue of David's great officers. 2 Sam. 20:26.

2. One of the heroes of David's guard. 2 Sam. 23:38; 1 Chron. 11:40.

3. Another of David's guard, a Tekoite, son of Ikkesh. 2 Sam. 23:26; 1 Chron. 11:28.

I'rad (ī'răd) (*fugitive*), son of Enoch; grandson of Cain, and father of Mehujael. Gen. 4:18.

I'ram (ī'ram) (*belonging to a city*), a leader of the Edomites, Gen. 36:43; 1 Chron. 1:54, *i. e.* the chief of a family or tribe.

I'ri (ī'rī), or **Ir** (*belonging to a city*), a Benjamite, son of Bela. 1 Chron. 7:7, 12.

Iri'jah (ĭ-rī'jah) (*Jehovah seeth*), son of Shelemiah, a captain in the ward, who met Jeremiah in the gate of Jerusalem called the "gate of Benjamin," accused him of being about to desert to the Chaldeans, and led him back to the princes. Jer. 37:13, 14.

Ir=na'hash (ĭr-nā'hăsh) (*serpent city*), a name which, like many other names of places, occurs in the genealogical lists of Judah. 1 Chron. 4:12.

I'ron (*conspicuous*), a city of Naphtali, Josh. 19:38. Probably the modern *Yarun*.

Iron is mentioned with brass as the earliest of known metals. Gen. 4:22. The book of Job contains passages which indicate that iron was a metal well known. Sheet-iron was used for cooking utensils. Ezek. 4:3; cf. Lev. 7:9. That it was plentiful in the time of David appears from 1 Chron. 22:3.

The market of Tyre was supplied with bright or wrought iron by the merchants of Dan and Javan. Ezek. 27:19. The Chalybes of the Pontus were celebrated as workers in iron in very ancient times. The product of their labor is supposed to be alluded to in Jer. 15:12 as being of superior quality. Specimens of Assyrian iron-work overlaid with bronze were discovered by Mr. Layard, and are now in the British Museum. Iron weapons of various kinds were found at Nimroud, but fell to pieces on exposure to the air.

Ir'peel (ir'pe-el) (*God heals*), one of the cities of Benjamin. Josh. 18:27. Probably the ruin *Rafat,* near Gibeon.

Ir-she'mesh (ir-shē'mesh) (*city of the sun*), a city of the Danites, Josh. 19:41, probably identical with Beth-shemesh.

I'ru (ī'rụ), the eldest son of the great Caleb, son of Jephunneh. 1 Chron. 4:15.

I'saac (ī'sak) (*laughter*), the son whom Sarah bore to Abraham, in the hundredth year of his age, at Gerar. (B.C. 1896.) In his infancy he became the object of Ishmael's jealousy; and in his youth the victim, in intention, of Abraham's great sacrificial act of faith. When forty years old he married Rebekah his cousin, by whom, when he was sixty, he had two sons, Esau and Jacob. Driven by famine to Gerar, he acquired great wealth by his flocks, but was repeatedly dispossessed by the Philistines of the wells which he sunk at convenient stations. After the deceit by which Jacob acquired his father's blessing, Isaac sent his son to seek a wife in Padan-aram; and all that we know of him during the last forty-three years of his life is that he saw that son, with a large and prosperous family, return to him at Hebron, Gen. 35:27, before he died there, at the age of 180 years. He was buried by his two sons in the cave of Machpelah. In the New Testament reference is made to the offering of Isaac, Heb. 11:17; James 2:21, and to his blessing his sons. Heb. 11:20. In Gal. 4:28–31 he is contrasted with Ishmael. In reference to the offering up of Isaac by Abraham, the primary doctrines taught are those of sacrifice and substitution, as the means appointed by God for taking away sin; and, as co-ordinate with these, the need of the obedience of faith, on the part of man, to receive the benefit. Heb. 11:17. The animal which God provided and Abraham offered was in the whole history of sacrifice the recognized type of "the Lamb of God, that taketh away the sins of the world." Isaac is the type of humanity itself, devoted to death for sin.

Isa'iah (ī-sā'iah), the prophet, son of Amoz. The Hebrew name signifies *Jehovah is salvation* and is synonymous with Joshua (Jesus) and Hosea. He prophesied concerning Judah and Jerusalem in the days of Uzziah, Jotham, Ahaz and Hezekiah, kings of Judah, Isa. 1:1, covering at least from the last years of Uzziah to the first of Manasseh —772–697 or 741–686 B.C. It is thought that he belonged to the royal family.

He was the greatest of the prophets, a statesman as well as a prophet-preacher, a man of wisdom, of eloquence, of literary genius, with divinely inspired insight and vision. He was married and had two sons. Rabbinical tradition says that Isaiah, in his old age, was sawn asunder in the trunk of a carob tree by order of Manasseh, to which it is supposed that reference is made in Heb. 11:37.

Isaiah, The Book of. "It may be safely asserted that nowhere else in the literature of the world have so many colossally great ideas been brought together within the limits of a single work. . . . Even in literary form the world has produced nothing greater than Isaiah." *Prof. Moulton.*

The book falls into two great divisions, each of which has several subdivisions.

1. Chapters 1–39 are chiefly historical, interspersed with songs and poems. It contains the most definite and magnificent prophecies of the Messiah to come. A new interest would be given to the reading of Isaiah if its poetic portions had been printed in poetic forms.

2. Chapters 40–66 are a collection of poems, printed as poems in the Revised Versions. They are concerned chiefly with assurances of return from the Babylonian Exile, with the conditions which make that return possible, and then, with this return as the basis and symbol, with visions of the final triumph of the kingdom of God. The prophecies were partly fulfilled to the Jews of that time, but the complete fulfilment has been going on ever since, and will

be realized when the kingdom of God has come, and his will be done on earth as it is in heaven.

The prophecies in the time of the Exile inspired the Jews with hope and courage and faith and love to God.

This second part is thought by many modern scholars to have been written not by Isaiah, who died almost a hundred years before the Exile began, but by a prophet or prophets in the latter part of the Exile whose main purpose was to show how Isaiah's prophecies had been fulfilled and to carry them on to still loftier heights. Of these chapters, 40–48 are considered to be certainly the work of a single prophet, while the remainder, though by different hands, has been set in order of date and of thought by a single wise and sympathetic editor. The argument for this conclusion is based upon the references to Cyrus as already come, a successful warrior on his way to attack Babylon; and the local color, language, style, and theology of the chapters. Their whole atmosphere is that of the Exile. They do not claim to be Isaiah's. In the original Jewish canon, Isaiah was placed after Jeremiah and Ezekiel. Prof. George Adam Smith holds that the only evidence for the Isaian authorship of chapters 40–66 is tradition, supported by a mistaken interpretation of New Testament citations; but after asserting this conclusion he emphatically adds: "Do we find them any the less wonderful or divine? Do they comfort less? Do they speak with less power to the conscience? Do they testify with more uncertain voice to our Lord and Saviour? Interpreted in connection with the history out of which they themselves say that God's Spirit drew them, these twenty-seven chapters become only more prophetic of Christ, and more comforting and instructive to men, than they were before."

On the other hand, though this second portion of the book does not formally claim to be Isaiah's, it contains no hint that it was written by another. Unbroken tradition, for more than twenty centuries, regards Isaiah as the author of the whole. The Septuagint, B.C. 250, and writers as early as the second century, distinctly attribute these last chapters to Isaiah. Indeed, as Delitzsch says in the last edition of his commentary on Isaiah, it is inconceivable that there should be a prophet or prophets who wrote in their master's style, but surpassed him in brilliance of genius, and splendor of imagination, and completeness of inspiration, who should yet be wholly unknown to history, utterly forgotten, "although they lived nearer to the collector than did the old prophet whom they had taken as their model."

Note that, whichever view is taken, no one questions the inspiration of all parts of the book; and as to its prophetic character, all agree that the marvelous foretelling of the Messiah was written many centuries before he appeared.

Is'cah (ĭs'kah), daughter of Haran the brother of Abram, and sister of Milcah and of Lot. Gen. 11:29. In the Jewish traditions she is identified with Sarai, but it is not likely.

Iscar'iot (ĭs-kär'ĭ-ot) (*man of Kerioth*). [JUDAS ISCARIOT.]

Ish'bah (ĭsh'bah) (*praising*), a man in the line of Judah, commemorated as the "father of Eshtemoa." 1 Chron. 4:17.

Ish'bak (ĭsh'băk), a son of Abraham and Keturah, Gen. 25:2; 1 Chron. 1:32, and the progenitor of a tribe of northern Arabia.

Ish'bi-be'nob (ĭsh'bi-bē'nob) (*my dwelling place is on a height*), one of the race of Philistine giants, who attacked David in battle, but was slain by Abishai. 2 Sam. 21:16, 17.

Ish-bo'sheth (ĭsh-bō'sheth) (*man of shame*), the youngest of Saul's four sons, and his legitimate successor. (B.C. 1055.) After the death of Saul, five years were spent in uniting the people under him, and then he "reigned two years." 2 Sam. 2:10. During these two years he reigned at Mahanaim, though only in name. The wars and negotiations with David were entirely carried on by Abner. 2 Sam. 2:12; 3:6, 12. The death of Abner deprived the house of Saul of its last remaining support. When Ish-bosheth heard of it, "his hands were feeble, and all the Israelites were troubled." He was murdered in his bed.

Ish'i (ĭsh'ī) (*salutary*). 1. A man of the descendants of Judah, son of Appaim, 1 Chron. 2:31; one of the great house of Hezron.

2. In a subsequent genealogy of Judah we find another Ishi, with a son Zoheth, 1 Chron. 4:20.

3. Head of a family of the tribe of Simeon. 1 Chron. 4 : 42.

4. One of the heads of the tribe of Manasseh on the east of Jordan. 1 Chron. 5 : 24.

Ish'i (ĭsh'ī) (*my husband*). This word occurs in Hos. 2 : 16. It is the Israelite term, in opposition to Baali, a synonymous word, because the word Baal had become associated with idolatry.

Ishi'ah (ĭsh-ī'-ah) (*Jehovah lends*), the fifth of the five sons of Izrahiah; one of the heads of the tribe of Issachar. 1 Chron. 7 : 3. The same name as JESIAH and ISSHIAH. R. V. always Isshiah.

Ishi'jah (ĭ-shī'jah) (*Jehovah lends*), a lay Israelite of the Bene-Harim who had married a foreign wife. Ezra 10 : 31. (B.C. 458.)

Ish'ma (ĭsh'mȧ) (*desolation*), a name in the genealogy of Judah. 1 Chron. 4 : 3.

Ish'mael (ĭsh'ma-el) (*may God hear*). 1. The son of Abraham by Hagar the Egyptian, his concubine; born when Abraham was fourscore and six years old. Gen. 16 : 15, 16. (B.C. 1910.) Ishmael was the first-born of his father. He was born in Abraham's house when he dwelt in the plain of Mamre; and on the institution of the covenant of circumcision, was circumcised, he being then thirteen years old. Gen. 17 : 25. With the institution of the covenant, God renewed his promise respecting Ishmael. He does not again appear in the narrative until the weaning of Isaac. At the great feast made in celebration of the weaning, " Sarah saw the son of Hagar the Egyptian, which she had borne unto Abraham, mocking," and urged Abraham to cast him and his mother out. Comforted by the renewal of God's promise to make of Ishmael a great nation, Abraham sent them away, and they departed and wandered in the wilderness of Beersheba. His mother took Ishmael " a wife out of the land of Egypt." Gen. 21 : 9–21. This wife of Ishmael was the mother of his twelve sons and one daughter. Of the later life of Ishmael we know little. He was present with Isaac at the burial of Abraham. He died at the age of 137 years. Gen. 25 : 17, 18. The sons of Ishmael peopled the north and west of the Arabian peninsula, and supposedly formed the chief element of the Arab nation, the wandering Bedouin tribes. They are now mostly Mohammedans, who look to him as their spiritual father, as the Jews look to Abraham. Their language, which is generally acknowledged to have been the Arabic commonly so called, has been adopted with insignificant exceptions throughout Arabia. The term " Ishmaelite " occurs on three occasions : Gen. 37 : 25, 27, 28 ; 39 : 1 ; Judges 8 : 24 ; Ps 83 · 6.

2. One of the sons of Azel, a descendant of Saul through Meribbaal or Mephibosheth. 1 Chron. 8 : 38 ; 9 : 44.

3. A man of Judah, father of Zebadiah. 2 Chron. 19 : 11.

4. Another man of Judah, son of Jehohanan; one of the captains of hundreds who assisted Jehoiada in restoring Joash to the throne. 2 Chron. 23 : 1.

5. A priest of the Bene-Pashur, who was forced by Ezra to relinquish his foreign wife. Ezra 10 : 22.

6. The son of Nethaniah; a member of the royal house of David, whose treachery forms one of the chief episodes of the history of the period immediately succeeding the first fall of Jerusalem. His exploits are related in Jer. 40 : 7–41 : 15 ; and 1 Kings 25 : 23–25. During the siege of the city he had fled across the Jordan, where he found a refuge at the court of Baalis. After the departure of the Chaldeans, Ishmael made no secret of his intention to kill the superintendent left by the king of Babylon and usurp his position. Of this Gedaliah was warned in express terms by Johanan and his companions, but notwithstanding entertained Ishmael and his followers at a feast, Jer. 41 : 1, during which Ishmael murdered Gedaliah and all his attendants. The same night he killed all Gedaliah's establishment, including some Chaldean soldiers who were there. For two days the massacre remained entirely unknown to the people of the town. On the second day eighty devotees were bringing incense and offerings to the ruins of the temple. At his invitation they turned aside to the residence of the superintendent, and there Ishmael and his band butchered nearly the whole number : ten only escaped by offering a heavy ransom for their lives. This done he descended to the town, surprised and carried off the daughters of King Zedekiah, who had been sent there by Nebuchadnezzar for safety, with their eunuchs and their

Chaldean guard, Jer. 41:10, 16, and all the people of the town, and made off with his prisoners to the country of the Ammonites. The news of the massacre had by this time got abroad, and Ishmael was quickly pursued by Johanan and his companions. He was attacked, two of his bravos slain, the whole of the prey recovered; and Ishmael himself, with the remaining eight of his people, escaped to the Ammonites.

Ish'maelite (ĭsh'ma-el-īte) (*descendant of Ishmael*). [ISHMAEL.]

Ishma'iah (ĭsh-ma'iah) (*Jehovah hears*), son of Obadiah; the ruler of the tribe of Zebulun in the time of King David. 1 Chron. 27:19.

Ish'me=elite (ĭs'/me-el-īte), 1 Chron. 2:17, and **Ish'me=elites** (*descendants of Ishmael*), Gen. 37:25, 27, 28; 39:1, the form in which the descendants of Ishmael are given in a few places in the Authorized Version.

Ish'merai (ĭsh'me-rāi) (*Jehovah keeps*), a Benjamite, one of the family of Elpaal. 1 Chron. 8:18.

I'shod (ĭ'shŏd) (*man of majesty*), one of the tribe of Manasseh on the east of Jordan, son of Hammoleketh. 1 Chron. 7:18.

Ish'pan (ĭsh'păn), a Benjamite, one of the family of Shashak. 1 Chron. 8:22.

Ish'=tob (ĭsh'tŏb). R. V. translates— "men of Tob." 2 Sam. 10:6, 8. See TOB.

Ish'uah (ĭsh'u-ah) (*resembling*), second son of Asher. Gen. 46:17.

Ish'uai (ĭsh'u-āi) (*resembling*), the third son of Asher. 1 Chron. 7:30. Called ISUI in Gen. 46:17.

Ish'ui (ĭsh'u-ī) (*resembling*), second son of Saul by his wife Ahinoam. 1 Sam. 14:49, comp. 50. (Died B.C. 1055.)

Isle. The radical sense of the Hebrew word seems to be "habitable places," as opposed to water, and in this sense it occurs in Isa. 42:15. Hence it means secondarily any maritime district, whether belonging to a continent or to an island: thus it is used of the shore of the Mediterranean, Isa. 20:6; 23:2, 6, and of the coasts of Elishah, Ezek. 27:7, *i. e.* of Greece and Asia Minor.

Ismachi'ah (ĭs-ma-kī'ah) (*Jehovah supports*), a Levite who was one of the overseers of offerings during the revival under King Hezekiah. 2 Chron. 31:13.

Isma'iah (ĭs-ma'īah) (*Jehovah hears*), a Gibeonite, one of the chiefs

of those warriors who joined David at Ziklag. 1 Chron. 12:4.

Is'pah (ĭs'pah) (*bald*), a Benjamite of the family of Beriah; one of the heads of his tribe. 1 Chron. 8:16.

Is'rael (ĭs'ra-el). 1. The name given, Gen. 32:28, to Jacob after his wrestling

A MONUMENT OF MERENPTAH
"The Pharaoh of the Exodus," with a reference to Israel, the first mention of the name and the people in extra-Biblical sources.

with the angel, Hos. 12:4, at Peniel. The meaning of the name has been a subject of much discussion. It may mean "Perseverer th God." Gesenius interprets Israel "soldier of God."

2. It became the national name of the twelve tribes collectively. They are so called in Ex. 3:16 and afterward.

3. It is used in a narrower sense, ex-

cluding Judah, in 1 Sam. 11:8; 2 Sam. 20:1; 1 Kings 12:16. Thenceforth it was assumed and accepted as the name of the northern kingdom.

4. After the Babylonian captivity, the returned exiles resumed the name Israel as the designation of their nation. The name Israel is also used to denote laymen, as distinguished from priests, Levites and other ministers. Ezra 6:16; 9:1; 10:25; Neh. 11:3, etc.

Is'rael, Kingdom of. I. *The kingdom.*—The prophet Ahijah of Shiloh, who was commissioned in the latter days of Solomon to announce the division of the kingdom, left one tribe (Judah) to the house of David, and assigned ten to Jeroboam. 1 Kings 11:31, 35. These were probably Joseph (= Ephraim and Manasseh), Issachar, Zebulun, Asher, Naphtali, Benjamin, Dan, Simeon, Gad and Reuben; Levi being intentionally omitted. Eventually the greater part of Benjamin, and probably the whole of Simeon and Dan, were included as if by common consent in the kingdom of Judah. With respect to the conquests of David, Moab appears to have been attached to the kingdom of Israel, 2 Kings 3.4; so much of Syria as remained subject to Solomon, see 1 Kings 11:24, would probably be claimed by his successor in the northern kingdom; and Ammon was at one time allied, 2 Chron. 20:1, we know not how closely or how early, with Moab. The seacoast between Accho and Japho remained in the possession of Israel. The whole population may perhaps have amounted to at least three and a half millions.

II. *The capitals.*—Shechem was the first capital of the new kingdom. 1

REPRESENTATION OF ISRAELITES on the Black Obelisk of Shalmaneser II. (See "Jehu," p. 296 and cut p. 608.)

Kings 12:25. Subsequently Tirzah became the royal residence, if not the capital, of Jeroboam, 1 Kings 14:17,

and of his successors, ch. 15:33; 16:8, 17, 23. Samaria was chosen by Omri. 1 Kings 16:24. Jezreel was probably only a royal residence of some of the Israelitish kings.

III. *History.*—The kingdom of Israel lasted 216 years, from B.C. 937 to B.C. 721. The detailed history of the kingdom will be found under the names of its nineteen kings. See chart of the kings of Judah and Israel, at the end of the work. A summary view may be taken in four periods: (*a*) B.C. 937–885. Jeroboam had not sufficient force of character in himself to make a lasting impression on his people. A king, but not a founder of a dynasty, he aimed at nothing beyond securing his present elevation. Baasha, in the midst of the army at Gibbethon, slew the son and successor of Jeroboam; Zimri, a captain of chariots, slew the son and successor of Baasha; Omri, the captain of the host, was chosen to punish Zimri; and after a civil war of four years he prevailed over Tibni, the choice of half the people. (*b*) B.C. 885–842. For forty-five years Israel was governed by the house of Omri. The princes of his house cultivated an alliance with the kings of Judah, which was cemented by the marriage of Jehoram and Athaliah. The adoption of Baal-worship led to a reaction in the nation, to the moral triumph of the prophets in the person of Elijah, and to the extinction of the house of Ahab in obedience to the bidding of Elisha. (*c*) 842–741. Unparalleled triumphs, but deeper humiliation, awaited the kingdom of Israel under the dynasty of Jehu. Hazael, the ablest king of Damascus, reduced Jehoahaz to the condition of a vassal, and triumphed for a time over both the disunited Hebrew kingdoms. Almost the first sign of the restoration of their strength was a war between them; and Jehoash, the grandson of Jehu, entered Jerusalem as the conqueror of Amaziah. Jehoash also turned the tide of war against the Syrians; and Jeroboam II., the most powerful of all the kings of Israel, captured Damascus, and recovered the whole ancient frontier from Hamath to the Dead Sea. This short-lived greatness expired with the last king of Jehu's line. (*d*) B.C. 741–721. Military violence, it would seem, broke off the hereditary succession after the obscure and probably convulsed reign of Zachariah.

An unsuccessful usurper, Shallum, is followed by the cruel Menahem, who, being unable to make head against the first attack of Assyria under Pul, became the agent of that monarch for the oppressive taxation of his subjects. Yet his power at home was sufficient to insure for his son and successor Pekahiah a ten-years reign, cut short by a bold usurper, Pekah. Abandoning the northern and transjordanic regions to the encroaching power of Assyria under Tiglath-pileser, he was very near subjugating Judah, with the help of Damascus, now the coequal ally of Israel. But Assyria interposing summarily put an end to the independence of Damascus, and perhaps was the indirect cause of the assassination of the baffled Pekah. The irresolute Hoshea, the next and last usurper, became tributary to his invader, Shalmaneser, betrayed the Assyrian to the rival monarchy of Egypt, and was punished by the loss of his liberty, and by the capture, after a three-years siege, of his strong capital, Samaria. Some gleanings of the ten tribes yet remained in the land after so many years of religious decline, moral debasement, national degradation, anarchy, bloodshed and deportation. Even these were gathered up by the conqueror and carried to Assyria, never again, as a distinct people, to occupy their portion of that goodly and pleasant land which their forefathers won under Joshua from the heathen. No doubt many of the kingdom of Israel joined the later kingdom of the Jews after the captivity, and became part of that kingdom. As the name "Israel," or "children of Israel" had been used before the division of the kingdom for the whole race, so after the destruction of the northern kingdom it was again used for the surviving portion of the descendants of Jacob, without distinction of tribe. It is so used by Paul. Rom. 10:1; 11:1; 2 Cor. 11: 22, etc., and also many times in the Gospels.

Is′raelite (*descendant of Israel*). In 2 Sam. 17:25, Ithra, the father of Amasa, is called "an Israelite," while in 1 Chron. 2:17 he appears as "Jether the Ishmaelite." The latter is undoubtedly the true reading.

Is′sachar (*there is a reward*). 1. The ninth son of Jacob and the fifth of Leah. Gen. 30:17, 18. At the descent into Egypt four sons are ascribed to him, who founded the four chief families of the tribe. Gen. 46:13; Num. 26:23, 25; 1 Chron. 7:1. The number of the fighting men of Issachar, when taken in the census at Sinai, was 54,400. During the journey they seem to have steadily increased. The allotment of Issachar lay above that of Manasseh. Josh. 19:17-23. In the words of Josephus, "it extended in length from Carmel to the Jordan, in breadth to Mount Tabor." This territory was, as it still is, among the richest land in Palestine. It is this aspect of the territory of Issachar which appears to be alluded to in the blessing of Jacob.

2. A Korhite Levite, one of the doorkeepers of the house of Jehovah, seventh son of Obed-edom. 1 Chron. 26:5.

Isshi′ah (ĭs-shī′ah) (*Jehovah lends*). 1. A descendant of Moses by his younger son Eliezer. 1 Chron. 24:21; comp. 23:17; 26:25.

2. A Levite of the house of Kohath and family of Uzziel. 1 Chron. 24:25.

Issue, Running. Lev. 15:2, 3; 22: 4; Num. 5:2; 2 Sam. 3:29. In Lev. 15:3 a distinction is introduced, which merely means that the cessation of the actual flux does not constitute ceremonial cleanness, but that the patient must bide the legal time, seven days, ver. 13, and perform the prescribed purifications and sacrifice, ver. 14.

Is′uah (ĭs′uah), second son of Asher. 1 Chron. 7:30. [ISHUAH.]

Is′ui (ĭs′u-ī), third son of Asher, Gen. 46:17, founder of a family called after him, though in the Authorized Version appearing as the JESHUITES. Num. 26: 44.

Ital′ian band. [ARMY.]

It′aly. This word is used in the New Testament, Acts 18:2; 27:1; Heb. 13: 24, in the usual sense of the period, *i. e.* in its true geographical sense, as denoting the whole natural peninsula between the Alps and the Straits of Messina.

I′thai (ī′thā-ī), a Benjamite, son of Ribai of Gibeah, one of the heroes of David's guard. 1 Chron. 11:31. [ITTAI.]

Ith′amar (ĭth′a-mär) (*is land of palms*), the youngest son of Aaron. Ex. 6:23. After the death of Nadab and Abihu, Lev. 10:1, Eleazar and Ithamar were appointed to succeed to their places in the priestly office. Ex. 28:1, 40-43; Num. 3:3, 4; 1 Chron.

24:2. In the distribution of services belonging to the tabernacle, and its transport on the march of the Israelites, the Gershonites and the Merarites were placed under the superintendence of Ithamar. Ex. 38:21; Num. 4:21-33. The high priesthood passed into the family of Ithamar in the person of Eli, but for what reason we are not informed.

Ith'iel (ĭth'i-el) (*God is with me*). 1. A Benjamite, son of Jesaiah. Neh. 11:7.

2. One of two persons—Ithiel and Ucal—to whom Agur ben-Jakeh delivered his discourse. Prov. 30:1.

Ith'mah (ĭth'măh) (*bereavement*), a Moabite, one of the heroes of David's guard. 1 Chron. 11:46.

Ith'nan (ĭth'nan) (*perennial*), one of the towns in the extreme south of Judah. Josh. 15:23. Its site is uncertain.

Ith'ra (ĭth'rà) (*abundance*), an Israelite, 2 Sam. 17:25, or Ishmaelite, 1 Chron. 2:17, the father of Amasa by Abigail, David's sister. Jether 3.

Ith'ran (ĭth'ran). 1. A son of Dishon, a Horite, Gen. 36:26; 1 Chron. 1:41, and probably a chief of a tribe of the Horim. Gen. 36:30. (B.C. about 1800.)

2. A descendant of Asher. 1 Chron. 7:30-40.

Ith'ream (ĭth're-am) (*abundance of people*), son of David, born to him in Hebron, and distinctly specified as the sixth, and as the child of Eglah, David's wife. 2 Sam. 3:5; 1 Chron. 3:3.

Ith'rite (ĭth'rīte), **The**, the designation of two of the members of David's guard, Ira and Gareb. 2 Sam. 23:38; 1 Chron. 11:40. They may have come from Jattir, in the mountains of Judah.

It'tah=ka'zin (ĭt'tah-kā'zin), one of the landmarks of the boundary of Zebulun. Josh. 19:13. It has not been identified.

It'tai (ĭt'ta-ī) (*companionable*). 1. "Ittai the Gittite," *i. e.* the native of Gath, a Philistine in the army of King David. He appears only during the revolution of Absalom. (B.C. 1023.) We first discern him on the morning of David's flight. The king urges him to return with the 600 men of his command. 2 Sam. 15:18, 19. But Ittai is firm; he is the king's slave, and wherever his master goes he will go. Accordingly he is allowed by David to proceed. When the army was num-

bered and organized by David at Mahanaim, Ittai again appears, now in command of a third part of the force. 2 Sam. 18:2, 5, 12.

2. Son of Ribai, from Gibeah of Benjamin; one of the thirty heroes of David's guard. 2 Sam. 23:29. Same as ITHAI.

Ituræ'a (ĭ-tu-rē'à) (*land of Jetur*), a small province on the northwestern border of Palestine, only mentioned in Luke 3:1. Jetur the son of Ishmael gave his name, like the rest of his brethren, to the little province he colonized. Gen. 25:15, 16. It adjoined or overlapped Trachonitis, and lay along the base of Lebanon. The territory occupied by the Itureans, was changed continually during their history, and the exact limits of the region intended are uncertain.

I'vah (ī'vah), or **A'va,** which is mentioned in Scripture twice, 2 Kings 18:34; 19:13; comp. Isa. 37:13, in connection with Hena and Sepharvaim, and once, 2 Kings 17:24, in connection with Babylon and Cuthah, was one of the cities conquered by the Assyrians. Its situation is unknown.

Ivory. The word translated "ivory" literally signifies the "tooth" of any animal, and hence more especially denotes the substance of the projecting tusks of elephants. The skilled workmen of Hiram, king of Tyre, fashioned the great ivory throne of Solomon, and overlaid it with pure gold. 1 Kings 10:18; 2 Chron. 9:17. The ivory thus employed was supplied by the caravans of Dedan, Isa. 21:13; Ezek. 27:15, or was brought, with apes and peacocks, by the navy of Tarshish. 1 Kings 10:22. The "ivory house" of Ahab, 1 Kings 22:39, was probably a palace, the walls of which were panelled with ivory, like the palace of Menelaus, described by Homer. *Odys.* iv. 73. Beds inlaid or veneered with ivory were in use among the Hebrews. Amos 6:4.

Iz'ehar, Num. 3:19. [IZHAR.]

Iz'eharites. A family of Kohathite Levites descended from Izhar, the son of Kohath. Num. 3:27. [IZHARITES.]

Iz'har (ĭz'här) (*fresh oil* or *shining*), son of Kohath, the son of Levi and ancestor of Korah. Ex. 6:18, 21; Num. 3:19; 16:1; 1 Chron. 6:2, 18. He was the founder of the family of the Izharites.

Iz'harites (ĭz'här-ītes). The descendants of Izhar. 1 Chron. 24:22; 26:23. This is more correct than the other spelling Izeharites.

Izrahi'ah (ĭz-ra-hī'ah) (*Jehovah will arise* or *shine*), a chieftain of Issachar. 1 Chron. 7:3.

Iz'rahite (ĭz'rāh-īte), The, the desig nation of Shamhuth. 1 Chron. 27:8. Its real force is probably Zerahite, that is, from the great Judaic family of Zerah.

Iz'ri (ĭz'rī), a Levite leader of the fourth course or ward in the service of the house of God. 1 Chron. 25:11. In ver. 3 he is called ZERI.

J

Ja′akan (jā′a-kan), the same as Jakan, the forefather of Bene-Jaakan. Deut. 10 : 6.

Jaako′bah (jȧ-ăk-o′bah) (*supplanting*), one of the princes of the families of Simeon. 1 Chron. 4 : 36.

Ja′ala (jȧ′ā-lȧ) (*wild she-goat*). Bene-Jaala were among the descendants of "Solomon's servants" who returned from Babylon with Zerubbabel. Neh. 7 : 58. The name also occurs as **Ja′alah** (jȧ′ā-lah). Ezra 2 : 56.

Ja′alam (jȧ′ā-lam), a son of Esau, Gen. 36 : 5, 14, 18; comp. 1 Chron. 1 : 35, and a head of a tribe of Edom.

Ja′anai (jȧ′ā-nai) (*Jehovah answers*), a chief man in the tribe of Gad. 1 Chron. 5 : 12.

Ja′are-or′egim (jȧ′är-e-ŏr′e-ğĭm) (*forests of the weavers*), 2 Sam. 21 : 19, a Bethlehemite, and the father of Elhanan who slew Goliath (not the man connected with David, but another of the same name). In the parallel passage, 1 Chron. 20 : 5, Jair is found instead of Jaare, and -oregim is omitted, having crept into the text from the line below.

Ja′asau (jā′a-sạu) (*Jehovah maketh*), one of the Bene-Bani who had married a foreign wife. Ezra 10 : 37. (B.C. 458.)

Jaa′siel (jȧ-a′sĭ-el) (*God maketh*), 1. Son of Abner. 1 Chron. 27 : 21.

2. One of David's mighty men. 1 Chron. 11 : 17.

Jaazani′ah (jȧ-ăz-a-nī′ah) (*Jehovah hears*). 1. One of the captains of the forces who accompanied Johanan ben-Kareah to pay his respects to Gedaliah at Mizpah, 2 Kings 25 : 23, and who appears afterwards to have assisted in recovering Ishmael's prey from his clutches. Comp. Jer. 41 : 11; 42 : 1; 43 : 2, 4, 5. Also called AZARIAH and JEZANIAH.

2. Son of Shaphan. Ezek. 8 : 11. One of the leaders in idolatry.

3. Son of Azur: one of the princes of the people against whom Ezekiel was directed to prophesy. Ezek. 11 : 1.

4. A Rechabite, son of a Jeremiah, not the prophet. Jer. 35 : 3.

Jaa′zer (jȧ-ā′zēr), or **Ja′zer** (*helpful*), a town on the east of Jordan, in or near to Gilead. Num. 32 : 1, 3; 1 Chron. 26 : 31. We first hear of it in possession of the Amorites, and as taken by Israel after Heshbon, and on their way from thence to Bashan. Num. 21 : 32. It seems to have given its name to a district of dependent or "daughter" towns, the "land of Jazer." Num. 32 : 1. The town is now called *Khurbet Sar*.

Jaazi′ah (jȧ-a-zī′ah) (*Jehovah comforts*), apparently a third son, or a descendant, of Merari the Levite. 1 Chron. 24 : 26, 27.

Jaa′ziel (jȧ-ā′zĭ-el) (*God consoleth*), one of the Levites appointed by David to perform the musical service before the ark. 1 Chron. 15 : 18. (B.C. 1042.)

Ja′bal (jā′bal) (*stream*), the son of Lamech and Adah, Gen. 4 : 20, and brother of Jubal. He is described as the father of such as dwell in tents and have cattle.

Jab′bok (jăb′bŏk) (*emptying*), a streaɯ which intersects the mountain range of Gilead, comp. Josh. 12 : 2, 5, and falls into the Jordan on the east about 25 miles north of the Dead Sea. It was anciently the border of the children of Ammon. Num. 21 : 24; Deut. 2 : 37; 3 : 16. It was on the south bank of the Jabbok that the interview took place between Jacob and Esau, Gen. 32 : 22; and this river afterward became, toward its western part, the boundary between the kingdoms of Sihon and Og. Josh. 12 : 2, 5. Its modern name is *Wady Zerka*.

Ja′besh (jā′besh) (*dry*). Father of Shallum, the fifteenth king of Israel. 2 Kings 15 : 10, 13, 14.

Jabesh-gilead, or Jabesh in the territory of Gilead, the territory east of the Jordan and north of Bashan, including Gad and the half tribe of Manasseh. Jabesh was in northern Gilead, in Manasseh, and was one of the chief cities of the region. It is first mentioned in Judges 21 : 8–14. Being attacked subsequently by Nahash the Ammonite, it gave Saul an opportunity of displaying his prowess in its defence. 1 Sam. 11 : 1–15. See 1 Sam. 31 : 11–13; 1 Chron. 10 : 11, 12. It was beyond the Jordan, six miles from Pella on the mountain road to Gerasa; where its name is doubtless preserved in the *Wady Yabis.*

Ja'bez (jā'bĕz) (*he makes sorrow*). **1.** Apparently a place at which the families of the scribes resided who belonged to the Kenites. 1 Chron. 2 : 55.

2. The name occurs again in the genealogies of Judah, 1 Chron. 4 : 9, 10, in a passage of remarkable detail inserted in a genealogy connected with Bethlehem, ver. 4.

Ja'bin (jā'bin) (*discerning*). **1.** King of Hazor, who organized a confederacy of the northern princes against the Israelites. Josh. 11 : 1–3. Joshua surprised the allied forces by the waters of Merom, ver. 7, and utterly routed them. During the ensuing wars Joshua again attacked Jabin, and burnt his city. Josh. 11 : 11–14.

2. A king of Hazor, whose general, Sisera, was defeated by Barak. Judges 4 : 2, 13, 24.

Jab'neel (jăb'ne-el) (*God causeth to build*). **1.** One of the points on the northern boundary of Judah, not quite at the sea, though near it. Josh. 15 : 11. There is no sign, however, of its ever having been occupied by Judah. Josephus attributes it to the Danites. There was a constant struggle going on between that tribe and the Philistines for the possession of all the places in the lowland plains, and it is not surprising that the next time we meet with Jabneel it should be in the hands of the latter. 2 Chron. 26 : 6. Uzziah dispossessed them of it and demolished its fortifications. Called also JABNEH. At the time of the fall of Jerusalem, A.D. 70, Jabneh was one of the most populous places of Judea. The modern village of *Yebna* stands about two miles from the sea, on a slight eminence just south of the *Nahr Rubin.*

2. One of the landmarks on the boundary of Naphtali, Josh. 19 : 33, in upper Galilee.

Jab'neh (jăb'neh). 2 Chron. 26 : 6. [JABNEEL.]

Ja'chan (jā'kan) (*troublous*), one of seven chief men of the tribe of Gad. 1 Chron. 5 : 13.

Ja'chin (jā'kin) (*he doth establish*). **1.** One of the two pillars which were set up "in the porch," 1 Kings 7 : 21, or before the temple, 2 Chron. 3 : 17, of Solomon. [BOAZ.]

2. Fourth son of Simeon, Gen. 46 : 10; Ex. 6 : 15; founder of the family of the Jachinites. Num. 26 : 12.

3. Head of the twenty-first course of priests in the time of David. 1 Chron. 9 : 10; 24 : 17; Neh. 11 : 10.

Jacinth, a precious stone, forming one of the foundations of the walls of the new Jerusalem. Rev. 21 : 20. Called *hyacinth* in the Revised Version. This is simply a different English rendering of the same Greek original. It is probably identical with the *ligure* of Ex. 28 : 19. The jacinth or hyacinth is a red variety of zircon, which is found in square prisms of a white, gray, red, reddish-brown, yellow or pale-green color. The expression in Rev. 9 : 17, "of jacinth," is descriptive simply of a dark-purple color. R. V. here gives "sapphire."

Ja'cob (*supplanter*), the second son of Isaac and Rebekah. He was born with Esau, probably at the well of Lahai-roi, about B.C. 1837. His history is related in the latter half of the book of Genesis. He bought the birthright from his brother Esau, and afterward acquired the blessing intended for Esau, by practising a well-known deceit on Isaac. Jacob did not obtain the blessing because of his deceit, but in spite of it. That which was promised he would have received in some good way; but Jacob and his mother, distrusting God's promise, sought the promised blessing in a wrong way, and received with it trouble and sorrow. Jacob, in his 78th year, was sent from the family home to avoid his brother, and to seek a wife among his kindred in Padan-aram. As he passed through Bethel, God appeared to him. After the lapse of twenty-one years he returned from Padan-aram with two wives, two concubines, eleven sons and a daughter, and large property. He escaped from the angry pursuit of Laban, from a meeting with Esau, and from the vengeance of the Canaanites provoked by the murder of Shechem;

and in each of these three emergencies he was aided and strengthened by the interposition of God, and in sign of the grace won by a night of wrestling with God his name was changed at Jabbok into Israel. Deborah and Rachel died before he reached Hebron; Joseph, the favorite son of Jacob, was sold into Egypt eleven years before the death of Isaac; and Jacob had probably exceeded his 130th year when he went thither. He was presented to Pharaoh, and dwelt for seventeen years in Rameses and Goshen, and died in his 147th year. His body was embalmed, carried with great care and pomp into the land of Canaan, and deposited with his fathers, and his wife Leah, in the cave of Mach-pelah.

The example of Jacob is quoted by the first and the last of the minor prophets. Hos. 12 : 4; Mal. 1 : 2. Besides the frequent mention of his name with those of the other two patriarchs, there are distinct references to the events in the life of Jacob in four books of the New Testament—John 1 : 51; 4 : 5, 12; Acts 7 : 12, 16; Rom. 9 : 11–13; Heb. 11 : 21; 12 : 16.

Ja'cob's Well, a deep spring in the vicinity of Sychar, which was either the same as Shechem, or a place near it. It was probably dug by Jacob, whose name it bears. On the curb of the well Jesus sat and discoursed with the Samaritan woman. John 4 : 5–26. It is situated about 2 miles east-southeast of Nablûs, the modern Shechem, at the foot of Mount Gerizim. It is about nine feet in diameter and 100 feet deep. At some seasons it is dry; at others it contains a few feet of water.

Ja'da (jā'dà) (*wise*), son of Onam and brother of Shammai, in the genealogy of the sons of Jerahmeel by his wife Atarah. 1 Chron. 2 : 28, 32.

Jada'u (jā-dā'ū), one of the Bene-Nebo who had taken a foreign wife. Ezra 10 : 43. (B.C. 458.) R. V. Iddo.

Jaddu'a (jăd-dū'à) (*known*). 1. Son and successor in the high priesthood of Jonathan or Johanan. He is the last of the high priests mentioned in the Old Testament, and probably altogether the latest name in the canon. Neh. 12 : 11, 22. Prof. Kent gives his date as from about 350 to the conquest of Palestine by Alexander in 331.

2. One of the chief of the people who sealed the covenant with Nehemiah. Neh. 10 : 21.

Ja'don (jā'dòn) (*he judgeth*), the Meronothite, who assisted to repair the wall of Jerusalem. Neh. 3 : 7. (B.C. 446.)

Ja'el (jā'ĕl) (*mountain goat*), the wife of Heber the Kenite. In the headlong rout which followed the defeat of the Canaanites by Barak, at Megiddo on the plain of Esdraelon, Sisera, their general, fled to the tent of the Kenite chieftainess, at Kedesh in Naphtali, four miles northwest of Lake Merom. He accepted Jael's invitation to enter, and she flung a mantle over him as he lay wearily on the floor. When thirst prevented sleep, and he asked for water, she brought him buttermilk in her choicest vessel. At last, with a feeling of perfect security, he fell into a deep sleep. Then it was that Jael took one of the great wooden pins which fastened down the cords of the tent, and with one terrible blow with a mallet dashed it through Sisera's temples deep into the earth. Judges 4 : 17–22; 5 : 24–27. She then met the pursuing Barak, and led him into her tent that she might in his presence claim the glory of the deed! Many have supposed that by this act she fulfilled the saying of Deborah, Judges 4 : 9; and hence they have supposed that Jael was actuated by some divine and hidden influence. But the Bible gives no hint of such an inspiration.

Ja'gur (jā'gŭr) (*lodging*), a town of Judah, one of those farthest to the south, on the frontier of Edom. Josh 15 : 21.

Jah (jäh) (*Jehovah*), the abbreviated form of Jehovah, used only in poetry. It occurs frequently in the Hebrew, but with a single exception, Ps. 68 : 4, is rendered "LORD" in the Authorized Version. The identity of Jah and Jehovah is strongly marked in two passages of Isaiah 12 : 2; 26 : 4. [JEHOVAH.]

Ja'hath (jā'hăth) (*grasping*). 1. Son of Libni, the son of Gershom, the son of Levi. 1 Chron. 6 : 20.

2. Head of a later house in the family of Gershom, being the eldest son of Shimei, the son of Laadan. 1 Chron. 23 : 10, 11.

3. A man in the genealogy of Judah, 1 Chron. 4 : 2, son of Reaiah ben-Shobal.

4. A Levite, son of Shelomoth. 1 Chron. 24 : 22.

5. A Merarite Levite in the reign of Josiah. 2 Chron. 34 : 12. (B.C. 623.)

Ja'haz (jā'hăz), also **Jaha'za, Jaha'zah** and **Jah'zah** (jäh'zah) (*trodden down*). Under these four forms is given in the Authorized Version the name of a place which in the Hebrew appears as *Yahatsah* and *Yahtsah*. At Jahaz the decisive battle was fought between the children of Israel and Sihon king of the Amorites. Num. 21 : 23; Deut. 2 : 32; Judges 11 : 20. It was in the allotment of Reuben. Josh. 13 : 18; 21 : 36, and was given to the Levites.

Jaha'zah (jā-hă'zà). Josh. 21 : 36; Jer. 48 : 21. [JAHAZ.]

Jahazi'ah (jà-ha-zī'ah) (*Jehovah sees*), son of Tikvah, apparently a priest. Ezra 10 : 15. R. V. Jahzeiah.

Jaha'ziel (jà-hà'zĭ-el) (*God sees*). 1. One of the heroes of Benjamin who joined David at Ziklag. 1 Chron. 12 : 4. (B.C. 1057.)

2. A priest in the reign of David. 1 Chron. 16 : 6.

3. A Kohathite Levite, third son of Hebron. 1 Chron. 23 : 19; 24 : 23.

4. Son of Zechariah, a Levite of the Bene-Asaph in the reign of Jehoshaphat. 2 Chron. 20 : 14. (B.C. 896.)

5. The "son of Jahaziel" was the chief of the Bene-Shecaniah who returned from Babylon with Ezra. Ezra 8 : 5.

Jah'dai (jäh'da-ĭ), a man who appears to be thrust abruptly into the genealogy of Caleb, as the father of six sons. 1 Chron. 2 : 47.

Jah'diel (jäh'dĭ-el) (*God giveth joy*), a chieftain of Manasseh on the east of Jordan. 1 Chron. 5 : 24.

Jah'do (jäh'dō) (*union*), a Gadite, 1 Chron. 5 : 14, son of Buz and father of Jeshishai.

Jah'leel (jäh'lĕ-el) (*wait for God*), the third of the three sons of Zebulun, Gen. 46 : 14; Num. 26 : 26; founder of the family of Jahleelites.

Jah'mai (jäh'ma-ī) (*may Jehovah protect*), a man of Issachar, one of the heads of the house of Tolah. 1 Chron. 7 : 2.

Jah'zah (jäh'zah). 1 Chron. 6 : 78. [JAHAZ.]

Jah'zeel (jäh'ze-el) (*God divides*), the first of the four sons of Naphtali, Gen. 46 : 24; founder of the family of the Jahzeelites. Num. 26 : 48.

Jah'zerah (iäh'ze-rah) (*may he lead back*), a priest of the house of Immer. 1 Chron. 9 : 12.

Jah'ziel (jäh'zĭ-el), the same as JAHZEEL. 1 Chron. 7 : 13.

Ja'ir (jä'ir) (*enlightener*). 1. A man who on his father's side was descended from Judah, and on his mother's from Manasseh. During the conquest he took the whole of the tract of Argob, Deut. 3 : 14, and in addition possessed himself of some nomad villages in Gilead, which he called after his own name Havoth-jair. Num. 32 : 41; 1 Chron. 2 : 22, 23.

2. Jair, the Gileadite, who judged Israel for two-and-twenty years. Judges 10 : 3–5. He had thirty sons, and possessed thirty cities in the land of Gilead, which, like those of their namesake, were called Havoth-jair.

3. A Benjamite, son of Kish and father of Mordecai. Esther 2 : 5.

4. The father of Elhanan, who was one of the heroes of David's army. 1 Chron. 20 : 5.

Ja'irite (jä'ir-īte) (*descendant of Jair*), **The.** Ira the Jairite was a priest (Authorized Version "chief ruler") to David. 2 Sam. 20 : 26.

Jai'rus (jà-ī'rus) (*Greek form of jair*). A ruler of a synagogue, probably in some town near the western shore of the Sea of Galilee, perhaps in Capernaum. Matt. 9 : 18; Mark 5 : 22; Luke 8 : 41. (A.D. 28.)

Ja'kan (jā'kan), son of Ezer the Horite. 1 Chron. 1 : 42. The same as JAAKAN. [And see AKAN.]

Ja'keh (jā'keh) (*pious*). Prov. 30. [AGUR.]

Ja'kim (jā'kim) (*God sets up*). 1. Head of the twelfth course of priests in the reign of David. 1 Chron. 24 : 12.

2. A Benjamite, one of the Bene-Shimhi. 1 Chron. 8 : 19.

Ja'lon (jā'lon), one of the sons of Ezra. 1 Chron. 4 : 17.

Jam'bres (jăm'brēs). [JANNES AND JAMBRES.]

James (*the Greek form of Jacob*). The name James occurs a number of times in the Gospels and Acts, and the identification of the men indicated involves points of dispute that can never be definitely settled. It is impossible to give any true discussion of the matter here. It seems best, therefore, to enumerate all who may possibly be different, indicating possible identifications with some of the main objections and leave the real discussion to books with more space at their command. One of the fullest discussions is in Hastings' "Dictionary of Christ and the Gospels." Articles "James" and "Brethren of the Lord."

1. JAMES THE SON OF ZEBEDEE, one of the twelve apostles. He was elder brother of the evangelist John. His mother's name was Salome. She was probably a sister of the Virgin Mary, making James the first cousin of Jesus. We first hear of him in A.D. 28, Mark 1 : 20, when at the call of the Master he left all, and became, once and forever, his disciple, in the spring of 28. Matt. 10 : 2; Mark 3 : 7; Luke 6 : 14; Acts 1 : 13. It would seem to have been at the time of the appointment of the twelve apostles that the name of Boanerges was given to the sons of Zebedee. The "sons of thunder" had a burning and impetuous spirit, which twice exhibits itself. Mark 10 : 35–37; Luke 9 : 54. On the night before the crucifixion James was present at the agony in the garden. On the day of the ascension he is mentioned as persevering, with the rest of the apostles and disciples, in prayer. Acts 1 : 13. Shortly before the day of the passover, in the year 44, he was put to death by Herod Agrippa I. Acts 12 : 1, 2.

2. JAMES THE SON OF ALPHÆUS, one of the twelve apostles (Matt. 10 : 3; Mark 3 : 18; Luke 6 : 15; Acts 1 : 13). The identification of this James is one of the most difficult problems in gospel history. Nothing more is said of him under this name. Matthew was "the son of Alphæus, and is considered by many as "most likely" a brother of James. He has been identified with both (3) and (4) but there is at least great doubt of this.

3. JAMES THE LESS (Mark 15 : 40; cf. Matt. 27 : 56; John 19 : 25). This common rendering "the less" comes from a mistake of Jerome in translating the Greek positive *mikros*, "little" (*i. e.* short of stature), by the Latin comparative *minor*, "less." Some arguments for reckoning (2), (3) and (4) as only one man rest on this mistake, and are therefore valueless. This James was the son of a Mary, very probably the wife of Clopas, and brother of a man named Joses. The identification with (2) rests on the supposition, "philolog-

ically impossible," that Alphæus and Clopas are two forms of the same name. We know nothing more of this James, under this name.

4. JAMES THE LORD'S BROTHER, mentioned by name in Matt. 13 : 55; Mk. 6 : 3 and several times in Acts and Epistles. He became the head of the church at Jerusalem, and was martyred between A.D. 60 and 70. He was the author of the Epistle bearing his name. He is often identified with (2). If so he was one of the twelve apostles, and not truly Jesus' brother. But he is distinctly called his brother in a large number of places, while in John 7 : 3, 5 it distinctly says that Jesus' "brethren" did not believe in him. This was over a year after the appointment of the twelve. Still more often is he identified with (3) who was not an apostle. The question of his relationship to Jesus would, however, rise in this case.

5. James in Luke 6 : 16, given in A. V. as "the brother" of Judas, is by R. V. and most scholars translated "the father" of Judas. Nothing more is known of him. The A. V. rendering has been used as argument for some of the other identifications.

James, The General Epistle of. The author of this epistle was in all probability James, "our Lord's brother." It was written from Jerusalem, which St. James does not seem to have ever left. It was probably written shortly before his martyrdom, A.D. 63. Its main object is not to teach doctrine, but to improve morality. Its style is remarkable, combining pure rhythmical Greek, with the fiery sternness and intensity of the Hebrew prophets. Its leading idea is that "faith without works is dead." He wrote for the Jewish Christians, whether in Jerusalem or abroad, to warn them against the sins to which as Jews they were most liable, and to console and exhort them under the sufferings to which as Christians they were most exposed.

Ja'min (*right hand*). 1. Second son of Simeon, Gen. 46 : 10; Ex. 6 : 15; 1 Chron. 4 : 24, founder of the family of the Jaminites. Num. 26 : 12.

2. A man of Judah, second son of Ram the Jerahmeelite. 1 Chron. 2 : 27.

3. One of the Levites who expounded the law to the people. Neh. 8 : 7.

Jam'lech (jam'lek), one of the chief

men of the tribe of Simeon. 1 Chron. 4 : 34.

Jan'na (jăn'nà), son of Joseph, and father of Melchi, in the genealogy of Christ. Luke 3 : 24.

Jan'nes (jăn'nes) and **Jam'bres**, according to the popular tradition the names of two Egyptian magicians who opposed Moses. Ex. 7 : 9–13; 2 Tim. 3 : 8, 9. (B.C. 1492.)

Jano'ah (jà-nō'àh) (*rest*), a place apparently in the north of Galilee, or the "land of Naphtali,"—one of those taken by Tiglath-pileser in his first incursion into Palestine. 2 Kings 15 : 29. It may be the modern *Yanuh*.

Jano'hah (jà-nō'hàh) (*rest*), a place on the boundary of Ephraim, Josh. 16 : 6, 7, east of Neapolis. A little less than twelve miles from *Nablûs*, and about southeast in direction, two miles from *Akrabeh*, is the village of *Yanûn*, doubtless identical with the ancient city of Janohah.

Ja'num (jā'num) (*slumber*), a town of Judah in the mountain district, apparently not far from Hebron. Josh. 15 : 53.

Ja'pheth (jā'feth) (*enlargement*), one of the three sons of Noah. The descendants of Japheth occupied the "isles of the Gentiles," Gen. 10 : 5—*i. e.* the coast lands of the Mediterranean Sea in Europe and Asia Minor—whence they spread northward over the whole continent of Europe and a considerable portion of Asia.

Japhi'a (jà-fī'à) (*splendid*). The boundary of Zebulun ascended from Daberath to Japhia, and thence passed to Gath-hepher. Josh. 19 : 12. *Yâfa*, two miles south of Nazareth, is likely to be identical with Japhia.

Japhi'a (*splendid*). 1. King of Lachish at the time of the conquest of Canaan by the Israelites. John 10 : 3. (B.C. 1450.)

2. One of the sons of David born to him in Jerusalem. 2 Sam. 5 : 15; 1 Chron. 3 : 7; 14 : 6.

Japh'let (jăf'lĕt) (*may he deliver*), a descendant of Asher through Beriah. 1 Chron. 7 : 32, 33.

Japh'leti (jăf'lē-tī) (*the Japhletite*). The boundary of the "Japhletite" is one of the landmarks on the south boundary line of Ephraim. Josh. 16 : 3.

Ja'pho (jā'fō) (*beauty*). Josh. 19 : 46. The Hebrew form for the better-known JOPPA.

Ja'rah (jā'rah) (*honey*), a descendant of Saul, 1 Chron. 9 : 42, comp. 40. Called Jehoadah in 8 : 36.

Ja'reb (jā'reb) (*contentious*), is a word used twice by Hosea (5 : 13; 10 : 6) as a designation of the king of Assyria. Various opinions have been expressed as to whether it is a proper name or a descriptive epithet. There is no king known by this name, but it may have been the original name of one who changed it at his accession. Sayce suggests Sargon II, but he is in the opinion of others later than the date of Hosea.

Ja'red (jā'red) (*descent*), one of the antediluvian patriarchs, and father of Enoch. Gen. 5 : 15, 16, 18–20; Luke 3 : 37. In the lists of Chronicles the name is given in the Authorized Version JERED.

Jaresi'ah (jăr-e-sī'ah) (*Jehovah nourishes*), a Benjamite, one of the Bene-Jeroham. 1 Chron. 8 : 27.

Jar'ha (jär'hà), the Egyptian servant of Sheshan of the tribe of Judah, to whom his master gave his daughter and heir in marriage. 1 Chron. 2 : 34, 35.

Ja'rib (jā'rib) (*adversary*). 1. Named in the list of 1 Chron. 4 : 24 only, as a son of Simeon. Probably the same as the JACHIN of Gen. 46 : 10.

2. One of the "chief men" who accompanied Ezra on his journey from Babylon to Jerusalem. Ezra 8 : 16. (B.C. 458.)

3. A priest of the house of Jeshua the son of Jozadak, who had married a foreign wife, and was compelled by Ezra to put her away. Ezra 10 : 18. (B.C. 458.)

Jar'muth (jär'mŭth) (*high*). 1. A town in the low country of Judah. Josh. 15 : 35. Its king, Piram, was one of the five who conspired to punish Gibeon for having made alliance with Israel, Josh. 10 : 3, 5, and who were routed at Beth-horon and put to death by Joshua at Makkedah, ver. 33. Its site is probably the modern *Yarmûk*.

2. A city of Issachar, allotted with its suburbs to the Gershonite Levites. Josh. 21 : 29. It is called in other lists RE-METH (Josh. 19 : 21) and RAMOTH (1 Chron. 6 : 73), these being in Hebrew synonyms of Jarmuth. Not identified.

Jaro'ah (ja-rō'ah) (*moon*), a chief man of the tribe of Gad. 1 Chron. 5 : 14.

Ja'shen (jā'shen) (*sleeping*). Bene-Jashen—"sons of Jashen"—are named in the catalogue of the heroes of David's guard in 2 Sam. 23 : 32.

Ja'sher (jā'shĕr), R. V. **Ja'shar, Book of** (*the book of the upright*), a book alluded to in two passages only of the Old Testament. Josh. 10 : 13 and 2 Sam. 1 : 18. It was probably written in verse; and it has been conjectured that it was a collection of ancient records of honored men or noble deeds. It is wholly lost.

Jasho'beam (jà-shō'be-am) (*let the people return*), named first among the chief of the mighty men of David. 1 Chron. 11 : 11. He came to David at Ziklag. His distinguishing exploit was that he slew 300 (or 800, 2 Sam. 23 : 8) men at one time. The same man is referred to under the name of Adino the Eznite in the parallel passage, 2 Sam. 23 : 8. But the reading in 1 Chron. is probably the correct one.

Jash'ub (jăsh'ŭb) (*he returns*). 1. The third son of Issachar, and founder of the family of the Jashubites. Num. 26 : 24; 1 Chron. 7 : 1. JOB in Gen. 46.

2. One of the sons of Bani, who had to put away his foreign wife. Ezra 10 : 29. (B.C. 458.)

Jash'ubi-le'hem (jash'ụ-bī-lē'hĕm), a person or a place named among the descendants of Shelah, the son of Judah by Bath-shua the Canaanitess. 1 Chron. 4 : 22.

Ja'siel (jā'sĭ-el) (*God made*), the last named on the list of David's heroes in 1 Chron. 11 : 47. R. V. "Jaasiel."

Ja'son (jā'son), called the Thessalonian, entertained Paul and Silas, and was in consequence attacked by the Jewish mob. Acts 17 : 5, 6, 7, 9. (A.D. 51.) He is probably the same as the Jason mentioned in Rom. 16 : 21.

Jasper, a precious stone frequently noticed in Scripture. It was the last of the twelve inserted in the high priest's breastplate, Ex. 28 : 20; 39 : 13, and the first of the twelve used in the foundations of the new Jerusalem. Rev. 21 : 19. The characteristics of the stone as far as they are specified in Scripture, Rev. 21 : 11, are that it "was most precious," and "like crystal;" we may also infer from Rev. 4 : 3 that it was a stone of brilliant and transparent light. Prof. Petrie, in Hastings' *Bible Dictionary,* calls it the dark green jasper, a favorite stone in Greece and Egypt. Cheyne considers it probable that the *opal* is the stone intended.

Jath'niel (jăth'nĭ-el) (*God bestoweth gifts*), a Korhite Levite, of the family of Meshelemiah. 1 Chron. 26 : 2.

Jat'tir (jăt'tir) (*pre-eminent*), a town of Judah in the mountain districts, Josh. 15 : 48, one of the group containing Socho, Eshtemoa, etc. See also Josh. 21 : 14; 1 Sam. 30 : 27; 1 Chron. 6 : 57. By Robinson it is identified with *'Attir,* six miles north of Molada and ten miles south of Hebron.

Ja'van (jā'văn). 1. A son of Japheth. Gen. 10 : 2, 4. Javan was regarded as the representative of the Greek race. The name was probably introduced into Asia by the Phœnicians, to whom the Ionians were naturally better known than any other of the Hellenic races, on account of their commercial activity and the high prosperity of their towns on the western coast of Asia Minor.

2. A town in the southern part of Arabia (*Yemen*), whither the Phœnicians traded. Ezek. 27 : 19.

Javelin. [ARMS.]

Ja'zer (jā'zēr). [JAAZER.]

Ja'ziz (jā'zĭz), a Hagerite who had charge of the flocks of King David. 1 Chron. 27 : 31.

Je'arim (jē'a-rĭm) (*forests*), **Mount,** a place named in specifying the northern boundary of Judah. Josh. 15 : 10. The boundary ran from Mount Seir to "the shoulder of Mount Jearim, which is Chesalon"—that is, Chesalon was the landmark on the mountain. *Kesla,* seven miles due west of Jerusalem, stands on a high point on the north slope of a lofty ridge, which is probably Mount Jearim.

Jcat'crai (jè-ăt'c-rāi), a Gershonite Levite, son of Zerah. 1 Chron. 6 : 21.

Jeberechi'ah (jè-bĕr-e-kī'ah) (*Jehovah blesses*), father of a certain Zechariah, in the reign of Ahaz, mentioned Isa. 8 : 2.

Je'bus (jē'bus) (*threshing-floor*). This name occurs only in Judges 19 : 10; 1 Chron. 11 : 4, 5, with the statement "the same is Jerusalem." It has therefore been commonly supposed an old name for that city. The Tel-el-Amarna tablets, however, call the city *Urusalim.* It is thought by many modern scholars to be a wrong inference from Jebusite, undoubtedly the name of the tribe occupying Jerusalem at the time of the conquest of the city by David.

Jeb'usi. R. V. Jebusite. Josh. 18 : 16, 28.

Jeb'usites (jĕb'u-sītes). One of the early tribes. They first appear in the invaluable report of the spies. Num. 13 : 29. When Jabin organized his rising against Joshua, the Jebusites joined him. Josh. 11 : 3. The tribe held Jerusalem, which lost its king in the slaughter of Beth-horon, Josh. 10 : 1, 5, 26; comp. 12 : 10, was sacked and burned by the men of Judah, Judges 1 : 21, and its citadel finally scaled and occupied by David. 2 Sam. **5 : 6.** The old inhabitants were not wholly expelled, for Araunah the Jebusite acted as an independent landowner in his well-known transaction with David. 2 Sam. 24 : 23; 1 Chron. 21 : 20–25. Solomon subjected the remnant of the Jebusites to bond service. 1 Kings 9 : 20.

Jecami'ah (jĕk-a-mī'ah) (*may Jehovah strengthen*). A son, or descendant of Jeconiah, that is, Jehoiachin, king of Judah. In R. V. Jekamiah. 1 Chron. 3 : 18.

Jecholi'ah (jĕk-o-lī'ah), wife of Amaziah king of Judah, and mother of Azariah or Uzziah his successor. 2 Kings 15 : 2.

Jechoni'as (jĕk-o-nī'as), the Greek form of Jeconiah, an altered form of JEHOIACHIN. Matt. 1 : 11.

Jecoli'ah (jĕk-o-lī'ah) the same as JECHOLIAH. 2 Chron. 26 : 3.

Jeconi'ah (jĕk-o-nī'ah). [See JEHOI-ACHIN.]

Jeda'iah (jè-dā'iah) (*Jehovah has cast*). 1. Head of the second course of priests, as they were divided in the time of David. 1 Chron. 24 : 7. Some of them survived to return to Jerusalem after the Babylonish captivity, as appears from Ezra 2 : 36; Neh. 7 : 39.

2. A priest in the time of Jeshua the high priest. Zech. 6 : 10, 14. (B.C. 536.)

Jeda'iah (jè-dā'iah). 1. A Simeonite, forefather of Zira. 1 Chron. 4 : 37.

2. Son of Harumaph; a man who did his part in the rebuilding of the wall of Jerusalem. Neh. 3 : 10. (B.C. 446.)

Jedi'ael (jĕd-ī'a-el) (*known of God*). 1. A chief patriarch of the tribe of Benjamin. 1 Chron. 7 : 6, 11. It has been assumed that Jediael is the same as Ashbel, Num. 26 : 38, but this is not certain.

2. Second son of Meshelemiah, a Levite. 1 Chron. 26 : 1, 2.

3. Son of Shimri; one of the heroes

of David's guard. 1 Chron. 11 : 45. Perhaps same as

4. One of the chiefs of the thousands of Manasseh who joined David on his march to Ziklag. 1 Chron. 12 : 20; comp. 1 Sam. 30. (B.C. 1055.)

Jedi'dah (jè-dī'dah), queen of Amon and mother of the good king Josiah. 2 Kings 22 : 1. (B.C. 648.)

Jedidi'ah (jĕd-ĭ-dī'ah) (*beloved of Jehovah*), **Jedid=jah** (*darling of Jehovah*), the name bestowed, through Nathan the prophet, on David's son Solomon. 2 Sam. 12 : 25.

Jed'uthun (jĕd'u-thūn) (*praising*), a Levite of the family of Merari, is probably the same as Ethan. Comp. 1 Chron. 15 : 17, 19 with 1 Chron. 16 : 41, 42; 25 : 1, 3, 6; 2 Chron. 35 : 15. His office was generally to preside over the music of the temple service. Jeduthun's name stands at the head of the 39th, 62d and 77th Psalms.

Jee'zer (jè-ē'zēr) (*father is help*), Num. 26 : 30, the name of a descendant of Manasseh and founder of the family of the Jeezerites. In parallel lists the name is given as ABI-EZER; in R. V. JEZER.

Je'gar=sahadu'tha (jē'gar-sā-hà-du'thà) (*heap of testimony*), the Aramæan name given by Laban the Syrian to the heap of stones which he erected as a memorial of the compact between Jacob and himself. Gen. 31 : 47. Galeed, a "witness heap," which is given as the Hebrew equivalent, does not exactly represent Jegar-sahadutha.

Jehale'leel (jè-ha-lē'le-el) (*he praises God*). Four men of the Bene-Jehaleleel are introduced abruptly into the genealogies of Judah. 1 Chron. 4 : 16.

Jehal'elel (jè-hal'e-lel) (*he praises God*), a Merarite Levite, father of Azariah. 2 Chron. 29 : 12.

Jehde'iah (*may Jehovah give joy*). 1. The representative of the Bene-Shubael, in the time of David. 1 Chron. 24 : 20.

2. A Meronothite who had charge of the she-asses of David. 1 Chron. 27 : 30.

Jehez'ekel (jè-hĕz'e-kĕl) (*God strengtheneth*), a priest to whom was given by David the charge of the twentieth of the twenty-four courses in the service of the house of Jehovah. 1 Chron. 24 : 16.

Jehi'ah (jè-hī'ah) (*may Jehovah live!*), "doorkeeper for the ark" at the time of its establishment in Jerusalem. 1 Chron. 15 : 24. (B.C. 1042.)

Jehi'el (jè-hi'el) (*may God live*). 1. One of the Levites appointed by David to assist in the service of the house of God. 1 Chron. 15 : 18, 20; 16 : 5.

2. One of the sons of Jehoshaphat king of Judah, put to death by his brother Jehoram. 2 Chron. 21 : 2, 4. (B.C. 850.)

3. One of the rulers of the house of God at the time of the reforms of Josiah. 2 Chron. 35 : 8. (B.C. 623.)

4. A Gershonite Levite, 1 Chron. 23 : 8, who had charge of the treasures, ch. 29 : 8.

5. A son of Hachmoni named in the list of David's officers, 1 Chron. 27 : 32, as "with the king's sons," whatever that may mean.

6. A Levite who took part in the restorations of King Hezekiah. 2 Chron. 29 : 14; 2 Chron. 31 : 13. (B.C. 726.)

7. Father of Obadiah, of the Bene-Joab. Ezra 8 : 9.

8. One of the Bene-Elam, father of Shechaniah. Ezra 10 : 2.

9. A member of the same family, perhaps the same man, who had to part with his wife. Ezra 10 : 26.

10. A priest, one of the Bene-Harim, who also had to put away his foreign wife. Ezra 10 : 21. (B.C. 458.)

Jehi'el (jè-hi'el), or **Jeiel** (*treasured of God*), a distinct name from the last. 1. A man described as father of Gibeon; a forefather of King Saul. 1 Chron. 9 : 35.

2. One of the sons of Hothan the Aroerite; a member of David's guard. 1 Chron. 11 : 44.

Jehi'eli (jè-hi'e-li) (*a Jehielite*), a family name from JEHIEL 4, a Gershonite Levite of the family of Laadan. 1 Chron. 26 : 21, 22.

Jehizki'ah (jè-hiz-ki'ah) (*Jehovah strengthens*), son of Shallum, one of the heads of the tribe of Ephraim in the time of Ahaz and Pekah. 2 Chron. 28 : 12; comp. 8, 13, 15.

Jeho'adah (jè-hò'a-dah), one of the descendants of Saul. 1 Chron. 8 : 36.

Jehoad'dan (jè-hò-ăd'dan), queen to King Joash, and mother of Amaziah of Judah. 2 Kings 14 : 2; 2 Chron. 25 : 1.

Jeho'ahaz (jè-hò'a-hăz) (*Jehovah hath grasped*). 1. The son and successor of Jehu, reigned 17 years, B.C. 815-798, over Israel in Samaria. His inglorious history is given in 2 Kings 13:

1-9. Throughout his reign, ver. 22, he was kept in subjection by Hazael king of Damascus. Jehoahaz maintained the idolatry of Jeroboam; but in the extremity of his humiliation he besought Jehovah, and Jehovah gave Israel a deliverer—probably either Jehoash, vs. 23 and 25, or Jeroboam II., 2 Kings 14: 24, 25.

2. Jehoahaz, otherwise called Shallum, son of Josiah, whom he succeeded as king of Judah. He was chosen by the people in preference to his elder (comp. 2 Kings 23 : 30, 31 and 36) brother, B.C. 609, and he reigned three months in Jerusalem. Pharaoh-necho sent to Jerusalem to depose him and to fetch him to Riblah. There he was cast into chains, and from thence he was taken into Egypt, where he died.

3. The name given, 2 Chron. 21 : 17, to Ahaziah, the youngest son of Jehoram king of Judah.

Jeho'ash (jè-hò'ash) (*Jehovah is strong*), the uncontracted form of Joash. 1. The eighth king of Judah; son of Ahaziah. 2 Kings 11 : 21; 12 : 1, 2, 4, 6, 7, 18; 14 : 13. [JOASH, 1.]

2. The twelfth king of Israel; son of Jehoahaz. 2 Kings 13 : 10, 25; 14 : 8, 9, 11, 13, 15, 16, 17. [JOASH, 2.]

Jehoha'nan (jè-hò-hă'nan) (*Jehovah is gracious*), a name contracted into Johanan and John. 1. A Korhite Levite, one of the doorkeepers to the tabernacle. 1 Chron. 26 : 3; comp. 26 : 1.

2. One of the principal men of Judah under King Jehoshaphat. 2 Chron. 17: 15; comp. 13 and 19. Perhaps same as

3. Father of Ishmael, one of the "captains of hundreds" whom Jehoiada the priest took into his confidence about the restoration of the line of Judah. 2 Chron. 23 : 1.

4. One of the Bene-Bebai who was forced to put away his foreign wife. Ezra 10 : 28. (B.C. 458.)

5. A priest, Neh. 12 : 13, during the high priesthood of Joiakim, ver. 12. (B.C. about 500.)

6. A priest who took part in the dedication of the wall of Jerusalem. Neh. 12 : 42. (B.C. 446.)

Jehoi'achin (jè-hoi'a-kĭn) (*Jehovah has appointed*), son of Jehoiakim, and for three months and ten days king of Judah. (B.C. 597.) At his accession Jerusalem was quite defenceless, and unable to offer any resistance to the army which Nebuchadnezzar sent to besiege it.

2 Kings 24 : 10, 11. In a very short time Jehoiachin surrendered at discretion; and he, and the queen-mother, and all his servants, captains and officers, came out and gave themselves up to Nebuchadnezzar, who carried them, with the harem and the eunuchs, to Babylon. 2 Kings 24 : 12; Jer. 29 : 2; Ezek. 17 : 12; 19 : 9. There he remained a prisoner, actually in prison and wearing prison garments, for 36 years, till the death of Nebuchadnezzar, when Evil-merodach, succeeding to the throne of Babylon, brought him out of prison, and made him sit at his own table. The time of his death is uncertain.

Jehoi′ada (jè-hoi′a-dà) (*Jehovah knows*). 1. Father of Benaiah, David's well-known warrior. 2 Sam. 8 : 18; 1 Kings 1 : 8, etc.; 2 : 25, etc.; 1 Chron. 18 : 17, etc. Without doubt the same as

2. Leader of the Aaronites, *i. e.* the priests; who joined David at Hebron. 1 Chron. 12 : 27.

3. According to 1 Chron. 27 : 34, son of Benaiah; but in all probability Benaiah the son of Jehoiada is meant. Probably an error in copying.

4. High priest at the time of Athaliah's usurpation of the throne of Judah, B.C. 842–836, and during the greater portion of the forty-years reign of Joash. He married Jehosheba; and when Athaliah slew all the seed royal of Judah after Ahaziah had been put to death by Jehu, he and his wife stole Joash from among the king's sons and hid him for six years in the temple, and eventually replaced him on the throne of his ancestors. [ATHALIAH.] The destruction of Baal-worship and the restoration of the temple were among the great works effected by Jehoiada. He died after 813 B.C. 2 Kings 11 : 1–12 : 16; 2 Chron. 22 : 10–24 : 14.

5. Son of Paseach, who assisted to repair the old gate of Jerusalem. Neh. 3 : 6.

Jehoi′akim (jè-hoi′a-kǐm) (*Jehovah raises up*), originally Eliakim, son of Josiah king of Judah. After deposing Jehoahaz, Pharaoh-necho set Eliakim, his elder brother, upon the throne, and changed his name to Jehoiakim, B.C. 608–597. For four years Jehoiakim was subject to Egypt. When Nebuchadnezzar defeated the Egyptians at Carchemish, B.C. 605, Nebuchadnezzar entered Jerusalem, received the submission of Jehoiakim, and probably took some cap-

tives and some of the precious vessels of the temple and carried them to the land of Shinar. Jehoiakim became tributary to Nebuchadnezzar after his invasion of Judah, and continued so for three years, but at the end of that time broke his oath of allegiance and rebelled against him. 2 Kings 24 : 1. Nebuchadnezzar sent against him numerous bands of Chaldeans, with Syrians, Moabites and Ammonites, 2 Kings 24 : 2, who cruelly harassed the whole country. Either the Babylonian king himself or his forces entered Jerusalem, and bound Jehoiakim and placed him in a cage to carry him to Babylon. Probably the purpose of taking him to Babylon was abandoned. Either in a skirmish or by assassination by some of his own oppressed subjects Jehoiakim came to a violent end in the eleventh year of his reign. His body was cast out ignominiously on the ground, and then was dragged away and buried "with the burial of an ass," without pomp or lamentation, "beyond the gates of Jerusalem." Jer. 22 : 18, 19; 36 : 30. All the accounts we have of Jehoiakim concur in ascribing to him a vicious and irreligious character. 2 Kings 23 : 37; 24 : 9; 2 Chron. 36 : 5. It was he who burnt the roll of the prophecy of Jeremiah, Jer. 36. He was succeeded by his son, Jehoiachin.

Jehoi′arib (jè-hoi′a-rǐb) (*Jehovah pleadeth*), head of the first of the twenty-four courses of priests. 1 Chron. 24 : 7.

Jehon′adab (jè-hŏn′a-dăb) (*whom Jehovah impels*) and **Jon′adab,** the son of Rechab, founder of the Rechabites, an Arab chief. When Jehu was advancing, after killing the king's sons, on the city of Samaria, he was suddenly met by Jehonadab, who joined with him in "slaying all that remained unto Ahab." 2 Kings 10 : 15–17.

Jehon′athan (jè-hŏn′a-than) (*Jehovah has given*). 1. Son of Uzziah; superintendent of certain of King David's storehouses. 1 Chron. 27 : 25.

2. One of the Levites who were sent by Jehoshaphat through the cities of Judah, with "the book of the law of the Lord," to teach the people. 2 Chron. 17 : 8. (B.C. 872.)

3. A priest, Neh. 12 : 18, the representative of the family of Shemaiah, ver. 6, when Joiakim was high priest. (B.C. about 500.)

Jeho′ram (jĕ-hō′ram) (*Jehovah is exalted*). 1. Second son of Ahab king of Israel, who succeeded his brother Ahaziah B.C. 853 and died B.C. 842. The alliance between the kingdoms of Israel and Judah, commenced by his father and Jehoshaphat, was very close throughout his reign. We first find him associated with Jehoshaphat and the king of Edom in a war against the Moabites. The three armies were in the utmost danger of perishing for want of water. The piety of Jehoshaphat suggested an inquiry of Jehovah, through Elisha. After reproving Jehoram, Elisha, for Jehoshaphat's sake, inquired of Jehovah, and received the promise of an abundant supply of water, and of a great victory over the Moabites; a promise which was immediately fulfilled. The allies pursued them with great slaughter into their own land, which they utterly ravaged and destroyed most of its cities. Kir-haraseth alone remained, and there the king of Moab made his last stand. An attempt to break through the besieging army having failed, he resorted to the desperate expedient of offering up his eldest son, as a burnt offering, upon the wall of the city, in the sight of the enemy. Upon this the Israelites retired and returned to their own land. 2 Kings 3. A little later, when war broke out between Syria and Israel, we find Elisha befriending Jehoram; but when the terrible famine in Samaria arose, the king immediately attributed the evil to Elisha, and determined to take away his life. The providential interposition by which both Elisha's life was saved and the city delivered is narrated 2 Kings 7, and Jehoram appears to have returned to friendly feeling toward Elisha. 2 Kings 8:4. It was soon after these events that the revolution in Syria predicted by Elisha took place, giving Jehoram a good opportunity of recovering Ramoth-gilead from the Syrians. He accordingly made an alliance with his nephew Ahaziah, who had just succeeded Joram on the throne of Judah, and the two kings proceeded to occupy Ramoth-gilead by force. The expedition was an unfortunate one. Jehoram was wounded in battle, and obliged to return to Jezreel to be healed of his wounds. 2 Kings 8:29; 9:14, 15. Jehu and the army under his command revolted from their allegiance to Jehoram, 2 Kings 9, and hastily marching to Jezreel, surprised Jehoram, wounded and defenceless as he was. Jehoram, going out to meet him, fell pierced by an arrow from Jehu's bow on the very plot of ground which Ahab had wrested from Naboth the Jezreelite; thus fulfilling to the letter the prophecy of Elijah. 1 Kings 21:29. Thus ended the dynasty of Omri. JORAM, 1.

2. Eldest son of Jehoshaphat, succeeded his father on the throne of Judah at the age of 32, and reigned eight years, from B.C. 851 to 843. As soon as he was fixed on the throne, he put his six brothers to death, with many of the chief nobles of the land. He then, probably at the instance of his wife Athaliah the daughter of Ahab, proceeded to establish the worship of Baal. A prophetic writing from the aged prophet Elijah, 2 Chron. 21:12, failed to produce any good effect upon him. The remainder of his reign was a series of calamities. First the Edomites, who had been tributary to Jehoshaphat, revolted from his dominion and established their permanent independence. Next Libnah, 2 Kings 8:22, rebelled against him. Then followed invasion by armed bands of Philistines and of Arabians, who stormed the king's palace, put his wives and all his children, except his youngest son Ahaziah, to death, 2 Chron. 22:1, or carried them into captivity, and plundered all his treasures. He died of a terrible disease. 2 Chron. 21:19, 20. JORAM, 2.

Jehoshab′eath (jĕ-hṓ-shăb′e-ăth) 2 Chron. 22:11. [See JEHOSHEBA.]

Jehosh′aphat (jĕ-hŏsh′a-făt) (*Jehovah hath judged*). 1. King of Judah, son of Asa, succeeded to the throne B.C. 875, when he was 35 years old, and reigned 25 years. His history is to be found among the events recorded in 1 Kings 15:24—2 Kings 8:16, or in a continuous narrative in 2 Chron. 17:1-21:3. He was contemporary with Ahab, Ahaziah and Jehoram. He was one of the best, most pious and prosperous kings of Judah, the greatest since Solomon. At first he strengthened himself against Israel; but soon afterward the two Hebrew kings formed an alliance. In his own kingdom Jehoshaphat ever showed himself a zealous follower of the commandments of God: he tried to put down the high places and groves in which the people of Judah burnt incense, and sent the wisest Levites through the cities and towns to instruct the people in true morality and religion. Riches and honors increased around him. He received tribute from the Philistines and Arabians, and kept up a large standing army in Jerusalem. It was probably about the 16th year of his reign, B.C. 854, when he became Ahab's ally in the great battle of Ramoth-gilead, for which he was severely reproved by Jehu. 2 Chron. 19:2. He built at Ezion-geber, with the help of Ahaziah, a navy designed to go to Tarshish or Ophir; but it was wrecked at Ezion-geber. Later in his reign he was engaged in two additional wars. He was miraculously delivered from a threatened attack of the people of Ammon, Moab and Seir. After this, perhaps, must be dated the war which Jehoshaphat, in conjunction with Jehoram king of Israel and the king of Edom, carried on against the rebellious king of Moab. 2 Kings 3. In his declining years the administration of affairs was placed, probably B.C. 854, in the hands of his son Jehoram.

2. Son of Ahilud, who filled the office of recorder or annalist in the courts of David, 2 Sam. 8:16, etc., and Solomon. 1 Kings 4:3.

3. One of the priests in David's time. 1 Chron. 15:24.

4. Son of Paruah; one of the twelve purveyors of King Solomon. 1 Kings 4:17.

5. Son of Nimshi and father of King Jehu. 2 Kings 9:2, 14.

Jehosh'aphat (jĕ-hŏsh'a-făt), **Valley of** (*valley of the judgment of Jehovah*), a valley mentioned by Joel only, as the spot in which, after the return of Judah and Jerusalem from captivity, Jehovah would gather all the heathen, Joel 3:2, and would there sit to judge them for their misdeeds to Israel, ch. 3:12. The scene of "Jehovah's judgment" has been localized, and the name has come down to us attached to that deep ravine which separates Jerusalem from the Mount of Olives, through which at one time the Kedron forced its stream. At what period the name "valley of Jehoshaphat" was first applied to this spot is unknown. It is not mentioned in the Bible or Josephus, but is first encountered in the middle of the fourth century. Both Moslems and Jews believe that the last judgment is to take place

there. The steep sides of the ravine, wherever a level strip affords the opportunity, are crowded—in places almost paved—by the sepulchres of the Moslems, or the simpler slabs of the Jewish tombs, alike awaiting the assembly of the last judgment. The name is generally confined by travelers to the upper part of the glen. Others suppose that the name is only an imaginary one, "the valley of the judgment of Jehovah" referring to some great victories of God's people in which judgment was executed upon the heathen; or perhaps, as Keil, etc., to the end of the world.

Jehosh'eba (jĕ-hŏsh'e-bà) (*Jehovah is an oath*), daughter of Joram king of Judah, and wife of Jehoiada the high priest. 2 Kings 11:2. She is called Jehoshabeath in Chronicles. She was instrumental in preserving the Davidic stock by concealing the infant Joash in a lumber-room of the palace. R. V. margin. She probably was the daughter, not of Athaliah, but of Joram by another wife. She is the only recorded instance of the marriage of a princess of the royal house with a high priest.

Jehosh'ua (jĕ-hŏsh'u-ah) (*Jehovah is salvation*). In this form is given the name of Joshua in Num. 13:16. Once more only the name appears by mistake, as

Jehosh'uah (jĕ-hŏsh'u-ah), in the genealogy of Ephraim. 1 Chron. 7:27.

Jeho'vah (*I am; the Eternal Living One*). The Scripture appellation of the supreme Being, usually interpreted as signifying self-derived and permanent existence. The Jews scrupulously avoided every mention of this name of God, substituting in its stead one or other of the words with whose proper vowel-points it may happen to be written. This custom, which had its origin in reverence, was founded upon an erroneous rendering of Lev. 24:16, from which it was inferred that the mere utterance of the name constituted a capital offence. According to Jewish tradition, it was pronounced but once a year, by the high priest on the day of atonement when he entered the holy of holies; but on this point there is some doubt. When Moses received his commission to be the deliverer of Israel, the Almighty, who appeared in the burning bush, communicated to him the name which he should give as the credentials of his mission: "And God said unto

Moses, I AM THAT I AM, אֶהְיֶה אֲשֶׁר אֶהְיֶה
(*ehyeh* *ăsher* *ehyeh*); and he said,
Thus shalt thou say unto the children
of Israel, I AM hath sent me unto you."
That this passage is intended to indicate
the etymology of Jehovah, as understood
by the Hebrews, no one has ventured to
doubt. While Elohim exhibits God displayed in his power as the creator and
governor of the physical universe, the
name Jehovah designates his nature as
he stands in relation to man, as the
only almighty, true, personal, holy Being,
a spirit and "the father of spirits,"
Num. 16:22; comp. John 4:24, who revealed himself to his people, made a
covenant with them, and became their
lawgiver, and to whom all honor and
worship are due.

Jeho'vah=ji'reh (je-hō'vah-ji'reh)
(*Jehovah will see* or *provide*), the name
given by Abraham to the place on which
he had been commanded to offer Isaac,
to commemorate the interposition of the
angel of Jehovah, who appeared to prevent the sacrifice, Gen. 22:14, and provided another victim.

Jeho'vah=nis'si (je-hō'vah-nĭs'sĭ)
(*Jehovah is my banner*), the name
given by Moses to the altar which he
built in commemoration of the discomfiture of the Amalekites. Ex. 17:15.

Jeho'vah=sha'lom (je-hō'vah-shā'lom)
(*Jehovah is peace*). The altar erected
by Gideon in Ophrah was so called in
memory of the salutation addressed to
him by the angel of Jehovah, "Peace
be unto thee." Judges 6:24.

Jehoz'abad (je-hŏz'a-băd) (*Jehovah
hath bestowed*). 1. A Korhite Levite,
second son of Obededom, and one of
the porters of the south gate of the
temple and of the storehouse there in
the time of David. 1 Chron. 26:4, 15.

2. A Benjamite, a high military officer,
said to be the captain of 180,000 armed
men, in the days of King Jehoshaphat.
2 Chron. 17:18. (B.C. 870.)

3. Son of Shomer or Shimrith, a Moabitish woman, who with another conspired against King Joash and slew him
in his bed. 2 Kings 12:21; 2 Chron. 24:
26. (B.C. 796.)

Jehoz'adak (je-hŏz'a-dăk) (*Jehovah
is righteous*), usually called Jozadak or
Josedech. He was the son of the high
priest Seraiah. 1 Chron. 6:14, 15.
When his father was slain at Riblah by
order of Nebuchadnezzar, 2 Kings 25:

18, 21, Jehozadak was led away captive
to Babylon. 1 Chron. 6:15. He himself never attained the high priesthood,
but he was the father of Jeshua the
high priest, and ancestor of all his successors till the pontificate of Alcimus.
Ezra 3:2; Neh. 12:26, etc.

Je'hu (je'hū) (*Jehovah is he*). 1.
The founder of the fifth dynasty of the
kingdom of Israel, son of Jehoshaphat,
son of Nimshi. Often called son of Nimshi. 2 Kings 9:2. He reigned over Israel
28 years, B.C. 842–815. His first appearance in history is when he heard the
warning of Elijah against the murderer
of Naboth. 2 Kings 9:25. In the
reigns of Ahaziah and Jehoram, Jehu
arose to importance. He was, under
the last-named king, captain of the host
in the siege of Ramoth-gilead. During
this siege he was anointed by Elisha's
servant, and told that he was appointed
to be king of Israel and destroyer of the
house of Ahab. 2 Kings 9:6, 7. The
army at once proclaimed him king, and
he set off full speed for Jezreel. Jehoram, who was lying ill in Jezreel,
came out to meet him, as it happened
on the fatal field of Naboth. 2 Kings
9:21–24. Jehu seized his opportunity,
and shot him through the heart. 2
Kings 9:24. Jehu himself advanced to
the gates of Jezreel and fulfilled the divine warning on Jezebel as already on
Jehoram. He then entered on a work
of extermination hitherto unparalleled
in the history of the Jewish monarchy.
All the descendants of Ahab that remained in Jezreel, together with the
officers of the court and the hierarchy
of Astarte, were swept away. His next
step was to secure Samaria. For the
pretended purpose of inaugurating anew
the worship of Baal, he called all the
Baalites together at Samaria. The vast
temple raised by Ahab, 1 Kings 16:32,
was crowded from end to end. The
chief sacrifice was offered, as if in the
excess of his zeal, by Jehu himself. As
soon as it was ascertained that all, and
none but, the idolaters were there, the
signal was given to eighty trusted
guards, and a sweeping massacre removed at one blow the whole heathen
population of the kingdom of Israel.
This is the last public act recorded of
Jehu. The remaining twenty-seven
years of his long reign are passed over
in a few words, in which two points
only are material:— He did not destroy

the calf-worship of Jeroboam:—The transjordanic tribes suffered much from the ravages of Hazael. 2 Kings 10 : 29–33. He was buried in state in Samaria, and was succeeded by his son Jehoahaz. 2 Kings 10 : 35. His name is the first Israelite king which appears in the Assyrian monuments. (See p. 280.)

2. Jehu son of Hanani; a prophet of Judah, but whose ministrations were chiefly directed to Israel. His father was probably the seer who attacked Asa. 2 Chron. 16 : 7. He must have begun his career as a prophet when very young. He first denounced Baasha, 1 Kings 16 : 1, 7, and then, after an interval of thirty years, reappeared to denounce Jehoshaphat for his alliance with Ahab. 2 Chron. 19 : 2, 3. He survived Jehoshaphat and wrote his life. ch. 20 : 34.

3. A man of Judah of the house of Hezron. 1 Chron. 2 : 38.

4. A Simeonite, son of Josibiah. 1 Chron. 4 : 35.

5. Jehu the Antothite was one of the chief of the heroes of Benjamin who joined David at Ziklag. 1 Chron. 12 : 3.

Jehub'bah (je-hŭb'bah), a man of Asher, son of Shamer or Shomer, of the house of Beriah. 1 Chron. 7 : 34.

Jehu'cal (je-hū'kal) (*Jehovah is able*), one of the two persons sent by King Zedekiah to Jeremiah to entreat his prayers and advice. Jer. 37 : 3.

Je'hud (je'hud) (*praise*), one of the towns of the tribe of Dan, Josh. 19 : 45, named between Baalath and Bene-berak. It is probably the modern *el-Yehudiyeh* 8 miles from Joppa.

Jehu'di (je-hū'dī) (*a Jew*), son of Nethaniah, a man employed by the princes of Jehoiakim's court to fetch Baruch to read Jeremiah's denunciation, Jer. 36 : 14, and then by the king to fetch the volume itself and read it to him, vs. 21, 23. (B.C. 605.)

Jehudi'jah (je-hū-dī'jah) (*the Jewess*). There is really no such name in the Hebrew Bible as that which our Authorized Version exhibits at 1 Chron. 4 : 18. If it is a proper name at all, it is Ha-jehudijah, like Hammelech, Hakkoz, etc.; and it seems to be rather an appellative, " the Jewess."

Je'hush (je'hŭsh), son of Eshek, a remote descendant of Saul. 1 Chron. 8 : 39. R. V. " Jeush."

Jei'el (je-ī'el) (*treasure of God*). 1.

A Reubenite of the house of Joel. 1 Chron. 5 : 7.

2. A Merarite Levite, one of the gatekeepers to the sacred tent. 1 Chron. 15 : 18. His duty was also to play the harp, ver. 21, or the psaltery and harp, 16 : 5, in the service before the ark. (B.C. 1042.)

3. A Gershonite Levite, one of the Bene-Asaph, forefather of Jahaziel in the time of King Jehoshaphat. 2 Chron. 20 : 14.

4. The scribe who kept the account of the numbers of King Uzziah's irregular predatory warriors. 2 Chron. 26 : 11. (B.C. 760.)

5. A Gershonite Levite, one of the Bene-Elizaphan. 2 Chron. 29 : 13. R. V. " Jeuel."

6. One of the chiefs of the Levites in the time of Josiah. 2 Chron. 35 : 9. (B.C. 623.)

7. One of the Bene-Adonikam who formed part of the caravan of Ezra from Babylon to Jerusalem. Ezra 8 : 13. R. V. " Jeuel."

8. A layman of the Bene-Nebo, who had taken a foreign wife and had to relinquish her. Ezra 10 : 43. (B.C. 458.)

Jekab'zeel (je-kăb'ze-el) (*God gathers*), a fuller form of the name of KABZEEL, the most remote city of Judah on the southern frontier. Neh. 11 : 25.

Jekame'am (jĕk-a-mē'am) (*who gathers the people together*), a Levite in the time of King David; one of the family of Hebron, the son of Kohath. 1 Chron. 23 : 19 ; 24 : 23.

Jekami'ah (jĕk-a-mī'ah) (*may Jehovah strengthen*), son of Shallum, in the line of Ahlai. 1 Chron. 2 : 41.

Jeku'thiel (je-ku'thĭ-el), a man recorded in the genealogies of Judah. 1 Chron. 4 : 18.

Jemi'ma (je-mī'mà) (*dove*), the eldest of the three daughters born to Job after the restoration of his prosperity. Job 42 : 14.

Jemu'el (jèm-ū'el) (*day of God*), the eldest son of Simeon. Gen. 46 : 10 ; Ex. 6 : 15.

Jeph'thae (jĕf'-thae), Heb. 11 : 32, the Greek form of the name JEPHTHAH.

Jeph'thah (jef'thah) (*he sets free*), a judge about B.C. 1116–1110. His history is contained in Judges 11 : 1–12 : 7. He was a Gileadite, the son of Gilead and a concubine. Driven by the legitimate sons from his father's inheritance, he went to Tob and became the head of a company of freebooters in a debatable land probably belonging to Ammon. 2 Sam. 10 : 6. This land was east of the Jordan and its situation is very uncertain. It is perhaps in the Hauran. His fame as a bold and successful captain was carried back to his native Gilead; and when the time was ripe for throwing off the yoke of Ammon, Jephthah consented to become the captain of the Gileadite bands, on the condition, solemnly ratified before the Lord in Mizpeh, that in the event of his success against Ammon he should still remain as their acknowledged head. Vowing his vow unto God, Judges 11: 31, that he would offer up as a burnt offering whatsoever should come out to meet him if successful, he went forth to battle. The Ammonites were routed with great slaughter; but as the conqueror returned to Mizpeh there came out to meet him his daughter, his only child, with timbrels and dancing. The father is heart-stricken; but the maiden asks only for a respite of two months in which to prepare for death. When that time was ended she returned to her father, who " did with her according to his vow." The tribe of Ephraim challenged Jephthah's right to go to war as he had done, without their concurrence, against Ammon. He first defeated them, then intercepted the fugitives at the fords of Jordan, and there put forty-two thousand men to the sword. He judged Israel six years, and died. It is generally conjectured that his jurisdiction was limited to the transjordanic region. That the daughter of Jephthah was really offered up to God in sacrifice is a conclusion which it seems impossible to avoid. But there is no word of approval, as if such a sacrifice was acceptable to God. Josephus well says that "the sacrifice was neither sanctioned by the Mosaic ritual nor acceptable to God." The vow and the fulfillment were the mistaken conceptions of a rude chieftain, not acts pleasing to God. Still, he is included among the heroes of faith in Heb. 11.

Jephun'neh (jè-fŭn'neh) (*it will be prepared*). 1. Father of Caleb the spy, appears to have belonged to an Edomitish tribe called Kenezites, from Kenaz their founder. See Num. 13 : 6, etc.; 32 : 12, etc.; Josh. 14 : 14, etc.; 1 Chron. 4 : 15.

2. A descendant of Asher, eldest of the three sons of Jether. 1 Chron. 7 : 38.

Je'rah (jĕ'räh) (*the moon*), the fourth in order of the sons of Joktan, Gen. 10 : 26; 1 Chron. 11 : 20, and the progenitor of a tribe of southern Arabia.

Jerah'meel (jè-räh'me-el) (*may God have compassion*). 1. First-born son of Hezron, the son of Pharez, the son of Judah, 1 Chron. 2 : 9, 25–27, 33, 42.

2. A Merarite Levite, the representative of the family of Kish, the son of Mahli. 1 Chron. 24 : 29; comp. 23 : 21.

3. Son of Hammelech, who was employed by Jehoiakim to make Jeremiah and Baruch prisoners, after he had burnt the roll of Jeremiah's prophecy. Jer. 36 : 26. (B.C. 605.)

Jerah'meelites (jè-räh'me-el-ītes) (*descendants of Jerahmeel*), **The,** tribe descended from the first of the foregoing persons. 1 Sam. 27 : 10. They dwelt in the south of Judah.

Je'red (jĕ'red) (*descent*). 1. Son of Mahalaleel and father of Enoch. 1 Chron. 1 : 2.

2. One of the descendants of Judah signalized as the "father"—*i. e.* the founder—" of Gedor." 1 Chron. 4 : 18.

Jer'emai (jĕr'e-māi), a layman, one of the Bene-Hashum, who was compelled by Ezra to put away his foreign wife. Ezra 10 : 33. (B.C. 458.)

Jeremi'ah (jĕr-e-mī'ah) (*whom Jehovah appoints*), was "the son of Hilkiah of the priests that were in Anathoth." Jer. 1 : 1.

1. *History.*—He was called very young (B.C. 626) to the prophetic office, and prophesied forty-two years; but we have hardly any mention of him during the eighteen years between his call and Josiah's death, or during the short reign of Jehoahaz. During the reigns of Jehoiakim and Jehoiachin, B.C. 607–597, he opposed the Egyptian party, then dominant in Jerusalem, and maintained that the only way of safety lay in accepting the supremacy of the Chaldeans. He was accordingly accused of treachery, and men claiming to be prophets had their " word of Jehovah" to set against his. Jer. 14 : 13; 23 : 17. As the danger from the Chaldeans became more threatening, the persecution against Jeremiah grew hotter, ch. 18. The people sought his life; then follows the scene in Jer.

19 : 10–13. He was set, however, "as a fenced brazen wall," ch. 15 : 20, and went on with his work, reproving king and nobles and people. The danger which Jeremiah had so long foretold at last came near. First Jehoiakim, and afterwards his successor Jehoiachin, were carried into exile, 2 Kings 24; but Zedekiah, B.C. 597–586, who was appointed by Nebuchadnezzar, was more friendly to the prophet, though powerless to help him. The approach of an Egyptian army, and the consequent departure of the Chaldeans, made the position of Jeremiah full of danger, and he sought to effect his escape from the city; but he was seized and finally thrown into a prison-pit to die, but was rescued. On the return of the Chaldean army he showed his faith in God's promises, and sought to encourage the people by purchasing the field at Anathoth which his kinsman Hanameel wished to get rid of. Jer. 32 : 6–10. At last the blow came. The city was taken, the temple burnt. The king and his princes shared the fate of Jehoiachin. The prophet gave utterance to his sorrow in the Lamentations. After the capture of Jerusalem, B.C. 586, by the Chaldeans, we find Jeremiah receiving better treatment; but after the death of Gedaliah, the people, disregarding his warnings, took refuge in Egypt, carrying the prophet with them. In captivity his words were sharper and stronger than ever. He did not shrink, even there, from speaking of the Chaldean king once more as "the servant of Jehovah." Jer. 43 : 10. After this all is uncertain, but he probably died in Egypt.

2. *Character.*—Canon Cook says of Jeremiah, "His character is most interesting. We find him sensitive to a most painful degree, timid, shy, hopeless, desponding, constantly complaining and dissatisfied with the course of events, but never flinching from duty. . . . Timid in resolve, he was unflinching in execution; as fearless when he had to face the whole world as he was dispirited and prone to murmuring when alone with God. Judged by his own estimate of himself, he was feeble, and his mission a failure; really, in the hour of action and when duty called him, he was in very truth 'a defenced city, and an iron pillar, and brazen walls against the whole land,' ch. 1 : 18. He was a noble example of the triumph of the moral over the physical nature."

It is not strange that he was desponding when we consider his circumstances. He saw the nation going straight to irremediable ruin, and turning a deaf ear to all warnings. "A reign of terror had commenced (in the preceding reign), during which not only the prophets but all who were distinguished for religion and virtue were cruelly murdered." "The nation tried to extirpate the religion of Jehovah;" "Idolatry was openly established," "and such was the universal dishonesty that no man trusted another, and society was utterly disorganized." How could one who saw the nation about to reap the awful harvest they had been sowing, and yet had a vision of what they might have been and might yet be, help indulging in "Lamentations"?

Jeremi'ah (jĕr-e-mī'ah). Seven other persons bearing the same name as the prophet are mentioned in the Old Testament:—1. Jeremiah of Libnah, father of Hamutal wife of Josiah. 2 Kings 23 : 31.

2, 3, 4. Three warriors—two of the tribe of Gad—in David's army. 1 Chron. 12 : 4, 10, 13.

5. One of the "mighty men of valor" of the transjordanic half-tribe of Manasseh. 1 Chron. 5 : 24.

6. A priest of high rank, head of the second or third of the twenty-one courses which are apparently enumerated in Neh. 10 : 2–8; 12 : 1, 12.

7. The father of Jazaniah the Rechabite. Jer. 35 : 3.

Jeremi'ah, Book of. "There can be little doubt that the book of Jeremiah grew out of the roll which Baruch wrote down at the prophet's mouth in the fourth year of Jehoiakim. ch. 36. This being destroyed by the king was immediately rewritten with additions. Apparently the prophets kept written records of their predictions, and collected into larger volumes such of them as were intended for permanent use."

In the present order we have two great divisions:—I. Chs. 1–45. Prophecies delivered at various times, directed mainly to Judah, or connected with Jeremiah's personal history. II. Chs. 46–51. Prophecies connected with other nations. Looking more closely into each

THE DOUBLE LINE OF WALLS AT JERICHO.
Excavated by the German Oriental Society.

of these divisions, we have the following sections: 1. Chs. 1–21, including prophecies from the thirteenth year of Josiah to the fourth of Jehoiakim; ch. 21 belongs to the later period. 2 Chs. 22–25. Shorter prophecies, delivered at different times, against the kings of Judah and the false prophets. Ch. 25 : 13, 14 evidently marks the conclusion of a series of prophecies; and that which follows, ch. 25 : 15–38, the germ of the fuller predictions in chs. 46–49, has been placed here as a kind of completion to the prophecy of the seventy years and the subsequent fall of Babylon. 3. Chs. 26–28. The two great prophecies of the fall of Jerusalem, and the history connected with them. 4. Chs. 29–31. The message of comfort for the exiles in Babylon. 5. Chs. 32–44. The history of the last two years before the capture of Jerusalem, and of Jeremiah's work in them and in the period that followed. 6. Chs. 46–51. The prophecies against foreign nations, ending with the great prediction against Babylon. 7. The supplementary narrative of ch. 52.

Jeremi'as (jĕr-e-mī'as), the Greek form of the name of Jeremiah the prophet. Matt. 16 : 14.

Jer'emoth (jĕr'e-mŏth) (*heights*). 1. A Benjamite chief, a son of the house of Beriah of Elpaal. 1 Chron. 8 : 14; comp. 12 to 18.

2. A Merarite Levite, son of Mushi. 1 Chron. 23 : 23.

3. Son of Heman; head of the fifteenth course of musicians in the divine service. 1 Chron. 25 : 22.

4. One of the sons of Elam, and,

5. One of the sons of Zattu, who had taken strange wives. Ezra 10 : 26, 27. (B.C. 458.)

6. The name which appears in the same list as "and Ramoth," Ezra 10 : 29.

Jer'emy (jĕr'e-mė), the prophet Jeremiah. Matt. 2 : 17; 27 : 9.

Jeri'ah (jė-rī'ah), a Kohathite Levite, chief of the great house of Hebron when David organized the service. 1 Chron. 23 : 19; 24 : 23. The same man is mentioned again as JERIJAH. 1 Chron. 26 : 31.

Jer'ibai (jĕr'ĭ-bāi) (*contentious*), one of the Bene-Elnaam, named among the heroes of David's guard. 1 Chron. 11 : 46.

Jer'icho (jĕr'ĭ-kō) (*place of fragrance*), a city of high antiquity, situated in a plain traversed by the Jordan, and exactly over against where that river was crossed by the Israelites under Joshua. Josh. 3 : 16. It was five miles west of the Jordan and seven miles northwest of the Dead Sea. It had a king. Its walls were so considerable that houses were built upon them, ch. 2 : 15. The spoil that was found in it betokened its affluence. Jericho is first mentioned as the city to which the two spies were sent by Joshua from Shittim. Josh. 2 : 1–21. It was assigned to Benjamin, and stood on the boundary between Ephraim and Benjamin, ch. 18 : 21, and from this time a long interval elapses before Jericho appears again upon the scene. Its second foundation under Hiel the Bethelite is recorded in 1 Kings 16 : 34. Once rebuilt, Jericho rose again slowly into consequence. In its immediate vicinity the sons of the prophets sought retirement from the world; Elisha " healed the spring of the waters;" and over against it, beyond Jordan, Elijah " went up by a whirlwind into heaven." 2 Kings 2 : 1–22. In its plains Zedekiah fell into the hands of the Chaldeans. 2 Kings 25 : 5; Jer. 39 : 5. In the return under Zerubbabel the "children of Jericho," 345 in number, are comprised. Ezra 2 : 34; Neh. 7 : 36. Under Herod the Great it again became an important place. He fortified it and built a number of new palaces, which he named after his friends. If he did not make Jericho his habitual residence, he at last retired thither to die, and it was in the amphitheatre of Jericho that the news of his death was announced to the assembled soldiers and people by Salome. Soon afterward the palace was burnt and the town plundered by one Simon, slave to Herod; but Archelaus rebuilt the former sumptuously, and founded a new town on the plain, that bore his own name; and, most important of all, diverted water from a village called Neæra to irrigate the plain which he had planted with palms. Thus Jericho was once more " a city of palms " when our Lord visited it. Here he restored sight to the blind. Matt. 20 : 30; Mark 10 : 46; Luke 18 : 35. Here the descendant of Rahab did not disdain the hospitality of Zacchæus the publican. Finally, between Jerusalem and Jericho was laid the scene of his story of the good Samaritan. The city was destroyed by Vespasian. The site of ancient (the first) Jericho is placed by Dr. Robinson in the immediate neighborhood of the fountain of Elisha; and that of the second (the city of the New Testament and of Josephus) at the opening of the *Wady Kelt* (Cherith), half an hour from the fountain.

of the elder Caleb's wives. 1 Chron. 2: 18.

Jerobo'am (jĕr-o-bō'am) (*whose people are many*). 1. The first king of the divided kingdom of Israel, B.C. 931–915, was the son of an Ephraimite of the name of Nebat. He was raised by

THE TELL OF JERICHO FROM THE WEST.
Showing the excavations made by the German Oriental Society.

The village identified with Jericho lies a mile and a half from the ancient site, and is called *er Riha*. It contains probably 300 inhabitants, indolent and licentious, and about 40 houses. Dr. Olin says it is the "meanest and foulest village of Palestine;" yet the soil of the plain is of unsurpassed fertility.

Je'riel (jĕ'rĭ-el) (*founded by God*), a man of Issachar, one of the six heads of the house of Tola. 1 Chron. 7: 2.

Jeri'jah (jė-rī'jah) (*founded by Jehovah*). [See JERIAH.]

Jer'imoth (jĕr'ĭ-mŏth) (*heights*). 1. Son or descendant of Bela. 1 Chron. 7: 7. He is perhaps the same as

2. One who joined David at Ziklag. 1 Chron. 12 : 5. (B.C. 1057.)

3. A son of Becher, 1 Chron. 7: 8, and head of a Benjamite house.

4. Son of Mushi, the son of Merari. 1 Chron. 24: 30. [JEREMOTH, 2.]

5. Son of Heman, head of the fifteenth ward of musicians. 1 Chron. 25: 4, 22. [JEREMOTH, 3.]

6. Son of Azriel, ruler of the tribe of Naphtali in the reign of David. 1 Chron. 27: 19. R. V. Jeremoth.

7. Son of King David, whose daughter Mahalath was one of the wives of Rehoboam, her cousin Abihail being the other. 2 Chron. 11: 18.

8. A Levite in the reign of Hezekiah. 2 Chron. 31: 13.

Jer'ioth (jĕr'ĭ-ŏth) (*curtains*), one

Solomon to the rank of superintendent over the taxes and labors exacted from the tribe of Ephraim. 1 Kings 11: 28. He made the most of his position, and at last was perceived by Solomon to be aiming at the monarchy. He was leaving Jerusalem, when he was met by Ahijah the prophet, who gave him the assurance that, on condition of obedience to his laws, God would establish for him a kingdom and dynasty equal to that of David. 1 Kings 11: 29–40. The attempts of Solomon to cut short Jeroboam's designs occasioned his flight into Egypt. There he was well received, found a patron in Shishak and married Ano, the elder sister of the

A SEAL FOUND AT MEGIDDO.
With the legend, "Of Shema, servant of Jeroboam" (perhaps Jeroboam II).

Egyptian queen Tahpenes. On hearing of the death of Solomon he returned to Shechem, where took place the conference with Rehoboam [REHOBOAM], and the final revolt which ended in the elevation of Jeroboam to the throne of the northern kingdom. Now occurred the fatal error of his policy. Fearing that the yearly pilgrimages to Jerusalem would undo all the work which he effected, he took the bold step of rending asunder the religious unity of the nation, which was as yet unimpaired. He caused two golden calves for the worship of Jehovah to be made and set up at the two extremities of his kingdom, one at Dan and the other at Bethel. It was while dedicating the altar at Bethel that a prophet from Judah suddenly appeared, who denounced the altar, and foretold its desecration by Josiah, and violent overthrow. The king, stretching out his hand to arrest the prophet, felt it withered and paralyzed, and only at the prophet's prayer saw it restored, and acknowledged his divine mission. Jeroboam was at constant war with the house of Judah, but the only act distinctly recorded is a battle with Abijah, son of Rehoboam, in which he was defeated. The calamity was severely felt; he never recovered from the blow, and soon after died, in the 22d year of his reign, 2 Chron. 13:20, and was buried in his ancestral sepulchre. 1 Kings 14:20.

2. Jeroboam II., the son of Joash, the fourth of the dynasty of Jehu. (B.C. 782–741.) The most prosperous of the kings of Israel. He repelled the Syrian invaders, took their capital city Damascus, 2 Kings 14:28, and recovered the whole of the ancient dominion from Hamath to the Dead Sea, ch. 14:25. Ammon and Moab were reconquered, and the transjordanic tribes were restored to their territory, 2 Kings 13:5; 1 Chron. 5:17–22; but it was merely an outward restoration.

Jer'oham (jĕr'o-hăm). 1. Father of Elkanah, the father of Samuel, of the house of Kohath. 1 Sam. 1:1; 1 Chron. 6:27, 34.

2. A Benjamite, and the founder of a family of Bene-Jeroham. 1 Chron. 8:27. Probably the same as

3. Father (or progenitor) of Ibneiah. 1 Chron. 9:8; comp. 3 and 9.

4. A descendant of Aaron, of the house of Immer, the leader of the sixteenth course of priests; son of Pashur, and father of Adaiah. 1 Chron. 9:12. He appears to be mentioned again in Neh. 11:12.

5. Jeroham of Gedor, some of whose sons joined David at Ziklag. 1 Chron. 12:7.

6. A Danite, whose son or descendant Azareel was head of his tribe in the time of David. 1 Chron. 27:22.

7. Father of Azariah, one of the "captains of hundreds" in the time of Athaliah. 2 Chron. 23:1.

Jerub'baal (jĕ-rŭb'ba-ăl) (*let Baal plead*), the surname of the judge Gideon, which he acquired in consequence of destroying the altar of Baal, when his father defended him from the vengeance of the Abi-ezrites. Judges 6:32.

Jerub'besheth (jĕ-rŭb'be-shĕth) (*let shame plead*), another name of Gideon. 2 Sam. 11:21.

Jer'uel (jĕr'u-el) (*founded by God*), **The wilderness of**, the place in which Jehoshaphat was informed by Jahaziel the Levite that he should encounter the hordes of Ammon, Moab and the Mehunims. 2 Chron. 20:16. It was in the vicinity of En-gedi.

Jeru'salem (*the habitation of peace* or *the city of peace*). The discussions of the meaning of the name have been superseded by the discovery among the Tel-el-Amarna of clay-tablet letters sent between Jerusalem and Egypt B.C. 1500, some of which show that the city at that time was called Jerusalem, sometimes shortened into Salem, and that Salem meant *Peace*. These letters, 7 or 8 in all, describe her condition in plaintive detail.

IMPORTANCE. Jerusalem stands first and supreme among all the cities of the world in its influence upon the hopes and destinies of mankind. Athens and Rome come next. The situation and surroundings of Jerusalem help us to understand much of her history as given in the Bible.

SITE AND SITUATION. Jerusalem stands in latitude 31° 46' 35" north, the same latitude as the northern end of the Dead Sea, and longitude 35° 13' 30" east of Greenwich. It is 32 miles distant from the sea and 18 from the Jordan, 20 from Hebron and 36 from Samaria.

"It was on the ridge, the broadest and most strongly-marked ridge of the backbone of the complicated hills which extend through the whole country from the plain of Esdraelon to the desert." To convey an idea of the position of

Jerusalem, we may say, roughly, that the city occupies the southern termination of a table-land which is cut off from the country round it on its west, south and east sides by ravines more than usually deep and precipitous. These ravines leave the level of the table-land, the one on the west and the other on the northeast of the city, and fall rapidly until they form a junction below its southeast corner. The eastern one—the valley of the Kedron, commonly called the valley of Jehoshaphat—runs nearly straight from north to south. But the western one—the valley promontory thus encircled is itself divided by a longitudinal ravine running up it from south to north, called the valley of the Tyropœon, rising gradually from the south, like the external ones, till at last it arrives at the level of the upper plateau, dividing the central mass into two unequal portions. Of these two, that on the west is the higher and more massive.

Just north of the city the central plateau turns to the west, and a spur runs toward the east and thence southeast and south at about 2680 feet, culminating in the Mount of Olives, and thence

JERUSALEM FROM THE NORTH.

of Hinnom—runs south for a time, and then takes a sudden bend to the east until it meets the valley of Jehoshaphat, after which the two rush off as one to the Dead Sea. How sudden is their descent may be gathered from the fact that the level at the point of junction —about a mile and a quarter from the starting-point of each—is more than 600 feet below that of the upper plateau from which they began their descent. So steep is the fall of the ravines, so trench-like their character, and so close do they keep to the promontory at whose feet they run, as to leave on the beholder almost the impression of the ditch at the foot of a fortress rather than of valleys formed by nature. The southward into a hill traditionally known as the Hill of Evil Counsel. These are the "mountains round about Jerusalem," forming a rough triangle of which the main ridge forms the western side. "The space they enclose is about 2½ miles north and south, by 1½ at its greatest breadth."

DEFENCES OF THE CITY. Jerusalem was an almost impregnable Gibraltar. The steep sides of the ravines on the east, the south and the west provided bulwarks against siege. The north was the only direction from which a foe could attack the city under the conditions of ancient warfare.

The city was situated outside of the great thoroughfares of Palestine through which passed the caravans of commerce and the march of armies between Assyria and Egypt.

Another peculiarity of the defence of Jerusalem is the fact that although the city is supplied by water from one perennial spring, and numerous cisterns and reservoirs receiving the rain-fall, the region around it where a besieging army would encamp, furnishes to the besiegers not much food, and scarcely any water. Geo. Adam Smith, in his *Jerusalem,* says: "The only point in the environs of the city where the lower, harder rocks now throw up water to the surface is in the Kidron valley immediately under the wall of Ophel; and this supply, secured for the City even in times of siege by a tunnel through the rock, was supplemented by the reservoirs for which Jerusalem has always been famous, and which were fed from the rain caught upon the multitude of her roofs. These gave the City when blockaded an advantage over most of her besiegers, who found no springs in her immediate neighborhood, and in several cases were ignorant of any even at a distance. To which fact we may attribute the brevity and failure of several blockades, as well as the unwillingness of every great invader to come near to Jerusalem till he had made sure of his base of supplies in the lower country round about."

The accompanying section across Palestine from west to east through Jerusalem, will help one to understand her defensible position.

THE SOURCE OF HER GREATNESS. Here was a city in a rocky out-of-the-way situation, with almost no commerce or business, with some natural resources, but bare of many of the necessaries of life, with some gardens and orchards, but with no rich surrounding farmland, avoided by the great avenues of trade. What has made her so great? She was the chosen city of the one true God, the centre of His worship and laws and revelation, with a mission to reveal Him to the world; the one great light in a world of darkness. Here His prophets taught. Here was the temple that expressed His character and here was the training and the prophecies that led up to the great central fact of human history, the coming of Jesus Christ, the scene of His Life, His Passion, His Cross, and His Grave. "Jerusalem re-

Outline showing the strong position of Jerusalem.

mained the religious centre of the earth, the home of faith, the goal of pilgrimages, the original of the Heavenly City which would one day descend from God among men."

HER EXPERIENCES OF AFFLICTION. "The bare catalogue of the disasters which have overtaken Jerusalem is enough to paralyze her topographer. It is singular, says Robinson, how amid all the terrific earthquakes with which Syria has been afflicted for so many centuries, the city of Jerusalem has

lapidation of prominent edifices; about eighteen reconstructions, embellishments and large extensions; the additions of suburbs, and the abandonment of parts of the habited area. There were also two intervals of silence, after Nebuchadnezzar and after Hadrian, during which the city lay almost, if not altogether desolate; five abrupt passages from one religion to another."—George Adam Smith's *Jerusalem*.

WALLS. The walls, built at different times, are some of them difficult to

Photo by Jan Wilga

THE DOME OF THE ROCK.

been comparatively spared. Still the immunity of Jerusalem was only comparative. Besides being visited at irregular intervals by fits and starts of earthquake, the city has suffered several convulsions of disastrous magnitude. One of these happened in Uzziah's reign. The account in Matthew's gospel of what happened at the Crucifixion at least implies the liability of Jerusalem to severe shocks during the first century of our era.

"Besides the earthquakes, the City has endured nearly twenty sieges and assaults of the utmost severity, some involving considerable, others a total destruction of her walls and buildings; almost twenty more blockades or military occupations, with the wreck or di-

trace. But the three great walls can best be understood by the accompanying plan.

Zion or Sion. The hill on the east, called Mount Moriah in 2 Chron. 3:1, the threshing floor which David bought of Ornan the Jebusite, became the Temple Mount. The southern part was called Ophel. Most scholars now regard this or the whole Temple hill as the famous hill of Zion, David's city, his original fortress which he captured from the Jebusites. Till a few years ago it was the general opinion that the southwest hill, the most massive and dominant of the heights of Jerusalem, was Zion, but the trend of opinion is now decidedly toward the whole or the southern part of the Temple hill. However, Hon. Selah Merrill, our Consul in Jerusalem for many years, in his book on Jerusalem, published in 1908, locates Zion on the western hill. Zion became also a general name for the whole city of *Jerusalem, and the daughter of Zion* was the personified city and her population.

THE CŒNACULUM or *Upper Room,* where the last supper was held, where the disciples met after the resurrection of Jesus, and where were the first scenes of the day of Pentecost, probably the

of London. The city receives this within seven months of the year, a quarter of it in January.

The private citizens had cisterns, which were supplied by the rain from the roofs; and the city had a water supply "perhaps the most complete and extensive ever undertaken by a city," and which would enable it to endure a long siege. These great reservoirs, 7 miles from Jerusalem, were a part of the water supply of the city. They are known as *Solomon's Pools.* The largest

APPROACH TO JERUSALEM.
From the railroad station on the southwest.

house of Mary, the mother of Mark. Sanday feels very certain that the place on the western hill, now occupied by Moslem buildings, is the site of the ancient Cœnaculum, surrounded by seven synagogues, and where "The Little Church" was formed. It was then in the most fashionable part of Jerusalem.

THE WATER SUPPLY. Jerusalem has only one natural perennial spring, the Fountain of the Virgin. All other sources of supply came from the rainfall, stored in private cisterns, public reservoirs, and three aqueducts. The average rainfall of Jerusalem is rather over 25 inches, about as much as that

is 200 yards long, 60 yards wide and 50 feet deep. To-day they are useless. It is not probable that they date back to the time of Solomon, and are generally considered Roman works.

The accompanying plan of Jerusalem, will be the best guide to the reservoirs of the city.

The Pool of Bethesda is generally regarded as situated near the Church of St. Anne, in the northeast, while others are equally strenuous in favor of the Virgin's Fountain with its intermittent flow.

Burial-grounds.—The main cemetery of the city seems from an early date to

JERUSALEM.
The Jaffa Gate.

have been where it is still—on the steep slopes of the valley of the Kedron. The site of the Tombs of the Kings is still disputed. The royal sepulchres were probably chambers containing separate recesses for the successive kings.

Gardens.— The king's gardens of David and Solomon seem to have been in the bottom formed by the confluence of the Kedron and Hinnom. Neh. 3:15. The Mount of Olives, as its name and the names of various places upon it seem to imply, was a fruitful spot. At

26:9; Jer. 31:38; Zech. 14:10. 4. Gate of Joshua, governor of the city. 2 Kings 23:8. 5. Gate between the two walls. 2 Kings 25:4; Jer. 39:4. 6. Horse gate. Neh. 3:28; 2 Chron. 23:15; Jer. 31:40. 7. Valley gate (*i. e.* opening on ravine of Hinnom). ' Chron. 26:9; Neh. 2:13, 15; 3:13. 8. Fish gate. 2 Chron. 33:14; Neh. 3:3; Zeph. 1:10. 9. Dung gate. Neh. 2:13; 3:13. 10. Sheep gate. Neh. 3:1, 32; 12:39. 11. East gate. Neh. 3:29. 12. Miphkad. Neh. 3:31. 13. Fountain

FORTRESS OF ANTONIA.
Site of the palace of Pilate.

its foot was situated the garden of Gethsemane. At the time of the final siege the space north of the wall of Agrippa was covered with gardens, groves and plantations of fruit trees, enclosed by hedges and walls; and to level these was one of Titus' first operations. We know that the gate Gennath (*i. e.* "of gardens") opened on this side of the city.

Gates.—The following is a list of the gates named in the Bible and by Josephus, with the references to their occurrence:—1. Gate of Ephraim. 2 Chron. 25:23; Neh. 8:16; 12:39. This is probably the same as the—2. Gate of Benjamin. Jer. 20:2; 37:13; Zech. 14:10. If so, it was 400 cubits distant from the—3. Corner gate. 2 Chron. 25:23;

gate (Siloam?). Neh. 12:37. 14. Water gate. Neh. 12:37. 15. Old gate. Neh. 12:39. 16. Prison gate. Neh. 12:39. 17. Gate Harsith (perhaps the Sun; Authorized Version East gate). Jer. 19:2. 18. First gate. Zech. 14:10. 19. Gate Gennath (gardens). Jos. *B. J.* v. 4, § 4. 20. Essenes' gate. Jos. *B. J.* 4, § 2. To these should be added the following gates of the temple:—Gate Sur, 2 Kings 11:6; called also gate of foundation. 2 Chron. 23:5. Gate of the guard, or behind the guard, 2 Kings 11:6, 19; called the high gate. 2 Kings 15:35; 2 Chron. 23:20; 27:3. Gate Shallecheth. 1 Chron. 26:16. At present the chief gates are—1. The Zion's gate and the dung gate, in the south wall. 2. St. Stephen's gate and the golden gate (now walled up), in the east wall; 3. The Damascus gate and 4. Herod's gate, in the north wall; and 5. The Jaffa gate, in the west wall.

Population.—The ordinary population of Jerusalem in Christ's time was doubtless about 25,000 to 30,000. During the festivals the number was greatly increased. There would be supposedly some 60,000 to 70,000 in the city when Titus came against it, as in consequence of the Passover, and of the Idumeans being admitted, the city was densely populated. Josephus says that at the siege of Jerusalem the population was 3,000,-000; but Tacitus' statement that it was 600,000 is nearer the truth. This last

THE TRADITIONAL VIA DOLOROSA.
By which Jesus was led to his crucifixion.

is certainly within the limits of possibility.

Streets, houses, etc.—Of the nature of these in the ancient city we have only the most scattered notices. The word "street" in the A. V. of 2 Chron. 29: 4; 32: 6; Ezra 10: 9; Neh. 8: 1, 3, 16, in all cases translated in the Revised Version "the broad place"; and the "open place of the first gate toward the east," must have been not "streets," in our sense of the word, so much as the open spaces found in eastern towns round the inside of the gates. Streets, properly so called, there were, Jer. 5: 1; 11: 13, etc.; but the name of only one, "the bakers' street," Jer. 37: 21, is preserved to us. The Via Dolorosa, or street of sorrows, is a part of the street through which Christ is supposed to have been led on his way to his crucifixion. To the houses we have even less clue; but there is no reason to suppose that in either houses or streets the ancient Jerusalem differed very materially from the modern.

Annals of the city.—If, as is probable, Salem is the same as Jerusalem, the first mention of Jerusalem is in Gen. 14: 18, about B.C. 1900. It is next mentioned in Josh. 10: 1, B.C. 1451. The first siege appears to have taken place almost immediately after the death of Joshua—about 1427 B.C. Judah and Simeon "fought against it and took it, and smote it with the edge of the sword, and set the city on fire." Judges 1: 8. In the fifteen centuries which elapsed between this siege and the siege and destruction of the city by Titus, A.D. 70, the city was besieged no fewer than seventeen times; twice it was razed to the ground, and on two other occasions its walls were levelled. In this respect it stands without a parallel in any city, ancient or modern. David captured the city very soon after becoming king of all Israel, and made it his capital, fortified and enlarged it. Solomon adorned the city with beautiful buildings, including the temple, but made no additions to its walls. The city was taken by the Philistines and Arabians in the reign of Jehoram, B.C. 844, and by the Israelites in the reign of Amaziah, B.C. 782. It was thrice taken by Nebuchadnezzar, in the years B.C. 607, 597 and 586, in the last of which it was utterly destroyed. Its restoration commenced under Cyrus, B.C. 538, and was completed under Artaxerxes I., who issued commissions for this purpose to Ezra, B.C. 457, and Nehemiah, B.C. 445. In B.C. 332 it was captured by Alexander the Great. Under the Ptolemies and the Seleucidæ the town was prosperous, until Antiochus Epiphanes sacked it, B.C. 170. In consequence of his tyranny, the Jews rose under the Maccabees, and Jerusalem became again independent, and retained its position until its capture by the Romans under Pompey, B.C. 63. The temple was subsequently plundered by Crassus, B.C. 54, and the city by the Parthians, B.C. 40. Herod took up his

a church on the supposed site of the holy sepulchre, A.D. 336. Justinian added several churches and hospitals about A.D. 532. It was taken by the Persians under Chosroes II. in A.D. 614. The dominion of the Christians in the holy city was now rapidly drawing to a close. In A.D. 637 the patriarch Sophronius surrendered to the khalif Omar in person. With the fall of the Abas-

THE SO-CALLED TOWER OF DAVID.

residence there as soon as he was appointed sovereign, and restored the temple with great magnificence. On the death of Herod it became the residence of the Roman procurators, who occupied the fortress of Antonia. The greatest siege that it sustained, however, was at the hands of the Romans under Titus, when it held out nearly five months, and when the town was completely destroyed, A.D. 70. Hadrian restored it as a Roman colony, A.D. 136, and among other buildings erected a temple of Jupiter Capitolinus on the site of the temple. He gave to it the name of Ælia Capitolina, thus combining his own family name with that of the Capitoline Jupiter. The emperor Constantine established the Christian character by the erection of

sides the holy city passed into the hands of the Fatimite dynasty, under whom the sufferings of the Christians in Jerusalem reached their height. About 1077 it fell into the hands of the Seljuk Turks, and the cruelty of these rulers led to the Crusades. It was taken by the Crusaders in 1099, and for eighty-eight years Jerusalem remained in the hands of the Christians. During this time the city increased greatly in prosperity, and was filled with churches and palaces, many of which still remain. In 1187 it was retaken by Saladin after a siege of several weeks. From 1229 to 1247 it was at least nominally in the possession of the Christians, but from 1247 to 1517 it was subject to the Sultan of Egypt. In 1517 it passed under the sway of the Ottoman sultan Selim I., whose successor Suliman built the present walls of the city in 1542. In 1825 there was a revolt against Turkish rule in the city. In 1832 it was

COIN TO COMMEMORATE THE CAPTURE OF JUDEA, A. D. 70.

taken by Mohammed Ali from Egypt, and in 1840, after the bombardment of Acre, it was again under the Turks until freed by the World War.

being an average depth of 30 to 40 feet throughout the whole town, while east of the temple in one place the shaft was sunk 120 feet before reaching the original rock. The modern wall, built in 1542, forms an irregular quadrangle about 2½ miles in circuit, with seven gates and 34 towers. It varies in height from 20 to 60 feet. In the older parts of the city especially the streets are narrow, ungraded crooked, and often filthy. The houses are of hewn stone, with flat roofs and frequent domes. There are few windows toward the street.

The most beautiful part of modern Jerusalem is the former temple area (Mount Moriah), "with its lawns and cypress trees, and its noble dome rising high above the wall." This enclosure, now called *Haram esh-Sherîf,* is 35 acres in extent, and is nearly a mile in circuit.

On the site of the ancient temple stands the Mosque of Omar, "perhaps the very noblest specimen of building-art in Asia." "It is the most prominent as well as the most beautiful building in the whole city." The mosque is an octagonal building, each side measuring 66 feet. It is surmounted by a dome, whose top is 170 feet from the ground.

The Church of the Holy Sepulchre, which is claimed, but without sufficient reason, to be upon the site of Calvary, is "a collection of chapels and altars of different ages and a unique museum of religious curiosities from Adam to Christ."

There has been a great change in Jerusalem during the past 40 years. Before the World War great progress had been made in excavation and exploration to clear up disputed questions, but much still remains to be accomplished. The changes are so

CHURCH OF THE HOLY SEPULCHRE.

Modern Jerusalem, called by the Arabs *el Khuds,* is built upon the ruins of ancient Jerusalem. The accumulated rubbish of centuries is very great, there great in every way that even the best available plans give little idea of it at the present moment. Settlements are found in almost every direction outside of the walls, as in the suburbs of modern cities. The World War freed it from the Turks, and it is now the capital of an almost independent Palestine. [See PALESTINE.] In 1838 there were probably about 3000 Jews in the city; by 1892 they had increased to 25,322. In the latter year the railroad was completed from Jaffa (Joppa) to Jerusalem. To-day the population is about 64,000, of which half are Jews.

Jeru'sha (jĕ-ru'shà) (*possessed*), daughter of Zadok and queen of Uzziah. 2 Kings 15 : 33.

Jeru'shah (jè-ru'shah) (*possessed*). 2 Chron. 27 : 1. The same as the preceding.

Jesa'iah (jè-sā'yah) (*salvation of Jehovah*). 1. Son of Hananiah, brother of Pelatiah and grandson of Zerubbabel. 1 Chron. 3 : 21.
2. A Benjamite. Neh. 11 : 7.

Jesha'iah (jè-shā'yah) (*salvation of Jehovah*). 1. One of the six sons of Jeduthun. 1 Chron. 25 : 3, 15.
2. A Levite in the reign of David, eldest son of Rehabiah, a descendant of Amram through Moses by his younger son Eliezer. 1 Chron. 26 : 25.
3. The son of Athaliah, and chief of the house of the Bene-Elam who returned with Ezra. Ezra 8 : 7. (B.C. 458.)
4. A Merarite who returned with Ezra. Ezra 8 : 19.

Jesh'anah (jĕsh'a-nah) (*old*), a town which, with its dependent villages, was one of the three taken from Jeroboam by Abijah. 2 Chron. 13 : 19. Probably the modern *Ain Sinia*, 3¼ miles north of Bethel.

Jeshare'lah (jè-shär-e'lah), son of Asaph, and head of the seventh of the twenty-four wards into which the musicians of the Levites were divided. 1 Chron. 25 : 14. [ASARELAH.]

Jesheb'eab (jè-shĕb'e-ăb) (*father's seat*), head of the fourteenth course of priests. 1 Chron. 24 : 13.

Je'sher (jè'shĕr) (*uprightness*), one of the sons of Caleb the son of Hezron by his wife Azubah. 1 Chron. 2 : 18.

Jesh'imon (jĕsh'ĭ-mŏn) (*a wilderness*), a name which occurs in Num. 21 : 20 and 23 : 28, in designating the position of Pisgah and Peor; both described

as "facing the Jeshimon." Perhaps the dreary, barren waste of hills lying immediately on the west of the Dead Sea.

Jeshish'ai (jè-shĭsh'a-ī) (*an old man*), one of the ancestors of the Gadites who dwelt in Gilead. 1 Chron. 5 : 14.

Jeshoha'iah (jĕsh-ó-hā'yah), a chief of the Simeonites, descended from Shimei. 1 Chron. 4 : 36.

Jesh'ua (jĕsh'u-à) (*Jehovah is salvation*), another form of the name Joshua or Jesus. 1. Joshua the son of Nun. Neh. 8 : 17. [JOSHUA.]
2. A priest in the reign of David, to whom the ninth course fell by lot. 1 Chron. 24 : 11.
3. One of the Levites in the reign of Hezekiah. 2 Chron. 31 : 15.
4. Son of Jehozadak, first high priest after the Babylonish captivity. B.C. 536. Jeshua was probably born in Babylon, whither his father Jehozadak had been taken captive while young. 1 Chron. 6 : 15, Authorized Version. He came up from Babylon in the first year of Cyrus, with Zerubbabel, and took a leading part with him in the rebuilding of the temple and the restoration of the Jewish commonwealth. The two prophecies concerning him in Zech. 3 and 6 : 9–15 point him out as an eminent type of Christ.
5. Head of a Levitical house, one of those which returned from the Babylonish captivity. Ezra 2 : 40; 3 : 9; Neh. 3 : 19; 8 : 7; 9 : 4, 5; 12 : 8, etc.
6. A branch of the family of Pahathmoab, one of the chief families, probably, of the tribe of Judah. Neh. 10 : 14; 7 : 11, etc.; Ezra 2 : 6; 10 : 30.

Jesh'ua (jĕsh'u-à) (*Jehovah is salvation*), one of the towns inhabited by the people of Judah after the return from captivity. Neh. 11 : 26. It is not mentioned elsewhere.

Jesh'uah (jĕsh'u-ah), a priest in the reign of David, 1 Chron. 24 : 11, the same as JESHUA, No. 2.

Jesh'urun (jĕsh'u-rŭn) (*the upright one*), and once by mistake in Authorized Version JESURUN, Isa. 44 : 2, a symbolical name for Israel in Deut. 32 : 15; 33 : 5, 26; Isa. 44 : 2. "The word is a name of endearment used in poetry for the nation of Israel with reference to the moral character which they were created to exhibit." It was formerly explained as "blessed" but with an idea of uprightness.

Jesi'ah (jĕ-sī'ah) (*Jehovah lends*).
1. A Korhite, one of the mighty men
who joined David's standard at Ziklag.
1 Chron. 12 : 6. (B.C. 1057.)
2. The second son of Uzziel, the son
of Kohath. 1 Chron. 23 : 20.

Jesim'iel (jĕ-sĭm'ĭ-el) (*God setteth
up*), a Simeonite chief of the family
of Shimei. 1 Chron. 4 : 36.

Jes'se (jĕs'se) (*wealthy*), the father
óf David, was the son of Obed, who
again was the fruit of the union of
Boaz and the Moabitess Ruth. His
great-grandmother was Rahab the Canaanite, of Jericho. Matt. 1 : 5. Jesse's
genealogy is twice given in full in the
Old Testament, viz., Ruth 4 : 18–22 and
1 Chron. 2 : 5-12. He is commonly designated as " Jesse the Bethlehemite," 1
Sam. 16 : 1, 18 ; 17 : 58 ; but his full title
is "the Ephrathite of Bethlehem Judah," ch. 17 : 12. He is an "old man"
when we first meet with him, 1 Sam.
17 : 12, with eight sons, ch. 16 : 10 ; 17 :
12, residing at Bethlehem. ch. 16 : 4, 5.
Jesse's wealth seems to have consisted
of a flock of sheep and goats, which
were under the care of David, ch. 16 :
11 ; 17 : 34, 35. After David's rupture
with Saul he took his father and his
mother into the country of Moab and
deposited them with the king, and there
they disappear from our view in the
records of Scripture. We are not told
who the wife of Jesse was.

Jes'ui (jĕs'u-ī), the son of Asher,
whose descendants the Jesuites were
numbered in the plains of Moab at the
Jordan of Jericho. Num. 26 : 44. He
is elsewhere called ISUI, Gen. 46 : 17,
and ISHUAI. 1 Chron. 7 : 30. R. V.
Ishvi.

Jes'uites (jĕs'u-ītes) (*the posterity
of Jesui*), **The**, a family of the tribe
of Asher. Num. 26 : 44.

Jes'urun (jĕs'u-rŭn). [JESHURUN.]

Je'sus (*Jehovah is salvation*). The
Greek form of the name Joshua or Jeshua.
It is used of—1. Joshua, the son of Nun.
Acts 7 : 45 ; Heb. 4 : 8, and of several
persons mentioned in the Apocrypha.
" It was a common name among the Jews
of the Greek-speaking period," as the
Hebrew form had been earlier.

Je'sus (jē'ṣus), called **Justus**, a
Christian who was with St. Paul at
Rome. Col. 4 : 11. (A.D. 60.)

Je'sus Christ. "The life and character of Jesus Christ," says Dr. Schaff,
"is the holy of holies in the history of
the world." 1. NAME.—The name *Jesus*
signifies *Jehovah is salvation*. It is the
Greek form of JEHOSHUA (Joshua).
The name *Christ* signifies *anointed*.
Jesus was both *priest* and *king*. Among
the Jews priests were anointed, as their
inauguration to their office. 1 Chron.
16 : 22. In the New Testament the name
Christ is used as equivalent to the Hebrew Messiah (*anointed*), John 1 : 41,
the name given to the long-promised
Prophet and King whom the Jews had
been taught by their prophets to expect.
Matt. 11 : 3 ; Acts 19 : 4. The use of
this name, as applied to the Lord, has
always a reference to the promises of
the prophets. The name of Jesus is
the proper name of our Lord, and that
of Christ is added to identify him with
the promised Messiah. Other names
are sometimes added to the names Jesus
Christ, thus, "Lord," "a king," "King
of Israel," "Emmanuel," "Son of
David," "chosen of God."

II. BIRTH.—Jesus Christ was born of
the Virgin Mary, God being his father,
at Bethlehem of Judea, six miles south
of Jerusalem. The date of his birth
was most probably in December, B.C. 5,
four years before the era from which
we count our years. That era was not
used till several hundred years after
Christ. The calculations were made by
a learned monk, Dionysius Exiguus, in
the sixth century, who made an error
of four years ; so that to get the exact
date from the birth of Christ we must
add four years to our usual dates ; *i. e.*
A.D. 1924 is really 1928 years since the
birth of Christ. It is also more than
likely that our usual date for Christmas,
December 25, is not far from the real
date of Christ's birth. Since the 25th
of December comes when the longest
night gives way to the returning sun on
his triumphant march, it makes an appropriate anniversary to mark the birth
of him who appeared in the darkest
night of error and sin as the true Light
of the world. At the time of Christ's
birth Augustus Cæsar was emperor of
Rome, and Herod the Great king of
Judea, but subject to Rome. God's providence had prepared the world for the
coming of Christ, and this was the fit-
test time in all its history. 1. All the
world was subject to one government,
so that the apostles could travel everywhere : the door of every land was open
for the gospel. 2. The world was at

peace, so that the gospel could have free course. 3. The Greek language was spoken everywhere with their other languages. 4. The Jews were scattered everywhere with synagogues and the Holy Scriptures,—the Old Testament.

III. EARLY LIFE.—Jesus, having a manger at Bethlehem for his cradle, at forty days old was taken to the temple at Jerusalem; and returning to Bethlehem, received a visit of adoration from the three wise men of the East. Soon after he was taken to Egypt to escape Herod's massacre of the infants there. After a few months stay there, Herod having died in April, B.C. 4, the family returned to their Nazareth home, where Jesus lived till he was about thirty years old, subject to his parents, and increasing " in wisdom and stature, and in favor with God and man." The only incident recorded of his early life is his going up to Jerusalem to attend the passover when he was twelve years old, and his conversation with the learned men in the temple. But we can understand the childhood and youth of Jesus better when we remember the surrounding influences amid which he grew. 1. The natural scenery was rugged and mountainous, but full of beauty. His home was in a country town, not in a large city, nor a secluded village. 2. The Roman dominion was galling. The people of God were subject to a foreign yoke. The taxes were heavy. Roman soldiers, laws, money, ever reminded them of their subjection, when they ought to be free and themselves the rulers of the world. When Jesus was ten years old, there was a great insurrection, Acts 5 : 37, in Galilee. He who was to be King of the Jews heard and felt all this. 3. The Jewish hopes of a Redeemer, of throwing off their bondage, of becoming the glorious nation promised in the prophets, were in the very air he breathed. The conversation at home and in the streets was full of them. 4. Within his view, and his boyish excursions, were many remarkable historic places,—rivers, hills, cities, plains,—that would keep in mind the history of his people and God's dealings with them. 5. His school training. From about B.C. 75 attendance on the elementary schools became compulsory. These schools were always in intimate connection with the synagogue, which was found in every considerable

village in the land. Here are a few of the innumerable popular sayings of the period : " Jerusalem was destroyed because the instruction of the young was neglected." " The world is only saved by the breath of the school-children." " Even for the rebuilding of the temple the schools must not be interrupted." 6. His home training. A child's first school was his home and his first teachers his parents. The boy was under the care of his mother till he was five years old. At five or six he was sent to the elementary school, where he was to learn the law, at first by extracts written on scrolls of the more important passages, the Shemà or creed of Deut. 6 : 4, the Hallel or festival psalms, Ps. 114, 118, 136, and by catechetical teaching in school. At twelve he became more directly responsible for his obedience to the law ; and on the day when he attained the age of thirteen, put on for the first time the phylacteries which were worn at the recital of his daily prayer. In addition to this, Jesus no doubt learned the carpenter's trade of his reputed father Joseph, and, as Joseph probably died before Jesus began his public ministry, he may have contributed to the support of his mother.

IV. PUBLIC MINISTRY.—All the leading events recorded of Jesus' life are given in the Chronological Table of the Life of Christ, in the APPENDIX at the end of this volume ; it is necessary only that here should be given a general survey.

Jesus began to enter upon his ministry when he was " about thirty years old ;" that is, he was not very far from thirty, older or younger. He is regarded as nearly thirty-one, in the tables of chronology referred to above and by most others. Having been baptized by John early in the winter of 26–27, he spent the larger portion of his first year in Judea and about the lower Jordan, till in December he went northward to Galilee through Samaria. The next year and a half, from December, A.D. 27, to October or November, A.D. 29, was spent in Galilee and northern Palestine, chiefly in the vicinity of the Sea of Galilee. In November, 29, Jesus made his final departure from Galilee, and the rest of his ministry was in Judea and Perea, beyond Jordan, till his crucifixion, April 7, A.D. 30. After three days he proved his divinity by rising from the dead ; and after appearing on eleven different occasions to his disciples during forty days, he finally ascended to heaven, where he is the living, ever-present, all-powerful Saviour of his people.

Jesus Christ, being both human and divine, is fitted to be the true Saviour of men. In this, as in every action and character, he is shown to be "the wisdom and power of God unto salvation." As human, he reaches down to our natures, sympathizes with us, shows us that God knows all our feelings, and weaknesses and sorrows and sins, brings God near to us, who otherwise could not realize the Infinite and Eternal as a father and friend. He is divine, in order that he may be an all-powerful, all-loving Saviour, able and willing to defend us from every enemy, to subdue all temptations, to deliver from all sin, and to bring each of his people, and the whole Church, into complete and final victory.

Jesus Christ is the centre of the world's history, as he is the centre of the Bible history and teachings.

Je'ther (jē'ther) (*abundance*). 1. Used for Jethro, the father-in-law of Moses. Ex. 4:18. Margin.

2. The first-born of Gideon's seventy sons. Judges 8:20.

3. The father of Amasa, captain-general of Absalom's army. 1 Kings 2:5. Jether is another form of ITHRA. 2 Sam. 17:25. He is described in 1 Chron. 2:17 as an Ishmaelite, which again is more likely to be correct than the "Israelite" of the Hebrew in 2 Sam. 17.

4. The son of Jada, a descendant of Hezron, of the tribe of Judah. 1 Chron. 2:32.

5. The son of Ezra. 1 Chron. 4:17.

6. The chief of a family of warriors of the line of Asher, and father of Jephunneh. 1 Chron. 7:38. He is probably the same as ITHRAN in the preceding verse.

Je'theth (jē'theth), one of the "dukes" who came of Esau. Gen. 36:40; 1 Chron. 1:51.

Jeth'lah (jĕth'lah), one of the cities of the tribe of Dan. Josh. 19:42.

Jeth'ro (jĕth'rô) (*his excellence*) was priest or prince of Midian. Moses married his daughter Zipporah. (B.C. 1530.) On account of his local knowledge his son was entreated to remain with the Israelites throughout their journey to Canaan. Num. 10:31, 33. He is called REUEL in Ex. 2:18, and RAGUEL in Num. 10:29, the same word in the original for both. Reuel is probably his proper name, and Jethro his official title.

Je'tur (jē'tŭr). Gen. 25:15; 1 Chron. 1:31; 5:19. [ITURÆA.]

Jeu'el (jē-ū'el), a chief man of Judah, one of the Bene-Zerah. 1 Chron. 9:6.

Je'ush (jē'ŭsh). 1. Son of Esau by Aholibamah the daughter of Anah, the son of Zebeon the Hivite. Gen. 36:5, 14, 18; 1 Chron. 1:35.

2. A Benjamite, son of Bilhan. 1 Chron. 7:10, 11.

3. A Gershonite Levite, of the house of Shimei. 1 Chron. 23:10, 11.

4. Son of Rehoboam king of Judah. 2 Chron. 11:18, 19.

Je'uz (jē'uz), head of a Benjamite house. 1 Chron. 8:10.

Jew (*a man of Judah*). This name was properly applied to a member of the kingdom of Judah after the separation of the ten tribes. The term first makes its appearance just before the captivity of the ten tribes. 2 Kings 16:6. After the return the word received a larger application. Partly from the predominance of the members of the old kingdom of Judah among those who returned to Palestine, partly from the identification of Judah with the religious ideas and hopes of the people, all the members of the new state were called Jews (Judeans), and the name was extended to the remnants of the race scattered throughout the nations. Under the name of "Judeans" the people of Israel were known to classical writers. (Tac. *H.* v. 2, etc.) In John's gospel the name "Jew" is used especially as antagonistic to our Lord. In this sense they were the blind followers of the Pharisees, scrupulous about traditions, but careless about those things Jesus taught as essentials. Everywhere in the New Testament it is also used in opposition to the Gentiles, proselytes or Samaritans. Mark 7:3; John 2:6, 13; 5:1, 7:2; etc. Also Rom. 1:16; 2:9, 10; Col. 3:11, etc. It was at the same time less expressive than *Israelite,* which brought out with especial clearness the privileges and hopes of the children of Jacob. 2 Cor. 11:22; John 1:47.

Jewel. [STONES, PRECIOUS.]

Jew'ess, a woman of Hebrew birth.

without distinction of tribe. Acts 16: 1; 24:24.

Jewish, of or belonging to Jews; an epithet applied to their rabbinical legends. Titus 1:14.

Jew'ry, the same word elsewhere rendered Judah and Judea. It occurs several times in the Apocrypha and the New Testament, but once only in the Old Testament—Dan. 5:13. Jewry is of frequent occurrence in Old English.

Jezani'ah (jĕz-a-nī'ah) (*Jehovah doth hearken*), the son of Hoshaiah the Maachathite, and one of the captains of the forces who had escaped from Jerusalem during the final attack of the beleaguering army of the Chaldeans. (B.C. 586.) When the Babylonians had departed, Jezaniah, with the men under his command, was one of the first who returned to Gedaliah at Mizpah. In the events which followed the assassination of that officer Jezaniah took a prominent part. 2 Kings 25:23; Jer. 40:8; 42:1. Called AZARIAH in Jer. 43:2 and JAAZANIAH in 2 Kings.

Jez'ebel (jĕz'e-bĕl) (*unmarried*), wife of Ahab king of Israel. She was a Phœnician princess, daughter of Ethbaal king of the Zidonians. In her hands her husband became a mere puppet. 1 Kings 21:25. The first effect of her influence was the immediate establishment of the Phœnician worship on a grand scale in the court of Ahab. At her table were supported no less than 450 prophets of Baal and 400 of Astarte. 1 Kings 16:31, 32; 18:19. The prophets of Jehovah were attacked by her orders and put to the sword. 1 Kings 18:13; 2 Kings 9:7. At last the people, at the instigation of Elijah, rose against her ministers and slaughtered them at the foot of Carmel. When she found her husband cast down by his disappointment at being thwarted by Naboth, 1 Kings 21:7, she wrote a warrant in Ahab's name, and sealed it with his seal. To her, and not to Ahab, was sent the announcement that the royal wishes were accomplished, 1 Kings 21:14, and on her accordingly fell the prophet's curse, as well as on her husband, 1 Kings 21:23; a curse fulfilled literally by Jehu, whose chariot-horses trampled out her life. 2 Kings 9:30–37.

Je'zer (jē'zēr) (*form*), the third son of Naphtali, Gen. 46:24; Num. 26:49; 1 Chron. 7:13, and father of the family of Jezerites.

Jezi'ah (jė-zī'ah), a descendant of Parosh, who had married a foreign wife. Ezra 10:25.

Je'ziel (jē'zĭ-el) (*assembly of God*), a Benjamite who joined David at Ziklag. 1 Chron. 12:3. (B.C. 1057.)

Jezli'ah (jĕz-lī'ah), a Benjamite of the sons of Elpaal. 1 Chron. 8:18.

Jezo'ar (jė-zō'ar), the son of Helah, one of the wives of Asher. 1 Chron. 4:7.

Jezrahi'ah (jĕzra-hī'ah) (*Jehovah will shine*), a Levite, the leader of the choristers at the solemn dedication of the wall of Jerusalem under Nehemiah. Neh. 12:42. (B.C. 446.)

Jez'reel (jĕz're-el) (*God soweth*). 1. A descendant of the father or founder of Etam, of the line of Judah. 1 Chron. 4:3.

2. The eldest son of the prophet Hosea. Hos. 1:4.

Jez'reel (jĕz're-el). 1. A city situated in the plain of the same name between Gilboa and Little Hermon, now generally called Esdraelon. [ESDRAELON.] It appears in Josh. 19:18, but its historical importance dates from the reign of Ahab, B.C. 876–854, who chose it for his chief residence. The situation of the modern village of *Zerin* still remains to show the fitness of his choice. In the neighborhood, or within the town probably, was a temple of Astarte, with an establishment of 400 priests supported by Jezebel. 1 Kings 16:33; 2 Kings 10:11. The palace of Ahab, 1 Kings 21:1; 18:46, probably containing his "ivory house," 1 Kings 22:39. was on the eastern side of the city, the harem being close by the gate, with windows overlooking the road thither. Comp. 1 Kings 21:1; 2 Kings 9:25, 30, 33. The vineyard of Naboth was here, and his execution took place here, or perhaps at Samaria. Still in the same eastern direction are two springs, "the dead spring" and *Ain Jelud,* both copious and good. The latter, probably from both its size and its situation, was known as "the fountain that was in Jezreel." 1 Sam. 29:1. With the fall of the house of Ahab the glory of Jezreel departed.

2. A town in Judah, in the neighborhood of the southern Carmel. Josh. 15:56. Here David in his wanderings took Ahinoam the Israelitess for his first wife. 1 Sam. 27:3; 30:5.

Jez'reelitess (jĕz're-el-ītess), a

woman of Jezreel. 1 Sam. 27:3; 30:5; 2 Sam. 2:2; 3:2; 1 Chron. 3:1.

Jib'sam (jïb'sam) (*fragrant*), one of the sons of Tola, the son of Issachar. 1 Chron. 7:2.

Jid'laph (jïd'laf) (*he weepeth*), a son of Nahor. Gen. 22:22.

Jim'na (jïm'nà), the first-born of Asher. Num. 26:44. He is elsewhere called in the Authorized Version JIM-NAH, Gen. 46:17, and IMNAH. 1 Chron. 7:30.

Jim'nah = JIMNA = IMNAH. Gen. 46:17.

Jim'nites, The, descendants of the preceding. Num. 26:44.

Jiph'tah (jïf'tah) (*he setteth free*), one of the cities of Judah in the maritime lowland, or Shefelah. Josh. 15:43. It has not yet been met with.

Jiph'thah=el (jïf'thah-ĕl), **The valley of**, a valley which served as one of the landmarks for the boundary of both Zebulun, Josh. 19:14, and Asher. Josh. 19:27. Dr. Robinson suggests that Jiphthah-el was identical with Jotapata, which survives in the modern *Jefat*, a village in the mountains of Galilee, halfway between the Bay of Acre and the Lake of Gennesareth, but many modern scholars dispute it.

Jo'ab (jō'ăb) (*Jehovah is father*), the most remarkable of the three nephews of David, the children of Zeruiah, David's sister. (B.C. 1053–1012.) Joab first appears after David's accession to the throne at Hebron. Abner slew in battle Asahel, the youngest brother of Joab; and when David afterward received Abner into favor, Joab treacherously murdered him. [ABNER.] There was now no rival left in the way of Joab's advancement, and at the siege of Jerusalem he was appointed for his prowess commander-in-chief—"captain of the host." In the wide range of wars which David undertook, Joab was the acting general. He was called by the almost regal title of "lord," 2 Sam. 11:11. In the entangled relations which grew up in David's domestic life he bore an important part, successfully re-instating Absalom in David's favor after the murder of Amnon. 2 Sam. 14:1–20. When the relations between father and son were reversed by the revolt of Absalom, Joab remained true to the king, taking the rebel prince's dangerous life in spite of David's injunction to spare him, and when no one else had

courage to act so decisive a part. 2 Sam. 18:2, 11–15. (B.C. 1023). The king transferred the command to Amasa, which so enraged Joab that he adroitly assassinated Amasa when pretending to welcome him as a friend. 2 Sam. 20:10. Friendly relations between himself and David seem to have existed afterward, 2 Sam. 24:2; but at the close of his long life, his loyalty, so long unshaken, at last wavered. "Though he had not turned after Absalom, he turned after Adonijah." 1 Kings 2:28. This probably filled up the measure of the king's long-cherished resentment. It is not, however, certain that he had the slightest thought of disloyalty to David himself. The revival of the pretensions of Adonijah after David's death was sufficient to awaken the suspicions of Solomon. Joab fled to the shelter of the altar at Gibeon, and was there slain by Benaiah.

2. One of the descendants of Kenaz. 1 Chron. 4:14.

3. The name of a family which returned with Zerubbabel and Ezra. Ezra 2:6; 8:9; Neh. 7:11.

Jo'ah (Jō'ah) (*Jehovah is brother*). 1. The son of Asaph, and chronicler or keeper of the records to Hezekiah. Isa. 36:3, 11, 22.

2. The son or grandson of Zimmah, a Gershonite. 1 Chron. 6:21.

3. The third son of Obed-edom, 1 Chron. 26:4, a Korhite, and one of the doorkeepers appointed by David.

4. A Gershonite, the son of Zimmah and father of Eden. 2 Chron. 29:12. Very possibly the same as 2.

5. The son of Joahaz, and annalist or keeper of the records to Josiah. 2 Chron. 34:8. (B.C. 623.)

Jo'ahaz (jō'a-hăz) (*Jehovah holds*), the father of Joah, the chronicler or keeper of the records to King Josiah. 2 Chron. 34:8.

Joa'nan (jō-ā'nan). In Revised Version for JOANNA, 1. Luke 3:27.

Joan'na (jō-an'na) (*Jehovah hath been gracious*) (in Revised Version spelled JOANAN). 1. Son of Rhesa, according to the text of Luke 3:27, one of the ancestors of Christ; but probably Rhesa is a title of Zerubbabel which has crept into the text, making Joanan, son of Zerubbabel, and the same as HANANIAH in 1 Chron. 3.19.

2. The name of a woman, occurring twice in Luke (8:3; 24:10), but evi-

dently denoting the same person. (A.D. 28–30.) In the first passage she is expressly stated to have been "wife of Chuza, steward of Herod," that is, Antipas, tetrarch of Galilee.

Jo'ash (jō'ăsh) (*Jehovah is strong*), contracted from JEHOASH. 1. Son of Ahaziah king of Judah (B.C. 843), and the only one of his children who escaped the murderous hand of Athaliah. After his father's sister Jehoshabeath, the wife of Jehoiada the high priest, had stolen him from among the king's sons, he was hidden for six years in the chambers of the temple. In the seventh year of his age and sixth of his concealment, a successful revolution, conducted by Jehoiada, placed him on the throne of his ancestors, and freed the country from the tyranny and idolatries of Athaliah. For at least twenty-three years, while Jehoiada lived, his reign was very prosperous; but after the death of Jehoiada, Joash fell into the hands of bad advisers, at whose suggestion he revived the worship of Baal and Ashtaroth. When he was rebuked for this by Zechariah, the son of Jehoiada, Joash caused him to be stoned to death in the very court of the Lord's house. Matt. 23:35. That very year Hazael king of Syria came up against Jerusalem, and carried off a vast booty as the price of his departure. Joash had scarcely escaped this danger when he fell into another and fatal one. Two of his servants conspired against him and slew him in his bed in the fortress of Millo. Joash's reign lasted forty years, from 836 to 796 B.C.

2. Son and successor of Jehoahaz on the throne of Israel from B.C. 798 to 782, and very possibly co-regent with his father before that time. 2 Kings 13:1, comp. with 12:1; 13:10. When he succeeded to the crown the kingdom was in a deplorable state from the devastations of Hazael and Ben-hadad, kings of Syria. On occasion of a friendly visit paid by Joash to Elisha on his death-bed, the prophet promised him deliverance from the Syrian yoke in Aphek. 2 Kings 13:14–19. He then bade him smite upon the ground, and the king smote thrice and then stayed. The prophet rebuked him for staying, and limited to three his victories over Syria. Accordingly Joash did defeat Ben-hadad three times on the field of battle, and recovered from him the cities which Hazael had taken from Jehoahaz. The other great military event of Joash's reign was the successful war with Amaziah king of Judah. He died in the fifteenth year of Amaziah king of Judah.

3. The father of Gideon, and a wealthy man among the Abi-ezrites. Judges 6:11.

4. Apparently a younger son of Ahab, who held a subordinate jurisdiction in the lifetime of his father. 1 Kings 22:26; 2 Chron. 18:25. (B.C. 854.)

5. A descendant of Shelah the son of Judah, but the passage naming him is not clear. 1 Chron. 4:22.

6. A Benjamite, son of Shemaah of Gibeah, 1 Chron. 12:3, who resorted to David at Ziklag.

7. One of the officers of David's household. 1 Chron. 27:28.

8. Son of Becher and head of a Benjamite house. 1 Chron. 7:8.

Jo'atham (jō'a-tham)=JOTHAM the son of Uzziah. Matt. 1:9.

Job (jōb) (R. V. *Iob*), the third son of Issachar, Gen. 46:13. Probably a copyist's error for the name *Jashub* which appears in another genealogy. 1 Chron. 7:1.

Job, the book of, stands as "the greatest poem in the world's great literatures."

ITS PURPOSE is to throw light upon the world-wide problem of the mystery of suffering in a world governed by the good God,—both in its relation to God, and its relation to man.

ITS LITERARY FORM is a dramatic poem in an epic story. Genung calls it "The Epic of the Inner Life."

It is almost universally agreed that the basis of the Book of Job was an historical fact; that Job was a real man who underwent such severe trials and disasters that they made a lasting impression upon his age, and the ages following. Ezekiel 14:14 and James 5:11, both mention Job.

The sad experience of Job, his conflict and his final victory were the most perfect and fitting groundwork for teaching in the most effective way the great divine truths about the darkest problem that faces mankind.

As the parable of the Prodigal Son has had vastly more power than the same truths told in a didactic way, and is a perfect vehicle of divine inspiration; so when we realize that the Book of

Job is a divinely inspired poem, drama or epic, founded on fact, and true to fact, to life, and to God, the whole book is lifted to a higher sphere, and given a more effective power.

The first two chapters and the last (from verse 7) are in prose; the rest of the book is poetic in form and expression.

AGE AND DATE. The period when Job lived, to which his personal story belongs, the scene of the drama, is almost universally understood to be the age of the patriarchs some two thousand years before Christ. But this gives no information as to the time when the book was written, any more than the date of "King Lear" or of "Julius Cæsar" tells us when Shakespeare wrote his plays.

The date of writing is placed by many modern scholars somewhere between Solomon and the Exile. But the whole atmosphere of the book, like that of Genesis, belongs to the days of the patriarchs. And there is not a single allusion or reference to anything that might not have existed in those early days.

THE AUTHOR is unknown.

UNITY. There are two views as to the unity of the book according as the student looks upon it—

1. From the literary and ethical standpoint the book is one complete and beautiful whole, by one inspired author of consummate genius, so Genung says—

"As a whole, the Book of Job is intelligible, and, indeed, easily intelligible; as a piece of patchwork it defies explanation."

2. From the critical standpoint, many scholars regard it as a composite work, by various writers at different times.

ITS STRUCTURE. The book consists of five parts or divisions, each of which presents one of the five possible solutions of the problem. Jesus Christ brought life and immortality to light, but so far as this problem is concerned, his message flows in these five channels. What in Job is twilight, in Jesus becomes the morning sun.

PART I. Chapters i and ii; the prose story on which the rest of the book is founded. Job is at home prosperous, good, peaceful. There are five scenes changing from earth to heaven. The persons are Jehovah, sons of God, the Adversary, Job, Job's wife and four messengers. The time is several weeks.

Job loses his property and his children, and is afflicted with a painful disease, and sits on the city ash heap outside the walls. The visions of heaven reveal the meaning of his misfortunes and the first solution of the problem, that *sometimes afflictions are sent as a test of character.*

PART II. Chapters iii–xxxi, in poetic form, present the great debate between Job and his three friends. Job sick and poor is on the ash mound, around which is an audience of neighbors, citizens, relatives, visitors, children; and a rabble. Three chiefs come to condole with Job, Eliphaz from Teman south of the Dead Sea, 200 miles from Uz. He was the oldest and wisest of the three, of dignified and noble character. Bildad, from Shuah near the Euphrates, a sage, of literary culture, quoting proverbs and traditions of the fathers. Zophar from Naamah 60 miles south of the Dead Sea, the ordinary good man of the day, uttering common thoughts in a commonplace way, somewhat sharp and bigoted.

There were three cycles of debate. The friends argue that Job's afflictions prove him to be a bad man, for a good God could not inflict such disasters on a righteous man. Job denies that he is bad. The friends regard this as a denial that God is good. They defend God at the expense of Job.

The second solution is *that sometimes suffering is the fruit and punishment of sin; but that no one knows enough to judge his fellow man, and to decide from the suffering how much, if any, is due to wrong-doing.*

PART III. THE ORATION OF ELIHU, Chapters xxxii–xxxvii. Poetic form except 32:1–5. Elihu was a young man who had been present during the discussion. He adds little that is new, but brings out into clear, shining vision what the friends only hinted at as subordinate to their main argument. Elihu shows that trouble and suffering are a discipline, one of the lessons in the school of life by which we are educated and trained in heavenly character.

His solution is *that suffering is a means of discipline even when sent or permitted for other ends, as for a test and punishment.*

NOTE that during the latter part of Elihu's oration there are signs of the coming of a storm, with wind, hail, snow, thunder and lightning, increasing in violence, till the storm has become a whirlwind, compelling Elihu to cease speaking, while Jehovah's presence is manifested by a brightness shining on the dark background of the storm, and out of the whirlwind comes a voice.

PART IV. THE VOICE FROM THE WHIRLWIND. Chapters xxxvii–xli. The voice describes the wonderful works of God, showing his infinite power, knowledge, wisdom and goodness, and that therefore man can trust him, even when he cannot understand the reasons for his doings. It is a training in faith. The fourth solution is *there are some troubles which are an insoluble mystery, but God has revealed Himself as so good, so wise, so powerful, such a loving Father, that we can rest our souls on him in perfect peace and faith and love.*

PART V. THE RESTORATION OF JOB. Chapter xlii, vs. 1–6, poetry; 7–17, prose. Job comes to the right mind and heart, is approved of God, and is restored to a larger, fuller, nobler life, with larger means for usefulness. The outward prosperity was a symbol and expression of his spiritual life and success, just as a perfect outward heaven is the natural place for those who have the perfect heavenly life. The fifth solution is *that every good man's life in the end is a success. With God's children there are no life-tragedies. There are dramas and lyric songs and epics, but no tragedies.*

Jo'bab (jō'băb) (*a desert*). 1. One of the sons of Joktan. Gen. 10 : 29; 1 Chron. 1 : 23.

2. One of the "kings" of Edom. Gen. 36 : 33, 34 : 1 Chron. 1 : 44, 45.

3. King of Madon; one of the northern chieftains who attempted to oppose Joshua's conquest, and were routed by him at the waters of Merom. Josh. 11 : 1 only.

4. Head of a Benjamite house. 1 Chron. 8 : 9.

Joch'ebed (jŏk'e-bed) (*Jehovah is glory*), the wife and at the same time the aunt of Amram and the mother of Moses and Aaron. Ex. 2 : 1; 6 : 20; Num. 26 : 59.

Jo'da (jō'dà), in Revised Version for JUDA. Luke 3 : 26.

Jo'ed (jō'ed), a Benjamite, the son of Pedaiah. Neh. 11 : 7.

Jo'el (jō'el) (*Jehovah is God*). 1. Eldest son of Samuel the prophet, 1

Sam. 8 : 2; 1 Chron. 6 : 33; 15 : 17, and father of Heman the singer.

2. In 1 Chron. 6 : 36, Authorized Version, Joel seems to be merely a corruption of Shaul in ver. 24.

3. A Simeonite chief. 1 Chron. 4 : 35.

4. A descendant of Reuben. 1 Chron. 5 : 4.

5. Chief of the Gadites, who dwelt in the land of Bashan. 1 Chron. 5 : 12.

6. The son of Izrahiah, of the tribe of Issachar. 1 Chron. 7 : 3.

7. The brother of Nathan of Zobah, 1 Chron. 11 : 38, and one of David's guard.

8. The chief of the Gershonites in the reign of David. 1 Chron. 15 : 7, 11.

9. A Gershonite Levite in the reign of David, son of Jehiel, a descendant of Laadan, and probably the same as the preceding. 1 Chron. 23 : 8; 26 : 22.

10. The son of Pedaiah, and a chief of the half-tribe of Manasseh west of Jordan, in the reign of David. 1 Chron. 27 : 20.

11. A Kohathite Levite in the reign of Hezekiah. 2 Chron. 29 : 12.

12. One of the sons of Nebo, who had married a foreign wife. Ezra 10 : 43. (B.C. 458.)

13. The son of Zichri, a Benjamite. Neh. 11 : 9.

14. The second of the twelve minor prophets, the son of Pethuel, who prophesied in Judah. His date is uncertain. The book of Joel contains a grand outline of the whole terrible scene, which was to be depicted more and more in detail by subsequent prophets. The proximate event to which the prophecy related was a public calamity, then impending on Judah, of a two-fold character—want of water, and a plague of locusts—and continuing for several years. The prophet exhorts the people to turn to God with penitence, fasting and prayer; and then, he says, the plague shall cease, and the rain descend in its season, and the land yield her accustomed fruit. Nay, the time will be a most joyful one; for God, by the outpouring of his Spirit, will extend the blessings of true religion to heathen lands. The prophecy is referred to in Acts 2.

Joe'lah (jō-ē'lah), son of Jeroham of Gedor. 1 Chron. 12 : 7.

Joe'zer (jō-ē'zēr) (*Jehovah is help*), a Korhite, one of David's captains. 1 Chron. 12 : 6. (B.C. 1057.)

Jog'behah (*lofty*), one of the cities on the east of Jordan which were built and fortified by the tribe of Gad when they took possession of their territory. Num. 32 : 35. Now *Jubeihah*.

Jog'li (*led into exile*), the father of Bukki, a Danite chief. Num. 34 : 22.

Jo'ha. 1. One of the sons of Beriah the Benjamite. 1 Chron. 8 : 16.

2. The Tizite, one of David's guard. 1 Chron. 11 : 45.

Joha'nan (jo-hā'nan) (*Jehovah is gracious*). 1. Son of Azariah, 1 and grandson of Ahimaaz the son of Zadok, and father of Azariah, 6. 1 Chron. 6 : 9, 10.

2. Son of Elioenai, the son of Neariah, the son of Shemaiah, in the line of Zerubbabel's heirs. 1 Chron. 3 : 24.

3. The son of Kareah, and one of the captains of the scattered remnants of the army of Judah, who escaped in the final attack upon Jerusalem by the Chaldeans. (B.C. 586.) After the murder of Gedaliah, Johanan was one of the foremost in the pursuit of his assassin, and rescued the captives he had carried off from Mizpah. Jer. 41 : 11–16. Fearing the vengeance of the Chaldeans, the captains, with Johanan at their head, notwithstanding the warnings of Jeremiah, retired into Egypt.

4. The first-born son of Josiah king of Judah. 1 Chron. 3 : 15.

5. A valiant Benjamite who joined David at Ziklag. 1 Chron. 12 : 4. (B.C. 1057.)

6. A Gadite warrior who followed David. 1 Chron. 12 : 12.

7. The father of Azariah (15), an Ephraimite in the time of Ahaz. 2 Chron. 28 : 12.

8. The son of Hakkatan, and chief of the Bene-Azgad who returned with Ezra. Ezra 8 : 12.

9. The son or more probably grandson of Eliashib, one of the chief Levites. Ezra 10 : 6; Neh. 12 : 23. R. V. Jehohanan.

10. The son of Tobiah the Ammonite. Neh. 6 : 18. R. V. Jehohanan.

John, the same name as Johanan, a contraction of Jehohanan. 1. One of the high priest's family, who, with Annas and Caiaphas, sat in judgment upon the apostles Peter and John. Acts 4 : 6.

2. The Hebrew name of the evangelist Mark. Acts 12 : 12, 25; 13 : 5, 13; 15 : 37.

John the apostle. THE TWO SOURCES of knowledge concerning him are : (1) The New Testament; (2) traditions.

HIS FAMILY DESCENT. His father's name was Zebedee, whose business was fishing in the Sea of Galilee. He seems to have been in comfortable circumstances, for he owned a boat and employed men to assist him (Matt. 4 : 21; Mark 1 : 20), and Salome, his wife, the mother of John, was one of the band of women who ministered to Jesus (Mark 15 : 40; 16 : 1).

HIS BIRTHPLACE AND EARLY HOME was Bethsaida (*house of fish, fishtown*), on the northern shore of the lake, near where the Jordan flows into it. Business led them often to be at Capernaum, the populous commercial emporium near the head of the lake.

DATE OF BIRTH. The exact date is unknown, but he is generally regarded as younger than Jesus. Probably he was born between A.D. 1 and 5.

PERIOD OF HIS LIFE. From the early fathers, who lived not far from his time, as Irenæus and Jerome, we learn that he lived to be 90 or 95 years old, and died in the early part of the reign of the Emperor Trajan, who began to reign A.D. 98. So that John's life extended over nearly the whole of the first century of the Christian era.

THE EVENTS OF HIS LIFE. He had a brother, James, who was one of the first Christian martyrs. During his early manhood he was a Galilean fisherman with his father. He was one of the first disciples of Jesus. He was one of the most prominent of the disciples during Christ's life, and during the early records of the church in the Acts. He was on friendly terms with the high priest (John 18 : 15). The latter part of the Acts concerns chiefly the work of St. Paul, but John was also doing his unrecorded work. " Tradition fixes on Ephesus as the scene of his later ministrations, and it is probable that the seven churches of Asia (in the vicinity of Ephesus) enjoyed his care (Rev. 1 : 11)."

WRITINGS. Five books of the New Testament are ascribed to him : The fourth Gospel, three Epistles, and the Book of Revelation.

CHARACTER. " It has become," says Canon Bentham, " a conventional rule in sacred art that because St. John speaks more about Love than the other apostles, and was specially beloved by his Master, he must have had a soft, feminine, sentimental countenance, without the wrinkles of age, betraying no conflict. Such a fancy is strangely contradicted by facts."

John was indeed the apostle of Love, but Love is "the greatest thing in the world," the most difficult, the most divine, the most manly and virile.

Jesus named John and his brother James, Boanerges (sons of thunder), because, according to *Muir* in Hastings' *Bible Dict.*, the name is "both descriptive and prophetic of the union of the passionate and vehement with the gentle and loving in their character, and the fact that once and again tempests of long-restrained emotion would burst forth out of the deep stillness of their strong, reserved natures." It is John's passionate affection that made him so indignant at the Samaritans who refused to receive Jesus that he would call down heaven's lightnings to blast them (Luke 9:54), that, in large part, made him ambitious to sit close to Jesus in his kingdom (Mark 10:37), and made him so courageous in the high priest's palace, while Peter the bold was denying his Lord.

"His natural vehemence, chastened by grace, became an element of strength and a glory." He blended the gentleness of the dove with the sublime force and vision of the eagle.

The lesson of John's character lies in the change wrought by Jesus in the expression and control of the strong forces of his soul, as they were gradually changed into his image from glory to glory, "the glory of the only begotten Son of God." All the tempestuousness, the threats, the ambitions, the narrowness are consumed in the perfectness of love.

John the Baptist was of the priestly race by both parents, for his father, Zacharias, was himself a priest of the course of Abia or Abijah, 1 Chron. 24:10, and Elisabeth was of the daughters of Aaron. Luke 1:5. His birth was foretold by an angel sent from God, and is related at length in Luke 1. The birth of John preceded by six months that of our Lord. John was ordained to be a Nazirite from his birth. Luke 1:15. Dwelling by himself in the wild and thinly-peopled region westward of the Dead Sea, he prepared himself for the wonderful office to which he had

been divinely called. His dress was that of the old prophets—a garment woven of camel's hair, 2 Kings 1:8, attached to the body by a leathern girdle. His food was such as the desert afforded—

THE JORDAN.
At the traditional site of Christ's baptism.

locusts, Lev. 11:22, and wild honey. Ps. 81:16. And now the long-secluded hermit came forth to the discharge of his office. His supernatural birth, his life, and the general expectation that some great one was about to appear, were sufficient to attract to him a great multitude from "every quarter." Matt. 3:5. Many of every class pressed forward to confess their sins and to be baptized. Jesus himself came from Galilee to Jordan to be baptized of John. [JESUS.] From incidental notices we learn that John and his disciples continued to baptize some time after our Lord entered upon his ministry. See John 3:23; 4:1; Acts 19:3. We gather also that John instructed his disciples in certain moral and religious duties, as fasting, Matt. 9:14; Luke 5:33, and prayer. Luke 11:1. But shortly after he had given his testimony to the Messiah, John's public ministry was brought to a close. In daring disregard of the divine laws, Herod Antipas had taken to himself Herodias, the wife of his brother Philip; and when John reproved him for this, as well as for other sins, Luke 3:19, Herod cast him into prison. (March, A.D. 28.) The place of his confinement was the castle of Machaerus, a fortress on the eastern shore of the

Dead Sea. It was here that reports reached him of the miracles which our Lord was working in Judea. Nothing but the death of the Baptist would satisfy the resentment of Herodias. A court festival was kept at Machaerus in honor of the king's birthday. After supper the daughter of Herodias came in and danced before the company, and so charmed was the king by her grace that he promised with an oath to give her whatsoever she should ask. Salome, prompted by her abandoned mother, demanded the head of John the Baptist. Herod gave instructions to an officer of his guard, who went and executed John in the prison, and his head was brought to feast the eyes of the adulteress whose sins he had denounced. His death is supposed to have occurred just before the third passover, in the course of the Lord's ministry. (March, A.D. 29.)

John, The Gospel of. The Books of John in the New Testament may be classed with the Book of Deuteronomy in the Old Testament, as "the storm centers of modern controversy." The questions at issue of date, authorship, and composition have no place in the ordinary uses of these writings, and hence are left for the large Bible Dictionaries. The majority of scholars favor the views given below.

I. AUTHOR. The Apostle John.

II. LANGUAGE. It was written in Greek, then known over the whole civilized world.

III. PLACE. Tradition is uniform, and generally accepted that it was written at Ephesus.

IV. DATE OF WRITING. The exact date is unknown, but it is generally regarded as written somewhere between A.D. 80 and 95. Plummer in the *Cambridge Bible* thinks that the first twenty chapters were written a considerable time before the Gospel was published, and that the last chapter was added some years later, and then the whole given to the church.

V. SOURCES. It was probably the record of the story of Jesus as preached by John for many years. John was the most intimate earthly friend of Jesus, so that on longer reflection and deeper experience, he saw the truth with new and truer light than was possible at the time the events took place.

VI. CHARACTERISTICS. 1. The object is expressed in John 20:31, to lead men to believe in Jesus (1) as the Messiah foretold in the Old Testament; and (2) as the eternal Son of God manifesting the Father in heaven.

2. It is the *latest of the Gospels,* taking the others for granted.

The contrast between John and the other three Gospels (called synoptics; *i. e.,* those which have a "general view" of the life of Christ) is plain even at the first glance.

The synoptic Gospels seem to have been the sifted and perfected record of the preaching of the apostles. They told the story over and over again as they preached. It was written at various times by several different persons as we learn from Luke. This statement of facts was the great need of the early church, till the facts were wrought into the hearts and memories and lives of the early Christians.

In time there came another need, both among the Jews and among the peoples permeated with Greek learning. Questions arose, errors would be promulgated, difficulties would arise. For instance, the Jews, as well as Christians, were very tenacious of the unity of God, but the question immediately arose how it was possible for Jesus to be the divine Son of God, and yet God be but one.

John states the fact so that all can see the truth. He proclaims the same truths taught by the other Gospels, but in different language for a different people. He who lived nearest the heart of Jesus recalls many of his teachings not reported by the others. John does not at this late day write a new Gospel, or new words of Jesus, but writes down what he had been preaching for more than half a century. It was this fact which made the wonderful perfection of the style and language of this Gospel, as well as its accuracy. It is said that Whitefield's sermons did not attain their perfect form till he had preached them forty times.

3. Its method is that of *signs* and *witness.* St. John selects only such miracles as were spiritual signs, not only helping the sick and needy ones, but illustrating and exhibiting some spiritual truth. His sayings are all of the nature of "Witness."

4. It is preëminently the gospel of the Teaching of Christ. It is a study rather than a biography. "Matthew shows the *fact,* John reveals the *truth.*"

The word "Father" occurs 140 times in this Gospel.

The name "Jesus" is found in John 242 times, 99 times more than in Matthew, and 158 times more than in Luke, showing how closely John keeps to his object of writing of the person of Jesus. He also uses other names of Jesus, as "the Son" 19 times, "the Son of God" 9 times, "the Son of man" 13 times, "the Life" 22 times, and "the Light" 25 times, besides the names "the Holy One of God," "the Lamb of God," and "the King of Israel." 333 times in all.

John, The First Epistle General of, is evidently by the author of the Fourth Gospel, having the same characteristic phraseology, and implying that his readers were acquainted with his Gospel. It was probably written from Ephesus, and most likely at the close of the first century. In the introduction, ch. 1:1-4, the apostle states the purpose of his epistle: it is to declare the word of life to those whom he is addressing, in order that he and they might be united in true communion with each other, and with God the Father and his Son Jesus Christ. His lesson throughout is that the means of union with God are, on the part of Christ, his atoning blood, ch. 1:7, 2:2, 3:5, 4:10, 14, 5:6, and advocacy, ch. 2:1; on the part of man, holiness, ch. 1:6, obedience, ch. 2:3, purity, ch. 3:3, faith, ch. 3:23; 4:3; 5:5, and above all love. ch. 2:7; 3:14; 4:7; 5:1.

John, The Second and Third Epistles of. The second epistle is addressed to an individual woman. One who had children, and a sister and nieces, is clearly indicated. According to one interpretation she is "the Lady Electa," to another, "the elect Kyria," to a third, "the elect Lady." The third epistle is addressed to Gaius. He was probably a convert of St. John, Epist. 3, 4, and a layman of wealth and distinction, Epist. 5, 6, in some city near Ephesus. The *object* of St. John in writing the second epistle was to warn the lady to whom he wrote against abetting the teaching known as that of Basilides and his followers, by perhaps an undue kindness displayed by her toward the preachers of the false doctrine. The third epistle was written for the purpose of commending to the kindness and hospitality of Gaius some Christians who were strangers in the place where he

lived. It is probable that these Christians carried this letter with them to Gaius as their introduction.

Joi'ada (joi'a-dà) (*Jehovah hath known*), son of the high priest Eliashib. Neh. 13:28.

Joi'akim (joi'a-kĭm), a high priest, son of the renowned Jeshua. Neh. 12:10.

Joi'arib (joi'a-rĭb). 1. A teacher who returned from Babylon with Ezra. Ezra 8:16. (B.C. 458.)

2. The founder of one of the courses of priests, elsewhere called in full JEHOIARIB. Neh. 12:6, 19.

3. A Shilonite—*i. e.* probably a descendant of Shelah the son of Judah. Neh. 11:5.

Jok'deam (jŏk'de-àm), a city of Judah, in the mountains, Josh. 15:56.

Jo'kim (jō'kim), one of the sons of Shelah the son of Judah. 1 Chron. 4:22.

Jok'meam (jŏk'me-ăm) (*the people is gathered*), a city of Ephraim, given with its suburbs to the Kohathite Levites. 1 Chron. 6:68. The situation of Jokmeam is to a certain extent indicated in 1 Kings 4:12 (Authorized Version JOKNEAM), where it is named with places which we know to have been in the Jordan valley at the extreme east boundary of the tribe.

Jok'neam (jŏk'ne-am) (*let the people possess*), a city of the tribe of Zebulun, allotted with its suburbs to the Merarite Levites. Josh. 21:34. Its modern site is *Tell Keimun,* an eminence which stands just below the eastern termination of Carmel.

Jok'shan (jŏk'shan) (*fowler*), a son of Abraham and Keturah, Gen. 25:2, 3; 1 Chron. 1:32, whose sons were Sheba and Dedan.

Jok'tan (jŏk'tan) (*small*), son of Eber, Gen. 10:25; 1 Chron. 1:19, and the father of the Joktanite Arabs. Gen. 10:30.

Jok'theel (jŏk'the-el) (*subdued by God*). 1. A city in the low country of Judah, Josh. 15:38, named next to Lachish.

2. "God-subdued," the title given by Amaziah to the cliff (Authorized Version Selah)—the stronghold of the Edomites, now Petra—after he had captured it from them. 2 Kings 14:7. The parallel narrative of 2 Chron. 25: 11-13 supplies fuller details.

Jo'na (jō'nà) (*a dove*) (Greek form

of Jonah), the father of the apostle Peter, John 1:42, who is hence addressed as Simon Bar-jona (*i. e.* son of Jona) in Matt. 16:17, A. V., in R. V. the form Jonah is used. In the R. V. of John the name John is substituted, on the authority of manuscripts.

Jon'adab (jŏn'a-dab). 1. Son of Shimeah and nephew of David. He is described as "very subtil." 2 Sam. 13: 3. His age naturally made him the friend of his cousin Amnon, heir to the throne. 2 Sam. 13:3. He gave him the fatal advice for ensnaring his sister Tamar. ch. 13:5, 6. Again, when, in a later stage of the same tragedy, Amnon was murdered by Absalom, and the exaggerated report reached David that all the princes were slaughtered, Jonadab was either already aware of or easily grasped the real state of the case. 2 Sam. 13:32, 33.

2. Jer. 35:6, 8, 10, 14, 16, 18, 19. [JEHONADAB.]

Jo'nah (jŏ'nah) (*dove*), the fifth of the minor prophets, was the son of Amittai, and a native of Gath-hepher. 2 Kings 14:25. He flourished before the close of the reign of Jeroboam II (832–770). He foretold in a time of bitter affliction, the recovery of the borders of Israel from Hamath in Syria to the Dead Sea; which was accomplished by Jeroboam, restoring Israel's territory to what it was in the golden days of Solomon. Beyond this we have no knowledge of him except the statements found in the book concerning him.

Jonah, the Book of, may be so named, not because he is the author, but because it is written concerning him, whoever is the author.

THE DATE of the story belongs to the reign of Jeroboam II.—about 800 B.C., whatever the date of writing.

There are two views among scholars, each with variations, as to the literary nature of the book. I. By many modern scholars it is regarded as "a prophetic story," an allegory or parable founded on fact, "linked to the name of a prophet of an earlier date, and composed in order to inculcate the lesson with which the narrative concludes." In this case the date of writing is supposed to be after the Exile. The reasons given are,—(1). The use of the past tense. "Nineveh *was* an exceeding great city" and therefore Nineveh was not in existence at the time the book was written.

(2) The use of late forms of language. (3) Nineveh remained in fact an idolatrous city to the end. (4) This theory avoids the difficulties arising from a man's living within a sea-monster's stomach for three days, and from the mourning and fasting of a whole city at the word of a stranger, while it teaches the same lessons as the historical facts.

II. The general view till of late, and still held by scholars, is that the book is historical, teaching by actual facts the lessons to be inculcated. The story on the face of it appears to be historical. The miraculous element is not impossible, and the occasion was worthy of it. The date of the events is not necessarily, nor usually, the date of the writing, so that the past tense "was," and late forms of language are no certain argument against the truth of the narrative. The time when Jonah lived was one of Assyrian decadence and weakness. There is no convincing or unanswerable argument against the historicity of the book.

NOTE that neither view denies the divine inspiration of the book. The Spirit can inspire a parable as well as a historical fact and its statement. Even the reference to Jonah by Jesus does not decide the question, any more than any preacher's reference to Hamlet or to giant Despair, prove whether they are historical or not.

ITS TEACHINGS. Jehovah was the rightful God of all nations, as He taught Abraham, and the Jews were God's chosen instrument to make Him known,—a duty they too often forgot. It is a missionary book. It shows that no nation can safely refuse its mission, to bring all men into the kingdom of God. The divine compassion of God enfolds all men in its loving arms.

Jo'nam (jŏ'nam) (*Jehovah hath been gracious*), the form given to JONAN in the Revised Version of Luke 3:30.

Jo'nan (jŏ'nan) (perhaps a contraction of Johanan, *Jehovah hath been gracious*), son of Eliakim, in the genealogy of Christ. Luke 3:30.

Jo'nas (jŏ'nas) (*a dove*). 1. The prophet Jonah. Matt. 12:39, 40, 41; 16: 4.

2. Father of Peter. John 21:15–17. [JONA.] R. V. translates *John*.

Jon'athan (jŏn'a-than), that is, "*Jehovah hath given*," the eldest son of

JAFFA (JOPPA) FROM THE SEA.

King Saul, and a young man when his father became king. He was a man of great strength and activity. 2 Sam. 1: 23. He was also famous as a warrior, as is shown by the courage he showed in attacking the garrison of the Philistines, in company with his armor-bearer only, slaying twenty men and putting an army to flight. 1 Sam. 14: 6–16. During the pursuit, Jonathan, who had not heard of the rash curse, ch. 14: 24, which Saul invoked on any one who ate before the evening, tasted the honey which lay on the ground. Saul would have sacrificed him; but the people interposed in behalf of the hero of that great day, and Jonathan was saved, ch. 14: 24–45. The chief interest of Jonathan's career is derived from the friendship with David, which began on the day of David's return from the victory over the champion of Gath, and continued till his death. Their last meeting was in the forest of Ziph, during Saul's pursuit of David. 1 Sam. 23: 16–18. From this time forth we hear no more till the battle of Gilboa. In that battle he fell. 1 Sam. 31: 2, 8. (B.C. 1055.) His ashes were buried first at Jabesh-gilead, ch. 31: 13, but were afterward removed with those of his father to Zelah in Benjamin. 2 Sam. 21 : 14. The news of his death occasioned the celebrated elegy of David. He left a son, Mephibosheth. [MEPHIBOSHETH.]

2. A nephew of David. 2 Sam. 21: 21; 1 Chron. 20: 7. He engaged in single combat with and slew a gigantic Philistine of Gath. 2 Sam. 21: 21.

3. The son of Abiathar, the high priest, is the last descendant of Eli of whom we hear anything. 2 Sam. 15: 36; 17: 15–21; 1 Kings 1: 42, 43. (B.C. 1023.)

4. One of David's heroes. 2 Sam. 23: 32; 1 Chron. 11: 34.

5. The son or descendant of Gershom the son of Moses. Judges 18: 30.

6. One of the Bene-Adin. Ezra 8: 6.

7. A priest, the son of Asahel, in the time of Ezra. Ezra 10: 15. (B.C. 458.)

8. A priest of the family of Melicu. Neh. 12: 14.

9. One of the sons of Kareah, and brother of Johanan. Jer. 40: 8. (B.C. 586.)

10. Son of Joiada, and his successor in the high priesthood. Neh. 12: 11, 22, 23.

11. Father of Zechariah, a priest who

blew the trumpet at the dedication of the wall. Neh. 12: 35.

Jo'nath=e'lem=recho'kim (jō'nath-ē'-lem-rė-kō'kim) (*the silent dove of them that are afar off*), a phrase found once only in the Bible, as a heading to the 56th psalm. Modern scholars regard this as in all probability the name of a melody to which this psalm is to be sung.

Jop'pa (jŏp'pà), or **Japho** (jăf'o) (*beauty*), now *Jaffa*, a town on the southwest coast of Palestine, in the portion of Dan. Josh. 19: 46. Having a harbor attached to it—though always, as still, a dangerous one—it became the port of Jerusalem in the days of Solomon, and has been ever since. Here Jonah "took ship to flee from the presence of his Maker." Here, on the house-top of Simon the tanner, "by the seaside," St. Peter had his vision of tolerance. Acts 11: 5. The existing town contains a population of about 50,-000 and is a very important town, partly from its trade and still more from the large number of pilgrims passing through every year to Jerusalem. It is the western terminus of the railroad to that city, which was completed in 1892. Although the harbor is poor it is one of the most active ports of the country.

Jo'rah (jō'rah) (*autumn rain*), the ancestor of a family of 112 who returned from Babylon with Ezra. Ezra 2: 18. In Neh. 7: 24 he appears under the name HARIPH, or more correctly the same family are represented as the Bene-Hariph, this being probably the true form.

Jor'ai (jō'rāi) (*whom Jehovah teaches*), one of the Gadites dwelling at Gilead in Bashan. 1 Chron. 5: 13.

Jo'ram (jō'ram) (*Jehovah is exalted*). 1. Son of Ahab king of Israel. [JEHORAM, 1.]

2. Son of Jehoshaphat; king of Judah. [JEHORAM, 2.]

3. A priest in the reign of Jehoshaphat. 2 Chron. 17: 8.

4. A Levite, descendant of Eliezer, in the time of David. 1 Chron. 26: 25.

5. Son of Toi king of Hamath. 2 Sam. 8: 10. [HADORAM.]

Jor'dan (jôr'dan) (*the descender*), is the one river of the "great plain" of Palestine—the "descender," if not "the river of God" in the book of Psalms, at least that of his chosen people throughout their history. There were very many fords in the northern portion, but south of the plain of Esdraelon there were few. There were fords over against Jericho, to which point the men of Jericho pursued the spies. Josh. 2 : 7; comp. Judges 3 : 28. Higher up were the fords or passages of Bethbarah, where Gideon lay in wait for the Midianites, Judges 7 : 24, and where the men of Gilead slew the Ephraimites, ch. 12 : 6. Jacob crossed the Jordan at some ford, Gen. 32 : 10. The question as to the positions of the various fords mentioned in the Bible is a disputed one. There were several well-known fords, in its lower portion. From their vicinity to Jerusalem these lower fords were much used. David, it is probable, passed over them in one instance to fight the Syrians. 2 Sam. 10 : 16, 17. Thus there were two customary places at which the Jordan was fordable; and it must have been at one of these, if not at both, that baptism was afterward administered by St. John and by the disciples of our Lord. The fords were rendered so much more precious in those days from two circumstances. First, it does not appear that there were then any bridges thrown over or boats regularly established on the Jordan; and secondly, because "Jordan overflowed all his banks all the time of harvest." Josh. 3 : 15. The channel or bed of the river became brimful, so that the level of the water and of the banks was then the same. Bridges were built in Roman times at several places, but there were probably none before that time,—at least none were mentioned. Dr. Selah Merrill speaks of a fine bridge near Tarichæa, just below the point where the Jordan leaves the lake of Galilee which doubtless existed in Christ's time. The last feature which remains to be noticed in the scriptural account of the Jordan is its frequent mention as a boundary: "over Jordan," "this" and "the other side," or "beyond Jordan," were expressions as familiar to the Israelites as "across the water," "this" and "the other side of the Channel" are to English ears. In one sense indeed, that is, in so far as it was the eastern boundary of the land of Canaan, it was the eastern boundary of the promised land. Num. 34 : 12. The Jordan rises from several sources near Panium (*Bâniâs*), and passes through the lakes of Merom (*Hûleh*) and Gen-

nesaret. The two principal features in its course are its descent and its windings. From the Lake of the Tiberias to the Dead Sea is about 65 miles; but if all the windings of the river are counted it reaches a total of 200 miles. From its fountain heads to the Dead Sea it rushes down one continuous inclined plane, only broken by a series of rapids or precipitous falls. Between the

THE JORDAN NEAR DAN.

Lake of Gennesaret and the Dead Sea there are about 27 rapids apart from whirlpools. The depression of the Lake of Gennesaret below the level of the Mediterranean is 682 feet, and that of the Dead Sea 1292 feet. The whole descent from its source to the Dead Sea is 2492 feet. Its width and depth vary exceedingly not only with the portion under consideration, but also with the season of the year. For this reason we find all varieties of estimates in different authorities. The only important tributaries to the Jordan below Gennesaret are the *Yarmûk* (Hieromax) and the *Zerka* (Jabbok). Not a single city ever crowned the banks of the Jordan. Still Bethshan and Jericho to the west, Gerasa, Pella and Gadara to the east of it were important cities, and caused a good deal of traffic between the two opposite banks. The physical features of the Ghor, through which the Jordan flows, are treated of under PALESTINE.

Jo'rim (jŏ'rim), son of Matthat, in the genealogy of Christ. Luke 3:29.

Jor'koam (jôr'ko-ăm), either a descendant of Caleb the son of Hezron, or the name of a place in the tribe of Judah. 1 Chron. 2:44.

Jos'abad (jŏs'a-băd), properly JOZABAD the Gederathite, one of the warriors of Benjamin who joined David at Ziklag. 1 Chron. 12:4. (B.C. 1057.)

Jos'aphat (jŏs'a-făt)=Jehoshaphat king of Judah. Matt. 1:8.

Jo'se (jŏ'sē) (another form of JOSES), son of Eliezer, in the genealogy of Jesus Christ. Luke 3:29. R. V. Jesus.

Jo'sech, the form of name given in the Revised Version for JOSEPH, in Luke 3:26. It is not found in the Old Testament.

Jos'edech (jŏs'e-dĕk)=JEHOZADAK (the father of Jeshua the high priest). Hag. 1:1, 12, 14; 2:2, 4; Zech. 6:11.

Jo'seph (jŏ'ṣef) (may he add). 1. The elder of the two sons of Jacob by Rachel. He was born in Padan-aram (Mesopotamia), about B.C. 1746 (Ussher). He is first mentioned when a youth, seventeen years old. Joseph brought the evil report of his brethren to his father, and they hated him because his father loved him more than he did them, and had shown his preference by making him a dress which appears to have been a long tunic with sleeves, worn by youths and maidens of the richer class. Gen. 37:2, 3. He dreamed a dream foreshadowing his future power, which increased the hatred of his brethren. Gen. 37:5-7. He was sent by his father to visit his brothers, who were tending flocks in the fields of Dothan. They resolved to kill him, but he was saved by Reuben, who persuaded the brothers to cast Joseph into a dry pit, to the intent that he might restore him to Jacob. The appearance of the Ishmaelites suggested his sale for "twenty pieces of silver," ver. 28. Sold into Egypt to Potiphar, Joseph prospered and was soon set over Potiphar's house, and "all he had he gave into his hand;" but incurring the anger of Potiphar's wife, ch. 39:7-13, he was falsely accused and thrown into prison, where he remained

at least two years, interpreting during this time the dreams of the cupbearer and the baker. Finally Pharaoh himself dreamed two prophetic dreams. Joseph, being sent for, interpreted them in the name of God, foretelling the seven years of plenty and the seven years of famine. Pharaoh at once appointed Joseph not merely governor of Egypt, but second only to the sovereign, and also gave him to wife Asenath, daughter of Potipherah priest of On (Hieropolis), and gave him a name or title, Zaphnathpaaneah. Joseph's first act was to go throughout all the land of Egypt. During the seven plenteous years there was a very abundant produce, and he gathered the fifth part and laid it up. When the seven good years had passed, the famine began. Gen. 41:54-57. [FAMINE.]

After the people had consumed all the grain they had stored themselves they were supplied by Joseph from the storehouses he had filled. First they gave money in return, when that was exhausted they gave away their cattle and finally themselves and their land. As a result all the land in Egypt, except that of the priests, became the property of the Pharaoh who received an annual rent of one-fifth of the produce from the former owners, who had thus become his tenants. (Gen. 47:13-26.) Now Jacob, who had suffered also from the effects of the famine, sent Joseph's brothers to Egypt for corn. The whole story of Joseph's treatment of his brethren is so graphically told in Gen. 42-45, and is so familiar, that it is unnecessary here to repeat it. On the death of Jacob in Egypt, Joseph carried him to Canaan, and laid him in the cave of Machpelah, the burying-place of his fathers. Joseph lived "a hundred and ten years," having been more than ninety in Egypt. Dying, he took an oath of his brethren that they should carry up his bones to the land of promise: thus showing in his latest action the faith, Heb. 11:22, which had guided his whole life. Like his father he was embalmed, "and he was put in a coffin in Egypt." Gen. 50:26. His trust Moses kept, and laid the bones of Joseph in his inheritance in Shechem, in the territory of Ephraim his offspring. His tomb is, according to tradition, about a stone's throw from Jacob's well.

2. Father of Igal, who represented the

tribe of Issachar among the spies. Num. 13 : 7.

3. An Israelite who had married a foreign wife. Ezra 10 : 42. (B.C. 458.)

4. A representative of the priestly family of Shebaniah. Neh. 12 : 14, in the days of Joiakim, about B.C. 500.

5. One of the ancestors of Christ, Luke 3 : 30, son of Jonan.

6. Another ancestor of Christ, son of Judah. Luke 3 : 26. In R. V. JOSECH.

7. Another, son of Mattathias. Luke 3 : 24.

8. Son of Heli, and reputed father of Jesus Christ. All that is told us of Joseph in the New Testament may be summed up in a few words. He was a just man, and of the house and lineage of David. He lived at Nazareth in Galilee. He espoused Mary, and before he took her home as his wife received the angelic communications recorded in Matt. 1 and 2. When Jesus was twelve years old Joseph and Mary took him with them to keep the passover at Jerusalem, and when they returned to Nazareth he continued to act as a father to the child Jesus, and was reputed to be so indeed. But here our knowledge of Joseph ends. That he died before our Lord's crucifixion is indeed tolerably certain, by what is related John 19 : 27, and perhaps Matt. 12 : 46 may imply that he was then dead. Probably the usual opinion is right, that he died before the beginning of Jesus' ministry. But where, when or how he died we know not.

9. Joseph of Arimathæa, a rich Israelite, probably a member of the Great Council or Sanhedrin. He is further characterized as "a good man and a just." Luke 23 : 50. He was Jesus' disciple, "but secretly for fear of the Jews." John 19 : 38. We are expressly told that he did not "consent to the counsel and deed" of his colleagues in conspiring to bring about the death of Jesus; but he seems to have lacked the courage to protest against their judgment. On the very evening of the crucifixion, when the triumph of the chief priests and rulers seemed complete, Joseph "went in boldly unto Pilate and craved the body of Jesus." Pilate consented. Joseph and Nicodemus then, having enfolded the sacred body in the linen shroud which Joseph had bought, consigned it to a tomb hewn in a rock, in a garden belonging to Joseph, and close to the place of crucifixion.

10. Joseph, called Barsabas, and surnamed Justus; one of the two persons chosen by the assembled church, Acts 1 : 23, as worthy to fill the place in the apostolic company from which Judas had fallen.

Jo'ses. 1. Son of Eliezer in the genealogy of Christ, Luke 3 : 29. The A. V. by mistake JOSE. The R. V. accepts another reading " Jesus."

2. One of the Lord's brethren. Matt. 13 : 55; Mark 6 : 3.

3. Joses Barnabas. Acts 4 : 36. [BARNABAS.]

Jo'shah (jō'shah), a prince of the house of Simeon. 1 Chron. 4 : 34, 38–41.

Josh'aphat (jŏsh'a-făt) (*Jehovah hath judged*), the Mithnite, one of David's guard. 1 Chron. 11 : 43.

Joshavi'ah (jŏsh-a-vī'ah), the son of Elnaam, and one of David's guard. 1 Chron. 11 : 46.

Joshbeka'shah (jŏsh-bek-a'shah), son of Heman, head of the seventeenth course of musicians. 1 Chron. 25 : 4, 24.

Josh'ua (jŏsh'u-à) (*Jehovah is salvation*). His name appears in the various forms of HOSHEA, OSHEA, JEHOSHUA, JESHUA and JESUS. 1. The son of Nun, of the tribe of Ephraim. 1 Chron. 7 : 27. He must have been born in Goshen, Egypt, where his parents were in slavery. He was nearly forty years old when he shared in the hurried triumph of the exodus. He is mentioned first in connection with the fight against Amalek at Rephidim, when he was chosen by Moses to lead the Israelites. Ex. 17 : 9. Soon afterward he was one of the twelve chiefs who were sent, Num. 13 : 17, to explore the land of Canaan, and one of the two, ch. 14 : 6, who gave an encouraging report of their journey. Moses, shortly before his death, was directed, Num. 27 : 18, to invest Joshua with authority over the people. God himself gave Joshua a charge by the mouth of the dying lawgiver. Deut. 31 : 14, 23. Under the direction of God again renewed, Josh. 1 : 1, Joshua assumed the command of the people at Shittim, sent spies into Jericho, crossed the Jordan, fortified a camp at Gilgal, circumcised the people, kept the passover, and was visited by the Captain of the Lord's host. The unexpectedness of the fall of Jericho made it more terrible to the Canaanites. In the great battle of Beth-horon the Amorites were signally routed, and the south country was open to the Israelites. Joshua returned to the camp at Gilgal, master of half of Palestine. He defeated the Canaanites under Jabin king of Hazor. In six years, six tribes, with thirty-one petty chiefs, were conquered. Joshua, now stricken in years, proceeded to make the division of the conquered land. Timnath-serah in Mount Ephraim was assigned as Joshua's peculiar inheritance. After an interval of rest, Joshua convoked an assembly from all Israel. He delivered two solemn addresses, recorded in Josh. 23, 24. He died at the age of 110 years, and was buried in his own city, Timnath-serah.

2. An inhabitant of Beth-shemesh, in whose field was the stone at which the milch-kine stopped when they drew the ark of God with the offerings of the Philistines from Ekron to Beth-shemesh. 1 Sam. 6 : 14, 18.

3. A governor of the city who gave his name to a gate of Jerusalem. 2 Kings 23 : 8. (In the reign of Josiah, B.C. 628.)

4. Jeshua the son of Jozadak. Hag. 1 : 1, 12, 14; Zech. 3 : 1, etc.

Josh'ua, Book of. Named from Joshua the son of Nun, who is the principal character in it. This book as the continuance of the history, is now joined by most modern scholars to the Pentateuch, and the whole six are termed the Hexateuch. They find the same interwoven threads in Joshua as in the earlier books.

It is probable that the book includes documents written by Joshua, since it is expressly stated of some portions that Joshua wrote "these words." The last verses, ch. 24 : 29–33, were obviously added at a later time. Some events, such as the capture of Hebron and Debir, Josh. 15 : 13–19 (see Judges 1 : 10–15), of Leshem, Josh. 19 : 47 (see Judges 18 : 7), and the joint occupation of Jerusalem, Josh. 15 : 63 (see Judges 1 : 21) probably did not occur till after Joshua's death.

The book consists of three parts: 1. *The Conquest of Canaan* (chs. 1–12), with its various campaigns, and the confirmation of the covenant on Mt. Ebal. 2. *The Settlement of Canaan* (chs. 13–22), with a description of the land and its allotment to the tribes. 3. *Joshua's Farewell address* (chs. 23, 24).

Josi'ah (jò-sī'ah) (*Jehovah supports*). 1. The son of Amon and Jedidah, succeeded his father B.C. 639, in the eighth year of his age, and reigned 31 years. His history is contained in 2 Kings 22 : 1–23 : 30; 2 Chron. 34, 35; and the first twelve chapters of Jeremiah throw much light upon the general character of the Jews in his day. The general keeper of his conscience during his youth seems to have been the high priest Hilkiah, but Josiah seems to have been a willing pupil. It says in 2 Chron. that he began in the eighth year of his reign to seek the Lord; and in his twelfth year began to destroy everywhere high places, groves, images and all outward signs and relics of idolatry. In his eighteenth year began the real reformation of his reign. The temple was restored under a special commission; and in the course of the repairs Hilkiah the priest found that book of the law of the Lord which quickened so remarkably the ardent zeal of the king. He was aided by Jeremiah the prophet in spreading through his kingdom the knowledge and worship of Jehovah. The great day of Josiah's life was the day of the passover in the eighteenth year of his reign. After this his endeavors to abolish every trace of idolatry and superstition were still carried on; but of the actual events of the next thirteen years we know nothing. When Pharaoh-necho went from Egypt to Carchemish to carry on his war against Assyria, Josiah opposed his march along the seacoast. Necho reluctantly paused and gave him battle in the valley of Esdraelon. Josiah was mortally wounded, and died before he could reach Jerusalem. He was buried with extraordinary honors.

2. The son of Zephaniah, at whose house took place the solemn and symbolical crowning of Joshua the high priest. Zech. 6 : 10.

Josi'as (jò-sī'as). Josiah, king of Judah. Matt. 1 : 10, 11.

Josibi'ah (jŏs-ĭ-bī'ah) (*Jehovah causes to dwell*), the father of Jehu, a Simeonite. 1 Chron. 4 : 35.

Josiphi'ah (jŏs-ĭ-fī'ah) (*Jehovah adds*), the father or ancestor of Shelomith, who returned with Ezra. Ezra 8 : 10.

Jot, the English form of the Greek iota, i. e., the smallest letter of the Greek alphabet. The Hebrew is *yod*, or *y* formed like a comma ('). It is used metaphorically to express the minutest thing.

Jot'bah (jŏt'bah) (*pleasantness*), the native place of Meshullemeth, the queen of Manasseh. 2 Kings 21:19.

Jot'bath (jŏt'bath) or **Jot'bathah** (jot'ba-thä) (*goodness*), Deut. 10:7; Num. 33:33, a desert station of the Israelites.

Jo'tham (jō'tham) (*Jehovah is perfect*). 1. The youngest son of Gideon, Judges 9:5, who escaped from the massacre of his brethren. His parable of the reign of the bramble is the earliest example of the kind.

2. The son of King Uzziah or Azariah and Jerushah. He was regent of the kingdom for some years during his father's leprosy, and sole king for about two years—B.C. 736–735. He was contemporary with Pekah and with the prophet Isaiah. His history is contained in 2 Kings 15 and 2 Chron. 27.

3. A descendant of Judah, son of Jahdai. 1 Chron. 2:47.

Joz'abad (joz'a-băd) (*Jehovah has bestowed*). 1. A captain of the thousands of Manasseh, who deserted to David before the battle of Gilboa. 1 Chron. 12:20. (B.C. 1055.)

2. A hero of Manasseh, like the preceding. 1 Chron. 12:20.

3. A Levite in the reign of Hezekiah. 2 Chron. 31:13.

4. A chief Levite in the reign of Josiah. 2 Chron. 35:9.

5. A Levite, son of Jeshua, in the days of Ezra. Ezra 8:33. (B.C. 458.) Probably identical with No. 7.

6. A priest of the sons of Pashur, who had married a foreign wife. Ezra 10:22.

7. A Levite among those who had married foreign wives, Ezra 10:23. He is probably identical with Jozabad the Levite, Neh. 8:7, and with Jozabad who presided over the outer work of the temple. Neh. 11:16. (B.C. 458.)

Joz'achar (jŏz'a-kär) (*Jehovah has remembered*), one of the murderers of Joash king of Judah. 2 Kings 12:21. The writer of the Chronicles, 2 Chron. 24:26, calls him ZABAD. (B.C. 796.)

Joz'adak (jŏz'a-dăk) (*Jehovah is righteous*). Ezra 3:2, 8; 5:2; 10:18; Neh. 12:26. The contracted form of Jehozadak.

Ju'bal (jŭ'bal), a son of Lamech by Adah, and the inventor of the "harp and organ." Gen. 4:21.

Jubilee (jū'bǐ-lē), **The year of.** 1. *The name.*—The name jubilee or *jubile*

is derived from the Hebrew *jobel*, the joyful shout or clangor of trumpets, by which the year of jubilee was announced.

2. *The time of its celebration.*—It was celebrated every fiftieth year, marking the half century; so that it followed the seventh sabbatic year, and for two years in succession the land lay fallow. It was announced by the blowing of trumpets on the day of atonement (about the 1st of October), the tenth day of the first month of the Israelites' civil year (the seventh of their ecclesiastical year).

3. *The laws connected with the jubilee.* —These embrace three points: (1) Rest for the soil. Lev. 25:11, 12. The land was to lie fallow, and there was to be no tillage as on the ordinary sabbatic year. The land was not to be sown, nor the vineyards and oliveyards dressed; and it was implied that neither the spontaneous fruits of the soil nor the produce of the vine and olive was to be gathered, but all was to be left for the poor, the slave, the stranger and the cattle. Ex. 23:10, 11. The law was accompanied by a promise of treble fertility in the sixth year, the fruit of which was to be eaten till the harvest sown in the eighth year was reaped in the ninth. Lev. 25:20–22. But the people were not debarred from other sources of subsistence, nor was the year to be spent in idleness. They could fish and hunt, take care of their bees and flocks, repair their buildings and furniture, and manufacture their clothing. (2) Reversion of landed property. The freehold of agricultural land could not be sold outright for in the jubilee every piece sold reverted to the owner or his heirs. The nominal sale amounted to a lease for the number of years to elapse before the next jubilee year, for the price was to be in proportion to the time. This applied to fields and houses in the country and to houses of the Levites in walled cities; but other houses in such cities, if not redeemed within a year from their sale, remained the perpetual property of the buyer. (3) The manumission of those Israelites who had become slaves for any reason and either had not served the six years after which they were by law allowed their freedom (Ex. 21:2-6) or had elected to remain with their masters after the expiration of the legal period.

4. *The reasons for the institution of the jubilee.*—It was to be a remedy for

those evils which accompany human society and human government; and had these laws been observed, they would have made the Jewish nation the most prosperous and perfect that ever existed. (1) The jubilee tended to abolish poverty. It prevented large and permanent accumulations of wealth. It gave unfortunate families an opportunity to begin over again with a fair start in life. It particularly favored the poor, without injustice to the rich. (2) It tended to abolish slavery, and in fact did abolish the slavery of the poorer Hebrews themselves; and it greatly mitigated it while it existed by removing at once the "terrible incubus of a life-long bondage," with its accompanying hopelessness. (3) "As an agricultural people, they would have much leisure; they would observe the sabbatic spirit of the year by using its leisure for the instruction of their families in the law, and for acts of devotion; and in accordance with this there was a solemn reading of the law to the people assembled at the feast of tabernacles."—*Smith's larger Dictionary.* (4) "This law of entail, by which the right heir could never be excluded, was a provision of great wisdom for preserving families and tribes perfectly distinct, and their genealogies faithfully recorded, in order that all might have evidence to establish their right to the ancestral property. Hence the tribe and family of Christ were readily discovered at his birth."

5. *Mode of celebration.*—"The Bible says nothing of the mode of celebration, except that it was to be proclaimed by trumpets, and that it was to be a sabbatic year. Tradition tells us that every Israelite blew nine blasts, so as to make the trumpet literally 'sound throughout the land,' and that from the feast of trumpets or new year till the day of atonement (ten days after), the slaves were neither manumitted to return to their homes, nor made use of by their masters, but ate, drank and rejoiced; and when the day of atonement came, the judges blew the trumpets, the slaves were manumitted to go to their homes, and the fields were set free."—*McClintock and Strong.*

6. *How long observed.*—Though very little is said about its observance in the Bible history of the Jews, yet it is referred to, and was no doubt observed with more or less faithfulness, till the Babylonish captivity.

Ju'cal (jŭ'kal) (*Jehovah is able*), son of Shelemiah. Jer. 38 : 1.

Ju'da (jŭ'dà) (*praised*). 1. Son of Joseph, in the genealogy of Christ. Luke 3 : 30.

2. Son of Joanna, or Hananiah. [HANANIAH, 8.] Luke 3 : 26. R. V. *Joda.*

3. One of the Lord's brethren, enumerated in Mark 6 : 3. R. V. *Judas.*

4. The patriarch Judah. Luke 3 : 33; Heb. 7 : 14; Rev. 5 : 5; 7 : 5.

Judæ'a (jŭ-dē'à) or **Jude'a** (from Judah), a territorial division first mentioned after the captivity. It is found in Dan. 5 : 13, Authorized Version "Jewry," and is alluded to in Neh. 11 : 3 (Authorized Version "Judah"). In the apocryphal books the word "province" is dropped, and throughout them and the New Testament the expressions are "the land of Judea," "Judea." In a wider sense, the term Judea was sometimes extended to the whole country of the Canaanites, its ancient inhabitants; and even in the Gospels we read of the coasts of Judea "beyond Jordan." Matt. 19 : 1; Mark 10 : 1. In Mark, however, the R. V. has "the borders of Judea and beyond Jordan." Judea was, in strict language, the name of the third district, west of the Jordan and south of Samaria. It was made a portion of the Roman province of Syria upon the deposition of Archelaus, the ethnarch of Judea, in A.D. 6, and was governed by a procurator, who was subject to the governor of Syria.

Ju'dah (jŭ'dà) (*praised*), the fourth son of Jacob and the fourth of Leah. Of Judah's personal character more traits are preserved than of any other of the patriarchs, with the exception of Joseph, whose life he in conjunction with Reuben saved. Gen. 37 : 26-28. During the second visit to Egypt for corn it was Judah who undertook to be responsible for the safety of Benjamin, ch. 43 : 3-10; and when, through Joseph's artifice, the brothers were brought back to the palace, he is again the leader and spokesman of the band. So too it is Judah who is sent before Jacob to smooth the way for him in the land of Goshen, ch. 46 : 28. This ascendency over his brethren is reflected in the last words addressed to him by his father. The families of Judah oc-

Photo by *Jan Wilga*

SCENE IN THE "WILDERNESS OF JUDAH."
According to legend this mountain was the place of the Forty Days'
Temptation of the Saviour.

cupy a position among the tribes similar to that which their progenitor had taken among the patriarchs. The numbers of the tribe at the census at Sinai were 74,600. Num. 1 : 26, 27. On the borders of the promised land they were 76,500. Num. 26 : 22. The boundaries and contents of the territory allotted to Judah are narrated at great length, and with greater minuteness than the others, in Josh. 15 : 20–63. The north boundary, for the most part coincident with the south boundary of Benjamin, began at the embouchure of the Jordan and ended on the west at Jabneel on the coast of the Mediterranean, four miles south of Joppa. On the east the Dead Sea, and on the west the Mediterranean, formed the boundaries. The southern line is hard to determine, since it is denoted by places many of which have not been identified. It left the Dead Sea at its extreme south end, and joined the Mediterranean at the *Wady el-Arish*. This territory is in length from north to south from 50 to 95 miles, and in breadth about 45.

Judah, Kingdom of. *Extent.*— When the disruption of Solomon's kingdom took place at Shechem, B.C. 937, only the tribe of Judah followed David, but almost immediately afterward the larger part of Benjamin joined Judah. A part, if not all, of the territory of Simeon, 1 Sam. 27 : 6; 1 Kings 19 : 3, comp. Josh. 19 : 1, 2, and of Dan, 2 Chron. 11 : 10, comp. Josh. 19 : 41, 42, was recognized as belonging to Judah; and in the reigns of Abijah and Asa the southern kingdom was enlarged by some additions taken out of the territory of Ephraim. 2 Chron. 13 : 19; 15 : 8; 17 : 2.

Advantages.—The kingdom of Judah possessed many advantages which secured for it a longer continuance than that of Israel. A frontier less exposed to powerful enemies, a soil less fertile, a population hardier and more united, a fixed and venerated centre of administration and religion, a hereditary aristocracy in the sacerdotal caste, an army always subordinate, a succession of kings which no revolution interrupted; so that Judah survived her more populous and more powerful sister kingdom by 135 years, and lasted from B.C. 937 to B.C. 586.

History.—The first three kings of Judah seem to have cherished the hope of re-establishing their authority over the ten tribes; for sixty years there was war between them and the kings of Israel. The victory achieved by the daring Abijah brought to Judah a temporary accession of territory. Asa appears to have enlarged it still further. Hanani's remonstrance, 2 Chron. 16 : 7, prepares us for the reversal by Jehoshaphat of the policy which Asa pursued toward Israel and Damascus. A close alliance sprang up with strange rapidity between Judah and Israel. Jehoshaphat, active and prosperous, commanded the respect of his neighbors; but under Amaziah Jerusalem was entered and plundered by the Israelites. Under Uzziah and Jotham, Judah long enjoyed prosperity, till Ahaz became the tributary and vassal of Tiglath-pileser. Already in the fatal grasp of Assyria, Judah was yet spared for a checkered existence of almost another century and a half after the termination of the kingdom of Israel. The consummation of the ruin came upon its people in the destruction of the temple by the hand of Nebuzar-adan, the "captain of the guard" of Nebuchadnezzar. B.C. 586. 2 Kings 25 : 8–21. There were 19 kings, all from the family of David.

Ju′das, the Greek form of the Hebrew name Judah, occurring in the LXX. and the New Testament. 1. The patriarch Judah. Matt. 1 : 2, 3.

2. A man residing at Damascus, in "the street which is called Straight," in whose house Saul of Tarsus lodged after his miraculous conversion. Acts 9 : 11.

Ju′das, surnamed Barsabas, a leading member of the apostolic church at Jerusalem, Acts 15 : 22, endued with the gift of prophecy, ver. 32, chosen with Silas to accompany Paul and Barnabas as delegates to the church at Antioch. (A.D. 50.) Later, Judas went back to Jerusalem.

Ju′das of Galilee, the leader of a popular revolt "in the days of the taxing" (*i. e.* the census, under the prefecture of P. Sulp. Quirinius, A.D. 6, or 7), referred to by Gamaliel in his speech before the Sanhedrin. Acts 5 : 37. According to Josephus, Judas was a Gaulonite of the city of Gamala; taking his name of Galilean either from his insurrection having had its rise in Galilee or because Gaulonitis was loosely attached to Galilee. The Gaulonites, as his followers were called, may be regarded as the doctrinal ancestors of the Zealots and Sicarii of later days.

Ju'das Iscar'iot (*Judas of Kerioth*). He is sometimes called "the son of Simon," John 6:71; 13:2, 26, but more commonly ISCARIOT. Matt. 10:4; Mark 3:19; Luke 6:16, etc. The name Iscariot has received many interpretations more or less conjectural; but the question is now practically settled as being from *Ish Kerioth*, i. e. "man of Kerioth," a town in the tribe of Judah. Josh. 15:25. Of the life of Judas before the appearance of his name in the lists of the apostles we know absolutely nothing. What that appearance implies, however, is that he had previously declared himself a disciple. He was drawn, as the others were, by the preaching of the Baptist, or his own Messianic hopes, or the "gracious words" of the new Teacher, to leave his former life, and to obey the call of the Prophet of Nazareth. The choice was not made, we must remember, without a prevision of its issue. John 6:64. The germs of the evil, in all likelihood, unfolded themselves gradually. The rules to which the twelve were subject in their first journey, Matt. 10:9, 10, sheltered him from the temptation that would have been most dangerous to him. The new form of life, of which we find the first traces in Luke 8:3, brought that temptation with it. As soon as the twelve were recognized as a body, travelling hither and thither with their Master, receiving money and other offerings, and redistributing what they received to the poor, it became necessary that some one should act as the steward and almoner of the small society, and this fell to Judas. John 12:6; 13:29. The Galilean or Judean peasant found himself entrusted with larger sums of money than before, and with this there came covetousness, unfaithfulness, embezzlement. Several times he showed his tendency to avarice and selfishness. This, even under the best of influences, grew worse and worse, till he betrayed his Master for thirty pieces of silver.

Why was such a man chosen to be one of the twelve?—(1) There was needed among the disciples, as in the Church now, a man of just such talents as Judas possessed,—the talent for managing business affairs. (2) Though he probably followed Christ at first from mixed motives, as did the other disciples, he had the opportunity of becoming a good and useful man. (3) It doubtless was included in God's plans that there should be thus a standing argument for the truth and honesty of the gospel; for if any wrong or trickery had been concealed, it would have been revealed by the traitor in self-defence. (4) Perhaps to teach the Church that God can bless and the gospel can succeed even though some bad men may creep into the fold.

What was Judas' motive in betraying Christ?—(1) Anger at the public rebuke given him by Christ at the supper in the house of Simon the leper. Matt. 26:6–16. (2) Avarice, covetousness, the thirty pieces of silver. John 12:6. (3) The reaction of feeling in a bad soul against the Holy One whose words and character were a continual rebuke, and who knew the traitor's heart. (4) A much larger covetousness,—an ambition to be the treasurer, not merely of a few poor disciples, but of a great and splendid temporal kingdom of the Messiah. He would hasten on the coming of that kingdom by compelling Jesus to defend himself. (5) Perhaps disappointment because Christ insisted on foretelling his death instead of receiving his kingdom. He began to fear that there was to be no kingdom, after all. (6) Perhaps, also, Judas "abandoned what seemed to him a failing cause, and hoped by his treachery to gain a position of honor and influence in the Pharisaic party."

The end of Judas.—(1) Judas, when he saw the results of his betrayal, "repented himself." Matt. 27:3–10. He saw his sin in a new light, and "his conscience bounded into fury." (2) He made ineffectual struggles to escape, by attempting to return the reward to the Pharisees; and when they would not receive it, he cast it down at their feet and left it. Matt. 27:5. But (*a*) restitution of the silver did not undo the wrong; (*b*) it was restored in a wrong spirit,—a desire for relief rather than hatred of sin; (*c*) he confessed to the wrong party, or rather to those who should have been secondary, and who could not grant forgiveness; (*d*) "compunction is not conversion." (3) The money was used to buy a burial-field for poor strangers. Matt. 27:6–10. (4) Judas himself, in his despair, went out and hanged himself, Matt. 27:5, at Acel-

22

dama, on the southern slope of the valley of Hinnom, near Jerusalem, and in the act he fell down a precipice and was dashed into pieces. Acts 1 : 18. "And he went to his own place." Acts 1 : 25. "A guilty conscience must find either hell or pardon." (5) Judas' repentance may be compared to that of Esau. Gen. 27 : 32-38; Heb. 12 : 16, 17. It is contrasted with that of Peter. Judas proved his repentance to be false by immediately committing another sin, suicide. Peter proved his to be true by serving the Lord faithfully ever after.

Ju'das Maccabæ'us. [MACCABEES.]

Ju'das or **Jude,** called also LEBBÆUS and THADDEUS, one of the twelve apostles. Matt. 10 : 3; Mark 3 : 18 · Luke 6 : 16; John 14 : 22; Acts 1 : 13. The A. V. in Luke and Acts have "Judas *the brother* of James." The R. V. text changes this to "*the son,*" though retaining the other reading in the margin. Nothing is certainly known of the later history of the apostle. Tradition connects him with the foundation of the church at Edessa.

Ju'das, the Lord's brother. Among the brethren of our Lord mentioned by the people of Nazareth. Matt. 13 : 55; Mark 6 : 3.

Jude, Epistle of. Its author was probably Jude, *i. e.* Judas, one of the brethren of Jesus. There are no clear data from which to determine its date or place of writing, but Hastings places it between A.D. 63 and 80, and thinks it was composed at Jerusalem, or at least in Palestine, and written to the church in Antioch of Syria. The object of the epistle is plainly enough announced ver. 3; the reason for this exhortation is given ver. 4. The remainder of the epistle is almost entirely occupied by a minute depiction of the adversaries of the faith. The epistle closes by briefly reminding the readers of the oft-repeated prediction of the apostles—among whom the writer seems not to rank himself—that the faith would be assailed by such enemies as he has depicted, vs. 17-19, exhorting them to maintain their own steadfastness in the faith, vs. 20, 21, while they earnestly sought to rescue others from the corrupt example of those licentious livers, vs. 22, 23, and commending them to the power of God in language which forcibly recalls the closing benediction of the epistle to the Romans. vs. 24, 25; cf.

Rom. 16 : 25-27. This epistle presents one peculiarity, which, as we learn from St. Jerome, caused its authority to be impugned in very early times—the supposed citation of apocryphal writings. vs. 9, 14, 15. The larger portion of this epistle, vs. 3-16, is almost identical in language and subject with a part of the Second Epistle of Peter. 2 Pet. 2 : 1-19.

Judges. The judges were temporary and special deliverers, sent by God to deliver the Israelites from their oppressors; not supreme magistrates, succeeding to the authority of Moses and Joshua. Their power only extended over portions of the country, and some of them were contemporaneous. The judge was not only the *vindicator,* the *punisher,* but also the *defender,* the *deliverer.* And "as the administration of justice was, in times of peace, the most important function of the chieftain or king, the noun is sometimes equivalent to *ruler.* . . . It is clear that the writer regarded these judges as a *succession of chiefs,* who arose in different parts of the land, *ruling with an authority* which was *personal and not hereditary.*"—*Prof. Geo. F. Moore, D.D.*

"They were more like Peter the Hermit and Jeanne d'Arc than like Roman dictators."

The nation had no fixed political capital, and the judge selected his own place of residence (Judg. 4 : 5; 10 : 1, 2). "He was surrounded by but little splendor, having no royal court, in the proper sense of the term."—*Johnson.* Even while the administration of Samuel gave something like a settled government to the south, there was scope for the irregular exploits of Samson on the borders of the Philistines; and Samuel at last established his authority as judge and prophet, but still as the servant of Jehovah, only to see it so abused by his sons as to exhaust the patience of the people, who at length demanded a *king,* after the pattern of the surrounding nations. A list of the judges, whose history is given under their respective names will be found in the APPENDIX under *Chronology.*

Judges, Book of. THE NAME. This book is so named because it is the record of the exploits of some of the leaders, heroes, champions, and deliverers of Israel during one marked period of their history, extending from the Conquest of Palestine to the period of the kings.

NUMBER. There were fifteen judges in all. Eight were military heroes, five seem to have led more peaceful lives; while Eli the high priest and Samuel the prophet stand apart with peculiar missions.

THE PERIOD OF THE JUDGES. According to 1 Kings 6 : 1, there were 480 years between the Exodus and the commencement of the Temple in the fourth year of Solomon's reign. Deducting from this the 40 years in the wilderness, 25 years of Joshua in Canaan, and 20 or 40 for Saul's reign, 40 for David's reign, and 3 years of Solomon's reign, the period of the judges would be 480 — 148 = 332 years (or 480 — 128 = 352 years), including the judgeships of Eli and Samuel up to the beginning of the reign of Saul. Of this about 280 years belong to the book of Judges. But if we add together the numbers given in Judges they amount to 410 years. For this and other reasons it is entirely probable that "the oppressions and deliverances were not successive, but, in part, synchronous. They were, in fact, without exception, local struggles; and it is not only conceivable, but highly probable, that while one part of the land was enjoying security under its judge, other tribes were groaning under the foreign yoke."— *Professor Moore.* While several of the events were thus occurring at the same time in different parts of the land, in other cases the judges ruled practically over the whole. "The judges formed temporary heads in particular centers, or over particular groups of tribes,— Barak, in the north of Israel, Gideon, in the center, Jephthah, on the east of Jordan, Samson, in the extreme southwest." —*Driver.*

THE CONSTRUCTION OF THE BOOK OF JUDGES. The book of the Judges consists of three parts :—

1. Judg. 1–2 : 5, giving a brief review of the wars immediately after the death of Joshua. Professors Driver, Moore, and others regard this period as a résumé of the conquest under Joshua, making the first statement, "After the death of Joshua it came to pass," to be a later addition, referring not to the immediately following events, but to the period of the judges as a whole. And they find many contradictions between the two accounts. But it seems more

scientific to take the account as it stands, and use the facts as given to us, and then there is no contradiction, but merely the differences of fact in two different periods.

2. From Judg. 2 : 6–16 : 31 we have a history of successive oppressions and deliverances by judges, not probably all in chronological order, but selected from the history to teach great religious lessons for the good of the nations.

3. Judg. 17–21 are an appendix throwing light on the social and religious life of the times; to which should be added the book of Ruth, which sheds a more beautiful and pleasing light over all.

A distinction must be made between the date of the events, the date of the first records of these events, and the date when the books were put into their present shape. There are the same differences in modern history. English history has been written over many times, and the latest historians use their predecessor's work as well as the earliest contemporary documents, and the history is, doubtless, the more exactly true on that account, and are readable by us, while the earlier ones could not well be read on account of the changes in language.

DATE. It is uncertain at what date the book of Judges was completed in its present form. Professor Moore thinks it was not till after the exile. But there were certainly earlier records, and, doubtless, written histories of these events not far from the time of their occurrence.

GENERAL PROSPERITY MINGLED WITH ADVERSITY. "It would be a mistake to suppose that there was nothing, during all the centuries covered by this book, but an unbroken series of apostasies and judgments. It would be as correct to infer from a modern criminal calendar that there were none but law-breakers in the country."—*Professor Green.* From a hasty glance at the records we get an impression, as we used to do from the histories of a generation ago, that most of the years were filled with wars and oppressions. But a careful study and a glance at the chronological chart, in the APPENDIX, shows that the times of peace and prosperity were much longer than the times of war and oppression. The intervals of peace naturally take up less space in the history than do the severer epochs of war and oppression, which mark sudden steps in the discipline of the people.

Judgment hall. The word *prætorium* is so translated five times in the Authorized Version of the New Testament, and in those five passages it denotes two different places. 1. In John 18 : 28, 33; 19 : 9, it is the residence which Pilate occupied when he visited Jerusalem. The site of Pilate's prætorium in Jerusalem has given rise to much dispute, some supposing it to be the palace of King Herod, others the tower of Antonia, which was then and long afterward the citadel of Jerusalem. 2. In Acts 23 : 35 Herod's judgment hall or prætorium in Cæsarea was doubtless a part of that magnificent range of buildings the erection of which by King Herod is described in Josephus. The word "palace," or "Cæsar's court," in the Authorized Version of Philip. 1 : 13, is a translation of the same word prætorium. It may here have denoted the quarters of that detachment of the prætorian guards which was in immediate attendance upon the emperor, and had barracks in Mount Palatine at Rome. The R. V. rendering here is "throughout the whole prætorian guard."

Ju'dith (jū'dĭth) (*object of praise*). The daughter of Beeri the Hittite, and wife of Esau. Gen. 26 : 34.

Ju'dith, The book of, one of the books of the Apocrypha, belongs to the earliest specimens of historical fiction. As to its authorship it probably belongs to the Maccabæan period, B.C. 175–135.

Ju'lia (jū'lià) (feminine of Julius), a Christian woman at Rome, possibly the wife of Philologus, in connection with whom she is saluted by St. Paul. Rom. 16 : 15. (A.D. 57.)

Ju'lius (jū'lǐ-us), the centurion of "Augustus' band," to whose charge St. Paul was delivered when he was sent prisoner from Cæsarea to Rome. Acts 27 : 1, 3. (A.D. 60.)

Ju'nia (jū'nià), a Christian at Rome, mentioned by St. Paul as one of his kinsfolk and fellow prisoners, of note among the apostles, and in Christ before St. Paul. Rom. 16 : 7. (A.D. 57.) R. V. *Junias.*

Juniper, 1 Kings 19 : 4, 5; Job 30 : 4; Ps. 120 : 4, the Hebrew *rothem* does not mean the cone-bearing tree known as juniper; but a sort of broom, doubtless the Arabic *ratam* or the *Retama Retem.* It is very abundant in the desert of Sinai, and affords shade and protection, in both heat and storm, to travelers. The rothem is a leguminous plant, and bears a white flower. It is found also in Spain, Portugal and Palestine. It grows like willow bushes along the shores of Spain. It is an erect shrub, with no main trunk, but many wand-like, slender branches, and is sometimes twelve feet high. Its use is very great in stopping the sand.

Ju'piter (jụ'pǐ'tẽr), the name of the supreme god of the Romans, corresponding to the Greek Zeus. The Olympian Zeus was the national god of the Hellenic race, as well as the supreme ruler of the heathen world, and as such formed the true opposite to Jehovah. Jupiter or Zeus is mentioned in two passages of the New Testament, on the occasion of St. Paul's visit to Lystra, Acts 14 : 12, 13, where the expression "Jupiter, which was before their city," means that his temple was outside the city. This god is said by some scholars to be a native Lycaonian god, whose Lycaonian name was represented in Greek by Zeus. Also in Acts 19 : 35, where the R. V. margin gives "heaven."

Ju'shab-he'sed (jū'shăb-hē'sed) (*loving kindness is returned*), son of Zerubbabel. 1 Chron. 3 : 20.

Jus'tus (jŭs'tus) (*just*). 1. A surname of Joseph, called Barsabas. Acts 1 : 23. (A.D. 30.)

2. A Christian at Corinth, with whom St. Paul lodged. Acts 18 : 7. (A.D. 51.) His name is given in full in the Revised Version as Titus Justus and attempts have been made to identify him with the traveling companion of Paul. It is not generally accepted, however, and some MSS. have *Titius Justus.*

3. A surname of Jesus, a friend of St. Paul. Col. 4 : 11. (A.D. 62.)

Jut'tah (jŭt'tah) (*stretched out*), a city in the mountain region of Judah, in the neighborhood of Maon and Carmel. Josh. 15 : 55. The place is now known as *Yutta.*

K

Kab'zeei (kăb'ze-el) (*gathered by God*), one of the "cities" of the tribe of Judah, Josh. 15:21, the native place of the great hero Benaiah ben-Jehoiada. 2 Sam. 23:20; 1 Chron. 11:22. After the captivity it was reinhabited by the Jews, and appears as Jekabzeel.

Ka'desh, Ka'desh=bar'ne=a (kā'desh-bär'ne-a), (*Kadesh* means *consecrated,* but there is no clue to the meaning of the word *Barnea.*) This place, the scene of Miriam's death, was the farthest point which the Israelites reached in their direct road to Canaan; it was also that whence the spies were sent, and where, on their return, the people broke out into murmuring, upon which their strictly penal term of wandering began. Num. 13:3, 26; 14:29-33; 20:1; Deut. 2:14. In Gen. 14:7, Kadesh is identified with En-mishpat, the "fountain of judgment." It has been supposed, from Num. 13:21, 26, and Num. 20, that there were two places of the name of Kadesh, one in the wilderness of Paran and the other in that of Zin; but it is more probable that only one place is meant, and that either the wilderness of Zin is a part of the larger one of Paran, or else that they run into each other without any precise boundary. There has been much doubt as to the exact site of Kadesh; but Rev. H. Clay Trumbull of Philadelphia, visiting the spot in 1881, succeeded in rendering almost certain that the site of Kadesh is *Ain Kadis* (spelled also *Gadis* and *Quadis*); "the very same name, letter for letter in Arabic and Hebrew, with the scriptural fountain of Kadesh—the 'holy fountain,' as the name means—which gushed forth when Moses smote the rock." It lies 40 miles south of Beersheba and 165 northeast of Horeb, immediately below the southern border of Palestine. It was discovered in 1842 by the Rev. J. Rowlands of Queen's College, Cambridge, England, whose dis-covery was endorsed by the great German geographer Ritter, by E. S. Palmer in his "Desert of the Exodus," and by the "Imperial Bible Dictionary." Dr. Trumbull thus describes it:—"It is an extensive oasis, a series of wells, the water of which flows out from under such an overhanging cliff as is mentioned in the Bible story; and it opens into a vast plain or wadi large enough to have furnished a camping-ground for the whole host of Israel. Extensive primitive ruins are on the hills near it. The plain or wadi, also called Quadis, is shut in by surrounding hills so as to make it a most desirable position for such a people as the Israelites on the borders of hostile territory—such a position as leaders like Moses and Joshua would have been likely to select. It was carpeted with grass and flowers. Fig trees laden with fruit were against its limestone hillsides. Shrubs in richness and variety abounded. Standing out from the mountain range at the northward of the beautiful oasis amphitheatre was the 'large single mass or small hill of solid rock' which Rowlands looked at as the cliff (sela) smitten by Moses to cause it to 'give forth its water' when its flowing had ceased. From beneath this cliff came the abundant stream. A well, walled up with time-worn limestone blocks, was the first receptacle of the water. Not far from this was a second well similarly walled, supplied from the same source. Around both these wells were ancient watering-troughs of limestone. Several pools, not walled up, were also supplied from the stream. The water was clear and sweet and abundant. Two of the pools were ample for bathing."

Kad'miel (kăd'mĭ-el) (*God is of old*), one of the Levites who with his family returned from Babylon with Zerubbabel. Ezra 2:40; Neh. 7:43. He and his house are mentioned in history

341

on three occasions—Ezra 3:9; Neh. 9: 4, 5; 10:9.

Kad'monites (kăd'mon-ītes) (*men of the East*), **The**, a people named in Gen. 15:19 only; one of the nations who at that time occupied the land (Canaan) promised to the descendants of Abram. The name is probably a synonym for the Bene-Kedem—the "children of the East," with no definite signification.

Kal'lai (kăl'la-ī) (*swift*), a priest in the days of Joiakim the son of Jeshua. He represented the family of Sallai. Neh. 12:20. (B.C. about 500.)

Ka'nah (kā'nah) (*a place of reeds*). 1. One of the places which formed the landmarks of the boundary of Asher; apparently next to Zidon-rabbah, or "great Zidon." Josh. 19:28. Probably the modern *Kana*, a few miles southeast of Tyre.

2. The river, a stream falling into the Mediterranean, which formed the division between the territories of Ephraim and Manasseh, the former on the south, the latter on the north. Josh. 16:8; 17: 9.

Kare'ah (kārē'ah) (*bald*), the father of Johanan and Jonathan, who supported Gedaliah's authority and avenged his murder. Jer. 40:8, 13, 15, 16; 41: 11, 13, 14, 16; 42:1, 8; 43:2, 4, 5.

Kar'kaa (kär'ka-ä) or **Karka'a**, one of the landmarks on the south boundary of the tribe of Judah. Josh. 15:3. Its site is unknown. R. V. Karka.

Kar'kor (kär'kôr) (*foundation*), the place in which Zebah and Zalmunna were again routed by Gideon, Judges 8: 10, must have been on the east of Jordan.

Kar'tah (kär'tah) (*city*), a town of Zebulun, allotted to the Merarite Levites. Josh. 21:34.

Kar'tan (kär'tan) (*double city*), a city of Naphtali, allotted to the Gershonite Levites. Josh. 21:32. In the parallel list of 1 Chron. 6 the name appears, ver. 76, in the more expanded form of KIRJATHAIM.

Kat'tath (kăt'tath), one of the cities of the tribe of Zebulun. Josh. 19:15. Sometimes identified with KARTAH and sometimes with KITRON.

Ke'dar (kē'där), the second in order of the sons of Ishmael, Gen. 25:13; 1 Chron. 1:29, and the name of a great tribe of Arabs settled on the northwest of the peninsula and on the confines of Palestine. The name is unknown to Arabic traditions, but it is said to be preserved in inscriptions found in Arabia, and it appears in the inscriptions of Assur-banipal. The "glory of Kedar" is recorded by the prophet Isaiah, Isa. 21:13–17, in the burden upon Arabia; and its importance may also be inferred from the "princes of Kedar" mentioned by Ezekiel, Ezek. 27:21, as well as the pastoral character of the tribe. They appear also to have been, like the wandering tribes of the present day, "archers" and "mighty men." Isa. 21:17; comp. Ps. 120:5. That they also settled in villages or towns we find from Isaiah. Isa. 42:11. The tribe seems to have been one of the most conspicuous of all the Ishmaelite tribes, and hence the rabbins call the Arabians universally by this name.

Ked'emah (kĕd'e-mah) (*eastward*), the youngest of the sons of Ishmael. Gen. 25:15; 1 Chron. 1:31.

Ked'emoth (kĕd'e-mŏth) (*beginnings*), one of the towns in the district east of the Dead Sea allotted to the tribe of Reuben, Josh. 13:18; given to the Merarite Levites. Josh. 21:37; 1 Chron. 6:79. It possibly conferred its name on the "wilderness," or uncultivated pasture land, "of Kedemoth." Num. 21:23; Deut. 2:26, 27, etc.

Ke'desh (kē'desh) (*a sanctuary*). 1. In the extreme south of Judah, Josh. 15: 23; probably not the same as Kadesh and Kadesh-barnea, although formerly so supposed.

2. A city of Issachar, allotted to the Gershonite Levites. 1 Chron. 6:72. Very possibly an error for *Kishion* which is found in the parallel passage Jos. 21:28. A. V. Kishon.

3. Kedesh; also Kedesh in Galilee; and once, Judges 4:6, Kedesh-naphtali, one of the fortified cities of the tribe of Naphtali, Josh. 19:37; appointed as a city of refuge, and allotted with its "suburbs" to the Gershonite Levites. Josh. 20:7; 21:32; 1 Chron. 6:76. It is mentioned among the cities whose kings were slain by Joshua, Josh. 12: 22. It was the residence of Barak, Judges 4:6, and there he and Deborah assembled the tribes of Zebulun and Naphtali before the conflict, being probably, as its name implies, a "holy place" of great antiquity. It was taken by Tiglath-pileser in the reign of Pekah. 2 Kings 15:29. It is identified with the village *Kades*, which lies four miles to

the northwest of the upper part of the waters of Merom.

Ked'ron (kĕd'rŏn), properly Kidron. [KIDRON.]

Kehel'athah (kė-hĕl'a-thath) (*assembly*), a desert encampment of the Israelites, Num. 33 : 22, of which nothing is known.

Kei'lah (kēi'lah), a city of the Shefelah, or lowland district of Judah. Josh. 15 : 44. Its main interest consists in its connection with David. 1 Sam. 23 : 7–13. The two halves of the "district of Keilah" were represented in Nehemiah's work of building the wall. *Kila*, a site with ruins, on the lower road from *Beit Jibrin* to Hebron is generally supposed to be the ancient Keilah, but it is disputed.

Kei'lah the Garmite, apparently a descendant of the great Caleb. 1 Chron. 4 : 19.

Kela'iah (kė-lā'yah)= KELITA. Ezra 10 : 23.

Kel'ita (kĕl'ĭ-tȧ) (*dwarf*), one of the Levites who returned with Ezra. Ezra 10 : 23. He, or another man of the same name, assisted in expounding the law, Neh. 8 : 7, and signed the covenant with Nehemiah. Neh. 10 : 10.

Kem'uel (kĕm'ū-ĕl) (*congregation of God*). 1. The son of Nahor by Milcah, and father of Aram. Gen. 22 : 21.

2. The son of Shiptan, and prince of the tribe of Ephraim; one of the twelve men appointed by Moses to divide the land of Canaan. Num. 34 : 24.

3. A Levite, father of Hashabiah, prince of the tribe in the reign of David. 1 Chron. 27 : 17.

Ke'nan (ke'nan) (*spear*)= CAINAN, the son of Enos. 1 Chron. 1 : 2.

Ke'nath (kē'nath) (*possession*), one of the cities of the east of Jordan, with its "daughter-towns" (Authorized Version "villages") taken possession of by a certain Nobah, who then called it by his own name. Num. 32 : 42.

Ke'naz (kē'năz). 1. Son of Eliphaz the son of Esau. He was one of the dukes of Edom. Gen. 36 : 15, 42; 1 Chron. 1 : 53.

2. One of the same family, a grandson of Caleb, according to 1 Chron. 4 : 15 (where see margin).

Ken'ezite (kĕn'ĕz-ītes) or **Ken'izzite** (*descendant of Kenaz*), Gen. 15 : 19, an Edomitish tribe. Num. 32 : 12; Josh. 14 : 6, 14.

Ken'ite, The, and **Ken'ites** (kĕn'ites) (*smiths*), **The**, inhabited the rocky and desert region between southern Palestine and the mountains of Sinai, east of the Gulf of Akabah. They were connected with the larger nation of Midian,—from the fact that Jethro, who in Exodus (see 2 : 15, 16; 4 : 19, etc.) is represented as dwelling in the land of Midian, and as priest or prince of that nation, is in Judges (1 : 16, 4 : 11) as distinctly said to have been a Kenite. The important services rendered by the sheikh of the Kenites to Moses during a time of great pressure and difficulty were rewarded by the latter with a promise of firm friendship between the two peoples. They seem to have accompanied the Hebrews during their wanderings, Num. 24 : 21, 22; Judges 1 : 16; but, the wanderings of Israel over, they forsook the neighborhood of the towns and betook themselves to freer air,— to "the wilderness of Judah, which is to the south of Arad." Judges 1 : 16. But one of the sheikhs of the tribe, Heber by name, had wandered north instead of south. Judges 4 : 11. The most remarkable development of this people is to be found in the sect or family of the Rechabites.

Ken'izzite. Gen. 15 : 19. [KENEZITE.]

Ke'ren-hap'puch (kĕr'en-hăp'puk) (*horn of antimony*), the youngest of the daughters of Job, born to him during the period of his reviving prosperity. Job 42 : 14.

Ke'rioth (kē'rĭ-oth) (*cities*). 1. A name which occurs among the lists of the towns in the southern district of Judah. Josh. 15 : 25. Probably the birthplace of Judas Iscariot. Properly Kerioth-Hezron, as in R. V. The same as HAZOR 3. Perhaps the modern *Karjetein*.

2. A city of Moab, named by Jeremiah, Jer. 48 : 24. Also in Amos 2 : 2, in A. V. Kirioth. Very possibly it should be translated "the cities."

Ke'ros (kē'ros), one of the Nethinim, whose descendants returned with Zerubbabel. Ezra 2 : 44; Neh. 7 : 47.

Kettle, a vessel for culinary or sacrificial purposes. 1 Sam. 2 : 14. The Hebrew word is also rendered "basket" in Jer. 24 : 2 (its usual translation) "caldron" in 2 Chron. 35 : 13, and "pot" in Job 41 : 20.

Ketu'rah (kė-tū'rah) (*incense*), the wife of Abraham after the death of

THE KIDRON VALLEY.

Sarah. Gen. 25:1; 1 Chron. 1:32. (B.C. after 1859.)

Key. The key of a native Oriental lock is a piece of wood, from seven

EGYPTIAN IRON KEY.

inches to two feet in length, fitted with wires or short nails, which, being inserted laterally into the hollow bolt which serves as a lock, raises other pins within the staple so as to allow the bolt to be drawn back. Keys were sometimes of bronze or iron, and so large that one was as much as a man could carry. They are used in Scripture as a symbol of authority and power. Giving keys to a person signifies the intrusting of him with an important charge. Matt. 16:19. In England in modern times certain officers of the government receive, at their induction into office, a golden key.

Kezi'a (kė-zī'ȧ) (*cassia*), the second of the daughters of Job born to him after his recovery. Job 42:14.

Ke'ziz (kē'zĭz) (*cut off*), **The valley of,** R. V. Emek-Keziz. One of the cities of Benjamin, Josh. 18:21, and the eastern border of the tribe.

Kib'roth=hatta'avah (kĭb'roth-hat-tā'a-vah), *i. e.* as in the margin, *the graves of lust,* a station of the Israelites in the wilderness, where, growing tired of manna and desiring flesh, they murmured, and God sent them quails in great abundance, but smote great numbers of them with a plague and they died. It was about a day's journey from Sinai. The traditional site is near the Gulf of Akabah and the *Wady el Hudherah* (Hazeroth). Num. 11:33.

Kib'zaim (kĭb'za-im) (*two heaps*), a city of Mount Ephraim, given up with its "suburbs" to the Kohathite Levites. Josh. 21:22. In the parallel list of 1 Chron. 6 JOKMEAM is substituted for Kibzaim. ver. 68.

Kid. [GOAT.]

Kid'ron (kĭd'ron) or **Ced'ron** (*turbid*), **The brook,** a torrent or valley, not a "brook," or, as in the margin of Revised Version, "ravine;" Gr. *winter torrent.* It was close to Jerusalem, between the city and the Mount of Olives. It is now commonly known as the "valley of Jehoshaphat." The channel of the valley is nothing more than the dry bed of a wintry torrent, bearing marks of being occasionally swept over by a large volume of water. It was crossed by David in his flight, 2 Sam. 15:23, comp. 30, and by our Lord on his way to Gethsemane. John 18:1; comp. Mark 14:26; Luke 22:39. The distinguishing peculiarity of the Kidron valley—mentioned in the Old Testament—is the impurity which appears to have been ascribed to it. In the time of Josiah it was the common cemetery of the city. 2 Kings 23:6; comp. Jer. 26:23.

Ki'nah (kī'nah) (*lamentation*), a city of Judah, on the extreme south boundary of the tribe, next to Edom. Josh. 15:22.

Kine, the plural of cow. [See BULL.]

King, "a chief ruler, one invested with supreme authority over a nation, tribe or country."—*Webster.* In the Bible the word does not necessarily imply great power of great extent of country. Many persons are called kings whom we should rather call chiefs or leaders. The word is applied in the Bible to God as the sovereign and ruler of the universe, and to Christ the Son of God as the head and governor of the Church.

The Hebrews were ruled by a king during a period of about 500 years previous to the destruction of Jerusalem, B.C. 586. The immediate occasion of the substitution of a regal form of government for that of judges seems to have been the siege of Jabesh-gilead by Nahash king of the Ammonites. 1 Sam. 11:1; 12:12. The conviction seems to have forced itself on the Israelites that they could not resist their formidable neighbor unless they placed themselves under the sway of a king, like surrounding nations. The original idea of a Hebrew king was twofold: first, that he should lead the people to battle in time of war; and, second, that he should execute judgment and justice to them in war and in peace. 1 Sam. 8:20. In both respects the desired end was attained. Besides being commander-in-chief of the army, supreme judge, and absolute master, as it were, of the lives of his subjects, the king exercised the power of imposing taxes on them, and of exacting from them personal service and labor. In addition to these earthly powers, the king of Israel had a more awful claim to respect and obedience. He was the vicegerent of Jehovah, 1 Sam. 10:1; 16:13, and as it were his son, if just and holy. 2 Sam. 7:14; Ps. 2:6, 7; 89:26, 27. He had been set apart as a consecrated ruler. Upon his head had been poured the holy anointing oil, which had hitherto been reserved exclusively for the priests of Jehovah. He had become, in fact, emphatically "the Lord's anointed." He had a court of Oriental magnificence. The king was dressed in royal robes, 1 Kings 22:10; 2 Chron. 18:9; his insignia were, a crown or diadem of pure gold, or perhaps radiant with precious gems, 2 Sam. 1:10; 12:30; 2 Kings 11:12; Ps. 21:3, and a royal sceptre. Those who approached him did him obeisance, bowing down and touching the ground with their foreheads, 1 Sam. 24:8; 2 Sam. 19:18; and this was done even by a king's wife, the mother of Solomon. 1 Kings 1:16. His officers and subjects called themselves his servants or slaves. He had a large harem, which was guarded by eunuchs. The law of succession to the throne is somewhat obscure, but it seems most probable that the king during his lifetime named his successor. At the same time, if no partiality for a favorite wife or son intervened, there would always be a natural bias of affection in favor of the eldest son.

Kings of Judah and Israel. For the list see table at the end of this volume.

Kings, First and Second Books of, originally only one book in the Hebrew canon, form in the LXX. and the Vulgate the third and fourth books of *Kings* (the books of Samuel being the first and second). It must be remembered that the division between the books of Kings and Samuel is equally artificial, and that in point of fact the historical books commencing with Judges and ending with 2 Kings present the appearance of one work, giving a continuous history of Israel from the time of Joshua to the death of Jehoiachin.

PERIOD. About 400 years from David's death and Solomon's accession to the destruction of the kingdom of Judah and the desolation of Jerusalem, with a supplemental notice of an event that occurred after an interval of twenty-six years—viz., the liberation of Jehoiachin from his prison at Babylon—and a still further extension to Jehoiachin's death, the time of which is not known, but which was probably not long after his liberation. The history therefore comprehends the whole time of the Israelitish monarchy, exclusive of the reigns of Saul and David.

RELATION TO FOREIGN NATIONS. As regards the affairs of foreign nations and the relation of Israel to them, the historical notices in these books, though in the earlier times scanty, are most valuable, and in striking accord with the latest additions to our knowledge of contemporary profane history.

CONFIRMATIONS. An important aid to a right understanding of the history in these books, and to the filling up of its outline, is to be found in the prophets, and especially in Isaiah and Jeremiah. Many other aids and confirmations have been discovered among the ruins of Nineveh, Babylon and elsewhere, such as the Black Obelisk, the Moabite Stone, the cylinders of Sennacherib, Cyrus, Nabonidus, and many others.

THE DATE (from internal considerations such as "unto this day," and references to the temple as still standing, and the monarchy still existing in David's line) is placed about B.C. 600, just before the exile, with later additions.

THE AUTHOR is unknown.

SOURCES OF INFORMATION.—There was a regular series of state annals for both the kingdom of Judah and that of Israel, which embraced the whole time comprehended in the books of Kings, or at least to the end of the reign of Jehoiakim. 2 Kings 24:5. Three of these are named in the history. The Book of the Acts of Solomon (1 Kings 11:41). The Book of the Annals of the Kings of Israel; the Annals or Chronicles are literally "acts of days," "the daily record of current events," mentioned fifteen times. The Book of the Annals (or Chronicles) of the Kings of Judah mentioned seventeen times. The author of Kings had these before him while he drew up his history, in which the reigns of the two kingdoms are harmonized and these annals constantly appealed to. But in addition to these national annals, there were also extant, at the time that the books of Kings were compiled, separate works of the several prophets who had lived in Judah and Israel.

PURPOSE OF THE BOOK, was to keep before the people the religious lessons which their divinely guided history was intended to teach. They were God's chosen people. Only by righteousness and obedience to God could they prosper and fulfil their mission; sin was certain to be punished, and righteousness to be rewarded in outward visible signs of its spiritual blessings. The history was a warning, a promise and a guide.

This religious purpose in no way reflects upon the truth of the history, but influenced the selection of facts. To falsify the history in any degree would in so far have destroyed its power, and hindered the very purpose for which it was written.

Kir (*fortress*) is mentioned by Amos, ch. 9:7, as the land from which the Syrians (Aramæans) were once "brought up;" *i. e.* apparently as the country where they had dwelt before migrating to the region north of Palestine. Several identifications have been proposed, none of which have sufficient plausibility to be generally accepted.

Kir (kīr) **of Moab** (*fortress of Moab*), one of the two chief strongholds of Moab, the other being Ar of Moab. The name occurs only in Isa. 15:1, though the place is probably referred to under the names of Kir-heres, Kir-haraseth, etc. It is almost identical with the name *Kerak,* by which the site of an important city in a high and very strong position at the southeast of the Dead Sea is known at this day. Its situation is truly remarkable. It is built upon the top of a steep hill, surrounded by a deep and narrow valley, which again is completely enclosed by mountains rising higher than the town and overlooking it on all sides.

Kir′har′aseth (kĭr-här′e-seth) (*brick fortress*), 2 Kings 3:25; **Kir=ha′resh,** Isa. 16:11; **Kir=har′eseth,** Isa. 16:7; **Kir=he′res.** Jer. 48:31, 36. These four names are all applied to one place, probably KIR OF MOAB.

Kiriatha′im (kĭr-ĭ-a-thā′im) (*two cities*), on the east of the Jordan, one of the places which were taken possession of and rebuilt by the Reubenites, and had fresh names conferred on them, Num. 32:37, and see 38, the first and last of which are known with some tolerable degree of certainty. It existed in the time of Jeremiah, Jer. 48:1, 23, and Ezekiel. Ezek. 25:9. In Numbers the Authorized Version gives the name KIRJATHAIM. By Eusebius it appears to have been well known. He describes it as a village entirely of Christians, ten miles west of Medeba. It may be the modern *Kureiyat* not far from Machærus.

Kir′ioth (kĭr′ĭ-ŏth) (*cities*), a place in Moab the palaces of which were threatened by Amos with destruction by fire, Amos 2:2; unless indeed the word means simply "the cities," which is probably the case also in Jer. 48:24. R. V. in both places has KERIOTH.

Kir′jath (kĭr′jath) (*a city*), the last of the cities enumerated as belonging to the tribe of Benjamin, Josh. 18:28, probably identical with the better-known place Kirjath-jearim.

Kirjatha′im (kĭr-ĭ-a-thā′im) (*two cities*), a town in Naphtali not mentioned in the original list of the possession allotted to the tribe, see Josh. 19:32-39, but inserted in the list of cities given to the Gershonite Levites in 1 Chron. 6:76, in place of KARTAN in the parallel catalogue, Kartan being probably only a contraction thereof. R. V. KIRIATHAIM.

Kir′jath=ar′ba (kĭr′jath-är′bà) (*the city of Arba*), an early name of the city which after the conquest is generally known as HEBRON. Josh. 14:15; Judges 1:10. The identity of Kirjatharba with Hebron is constantly asserted. Gen. 23:2; 35:27; Josh. 14:15; 15:13, 54; 20:7; 21:11.

Kir′jath=a′rim (kĭr′jath-ā′rim) (*city of forests*), an abbreviated form of the name Kirjath-jearim, which occurs only in Ezra 2:25.

Kir′jath=ba′al (kĭr′jath-bā′al). [KIR-JATH-JEARIM.]

Kir′jath=hu′zoth (kĭr′jath-hū′zoth) (*city of streets*), a place to which Balak accompanied Balaam immediately after his arrival in Moab, Num. 22:39, and which is nowhere else mentioned. It appears to have lain between the Arnon (*Wady Mojeb*) and Bamoth-baal. Comp. vs. 36 and 41.

Kir′jath=je′arim (kĭr′jath-jē′a-rim) (*the city of forests*), first mentioned as one of four cities of the Gibeonites, Josh. 9:17; it next occurs as one of the landmarks of the northern boundary of Judah, ch. 15:9, and as the point at which the western and southern boundaries of Benjamin coincided, ch. 18:14, 15; and in the last two passages we find that it bore another, perhaps earlier, name—that of the great Canaanite deity

Baal, namely BAALAH and KIRJATH-BAAL. At this place the ark remained for twenty years. 1 Sam. 7 : 2. At the close of that time Kirjath-jearim lost its sacred treasure, on its removal by David to the house of Obed-edom the Gittite. 1 Chron. 13 : 5, 6; 2 Chron. 1 : 4; 2 Sam. 6 : 2, etc. To Eusebius and Jerome it appears to have been well known. They describe it as a village at the ninth mile between Jerusalem and Diospolis (Lydda). These requirements are considered by many exactly fulfilled in the small modern village of *Kuriet-el-Enab*—now usually known as *Abû Gosh*, from the robber chief whose headquarters it was—on the road from Jaffa to Jerusalem, though Conder disputes it.

Kir'jath=san'nah (kĭr'jath-săn'nah). [DEBIR.]

Kir'jath=se'pher (kĭr'jath-sē'fĕr). Josh. 15 : 15, 16; Judges 1 : 11, 12. [DEBIR.]

Kish (kĭsh) (*a bow*). 1. The father of Saul; a Benjamite of the family of Matri. 1 Sam. 9 : 1; 10 : 21.

2. Son of Jehiel and uncle to the preceding. 1 Chron. 9 : 36.

3. A Benjamite, great-grandfather of Mordecai. Esther 2 : 5.

4. A Merarite of the house of Mahli, of the tribe of Levi. 1 Chron. 23 : 21, 22; 24 : 28, 29.

Kish'i (kĭsh'ī), a Merarite, and father or ancestor of Ethan the minstrel. 1 Chron. 6 : 44. The parallel passage has Kushaiah, which is probably correct.

Kish'ion (kĭsh'ī-ŏn) (*hardness*), one of the towns on the boundary of the tribe of Issachar, Josh. 19 : 20, which with its suburbs was allotted to the Gershonite Levites. Josh. 21 : 28. **Ki'shon.** [KISHION.]

Ki'shon (kī'shŏn) (*winding*), **The river,** a torrent or winter stream of central Palestine, the scene of two of the grandest achievements of Israelitish history—the defeat of Sisera, Judges 4, and the destruction of the prophets of Baal by Elijah. 1 Kings 18 : 40. The *Nahr-el-Mukûtta*, the modern representative of the Kishon, is the drain by which the waters of the plain of Esdraelon and of the mountains which enclose that plain find their way through the plain of Acre to the Mediterranean. The part of the Kishon at which the prophets of Baal were slaughtered by Elijah was doubtless close below the spot on Carmel where the sacrifice had taken place.

Ki'son (kī'sŏn) (*winding*), an inaccurate mode of representing the name Kishon. Ps. 83 : 9.

Kiss. Kissing the lips by way of affectionate salutation was customary among near relatives of both sexes, in both patriarchal and later times. Gen. 29 : 11; Cant. 8 : 1. Between individuals of the same sex, and in a limited degree between those of different sexes, the kiss on the cheek as a mark of respect or an act of salutation has at all times been customary in the East, and can hardly be said to be extinct even in Europe. In the Christian Church the kiss of charity was practised not only as a friendly salutation, but as an act symbolical of love and Christian brotherhood. Rom. 16 : 16; 1 Cor. 16 : 20; 2 Cor. 13 : 12; 1 Thess. 5 : 26; 1 Peter 5 : 14. It was embodied in the earlier Christian offices, and has been continued in some of those now in use. Among the Arabs the women and children kiss the beards of their husbands or fathers. The superior returns the salute by a kiss on the forehead. In Egypt an inferior kisses the hand of a superior, generally on the back, but sometimes, as a special favor, on the palm also. To testify abject submission, and in asking favors, the feet are often kissed instead of the hand. The written decrees of a sovereign are kissed in token of respect; even the ground is sometimes kissed by Orientals in the fullness of their submission. Gen. 41 : 40 (marg.); 1 Sam. 24 : 8; Ps. 72 : 9, etc. Kissing is spoken of in Scripture as a mark of respect or adoration to idols. 1 Kings 19 : 18; Hos. 13 : 2.

Kite (Heb. *ayyâh*), a rapacious and keen-sighted bird of prey belonging to the hawk family. The Hebrew word thus rendered occurs in three passages —Lev. 11 : 14; Deut. 14 : 13; Job 28 : 7. In the two former it is translated "kite" in the Authorized Version, in the latter "vulture," in all the R. V. gives "falcon." The Hebrew word *dayyah* in the same reference in Lev. and Deut. is translated "vulture" in the A. V. and "kite" in the R. V. Both names are probably generic. It is enumerated among the twenty names of birds mentioned in Deut. 14 which were considered unclean by the Mosaic law and forbidden to be used as food by the Israelites.

Kith'lish (kĭth'lish), one of the towns of Judah, in the Shefelah or lowland. Josh. 15 : 40.

Kit'ron (kĭt'ron), one of the towns from which Zebulun did not expel the Canaanites. Judges 1 : 30. In the Talmud it is identified with "Zippori," *i. e.* Sepphoris, now *Seffurieh*, but the identity is denied by many modern scholars.

Kit'tim (kĭt'tim). Twice written in the Authorized Version for Chittim. Gen. 10 : 4; 1 Chron. 1 : 7.

Kneading=troughs. [BREAD.]

Knife. 1. The knives of the Egyptians, and of other nations in early times, were probably only of hard stone, and the use of the flint or stone knife was sometimes retained for sacred purposes after the introduction of iron and steel. 2. In their meals the Jews, like other Orientals, made little use of knives, but they were required both for slaughtering animals, either for food or sacrifice, and for cutting up the carcass. Lev. 7 : 33, 34; 8 : 15, 20, 25; 9 : 13; Num. 18 : 18; 1 Sam. 9 : 24, etc. 3. Smaller knives were in use for paring fruit (Josephus) and for sharpening pens. Jer. 36 : 23. 4. The razor (perhaps not differing from other knives) was often used for Naziritic purposes, for which a special chamber was reserved in the temple. Num. 6 : 5, 9, 19; Ezek. 5 : 1, etc. 5. The pruning-hooks of Isa. 18 : 5 were probably like modern sickles or reaping hooks. 6. The lancets of the priests of Baal were doubtless pointed knives. 1 Kings 18 : 28.

Knop, a word employed in the Authorized Version to translate two terms which refer to some architectural or ornamental object, which have nothing in common. 1. *Caphtor.*—This occurs in the description of the candlestick of the sacred tent in Ex. 25 : 31–36 and 37 : 17–22. 2. The second term, *Peka'im,* is found only in 1 Kings 6 : 18 and 7 : 24. The word no doubt signifies some globular thing resembling a small gourd or an egg, though as to the character of the ornament we are quite in the dark.

Ko'a (kō'à), is a word which occurs only in Ezek. 23 : 23. A people named between Babylonians and Assyrians. Driver considers them as probably the *Kuti,* often mentioned in the Assyrian

inscriptions who lived north of Babylon. (Hastings' *Bible Dictionary.*)

Ko'hath (kō'hath) (*assembly*), second of the three sons of Levi, from whom the three principal divisions of the Levites derived their origin and their name. Gen. 46 : 11; Ex. 6 : 16. In the journeyings of the tabernacle the sons of Kohath (Kohathites) had charge of the most holy portions of the vessels. Num. 4. Of the personal history of Kohath we know nothing, except that he came down to Egypt with Levi and Jacob, Gen. 46 : 11, that his sister was Jochebed, Ex. 6 : 20, and that he lived to the age of 133 years. Ex. 6 : 18.

Kola'iah (kŏl-ā'iah) (*voice of Jehovah*). 1. A Benjamite whose descendants settled in Jerusalem after the return from the captivity. Neh. 11 : 7.

2. The father of Ahab the false prophet, who was burnt by the king of Babylon. Jer. 29 : 21.

Ko'rah (kō'rah) (*baldness*). 1. Third son of Esau by Aholibamah. Gen. 36 : 5, 14, 18; 1 Chron. 1 : 35. He was born in Canaan before Esau migrated to Mount Seir, Gen. 36 : 5–9, and was one of the "dukes" of Edom.

2. Another Edomitish "duke" of this name, sprung from Eliphaz, Esau's son by Adah. Gen. 36 : 16.

3. One of the "sons of Hebron," in 1 Chron. 2 : 43.

4. Son of Izhar the son of Kohath the son of Levi. He was leader of the famous rebellion against Moses and Aaron in the wilderness, for which he paid the penalty of perishing with his followers by an earthquake and flames of fire. Num. 16; 26 : 9–11. The particular grievance which rankled in the mind of Korah and his company was their exclusion from the office of the priesthood, and their being confined—those among them who were Levites—to the inferior service of the tabernacle. Korah's position as leader in this rebellion was evidently the result of his personal character, which was that of a bold, haughty and ambitious man. (B.C. 1490.) In the New Testament (Jude 11) Korah is coupled with Cain and Balaam.

Kor'ahite, 1 Chron. 9 : 19, 31, **Kor'hite,** or **Kor'athite** (kôr'ath-īte), that portion of the Kohathites who were descended from Korah. They were an important branch of the singers, 2 Chron. 20:19; hence we find eleven psalms (or twelve, if Ps. 43 is included under the same title as Ps. 42) dedicated or assigned to the sons of Korah, viz., Ps. 42, 44–49, 84, 85, 87, 88. These are said to have been taken from "the hymn book of the Korahite choir."

Ko're (kō'rè) (*partridge*). 1. A Korahite, ancestor of Shallum and Meshelemiah, chief porters in the reign of David. 1 Chron. 9:19; 26:1.

2. Son of Imnah, a Levite in the reign of Hezekiah. He had charge of the offerings. 2 Chron. 31:14.

3. In the Authorized Version of 1 Chron. 26:19, "the sons of Kore" (following the Vulgate *Core*) should properly be "the sons of the Korahites."

Koz (kŏz) (*thorn*), Ezra 2:61; Neh. 3:4, 21 = Coz = Hakkoz.

Kusha'iah (kṳ-shā'yah), the same as Kish or Kishi, the father of Ethan the Merarite. 1 Chron. 15:17.

L

La'adah (lā'a-dah) (*order*), the son of Shelah and grandson of Judah. 1 Chron. 4 : 21.

La'adan (lā'a-dan) (*well-ordered*). 1. An Ephraimite, ancestor of Joshua the son of Nun. 1 Chron. 7 : 26.

2. The son of Gershom, elsewhere called LIBNI. 1 Chron. 23 : 7, 8, 9; 26 : 21.

La'ban (lā'ban) (*white*). 1. Son of Bethuel, brother of Rebekah and father of Leah and Rachel. The elder branch of the family remained at Haran, Mesopotamia, when Abraham removed to the land of Canaan, and it is there that we first meet with Laban, as taking the leading part in the betrothal of his sister Rebekah to her cousin Isaac. Gen. 24 : 10, 29–60; 27 : 43; 29 : 5. The next time Laban appears in the sacred narrative it is as the host of his nephew Jacob at Haran. Gen. 29 : 13, 14. [JACOB.] Jacob married Rachel and Leah, daughters of Laban, and remained with him 20 years, B.C. 1760–1740 (Ussher). But Laban's dishonest and overreaching practice toward his nephew shows from what source Jacob inherited his tendency to sharp dealing. Nothing is said of Laban after Jacob left him.

2. One of the landmarks named in the obscure and disputed passage Deut. 1 : 1. The mention of Hazeroth has perhaps led to the conjecture that it is identical with LIBNAH. Num. 33 : 20.

La'chish (lā'kish), a city lying southwest of Jerusalem on the borders of Simeon, and belonging to the Amorites, the king of which joined with four others, at the invitation of Adoni-zedek king of Jerusalem, to chastise the Gibeonites for their league with Israel. Josh. 10 : 3, 5. They were routed by Joshua at Beth-horon, and the king of Lachish fell a victim with the others under the trees at Makkedah, ver. 26. The destruction of the town shortly followed the death of the king, vs. 31–33.

In the special statement that the attack lasted two days, in contradistinction to one (see ver. 35), we gain our first glimpse of that strength of position for which Lachish was afterward remarkable. Lachish was one of the cities for-

TELL EL-HESY.
Site of the ancient Lachish.

tified and garrisoned by Rehoboam after the revolt of the northern kingdom. 2 Chron. 11 : 9. In the reign of Hezekiah it was one of the cities taken by Sennacherib. This siege is considered by Layard and Hincks to be depicted on the slabs found by the former in one of the chambers of the palace at Kouyunjik, and now in the British Museum. After the return from captivity, Lachish with its surrounding "fields" was reoccupied by the Jews. Neh. 11 : 30. Its identification with *Tell el-Hesy* is practically certain. Excavation has laid bare the wall of the ancient city, as well as later constructions, believed to belong to the time of the Divided Kingdom. Ten towns seem to have occupied the place in succession.

La'el (lā'el) (*of God*), the father of Eliasaph. Num. 3 : 24.

La'had (lā'hăd) (*oppression*), son of Jahath, one of the descendants of Judah. 1 Chron. 4 : 2.

Lahai'-roi (là-hā'roi) (*the living one who seeth me*), **The well.** In this form is given in the Authorized Version of Gen. 24: 62 and 25: 11 the name of the famous well of Hagar's relief, in the oasis of verdure round which Isaac afterward resided. It was southwest of Beersheba.

Lah'mam (läh'mam), a town in the lowland district of Judah. Josh. 15: 40. Possibly *el-Lahm* near *Beit Jibrin*.

Lah'mi (läh'mĭ), the brother of Goliath the Gittite, slain by Elhanan the son of Jair. 1 Chron. 20: 5, but the parallel in 2 Sam. 21: 19 substitutes "Bethlehemite." One or the other text is corrupt.

La'ish (lā'ish) (*lion*), the city which was taken by the Danites, and under its new name of Dan became famous as the northern limit of the nation. Judges 18: 7, 14, 27, 29. [DAN.] It was near the sources of the Jordan. In the Authorized Version Laish is again mentioned in the account of Sennacherib's march on Jerusalem. Isa. 10: 30. This Laish is probably the small village Laishah, lying between Gallim and Anathoth in Benjamin, of which hitherto no traces have been found.

La'ish (lā'ish) (*lion*), father of Phaltiel, to whom Saul had given Michal, David's wife. 1 Sam. 25: 44; 2 Sam. 3: 15.

La'kum (lā'kŭm), properly **Lak'kum,** one of the places which formed the landmarks of the boundary of Naphtali. Josh. 19: 33.

Lambs are the young of sheep, but originally included also the young of goats. They formed an important part of almost every sacrifice. Ex. 29: 38–41; Num. 28: 9, 11; 29: 2, 13–40, etc. [On the paschal lamb see PASSOVER.]

La'mech (lā'mek). 1. The fifth lineal descendant from Cain. Gen. 4: 18–24. He is the only one except Enoch, of the posterity of Cain, whose history is related with some detail. His two wives, Adah and Zillah, and his daughter Naamah, are, with Eve, the only antediluvian women whose names are mentioned in Genesis. His three sons, Jabal, Jubal and Tubal-cain, are celebrated in Scripture as authors of useful inventions. The remarkable poem which Lamech uttered may perhaps be regarded as Lamech's song of exultation on the invention of the sword by his son Tubalcain, in the possession of which he fore-saw a great advantage to himself and his family over any enemies.

2. The father of Noah. Gen. 5: 29.

Lamentations. The book of, consists of five elegiac poems.

ITS SUBJECT is the sufferings of the people of Judah and Jerusalem during the final siege and destruction of the city and the Temple. The end of hope seemed to have come.

THE DATE of the subject is therefore between 606–586 B.C. The date of writing may be later, but some time during the Exile.

STRUCTURE is a series of acrostic poems, each chapter being a poem, and in the Revised Versions printed in poetic form. Chapters 1, 2, 4 and 5 have each 22 verses, one for each letter in the Hebrew alphabet. The verses in the first four chapters are arranged in alphabetical order, in the Hebrew original, verse 1, beginning A, verse 2 with B, etc., except that in chapter 3, three verses begin with A, the next three with B, and so on, 66 verses in all. Chapter 5 has no alphabetical arrangement.

AUTHOR. The book is anonymous, but most scholars attribute the first four poems to Jeremiah. *Contents.*—The book consists of five chapters, each of which, however, is a separate poem, complete in itself, and having a distinct subject, but brought at the same time under a plan which includes them all. Jeremiah was not merely a patriot-poet, weeping over the ruin of his country; he was a prophet who had seen all this coming, and had foretold it as inevitable. There are perhaps few portions of the Old Testament which appear to have done the work they were meant to do more effectually than this. The book has supplied thousands with the fullest utterance for their sorrows in the critical periods of national or individual suffering. We may well believe that it soothed the weary years of the Babylonian exile. It enters largely into the order of the Latin Church for the services of passion-week. On the ninth day of the month of Ab (July–August), the Lamentations of Jeremiah were read, year by year, with fasting and weeping, to commemorate the misery out of which the people had been delivered.

Lamp. 1. That part of the golden candlestick belonging to the tabernacle which bore the light; also of each of the ten candlesticks placed by Solomon in the temple before the holy of holies. Ex. 25:37; 1 Kings 7:49; 2 Chron. 4: 20; 13:11; Zech. 4:2. The lamps were lighted every evening and cleansed every morning. Ex. 30:7, 8.

2. A torch or flambeau, such as was carried by the soldiers of Gideon. Judges 7:16, 20; comp. 15:4. The use in marriage processions of lamps fed

LAMP WITH CHRISTIAN INSCRIPTION.

with oil is alluded to in the parable of the ten virgins. Matt. 25:1. Modern Egyptian lamps consist of small glass vessels with a tube at the bottom containing a cotton wick twisted around a piece of straw. For night travelling, a lantern composed of waxed cloth strained over a sort of cylinder of wire rings, and a top and bottom of perforated copper. This would, in form at least, answer to the lamps within pitchers of Gideon.

"The Hebrews, like the ancient Greeks and Romans, as well as the modern Orientals, were accustomed to burn lamps all night. This custom, with the effect produced by their going out or being extinguished, supplies various figures to the sacred writers. 2 Sam. 21: 17; Prov. 13:9; 20:20. On the other hand, the keeping up of a lamp's light is used as a symbol of enduring and unbroken succession. 1 Kings 11:36; 15:4; Ps. 132:17."

Lancet. This word is found in 1 Kings 18:28 only. The Hebrew term is *romach,* which is elsewhere rendered, and appears to mean a javelin or light spear. In the original edition of the Authorized Version (1611) the word is "lancers."

Lantern (so called for its shining) occurs only in John 18:3. Lanterns were much employed by the Romans in military operations. Two, of bronze, have been found among the ruins of Herculaneum and Pompeii. They are cylindrical, with translucent horn sides, the lamp within being furnished with an extinguisher.

Laodice′a (lā′ŏd-ĭ-çē′à) (*pertaining to Laodice*), a town in the Roman province of Asia, situated in the valley of the Mæander, on a small river called the Lycus, with Colossæ and Hierapolis a few miles distant. Built, or rather rebuilt, by one of the Seleucid monarchs, and named in honor of his wife, Laodicea became under the Roman government a place of some importance. Its trade was considerable; it lay on the line of a great road; and it was the seat of a *conventus*. Rev. 3:17 indicates both its wealth and its pride. Christianity was introduced into Laodicea, not, however, as it would seem, through the direct agency of St. Paul. We have good reason for believing that when, in writing from Rome to the Christians of Colossæ, he sent a greeting to those of Laodicea, he had not personally visited either place. But the preaching of the gospel at Ephesus, Acts 18:19–19:41, must inevitably have resulted in the formation of churches in the neighboring cities, especially where Jews were settled; and there were Jews in Laodicea. In subsequent times it became a Christian city of eminence, the see of a bishop and a meeting-place of councils. The Mohammedan invaders destroyed it, and it is now a scene of utter desolation, as was prophesied in Rev. 3:14–22; and the extensive ruins near *Denislu* justify all that we read of Laodicea in Greek and Roman writers. Another biblical subject of interest is connected with Laodicea. From Col. 4: 16 it appears that St. Paul wrote a letter to this place when he wrote the letter to Colossæ. Ramsay in Hastings' *Bible Dictionary* thinks that it was perhaps the same as the Epistle to the Ephesians, which was a circular letter sent to Laodicea among other places. The apocryphal *Epistola ad Laodicenses* is a late and clumsy forgery.

Laodice′ans (lā′ŏd-ĭ-çē′anş), the inhabitants of Laodicea. Col. 4:16; Rev. 3:14.

Lap′idoth (lăp′i-dŏth) (*torches*), the husband of Deborah the prophetess. Judges 4:4.

Lapwing (Heb. *dukiphath*) occurs only in Lev. 11:19 and in the parallel passage of Deut. 14:18, amongst the list of those birds which were forbidden by the law of Moses to be eaten by the Israelites. Commentators generally agree that the *hoopoe* is the bird intended.

23

The hoopoe is an occasional visitor to England, arriving for the most part in the autumn. Its crest is very elegant; each of the long feathers forming it is tipped with black.

LAPWING OR HOOPOE.

Lase'a (là-sē'à), Acts 27:8, a city of Crete, the ruins of which were discovered in 1856, a few miles to the eastward of Fair Havens.

La'sha (lā'shà) (*fissure*), a place noticed in Gen. 10:19 as marking the limit of the country of the Canaanites. It lay somewhere in the southeast of Palestine. Jerome and other writers identify it with Callirrhoë, a spot famous for hot springs, near the eastern shore of the Dead Sea, but the site is disputed.

Lashar'on (lā-shâr'on), one of the Canaanite towns whose kings were killed by Joshua. Josh. 12:18. It may be a corruption of the expression "king of Aphek in Sharon."

Latchet, the thong or fastening by which the sandal was attached to the foot. It occurs in the proverbial expression in Gen. 14:23, and is there used to denote something trivial or worthless. Another semi-proverbial expression in Luke 3:16 points to the fact that the office of bearing and unfastening the shoes of great personages fell to the meanest slaves.

Lat'in, the language spoken by the Romans, is mentioned only in John 19:20 and Luke 23:38.

Lat'in Versions. [See VULGATE, THE.]

Lattice. This word is used for a latticed window or simply a network placed before a window or balcony. Perhaps the network through which Ahaziah fell and received his mortal injury was on the parapet of his palace. 2 Kings 1:2. The latticed window is much used in warm eastern countries. It frequently projects from the wall (like our bay windows), and is formed of reticulated work, often highly ornamental, portions of which are hinged so that they may be opened or shut at pleasure. The object is to keep the apartments cool by intercepting the direct rays of the sun, while the air is permitted to circulate freely. [See HOUSE and WINDOW.]

Laver. 1. In the tabernacle, a vessel of brass containing water for the priests to wash their hands and feet before offering sacrifice. It stood in the court between the altar and the door of the tabernacle. Ex. 30:19, 21. It rested on a basis, *i. e.* a foot, which, as well as the laver itself, was made from the mirrors of the women who assembled at the door of the tabernacle court. Ex. 38:8. The form of the laver is not specified, but may be assumed to have been circular. Like the other vessels belonging to the tabernacle, it was, together with its "foot," consecrated with oil. Lev. 8:10, 11.

2. In Solomon's temple, besides the great molten sea, there were ten lavers

A BRAZEN LAVER ON WHEELS.

of brass, raised on bases, 1 Kings 7:27, 39, five on the north and five on the south side of the court of the priests. They were used for washing the animals to be offered in burnt offerings. 2 Chron. 4:6.

Law. The word is properly used, in

Scripture as elsewhere, to express a definite commandment laid down by any recognized authority; but when the word is used with the article, and without any words of limitation, it refers to the expressed will of God, and in nine cases out of ten to the Mosaic law, or to the Pentateuch of which it forms the chief portion. The Hebrew word *tôrâh* (law) lays more stress on its moral authority, as teaching the truth and guiding in the right way; the Greek νόμος (law), on its constraining power as imposed and enforced by a recognized authority. The sense of the word, however, extends its scope and assumes a more abstract character in the writings of St. Paul. *Nomos*, when used by him with the article, still refers in general to the law of Moses; but when used without the article, so as to embrace any manifestation of "law," it includes all powers which act on the will of man by compulsion, or by the pressure of external motives, whether their commands be or be not expressed in definite forms. The occasional use of the word "law" (as in Rom. 3:27, "law of faith") to denote an *internal* principle of action does not really mitigate against the general rule. It should also be noticed that the title "the Law" is occasionally used loosely to refer to the whole of the Old Testament, as in John 10:34, referring to Ps. 82:6; in John 15:25, referring to Ps. 35:19; and in 1 Cor. 14:21, referring to Isa. 28:11, 12.

The article "Law of Moses" is to be omitted for most weighty reasons. The whole subject is so much disputed that it would not be possible to give in the space available anything which would be of any real value to the reader. Hastings' *Bible Dictionary* gives about 36 columns to the subject,—and that is only one opinion out of the many brought forward with equal plausibility. Besides, unless the matter were copied bodily from another source it would be impossible in less time than months to do any justice to it.

For these reasons among others, we omit it.

Lawyer. The title "lawyer" is generally supposed to be equivalent to the title "scribe." The scribes expounded the law in the synagogues and schools. [See SCRIBES.]

Laying on of hands. In the Old Testament. (1) Used as a symbol of benediction, Gen. 48:14. (2) A part of the sacrificial system, Ex. 29:10, 15, 19, etc. (3) Witnesses laid their hands on the head of a person charged with a capital offence. (4) The tribe of Levi were consecrated by the laying on of hands. In (1) it may have meant the imparting of a personal gift. The others had as their prominent thought devotion to God of the object upon which the hands are laid,—dedication to his service, or deliverance to the judgment decreed by him. In the New Testament the meaning is much the same. Jesus used it in the blessing of little children, and of the Eleven; and as a sign in his miracles of healing. The apostles used it when the Holy Ghost was imparted, and in the Christian Church was especially used in setting apart men to the ministry and to other holy offices. It is a symbolical act expressing the imparting of spiritual authority and power.

Laz'arus (lăz'a-rus) (*God hath helped*), another form of the Hebrew name Eleazar. 1. Lazarus of Bethany, the brother of Martha and Mary. John 11:1. All that we know of him is derived from the Gospel of St. John, and that records little more than the facts of his death and resurrection. The language of John 11:1 implies that the sisters were the better known. Lazarus is "of Bethany, of the village of Mary and her sister Martha." From this and from the order of the three names in John 11:5 we may reasonably infer that Lazarus was the youngest of the family. All the circumstances of John 11 and 12 point to wealth and social position above the average. The fact that Jesus did not arrive until Lazarus had been four days buried proved the miracle. If he had come in three days it might have been a swoon in the place of death; but after the fourth day decomposition had set in.

2. The name of a poor man in the well-known parable of Luke 16:19–31. The name of Lazarus has been perpetuated in an institution of the Christian Church. The leper of the Middle Ages appears as a *lazzaro*. The use of *lazaretto* and *lazar-house* for the leper hospitals then founded in all parts of western Christendom, no less than that of *lazaroni* for the mendicants of Italian towns, is an indication of the effect of the parable upon the mind of Europe in the Middle Ages, and thence upon its later speech.

It is, however, impossible that this Lazarus should have been a leper both from the description of his state and from the fact that he lay close to the rich man's door—for lepers were forced to stay far away from the homes of men.

Lead. This is one of the most common of metals, found generally in veins of rocks, though seldom in a metallic state, and most commonly in combination with sulphur. It was early known to the ancients, and the allusions to it in Scripture indicate that the Hebrews were well acquainted with its uses. The rocks in the neighborhood of Sinai yielded it in large quantities, and it was found in Egypt. In Job 19 : 24 the allusion is supposed to be to the practice of carving inscriptions upon stone and pouring molten lead into the cavities of the letters, to render them legible and at the same time preserve them from the action of the air.

Leaf, Leaves. The word occurs in the Authorized Version either in singular or plural number in three different senses. (1) Leaf of a tree. The righteous are often compared to green leaves. Jer. 17 : 8. The ungodly, on the other hand, are "as an oak whose leaf fadeth." Isa. 1 : 30. (2) Leaves of doors. The large doors of the temple, and probably any other large building, were made to fold, so that for ordinary occasions the priests could pass in and out without opening the entire door. (3) Leaves of a book or roll occurs in this sense only in Jer. 36 : 23. The Hebrew word (literally *doors*) would perhaps be more correctly translated *columns*.

Le'ah (lē'ah) (*wild cow*), the daughter of Laban. Gen. 29 : 16. The dullness or weakness of her eyes was so notable that it is mentioned as a contrast to the beautiful form and appearance of her younger sister Rachel. Her father took advantage of the opportunity which the local marriage rite afforded to pass her off in her sister's stead on the unconscious bridegroom, and excused himself to Jacob by alleging that the custom of the country forbade the younger sister to be given first in marriage. Jacob's preference of Rachel grew into hatred of Leah after he had married both sisters. Leah, however, bore to him in quick succession Reuben, Simeon, Levi, Judah, then Issachar, Zebulun and Dinah, before Rachel had a child. She died some time after Jacob reached the south country in which his father Isaac lived. She was buried in the family grave in Machpelah, near Hebron. Gen. 49 : 31.

Leasing (*falsehood*). This word is retained in the Authorized Version of Ps. 4 : 2; 5 : 6, from the older English versions; but the Hebrew word of which it is the rendering is elsewhere almost uniformly translated "lies." Ps. 40 : 4; 58 : 3, etc.

Leather. The notices of leather in the Bible are singularly few; indeed the word occurs but twice in the Authorized Version, and in each instance in reference to the same object, a girdle. 2 Kings 1 : 8; Matt. 3 : 4. There are, however, other instances in which the word "leather" might with propriety be substituted for "skin." Lev. 11 : 32; 13 : 48; Num. 31 : 20. Though the material itself is seldom noticed, yet we cannot doubt that it was extensively used by the Jews; shoes, bottles, thongs, garments, ropes and other articles were made of it. The art of tanning, however, was held in low esteem by the Jews.

Leaven. Various substances were known to have fermenting qualities; but the ordinary leaven consisted of a lump of old dough in a high state of fermentation, which was mixed into the mass of dough prepared for baking. The use of leaven was strictly forbidden in all offerings made to the Lord by fire. During the passover the Jews were commanded to put every particle of leaven from the house. The most prominent idea associated with leaven is connected with the *corruption* which it had undergone, and which it communicated to bread in the process of fermentation. It is to this property of leaven that our Saviour points when he speaks of the "leaven (*i. e.* the corrupt doctrine) of the Pharisees and of the Sadducees," Matt. 16 : 6; and St. Paul, when he speaks of the "old leaven." 1 Cor. 5 : 7. Another quality in leaven is noticed in the Bible, namely, its secretly penetrating and diffusive power. In this respect it was emblematic of moral influence generally, whether good or bad; and hence our Saviour adopts it as illustrating the growth of the kingdom of heaven in the individual heart and in the world at large: because (1) its source is from without; (2) it is secret in its operation; (3) it spreads by contact of particle with particle; (4) it is widely diffusive, one particle of leaven being able to change any number of particles of flour; and because (5) it does not act like water, moistening a certain amount of flour, but is like a plant, changing the particles it comes in contact with into its own nature, with like propagating power.

Leb'ana (lĕb'a-nà) (*white*), one of the Nethinim whose descendants returned from Babylon with Zerubbabel. Neh. 7 : 48. He is called **Leb'anah** (*white*) in Ezra 2 : 45.

Leb'anon (lĕb'a-non), a mountain range in the north of Palestine. The name Lebanon signifies *white,* and was applied either on account of the snow which, during a great part of the year, covers its whole summit, or on account of the white color of its limestone cliffs and peaks. It is the "white mountain"—the Mont Blanc of Palestine. Lebanon is represented in Scripture as lying upon the northern border of the land of Israel. Deut. 1: 7; 11 : 24; Josh. 1 : 4. Two distinct ranges bear this name. They run for nearly 90 miles in parallel lines from southwest to northeast, enclosing between them a long, fertile valley from five to eight miles wide, anciently called *Cœle-Syria.* The western range is the "Libanus" of the old geographers and the Lebanon of Scripture. The eastern range was called "Anti-Libanus" by geographers, and "Lebanon toward the sunrising" by the sacred writers. Josh. 13 : 5.

1. *Lebanon*—the western range—commences on the south of the deep ravine of the *Litâny,* the ancient river Leontes, which drains the valley of Cœle-Syria, and falls into the Mediterranean five miles north of Tyre. It runs northeast in a straight line parallel to the coast, to the opening from the Mediterranean into the plain of Emesa, called in Scripture the "entrance of Hamath." Num. 34 : 8. Here *Nehr el-Kebîr*—the ancient river Eleutherus—sweeps round its northern end, as the Leontes does round its southern. The average elevation of the range is from 6000 to 8000 feet; but two peaks rise considerably higher. On the summits of both these peaks the snow remains in patches during the whole summer. The line of cultivation runs along at the height of about 6000 feet; and below this the features of the western slopes are entirely different. The rugged limestone banks are scantily clothed with the evergreen oak, and the sandstone with pines; while every available spot is carefully cultivated. The cultivation is wonderful, and shows what all Syria might be if under a good government. Fig trees cling to the naked rock; vines are trained along narrow ledges; long ranges of mulberries, on terraces like steps of stairs, cover the more gentle declivities; and dense groves of olives fill up the bottoms of the glens. Hundreds of villages are seen—here built among labyrinths of rocks, there clinging like swallows' nests to the sides of cliffs; while convents, no less numerous, are perched on the top of every peak. The vine is still largely cultivated in every part of the mountain. Lebanon also abounds in olives, figs and mulberries; while some remnants exist of the forests of pine, oak and cedar which formerly covered it. 1 Kings 5 : 6; Ezra 3 : 7; Ps. 29 : 5; Isa. 14 : 8. Considerable numbers of wild beasts still inhabit its retired glens and higher peaks; jackals, hyænas, wolves and panthers. Bears are no longer abundant. 2 Kings 14 : 9; Cant. 4 : 8; Hab. 2 : 17. Along the base of Lebanon runs the irregular plain of Phœnicia—nowhere more than two miles wide, and often interrupted by bold rocky spurs that dip into the sea. The main ridge of Lebanon is composed of Jura limestone, and abounds in fossils. Long belts of more recent sandstone run along the western slopes, which are in places largely impregnated with iron. Lebanon was originally inhabited by the Hivites and Giblites. Josh. 13: 5, 6; Judges 3 : 3. The whole mountain range was assigned to the Israelites, but was never conquered by them. Josh. 13: 2–6; Judges 3 : 1–3. During the Jewish monarchy it appears to have been subject to the Phœnicians. 1 Kings 5 : 2–6; Ezra 3 : 7. From the Greek conquest until modern times Lebanon had no separate history.

2. *Anti-Lebanon.*—The main chain of Anti-Lebanon commences in the plateau of Bashan, near the parallel of Cæsarea Philippi, runs north to Hermon, and then northeast in a straight line till it sinks down into the great plain of Emesa, not far from the site of Riblah. Hermon is the loftiest peak; the next highest is a few miles north of the site of Abila, beside the village of *Bludân,*

and has an elevation of about 8090 feet. The rest of the ridge averages about 5000 feet; it is in general bleak and barren, with shelving gray declivities, gray cliffs and gray rounded summits. Here and there we meet with thin forests of dwarf oak and juniper. The western slopes descend abruptly into the *Bukâ'a;* but the features of the eastern are entirely different. Three side ridges here radiate from Hermon, like the ribs of an open fan, and form the supporting walls of three great terraces. Anti-Libanus is only once distinctly mentioned in Scripture, where it is accurately described as "Lebanon toward the sunrising." Josh. 13 : 5.

Leb'aoth (lĕb'a-ŏth) (*lionesses*), a town which forms one of the last group of the cities of "the south" in the enumeration of the possessions of Judah, Josh. 15 : 32; probably identical with Beth-lebaoth.

Lebbæ'us (lĕb-bē'ŭs), one name of Jude, who was one of the twelve apostles. Matt. 10 : 3. R. V. omits, as there seems to be no ground for its insertion.

Lebo'nah (lĕ-bō'nah) (*frankincense*), a place named in Judges 21 : 19 only. Lebonah has survived to our times under the almost identical form of *el-Lubban.* It lies to the west of and close to the *Nablûs* road, about eight miles north of *Beitin* (Bethel) and three miles from *Seilum* (Shiloh).

Le'cah (lē'cah), a name mentioned in the genealogies of Judah, 1 Chron. 4 : 21 only, as one of the descendants of Shelah, the third son of Judah by the Canaanites Bath-shua.

COMMON LEEK.

Leeks (Heb. *chât-sîr*). The leek was a bulbous vegetable resembling the onion. Its botanical name is *Allium porrum.* The Israelites in the wilderness longed for the leeks and onions of Egypt. Num. 11:5. The word *châtsîr,* which in Num. 11:5 is translated *leeks,* occurs twenty times in the Hebrew text. The Hebrew term, which commonly denotes *grass,* is derived from a root signifying "to

be green," and may therefore stand in this passage for any green food—lettuce, endive, etc.; it would thus be applied somewhat in the same manner as we use the term "greens;" yet as the *châtsîr* is mentioned together with onions and garlic in the text, and as the most ancient versions unanimously understand *leeks* by the Hebrew word, we may be satisfied with our own translation, which the R. V. has retained.

Lees, the coarser parts of a liquor, its sediment or dregs. "Wine on the lees" means a generous, full-bodied liquor. Isa. 25 : 6. Before the wine was consumed, it was necessary to strain off the lees; such wine was then termed "well refined." Isa. 25 : 6. To drink the lees, or "dregs," was an expression for the endurance of extreme punishment. Ps. 75 : 8.

Legion, the chief subdivision of the Roman army, containing about 6000 infantry, with a contingent of cavalry. The term does not occur in the Bible in its primary sense, but appears to have been adopted in order to express any large number, with the accessory ideas of order and subordination. Matt. 26 : 53; Mark 5 : 9.

Le'habim (lē'hȧ-bĭm), occurring only in Gen. 10 : 13 and 1 Chron. 1 : 11, the name of a Mizraite people or tribe. The name is very similar to Lubim, which was most probably the ancient name of Libya. These primitive Libyans appear to have inhabited the northern part of Africa to the west of Egypt, though latterly driven from the coast by the Greek colonists of the Cyrenaica.

Le'hi (lē'hī) (*jaw bone*), a place in Judah, probably on the confines of the Philistines' country, between it and the cliff Etam; the scene of Samson's well-known exploit with the jaw bone. Judges 15 : 9, 14, 19. Several identifications have been suggested, but none with great plausibility.

Lem'uel (lĕm'ū-el) (*dedicated to God*), the name of an unknown king to whom his mother addressed the prudential maxims contained in Prov. 31 : 1-9. The rabbinical commentators identified Lemuel with Solomon. Most modern scholars regard him as king, or chief of Massa, in Arabia. But all identifications are pure guess.

Lentils (Heb. *'ădâshîm*), a leguminous plant bearing seeds resembling small beans. The red pottage which

Jacob prepared and for which Esau sold his birthright was made from them. Gen. 25 : 34. There are three or four kinds of lentils, all of which are much esteemed in those countries where they

LENTILS.

are grown, viz., the south of Europe, Asia and north Africa. The red lentil is still a favorite article of food in the East. Lentils are thoroughly wholesome and not at all unpalatable, being found on the tables of rich as well as poor. Lentil bread is eaten by the poor of Egypt.

Leopard (Heb. *nâmêr*) is invariably

THE SYRIAN LEOPARD.

given by the Authorized Version as the translation of the Hebrew word, which occurs in the seven following passages: Cant. 4 : 8; Isa. 11 : 6; Jer. 5 : 6; 13 : 23; Dan. 7 : 6; Hos. 13 : 7; Hab. 1 : 8. *Leopard* occurs also of the body of the creature described in Rev. 13 : 2. The hilly ranges of Lebanon were in ancient times frequented by these animals. They are now not uncommonly seen in and about Lebanon and the southern maritime mountains of Syria. Under the name *nâmêr*, it is probable that another animal, namely the cheetah (*Felis jubata*), may be included; which is tamed by the Mohammedans of Syria, who employ it in hunting gazelle.

Leper, Leprosy. There is great difficulty in determining in all cases the exact disease intended by these words. The word "leprosy" is used as the equivalent of three different foreign words,—the Hebrew *Zaraath*, the Greek *elephas* and *elephantiasis*. The subject is still more difficult because the last of these terms is now used for a very different disease from that described by Greek medical writers. Without doubt a large number of skin diseases were classed together by the people of the East in Scripture times. This is not strange, for it is only within the present generation that the medical fraternity has fully understood many of them. The Hebrew term, which is the word in use in the Old Testament must have denoted a large number of skin diseases, because neither true leprosy nor any other known disease displays all the symptoms described. The only alternative to this would be the total disappearance of the diseases described. The Septuagint uses for this Hebrew word the Greek word *lepra*, which is used by the Greeks themselves as the name of a disease called *psoriasis*, neither contagious, dangerous nor incurable. In Lev. 13, there are directions for the treatment of leprosy which seem to render necessary the inclusion of these varieties of skin diseases as well as of true leprosy. The principal ones are probably *psoriasis*, "a leper as white as snow;" *favus*, common among Eastern Jews to-day; *ringworm* and *vitiligo*.

It is, however, an undoubted fact that true leprosy in some one of its forms was found in Palestine and Egypt during Old Testament times, as well as in New Testament times, and even to-day.

The Egyptian bondage, with its studied degradations and privations, and especially the work of the kiln under an Egyptian sun, must have had a frightful tendency to generate this class of disorders. The sudden and total change of food, air, dwelling and mode of life, caused by the Exodus, to this nation of newly-emancipated slaves, may possibly have had a further tendency to produce skin disorders, and severe repressive measures may have been required in the desert-moving camp to secure the public health or to allay the panic of infection. It is now undoubted that the "leprosy" of modern Syria, and which has a wide range in Spain, Greece and Norway, is the *Elephantiasis græcorum*. It is said to have been brought home by the crusaders into the various countries of western and northern Europe. But it was in Britain before the date of the first crusade, as the leper-house at Canterbury was founded in 1096, the year of the starting of the crusade. The ultimate cause of leprosy was demonstrated by Hansen (1871) as a microbe somewhat like the tubercle bacillus. It occurs sporadically, proving other causes than contagion; what they are, however, has never been proved. It is not a common disease, even in Palestine, but appears more so than it is for several reasons. (1) the association of the disease with the Bible and with Christ; causing a larger notice of it among Christian people everywhere; (2) the repulsive appearance caused by it, so that a few cases impress themselves indelibly on the observer, and (3) because practically all the lepers are segregated, and their villages are often visited by travelers.

True leprosy manifests itself in three forms: (1) the *tubercular,* the most repulsive form; (2) the *anæsthetic,* less horrible and less fatal; and (3) the *mixed* form, into which the sufferer always falls at last, unless the disease is arrested. In the tubercular form it "began with little specks on the eyelids and on the palms of the hands, and gradually spread over different parts of the body; bleaching the hair white wherever it showed itself, crusting the affected parts with shining scales, and causing swellings and sores. From the skin it slowly ate its way through the tissues, to the bones and joints, and even to the marrow, rotting the whole body piecemeal. The lungs, the organs of speech and hearing, and the eyes, were attacked in turn, till at last consumption or dropsy brought welcome death."

The Jews regarded leprosy as a contagious disease, and also thought that it was hereditary. It is not hereditary, however, as children of lepers removed to healthy surroundings at an early age rarely have the disease. The Leprosy Commission in India could discover a history of heredity in only 5%. Very probably the greater part of the cases formerly supposed hereditary were caused by contagion. For there is little doubt that it is contagious. It is not contagious like scarlet fever or smallpox, but it can "be communicated by the inoculation of the blood with the morbid secretions of an affected person." "Leprosy is no more dangerous than consumption. Persons in a street car are very much more likely to contract tuberculosis from the expectoration of a consumptive than to get leprosy from the presence of a leper."—*Dr. G. H. Fox, in Medical Record.* It is a well-established fact that when leprosy has once gained for itself a foothold in any locality, it is apt to remain there and spread. But experience has shown that there is little or no danger of infection from leprosy to persons of cleanly habits. The disease spreads among the natives because they do not fear it, but live in intimate contact with lepers, just as if they were not diseased. Even attendants upon lepers do not necessarily contract the disease if they exercise a reasonable amount of care. Leprosy is practically incurable by human skill, although under favorable circumstances there have been several cures, even in advanced stages, says Dr. Fox in his report to the New York Health Department (1896). "But that man was carefully treated in the hospital, and he received all the comforts of life, whereas, if he had been locked up in a lazaretto, and his food handed to him through a hole, probably he would have died. The great difficulty in curing leprosy is that as soon as a person learns that he has it he is made to believe that all hope is gone. He is treated as a doomed man and made to believe that he is an object to be shunned by everybody."—*Dr. Fox.*

One of the saddest things about the leprosy is the necessary separation from the healthy and clean. (See *Ben Hur.*) In the Sandwich Islands the lepers are all sent to one of the islands, called Molokai, by the board of health; but there is intense opposition to it by many of the natives, on account of the separation from family and friends. Again, Rev. S. E. Bishop, of Honolulu, says: "Lepers themselves appear to especially revolt against submitting to any distinction when at large, but seem inclined to push themselves upon their neighbors, and to resent their personal contact being shunned." Mr. Scully, who lives in South Africa, has written a touching tale of the lepers in that country. He writes that the story is founded on fact. Most vividly he describes how awful was the separation of the lepers from all that they loved, so that one man led a company of lepers to a precipice to destroy himself and them by sudden death, rather than go into the leper colony.

Leprosy in the house, or in garments. —The same word leprosy is used in the law of Leviticus 13, 14, to denote something appearing in the walls of houses, or in the garments of wool, linen or leather. This, in all probability, means a sort of fungus from some source or other, which if left to itself would destroy the material. If it has gone so far as to be irremediable the article is to be destroyed. In the case of the house it may mean the formation of calcium nitrate from the action of decaying animal matter on the lime of the plaster. In all cases it seems a result of lack of cleanliness.

Leprosy as a type of sin.—Leprosy is a remarkable type of sin and its fruits, in certain aspects; as intemperance is a type of sin and the ruin it causes, from another point of view. The visible effect on the body illustrates the effect of sin upon the soul. Sin, like leprosy, is a most loathsome, polluting, deforming, unclean thing. "Leprosy is God's language by which he describes sin as it appears in his sight."

1. It is a loathsome, defiling disease in its later stages. In the Gospels the word used for curing the leprosy, in every case but one, is *cleansing.*

2. In the early stages there are often few symptoms and little discomfort. Rev. Dr. S. E. Bishop, of the Hawaiian Islands, says it is not virulent, acute, or even painful, *except in its later stages.* The *Encyc. Biblica* says that a large part of all leprosy, perhaps half, wants the more obvious characteristics. A person may be truly leprous and have nothing to show for it on the face or hands. Many cases have only blanched or discolored patches of the skin.

3. The progress is slow, especially in the early stages. "There are cases on record of persons who lived as lepers forty years." The average duration of one form is nine years, but of the more common form in the East it is eighteen and one-half years. "It is, therefore, easy to understand how a great general like Naaman might retain his office, though a leper."

4. It is contagious by intimate contact, but there is almost no danger to those of cleanly habits.

5. It is almost incurable, probably entirely so in Bible times.

Le′shem (lē′shem), another form of Laish, afterward Dan, occurring in Josh. 19 : 47.

Letu′shim (lētū′shĭm) (*hammered*), the name of the second of the sons of Dedan son of Jokshan. Gen. 25 : 3.

Leum′mim (lē-ŭm′mim) (*peoples*), the name of the third of of the descendants of Dedan son of Jokshan, Gen. 25 : 3, being in the plural form, like his brethren, Asshurim and Letushim.

Le′vi (lē′vī). 1. The name of the third son of Jacob by his wife Leah. The meaning of the name is uncertain. In Gen. 29 : 34 it seems to be interpreted as from *lâvâh* "to adhere," but several other meanings are found by modern scholars. Levi, with his brother Simeon, avenged with a cruel slaughter the outrage of their sister Dinah. [DINAH.] Levi, with his three sons, Gershon, Kohath and Merari, went down to Egypt with his father Jacob. Gen. 46 : 11. When Jacob's death draws near, and the sons are gathered round him, Levi and Simeon hear the old crime brought up again to receive its sentence. They no less than Reuben, the incestuous first-born, had forfeited the privileges of their birthright. Gen. 49 : 5–7.

2. Two of the ancestors of Jesus. Luke 3 : 24, 29.

3. Son of Alphæus; one of the apos-

tles. Mark 2:14; Luke 5:27, 29. [MATTHEW.]

Leviathan (le-vī'a-than), occurs five times in the text of the Authorized Version, and once in the margin of Job 3:8, where the text has "mourning." In the Hebrew Bible the word *livyathan*, which is, with the foregoing exception, always left untranslated in the Authorized Version, is found only in the following passages: Job 3:8; 41:1; Ps. 74:14; 104:26; Isa. 27:1. In Job 41:1 and Ps. 74:14 the crocodile is without doubt the animal intended. The context of Ps. 104:26 seems to show that in this passage the name represents some animal of the whale tribe, which is common in the Mediterranean; but it is somewhat uncertain what animal is denoted in Isa. 27:1 and Job 3:8. On the whole modern commentators are inclined to believe them poetical references based upon the mythological "dragon."

Le'vites (le'vītes) (*descendants of Levi*). Sometimes the name extends to the whole tribe, the priests included, Ex. 6:25; Lev. 25:32; Num. 35:2; Josh. 21:3, 41, etc.; sometimes only to those members of the tribe who were not priests, and as distinguished from them. Sometimes again it is added as an epithet of the smaller portion of the tribe, and we read of "the priests the Levites." Josh. 3:3; Ezek. 44:15. The history of the tribe and of the functions attached to its several orders is essential to any right apprehension of the history of Israel as a people. It will fall naturally into four great periods:—

The time of the Exodus.—There is no trace of the consecrated character of the Levites till the institution of a hereditary priesthood in the family of Aaron, during the first withdrawal of Moses to the solitude of Sinai. Ex. 24:1. The next extension of the idea of the priesthood grew out of the terrible crisis of Ex. 32. The tribe stood forth separate and apart, recognizing even in this stern work the spiritual as higher than the natural. From this time they occupied a distinct position. The tribe of Levi was to take the place of that earlier priesthood of the first-born as representatives of the holiness of the people. As the tabernacle was the sign of the presence among the people of their unseen King, so the Levites were, among the other tribes of Israel, as the royal guard that waited exclu-

sively on him. Their service began at 25 years of age as assistants to the priests, and at 30 as carriers of the tabernacle. Num. 4:23, 30, 35; 8:24. At fifty they were to be free from all duties but those of superintendence. Num. 8:25, 26. The Kohathites were to bear all the vessels of the sanctuary, the ark itself included. Num. 3:31; 4:15; Deut. 31:25. The Gershonites had to carry the tent-hangings and curtains. Num. 4:22–26. The heavier burden of the boards, bars and pillars of the tabernacle fell on the sons of Merari. The Levites were to have no territorial possessions. In place of them they were to receive from the others the tithes of the produce of the land, from which they, in their turn, offered a tithe to the priests, as a recognition of their higher consecration. Num. 18:21, 24, 26; Neh. 10:37. Distinctness and diffusion were both to be secured by the assignment to the whole tribe of forty-eight cities; each with an outlying "suburb," Num. 35:2, of meadow-land for the pasturage of their flocks and herds. Six of these were to be selected as cities of refuge. Through the whole land the Levites were to take the place of the old household priests, sharing in all festivals and rejoicings. Deut. 12:19; 14:26, 27; 26:11. Every third year they were to have an additional share in the produce of the land. Deut. 14:28; 26:12. To "the priests the Levites" was to belong the office of preserving, transcribing and interpreting the law. Deut. 17:9–12; 31:25, 26.

The Monarchy.—When David's kingdom was established, there came a fuller organization of the whole tribe. Their position in relation to the priesthood was once again definitely recognized. In the worship of the tabernacle under David, as afterward in that of the temple, the Levites were divided into (1) Assistants to the priests; (2) Judges and scribes; (3) Gate keepers; (4) Musicians. They lived for the greater part of the year in their own cities, and came up at fixed periods to take their turn of work. 1 Chron. 24–26. The educational work which the Levites received for their peculiar duties, no less than their connection, more or less intimate, with the schools of the prophets, would tend to make them the teachers of the others, the transcribers and interpreters of the law, the chroniclers of the times in which they lived. Thus they became to the Israelites what ministers and teachers are to the people now, and this teaching and training the people in morality and religion was no doubt one of the chief reasons why they were set apart by God from the people, and yet among the people. The revolt of the ten tribes, and the policy pursued by Jeroboam, who wished to make the priests the creatures and instruments of the king, and to establish a provincial and divided worship, caused them to leave the cities assigned to them in the territory of Israel, and gather round the metropolis of Judah. 2 Chron. 11:13, 14. In the kingdom of Judah they were, from this time forward, a powerful body, politically as well as ecclesiastically.

After the Captivity.—During the period that followed the captivity the Levites contributed to the formation of the so-called Great Synagogue. They, with the priests, formed the majority of the permanent Sanhedrin, and as such had a large share in the administration of justice even in capital cases. They appear but seldom in the history of the New Testament.

Leviticus so named because it relates principally to the duties of the Levites and priests as the guides and teachers of the people in their religious life. In early Jewish literature it is called The Law of Priests; The Book of Priests. According to the higher critics it belongs in its entirety to the priestly school of the writers of the Hexateuch.

LITERARY STRUCTURE. The 27 chapters fall readily apart into four divisions.

1. *The Law of Sacrifice,* chs. 1–7, as a visible means of expressing and cultivating the religious feelings of worship, forgiveness, devotion, consecration; "sign-posts pointing to the Perfect Sacrifice."

2. *The Consecration of the Priesthood,* chs. 8–10, as the ministers of God, leaders and teachers of the religious and moral life of the people.

3. *The Law of the Clean and the Unclean* with an Appendix on the Day of Atonement, chs. 11–16: This section emphasizes by symbols the distinction between right and wrong. It shows the moral value of right care of the body, of health, and sanitary laws, of simple living.

4. *The Law of Holiness,* chs. 17–27,

with an appendix on vows. There is a unique sense of the majesty and holiness of God, with its corollary of the holiness of his people. Thus one of the most notable features of the book is what may be called its spiritual meaning. That so elaborate a ritual looked beyond itself we cannot doubt. It was a prophecy of things to come; a shadow whereof the substance was Christ and his kingdom. We may not always be able to say what the exact relation is between the type and the antitype; but we cannot read the Epistle to the Hebrews and not acknowledge that the Levitical priests "served the pattern and type of heavenly things;" that the sacrifices of the law pointed to and found their interpretation in the Lamb of God; that the ordinances of outward purification signified the true inner cleansing of the heart and conscience from dead works to serve the living God. One idea—HOLINESS—moreover penetrates the whole of this vast and burdensome ceremonial, and gives it a real glory even apart from any prophetic significance.

THE DATE of the book is the first year of the Exodus, at Mt. Sinai. It is not impossible that additions may have been made to the original law as new circumstances require. But the fact that the Israelites did not always live up to these requirements is no proof of their late date, for they were the ideal and rule of the nation; just as the gospels are the ideal of Christian nations, although no nation has lived up to its principles.

Several similar laws to those of Leviticus are found in the code of Hammurabi, in the days of Abraham.

Lib'anus. [LEBANON.]

Lib'ertines (lĭb'er-tīnĕṣ). This word, which occurs once only in the New Testament—Acts 6:9—is the Latin *libertini,* that is, "freedmen." They were probably Jews who, having been taken prisoners by Pompey and other Roman generals in the Syrian wars, had been reduced to slavery, and had afterward been emancipated, and returned, permanently or for a time, to the country of their fathers.

Lib'nah (lĭb'nah) (*white*). 1. A royal city of the Canaanites which lay in the southwest part of the Holy Land, taken by Joshua immediately after the rout of Beth-horon. Josh. 10. It was near Lachish, west of Makkedah. It was appropriated with its "suburbs" to the priests. Josh. 21:13; 1 Chron. 6:57. In the reign of Jehoram the son of Jehoshaphat it "revolted" from Judah at the same time with Edom. 2 Kings 8:22; 2 Chron. 21:10. Sennacherib the king of Assyria attacked it in the time of Hezekiah, 2 Kings 19:8; Is. 37:8. It was later occupied by Jewish families, for Josiah married a daughter of Jeremiah of Libnah (2 Kings 23:31; 24:18). This is the latest known reference to the place. It was probably near *Beit Jibrin*, but is not identified.

2. One of the stations at which the Israelites encamped on their journey between the wilderness of Sinai and Kadesh. Num. 33:20, 21.

Lib'ni (lĭb'nī) (*white*). 1. The eldest son of Gershon the son of Levi, Ex. 6:17; Num. 3:18; 1 Chron. 6:17, 20, and ancestor of the family of the Libnites.

2. The son of Mahli or Mahali, son of Merari, 1 Chron. 6:29, as the text at present stands. It is probable, however, that he is the same with the preceding, and that something has been omitted. Comp. ver. 29 with 20, 42.

Lib'ya (lĭb'ĭ-à). This name occurs only in Acts 2:10. It is applied by the Greek and Roman writers to the African continent, generally, however, excluding Egypt.

Lice (Heb. *kinnam, kinnîm*). This word occurs in the Authorized Version only in Ex. 8:16–18 and in Ps. 105:31, both of which passages have reference to the third great plague of Egypt. The Hebrew word has given occasion to whole pages of discussion. Some commentators suppose that gnats are the animals intended by the original word; while, on the other hand, the Jewish rabbis, Josephus and others, are in favor of the translation of the Authorized Version. The R. V. margin gives *sand-flies or fleas*. Lice are exceedingly common among the uncleanly people of the East. The better classes of the Egyptians were unusually cleanly, and would feel a plague of lice most sorely.

Lieutenants. The Hebrew *achash darpan* was the official title of the satraps or viceroys who governed the provinces of the Persian empire; it is rendered "prince" in Dan. 3:2; 6:1. The R. V. has *satrap* in all cases.

Lign aloes. [ALOES.]

Ligure (Heb. *leshem*), a precious stone mentioned in Ex. 28:19; 39:12 as the first in the third row of the high priest's breastplate. It is impossible to say, with any certainty, what stone is denoted by the Hebrew term. The R. V. has *Jacinth.* Hastings' *Bible Dictionary* rather favors the yellow quartz or agate.

Lik'hi (lĭk'hī) (*learned*), a Manassite, son of Shemidah the son of Manasseh. 1 Chron. 7:19.

Lily (Heb. *shûshân, shôshan, shôshan-*

SCARLET LILY.

nâh). Although there is little doubt that the Hebrew word denotes some plant of the lily species, it is by no means certain what individual of this class it specially designates. The plant

LILY OF PALESTINE.

must have been a conspicuous object on the shores of the Lake of Gennesaret, Matt. 6 : 28; Luke 12 : 27; it must have flourished in the deep broad valleys of Palestine, Cant. 2 : 1, among the thorny shrubs, *ib.* 2 : 2, and pastures of the desert, *ib.* 2 : 16; 4 : 5; 6 : 3, and in gardens, *ib.* 6 : 2; and must have been remarkable for its luxuriant growth. Hos. 14 : 5. That its flowers were brilliant in color would seem to be indicated in Matt. 6 : 28, where it is compared with the gorgeous robes of Solomon; and that this color was scarlet or purple is implied in Cant. 5 . 13. There were many species of liliaceous blossoms in Palestine, some exceedingly gorgeous in color, and some exquisitely fragrant. "In late winter the regions over which Jesus walked are clothed most gorgeously. Most conspicuous, perhaps, are the great blue and red flowers of the order *Ranunculaceæ,* where the anemone and the ranunculus grow together. They are not small things, like our buttercups, but great wide flowers of two inches or more in diameter, carpeting the ground with patches as gorgeous as masses of our brilliant verbenas. They grow everywhere; and, like the other herbs, are glorious one day, and the next day literally cast into the oven to bake the peasant's bread."—*Isaac Hall, D. D.*

Thomson, in "The Land and the Book," speaks of a splendid iris, which he calls the *Hûleh lily.* "This Hûleh lily is very large; and the three inner petals meet above, and form a gorgeous canopy, such as art never approached, and king never sat under, even in his utmost glory. And when I met this incomparable flower, in all its loveliness, among the oak woods around the north base of Tabor and on the hills of Nazareth, where our Lord spent his youth, I felt assured that it was to this he referred."

It is very probable that the term *lily* here is general, not referring to any particular species, but to a large class of flowers growing in Palestine, and resembling the lily, as the tulip, iris, gladiolus, etc.

Lime, the substance obtained from limestone, shells, etc., by heat. It is noticed only three times in the Bible, viz., in Deut. 27 : 2 (where it is translated *plaster*), Isa. 33 : 12, and Amos 2 : 1.

Linen, cloth made from flax. Several different Hebrew words are rendered linen, which may denote different fabrics of linen or different modes of manufacture. Egypt was the great centre of the linen trade. Some linen, made from the Egyptian *byssus,* a flax that grew on the banks of the Nile, was exceedingly soft and of dazzling whiteness. This linen has been sold for twice its weight in gold. Sir J. G. Wilkinson says of it, "The quality of the fine linen fully justifies all the praises of antiquity, and excites equal admiration at the present day, being to the touch comparable to silk, and not inferior in texture to our finest cambric."

Lintel, the beam which forms the upper framework of a door. Ex. 12 : 22.

Li'nus, a Christian at Rome, known to St. Paul and to Timothy, 2 Tim. 4 : 21, who was the first bishop of Rome after the apostles. (A.D. 64.)

Lion. "The most powerful, daring and impressive of all carnivorous animals, the most magnificent in aspect and awful in voice." At present lions do not exist in Palestine; but they must in ancient times have been numerous. The lion of Palestine was in all probability the Asiatic variety, described by Aristotle and Pliny as distinguished by its short curly mane, and by being shorter

THE ASIATIC LION.

and rounder in shape, like the sculptured lion found at Arban. It was less daring than the longer maned species, but when driven by hunger it not only ventured to attack the flocks in the desert in presence of the shepherd, 1 Sam. 17 : 34; Isa. 31 : 4, but laid waste towns and villages, 2 Kings 17 : 25, 26; Prov. 22 : 13; 26 : 13, and devoured men. 1 Kings 13 :

24; 20 : 36. Among the Hebrews, and throughout the Old Testament, the lion was the achievement of the princely tribe of Judah, while in the closing book of the canon it received a deeper significance as the emblem of him who "prevailed to open the book and loose the seven seals thereof." Rev. 5 : 5. On the other hand its fierceness and cruelty rendered it an appropriate metaphor for a fierce and malignant enemy, Ps. 7 : 2; 22 : 21; 57 : 4; 2 Tim. 4 : 17, and hence for the archfiend himself. 1 Peter 5 : 8.

Lizard (Heb. *letââh.* Lev. 11 : 30). Lizards of various kinds abound in Egypt, Palestine and Arabia. What

LIZARD.

species of lizard is intended by the Hebrew word we have no means of deciding. There are several common species; the green lizard, the sand lizard, the wall lizard, and others. The *Gecko* or fan-footed lizard is thought by some to be intended here, but the R. V. uses that word as the translation of *anakah.* All the lizard tribe seem to have been regarded as unclean.

Lo=am'mi (lō-ăm'mī) (*not my people*), the figurative name given by the prophet Hosea to his second son by Gomer the daughter of Diblaim, Hos. 1 : 9, to denote the rejection of the kingdom of Israel by Jehovah. Its significance is explained in vs. 9, 10.

Loan. In the early days of the Hebrew nation loans were not sought for the purpose of obtaining capital, but for the necessaries of life. For this reason, probably, the law strictly forbade any interest to be taken for a loan to any poor person. This prohibition was limited to Hebrews only, from whom, of whatever rank, no interest was on any pretence to be exacted. Relief to the poor by way of loan was enjoined, and excuses for evading this duty were forbidden. Ex. 22 : 25; Lev. 25 : 35, 37. As commerce increased, the practice of interest, and so also of suretyship, grew up; but the exaction of it from a Hebrew appears to have been regarded to a late period as discreditable. Ps. 15 : 5; Prov. 6 : 1, 4; 11 : 15; 17 : 18; 20 : 16; 22 : 26; Jer. 15 : 10; Ezek. 18 : 13. Systematic breach of the law in this respect was corrected by Nehemiah after the return from captivity. Neh. 5 : 1–13. The money-changers, who had seats and tables in the temple, were traders whose profits arose chiefly from the exchange of money with those who came to pay their annual half-shekel. The Jewish law did not forbid temporary bondage in the case of debtors, but it forbade a Hebrew debtor to be detained as a bondman longer than the seventh year, or at farthest the year of jubilee. Ex. 21 : 2; Lev. 25 : 39, 42; Deut. 15 : 9.

Loaves. [BREAD.]

Lock. Where European locks have not been introduced, the locks of eastern houses are usually of wood, and consist of a partly hollow bolt from fourteen inches to two feet long for external

ANCIENT LOCK.

doors or gates, or from seven to nine inches for interior doors. The bolt passes through a groove in a piece attached to the door into a socket in the door-post.

Locust, a well-known insect, of the grasshopper family, which commits terrible ravages on vegetation in the countries which it visits. Their color is generally brown bordering on green. They are often as much as three or four inches long when full grown. The most destructive of the locust tribe that occur in the Bible lands are the *Œdipoda migratoria* and the *Acridium peregrinum;* and as both these species occur in Syria and Arabia, etc., it is most probable that one or other is denoted in those passages which speak of the dreadful devastations committed by these insects. At least nine different names are used in the Bible in speaking, but it is not certain that any distinction in species is intended. Locusts occur in great numbers, and sometimes obscure the sun. Ex. 10:15; Judges 6: 5; Jer. 46:23. Their voracity is alluded to in Ex. 10:12, 15; Joel 1:4, 7. They make a fearful noise in their flight. Joel 2:5; Rev. 9:9. Their ir-

LOCUSTS.

resistible progress is referred to in Joel 2:8, 9. They enter dwellings, and devour even the woodwork of houses. Ex. 10:6; Joel 2:9, 10. They do not fly in the night. Nah. 3:17. The sea destroys the greater number. Ex. 10: 19; Joel 2:20. The flight of locusts is thus described by M. Olivier (*Voyage dans l'Empire Othoman*, ii. 424): "With the burning south winds (of Syria) there come from the interior of Arabia and from the most southern parts of Persia clouds of locusts (*Acridium peregrinum*), whose ravages to these countries are as grievous and nearly as sudden as those of the heaviest hail in Europe. We witnessed them twice. It is difficult to express the effect produced on us by the sight of the whole atmosphere filled on all sides and to a great height by an innumerable quantity of these insects, whose flight was slow and uniform, and whose noise resembled that of rain: the sky was darkened, and the light of the sun considerably weakened. In a moment the terraces of the houses, the streets, and

all the fields were covered by these insects, and in two days they had nearly devoured all the leaves of the plants. Happily they lived but a short time, and seemed to have migrated only to reproduce themselves and die; in fact, nearly all those we saw the next day had paired, and the day following the fields were covered with their dead bodies." The only mention of locusts in the New Testament is as an article of food. John the Baptist used them when in the wilderness, Matt. 3:4. "Locusts have been used as food from the earliest times. Herodotus speaks of a Libyan nation who dried their locusts in the sun and ate them with milk. The more common method, however, was to pull off the legs and wings and roast them in an iron dish. Then they were thrown into a bag, and eaten like parched corn, each one taking a handful when he chose." Sometimes the insects are ground and pounded, and then mixed with flour and water and made into cakes, or they are salted and then eaten; sometimes smoked; sometimes boiled or roasted; again, stewed, or fried in butter. They are now eaten only by the Bedouins, and the very poorest of the people. They resemble shrimps in taste.

Lod. [LYDDA.]

Lo=de'bar (lŏ-dē'bär) (*without pasture*), a place named with Mahanaim, Rogelim and other transjordanic towns, 2 Sam. 17:27, and therefore no doubt on the east side of the Jordan. It was the retreat of Mephibosheth until he was summoned to the court of David. 2 Sam. 9:4, 5.

Lodge, To. This word, with one exception only, has, at least in the narrative portions of the Bible, almost invariably the force of "passing the night."

Log. [WEIGHTS AND MEASURES.]

Lo'is (lō'ĭs) (*agreeable*), the grandmother of Timothy, and doubtless the mother of his mother, Eunice. 2 Tim. 1:5. It seems likely that Lois had resided long at Lystra; and almost certain that from her, as well as from Eunice, Timothy obtained his intimate knowledge of the Jewish Scriptures. 2 Tim. 3:15.

Looking=glasses. [MIRRORS.]

Lord. [GOD.]

Lord's day, The (ἡ Κυριακὴ Ἡμέρα, Rev. 1:10 only), the weekly festival of our Lord's resurrection, and identified with "the first day of the week," or "Sunday," of every age of the Church. Scripture says very little concerning this day; but that little seems to indicate that the divinely-inspired apostles, by their practice and by their precepts, marked the first day of the week as a day for meeting together to break bread, for communicating and receiving instruction, for laying up offerings in store for charitable purposes, for occupation in holy thought and prayer. [See SAB-BATH.]

Lord's Prayer, the prayer which Jesus taught his disciples. Matt. 6: 9-13; Luke 11: 2-4. "In this prayer our Lord shows his disciples how an infinite variety of wants and requests can be compressed into a few humble petitions. It embodies every possible desire of a praying heart, a whole world of spiritual requirements; yet all in the most simple, condensed and humble form, resembling, in this respect, a pearl on which the light of heaven plays."—*Lange.*

"A peasant child can understand enough of it to make it the expression of his daily needs. The ripest scholar, philosopher and saint cannot exhaust its possibilities of meaning."

It is a summary of all other prayers.

It is a guide and model of prayer; not intended to supersede other prayers, not to be an exclusive form of prayer, but to express the true spirit of prayer, to show the emphasis which should be laid upon the different things we desire when we pray, and to form the channel in which our feelings and desires should naturally flow toward God.

The prayer asks for the fulfilment of the teachings of Christ, and corresponds to the duties enforced in the decalogue and in the Sermon on the Mount.

Beginning with the Person to whom we should pray, there follow the three classes of petitions which include the needs of our life, while the close gives us the assurance of the answer.

The Hearer and answerer of prayer.
Our Father which art in Heaven,

I. *The aim, ideal and supreme desire.*

　Hallowed be thy name
　Thy kingdom come
　Thy will be done
On earth as it is in heaven.

(This last clause belongs to all the three petitions, and not to the last alone.)

II. *The Material basis.*

　Give us this day our daily bread.

III. *Deliverance from evil.*

　And *forgive us* our debts
　As *we forgive* our debtors
　And lead us not into *temptation*
　But *deliver* us from evil.

The power that can give the answer
For thine is the *Kingdom*
　　　And the *Power*
　　　And the *glory*
Forever. Amen.

FATHER expresses the thought of God which makes it easiest to go to him in prayer.

THE FIRST PETITION expresses the true aim of all true prayer, the ideal we should seek first in all our living and praying, for ourselves and for all men.

THE SECOND PETITION includes all that we need of worldly good; the material training through which we can gain the true aim, always secondary to that purpose; and of which the world can safely have the most in proportion to its spiritual attainment.

THE THIRD SERIES of petitions expresses the need of every sinful soul, and the essential conditions by which the highest good can be reached.

THE DOXOLOGY gives us the assurance of an answer to our prayer, for God rules over all, he has all power, and the answer to our prayer will cause God's glory, the outshining of his real nature, to be revealed. (The doxology, "for thine is the kingdom," etc., is wanting in many manuscripts. It is omitted in the Revised Version; but it nevertheless has the authority of some manuscripts, and is truly biblical, almost every word being found in 1 Chron. 29: 11; and is a true and fitting ending for prayer.)

Lord's Supper. The words which thus describe the great central act of the worship of the Christian Church occur but in a single passage of the New Testament—1 Cor. 11: 20. 1. *Its institution.* —It was instituted on that night when Jesus and his disciples met together to eat the passover, Matt. 26: 19; Mark 14: 16; Luke 22: 13, probably on Thursday evening, April 6, A.D. 30. It was probably instituted at the *third cup* (the cup of blessing) of the passover, Jesus taking one of the unleavened cakes used at that feast and breaking it and giving it to his disciples with the cup. The narratives of the Gospels show how strongly the disciples were impressed with the words which had given a new meaning to the old familiar acts. They had looked on the bread and the wine as memorials of the deliverance from Egypt. They were now told to partake of them "in remembrance" of their Master and Lord. The words "This is my body" gave to the unleavened bread a new character. They had been prepared for language that would otherwise have been so startling, by the teaching of John 6: 32–58, and they were thus taught to see in the bread that was broken the witness of the closest possible union and incorporation with their Lord. The cup, which was "the new testament in his blood," would remind them, in like manner, of the wonderful prophecy in which that new covenant had been foretold. Jer. 31: 31–34. "Gradually and progressively he had prepared the minds of his disciples to realize the idea of his death as a sacrifice. He now gathers up all previous announcements in the institution of this sacrament."—*Cambridge Bible.* The festival had been annual. No rule was given as to the time and frequency of the new feast that thus supervened on the old, but the command "Do this as oft as ye drink it," 1 Cor. 11: 25, suggested the more continual recurrence of that which was to be their memorial of one whom they would wish never to forget. Luke, in the Acts, describes the baptized members of the Church as continuing steadfast in or to the teaching of the apostles, in fellowship with them and with each other, and *in breaking of bread* and in prayers. Acts 2: 42. We can scarcely doubt that this implies that the chief actual meal of each day was one in which they met as brothers, and which was either preceded or followed by the more solemn commemorative acts of the breaking of the bread and the drinking of the cup. It will be convenient to anticipate the language and the thoughts of a somewhat later date, and to say that, apparently, they thus united every day the Agapè or feast of love with the celebration of the Eucharist. At some time, before or after the

meal of which they partook as such, the bread and the wine would be given with some special form of words or acts, to indicate its character. New converts would need some explanation of the meaning and origin of the observance. What would be so fitting and so much in harmony with the precedents of the paschal feast as the narrative of what had passed on the night of its institution? 1 Cor. 11: 23–27.

2. *Its significance.*—The Lord's Supper is a reminder of the leading truths of the gospel: (1) Salvation, like this bread, is the gift of God's love. (2) We are reminded of the life of Christ —all he was and did and said. (3) We are reminded, as by the passover, of the grievous bondage of sin from which Christ redeems us. (4) It holds up the atonement, the body of Christ broken, his blood shed, for us. (5) In Christ alone is forgiveness and salvation from sin, the first need of the soul. (6) Christ is the food of the soul. (7) We must partake by faith, or it will be of no avail. (8) We are taught to distribute to one another the spiritual blessings God gives us. (9) By this meal our daily bread is sanctified. (10) The most intimate communion with God in Christ. (11) Communion with one another. (12) It is a feast of joy. "Nothing less than the actual joy of heaven is above it." (13) It is a prophecy of Christ's second coming, the perfect triumph of his kingdom. (14) It is holding up before the world the cross of Christ; not a selfish gathering of a few saints, but a proclamation of the Saviour for all. Why did Christ ordain *bread* to be used in the Lord's Supper, and not a *lamb?* Canon Walsham How replies, "Because the types and shadows were to cease when the real Sacrifice was come. There was to be no more shedding of blood when once his all-prevailing blood was shed. There must be nothing which might cast a doubt upon the all-sufficiency of *that.*" Then, the Lamb being sacrificed once for all, what is needed is to teach the world that Christ is now the bread of life. Perhaps also it was because bread was more easily provided, and fitted thus more easily to be a part of a universal ordinance.

3. *Was it a permanent ordinance?*— "'Do this in remembrance of me' points to a permanent institution. The

command is therefore binding on all who believe in Christ; and disobedience to it is sin, for the unbelief that keeps men away is one of the worst of sins." "The subsequent practice of the apostles, Acts 2 : 42, 46; 20 : 7, and still more the fact that directions for the Lord's Supper were made a matter of special revelation to Paul, 1 Cor. 11: 23, seem to make it clear that Christ intended the ordinance for a perpetual one, and that his apostles so understood it."

4. *Method of observance.*—"The original supper was taken in a private house, an upper chamber, at night, around a table, reclining, women excluded, only the ordained apostles admitted. None of these conditions are maintained to-day by any Christian sect." But it must be kept with the same spirit and purpose now as then.

Lo=ruha′mah (lō-ru̯-hā′mah) (*not having obtained mercy*), the name of the daughter of Hosea the prophet, given to denote the utterly ruined condition of the kingdom of Israel. Hos. 1: 6.

Lot (*veil* or *covering*), the son of Haran, and therefore the nephew of Abraham. Gen. 11: 27, 31. His sisters were Milcah the wife of Nahor, and Iscah, by some identified with Sarah. Haran died before the emigration of Terah and his family from Ur of the Chaldees, ver. 28, and Lot was therefore born there. He removed with the rest of his kindred to Charran (B.C. 1926 [Ussher]) and again subsequently with Abraham and Sarai to Canaan, ch. 12 : 4, 5. With them he took refuge in Egypt from a famine, and with them returned, first to the "south," ch. 13 : 1, and then to their original settlement between Bethel and Ai, vs. 3, 4. But the pastures of the hills of Bethel, which had with ease contained the two strangers on their first arrival, were not able any longer to bear them, so much had their possessions of sheep, goats and cattle increased. Accordingly they separated, Lot choosing the fertile plain of the Jordan, and advancing as far as Sodom. Gen. 13 : 10–14. The next occurrence in the life of Lot is his capture by the four kings of the east and his rescue by Abram, ch. 14. The last scene preserved to us in the history of Lot is too well known to need repetition. He was still living in Sodom, Gen. 19, from which he was rescued by some angels on the day of its final overthrow. He fled first

to Zoar, in which he found a temporary refuge during the destruction of the other cities of the plain. Where this place was situated is not known with certainty. [ZOAR.] The end of Lot's wife is commonly treated as one of the difficulties of the Bible; but it surely need not be so. It cannot be necessary to create the details of the story where none are given. On these points the record is silent. The value and the significance of the story to us are contained in the allusion of Christ. Luke 17: 32. Later ages have not been satisfied so to leave the matter, but have insisted on identifying the "pillar" with some one of the fleeting forms which the perishable rock of the south end of the Dead Sea is constantly assuming in its process of decomposition and liquefaction. Lot's character is in strong contrast with that of Abraham. He is selfish, weak and worldly; in personal character "righteous" and deemed by God worthy of a special deliverance, he was nevertheless willing for the sake of luxury and ease to dwell in the midst of temptation. His descendants were the Moabites and Ammonites.

Lot (literally *a pebble*). The custom of deciding doubtful questions by lot is one of great extent and high antiquity. Among the Jews lots were used with the expectation that God would so control them as to give a right direction to them. They were very often used by God's appointment. "As to the mode of casting lots, we have no certain information. Probably several modes were practised." "Very commonly among the Latins little counters of wood were put into a jar with so narrow a neck that only one could come out at a time. After the jar had been filled with water and the contents shaken, the lots were determined by the order in which the bits of wood, representing the several parties, came out with the water. In other cases they were put into a wide open jar, and the counters were drawn out by the hand. Sometimes again they were cast in the manner of dice. The soldiers who cast lots for Christ's garments undoubtedly used these dice."— *Lyman Abbott.*

Lo′tan (lō′tan) (*covering*), the eldest son of Seir the Horite. Gen. 36 : 20, 22, 29; 1 Chron. 1: 38, 39.

Lots, Feast of. [PURIM.]

Love feasts (*Agapè*), 2 Pet. 2: 13;

Jude 12, an entertainment in which the poorer members of the church partook, furnished from the contributions of Christians resorting to the eucharistic celebration, but whether before or after may be doubted. The true account of the matter is probably that given by Chrysostom, who says that after the early community of goods had ceased the richer members brought to the church contributions of food and drink, of which, after the conclusion of the services and the celebration of the Lord's Supper, all partook together, by this means helping to promote the principle of love among Christians. The intimate connection, especially in early times, between the Eucharist itself and the love feasts has led some to speak of them as identical. The love feasts were forbidden to be held in churches by the Council of Laodicea, A.D. 320; but in some form or other they continued to a much later period. They still exist in the Greek church. The Wesleyan love-feast was a deliberate attempt at their revival.

Lu'bim (lŭ'bĭm), a nation mentioned as contributing, together with Cushites and Sukkiim, to Shishak's army, 2 Chron. 12:3; and apparently as forming with Cushites the bulk of Zerah's army, 2 Chron. 16:8, spoken of by Nahum, ch. 3:9, with Put or Phut, as helping No-amon (Thebes), of which Cush and Egypt were the strength. They are most probably the same as LEHABIM, and represent the primitive Libyans, who lived west of Egypt.

Lu'cas. Phil. 24. [LUKE.]

Lu'cifer (*light-bearer* or *shining one*), found in Isa. 14:12, coupled with the epithet "son of the morning," clearly signifies a "bright star," and probably what we call the morning star. In this passage it is a symbolical representation of the king of Babylon in his splendor and in his fall. Its application, from St. Jerome downward, to Satan in his fall from heaven arises from an erroneous supposition that Christ's words in Luke 10:18 were intended as an explanation of the passage in Isaiah.

Lu'cius (lŭ'shŭs). 1. A kinsman or fellow tribesman of St. Paul, Rom. 16:21, by whom he is said by tradition to have been ordained bishop of the church of Cenchreæ. He is thought by some to be the same with Lucius of Cyrene. 2. Lucius of Cyrene is first mentioned

in the New Testament in company with Barnabas, Simeon called Niger, Manaen and Saul, who are described as prophets and teachers of the church at Antioch. Acts 13:1. Whether Lucius was one of the seventy disciples is quite a matter of conjecture; but it is highly probable that he formed one of the congregation to whom St. Peter preached on the day of Pentecost, Acts 2:10; and there can hardly be a doubt that he was one of "the men of Cyrene" who, being "scattered abroad upon the persecution that arose about Stephen," went to Antioch preaching the Lord Jesus. Acts 11:19, 20.

Lud, the fourth name in the list of the children of Shem, Gen. 10:22; comp. 1 Chron. 1:17, supposed by many to have been the ancestor of the Lydians, though the Lydians do not seem to have been Semites. Still further explorations may disclose the fact of a Semitic founder of the original Lydia.

Lu'dim (lŭ'dim), Gen. 10:13; 1 Chron. 1:11, a Mizraite people or tribe, descended from Ludim the son of Mizraim. It is probable that the Ludim were settled to the west of Egypt, perhaps farther than any other Mizraite tribe. Lud and the Ludim are mentioned in four passages of the prophets —Isa. 66:19; Jer. 46:9; Ezek. 27:10; 38:5. The mentions of these peoples are so confused that it is impossible to make any true distinction between them. There must, however, have been two peoples.

Lu'hith (lŭ'hith), **The ascent of, a** place in Moab, occurs only in Isa. 15:5 and the parallel passage of Jeremiah. Jer. 48:5. In the days of Eusebius and Jerome a village of the same name was known, which stood between Areopolis (Rabbath-moab) and Zoar.

Luke or **Lu'cas,** is an abbreviated form of Lucanus. It is not to be confounded with Lucius, Acts 13:1; Rom. 16:21, which belongs to a different person. The name Luke occurs three times in the New Testament—Col. 4:14; 2 Tim. 4:11; Phil. 24—and probably in all three the third evangelist is the person spoken of. Combining the traditional element with the scriptural, we are able to trace the following dim outline of the evangelist's life.

His parents were probably from Antioch of Syria, and possibly he was born there.

He was a Gentile Christian, as we learn from Col. 4, v. 11 compared with v. 14.

He was a physician. Dr. Hobart on *The Medical Language of Luke* shows that his language in speaking of diseases confirms the statement that he was "the beloved physician."

It is possible that this was one reason why he was so frequently the companion of Paul in his journeys and his imprisonment.

His writings show that he was a man of culture, for "he had a command of good Greek not possessed by any of the other evangelists," and the preface to his Gospel is "the most finished piece of writing that is to be found in the New Testament."

He was the Author of the third Gospel, and of the Acts of the Apostles, and these show that he was an author of "the first rank, and of consummate artistic skill."

The date of his conversion is uncertain. He joined St. Paul at Troas, and shared his journey into Macedonia. The sudden transition to the first person plural in Acts 16:10 is most naturally explained, after all the objections that have been urged, by supposing that Luke, the writer of the Acts, formed one of St. Paul's company from this point. As far as Philippi the evangelist journeyed with the apostle. The resumption of the third person on Paul's departure from that place, Acts 17:1, would show that Luke was now left behind.

He accompanied Paul on his voyage to Rome, and remained with him at least during a part of his imprisonment. "If Paul wrote 2 Timothy during a second imprisonment at Rome, then Luke must have been with him again, for the apostle says in that letter, 'only Luke is with me' (iv. 11). It was a time of danger and sorrow. . . . Thus the last glimpse we have of the evangelist reveals him in the light of a loyal friend whose fidelity is exceptionally apparent in a scene of great peril." Prof. Adeney, in *The New Century Bible*.

Luke, Gospel of. The third Gospel is ascribed, by the general consent of ancient Christendom, to "the beloved physician," Luke, the friend and companion of the apostle Paul. DATE OF THE GOSPEL OF LUKE.—From Acts 1:1 it is clear that the Gospel described as "the former

treatise" was written before the Acts of the Apostles; but how much earlier is uncertain. Acts was probably written not later than A.D. 63.

CHARACTERISTICS. Renan calls Luke's Gospel, "the most beautiful book that has ever been written." Not only does the narrative "flow with an ease and grace unmatched by any other N. T. historical writing," but the subject matter, the life of Christ "is at once the most important, the most interesting, and the most fascinating of all topics of historical and literary study." His narratives are full of movement.

Luke is especially full on birth and infancy of Jesus.

In describing the most wonderful religious revival the world has ever known accompanied by a great outburst of song, Luke records five—the *Beatitude* of Elisabeth, the *Magnificat* of Mary, the *Benedictus* of Zacharias, the *Gloria in Excelsis* of the angels, and the *Nunc Dimittis* of Simeon. Two were by men, and two by women, and one by angels. None of these are found in the other Gospels. This gives a joyous, praise-giving character to his Gospel. "It is quicker to discover the brighter side of the topics it deals with." His Gospel is emphatically one of glad tidings of great joy. "Luke contains more social festivities," more occasions on which Jesus accepts hospitality, than the other Gospels.

More than half of Luke's Gospel consists of matter not found in the other evangelists; representing the contents by 100, Luke has 59 peculiarities and 41 coincidences with the other Gospels.

SOURCES. There were many narratives of the life of our Lord current at the early time when Luke wrote his Gospel from which he derived the facts he records, weaving them together in his own systematic way. He sought information from every reliable source.

He uses secular history and contemporary facts as a setting for the Gospel story, thus rendering the truth of his narrative to be easily tested. Far more than others he made references to the institutions, customs, geography, history and rulers of the times when he wrote.

THE GOSPEL FOR THE GREEK. Professor Gregory in his "Why Four Gospels," says that Luke wrote for Greek readers, and therefore the character and needs of the Greeks furnish the key to this

Gospel. The Greek was the representation of reason and humanity. He looked upon himself as having the mission of perfecting man. He was intellectual, cultured, not without hope of a higher world. Luke's Gospel therefore presented the character and career of Christ as answering the conception of a perfect and divine humanity. Reason, beauty, righteousness and truth are exhibited as they meet in Jesus in their full splendor. Jesus was the Saviour of all men, redeeming them to a perfect and cultured manhood.

Lunatics (from the Latin *Luna,* the moon, because insane persons, especially those who had lucid intervals, were once supposed to be affected by the changes of the moon). This word is used twice in the New Testament—Matt. 4:24; 17:15. (Translated *epileptic* in the Revised Version.) It is evident that the word itself refers to some disease affecting both the body and the mind, which might or might not be a sign of possession. By the description of Mark 9:17-26 it is concluded by many, including the Revisers, that epilepsy was intended. The conclusion is, however, disputed by others, who think the word includes much more than that.

Many other cases of so-called "possession" must be explained by the same or a similar disease to the one actually translated lunatic; and not all can be explained by epilepsy.

Luz (lŭz) (*almond*). It seems impossible to discover with precision whether Luz and Bethel represent one and the same town—the former the Canaanite, the latter the Hebrew, name—or whether they were distinct places, though in close proximity. The most probable conclusion is that the two places were, during the times preceding the conquest, distinct, Luz being the city and Bethel the pillar and altar of Jacob; that after the destruction of Luz by the tribe of Ephraim the town of Bethel arose. When the original Luz was destroyed, through the treachery of one of its inhabitants, the man who had introduced the Israelites into the town went into the "land of the Hittites" and built a city, which he named after the former one. Judges 1:26. Its situation is unknown, though several unproved identifications have been made.

Lycao'nia (lўk-a-ō'nĭ-a) (*land of Lycaon,* or *wolf-land*), a district of Asia Minor. From what is said in Acts 14:11 of "the speech of Lycaonia," it is evident that the inhabitants of the district, in St. Paul's day, spoke something very different from ordinary Greek. Whether this language was some Syrian dialect or a corrupt form of Greek has been much debated. The fact that the Lycaonians were familiar with the Greek mythology is consistent with either supposition. Lycaonia is for the most part a dreary plain, bare of trees, destitute of fresh water, and with several salt lakes. "Cappadocia is on the east, Galatia on the north, Phrygia on the west and Cilicia on the south." Among its chief cities are Derbe, Lystra and Iconium.— After the provincial system of Rome had embraced the whole of Asia Minor, the boundaries of the provinces were variable; and Lycaonia was, politically, sometimes in Cappadocia, sometimes in Galatia. Paul visited it three times in his missionary tours.

Ly'cia (lў'shà) (*land of Lycus*) is the name of that southwestern region of the peninsula of Asia Minor which is immediately opposite the island of Rhodes. The Lycians were incorporated in the Persian empire, and their ships were conspicuous in the great war against the Greeks (Herod. vii. 91, 92). After the death of Alexander the Great, Lycia was included in the Greek Seleucid kingdom, and was a part of the territory which the Romans forced Antiochus to cede. It was not till the reign of Claudius that Lycia became part of the Roman provincial system. Such seems to have been the condition of the district when St. Paul visited the Lycian towns of Patara, Acts 21:1, and Myra. Acts 27:5. In 74 A.D. it was united with Pamphylia as a double province.

Lyd'da (lĭd'dà), the Greek form of the name, Acts 9:32, 35, 38, which appears in the Hebrew records as Lod, a town of Benjamin, founded by Shamed or Shamer. 1 Chron. 8:12; Ezra 2:33; Neh. 7:37; 11:35. It is still called *Lûdd,* and stands in part of the great maritime plain which anciently bore the name of Sharon. It is about ten miles from Joppa, and is the first town on the northernmost of the two roads between that place and Jerusalem. It was burned in the time of Nero, taken by Vespasian in 68 A.D., and after the fall of Jerusalem became one of the chief seats of Rabbinical learning. One of its chief claims to interest is its connection with St. George, who was martyred there in 303. It is now a village of about 300 to 400 inhabitants, and the Cathedral of St. George is a mosque.

Lyd′ia (lĭd′i-à) (*land of Lydus*), a maritime province in the west of Asia Minor, bounded by Mysia on the north, Phrygia on the east, and Caria on the south. It is enumerated among the districts which the Romans took away from Antiochus the Great after the battle of Magnesia in B.C. 190, and transferred to Eumenus II. king of Pergamus. Lydia is included in the "Asia" of the New Testament. Rev. 1 : 1.

Lyd′ia (lĭd′i-à), the first European convert of St. Paul, and afterward his hostess during his first stay at Philippi. Acts 16 : 14, 15; also 40. (A.D. 50 or 51.) She was a Jewish proselyte at the time of the apostle's coming; and it was at the Jewish Sabbath-worship by the side of a stream, ver. 13, that the preaching of the gospel reached her heart. Her native place was Thyatira, in the province of Asia, ver. 14; Rev. 2 : 18. Thyatira was famous for its dyeing works; and Lydia was connected with this trade, as a seller either of dye or of dyed goods. We infer that she was a person of considerable wealth.

Lysa′nias (lĭ-sā′ni-as) (*that drives away sorrow*), mentioned by St. Luke in one of his chronological passages, ch. 3 : 1, as being tetrarch of Abilene (*i. e.* the district round Abila) in the thirteenth year of Tiberius (A.D. 26), at the time when Herod Antipas was tetrarch of Galilee and Herod Philip tetrarch of Ituræa and Trachonitis.

Lys′ias, Clau′dius (lўs′i-ăs, klạu′dĭ-ŭs), a chief captain of the band, that is, military tribune of the Roman cohort who rescued St. Paul from the hands of the infuriated mob at Jerusalem, and sent him under a guard to Felix, the governor or proconsul of Cæsarea. Acts 21 : 31, *seq.:* 23 : 26; 24 : 7. (A.D. 57.)

Lys′tra (lĭs′trà). This place has two points of interest in connection respectively with St. Paul's first and second missionary journeys: (1) as the place where divine honors were offered to him, and where he was presently stoned, Acts 14; (2) as the home of his chosen companion and fellow missionary Timotheus. Acts 16 : 1. Lystra was a city in Lycaonia about 18 miles south of Iconium. Little is known of its history. Even the fact that it was a Roman colony was unknown until 1888, when an inscription proving it was discovered. The ruins of the city were found about a mile northwest from the present village of *Khatyn Serai.*

M

Ma'acah (mā'a-kah) (*oppression*).
1. The mother of Absalom. 2 Sam. 3:
3. Also called MAACHAH.
2. A small Aramean kingdom in Gaulanitis the modern *Jaulan* east of the sea of Galilee. In 1 Chron. 19:6 it is called Syria-maachah. R. V. Aram-maacah. They took part in the war of the Ammonites against David. 2 Sam. 10:6.

Ma'achah (mā'a-kah) (*oppression*).
1. The daughter of Nahor by his concubine Reumah. Gen. 22:24.
2. The father of Achish, who was king of Gath at the beginning of Solomon's reign. 1 Kings 2:39. Perhaps the same as MAOCH.
3. The favorite wife of Rehoboam, and mother of Abijah. 1 Kings 15:2; 2 Chron. 11:20–22. In 1 Kings 15:2 she is called the daughter of Absalom, and in 2 Chron. 13:2. "Michaiah the daughter of Uriel of Gibeah." In view of this and the fact that Absalom's only daughter was named Tamar, Maachah is supposed by many to have been the grand-daughter of Absalom. Until the reign of her grandson Asa she occupied at the court of Judah the high position of "king's mother," comp. 1 Kings 15: 13; but she was removed at the time of his reforms because of her idolatrous habits. 2 Chron. 15:16.
4. The concubine of Caleb the son of Hezron. 1 Chron. 2:48.
5. The daughter of Talmai king of Geshur, and mother of Absalom, 1 Chron. 3:2; also called MAACAH in 2 Sam. 3:3.
6. The wife of Machir the Manassite. 1 Chron. 7:15, 16.
7. The wife of Jehiel, father or founder of Gibeon. 1 Chron. 8:29; 9: 35.
8. The father of Hanan, one of the heroes of David's body-guard. 1 Chron. 11:43.

9. A Simeonite, father of Shephatiah, prince of his tribe in the reign of David. 1 Chron. 27:16.

Maach'athi (mà-ăk'a-thī) (*oppression*) and **Maach'athites, The,** two words which denote the inhabitants of the small kingdom of Maachah. Deut. 3:14; Josh. 12:5; 13:11, 13; 2 Sam. 23: 34; 2 Kings 25:23; Jer. 40:8.

Maada'i, or **Maad'ai** (mà-ăd'ā-ī), one of the sons of Bani, who had married a foreign wife. Ezra 10:34.

Maadi'ah (mā'a-dī'à), one of the priests who returned with Zerubbabel, Neh. 12:5; elsewhere (ver. 17) called MOADIAH.

Maa'i (mà-ā'ī), one of the Bene-Asaph who took part in the solemn musical service by which the wall of Jerusalem was dedicated. Neh. 12:36.

Ma'aleh-acrab'bim (mà'ăl-eh-à-krăb'bim) (*ascent of scorpions*), Josh. 15 : 3, the full form of the name given as AKRABBIM in Num. 34:4.

Ma'arath (mā'a-răth) (*a place bare of trees*), one of the towns of Judah, in the district of the mountains. Josh. 15:59. It is doubtless north of Hebron and may possibly be *Beit Ummar.*

Maase'iah (mā-a-sē'yah) (*work of Jehovah*). 1. A descendant of Jeshua the priest, who had married a foreign wife. Ezra 10:18. Foreign wives had also been taken by
2. A priest, of the sons of Harim. Ezra 10:21; by
3. A priest, of the sons of Pashur. Ezra 10:22; and by
4. One of the laymen, a descendant of Pahath-moab. Ezra 10:30.
5. The father of Azariah. Neh. 3:23.
6. One of those who stood on the right hand of Ezra when he read the law to the people. Neh. 8:4.
7. A Levite who assisted on the same occasion. Neh. 8:7.

375

8. One of the heads of the people whose descendants signed the covenant with Nehemiah. Neh. 10:25.

9. Son of Baruch and descendant of Judah. Neh. 11:5.

10. A Benjamite, ancestor of Sallu. Neh. 11:7.

11. Two priests or Levites of this name are mentioned, Neh. 12:41, 42, as taking part in the musical service which accompanied the dedication of the wall of Jerusalem under Ezra. Perhaps the same as No. 6 and 7.

12. Father of Zephaniah, who was a priest in the reign of Zedekiah. Jer. 21:1; 29:25; 37:3.

13. Father of Zedekiah the false prophet. Jer. 29:21.

14. One of the Levites of the second rank, appointed by David to sound " with psalteries on Alamoth." 1 Chron. 15:18, 20.

15. The son of Adaiah, and one of the captains of hundreds in the reign of Joash king of Judah. 2 Chron. 23:1.

16. An officer of high rank in the reign of Uzziah. 2 Chron. 26:11.

17. The "king's son," killed by Zichri the Ephraimitish hero in the invasion of Judah by Pekah king of Israel, during the reign of Ahaz. 2 Chron. 28:7.

18. The governor of Jerusalem in the reign of Josiah. 2 Chron. 34:8.

19. The son of Shallum, a Levite of high rank in the reign of Jehoiakim. Jer. 35:4; comp. 1 Chron. 9:19.

20. A priest; ancestor of Baruch and Seraiah, the sons of Neriah. Jer. 32:12; 51:59. R. V. "Mahseiah."

Maas'iai (mā-ăs'i-ī) (*work of Jehovah*), a priest who dwelt in Jerusalem. 1 Chron. 9:12.

Ma'ath (mā'ath), son of Mattathias in the genealogy of Jesus Christ. Luke 3:26.

Ma'az (mā'az) (*wrath*), son of Ram, the first-born of Jerahmeel. 1 Chron. 2:27.

Maazi'ah (mā-a-zī'ah) (*consolation of Jehovah*). 1. One of the priests who signed the covenant with Nehemiah. Neh. 10:8.

2. A priest in the reign of David, head of the twenty-fourth course. 1 Chron. 24:18.

Mac'cabees (*a hammer*), **The.** This title, which was originally the surname of Judas, one of the sons of Mattathias, was afterward extended to the heroic family of which he was one of the no-

blest representatives. *Asmonæans* or *Hasmonæans* is the proper name of the family, which is derived from Cashmon, great-grandfather of Mattathias. The Maccabees were a family of Jews who resisted the authority of Antiochus Epiphanes king of Syria and his successors, who had usurped authority over the Jews, conquered Jerusalem, and strove to introduce idolatrous worship. The standard of independence was first raised by Mattathias, who was already advanced in years when the rising was made, and who did not long survive the fatigues of active service. He died B.C. 166, having named Judas—apparently his third son—as his successor in directing the war of independence. After gaining several victories over the generals of Antiochus, Judas was able to occupy Jerusalem, except the "tower," and purified the temple exactly three years after its profanation. Nicanor was defeated, first at Capharsalama, and again in a decisive battle at Adasa, B.C. 161, where he was slain. This victory was the greatest of Judas' successes, and

SILVER SHEKEL OF SIMON MACCABEUS.

practically decided the question of Jewish independence; but shortly after Judas fell at Elasa, fighting at desperate odds against the invaders. After the death of Judas, Jonathan his brother succeeded to the command, and later assumed the high-priestly office. He was killed by the Syrians in B.C. 143, and was succeeded by Simon, the last remaining brother of the Maccabæan family, who was ethnarch and high priest; finished winning the independence of his kingdom; and was assassinated by his son-in-law in B.C. 135. On the death of Simon, Johannes Hyrcanus, one of his sons, at once assumed the government, B.C. 135, and after a prosperous reign met with a peaceful death B.C. 105. His eldest son, Aristobulus I., who succeeded him B.C. 105–104, was the first who assumed the kingly title, though Simon had enjoyed the fullness of the kingly power. Alexander Jannæus was the next successor, B.C. 104–78. Aristobulus II. and Hyrcanus II, engaged in a civil war on the death of their mother, Alexandra, who was queen, B.C. 78–69, resulting in the dethronement of Aristobulus II, B.C. 69–63, and the succession of Hyrcanus under Roman rule, but without his kingly title, B.C. 63–40. Antipater, the father of Herod the Great, was more and more the real ruler, until in B.C. 40, Herod assumed the kingdom under Rome, and the Hasmonæan dynasty was at an end.

Mac'cabees, Books of. Four books which bear the common title of "Maccabees" are found in some MSS. of the LXX. Two of these were included in the early current Latin versions of the Bible, and thence passed into the Vulgate. As forming part of the Vulgate they were received as canonical by the Council of Trent, and retained among the *Apocrypha* by the reformed churches. The two other books obtained no such wide circulation, and have only a secondary connection with the Maccabæan history. 1. THE FIRST BOOK OF MACCABEES contains a history of the patriotic struggle of the Jews in resisting the oppressions of the Syrian kings, from the first resistance of Mattathias to the settled sovereignty and death of Simon, a period of thirty-three years—B.C. 168–135. The great marks of trustworthiness are everywhere conspicuous. The testimony of antiquity leaves no doubt that the book was first written in Hebrew. Its whole structure points to Palestine as the place of its composition. There is, however, considerable doubt as to its date, though it was probably between B.C. 105 and 64. The date and person of the Greek translator are wholly undetermined.

2. THE SECOND BOOK OF MACCABEES.— The history of the second book of Maccabees begins some years earlier than that of the first book, and closes with the victory of Judas Maccabæus over Nicanor; from B.C. 176 to B.C. 161. It is professedly an abridgment of the large work of Jason of Cyrene, and is much less trustworthy than the first book. The date of writing is very uncertain.

3. THE THIRD BOOK OF MACCABEES contains the history of events which preceded the great Maccabæan struggle, beginning with B.C. 217.

4. THE FOURTH BOOK OF MACCABEES

is a moral treatise, illustrated by stories of the Maccabees and their times, of no historical value.

Macedo'nia (măs-e-dō'nĭ-à), a large and celebrated country lying north of Greece between that country and the Balkans. This region with a mountainous interior rearing a hardy population, its fertile plains and extensive seaboard exercised under its noted kings, Philip and Alexander, a surprising influence over the history of the world. The Macedonia of the New Testament is the Roman Province, which included also parts of Illyria and Thessaly, and was governed by a proconsul, who

COIN OF MACEDON
HEAD OF ALEXANDER THE GREAT.

had his headquarters at Thessalonica, now *Salonica*. It was a part of Turkey until the Balkan war gave it to Greece. It was the first part of Europe which received the gospel directly from St. Paul, and an important scene of subsequent missionary labors. The character of the Christians of Macedonia is set before us in Scripture in a very favorable light. The candor of the Bereans is highly commended, Acts 17 : 11; the Thessalonians were evidently objects of St. Paul's peculiar affection, 1 Thess. 2 : 8, 17–20; 3 : 10; and the Philippians, besides their general freedom from blame, are noted as remarkable for their liberality and self-denial. Philip. 4 : 10, 14–19; see 2 Cor. 9 : 2; 11 : 9.

Machæ'rus (mă-kæ'rŭs), a castle built by Alexander Jannæus and restored by Herod Antipas, who used it as a residence. It was on the southern border of their Perean dominions, nine miles east of the northern end of the Dead Sea. Here John the Baptist was imprisoned, and here was held the feast where the daughter of Herodias, at whose request John was beheaded, danced before the king.

Mach'banai (măk'ba-nī), one of the lion-faced warriors of Gad, who joined the fortunes of David when living in retreat at Ziklag. 1 Chron. 12:13.

Mach'benah (măch'bēnah) (*bond*), Sheva, the father of Machbenah, is named in the genealogical list of Judah as the offspring of Maachah, the concubine of Caleb ben-Hezron. 1 Chron. 2:49.

Ma'chi (mā'kī), the father of Geuel the Gadite, who went with Caleb and Joshua to spy out the land of Canaan. Num. 13:15.

Ma'chir (mā'kĭr) (*sold*). 1. The eldest son, Josh. 17:1, of the patriarch Manasseh by an Aramite or Syrian, 1 Chron. 7:14. At the time of the conquest the family of Machir had become very powerful, and a large part of the country on the east of Jordan was subdued by them. Num. 32:39; Deut. 3:15.

2. The son of Ammiel, a powerful sheikh of one of the transjordanic tribes, who rendered essential service to the cause of Saul and of David successively. 2 Sam. 9:4, 5; 17:27-29.

Ma'chirites (mā'kĭr-ītes), The, the descendants of Machir the father of Gilead. Num. 26:29.

Machnade'bai (măk-na-dē'bī), one of the sons of Bani who put away his foreign wife at Ezra's command. Ezra 10:40.

Machpe'lah (măk-pē'lah) (*double*). [HEBRON.]

Ma'dai (mā'dī), Gen. 10:2, is usually called the third son of Japhet, and the progenitor of the Medes.

Ma'dian (mā'dĭ-an). Acts 7:29. [MIDIAN.]

Madman'nah (măd-măn'nah) (*dunghill*), one of the towns in the south district of Judah. Josh. 15:31. In the time of Eusebius and Jerome it was called Menois, and was not far from Gaza. The first stage southward from Gaza is now *el-Minyây,* which is perhaps the modern representative of Menois, and therefore of Madmannah.

Mad'men (*dunghill*), a place in Moab, threatened with destruction in the denunciations of Jeremiah. Jer. 48:2.

Madme'nah (măd-mē'nah) (*dunghill*), one of the Benjamite villages north of Jerusalem, the inhabitants of which were frightened away by the approach of Sennacherib along the northern road. Isa. 10:31.

Madness in the Old Testament is regarded as produced by a spirit sent from God (1 Sam. 16:14; 18:10), and closely allied with the spirit of prophecy (1 Sam. 10:6 ff.). For this reason madmen were at that time, as now in the East, looked upon as in some sense sacred. In the Gospels the reverse is true, the disorder being directly attributed to demonic influence.

Ma'don (mā'dŏn) (*strife*), one of the principal cities of Canaan before the conquest, probably in the north. Its king joined Jabin and his confederates in their attempt against Joshua at the waters of Merom, and like the rest was killed. Josh. 11:1; 12:19.

Mag'adan (măg'ădăn) (*a tower*). The name given in the Revised Version of Matt. 15:39 for Magdala. It is probably another name for the same place, or it was a village so near it that the shore where Christ landed may have belonged to either village.

Mag'bish (măg'bĭsh) (*congregating*), a proper name in Ezra 2:30, but whether of a man or of a place is doubtful; probably the latter, as all the names from Ezra 2:20 to 34, except Elam and Harim, are names of places.

Mag'dala (măg'da-là) (*a tower*). The chief MSS. and versions give the name as MAGADAN, as in the Revised Version, Matt. 15:39. In the parallel narrative of St. Mark, ch. 8:10, we find the "parts of Dalmanutha," which must refer to the same district, but not necessarily to the same place. By the best information attainable now it seems probable that it is the district west of the Sea of Galilee, and Magdala or Magadan is the present *el-Mejdel,* the traditional, and generally accepted, home of Mary Magdalene. This is a miserable little Moslem village, of twenty huts, on the water's edge at the southeast corner of the plain of Gennesareth. It is now the only inhabited place on this plain.

Mag'diel (măg'dĭ-el) (*honor of God*), one of the "dukes" of Edom, descended from Esau. Gen. 36:43; 1 Chron. 1:54.

Ma'gi (called in the Bible *wise men*). 1. In Jer. 39:3, 13 the officer *Rab Mag,* "chief of the Magi," is named among the princes of Nebuchadnezzar sent to Jerusalem. This is the only reference to the Magi in the Old Testament. The traditional account of the Magi, culled largely from Herodotus, is "that they were a Median race who acted as priests of the Persians, but whose persistence as a race is frequently attested and occasionally causes violent conflicts." They were priests of Zoroaster, giving their time largely to astrology, the interpretation of dreams, natural science and medicine. There are some difficulties in this account; but no better one has yet been found. Daniel probably held the office of Rab-mag.

2. The word presented itself to the Greeks as connected with a foreign system of divination, and it soon became a byword for the worst form of imposture. This is the predominant meaning of the word as it appears in the New Testament. Acts 8 : 9; 13 : 8.

3. In one memorable instance the word retains its better meaning. In the Gospel of St. Matthew, ch. 2:1–12, the Magi appear as "wise men"—properly Magians—who were guided by a star from "the east" to Jerusalem, where they suddenly appeared in the days of Herod the Great, inquiring for the new-born king of the Jews, whom they had come to worship. According to a late tradition, the Magi are represented as three kings, named Gaspar, Melchior and Belthazar, who take their place among the objects of Christian reverence, and are honored as the patron saints of travelers. There is a great difference of opinion as to the country from which they came, but the general trend of opinion seems to be in favor of Persia, or a neighboring region. An objection to the story that the visit of such men would be noticed in other writings of the time, is answered by the fact of the desire of Herod to keep it secret. There were several reasons why these Magi should seek a king of the Jews at this time. (1) They were worshippers of one God, regarding the sun as his nearest symbol, and fire man's best way of representing the sun. (2) There was a general expectation of the coming of a "great king who was to rise from among the Jews. It had fermented in the minds of men, heathen as well as Jews, and would have led them to welcome Jesus as the Christ had he come in accordance with their expectation." Virgil, who lived a little before this, owns that a child from heaven was looked for, who should restore the golden age and take away sin. (3) This expectation arose largely from the dispersion

of the Jews among all nations, carrying with them the hope and the promise of a divine Redeemer. Isa. 9, 11; Dan. 7. (4) Daniel himself was a prince and chief among this very class of wise men. His prophecies were made known to them; and the calculations by which he pointed to the very time when Christ should be born became, through the book of Daniel, a part of their ancient literature.

Magic, Magicians. Magic is "the science or practice of evoking spirits or educing the occult powers of nature to produce effects apparently supernatural." It formed an essential element in many ancient religions, especially among the Persians, Chaldeans and Egyptians. During the plagues in Egypt the magicians appear. Ex. 7:11; 8:18, 19. Balaam also practised magic. Num. 22: 7. The practice of magic was forbidden by the law of the Hebrews. The magical practices which obtained among the Hebrews were therefore borrowed from the nations around. From the first entrance into the land of promise until the destruction of Jerusalem we have constant glimpses of magic practised in secret, or resorted to not alone by the common but also by the great. Saul banished all the workers of magic (1 Sam. 28:3), but himself consulted the witch of Endor when in dread before the battle of Gilboa. There is every reason to think that the prohibition of the practice of magic by the Jews did not in the least arise from their disbelief in it. They manifestly had great faith in it, arising from their belief in the existence of demons. But a reliance on the power of demons was regarded by the best of the people as apostasy from God. Later rabbis allowed the study though not advocating the practice of magic.

Ma'gog (mā'gŏg). In Gen. 10:2 Magog appears as the second son of Japheth; in Ezek. 38:2; 39:1, 6 it appears as a country or people of which Gog was the prince. The notices of Magog would lead us to fix a northern locality: it is expressly stated by Ezekiel that he was to come up from "the sides of the north," Ezek. 39:2, from a country adjacent to that of Togarmah or Armenia, ch. 38: 6, and not far from "the isles" or maritime regions of Europe, ch. 39: 6. The people of Magog further appear as having a force of cavalry, Ezek. 38 : 15, and as armed with the bow, ch. 39 : 3. Josephus identifies them with the Scythians, and the identification is generally accepted. But it must be remembered that "the term Scythian was used vaguely to denote almost any northern population about which little was known."

Ma'gor=mis'sabib (mā'gôr-mĭs'sa-bĭb) (*terror on every side*), the name given by Jeremiah to Pashur the priest when he smote him and put him in the stocks for prophesying against the idolatry of Jerusalem. Jer. 20 : 3.

Mag'piash (măg'pĭ-ăsh), one of the heads of the people who signed the covenant with Nehemiah. Neh. 10 : 20.

Ma'halah (mà'hā-lah) (*sickness*), one of the three children of Hammoleketh the sister of Gilead. 1 Chron. 7 : 18. R. V. has, correctly, "Mahlah."

Maha'lale=el (mà-hā'la-lē-el) (*praise of God*). 1. The fourth in descent from Adam, according to the Sethite genealogy, and son of Cainan. Gen. 5 : 12, 13, 15–17; 1 Chron. 1 : 2; Luke 3 : 37, Revised Version.

2. A descendant of Perez or Pharez the son of Judah. Neh. 11 : 4.

Ma'halath (mā'ha-lath) (*sickness, anxiety*). 1. The daughter of Ishmael, and one of the wives of Esau. Gen. 28 : 9.

2. One of the eighteen wives of King Rehoboam, apparently his first. 2 Chron. 11 : 18 only. She was her husband's cousin, being the daughter of King David's son Jerimoth.

Mahalath, the title of Ps. 53, and **Mahalath Leannoth**, the title of Ps. 88. The meaning of these words is uncertain. It may mean the name of the tune, the sadness of the melody, or refer to a musical instrument.

Ma'hali (mā'ha-lī) (*sick*), **Mah'li** (mā'ha-lī), the son of Merari. Ex. 6 : 19.

Mahana'im (mā'hà-nā'im), a town on the east of the Jordan. The name signifies *two hosts* or *two camps*, and was given to it by Jacob, because he there met "the angels of God." Gen. 32 : 1, 2. We next meet with it in the records of the conquest. Josh. 13 : 26, 30. It was within the territory of Gad, Josh. 21 : 38, 39, and therefore on the south side of the torrent Jabbok. The town with its "suburbs" was allotted to the service of the Merarite Levites. Josh. 21 : 39; 1 Chron. 6 : 80. Maha-naim had become in the time of the

monarchy a place of mark. 2 Sam. 2 : 8, 12. David took refuge there when driven out of the western part of his kingdom by Absalom. 2 Sam. 17 : 24; 1 Kings 2 : 8. Mahanaim was the seat of one of Solomon's commissariat officers, 1 Kings 4 : 14, and it is alluded to in the song which bears his name. Ch. 6 : 13. The site is uncertain, several identifications being given and disputed.

Ma'haneh=dan (mā'hà-neh-dăn) (*camp of Dan*), spoken of as "behind," that is, west of Kirjath-jearim, Judges 18 : 12, and as "between Zorah and Eshtaol," ch. 13 : 25.

Ma'harai (mā'hăr-ī) (*impetuous*), 2 Sam. 23 : 28; 1 Chron. 11 : 30; 27 : 13, an inhabitant of Netophah in the tribe of Judah, the modern *Beit Netlif*, and one of David's captains.

Ma'hath (mā'hăth) (*seizing*). 1. A Kohathite of the house of Korah. 1 Chron. 6 : 35.

2. Also a Kohathite, in the reign of Hezekiah. 2 Chron. 29 : 12; 31 : 13.

Ma'havite (mā'hăv-īte), **The**, the designation of Eliel, one of the warriors of David's guard, whose name is preserved in the catalogue of 1 Chron. 11 : 46 only. Probably it is an error, as "the word is plural and yet joined to the singular."

Maha'zioth (mà-hā'zĭ-ŏth) (*visions*), one of the fourteen sons of Heman the Kohathite. 1 Chron. 25 : 4, 30.

Ma'her=shal'al=hash'=baz (mā'hĕr-shăl'al-hăsh'băz) (*spoil speedeth, prey hasteth*), a son of Isaiah whose name was given by divine direction to indicate that Damascus and Samaria were soon to be plundered by the king of Assyria. Isa. 8 : 1–4.

Mah'lah (mäh'là) (*sickness*), the eldest of the five daughters of Zelophehad the grandson of Manasseh. Num. 27 : 1–11.

Mah'li (mäh'lī) (*sick*). 1. Son of Merari, the son of Levi and ancestor of the family of the Mahlites. Num. 3 : 20; 1 Chron. 6 : 19, 29; 24 : 26.

2. Son of Mushi and grandson of Merari. 1 Chron. 6 : 47; 23 : 23; 24 : 30.

Mah'lon (mäh'lon) (*sickly*), the first husband of Ruth; son of Elimelech and Naomi. Ruth 1 : 2, 5; 4 : 9, 10.

Ma'hol (mā'hŏl) (*dance*), the father of three of the four men most famous for wisdom next to Solomon himself. 1 Kings 4 : 31. Comp. 1 Chron. 2 : 6.

Ma'kaz (mā'kăz) (*end*), a place, apparently a town, named once only—1 Kings 4:9—in the specification of the jurisdiction of Solomon's commissariat officer, Ben-Dekar. Makaz has not been discovered.

Makhe'loth (măk-hē'loth), a place mentioned in Num. 33:25 as that of a desert encampment of the Israelites. The same Hebrew word is used in Ps. 68:26, and translated "congregations."

Makke'dah (măk-kē'dah), a place memorable in the annals of the conquest of Canaan as the scene of the execution by Joshua of the five confederate kings, Josh. 10:10–30, who had hidden themselves in a cave at this place. It was a royal city of the Canaanites, in the plains of Judah. Conder identifies it with the modern *el-Moghâr*, 25 miles northwest of Jerusalem, where there are numerous caves.

Mak'tesh (măk'tesh) (*a mortar*), a place evidently in Jerusalem, the inhabitants of which are denounced by Zephaniah. Zeph. 1:11. Ewald conjectures that it was the "Phœnician quarter" of the city.

Mal'a=chi (măl'a-kī) (*my messenger*) is the author of the last book in the Old Testament. Nothing is known of him beyond what may be learned from nis book.

His prophecy belongs to the times of Nehemiah, near the time of Nehemiah's second visit to Jerusalem, about B.C. 432. It was an effort to aid in the great reforms then needed. Malachi believed in a spiritual worship as the one essential of true religion. But the system of temple ritual and sacrifices was in existence, and the prophet recognizes it as a means of educating the people into the spiritual life.

Mal'cham (măl'kăm), in R. V. Malcam. 1. A Benjaminite, son of Shaharahim and Hodesh. 1 Chron. 8:9.

2. One of the false gods adopted by the people of Judah. Zeph. 1:5. It is given also in the R. V. of Jer. 49:1, where the A. V. has "their king," as the chief deity of the Ammonites.

Malchi'ah (măl-kī'à). 1. A royal prince into whose dungeon the prophet Jeremiah was cast. Jer. 38:6. Very probably the one named in verse 1, as the father of Pashur; and in Jer. 21:1, where the A. V. has Melchiah. R. V. Malchiah.

2. A Gershonite Levite. 1 Chron. 6:40.

3. A descendant of Aaron. His family had grown to a father's house in the time of David and became the fifth of the courses into which David divided the priests. 1 Chron. 24:1, 6, 9. Apparently members of one branch of his family, the house of Pashur, returned with Zerubbabel from Babylon. Ezra 2:38. He is probably referred to in 1 Chron. 9:12, where a priestly line is traced back to a Malchijah, and in Neh. 11:12. Not the same as 1.

4. A son of Parosh who put away his foreign wife. Ezra 10:25.

5. A son of Harim who also put away his wife. Ezra 10:31.

6. A son of Rechab who repaired a part of the wall of Jerusalem. Neh. 3:14.

7. A goldsmith who repaired part of the wall. Neh. 3:31.

8. One of the Levites who assisted Ezra when the law was explained to the people. Neh. 8:14.

R. V. usually Malchijah.

Mal'chiel. A son of Beriah, and grandson of Asher, and founder of a tribal family. Gen. 46:17; Num. 26:45.

Malchi'jah. 1. An ancestor of one of the priests who returned with Zerubbabel from Babylon. 1 Chron. 9:12. Probably the same as Malchiah 3.

2. A son of Parosh who put away his foreign wife. Ezra 10:25. Not the same as Malchiah 4.

3. A son of Harim who repaired a part of the wall of Jerusalem. Neh. 3:11. Probably the same as Malchiah 5.

4. A priest who with others officiated at the dedication of the wall of Jerusalem. Neh. 12:42. Perhaps the same as Malchiah 8.

Malchi'ram. A son of king Jehoiachin. 1 Chron. 3:18.

Mal'chi=shu'a (măl'kĭ-shụ'à) (*the king is wealth*), one of the sons of King Saul. 1 Sam. 14:49; 31:2; 1 Chron. 8:33; 9:39.

Mal'chus (măl'kus) (*king*), the name of the servant of the high priest whose right ear Peter cut off at the time of the Saviour's apprehension in the garden. Matt. 26:51; Mark 14:47; Luke 22:49–51; John 18:10.

Male'leel (mà-lē'le-el), the son of Cainan. Gen. 5:12, marg.; Luke 3:37. MAHALEEL.

Mal'lothi (măl'lŏ-thī), a Kohathite, one of the fourteen sons of Heman the singer. 1 Chron. 25:4, 26.

Mal'luch (măl'luk) (*counsellor*). 1. A Levite of the family of Merari, and ancestor of Ethan the singer. 1 Chron. 6:44.
2. One of the sons of Bani. Ezra 10:29, and
3. One of the descendants of Harim, Ezra 10:32, who had married foreign wives.
4. A priest or family of priests. Neh. 10:4, and
5. One of the heads of the people who signed the covenant with Nehemiah. Neh. 10:27.
6. One of the families of priests who returned with Zerubbabel, Neh. 12:2; probably the same as No. 4.

Mammon (măm'mon) (*riches*), Matt. 6:24; Luke 16:9, used as the personification of worldliness, or wealth as a reason for worldliness.

Mam're (măm're) (*strength, fatness*), an ancient Amorite, who with his brothers, Eshcol and Aner, was in alliance with Abram, Gen. 14:13, 24, and under the shade of whose oak grove the patriarch dwelt in the interval between his residence at Bethel and at Beersheba. ch. 13:18; 18:1. In the subsequent chapters Mamre is a mere local appellation, ch. 23:17, 19; 25:9; 49:30; 50:13.

Man. There are several Hebrew words translated "man." 1. *Adam*, usually used as the generic term corresponding to Latin Homo (Gen. 5:2; Job 5:7). 2. *Ish.* Man as distinguished from woman—husband. Latin Vir. (Gen. 3:6). 3. *Geber* from the root "to be strong," a mighty man, as opposed to the weaker, woman (Deut. 22:5). 4. *Methim*, male, masculine—men as distinguished from both women and children (Deut. 2:34).

Man'aen (măn'a-ĕn) (*comforter*) is mentioned in Acts 13:1 as one of the teachers and prophets in the church at Antioch at the time of the appointment of Saul and Barnabas as missionaries to the heathen. He is said to have been brought up with Herod Antipas. He was probably his foster-brother.

Man'ahath (măn'a-hăth) (*rest*), a place named in 1 Chron. 8:6 only, in connection with the genealogies of the tribe of Benjamin.

Man'ahath (măn'a-hăth) (*rest*), one of the sons of Shobal, and descendant of Seir the Horite. Gen. 36:23; 1 Chron. 1:40.

Mana'hethites (mà-nā'heth-ītes) (*inhabitants of Manahath*), **The.** "Half the Manahethites" are named in the genealogies of Judah as descended from Shobal, the father of Kirjath-jearim, 1 Chron. 2:52, and half from Salma, the founder of Bethlehem, ver. 54.

Manas'seh (mà-năs'seh) (*making to forget*). 1. The eldest son of Joseph, Gen. 41:51; 46:20, born about 1715 B.C. before the beginning of the famine. He was placed after his younger brother, Ephraim, by his grandfather, Jacob, when he adopted them into his own family, and made them heads of tribes. In the division of the promised land half of the tribe of Manasseh settled east of the Jordan, in the district embracing the hills of Gilead with their inaccessible heights and impassable ravines, and the almost impregnable tract of Argob. Josh. 13:29-31. Here they throve exceedingly, pushing their way northward over the rich plains of Jaulân and Jedûr to the foot of Mount Hermon. 1 Chron. 5:23. They were among the first carried away by Pul and Tiglath-pileser, and settled in the Assyrian territories. 1 Chron. 5:25, 26. The other half tribe settled to the west of the Jordan, north of Ephraim. Josh. 17.
2. The fourteenth king of Judah, son of Hezekiah, 2 Kings 21:1, ascended the throne at the age of twelve, and reigned 55 years, from B.C. 697 to 641. His accession was the signal for an entire change in the religious administration of the kingdom. The foreign religions of Assyria and Babylon, the Canaanitish Baal and Asherah worship, were blended with the popular religion of Israel. There seems to have been a systematic religious persecution, the victims of which were those who, retaining their fidelity to Jehovah, opposed his reactionary measures. The Babylonian alliance which the king formed against Assyria resulted in his being made prisoner and carried off to Babylon in the twenty-second year of his reign, according to a Jewish tradition. There his eyes were opened and he repented, and his prayer was heard and the Lord delivered him, 2 Chron. 33:12, 13, and he returned after some uncertain interval of time to Jerusalem. The altar of the Lord was again restored, and peace offerings and thank offerings were sacrificed to Jehovah. 2 Chron. 33:15, 16.
3. One of the descendants of Pahath-

moab, who in the days of Ezra had married a foreign wife. Ezra 10:30.

4. One of the laymen, of the family of Hashum, who put away his foreign wife at Ezra's command. Ezra 10:33.

Manas'ses (mà-năs'sēs). 1. Manasseh, king of Judah. Matt. 1:10.

2. Manasseh the son of Joseph. Rev. 7:6.

Manas'sites (mà-năs'ītes), **The,** that is, the members of the tribe of Manasseh. Deut. 4:43; Judges 12:4; 2 Kings 10:33.

Mandrakes (Heb. *dudâim*) are mentioned in Gen. 30:14, 15, 16, and in Cant. 7:13. The Hebrew word means "love-plants." The mandrake, *Mandragora officinarum,* is closely allied to the well-known deadly nightshade, *Atropa belladonna,* and belongs to the order *Solanaceæ,* or potato family. It grows in the Jordan valley and along the

THE MANDRAKE.

rivers running into it, in the plains of Moab and Gilead, and in Galilee. It grows low like lettuce with wavy dark green leaves, somewhat resembling the tobacco plant. The root is usually forked, and is often made to assume a resemblance to a human being. The flowers are violet, white or deep blue. Its fruit when ripe (early in May) is globular, ruddy or yellow, resembling a small tomato, and of a most agreeable odor (to Orientals more than to Europeans) and an equally agreeable taste. The Arabs call it "devil's apple," from its power to excite voluptuousness. The ancients believed that the root gave a demoniacal shriek when pulled up, and

the one who touched it died. It is a powerful narcotic.

Maneh (mā'neh). [WEIGHTS AND MEASURES.]

Manger. This word occurs only in Luke 2:7, 12, 16, in connection with the birth of Christ. It means a crib or feeding-trough, and doubtless was used for that purpose in the cave-stable in which Jesus was born. "They were usually built of small stones and mortar in the shape of a box." The same Greek word is used in Luke 13:15 and is there rendered "stall," instead of "manger."

Manna (*what is this?*) (Heb. *mân*). The most important passages of the Old Testament on this topic are the following: Ex. 16:14–36; Num. 11:7–9; Deut. 8:3, 16; Josh. 5:12; Ps. 78:24, 25. From these passages we learn that the manna came every morning except the Sabbath, in the form of a small round seed resembling the hoar frost; that it must be gathered early, before the sun

TAMARISK OR MANNA TREE OF THE SINAITIC PENINSULA.

became so hot as to melt it; that it must be gathered every day except the Sabbath; that the attempt to lay aside for a succeeding day, except on the day immediately preceding the Sabbath, failed by the substance becoming wormy and offensive; that it was prepared for food by grinding and baking; that its taste was like fresh oil, and like wafers made with honey, equally agreeable to all palates; that the whole nation subsisted upon it for forty years; that it suddenly ceased when they first got the new corn of the land of Canaan; and that it was always regarded as a miraculous gift directly from God, and not as a product of nature. The natural products of the Arabian deserts and other Oriental regions which bear the name of manna have not the qualities or uses ascribed to the manna of Scripture. The latter substance was undoubtedly wholly miraculous, and not in any respect a product of nature, though its name may have come from its resemblance to the natural manna. The substance now called manna in the Arabian desert through which the Israelites passed is collected in the month of June from the *tarfa* or tamarisk shrub (*Tamarix gallica*). It drops from the thorns on the sticks and leaves with which the ground is covered, and must be gathered early in the day or it will be melted by the sun. The Arabs cleanse and boil it, strain it through a cloth and put it in leathern bottles; and in this way it can be kept uninjured for several years. They use it like honey or butter with their unleavened bread, but never make it into cakes or eat it by itself. The entire yield of the whole peninsula is less than 1000 pounds in the best years, making the supply of 300 tons a day for 40 years miraculous, even did this substance fulfil other conditions. Other kinds are also found in smaller quantities, some produced by the puncture of an insect. The manna of European commerce comes mostly from Calabria. It is a "sickly smelling, sweet, laxative exudation from the flowering ash, *Fraxinus ornus* and *Fraxinus rotundifolia.*"

Mano'ah (mà-nō'ah) (*rest*), the father of Samson; a Danite, native of the town of Zorah. Judges 13:2. [SAMSON.]

Manslayer, one who kills another unintentionally, and is thus distinguished from a murderer, who kills with malice aforethought. The cases of manslaughter mentioned in Scripture appear to be a sufficient indication of the intention of the lawgiver. 1. Death by a blow in a sudden quarrel. Num. 35:22. 2. Death by a stone or missile thrown at random. Num. 35:22, 23. 3. By the blade of an axe flying from its handle. Deut. 19:5. In all these and the like cases the man-

slayer was allowed to retire to a city of refuge.

Mantle, the word employed in the Authorized Version to translate no less than four Hebrew terms, entirely distinct in both derivation and meaning. 1. Judges 4:18, the garment with which Jael covered Sisera; mar. "blanket." 2. The word rendered "mantle" in 1 Sam. 15:27; 28:14; Ezra 9:3, 5, etc., is in other passages of the Authorized Version rendered "coat," "cloak" and "robe." The American Revision has "robe" throughout. 3. Isa. 3:22 only. An article of a lady's dress, probably the wide upper tunic with sleeves. 4. Probably a robe of office or state. It is used five times of Elijah's mantle (1 Kings 19:13, 19; 2 Kings 2:8, 13, 14) which was apparently of hair. It may well have been of sheepskin, such as is worn by the modern dervishes. The same word is used in Joshua 7:21, 24, of the Babylonish "garment" which tempted Achan, and in Jonah 3:6, of the "robe" of the king of Nineveh.

Ma'och (mā'ŏk) (*oppression*), the father of Achish king of Gath, with whom David took refuge. 1 Sam. 27:2. Perhaps the same as MAACHAH, 2.

Ma'on (mā'on) (*habitation*), one of the cities of the tribe of Judah, in the district of the mountains. Josh. 15:55. Its interest for us lies in its connection with David. 1 Sam. 23:24, 25. The name of Maon still exists in *Maîn,* a lofty conical hill, south of and about 8 miles distant from Hebron.

Ma'onites (mā'on-ītes), **The,** a people mentioned in one of the addresses of Jehovah to the repentant Israelites, Judges 10:12; elsewhere in the Authorized Version called Mehunim.

Ma'ra (mā'rà) (*sad, bitter*), the name which Naomi adopted in the exclamation forced from her by the recognition of her fellow citizens at Bethlehem. Ruth 1:20.

Ma'rah (mā'rà) (*bitterness*), a place which lay in the wilderness of Shur or Etham, three days journey distant, Ex. 15:23; Num. 33:8, from the place at which the Israelites crossed the Red Sea, and where was a spring of bitter water, sweetened subsequently by the casting in of a tree which "the Lord showed" to Moses. *Howarah,* distant 16½ hours (47 miles) from *Ayoun Mousa,* the "Wells of Moses," the Israelites' first encampment, has been by many identified with it, apparently because it is the bitterest water in the neighborhood.

Mar'alah (măr'a-lah) (*trembling*), one of the landmarks on the boundary of the tribe of Zebulun. Josh. 19 : 11.

Marana'tha (măr'an-ä'thä), an Aramaic or Syriac expression used by St. Paul at the conclusion of his First Epistle to the Corinthians, ch. 16 : 22, signifying " our Lord cometh."

Marble. The Hebrew *shêsh*, the generic term for marble, may probably be taken to mean almost any shining stone. The so-called marble of Solomon's architectural works may thus have been limestone. There can be no doubt that Herod both in the temple and elsewhere employed true marble. The marble pillars and tesseræ of various colors of the palace at Susa came doubtless from Persia. Esther 1 : 6.

Marcheshvan. [MONTH.]

Mar'cus (măr'kus), the evangelist Mark. Col. 4 : 10; Phil. 24; 1 Pet. 5 : 13. [MARK.]

Mare'shah (*at the head*), one of the cities of Judah in the low country, Josh. 15 : 44. It was one of the cities fortified and garrisoned by Rehoboam after the rupture with the northern kingdom. 2 Chron. 11 : 8. Near it was fought the great battle between Asa and Zerah. 2 Chron. 14 : 9-12. It is mentioned once or twice by Josephus and in the history of the Maccabæan war of independence. It was in ruins in the fourth century, when Eusebius and Jerome describe it as in the second mile from Eleutheropolis, or *Beit Jibrin*. The present ruin Merash no doubt represents this ancient city.

Mark, one of the evangelists, and author of the Gospel bearing his name. Hastings' *Dictionary of Christ and the Gospels* regards the identity of John Mark of Acts with the Mark of Paul's Epistles, as clearly proved; and states that there is no reason to doubt that the same Mark was the author of the second Gospel. Marcus was his Latin surname. His Jewish name was John, which is the same as Johanan (*Jehovah is gracious*). We can almost trace the steps whereby the former became his prevalent name in the Church. " John, whose surname was Mark," in Acts 12 : 12, 25 ; 15 : 37, becomes " John " alone in Acts 13 : 5, 13, " Mark " in Acts 15 : 39,

and thenceforward there is no change. Col. 4 : 10; Phil. 24; 2 Tim. 4 : 11. The evangelist was the son of a certain Mary, a Jewish matron of some position who dwelt at Jerusalem, Acts 12 : 12, and was probably born of a Hellenistic family in that city. Of his father we know nothing ; but we do know that the future evangelist was cousin of Barnabas of Cyprus, the great friend of St. Paul. His mother would seem to have been intimately acquainted with St. Peter, and it was to her house, as to a familiar home, that the apostle repaired, A.D. 44, after his deliverance from prison. Acts 12 : 12. This fact accounts for St. Mark's intimate acquaintance with that apostle, to whom also he probably owed his conversion, for St. Peter calls him his son. 1 Pet. 5 : 13. We hear of him for the first time in Acts 12 : 25, where we find him accompanying Paul and Barnabas on their return from Jerusalem to Antioch, A.D. 46. He next comes before us on the occasion of the earliest missionary journey of the same apostles, A.D. 47, when he joined them as their " minister or assistant." Acts 13 : 5. With them he visited Cyprus; but at Perga in Pamphylia, Acts 13 : 13, when they were about to enter upon the more arduous part of their mission, he left them, and, for some unexplained reason, returned to Jerusalem to his mother and his home. On Professor Ramsay's theory that Paul at this time was sick with malarial fever, it is quite possible that John Mark, too, was attacked with the depressing malarial fever, and felt unable to go through the rough experiences that lay before them, while at the same time this sickness emphasized all the other reasons. Paul went on with his work in spite of his sickness, and he thought that the more delicate young man should do the same. But while Paul on his next journey was unwilling to risk having Mark for his attendant, yet he was restored later to Paul's friendship and confidence, for we find him at Paul's side during that apostle's first imprisonment at Rome, A.D. 61–63, and he is acknowledged by him as one of his few fellow laborers who had been a " comfort " to him during the weary hours of his imprisonment. Col. 4 : 10, 11; Phil. 24. We next have traces of him in 1 Pet. 5 : 13: " The church that is in Babylon . . . saluteth you, and so doth Marcus my

25

son." From this we infer that he joined his spiritual father, the great friend of his mother, at Babylon. From Babylon he would seem to have returned to Asia Minor; for during his second imprisonment, A.D. 66, St. Paul, writing to Timothy, charges him to bring Mark with him to Rome, on the ground that he was "profitable to him for the ministry." 2 Tim. 4:11. From this point we gain no further information from the New Testament respecting the evangelist. It is most probable, however, that he did join the apostle at Rome, whither also St. Peter would seem to have proceeded, and suffered martyrdom along with St. Paul. After the death of these two great pillars of the Church, ecclesiastical tradition affirms that St. Mark visited Egypt, founded the church of Alexandria, and died by martyrdom.

Mark, Gospel of. There has been a decisive change in these later years as to the relation of Mark's Gospel to the others. For centuries it had been regarded as a condensation, or abbreviation of the Gospel according to Matthew. Now scholars look upon it as the oldest of the Gospels, and one of the sources from which the other writers drew their material.

The last twelve verses are an appendix, perhaps by Mark himself, "having once had an independent existence, and being added later to the Gospel to supply a lost leaf." Hence in the Revision these verses are separated by a space from the preceding verses; but this does not affect our faith in their truth or inspiration.

DATE WRITTEN.—Upon this point nothing absolutely certain can be affirmed, and the Gospel itself affords us no information. The most direct testimony is that of Irenæus, who says it was after the death of the apostles Peter and Paul. We may conclude, therefore, that this Gospel was not written before A.D. 63. Again we may as certainly conclude that it was not written after the destruction of Jerusalem, for it is not likely that he would have omitted to record so remarkable a fulfilment of our Lord's predictions. Hence A.D. 63–68 becomes our limit, but nearer than this we cannot go. PLACE OF WRITING.—The many Latin words in Greek form, used by Mark, indicate that his book may have been originally published, as tradition states, at Rome. SOURCES OF INFORMA-

TION.—Mark was not one of the twelve; and there is no reason to believe that he was an eye and ear witness to many of the events which he has recorded; but an almost unanimous testimony of the early fathers indicates Peter as the source of his information. The most important of these testimonies is that of Papias, who says, "He, the presbyter (John), said, Mark, being the interpreter of Peter, wrote exactly whatever he remembered." Peter told the story of what he had seen Jesus do, and heard him teach, a story he must have told many times in the hearing of Mark. But besides this, reports from the other apostles must have been in circulation among the churches, many of which, according to Luke, were put in writing.

FOR WHOM THE BOOK WAS WRITTEN. —The traditional statement is that it was intended primarily for Gentiles, and especially for those at Rome. A review of the Gospel itself confirms this view. CHARACTERISTICS.—Mark's Gospel is occupied almost entirely with the ministry in Galilee and the events of the passion week. It is the shortest of the four Gospels, and contains almost no incident or teaching which is not contained in one of the other two synoptists; but it is by far the most vivid and dramatic in its narratives, and their pictorial character indicates not only that they were derived from an eye and ear witness, but also from one who possessed the observation and the graphic artistic power of a natural orator, such as Peter emphatically was. One peculiarity strikes us the moment we open it,—the absence of any genealogy of our Lord. This is the key to much that follows. It is not the design of the evangelist to present our Lord to us, like St. Matthew, as the Messiah, "the son of David and Abraham," ch. 1:1, or, like St. Luke, as the universal Redeemer, "the son of Adam, which was the son of God." ch. 3:38. His design is to present him to us as the conquering Saviour, the incarnate and wonderworking Son of God, living and acting among men; to portray him in the fullness of his living energy.

Market=places, Matt. 20:3; Mark 12:38; Luke 7:32; Acts 16:19, any open place of public resort in cities or towns where public trials and assemblies were held and goods were exposed for sale. The *Agora* or *Forum* of a Greek or

Roman town was not only the market-place but the meeting place, for business or discussion on any subject.

Market of Ap'pius. Acts 28 : 15. In the Revised Version for Appii Forum of the Authorized Version, which see.

Ma'roth (mā'roth) (*bitternesses*), one of the towns of the western lowland of Judah. Micah 1 : 12.

Marriage. 1. *Its origin and history.* —The institution of marriage dates from the time of man's original creation. Gen. 2 : 18–25. From Gen. 2 : 24 we may evolve the following principles : (1) The unity of man and wife, as implied in her being formed out of man. (2) The indissolubleness of the marriage bond, except on the strongest grounds. Comp. Matt. 19 : 9. (3) Monogamy, as the original law of marriage. (4) The social equality of man and wife. (5) The subordination of the wife to the husband. 1 Cor. 11 : 8, 9 ; 1 Tim. 2 : 13. (6) The respective duties of man and wife. In the patriarchal age polygamy prevailed, Gen. 16 : 4 ; 25 : 1, 6 ; 28 : 9 ; 29 : 23, 28 ; 1 Chron. 7 : 14, but to a great extent divested of the degradation which in modern times attaches to that practice. Divorce also prevailed in the patriarchal age, though but one instance of it is recorded. Gen. 21 : 14. The Mosaic law discouraged polygamy, restricted divorce, and aimed to enforce purity of life. It was the best civil law possible at the time, and sought to bring the people up to the pure standard of the moral law. In the post-Babylonian period monogamy appears to have become more prevalent than at any previous time. The practice of polygamy nevertheless still existed ; Herod the Great had no less than nine wives at one time. The abuse of divorce continued unabated. Our Lord and his apostles re-established the integrity and sanctity of the marriage bond by the following measures ; (*a*) By the confirmation of the original charter of marriage as the basis on which all regulations were to be framed. Matt. 19 : 4, 5. (*b*) By the restriction of divorce to the case of fornication, and the prohibition of re-marriage in all persons divorced on improper grounds. Matt. 5 : 32 ; 19 : 9 ; Rom. 7 : 3 ; 1 Cor. 7 : 10, 11. (*c*) By the enforcement of moral purity generally, Heb. 13 : 4, etc., and especially by the formal condemnation of fornication. Acts 15 : 20.

2. *The conditions of legal marriage.*— In the time of the patriarchs marriage with aliens was protested against. When the Israelites returned from the exile in Egypt they were commanded to have no marriage with the idolatrous tribes of Canaan, exceptions being made only in the case of Edomites and Egyptians. But the command was not obeyed. Common people and rulers alike married members of other nations. Even David himself married out of Israel (2 Sam. 3 : 3). Under Nehemiah the law was revived and enforced with great stringency (Neh. 13). The regulations relative to marriage between Israelites and Israelites were based on considerations of relationship. The most important passage relating to these is contained in Lev. 18 : 6–18, wherein we have in the first place a general prohibition against marriage between a man and the "flesh of his flesh," and in the second place special prohibitions against marriage with a mother, stepmother, sister or half-sister, whether "born at home or abroad," granddaughter, aunt, whether by consanguinity on either side or by marriage on the father's side, daughter-in-law, brother's wife, stepdaughter, wife's mother, stepgranddaughter, or wife's sister during the lifetime of the wife. An exception is subsequently made, Deut. 25 : 5–9, in favor of marriage with a brother's wife in the event of his having died childless. The law which regulates this has been named the "levirate," from the Latin *levir,* "brother-in-law."

3. *The modes by which marriage was effected.*—The choice of the bride devolved not on the bridegroom himself, but on his relations or on a friend deputed by the bridegroom for this purpose. The consent of the maiden was sometimes asked, Gen. 24 : 58 ; but this appears to have been subordinate to the previous consent of the father and the adult brothers. Gen. 24 : 51 ; 34 : 11. Occasionally the whole business of selecting the wife was left in the hands of a friend. The selection of the bride was followed by the betrothal, which was a formal proceeding undertaken by a friend or legal representative on the part of the bridegroom and by the parents on the part of the bride ; it was confirmed by oaths, and accompanied with presents to the bride. The presents paid by the groom, were a relic of

a purchase of the bride as in some of the less civilized portions of the world to-day. On the other hand a father was bound to provide a dowry for his daughter either in money or land or jewelry, now the common form. The act of betrothal was celebrated by a feast, and among the more modern Jews it is the custom in some parts for the bridegroom to place a ring on the bride's finger. Between the betrothal and the marriage a varying interval elapsed. During this period the bride-elect lived with her friends, and all communication between herself and her future husband was carried on through the medium of a friend deputed for the purpose, termed the "friend of the bridegroom." John 3 : 29. She was virtually regarded as the wife of her future husband; hence faithlessness on her part was punishable with death, Deut. 22 : 23, 24, the husband having, however, the option of "putting her away." Deut. 24 : 1; Matt. 1 : 19. The essence of the marriage ceremony consisted in the removal of the bride from her father's house to that of the bridegroom or his father. The bridegroom prepared himself for the occasion by putting on a festive dress. The bride was veiled. Trumbull ("Studies in Oriental Social Life") speaks of a bride vested from head to foot in a red cashmere shawl so thick that she could see nothing, but was led by her friends. Her robes were white. Rev. 19 : 8, and sometimes embroidered with gold thread, Ps. 45 : 13, 14, and covered with perfumes, Ps. 45 : 8; she was further decked out with jewels. Isa. 49 : 18; 61 : 10; Rev. 21 : 2. When the fixed hour arrived, which was generally late in the evening, the bridegroom set forth from his house, attended by his groomsmen and friends, Judg. 14 : 11; Matt. 9 : 15, preceded by a band of musicians or singers, Jer. 7 : 34; 16 : 9, and accompanied by persons bearing flambeaux, Jer. 25 : 10; Matt. 25 : 7; Rev. 18 : 23, and took the bride with the friends to his own house. At the house a feast was prepared, to which all the friends and neighbors were invited, Gen. 29 : 22; Matt. 22 : 1–10; Luke 14 : 8; John 2 : 2, and the festivities were protracted for seven or even fourteen days. Gen. 29 : 27; Judges 14 : 12. The guests were provided by the host with fitting robes, Matt. 22 : 11, and the feast was enlivened with riddles.

Judges 14 : 12, and other amusements. The last act in the ceremonial was the conducting of the bride to the bridal chamber, Joel 2 : 16. The bride was still completely veiled, so that the deception practised on Jacob, Gen. 29 : 23, was not difficult. A newly-married man was exempt from military service, or from any public business which might draw him away from his home, for the space of a year, Deut. 24 : 5; a similar privilege was granted to him who was betrothed. Deut. 20 : 7.

4. *The social and domestic conditions of married life.*—The wife must have exercised an important influence in her own home. She appears to have taken her part in family affairs, and even to have enjoyed a considerable amount of independence. Judges 4 : 18; 1 Sam. 25 : 14; 2 Kings 4 : 8, etc. In the New Testament the mutual relations of husband and wife are a subject of frequent exhortation. Eph. 5 : 22, 33; Col. 3 : 18, 19; Titus 2 : 4, 5; 1 Pet. 3 : 1–7. The duties of the wife in the Hebrew household were multifarious: in addition to the general superintendence of the domestic arrangements, such as cooking, from which even women of rank were not exempt, Gen. 18 : 6; 2 Sam. 13 : 8, and the distribution of food at meal times, Prov. 31 : 15, the manufacture of the clothing and of the various fabrics required in her home devolved upon her, Prov. 31 : 13, 21, 22; and if she were a model of activity and skill, she produced a surplus of fine linen shirts and girdles, which she sold, and so, like a well-freighted merchant ship, brought in wealth to her husband from afar. Prov. 31 : 14, 24. The legal rights of the wife are noticed in Ex. 21 : 10 under the three heads of food, raiment, and duty of marriage or conjugal right.

5. *The allegorical and typical allusions to marriage* have exclusive reference to one object, viz., to exhibit the spiritual relationship between God and his people. In the Old Testament Isa. 54 : 5; Jer. 3 : 14; Hos. 2 : 19. In the New Testament the image of the bridegroom is transferred from Jehovah to Christ, Matt. 9 : 15; John 3 : 29, and that of the bride to the Church. 2 Cor. 11 : 2; Rev. 19 : 7; 21 : 2, 9.

Mars' Hill, also known by the name of Areopagus, of which *hill of Ares* (*Mars*) is a translation. The Areopagus was a rocky height in Athens, opposite the western end of the Acropolis. It rises gradually from the northern end, and terminates abruptly on the south, over against the Acropolis, at which point it is about fifty or sixty feet above the valley. The spot is memorable as the place of meeting of the Council of Areopagus. This body existed as a "certain philosophers of the Epicureans and Stoics" brought him up from the valley, probably by the stone steps, to the Areopagus above, that they might listen to him more conveniently.

Mar'sena (mär'se-nȧ), one of the seven princes of Persia, "wise men which knew the times," which saw the

THE AREOPAGUS (MARS' HILL) AT ATHENS.

criminal tribunal before the time of Solon, and was the most ancient and venerable of all the Athenian courts. It consisted of all persons who had held the office of archon, and who were members of the council for life unless expelled for misconduct. Before the time of Solon the court tried only cases of willful murder, wounding, poison, and arson; but he gave it extensive powers of a censorial and political nature. The council continued to exist even under the Roman emperors. Sixteen worn steps cut in the rock lead up to the summit, and a few remnants of the seats remain. The Areopagus possesses peculiar interest to the Christian as the spot from which St. Paul delivered his memorable address to the men of Athens. Acts 17: 22–31. St. Paul "disputed daily" in the "market" or agora, Acts 17: 17, which was situated south of the Areopagus in the valley lying between this and the hills of the Acropolis, the Pnyx and the Museum. Attracting more and more attention.

king's face and sat first in the kingdom. Esther 1: 14.

Mar'tha (*lady*), the sister of Lazarus and Mary. [LAZARUS.] The facts recorded in Luke 10 and John 11 indicate a character devout after the customary Jewish type of devotion, sharing in Messianic hopes and accepting Jesus as the Christ. When she first comes before us, Luke 10: 38, her spirit is "cumbered with much serving," is "careful and troubled about many things." Her love, though imperfect in its form, is yet recognized as true, and she has the distinction of being one whom Jesus loved. John 11: 5. Her position is obviously that of the elder sister, the head and manager of the household. Since the supper is said in Matthew and Mark to have been held in "the house of Simon the leper" it is suggested that Martha, the head of the house, may have been his wife or widow. In the supper at Bethany, John 12: 2, the old character shows itself still, but it has been freed from evil. She is no longer "cumbered," no longer impatient. Activity has been calmed by trust.

Ma'ry of Cle'ophas. So in Authorized Version, but accurately "of Clopas," whether "wife" as supplied by the translators, or "daughter" as suggested by some scholars is not certain. John 19:25. There is also considerable uncertainty as to her identification with "Mary the mother of James" (Matt. 27:56) and "the other Mary" (Matt. 28:1). If she was the *daughter* of Clopas she might easily be the mother of "James the son of Alphæus." (For a fuller discussion see JAMES.)

Ma'ry Magdale'ne. Different explanations have been given of this name; but the most natural is that she came from the town of Magdala. She appears before us for the first time in Luke 8:2, among the women who "ministered unto him of their substance." All appear to have occupied a position of comparative wealth. With all the chief motive was that of gratitude for their deliverance from "evil spirits and infirmities." Of Mary it is said specially that "seven devils went out of her," and the number indicates a *possession* of more than ordinary malignity. She was present during the closing hours of the agony on the cross. John 19:25. She remained by the cross till all was over, and waited till the body was taken down and placed in the garden sepulchre of Joseph of Arimathæa, Matt. 27:61; Mark 15:47; Luke 23:55, when she, with others "bought sweet spices that they might come and anoint" the body. Mark 16:1. The next morning accordingly, in the earliest dawn, Matt. 28:1; Mark 16:2, they came to the sepulchre. Mary Magdalene had been to the tomb and had found it empty, and had seen the "vision of angels." Matt. 28:5; Mark 16:5. To her first of all Jesus appeared after his resurrection. John 20:14, 15. Mary Magdalene has become the type of a class of repentant sinners; but there is no authority for identifying her with the "sinner" who anointed the feet of Jesus in Luke 7:36–50; neither is there any authority for the supposition that Mary Magdalene is the same as the sister of Lazarus. Neither of these theories has the slightest foundation in fact.

Ma'ry, mother of Mark, Col. 4:10, was aunt to Barnabas. Acts 4:36; 12:12. She was among the earliest disciples, and lived at Jerusalem. She gave up her house to be used as one of the chief places of meeting. The fact that Peter went to that house on his release from prison, Acts 12:12, indicates that there was some special intimacy between them. There is a tradition that the place of meeting of the disciples, and hence Mary's house, was on the upper slope of Zion, and that it was here that the Holy Ghost came upon the disciples with tongues of flame on the day of Pentecost.

Ma'ry, sister of Lazarus. She and her sister Martha appear in Luke 10:40 as receiving Christ in their house. Mary sat listening eagerly for every word that fell from the divine Teacher. She had chosen the good part, the "one thing needful." The same character shows itself in the history of John 11. Her grief was deeper, but less active. Her first thought, when she saw the Teacher in whose power and love she had trusted, was one of complaint. But the great joy and love which her brother's return to life called up in her poured themselves out in larger measure than had been seen before. The treasured alabaster box of ointment was brought forth at the final feast of Bethany. John 12:3.

Ma'ry the virgin, the mother of our Lord. There is no person perhaps in sacred or profane history around whom so many legends have been grouped as the Virgin Mary; and there are few whose authentic history is more concise. She was, like Joseph, of the tribe of Judah and of the lineage of David. Ps. 132:11; Luke 1:32; Rom. 1:3. She was connected by marriage, Luke 1:36, with Elisabeth, who was of the tribe of Levi and of the lineage of Aaron. This is all that we know of her antecedents. She was betrothed to Joseph of Nazareth; but before her marriage she became with child by the Holy Ghost, and became the mother of Jesus Christ, the Saviour of the world. Her history at this time, her residence at Bethlehem, flight to Egypt, and return to her early home at Nazareth, are well known. Four times only does she appear after the commencement of Christ's ministry. These four occasions are—1. The marriage at Cana in Galilee took place in the three months which intervened between the baptism of Christ and the passover of the year 27. Mary was present, and witnessed the first miracle performed by Christ, when he turned the water into wine. She had probably become a widow before this time. 2. The next time that she is brought before us we find her at Capernaum, where she, with other relatives, had gone to inquire about the strange stories they had heard of her son Jesus. They sought an audience with our Lord, which was not granted, as he refused to admit any authority on the part of his relatives, or any privilege on account of their relationship. 3. The next scene in Mary's life brings us to the foot of the cross. With almost his last words Christ commended his mother to the care of him who had borne the name of the disciple whom Jesus loved: "Woman, behold thy son." And from that hour St. John assures us that he took her to his own abode. So far as Mary is portrayed to us in Scripture, she is, as we should have expected, the most tender, the most faithful, humble, patient and loving of women, but a woman still. 4. In the days succeeding the ascension of Christ Mary met with the disciples in the upper room, Acts 1: 14, waiting for the coming of the Holy Spirit with power.

Ma'ry, a Roman Christian who is greeted by St. Paul in his Epistle to the Romans, ch. 16: 6, as having toiled hard for him.

Mas'chil (măs'kĭl), the title of thirteen Psalms: 32, 42, 44, 45, 52–55, 74, 78, 88, 89, 142. In Ps. 47: 7 the Hebrew word is translated "understanding." It is variously explained as meaning (1) a didactic poem. (2) A reflective poem or (3) with reference to skill in music.

Mash, one of the sons of Aram. Gen. 10: 23. In 1 Chron. 1: 17 the name appears as Meshech. The name is found in the Assyrian inscriptions in discussing the Arabian campaign of Asshur-bani-pal. Its signification is not determined.

Ma'shal (mā'shal), the same as Misheal or Mishal. 1 Chron. 6: 74.

Mas'rekah (măs're-kah), an ancient place, the native spot of Samlah, one of the old kings of the Edomites. Gen. 36: 36; 1 Chron. 1: 47.

Mas'sa (măs'sà) (*burden*), a son of Ishmael. Gen. 25: 14; 1 Chron. 1: 30. The tribe descended from him has been identified with the *Masani* an Arab tribe near the Persian gulf. The Assyrian inscriptions give a similar name which is

variously interpreted, but generally understood as Arabs.

Mas'sah (măs'sah) (*proving, testing*), a name given to the spot, also called Meribah, where the Israelites tempted Jehovah. Ex. 17: 7; Ps. 95: 8, 9; Heb. 3: 8.

Mathu'sala (mà-thu'sa-là)= METHU-SELAH, the son of Enoch. Luke 3: 37.

Ma'tred (mā'tred) (*driving forward*), a daughter of Mezahab and mother of Mehetabel, who was wife of Hadar or Hadad of Pau, king of Edom. Gen. 36: 39; 1 Chron. 1: 50.

Ma'tri (mā'trī) (*rainy*), a family of the tribe of Benjamin, to which Saul the king of Israel belonged. 1 Sam. 10: 21.

Mat'tan (măt'tan) (*a gift*). 1. The priest of Baal slain before his altars in the idol temple at Jerusalem. 2 Kings 11: 18; 2 Chron. 23: 17. He probably accompanied Athaliah from Samaria.
2. The father of Shephatiah. Jer. 38: 1.

Mat'tanah (măt'ta-nah) (*gift*), a station in the latter part of the wanderings of the Israelites. Num. 21: 18, 19. Its situation is unknown.

Mattani'ah (măt'ta-nī'ah) (*gift of Jehovah*). 1. The original name of Zedekiah king of Judah, which was changed when Nebuchadnezzar placed him on the throne. 2 Kings 24: 17.
2. A Levite singer of the sons of Asaph. 1 Chron. 9: 15. He or his family was leader of the temple choir after its restoration, Neh. 11: 17; 12: 8, in the time of Nehemiah, and took part in the musical service which accompanied the dedication of the wall of Jerusalem. Neh. 12: 25, 35.
3. A descendant of Asaph, and ancestor of Jahaziel the Levite, in the reign of Jehoshaphat. 2 Chron. 20: 14. Probably this should be identified with (2) in which case it would certainly mean the family name.
4. One of the sons of Elam. Ezra 10: 26, who with
5. One of the sons of Zattu. Ezra 10: 27, and
6. A descendant of Pahath-moab, Ezra 10: 30, and
7. One of the sons of Bani, Ezra 10: 37, all put away their foreign wives at Ezra's command.
8. A Levite, father of Zaccur and ancestor of Hanan the under-treasurer who had charge of the offerings for the

Levites in the time of Nehemiah. Neh. 13:13.

9. One of the fourteen sons of Heman, whose office it was to blow the horns in the temple service as appointed by David. 1 Chron. 25:4, 16.

10. A descendant of Asaph the Levite minstrel, who assisted in the purification of the temple in the reign of Hezekiah. 2 Chron. 29:13.

Mat'tatha (măt'ta-thah), or **Mat= tathah** (*gift of Jehovah*), probably a contraction of Mattathiah. 1. Son of Nathan and grandson of David, in the genealogy of Christ. Luke 3:31.

2. An Israelite, son of Hashun, who divorced his Gentile wife after the return from Babylon. Ezra 10:33.

Mattathi'as (măt'ta-thī'as) (*gift of Jehovah*), the Greek form of Mattathiah. Two names given in the genealogy of Christ. Luke 3:25, 26.

Mat'tenai (măt'tē-nī) (*bestowment*), a contraction of Mattaniah. 1. Two Israelites who divorced their Gentile wives after the return from the Babylonish captivity. Ezra 10:33, 37.

2. A priest, son of Joiarib, in the time of Joiakim. Neh. 12:19. (B.C. about 500.)

Mat'than (măt'than) (*gift*), grandfather of Joseph the husband of the Virgin Mary. Matt. 1:15.

Mat'that (măt'that) (*gift*), a form of the name Matthan. 1. Son of Levi, in the genealogy of Christ. Luke 3:29.

2. Grandfather of Joseph the husband of the Virgin Mary. Luke 3:24.

Mat'thew (măth'thū) (*gift of Jehovah*). A contraction, as is also Matthias, of Mattathias. His original name was Levi, and his name Matthew was probably adopted as his new apostolic name. He was a Jew. His father's name was Alphæus. His home was at Capernaum. His business was the collection of dues and customs from persons and goods crossing the Sea of Galilee, or passing along the great Damascus road which ran along the shore between Bethsaida Julius and Capernaum. Christ called him from this work to be his disciple. The fact that he was called a "publican" indicates only that he was collector for the Roman government, and therefore hated by the Jews; it infers nothing necessarily as to his personal character. He appears to have been a man of wealth, for he made a great feast in his own house, perhaps in order to in- troduce his former companions and friends to Jesus. His business would tend to give him a knowledge of human nature, and accurate business habits, and of how to make a way to the hearts of many publicans and sinners not otherwise easily reached. He is mentioned by name, after the resurrection of Christ, only in Acts 1:13; but he must have lived many years as an apostle, since he was the author of the Gospel of Matthew, which was written more than 30 years later. It is probable that "Matthew remained at Jerusalem until the general dispersion of the church there on the outbreak of the Jewish war. According to Eusebius it was at this time, when about to depart to distant lands to preach the Gospel, that he left as a memorial to his Palestinean converts the story of the New Covenant (*i. e.* Testament), committed to writing in their own tongue, the Aramaic or Hebrew dialect."

Mat'thew, Gospel of. AUTHORSHIP. —That this Gospel was written by the apostle Matthew there is no reason to doubt. Seventeen independent witnesses of the first four centuries attest its genuineness. ORIGINAL LANGUAGE.—The testimony of the early Church is unanimous that Matthew wrote originally in the Hebrew language. On the other hand, doubt is thrown over this opinion, both by an examination of the statements of the fathers and by a consideration of peculiar forms of language employed in the Gospel itself. The question is unsettled, the best scholars not agreeing in their judgment concerning it. If there was a Hebrew original, it disappeared at a very early age. The Greek Gospel which we now possess was, it is almost certain, written in Matthew's lifetime; and it is not at all improbable that he wrote the Gospel in both the Greek and Hebrew languages. It is almost certain that our Lord spoke in Greek with foreigners, but with his disciples and the Jewish people in Aramaic (a form of language closely allied to the Hebrew). The Jewish historian Josephus furnishes an illustration of the fate of the Hebrew original of Matthew. Josephus himself informs us that he wrote his great work, "The History of the Jewish Wars," originally in Hebrew, his native tongue, for the benefit of his own nation, and he afterward translated it into Greek. No notices of the Hebrew original now survive. Irenæus relates that Matthew wrote his Gospel while Peter and Paul were preaching, and founding the Church at Rome, *after* A.D. 61. It was published *before* the destruction of Jerusalem. Hastings says that about 68 or 69 seems the best date. We would place our present Gospel between A.D. 60 and 66. If there was an original Hebrew Gospel, an earlier date belongs to it.—*Ellicott.* CHARACTERISTICS.—This Gospel was probably written in Palestine for Jewish Christians. It is an historical proof that Jesus is the Messiah. Matthew is the Gospel for the Jew. It is the Gospel of Jesus, the Messiah of the prophets. This Gospel takes the life of Jesus as it was lived on earth, and his character as it actually appeared, and places them alongside the life and character of the Messiah as sketched in the prophets, the historic by the side of the prophetic, that the two may appear in their marvellous unity and in their perfect identity. The arrangement of his book is topical rather than chronological. Only the general outline of the first part is given in the exact order of events. The latter part follows more nearly the order in which the events took place, but the selection is still in the form of grouping the teachings and the miracles. Thus he emphasizes and illustrates the instructions and truths about the kingdom of heaven, and shows their connection and meaning in the life and work of Christ. This method is especially apparent in the collection of teachings called the Sermon on the Mount, occupying three chapters; and the group of miracles in chapters eight and nine, proving the teacher's authority, and illustrating his teachings and his mission; and in chapter ten, embodying his personal instructions to his disciples.

Matthi′as (măth-thī′as) (*gift of Jehovah*), the apostle elected to fill the place of the traitor Judas. Acts 1:26. All beyond this that we know of him for certainty is that ne had been a constant attendant upon the Lord Jesus during the whole course of his ministry; for that was the condition of election. Tradition numbers him among the 70 and some suggest him to have been Nathanael. Tradition also says that he preached the gospel and suffered martyrdom in Ethiopia.

Mattithi′ah (măt′tĭ-thī′ä) (*gift of Jehovah*). 1. A Levite who presided over the offerings made in the pans. 1 Chron. 9:31; comp. Lev. 6:20, etc.

2. One of the Levites appointed by David to minister before the ark with harps to lead the choir. 1 Chron. 15: 18, 21; 16:5; 25:3, 21.

3. One of the family of Nebo who had married a foreign wife, in the days of Ezra. Ezra 10:43.

4. Probably a priest, who stood at the right hand of Ezra when he read the law to the people. Neh. 8:4.

Mattock. Isaiah 7:25. The tool used in Arabia for loosening the ground, described by Niebuhr, answers generally to our mattock or grubbing-axe, *i. e.* a single-headed pickaxe. The ancient Egyptian hoe was of wood, and answered for hoe, spade and pick.

MATTOCK OR EGYPTIAN HOE. (*After Wilkinson.*)

Maul, a sort of battleaxe or hammer, used as an implement of war. Prov. 25:18.

Mauzzim (māŭz′zĭm). The marginal note to the Authorized Version of Dan. 11:38, "the god of forces," gives as the equivalent of the last word "mauzzim or gods protectors, or munitions." There can be little doubt that mauzzim is to be taken in its literal sense of "fortresses," just as in Dan. 11:19, 39; "the god of fortresses" being then the deity who presided over strongholds. There is not sufficient evidence to justify a decision as to what god is intended. Such as there is seems to make the choice lie between Jupiter Capitolinus (Livy xli. 20), and Zeus Polieus the family god of the Seleucids.

Mazzaroth (măz′za-rŏth) (*the twelve signs*). The margins of both Versions of Job 38:32 give *Mazzaroth* as the name of the twelve signs of the zodiac.

Meadow. 1. In Genesis 41:2, 18, meadow is the translation of a word of Egyptian origin probably meaning reed-grass as it is translated in the R. V. The same word is translated "flag" in the text of Job 8:11. 2. In Judges 20: 33 the sense of the Hebrew word translated *meadow* is doubly uncertain. The most plausible interpretation is that of the Peshito-Syriac, which by a slight difference in the vowel-points makes the word *mearah,* "the cave."

Me'ah (mē'ah) (*a hundred*), **The tower of,** properly as in R. V. "Hammeah," one of the towers of the wall of Jerusalem when rebuilt by Nehemiah, Neh. 3:1; 12:39, appears to have been situated somewhere at the northeast part of the city, and perhaps guarded the temple area.

Meals. Our information on the subject of meals is but scanty. The early Hebrews do not seem to have given special names to their several meals, for the terms rendered "dine" and "dinner" in the Authorized Version (Gen. 43:16; Prov. 15:17) are in reality general expressions, which might more correctly be rendered "eat" and "portion of food." In the New Testament "dinner" and "supper," Luke 14:12; John 21:12, are more properly "breakfast" and "dinner." There is some uncertainty as to the hours at which meals were taken; the Egyptians undoubtedly took their principal meal at noon, Gen. 43:16; laborers took a light meal at that time. Ruth 2:14; comp. ver. 18. The Jews rather followed the custom that prevails among the Bedouins, and made their principal meal after sunset, and a lighter meal at about 9 or 10 A.M. The old Hebrews were in the habit of *sitting.* Gen. 27:19; Judges 19:6; 1 Sam. 20:5, 24; 1 Kings 13:20. The table was in this case but slightly elevated above the ground, as is still the case in Egypt. As luxury increased, the practice of sitting was exchanged for that of reclining. In the time of our Saviour, reclining was the universal custom. As several guests reclined on the same couch, each overlapped his neighbor, as it were, and rested his head on or near the breast of the one who lay behind him; he was then said to "lean on the bosom" of his neighbor. John 13:23; 21:20. The ordinary arrangement of the couches was in three sides of a square, the fourth being left open for the servants to bring up the dishes. Women took their meals with men, occasionally at least (Ruth 2:14; 1 Sam. 1:4; Job 1:4), etc. Before commencing the meal the guests washed their hands. This custom was founded on natural decorum: not only was the hand the substitute for our knife and fork, but the hands of all the guests were dipped into one and the same dish. Another preliminary step

was the grace or blessing, of which we have but one instance in the Old Testament—1 Sam. 9:13—and more than one pronounced by our Lord himself in the New Testament—Matt. 15:36; Luke 9:16; John 6:11. The mode of taking the food differed in no material point from the modern usages of the East. Generally there was a single dish, into which each guest dipped his hand. Matt. 26:23. Occasionally separate portions were served out to each. Gen. 43:34; Ruth 2:14; 1 Sam. 1:4. A piece of bread was held between the thumb and two fingers of the right hand, and was dipped either into a bowl of melted grease (in which case it was termed "a sop," John 13:26) or into the dish of meat, whence a piece was conveyed to the mouth between the layers of bread. At the conclusion of the meal, grace was again said in conformity with Deut. 8:10, and the hands were again washed. On state occasions more ceremony was used, and the meal was enlivened in various ways. A sumptuous repast was prepared; the guests were previously invited, Esther 5:8; Matt. 22:3, and on the day of the feast a second invitation was issued to those that were bidden. Esther 6:14; Prov. 9:3; Matt. 22:4. The visitors were received with a kiss, Luke 7:45; water was furnished for them to wash their feet with, Luke 7:44; the head, the beard, the feet, and sometimes the clothes, were perfumed with ointment, Ps. 23:5; John 12:3; on special occasions robes were provided, Matt. 22:11, and the head was decorated with wreaths. Isa. 28:1. The regulation of the feast was under the superintendence of a special officer, John 2:8 (Authorized Version "governor of the feast"), whose business it was to taste the food and the liquors before they were placed on the table, and to settle about the toasts and amusements; he was generally one of the guests and might therefore take part in the conversation.

The places of the guests were settled according to their respective rank, Gen. 43:33; Mark 12:39; portions of food were placed before each, 1 Sam. 1:4, the most honored guests receiving either larger, Gen. 43:34, or more choice, 1 Sam. 9:24, portions than the rest. The meal was enlivened with music, singing and dancing, 2 Sam. 19:35, or with riddles, Judges 14:12; and amid these entertainments the festival was prolonged for several days. Esther 1:3, 4.

Mea'rah (mē-ā'rah) (*a cave*), a place named in Josh. 13:4 only. Probably a place not far from Sidon. Site unknown. Possibly *Mogheiriyeh*, 6 miles northeast of Sidon.

Measures. [WEIGHTS AND MEASURES.]

Meat. In accordance with usage when the A. V. was made, the word "meat" means food in general. Animal food is uniformly translated "flesh." The only real ambiguity caused by the change in usage is in the MEAT-OFFERING, which contained no flesh.

Meat offering. R. V. "Meal-offering." The law or ceremonial of the meat offering is described in Lev. 2 and 6:14-23. It was to be composed of fine flour, seasoned with salt and mixed with oil and frankincense, but without leaven; and it was generally accompanied by a drink offering of wine. A portion of it, including all the frankincense, was to be burnt on the altar as "a memorial;" the rest belonged to the priest; but the meat offerings offered by the priests themselves were to be wholly burnt. Its meaning appears to be exactly expressed in the words of David, 1 Chron. 29:10-14. It will be seen that this meaning involves neither of the main ideas of sacrifice—the atonement for sin and self-dedication to God. It takes them for granted, and is based on them. Rather it expresses gratitude and love to God as the giver of all. Accordingly the meat offering, properly so called, seems always to have been a subsidiary offering, needing to be introduced by the sin offering, which represented the one idea, and to have formed an appendage to the burnt offering, which represented the other. The unbloody offerings offered alone did not properly belong to the regular meat offering; they were usually substitutes for other offerings. Comp. Lev. 5:11; Num. 5:15.

Mebun'nai (mē-bŭn'nī) (*built*). In this form appears, in one passage only —2 Sam. 23:27—the name of one of David's guard, who is elsewhere called SIBBECHAI, 2 Sam. 21:18; 1 Chron. 20:4, or SIBBECAI, 1 Chron. 11:29; 27:11.

Meche'rathite (mē-kē'rath-īte), **The,** a person connected with Mecherah, a name which does not occur alone. 1 Chron. 11:36. In the parallel list of 2 Sam. 23:34 the name appears, with

other variations, as "the Maachathite."

Me'dad (mē'dad) (*love*). [ELDAD AND MEDAD.]

Me'dan (mē'dan) (*object of worship*), a son of Abraham and Keturah. Gen. 25:2; 1 Chron. 1:32.

Med'eba (mĕd'e-bà) (*water of rest*), a town on the eastern side of Jordan, first alluded to in Num. 21:30. It was in the *Mishor* plain, or tableland near to Heshbon.

It originally belonged to Moab; but was taken from them by the Amorites; and from them by the Israelites and assigned to Reuben (Josh. 13:9-16). According to the Moabite stone it was again in the possession of Moab in the reign of Ahab. In the time of Ahaz Medeba was a sanctuary of Moab. Isa. 15:2. It has retained its name down to our own times, and lies about 6 miles south of *Heshbon*.

Medes (mēdeṣ), **Me'dia** (mē'dĭ-à). Media lay north of Persia proper, south of the Caspian Sea, southeast of Armenia, east of Assyria. Its length was about 600 miles, its breadth about 250. "A great part of Media proper was a tableland 3000 feet high. The rest consisted of 7 parallel mountain chains with fertile and well-watered valleys between." The early inhabitants may have been neither Aryan nor Semitic, but they were apparently conquered by the Aryan *Madai* (Gen. 10:2; cp. Herod, 7, 62). We find a notice of the Medes in the primitive Babylonian history of Berosus, who says that the Medes conquered Babylon at a very remote period (*cir.* B.C. 2458), and that eight Median monarchs reigned there consecutively, over a space of 224 years. The deepest obscurity hangs, however, over their whole history until their first appearance among the enemies of Assyria, about B.C. 840. From that time we read of several expeditions against them resulting in their becoming tributary to Assyria; and later they were more thoroughly under Assyrian control. Near the middle of the seventh century B.C. the Median kingdom was consolidated, and became formidable to its neighbors; but previous to this time it was not under the dominion of a single powerful monarch, but was ruled by a vast number of petty chieftains. Cyaxares, Median monarch, took Nineveh and conquered Assyria B.C. 606, uniting for the purpose with Nabopolassar the king of Babylonia. The two divided the territory proper, Media having as its share Assyria and the countries north and east of it. The Median Empire only lasted during the reign of Cyaxares and his son Astyages, when it was overthrown by the Persians under Cyrus, B.C. 558, who captured its king. The treatment of the Medes by the victorious Persians was not that of an ordinary conquered nation. Medes were appointed to stations of high honor and importance under Cyrus and his successors. The two nations seem blended into one, and we often find reference to this kingdom as that of the "Medes and Persians." Dan. 5:28; 6: 8, 12, 15. The references to the Medes in the canonical Scriptures are not very numerous, but they are striking. We first hear of certain "cities of the Medes," in which the captive Israelites were placed by "the king of Assyria" on the destruction of Samaria, B.C. 721. 2 Kings 17:6; 18:11. Soon afterward Isaiah prophesies the part which the Medes shall take in the destruction of Babylon, Isa. 13:17; 21:2; which is again still more distinctly declared by Jeremiah, Jer. 51:11, 28, who sufficiently indicates the independence of Media in his day, ch. 25:25. Daniel relates the fact of the Medo-Persic conquest, Dan. 5:28, 31, giving an account of the reign of Darius the Mede, who appears to have been made viceroy by Cyrus. Dan. 6:1–28. After the destruction of the Persian Empire Media seems to have been divided into two parts, *Media Atropatene* (from the satrap, Atropates) corresponding nearly to the modern *Azerbijan,* and *Media Magna* to the south and east, including some of *Kurdistan.* There were two cities named Ecbatana, capitals of the two divisions; but the southern (the Achmetha of Ezra 6:2–5) was the most important.

Me'dian (mē'dĭ-an), **The.** Darius, "the son of Ahasuerus, of the seed of the Medes," Dan. 9:1, or "the Mede," ch. 11:1, is thus denoted in Dan. 5:31; A. V. R. V. has Darius the Mede.

Medicine. Egypt was the earliest home of medical knowledge and skill. Compared with the wild countries around them, the Egyptians must have seemed incalculably advanced. The process of embalming in its fullest form, must have required a knowledge of anatomy and of chemistry. Repre-

sentations of early Egyptian surgery apparently occur on some of the monuments of Beni-Hassan. The teeth of the mummies when opened show a dentistry which would bear comparison with a great part of what is done to-day. Herodotus says (ii. 84) that every part of the body was studied by a distinct practitioner. The reputation of Egypt's practitioners in historical times was such that both Cyrus and Darius sent to that country for physicians or surgeons. Of midwifery we have a distinct notice, Ex. 1:15, and of women as its practitioners, which fact may also be verified from the sculptures. The scrupulous attention paid to the dead was favorable to the health of the living. In early Egypt the physicians were priests and the knowledge of medicine was kept as their exclusive privilege. No traces of any system of medical education in Palestine in Bible times are found, and allusions to physicians are few. Those in the Old Testament were priests or prophets as well as healers. (Lev. 13; 1 Kings 14:2; 17:18; 2 Kings 4:22; 20:7). Very few allusions are very appreciative. St. Luke, "the beloved physician," who practised at Antioch, could hardly have failed to be conversant with all the leading opinions current down to his own time. Until a comparatively late period the ceremonial uncleanness from touching the dead prevented the Jewish physicians from thoroughly understanding anatomy. The first beginning of dissection was by Rabbi Ishmael in A.D. 100. Among the diseases mentioned in the Bible are blindness, arising from (1) ophthalmia (Lev. 26:16; and perhaps Gen. 29:17), a common disease to-day in Syria and Egypt, through the sun-glare, dust and dirt, or (2) from age (1 Sam. 3:2; 4:15, etc.). The "burning boil," Lev. 13:23, is merely marked by the notion of an effect resembling that of fire, like our "carbuncle." The diseases rendered "scab" and "scurvy" in Lev. 21:20; 22:22; Deut. 28:27, may be almost any skin disease; perhaps "favus." The "botch (*shechin*) of Egypt," Deut. 28:27, is so vague a term as to yield a most uncertain sense. In Deut. 28:35 is mentioned a disease attacking the "knees and legs," consisting in a "sore botch which cannot be healed," but extended, in the sequel of the verse, from the "sole of the foot to the top of the head." The *Elephantiasis græcorum* is what now passes under the name of "leprosy." [LEPROSY.] The case of the widow's son restored by Elisha, 2 Kings 4:19, was probably one of sunstroke. The palsy meets us in the New Testament only, and in features too familiar to need special remark. Palsy, gangrene and cancer were common in all the countries familiar to the scriptural writers, and neither differs from the modern disease of the same name. Mention is also made of the bites and stings of poisonous reptiles. Num. 21: 6. Among surgical instruments or pieces of apparatus the following only are alluded to in Scripture: A cutting instrument, probably a flint knife, Ex. 4:25; Josh. 5:2. The "awl" of Ex. 21:6 was probably a surgical instrument. The "roller to bind" of Ezek. 30:21 was for a broken limb, and is still used. Ex. 30:23-25 is a prescription in form. An occasional trace occurs of some chemical knowledge, *e. g.* the calcination of the gold by Moses, Ex. 32:20; the effect of "vinegar upon natron," Prov. 25:20; comp. Jer. 2:22. The mention of "the apothecary," properly, however, "perfumer," Ex. 30:35; Eccles. 10:1, and of the merchant in "powders," Cant. 3:6, indicates a knowledge of chemistry. Among the favorite external remedies have always been the application of oil, or of oil and wine, and the bath, whether of oil or water. There were special occasions on which the bath was ceremonially enjoined. The Pharisees and Essenes aimed at scrupulous strictness in all such rules. Matt. 15:2; Mark 7:5; Luke 11:38. River-bathing was common, but houses soon began to include a bathroom. Lev. 15:13; 2 Sam. 11:2; 2 Kings 5:10.

Megid'do (mė-gĭd'dò) (*place of troops*) was an old Canaanitish capital in Issachar, but assigned to Manasseh, who did not drive out the original inhabitants. It commanded one of those passes from the north into the hill country which were of such critical importance on various occasions in the history of the Israelites. The first mention occurs in Josh. 12:21, where Megiddo appears as the city of one of the kings whom Joshua defeated on the west of the Jordan. The song of Deborah brings the place vividly before us, as the scene of the great conflict between Sisera and Barak. When Pharaoh-necho came from Egypt against the king of Assyria, Josiah joined the latter, and was slain at Megiddo. 2 Kings 23:29; 2 Chron. 35:22-24. The common identification of Megiddo, is on the plain of Esdraelon, on a spur about 6 miles from Carmel. This is the modern *el-Lejjûn*, which is undoubtedly the Legio of Eusebius and Jerome. There is a copious stream flowing down the gorge, and turning some mills before joining the Kishon. Here are probably the "waters of Megiddo" of Judges 5:19. Other locations are, however, favored by Thomson and Conder. (See cut p. 398.)

Mehet'abeel (me-hĕt'a-be-el) (*God benefits*), another and less correct form of Mehetabel. The ancestor of Shemaiah the prophet who was hired against Nehemiah by Tobiah and Sanballat. Neh. 6:10.

Mehet'abel (me-hĕt'a-bĕl) (*God benefits*), the daughter of Matred, and wife of Hadad king of Edom. Gen. 36:39.

Mehi'da (mė-hī'dà) (*conjunction*), a family of Nethinim, the descendants of Mehida, returned from Babylon with Zerubbabel. Ezra 2:52; Neh. 7:54.

Me'hir (mē'hïr) (*price*), the son of Chelub the brother of Shuah. 1 Chron. 4:11.

Meho'lathite (me-hō'lath-īte), The, a word occurring once only—1 Sam. 18: 19. It no doubt denotes that Adriel belonged to a place called Meholah.

Mehu'jael (me-hū'ja-el) (*smitten by God*), the son of Irad, and fourth in descent from Cain. Gen. 4:18.

Mehu'man (me-hū'man), one of the seven eunuchs of Ahasuerus. Est. 1:10.

Mehu'nim (me-hū'nim) (*people of Maon*). R. V. "Meunim."
A people against whom King Uzziah waged a successful war. 2 Chron. 26: 7. The name is the plural of MAON. Another notice of the Mehunim is found in 1 Chron. 4:41. Here they are spoken of as a pastoral people, quiet and peaceable, dwelling in tents near Gedor. The Authorized Version treats the word here as an ordinary noun, and renders it "habitations." The latest appearance of the name in the Bible is in the lists of those who returned from the captivity with Zerubbabel. Ezra 2:50; Neh. 7:52.

Me=jar′kon (mĕ-jär′kon) (*waters of yellowness*), a town in the territory of Dan, Josh. 19:46 only, in the neighborhood of Joppa.

Meko′nah (me-kō′nà) (*foundation*), one of the towns which were reinhabited after the captivity by the men of Judah. Neh. 11:28.

Melati′ah (mĕl-atī′ah) (*Jehovah hath delivered*), a Gibeonite who assisted in rebuilding the wall of Jerusalem. Neh. 3:7.

Mel′chi (mĕl′kī). **1.** The son of

Mel′chi=shu′a (mĕl′kī-shu′à), a son of Saul. 1 Sam. 14:49; 31:2. Elsewhere correctly given Malchi-shua.

Melchiz′edek (mĕl-kĭz′e-dĕk) (*king of righteousness*), king of Salem and priest of the most high God, who met Abram in the valley of Shaveh, which is the king's vale, brought out bread and wine, blessed him, and received tithes from him. Gen. 14:18–20. The other places in which Melchizedek is mentioned are Ps. 110:4, where Messiah is described as a priest forever,

TELL EL-MUTESELLINE FROM THE NORTH.
The Ancient Megiddo.

WALLS OF MEGIDDO.

Section, uncovered by excavation, of the walls of ancient Megiddo, exhibiting the height and strength of the fortifications of the cities of Canaan. (The figures are in metres.)

Janna, and ancestor of Joseph in the genealogy of Jesus Christ. Luke 3:24. **2.** The son of Addi in the same genealogy. Luke 3:28.

Melchi′ah (mĕl-kī′à) (*Jehovah is king*), a priest, the father of Pashur. Jer. 21:1.

Melchis′edec (mĕl-kĭz′e-dĕk) (*king of righteousness*). Heb. 5, 6, 7. [MEL-CHIZEDEK.]

"after the order of Melchizedek," and Heb. 5, 6, 7, where these two passages of the Old Testament are quoted, and the typical relation of Melchizedek to our Lord is stated at great length. Salem is most probably Jerusalem [SALEM] which is called on the Tel-el-Amarna Tablets *Uru-Salim* or city of Salim. In this case Shaveh would be the "king's dale," where Absalom later set up his pillar. There are interesting statements with regard to the king of Uru-Salim on the Tel-el-Amarna tablets. He begs for help from Egypt, saying "that he was not like the other Egyptian governors in Palestine, nor had he received his crown by inheritance from his father or mother; it had been conferred on him by 'the mighty king,'" who is distinguished from the king of Egypt, and thought by some to mean "the Most High God." However it is explained there is a striking similarity to the priest-king Melchizedek, and the description in Heb. 7 : 3. There is something surprising and mysterious in the first appearance of Melchizedek, and in the subsequent reference to him. Bearing a title which Jews in after ages would recognize as designating their own sovereign, bearing gifts which recall to Christians the Lord's Supper, this Canaanite crosses for a moment the path of Abram, and is unhesitatingly recognized as a person of higher spiritual rank than the friend of God. Disappearing as suddenly as he came, he is lost to the sacred writings for a thousand years. Jewish tradition pronounces Melchizedek to be a survivor of the deluge, the patriarch Shem. The "order of Melchizedek," in Ps. 110 : 4, is explained to mean "manner" = likeness in official dignity = a king and priest. The relation between Melchizedek and Christ as type and antitype is made in the Epistle to the Hebrews to consist in the following particulars: Each was a priest (1) not of the Levitical tribe; (2) superior to Abraham; (3) whose beginning and end are unknown; (4) who is not only a priest, but also a king of righteousness and peace.

Me′lea (mē′le-à), the son of Menan, and ancestor of Joseph in the genealogy of Jesus Christ. Luke 3 : 31.

Me′lech (mē′lek), the second son of Micah, the son of Merib-baal or Mephibosheth. 1 Chron. 8 : 35 ; 9 : 41.

Mel′icu (mĕl′i-cū), the same as MALLUCH 6. Neh. 12 : 14; comp. ver. 2.

Mel′ita (mĕl′ĭ-tà), the modern *Malta.* This island lies in the Mediterranean 60 miles south of Cape Passaro in Sicily. It is 17 miles long by 9 broad in its widest parts. It is naturally a barren rock, with no high mountains, but has been rendered fertile by industry and toil. It is famous for its honey and fruits. It is now in the hands of the English. This island has an illustrious place in Scripture as the scene of that shipwreck of St. Paul which is described in such minute detail in the Acts of the Apostles. Acts 27. The wreck probably happened at the place traditionally known as St. Paul's Bay, an inlet with a creek two miles deep and one broad. Mr. Smith of Jordan Hill, in his "Voyage and Shipwreck of St. Paul," the first published work in which it was thoroughly investigated from a sailor's point of view confirms the opinion of the identity of Malta and Melita. The fact that no vipers are found in the island now does not preclude the possibility of there being some in wilder ancient times. As regards the condition of the island of Melita, when St. Paul was there it was a dependency of the Roman province of Sicily. Its chief officer (under the governor of Sicily) appears from inscriptions to have had the title of πρῶτος Μελιταίων, or *Primus Melitensium,* and this is the very phrase which Luke uses. Acts 28 : 7. Melita, from its position in the Mediterranean and the excellence of its harbors, has always been important in both commerce and war. It was a settlement of the Phœnicians at an early period, and their language, in a corrupted form, was still spoken there in St. Paul's day.

Melons (Heb. *abattichîm*) are mentioned only in Num. 11 : 5. By the Hebrew word we are probably to understand both the melon (*Cucumis melo*) and the watermelon (*Cucurbita citrullus*). Melons of excellent quality are still produced in Egypt, Palestine and Syria. The watermelons of Jaffa are specially prized.

Melzar (mĕl′zar) (*steward*). The Authorized Version is wrong in regarding melzar as a proper name; it is rather an official title, Dan. 1 : 11, 16; the reading, "the steward," of the R. V. and the A. V. margin, is therefore more correct.

Mem′phis (mĕm′fĭs) (*the good abode*), a city of ancient Egypt, situated on the western bank of the Nile, about nine miles south of Cairo and five from the great pyramids and the sphinx. It is mentioned by Isaiah, Isa. 19 : 13, Jeremiah, Jer. 2 : 16; 46 : 14, 19, and Ezekiel. Ezek. 30 : 13, 16, under the name of Noph; by Hosea (9 : 6) as

Memphis. (Hebrew, *Moph.*) It is said to have been built by Menes, the first historical king who lived before 3000 B.C. Successive kings built new suburbs, till it is impossible to determine where the original city was. In the end it extended 17 miles from north to south along the Nile, and was probably 3 miles broad. The temple of Apis was one of the most noted structures of Memphis. It stood opposite the southern portico of the temple of Ptah; and Psammetichus, who built that gateway, also erected in front of the sanctuary of Apis a magnificent colonnade, supported by colossal statues or Osiride pillars, such as may still be seen at the temple of Medeenet Habou at Thebes. Herod. ii. 153. Through this colonnade the Apis was led with great pomp upon state occasions. At Memphis was the reputed burial-place of Isis; it had also a temple to that "myriad-named" divinity. Memphis had also its Serapeium, which probably stood in the western quarter of the city. The sacred cubit and other symbols used in measuring the rise of the Nile were deposited in the temple of Serapis. The Necropolis, adjacent to Memphis, was on a scale of grandeur corresponding with the city itself. Usually travelers only visit the most remarkable group of royal tombs, the pyramids, that at Gizeh. But there are some 50 others, smaller or more dilapidated. The "city of the pyramids" is a title of Memphis in the hieroglyphics upon the monuments. Memphis long held its place as a capital; and for centuries a Memphite dynasty ruled over all Egypt. The third, fourth, sixth, seventh and eighth dynasties of the old empire are regarded by good authorities as Memphite, reaching through a period of about 1000 years. The city's overthrow was distinctly predicted by the Hebrew prophets. Isa. 19: 13; Jer. 46: 19. The latest of these predictions was uttered nearly 600 years before Christ, and half a century before the invasion of Egypt by Cambyses (*cir.* B.C. 525). Herodotus informs us that Cambyses, enraged at the opposition he encountered at Memphis, committed many outrages upon the city. The city never recovered from the blow. The rise of Alexandria hastened its decline. The caliph conquerors founded Fostát (old Cairo) upon the opposite bank of the Nile, a few miles north of Memphis, and brought materials from the old city to build their new capital, A.D. 638. At length so complete was the ruin of Memphis that for a long time its very site was lost. Recent explorations have brought to light many of its antiquities.

Memu'can (me-mū'kan), one of the seven princes of Persia in the reign of Ahasuerus, who "saw the king's face," and sat first in the kingdom. Esther 1: 14, 16, 21.

Men'ahem (men'a-hĕm) (*comforter*), son of Gadi, who slew the usurper Shallum, and seized the vacant throne of Israel, B.C. 741. His reign is briefly recorded in 2 Kings 15: 14-22. He maintained the calf-worship of Jeroboam. The contemporary prophet Hosea has left a melancholy picture of the ungodliness, demoralization and feebleness of Israel. Menahem reigned B.C. 741-737, his date being better fixed than some of the rest, because of the tribute given by him to Assyria B.C. 738, as recorded in the Assyrian sculptures. This was soon after he seized the throne.

Me'nan (me'nan) (called Menna in the Revised Version), one of the ancestors of Joseph in the genealogy of Jesus Christ. Luke 3: 31.

Mene (me'ne) (*numbered*), the first word of the mysterious inscription written upon the wall of Belshazzar's palace, in which Daniel read the doom of the king and his dynasty. Dan. 5: 25, 26.

Me'ni (me'ni) (*fate, fortune*). Isa. 65: 11. This word is the name of an object of idolatrous worship cultivated by the Jews in Babylon.

Men'na. In the Revised Version of Luke 3: 31 for Menan.

Meon'enim (me-ŏn'e-nim), **The plain of.** More correctly as in R. V. "the oak of Meonenim"—and better still as in R. V. margin "the augurs' oak," (or terebinth), Judges 9: 37.

Meon'othai (me-ŏn'o-thī) (*my habitations*), one of the sons of Othniel, the younger brother of Caleb. 1 Chron. 4: 14.

Meph'a-ath (mĕf'a-ăth) (*splendor, beauty*), a city of the Reubenites, one of the towns dependent on Heshbon, Josh. 13: 18, lying in the district of the Mishor, comp. ver. 17 and Jer. 48: 21. It was one of the cities allotted with their suburbs to the Merarite Levites. Josh. 21: 37; 1 Chron. 6: 79. Its site is uncertain.

Mephib'osheth (mĕ-fĭb'o-shĕth) (*destroying shame*), the name borne by two members of the family of Saul—his son and his grandson. 1. Saul's son by Rizpah the daughter of Aiah, his concubine. 2 Sam. 21:8. He and his brother Armoni were among the seven victims who were surrendered by David to the Gibeonites, and by them crucified to avert a famine from which the country was suffering.

2. The son of Jonathan, grandson of Saul and nephew of the preceding; called also Merib-baal. 1 Chron. 8:34. His life seems to have been, from beginning to end, one of trial and discomfort. When his father and grandfather were slain on Gilboa he was an infant but five years old. At this age he met with an accident which deprived him for life of the use of both feet. 2 Sam. 4:4. After this he found a home with Machir ben-Ammiel, a powerful Gadite, who brought him up, and while here was married. Later on David invited him to Jerusalem, and there treated him and his son Micha with the greatest kindness. From this time forward he resided at Jerusalem. Of Mephibosheth's behavior during the rebellion of Absalom we possess two accounts—his own, 2 Sam. 19:24–30, and that of Ziba, 2 Sam. 16:1-4. They are naturally at variance with each other. In consequence of the story of Ziba, he was rewarded by the possessions of his master. Mephibosheth's story—which, however, he had not the opportunity of telling until several days later, when he met David returning to his kingdom at the western bank of Jordan—was very different from Ziba's. That David did not disbelieve it is shown by his revoking the judgment he had previously given. That he did not entirely reverse his decision, but allowed Ziba to retain possession of half the lands of Mephibosheth, is probably due partly to weariness at the whole transaction, but mainly to the conciliatory frame of mind in which he was at that moment. "Shall there any man be put to death this day?" is the keynote of the whole proceeding.

Me'rab (me'răb) (*increase*), the elder daughter of King Saul. 1 Sam. 14:49. In accordance with the promise which he made before the engagement with Goliath, ch. 17:25, Saul betrothed Merab to David, ch. 18:17. The promise was ignored, however, and Merab

was married to Adriel the Meholathite, to whom she bore five sons. 1 Sam. 18:19; 2 Sam. 21:8.

Mera'iah (me-rā'iah) (*contumacy*), a priest in the days of Joiakim. Neh. 12:12.

Mera'ioth (mĕ-rā'ioth) (*rebellious*). 1. A descendant of Eleazar the son of Aaron, and head of a priestly house. 1 Chron. 6:6, 7, 52.

2. Another priest who comes between Zadok and Ahitub in the genealogy of Azariah. 1 Chron. 9:11; Neh. 11:11.

3. The head of one of the houses of priests, which in the time of Joiakim the son of Jeshua was represented by Helkai. Neh. 12:15.

Mera'ri (me-rā'rī), **Mera'rites** (mĕ-rā'rītes) (*bitter, unhappy*), third son of Levi, and head of the third great division of the Levites, the Merarites. Gen. 46:8, 11. At the time of the Exodus and the numbering in the wilderness, the Merarites consisted of two families, the Mahlites and the Mushites. Their chief at that time was Zuriel. Their charge was the boards, bars, pillars, sockets, pins and cords of the tabernacle and the court, and all the tools connected with setting them up. In the division of the land by Joshua, the Merarites had twelve cities assigned to them, out of Reuben, Gad and Zebulun. Josh. 21:7, 34–40; 1 Chron. 6:63, 77–81. In the days of Hezekiah the Merarites were still flourishing. 2 Chron. 29:12, 15.

Meratha'im (mĕr-a-thā'im) (*double rebellion*), **The land of,** alluding to the country of Babylonia. Its significance is unknown. Jer. 50:21.

Mercu'rius (mĕr-kū'rĭ-us), properly Hermes, the Greek deity, whom the Romans identified with their Mercury, the god of commerce and bargains. Hermes was the son of Zeus (Jupiter) and Maia the daughter of Atlas, and is constantly represented as the companion of his father in his wandering upon earth. The episode of Baucis and Philemon, Ovid, *Metam.* viii. 620–724, appears to have formed part of the folk-lore of Asia Minor, and strikingly illustrates the readiness with which the simple people of Lystra recognized in Barnabas and Paul the gods who, according to their wont, had come down in the likeness of men. Acts 14:11.

Mer'cury, Acts 14:12, the translation of the above in the Revised Version.

Mercy=seat. Ex. 25:17; 37:6; Heb.

9 : 5. The lid of the ark of the covenant. It was a solid plate of gold, 2½ cubits long by 1½ cubits wide on each end of which were figures of cherubim, and represented a kind of throne of God, where he would hear prayer and from which he spoke words of comfort. It was that whereon the blood of the yearly atonement was sprinkled by the high priest; and in this relation it is doubtful whether the sense of the word in the Hebrew is based on the material fact of its "covering" the ark, or derived from this notion of its reference to the "covering" (*i. e.* atonement) of sin.

Me'red (mē'red) (*rebellion*). This name occurs in a fragmentary genealogy in 1 Chron. 4 : 17, 18, as that of one of the sons of Ezra.

Mer'emoth (mĕr'ĕ-mōth) (*elevations*). 1. Son of Uriah or Urijah the priest, of the family of Koz or Hakkoz, the head of the seventh course of priests as established by David. In Ezra 8 : 33 Meremoth is appointed to weigh and register the gold and silver vessels belonging to the temple. In the rebuilding of the wall of Jerusalem under Nehemiah we find Meremoth taking an active part. Neh. 3 : 4, 21. 2. A layman of the sons of Bani, who had married a foreign wife. Ezra 10 : 36. 3. A priest, or more probably a family of priests, who sealed the covenant with Nehemiah. Neh. 10 : 5. Perhaps same as 1.

Me'res (mē'rēz), one of the seven counsellors of Ahasuerus. Esther 1 : 14.

Mer'ibah (mĕr'i-bah) (*strife, contention*). In Ex. 17 : 7 we read, "he called the name of the place Massah and Meribah," where the people murmured and the rock was smitten. [For the situation see REPHIDIM.] The name is also given to Kadesh, Num. 20 : 13, 24; 27 : 14; Deut. 32 : 51 (Meribah-kadesh), because there also the people, when in want of water, strove with God.

Merib=ba'al (mĕr-ĭb-bā'ăl) (*contender against Baal*). 1 Chron. 8 : 34; 9 : 40. [See MEPHIBOSHETH, 2.]

Mer'odach (mer'ō-dăk), Jer. 50 : 2, identical with the famous Babylonian Bel or Belus, the word being probably at first a mere epithet of the god, which by degrees superseded his proper appellation.

Mer'odach=bal'adan (mer'ō-dăk-băl'-a-dăn) (*Merodach hath given a son*), is mentioned as king of Babylon in the days of Hezekiah both in 2 Kings 20 : 12, and in Isaiah 39 : 1. In the former place he is called Berodach-baladan, the son of Baladan. The name of Merodach-baladan has been recognized in the Assyrian inscriptions. It appears there were two reigns of this king, the first from B.C. 721 to B.C. 709, when he was deposed; and the second after his recovery of the throne in B.C. 702, which lasted only half a year. About B.C. 711 he saw the danger he was in from Assyria and sent an embassy to rulers in the west proposing an alliance. That to Hezekiah was ostensibly to congratulate him on his recovery. Before the alliance could be perfected the blow had fallen, and he was deposed.

Me'rom (mē'rom), **The, waters of,** a lake formed by the river Jordan, about 11 miles north of the Sea of Galilee. It is a place memorable in the history of the conquest of Palestine. Here Joshua completely routed the confederacy of the northern chiefs under Jabin. Josh. 11 : 5, 7. It is a remarkable fact that though by common consent "the waters of Merom" are identified with the lake through which the Jordan runs between Banias and the Sea of Galilee—the *Bahr el-Hûleh* of the modern Arabs—yet that identity cannot be proved by any ancient record. In form the lake is not far from a triangle, the base being at the north and the apex at the south. It measures about 3 miles in each direction, and 11 to 16 feet deep. The water is clear and sweet; it is covered in parts by a broad-leaved plant, and abounds in water-fowl. The northern part is a dense swamp of papyrus reeds, as large as the lake itself. See "Rob Roy on the Jordan."

Meron'othite (mĕ-rŏn'ōthīte), **The,** that is, the native of a place called probably Meronoth, of which, however, no further traces have yet been discovered. Two Meronothites are named in the Bible—1. Jehdeiah, 1 Chron. 27 : 30; 2. Jadon. Neh. 3 : 7.

Me'roz (mē'rŏz) (*refuge*), a place, Judges 5 : 23, denounced because its inhabitants had refused to take any part in the struggle with Sisera. Its real position is unknown, though the site *el-Murussus* 9 miles east of Jezreel is thought to answer the conditions.

Me'sech (mĕ'sek), **Me'shech,** a son of Japhet, Gen. 10:2; 1 Chron. 1:5, and the progenitor of a race frequently noticed in Scripture in connection with Tubal, Magog and other northern nations. They appear as allies of Gog, Ezek. 38:2, 3; 39:1, and as supplying the Tyrians with copper and slaves. Ezek. 27:13. Both the name and the associations are in favor of the identification of Meshech with the *Moschi,* a people on the borders of Colchis and Armenia.

Me'sha. 1. The name of one of the geographical limits of the Joktanites when they first settled in Arabia. Gen. 10:30.

2. The king of Moab who was tributary to Ahab, 2 Kings 3:4; but when Ahab fell at Ramoth-gilead, Mesha refused to pay tribute to his successor, Ahaziah. When Jehoram succeeded to the throne of Israel, one of his first acts was to secure the assistance of Jehoshaphat, his father's ally, in reducing the Moabites to their former condition of tributaries. The Moabites were defeated, and the king took refuge in his last stronghold, and defended himself with the energy of despair. With 700 fighting men he made a vigorous attempt to cut his way through the beleaguering army, and when beaten back, he withdrew to the wall of his city, and there, in sight of the allied host, offered his first-born son, his successor in the kingdom, as a burnt offering to Chemosh, the ruthless fire-god of Moab. His bloody sacrifice had so far the desired effect that the besiegers retired from him to their own land. The famous Moabite Stone, contains inscriptions concerning King Mesha and his wars, which confirm the Bible account.

3. The eldest son of Caleb the son of Hezron. 1 Chron. 2:42.

4. A Benjamite, son of Shaharaim by his wife Hodesh, who bore him in the land of Moab. 1 Chron. 8:9.

Me'shach (mĕ'shak) (*guest of a king*), the name given to Mishael, one of the companions of Daniel, who with three others was chosen from among the captives to be taught, Dan. 1:4, and qualified to "stand before" King Nebuchadnezzar, Dan. 1:5, as his personal attendants and advisers. Dan. 1:20. But notwithstanding their Chaldean education, these three young Hebrews were strongly attached to the religion of their fathers; and their refusal to join in the worship of the image on the plain of Dura gave a handle of accusation to the Chaldeans. The rage of the king, the swift sentence of condemnation passed upon the three offenders, their miraculous preservation from the fiery furnace heated seven times hotter than usual, the king's acknowledgment of the God of Shadrach, Meshach and Abed-, nego, with their restoration to office, are written in the third chapter of Daniel, and there the history leaves them.

Meshelemi'ah (mĕ-shĕl-e-mī'ah) (*Jehovah recompenses*), a Korhite porter or gate-keeper of the house of Jehovah. 1 Chron. 9:21; 26:1, 2, 9. In 1 Chron. 26:14 he is called Shelemiah.

Meshez'abeel (mĕ-shĕz'a-be-el) (*God sets free*). 1. Ancestor of Meshullam, who assisted Nehemiah in rebuilding the wall of Jerusalem. Neh. 3:4.

2. One of the "heads of the people," probably a family, who sealed the covenant with Nehemiah. Neh. 10:21.

3. The father of Pethahiah, and descendant of Zerah the son of Judah. Neh. 11:24.

Meshil'lemith (mĕ-shĭl'le-mĭth) (*recompense*), the son of Immer, a priest. Neh. 11:13; 1 Chron. 9:12.

Meshil'lemoth (mĕ-shĭl'le-mōth) (*recompense*). 1. An Ephraimite, one of the chiefs of the tribe in the reign of Pekah. 2 Chron. 28:12.

2. The same as MESHILLEMITH. Neh. 11:13.

Meshul'lam (mĕ-shŭl'lam) (*friend*). 1. Ancestor of Shaphan the scribe. 2 Kings 22:3.

2. The son of Zerubbabel. 1 Chron. 3:19.

3. A Gadite in the land of Bashan. 1 Chron. 5:13.

4. A Benjamite, of the sons of Elpaal. 1 Chron. 8:17.

5. A Benjamite, father of Sallu. 1 Chron. 9:7; Neh. 11:7

6. A Benjamite who lived at Jerusalem after the captivity. 1 Chron. 9:8.

7. The same as Shallum, who was high priest probably in the reign of Amon, and father of Hilkiah. 1 Chron. 9:11; Neh. 11:11.

8. A priest, son of Meshillemith or Meshillemoth the son of Immer, and ancestor of Maasai or Amashai. 1 Chron. 9:12; comp. Neh. 11:13.

9. A Kohathite or a family of Kohath-

ite Levites, in the reign of Josiah. 2 Chron. 34 : 12.

10. One of the "heads" sent by Ezra to Iddo, "the head," to gather together the Levites to join the caravan about to return to Jerusalem. Ezra 8 : 16.

11. A chief man who opposed abolishing the marriages which some of the people had contracted with foreign wives. Ezra 10 : 15.

12. One of the descendants of Bani, who had married a foreign wife and put her away. Ezra 10 : 29.

13. Neh. 3 : 30; 6 : 18. The son of Berechiah, who assisted in rebuilding the wall of Jerusalem. Neh. 3 : 4.

14. The son of Besodeiah: he assisted Jehoiada the son of Paseah in restoring the old gate of Jerusalem. Neh. 3 : 6.

15. One of those who stood at the left hand of Ezra when he read the law to the people. Neh. 8 : 4.

16. A priest or family of priests who sealed the covenant with Nehemiah. Neh. 10 : 7.

17. One of the heads of the people who did so. Neh. 10 : 20.

18. A priest in the days of Joiakim the son of Jeshua, and representative of the house of Ezra. Neh. 12 : 13.

19. Also a priest, head of the priestly family of Ginnethon. Neh. 12 : 16.

20. A family of porters, descendants of Meshullam, Neh. 12 : 25.

21. One of the princes of Judah at the dedication of the wall of Jerusalem. Neh. 12 : 33.

Meshul'lemeth (mé-shŭl'le-mĕth) (*friend*), the daughter of Haruz of Jotbah, wife of Manasseh king of Judah, and mother of Amon. 2 Kings 21 : 19.

Meso'baite (mé-sō'ba-ite), **The,** a title attached to the name of Jasiel. 1 Chron. 11 : 47. It is impossible to decide to what it refers.

Mesopota'mia (mĕs-o-pŏ-tā'mĭ-à) (*between the rivers*), the entire country between two rivers, the Tigris and the Euphrates, the Greek name for that known earlier by the name of *Aram-Naharaim*. *Padan* (or Paddan) *Aram* was a name applied to the northern portion. We first hear of Mesopotamia in Scripture as the country where Nahor and his family settled after quitting Ur of the Chaldees. Gen. 24 : 10. Here lived Bethuel and Laban; and hither Abraham sent his servants to fetch Isaac a wife. Gen. 24 : 38. Hither too, a century later, came Jacob on the same errand; and hence he returned with his two wives after an absence of twenty-one years. After this we have no mention of Mesopotamia till the close of the wanderings in the wilderness. Deut. 23 : 4. About half a century later we find, for the first and last time, Mesopotamia the seat of a powerful monarchy, which oppressed the Israelites. Judges 3. Finally, the children of Ammon, having provoked a war with David, "sent a thousand talents of silver to hire them chariots and horsemen out of Mesopotamia, and out of Syria-maachah, and out of Zobah." 1 Chron. 19 : 6. According to the Assyrian inscriptions Mesopotamia was inhabited in the early times of the empire, by a vast number of petty tribes, each under its own prince. The Assyrian monarchs contended with these chiefs at great advantage, and by the time of Jehu, B.C. 838, had fully established their dominion over them. On the destruction of the Assyrian empire, Mesopotamia seems to have been divided between the Medes and the Babylonians. The conquests of Cyrus brought it wholly under the Persian yoke; and thus it continued to the time of Alexander. After 1516 it was a part of the Turkish empire until the time of the World War. It then came under British mandate with a native king, chosen directly by the people, as a constitutional sovereign. Its present name is *The Kingdom of Iraq*. In 1920 the kingdom had a population of about 3,000,000, of which about 250,000 were in the capital city of Baghdad. It is full of ruins and mounds of ancient cities, some of which are now throwing much light on the Scripture.

Messi'ah (mĕs-sī'ah) (*anointed*). This word answers to the word *Christ* (Χριστός) in the New Testament, and is applicable in its first sense to any one anointed with the holy oil. The kings of Israel were called *anointed*, from the mode of their consecration. 1 Sam. 2 : 10, 35; 12 : 3, 5, etc. This word also refers to the expected Prince of the chosen people who was to complete God's purposes for them and to redeem them, and of whose coming the prophets of the old covenant in all time spoke. He was the Messiah, the *Anointed*, i. e. consecrated as the king and prophet by God's appointment. The word is twice used in the New Testament of Jesus. John 1 : 41; 4 : 25; Authorized Version

"Messias." The earliest gleam of the gospel is found in the account of the fall. Gen. 3 : 15. The blessings in store for the children of Shem are remarkably indicated in the words of Noah. Gen. 9 : 26. Next follows the promise to Abraham. Gen. 12 : 2, 3. A great step is made in Gen. 49 : 10. This is the first case in which the promises distinctly centre in one person. The next passage usually quoted is the prophecy of Balaam. Num. 24 : 17–19. The prophecy of Moses, Deut. 18 : 18, claims attention. Passages in the Psalms are numerous which are applied to the Messiah in the New Testament; such as Ps. 2, 16, 22, 40, 110. The advance in clearness in this period is great. The name of Anointed, *i. e.* King, comes in, and the Messiah is to come of the lineage of David. He is described in his exaltation with his great kingdom that shall be spiritual rather than temporal. Ps. 2, 21, 40, 110. In other places he is seen in suffering and humiliation. Ps. 16, 22, 40. Later on the prophets show the Messiah as a king and ruler of David's house, who should come to reform and restore the Jewish nation and purify the Church, as in Isa. 11, 40–66. The blessings of the restoration, however, will not be confined to Jews; the heathen are made to share them fully. Isa. 2, 66. The passage of Micah 5 : 2 (comp. Matt. 2 : 6) left no doubt in the mind of the Sanhedrin as to the birthplace of the Messiah. The lineage of David is again alluded to in Zech. 12 : 10–14. The coming of the Forerunner and of the Anointed is clearly revealed in Mal. 3 : 1; 4 : 5, 6. The Pharisees and those of the Jews who expected Messiah at all looked for a temporal prince only. The apostles themselves were infected with this opinion till after the resurrection. Matt. 20 : 20, 21; Luke 24 : 21; Acts 1 : 6. Gleams of a purer faith appear in Luke 2 : 30; 23 : 42; John 4 : 25.

Messi′as (mĕs-sī′as) (*anointed*), the Greek form of Messiah. John 1 : 41; 4 : 25.

Metals. The metals in use in ancient times were gold, silver, iron, lead, copper and tin. One of the earliest geographical definitions is that which describes the country of Havilah as the land which abounded in *gold,* and the gold of which was good. Gen. 2 : 11, 12. "Abram was very rich in cattle, in silver, and in gold," Gen. 13 : 2; silver, as will be shown hereafter, being the medium of commerce, while gold existed in the shape of ornaments, during the patriarchal ages. *Tin* is first mentioned Num. 31 : 22, and *lead* is used to heighten the imagery of Moses' triumphal song. Ex. 15 : 10. Whether the ancient Hebrews were acquainted with *steel,* properly so called, is uncertain; the words so rendered in the Authorized Version, 2 Sam. 22 : 35; Job 20 : 24; Ps. 18 : 34; Jer. 15 : 12, are in all other passages translated *brass* and the R. V. corrects these themselves to *brass.* It is supposed that the Hebrews used the mixture of copper and tin known as *bronze,* rather than brass as we know it. The great abundance of gold in early times is indicated by its entering into the composition of all articles of ornament and almost all of domestic use. The Hebrews obtained their principal supply from the south of Arabia and the commerce of the Persian Gulf. Josh. 7 : 21. Among the spoils of the Midianites taken by the Israelites in their decisive victory when Balaam was slain were ear-rings and jewels to the amount of 16,750 shekels of gold, Num. 31 : 48–54, equal in value to either about $81,000 or $162,000 according to the standard in use. This does not take into account the greater purchasing value then. Seventeen hundred shekels of gold (worth about $8000 to $16,000) in nose jewels (Authorized Version " ear-rings ") alone were taken by Gideon's army from the slaughtered Midianites. Judges 8 : 26. But the amount of treasure accumulated by David from spoils taken in war is so enormous that we are tempted to conclude the numbers exaggerated. Though gold was thus common, silver appears to have been the ordinary medium of commerce. The first commercial transaction of which we possess the details was the purchase of Ephron's field by Abraham for 400 shekels of *silver.* Gen. 23 : 16. The accumulation of wealth in the reign of Solomon was so great that silver was but little esteemed. 1 Kings 10 : 21, 27. Brass, or more properly copper, was a native product of some parts of Palestine. Deut. 8 : 9; Job 28 : 2. It was plentiful in the days of Solomon, and the quantity employed in the temple could not be estimated, it was so great. 1 Kings 7 : 47. No allusion is found to zinc; but tin was well known. Arms, 2 Sam. 21 : 16; Job 20 : 24; Ps. 18 : 34, and armor, 1 Sam. 17:5, 6, 38, were made of copper, which was capable of being so wrought as to admit of a keen and hard edge. Iron was found in the hills at the foot of Lebanon.

Me'theg=am'mah (mē'theg-am'mah) (*bridle of the mother city*), a place which David took from the Philistines, apparently in his last war with them. 2 Sam. 8:1. Ammah may be taken as meaning " mother-city " or " metropolis," comp. 2 Sam. 20:19, and Metheg-ha-Ammah " the bridle of the mother-city " —viz. of Gath, the chief town of the Philistines.

Methu'sael (mė-thụ'sa-el) (*man of God*), the son of Mehujael, fourth in descent from Cain, and father of Lamech. Gen. 4:18.

Methu'selah (mė-thụ'se-lah) (*man of the dart*), the son of Enoch, sixth in descent from Seth, and father of Lamech. Gen. 5:25–27.

Meu'nim (mė-ū'nim) (*people of Maon*). Neh. 7:52. Elsewhere given in Authorized Version as Mehunim and Mehunims.

Mez'ahab (mĕz'a-häb) (*waters of gold*), the father of Matred and grandfather of Mehetabel, who was wife of Hadar or Hadad, king of Edom. Gen. 36:39; 1 Chron. 1:50.

Mi'amin (mĭ'a-min) (*from the right hand*). 1. A layman of Israel who had married a foreign wife and put her away at the bidding of Ezra. Ezra 10:25.

2. A priest or family of priests who went up from Babylon with Zerubbabel. Neh. 12:5.

Mib'har (mĭb'här) (*choice*), one of David's heroes in the list given in 1 Chron. 11:38.

Mib'sam (mĭb'sam) (*sweet odor*). 1. A son of Ishmael. Gen. 25:13; 1 Chron. 1:29.

2. A son of Simeon. 1 Chron. 4:25.

Mib'zar (mĭb'zar) (*fortress*), one of the " dukes " of Edom. Gen. 36:42; 1 Chron. 1:53.

Mi'cah (mĭ'kah) (*who is like Jehovah?*), an abbreviation of " Micaiah." 1. An Israelite whose familiar story is preserved in the 17th and 18th chapters of Judges. Micah is evidently a devout believer in Jehovah, and yet so completely ignorant is he of the law of Jehovah that the mode which he adopts of honoring him is to make a molten and graven image, teraphim or images of domestic gods, and to set up an un-authorized priesthood, first in his own family, Judges 17:5, and then in the person of a Levite not of the priestly line. ver. 12. A body of 600 Danites break in upon and steal his idols from him.

2. The sixth in order of the minor prophets. He is called the Morasthite, that is, a native of Moresheth, or Moresheth-Gath, an unidentified site in Judah, near the Philistine country. Micah exercised the prophetical office during the reigns of Jotham, Ahaz and Hezekiah, kings of Judah. He was contemporary with Hosea and Amos during the part of their ministry in Israel, and with Isaiah in Judah.

3. A descendant of Joel the Reubenite. 1 Chron. 5:5.

4. The son of Meribbaal or Mephibosheth, the son of Jonathan. 1 Chron. 8:34, 35; 9:40, 41. [MICHA.]

5. A Kohathite Levite, the eldest son of Uzziel the brother of Amram. 1 Chron. 23:20.

6. The father of Abdon, a man of high station in the reign of Josiah. 2 Chron. 34:20.

Mi'cah, The book of, was written during the time of Isaiah. The prophecies were written at different times, or the collection of prophecies included other authors. The contents and style are very diverse, but either theory will account for the diversity. Three sections of this work represent three natural divisions of the prophecy—1, 2; 3–5; 6, 7—each commencing with rebukes and threatening and closing with a promise. The first section opens with a magnificent description of the coming of Jehovah to judgment for the sins and idolatries of Israel and Judah, ch. 1:2–4, and the sentence pronounced upon Samaria, vs. 5–9, by the Judge himself. The sentence of captivity is passed upon them, Micah 2:10, but is followed instantly by a promise of restoration and triumphant return, ch. 2:12, 13. The second section is addressed especially to the princes and heads of the people: their avarice and rapacity are rebuked in strong terms; but the threatening is again succeeded by a promise of restoration. In the last section, chs. 6, 7, Jehovah, by a bold poetical figure, is represented as holding a controversy with his people, pleading with them in justification of his conduct toward them and the reasonableness of his requirements.

The whole concludes with a triumphal song of joy at the great deliverance, like that from Egypt, which Jehovah will achieve, and a full acknowledgment of his mercy and faithfulness to his promises. vs. 16–20. The last verse is reproduced in the song of Zacharias, Luke 1:72, 73. Micah's prophecies are distinct and clear. He it is who says that the Ruler shall spring from Bethlehem. ch. 5:2. His style has been compared with that of Hosea and Isaiah. His diction is vigorous and forcible, sometimes obscure from the abruptness of its transitions, but varied and rich.

Mica′iah (mī-kā′yà) (*who is like Jehovah?*). Micaiah, the son of Imlah, was a prophet of Samaria, who in the last year of the reign of Ahab king of Israel predicted his defeat and death, B.C. 855. 1 Kings 22:1–35; 2 Chron. 18.

Mi′cha (mī′ka) (*who is like Jehovah?*). 1. The son of Mephibosheth. 2 Sam. 9:12. [MICAH.]

2. A Levite who signed the covenant with Nehemiah. Neh. 10:11.

3. The father of Mattaniah, a Gershonite Levite and descendant of Asaph. Neh. 11:17, 22.

Mi′chael (mī′kĕl) (*who is like God?*). 1. An Asherite, father of Sethur, one of the twelve spies. Num. 13:13.

2. One of the Gadites who settled in the land of Bashan. 1 Chron. 5:13.

3. Another Gadite, ancestor of Abihail. 1 Chron. 5:14.

4. A Gershonite Levite, ancestor of Asaph. 1 Chron. 6:40.

5. One of the five sons of Izrahiah, of the tribe of Issachar. 1 Chron. 7:3.

6. A Benjamite of the sons of Beriah. 1 Chron. 8:16.

7. One of the captains of the "thousands" of Manasseh who joined David at Ziklag. 1 Chron. 12:20.

8. The father or ancestor of Omri, chief of the tribe of Issachar in the reign of David. 1 Chron. 27:18.

9. One of the sons of Jehoshaphat who were murdered by their elder brother, Jehoram. 2 Chron. 21:2, 4.

10. The father or ancestor of Zebadiah, of the sons of Shephatiah. Ezra 8:8.

11. "One," or "the first," of the chief princes" or archangels, Dan. 10:13; comp. Jude 9, described in Dan. 10:21 as the "prince" of Israel, and in ch. 12:1 as "the great prince which standeth" in time of conflict "for the children of thy people." In Rev. 12:7 he is the leader of the hosts of God in war.

Mi′chah (mī′kah) (*who is like Jehovah?*), eldest son of Uzziel the son of Kohath, 1 Chron. 24:24, 25; called MICAH in 1 Chron. 23:20.

Micha′iah (mī-kā′yà) (*who is like Jehovah?*). 1. Same as MICAH 6. 2 Kings 23:12.

2. Same as MICHA 3. 1 Chron. 9:15; Neh. 12:35.

3. One of the priests at the dedication of the wall of Jerusalem. Neh. 12:41.

4. The daughter of Uriel of Gibeah, wife of Rehoboam and mother of Abijah king of Judah. 2 Chron. 13:2. [MAACHAH, 3.]

5. One of the princes of Jehoshaphat whom he sent to teach the law of Jehovah in the cities of Judah. 2 Chron. 17:7.

6. The son of Gemariah. He is only mentioned on one occasion. Jer. 36:11, 13, 14.

Mi′chal (mī′kal), the younger of Saul's two daughters, 1 Sam. 14:49, who married David. The price fixed on Michal's hand was no less than the slaughter of a hundred Philistines. David by a brilliant feat doubled the tale of victims, and Michal became his wife. Shortly afterward she saved David from the assassins whom her father had sent to take his life. 1 Sam. 19:11–17. When the rupture between Saul and David had become open and incurable, she was married to another man, Phalti or Phaltiel of Gallim. 1 Sam. 25:44. After the death of her father and brothers at Gilboa, David compelled her new husband to surrender Michal to him. 2 Sam. 3:13–16. How Michal comported herself in the altered circumstances of David's household we are not told; but it is plain from the subsequent occurrences that something had happened to alter the relations of herself and David, for on the day of David's greatest triumph, when he brought the ark of Jehovah to Jerusalem, we are told that "she despised him in her heart." All intercourse between her and David ceased from that date. 2 Sam. 6:20–23. Her name appears, 2 Sam. 21:8, as the mother of five of the grandchildren of Saul. Given as Merab in 1 Sam. 18:19.

Mich′mas, or **Mich′mash** (mĭk′mash) (*hidden*), a town which is known to us almost solely by its connection with the

MIC 408 MIG

Philistine war of Saul and Jonathan. 1 Sam. 13, 14. It has been identified with great probability in a village which still bears the name of *Mŭkhmas,* about seven miles north of Jerusalem. The place was thus situated in the very middle of the tribe of Benjamin. In the invasion of Sennacherib in the reign of Hezekiah, it is mentioned by Isaiah, Isa. 10:28. After the captivity the men of the place returned. Ezra 2:27; Neh. 7:31. At a later date it became the residence of Jonathan Maccabæus and the seat of his government. 1 Macc. 9:73. In the time of Eusebius and Jerome it was "a very large village, retaining its ancient name, and lying near Ramah in the district of Ælia (Jerusalem), at nine miles distance therefrom." Immediately below the village the great wady spreads out to a considerable width—perhaps half a mile; and its bed is broken up into an intricate mass of hummocks and mounds, two of which, before the torrents of three thousand winters had reduced and rounded their forms, were probably the two "teeth of cliff"—the Bozez and Seneh of Jonathan's adventure.

Mich'methah (mĭk'me-thah), a place which formed one of the landmarks of the boundary of the territories of Ephraim and Manasseh on the western side of Jordan. Josh. 17:7. The position of the place must be somewhere on the east of and not far distant from Shechem.

Mich'ri (mĭch'rĭ) (*worthy of price*), ancestor of Elah, one of the heads of the fathers of Benjamin. 1 Chron. 9:8.

Michtam (mĭk'tam) (*inscription*). This word occurs in the titles of six psalms (16, 56–60), all of which are ascribed to David. The marginal reading of our Authorized Version is "*a golden* psalm," while in the Geneva version it is described as "a certain tune." A more general opinion is, a carefully wrought out memorial psalm, like an inscription.

Mid'din (mĭd'din) (*extensions*), a city of Judah, Josh. 15:61, one of the six specified as situated in the district of "the midbar," "wilderness."

Mid'ian (mĭd'ĭ-an) (*strife*), a son of Abraham and Keturah, Gen. 25:2; 1 Chron. 1:32; progenitor of the Midianites, or Arabians dwelling principally in the desert north of the peninsula of Arabia. Southward they extended along the eastern shore of the Gulf of Eyleh (*Sinus Ælaniticus*): and northward they stretched along the eastern frontier of Palestine. The "land of Midian," the place to which Moses fled after having killed the Egyptian, Ex. 2:15, 21, or the portion of it specially referred to, was probably the peninsula of Sinai. The character of the Midianites is differently portrayed in different accounts. Jethro, priest of Midian, the Midianite father-in-law of Moses, and Hobab his son were good friends to the Israelites during their wanderings, and their descendants, under the name of Kenites, were united with Israel during the later history. 1 Sam. 15:6. Elsewhere they are spoken of as a nation of idolaters on whom Israel must take vengeance. It seems probable that the name was applied to a large number of tribes, some of whom were peaceful and quiet, while others were idolatrous, roving and warlike. The influence of these latter Midianites on the Israelites was clearly most evil, and directly tended to lead them from the injunctions of Moses. The events at Shittim occasioned the injunction to vex Midian and smite them. After a lapse of some years, the Midianites appear again as the enemies of the Israelites, oppressing them for seven years, but are finally defeated with great slaughter by Gideon. [GIDEON.] The Midianites are described as true Arabs, and possessed cattle and flocks and camels as the sand of the seashore for multitude. The spoil taken in the war of both Moses and of Gideon is remarkable. Num. 31:52; Judges 8:21, 24–26. We have here a wealthy Arab nation, living by plunder, delighting in finery; and, where forays were impossible, carrying on the traffic southward into Arabia, the land of gold—if not naturally, by trade—and across to Chaldea, or into the rich plains of Egypt.

Mig'dal-el (mĭg'dal-el) (*tower of God*), one of the fortified towns of the possession of Naphtali, Josh. 19:38 only, possibly deriving its name from some ancient tower—the "tower of El," or God. Some identify it with *Mujeidil,* about 12 miles northwest of Kedesh.

Mig'dal-gad (mĭg'dal-găd) (*tower of Gad*), a city of Judah, Josh. 15:37, in the district of the Shefelah, or maritime lowland.

Mig'dol (mĭg'dol) (*tower*), the name of one or two places on the eastern frontier of Egypt. 1. A Migdol is mentioned in the account of the Exodus, Ex. 14:2; Num. 33:7, 8, near the head of the Red Sea.

2. A Migdol is spoken of by Jeremiah and Ezekiel. The latter prophet mentions it as a boundary-town, evidently on the eastern border. Ezek. 29:10; 30:6. In the prophecy of Jeremiah the Jews in Egypt are spoken of as dwelling at Migdol. Jer. 44:1.

Mig'ron (mĭg'rŏn), a town or a spot in the neighborhood of Gibeah. 1 Sam. 14:2. Migron is also mentioned in Sennacherib's approach to Jerusalem. Isa. 10:28. The former may be an error for "by the threshing-floor."

Mij'amin (mĭj'a-mĭn) (*from the right hand*). 1. The chief of the sixth of the twenty-four courses of priests established by David. 1 Chron. 24:9.

2. A family of priests who signed the covenant with Nehemiah; probably the descendants of the preceding. Neh. 10:7.

Mik'loth (mĭk'lŏth) (*staves*). 1. One of the sons of Jehiel, the father or prince of Gibeon, by his wife Maachah. 1 Chron. 8:32; 9:37, 38.

2. The leader of the second division of David's army. 1 Chron. 27:4.

Mikne'iah (mĭknē'iah) (*possession of Jehovah*), one of the Levites of the second rank, gatekeepers of the ark, appointed by David to play in the temple band "with harps upon Sheminith." 1 Chron. 15:18, 21.

Mil'alai (mĭl'a-lī) (*eloquent*), probably a Gershonite Levite of the sons of Asaph, who assisted at the dedication of the walls of Jerusalem. Neh. 12:36.

Mil'cah (mĭl'kah) (*counsel*). 1. Daughter of Haran and wife of her uncle Nahor, Abraham's brother, to whom she bore eight children. Gen. 11:29; 22:20, 23; 24:15, 24, 47.

2. The fourth daughter of Zelophehad. Num. 26:33; 27:1; 36:11; Josh. 17:3.

Mil'com (mĭl'kom). [MOLECH.]

Mile, a Roman measure of length, equal to 1618 English yards—4854 feet, or about nine-tenths of an English mile. It is only once noticed in the Bible, Matt. 5:41, the usual method of reckoning both in the New Testament and in Josephus being by the stadium.

Mile'tus (mī-lē'tus), Acts 20:15, 17, less correctly called Miletum in 2 Tim. 4:20. It lay on the coast, 36 miles to the south of Ephesus, a day's sail from Trogyllium. Acts 20:15. By land, however, in the time of the apostles, a long circuit of nearly 70 miles was necessary between Ephesus and Miletus. Moreover, to those who are sailing from the north it is in the direct line for Cos. The site of Miletus has now receded several miles from the coast, and even in the apostles' time it must have lost its strictly maritime position. Miletus was far more famous five hundred years before St. Paul's day than it ever became afterward. In early times it was the most flourishing city of the Ionian Greeks. In the natural order of events it was absorbed in the Persian empire. After a brief period of spirited independence, it received a blow from which it never recovered, in the siege conducted by Alexander when on his eastern campaign. But still it held, even through the Roman period, the rank of a second-rate trading town, and Strabo mentions its four harbors. At this time it was politically in the province of Asia, though Caria was the old ethnological name of the district in which it was situated. All that is left now is a small Turkish village called *Melas*, near the site of the ancient city.

Milk. As an article of diet, milk holds a more important position in eastern countries than with us. It is not a mere adjunct in cookery, or restricted to the use of the young, although it is naturally the characteristic food of childhood, both from its simple and nutritive qualities, 1 Pet. 2:2, and particularly as contrasted with meat, 1 Cor. 3:2; Heb. 5:12; but beyond this it is regarded as substantial food adapted alike to all ages and classes. Not only the milk of cows, but of sheep, Deut. 32:14, of camels, Gen. 32:15, and of goats, Prov. 27:27, was used; the latter appears to have been most highly prized.

Mill. The mills of the ancient Hebrews probably differed but little from those at present in use in the East. These consist of two circular stones, each about eighteen inches or two feet in diameter, the lower of which is fixed. It has a peg in the centre about which the upper stone revolves. The upper stone is turned by an upright handle near the outer edge. The grain is put into the central hole, and comes out as flour between the two stones at the edge, and is caught by a cloth or dish. It is worked by women, sometimes singly and sometimes two together, according to the size of the mill. They are usually seated on the bare ground, Isa. 47:1, 2, facing each other; both have hold of the handle by which the upper is turned round on the "nether" millstone. The proverb of our Saviour, Matt. 24:41, is true to life, for *women* only grind. In ancient times it was esteemed work fit only for women, slaves and prisoners. So essential were millstones for daily domestic use that they were forbidden to be taken in pledge. Deut. 24:6. There were also larger mills that could only be turned by cattle or asses. Allusion to one of these is made in Matt. 18:6. With the movable upper millstone of the hand-mill the woman of Thebez broke Abimelech's skull. Judges 9:53.

Millet, a kind of grain. A number of species are cultivated in the East. When green it is used as fodder, and

MILLET.

for bread when ripe. Ezek. 4:9. It is probable that both the *Sorghum vulgare* and the *Panicum miliaceum* were used, and the Hebrew *dôchan* may denote either of these plants.

Mil'lo (mĭl'lò) (*a filling up*), a place in ancient Jerusalem. Both name and place seem to have been already in existence when the city was taken from the Jebusites by David. 2 Sam. 5:9; 1 Chron. 11:8. Its repair or restoration was one of the great works for which

Solomon raised his "levy," 1 Kings 9: 15, 24; 11:27; and it formed a prominent part of the fortifications by which Hezekiah prepared for the approach of the Assyrians. 2 Chron. 32:5.

Mil'lo, The house of. 1. Apparently a family or clan, mentioned in Judges 9:6, 20 only, in connection with the men or lords of Shechem.

2. The spot at which King Joash was murdered by his slaves. 2 Kings 12:20.

Mina. [WEIGHTS AND MEASURES.]

Mines, Mining. A highly-poetical description given by the author of the book of Job of the operations of mining as known in his day is the only record of the kind which we inherit from the ancient Hebrews. Job 28:1–11. In the *Wady Maghârah,* "the valley of the cave," are still traces of the Egyptian colony of miners who settled there for the purpose of extracting copper from the freestone rocks, and left their hieroglyphic inscriptions upon the face of the cliff. The ancient furnaces are still to be seen, and on the coast of the Red Sea are found the piers and wharves whence the miners shipped their metal in the harbor of *Abu Zelimeh.* Three methods were employed for refining gold and silver: (1) by exposing the fused metal to a current of air; (2) by keeping the alloy in a state of fusion and throwing nitre upon it; and (3) by mixing the alloy with lead, exposing the whole to fusion upon a vessel of boneashes or earth, and blowing upon it with bellows or other blast. There seems to be reference to the latter in Ps. 12:6; Jer. 6:28–30; Ezek. 22:18–22. The chief supply of silver in the ancient world appears to have been brought from Spain. The Egyptians evidently possessed the art of working bronze in great perfection at a very early time, and much of the knowledge of metals which the Israelites had must have been acquired during their residence among them. Of tin there appears to have been no trace in Palestine. Iron is found at the southern base of Lebanon, and the mines are still worked there, though in a very simple, rude manner.

Min'iamin (mĭn'ĭa-mĭn) (*from the right hand*). 1. A Levite in the reign of Hezekiah. 2 Chron. 31:15.

2. The same as Miamin 2 and Mijamin 2. Neh. 12:17.

3. One of the priests at the dedication of the wall of Jerusalem. Neh. 12:41.

Minister. This term is used in the Authorized Version to describe various officials of a religious and civil character. Its meaning, as distinguished from servant, is a voluntary attendant on another. In the Old Testament it is applied (1) to an attendance upon a person of high rank, Ex. 24:13; Josh. 1:1; 2 Kings 4:43 (servitor); (2) to the *attachés* of a royal court, 1 Kings 10:5; 2 Chron. 22:8; (3) to the priests and Levites. Ezra 8:17; Neh. 10:36; Isa. 61:6; Ezek. 44:11; Joel 1: 9, 13. One term in the New Testament betokens a subordinate public administrator, Rom. 13:6; 15:16; Heb. 8:2, one who performs certain gratuitous public services. A second term contains the idea of actual and personal attendance upon a superior, as in Luke 4:20. The minister's duty was to open and close the building, to produce and replace the books employed in the service, and generally to wait on the officiating priest or teacher. A third term, *diakonos* (from which comes our word deacon), is the one usually employed in relation to the ministry of the gospel: its application is twofold,—in a general sense to indicate ministers of any order, whether superior or inferior, and in a special sense to indicate an order of inferior ministers. [DEACON.]

Min'ni (mĭn'nĭ), Jer. 51:27; already noticed as a portion of Armenia. [ARMENIA.]

Min'nith (mĭn'nith), a place on the east of the Jordan, named as the point to which Jephthah's slaughter of the Ammonites extended. Judges 11:33. The "wheat of Minnith" is mentioned in Ezek. 27:17 as being supplied by Judah and Israel to Tyre; but there is nothing to indicate that the same place is intended, and indeed the word is believed by some not to be a proper name.

Minstrel. The Hebrew word in 2 Kings 3:15 properly signifies a player upon a stringed instrument like the harp or lyre, on which David played before Saul, 1 Sam. 16:16; 18:10; 19:9. The "minstrels" in Matt. 9:23 were the flute-players who were employed as professional mourners, to whom frequent allusion is made. 2 Chron. 35: 25; Eccles. 12:5; Jer. 9:17–20.

Mint. This name occurs only in Matt. 23:23 and Luke 11:42, as one of those herbs the tithe of which the Jews were most scrupulously exact in

paying. The horsemint, *M. Sylvestris,* and several other species of mint are common in Syria.

Miph'kad (mĭf'-kad) (*appointed place*), **The gate,** one of the gates of Jerusalem. Neh. 3: 31. It was probably somewhere east or northeast of the temple.

MINT.

Miracles. In the New Testament Miracles are described by four names, Signs, Works, Wonders, Powers.

They are *Signs* of the presence and power of God, of the truth of divine revelation, of the love and heart of the Father, of the credentials of his messengers.

Works, all of them are the doings of God, works worthy of Him, works of kindness and love, direct acts of God.

Wonders, astonishing manifestations of God, attracting men's attention to him, his nature and his promises.

Powers revealing the almighty power of God to save and help in time of trouble.

Miracles are evidences and proofs that Jesus bears a true message from the Father. Jesus continually calls attention to them as proofs and steppingstones to a higher and more spiritual faith.

It is said that instead of being an aid to faith, they are a hindrance to believing in the Gospels. It is indeed easier to believe that Jesus was a mere man, and did only what man can do; but then your faith does not amount to much, does not include much.

The objections to miracles and difficulties arising from them arise from the scientific doctrine of the uniformity of the laws of nature, and from our experience and observation of daily life. But they all arise from a false definition of what a miracle is, or a disbelief in a personal God.

A miracle is not the breaking of a law of nature, it is not an interference with or suspension of the unchanging uniformity of the laws of the universe. It is simply a personal God putting his will into the laws of nature; it is God's doing with his infinite power, the same *quality* of action, though vastly greater in degree, that we do every hour when we exert our personal will amid the forces of nature. I lift up a book, I turn on the water from the waterworks and make a shower on my parched lawn or garden. I stop a part of the machinery in the factory and rescue a child caught in its wheels. These acts break no law of nature, they suspend none, they change none, neither in the natural nor in the spiritual world.

All civilization is the result of man's putting his will into the uniform laws of nature. He can do it because the laws are uniform, and he believes them to be unchanging. The doctor puts his will into the laws of nature, which, if left to work out their natural result, would take away his patient's life, and by using the laws of nature cures the patient.

It is absurd to suppose that God cannot do what his children are doing every day. The believer in miracles and in the answer to prayer, stands by the side of the scientist in his belief in the uniform action of the laws of God in nature.

The miracles reported in the Bible are worthy of God and of his cause on earth. Three marks test their truth: (1) They are wrought by good men (2) in attestation of a message which, while beyond our knowledge, does not contradict our conscience and reason, but is in harmony with the other words of God. (3) They are worthy of God, helpful, useful, a blessing, never done merely to startle and excite wonder, but are expressions of God's holy character, his love, tenderness, pity, goodwill to men.

Every miracle is a visible picture before men of the character of God, of the nature of the gospel, of the loving kindness of our Saviour, of his power to help, of the wonders of grace he can work in our hearts, of his power to deliver from the diseases of sin. There were many miracles, of all kinds, to show that Jesus has power over all kinds of diseases, all the many forms of evil of which they are a type, over demons, over the forces of nature.

The work of God in Christ in bestowing spiritual life, in renewing the soul through the Holy Spirit, in guiding his people individually, and as the representatives of the kingdom of God, partakes of the nature of a miracle, for it is the personal will of God working upon men through the laws of their spiritual nature. So that Professor Drummond may well say: "When a man declares to me, 'I cannot believe in miracles,' I reply, 'I can, because I have witnessed them.' 'When and where?' 'On a certain street in this city is a man who was a week ago given over to every form of vice and brutality, and who is now a good citizen, an honest workman, a kind husband, a loving father, a pure, upright man. Surely that is such a miracle as makes me forever believe in the possibility of miracles.'"

Jesus in his nature is the supreme miracle. "The achievement of Christ in founding by his single will and power a structure so durable and so universal (as Christianity and all it has done for the world) is like no other achievement which history records." Only a divine man could have done it, and to such a being miracles are the natural outcome.

Mir'iam (mĭr'ĭ-am) (*rebellion*), the sister of Moses, the eldest of the family. She first appears, probably as a young girl, watching her infant brother's cradle in the Nile, Ex. 2 : 4, and suggesting her mother as a nurse, ver. 7. After the crossing of the Red Sea "Miriam the prophetess" is her acknowledged title, ch. 15 : 20. The prophetic power showed itself in her under the same form as that which it assumed in the days of Samuel and David,—poetry, accompanied with music and processions, ch. 15 : 1–19. She took the lead, with Aaron, in the complaint against Moses for his marriage with a Cushite, Num. 12 : 1, 2, and for this was attacked with leprosy. This stroke and its removal, which took place at Hazeroth, form the last public event of Miriam's life, ch. 12 : 1–15. She died toward the close of the wanderings at Kadesh, and was buried there, ch. 20 : 1.

Mir'ma (*fraud*), a Benjamite, born in the land of Moab. 1 Chron. 8 : 10.

Mirror. Ex. 38 : 8; Job 37 : 18. The Hebrew women on coming out of Egypt probably brought with them mirrors like those which were used by the Egyptians, and were made of a mixed metal, chiefly copper, wrought with admirable skill.

and susceptible of a bright lustre. 1 Cor. 13 : 12.

Mis'gab (mĭs'găb), a place in Moab. Jer. 48 : 1. The same Hebrew word is used in Isa. 25 : 12, and translated in both A. V. and R. V. "high fort." Perhaps it should be so translated in Jeremiah.

Mish'ael (mĭsh'a-el). 1. One of the sons of Uzziel, the uncle of Aaron and Moses. Ex. 6 : 22. When Nadab and Abihu were struck dead for offering strange fire, Mishael and his brother Elzaphan, at the command of Moses, removed their bodies from the sanctuary, and buried them without the camp, their loose-fitting tunics serving for winding-sheets. Lev. 10 : 4, 5.
2. One of those who stood at Ezra's left hand when he read the law to the people. Neh. 8 : 4.

Mi'shal (mi'shăl), or **Mi'sheal** (*prayer*), one of the towns in the territory of Asher, Josh. 19 : 26, allotted to the Gershonite Levites, ch. 21 : 30.

Mi'sham (mi'shăm) (*swiftness*), a Benjamite, son of Elpaal and descendant of Shaharaim. 1 Chron. 8 : 12.

Mish'ma (mĭsh'mȧ) (*hearing*). 1. A son of Ishmael and brother of Mibsam. Gen. 25 : 14; 1 Chron. 1 : 30.
2. A son of Simeon, 1 Chron. 4 : 25.

Mishman'nah (mĭsh-măn'nah) (*fatness*), the fourth of the twelve lion-faced Gadites who joined David at Ziklag. 1 Chron. 12 : 10.

Mish'raites (mĭsh'ra-ītes), **The,** the fourth of the four " families of Kirjathjearim," *i. e.* colonies proceeding therefrom and founding towns. 1 Chron. 2 : 53.

Mis'pereth (mĭs'pe-rĕth), one of those who returned with Zerubbabel and Jeshua from Babylon. Neh. 7 : 7. [Mizpar.]

Mis'rephoth=ma'im (mĭs're-fŏth-mā'im), a place in northern Palestine. It is commonly and probably correctly identified with a collection of springs called *Ain-Musheirifeh,* on the seashore close under the *Ras en-Nakhura,* or the Ladder of Tyre. Josh. 11 : 8.

Mite, a coin current in Palestine in the time of our Lord. Mark 12 : 41–44; Luke 21 : 1–4. It seems in Palestine to have been the smallest piece of money (worth about one-eighth of a cent), being the half of the farthing. From St. Mark's explanation, " two mites, which make a farthing," ver. 42. it may per-

BRONZE LEPTON.
(Mite, Mark 12 : 42) equals ⅛ cent.

haps be inferred that the farthing was the commoner coin.

Mith'cah (mĭth'kah) (*sweetness*), the name of an unknown desert encampment of the Israelites. Num. 33 : 28, 29.

Mith'nite (mĭth'nīte), **The,** the designation of Joshaphat, one of David's guard in the catalogue of 1 Chron. 11 : 43.

Mith'redath (mĭth're-dăth) (*given by Mithra*). 1. The treasurer of Cyrus king of Persia, to whom the king gave the vessels of the temple. Ezra 1 : 8.
2. A Persian officer stationed at Samaria. Ezra 4 : 7. Both these are given in the Apocrypha as Mithridates.

Mitre (something rolled around the head), the turban or headdress of the

MITRE.

high priest, made of fine linen cloth, eight yards long, folded around the head. On the front was a gold plate on which was inscribed *Holiness to the Lord.* Ex. 28 : 4, 37, 39; 39 : 28, 30; Lev. 8 : 9.

Mityle'ne (mĭt'ў-lē'ne), the chief town of Lesbos, an island of the Ægean Sea, about 10 or 12 miles from the coast of Asia Minor. The city is situated on the east coast of the island. Mitylene is the intermediate place where St.

Paul stopped for the night between Assos and Chios. Acts 20:14, 15. The town itself was celebrated in Roman times for the beauty of its buildings. In St. Paul's day it had the privileges of a free city. It now has a population of about 150,000.

Mixed multitude. When the Israelites journeyed from Rameses to Succoth, the first stage of the exodus from Egypt, there went up with them "a mixed multitude." Ex. 12:38; Num. 11:4. They were probably the offspring of marriages contracted between the Israelites and the Egyptians; and the term may also include all those who were not of pure Israelite blood. In Exodus and Numbers it probably denoted the miscellaneous hangers-on of the Hebrew camp, whether they were the issue of spurious marriages with Egyptians or were themselves Egyptians, or belonging to other nations. The same happened on the return from Babylon, and in Neh. 13:3 (comp. vs. 23–30) a slight clue is given by which the meaning of the "mixed multitude" may be more definitely ascertained.

Mi'zar (mĭ'zar) (*small*), **The hill,** Ps. 42:6. If this is a proper name it must have been a mountain or hill in the vicinity of, or a part of, Hermon. Some, however, think it should be translated "little" and then might refer to Mt. Zion, a small mountain compared to Hermon; then the reading would be "I remember thee, thou little mountain, from the land of Jordan and the Hermons."

Miz'pah (mĭz'pah) and **Miz'peh** (mĭz'peh) (*a watch-tower*), the name of several places in Palestine. 1. The earliest of all, in order of the narrative, is the heap of stones piled up by Jacob and Laban, Gen. 31:48, on Mount Gilead, ver. 25, to serve both as a witness to the covenant then entered into and as a landmark of the boundary between them, ver. 52. On this natural watch-tower did the children of Israel assemble for the choice of a leader to resist the children of Ammon. Judges 10:17. There the fatal meeting took place between Jephthah and his daughter on his return from the war, ch. 11:34. The position of this Mizpah is doubtful. It must have been north of the Jabbok, and held a commanding situation. A very possible site is *Jerash,* the ancient *Gerasa.*

2. A second Mizpeh, on the east of Jordan, was the Mizpeh-moab, where the king of that nation was living when David committed his parents to his care. 1 Sam. 22:3.

3. A third was "the land of Mizpeh," or more accurately "of Mizpah," the residence of the Hivites who joined the northern confederacy against Israel, headed by Jabin king of Hazor. Josh. 11:3. No other mention is found of this district in the Bible, unless it be identical with—

4. The valley of Mizpeh, to which the discomfited hosts of the same confederacy were chased by Joshua, Josh. 11:8; perhaps identical with the great country of Cœle-Syria.

5. Mizpeh, a city of Judah, Josh. 15:38, in the district of the Shefelah or maritime lowland.

6. Mizpeh, in Joshua and Samuel; elsewhere Mizpah, a "city" of Benjamin, not far from Jerusalem. Josh. 18:26; 1 Kings 15:22; 2 Chron. 16:6; Neh. 3:7. It was one of the places fortified by Asa against the incursions of the kings of northern Israel, 1 Kings 15:22; 2 Chron. 16:6; Jer. 41:10; and after the destruction of Jerusalem it became the residence of the superintendent appointed by the king of Babylon, Jer. 40:7, etc., and the scene of his murder and of the romantic incidents connected with the name of Ishmael the son of Nethaniah. It was one of the three holy cities which Samuel visited in turn as judge of the people, 1 Sam. 7:6, 16, the other two being Bethel and Gilgal. With the conquest of Jerusalem and the establishment there of the ark, the sanctity of Mizpah, or at least its reputation, seems to have declined. From Mizpah the city or the temple was visible. It is very possibly either *Neby Samwil,* or some point on the high ridge north of *Shafat,* which overlooks Jerusalem.

Miz'par (mĭz'pär) (*number*); properly **Mispar,** the same as MISPERETH. Ezra 2:2.

Miz'peh. [MIZPAH.]

Miz'raim (mĭz'ra-im), the usual name of Egypt in the Old Testament, the dual of *Misru,* which is less frequently employed. Mizraim first occurs in the account of the Hamites in Gen. 10. In the use of the name Mizraim for Egypt there can be no doubt that the dual indicates the two regions, upper and lower Egypt, into which the country has always been divided by nature as well as by its inhabitants.

Miz'zah (miz'zah) (*fear*), son of Reuel and grandson of Esau. Gen. 36: 13, 17; 1 Chron. 1: 37.

Mna'son (nā'son). Acts 21: 16. An "early" disciple; that is, probably from the time of Pentecost. Paul and his companions lodged with him on his last visit to Jerusalem. He was a Cyprian by birth, and may have been a friend of Barnabas. Acts 4: 36.

Mo'ab (mō'ab), **Mo'abites.** Moab was the son of Lot's eldest daughter, the progenitor of the Moabites. Zoar was the cradle of the race of Lot. From this centre the brother tribes spread themselves. The Moabites first inhabited the rich highlands which crown the eastern side of the chasm of the Dead Sea, extending as far north as Heshbon, from which country they expelled the Emims, the original inhabitants, Deut. 2: 11; but they themselves were afterward driven southward by the warlike Amorites, who had crossed the Jordan, and were confined to the country south of the river Arnon, which formed their northern boundary. Num. 21: 13; Judges 11: 18. They refused permission to cross their land to the Israelites on their way to the promised land although friendly commercially. Frightened at the host when in his vicinity Balak their king hired Balaam to curse them (Num. 22–24; Deut. 23: 3–6) and the Moabites later led them into idolatry (Num. 25). The Israelites were not allowed to attack the Moabites (Deut. 2: 9, 19) but conquered the Amorites, who occupied the country from which the Moabites had been so lately expelled. After the conquest of Canaan the relations of Moab with Israel were of a mixed character, sometimes warlike and sometimes peaceable. With the tribe of Benjamin they had at least one severe struggle, in union with their kindred the Ammonites. Judges 3: 12–30. The story of Ruth, on the other hand, testifies to the existence of a friendly intercourse between Moab and Bethlehem, one of the towns of Judah. By his descent from Ruth, David may be said to have had Moabite blood in his veins. He committed his parents to the protection of the king of Moab, when hard pressed by Saul. 1 Sam. 22: 3, 4. But here all friendly relations stop forever. The next time

the name is mentioned is in the account of David's war, who made the Moabites tributary. 2 Sam. 8: 2; 1 Chron. 18: 2. They were subject to Omri and his son Ahab, at whose death they refused to pay tribute and asserted their independence, making an alliance for an attack upon Judah, which failed (2 Chron. 20: 1–30). Israel, Judah and Edom finally united in an attack on Moab, resulting in the complete overthrow of the Moabites. Falling back into their own country, they were followed and their cities and farms destroyed. Finally, shut up within the walls of his own capital, the king, Mesha, in the sight of the thousands who covered the sides of that vast amphitheatre, killed and burnt his child as a propitiatory sacrifice to the cruel gods of his country. Isaiah, chs. 15, 16, 25: 10–12, predicts the utter annihilation of the Moabites; and they are frequently denounced by the subsequent prophets. For the religion of the Moabites see CHEMOSH; MOLECH; PEOR. The country is now a wilderness. The line between the arable land and the Arabian desert on the east is quite indeterminate. There are many ruined villages and cities, but only a small nomadic population. There is little real cultivation, but there are occasional fields of grain and considerable pasture land. A great part of the country is treeless.

Mo'abite Stone, The. In the year 1868 Rev. F. Klein, of the Church Missionary Society at Jerusalem, found at *Dhiban* (the biblical Dibon), in Moab, a remarkable stone, since called the Moabite Stone. It was lying on the ground, with the inscription uppermost, and measures about 3 feet 9 inches long, 2 feet wide and 1 foot 2 inches thick. It is a very heavy, compact black basalt. There was a rivalry between the Berlin and Paris Museums for its possession, which ran it up to a nearly prohibitory price. Then the Arabs fell to fighting over the expected money. The dispute settled nothing, so kindling a fire under the stone, and pouring water on it when it was hot, they broke it into fragments." —*Davis' Bible Dictionary.* An impression had previously been made of the inscription, but it was broken, and not of much use. Later other impressions were taken of the various fragments. Finally the fragments were purchased by the French government for 32,000 francs, were joined together, and are in the Louvre in Paris. The engraved face is about the shape of an ordinary gravestone, rounded at the top. On this stone is the record, 34 lines, in the Phœnician characters, of the wars of Mesha, king of Moab, with Israel (2

THE MOABITE STONE.

Kings 3 : 4), and his victory over the Israelites in the time of Ahab. (B.C. 875.) It speaks of King Omri and other names of places and persons mentioned in the Bible, and belongs to this exact period of Jewish and Moabite history. The names given on the Moabite Stone, engraved by one who knew them in daily life, are, in nearly every case, identical with those found in the Bible itself, and testify to the wonderful integrity with which the Scriptures have been preserved. " The inscription reads like a leaf taken out of a lost book of Chronicles. The expressions are the same; the names of gods, kings and of towns are the same."

Moadi'ah (mō-a-dī'ah), Neh. 12 : 17. Called MAADIAH in Neh. 12 : 5.

Mo'din (mō'din), a place not mentioned in either the Old or the New Testament, though rendered immortal by its connection with the history of the Jews in the interval between the two. The place was known without question down to the 4th century, A.D. Then all trace was lost, and various sites are now suggested. *El-Medyeh*, about 6 miles from Lydda, seems the most probable location. There are ruins there which might be those of the tomb of the Maccabees, among others.

Mol'adah (mŏl'a-dah) (*birth, race*), a city in the extreme south of Judah, assigned to the Simeonites. Josh. 15 : 26; 19 : 2. In the latter tribe it remained at any rate till the reign of David, 1 Chron. 4 : 28, but by the time of the captivity it seems to have come back into the hands of Judah, by whom it was reinhabited after the captivity. Neh. 11 : 26. Robinson places it at *el-Milh*, which is about 7 English miles from *Tell Arad*, 22 from Hebron, and 14 east of Beersheba. This site is, however, disputed.

Mole. 1. *Tinshemeth*. Lev. 11 : 30. It is probable that the animals mentioned with the *tinshemeth* in the above passage denote different kinds of lizards; perhaps, therefore, the chameleon is the animal intended. Many scholars, however, still consider "mole" nearer the true meaning; probably the Greek *Aspalax*, not the true mole but a kind of blind mole-rat, from 8 to 12 inches long, feeding on vegetables, and burrowing like a mole, but on a larger scale.

2. *Chaphôr pêrôth* is rendered "moles" in Isa. 2 : 20. The word means burrowers, hole-diggers, and may designate any of the small animals, as rats and weasels, which burrow among ruins. It is very likely the mole-rat, which is very common in Palestine. It resembles the mole in appearance, but is not of the same order.

Mo'lech (mō'lĕk) (*king*). The fire-god Molech was the tutelary deity of the children of Ammon, and essentially identical with the Moabitish Chemosh. Fire-gods appear to have been common to all the Canaanite, Syrian and Arab tribes, who worshipped fire under an outward symbol, with the most inhuman rites. According to Jewish tradition, the image of Molech was of brass, hollow within, and was situated without Jerusalem. Many instances of human sacrifices are found in ancient writers, which may be compared with the description in the Old Testament of the manner in which Molech was worshipped. Molech was the lord and master of the Ammonites; their country was his possession, Jer. 49:1, as Moab was the heritage of Chemosh. His priests were men of rank, Jer. 49:3, taking precedence of the princes. The priests of Molech, like those of other idols, were called Chemarim. 2 Kings 23:5; Hos. 10:5; Zeph. 1:4. Solomon erected an altar to this god; Ahaz burnt children at his altar; and Manasseh made at least one of his sons pass through the fire. (1 Kings 11:7; 2 Kings 21:6; 2 Chron. 28:3). Josiah

evidence of the use of *coined money* by the Hebrews before the return from the Babylonian captivity; but silver was used for money, in quantities determined by weight, at least as early as the time of Abraham; and its earliest mention is in the generic sense of the price paid for a slave. Gen. 17:13. The 1000 *pieces of silver* paid by Abimelech to Abraham, Gen. 20:16, and the 20 *pieces of silver* for which Joseph was sold to the Ishmaelites, Gen. 37:28, were probably rings such as we see on

THE PALESTINIAN MOLE (*Spalax typhilus*).

destroyed and defiled these high places. The name was also written Malcam, Milcom and Moloch.

Mo'lid (mō'lĭd) (*begetter*), the son of Abishur by his wife Abihail, and descendant of Jerahmeel. 1 Chron. 2:29.

Mo'loch (mō'lŏk). The same as MOLECH.

Money. 1. *Uncoined money.*—It is well known that ancient nations that were without a coinage weighed the precious metals, a practice represented on the Egyptian monuments, on which gold and silver are shown to have been kept in the form of rings. We have no

the Egyptian monuments in the act of being weighed. In the first recorded transaction of commerce, the cave of Machpelah is purchased by Abraham for 400 shekels of silver. The shekel weight of silver was the unit of value through the whole age of Hebrew history, down to the Babylonian captivity.

2. *Coined money.*—After the captivity we have the earliest mention of *coined money*, in allusion, as might have been expected, to the Persian coinage, the gold *daric* (Authorized Version *dram*). Ezra 2:69; (cf. 8:27); Neh. 7:70, 71, 72. [DARIC.] No native Jewish coinage

appears to have existed till Antiochus VII. Sidetes granted Simon Maccabæus the license to coin money, B.C. 140; and it is now generally agreed that the oldest

THE PERSIAN (or golden) DARIC.

Jewish *silver coins* belong to this period. They are shekels and half-shekels, of the weight of 220 and 110 grains. With this silver there was associated

DENARIUS OF CÆSAR.

a *copper* coinage. The abundant money of Herod the Great, which is of a thoroughly Greek character, and of copper only, seems to have been a continuation

JEWISH HALF-SHEKEL, the coin in which the Temple tax was paid — "tribute money" (Matt. 17:27) — value, 32 cents.

of the copper coinage of the Maccabees, with some adaptation to the Roman standard. In the money of the New Testament we see the native copper

ASSARION (farthing). Actual size.

coinage side by side with the Græco-Roman copper, silver and gold. The coins mentioned by the evangelists, are the following: The *didrachm,* A. V.

"tribute money"; R. V. "half-shekel." Matt. 17:24. *Stater,* A. V. "piece of money"; R. V. "shekel"; Matt. 17:27. A Roman coin worth 64 cents, about

JEWISH SHEKEL.

the same value as the Jewish coined shekel. The *denarius,* or Roman penny, rather better translated in the R. V. shilling, as well as the Greek *drachma,* then of about the same weight, are spoken of as current coins. Matt. 22: 15–21; Luke 20:19–25. They were worth about 16 cents. Of copper coins the *farthing* and its half, the *mite,* are spoken of, and these probably formed the chief native currency. The Roman farthing (*quadrans*) was a brass coin worth ¼ of a cent. The Greek *farthing* (*as* or *assarion*) was worth four Roman farthings, *i. e.* about one cent. A *mite* was half a farthing, and therefore was worth about ⅛ of a cent. See table of *Jewish weights and measures* and *Money,* in APPENDIX.

Money=changers. Matt. 21:12; Mark 11:15; John 2:15. Money-changers were a necessity because coins of so many countries were in use; and especially because Jews came from all parts of the world with the money which belonged to the country where they lived, and often not current in any other land. Moreover, according to Ex. 30:13–15, every Israelite who had reached or passed the age of twenty must pay into the sacred treasury, whenever the nation was numbered, a half-shekel as an offering to Jehovah. The money-changers whom Christ, for their impiety, avarice and fraudulent dealing, expelled from the temple were the dealers who supplied half-shekels, for such a premium as they might be able to exact, for they were required to pay their tribute or ransom money in the Hebrew coin.

Month. From the time of the institution of the Mosaic law downward, the month was a lunar one. The cycle of religious feasts commencing with the

MON 419 MOR

passover depended not simply on the month, but on the moon; the 14th of Abib was coincident with the full moon; and the new moons themselves were the occasions of regular festivals. Num. 10: 10; 28:11–14. The commencement of the month was generally decided by observation of the new moon. The usual number of months in a year was twelve, as implied in 1 Kings 4:7; 1 Chron. 27: 1–15; but since twelve lunar months would make but 354½ days, the years would be short twelve days of the true year, and therefore it follows as a matter of course that an additional month must have been inserted about every third year, which would bring the number up to thirteen. No notice, however, is taken of this month in the Bible. In the modern Jewish calendar the intercalary month is introduced seven times in every nineteen years. The usual method of designating the months was by their numerical order, e. g. "the second month," Gen. 7:11, "the fourth month," 2 Kings 25:3; and this was generally retained even when the names were given, e. g. "in the month Zif, which is the second month." 1 Kings 6:1. The names of the months belong to two distinct periods. In the first place we have those peculiar to the period of Jewish independence, of which four only, are including Abib, which we hardly regard as a proper name, are mentioned, viz.: Abib, in which the passover fell, Ex. 13:4; 23:15; 34:18; Deut. 16:1, and which was established as the first month in commemoration of the Exodus, Ex. 12:2; Zif, the second month, 1 Kings 6:1, 37; Bul, the eighth, 1 Kings 6:38; and Ethanim, the seventh, 1 Kings 8:2. In the second place we have the names which prevailed subsequent to the Babylonish captivity; of these the following seven appear in the Bible: Nisan, the first, Neh. 2:1; Esther 3: 7; Sivan, the third, Esther 8:9; Elul, the sixth, Neh. 6:15; Chisleu or more correctly, Chislev, the ninth, Neh. 1:1; Zech. 7:1; Tebeth, the tenth, Esther 2:16; Sebat or more exactly, Shebat, the eleventh, Zech. 1:7; and Adar, the twelfth. Esther 3:7; 8:12 and 9:21. The names of the remaining five occur in the Talmud and other works. They were: Iyar, the second, Targum, 2 Chron. 30:2; Tammuz, the fourth; Ab, the fifth; Tisri, the

seventh; and Marchesvan, the eighth. The name of the intercalary month was Ve-adar, i. e. the additional Adar. The identification of the Jewish months with our own cannot be effected with precision on account of the variations that must inevitably exist between the lunar and the solar month. Nisan (or Abib) answers to April; Zif or Iyar to May; Sivan to June; Tammuz to July; Ab to August; Elul to September; Ethanim or Tisri to October; Bul or Marchesvan to November; Chislev to December; Tebeth to January; Shebat to February; and Adar to March. In the APPENDIX is given a table of the Jewish months and the exact corresponding days of our months, for two years.

The Jews of our time begin their year in September, with Tisri, so that there are two Jewish years recognized. But in the Old Testament the year almost without exception begins in the spring with Abib (Nisan).

Moon. The moon held an important place in the kingdom of nature, as known to the Hebrews. Conjointly with the sun, it was appointed "for signs and for seasons, and for days and years;" though in this respect it exercised a more important influence, if by the "seasons" we understand the great religious festivals of the Jews, as is particularly stated in Ps. 104:19. The worship of the moon prevailed extensively among the nations of the East, and under a variety of aspects. It was one of the only two deities which commanded the reverence of all the Egyptians. The worship of the heavenly bodies is referred to in Job 31:26, 27, and Moses directly warns the Jews against it. Deut. 4:19. In the figurative language of Scripture, the moon is frequently noticed as presaging events of the greatest importance through the temporary or permanent withdrawal of its light. Isa. 13:10; Joel 2:31; Matt. 24:29; Mark 13:24.

Moon, New. [NEW MOON.]

Mor'asthite (mō'ras-thīte), **The,** that is, the native of a place named Moresheth. It occurs twice—Jer. 26:18; Micah 1:1—each time as the description of the prophet Micah.

Mor'decai (môr'de-kī) (either Persian, meaning *little man,* or Babylonian, = *a worshipper of Merodach*), the deliverer, under divine Providence, of the Jews from the destruction plotted against them by Haman the chief minister of Xerxes; the institutor of the feast of Purim. The incidents of his history are too well known to need to be dwelt upon. [ESTHER.] Three things are predicated of Mordecai in the book of Esther: (1) That he lived in Shushan; (2) That his name was Mordecai, son of Jair, son of Shimei, son of Kish the Benjamite who was taken captive with Jehoiachin; (3) That he brought up Esther.

Mo′reh (mō′reh) (*teacher*). 1. The plain or plains (or, as it should rather be rendered, the oak or oaks) of Moreh. The oak (or terebinth) of Moreh was the first recorded halting-place of Abram after his entrance into the land of Canaan. Gen. 12:6. It was at the "place of Shechem," close to the mountains of Ebal and Gerizim. Deut. 11:30; comp. Judg. 9:6.

2. The hill of Moreh, at the foot of which the Midianites and Amalekites were encamped before Gideon's attack upon them. Judges 7:1. It is not positively identified, but probably lay in the valley of Jezreel, rather on the north side of the valley, and north also of the eminence on which Gideon's little band of heroes was clustered. A suggestion is *Jebel ed-Duhy*, the "Little Hermon" of the modern travelers.

Mor′esheth=gath (mŏr′esh-eth-gath) (*possession of Gath*), a place named by the prophet Micah. Micah 1:14. The prophet was himself a native of a place called Moresheth.

Mori′ah (mȯ-rī′ah). 1. *The land of Moriah.*—On "one of the mountains" in this district took place the sacrifice of Isaac. Gen. 22:2. A tradition first given by Josephus that this mountain was the one afterwards the site of the Temple has long had credence. There are many however who dispute it.

2. *Mount Moriah.*—The elevation on which Solomon built the temple, where God appeared to David "in the threshing-floor of Araunah the Jebusite." It is the eastern eminence of Jerusalem. The top was levelled by Solomon, and immense walls were built around it from the base to enlarge the level surface for the temple area.

Mortar, "a wide-mouthed vessel in form of an inverted bell, in which substances are pounded or bruised with a pestle."—*Webster.* The simplest and probably most ancient method of preparing grain for food was by pounding it between two stones. The Israelites in the desert appear to have possessed mortars and handmills among their necessary domestic utensils. When the manna fell they gathered it, and either ground it in the mill or pounded it in the mortar till it was fit for use. Num. 11:8. So in the present day stone mortars are used by the Arabs to pound wheat for their national dish *kibby*. Another word occurring in Prov. 27:22 probably denotes a mortar of a larger kind in which grain was pounded: "Though thou shouldest bray a fool in a mortar among wheat with a pestle, yet will not his foolishness depart from him." Grain may be separated from its husk and all its good properties preserved by such an operation, but the fool's folly is so essential a part of himself that no analogous process can remove it from him. Such seems the natural interpretation of this remarkable proverb. The language is intentionally exaggerated, and there is no necessity for supposing an allusion to a mode of punishment by which criminals were put to death by being pounded in a mortar. A custom of this kind existed among the Turks, but there is no distinct trace of it among the Hebrews. Such, however, is supposed to be the reference in the proverb by Mr. Roberts, who illustrates it from his Indian experience.

Mortar. Gen. 11:3; Ex. 1:14; Lev. 14:42, 45; Isa. 41:25; Ezek. 13:10, 11, 14, 15; 22:28; Nah. 3:14. The various compacting substances used in Oriental buildings appear to be—1. Bitumen, as in the Babylonian structures; 2. Common mud or moistened clay; 3. A very firm cement compounded of sand and lime, well pounded, sometimes mixed and sometimes coated with oil, so as to form a surface almost impenetrable to wet or the weather. In Assyria and also Egyptian brick buildings, stubble or straw, as hair or wool among ourselves, was added to increase the tenacity.

Mose′rah (mȯ-sē′rà) (*bonds*), Deut. 10:6, apparently the same as Moseroth, Num. 33:30, its plural form, the name of a place near Mount Hor.

Mo′ses (mō′zez) (from Egyptian *mes* or *mesu; extraction, a son.* Formerly thought from Coptic "saved from the water"), the legislator of the Jewish people, and in a certain sense the founder of the Jewish religion.

The history of Moses as given in the Pentateuch, naturally divides itself into three periods of 40 years each. Moses was born at Goshen in Egypt, B.C. 1571, if we accept Ussher's date for the Exodus. The story of his birth is thoroughly Egyptian in its scene. His mother made extraordinary efforts for his preservation from the general destruction of the male children of Israel. For three months the child was concealed in the house. Then his mother placed him in a small boat or basket of papyrus, closed against the water by bitumen. This was placed among the aquatic vegetation by the side of one of the canals of the Nile. The sister lingered to watch her brother's fate. The Egyptian princess, who, tradition says, was a childless wife, came down to bathe in the sacred river. Her attendant slaves followed her. She saw the basket in the flags, and ordered it to be opened. The cry of the child moved the princess to compassion. She determined to rear it as her own. The sister was at hand to recommend a Hebrew nurse, the child's own mother. Here was the *first part* of Moses' training,—a training at home in the true religion, in faith in God, in the promises to his nation, in the life of a saint,—a training which he never forgot, even amid the splendors and gilded sin of Pharaoh's court. The child was adopted by the princess. From this time for many years Moses must be considered as an Egyptian. As an Egyptian prince he must have a princely education; and he became "learned in all the wisdom of the Egyptians" (Acts 7:22), who were then unsurpassed in civilization and learning by any people in the world. This was the *second part* of Moses' training, fitting him for high office, and for leadership.

The second period of Moses' life began when he was forty years old. Seeing the sufferings of his people, Moses determined to go to them as their helper, and made his great life-choice, to be their guide and deliverer. Heb. 11:25, 26. Seeing an Israelite illtreated by an Egyptian, and thinking that they were alone, he slew the Egyptian, and buried the corpse in the sand. But the people soon showed themselves unfitted as yet to obtain their freedom, nor was Moses yet fitted to be their leader. He was compelled to leave Egypt when the slaying of the Egyptian became known, and he fled to the land of Midian, in the southern and southeastern part of the Sinai peninsula. There, wearied, he sat down by a well where the Midianite herdsmen were watering their sheep. He aided the daughters of Jethro, and by this means was introduced to Jethro, who was a priest. He gave him hospitality and employment, and also one of his daughters to wife. For forty years Moses communed with God and with nature, and enjoyed intimate association with Jethro, a man of sound judgment (Ex. 18). This was the *third process* of his training for his work; and from this training he learned infinitely more than from Egypt. One advantage of this life was the familiarity it gave him with the desert, its roads and its resources. Finally God met him on Horeb, appearing in a burning bush, and, communicating with him, appointed him to be the leader and deliverer of his people.

Now begins the third period of forty years in Moses' life. He meets Aaron, his brother, as promised, whom God permitted to be the spokesman, and together they return to Goshen in Egypt. From this time the history of Moses is the history of Israel. Aaron spoke and acted for Moses, and was the permanent inheritor of the sacred staff of power. But Moses was the inspiring soul behind. He is incontestably the chief personage of the history, in a sense in which no one else is described before or since. He was led into a closer communion with the invisible world than was vouchsafed to any other in the Old Testament. On approaching Palestine the office of the leader becomes blended with that of the general or the conqueror. By Moses the spies were sent to explore the country. Against his advice took place the first disastrous battle at Hormah. To his guidance is ascribed the circuitous route by which the nation approached Palestine from the east, and to his generalship the two successful campaigns in which Sihon and Og were defeated. The narrative is told so briefly that we are in danger of forgetting that at this last stage of his life Moses must have been as much a conqueror and victorious soldier as was Joshua.

HIS CHARACTER. Moses stands among

the few greatest men in all history. In every direction he was great and good.

1. As a PROPHET. A prophet is one who speaks and acts under the direction of God, the medium through which God reveals his will to men.

2. As a SAINT. Moses' goodness shines as brightly as his greatness. He was unselfish. He devoted himself at every cost to the good of his people. He encountered every danger for their sakes. He was willing to die to save them. He was the embodiment of love to God and love to man. By seeing God face to face he was becoming transformed into his spiritual likeness.

3. HIS MEEKNESS. Moses was in a sense peculiar to himself the founder and representative of his people; and in accordance with this complete identification of himself with his nation is the only strong personal trait which we are able to gather from his history. Num. 12 : 3. The word "meek" is hardly an adequate reading of the Hebrew term, which should be rather "much enduring." It represents what we should now designate by the word "disinterested." All that is told of him indicates a withdrawal of himself, a preference of the cause of his nation to his own interests, which makes him the most complete example of Jewish patriotism.

4. HIS IMPERFECTION. Two or three times some fault is attributed to Moses, as every saint has failed in some point at some time. There is no garden but has some weeds. But the most unjust thing we can do is to measure its value by its weeds and not by its fruits. " By their *fruits* ye shall know them." Moses' few faults are such that they would never be noticed at all in a worldly man. They are like a broken limb on a tree loaded with magnificent fruit. All God's works through men are done by imperfect instruments.

5. As a STATESMAN. "Inspiration apart, Moses possessed all those endowments and qualities which form the consummate statesman and chief magistrate : an intellect of the highest order; a perfect mastery of all the civil wisdom of the age; a penetrating, comprehensive, and sagacious judgment; great promptness and energy in action; patriotism which neither ingratitude, ill treatment nor rebellion could quench, or even cool; a commanding and per-suasive eloquence; a hearty love of truth; an incorruptible virtue; an entire freedom from selfish ambition; an invincible hatred of tyranny and injustice; a patient endurance of toil; a courageous contempt of danger; and a greatness of soul in which he has never been surpassed by the most admired heroes of ancient or modern times. Comprehensiveness, grasp, force, sagacity were the predominant characteristics of his mind; magnanimity, disinterestedness, an enthusiastic devotion to liberty, and an ardent but rational piety, the leading qualities of his heart."

6. As a GENERAL Moses delivered his people from the most powerful nation on earth; maintained them amid the perils of the desert for forty years, and led them in confidence against a country settled by fierce tribes, which they conquered.

7. As a LAWGIVER. However much may have been added by the development of the people, like the amendments to the Constitution and laws of the United States, yet through Moses was instituted the great system of civil and religious law.

8. As a POET. The two songs in Deuteronomy 32 and 33, and Psalm 90.

9. As an ORATOR. The great orations in Deuteronomy stand among the few greatest masterpieces of eloquence in the world's history, if not at their head.

CLOSE OF HIS LIFE. The song and the blessing of the tribes conclude the farewell, chs. 32, 33. And then comes the mysterious close. He is told that he is to see the good land beyond the Jordan, but not to possess it himself. He ascends the mount of Pisgah and stands on Nebo, one of its summits, and surveys the four great masses of Palestine west of the Jordan, so far as it can be discerned from that height. The view has passed into a proverb for all nations. "So Moses the servant of Jehovah died there in the land of Moab, according to the word of Jehovah. And he buried him in a 'ravine' in the land of Moab, 'before' Beth-peor : but no man knoweth of his sepulchre unto this day. . . . And the children of Israel wept for Moses in the plains of Moab thirty days." Deut. 34 : 5, 6, 8. This is all that is said in the sacred record.

Moses is spoken of as a likeness of Christ; and as this is a point of view which has been almost lost in the Church, compared with the more familiar comparisons of Christ to Adam, David, Joshua, and yet has as firm a basis in fact as any of them, it may be well to draw it out in detail. (1) Moses is, as it would seem, the only character of the Old Testament to whom Christ expressly likens himself: "Moses wrote of me." John 5:46. It suggests three main points of likeness: (a) Christ was, like Moses, the great prophet of the people—the last, as Moses was the first. (b) Christ, like Moses, is a lawgiver: "Him shall ye hear." (c) Christ, like Moses, was a prophet out of the midst of the nation, "from their brethren." As Moses was the entire representative of his people, feeling for them more than for himself, absorbed in their interests, hopes and fears, so, with reverence be it said, was Christ. (2) In Heb. 3:1-19; 12:24-29; Acts 7:37, Christ is described, though more obscurely, as the Moses of the new dispensation—as the apostle or messenger or mediator of God to the people—as the controller and leader of the flock or household of God. (3) The details of their lives are sometimes, though not often, compared. Acts 7:24-28, 35.

Moth. By the Hebrew word we are certainly to understand some species of clothes-moth (*tinea*). Reference to the destructive habits of the clothes-moth is made in the Bible; reference being made to its destruction of clothing (Job 13:28; Matt. 6:19; Jas. 5:2); its feeding on wool (Isa. 51:8) and building for itself a frail covering from it (Job 27:18). There are many kinds of moths, the clothes-moth in its larva state being the one which creates this havoc.

Mother. The superiority of the Hebrew over all contemporaneous systems of legislation and of morals is strongly shown in the higher estimation of the mother in the Jewish family, as contrasted with modern Oriental as well as ancient Oriental and classical usage. The king's mother, as appears in the case of Bath-sheba, was treated with special honor. Ex. 20:12; Lev. 19:3; Deut. 5:16; 21:18, 21; 1 Kings 2:19; Prov. 10:1; 15:20; 17:25; 29:15; 31:1, 30.

Mount, Mountain. The Hebrew word *har*, like the English "mountain," is employed for both single eminences more or less isolated, such as Sinai, Ger-

izim, Ebal, Zion and Olivet, and for ranges, such as Lebanon. It is also applied to a mountainous country or district.

Mourning. One marked feature of Oriental mourning is what may be called its studied publicity and the careful observance of the prescribed ceremonies. Gen. 23:2; Job 1:20; 2:12. 1. Among the particular forms observed the following may be mentioned: (a) Rending the clothes. Gen. 37:29, 34; 44:13; 2 Sam. 3:31; Jer. 6:26, etc. (b) Dressing in sackcloth. Gen. 37:34; 2 Sam. 3:31; 21:10; Joel 1:8, etc. (c) Ashes, dust or earth sprinkled on the person. 2 Sam. 13:19; 15:32, etc. (d) Black or sad-colored garments. 2 Sam. 14:2; Jer. 8:21, etc. (e) Removal of ornaments or neglect of person. 2 Sam. 19:24, etc. (f) Shaving the head, plucking out the hair of the head or beard. Ezra 9:3; Jer. 7:29, etc. (g) Laying bare some part of the body. Isa. 20:2; 47:2, etc. (h) Fasting or abstinence in meat and drink. 2 Sam. 1:12; 3:35; 12:16, 22, etc. (i) Weeping and lamenting. 2 Sam. 1:17; 18:33; Joel 1:8, 13. (k) Covering the lower part of the face, and sometimes the head, in token of silence. 2 Sam. 15:30; 19:4. (l) Cutting the flesh. Deut. 14:1; Jer. 16:6, 7; 41:5; beating the body. Ezek. 21:12; Jer. 31:19. (m) Employment of persons hired for the purpose of mourning. Eccles. 12:5; Jer. 9:17; Amos 5:16; Matt. 9:23. (n) Akin to the foregoing usage the custom for friends or passers-by to join in the lamentations of bereaved or afflicted persons. Gen. 50:3; Judges 11:40; Job 2:11; 30:25, etc. (o) The sitting or lying posture in silence indicative of grief. Judges 20:26; 2 Sam. 12:16, etc. (p) Mourning feast and cup of consolation. Jer. 16:7, 8. Often several of these modes of mourning were combined by those mourning. 2. The period of mourning varied. The ordinary time was seven days. The period for Aaron and Moses was thirty days (Num. 20:29; Deut. 34:8), and for Jacob seventy days in Egypt (including however the forty days of the embalming) (Gen. 50:3) and seven days on arrival in Canaan (Gen. 50:10).

With the practices above mentioned, Oriental and other customs, ancient and modern, in great measure agree. Arab men are silent in grief, but the women scream, tear their hair, hands and face, and throw earth or sand on their heads. Both Mohammedans and Christians in Egypt hire wailing-women, and wail at stated times. Burckhardt says the women of Atbara in Nubia shave their heads on the death of their nearest relatives—a custom prevalent also among several of the peasant tribes of upper Egypt. He also mentions wailing-women, and a man in distress besmearing his face with dirt and dust in token of grief. In the "Arabian Nights" are frequent allusions to similar practices. It also mentions ten days and forty days as periods of mourning. Lane, speaking of the modern Egyptians, says, "After death the women of the family raise cries of lamentation called *welweléh* or *wilwál,* uttering the most piercing shrieks, and calling upon the name of the deceased, 'Oh, my master! Oh, my resource! Oh, my misfortune! Oh, my glory!' See Jer. 22:18. The females of the neighborhood come to join with them in this conclamation: generally, also, the family send for two or more *neddâbehs* or public wailing-women. Each brings a tambourine, and beating them they exclaim, 'Alas for him!' The female relatives, domestics and friends, with their hair dishevelled and sometimes with rent clothes, beating their faces, cry in like manner, 'Alas for him!' These make no alteration in dress, but women, in some cases, dye their shirts, head-veils and handkerchiefs of a dark-blue color. They visit the tombs at stated periods."

Mouse. The name of this animal occurs in Lev. 11:29; 1 Sam. 6:4, 5; Isa. 66:17. The Hebrew word is in all probability generic, and is not intended to denote any particular species of mouse. The original word denotes a field-ravager, and may therefore comprehend any destructive rodent. Tristram found twenty-five species of mice in Palestine. It is probable that in 1 Sam. 6:5 the expression "the mice that mar the land" includes and more particularly refers to the short-tailed field-mice (*Arvicola avalis*), which cause great destruction to the grain-lands of Syria.

Mowing. As the great heat of the climate in Palestine and other similarly-situated countries soon dries up the herbage itself, hay-making in our sense

of the term is not in use. The "king's mowings," Amos 7:1, may perhaps refer to some royal right of early pasturage for the use of the cavalry.

Mo'za (mō′zà) (*fountain*). 1. Son of Caleb the son of Hezron. 1 Chron. 2:46.

2. Son of Zimri and descendant of Saul. 1 Chron. 8:36, 37; 9:42, 43.

Mo'zah (mō′zah) (*fountain*), one of the cities in the allotment of Benjamin, Josh. 18:26 only, named between Cephirah and Rekem. Possibly *Beit Mizzeh,* 5 miles northwest of Jerusalem.

Mulberry trees (Heb. *becâîm*). Mention of these is made only in 2 Sam. 5:23, 24 and 1 Chron. 14:14. We are quite unable to determine what kind of tree is denoted by the Hebrew word. Some believe pear trees are meant; others the aspen or poplar, whose leaves tremble and rustle with the slightest breeze, even when the breeze is not otherwise perceptible. It may have been to the rustling of these leaves that the "going in the tree tops" refers. 2 Sam, 5:23, 24.

Mule, a hybrid animal, the offspring of a horse and an ass. The mule is a remarkably hardy, patient, obstinate, sure-footed animal, living, ordinarily, twice as long as a horse. It was forbidden to the Israelites to breed mules, but sometimes they imported them. David and other kings rode on mules. (2 Sam. 13:29; 18:9; 1 Kings 1:33). Ezra's company brought 245 from Babylon. They are now universally used in Bible lands.

Mup'pim (mŭp′pĭm), a Benjamite, and one of the fourteen descendants of Rachel who belonged to the original colony of the sons of Jacob in Egypt. Gen. 46:21. (B.C. 1706.) In Num. 26:39 the name is given as SHUPHAM.

Murder. The law of Moses, while it protected the accidental homicide, defined with additional strictness the crime of murder. It prohibited compensation or reprieve of the murderer, or his protection if he took refuge in the refuge city, or even at the altar of Jehovah. Ex. 21:12, 14; Lev. 24:17, 21; 1 Kings 2:5, 6, 31. The duty of executing punishment on the murderer is in the law expressly laid on the "Avenger of blood;" but the question of guilt was to be previously decided by the Levitical tribunal. In regal times the duty of execution of justice on a murderer seems to have been assumed to some extent by the sovereign, as was also the privilege of pardon. 2 Sam. 13:39; 14:7, 11; 1 Kings 2:34. It was lawful to kill a burglar taken at night in the act, but unlawful to do so after sunrise. Ex. 22:2, 3.

Mu'shi (mū'shī), the son of Merari the son of Levi. Ex. 6:19; Num. 3: 20; 1 Chron. 6:19, 47; 23:21, 23; 24: 26, 30.

Music. 1. *The most ancient music.*— The inventor of musical instruments, like the first poet and the first forger of metals, was a Cainite. We learn from Gen. 4:21 that Jubal the son of Lamech was "the father of all such as handle the harp and organ," that is, of all players upon stringed and wind instruments. The first mention of music in the times after the deluge is in the narrative of Laban's interview with Jacob, Gen. 31:27; and Job 21:12 refers to music as a common feature in a prosperous life. On the banks of the Red Sea Moses and the children of Israel sang their triumphal song of deliverance from the hosts of Egypt; and Miriam, in celebration of the same event, exercised one of her functions as a prophetess by leading a procession of the women of the camp, chanting in chorus the burden of the song of Moses. The song of Deborah and Barak is cast in a distinctly metrical form, and was probably intended to be sung with a musical accompaniment as one of the people's songs. The simpler impromptu with which the women from the cities of Israel greeted David after the slaughter of the Philistines was apparently struck off on the spur of the moment, under the influence of the wild joy with which they welcomed their national champion, "the darling of the sons of Israel." 1 Sam. 18:6, 7. Up to this time we meet with nothing like a systematic cultivation of music among the Hebrews, but the establishment of the schools of the prophets appears to have supplied this want. Whatever the students of these schools may have been taught, music was an essential part of their practice. Professional musicians soon became attached to the court.

2. *The golden age of Hebrew music.*— David seems to have gathered round him "singing men and singing women." 2

Sam. 19:35. Solomon did the same, Eccles. 2:8, adding to the luxury of his court by his patronage of art, and obtaining a reputation himself as no mean composer. 1 Kings 4:32. But the temple was the great school of music, and it was consecrated to its highest service in the worship of Jehovah. Before, however, the elaborate arrangements had been made by David for the temple choir, there must have been a considerable body of musicians throughout the country. 2 Sam. 6:5. David chose 4000 musicians from the Levites. Of these musicians 288 were specially trained for leaders. 1 Chron. 25:6, 7. The whole number was divided into 24 courses, each of which would thus consist of a full band of 154 musicians, presided over by a body of 12 specially-trained leaders, under one of the twenty-four sons of Asaph, Heman or Jeduthun as conductor. The leaders appear to have played on the cymbals, perhaps to mark the time. 1 Chron. 15:19; 16: 5. These great choirs answered one to another in responsive singing; thus the temple music must have been grand and inspiring beyond anything known before that time.

3. *Character of Hebrew music.*—As in all Oriental nations, the music of the Hebrews was melody rather than harmony, which latter in our sense of the term was then unknown. All, old and young, men and maidens, singers and instruments, appear to have sung one part only in unison, or in octaves. "The beauty of the music consisted altogether in the melody;" but this with so many instruments and voices was so charming that "the whole of antiquity is full of the praises of this music. By its means battles were won, cities conquered, mutinies quelled, diseases cured."

4. *Uses of music.*—In the private as well as in the religious life of the Hebrews music held a prominent place. The kings had their court musicians, 2 Chron. 35:25; Eccles. 2:8; and in the luxurious times of the later monarchy the effeminate gallants of Israel amused themselves with devising musical instruments while their nation was perishing "as Nero fiddled while Rome was burning." But music was also the legitimate expression of mirth and gladness. The bridal processions as they passed through the streets were accompanied with

music and song. Jer. 7 : 34. The music of the banquets was accompanied with songs and dancing. Luke 15 : 25. The triumphal processions which celebrated a victory were enlivened by minstrels and singers. Ex. 15 : 1, 20; Judges 5 : 1; 11 : 34. There were also religious songs. Isa. 30 : 29; James 5 : 13. Love songs are alluded to in Ps. 45, title, and Isa. 5 : 1. There were also the doleful

Egyptians had a long drum, of wood or copper, 2½ feet long, resembling the tom-tom of India, and beaten by the hand. Another form was shaped like a cask with bulging centre, and was made of copper. It was of the same length as the other, but larger around, and was beaten with sticks. Another drum was more like our kettle-drum; and one of these, the rabbins say, was

ASSYRIAN BAND.

songs of the funeral procession, and the wailing chant of the mourners. The grape-gatherers sang at their work, and the women sang as they toiled at the mill, and on every occasion the land of the Hebrews during their national prosperity was a land of music and melody.

Musical instruments of the Hebrews. There has been great obscurity as to the instruments of music in use among the Hebrews, but the discoveries on the monuments of Egypt and Assyria have thrown much light upon their form and nature.

I. STRINGED INSTRUMENTS.—1. The *kinnor,* the harp or lyre. [See illustration.] 2. The *nebel* or *psaltery,* the name of various large instruments of the harp kind. 3. The *sackbut,* probably the Latin *Sambuca,* a harp-like instrument of four strings and of triangular form. Some have considered the terms *Mahalath* and *Gittith* found in the titles of several of the Psalms to be musical instruments, and have gone so far as to describe them. While the idea has not been really confuted there is too much doubt to warrant any description.

II. INSTRUMENTS OF PERCUSSION.—1. The *tabret* or *timbrel* (*toph*), a form of tambourine, a narrow hoop covered with a tightened skin, and struck with the hand. On the Egyptian monuments are three kinds—the circular, the square, and another formed by two squares separated by a bar. 2. The *drum.* Of this there were many varieties, some of them resembling modern drums. The

placed in the temple court to call the priests to prayer, and could be heard from Jerusalem to Jericho. 3. *Bells* (*paamon*), attached to the high priest's dress, and rung by striking against the knobs, shaped like pomegranates, which were hung near them. 4. *Cymbals.* The earliest cymbals were probably finger-cymbals, castanets,—small plates of metal fastened to the thumb and

EGYPTIAN PICTURE OF A BEDOUIN PLAYING THE LYRE.

middle finger, and struck together. Afterward there were the large cymbals played with both hands. 5. *Systra* (*menaanim*), 2 Sam. 6:5, there translated "cornets" in the A. V. but "cas-

I. EGYPTIAN HARPS.

tanets" in the R. V. The systrum was a carved bronze or copper frame, with a handle, in all from 8 to 18 inches long, with movable rings and bar;. It was

II. INSTRUMENTS OF PERCUSSION.

shaken with the hand, and the rings and bars made a piercing metallic sound by

striking against the bronze frame. 6. The *shalishim*, 1 Sam. 18:6, a musical instrument used for accompanying the dance, and several times translated dancing. Ps. 150:3, 4, 5. It is doubtful what instrument is intended. Many consider that it was either a triangle with a metallic rim or frame, sometimes with a handle, and small bells attached to it, a systrum with three parallel bars across it on which were strung metallic

III. WIND INSTRUMENTS.

rings or plates. It was held in the hand, and was played by the women at weddings and merry-makings.

III. WIND INSTRUMENTS.—1. The *ugab*, translated "organ" in Gen. 4:21, A. V. and "pipe" in R. V. The meaning is very uncertain. It is considered by different authorities as a *pipe, bagpipe, Pan's pipe, syrinx,* or as a general term for a wind instrument. Each authority brings strong objections to all but the one he selects. 2. The *horn*, in the form of an animal's horn even when made of metal, but originating in the use of the horns of cattle. 3. The *trumpet* (*shophar*), same as the horn. 4. The *straight trumpet* reserved for the priests. 5. The *flute* (*halil,* meaning "bored through"), a pipe perforated with holes, originally made from reeds, but afterward of wood, bone, horn or ivory. It was chiefly consecrated to joy or pleasure. 6. The *flute,* alluded to in Dan. 3:5; probably the *syrinx.* Perhaps the same as the *ugab*. 7. The *dulcimer.* Dan. 3:5, the *Symphonia,* perhaps the bagpipe. The *modern* dulcimer is a triangular instrument strung with about 50 brass wires, and played upon with little sticks or metallic rods. It more resembles the ancient psaltery than the dulcimer of Dan. 3:5.

Mustard is mentioned in Matt. 13: 31; 17:20; Mark 4:31; Luke 13:19; 17:6. It is generally agreed that the mustard tree of Scripture is the black mustard (*Sinapis nigra*). The objection commonly made against any *sinapis* being the plant of the parable is that the seed grew into "a tree," in which the fowls of the air are said to come and lodge. As to this objection, it is urged with great truth that the expression is figurative and Oriental, and that in a proverbial simile no literal accuracy is to be expected. It is an error, for which

THE MUSTARD PLANT.

the language of Scripture is not accountable, to assert that the passage implies that birds "built their nests" in the tree: the Greek word has no such meaning; the word merely means "to settle or rest upon" anything for a longer or shorter time; nor is there any occasion to suppose that the expression "fowls of the air" denotes any other than the smaller *insessorial* kinds— linnets, finches, etc. Hiller's explanation is probably the correct one,—that the birds came and settled on the mustard-plant for the sake of the seed, of which they are very fond. Dr. Thomson also

says he has seen the wild mustard on the rich plain of Akkar as tall as the horse and the rider. If, then, the wild plant on the *rich plain* of Akkar grows as high as a man on horseback, it might attain to the same or a greater height when in a cultivated garden. The expression "which is indeed the least of all seeds" is in all probability hyperbolical, to denote a very small seed indeed, as there are many seeds which are smaller than mustard. "The Lord in his popular teaching," says Trench ("Notes on Parables," 108), "adhered to the popular language;" and the mustard-seed was used proverbially to denote anything very minute; or it may mean that it was the smallest of all *garden* seeds, which it is in truth.

Muth=labben (mūth-lăb'bĕn). "To the chief musician upon Muth-labben" is the title of Ps. 9, which has given rise to infinite conjecture. Most moderns think *Muth-labben* to be the opening words of an air or song to the melody of which the Psalm is to be sung. Possibly to the tune "Death of the son" or "Death makes wise."

My'ra (mī'rà), an important town in Lycia, on the southwest coast of Asia Minor, on the river Andriacus, 2½ miles from its mouth, referred to in Acts 27:5. Myra (now called *Dembra*) is remarkable still for its remains of various periods of history.

Myrrh. This substance is mentioned in Ex. 30:23 as one of the ingredients of the "oil of holy ointment;" in Esther 2:12, as one of the substances used in the purification of women; in Ps. 45:8, Prov. 7:17, and in several passages in Canticles, as a perfume. The Greek occurs in Matt. 2:11 among the gifts brought by the wise men to the infant Jesus; and in Mark 15:23 it is said that "wine mingled with myrrh" was offered to, but refused by, our Lord on the cross. Myrrh was also used for embalming. See John 19:39 and Herod. ii. 86. The *Balsamodendron myrrha,* which produces the myrrh of commerce, has a wood and bark which emit a strong odor; the gum which exudes from the bark is at first oily, but becomes hard by exposure to the air. This myrrh is in small yellowish or white globules or tears. The tree is small, with a stunted trunk, covered with light-gray bark. It is found in Arabia Felix. The myrrh of Gen. 37:

25 was probably *ladanum,* a highly-fragrant resin and volatile oil used as a cosmetic, and stimulative as a medicine. It is yielded by the *cistus,* known in Europe as the rock rose, a shrub with rose-colored flowers, growing in Pales-

MYRRH.

tine and along the shores of the Mediterranean. For wine mingled with myrrh see GALL.

Myrtle, a plant mentioned in Neh. 8: 15; Isa. 41:19; 55:13; Zech. 1:8, 10, 11. The modern Jews still adorn with myrtle the booths and sheds at the feast of tabernacles. Formerly, as we learn from Nehemiah, Neh. 8:15, myrtles grew on the hills about Jerusalem. The *Myrtus communis* is the kind denoted

by the Hebrew word. It is a shrub or low tree, sometimes ten feet high, with green shining leaves, and snow-white flowers bordered with purple, " which emit a perfume more exquisite than that of the rose." The seeds of the

MYRTLE.

myrtle, dried before they are ripe, form our allspice. The plant is common in Palestine to-day.

Mys′ia (mĭs′ĭà), Acts 16:7, 8, the name customarily used for the northwestern part of Asia Minor, bounded on the east and south by Bithynia, Phrygia and Lydia. Its boundaries were vague and undeterminable.

N

Na'am (nā'am) (*pleasantness*), one of the sons of Caleb the son of Jephunneh. 1 Chron. 4:15.

Na'amah (nā'a-mah) (*pleasant*). 1. One of the four women whose names are preserved in the records of the world before the flood; all except Eve being Cainites. She was daughter of Lamech by his wife Zillah, and sister, as is expressly mentioned, to Tubal-cain. Gen. 4:22 only.

2. Mother of King Rehoboam. 1 Kings 14:21, 31; 2 Chron. 12:13. In each of these passages she is distinguished by the title "the (not 'an,' as in Authorized Version) Ammonitess." She was therefore one of the foreign women whom Solomon took into his establishment. 1 Kings 11:1.

Na'amah (nā'a-mah), one of the towns of Judah in the district of the lowland or Shefelah. Josh. 15:41. It is proposed to identify it with *Naneh*, a small mud village 6 miles south of Lydda.

Na'aman (nā'a-man) (*pleasantness*). 1. "Naaman the Syrian." Luke 4:27. Naaman was commander-in-chief of the army of Syria, and was nearest to the person of the king, Ben-hadad II., whom he accompanied officially and supported when he went to worship in the temple of Rimmon, 2 Kings 5:18, at Damascus, the capital, about B.C. 840. A Jewish tradition apparently accepted by Josephus, which may very well be a genuine one, identifies him with the archer whose arrow, whether at random or not, struck Ahab with his mortal wound. The expression in 2 Kings 5:1 is remarkable—"because that by him Jehovah had given deliverance to Syria." Whatever the particular exploit referred to was, it had given Naaman a great position at the court of Ben-hadad. Naaman was afflicted with a leprosy which had hitherto defied cure. A little Israelitish captive maiden tells him of the fame and skill of Elisha, and he is cured by him by following his simple directions to bathe in the Jordan seven times. See 2 Kings 5:14. His first business after his cure is to thank his benefactor and gratefully acknowledge the power of the God of Israel, and promise "henceforth to offer neither burnt offering nor sacrifice unto other gods, but unto the Lord."

2. One of the family of Benjamin who came down to Egypt with Jacob, as read in Gen. 46:21. He was the son of Bela, and head of the family of the Naamites. Num. 26:40; 1 Chron. 8:3, 4. (B.C. 1706.)

Na'amathite (nā'a-math-īte), the gentilic name of one of Job's friends, Zophar the Naamathite. Job 2:11; 11:1; 20:1; 42:9. There is no other trace of this name in the Bible, and the town whence it is derived is unknown. But as Uz was in Arabia, probably the Naamah where he lived was on the Arabian borders of Syria.

Na'amites (nā'a-mītes), **The,** the family descended from Naaman, the grandson of Benjamin. Num. 26:40 only.

Na'arah (nā'a-rȧ) (*a maiden*), the second wife of Ashur; a descendant of Judah. 1 Chron. 4:5, 6.

Na'arai (nā'a-rā-ī), one of the valiant men of David's armies. 1 Chron. 11:37. In 1 Chron. he is called the son of Ezbai, but in 2 Sam. 23:35 he appears as "Paarai the Arbite." It is impossible to decide between the readings.

Na'aran (nā'a-răn), a city of Ephraim, which 1 Chron. 7:28 mentions as the eastern limit of the tribe. It is very probably identical with Naarath, or more accurately Naarah.

Na'arath (nā'a-răth) (properly Naarah), a place named, Josh. 16:7 only, as one of the landmarks on the southern boundary of Ephraim. It appears to have lain between Ataroth and Jericho, in the Jordan valley. Eusebius and

Jerome speak of it as if well known to them—"Naorath, a small village of the Jews, five miles from Jericho." The modern village of *el-Aujah* is a suitable identification.

Naash'on (na-āsh'on). [NAHSHON.]

Naas'son (na-ăs'sŏn) (*enchanting*), the Greek form of the name NAHSHON. Matt. 1 : 4, Luke 3 : 32, only.

Na'bal (nā'bal) (*foolish*), a sheepmaster on the confines of Judea and the desert, in that part of the country which bore from its great conqueror the name of Caleb. He was a resident of Carmel near to Ziph, and a descendant of Caleb. 1 Sam. 25 : 3, 5; 30 : 14.' (B.C. about 1059.) His residence was on the southern Carmel, in the pasture lands of Maon. His wealth, as might be expected from his abode, consisted chiefly of sheep and goats. David was living in the desert adjoining, and levying tribute on the large sheepmasters as reward for his protection. 1 Sam. 25 : 7, 15, 16. Once a year there was a grand shearing-feast on Carmel, "like the feast of a king," ch. 25 : 2, 4, 36. It was on one of these occasions that ten young men of David's band came to ask the tribute, in the courteous language of the East, "whatsoever cometh into thy hand for thy servants and for *thy son* David." The great sheepmaster peremptorily refused with insulting words as to masterless men in the district. The moment that the messengers were gone, the shepherds that stood by perceived the danger that their master and themselves would incur. To Nabal himself they durst not speak, ch. 25 : 17. To his wife, as to the good angel of the household, one of the shepherds told the state of affairs. She, with the expected tribute and doubtless the additional offerings usual on such occasions, with her attendants running before her, rode down the hill toward David's encampment. David had already made the fatal vow of extermination, ch. 25 : 22. At this moment, as it would seem, Abigail appeared, threw herself on her face before him, and poured forth her petition in language which in both form and expression almost assumes the tone of poetry. She returned with the news of David's recantation of his vow. Nabal was then at the height of his orgies, and his wife dared not communicate to him either his danger or

his escape, ch. 25 : 36. At break of day she told him both. The stupid reveller was suddenly roused to a sense of that which impended over him. "His heart died within him, and he became as a stone." It was as if a stroke of apoplexy or paralysis had fallen upon him. Ten days he lingered, "and the Lord smote Nabal, and he died," ch. 25 : 37, 38. Abigail shortly after became David's wife.

Na'both (nā'bŏth), the victim of Ahab and Jezebel, was the owner of a small vineyard at Jezreel, close to the royal palace of Ahab. 1 Kings 21 : 1, 2. (B.C. 854.) It thus became an object of desire to the king, who offered an equivalent in money or another vineyard in exchange for this. Naboth, in the independent spirit of a Jewish landholder, refused: "The Lord forbid it me that I should give the inheritance of my fathers unto thee." Ahab knowing the temper of his people was about to yield, when Jezebel, a foreigner with Phœnician ideas of royal authority, took the matter into her own hands. A fast was proclaimed, as on the announcement of some impending calamity. Naboth was "set on high" in the public place of Samaria; two men of worthless character accused him of having "cursed God and the king." He and his children, 2 Kings 9 : 26, were dragged out of the city and stoned the same night. For the signal retribution taken on this judicial murder—a remarkable proof of the high regard paid in the old dispensation to the claims of justice and independence—see AHAB; JEHU; JEZEBEL.

Na'chon's (nā'kŏn) **threshing=floor**, the place at which the ark had arrived in its progress from Kirjath-jearim to Jerusalem, when Uzzah lost his life in his too-hasty zeal for its safety. 2 Sam. 6 : 6. (B.C. 1042.)

Na'chor (nā'kŏr). [NAHOR.]

Na'dab (nā'dăb) (*liberal*). 1. The eldest son of Aaron and Elisheba. Ex. 6 : 23; Num. 3 : 2. He, his father and brother, and seventy elders of Israel were led out from the midst of the assembled people, Ex. 24 : 1, and were commanded to stay and worship God "afar off," below the lofty summit of Sinai, where Moses alone was to come near to the Lord. Subsequently, Lev. 10 : 1, Nadab and his brother were struck dead before the sanctuary by fire from the Lord. Their offence was kindling the incense in their censers with "strange" fire, *i. e.* not taken from that which burned perpetually, Lev. 6: 13, on the altar. (B.C. 1490.)

2. King Jeroboam's son, who succeeded to the throne of Israel B.C. 915, and reigned two years. 1 Kings 15: 25–31. At the siege of Gibbethon a conspiracy broke out in the midst of the army, and the king was slain by Baasha, a man of Issachar. This fulfilled the threatenings of Jehovah against Jeroboam and his house.

3. A son of Shammai, 1 Chron. 2 : 28, of the tribe of Judah.

4. A son of Gibeon, 1 Chron. 8 : 30; 9 : 36, of the tribe of Benjamin.

Nag'gai (năg'gā-ī) (*illuminating*), the true form of NAGGE.

Nag'ge (năg'ge), one of the ancestors of Christ. Luke 3 : 25.

Nahal'al (nà-hăl'al) (*pasture*), one of the cities of Zebulun, given with its "suburbs" to the Merarite Levites. Josh. 21 : 35. It is the same which in Josh. 19 : 15 is inaccurately given in the Authorized Version as Nahallal, the Hebrew being in both cases identical. In Judges 1 : 30 it is called NAHALOL. It is identified with the modern *Malul*, a village 3½ miles west of Nazareth. Another site proposed is *Ain Mahil* a little north of Nazareth.

Naha'liel (nà-hā'lĭ-el) (*torrent-valley of God*), one of the halting-places of Israel in the latter part of their progress to Canaan. Num. 21 : 19. It lay "beyond," that is, north of, the Arnon, ver. 13. It may be either on *Wady Waleh*, a tributary to the Arnon, or *Wady Zerka Main*, which flows into the Dead Sea.

Nahal'ol. [NAHALAL.]

Naham (nā'hăm) (*consolation*), the brother of the wife of Hodiah. The translation in the A. V. is impossible. 1 Chron. 4 : 19.

Naham'ani (nà-hăm'a-nī) (*merciful*), a chief man among those who returned from Babylon with Zerubbabel and Jeshua. Neh. 7 : 7. (B.C. 536.)

Na'harai (nā'hăr-ī) (*snoring*), the armor-bearer of Joab, called NAHARI in the Authorized Version of 2 Sam. 23 : 37. He was a native of Beeroth. 1 Chron. 11 : 39.

Na'hari. The same as NAHARAI. 2 Sam. 23 : 37. In the original edition of 1611 the name is correctly given as "Naharai the Berothite."

Na'hash (nā'hăsh) (*serpent*). **1.** King of the Ammonites who dictated to the inhabitants of Jabesh-gilead that cruel alternative of the loss of their right eyes or slavery, which roused the swift wrath of Saul, and caused the destruction of the Ammonite force. 1 Sam. 11 : 2–11. (B.C. 1092.) Either the same Nahash or his son "Nahash the father of Hanun" rendered David some special and valuable service, which David was anxious for an opportunity of requiting. 2 Sam. 10 : 2.

2. A person mentioned once only—2 Sam. 17 : 25—in stating the parentage of Amasa, the commander-in-chief of Absalom's army. Amasa is there said to have been the son of a certain Ithra by Abigail, "daughter of Nahash and sister to Zeruiah." Some consider him the same as the preceding.

Na'hath (nā'hăth) (*rest*). **1.** One of the "dukes" of Edom, eldest son of Reuel the son of Esau. Gen. 36 : 13, 17; 1 Chron. 1 : 37.

2. A Kohathite Levite, son of Zophai. 1 Chron. 6 : 26. Elsewhere called TOAH, and TOHU.

3. A Levite in the reign of Hezekiah. 2 Chron. 31 : 13.

Nah'bi (näh'bī) (*hidden*), the son of Vophsi, a Naphtalite, and one of the twelve spies. Num. 13 : 14.

Na'hor (nā'hôr) (*snorting*), the name of two persons in the family of Abraham. **1.** His grandfather; the son of Serug and father of Terah. Gen. 11 : 22–25.

2. Grandson of the preceding, son of Terah and brother of Abraham and Haran. Gen. 11 : 26, 27. He married Milcah, the daughter of his brother Haran; and when Abraham and Lot migrated to Canaan, Nahor remained behind in the land of his birth, on the eastern side of the Euphrates.

Nah'shon (näh'shŏn), or **Naash'on** (*enchanting*), son of Amminadab, and prince of the children of Judah (as he is styled in the genealogy of Judah, 1 Chron. 2 : 10) at the time of the first numbering in the wilderness. Ex. 6 : 23; Num. 1 : 7, etc. His sister, Elisheba, was wife to Aaron, and his son, Salmon, was husband to Rahab after the taking of Jericho. He died in the wilderness, according to Num. 26 : 64, 65.

Na'hum (nā'hum) (*consolation*). Nahum, called "the Elkoshite," is the seventh in order of the minor prophets.

His personal history is quite unknown. The site of Elkosh, his native place, is disputed, some placing it in Galilee, others in Assyria. The imagery of his prophecy is such as would be natural to an inhabitant of Palestine, Nah. 1 : 4, to whom the rich pastures of Bashan, the vineyards of Carmel and the blossoms of Lebanon were emblems of all that was luxuriant and fertile. The language employed in ch. 1 : 15; 2 : 2 is appropriate to one who wrote for his countrymen in their native land. Hastings thinks that most probably Elkosh was the modern *Beit-Jibrin,* half way between Jerusalem and Gaza. McClintock and Strong come to the conclusion that Nahum was a native of Galilee, that at the captivity of the ten tribes he escaped into Judah, and prophesied in the reign of Hezekiah.

Nahum, Book of. DATE. It is certain that the prophecy was written before the final downfall of Nineveh and its capture by the Medes and Chaldeans, B.C. 606. The allusions to the Assyrian power imply that it was still unbroken, ch. 1 : 12; 2 : 8, 13; 3 : 15–17. And as the prophet reports the destruction of No-ammon the capital of Upper Egypt by the Assyrians, which took place B.C. 664, his book must have been written between these two dates, in the reigns of Manasseh or Josiah. PLACE. He probably wrote his prophecy either in Jerusalem or its neighborhood. The subject of the prophecy is, in accordance with the superscription, " the burden of Nineveh," the destruction of which he predicts. As a poet Nahum occupies a high place in the first rank of Hebrew literature. His style is clear and uninvolved, though pregnant and forcible; his diction sonorous and rhythmical, the words re-echoing to the sense. Comp. 2 : 4; 3 : 3.

Nail. The translation of three Hebrew words. 1. A finger nail. Deut. 21 : 12; Dan. 4 : 33.

2. A tent-peg. Judges 4 : 21. Tent-pegs were usually of wood and of large size; but sometimes, as was the case with those used to fasten the curtains of the tabernacle, they were of metal. Ex. 27 : 19; 38 : 20.

3. A nail, primarily a point, commonly of metal. We are told that David prepared iron for the nails to be used in the temple; and as the Holy of Holies was plated with gold, the nails for fastening the plates were probably of gold.

Na'in (nā'in) (*beauty*), a village of Galilee, the gate of which is made illustrious by the raising of the widow's son. Luke 7 : 12. The modern *Nein* is situated on the northwestern edge of the " Little Hermon," or *Jebel-ed-Dûhy,* where the ground falls into the plain of Esdraelon. The entrance to the place, where our Saviour met the funeral, must probably always have been up the steep ascent from the plain; and here, on the west side of the village, the rock is full of sepulchral caves.

Na'ioth (nā'yoth) (*habitations*), or more fully, " Naioth in Ramah," a place of Mount Ephraim, in which Samuel and David took refuge together after the latter had made his escape from the jealous fury of Saul. 1 Sam. 19 : 18, 19, 22, 23; 20 : 1. An explanation generally accepted is the huts or dwellings of a school or college of prophets over which Samuel presided, as Elisha did over those at Gilgal and Jericho. This is disputed by some modern scholars, *e. g.* Driver, partly on philological grounds.

Names. 1. *Names of places.*—These may be divided into two general classes —descriptive and historical. The former are such as mark some peculiarity of the locality, usually a natural one, *e. g.* Sharon, " plain;" Gibeah, " hill;" Ramah, " height." Of the second class of local names, some were given in honor of individual men, *e. g.* the city Enoch, Gen. 4 : 17, etc. More commonly, however, such names were given to perpetuate the memory of some important historic occurrence. Bethel perpetuated through all Jewish history the early revelations of God to Jacob. Gen. 28 : 19; 35 : 15. So Jehovah-jireh, Gen. 22 : 14; Mahanaim, Gen. 32 : 2; Peniel, Gen. 32 : 30, etc. In compounds for the names of towns or other localities, some of the most common terms employed were *Kir,* a " wall " or " fortress;" *Kirjath,* " city;" *En,* " fountain;" *Beer,* " a well," etc. The names of countries were almost universally derived from the name of the first settlers or earliest historic population. Many of the names in common use in Palestine, and once supposed Israelitish, with a decipherable meaning, have been found on the Tel-el-Amarna tablets; showing their existence by name before the entrance of Israel. This is an indication that still other names may be of Canaanitish origin. Among these is Jerusalem.

2. *Names of persons.*—Among the Hebrews each person received but a single name. In the case of boys this was conferred upon the eighth day, in connection with the rite of circumcision. Luke 1:59; comp. Gen. 17:5-14. To distinguish an individual from others of the same name it was customary to add to compounded either (1) with terms denoting relationship, as *Abi* or *Ab*, father, as Abihud, "father of praise," Abimelech, "father of the king;" Ben, son, as Benoni, "son of my sorrow," Benjamin, "son of the right hand;" or (2) nouns denoting natural life, as *am*, "people," *melech*, "king;" or (3) with names of God, as *El*, "God," and *Jah* or *Ja*, shortened from "Jehovah." Among the

RUINS OF NAIN.

his own proper name that of his father or ancestors. Sometimes the mother's was used instead. Simple names in Hebrew, as in all languages, were largely borrowed from nature; *e. g.* Deborah, "bee;" Tamar, "a palm tree;" Jonah, "dove." Many names of women were derived from those of men by change of termination; *e. g.* Hammelech, "the king;" Hammoleketh, "the queen." The majority of compound names have special religious or social significance, being Oriental nations, it is customary to mark one's entrance into a new relation by a new name, in which case the acceptance of the new name involves the acknowledgment of the sovereignty of the namegiver. Examples of this are Abraham, Gen. 17:5; Sarah, Gen. 17:15; Israel, as the designation of the spiritual character, in place of Jacob, which designated the natural character. Gen. 32:28.

Na′omi, or **Nao′mi** (nȧ-ō′mī) (*pleas-*

ant), the wife of Elimelech and mother-in-law of Ruth, Ruth 1 : 2, etc., probably in the time of Gideon. Naomi left Judea with her husband and two sons, in a time of famine, and went to the land of Moab. Here her husband and sons died, and she later returned to Bethlehem with Ruth.

Na'phish (nā'fish) (*respiration*), the last but one of the sons of Ishmael. Gen. 25 : 15; 1 Chron. 1 : 31.

Naph'tali (năf'ta-lī) (*wrestling*), the sixth son of Jacob; the second child borne to him by Bilhah, Rachel's slave. His birth and the bestowal of his name are recorded in Gen. 30 : 8. When the census was taken at Mount Sinai the tribe of Naphtali numbered no less than 53,400 fighting men, Num. 1 : 43; 2 : 30; but when the borders of the promised land were reached, its numbers were reduced to 45,400. Num. 26 : 48–50. During the march through the wilderness Naphtali occupied a position on the north of the sacred tent with Dan and Asher. Num. 2 : 25–31. In the apportionment of the land, the tribe was given some of the finest land in Palestine. Its northern boundary was the boundary of Israel—on the east the Jordan, on the west and south Asher, Zebulun and Issachar. It was a part of Galilee in the time of Christ, and included the cities of Chorazin, Capernaum and Tiberias.

Naph'tali (năf'ta-lī), **Mount**, the northernmost portion of the central range of western Palestine, Josh. 20 : 7, answering to "Mount Ephraim" in the centre and "Mount Judah" in the south of Palestine.

Naph'tuhim (năf'tu-hĭm), a Mizraite (Egyptian) nation or tribe, mentioned only in the account of the descendants of Noah. Gen. 10 : 13; 1 Chron. 1 : 11. If we may judge from their position in the list of the Mizraites, the Naphtuhim were probably settled, at first, either in Egypt or immediately to the west of it.

Napkin. [HANDKERCHIEF.]

Narcis'sus (när-cĭs'sus), a dweller at Rome, Rom. 16 : 11, some members of whose household were known as Christians to St. Paul. Some have assumed the identity of this Narcissus with the secretary of the emperor Claudius.

Nard. [SPIKENARD.]

Na'than (nā'than) (*he has given*). 1. An eminent Hebrew prophet in the reigns of David and Solomon. He first appears in the consultation with David about the building of the temple. 2 Sam. 7 : 2, 3, 17. He next comes forward as the reprover of David for the sin with Bath-sheba; and his famous apologue on the rich man and the ewe lamb, which as the only direct example of his prophetic power, shows it to have been of a very high order. 2 Sam. 12 : 1–12.

2. A son of David; one of the four who were borne to him by Bath-sheba. 1 Chron. 3 : 5; 14 : 4; 2 Sam. 5 : 14. The line of Mary ran through Nathan, Luke 3 : 31, while it is through Solomon that Joseph, the husband of Mary, was descended from David. Matt. 1 : 6.

3. Father of one and brother of another one of the members of David's guard. 2 Sam. 23 : 36; 1 Chron. 11 : 38.

4. One of the head men who returned from Babylon with Ezra on his second expedition. Ezra 8 : 16. It is not impossible that he may be the same as

5. The "son of Bani." Ezra 10 : 39.

Nathan'ael (nà-thăn'a-el) (*God has given*), a disciple of Jesus Christ, concerning whom, under that name at least, we learn from Scripture little more than his birthplace, Cana of Galilee, John 21 : 2, and his simple, truthful character. John 1 : 47. The name does not occur in the first three Gospels; but it is commonly believed that Nathanael and Bartholomew are the same person. The evidence for that belief is as follows: St. John, who twice mentions Nathanael, never once introduces the name of Bartholomew at all. St. Matthew, Matt. 10 : 3, St. Mark, Mark 3 : 18, and St. Luke, Luke 6 : 14, all speak of Bartholomew, but never of Nathanael. But the identification was not made till the 9th century, and it may not be correct. It was Philip who first brought Nathanael to Jesus, just as Andrew had brought his brother Simon.

Na'than=me'lech (nā'than-mē'lek) (*Melech*, i. e. *the king gave*), a eunuch (Authorized Version "chamberlain") in the court of Josiah. 2 Kings 23 : 11. (B.C. 628.)

Na'um (nā'um) (*consolation*), son of Esli and father of Amos, in the genealogy of Christ, Luke 3 : 25.

Nave (Heb. *gao*), anything convex or arched. It is rendered once only in the plural, "naves," 1 Kings 7 : 33, meaning the centres of the wheels in which the spokes are inserted, *i. e.* the hubs.

Nazarene' (năz-a-rēne'), an inhabitant of Nazareth. This appellative is applied to Jesus in many passages in the New Testament. This name, made striking in so many ways, and which, if first given in scorn, was adopted and gloried in by the disciples, we are told in Matt. 2 : 23 possesses a prophetic significance. Its application to Jesus, in consequence of the providential arrangements by which his parents were led to take up their abode in Nazareth, was the filling out of the predictions in which the promised Messiah is described as a *nêtser, i. e.* a *shoot, sprout,* of Jesse, a humble and despised descendant of the decayed royal family. Isa. 11 : 1. He is frequently termed the Branch, which has much the same meaning. Jer. 23 : 5; 33 : 15; Zech. 3 : 8; 6 : 12.

Once, Acts 24 : 5, the term *Nazarenes* is applied to the followers of Jesus by way of contempt. The name still exists in Arabic as the ordinary designation of Christians.

THE FOUNTAIN OF THE VIRGIN AT NAZARETH.

Naz'areth (năz'a-rĕth) (*verdant, off-shoot*), the ordinary residence of our Saviour, is not mentioned in the Old Testament, but occurs first in Matt. 2: 23. It is not even mentioned in Josephus, a fact explained by some as indicating its recent origin, or small size; by others as merely the result of its secluded position. It derives its celebrity from its connection with the history of Christ, and in that respect has a hold on the imagination and feelings of men which it shares only with Jerusalem and Bethlehem. It is situated among the hills which constitute the south ridges of Lebanon, just before they sink down into the plain of Esdraelon. It must have been a place of considerable importance in the time of Christ, as the word *Polis,* "city" is always used of it, and not *kome,* "village." Merrill represents it as a city of 15,000 to 20,000 inhabitants. Of the identification of the ancient site there can be no doubt. The name of the present village is *en-Nâzirah,* the same, therefore, as of old; it is on a hill or mountain, Luke 4:29; it is within the limits of the province of Galilee, Mark 1:9; it is near Cana, according to the implication in John 2:1, 2, 11; a precipice exists in the neighborhood. Luke 4:29. The modern Nazareth belongs to the better class of eastern villages. It has a population of about 7500; a few are Mohammedans, the rest Latin and Greek Christians. Near this town Napoleon once encamped (1799), after the battle of Mount Tabor. The expression used in John 1: 47 to the disparagement of Nazareth less probably refers to any particular viciousness of Nazareth, than to the surprise felt by Nathanael that the Messiah-King could come from such an insignificant place. Above the town are several rocky ledges, over which a person could not be thrown without almost certain destruction. There is one very remarkable precipice, almost perpendicular and forty or fifty feet high, near the Maronite church, which may well be supposed to be the identical one over which his infuriated fellow townsmen attempted to hurl Jesus.

Naz'arite (năz'a-rīte), more properly **Naz'irite** (*one separated*), one of either sex who was bound by a vow of a peculiar kind to be set apart from others for the service of God. The obligation was either for life or for a de-

fined time. There is no notice in the Pentateuch of Nazirites for life; but the regulations for the vow of a Nazirite of days are given Num. 6:1-21. The Nazirite, during the term of his consecration, was bound to abstain from wine, grapes, with every production of the vine, and from every kind of intoxicating drink. He was forbidden to cut the hair of his head, or to approach any dead body, even that of his nearest relation. When the period of his vow was fulfilled, he was brought to the door of the tabernacle, and was required to offer a he lamb for a burnt offering, a ewe lamb for a sin offering, and a ram for a peace offering, with the usual accompaniments of peace offerings, Lev. 7:12, 13, and of the offering made at the consecration of priests. Ex. 29:2; Num. 6:15. He brought also a meat offering and a drink offering, which appear to have been presented by themselves as a distinct act of service. ver. 17. He was to cut off the hair of "the head of his separation" (that is, the hair which had grown during the period of his consecration) at the door of the tabernacle, and to put it into the fire under the sacrifice on the altar. Of the Nazirites for life three are mentioned in the Scriptures—Samson, Samuel and St. John the Baptist. The only one of these actually called a Nazirite is Samson. The regulations governing them are not exactly the same as those governing the Nazirite of days. We do not know whether the vow for life was ever voluntarily taken by the individual. In all the cases mentioned in the sacred history, it was made by the parents before the birth of the Nazirite himself. The consecration of the Nazirite bore a striking resemblance to that of the high priest. Lev. 21:10-12. The meaning of the Nazirite vow has been regarded in different lights. It may be regarded as an act of self-sacrifice. That it was essentially a sacrifice of the person to the Lord is obviously in accordance with the terms of the law. Num. 6:2. The man was separated from his brethren that he might be peculiarly devoted to the Lord. They were more numerous than the references in the Old Testament would lead one to think. Amos 2:11 shows their existence late in the history; while Acts 21:23 doubtless refers to the same thing.

Ne'ah (nē'ah) (*emotion*), a place

NAZARETH.

Photo by Jan Wilga

which was one of the landmarks on the boundary of Zebulun. Josh. 19:13 only. It has not been identified.

Neap'olis (né-ăp'o-lĭs) (*new city*) is the place in northern Greece where Paul and his associates first landed in Europe, Acts 16:11, where, no doubt, he landed also on his second visit to Macedonia, Acts 20:1, and whence certainly he embarked on his last journey through that province to Troas and Jerusalem. Acts 20:6. Philippi being an inland town, Neapolis was evidently the port, and is represented by the present *Kavalla*. Kavalla is a city of 4000 or 5000 inhabitants, Greeks and Turks. Neapolis was ten miles from Philippi, on a high rocky promontory jutting out into the Ægean Sea, while a temple of Diana crowned the hill-top.

Neari'ah (nē'a-rī'ah). 1. One of the sons of Shemaiah in the line of the royal family of Judah after the captivity. 1 Chron. 3:22, 23.

2. A son of Ishi, and one of the captains of the 500 Simeonites who, in the days of Hezekiah, drove out the Amalekites from Mount Seir. 1 Chron. 4:42.

Neba'i (nĕb-a'ī), a family of the heads of the people who signed the covenant with Nehemiah. Neh. 10:19.

Neba'ioth, Neba'joth (nė-bā'yoth) (*heights*), the "first-born of Ishmael," Gen. 25:13; 1 Chron. 1:29, and father of a pastoral tribe named after him, the "rams of Nebaioth" being mentioned by the prophet Isaiah, Isa. 60:7, with the flocks of Kedar. From the days of Jerome this people has been identified with the Nabathæans of Greek and Roman history who took possession of Mount Seir in the 4th century B.C., and spread thence over the entire region east of the Jordan. Petra was their capital. Some modern scholars, however, reject this identification.

Nebal'lat (nė-băl'lat), a town of Benjamin, one of those which the Benjamites reoccupied after the captivity. Neh. 11:34.

Ne'bat (nē'băt), the father of Jeroboam I, 1 Kings 11:26; 12:2, 15, etc., is described as an Ephraimite of Zereda.

Ne'bo (nē'bó) (*prophet*), **Mount,** the mountain from which Moses took his first and last view of the promised land. Deut. 32:49; 34:1. It is described as in the land of Moab, facing Jericho; the head or summit of a moun-

tain called Pisgah, which again seems to have formed a portion of the general range of Abarim. Notwithstanding the minuteness of this description, it is only recently that any one has succeeded in pointing out any spot which answers to Nebo. Tristram identifies it with a peak (*Jebel Nebbah*) of the Abarim or Moab mountains, about five miles southwest of Heshbân (Heshbon) and about 9½ west of the northeast end of the Dead Sea. From the western summit, *Siaghah,* the whole of the Jordan valley opens out to view, and could well be called "all the land."

Ne'bo. 1. A town of Reuben on the east side of Jordan. Num. 32:3, 38. In the remarkable prophecies given by Isaiah, Isa. 15:2, and Jeremiah, Jer. 48:1, 22, concerning Moab, Nebo is mentioned in the same connection as before, but in the hands of Moab. Eusebius and Jerome identify it with Nobah or Kenath, and place it eight miles south of Heshbon. Others identify it with some ruins on Mount Nebo.

2. The children of Nebo returned from Babylon with Zerubbabel. Ezra 2:29; 10:43; Neh. 7:33. The name occurs between Bethel and Ai and Lydda, which implies that it was situated in the territory of Benjamin to the northwest of Jerusalem. This is possibly the modern *Beit-Nûbah*, about 12 miles northwest by west of Jerusalem, 8 from Lydda.

3. Nebo, which occurs both in Isaiah, Isa. 46:1, and Jeremiah, Jer. 48:1, as the name of a Chaldean god, is a well-known deity of the Babylonians and Assyrians. He was the god who presided over learning and letters. His general character corresponds to that of the Egyptian Thoth, the Greek Hermes and the Latin Mercury. In Babylonia Nebo held a prominent place from an early time. The ancient town of Borsippa was especially under his protection, and the great temple here, the modern *Birs-Nimrûd,* was dedicated to him from a very remote age. He was the tutelar god of the most important Babylonian kings, in whose names the word *Nabu* or Nebo appears as an element.

Nebuchadnez'zar (nĕb-u-kad-nĕz'-zar), or **Nebuchadrez'zar** (*O Nebo protect the landmark*), was one of the greatest and most powerful of the Babylonian kings. He was the son and successor of Nabopolassar, the founder of the Babylonian empire. In the lifetime of his father, Nebuchadnezzar led an army against Pharaoh-necho, king of Egypt, defeated him at Carchemish, B.C. 605, in a great battle, Jer. 46:2–12, recovered Cœle-Syria, Phœnicia and Palestine, took Jerusalem, Dan. 1:1, 2, pressed forward to Egypt, and was engaged in that country or upon its borders when intelligence arrived which recalled him hastily to Babylon. Nabopolassar, after reigning twenty-one years, had died and the throne was vacant. In alarm about the succession Nebuchadnezzar returned to the capital, accompanied only by his light troops; and crossing the desert, probably by way of Tadmor or Palmyra, reached Babylon before any disturbance had arisen, and entered peaceably on his kingdom, B.C. 604. Within three years of Nebuchadnezzar's first expedition into Syria and Palestine, disaffection again showed itself in those countries. Jehoiakim, who, although threatened at first with captivity, 2 Chron. 36:6, had been finally maintained on the throne as a Babylonian vassal, after three years of service "turned and rebelled" against his suzerain, probably trusting to be supported by Egypt. 2 Kings 24:1. Not long afterward Phœnicia seems to have broken into revolt, and the Chaldean monarch once more took the field in person, and marched first of all against Tyre. Having invested that city and left a portion of his army there to continue the siege, he proceeded against Jerusalem, which submitted without a struggle. According to Josephus, who is here our chief authority, Nebuchadnezzar punished Jehoiakim with death, comp. Jer. 22:18, 19 and 36:30, but placed his son Jehoiachin upon the throne. Jehoiachin reigned only three months; for, on his showing symptoms of disaffection, Nebuchadnezzar came up against Jerusalem for the third time, deposed the young prince (whom he carried to Babylon, together with a large portion of the population of the city and the chief of the temple treasures), and made his uncle, Zedekiah, king in his room. Tyre still held out; and it was not till the thirteenth year from the time of its first investment that the city of merchants fell, B.C. 585. Ere this happened, Jerusalem had been totally destroyed. Nebuchadnezzar had

commenced the final siege of Jerusalem in the ninth year of Zedekiah—his own seventeenth year (B.C. 588)—and took it two years later, B.C. 586. Zedekiah escaped from the city, but was captured near Jericho, Jer. 39:5, and brought to Nebuchadnezzar at Riblah in the territory of Hamath, where his eyes were put out by the king's order, while his sons and his chief nobles were slain. Nebuchadnezzar then returned to Babylon with Zedekiah, whom he imprisoned for the remainder of his life. The military successes of Nebuchadnezzar can-

INSCRIPTION ON A BRICK OF NEBUCHADNEZZAR.

not be traced minutely beyond this point. It may be gathered from the prophetical Scriptures and from Josephus that the conquest of Jerusalem was rapidly followed by the fall of Tyre and the complete submission of Phœnicia, Ezek. 26–28; after which the Babylonians carried their arms into Egypt, and inflicted severe injuries on that fertile country. Jer. 46:13–26; Ezek. 29:2–20. We are told that the first care of Nebuchadnezzar, on obtaining quiet possession of his kingdom after the first Syrian expedition, was to rebuild the temple of Bel (*Bel-Merodach*) at Babylon out of the spoils of the Syrian war. He next proceeded to strengthen and beautify the city, which he renovated throughout and surrounded with several lines of fortifications, himself adding one entirely new quarter. Having finished the walls and adorned the gates magnificently, he constructed a new palace. In the grounds of this palace he formed the celebrated "hanging garden," which the Greeks placed among the seven wonders of the world. But he did not confine his efforts to the ornamentation and improvement of his capital. Throughout the empire, at Borsippa, Sippara, and a multitude of other places, he built or rebuilt cities, repaired temples, constructed quays, reservoirs, canals and aqueducts, on a scale of grandeur and magnificence surpassing everything of the kind recorded in history, unless it be the constructions of one or two of the greatest Egyptian monarchs. The wealth, greatness and general prosperity of Nebuchadnezzar are strikingly placed before us in the book of Daniel. Toward the close of his reign the glory of Nebuchadnezzar suffered a temporary eclipse. As a punishment for his pride and vanity, that strange form of madness was sent upon him which the Greeks called Lycanthropy, wherein the sufferer imagines himself a beast, and, quitting the haunts of men, insists on leading the life of a beast. Dan. 4:33. This strange malady is thought by some to receive illustration from an inscription which speaks of a period of four years during which he took no part in public affairs. After an interval of four or perhaps seven years, Dan. 4:16, Nebuchadnezzar's malady left him. We are told that "his reason returned, and for the glory of his kingdom his honor and brightness returned;" and he "was established in his kingdom, and excellent majesty was added to him." Dan. 4:36. He died in the year B.C. 561, at an advanced age (eighty-three or eighty-four), having reigned forty-three years. A son, Evil-merodach, succeeded him.

Nebushas'ban (něb-u-shǎs'ban) (*Nebo, save me*), one of the officers of Nebuchadnezzar at the time of the capture of Jerusalem. He was Rab-saris, *i. e.* chief of the eunuchs. Jer. 39:13. Nebushasban's office and title were the same as those of Ashpenaz, Dan. 1:3. There were probably several who held the same office. See Jer. 39:3.

Nebuzar-a'dan (něb-u-zär-ā'dan) (*Nebo hath given offspring*), the captain of Nebuchadnezzar's body guard. On the capture of Jerusalem he was left by Nebuchadnezzar in charge of the city. Comp. Jer. 39:11. He seems to have quitted Judea when he took down the chief people of Jerusalem to his master at Riblah. 2 Kings 25:18–20. In five years he again appeared.

Jer. 52:30. Nebuchadnezzar in his twenty-third year made a descent on the regions east of Jordan, including the Ammonites and Moabites, who escaped when Jerusalem was destroyed. Thence he proceeded to Egypt, and either on the way thither or on the return, Nebuzar-adan again passed through the country and carried off more captives.

Ne'cho (nē'kò). 2 Chron. 35:20, 22; 36:4. [PHARAOH-NECHO.]

Nedabi'ah (něd-a-bī'ah) (*Jehovah hath impelled*), one of the sons of Jeconiah or Jehoiachin, king of Judah. 1 Chron. 3:18.

Neginah (něg'ĭ-nah) (*stringed instrument*), the singular of *Neginoth*. It occurs in the title of several psalms. It is the general term by which all stringed instruments are described. "The chief musician on *Neginoth*" was, therefore, the conductor of that portion of the temple choir who played upon the stringed instruments.

Neginoth. [NEGINAH.]

Nehel'amite (nè-hěl'a-mīte), **The,** the designation of a man named Shemaiah, a false prophet, who opposed Jeremiah. Jer. 29:24, 31, 32. The name is no doubt formed from that either of Shemaiah's native place or the progenitor of his family; which of the two is uncertain.

Nehemi'ah (nēhe-mī'ah) (*Jehovah hath consoled*). 1. Son of Hachaliah, and apparently of the tribe of Judah. All that we know certainly concerning him is contained in the book which bears his name. We first find him at Shushan, the winter residence of the kings of Persia, in high office as the cupbearer of King Artaxerxes Longimanus. In the twentieth year of the king's reign, *i. e.* B.C. 445, certain Jews arrived from Judea, and gave Nehemiah a deplorable account of the state of Jerusalem. He immediately conceived the idea of going to Jerusalem to endeavor to better their state, and obtained the king's consent to his mission. Having received his appointment as governor of Judea, he started upon his journey, being under promise to return to Persia within a given time. Nehemiah's great work was rebuilding, for the first time since their destruction by Nebuzar-adan, the walls of Jerusalem, and restoring that city to its former state and dignity as a fortified town. To this great object therefore Nehemiah directed his whole energies without an hour's unnecessary delay. In a wonderfully short time the walls seemed to emerge from the heaps of burnt rubbish, and to encircle the city as in the days of old. It soon became apparent how wisely Nehemiah had acted in hastening on the work. On his very first arrival, as governor, Sanballat and Tobiah had given unequivocal proof of their mortification at his appointment; but when the restoration was seen to be rapidly progressing, their indignation knew no bounds. They made a great conspiracy to fall upon the builders with an armed force and put a stop to the undertaking. The project was defeated by the vigilance and prudence of Nehemiah. Various stratagems were then resorted to to get Nehemiah away from Jerusalem, and if possible to take his life; but that which most nearly succeeded was the attempt to bring him into suspicion with the king of Persia, as if he intended to set himself up as an independent king as soon as the walls were completed. The artful letter of Sanballat so far wrought upon Artaxerxes that he issued a decree stopping the work till further orders. It is probable that at the same time he recalled Nehemiah, or perhaps his leave of absence had previously expired. But after a delay, perhaps of several years, he was permitted to return to Jerusalem and to crown his work by repairing the temple and dedicating the walls. During his government Nehemiah firmly repressed the exactions of the nobles and the usury of the rich, and rescued the poor Jews from spoliation and slavery. He refused to receive his lawful allowance as governor from the people, in consideration of their poverty, during the whole twelve years that he was in office, but kept at his own charge a table for 150 Jews, at which any who returned from captivity were welcome. He made most careful provision for the maintenance of the ministering priests and Levites, and for the due and constant celebration of divine worship. He insisted upon the sanctity of the precincts of the temple being preserved inviolable, and peremptorily ejected the powerful Tobiah from one of the chambers which Eliashib had assigned to him. With no less firmness and im-

partiality he expelled from all sacred functions those of the high priest's family who had contracted heathen marriages, and rebuked and punished those of the common people who had likewise intermarried with foreigners; and lastly, he provided for keeping holy the Sabbath day, which was shamefully profaned by many, both Jews and foreign merchants, and by his resolute conduct succeeded in repressing the lawless traffic on the day of rest. Beyond the thirty-second year of Artaxerxes, to which Nehemiah's own narrative leads us, we have no account of him whatever.

2. One of the leaders of the first expedition from Babylon to Jerusalem under Zerubbabel. Ezra 2:2; Neh. 7:7.

3. Son of Azbuk and ruler of the half part of Beth-zur, who helped to repair the wall of Jerusalem. Neh. 3:16.

Nehemi′ah (nĕhe-mī′ah), **The book of,** like the preceding one of Ezra, is clearly and certainly not all by the same hand. [EZRA, BOOK OF.] By far the most important portion, indeed, is the work of Nehemiah; but other portions are either extracts from various chronicles and registers or supplementary narratives and reflections, some apparently by Ezra, others, perhaps, the work of the same person who inserted the latest genealogical extracts from the public chronicles. The main history contained in the book of Nehemiah covers about twelve years, viz., from the twentieth to the thirty-second year of Artaxerxes Longimanus, i. e. from B.C. 445 to 433. The whole narrative gives us a graphic and interesting account of the state of Jerusalem and the returned captives in the writer's times, and, incidentally, of the nature of the Persian government and the condition of its remote provinces. The book of Nehemiah has always had an undisputed place in the Canon, being included by the Hebrews under the general head of the book of Ezra, and, as Jerome tells us in the *Prolog. Gal.,* by the Greeks and Latins under the name of the second book of Ezra.

Nehiloth (nĕ′hī-lŏth). The title of Ps. 5 in the Authorized Version is rendered "To the chief musician upon *Nehiloth.*" It is most likely that *nehiloth* is the general term for perforated wind-instruments of all kinds, as *negi-*

noth denotes all manner of stringed instruments.

Ne'hum (nē'hum) (*consolation*), one of those who returned from Babylon with Zerubbabel. Neh. 7:7.

Nehush'ta (nè-hŭsh'tà), the daughter of Elnathan of Jerusalem, wife of Jehoiakim and mother of Jehoiachin, kings of Judah. 2 Kings 24:8.

Nehush'tan (nè-hŭsh'tan) (*a thing of brass*), the name by which the brazen serpent made by Moses in the wilderness, Num. 21:9, was worshipped in the time of Hezekiah. 2 Kings 18:4. It is evident that our translators by their rendering "and he called it Nehushtan" understood that the subject of the sentence is Hezekiah, and that when he destroyed the brazen serpent he gave it the name Nehushtan, "a brazen thing," in token of his utter contempt. But it is better to understand the Hebrew as referring to the name by which the serpent was generally known, the subject of the verb being indefinite—"and one called it 'Nehushtan.'"

Nei'el (nè-ī'el) (*moved by God*), a place which formed one of the landmarks of the boundary of the tribe of Asher. Josh. 19:27 only. It occurs between Jiphthah-el and Cabul. It is not identified. But if the common identifications of Jiphthah-el and Cabul are correct, it may possibly be represented by *Mî'ar*, a village conspicuously placed on a lofty mountain brow, just halfway between the two.

Ne'keb (nē'keb) (*cavern*), one of the towns on the boundary of Naphtali. Josh. 19:33. It lay between Adami and Jabneel. A great number of commentators have taken this name as being connected with the preceding, —"Adami-nekeb." The Talmud called it Siadatha and Conder suggests an identification with *Seiyadeh*, near Tiberias.

Neko'da (nè-kō'dà) (*distinguished*). 1. The descendants of Nekoda returned among the Nethinim after the captivity. Ezra 2:48; Neh. 7:50.

2. The sons of Nekoda were among those who went up after the captivity from Tel-melah, Tel-harsa, and other places, but were unable to prove their descent from Israel. Ezra 2:60; Neh. 7:62.

Nem'uel (něm'ūĕl). 1. A Reubenite,

son of Eliab and eldest brother of Dathan and Abiram. Num. 26:9.

2. The eldest son of Simeon, Num. 26:12; 1 Chron. 4:24, from whom were descended the family of the Nemuelites. In Gen. 46:10 he is called JEMUEL.

Ne'pheg (nē'fĕg) (*sprout*). 1. One of the sons of Izhar the son of Kohath. Ex. 6:21.

2. One of David's sons born to him in Jerusalem. 2 Sam. 5:15; 1 Chron. 3:7; 14:6.

Ne'phish (nè-fish), an inaccurate variation (found in 1 Chron. 5:19 only) of the name Naphish.

Nephish'esim (nè-fish'e-sĭm) (*expanded ones*). The children of Nephishesim were among the Nethinim who returned with Zerubbabel. Neh. 7:52.

Neph'thalim (nĕf'tha-lĭm), a form of the name Naphtali. Tob. 7:3; Matt. 4:13, 15; Rev. 7:6.

Neph'toah (nĕf'to-ah), or **Nephto'ah** (*opening*), **The water of.** The spring or source of the water or (inaccurately) waters of Nephtoah was one of the landmarks in the boundary line which separated Judah from Benjamin. Josh. 15:9; 18:15. It lay northwest of Jerusalem, in which direction it seems to have been satisfactorily identified in *Ain Lifta,* a spring situated a little distance above the village of the same name.

Nephu'sim (nè-fū'sim), the same as Nephishesim, of which name according to Gesenius it is the proper form. Ezra 2:50.

Ner (*light* or *lamp*), the father of Abner, the chief of the army under Saul and his son Ishbosheth. There is quite a difference of opinion as to his relationship to Saul. Some consider Ner Saul's uncle and Abner his first cousin. Others that Abner himself was Saul's uncle. Still others consider there might be two men of the name (1) the father of Abner, (2) the grandfather of Saul, who would be identical with (1) if Abner were considered Saul's uncle. 1 Sam. 14:51; 1 Chron. 8:33; 9:35, 36.

Ne'reus (nē're-ŭs), a Christian at Rome, saluted by St. Paul. Rom. 16:15. According to tradition he was beheaded at Terracina, probably in the reign of Nerva.

Ner'gal (nēr'gal), one of the chief

Assyrian and Babylonian deities, seems to have corresponded closely to the classical Mars. 2 Kings 17:30. It is conjectured that he may represent the deified Nimrod.

Ner'gal=share'zer (nĕr'gal-shà-rē'zer) (*O Nergal, defend the king*), occurs only in Jer. 39:3 and 13. One of the "princes of the king of Babylon" who accompanied Nebuchadnezzar on his last expedition against Jerusalem. He had the honorable distinction of Rab-mag, probably meaning *chief of the Magi* [see RAB-MAG]. In sacred Scripture he appears among the persons who, by command of Nebuchadnezzar, released Jeremiah from prison. He is usually considered, though against some opposition, as one who not long afterward mounted the Babylonian throne. This latter is the same as the monarch called Neriglissar or Neriglissor, who murdered Evil-merodach, the son of Nebuchadnezzar, and succeeded him upon the throne. His reign lasted from B.C. 559 to B.C. 556.

Ne'ri (nē'rī), short form for NERIAH, son of Melchi and father of Salathiel, in the genealogy of Christ. Luke 3:27.

Neri'ah (nè-rī'ah) (*lamp of Jehovah*), the son of Maaseiah and father of Baruch and Seraiah. Jer. 32:12.

Net. [See FISHING.]

Nethan'eel (nė-thăn'e-el) (*given of God*). 1. The son of Zuar, and prince of the tribe of Issachar at the time of the Exodus. Num. 1:8; 2:5; 7:18. (B.C. 1491.)

2. The fourth son of Jesse and brother of David. 1 Chron. 2:14.

3. A priest in the reign of David who blew the trumpet before the ark when it was brought from the house of Obed-edom. 1 Chron. 15:24. (B.C. 1042.)

4. A Levite, father of Shemaiah the scribe. 1 Chron. 24:6.

5. A son of Obed-edom. 1 Chron. 26:4.

6. One of the princes of Judah whom Jehoshaphat sent to teach in the cities of his kingdom. 2 Chron. 17:7. (B.C. 870.)

7. A chief of the Levites in the reign of Josiah. 2 Chron. 35:9. (B.C. 628.)

8. A priest of the family of Pashur, in the time of Ezra, who had married a foreign wife. Ezra 10:22. (B.C. 458.)

9. The representative of the priestly family of Jedaiah in the time of Joiakim. Neh. 12:21.

10. A Levite, of the sons of Asaph, who with his brethren played upon the musical instruments of David at the dedication of the wall of Jerusalem under Ezra and Nehemiah. Neh. 12:36. (B.C. 446.)

Nethani'ah (nĕth-a-nī'ah) (*given of Jehovah*). 1. The son of Elishama, and father of Ishmael who murdered Gedaliah. 2 Kings 25:23, 25.

2. One of the four sons of Asaph the minstrel. 1 Chron. 25:12.

3. A Levite in the reign of Jehoshaphat. 2 Chron. 17;8. (B.C. 870.)

4. The father of Jehudi. Jer. 36:14. (B.C. 638.)

Neth'inim (nĕth'ĭ-nĭm) (*given, dedicated*). As applied specifically to a distinct body of men connected with the services of the temple, this name first meets us in the later books of the Old Testament—in 1 Chronicles, Ezra and Nehemiah. The word and the ideas embodied in it may, however, be traced to a much earlier period. As derived from the verb *nâthan, i. e.* give, set apart, dedicate, it was applied to those who were specially appointed to the liturgical offices of the tabernacle. At the close of the campaign against the Midianites captives from them were given by Moses to the Levites for the menial work of the tabernacle. Num. 31:47. This disposition to devolve the more laborious offices of the ritual upon slaves of another race showed itself again in the treatment of the Gibeonites. Josh. 9:27. The number of these was likely to be quite inadequate for the greater stateliness of the new worship at Jerusalem. It is to this period accordingly that the origin of the class bearing this name may be traced. The Nethinim were those "whom David and the princes appointed (Heb. *gave*) for the service of the Levites." Ezra 8:20. At this time the Nethinim probably lived within the precincts of the temple, doing its rougher work and so enabling the Levites to take a higher position as the religious representatives and instructors of the people. The example set by David was followed by his successors, the principal references to them being in Ezra and Nehemiah.

Neto'phah (nė-tō'fà) (*dropping*), a town the name of which occurs only in the catalogue of those who returned with Zerubbabel from the captivity. Ezra 2 : 22; Neh. 7 : 26. But, though not directly mentioned till so late a period, Netophah was really a much older place. Two of David's guard, 2 Sam. 23 : 28; 1 Chron. 27 : 13, 15, were Netophathites. The "villages of the Netophathites" were the residence of the Levites. 1 Chron. 9 : 16. From another notice we learn that the particular Levites who inhabited these villages were singers. Neh. 12 : 28. To judge from Neh. 7 : 26 the town was in the neighborhood of, or closely connected with, Bethlehem. A suggested site is *Khurbet umm-Tobah*, between Jerusalem and Bethlehem, another, *Beit Netlif* at the entrance to the Vale of Elah.

Nethoph'athite (nė-tŏf'a-thīte), an inhabitant of Netophah. 1 Chron. 25 : 4.

Nettle, a well-known plant covered with minute sharp hairs, containing a poison that produces a painful, stinging

THE NETTLE OF PALESTINE.

sensation. It grows on neglected ground. Isa. 34 : 13; Hos. 9 : 6. A different Hebrew word in Job 30 : 7; Prov. 24 : 31; Zeph. 2 : 9 seems to indicate a different species.

New Moon. The first day of the lunar month was observed as a holy day. In addition to the daily sacrifice there were offered two young bullocks, a ram and seven lambs of the first year as a burnt offering, with the proper meat offerings and drink offerings, and a kid as a sin offering. Num. 28 : 11–15. As on the Sabbath, trade and handicraft work were stopped, Amos 8 : 5, and the temple was opened for public worship. Isa. 66 : 23; Ezek. 46 : 3. The trumpets were blown at the offering of the special sacrifices for the day, as on the solemn festivals. Num. 10 : 10; Ps. 81 : 3. It was an occasion for state banquets. 1 Sam. 20 : 5–24. The mentions of the new moons show that they were regarded as a peculiar class of holy days, distinguished from the solemn feasts and the Sabbaths. 1 Chron. 23 : 31; 2 Chron. 2 : 4; 8 : 13; 31 : 3; Ezra 3 : 5; Neh. 10 : 33; Ezek. 45 : 17. The seventh new moon of the religious year, being that of Tisri, commenced the civil year, and had a significance and rites of its own, in addition to the usual worship on the day of the new moon. Lev. 23 : 24, 25; Num. 29 : 1–6. "After the exile this celebration assumed the character of a new year's festival." The usual religious observance of the day of the new moon may plainly be regarded as the consecration of a natural division of time.

New Testament. The name Testament is derived from the Latin *Testamentum,* an erroneous translation of the Greek and Hebrew words meaning Covenant, used to designate the Old and the New *Dispensations*. Hence the Revisions have altered the word "Testament" in the common version to "Covenant." There are 27 books in the New Testament, 4 Gospels, 22 Epistles and Revelation.

THE HISTORY OF THE WRITTEN TEXT.—The early history of the apostolic writings externally, as far as it can be traced, is the same as that of other contemporary books. St. Paul, like Cicero or Pliny, often employed the services of an amanuensis, to whom he dictated his letters, affixing the salutation "with his own hand." 1 Cor. 16 : 21; 2 Thess. 3 : 17; Col. 4 : 18. The originals seem to have soon perished.

In the natural course of things the apostolic autographs would be likely to perish soon. The material which was commonly used for letters, the papyrus paper, to which St. John incidentally alludes, 2 John 12, comp. 3 John 13, was singularly fragile, and even the stouter kinds, likely to be used for the historical books, were not fitted to bear constant use. The papyrus fragments which have come down to the present time have been preserved under peculiar circumstances, as at Herculaneum or in the Egyptian tombs.

In the time of the Diocletian persecution, A.D. 303, copies of the Christian Scriptures were sufficiently numerous to furnish a special object for persecutors, who searched for copies of the Christian writings to destroy them. Owing to the destruction thus caused, but still more from the natural effects of time, no MS. of the New Testament of the first three centuries remains. But though no fragment of the New Testament of the first century still remains, the Italian and Egyptian papyri, which are of that date, give a clear notion of the caligraphy of the period. In these the text is written in columns, rudely divided, in UNCIALS, in separate capital letters printed with a pen, without any punctuation or division of words; and there is no trace of accents or breathings. These manuscripts are called *Uncials*. The elder of the church at Ephesus, when he arose to read Paul's letter to that church, " must have held in his hand a roll of white or yellow material about 4 feet in length and some 10 inches in height. The Acts of the Apostles might have formed a portly roll of 30 feet, or might even have been divided into two or more sections."

Uncial Manuscripts are the oldest, the rarest and most important. Only two contain all the books of the New Testament; and there are only 112 in all including even the smallest fragments. These are the only New Testament manuscripts from the fourth to the ninth century.

CURSIVES are manuscripts written in smaller letters in a more or less running hand. They range from the ninth to the fifteenth century when printing was invented. Every great library possesses some of them, and 2429 are known to exist.

As soon as definite controversies arose among Christians, the text of the New Testament assumed its true importance. Several very important conclusions follow from this earliest appearance of textual criticism. It is in the first place evident that various readings existed in the books of the New Testament at a time prior to all extant authorities. History affords no trace of the pure apostolic originals. Again, from the

preservation of the first variations noticed, which are often extremely minute, in one or more of the primary documents still left, we may be certain that no important changes have been made in the sacred text which we cannot now detect.

Passing from these isolated quotations, we find the first great witnesses to the apostolic text in the early Syriac and Latin versions, and in the rich quotations of Clement of Alexandria († *cir.* A.D. 220) and Origen (A.D. 184–254). From the extant works of Origen alone no inconsiderable portion of the whole New Testament might be transcribed; and his writings are an almost inexhaustible storehouse for the history of the text. There can be no doubt that in Origen's time the variations in the New Testament MSS. were beginning to lead to the formation of specific groups of copies. The most ancient MSS. and versions now extant exhibit the characteristic differences which have been found to exist in different parts of the works of Origen. These cannot have had their source later than the beginning of the third century, and probably were much earlier. Bengel was the first (1734) who pointed out the affinity of certain groups of MSS., which, as he remarks, must have arisen before the first versions were made. The honor of carefully determining the relations of critical authorities for the New Testament text belongs to Griesbach. According to him two distinct recensions of the Gospels existed at the beginning of the third century—the *Alexandrine* and the *Western.* A MS. of the fourth century, the *Codex Vaticanus,* may be taken as a type. The writing is in elegant continuous uncials (capitals), in three columns, without initial letters or *iota subscript or adscript.* A small interval serves as a simple punctuation; and there are no accents or breathings by the hand of the first writer, though these have been added subsequently. *Uncial* writing continued in general use till the middle of the tenth century. From the eleventh century downward *cursive* writing prevailed. The earliest cursive biblical MS. is dated 964 A.D. The MSS. of the fourteenth and fifteenth centuries abound in the contractions which afterward passed into the early printed books. The oldest MSS. are written on the thinnest and finest vellum; in later copies the parchment is thick and coarse. Papyrus was very rarely used after the ninth century. In the tenth century cotton paper was generally employed in Europe; and one example at least occurs of its use in the ninth century. In the twelfth century the common linen or rag paper came into use. One other kind of material requires notice—re-dressed parchment, called *palimpsests*. Even at a very early period the original text of a parchment MS. was often erased, that the material might be used afresh. In lapse of time the original writing frequently reappeared in faint lines below the later text, and in this way many precious fragments of biblical MSS., which had been once obliterated for the transcription of other works, have been recovered. A complete description of these MSS. is given in the great critical editions of the New Testament. Here those only can be briefly noticed which are of primary importance.

The Codex Sinaiticus at St. Petersburg, the latest discovered and the most complete, was obtained by Tischendorf from the convent of St. Catherine, Mount Sinai, in 1859. The New Testament is entire, and the Epistle of Barnabas and parts of the Shepherd of Hermas are added. It is probably the oldest of the MSS. of the New Testament and of the fourth century.

Codex Alexandrinus (Brit. Mus.), a MS. of the entire Greek Bible, with the Epistles of Clement added. It was given by Cyril Lucar, patriarch of Constantinople, to Charles I. in 1628, and is now in the British Museum. It contains the whole of the New Testament, with some chasms. It was probably written in the first half of the fifth century.

Codex Vaticanus (1209), a MS. of the entire Greek Bible, which seems to have been in the Vatican Library almost from its commencement (*cir.* A.D. 1450). It contains the New Testament entire to Heb. 9:14, καθα: the rest of the Epistle to the Hebrews, the Pastoral Epistles and the Apocalypse were added in the fifteenth century. The MS. is assigned to the fourth century.

Codex Ephraemi rescriptus (Paris, *Bibl. Imp.* 9), a palimpsest MS. which contains fragments of the LXX. and of every part of the New Testament. In the twelfth century the original writing was effaced and some Greek writings of Ephraem Syrus were written over it. The MS. was brought to Florence from the East at the beginning of the sixteenth century, and came thence to Paris with Catherine de Medici. The only entire books which have perished are 2 Thess. and 2 John.

VARIATIONS. Having surveyed in outline the history of the transmission of the written text and the chief characteristics of the MSS. in which it is preserved, we are in a position to consider the extent and nature of the variations which exist in different copies. It is impossible to estimate the number of these exactly, but they cannot be less than 150,000 in all, though of these a very large proportion consists of differences of spelling and isolated aberrations of scribes, and of the remainder comparatively few alterations are sufficiently well supported to create reasonable doubt as to the final judgment. Probably there are not more than 1600–2000 places in which the true reading is a matter of uncertainty. Various readings are due to different causes: some arose from accidental variations. Many are mere variations of spelling, such as we see in comparing the English and American revisions, as judgement and judgment, Neighbour and neighbor; other variations are due to errors of *sight*. Others may be described as errors of *impression* or *memory*. The copyist, after reading a sentence from the text before him, often failed to reproduce it exactly. Variations of order are the most frequent and very commonly the most puzzling questions of textual criticism. Examples occur in every page, almost in every verse, of the New Testament. The number of readings which seem to have been altered for distinctly dogmatic reasons is extremely small. In spite of the great revolutions in thought, feeling and practice through which the Christian Church passed in fifteen centuries, the copyists of the New Testament faithfully preserved, according to their ability, the sacred trust committed to them. There is not any trace of intentional revision designed to give support to current opinions. Matt. 17:21, Mark 9:29, 1 Cor. 7:5, need scarcely be noticed. There are no variations which change any doctrine or great truth. The great mass of various readings are simply variations in form.

There are, however, one or two greater variations of a different character. The most important of these are Mark 16 : 9–end; John 7 : 53–8 : 12; Rom. 16 : 25–27. The second stands quite by itself; and there seems to be little doubt that it contains an authentic narrative, but not by the hand of St. John. The two others, taken in connection with the last chapter of St. John's Gospel, suggest the possibility that the apostolic writings may have undergone in some cases authoritative revision. Manuscripts, it must be remembered, are but one of the three sources of textual criticism. The versions and patristic quotations are scarcely less important in doubtful cases.

THE HISTORY OF THE PRINTED TEXT.—The first complete book produced by the printing press was the Bible in 1456. It was in Latin, the language of literature in western Europe.

The following are the earliest editions: 1. *The Complutensian Polyglot,* so called because it was printed at Complutum in Spain. The glory of printing the first Greek Testament is due to the princely Cardinal Ximenes. This great prelate as early as 1502 engaged the services of a number of scholars to superintend an edition of the whole Bible in the original Hebrew and Greek, with the addition of the Chaldee Targum of Onkelos, the LXX. version and the Vulgate. The volume containing the New Testament was printed first, and was completed on January 10, 1514. The whole work was not finished till July 10, 1517. 2. *The edition of Erasmus.*—The edition of Erasmus was the first *published* edition of the New Testament. Erasmus had paid considerable attention to the study of the New Testament, when he received an application from Froben, a printer of Basle with whom he was acquainted, to prepare a Greek text for the press. The request was made on April 17, 1515, and the whole work was finished in February, 1516. 3. *The edition of Stephens.*—The scene of our history now changes from Basle to Paris. In 1543, Simon de Colines (Colinæus) published a Greek text of the New Testament, corrected in about 150 places on fresh MS. authority. Not long after it appeared, R. Estienne (Stephanus) published his first edition (1546), which was based on a collation of MSS. in the Royal Library with the

Complutensian text. 4. *The editions of Beza and Elzevir.*—The Greek text of Beza (dedicated to Queen Elizabeth) was printed by H. Stephens in 1565, and a second edition in 1576; but the chief edition was the third, printed in 1582, which contained readings from *Codex Bezæ* and *Codex Claromontanus.*

The literal sense of the apostolic writings must be gained in the same way as the literal sense of any other writings —by the fullest use of every appliance of scholarship, and the most complete confidence in the necessary and absolute connection of words and thoughts. No variation of phrase, no peculiarity of idiom, no change of tense, no change of order, can be neglected. The truth lies in the whole expression, and no one can presume to set aside any part as trivial or indifferent. The importance of investigating most patiently and most faithfully the literal meaning of the sacred text must be felt with tenfold force when it is remembered that the literal sense is the outward embodiment of a spiritual sense, which lies beneath and quickens every part of Holy Scripture.

New Year. [TRUMPETS, FEAST OF.]

Nezi'ah (nĕ-zī'ah) (*illustrious*). The descendants of Neziah were among the Nethinim who returned with Zerubbabel. Ezra 2 : 54; Neh. 7 : 56.

Ne'zib (nē'zib) (*garrison*), a city of Judah, Josh. 15 : 43 only, in the district of the Shefelah or lowland, one of the same group with Keilah and Mareshah. To Eusebius and Jerome it was evidently known. They place it on the road between Eleutheropolis and Hebron, seven or nine miles from the former, and there it still stands under the almost identical name of *Beit Nûsib.*

Nib'haz (nib'hăz) (*the barker*), a deity of the Avites, introduced by them into Samaria in the time of Sargon. 2 Kings 17 : 31. The rabbins derived the name from a Hebrew root *nâbach*, "to bark," and hence assigned to it the figure of a dog, or a dog-headed man. But there is no reason to think them correct, and any identification is regarded as hopeless by modern scholars.

Nib'shan (nĭb'shăn) (*soft soil*), one of the six cities of Judah, Josh. 15 : 62, which were in the wilderness.

Nica'nor (nĭ-kā'nor) (*conqueror*). One of the first seven deacons. Acts 6 : 5. Nothing more is known of him.

Nicode'mus (nĭk-o-dē'mus) (*conqueror of the people*), a Pharisee, a ruler of the Jews and a teacher of Israel, John 3 : 1, 10, whose secret visit to our Lord was the occasion of the discourse recorded only by St. John. In Nicodemus a noble candor and a simple love of truth shine out in the midst of hesitation and fear of man. He finally became a follower of Christ, defended him in the Sanhedrin, of which he was a member (John 7 : 50–52), and after the crucifixion came with Joseph of Arimathæa to take down and embalm the body of Jesus. John 19 : 39. The time and manner of his own death are unknown.

Nicola'itans (nĭk-o-lā'ĭ-tanṣ) (*followers of Nicolas*), a sect mentioned in Rev. 2 : 6, 15, whose deeds were strongly condemned. They may have been identical with those who held the doctrine of Balaam. They seem to have held that it was lawful to eat things sacrificed to idols, and to commit the immoral excesses of the heathen, in opposition to the decree of the Church rendered in Acts 15 : 20, 29. Mingling themselves in the orgies of idolatrous feasts, they brought the impurities of those feasts into the meetings of the Christian Church. And all this was done, it must be remembered, not simply as an indulgence of appetite, but as a part of a system, supported by a "doctrine," accompanied by the boast of a prophetic illumination. 2 Pet. 2 : 1.

Nic'olas (nĭk'o-lăs) (*victor of the people*), Acts 6 : 5, a native of Antioch and a proselyte to the Jewish faith. When the church was still confined to Jerusalem, he became a convert; and being a man of honest report, full of the Holy Ghost and of wisdom, he was chosen by the whole multitude of the disciples to be one of the first seven deacons, and was ordained by the apostles. He is very likely the one from whom the Nicolaitans claimed to have derived their doctrines. But there is no proof that he actually taught them. All heretics of that day were very anxious to father their peculiar beliefs on an apostle or a prominent officer of the church. The traditions in their details are of no value.

Nicop'olis (ni-kŏp'o-lis) (*city of victory*) is mentioned in Titus 3 : 12 as the place where St. Paul was intending to pass the winter. Nothing is to be found in the epistle itself to determine which Nicopolis is here intended. One Nicopolis was in Thrace, near the borders of Macedonia. The subscription (which, however, is of no authority) fixes on this place, calling it the Macedonian Nicopolis. But there is little doubt that Jerome's view is correct, and that the Pauline Nicopolis was the celebrated city of Epirus. This city (the "city of victory") was built by Augustus in memory of the battle of Actium. It was on a peninsula to the west of the bay of Actium.

Ni'ger (nī'jer) (*black*) is the additional or distinctive name given to the Simeon who was one of the teachers and prophets in the church at Antioch. Acts 13 : 1.

Night. [DAY.]

Night=hawk. The Hebrew word so translated, Lev. 11 : 16; Deut. 14 : 15, is impossible to identify. It may be the night jar. The Septuagint and Vulgate identify it with the owl.

Nile, the great river of Egypt. In the Authorized Version it is spoken of under the name of Shihor or SIHOR and the "river of Egypt." Gen. 15 : 18. At Khartoom, the capital of Nubia, is the junction of the two great branches, the White Nile and the Blue Nile, so called from the color of the clay which tinges their waters. The Blue Nile rises in the mountains of Abyssinia, and is the chief source of the deposit which the Nile brings to Egypt. The White Nile is the larger branch. Its true beginning is in the river Kagera, 3° south of the equator, flowing into the Lake Victoria Nyanza. The total length of the Nile is therefore about 4000 miles. From the First Cataract, at Syene, the river flows smoothly at the rate of two or three miles an hour, with a width of half a mile, to Cairo. A little north of Cairo it divides into two branches, one flowing to Rosetta and the other to Damietta, from which places the mouths are named. Originally there were seven of these mouths, but the rest have been filled up by the deposit brought down from the upper course of the river. The great peculiarity of the river is its annual overflow, caused by the periodical tropical rains. Egypt is said to be "the gift of the Nile"; and it is very certain that were the overflow to cease famine would be the result. Something of this sort is doubtless the cause of the famine in the time of Joseph, and those of later years. Modern enterprise is attempting to guard against this, and provide a natural and uniform supply of water by the great dam at Assouan, which is to hold back any surplus ready for a later year of deficit. The monuments and the narratives of ancient writers show us in the Nile of Egypt in old times a stream bordered by flags and reeds, the covert of abundant wild fowl, and bearing on its waters the fragrant flowers of the various-colored lotus. Now in Egypt scarcely any reeds or waterplants—the famous papyrus being nearly if not quite extinct, and the lotus almost unknown—are to be seen, excepting in the marshes near the Mediterranean. Of old the great river must have shown a more fair and busy scene than now. Boats of many kinds were ever passing along it, by the painted walls of temples and the gardens that extended around the light summer pavilions, from the pleasure-galley, with one great square sail, white or with variegated pattern and many oars, to the little papyrus skiff dancing on the water and carrying the seekers of pleasure where they could shoot with arrows or knock down with the throw-stick the wild fowl that abounded among the reeds, or engage in the dangerous chase of the hippopotamus or the crocodile. The Nile is constantly before us in the history of Israel in Egypt.

Nim'rah (nim'rah) (*leopard*), a place mentioned by this name in Num. 32:3

A SCENE ON THE NILE.

only. Given as BETH-NIMRAH, ver. 36. It belonged to the tribe of Gad. It was east of the Jordan, and if Jerome's identification is correct it is the same as NIMRIM, and is represented by the ruined mound *Tell Nimrin* opposite Jericho.

Nim'rim (nim'rim), **The waters of,** a stream or brook within the country of Moab, which is mentioned in the denunciations of that nation by Isaiah, Isa. 15:6, and Jeremiah. Jer. 48:34. Opinions differ as to its identification. That with NIMRAH has been given. Another is with *Wady Nemeirah* eight miles from Zoar.

Nim'rod (nĭm'rŏd), a Cushite, a mighty hunter, and a powerful monarch mentioned in Gen. 10:8 ff. It is hard to determine the identity of this man. According to the account in Genesis he established an empire in Shinar (the classical Babylonia), the chief towns being Babel, Erech, Accad and Calneh; and that he extended this empire northward along the course of the Tigris over Assyria, where he founded a second group of capitals, Nineveh, Rehoboth, Calah and Resen. He is sometimes thought the same as the Babylonian king Izdubar or Gilgamesh, around whose name many legends have gathered. Others regard him as Merodach who was later deified.

Nim'shi (nĭm'shī), the grandfather of Jehu, who is generally called "the *son* of Nimshi." 1 Kings 19:16; 2 Kings 9:2, 14, 20; 2 Chron. 22:7.

Nin'eveh (nĭn'e-veh), the capital of the ancient kingdom and empire of Assyria. The name appears to be compounded from that of an Assyrian deity, "Nina," probably the original of Ninos, who in the Greek myth was the founder of the city. It is first mentioned in the Old Testament as founded by Nimrod. Gen. 10:11. Hence Assyria was subsequently known to the Jews as "the land of Nimrod," cf. Micah 5:6. The kingdom of Assyria and of the Assyrians is referred to in the Old Testament as connected with the Jews at a very early period, as in Num. 24:22, 24. It was probably founded by a colony from Babylonia, as far back as the year 2000 B.C., if not earlier. Records are found for that date. For its history see the article ASSYRIA. Jonah was sent to preach to the king and people of Nineveh. Nahum prophesied its complete destruction, so that it should not again rise from its ruins, while Zephaniah gives the fullest and most poetical picture of Nineveh's ruined and deserted condition. This is the last mention of Nineveh as an *existing* city. The destruction of Nineveh occurred B.C. 606. The city was then laid waste, its monuments destroyed, and its inhabitants scattered or carried away into captivity. It never rose again from its ruins. This total disappearance of Nineveh is fully confirmed by the records of profane history.

THE SITE OF THE CITY. Nineveh is situated on the eastern bank of the river Tigris, 550 miles from its mouth and 250 miles north of Babylon. Previous to recent excavations and researches, the ruins which occupied the presumed site of Nineveh seemed to consist of mere shapeless heaps or mounds of earth and rubbish. Unlike the vast masses of brick masonry which mark the site of Babylon, they showed externally no signs of artificial construction, except perhaps here and there the traces of a rude wall of sun-dried bricks. Some of these mounds were of enormous dimensions, looking in the distance rather like natural elevations than the work of men's hands. They differ greatly in form, size and height. Some are mere conical heaps, varying from 50 to 150 feet high; others have a broad flat summit, and very precipitous cliff-like sides furrowed by deep ravines worn by the winter rains. The first investigations of the site of Nineveh were made by Rich, English resident at Bagdad, who in 1820 made a survey of the mound called Kouyunjik, and became convinced that it concealed the ruins of Nineveh. Others, notably the Frenchman Botta, continued the explorations at other points near by, and considerable differences of opinion existed as to the true site of Nineveh proper; also as to whether the various mounds were the remains of distinct cities, or of various portions and suburbs of the same city. Layard between 1845 and 1850 began operations at Nimroud, 18 miles south of Kouyunjik; then he made excavations at the latter place itself, which proved conclusively that it was Nineveh itself. Later discoveries have brought to light many ruins, inscriptions, etc., throwing much light on the history.

DESCRIPTION OF THE CITY. The principal ruins are—(1) the group immediately opposite Mosul, including the great mounds of *Kouyunjik* and *Nebbi Yunus*, which are proved the site of Nineveh proper; (2) that near the junction of the Tigris and Zab, comprising the mounds of *Nimroud* and *Athur*, or Calah; (3) *Khorsabad*, about ten miles to the east of the former river; (4) *Shereef Khan*, about 5½ miles to the north of Kouyunjik; and (5) *Selamiyah,* three miles to the north of Nimroud. These were all, without much doubt, included within the great city—those farthest away being the magnificent palaces in the suburbs. We find by the remains that the city was rectangular in shape, surrounded by a wall pierced with gates and protected by towers. This wall enclosed about 1800 acres, and had a circumference of about 7½ miles, being about 3 miles long, and very narrow.

The statement in Jonah 4:11 that Nineveh contained "more than six score thousand" infants, would indicate a population of about 600,000. Captain Jones, who surveyed the site in 1853, reckons a possible population of only about 175,000. Traditions of the first century B.C. give its size as much larger than Babylon. Probably the older writers reckoned in the "suburbs" as a part of the city,—since they belonged to the people of Nineveh—as we used to say "Greater New York" before the actual union of the cities and towns. The Assyrian edifices were built upon artificial mounds or platforms, varying in height often from 30 to 50 feet. This platform was probably faced with stone masonry, remains of which were discovered at Nimroud, and broad flights of steps or inclined ways led up to its summit. Although only the general plan of the ground-floor can now be traced, it is evident that the palaces had several stories built of wood and sun-dried bricks, which, when the building was deserted and allowed to fall to decay, gradually buried the lower chambers with their ruins, and protected the sculptured slabs from the effects of the weather. The depth of soil and rubbish above the alabaster slabs varied from a few inches to about 20 feet. It is to this accumulation of rubbish above them that the bas-reliefs owe their extraordinary preservation. The portions of the edifices still remaining consist of halls, chambers and galleries, opening for the most part into large uncovered courts. The wall above the wainscoting of alabaster was plastered, and painted with figures and ornaments. The sculptures, with the exception of the human-headed lions and bulls, were for the most part in low relief. The colossal figures usually represent the king, his attendants and the gods; the smaller sculptures, which either cover the whole face of the slab or are divided into two compartments by bands of inscriptions, represent battles, sieges, the chase, single combats with wild beasts, religious ceremonies, etc., etc. All refer to public or national events; the hunting-scenes evidently recording the prowess and personal valor of the king as the head of the people—"the mighty hunter before the Lord." The sculptures appear to have been painted, remains of color having been found on most of them. Thus decorated without and within, the Assyrian palaces must have displayed a barbaric magnificence, not, however, devoid of a certain grandeur and beauty which probably no ancient or modern edifice has exceeded. These great edifices, the depositories of the national records, appear to have been at the same time the abode of the king and the temple of the gods.

THE LITERATURE OF NINEVEH. In the ruins of Nineveh have been found the remains of an ancient library written on stone tablets. These leaves or tablets were from an inch to a foot square, made of terra-cotta clay, on which when soft the inscriptions were written; the tablets were then hardened and placed upon the walls of the library rooms, so as to cover the walls. Judging from the fragments discovered this royal library must have contained over 10,000 tablets, including almost every subject in ancient literature. The character employed was the arrow-headed or cuneiform—so called from each letter being formed by marks or elements resembling an arrow-head or a wedge. It was begun by Shalmaneser B.C. 860; his successors added to it, and Sardanapalus (B.C. 673) almost doubled it. Stories or subjects were begun on tablets, and continued on tablets of the same size sometimes to the number of one hundred. Some of the most interesting of these give accounts of the creation and of the deluge, and all agree with or confirm the Bible. One of the most important inscriptions discovered in connection with biblical history is that upon a pair of colossal human-headed bulls from Kouyunjik, now in the British Museum, containing the records of Sennacherib, and describing, among other events, his wars with Hezekiah. It is accompanied by a series of bas-reliefs believed to represent the siege and capture of Lachish. The people of Nineveh spoke a Semitic dialect, connected with the Hebrew and with the so-called Chaldee of the books of Daniel and Ezra. This agrees with the testimony of the Old Testament.

Nin'evites (nĭn'e-vītes), the inhabitants of Nineveh. Luke 11:30.

Ni'san. [MONTH.]

Nis'roch (nĭs'rŏk), an idol of Nineveh, in whose temple Sennacherib was worshipping when assassinated by his sons, Adrammelech and Sharezer. 2 Kings 19:37; Isa. 37:38. This idol has been identified with the eagle-headed human figure, which is one of the most prominent on the earliest Assyrian monuments, and is always represented as contending with and conquering the lion or the bull. Some of the later scholars, however, consider it a Hebrew corruption of the name Ashur, the national god of Assyria.

Nitre. Mention of this substance is made in Prov. 25:20—"and as vinegar upon nitre"—and in Jer. 2:22. The article denoted is not that which we now understand by the term *nitre, i. e.* nitrate of potash—"saltpetre"—but the *nitrum* of the Latins and the *natron* or native carbonate of soda of modern chemistry. Natron was and still is used by the Egyptians for washing linen. The value of soda in this respect is well known. This explains the passage in Jeremiah. Natron is found in great abundance in the well-known soda lakes of Egypt.

No. [NO-AMON.]

Noadi'ah (no-a-dī'ah) (*meeting with Jehovah*). 1. A Levite, son of Binnui, who with Meremoth, Eleazar and Jozabad weighed the vessels of gold and silver belonging to the temple which were brought back from Babylon. Ezra 8:33. (B.C. 459.)

2. The prophetess Noadiah joined Sanballat and Tobiah in their attempt to intimidate Nehemiah. Neh. 6:14. (B.C. 446.)

No'ah (nō'ah) (*rest*), the tenth in descent from Adam, in the line of Seth, was the son of Lamech and grandson of Methuselah. (B.C. 2948–1998, Ussher.) We hear nothing of Noah till he is 500 years old, when it is said he begat three sons, Shem, Ham and Japhet. In consequence of the grievous and hopeless wickedness of the world at this time, God resolved to destroy it. Of Noah's life during this age of almost universal apostasy we are told but little. It is merely said that he was a righteous man and perfect in his generations (*i. e.* among his contemporaries), and that he, like Enoch, walked with God. St. Peter calls him "a preacher of righteousness." 2 Pet. 2:5. Besides this we are merely told that he had three sons, each of whom had married a wife; that he built the ark in accordance with divine direction; and that he was 600 years old when the flood came. Gen. 7:6.

The ark.—The same Hebrew word is used for the Ark of Noah, and for that in which the infant Moses was laid. This "chest" or "boat" was to be made of gopher wood, probably cypress, which both for its lightness and its durability was employed by the Phœnicians for building their vessels. The planks of the ark, after being put together, were to be protected by a coating of pitch, or rather bitumen, both inside and outside, to make it water-tight, and perhaps also as a protection against the attacks of marine animals. The ark was to consist of a number of "nests" or small compartments, with a view, no doubt, to the convenient distribution of the different animals and their food. These were to be arranged in three tiers, one above another; "with lower, second and third (stories) shalt thou make it." Means were also to be provided for letting light into the ark. There was to be a door; this was to be placed in the side of the ark. Of the shape of the ark nothing is said, but its dimensions are given. It was to be 300 cubits in length, 50 in breadth and 30 in height. Taking 21 inches for the cubit, the ark would be 525 feet in length, 87 feet 6 inches in breadth and 52 feet 6 inches in height. This is very considerably larger than the most of the vessels we usually see, but not as large as some modern ships. It should be remembered that this huge structure was only intended to float on the water, and was not in the proper sense of the word a ship. It had neither mast, sail nor rudder; it was in fact nothing but an enormous floating house, or rather oblong box. The inmates of the ark were Noah and his wife and his three sons with their wives. Noah was directed to take also animals of all kinds into the ark with him, that they might be preserved alive. Many discussions on this point are given in fuller treatises. Most of the objections raised to the Bible narrative are based on the supposition that Noah would try to obtain specimens of every existing animal. The more natural supposition seems to be that only those which were useful to man were preserved, and that no wild animals were taken into the ark. There erful and impressive description is given of the appalling catastrophe. The waters of the flood increased for a period of 190 days (40+150, comparing Gen. 7: 12 and 24); and then "God remembered Noah," and made a wind to pass over the earth, so that the waters were assuaged. The ark rested on the seventeenth day of the seventh month on the mountains of Ararat. After this the

THE BABYLONIAN DELUGE STORY.
The eleventh tablet of the Gilgamesh epic.

would then be no difficulty from the great number of different species of animal life existing in the world.

The flood.—The ark was finished, and all its living freight was gathered into it as a place of safety. Jehovah shut him in, says the chronicler, speaking of Noah; and then there ensued a solemn pause of seven days before the threatened destruction was let loose. At last the flood came; the waters were upon the earth. A very simple but very pow- waters gradually decreased till the first day of the tenth month, when the tops of the mountains were seen; but Noah and his family did not disembark till they had been in the ark over a year. Whether the flood was universal or partial has given rise to much controversy. The language of the book of Genesis does not compel us to suppose that the whole surface of the globe was actually covered with water. It is natural to suppose that the writer, when he speaks of "all flesh," "all in whose nostrils was the breath of life," refers only to his own locality. This sort of language is common enough in the Bible when only a small part of the globe is intended. Thus, for instance, it is said that "*all countries* came into Egypt to Joseph to buy corn;" and that "a decree went out from Cæsar Augustus that *all the world* should be taxed." The language must be understood in the sense it would bear to the authors. The world as then known was very small—travel was much circumscribed. The eye witnesses who handed down the story saw no part omitted, they met no survivors. The truth of the Bible would not be shaken were the flood to be limited to a comparatively small area in Asia. There are traditions held by people all over the globe which have preserved the memory of a great and destructive flood, from which but a small part of mankind escaped. They seem to point back to a common centre, whence they were carried by the different families of man as they wandered east and west, but may be explained otherwise. The traditions which come nearest to the biblical account are those of the nations of western Asia. Foremost among these is the Chaldean. Other notices of a flood may be found in the Phœnician mythology. There is a medal or coin

branch between its feet. Before the vessel are represented the same pair as having just quitted it and got upon the dry land. Singularly enough, too, on some specimens of this medal the letters NΩ or NΩE have been found on the vessel, as in the cut on this page. Tayler Lewis deduces "the partial extent of the flood from the very face of the Hebrew text." "Earth," where it speaks of "all the earth," often is, and here should be, translated "land," the home of the race, from which there appears to have been little inclination to wander. Even after the flood God had to *compel* them to disperse. "Under the whole heavens" simply includes the horizon reaching around "all the land" —the visible horizon. We still use the words in the same sense, and so does the Bible. Nearly all commentators now agree on the partial extent of the deluge. And very many of them suppose it to have taken place in that part of Asia which includes the modern Mount Ararat.

After the flood.—Noah's first act after he left the ark was to build an altar and to offer sacrifices. Then follows the blessing of God upon Noah and his sons. Noah is clearly the head of a new human family, the representative of the whole race. It is as such that God makes his covenant with him; and hence selects a *natural* phenomenon as the sign of that covenant. The bow in the cloud, seen by every nation under heaven, is an unfailing witness to the truth of God. Noah now for the rest of his life betook himself to agricultural pursuits. It is particularly noticed that he planted a vineyard. Whether in igno-

APAMEAN COIN SHOWING THE WORD "NOE" ON THE ARK.

of Apamea in Phrygia, struck as late as the time of Septimius Severus, in which the Phrygian deluge is commemorated. This medal represents a kind of square vessel floating in the water. Through an opening in it are seen two persons, a man and a woman. Upon the top of this chest or ark is perched a bird, whilst another flies toward it carrying a

rance of its properties or otherwise we are not informed, but he drank of the juice of the grape till he became intoxicated and shamefully exposed himself in his own tent. One of his sons, Ham, mocked openly at his father's disgrace. The others, with dutiful care and reverence, endeavored to hide it. When he recovered from the effects of his intoxication, he declared that a curse should rest upon the sons of Ham. With the curse on his youngest son was joined a blessing on the other two. After this prophetic blessing we hear no more of the patriarch but the sum of his years, 950.

No'ah (nō'ah) (*motion*), one of the five daughters of Zelophehad. Num. 26: 33; 27:1; 36:11; Josh. 17:3. (B.C. 1450.)

No=a'mon (nō-ā'mŏn) (*city of Amon*), Nah. 3:8; **No,** Jer. 46:25; Ezek. 30:14, 15, 16, a city of Egypt, better known under the name of Thebes, the ancient and splendid metropolis of upper Egypt. The second part of the first form is the name of *Amon*, the

Nob (nŏb), 1 Sam. 22:19; Neh. 11: 32, a sacerdotal city in the tribe of Benjamin, and situated on some eminence near Jerusalem. It was one of the places where the ark of Jehovah was kept for a time during the days of its wanderings. 1 Sam. 21:1-6. But the event for which Nob was most noted in the Scripture annals was a frightful massacre which occurred there in the reign of Saul. 1 Sam. 22:17-19.

No'bah (nō'bah) (*barking*), an Israelite warrior, Num. 32:42, who during the conquest of the territory on the east of Jordan possessed himself of the town of Kenath and the villages or hamlets dependent upon it, and gave them his own name. (B.C. 1450.) For

SITE OF NOB.

chief divinity of Thebes. Nahum refers to the capture and sack of Thebes, probably in Assurbanipal's last invasion, B.C. 663. The description of No-amon as "situate among the rivers, the waters round about it" (Nah. *l. c.*), remarkably characterizes Thebes. It lay on both sides of the Nile, and was celebrated for its hundred gates, for its temples, obelisks, statues, etc. It was emphatically the city of temples, in the ruins of which many monuments of ancient Egypt are preserved. The plan of the city was a parallelogram, two miles from north to south and four from east to west, but none suppose that in its glory it really extended 33 miles along both sides of the Nile. Thebes was destroyed by Ptolemy, B.C. 81, and since then its population has dwelt in villages only.

a certain period after the establishment of the Israelite rule the new name remained, Judges 8:11; but it is not again heard of, and the original appellation, as is usual in such cases, appears to have recovered its hold, which it has since retained; for in the slightly-modified form of *Kunawât* it is the name of the place to the present day.

Nod (nŏd) (*wandering*), the land to which Cain fled after the murder of Abel. Gen. 4:16.

No'dab (nō'dab) (*nobility*), the name of an Arab tribe mentioned only in 1 Chron. 5:19, in the account of the war of the Reubenites against the Hagarites.

No'e. [NOAH.]

No'gah (nō'gah) (*splendor*), one of the thirteen sons of David who were born to him in Jerusalem. 1 Chron. 3: 7; 14:6.

No'hah (nō'hah) (*rest*), the fourth son of Benjamin. 1 Chron. 8:2.

Non (*fish*). Nun, the father of Joshua. 1 Chron. 7:27.

Noph (nŏf). [MEMPHIS.]

No'phah (nō'fah) (*blast*), a place mentioned only in Num. 21:30, in the remarkable song apparently composed by the Amorites after their conquest of Heshbon from the Moabites, and therefore of an earlier date than the Israelite invasion. It is named with Dibon and Medeba, and was possibly in the neighborhood of Heshbon. A name very similar to Nophah is Nobah, which is twice mentioned. Ewald decides that Nophah is identical with the latter of these.

Nose=jewel, Isa. 3:21, a ring of metal, sometimes of gold or silver, passed usually through the right nostril, and worn by way of ornament by women in the East. Upon it are strung beads, coral or jewels. In Egypt it is

NOSE-JEWELS WORN IN THE EAST.

now almost confined to the lower classes. This jewel is meant by "ear-ring," in Gen. 24:22; Ex. 35:22; and "jewel on the forehead" in Ezek. 16:12.

Number. Like most Oriental nations, it is probable that the Hebrews in their written calculations made use of the letters of the alphabet. That they did so in post-Babylonian times we have conclusive evidence in the Maccabæan coins; and it is highly probable that this was the case also in earlier times. Although it is certain that the words were often spelled out, the fact that signs were *often*, though not universally, used, would be enough to account for all the discrepancies in numbers found in the Old Testament. Numbers are often given approximately, as writers give them to-day. They are also used symbolically and conventionally. Certain

numbers, as 7, 10, 40, 100, were regarded as giving the idea of completeness. Such approximation is extremely common among eastern nations, who have a prejudice against counting their possessions accurately. 1. *Seven* is used in an exact sense, as in the case of the seven days in the week (Gen. 2:2; Ex. 20:10), but more often either symbolically or to give the idea of completeness. It was early a sacred number, perhaps because of the sanctity of the Sabbath. It is so frequent as to make a selection only of instances necessary, *e. g. seven fold*, Gen. 4:15; *seven times, i. e.* completely, Lev. 26:24; Ps. 12:6; *seven* (*i. e.* many) *ways*, Deut. 28:25. 2. *Ten* as a preferential number is exemplified in the Ten Commandments and the law of tithe. 3. *Seventy*, as compounded of 7×10, appears frequently, *e. g. seventy fold*. Gen. 4:24; Matt. 18:22. Its definite use appears in the offerings of 70 shekels, Num. 7:13, 19 ff.; the 70 elders, ch. 11:16; 70 years of captivity. Jer. 25:11. 4. *Five* appears in the table of punishments, or legal requirements, Ex. 22:1; Lev. 5:16; 22:14; 27:15; Num. 5:7; 18:16, and in the five empires of Daniel. Dan. 2. 5. *Four* is used in reference to the 4 winds, Dan. 7:2, and the so-called 4 corners of the earth; the 4 creatures, each with 4 wings and 4 faces, of Ezekiel, Ezek. 1:5 ff.; 4 rivers of Paradise, Gen. 2:10; 4 beasts, Dan. 7 and Rev. 4:6; the 4 equal-sided temple-chamber. Ezek. 40:47. 6. *Three* was very often used for a small total. 7. *Twelve* (3×4) appears in 12 tribes, 12 stones in the high priest's breastplate, 12 apostles, 12 foundation-stones, and 12 gates. Rev. 21:19–21. 8. Lastly, the mystic number 666. Rev. 13:18.

Num'bers, the fourth book of the law or Pentateuch. It takes its name in the LXX. and Vulgate (whence our "Numbers") from the double numbering or census of the people; the first of which is given in chs. 1–4, and the second in ch. 26. *Contents.*—The book may be said to contain generally the history of the Israelites from the time of their leaving Sinai, in the second year after the Exodus, till their arrival at the borders of the promised land, in the fortieth year of their journeyings. It consists of the following principal divisions: 1. The preparations for the departure from Sinai. Num. 1:1–10:10. 2. The journey from Sinai to the borders of Canaan. ch. 10:11-14:45. 3. A brief notice of laws given and events which transpired during the thirty-seven years wandering in the wilderness. ch. 15:1-19:22. 4. The history of the last year, from the second arrival of the Israelites in Kadesh till they reached "the plains of Moab by Jordan near Jericho." ch. 20:1-36:13. The book of Numbers is rich in fragments of ancient poetry, some of them of great beauty and all throwing an interesting light on the character of the times in which they were composed. Such, for instance, is the blessing of the high priest. ch. 6:24-26. Such too are chants which were the signal for the ark to move when the people journeyed, and for it to rest when they were about to encamp. In 21:14 ff. we have a passage cited from a book called the "Book of the Wars of Jehovah." This was probably a collection of ballads and songs composed on different occasions by the watch-fires of the camp, and for the most part, though not perhaps exclusively, in commemoration of the victories of the Israelites over their enemies.

Nun (*fish*), the father of the Jewish captain Joshua. Ex. 33:11, etc. His genealogical descent from Ephraim is recorded in 1 Chron. 7.

Nurse. In ancient times the position of the nurse, wherever one was maintained, was one of much honor and importance. See Gen. 24:59; 35:8; 2 Sam. 4:4; 2 Kings 11:2. The same term is applied to a foster-father or mother, *e. g.* Num. 11:12; Isa. 49:23; 60:16.

Nuts are mentioned among the good things of the land which the sons of Israel were to take as a present to Joseph in Egypt. Gen. 43:11. There can scarcely be a doubt that the Hebrew word, here translated "nuts," denotes the fruit of the pistachio tree (*Pistacia vera*), for which Syria and Palestine

PISTACHIO NUTS.

have been long famous. In Cant. 6:11 a different Hebrew word is translated "nuts." In all probability it here refers to the *walnut tree*. According to Josephus the walnut tree was formerly common, and grew most luxuriantly around the Lake of Gennesareth.

Nym'phas (nĭm'fas) (*sacred to the Muses*), a wealthy and zealous Christian in Laodicea. Col. 4:15. (A.D. 60.)

O

Oak (Heb. *strong* or *prominent*). There is much difficulty in determining the exact meanings of the several varieties of the term mentioned above. Sometimes, evidently, the terebinth or elm is intended, and at others the oak. There are a number of varieties of oak in Palestine. Dr. Robinson contends that the oak is generally intended, and that it is a very common tree in the East. Oaks grow to a large size, reach an old age, and are every way worthy the venerable associations connected with the tree. Two oaks, *Quercus coccifera* and *Q. ægilops*, are well worthy of the name of mighty trees; though it is equally true that over a greater part of the country the oaks of Palestine are at present merely bushes.

Oath. The principle on which an oath is held to be binding is incidentally laid down in Heb. 6:16, viz. as an ultimate appeal to divine authority to ratify an assertion. On the same principle, that oath has always been held most binding which appealed to the highest authority, as regards both individuals and communities. As a consequence of this principle, appeals to God's name on the one hand, and to heathen deities on the other, are treated in Scripture as tests of allegiance. Ex. 23:13; Deut. 12:3; 29:12, etc. So also the sovereign's name is sometimes used as a form of obligation. Gen. 42:15; 2 Sam. 11:11; 14:19. Other forms of oath, serious or frivolous, are mentioned, some of which are condemned by our Lord. Matt. 5:33; 23:16–22; and see James 5:12. There is, however, a world-wide difference between a solemn appeal to God and profane swearing. The forms of adjuration mentioned in Scripture are—1. Lifting up the hand. Witnesses laid their hands on the head of the accused. Gen. 14:22; Lev. 24:14; Deut. 17:7; Isa. 3:7. 2. Putting the hand under the thigh of the person to whom the promise was made. Gen. 24:2; 47:29. 3. Oaths were sometimes taken before the altar, or, as some understand the passage, if the persons were not in Jerusalem, in a position looking toward the temple. 1 Kings 8:31; 2 Chron. 6:22. 4. Dividing a victim and passing between or distributing the pieces. Gen. 15:10, 17; Jer. 34:18. As the sanctity of oaths was carefully inculcated by the law, so the crime of perjury was strongly condemned; and to a false witness the same punishment was assigned which was due for the crime to which he testified. Ex. 20:7; Lev. 19:12.

Obadi'ah (ō-ba-dī'ah) (*worshipper of Jehovah*). 1. A man whose sons are enumerated in the genealogy of the tribe of Judah. 1 Chron. 3:21.

2. A descendant of Issachar and a chief man of his tribe. 1 Chron. 7:3.

3. One of the six sons of Azel, a descendant of Saul. 1 Chron. 8:38; 9:44.

4. A Levite, son of Shemaiah, and descended from Jeduthun. 1 Chron. 9:16; Neh. 12:25.

5. The second of the lion-faced Gadites who joined David at Ziklag. 1 Chron. 12:9.

6. One of the princes of Judah in the reign of Jehoshaphat. 2 Chron. 17:7. (B.C. 867.)

7. The son of Jehiel, of the sons of Joab, who came up in the second caravan with Ezra. Ezra 8:9.

8. A priest, or family of priests, who sealed the covenant with Nehemiah. Neh. 10:5.

9. An officer of high rank in the court of Ahab. 1 Kings 18:3. He was a devout worshipper of Jehovah, and at the peril of his life concealed over a hundred prophets during the persecution by Jezebel. 1 Kings 18:3–16. (B.C. 862.)

10. The father of Ishmaiah, who was chief of the tribe of Zebulun in David's reign. 1 Chron. 27:19.

11. A Merarite Levite in the reign of

Josiah, and one of the overseers of the workmen in the restoration of the temple. 2 Chron. 34:12. (B.C. 623.)

12. The fourth of the twelve minor prophets. We know nothing of him except what we can gather from the short book which bears his name. The question of his date must depend upon the interpretation of the 11th verse of his prophecy. See below.

Obadiah, Book of, is the shortest book in the Old Testament, consisting of one chapter of 21 verses. It is a sustained denunciation of the Edomites, melting into a vision of the future glories of Zion when the arm of the Lord should have wrought her deliverance and have repaid double upon her enemies. There is a close resemblance between vs. 1–9 and Jeremiah 49:7–22, which leads to critical questions depending on which was written first.

Critics see two distinct prophecies in the book, the first including vs. 1–9, the other vs. 10–21, with a difference in style, and in tense, and therefore written at different dates. Verses 1–9 belong to the time of the destruction of Jerusalem by Nebuchadnezzar, B.C. 586, and vs. 10–21 to the early part of the exile, not long after the fall of Jerusalem. To this latter date George Adam Smith assigns the book.

O'bal (ō'bal), a son of Joktan, and, like the rest of his family, apparently the founder of an Arab tribe. Gen. 10:28. In 1 Chron. 1:22 the name is written EBAL.

O'bed (ō'bed) (*serving*). 1. Son of Boaz and Ruth the Moabitess and father of Jesse. Ruth 4:17. The circumstances of his birth, which make up all that we know about him, are given with much beauty in the book of Ruth. The name of Obed occurs only Ruth 4:17, and in the four genealogies, Ruth 4:21, 22; 1 Chron. 2:12; Matt. 1:5; Luke 3:32.

2. A descendant of Jarha, the Egyptian slave of Sheshan, in the line of Jerahmeel. 1 Chron. 2:37, 38.

3. One of David's mighty men. 1 Chron. 11:47.

4. One of the gate-keepers of the temple; son of Shemaiah the first-born of Obed-edom. 1 Chron. 26:7.

5. Father of Azariah, one of the captains of hundreds who joined with Jehoiada in the revolution by which Athaliah fell. 2 Chron. 23:1.

O'bed=e'dom (ō'bed-ē'dom) (*servant of Edom*). 1. A Gittite, 2 Sam. 6:10, 11, that is, probably, a native either of Gath or of the Levitical city of Gathrimmon. (B.C. 1042.) After the death of Uzzah, the ark, which was being conducted from the house of Abinadab in Gibeah to the city of David, was carried aside into the house of Obed-edom, where it continued three months. It was brought thence by David. 2 Sam. 6:12; 1 Chron. 15:25. He is also described as a Levite. If so he was doubtless identical with Obed-edom the Korahite. (No. 3 below.)

2. A Levite of the second degree who with others was a gate-keeper for the Ark, 1 Chron. 15:18; and was a musician appointed to play the harp to lead the singing. 1 Chron. 15:21; 16:5.

3. A Levite who also served as doorkeeper, 1 Chron. 15:24. Probably the same as Obed-edom, the son of Jeduthun. 1 Chron. 16:38, and Obed-edom the Korahite, 1 Chron. 26:1, 4, 8, 15. The same family was on duty in the reign of Amaziah. 2 Chron. 25:24. There is considerable difference of opinion as to the identification of the different men by this name.

O'bil (ō'bil) (*keeper of the camels*), a keeper of the herds of camels in the reign of David. 1 Chron. 27:30.

Oblation. [SACRIFICE.]

O'both (ō'both) (*water skins*), one of the encampments of the Israelites, east of Moab. Num. 21:10; 33:43. Its exact site is unknown, but it was in the neighborhood of Moab.

Oc'ran (ok'ran) (*troubled*), an Asherite, father of Pagiel. Num. 1:13.

O'ded (ō'ded) (*restoring*). 1. The father of Azariah the prophet, in the reign of Asa. 2 Chron. 15:1.

2. A prophet of Jehovah in Samaria, at the time of Pekah's invasion of Judah. 2 Chron. 28:9. He pleaded that the opposing armies were brothers, and obtained a cessation of hostilities.

Offerings. [SACRIFICE.]

Officer. It is obvious that most, if not all, of the Hebrew words rendered "officer" are either of an indefinite character or are synonymous terms for functionaries known under other and more specific names, as "scribe," "eunuch," etc. The two words so rendered in the New Testament denote—1. An inferior officer of a court of justice, a messenger or bailiff, like the Roman viator or lictor. Matt. 5 : 25; Acts 5 : 22. 2. Officers whose duty it was to register and collect fines imposed by courts of justice. Luke 12 : 58, 59.

Og (ŏg), an Amoritish king of Bashan, whose rule extended over sixty cities. Josh. 13 : 12. He was one of the last representatives of the giant race of Rephaim, and was, with his children and his people, defeated and exterminated by the Israelites at Edrei immediately after the conquest of Sihon. Num. 21 : 20, 32–35; 32 : 33; Deut. 3 : 1–13; 1 : 4; 4 : 47; 31 : 4; Josh. 2 : 10; 9 : 10; 13 : 12, 30. The belief in Og's enormous stature is corroborated by an allusion to his iron bedstead (or sarcophagus) preserved in "Rabbath of the children of Ammon." Deut. 3 : 11. (B.C. 1451.)

Oil. Of the numerous substances, animal and vegetable, which were known to the ancients as yielding oil, the olive berry is the one of which most frequent mention is made in the Scriptures. 1. *Gathering.*—The olive berry was either gathered by hand or shaken off carefully with a light reed or stick. 2. *Pressing.* —In order to make oil, the fruit was either bruised in a mortar, crushed in a press loaded with wood or stones, ground in a mill, or trodden with the feet. The "beaten" oil of Ex. 27 : 20; 29 : 40; Lev. 24 : 2; Num. 28 : 5 was probably made by bruising in a mortar. It was used—(1) As food. Dried wheat, boiled with either butter or oil, but generally the former, is a common dish for all classes in Syria. Ex. 29 : 2. (2) Cosmetic. Oil was used by the Jews for anointing the body, *e. g.* after the bath, and giving to the skin and hair a smooth and comely appearance, *e. g.* before an entertainment. 2 Sam. 14 : 2. (3) Medicinal. Isaiah alludes to the use of oil in medical treatment. Isa. 1 : 6; see also Mark 6 : 13; Luke 10 : 34; James 5 : 14. (4) For light. Ex. 25 : 6; Matt. 25 : 3. The oil for "the light" was expressly ordered to be olive oil, beaten. Ex. 27 : 20. (5) Ritual. Oil was poured on or mixed with the flour or meal used in offerings. Ex. 29 : 7; 37 : 29; 40 : 9; Lev. 2 : 1, 4–7. Kings, priests and prophets were anointed with oil or ointment, Lev. 8 : 12. (6) In offerings. As so important a necessary of life, the Jew was required to include oil among his first-fruit offerings. Num. 18 : 12. Tithes of oil were also required. Deut. 12 : 17. [OLIVE.]

Oil tree (Heb *ēts shemen*). The Hebrew words occur in Neh. 8 : 15 (Authorized Version "pine branches"), 1 Kings 6 : 23 ("olive tree," R. V. "olive wood"), and in Isa. 41 : 19 ("oil tree"). From the passage in Nehemiah, where the *ēts shemen* is mentioned as distinct from the olive tree, it may perhaps be identified with the *zackum* tree of the Arabs, the *Balanites ægyptiaca*, a well-known and abundant shrub or small tree in the plain of Jordan. The zackum oil is held in high repute by the Arabs for its medicinal properties. [OLIVE.]

Ointment. An oily or unctuous substance, usually compounded of oil with various spices and resins and aromatics, and preserved in small alabaster boxes or cruses, in which the delicious aroma was best preserved. Some of the ointments have been known to retain their fragrance for several hundred years. They were a much-coveted luxury, and often very expensive. 1. *Cosmetic.*— The Greek and Roman practice of anointing the head and clothes on festive occasions prevailed also among the Egyptians, and appears to have had place among the Jews. Ruth 3 : 3. 2. *Funereal.*—Ointments were used among the Jews to anoint dead bodies and the clothes in which they were wrapped. Matt. 26 : 12. 3. *Medicinal.*—Ointment formed an important feature in medical treatment. Jer. 8 : 22; Rev. 3 : 18, etc. 4. *Ritual.*—Besides the oil used in many ceremonial observances, a special ointment was appointed to be used in consecration. Ex. 30 : 23, 33. The Hebrew word for "oil" is sometimes translated ointment. A person whose business it was to compound ointments in general was called an "apothecary." R. V. mar. "perfumer." Neh. 3 : 8. The work was sometimes carried on by woman "confectionaries." 1 Sam. 8 : 13. R. V. mar. "perfumers."

Old Testament. Properly the Old Covenant, or the relations of man with God before the coming of Christ. It describes the training of man in religion.

CLASSIFICATION. It consists of 39 books. These are with us divided into three classes—17 Historical, 17 Prophetic, and 5 Poetical. Poems are quoted in the historical books, and much of the prophetical is in poetic form. The Jews also made three divisions, but with a different classification: (1) The

Law, comprising the 5 books of the Pentateuch; (2) The Prophets, comprising all the prophets except Daniel, and the historical books except Chronicles, Ezra and Nehemiah; (3) The Hagiographa, or sacred writings, comprising all the other books of the Old Testament, books of the most heterogeneous sorts, poetry, ethics, philosophy, prophecy.

FORM OF THE BOOKS. As regards the form in which the sacred writings were preserved, there can be little doubt that the text was ordinarily written on skins, rolled up into volumes, like the modern synagogue rolls.

THE LANGUAGE. The whole Old Testament was originally written in the Hebrew language, except certain short passages which are in Aramaic (one branch of the Syriac), viz., Ezra 4:8; 6:18; 7:12-26; Jer. 10:11; Dan. 2:4-7: 28. The letters of the two languages are the same in both languages, just as the letters of English and French and Latin.

One of the difficulties in understanding the true meaning of the Hebrew lies in the fact that originally the writing consisted of consonants only, the vowels to be vocalized in speech being taught orally, as we learn to pronounce the consonants, cts., lbs., "cents" and "pounds." We can see the difficulty more clearly if we take the consonants which are translated "raven" in the story of Elijah, and see how many different Hebrew words have exactly the same. The first consonant of the three is merely a sign to show that some vowel is to be understood.

ōReB = raven; āRoB = gadfly; ēRaB = Arabian; ERĕB' = wolf; ĕRĕB = evening; ōRBō = name *of a village;* in plural, *inhabitants of Orbo.* So with three English consonants, different vowels entirely change the meaning, as G-R-T might mean GReaT, GReeT, GiRT, GRiT, GRaTe, eGReT, GRoTe (the historian). Therefore, says Farrar, "It is as perfectly open to any one who chooses to say that 'Arabians,' or 'Orebites,' or 'merchants,' or 'people of the rock Oreb' fed Elijah, as to say that the 'raven' did so."

Between the seventh and tenth centuries of the Christian era certain Jewish scholars called Masoretes (from Masorah = tradition) resident chiefly at Tiberias on the sea of Galilee, placed under these consonants the signs which indicated the vowel sounds belonging according to tradition to the consonants.

FORMS OF LITERATURE. Almost every form of literature is employed in the Old Testament, prose, poetry, history, story, parable, drama, dialogue, lyric, epic, oratory, proverb, epigram, satire, hymns, songs, visions, symbols. And each form must be interpreted according to its own laws; or error will result. Every great truth is presented in various forms, in order that it may be seen from every point of view. No one form of language can make it clearly understood.

EVOLUTION OR DEVELOPMENT. The story of the Old Testament is the history of the gradual teaching and unfolding of the great truths of religion, as far and as fast as the people were able to understand. What is necessary for the childhood of the race, is not the fulness of the truth for its manhood. The method of dealing with its childhood, its ignorant and untrained age, is not the one used as the race or as God's people grew in intelligence. To realize this is to avoid many of the mistakes and misunderstandings of the morality of the Old Testament.

THE HIGHER CRITICISM has been very busy with the Old Testament. Perhaps the most help it has given to the average reader is the viewing of every book in its own place in the history. No one can understand a prophet's message without realizing the circumstance in which and the people to which it was delivered.

MANUSCRIPTS.—The Old Testament MSS. known to us fall into two main classes: synagogue rolls and MSS. for private use. Of the latter, some are written in the square, others in the rabbinic or cursive, character. The synagogue rolls contain, separate from each other, the Pentateuch, the Haphtaroth or appointed sections of the Prophets, and the so-called Megilloth, viz. Canticles, Ruth, Lamentations, Ecclesiastes and Esther. Private MSS. in the square character are in the book form, either on parchment or on paper, and of various sizes, from folio to 12mo. Some contain the Hebrew text alone; others add the Targum, or an Arabic or other translation, either interspersed with the text or in a separate column, occasionally in the margin. The upper and lower margins are generally occupied by the Masorah, sometimes by rabbinical commentaries, etc. The date of a MS. is ordinarily given in the subscription; but as the subscriptions are often concealed in the Masorah or elsewhere, it is occasionally difficult to find them; occasionally also it is difficult to decipher them. No satisfactory criteria have been yet established by which the ages of MSS. are to be determined. Few existing MSS. are supposed to be older than the twelfth century. Kennicott and Bruns assigned one of their collation (No. 590) to the tenth century; De Rossi dates it A.D. 1018; on the other hand, one of his own (No. 634) he adjudges to the eighth century. Since the days of Kennicott and De Rossi modern research has discovered MSS. beyond the limits of Europe. Of many of these there seems no reason to suppose that they will add much to our knowledge of the Hebrew text. It is different with the MSS. examined by Pinner at Odessa. One of these MSS. (A, No. 1), a Pentateuch roll, unpointed, brought from Derbend in Daghestan, appears by the subscription to have been written previous to A.D. 580, and if so is the oldest known biblical Hebrew MS. in existence. The forms of the letters are remarkable. Another MS. (B, No. 3) containing the Prophets, on parchment, in small folio, although only dating, according to the inscription, from A.D. 916, and furnished with a Masorah, is a yet greater treasure. Its vowels and accents are wholly different from those now in use, both in form and in position, being all above the letters: they have accordingly been the theme of much discussion among Hebrew scholars. 3. *Printed text.*—The history of the printed text of the Hebrew Bible commences with the early Jewish editions of the separate books. First appeared the Psalter, in 1477, probably at Bologna, in 4to, with Kimchi's commentary interspersed among the verses. Only the first four psalms had the vowel-points, and these but clumsily expressed. At Bologna there subsequently appeared, in 1482, the Pentateuch, in folio, pointed, with the Targum and the commentary of Rashi; and the five Megilloth (Ruth—Esther), in folio, with the commentaries of Rashi and Aben Ezra. From Soncino, near Cremona, issued in 1486 the Prophetæ priores (Joshua—Kings), folio, un-pointed, with Kimchi's commentary. The honor of printing the first entire Hebrew Bible belongs to the above-mentioned town of Soncino. The edition is in folio, pointed and accentuated. Nine copies only of it are now known, of which one belongs to Exeter College, Oxford. This was followed, in 1494, by the 4to or 8vo edition printed by Gersom at Brescia, remarkable as being the edition from which Luther's German translation was made. After the Brescian, the next primary edition was that contained in the Complutensian Polyglot, published at Complutum (Alcala) in Spain, at the expense of Cardinal Ximenes, dated 1514-17, but not issued till 1522. To this succeeded an edition which has had more influence than any on the text of later times—the Second Rabbinical Bible, printed by Bomberg at Venice, 4 vols. fol., 1525-6. The editor was the learned Tunisian Jew R. Jacob ben Chaim. The great feature of his work lay in the correction of the text by the precepts of the Masorah, in which he was profoundly skilled, and on which, as well as on the text itself, his labors were employed. The Hebrew Bible which became the standard to subsequent generations was that of Joseph Athias, a learned rabbi and printer at Amsterdam. His text was based on a comparison of the previous editions with two MSS.; one bearing date 1299, the other a Spanish MS. boasting an antiquity of 900 years. It appeared at Amsterdam, 2 vols. 8vo, 1661. 4. *Principles of criticism.*—The method of procedure required in the criticism of the Old Testament is widely different from that practised in the criticism of the New Testament. Our Old Testament textus receptus is a far more faithful representation of the genuine Scripture; but, on the other hand, the means of detecting and correcting the errors contained in it are more precarious, the results are more uncertain, and the ratio borne by the value of the diplomatic evidence of MSS. to that of a good critical judgment and sagacity is greatly diminished. It is indeed to the direct testimony of the MSS. that, in endeavoring to establish the true text, we must first have recourse. The comparative purity of the Hebrew text is probably different in different parts of the Old Testament.

II. QUOTATIONS FROM THE OLD TESTA-

MENT IN THE NEW TESTAMENT.—The New Testament quotations from the Old form one of the outward bonds of connection between the two parts of the Bible. They are manifold in kind. In the quotations of all kinds from the Old Testament in the New, we find a continual variation from the *letter* of the older Scriptures. To this variation three causes may be specified as having contributed: First, all the New Testament writers quoted from the Septuagint; correcting it indeed more or less by the Hebrew, especially when it was needful for their purpose; occasionally deserting it altogether; still abiding by it to so large an extent as to show that it was the primary source whence their quotations were drawn. Secondly, the New Testament writers must have frequently quoted f r o m memory. Thirdly, combined with this there was an alteration of conscious or unconscious d e s i g n. Sometimes the object of this was to obtain increased f o r c e. Sometimes a n Old Testament passage is abridged, and in the abridgment so adjusted, by a little alteration, as to present an aspect of completeness, and yet omit what is foreign to the immediate purpose. Acts 1:20; 1 Cor. 1:31. At other times a passage is enlarged by the incorporation of a passage from another source: thus in Luke 4:18, 19, although the contents are professedly those read by our Lord from Isa. 61, we have the words "to set at liberty them that are bruised," introduced from Isa. 58:6 (Sept.); similarly i n Rom. 11:8, Deut. 29:4 is combined with Isa. 29:10. I n some cases still greater liberty of alteration is assumed. In some places, again, the actual words of the original are taken up, but employed with a new meaning. Almost more remarkable than any alteration in the quotation itself is the circumstance that in Matt. 27:9 Jeremiah should be named as the author of a prophecy really delivered by Zechariah; the reason being that the prophecy is based upon that in Jer. 18, 19, and that without a reference to this original source the most essential features of the fulfilment of Zechariah's prophecy would be misunderstood.

Olive. The olive was among the most abundant and characteristic vegetation of Judea. The olive tree grows freely almost everywhere on the shores of the Mediterranean, but it was peculiarly abundant in Palestine. See Deut. 6:11; 8:8; 28:40. Oliveyards are a matter of course in descriptions of the country, like vineyards and cornfields. Judges 15:5; 1 Sam. 8:14. The kings had very extensive ones. 1 Chron. 27:28. Even now the tree is very abundant in the country. Almost every village has its olive grove. Cer-

OLIVE BRANCHES AND OLIVES.

tain districts may be specified where at various times this tree has been very luxuriant. The cultivation of the olive tree had the closest connection with the domestic life of the Israelites, 2 Chron. 2:10, their trade, Ezek. 27:17; Hos. 12:1, and even their public ceremonies and religious worship. In Solomon's temple the cherubim were "of olive tree," 1 Kings 6:23, as also the doors, vs. 31, 32, and the posts. ver. 33. For the various uses of olive oil see OIL. The wind was dreaded by the cultivator of the olive, for the least ruffling of a breeze is apt to cause the flowers to fall. Job 15:33. It is needless to add that the locust was a formidable enemy of the olive. It happened not unfrequently that hopes were disappointed, and that "the labor of the olive failed." Hab. 3:17. As to the growth of the tree, it thrives best in warm and sunny situations. It is of moderate height, growing from 20 to 40 feet high, with knotty gnarled trunk and a smooth ash-colored bark. In general appearance it resembles the apple tree; in leaves and stems, the willow. The flowers are white and appear in June. The fruit is like a plum in shape, but much smaller,

Those who see olives for the first time are occasionally disappointed by the dusty color of their foliage; but those who are familiar with them find an inexpressible charm in the rippling changes of their slender gray-green leaves. (See Ruskin's "Stones of Venice," iii. 175–177.) The olive furnishes the basis of one of Paul's allegories. Rom. 11:16–25. The Gentiles are the "wild olive" grafted in upon the "good olive," to which once the Jews belonged, and with which they may again be incorporated. Olive trees were so abundant in Galilee that at the siege of Jotapata by Vespasian the Roman army

OLIVE TREE AND OIL PRESS.

and at first is green, but gradually becomes purple, and even black, with a hard stony kernel, and is remarkable from the outer fleshy part being that in which much oil is lodged, and not, as is usual, in the seed. The fruit ripens from August to September. It is sometimes eaten green, but its chief value is in its oil. The wood is hard, fine, beautifully veined, and is often used for cabinet work. It grows slowly, but lives to an immense age. Its look is singularly indicative of tenacious vigor; and this is the force of what is said in Scripture of its "greenness," as emblematic of strength and prosperity. The leaves, too, are not deciduous.

were driven from the ascent of the walls by hot olive oil poured upon them and scalding them underneath their armor.—Josephus, *Wars,* 3:7:28.

Olives, Mount of. The term "Mount of Olives" occurs in the Old Testament in Zech. 14:4 only. In 2 Sam. 15:30 it is called "Olivet;" literally as in R. V. "Olives." The word "Mount" is supplied in each case by the translators, in other places simply "the mount," Neh. 8:15, "the mount that is before Jerusalem," 1 Kings 11: 7, or "the mountain which is on the east side of the city." Ezek. 11:23. In the New Testament the usual form is "the Mount of Olives." It is called also "Olivet." Acts 1 : 12. This mountain is the well-known eminence on the east of Jerusalem, intimately connected with some of the gravest events of the history of the Old Testament and the New Testament, the scene of the flight of David and the triumphal progress of the Son of David, of the idolatry of Solomon, and the agony and betrayal of Christ. It is a ridge of rather more than a mile in length, running in general direction north and south, covering the whole eastern side of the city. At its northern end the ridge bends round to the west, so as to form an enclosure to the city on that side also. On the north a space of nearly a mile of tolerably level surface intervenes between the walls of the city and the rising ground; on the east the mount is close to the walls, parted only by the narrow ravine of the Kidron. It is this portion which is the real Mount of Olives of the history. In general height it is not very much above the city: 200 feet higher than the temple mount, 2637 feet above sea-level. It is rounded, swelling and regular in form. Proceeding from north to south there occur four independent summits, called —1, "Galilee," or "Scopus;" 2, "Mount of Ascension;" 3, "Prophets" —subordinate to the last and almost a part of it; 4, "Mount of Offence." 1. Of these the central one—the "Mount of Ascension"—is the most important. Three paths lead from the valley to the summit—one on the north, in the hollow between the two crests of the hill, another over the summit, and a third winding around the southern shoulder, still the most frequented and the best. The central hill, which we are now considering, purports to contain the sites of some of the most sacred and impressive events of Christian history. The majority of these sacred spots now command little or no attention; but three still remain, sufficiently sacred—if authentic—to consecrate any place. These are—(1) Gethsemane, at the foot of the mount; (2) The spot from which our Saviour ascended on the summit; (3) The place of the lamentation of Christ over Jerusalem, halfway up. Of these, Gethsemane is the only one which has any claim to be authentic. [GETHSEMANE.] 2. Next to the central summit, on the southern side, is a hill remarkable only for the

fact that it contains the "singular catacomb" known as the "Tombs of the Prophets," probably in allusion to the words of Christ. Matt. 23 : 29. 3. The most southern portion of the Mount of Olives is that usually known as the "Mount of Offence," *Mons Offensionis.* It rises next to that last mentioned. The title "Mount of Offence," or "Scandal," was bestowed on the supposition that it is the "Mount of Corruption" on which Solomon erected the high places for the gods of his foreign wives. 2 Kings 23 : 13; 1 Kings 11 : 7. The southern summit is considerably lower than the centre one. 4. There remains "Galilee," the "Scopus" of Josephus, about 400 yards from the "Mount of Ascension." It stands directly opposite the northeast corner of Jerusalem, and is approached by the path between it and the "Mount of Ascension." The presence of a number of churches and other edifices must have rendered the Mount of Olives, during the early and middle ages of Christianity, entirely unlike what it was in the time of the Jewish kingdom or of our Lord. Except the high places on the summit, the only buildings then to be seen were probably the walls of the vineyards and gardens and the towers and presses which were their invariable accompaniment. But though the churches are nearly all demolished, there must be a considerable difference between the aspect of the mountain now and in those days when it received its name from the abundance of its olive groves. It does not now stand so preeminent in this respect among the hills in the neighborhood of Jerusalem. It is only in the deeper and more secluded slope leading up to the northernmost summit that these venerable trees spread into anything like a forest. The cedars commemorated by the Talmud and the date-palms implied in the name Bethany have fared still worse; there is not one of either to be found within many miles. Two religious ceremonies performed there must have done much to increase the numbers who resorted to the mount. The appearance of the new moon was probably watched for, certainly proclaimed, from the summit. The second ceremony referred to was the burning of the *red heifer.* This solemn ceremonial was enacted on the central mount, and in a spot so carefully specified that it

MOUNT OF OLIVES.

Photo by Jan Wilga

would seem not difficult to fix it. It was due east of the sanctuary, and at such an elevation on the mount that the officiating priest, as he slew the animal and sprinkled her blood, could see the façade of the sanctuary through the east gate of the temple.

Ol'ivet (*olive-yard*). 2 Sam. 15:30; Acts 1:12. [OLIVES, MOUNT OF.]

Olym'pas, a Christian at Rome. Rom. 16:15. (A.D. 60.)

O'mar (ō'mar) (*eloquent, talkative*), son of Eliphaz the first-born of Esau. Gen. 36:11, 15; 1 Chron. 1:36.

Ome'ga (ō-mē'gà), or **o'mega,** the last letter of the Greek alphabet. It is used metaphorically to denote the end of anything. Rev. 1:8, 11.

Omer. [WEIGHTS AND MEASURES.]

Om'ri (ŏm'rī). 1. Originally "captain of the host" to Elah, was afterward himself king of Israel, and founder of the third dynasty. (B.C. 885.) Omri was engaged in the siege of Gibbethon, situated in the tribe of Dan, which had been occupied by the Philistines. As soon as the army heard that Zimri had murdered Elah, they proclaimed Omri king. Thereupon he broke up the siege of Gibbethon, and attacked Tirzah, where Zimri was holding his court as king of Israel. The city was taken, and Zimri perished in the flames of the palace, after a reign of seven days. Omri, however, was not allowed to establish his dynasty without a struggle against Tibni, whom "half the people," 1 Kings 16:21, desired to raise to the throne. The civil war lasted four years. Comp. 1 Kings 16:15 with 23. After he was firmly on the throne he transferred the capital to Samaria which he built for the purpose. He seems to have been a vigorous and unscrupulous ruler, anxious to strengthen his dynasty by intercourse and alliances with foreign states. The length of his reign is disputed. It is generally called 12 years, but the date of the beginning of the 12 years is uncertain. Some think he reigned considerably longer, some of the time generally reckoned to his son Ahab belonging to him. He conducted a vigorous and very successful campaign against the Moabites which is mentioned on the Moabite Stone.

2. One of the sons of Becher the son of Benjamin. 1 Chron. 7:8.

3. A descendant of Pharez the son of Judah. 1 Chron. 9:4.

4. Son of Michael, and chief of the tribe of Issachar in the reign of David. 1 Chron. 27:18.

On, the son of Peleth, and one of the chiefs of the tribe of Reuben, who took part with Korah, Dathan and Abiram in their revolt against Moses. Num. 16:1. (B.C. 1491.) His name does not again appear in the narrative of the conspiracy, nor is he alluded to when reference is made to the final catastrophe; it is therefore thought by some to be a misreading.

On (*light*), a town of lower Egypt, called BETH-SHEMESH in Jer. 43:13. On is better known under its Greek name Heliopolis or "city of the Sun." It was situated on the east side of the Pelusiac branch of the Nile, just below the point of the Delta, and about twenty miles northeast of Memphis. The chief object of worship at Heliopolis was the sun, whose temple, described by Strabo, is now only represented by the single beautiful obelisk, of red granite, 68 feet 2 inches high above the pedestal, which has stood for more than 4000 years, having been erected by Usirtesen, the second king of the twelfth dynasty. Heliopolis was anciently famous for its learning, and Eudoxus and Plato studied under its priests. The first mention of this place in the Bible is in the history of Joseph, to whom we read Pharaoh gave "to wife Asenath the daughter of Potipherah priest of On." Gen. 41:45, comp. ver. 50, and 46:20. On is to be remembered not only as the home of Joseph, but as the traditional place to which his far-off namesake took Mary and the babe Jesus in the flight to Egypt. The two famous obelisks, long called "Cleopatra's Needles," one of which now stands in London and the other in Central Park in New York city, once stood before this city, and were seen by the children of Israel before the Exodus having been quarried at Syene on the Nile, erected at On (Heliopolis) by Thothmes III., B.C. 1500 (?), and inscriptions added by Rameses II. (Sesostris) two hundred years later. They were taken to Alexandria by Augustus Cæsar A.D. 23, from which they were removed to their present places.

O'nam (ō'nam) (*strong*). 1. One of the sons of Shobal the son of Seir. Gen. 36:23; 1 Chron. 1:40.

2. The son of Jerahmeel by his wife Atarah. 1 Chron. 2:26, 28.

O'nan (ō'nan) (*strong*), the second son of Judah by the Canaanitess, "the daughter of Shua." Gen. 38:4; 1 Chron. 2:3. "What he did was evil in the eyes of Jehovah, and he slew him also," as he had slain his elder brother. Gen. 38:9. His death took place before the family of Jacob went down into Egypt. Gen. 46:12; Num. 26:19.

Ones'imus (ō-nĕs'ĭmŭs) (*profitable, useful*), the name of the servant or slave in whose behalf Paul wrote the Epistle to Philemon. He was a native, or certainly an inhabitant, of Colosse. Col. 4:9. (A.D. 61.) He fled from his master and escaped to Rome, where he was led to embrace the gospel through Paul's instrumentality. After his conversion the most happy and friendly relations sprung up between the teacher and disciple.

Onesiph'orus (ŏn-e-sĭf'o-rŭs) (*bringing profit*) is named twice only in the New Testament, viz. 2 Tim. 1:16–18 and 4:19. Paul mentions him in terms of grateful love as having a noble courage and generosity in his behalf, amid his trials as a prisoner at Rome, when others from whom he expected better things had deserted him. 2 Tim. 4:16. Probably other members of the family were also active Christians. 2 Tim. 4:19. It is evident from 2 Tim. 1:18 that Onesiphorus had his home at Ephesus. (A.D. 64.)

Oni'as (ŏnī'as), the name of five high priests in the period between the Old and the New Testament. They are only mentioned in the Apocrypha.

Onion. This product is mentioned only in Num. 11:5, as one of the good things of Egypt of which the Israelites regretted the loss. Onions have been from time immemorial a favorite article of food among the Egyptians. The onions of Egypt are much milder in flavor and less pungent than those of this country.

O'no (ō'nö) (*strong*), one of the towns of Benjamin, is first found in 1 Chron. 8:12. A plain was attached to the town, called "the plain of Ono," Neh. 6:2, perhaps identical with the "valley of craftsmen." Neh. 11:35. It is the modern *Kefr Ana* north of Lydda.

Onycha (ŏn'ĭkà), spoken of in Ex. 30:34, was one of the ingredients of the sacred perfume. It consists of the shells of several kinds of mussels, which when burned emit a strong odor.

Onyx (*a finger-nail*) is the translation of the Hebrew *shôham;* but there is some doubt as to its signification. Some writers believe that the "beryl" is intended; while others favor "carbuncle" "chalcedony" or "turquoise;" but the balance of authority is in favor of some variety of the onyx. The onyx varies greatly in value, according to the size, variety or special beauty. White and reddish stripes alternating form the *sardonyx;* white and reddish gray, the *chalcedony.* When polished it has a fine lustre and is easily engraved. It was much used for signets during the Roman period. Ex. 28:9, 20; 35:9; Ezek. 28:13.

O'phel (ō'fel) (*hill*), a part of ancient Jerusalem. Ophel was the swelling declivity by which the mount of the temple slopes off on its southern side into the valley of Hinnom—a long, narrowish, rounded spur or promontory, which intervenes between the mouth of the central valley of Jerusalem (the Tyropœon) and the Kidron, or valley of Jehoshaphat. Halfway down it on its eastern face is the "Fount of the Virgin," so called; and at its foot the lower outlet of the same spring—the Pool of Siloam. In 2 Chron. 27:3 Jotham is said to have built much "on the wall of Ophel." Manasseh, among his other defensive works, "compassed about Ophel." 2 Chron. 33:14. It appears to have been near the "watergate," Neh. 3:26, and the "great tower that lieth out." ver. 27. It was evidently the residence of the Nethinim. Neh. 11:21.

O'phir (ō'fĭr). 1. The eleventh in order of the sons of Joktan. Gen. 10:29; 1 Chron. 1:23.

2. A seaport or region from which the Hebrews in the time of Solomon obtained gold. The gold was proverbial for its fineness, so that "gold of Ophir" is several times used as an expression for fine gold, 1 Chron. 29:4; Job 28:16; Ps. 45:9; Isa. 13:12; and in one passage, Job 22:24, the word "Ophir" by itself is used for gold of Ophir, and for gold generally. In addition to gold, the vessels brought from Ophir almug wood and precious stones. The precise geographical situation of Ophir has long been a subject of doubt and discussion. The two countries which

have divided the opinions of the learned have been Arabia and India, while some have placed it in Africa. In five passages Ophir is mentioned by name—1 Kings 9:28; 10:11; 22:48; 2 Chron. 8:18; 9:10. If the three passages of the book of Kings are carefully examined, it will be seen that all the information given respecting Ophir is that it was a place or region accessible by sea from Ezion-geber on the Red Sea, from which imports of gold, almug trees and precious stones were brought back by the Tyrian and Hebrew sailors. The author of the tenth chapter of Genesis certainly regarded Ophir as the name of some city, region or tribe in Arabia. It is almost certain that the Ophir of Genesis is the Ophir of the book of Kings, although it cannot be proved to be so. The characteristics of Arabia as found by modern investigation seem to prove Ophir was in southern Arabia, upon the border of the Indian Ocean; for even if all the things brought over in Solomon's ships are not now found in Arabia, but are found in India, yet there is evidence that many now unknown once were known in Arabia; and, moreover, Ophir may not have been the original place of production of some of them, but the great market for traffic in them.

Oph′ni (ŏf′nĭ), a town of Benjamin, mentioned in Josh. 18:24. It may be the same as the Gophna of Josephus, a place which at the time of Vespasian's invasion was apparently so important as to be second only to Jerusalem. This still survives in the modern *Jufna*, 2½ miles northwest of Bethel.

Oph′rah (ŏf′rah) (*fawn*). 1. A town in the tribe of Benjamin. Josh. 18:23; 1 Sam. 13:17. Jerome places it five miles east of Bethel. It is perhaps *et-Taiyibeh*, a small village on the crown of a conspicuous hill, four miles east-northeast of *Beitin* (Bethel).

2. More fully, OPHRAH OF THE ABI-EZRITES, the native place of Gideon, Judges 6:11, and the scene of his exploits against Baal, ver. 24; his residence after his accession to power, ch. 9:5, and the place of his burial in the family sepulchre, ch. 8:32. It was probably in Manasseh, ch. 6:15, and not far distant from Shechem. Judges 9:1, 5.

3. The son of Meonothai. 1 Chron. 4:14.

Orchard. [GARDEN.]

O′reb (ō′reb) (*raven*), one of the chieftains of the Midianite host which invaded Israel, and was defeated and driven back by Gideon. Judges 7:25. Isaiah, Isa. 10:26, refers to the magnitude of this disaster. Comp. Ps. 83.

O′reb, The rock, the "raven's crag," the spot, east of Jordan, at which the Midianite chieftain Oreb, with thousands of his countrymen, fell by the hand of the Ephraimites, and which probably acquired its name therefrom. It is mentioned in Judges 7:25; Isa. 10:26.

O′ren (ō′ren) (*fir tree*), one of the sons of Jerahmeel, the first-born of Hezron. 1 Chron. 2:25.

Organ. Gen. 4:21; Job 21:12; 30:31; Ps. 150:4. The Hebrew word thus rendered probably denotes a pipe or perforated wind-instrument. In Gen. 4:21 it appears to be a general term for all wind-instruments. In Job 21:12 are enumerated three kinds of musical instruments which are possible, under the general terms of the timbrel, harp and *organ*. Some identify it with the pandean pipe or syrinx, an instrument of unquestionably ancient origin, and common in the East. [See MUSIC.]

Ori′on (ô-rī′on), a large and bright constellation visible in all latitudes. It is named after a mythical personage of the Greeks, of gigantic stature, and "the handsomest man in the world." The Arabs called it "the giant," referring to Nimrod, the mighty hunter, who was fabled to have been bound in the sky for his impiety. Job 9:9. Also alluded to in Job 38:31.

Ornaments, Personal. The number, variety and weight of the ornaments ordinarily worn upon the person form one of the characteristic features of Oriental costume, in both ancient and modern times. The monuments of ancient Egypt exhibit the persons of ladies loaded with rings, earrings of very great size, anklets, armlets, bracelets of the most varied forms, richly-ornamented necklaces, and chains of various kinds. There is sufficient evidence in the Bible that the inhabitants of Palestine were equally devoted to finery. In the Old Testament, Isaiah, Isa. 3:18–23, supplies us with a detailed description of the articles with which the luxurious women of his day were decorated.

Eliezer decorated Rebekah with "a golden nose-ring of half a shekel (¼ oz.) weight, and two bracelets for her hands

ANKLETS.

of ten shekels (4½ oz.) weight of gold." Gen. 24:22. Earrings were worn by Jacob's wives. Gen. 35:4. The number of personal ornaments worn by the

wife of Chilion son of Naomi, and thereby sister-in-law to Ruth. Ruth 1: 4, 14. Probably about the time of Gideon.

O'shea (ō'shē-à). [JOSHUA.]

Osprey. The Hebrew word occurs in Lev. 11:13 and Deut. 14:12, as the name of some unclean bird. It is probably the osprey (*Pandion haliaetus*).

Ossifrage (*the bone-breaker*). The Hebrew word occurs, as the name of an unclean bird, in Lev. 11:13 and Deut. 14:12. It is probably the *lammergeyer*, or bearded vulture as it is sometimes called, one of the largest of the birds of prey. It derives its name from its practice of dropping tortoises and bones from a height in order to break them and get at their contents.

Ostrich, a large bird, native of Africa and Arabia, nearly ten feet high, having a long neck and short wings. It seeks retired places, Job 30:29; Lam. 4:3, and has a peculiar mournful cry that is sometimes mistaken by the Arabs for that of the lion. Micah 1:8. In Job 39:13-18 will be found a description of the bird's habits. The eggs are laid in a hole scratched in the sand, perhaps 6 feet in diameter; the eggs are then covered over to the depth of about a foot, and are, in the case of those birds which are found within the tropics, generally left for the greater part of the

ASSYRIAN AND EGYPTIAN ORNAMENTS.

Egyptians, particularly by the females, is incidentally noticed in Ex. 3:22.

Or'nan (ôr'nan). 1 Chron. 21:15; 2 Chron. 3:1. [ARAUNAH.]

Or'pah (ôr'pah), a Moabite woman,

day to the heat of the sun, the parent-birds taking their turns at incubation during the night. The habit of the ostrich leaving its eggs to be matured by the sun's heat is usually appealed to in order to confirm the scriptural account, "she leaveth her eggs to the earth"; but this is probably the case only with the tropical birds. The true explanation of this passage may be that some of the eggs are left exposed around the nest for the nourishment of the young birds. It is a general belief among the Arabs that the ostrich is a very stupid bird; indeed they have a proverb, "stupid as an ostrich." As is well known, the ostrich will swallow almost any substance, iron, stones, and even has been known

THE OSTRICH.

to swallow "several leaden bullets scorching hot from the mould." But in many other respects the ostrich is not as stupid as this would indicate, and is very hard to capture. It is the largest of all known birds, and perhaps the swiftest of all runners. The feathers so much prized are the long white plumes of the wings. The best are brought from Barbary and the west coast of Africa.

Oth'ni (ŏth'nī) (*lion of* [God]), son of Shemaiah, the first-born of Obededom. 1 Chron. 26:7.

Oth'niel (ŏth'nĭ-el) (*lion of God*), son of Kenaz and younger brother of Caleb. Josh. 15:17; Judges 1:13; 3:9; 1 Chron. 4:13. (B.C. 1450.) The first mention of Othniel is on occasion of the taking of Kirjath-sepher, or Debir as it was afterward called. Caleb promised to give his daughter Achsah to whosoever should assault and take the city. Othniel won the prize. The next mention of him is in Judges 3:9, where he appears as the first judge of Israel after the death of Joshua, and the deliverer of his countrymen from the oppression of Chushan-rishathaim. Judges 3:8-9.

Oven. The eastern oven is of two kinds—fixed and portable. The former is found in towns, where regular bakers are employed. Hos. 7:4. It is now in a more or less perfect state the common oven in use in Palestine. It consists of a hole in the ground, plastered with cement which will resist the action of fire. The latter consists of a large jar

AN EASTERN OVEN.

made of clay, about three feet high and widening toward the bottom, with a hole for the extraction of the ashes. Each household possessed such an article, Ex. 8:3; and it was only in times of extreme dearth that the same oven sufficed for several families. Lev. 26: 26. It was heated with dry twigs and grass, Matt. 6:30, and the loaves were placed both inside and outside of it.

Owl. There are five Hebrew words translated "owl" in the Authorized Version of the Old Testament. 1. *Bath hayyaanah*, Lev. 11:16. Correctly in R. V. "ostrich." 2. *Yanshuph*, Lev. 11: 17; Deut. 14:16; Is. 34:11. This is variously interpreted. The Septuagint renders it "ibis." 3. *Kos*, Lev. 11:17; Deut. 14:16; Ps. 102:6. Without doubt some sort of owl. 4. *Kippoz*, Is. 34:15. R. V. "Arrowsnake." 5. *Lilith*, Is. 34: 14. R. V. "Screech owl."

A PAGE OF THE OXYRHYNCHUS PAPYRI.

Part of a sheet from a papyrus book containing verses 1–9, 12, 14–20 of the first chapter of St. Matthew's Gospel. From the style of the writing it may probably be assigned to the third century and may thus be a fragment of the oldest known manuscript of the New Testament.

OWL.

Ox. There was no animal in the rural economy of the Israelites, or indeed in that of the ancient Orientals generally, that was held in higher esteem than the ox; and deservedly so, for the ox was *the* animal upon whose

SYRIAN CATTLE.

patient labors depended all the ordinary operations of farming. Cattle were used for ploughing. Deut. 22 : 10; 1 Kings 19 : 19, etc.; for treading out grain, Deut. 25 : 4; Hos. 10 : 11, etc.; for draught purposes, when they were generally yoked in pairs, Num. 7 : 3; 1 Sam. 6 : 7, etc.; as beasts of burden, 1 Chron. 12 : 40; their flesh was eaten, Deut. 14 : 4; 1 Kings 1 : 9; etc.; they were used in the sacrifices; cows supplied milk, butter, etc. Deut. 32 : 14; 2 Sam. 17 : 29; Isa. 7 : 22. Connected with the importance of oxen in the rural economy of the Jews is the strict code of laws which was mercifully enacted by God for their protection and preservation. The ox that threshed the grain was by no means to be muzzled; he was to enjoy rest on the Sabbath as well as his master. Ex. 23 : 12; Deut. 5 : 14. It seems clear from Prov. 15 : 17 and 1 Kings 4 : 23 that cattle were sometimes stall-fed, though as a general rule it is probable that they fed in the plains or on the hills of Palestine. The cattle that grazed at large in the open country would no doubt often become fierce and wild, for it is to be remembered that in primitive times the lion and other wild beasts of prey roamed about Palestine. Hence the force of the Psalmist's complaint of his enemies. Ps. 22 : 12.

Oxyrhyn'chus (ŏk-sĭ-ring'kus). Ancient name of a town in Egypt, now called Belmesa. It is now merely a heap of mounds which cover an area once occupied by a few Egyptian towns. These mounds have lately been opened and explored and rich finds of papyri have resulted containing many treasures of lost classical and early Christian literature. The Greek papyri which were found include a 3rd century fragment of so-called "Logia" or "Sayings of Jesus." Among the Latin papyri is a fragment containing the largest piece of the New Testament yet discovered, namely: The Epistle to the Hebrews.

O'zem (ō'zem). 1. The sixth son of Jesse, the next eldest above David. 1 Chron. 2 : 15.

2. Son of Jerahmeel. 1 Chron. 2 : 25.

Ozi'as (ō-zī'as) (*strength from Jehovah*). Uzziah, king of Judah. Matt. 1 : 8, 9.

Oz'ni (ŏz'nī) (*attentive*), one of the sons of Gad, Num. 26 : 16; founder of the family of the Oznites. Num. 26 : 16.

P

Pa'arai (pā'a-rī). In the list of 2 Sam. 23 : 35, "Paarai the Arbite" is one of David's mighty men. In 1 Chron. 11 : 37 he is called "Naarai the son of Ezbai."

Pa'dan (pā'dan). Padan-aram. Gen. 48 : 7.

Pa'dan=a'ram (pā'dan-ā'ram). By this name, which signifies *the plain* or *field of Aram,* i. e. *Syria,* the Hebrews designated the tract of country which they otherwise called Aram-naharaim, "Aram of the two rivers," the Greek Mesopotamia, Gen. 24 : 10, and "the field (Authorized Version, 'country') of Syria." Hos. 12 : 12. The term was perhaps more especially applied to the northern portion of Mesopotamia. It is elsewhere called PADAN simply. Gen. 48 : 7. Abraham obtained a wife for Isaac from Padan-aram. Gen. 25 : 20. Jacob's wives were also from Padan-aram. Gen. 28 : 2, 5, 6, 7; 31 : 18; 33 : 18.

Pa'don (pā'dŏn) (*redemption*), the ancestor of a family of Nethinim who returned with Zerubbabel. Ezra 2 : 44; Neh. 7 : 47.

Pa'gi=el (pā'gi-el) (*a meeting with God*), the son of Ocran and chief of the tribe of Asher at the time of the exodus. Num. 1 : 13; 2 : 27; 7 : 72, 77; 10 : 26. (B.C. 1491.)

Pa'hath=mo'ab (pā'hath-mō'ab) (*governor of Moab*), head of one of the chief houses of the tribe of Judah. Of the individual or the occasion of his receiving so singular a name nothing is known certainly; but as we read in 1 Chron. 4 : 22 of a family of Shilonites, of the tribe of Judah, who in very early times "had dominion in Moab," it may be conjectured that this was the origin of the name.

Pa'i (*bleating*). [PAU.]

Paint (as a cosmetic). The use of cosmetic dyes has prevailed in all ages in eastern countries. We have abundant evidence of the practice of painting the eyes both in ancient Egypt and in Assyria; and in modern times no usage is more general. It does not appear, however, to have been by any means universal among the Hebrews. The notices of it are few; and in each instance it seems to have been used as a meretricious art, unworthy of a woman of high character. The Bible gives no indication of the substance out of which the dye was formed. The old versions agree in pronouncing the dye to have been produced from antimony. Antimony is still used for the purpose in Arabia and in Persia, but in Egypt the *kohl* is a soot produced by burning either a kind of frankincense or the shells of almonds. The dye-stuff was moistened with oil and kept in a small jar. Whether the custom of staining the hands and feet, particularly the nails, now so prevalent in the East, was known to the Hebrews is doubtful. Painting as an art was not cultivated by the Hebrews, but they decorated their buildings with paint.

Palace. Palace in the Bible, in the singular and plural, is the rendering of several words of diverse meaning. 1 Chron. 29 : 1; Ezra 4 : 14; Amos 4 : 3, etc. It often designates the royal residence, and usually suggests a fortress or battlemented house. The word occasionally included the whole city, as in Esther 9 : 12; and again, as in 1 Kings 16 : 18, it is restricted to a part of the royal apartments. It is applied, as in 1 Chron. 29 : 1, to the temple in Jerusalem. The site of the palace of Solomon was almost certainly in the city itself, on the brow opposite to the temple, and overlooking it and the whole city of David. It is impossible, of course, to be at all certain what was either the form or the exact disposition of such a palace. When there are taken into connection with the royal residence all the offices and public rooms besides the residences for the chief palace officials, it reaches

475

the dimensions of a city. The principal building situated within the palace was, as in all eastern palaces, the great hall of state and audience, called "the house of the forest of Lebanon," apparently from the four rows of cedar pillars by which it was supported. It was 100 cubits (175 feet) long, 50 (87½ feet) wide, and 30 (52½ feet) high. Next in importance was the hall or "porch of judgment," a quadrangular building supported by columns, as we learn from Josephus, which apparently stood on the other side of the great court, opposite the house of the forest of Lebanon. The third edifice is merely called a "porch of pillars." Its dimensions were 50 by 30 cubits. Its use cannot be considered as doubtful, as it was an indispensable adjunct to an eastern palace. It was the ordinary place of business of the palace, and the reception-room when the king received ordinary visitors, and sat, except on great state occasions, to transact the business of the kingdom. Behind this, we are told, was the inner court, adorned with gardens and fountains, and surrounded by cloisters for shade; and there were other courts for the residence of the attendants and guards, and for the women of the harem. Apart from this palace, but attached, as Josephus tells us, to the hall of judgment, was the palace of Pharaoh's daughter—too proud and important a personage to be grouped with the ladies of the harem, and requiring a residence of her own. The recent discoveries at Nineveh have enabled us to understand many of the architectural details of this palace, which before they were made were nearly wholly inexplicable. Solomon constructed an ascent from his own house to the temple, "the house of Jehovah," 1 Kings 10:5, which was a subterranean passage 250 feet long by 42 feet wide, of which the remains may still be traced.

Pa′lal (pā′lal) (*judge*), the son of Uzai, who assisted in restoring the walls of Jerusalem in the time of Nehemiah. Neh. 3:25. (B.C. 446.)

Palesti′na (păl-es-tī′nà) and **Pal′- estine.** These two forms occur in the Authorized Version but four times in all, always in poetical passages; the first in Ex. 15:14 and Isa. 14:29, 31; the second, Joel 3:4. In each case the Hebrew is *Pelesheth*, a word found, besides the above, only in Ps. 60:8; 83:

7; 87:4 and 108:9, in all which our translators have rendered it by "Philistia" or "Philistines." Palestine in the Authorized Version really means nothing but *Philistia*. The original Hebrew word *Pelesheth* to the Hebrews signified merely the long and broad strip of maritime plain inhabited by their encroaching neighbors; nor does it appear that at first it signified more to the Greeks. As lying next the sea, and as being also the high road from Egypt to Phœnicia and the richer regions north of it, the Philistine plain became sooner known to the western world than the country farther inland, and was called by them Syria Palestina —Philistine Syria. From thence it was gradually extended to the country farther inland, till in the Roman and later Greek authors, both heathen and Christian, it became the usual appellation for the whole country of the Jews, both west and east of Jordan. The word is now so commonly employed in our more familiar language to designate the whole country of Israel that, although biblically a misnomer, it has been chosen here as the most convenient heading under which to give a general description of THE HOLY LAND, embracing those points which have not been treated under the separate headings of cities or tribes. This description will most conveniently divide itself into three sections:—I. The Names applied to the country of Israel in the Bible and elsewhere. II. The Land: its situation, aspect, climate, physical characteristics in connection with its history, its structure, botany and natural history. III. The History of the country; which, however, is so fully given under its various headings throughout the work that it is unnecessary to recapitulate it here.

I. THE NAMES.—Palestine, then, is designated in the Bible by more than one name. 1. During the patriarchal period, the conquest and the age of the judges, and also where those early periods are referred to in the later literature (as Ps. 105:11), it is spoken of as "Canaan," or more frequently "the land of Canaan," meaning thereby the country west of the Jordan, as opposed to "the land of Gilead," on the east. 2. During the monarchy the name usually, though not frequently, employed is "land of Israel." 1 Sam. 13:19. 3. Between the captivity and the time of our Lord the name "Judea" had extended itself from the southern portion to the whole of the country, and even that beyond the Jordan. Matt. 19 : 1. 4. The Roman division of the country hardly coincided with the biblical one, and it does not appear that the Romans had any distinct name for that which we understand by Palestine. 5. Soon after the Christian era we find the name Palestina in possession of the country. 6. The name most frequently used throughout the middle ages, and down to our own time, is *Terra Sancta*—the Holy Land.

II. THE LAND.—The Holy Land is not in size or physical characteristics proportioned to its moral and historical position as the theatre of the most momentous events in the world's history. Western Palestine, Palestine proper according to common usage of the name, is but a strip of country about the size of Wales, about 145 miles in length and barely 40 in average breadth, on the very frontier of the East, hemmed in between the Mediterranean Sea on the one hand and the enormous trench of the Jordan valley on the other, by which it is effectually cut off from the mainland of Asia behind it. On the north it is shut in by the high ranges of Lebanon and Anti-Lebanon, and by the chasm of the Litany. On the south it is no less enclosed by the arid and inhospitable deserts of the upper parts of the peninsula of Sinai. Eastern Palestine, rightly to be considered a part of the country, since it was settled by the Hebrews, extended to the Syrian desert. 1. *Its position.*—Its position on the map of the world—as the world was when the Holy Land first made its appearance in history—is a remarkable one. It is on the very outpost—on the extremest western edge of the East. On the shore of the Mediterranean it stands, as if it had advanced as far as possible toward the west, separated therefrom by that which, when the time arrived, proved to be no barrier, but the readiest medium of communication —the wide waters of the "great sea." Thus it was open to all the gradual influences of the rising communities of the West, while it was saved from the retrogression and decrepitude which have ultimately been the doom of all purely eastern states whose connections were limited to the East only.

There was one channel, and but one, by which it could reach and be reached by the great Oriental empires. The only road by which the two great rivals of the ancient world could approach one another—by which alone Egypt could get to Assyria and Assyria to Egypt— lay along the broad flat strip of coast which formed the maritime portion of the Holy Land, and thence by the plain of the Lebanon to the Euphrates. Because of this the Holy Land became (like the Netherlands in Europe) the convenient arena on which in successive ages the hostile powers who contended for the empire of the East fought their battles.

2. *Physical features.*—Palestine is essentially a mountainous country. Not that it contains independent mountain chains, as in Greece, for example, but that every part of the highland is in greater or less undulation. But it is not only a mountainous country. The mass of hills which occupies the centre of the country is bordered or framed on both sides, east and west, by a broad belt of lowland, sunk deep below its own level. The slopes or cliffs which form, as it were, the retaining walls of this depression are furrowed and cleft by the torrent beds which discharge the waters of the hills and form the means of communication between the upper and lower level. On the west this lowland interposes between the mountains and the sea, and is the plain of Philistia and of Sharon. On the east it is the broad bottom of the Jordan valley, deep down in which rushes the one river of Palestine to its grave in the Dead Sea. Such is the first general impression of the physiognomy of the Holy Land. It is a physiognomy compounded of the three main features already named—the plains, the highland hills, and the torrent beds: features which are marked in the words of its earliest describers, Num. 13 : 29; Josh. 11 : 16; 12 : 8, and which must be comprehended by every one who wishes to understand the country and the intimate connection existing between its structure and its history. About halfway up the coast the maritime plain is suddenly interrupted by a long ridge thrown out from the central mass, rising considerably above the general level and terminating in a bold promontory on the very edge of the Mediterranean. This ridge is Mount

Carmel. On its upper side, the plain, as if to compensate for its temporary displacement, invades the centre of the country, and forms an undulating hollow right across it from the Mediterranean to the Jordan valley. This central lowland, which divides with its broad depression the mountains of Ephraim from the mountains of Galilee, is the plain of Esdraelon or Jezreel, the great battle-field of Palestine. North of Carmel the lowland resumes its position by the seaside till it is again interrupted and finally put an end to by the northern mountains, which push their way out of the sea, ending in the white promontory of the *Ras Nakhûra*. Above this is the ancient Phœnicia. The country thus roughly portrayed is to all intents and purposes the whole land of Israel. The northern portion is Galilee; the centre, Samaria; the south, Judea. This is the land of Canaan which was bestowed on Abraham,—the covenanted home of his descendants. The highland district, surrounded and intersected by its broad lowland plains, preserves from north to south a remarkably even and horizontal profile. Its average height may be taken as 1500 to 1800 feet above the Mediterranean. It can hardly be denominated a plateau; yet so evenly is the general level preserved, and so thickly do the hills stand behind and between one another, that, when seen from the coast or the western part of the maritime plain, it has quite the appearance of a wall. This general monotony of profile is, however, relieved at intervals by certain centres of elevation. Between these elevated points runs the watershed of the country, sending off on either hand—to the Jordan valley on the east and the Mediterranean on the west—the long, tortuous arms of its many torrent beds. The valleys on the two sides of the watershed differ considerably in character. Those on the east are extremely steep and rugged; the western valleys are more gradual in their slope.

3. *Fertility.*—When the highlands of the country are more closely examined, a considerable difference will be found to exist in the natural condition and appearance of their different portions. The south, as being nearer the arid desert and farther removed from the drainage of the mountains, is drier and less productive than the north. The tract below Hebron, which forms the link between the hills of Judah and the desert, was known to the ancient Hebrews by a term originally derived from its dryness—*Negeb*. This was the south country. As the traveler advances north of this tract there is an improvement; but perhaps no country equally cultivated is more monotonous, bare or uninviting in its aspect than a great part of the highlands of Judah and Benjamin during the larger portion of the year. The spring covers even those bald gray rocks with verdure and color, and fills the ravines with torrents of rushing water; but in summer and autumn the look of the country from Hebron up to Bethel is very dreary and desolate. At Jerusalem this reaches its climax. To the west and northwest of the highlands, where the sea-breezes are felt, there is considerably more vegetation. Hitherto we have spoken of the central and northern portions of Judea. Its eastern portion—a tract some nine or ten miles in width by about thirty-five in length, which intervenes between the centre and the abrupt descent to the Dead Sea—is far more wild and desolate, and that not for a portion of the year only, but throughout it. This must have been always what it is now—an uninhabited desert, because uninhabitable. No descriptive sketch of this part of the country can be complete which does not allude to the caverns, characteristic of all limestone districts, but here existing in astonishing numbers. Every hill and ravine is pierced with them, some very large and of curious formation—perhaps partly natural, partly artificial—others mere grottos. Many of them are connected with most important and interesting events of the ancient history of the country. Especially is this true of the district now under consideration. Machpelah, Makkedah, Adullam, Engedi, names inseparably connected with the lives, adventures and deaths of Abraham, Joshua, David and other Old-Testament worthies, are all within the small circle of the territory of Judea. The bareness and dryness which prevail more or less in Judea are owing partly to the absence of wood, partly to its proximity to the desert, and partly to a scarcity of water arising from its distance from the Lebanon. But to this discouraging aspect there are some important exceptions. The valley of *Ur-*

tâs, south of Bethlehem, contains springs which in abundance and excellence rival even those of *Nablûs;* the huge "Pools of Solomon" are enough to supply a district for many miles round them; and the cultivation now going on in that neighborhood shows what might be done with a soil which requires only irrigation and a moderate amount of labor to evoke a boundless produce. It is obvious that in the ancient days of the nation, when Judah and Benjamin possessed the teeming population indicated in the Bible, the condition and aspect of the country must have been very different. Of this there are not wanting sure evidences. There is no country in which the ruined towns bear so large a proportion to those still existing. Hardly a hill-top of the many within sight that is not covered with vestiges of some fortress or city. But, besides this, forests appear to have stood in many parts of Judea until the repeated invasions and sieges caused their fall; and all this vegetation must have reacted on the moisture of the climate, and, by preserving the water in many a ravine and natural reservoir where now it is rapidly dried by the fierce sun of the early summer, must have influenced materially the look and the resources of the country. Advancing northward from Judea, the country (Samaria) becomes gradually more open and pleasant. Plains of good soil occur between the hills, at first small, but afterward comparatively large. The hills assume here a more varied aspect than in the southern districts, springs are more abundant and more permanent, until at last, when the district of *Jebel Nablûs* is reached—the ancient Mount Ephraim—the traveler encounters an atmosphere and an amount of vegetation and water which are greatly superior to anything he has met with in Judea, and even sufficient to recall much of the scenery of the West. Perhaps the springs are the only objects which in themselves, and apart from their associations, really strike an English traveler with astonishment and admiration. Such glorious fountains as those of *Ain-jalûd* or the *Ras el-Mukâtta*—where a great body of the clearest water wells silently but swiftly out from deep blue recesses worn in the foot of a low cliff of limestone rock, and at once forms a considerable stream—are rarely to be met with out

of irregular, rocky, mountainous countries, and being such unusual sights, can hardly be looked on by the traveler without surprise and emotion. The valleys which lead down from the upper level in this district to the valley of the Jordan are less precipitous than in Judea. The eastern district of the *Jebel Nablûs* contains some of the most fertile and valuable spots in the Holy Land. Hardly less rich is the extensive region which lies northwest of the city of Shechem (*Nablûs*), between it and Carmel, in which the mountains gradually break down into the plain of Sharon. But with all its richness and all its advance on the southern part of the country, there is a strange dearth of natural wood about this central district. It is this which makes the wooded sides of Carmel and the park-like scenery of the adjacent slopes and plains so remarkable. No sooner, however, is the plain of Esdraelon passed than a considerable improvement is perceptible. The low hills which spread down from the mountains of Galilee, and form the barrier between the plains of Akka and Esdraelon, are covered with timber, of moderate size it is true, but of thick, vigorous growth, and pleasant to the eye. Eastward of these hills rises the round mass of Tabor, dark with its copses of oak, and set off by contrast with the bare slopes of *Jebel ed-Duhy* (the so-called "Little Hermon") and the white hills of Nazareth. A few words must be said in general description of the maritime lowland, which intervenes between the sea and the highlands. This region, only slightly elevated above the level of the Mediterranean, extends without interruption from *el-Arish,* south of Gaza, to Mount Carmel. It naturally divides itself into two portions, each of about half its length; the lower one the wider, the upper one the narrower. The lower half is the plain of the Philistines—Philistia. The upper part is the plain of Sharon, or Saron. The Philistine plain is on an average 15 or 16 miles in width from the coast to the beginning of the belt of hills which forms the gradual approach to the high land of the mountains of Judah. The larger towns, as Gaza and Ashdod, which stand near the shore, are surrounded with huge groves of olive, sycamore and palm, as in the days of King David. 1 Chron. 27:28. The whole plain appears to consist of brown loamy soil, light but rich, and almost without a stone. It is now, as it was when the Philistines possessed it, one enormous grainfield; an ocean of wheat covers the wide expanse between the hills and the sand dunes of the seashore, without interruption of any kind—no break or hedge, hardly even a single olive tree. Its fertility is marvelous; for the prodigious crops which it raises are produced, and probably have been produced almost year by year for the last forty centuries, without any of the appliances which we find necessary for success. The plain of Sharon is much narrower than Philistia. It is about 10 miles wide from the sea to the foot of the mountains, which are here of a more abrupt character than those of Philistia, and without the intermediate hilly region there occurring. The one ancient port of the Jews, the "beautiful" city of Joppa, was at the southern boundary. Roads led from these various cities to each other, to Jerusalem, Neapolis and Sebaste in the interior, and to Ptolemais and Gaza on the north and south. The commerce of Damascus, and, beyond Damascus, of Persia and India, passed this way to Egypt, Rome and the infant colonies of the West; and that traffic and the constant movement of troops backward and forward must have made this plain, at the time of Christ, one of the busiest and most populous regions of Syria.

4. *The Jordan valley.*—The characteristics already described are hardly peculiar to Palestine. But there is one feature, as yet only alluded to, in which she stands alone. This feature is the Jordan—the one river of the country. The river is elsewhere described [JORDAN]; but it and the valley through which it rushes down its extraordinary descent must be here chiefly characterized. This valley begins with the river at its remotest springs of *Hasbeiya*, on the northwest side of Hermon, and accompanies it to the lower end of the Dead Sea, a length of about 150 miles. During the whole of this distance its course is straight and its direction nearly due north and south. The springs of Hasbeiya are 1700 feet above the level of the Mediterranean, and the northern end of the Dead Sea is 1292 feet below it, so that between these two points the valley falls with more or less regularity through a height of almost 3000 feet. But though the *river* disappears at this point, the *valley* still continues its descent below the waters of the Dead Sea, so that the bottom of this extraordinary crevasse is actually more than 2600 feet below the surface of the ocean. In width the valley varies. In its upper and shallower portion, as between Banias and the lake of Merom (*Hûleh*), it is about five miles across. Between the lake of Merom and the Sea of Galilee it contracts, and becomes more of an ordinary ravine or glen. It is in its third and lower portion that the valley assumes its more definite and regular character. During the greater part of this portion it is about ten miles wide from the one wall to the other. North of Jericho the valley becomes twelve miles broad —a breadth which it thenceforward retains to the southern extremity of the Dead Sea. Buried as it is between such lofty ranges, and shielded from every breeze, the climate of the Jordan valley is extremely hot and relaxing. Its enervating influence is shown by the inhabitants of Jericho. All the irrigation necessary for the cultivation which formerly existed is obtained from the torrents of the western mountains. For all purposes to which a river is ordinarily applied the Jordan is useless. The Dead Sea, which is the final receptacle of the Jordan, is described elsewhere. [SEA, THE SALT.]

5. *Climate.*—The climate of Palestine presents more variety than that of any other country of its size. The traveler in a short journey of a hundred miles passes from the Alpine snows of Mt. Hermon to the tropical plains of the Dead Sea region. Its plants and animals range from those of northern Europe to those of Africa. Ice, snow and hail are named; sun stroke and desert winds; while on the hills near Bethlehem shepherds with their flocks could pass a December night in the open air. As in the time of our Saviour, Luke 12: 54, the rains come chiefly from the south or southwest. They commence at the end of October or beginning of November and continue with greater or less constancy till the end of February or March. It is not a heavy, continuous rain so much as a succession of severe showers or storms, with intervening periods of fine, bright weather. Between April and November there is,

with the rarest exceptions, an uninterrupted succession of fine weather and skies without a cloud. Thus the year divides itself into two and only two seasons—as indeed we see it constantly divided in the Bible—"winter and summer," "cold and heat," "seed-time and harvest."

6. *Botany.*—The botany of Syria and Palestine differs but little from that of Asia Minor, which is one of the most rich and varied on the globe. Among trees the oak is by far the most prevalent. The trees of the genus *Pistacia* rank next to the oak in abundance, and of these there are three species in Syria. There is also the carob or locust tree (*Ceratonia siliqua*), the pine, sycomore, poplar and walnut. Of planted trees and large shrubs the first in importance is the vine, which is most abundantly cultivated all over the country, and produces, as in the time of the Canaanites, enormous bunches of grapes. This is especially the case in the southern districts, those of Eschol being still particularly famous. Next to the vine, or even in some respects its superior in importance, ranks the olive, which nowhere grows in greater luxuriance and abundance than in Palestine, where the olive orchards form a prominent feature throughout the landscape, and have done so from time immemorial. The fig forms another most important crop in Syria and Palestine. Besides these are the almond, pomegranate, orange, pear, banana, quince and mulberry among fruit trees. Of vegetables there are many varieties, as the egg plant, pumpkin, asparagus, lettuce, melon and cucumber. Palestine is especially distinguished for its wild flowers, of which there are more than five hundred varieties. The geranium, pink, poppy, narcissus, honeysuckle, oleander, jessamine, tulip and iris are abundant. The various grains are also very largely cultivated.

7. *Zoology.*—It will be sufficient in this article to give a general survey of the fauna of Palestine, as the reader will find more particular information in the several articles which treat of the various animals under their respective names. Jackals and foxes are common; the hyena and wolf are also occasionally observed; the lion is no longer a resident in Palestine or Syria. A species of squirrel which the Arabs term *orki-*
31

daun, "the leaper," has been noticed on the lower and middle parts of Lebanon. Two kinds of hare, rats and mice, which are said to abound, the jerboa, the porcupine, the short-tailed field-mouse, may be considered as the representatives of the *Rodentia*. Of the *Pachydermata*, the wild boar, which is frequently met with on Tabor and Little Hermon, appears to be the only living wild example. There does not appear to be at present any wild ox in Palestine. Of domestic animals we need only mention the Arabian or one-humped camel, the ass, the mule and the horse, all of which are in general use. The buffalo (*Bubalus buffalo*) is common. The ox of the country is small and unsightly in the neighborhood of Jerusalem, but in the richer pastures the cattle, though small, are not unsightly. The common sheep of Palestine is the broadtail, with its varieties. Goats are extremely common everywhere. Palestine abounds in numerous kinds of birds. Vultures, eagles, falcons, kites, owls of different kinds, represent the *Raptorial* order. In the south of Palestine especially, reptiles of various kinds abound. It has been remarked that in its physical character Palestine presents on a small scale an epitome of the natural features of all regions, mountainous and desert, northern and tropical, maritime and inland, pastoral, arable and volcanic.

8. *Antiquities.*—In the preceding description allusion has been made to many of the characteristic features of the Holy Land; but it is impossible to close this account without mentioning a defect which is even more characteristic—its lack of monuments and personal relics of the nation which possessed it for so many centuries and gave it its claim to our veneration and affection. When compared with other nations of equal antiquity—Egypt, Greece, Assyria —the contrast is truly remarkable. In Egypt and Greece, and also in Assyria, as far as our knowledge at present extends, we find a series of buildings reaching down from the most remote and mysterious antiquity, a chain of which hardly a link is wanting, and which records the progress of the people in civilization, art and religion, as certainly as the buildings of the mediæval architects do that of the various nations of modern Europe. In Palestine there are but few remains of any

sort. At Lachish pottery and flint instruments have been found dating back, probably to the times of the Egyptian or the Hittite occupation. Rude stone monuments like cromlechs are numerous in ancient Moab and even farther north, —but none are found in western Palestine. It is perhaps not too much to say of Palestine proper, the portion actually under the control of Israel, that there does not exist a single edifice or part of an edifice of which we can be sure that it is of a date anterior to the Christian era. And as with the buildings, so with other memorials. With one exception, the museums of Europe do not possess a single piece of pottery or metal work, a single weapon or household utensil, an ornament or a piece of armor, of Israelite make, which can give us the least conception of the manners or outward appliances of the nation before the date of the destruction of Jerusalem by Titus. The coins form the single exception. M. Renan has named two circumstances which must have had a great effect in suppressing art or architecture amongst the ancient Israelites, while their very existence proves that the people had no genius in that direction. These are (1) the prohibition of sculptured representations of living creatures, and (2) the command not to build a temple anywhere but at Jerusalem.

Pal′lu (păl′lu) (*distinguished*), the second son of Reuben, father of Eliab, Ex. 6:14; Num. 26:5, 8; 1 Chron. 5:3, and founder of the family of

Pal′luites (păl′lu-ites), **The.** Num. 26:5.

Palmer-worm (Heb. *gâzâm*) occurs Joel 1:4; 2:25; Amos 4:9. Many regard it as a stage of the locust—as none of the moth or butterfly larvae now found in Syria are greatly harmful. The word *palmer-worm* is an old name for some species of caterpillar.

Palm tree (Heb. *tâmâr*). Under this generic term many species are botanically included; but the palm of Scripture is the date palm, the *Phœnix dactylifera* of Linnæus. While this tree was abundant generally in the Levant, it was regarded by the ancients as peculiarly characteristic of Palestine and the neighboring regions, though now it is rare. It may grow to the height of 50 to 100 feet, usually from 60 to 80. Its trunk is straight, tall and unbroken, termi-

nating in a crown of emerald-green plumes, like a diadem of gigantic ostrich-feathers; these leaves are from 6 to 12 feet long, often even more, droop slightly at the ends, and whisper musically in the breeze. The palm is, in truth, a beautiful and most useful tree. Its fruit is the daily use of millions; from them, and from the sap of the tree wine is prepared. Even the seeds are ground and fed to camels. The fibres of the base of its leaves are woven into ropes and rigging; its tall stem supplies a valuable timber; its

PALM TREE, showing fruit.

leaves are manufactured into brushes, mats, bags, couches and baskets. This one tree supplies almost all the wants of the Arab or Egyptian. Many places are mentioned in the Bible as having connection with palm trees; Elim, where grew three score and ten palm trees, Ex. 15:27. Jericho was the city of "palm trees." Deut. 34:3. Hazezon-tamar, possibly means "the felling of the palm tree." There is also Tamar, "the palm." Ezek. 47:19. Bethany means the "house of dates." The word Phœnicia, which occurs twice in the New Testament—Acts 11:19; 15:3—is in all probability derived from the Greek word for a palm. The striking appearance of the tree, its uprightness and beauty, would naturally suggest the giving of its name occasionally to women. Gen. 38:6; 2 Sam. 13:1; 14:27. There is in the Psalms, 92:12, the familiar comparison, "The righteous shall flourish like the palm tree," which suggests a world of illustration, whether respect be had to the orderly and regular aspect of the tree, its fruitfulness, the perpetual greenness of its foliage, or the height at which the foliage grows, as far as possible from earth and as near as possible to heaven. The passage in Rev. 7:9, where the glorified of all nations are described as "clothed with white robes and palms in their hands," might seem to us a purely classical image; but palm branches, that is, the long plumes, were used by the Jews in token of victory and peace. To these points of comparison may be added, its principle of growth: it is an endogen, and grows from within; its usefulness: the Syrians enumerating 360 different uses to which it may be put; and the statement that it bears its best fruit in old age. It is curious that this tree, once so abundant in Judea, is now comparatively rare, except in the Philistine plain and in the old Phœnicia about *Beyrout,* though it is being cultivated anew around Jericho.

Palsy (contracted from paralysis). The loss of sensation or the power of motion, or both, in any part of the body. The infirmities included under this name in the New Testament were various:—1. The paralytic shock affecting the whole body, or apoplexy. 2. That affecting only one side. 3. Affecting the whole system below the neck. 4. Catalepsy, caused by the contraction of the muscles in the whole or a part of the body. This was very dangerous and often fatal. The part affected remains immovable, and diminishes in size and dries up. A hand thus affected was called "a withered hand." Matt. 12:10-13. 5. Cramp. This was a most dreadful disease, caused by the chills of the nights. The limbs remain immovably fixed in the same position as when seized by it, and the person seems like one suffering torture. It is frequently followed in a few days by death. Several paralytics were cured by Jesus. Matt. 4:24; 8:6, 13, etc.

Pal'ti (păl'tĭ) (*deliverance by* [God]).

1. The Benjamite spy, son of Raphu. Num. 13:9. 2. See PHALTI. (B.C. 1490.)

Pal'tiel (păl'tĭ-el) (*deliverance by God*). 1. The son of Azzan and prince of the tribe of Issachar. Num. 34:26. He was one of the twelve appointed to divide the land of Canaan among the tribes west of Jordan. (B.C. 1450.) 2. See PHALTIEL.

Pal'tite (păl'tīte), **The.** Helez "the Paltite" is named in 2 Sam. 23:26 among David's mighty men.

Pamphyl'ia (păm-fĭl'ĭ-à) (*of every tribe*), one of the coast-regions in the south of Asia Minor, having Cilicia on the east and Lycia on the west. In St. Paul's time it was not only a regular province, but the emperor Claudius had united Lycia with it, and perhaps also a part of Pisidia. It was in Pamphylia that St. Paul first entered Asia Minor, after preaching the gospel in Cyprus. He and Barnabas sailed up the river Cestrus to Perga. Acts 13:13. The two missionaries finally left Pamphylia by its chief seaport, Attalia. Many years afterward St. Paul sailed near the coast. Acts 27:5.

Pan. Of the words so rendered in the Authorized Version, one or two seem to imply a shallow pan or plate, such as is used by the Bedouins and Syrians for baking or dressing rapidly their cakes of meal, such as were used in legal oblations; the others, a deeper vessel or caldron for boiling meat, placed during the process on three stones; or in other cases for ashes.

Pannag, an article of commerce exported from Palestine to Tyre, Ezek. 27:17, the nature of which is a pure matter of conjecture, as the term occurs nowhere else. It is explained by some as a sort of pastry, or confection.

Paper. [WRITING.]

Pa'phos (pā'fos), a town at the west end of Cyprus, connected by a road with Salamis at the east end. Its foundation is ascribed to the legendary Kinyras. Paul and Barnabas traveled, on their first missionary expedition, "through the isle," from the latter place to the former. Acts 13:6. The celebrity of the city was due to the worship of the "Paphian goddess" identified by the Greeks with Aphrodite. Her temple, however, was at "Old Paphos," now called *Kuklia.* The harbor and the chief town were at "New Paphos," ten miles to the northwest. The place is still called *Baffa*.

Parable. The word parable is in Greek *parabolé*, which signifies *placing beside* or *together*, a *comparison*. A parable is therefore literally a placing beside, a comparison, a similitude, an illustration of one subject by another.— As used in the Old Testament it had a very wide application, being applied sometimes to the shortest proverbs, 1 Sam. 10:12; 24:13; 2 Chron. 7:20, sometimes to dark prophetic utterances, Num. 23:7, 18; 24:3; Ezek. 20:49, sometimes to enigmatic maxims, Ps. 78:2; Prov. 1:6, or metaphors expanded into a narrative. Ezek. 12:22. In the New Testament itself the word is used with a like latitude in Matt. 24:32; Luke 4:23; Heb. 9:9. It was often used in a more restricted sense to denote a short narrative under which some important truth is veiled. Of this sort were the parables of Christ. The parable differs from the fable (1) in excluding brute and inanimate creatures passing out of the laws of their nature, and speaking or acting like men; (2) in its higher ethical significance. It differs from the allegory in that the latter, with its direct personification of ideas or attributes, and the names which designate them, involves really no comparison. The virtues and vices of mankind appear as in a drama, in their own character and costume. It differs from the apologue " in that it deals with events which, though fictitious, might reasonably have happened in nature." The allegory is self-interpreting; the parable demands attention, insight, sometimes an actual explanation. It differs from a proverb in that it must include a similitude of some kind, while the proverb may assert, without a similitude, some wide generalization of experience. Jesus used the parabolic form of preaching at every period of his teaching; but there came a time when a distinct change took place, and a larger place was given to parables in his public ministry. The direct teaching was met with scorn, unbelief, hardness, and he seemed for a time to abandon it for that which took the form of parables. The worth of parables as instruments of teaching lies in their being at once a test of character and in their presenting each form of character with that which, as a

penalty or blessing, is adapted to it. They withdraw the light from those who love darkness. They protect the truth which they enshrine from the mockery of the scoffer. They leave something even with the careless which may be interpreted and understood afterward. They reveal, on the other hand, the seekers after truth. These ask the meaning of the parable, and will not rest until the teacher has explained it. In this way the parable did its work, found out the fit hearers and led them on. In most of the parables it is possible to trace something like an order. 1. There is a group which have for their subject the laws of the divine kingdom. Under this head we have the sower, Matt. 13, Mark 4, Luke 8; the wheat and the tares, Matt. 13, etc. 2. When the next parables meet us they are of a different type and occupy a different position. They are drawn from the life of men rather than from the world of nature. They are such as these —the two debtors, Luke 7; the merciless servant, Matt. 18; the good Samaritan, Luke 10, etc. 3. Toward the close of our Lord's ministry the parables are again theocratic, but the phase of the divine kingdom on which they chiefly dwell is that of its final consummation. In interpreting parables note—(1) The analogies must be real, not arbitrary; (2) The parables are to be considered as parts of a whole, and the interpretation of one is not to override or encroach upon the lessons taught by others; (3) The direct teaching of Christ presents the standard to which all *our* interpretations are to be referred. See APPENDIX for list of Parables.

Par'adise. This is a word of Persian origin, and is used in the Septuagint as the translation of Eden. It means " an orchard of pleasure and fruits," a " garden " or " pleasure ground," something like an English *park*. It is applied figuratively to the celestial dwelling of the righteous, in allusion to the garden of Eden. 2 Cor. 12:4; Rev. 2:7. It has thus come into familiar use to denote both that garden and the heaven of the just.

Pa'rah (pā'rah) (*heifer*), one of the cities in the territory allotted to Benjamin, named only in the lists of the conquest. Josh. 18:23. Now the ruin *Farah* about 5 miles from Jerusalem.

Pa'ran (pā'ran), **El=pa'ran** (*place of*

caverns), a desert or wilderness, apparently bounded on the north by Palestine, on the east by Edom, and on the south by the desert of Sinai. The notices of it are however not distinct enough to exactly determine its boundaries. The first notice of Paran is in connection with the invasion of the confederate kings. Gen. 14:6. The detailed itinerary of the children of Israel in Num. 33 does not mention Paran because it was the name of a wide region; but the many stations in Paran are recorded, vss. 17-36, and probably all the eighteen stations there mentioned between Hazeroth and Kadesh were in Paran. Through this very wide wilderness, from pasture to pasture as do modern Arab tribes, the Israelites wandered in irregular lines of march. This region through which the Israelites journeyed so long is now called by the name it has borne for ages—*Bedu et-Tih*, "the wilderness of wandering." "Mount" Paran occurs only in two poetic passages, Deut. 33:2; Hab. 3:3. It probably denotes the northwestern member of the Sinaitic mountain group which lies adjacent to the *Wady Teiran*. It is probably the ridge or series of ridges lying on the northeastern part of the desert of Paran, not far from Kadesh.

Par'bar, a word occurring in Hebrew and Authorized Version only in 1 Chron. 26:18. Parbar was probably a precinct some where on the west side of the temple enclosure, where six gate keepers were stationed. It was perhaps a colonnade, but contained chambers for the officials and stalls for the cattle. See 2 Kings 23:11, where the same Hebrew word, used in the plural, is rendered in the R. V. by "colonnades." In later Hebrew the word is occasionally used of "suburbs" and that is the rendering in the A. V. of 2 Kings 23:11. But that is not considered the correct translation by modern scholars.

Parchment. [WRITING.]

Parlor, a word in English usage meaning the common room of the family, and hence probably in Authorized Version denoting the king's audience-chamber, so used in reference to Eglon. Judges 3:20-25.

Parmash'ta (pär-măsh'tà) (*superior*), one of the ten sons of Haman slain by the Jews in Shushan. Esther 9:9. (B.C. 473.)

Par'menas (pär'me-nas) *(faithful)*, one of the seven deacons, "men of honest report, full of the Holy Ghost and wisdom." Acts 6:5. There is a tradition that he suffered martyrdom at Philippi in the reign of Trajan.

Par'nach (pär'năk), father or ancestor of Elizaphan prince of the tribe of Zebulun. Num. 34:25.

Pa'rosh (pä'rŏsh) (*flea*). The descendants of Parosh, in number 2172, returned from Babylon with Zerubbabel. Ezra 2:3; Neh. 7:8. Another detachment of 150 males, with Zechariah at their head, accompanied Ezra. Ezra 8:3. They assisted in the building of the wall of Jerusalem, Neh. 3:25, and signed the covenant with Nehemiah. Neh. 10:14.

Parshan'datha (pär-shăn'da-thà) (*given by prayer*), the eldest of Haman's ten sons who were slain by the Jews in Shushan. Esther 9:7. (B.C. 473.)

Par'thians (pär'thĭ-anş). This name occurs only in Acts 2:9, where it designates Jews settled in Parthia. Parthia was a mountainous district situated south of the Caspian sea, and nearly corresponding with the modern Persian province of Khorasan. The ancient Parthians are called a "Scythic" race, and probably belonged to the great Turanian family. After being subject in succession to the Persians and the Seleucidæ, they revolted in B.C. 256, and under Arsaces succeeded in establishing their independence. Parthia, in the mind of the writer of the Acts, would designate this empire, which extended from India to the Tigris and from the Chorassman desert to the shores of the Southern Ocean; hence the prominent position of the name Parthians in the list of those present at Pentecost. Parthia was a power almost rivalling Rome—the only existing power which had tried its strength against Rome and not been worsted in the encounter. The Parthian dominion lasted for nearly five centuries, commencing in the third century before and terminating in the third century after our era.

Partridge (Heb. *kôrê*) occurs only 1 Sam. 26:20 and Jer. 17:11. David's comparison of himself to a partridge is exactly suited by the *Caccabis Chukar* or red-legged partridge, a larger variety of the Greek partridge, and the *Ammoperdix Heyii*, the sand partridge, both of which are common in Palestine. The *Chukar* is the most common. In every part of the hill country it abounds, and its ringing call-note in early morning echoes from cliff to cliff alike amid the barrenness of the hills of Judea and in the glens of the forest

THE GREEK PARTRIDGE.

of Carmel. The flesh of the partridge and the eggs are highly esteemed as food, and the search for the eggs at the proper time of the year is made a regular business.

Paru'ah (păr-ṳ'ah) (*flourishing*), the father of Jehoshaphat, Solomon's commissariat officer in Issachar. 1 Kings 4:17.

Parva'im (pär-vā'ĭm), the name of an unknown place or country whence the gold was procured for the decoration of Solomon's temple. 2 Chron. 3:6. We may notice the conjecture that it is derived from the Sanscrit *pûrva*, "eastern," and is a general term for the east.

Pa'sach (pā'săch) (*divider*), son of Japhlet, of the tribe of Asher. 1 Chron. 7:33.

Pas=dam'mim (păs-dăm'mim). [EPHES-DAMMIM.]

Pase'ah (pȧ-sē'ah) (*lame*). 1. Son of Eshton, in an obscure fragment of the genealogies of Judah. 1 Chron. 4:12.

2. The "sons of Paseah" were among the Nethinim who returned with Zerubbabel. Ezra 2:49.

Pash'ur (păsh'ur). 1. One of the families of priests of the chief house of Malchijah. 1 Chron. 9:12; 24:9; Neh. 11:12; Jer. 21:1; 38:1. In the time of Nehemiah this family appears to have become a chief house, and its head the head of a course. Ezra 2:38; Neh. 7:

41; 10:3. The individual from whom the family was named was probably Pashur the son of Malchiah, who in the reign of Zedekiah was one of the chief princes of the court. Jer. 38:1. (B.C. 607.) He was sent, with others, by Zedekiah to Jeremiah at the time when Nebuchadnezzar was preparing his attack upon Jerusalem. Jer. 21. Again, somewhat later, Pashur joined with several other chief men in petitioning the king that Jeremiah might be put to death as a traitor. Jer. 38:4.

2. Another person of this name, also a priest, and "chief governor of the house of the Lord," is mentioned in Jer. 20:1. He is described as "the son of Immer," 1 Chron. 24:14, probably the same as Amariah. Neh. 10:3; 12:2, etc. In the reign of Jehoiakim he showed himself as hostile to Jeremiah as his namesake the son of Malchiah did afterward, and put him in the stocks by the gate of Benjamin. For this indignity to God's prophet Pashur was told by Jeremiah that his name was changed to Magor-missabib (*terror on every side*), and that he and all his house should be carried captives to Babylon and there die. Jer. 20:1–6. Some think these are 4 distinct men.

Passage. Used in the plural, Jer. 22:20, probably to denote the mountain region of Abarim, on the east side of Jordan. It also denotes a river ford or a mountain gorge or pass.

Pass'over, the first of the three great annual festivals of the Israelites, celebrated in the month Nisan (March-April), from the 14th to the 21st. Strictly speaking the Passover only applied to the *paschal supper*, and the feast of unleavened bread followed, which was celebrated to the 21st. (For the corresponding dates in our month, see *Jewish calendar* in the Appendix to this volume.) The following are the principal passages in the Pentateuch relating to the Passover: Ex. 12:1–51; 13:3–10; 23:14–19; 34:18–26; Lev. 23:4–14; Num. 9:1–14; 28:16–25; Deut. 16:1–6.

Why instituted.—This feast was instituted by God to commemorate the deliverance of the Israelites from Egyptian bondage and the sparing of their first-born when the destroying angel smote the first-born of the Egyptians. The deliverance from Egypt was regarded as the starting-point of the Hebrew nation. The Israelites were then raised from the condition of bondmen under a foreign tyrant to that of a free people owing allegiance to no one but Jehovah. The prophet in a later age spoke of the event as *a creation* and *a redemption* of the nation. God declares himself to be "the Creator of Israel." The Exodus was thus looked upon as the birth of the nation; the Passover was its annual birthday feast. It was the yearly memorial of the dedication of the people to him who had saved their first-born from the destroyer, in order that they might be made holy to himself.

First celebration of the Passover.—On the tenth day of the month, the head of each family was to select from the flock either a lamb or a kid, a male of the first year, without blemish. If his family was too small to eat the whole of the lamb, he was permitted to invite his nearest neighbor to join the party. On the fourteenth day of the month he was to kill his lamb, while the sun was setting. He was then to take blood in a basin, and with a sprig of hyssop to sprinkle it on the two side-posts and the lintel of the door of the house. The lamb was then thoroughly roasted, whole. It was expressly forbidden that it should be boiled, or that a bone of it should be broken. Unleavened bread and bitter herbs were to be eaten with the flesh. No male who was uncircumcised was to join the company. Each one was to have his loins girt, to hold a staff in his hand, and to have shoes on his feet. He was to eat in haste, and it would seem that he was to stand during the meal. The number of the party was to be calculated as nearly as possible, so that all the flesh of the lamb might be eaten; but if any portion of it happened to remain, it was to be burned in the morning. No morsel of it was to be carried out of the house. The lambs were selected, on the fourteenth they were slain and the blood sprinkled, and in the following evening, after the fifteenth day of the month had commenced, the first paschal meal was eaten. At midnight the first-born of the Egyptians were smitten. The king and his people were now urgent that the Israelites should start immediately, and readily bestowed on them supplies for the journey. In such haste did the Israelites depart, on that very day, Num. 33: 3, that they packed up their kneading-troughs containing the dough prepared for the morrow's provisions, which was not yet leavened.

Observance of the Passover in later times.—As the original institution of the Passover in Egypt preceded the establishment of the priesthood and the regulation of the service of the tabernacle, it necessarily fell short in several particulars of the observance of the festival according to the fully-developed ceremonial law. The head of the family slew the lamb in his own house, not in the holy place; the blood was sprinkled on the doorway, not on the altar. But when the law was perfected, certain particulars were altered in order to assimilate the Passover to the accustomed order of religious service. In the twelfth and thirteenth chapters of Exodus there are not only distinct references to the observance of the festival in future ages (*e. g.* 12: 2, 14, 17, 24–27, 42; 13: 2, 5, 8–10), but there are several injunctions which were evidently not intended for the first Passover, and which indeed could not possibly have been observed. Besides the private family festival, there were public and national sacrifices offered each of the seven days of unleavened bread. Num. 28: 19. On the second day also the first-fruits of the barley harvest were offered in the temple. Lev. 23: 10. In the later notices of the festival in the books of the law there are particulars added which appear as modifications of the original institution. Lev. 23: 10–14; Num. 28: 16–25; Deut. 16: 1–6. Hence it is not without reason that the Jewish writers have laid great stress on the distinction between "the Egyptian Passover" and "the perpetual Passover."

Mode and order of the paschal meal.—All work except that belonging to a few trades connected with daily life was suspended for some hours before the evening of the 14th Nisan. It was not lawful to eat any ordinary food after midday. No male was admitted to the table unless he was circumcised, even if he were of the seed of Israel. Ex. 12: 48. It was customary for the number of a party to be not less than ten. They were organized indiscriminately and the number fixed beforehand. When the meal was prepared, the family was placed round the table, the head of the family taking a place of honor, probably somewhat raised above the rest. When the party was arranged the first cup of wine was filled, and a blessing was asked by the head of the family on the feast, as well as a special one on the cup. The bitter herbs were then placed on the table, and a portion of them eaten, either with or without the sauce. The unleavened bread was handed round next, and afterward the lamb was placed on the table in front of the head of the family. The paschal lamb could be legally slain and the blood and fat offered only in the national sanctuary. Deut. 16:2. Before the lamb was eaten the second cup of wine was filled, and the son, in accordance with Ex. 12:26, asked his father the meaning of the feast. In reply, an account was given of the sufferings of the Israelites in Egypt and of their deliverance, with a particular explanation of Deut. 26:5, and the first part of the Hallel (a contraction from *Hallelujah*), Ps. 113, 114, was sung. This being gone through, the lamb was carved and eaten. The third cup of wine was poured out and drunk, and the fourth followed the second part of the Hallel, Ps. 115 to 118. The Israelites who lived in the country appear to have been accommodated at the feast by the inhabitants of Jerusalem in their houses, so far as there was room for them. Matt. 26:18; Luke 22:10-12. Those who could not be received into the city encamped without the walls in tents, as the pilgrims now do at Mecca.

The Passover as a type.—The Passover was not only commemorative but also typical. "The deliverance which it commemorated was a type of the great salvation it foretold." No other shadow of good things to come contained in the law can vie with the festival of the Passover in expressiveness and completeness. (1) The paschal lamb must of course be regarded as the leading feature in the ceremonial of the festival. The lamb slain typified Christ the "Lamb of God," slain for the sins of the world. Christ "our Passover is sacrificed for us." 1 Cor. 5:7. (2) The unleavened bread ranks next in importance to the paschal lamb. The bread of the first passover was unleavened, and having no leaven in their houses the dough carried away in their hurried flight was unleavened. Henceforth unleavened bread was associated in their minds with the hurried flight from Egypt as well as the thought of sincerity and truth, which was the es-

sential idea. (3) The offering of the omer or first sheaf of the harvest, Lev. 23:10-14, signified deliverance from winter, the bondage of Egypt being well considered as a winter in the history of the nation. (4) The consecration of the first-fruits, the first-born of the soil, is an easy type of the consecration of the first-born of the Israelites, and of our own best selves, to God. Further than this (1) the Passover is a type of deliverance from the slavery of sin. (2) It is the passing over of the doom we deserve for our sins, because the blood of Christ has been applied to us by faith. (3) The sprinkling of the blood upon the door-posts was a symbol of open confession of our allegiance and love. (4) The Passover was useless unless eaten; so we live upon the Lord Jesus Christ. (5) It was eaten with bitter herbs, as we must eat our passover with the bitter herbs of repentance and confession, which yet, like the bitter herbs of the Passover, are a fitting and natural accompaniment. (6) As the Israelites ate the Passover all prepared for the journey, so do we with a readiness and desire to enter the active service of Christ, and to go on the journey toward heaven.

Pat'ara (păt'a-rà), a city situated on the southwestern shore of Lycia, not far from the left bank of the river Xanthus. The coast here is very mountainous and bold. Immediately opposite is the island of Rhodes. Patara was practically the seaport of the city of Xanthus, which was ten miles distant. These notices of its position and maritime importance introduce us to the single mention of the place in the Bible— Acts 21:1, 2.

Path'ros (păth'ros) (*region of the south*), a part of Egypt, and a Mizraite tribe whose people were called Pathrusim. In the list of the Mizraites the Pathrusim occur after the Naphtuhim and before the Casluhim; the latter being followed by the notice of the Philistines and by the Caphtorim. Gen. 10:13, 14; 1 Chron. 1:12. Pathros is mentioned in the prophecies of Isaiah, Isa. 11:11, Jeremiah, Jer. 44:1, 15, and Ezekiel. Ezek. 29:14; 30:13-18. It was probably part or all of upper Egypt, and we may trace its name in the Pathyrite nome, in which Thebes was situated.

Pathru'sim (păth-rū'şĭm) (people of Pathros. [PATHROS.]

Pat'mos (păt'mos), Rev. 1: 9, a rugged and bare island in the Ægean Sea off the coast of Asia Minor, and 30 miles south of Samos and 24 west of Asia Minor. It was the scene of the banishment of St. John in the reign of Domitian, A.D. 95. Patmos is divided into two nearly equal parts, a northern and a southern, by a very narrow isthmus, where, on the east side, are the harbor and the town. On the hill to the south, crowning a commanding height, is the celebrated monastery which bears the name of "John the Divine." Halfway up the ascent is the cave or grotto where tradition says that St. John received the Revelation.

Patriarch (*father of a tribe*), the name given to the head of a family or tribe in Old Testament times. In common usage the title of patriarch is assigned especially to those whose lives are recorded in Scripture previous to the time of Moses, as Adam, Abraham, Isaac and Jacob. In the early history of the Hebrews we find the patriarchal or paternal form of government, the founder of the tribe possessing authority over his children and his children's children so long as he lived, whatever new connections they might form. When the father died the power descended to his eldest son, or the eldest lineal male descendant. He was honored as the central point of connection, and as the representative of the whole kindred. The head of each several family into which the increasing tribe expanded held authority over his dependents, under the head of the entire tribe. After the destruction of Jerusalem, patriarch was the title of the chief religious rulers of the Jews in Asia; and in early Christian times it became the designation of the bishops of Rome, Constantinople, Alexandria, Antioch and Jerusalem.

Pat'robas (păt'ro-bas), a Christian at Rome to whom St. Paul sends his salutation. Rom. 16: 14. Like many other names mentioned in Rom. 16, this was borne by at least one member of the emperor's household. Suet. *Galba.* 20; Martial, *Ep.* ii. 32, 3. (A.D. 57.)

Pau (pā'u) (*bleating*) (but in 1 Chron. 1: 50, PAI), the capital of Hadar king of Edom. Gen. 36: 39. Its position is unknown.

Paul (*small, little*). Nearly all the original materials for the life of St. Paul are contained in the Acts of the Apostles and in the Pauline epistles. Paul was born in Tarsus, a city of Cilicia, very likely about B.C. 1. His Jewish name was Saul, and his Latin name, to which as a Roman citizen he was entitled, was Paul. The latter was exclusively used after he became the apostle to the Gentiles. Of his parents we know nothing, except that his father was of the tribe of Benjamin, Philip. 3: 5, and a Pharisee, Acts 23: 6; that he had acquired by some means the Roman franchise ("I was free born," Acts 22: 28), and that he was settled in Tarsus. At Tarsus Paul must have learned to use the Greek language with freedom and mastery in both speaking and writing. He was sent to Jerusalem for his education, "at the feet of Gamaliel," one of the most eminent of all the doctors of the law. Saul was yet "a young man," Acts 7: 58, at Stephen's martyrdom. Among those who disputed with Stephen were some "of them of Cilicia." We naturally think of Saul as having been one of these, when we find him afterward keeping the clothes of those who stoned Stephen.

Saul's conversion. A.D. 36.—The persecutor was to be converted. Having undertaken to follow up the believers "unto strange cities," Saul naturally turned his thoughts to Damascus. What befell him as he journeyed thither is related in detail three times in the Acts, first by the historian in his own person, then in the two addresses made by St. Paul at Jerusalem and before Agrippa. The sudden light from heaven; the voice of Jesus speaking with authority to his persecutor; Saul struck to the ground, blinded, overcome; the three-days suspense; the coming of Ananias as a messenger of the Lord, and Saul's baptism, were the leading features of the great event. It was in Damascus that he was received into the church by Ananias, and here, to the astonishment of all his hearers, he proclaimed Jesus in the synagogues, declaring him to be the Son of God. The narrative in the Acts tells us simply that he was occupied in this work, with increasing vigor, for "many days," up to the time when imminent danger drove him from Damascus. From the Epistle to the Galatians, Gal. 1: 17, 18, we learn that Saul went after his conversion into Arabia, and returned from thence to Damascus. We know nothing whatever of this visit to

Arabia; but upon his departure from Damascus we are again upon historical ground, and have the double evidence of St. Luke in the Acts and of the apostle in his Second Epistle to the Corinthians. According to the former, the *Jews* lay in wait for Saul, intending to kill him, and watched the gates of the city that he might not escape from them. Knowing this, the disciples took him by night and let him down in a basket from the wall. Having escaped from Damascus, Saul betook himself to Jerusalem (A.D. 38), and there "assayed to join himself to the disciples; but they were all afraid of him, and believed not that he was a disciple." Barnabas' introduction removed the fears of the apostles, and Saul "was with them coming in and going out at Jerusalem." But it is not strange that the former persecutor was soon singled out from the other believers as the object of a murderous hostility. He, therefore, betook himself to his native city, Tarsus. Later (perhaps 43 A.D.) Barnabas was sent on a special mission to Antioch. As the work grew under his hands, he felt the need of help, went himself to Tarsus to seek Saul, and succeeded in bringing him to Antioch. There they labored together unremittingly for "a whole year." All this time Saul was subordinate to Barnabas. In B.C. 44 the Holy Ghost spoke to the leaders of the church: "Separate me Barnabas and Saul for the work whereunto I have called them." So after fasting and prayer they laid their hands on them, and so they departed.

The first missionary journey. A.D. 47–49.—Barnabas and Saul began their work in Cyprus, "to Jews only." After going through the island, from Salamis to Paphos, they preached in the latter place to the Proconsul, Sergius Paulus, who was converted. Here comes the incident of Elymas. Saul here began to use his Gentile name Paul, and began to take precedence of Barnabas. From Paphos "Paul and his company" set sail for the mainland, and arrived at Perga in Pamphylia. Here the heart of their companion John failed him, and he returned to Jerusalem. From Perga they traveled to Antioch in Pisidia. Rejected by the Jews, they turned from them to the Gentiles. At Antioch now, as in every city afterward, the unbelieving Jews used their influence with

their own adherents among the Gentiles to persuade the authorities or the populace to persecute the apostles and to drive them from the place. Paul and Barnabas now traveled to Iconium, where the occurrences at Antioch were repeated, and from thence to the Lycaonian country which contained the cities Lystra and Derbe. At Lystra the healing of a cripple took place, on which account the people took the apostles for gods, calling Barnabas, who was of the more imposing presence, Jupiter, and Paul, who was the chief speaker, Mercurius. Although the people of Lystra had been so ready to worship Paul and Barnabas, the repulse of their idolatrous instincts appears to have provoked them, and they allowed themselves to be persuaded into hostility by Jews who came from Antioch and Iconium, so that they attacked Paul with stones, and thought they had killed him. He recovered, however, as the disciples were standing around him, and went again into the city. The next day he left it with Barnabas, and went to Derbe, and thence they returned once more to Lystra, and so to Iconium and Antioch, appointing "elders" in every church. Then they came down to the coast, and from Attalia they sailed home to Antioch in Syria, where they related the successes which had been granted to them, and especially the "opening of the door of faith to the Gentiles."

The council at Jerusalem.—Upon that missionary journey follows most naturally the next important scene which the historian sets before us—the council held at Jerusalem to determine the relations of Gentile believers to the law of Moses. Acts 15:1–29; Gal. 2.

Second missionary journey. A.D. 50–52. At the beginning of the next journey came the memorable difference of opinion between Paul and Barnabas, Acts 15:35–40. Barnabas and Mark went to Cyprus. Paul with a new companion Silas went through Syria and Cilicia, visiting the churches, and so came to Derbe and Lystra. Here they find Timotheus, who had become a disciple on the former visit of the apostle. Him St. Paul took and circumcised. After some time in Galatia he was "forbidden" to preach in Asia—so passed by portions they would otherwise have visited and came down to Troas. St. Paul saw in a vision a man of Macedonia, who besought him, saying, "Come over into Macedonia and help us." The party, therefore, probably joined by Luke ("we") immediately set sail from Troas, touched at Samothrace, then landed on the continent at Neapolis, and thence journeyed to Philippi. The first convert in Macedonia was Lydia, an ing the magistrates sent word to the prison that the men might be let go; but Paul held out for their rights as Roman citizens. The magistrates, in great alarm, saw the necessity of humbling themselves. They came and begged them to leave the city. Paul and Silas consented to do so, and, after pay-

TRADITIONAL PORTRAITS OF PETER AND PAUL.

These portraits are copied, same size as the original, from the bottom of a gilded glass cup found in the catacombs of St. Sebastian at Rome. The earliest interments by the Christians in the Roman catacombs included, besides Christian symbols, some objects of pagan regard. This having been the case in the section in which the glass cup bearing the group of the Saviour, Paul and Peter was discovered, it seems conclusive that the age was probably the fourth, if not the third, century. The absence of the nimbus (glory or circle) about the heads of Peter and Paul, and its presence around the Saviour's, may indicate the third century or early in the fourth; for the nimbus was generally used around the heads of all saints and divine persons in the latter part of the fourth century. Tertullian speaks of glass cups as used in sacramental services, as also does Eusebius. In this picture the Saviour is represented as presenting a crown of life to the apostles; the inscription is a prayer of the friends of the dead, who was laid in the tomb in the faith of Christ, and may be paraphrased, " Friendship's blessing; may you live forever with thy (Saviour)."

Asiatic woman, at Philippi. Acts 16: 13, 14. At Philippi Paul and Silas were arrested, beaten and put in prison, having cast out the spirit of divination from a female slave who had brought her masters much gain by her power. The narrative tells of the earthquake, the jailer's terror, his conversion and baptism. Acts 16: 26-34. In the morn- ing a visit to "the brethren" in the house of Lydia, they departed. Leaving St. Luke at Philippi, Paul and Silas traveled through Amphipolis and Apollonia, and stopped again at Thessalonica. Here again, as in Pisidian Antioch, the envy of the Jews was excited, and the mob assaulted the house of Jason, with whom Paul and Silas were staying as guests, and, not finding them, dragged Jason himself and some other brethren before the magistrates. After these signs of danger the brethren immediately sent away Paul and Silas by night. They next came to Berea. Here they found the Jews more noble than those at Thessalonica had been. Accordingly they gained many converts, both Jews and Greeks; but the Jews of Thessalonica, hearing of it, sent emissaries to stir up the people, and it was thought best that Paul should himself leave the city. Some of the brethren went with him as far as Athens. Here the apostle delivered that wonderful discourse reported in Acts 17: 22–31. He gained but few converts at Athens, and soon took his departure and went to Corinth, where he became acquainted with Aquila and Priscilla, and where Silas and Timothy joined him. The two epistles to the Thessalonians—and these alone—belong to the present missionary journey. They were written from Corinth A.D. 51, 52. The Jews of Corinth accused Paul to the proconsul Gallio of being an innovator in religion. But Gallio perceived at once, before Paul could "open his mouth" to defend himself, that the movement was due to Jewish prejudice, and refused to go into the question. Then a singular scene occurred. The Corinthian spectators, either favoring Paul or actuated only by anger against the Jews, seized on the principal person of those who had brought the charge, and beat him before the judgment-seat. Gallio left these religious quarrels to settle themselves. The apostle, therefore, was not allowed to be "hurt," and remained some time longer at Corinth unmolested, and accomplished a good work. In A.D. 52, he left for Jerusalem, wishing to attend a festival there. From Jerusalem the apostle went almost immediately down to Antioch, thus returning to the same place from which he had started with Silas.

Third missionary journey, including the stay at Ephesus. A.D. 53–57. Acts 18: 23–21: 17.—St. Paul "spent some time" at Antioch, and during this stay, as we are inclined to believe, his collision with St. Peter, Gal. 2: 11–14, took place. When he left Antioch, he "went over all the country of Galatia and Phrygia in order, strengthening all the disciples," and giving orders concerning the collection for the saints. 1 Cor. 16: 1. From the upper districts of Phrygia he came down to Ephesus. Here he entered upon his usual work preaching three months in the synagogue, and for two years thereafter in "the school of Tyrannus," probably a lecture hall. During this time many things occurred of which the historian of the Acts chooses two examples, the triumph over magical arts and the great disturbance raised by the silversmiths who made shrines for Diana—among which we are to note further the writing of the First Epistle to the Corinthians, probably in the spring of A.D. 57. He sent Titus to Corinth to see and report the condition of affairs there. On his return with good news Paul wrote the second Epistle to the Corinthians, in the autumn of the same year, and sent it by the hands of Titus and two other brethren. After writing this epistle, St. Paul traveled through Macedonia, perhaps to the borders of Illyricum, Rom. 15: 19, and then went to Corinth. While in Greece Paul wrote the Epistle to the Galatians, and that to the Romans, both in the autumn of A.D. 57. The writing of Romans at Corinth has never been doubted, being confirmed from passages in the letter itself. Paul now starts on his last journey to Jerusalem, intending to go by sea. But he was made aware of some plot of the Jews for his destruction, to be carried out through this voyage; so he changed his route. Several brethren were associated with him in this expedition, the bearers, no doubt, of the collections made in all the churches for the poor at Jerusalem. These were sent on by sea, and probably the money with them, to Troas, where they were to await Paul. He went round by way of Philippi, where Luke joined him, to Troas where the incident of Eutychus occurred, and thence to Assos. At Assos he went on board again. At Miletus, there was time to send to Ephesus, and the elders of the church were invited to come down to him there. At Tyre Paul and his company spent seven days. From Tyre they sailed to Ptolemais, where they spent one day, and from Ptolemais proceeded, apparently by land, to Cæsarea. They now "tarried many days" at Cæsarea. During this interval the prophet Agabus, Acts 11: 28, came down from Jerusalem, and crowned the previous intimations of danger with a prediction expressively delivered. At this stage a final effort was made to dissuade Paul from going up to Jerusalem, by the Christians of Cæsarea and by his traveling companions. After a while they went up to Jerusalem and were gladly received by the brethren. This is St. Paul's fifth and last visit to Jerusalem.

St. Paul's imprisonment: Jerusalem. Spring, A.D. 57.—Paul's preaching to the Gentiles had made him especially obnoxious to the Jewish leaders. He was now approaching a crisis in the long struggle, and the shadow of it has been made to rest upon his mind throughout his journey to Jerusalem. He came "ready to die for the name of the Lord Jesus," but he came expressly to prove himself a faithful Jew, and this purpose is shown at every point of his history. Certain Jews from "Asia," who had come up for the pentecostal feast, and who had a personal knowledge of Paul, saw him in the temple. They set upon him at once, and stirred up the people against him. There was instantly a great commotion; Paul was dragged out of the temple, the doors of which were immediately shut, and the people, having him in their hands, were proposing to kill him. Paul was rescued from the violence of the multitude by the Roman officer, who made him his own prisoner, causing him to be chained to two soldiers, and then proceeded to inquire who he was and what he had done. The inquiry only elicited confused outcries, and the "chief captain" seems to have imagined him a certain Egyptian pretender who had recently stirred up a considerable rising of the people. The account in Acts, 21: 34–40, tells us with graphic touches how St. Paul obtained leave and opportunity to address the people in a discourse which is related at length. Until the hated word of a mission to the Gentiles had been spoken, the Jews had listened to the speaker. "Away with such a fellow from the earth," the multitude now shouted; "it is not fit that he should live." The Roman commander, seeing the tumult that arose, might well conclude that St. Paul had committed some heinous offence; and carrying him off, he gave orders that he should be forced by scourging to confess his crime. Again the apostle took advantage of his Roman citizenship to

protect himself from such an outrage. The chief captain set him free from bonds, but on the next day called together the chief priests and the Sanhedrin, and brought Paul as a prisoner before them. When a plot of more than forty of the Jews who had bound themselves under a curse neither to eat nor drink until they had killed Paul was discovered, St. Paul was hurried away from Jerusalem. The chief captain, Claudius Lysias, determined to send him to Cæsarea to Felix, the governor or procurator of Judea. He therefore put him in charge of a strong guard of soldiers, who took him by night as far as Antipatris. From thence a smaller detachment conveyed him to Cæsarea, where they delivered up their prisoner into the hands of the governor.

Imprisonment at Cæsarea. A.D. 58–59. —St. Paul was henceforth, to the end of the period embraced in the Acts, if not to the end of his life, in Roman custody. This custody was in fact a protection to him, without which he would have fallen a victim to the animosity of the Jews. He seems to have been treated throughout with humanity and consideration. The governor before whom he was now to be tried, according to Tacitus and Josephus, was a mean and dissolute tyrant. After hearing St. Paul's accusers and the apostle's defence, Felix made an excuse for putting off the matter, and gave orders that the prisoner should be treated with indulgence, and that his friends should be allowed free access to him. After a while he heard him again. St. Paul remained in custody until Felix left the province. The unprincipled governor had good reason to seek to ingratiate himself with the Jews; and to please them, he handed over Paul, as an untried prisoner, to his successor, Festus. Upon his arrival in the province, Festus went up without delay from Cæsarea to Jerusalem, and the leading Jews seized the opportunity of asking that Paul might be brought up there for trial, intending to assassinate him by the way. But Festus would not comply with their request. He invited them to follow him on his speedy return to Cæsarea, and a trial took place there, closely resembling that before Felix. The proposal that he should go to Jerusalem for trial was the occasion of

St. Paul's appeal to Cæsar. The appeal having been allowed, Festus took advantage of an opportunity which offered itself in a few days to seek some help as to the report to be sent with him. The Jewish prince Agrippa arrived with his sister Berenice on a visit to the new governor, and Agrippa expressed a desire to hear Paul himself. Accordingly Paul conducted his defence before the king; and when it was concluded Festus and Agrippa, and their companions, consulted together, and came to the conclusion that t h e accused w a s g u i l t y o f nothing that d e s e r v e d d e a t h o r imprisonment. And Agrippa's final answer to the inquiry of Festus was, "This man might have been set at liberty, if he had not appealed unto Cæsar."

The voyage to Rome and shipwreck. Autumn, A.D. 59–60. "Paul a n d certain other prisoners," were sent i n t h e custody o f a centurion named Julius, i n t o Italy, a n d amongst t h e company whether by favor or from any other reason, we find Luke, who in chapters 27 and 28 gives a graphic description o f the voyage to Rome and t h e shipwreck on the island of Melita o r Malta. After a three-months stay in Malta the soldiers and their prisoners left i n a n Alexandrian ship f o r Italy. A t Puteoli they found "brethren," for it was an important place, a n d especially a chief port for the traffic between Alexandria a n d Rome; and by these brethren they were exhorted to stay a while with them. Permission seems to have been granted by the centurion; and whilst they were spending seven days at Puteoli news of the apostle's arrival was sent to Rome. (Spring, A.D. 60.)

First imprisonment of St. Paul at Rome. A.D. 60–62.—On their arrival at Rome the centurion delivered up his prisoners into the proper custody, that of the prætorian prefect. Paul was at once treated with special consideration, and was allowed to dwell by himself with the soldier who guarded him. He was now therefore free "to preach the gospel to them that were at Rome also;" and proceeded without delay to act upon his rule—"to the Jews first." But as of old, the reception of his message by the Jews was not favorable. He turned, therefore, again to the Gentiles, and for two years he dwelt in his own hired house. These are the last words of the Acts.

Period of the later epistles.—To the imprisonment belongs the group of letters to Philemon, to the Colossians, to the Ephesians and to the Philippians. According to the general opinion the apostle was liberated from imprisonment at the end of two years, having been acquitted by Nero A.D. 63, and left Rome. He spent some time in visits to Macedonia, Greece, Asia Minor and Spain, and during the latter part of this time wrote the letters to Timothy and Titus from Macedonia. After these were written he was apprehended again and sent to Rome.

Second imprisonment at Rome. A.D

THE APPIAN WAY.
St. Paul probably took this road on his journey to Rome.

66–67.—The apostle appears now to have been treated not as an honorable state prisoner, but as a felon, 2 Tim. 2:9; but he was allowed to write the second letter to Timothy, A.D. 67. For what remains we have the concurrent testimony of ecclesiastical antiquity that he was beheaded at Rome, by Nero, in the great persecutions of the Christians by that emperor, A.D. 67 or 68.

Pavement. [GABBATHA.]

Pavilion, a temporary movable tent or habitation. 1. *Sôk,* properly an enclosed place, also rendered "tabernacle," "covert" and "den;" once only "pavilion." Ps. 27:5. Among the Egyptians pavilions were built in a similar style to houses, though on a smaller scale, in various parts of the country, and in the foreign districts through which the Egyptian armies passed, for the use of the king. 2. *Sukkah,* usually "tabernacle" and "booth." 3. *Shaphrûr,* a word used once only, in Jer. 43:10, to signify glory or splendor, and hence probably to be understood of the splendid covering of the royal throne. R. V. "glittering pavilion."

Peacocks (Heb. *tukkîyyîm*). Among the natural products which Solomon's

THE PEACOCK.

fleet brought home to Jerusalem, mention is made of "peacocks," 1 Kings 10: 22; 2 Chron. 9:21, which is probably the correct translation. The Hebrew word may be traced to the Tamul or Malabaric *togei,* "peacock."

Pearl (Heb. *gâbîsh*). The Hebrew word in Job 28:18 probably means "crystal." Pearls, however, are frequently mentioned in the New Testament, Matt. 13:45; 1 Tim. 2:9; Rev. 17:4; 21:21, and were considered by the ancients among the most precious of gems, and were highly esteemed as or-

PEARL OYSTER.

naments. The kingdom of heaven is compared to a "pearl of great price." In Matt. 7:6 pearls are used metaphorically for anything of value, or perhaps more especially for "wise sayings." The finest specimens of the pearl are yielded by the pearl oyster (*Avicula margaritifera*), still found in abundance in the Persian Gulf and near the coasts of Ceylon, Java and Sumatra. The oysters grow in clusters on rocks in deep water, and the pearl is found inside the shell, and is the result of a diseased secretion caused by the introduction of foreign bodies, as sand, etc., between the mantle and the shell. They are obtained by divers trained to the business. In the pearl fisheries of Ceylon and Coromandel March or April is the time for pearl fishing. A single shell may contain from eight to twenty pearls. The size of a good Oriental pearl varies from that of a pea to about three times that size.

Ped'ahel (pĕd'a-hĕl) (*God hath saved*), the son of Ammihud, and prince of the tribe of Naphtali. Num. 34:28.

Pedah'zur (pė-däh'zur) (*the rock*) (i. e. *God hath saved*), father of Gamaliel, the chief of the tribe of Manasseh at the time of the Exodus. Num. 1:10; 2:20; 7:54, 59; 10:23.

Peda'iah (pė-dā'yah) (*Jehovah has redeemed*). 1. The father of Zebudah, mother of King Jehoiakim. 2 Kings 23: 36.

2. The brother of Salathiel or Shealtiel. 1 Chron. 3: 17–19. In 1 Chron. 3: 19 he is named as father of Zerubbabel, who is usually called the "son of Shealtiel." Probably he was legal son of Shealtiel, though son of Pedaiah, by Levirate marriage, in consequence of the failure of issue in the direct line.

3. Son of Parosh, that is, one of the family of that name, who assisted Nehemiah in repairing the walls of Jerusalem. Neh. 3 : 25. (B.C. about 446.)

4. Apparently a priest; one of those who stood on the left hand of Ezra when he read the law to the people. Neh. 8 : 4. (B.C. 445.)

5. A Benjamite, ancestor of Sallu. Neh. 11 : 7.

6. A Levite in the time of Nehemiah, Neh. 13 : 13.

7. The father of Joel, prince of the half tribe of Manasseh in the reign of David. 1 Chron. 27 : 20.

Pe'kah (pē'kah) (*open-eyed*), son of Remaliah, originally a captain of Pekahiah, king of Israel, murdered his master, seized the throne, and became the 18th sovereign of the northern kingdom, B.C. 736–729. Under his predecessors Israel had been much weakened through the payment of enormous tribute to the Assyrians (see especially 2 Kings 15: 20), and by internal wars and conspiracies. Pekah seems to have steadily applied himself to the restoration of its power. Judah, now under Jotham, may have been asked to join, but no mention is made of the fact. Either by original intention or in consequence of Jotham's refusal, the allied armies began an attempt to force Judah to join them. Just as the campaign opened Jotham died (B.C. 735), and the youthful Ahaz succeeded him. The history of the war is found in 2 Kings 16 and 2 Chron. 28. It is famous as the occasion of the great prophecies in Isa. 7–9. Its chief result was the Jewish port of Elath on the Red Sea; but the unnatural alliance of Damascus and Samaria was punished through the complete overthrow of the ferocious confederates by Tiglath-pileser whom Ahaz had summoned to his aid. The kingdom of Damascus was finally suppressed and Rezin put to death, while Pekah was deprived of at least half his kingdom,

including all the northern portion and the whole district to the east of Jordan. Pekah himself, now fallen into the position of an Assyrian vassal, was of course compelled to abstain from further attacks on Judah. By the connivance, if not by the direct instigation of Tiglath-pileser he was killed by Hoshea the son of Elah in 729 B.C.

Pekahi'ah (pĕk-a-hī'ah) (*whose eyes Jehovah opened*), son and successor of Menahem, was the 17th king of the separate kingdom of Israel, B.C. 737–736. After a brief reign of scarcely two years a conspiracy was organized against him by Pekah, who murdered him and seized the throne. 2 Kings 15 : 23–26.

Pe'kod (pē'kod), an appellative applied to the Chaldeans. Jer. 50 : 21; Ezek. 23 : 23. In the Assyrian inscriptions the name of a people called *Pukudu* appears, and it probably refers to them.

Pela'iah (pē-lā'iah) (*distinguished by Jehovah*). 1. A son of Elioenai, of the royal line of Judah. 1 Chron. 3 : 24.

2. One of the Levites who assisted Ezra in expounding the law. Neh. 8 : 7. He afterward sealed the covenant with Nehemiah. Neh. 10 : 10. (B.C. 445.)

Pelali'ah (pĕl-a-lī'ah) (*Jehovah hath judged*), the son of Amzi and ancestor of Adaiah. Neh. 11 : 12.

Pelati'ah (pĕl-a-tī'ah) (*Jehovah hath set free* (*or delivered*). 1. Son of Hananiah the son of Zerubbabel. 1 Chron. 3 : 21.

2. One of the captains of the marauding band of Simeonites who in the reign of Hezekiah made an expedition to Mount Seir and smote the Amalekites. 1 Chron. 4 : 42.

3. One of the heads of the people, and probably the name of a family who sealed the covenant with Nehemiah. Neh. 10 : 22. Perhaps the same as 1.

4. The son of Benaiah, and one of the princes of the people against whom Ezekiel was directed to utter the words of doom recorded in Ezek. 11 : 5–12, because he misled the people.

Pe'leg (pe'lĕg) (*division, part*), son of Eber and brother of Joktan. Gen. 10 : 25; 11 : 16. The only incident connected with his history is the statement that "in his days was the earth divided," an event embodied in the meaning of his name—"division." It may refer to the separation of the children of Eber, or to that caused by the confusion of tongues at the Tower of Babel.

Pe'let (pē'let) (*liberation*). 1. A son of Jahdai in an obscure genealogy. 1 Chron. 2: 47.

2. The son of Azmaveth, possibly a native of the place of that name. One of David's heroes. 1 Chron. 12: 3.

Pe'leth (pē'leth) (*swiftness*). 1. The father of On the Reubenite, who joined Dathan and Abiram in their rebellion. Num. 16: 1. (B.C. 1490.) Perhaps more correctly Pallu.

2. Son of Jonathan, and a descendant of Jerahmeel. 1 Chron. 2: 33.

Pel'ethites (pēl'eth-ītes). [CHERETHITES.]

Pelican (Heb. *kâath,* sometimes translated "cormorant," as Isa. 34: 11; Zeph. 2: 14, though in the margin correctly rendered "pelican"), a voracious waterbird, found most abundantly in tropical regions. It is equal to the swan in size. It has a flat bill, fifteen inches long, and the female has under the bill a pouch, capable of great distension. It is capacious enough to hold fish sufficient for the dinner of half a dozen men. The young are fed from this pouch, which is emptied of the food by pressing the pouch against the breast. The pelican's bill has a crimson tip, and the contrast of this red tip against the white breast probably gave rise to the tradition that the bird tore her own breast to feed her young with her blood. The flesh of the pelican was forbidden to the Jews. Lev. 11: 18. The psalmist, in comparing his pitiable condition to the pelican, Ps. 102: 6, probably has reference to its general aspect as it sits in apparent melancholy mood, with its bill resting on its breast.

Pel'onite (pĕl'o-nīte), **The.** Two of David's mighty men, Helez and Ahijah, are called Pelonites. 1 Chron. 11: 27, 36. From 1 Chron. 27: 10 it appears that the former was of the tribe of Ephraim, and "Pelonite" would therefore be an appellation derived from his place of birth or residence or very possibly a corruption of the text. "Ahijah the Pelonite" appears in 2 Sam. 23: 34 as "Eliam the son of Ahithophel the Gilonite," of which the former is a corruption.

Pen. [WRITING.]

Peni'el (*face of God*), the name which Jacob gave to the place in which he had wrestled with God: "He called

32

the name of the place 'face of El,' for I have seen Elohim face to face." Gen. 32: 30. It has been generally supposed that Penuel in Gen. 32: 31, is another form of the same name. But the celebrated traveller Agnes Smith Lewis, D.D., after having been carefully over the ground, decided that *Peniel* is a ford over the Jabbok, while *Penuel* is a mountain. Jacob crossed over the ford Peniel, then as "he passed over" the mountain "Penuel, the sun rose upon him." On either side, of the Peniel ford, called the Mispeh ford, is a meadow full of rank grass and flowers, above the *Wady es Zerka*. Below this point the stream winds between steep mountains. It was a fitting place for the scenes in the life of Jacob, described in Genesis 32.

Penin'nah (pĕ-nĭn'nah) (*coral,* or *pearl*), one of the two wives of Elkanah, the father of Samuel. 1 Sam. 1: 2.

Penny, Pennyworth. In the New Testament "penny," either alone or in the compound "pennyworth," occurs as the rendering of the Roman *denarius*. Matt. 20: 2; 22: 19; Mark 6: 37; 12: 15; Luke 20: 24; John 6: 7; Rev. 6: 6. The denarius was the chief Roman silver coin, and was worth about 16 cents.

Pen'tateuch, The, is the Greek name given to the five books commonly called the "five books of Moses." This title is derived from *Pente,* five, and *teuchos,* which, meaning originally "vessel," "instrument," etc., came in Alexandrine Greek to mean "book," hence *the five-fold book*. In the time of Ezra and Nehemiah it was called "the law of Moses," Ezra 7: 6, or "the book of Moses," Neh. 8: 1, or simply "the book of Moses." 2 Chron. 25: 4; 35: 12; Ezra 6: 18; Neh. 13: 1. This was beyond all reasonable doubt our existing Pentateuch. The Jews usually called the whole by the name of *Torah, i. e.* "the Law," or *Torath Mosheh,* "the Law of Moses." The division of the whole work into five parts was probably made by the Greek translators; for the titles of the several books are not of Hebrew but of Greek origin. The Hebrew names are merely taken from the first words of each book, and in the first instance only designated particular *sections* and not whole books. The MSS. of the Pentateuch form a single roll or volume, and are divided, not into books but into the larger and smaller sections. The five books of the Pentateuch form a consecutive whole. The work, beginning with the record of

The Pentateuch is now one of the great battle grounds of criticism and interpretation, concerning which it may be wise to make some statement. Till the middle of the last century it was the

PENTATEUCH AT SHECHEM.

creation and the history of the primitive world, passes on to deal more especially with the early history of the Jewish family, and finally concludes with Moses' last discourses and his death

general opinion of both Jews and Christians that the whole of the Pentateuch was written by Moses, with the exception of a few manifestly later additions,—such as the 34th chapter of Deuteronomy, which gives the account of Moses' death. Since then there has been a wide difference of opinion.

Many scholars still regard Moses as the chief author and the accounts given in the Pentateuch as real history.

The popular Biblical scholarship of the day attributes very little of the Pentateuch to Moses.

It has made a revolutionary reconstruction of the history of Israel and its development, very different from that which appears in the continuous narrative as arranged by the Jews in our present Scriptures. It claims to have made a new Bible of the Old Testament, better and truer than that of the old arrangement.

It regards the early narratives as consisting more or less largely of legends and myths and traditions, not of real history, but often with a substratum of history.

It finds in the Old Testament history three or four narratives, and claims 1. that they were written at different dates, interwoven together as we have them, at a late period of Israelitish history, but including many ancient documents; as we sometimes see the four Gospels interwoven into one continuous narrative or diatessaron;

2. that these narratives they have separated, and enabled each to tell its own distinct story;

3. that thus arranged there are many contradictions between the different accounts, and errors of statement, which do not for the most part appear such in the continuous narrative.

The lateness of the date at which they regard the various narratives as finally written, favors the unreliability of the stories as true history.

It claims that much that we find here came from Babylonian influence.

The more moderate critics of this school believe in a real inspiration and a real revelation from God, as Professor Budde, the eminent German critic, writes that as for himself his "belief in a genuine revelation of God in the Old Testament remains rock-fast." They teach that the legends, myths, and traditions of the far-off past were transformed and inspired by God to convey great religious truths. The history of Israel is the record of "a divine guidance in the strictest sense supernatural and unique."

They claim that while the faith of not a few has been shaken by these new views, yet "that those who have been led into unbelief by modern criticism are not to be compared in number with those who have fallen from faith over the edge of the opposite extreme;" that great numbers are helped by it out of their doubts and perplexities occasioned by "its discrepancies, pitiless tempers, rigorous laws, atrocities narrated and sanctioned by its laws," and its seeming conflict with modern science. They claim that all these difficulties are removed by the conclusion that in the early portions of the Bible "we are handling not history, but tradition."

On the other hand the intelligent moderate conservatives accept all the *facts* brought to notice by the higher critics, but interpret them in a different way.

They believe in the historical method and the light it has thrown upon the Pentateuch.

They believe in a progressive revelation, and a gradual development in the history of Israel under divine guidance.

They believe in the general fact of the composite nature of the Pentateuch.

They believe that there have been revisions, editings, translations, even as we have seen all through the history of the Bible, down to our latest revisions.

They believe that God uses all the various forms of literature,—poetry, story, allegory, parable, as well as history, prophecy, and statements of fact, —to convey his revelation of truth to man, and that this has thrown much light on the Bible, and avoids the difficulties which have arisen from confounding together the different forms of literature.

They accept the general truth of the historical statements of the Pentateuch; and see that nearly all the contradictions which throw a doubt over the truth of the stories, are not in the narrative as it stands, but are made by separating the narrative into different stories and then contrasting them, as if each of the separated stories was the whole of that story. History is not made in that way. Take, for instance, Tatian's Diatessaron.

They believe that the Bible, as now arranged, more truly expresses, as a whole, the real historic religious development of man and of Israel,—one divine plan running through the whole, —a divine revelation early in the history of man, but growing fuller and brighter as the centuries moved on and the people could receive it, while along with this the written history records the tortuous and often reversionary struggles of the people under the divine training to live up to it; very much as the history of Christianity records the struggles and training of its adherents to live up to the original revelation in Jesus Christ, with all their reverses, neglects, and moral falls.

As to the doubts, perplexities, and moral difficulties which the higher critics claim to remove from the younger generation, they are all, or nearly all, equally removed by the positions held as common ground by both schools, without involving them in the atmosphere of unreality and legend which the "Higher Criticism" throws around them.

Both schools are seeking the truth. Both are open minded to light from every source. Both are looking for new light to break forth upon and from the Bible as claimed the old Puritan, John Robinson. To the question Professor Cheyne asks, "Has the clock stopped in Bible criticism?" the answer of both schools would be an emphatic "No." But the conservatives think the higher critics have sometimes moved the hands of that clock faster than the Sun of Truth moves, and they would like to keep the hands with the sun.

Pen'tecost, that is, *the fiftieth day* (from a Greek word meaning fiftieth), or Harvest Feast, or Feast of Weeks, may be regarded as a supplement to the Passover. It lasted for but one day. From the sixteenth of Nisan seven weeks were reckoned inclusively, and the next or fiftieth day was the day of Pentecost, which fell on the sixth of Sivan (about the end of May). Ex. 23: 16; 34: 22; Lev. 23: 15–22; Num. 28. See *Jewish calendar* at the end of this volume. The Pentecost was the Jewish harvest-home, and the people were especially exhorted to rejoice before Jehovah with their families, their servants, the Levite within their gates, the stranger, the fatherless and the widow, in the place chosen by God for his name, as they brought a free-will offering of their hand to Jehovah their God. Deut. 16: 10, 11. The great feature of the celebration was the presentation of the *two loaves,* made from the firstfruits of the wheat harvest. With the loaves two lambs were offered as a peace offering, and all were waved before Jehovah, and given to the priests; the loaves, being leavened, could not be offered on the altar. The other sacrifices were, a burnt offering of a young bullock, two rams and seven lambs, with a meal and drink offering, and a kid for a sin offering. Lev. 23: 18, 19. Till the pentecostal loaves were offered, the produce of the harvest might not be eaten, nor could any other first-fruits be offered. The whole ceremony was the completion of that dedication of the harvest to God as its giver, and to whom both the land and the people were holy, which was begun by the offering of the wave-sheaf at the Passover. The interval is still regarded as a religious season. The Pentecost is the only one of the three great feasts which is not mentioned as the memorial of events in the history of the Jews. The Jews of the post-biblical period held that it celebrated the fact that the law was given from Sinai on the fiftieth day after the deliverance from Egypt. Comp. Ex. 12 and 19. But there is no conclusive proof that the giving of the law was on the 50th day after the Passover. Such a connection is not mentioned in the Old Testament, nor by Josephus or Philo, and is doubtless incorrect. In the Christian church Pentecost is the memorial of the coming of the Holy Spirit upon the disciples at Jerusalem after the Ascension of Christ. Acts 2.

Penu'el, a mountain or height near the Peniel ford of the Jordan, on the south. The accounts in Judges 8: 8–17, and 1 Kings 12: 25, confirm this view. "It was a city whose chief feature was a strong tower or castle." See PENIEL.

Pe'or (pē'or) (*cleft*), a mountain peak in Moab belonging to the Abarim range, and near Pisgah, to which, after having ascended Pisgah, the prophet Balaam was conducted by Balak that he might look upon the whole host of Israel and curse them. Num. 23: 14, 28. In four passages—Num. 25: 18 twice; 31: 16; Josh. 22: 17—Peor occurs as a contraction for Baal-peor. [BAAL.]

Per'azim (pĕr'a-zĭm) (*a breach*), **Mount,** a name which occurs in Isa. 28: 21 only—unless the place which it designates is identical with the Baal-perazim mentioned as the scene of one of David's victories over the Philistines, which was in the valley of Rephaim, south of Jerusalem, on the road to Bethlehem.

Pere'a. A name for the country "beyond Jordan" often used by Josephus, and adopted by all modern writers. It is not found in the Scriptures themselves.

Pe'resh (pē'rĕsh) (*distinction*), the son of Machir by his wife Maachah. 1 Chron. 7:16.

Pe'rez (pē'rĕz) (*breach*). The "children of Perez," or PHAREZ, the son of Judah, appear to have been a family of importance for many centuries. 1 Chron. 27:3; Neh. 11:4, 6.

Pe'rez-uz'za (pē'rez-ŭz'zà) (*breach of Uzzah*), 1 Chron. 13:11, and **Perez-uzzah**, 2 Sam. 6:8, the title which David conferred on the threshing-floor of Nachon in commemoration of the sudden death of Uzzah. (B.C. 1042.)

Perfumes. The free use of perfumes was peculiarly grateful to the Orientals, Prov. 27:9, as masking the odor of the body so liable to be offensive in a hot climate. The Hebrews manufactured their perfumes chiefly from spices imported from Arabia, though to a certain extent also from aromatic plants growing in their own country. Perfumes entered largely into the temple service, in the two forms of incense and ointment. Ex. 30:22–38. Nor were they less used in private life; not only were they applied to the person, but to garments, Ps. 45:8; Cant. 4:11, and to articles of furniture, such as beds. Prov. 7:17.

Per'ga (pĕr'gà) (*earthy*), a city of Pamphylia, Acts 13:13, is situated near the river Cestrus, at a distance of 60 stadia (7½ miles) from its mouth, and celebrated in antiquity for the worship of a goddess identified with the Greek Artemis, but more like the Ephesian.

Per'gamos (pĕr'ga-mŏs) (in Revised Version *Pergamum*) (*citadel, berg*), a city of Mysia, about 3 miles to the north of the river Caicus, and 20 miles from its present mouth. It was the residence of a dynasty of Greek princes founded after the time of Alexander the Great, and usually called the Attalic dynasty, from its founder Attalus. The sumptuousness of the Attalic princes had raised Pergamos to the rank

of the first city in Asia as regards splendor. The city was noted for its vast library, second only to that of Alexandria; and afterwards added to it. Here were splendid temples of Zeus or Jupiter, Athene, Dionysos or Apollo and Æsculapius. One of "the seven churches of Asia" was in Pergamos. Rev. 1:11; 2:12–17. It is called "Satan's seat" by John, which some suppose to refer to the worship of Æsculapius, from the *serpent* being his characteristic emblem. Others to the fact that it was a centre for the worship of the emperor, while still others refer it to the persecutions of Christians, which was the work of Satan. The modern name of the city is *Bergama*.

Peri'da (pé-rī'dà) (*grain, kernel*). The children of Perida returned from Babylon with Zerubbabel. Neh. 7:57.

Per'izzite, The, and **Per'izzites** (pĕr'ĭz-zītes), one of the nations inhabiting the land of promise before and at the time of its conquest by Israel. (B.C. 1450.) They are continually mentioned in the formula so frequently occurring to express the promised land. Gen. 15:20; Ex. 3:8, 17; 23:23; 33:2; 34:11. The notice in the book of Judges appears to locate them in the central or southern part of the Holy Land. The signification of the name is not by any means clear. It possibly meant rustics, dwellers in open, unwalled villages, which are denoted by a word similar to this.

Per'sia (pĕr'zià), **Per'sians.** Persia proper was a tract of no very large dimensions on the east side of the Persian Gulf, which is still known as *Fars*, a corruption of the ancient appellation. This tract was bounded on the west by Elam, on the north by Media, on the south by the Persian Gulf and on the east by Carmania. But the name is more commonly applied, both in Scripture and by profane authors, to the entire tract which came by degrees to be included within the limits of the Persian empire, which extended at one time from India to the Mediterranean, and from the Danube and Black Sea to the Arabian and Nubian deserts. The Persians were of the same race as the Medes, both being branches of the great Aryan stock.

1. *Character of the nation.*—The Persians were a people of lively and impressible minds, brave and impetuous in war,

witty, passionate, for Orientals truthful, not without some spirit of generosity, and of more intellectual capacity than the generality of Asiatics. In the times anterior to Cyrus they were noted for the simplicity of their habits, which offered a strong contrast to the luxuriousness of the Medes; but from the date of the Median overthrow this simplicity began to decline. Polygamy was commonly practised among them. They were fond of the pleasures of the table, especially of drinking. In war they fought bravely, but without proper discipline.

2. *Religion.*—Zoroastrianism, the religion which the Persians brought with them into Persia proper, seems to have been of a very simple character, differing from natural religion in little except that it was deeply tainted with Dualism. Like the other Aryans, the Persians worshipped one supreme God. They had few temples, and no altars or images, their religion being spiritual, recognizing the distinction between God and nature, and between spirit and matter. Its fundamental ethical principle was the essential contradiction between good and evil, light and darkness. It taught the duty of man to eradicate evil and cultivate good, and to strive after holiness in thought, word, and deed, which will be rewarded by immortality and heaven. It paid homage to fire, air, earth and water as the creation of their supreme deity.—*Condensed from Davis' Bible Dictionary.*

3. *Language.*—The Ancient Persian language was remotely akin to the Sanscrit, or ancient language of India. Later it approached Aramaic. Modern Persian is its degenerated representative, being largely impregnated with Arabic.

4. *History.*—The history of Persia begins with the revolt from the Medes and the accession of Cyrus the Great, about B.C. 550. Cyrus defeated Crœsus, and added the Lydian empire to his dominions. This conquest was followed closely by the submission of the Greek settlements on the Asiatic coast, and by the reduction of Caria and Lycia. The empire was soon afterward extended greatly toward the northeast and east. In B.C. 539 or 538, Babylon was attacked, and after a stout defence fell into the hands of Cyrus. This victory first brought the Persians into contact with the Jews. The conquerors found in Babylon an oppressed race—like themselves abhorrers of idols, and professors of a religion in which to a great extent they could sympathize. This race Cyrus determined to restore to their own country: which he did by the remarkable edict recorded in the first chapter of Ezra. Ezra 1 : 2–4. He was slain in an expedition against the Massagetæ or the Derbices, about B.C. 529. Under his son and successor, Cambyses, the conquest of Egypt took place, B.C. 525. Gomates, the false Smerdis, Cambyses' successor, reversed the policy of Cyrus with respect to the Jews, and forbade by an edict the further building of the temple. Ezra 4 : 17–22. He reigned but seven months, and was succeeded by Darius. Appealed to, in his second year, by the Jews, who wished to resume the construction of their temple, Darius not only granted them this privilege, but assisted the work by grants from his own revenues, whereby the Jews were able to complete the temple as early as his sixth year. Ezra 6 : 1–15. Darius was succeeded by Xerxes, the Ahasuerus of Esther. Artaxerxes, the son of Xerxes, reigned for forty years after his death, and is beyond doubt the king of that name who stood in such a friendly relation toward Ezra. Ezra 7 : 11–28, and Nehemiah. Neh. 2 : 1–9, etc. He is the last of the Persian kings who had any special connection with the Jews. Darius Codomannus, B.C. 336, is probably the "Darius the Persian" who is mentioned in Nehemiah 12 : 22.

After some centuries of independent existence Persia came under Mohammedan rule. Some of the bolder spirits refused to submit to Mohammedan domination and fled to the mountains, from which they gradually made their way into India and formed the section of its inhabitants called the Parsees. They are prosperous, and loyal to the English. Modern Persia has been long nominally independent under the rule of a despotic Shah. Since 1909 there has been much unrest and at this time there is a liberal government. The estimated population is about 10,000,000.

Per′sis (pĕr′sis) (*a Persian woman*), a Christian woman at Rome, Rom. 16 : 12, whom St. Paul salutes and praises for her work. (A.D. 57.)

Peru′da (pé-rṳ′dà). The same as PERIDA. Ezra 2 : 55.

Pestilence. [PLAGUE, THE.]

Pe'ter (pē'tēr) (*a rock or stone*). The original name of this disciple was Simon, *i. e.* "hearing." He was the son of a man named Jonas (R. V. sometimes John), Matt. 16:17; John 1:42; 21:16, and was brought up in his father's occupation, that of a fisherman. He and his brother Andrew were partners of John and James, the sons of Zebedee, who had hired servants. Peter was probably born in Bethsaida. When first known in the Gospels he was married and living at Capernaum, in his own house, which must have been rather a large one, since he received in it not only our Lord and his fellow disciples, but multitudes who were attracted by the miracles and preaching of Jesus. Peter was probably between thirty and forty years of age at the date of his call to become a follower of Jesus. He and his brother Andrew, together with their partners James and John, the sons of Zebedee, were disciples of John the Baptist when he was first called by our Lord. The particulars of this call are related with graphic minuteness by St. John. It was upon this occasion that Jesus gave Peter the name Cephas, a Syriac word answering to the Greek Petros and signifying a stone or rock. John 1:35–42. It did not denote the character he then had, but what our Lord perceived he was capable of becoming. It was a prophecy of his future. The second call, to constant companionship with Christ, over a year later, is recorded by the other three evangelists. It took place on the Sea of Galilee near Capernaum, where the four disciples, Peter and Andrew, James and John, were fishing. Some time was passed afterward in attendance upon our Lord's public ministrations in Galilee, Decapolis, Peræa and Judea. The selection of the Twelve Apostles as distinct from the other disciples was several months later still. See Matt. 10:2–4; Mark 3:13–19 (the most detailed account); Luke 6:13–16. From this time there can be no doubt that Peter held the first place among the apostles, to whatever cause his precedence is to be attributed. He is named first in every list of the apostles; he is generally addressed by our Lord as their representative; and on the most solemn occasions he speaks in their name. The distinction which he received, and it may be his con-

sciousness of ability, energy, zeal and absolute devotion to Christ's person, seem to have developed a natural tendency to rashness and forwardness bordering upon presumption. In his affection and self-confidence Peter ventured to reject as impossible the announcement of the sufferings and humiliation which Jesus predicted, and heard the sharp words, "Get thee behind me, Satan; thou art an offence unto me; for thou savorest not the things that be of God, but those that be of men." It is remarkable that on other occasions when St. Peter signalized his faith and devotion, he displayed at the time, or immediately afterward, a more than usual deficiency in spiritual discernment and consistency. Toward the close of our Lord's ministry Peter's characteristics become especially prominent. At the last supper Peter seems to have been particularly earnest in the request that the traitor might be pointed out. After the supper his words drew out the meaning of the significant act of our Lord in washing his disciples' feet. Then too it was that he made those repeated protestations of unalterable fidelity, so soon to be falsified by his miserable fall. On the morning of the resurrection we have proof that Peter, though humbled, was not crushed by his fall. He and John were the first to visit the sepulchre; he was the first who entered it. We are told by Luke and by Paul that Christ appeared to him first among the apostles. In John 21 we have the account of a full re-instatement into the place of an apostle. From this time he became what his name signified, a rock—and his boldness in face of persecution formed a sharp contrast with his previous timidity.

The first part of the Acts of the Apostles is occupied by the record of transactions in nearly all of which Peter stands forth as the recognized leader of the apostles. He is the most prominent person in the greatest event after the resurrection, on the day of Pentecost. He performed the first Christian miracle, and conducted the defence when the Christian leaders were brought before the Sanhedrin. When the gospel was first preached beyond the precincts of Judea, he and John were at once sent by the apostles to confirm the converts at Samaria. Henceforth he remains prominent, but not exclusively prominent, among the propagators of the gospel. The most signal transaction after the day of Pentecost was the baptism of Cornelius, by Peter. The establishment of a church in great part of Gentile origin at Antioch, and the mission of Barnabas, between whose family and Peter there were the bonds of near intimacy, set the seal upon the work thus inaugurated by Peter. This transaction was soon followed by the imprisonment of our apostle. His miraculous deliverance marks the close of this second great period of his ministry. The special work assigned to him was completed. From that time we have no continuous history of him.

Peter was probably employed for the most part in building up and completing the organization of Christian communities in Palestine and the adjoining districts. He traveled about preaching the gospel, accompanied by his wife (1 Cor. 9:5) and visited Antioch in Syria certainly (Gal. 2:11). He is thought by many to have gone to Corinth (1 Cor. 1:12; and Eusebius). It is certainly possible that he went to the far east (1 Pet. 5:13). It may be considered as a settled point that he did not visit Rome before the last year of his life; but there is satisfactory evidence that he and Paul were the founders of the church at Rome, and suffered death in that city. The time and manner of the apostle's martyrdom are less certain. According to the early writers, he suffered at or about the same time with Paul, and in the Neronian persecution, A.D. 67, 68. All agree that he was crucified. Origen says that Peter felt himself to be unworthy to be put to death in the same manner as his Master, and was therefore, at his own request, crucified with his head downward. The apostle is said to have employed interpreters. Of far more importance is the statement that Mark wrote his Gospel under the teaching of Peter, or that he embodied in that Gospel the substance of our apostle's oral instructions. [MARK.] The only written documents which Peter has left are the First Epistle—about which no doubt has ever been entertained in the Church—and the Second, which has been a subject of earnest controversy.

Peter, First Epistle of. The external evidence of authenticity of this epistle is of the strongest kind; and the internal is equally strong.

To WHOM ADDRESSED. It was addressed to the churches of Asia Minor, which had for the most part been founded by Paul and his companions, hence chiefly to Gentile Christians.

PLACE OF WRITING. Supposing it to have been written at Babylon, 1 Pet. 5:13, it is a probable conjecture that Silvanus, by whom it was transmitted to those churches, had joined Peter after a tour of visitation, and that his account of the condition of the Christians in those districts determined the apostle to write the epistle. On the question of this epistle having been written at Babylon commentators differ. " Some refer it to the famous Babylon in Asia, which after its destruction was still inhabited by a Jewish colony; others understand it mystically of heathen Rome, in which sense 'Babylon' is certainly used in the Apocalypse of John."—*Schaff*.

THE DATE. From its copious use of Paul's letter to the Ephesians, written in A.D. 62 or 63, and the death of Peter in A.D. 67, the time of writing this epistle must lie between these dates.

CHARACTERISTICS. "The style in which the letter is written is at once simple, striking and forcible, abounding in sudden and abrupt transitions, and admirably reflecting the character of the writer. It is filled to a remarkable degree with reminiscences of earlier Christian writings, particularly of the Epistles to the Romans, Ephesians and James."—*Prof. Warfield*.

THE OBJECTS of the epistle were—1. To comfort and strengthen the Christians in a season of severe trial. 2. To enforce the practical and spiritual duties involved in their calling. 3. To warn them against special temptations attached to their position. 4. To remove all doubt as to the soundness and completeness of the religious system which they had already received. Such an attestation was especially needed by the Hebrew Christians, who were wont to appeal from Paul's authority to that of the elder apostles, and above all to that of Peter. The last, which is perhaps the very principal object, is kept in view throughout the epistle, and is distinctly stated ch. 5:12. The harmony of such teaching with that of Paul is sufficiently obvious. Peter belongs to the school, or, to speak more correctly, is the leader of the school, which at once vindicates the unity of the law and the gospel, and puts the superiority of the latter on its true basis—that of spiritual development.

Peter, Second Epistle of. The genuineness of this Epistle has been in dispute from the early ages. The author represents himself as Simon Peter (1: 1), as being present at the transfiguration (1: 16) as warned by Christ of his death (1: 14). Only strong reasons should overcome this testimony. Others infer from the difference in style, from the fact that there is no certain knowledge of the existence of this Epistle till far into the second century, that this is not a letter by St. Peter, but was written by some unknown writer in his name. If written by Peter the date is probably not far from A.D. 67. If by some other writer, it is dated about A.D. 175 by Hastings' B. D. The following is a brief outline of the contents of this epistle: The customary opening salutation is followed by an enumeration of Christian blessings and exhortation to Christian duties, ch. 1: 1– 13. Referring then to his approaching death, the apostle assigns as grounds of assurance for believers his own personal testimony as eye-witness of the transfiguration, and the sure word of prophecy—that is, the testimony of the Holy Ghost, vs. 14–21. The danger of being misled by false prophets is dwelt upon with great earnestness throughout the second chapter, which is almost identical in language and subject with the Epistle of Jude. The overthrow of all opponents of Christian truth is predicted in connection with prophecies touching the second advent of Christ, the destruction of the world by fire, and the promise of new heavens and a new earth wherein dwelleth righteousness, ch. 3.

Pethahi'ah (pĕth-a-hī'ah) (*Jehovah hath set free*). 1. A priest, over the nineteenth course in the reign of David. 1 Chron. 24: 16.

2. A Levite in the time of Ezra, who had married a foreign wife. Ezra 10: 23. He is probably the same who is mentioned in Neh. 9: 5. (B.C. 458.)

3. The son of Meshezabeel, and descendant of Zerah. Neh. 11: 24.

Pe'thor (pē'thôr) (*cleft, opening*), a town of Mesopotamia, where Balaam

resided, and situated "upon the river," the Euphrates. Num. 22: 5; Deut. 23: 4. It is no doubt the city *Pitru* named by Shalmaneser in his inscriptions and Pedru named before by Thothmes III. In that case it was situated both on the *Sagur,* the modern *Sajur* and on the Euphrates, and so at their junction about 60 miles northeast of Aleppo.

Pethu'el (pė-thū'el), the father of the prophet Joel. Joel 1: 1.

Peul'thai (pė-ŭl'thā), properly Peullethai, the eighth son of Obed-edom. 1 Chron. 26: 5.

Pha'lec (fā'lek) (*division*). Peleg the son of Eber, Luke 3: 35.

Phal'lu (făl'lū) (*distinguished*). Pallu the son of Reuben is so called in the Authorized Version of Gen. 46: 9.

Phal'ti (făl'tī) (*deliverance*), the son of Laish of Gallim, to whom Saul gave Michal in marriage after his mad jealousy had driven David forth as an outlaw. 1 Sam. 25: 44. In 2 Sam. 3: 15 he is called PHALTIEL. With the exception of this brief mention of his name, and the touching little episode in 2 Sam. 3: 16, nothing more is heard of Phalti. (B.C. 1061.) R. V. Palti and Paltiel.

Phal'tiel (făl'ti-el). The same as Phalti. 2 Sam. 3: 15.

Pha'nuel (fā'nū-el) (*face of God*), the father of Anna, the prophetess of the tribe of Aser. Luke 2: 36.

Phar'aoh (fā'rō), the common title of the kings of Egypt in the Bible means "The Great House" which corresponds to our "The Sublime Porte" or "The Holy See," and was used as a term of reverence for the king. Several kings are mentioned in the Bible merely by this title, and it is well to attempt to discriminate between them, although in the case of the earlier ones it is impossible to do so with certainty.

1. *The Pharaoh of Abraham,* Gen. 12: 15. It is impossible to identify this king. Were it possible to determine the exact date of Abraham's visit it would still be extremely uncertain which Pharaoh was on the throne. Ussher gives the date of his visit as B.C. 1921. Beecher in his "Dated Events of the Old Testament" reckons it as B.C. 1927, which is practically the same. He argues from the kindly reception to Abraham that Pharaoh was one of the Shepherd Kings or Hyksos.

2. *The Pharaoh of Joseph,* Gen. 41.— This Pharaoh has been considered as

one of the Shepherd Kings, but it does not seem probable that their rule extended to so late a date. Beecher names as a possibility Amenhotep II, of the 18th dynasty, and gives the date as 1736 B.C. practically the same as Ussher's—1729 B.C.

3. *The Pharaoh of the oppression,* Ex. 1:8. Apparently a different dynasty from 2. There were probably several who oppressed Israel, but the one under whom it reached its climax is usually considered to be Rameses II, although there is not a unanimity of opinion on the point. One great difficulty with regard to the acceptance of Rameses II as this king was the late date assigned to him, the middle of the 14th century B.C., bringing the date of the Exodus down to about 1300 B.C. Beecher, however, reconciles the dates by bringing Rameses nearly 100 years earlier, and bringing the Exodus within a very few years of the date given by

HEAD OF MUMMY OF RAMESES II, "The Pharaoh of the Oppression."

Ussher. Rameses' mummy has been found, and identified.

4. *The Pharaoh of the Exodus,* Ex. 5:1. If the Pharaoh of the oppression was Rameses II, that of the Exodus was Menephthah, his son. Some inscriptions have been found indicating some unusual disturbance during his reign, and also the death of his first born son under peculiar circumstances. The finding of the mummy of this king was by some regarded as decisive proof against the claim that he was ruler at

this time. His army was overwhelmed, but there is no proof that the Scripture account is intended to convey the idea that the king himself was drowned. Any such occurrence as the pursuit re-

STATUE OF RAMESES II, "The Pharaoh of the Oppression."

ferred to would be spoken of as the pursuit "of Pharaoh."

5. *Pharaoh, father-in-law of Mered.*—In the genealogies of the tribe of Judah, mention is made of the daughter of a Pharaoh married to an Israelite—"Bithiah the daughter of Pharaoh, which Mered took." 1 Chron. 4:18. No indication of even the period is now obtainable.

6. *Pharaoh, brother-in-law of Hadad the Edomite.*—This king gave Hadad, as his wife, the sister of his own wife, Tahpenes. 1 Kings 11:18–20. At this period there were two contemporaneous dynasties, so that the power of Egypt was weak and there are no monuments. So it is impossible to identify him.

7. *Pharaoh, father-in-law of Solomon.*—The mention that the queen was brought into the city of David while Solomon's house and the temple and the city wall were building shows that the marriage took place not later than the 11th year of the king, when the temple was finished. 1 Kings 3:1; 6:1, 37, 38.

8. *Shishak,* "king of Egypt" who took Jerusalem in the reign of Rehoboam. 1 Kings 14:25. [SHISHAK.]

9. *So,* "king of Egypt," the contem-

porary of Hoshea, king of Israel. 2
Kings 17 : 4. [So.]

10. *Pharaoh, the opponent of Sennacherib.*—This Pharaoh, Isa. 36 : 6, is *Tirhakah,* the last king of the 25th, or
Ethiopian dynasty.

11.. *Pharaoh-necho.*—Also called Necho. This king was the second king
of the Saïte twenty-sixth dynasty. Herodotus calls him Nekos, and assigns to
him a reign of sixteen years, which is
confirmed by the monuments. He seems
to have been an enterprising king, as he
is related to have attempted to complete the canal connecting the Red Sea
with the Nile, and to have sent an expedition of Phœnicians to circumnavigate Africa, which was successfully accomplished. At the commencement of
his reign, B.C. 610, he made war against
the king of Assyria, and, being encountered on his way by Josiah, defeated
and slew the king of Judah at Megiddo in B.C. 608. 2 Kings 23 : 29, 30; 2
Chron. 35 : 20–24. Necho seems to have
soon returned to Egypt. Perhaps he
was on his way thither when he deposed
Jehoahaz. The army was probably
posted at Carchemish, and was there
defeated by Nebuchadnezzar in the
fourth year of Necho, B.C. 604, that
king not being, as it seems, then at its
head. Jer. 46 : 1, 2, 6, 10. This battle
led to the loss of all the Asiatic dominions of Egypt. 2 Kings 24 : 7.

12. *Pharaoh-hophra.*—The next king
of Egypt mentioned in the Bible is Pharaoh-hophra, the second successor of
Necho, from whom he was separated by
the six-years reign of Psammetichus II.
He came to the throne about B.C. 588,
and ruled nineteen years. Herodotus,
who calls him Apries, makes him son of
Psammetichus II, whom he calls Psam-
mis, and great-grandson of Psammetichus I. In the Bible it is related that
Zedekiah, the last king of Judah, was
aided by a Pharaoh against Nebuchadnezzar, in fulfilment of a treaty, and
that an army came out of Egypt, so
that the Chaldeans were obliged to raise
the siege of Jerusalem. The city was
first besieged in the ninth year of
Zedekiah, B.C. 588, and was captured in
his eleventh year, B.C. 586. It was evidently continuously invested for a length
of time before it was taken, so that it
is most probable that Pharaoh's expedition took place during 587 or 586. The
Egyptian army returned without effecting its purpose. Jer. 37 : 5–8: Ezek. 17 :
11–18; comp. 2 Kings 25 : 1–4. No subsequent Pharaoh is mentioned in Scripture, but there are predictions doubtless referring to the misfortunes of
later princes until the second Persian
conquest.

Pharaoh's daughter. Three Egyptian princesses, daughters of Pharaohs,
are mentioned in the Bible :—1. The pre-

EGYPTIAN PRINCESS.

server of Moses, daughter of the
Pharaoh who first oppressed the Israelites. Ex. 2 : 5–10. Josephus gives her
name as *Thermuthis* and Eusebius as
Merris.

2. Bithiah, wife of Mered, an Israelite,
daughter of a Pharaoh of an uncertain
period. 1 Chron. 4 : 18.

3. A wife of Solomon. 1 Kings 3 : 1;
7 : 8; 9 : 24.

Pharaoh, The wife of. The wife
of one Pharaoh, the king who received
Hadad the Edomite, is mentioned in
Scripture. She is called " queen," and
her name, Tahpenes, is given. [TAH-
PENES; PHARAOH, 6.]

Pha′res (fă′rĕz), **Pha′rez** or **Pe′rez,**
the son of Judah. Matt. 1 : 3; Luke 3 :
33.

Pha′rez (Perez, 1 Chron. 27 : 3; Pha-
res, Matt. 1 : 3; Luke 3 : 33, the twin
son, with Zarah or Zerah, of Judah
and Tamar his daughter-in-law. The
circumstances of his birth are detailed
in Gen. 38. Pharez occupied the rank
of Judah's second son, and from two of
his sons sprang two new chief houses,
those of the Hezronites and Hamulites.
From Hezron's second son Ram, or
Aram, sprang David and the kings of

Judah, and eventually Jesus Christ. Ruth 4 : 18. In the reign of David the house of Pharez seems to have been eminently distinguished.

Phar'isees, a religious party or school among the Jews at the time of Christ, so called from *perîshîn,* the Aramaic form of the Hebrew word *perûshim,* "the separated ones." The name may have been given them by their enemies,—it is not certain. It indicates a separation from other Israelites as well as from the Gentiles. A name they gave themselves was *Haberim* "associates." The chief sects among the Jews were the *Pharisees,* the *Sadducees* and the *Essenes,* who may be described respectively as the Formalists, the Freethinkers and the Puritans. A knowledge of the opinions and practices of the Pharisees at the time of Christ is of great importance for entering deeply into the genius of the Christian religion. A cursory perusal of the Gospels is sufficient to show that Christ's teaching was in some respects thoroughly antagonistic to theirs. He denounced them in the bitterest language; see Matt. 5 : 20; 15 : 7, 8; 16 : 6, 11, 12; 23 : 5, 13, 14, 15, 23; Mark 7 : 6; Luke 11 : 42–44. To understand the Pharisees is by contrast an aid toward understanding the spirit of uncorrupted Christianity.

1. They were founded in the period just before the Maccabæan War, as a protest against the Hellenistic influence that was becoming very strong. After obtaining religious freedom they withdrew from the other patriotic parties, to assure themselves of the complete separation. Surviving the Temple and the State they bent their energies to a strict keeping of the law, using political means for its preservation when it seemed to them wise. Their excessive strictness led them to formulate more detailed rules, originally as exegesis of the Law of Moses, later as binding as the original law itself. The first portion of the Talmud, called the Mishna or "second law," contains this additional, or oral law. It is a digest of the Jewish traditions and a compendium of the whole ritual law, and it came at length to be esteemed far above the sacred text.

2. While it was the aim of Jesus to call men to the law of God itself as the supreme guide of life, the Pharisees, upon the pretence of maintaining it intact, multiplied minute precepts and distinctions to such an extent that the whole life of the Israelite was hemmed in and burdened on every side by instructions so numerous and trifling that the law was almost if not wholly lost sight of. These "traditions," as they were called, had long been gradually accumulating. Of the trifling character of these regulations innumerable instances are to be found in the Mishna. Such were their washings before they could eat bread, and the special minuteness with which the forms of this washing were prescribed; their bathing when they returned from the market; their washing of cups, pots, brazen vessels, etc.; their fastings twice in the week, Luke 18 : 12; such were their tithings, Matt. 23 : 23; and such, finally, were those minute and vexatious extensions of the law of the Sabbath which must have converted God's gracious ordinance of the Sabbath's rest into a burden and a pain. Matt. 12 : 1–13; Mark 3 : 1–6; Luke 13 : 10–17. See also Matt. 15 : 2, 3, 5, for Jesus' teaching.

3. It was a leading aim of the Redeemer to teach men that true piety consisted not in forms, but in substance, not in outward observances, but in an inward spirit. The whole system of Pharisaic piety led to exactly opposite conclusions. Jesus taught humility; but the Pharisees sought mainly to attract the attention and to excite the admiration of men. Matt. 6 : 2, 5, 16; 23 : 5, 6; Luke 14 : 7. Indeed the whole spirit of their religion was summed up, not in confession of sin and in humility, but in a proud self-righteousness at variance with any true conception of man's relation to either God or his fellow creatures.

4. They looked with contempt upon every nation but their own, Luke 10; 29, and included in this contempt the common people of their own nation, and the Sadducees. Finally, instead of endeavoring to fulfil the great end of the dispensation whose truths they professed to teach, and thus bringing men to the Hope of Israel, they devoted their energies to making converts to their own narrow views, who with all the zeal of proselytes were more exclusive and more bitterly opposed to the truth than they were themselves. Matt. 23 : 15.

5. The Pharisees at an early day secured the popular favor, and thereby acquired considerable political influence. In the time of Christ they were the religious power in Palestine, though the priesthood belonged to the sect of the

Sadducees. They took a prominent part in the death of Jesus. Mark 3 : 6; John 11 : 47-57. From that time began their decline. The bulk of the common people believed as the Pharisees, but they themselves were a "close" association, numbering about 6000 to 7000.

6. One of the fundamental doctrines of the Pharisees was a *belief in a future state*. They appear to have believed in a resurrection of the dead, very much in the same sense as the early Christians. They also believed in predestination and free will, much as St. Paul taught those doctrines.

7. It is proper to add that it would be a great mistake to suppose that the Pharisees were wealthy and luxurious, much more that they had degenerated into vice. Josephus compared the Pharisees to the sect of the Stoics. He says that they lived frugally, in no respect giving in to luxury. We are not to suppose that there were not many individuals among them who were upright and pure, for there were such men as Nicodemus, Gamaliel, Joseph of Arimathæa and Paul. See Acts 5 : 34; 23 : 6; 26 : 5-7; Phil. 3 : 5.

Pha'rosh (fā'rŏsh). Ezra 8 : 3. [See PAROSH.]

Phar'par (fär'par) (*swift*), the second of the "two rivers of Damascus" —Abana and Pharpar—alluded to by Naaman. 2 Kings 5 : 12. There is still doubt as to the identity of the Pharpar. It is commonly believed, however, that of the two principal streams now found in the district of Damascus, the *Barada* and the *Awaj*, the former is the Abana and the latter the Pharpar. The Awaj rises on the southeast slopes of Hermon, and flows into the most southerly of the three lakes or swamps of Damascus.

Phar'zites (fär'zītes), **The**, the descendants of Parez the son of Judah. Num. 26 : 20.

Phase'ah (fà-sē'ah). Neh. 7 : 51. [PASEAH, 2.]

Phe'be (fē'bè). [PHŒBE.]

Pheni'ce (fé-nī'sè) (Acts 27 : 12, more properly Phœnix, as it is translated in the Revised Version), the name of a haven in Crete on the south coast. It is the modern *Lutró*. [See PHŒNICE; PHŒNICIA.]

Phi'col (fī'kol), chief captain of the army of Abimelech, king of the Philistines of Gerar in the days of both Abraham, Gen. 21 : 22, 32, and Isaac, Gen. 26 : 26.

Philadel'phia (*brotherly love*), a town in the eastern part of Lydia, 28 miles southeast of Sardis, and built by Attalus II, king of Pergamos, who died B.C. 138. It was situated on the lower slopes of Tmolus, and is still represented by a town called *Ala-shehr*, "the reddish city." (By a mistake due to ignorance of Turkish, older travelers reported its name as Allah-shehr, city of God.) Its elevation is 650 feet above the sea. The original population of Philadelphia seems to have been Macedonian; but there was, as appears from Rev. 3 : 9, a synagogue of Hellenizing Jews there, as well as a Christian church. It was the seat of one of "the seven churches of Asia." Strabo describes the locality as subject to constant earthquakes, which rendered even the town walls of Philadelphia unsafe. This is however deemed an exaggeration by those who have lived there in modern times. The ancient walls are still standing and many of the buildings. The church was highly commended. Rev. 3 : 7-13. Even Gibbon bears the following well-known testimony to the truth of the prophecy, "Because thou hast kept the word of my patience, I also will keep thee in the hour of temptation": "At a distance from the sea, forgotten by the (Greek) emperor, encompassed on all sides by the Turks, her valiant citizens defended their religion and freedom above fourscore years. Among the Greek colonies and churches of Asia, Philadelphia is still erect, a column in a scene of ruins." The modern town has about 21,000 inhabitants, a large proportion Christian. A few ruins are found, including remains of a wall and about twenty-five churches. In one place are four strong marble pillars, which once supported the dome of a church. One of the old mosques is believed by the native Christians to have been the church in which assembled the primitive Christians addressed in the Apocalypse. It is in the part of Asia left under the control of Turkey by the arrangements at the close of the World War.

Phile'mon (fī-lē'mon), the name of the Christian to whom Paul addressed his epistle in behalf of Onesimus. He was a native probably of Colosse, or at all events lived in that city when the apostle wrote to him: first, because

Onesimus was a Colossian, Col. 4:9; and secondly, because Archippus was a Colossian, Col. 4:17, whom Paul associates with Philemon at the beginning of his letter. Phil. 1, 2. Apphia may have been his wife, and Archippus his son. It is evident from the letter to him that Philemon was a man of property and influence, since he is represented as the head of a numerous household, and as exercising an expensive liberality toward his friends and the poor in general. It is probable that his conversion took place during Paul's stay at Ephesus (Acts 19:10), for Paul's work there doubtless extended to the cities of the valley of the Lycus of which Colosse was one. It is evident that on becoming a disciple he gave no common proof of the sincerity and power of his faith. His character, as shadowed forth in the epistle to him, is one of the noblest which the sacred record makes known to us.

Philemon, The Epistle of Paul to, is one of the letters which the apostle wrote during his first captivity at Rome, A.D. 62 or early in A.D. 63. Nothing is wanted to confirm the genuineness of the epistle: the external testimony is unimpeachable; nor does the epistle itself offer anything to conflict with this decision. The occasion of the letter was that Onesimus, a slave of Philemon, had run away from him to Rome, either desiring liberty or, as some suppose, having committed theft. Phil. 18. Here he was converted under the instrumentality of Paul. The latter, intimately connected with the master and the servant, was naturally anxious to effect a reconciliation between them. He used his influence with Onesimus, ver. 12, to induce him to return to Colosse and place himself again at the disposal of his master. On his departure, Paul put into his hand this letter as evidence that Onesimus was a true and approved disciple of Christ, and entitled as such to be received, not as a servant, but above a servant, as a brother in the faith. The Epistle to Philemon has some peculiar features, which distinguish it from all the other epistles. It is a strictly private letter written to an individual friend. The writer had peculiar difficulties to overcome; but Paul, it is confessed, has shown a degree of self-denial and a tact in dealing with them which in being equal to the occasion could hardly be greater.

Phile'tus (fīlē'tus) (*worthy of love*), possibly a disciple of Hymenæus, with whom he is associated in 2 Tim. 2:17, and who is named without him in an earlier epistle. 1 Tim. 1:20 (A.D. 58-64.) They appear to have been persons who believed the Scriptures of the Old Testament, but misinterpreted them, allegorizing away the doctrine of the resurrection, and resolving it all into figure and metaphor. The delivering over unto Satan is not fully understood. It was probably the highest form of excommunication where the person was not only cut off from Christian privileges, but also subject to suffering or even death. It was only pronounced by an apostle, or one especially delegated by him. 1 Cor. 5:3-5. See also analogous cases, Acts 5 and 13:11.

Phil'ip (fîl'ĭp) (*lover of horses*) **the apostle** was of Bethsaida, the city of Andrew and Peter, John 1:44, and apparently was among the Galilean peasants of that district who flocked to hear the preaching of the Baptist. The statement that Jesus *found* him, John 1:43, implies a previous seeking. In the lists of the twelve apostles, in the Synoptic Gospel, his name is as uniformly at the head of the second group of four as the name of Peter is at that of the first, Matt. 10:3; Mark 3:18; Luke 6:14. Philip apparently was among the first company of disciples who were with the Lord at the commencement of his ministry, at the marriage at Cana, on his first appearance as a prophet in Jerusalem. John 2. He it was who brought to Jesus his friend Nathanael. The first three Gospels tell us nothing more of him individually. St. John, with his characteristic fullness of personal reminiscences, records a few significant utterances. John 6:5-9; 12:20-22; 14:8. He is among the company of disciples at Jerusalem after the ascension, Acts 1:13, and on the day of Pentecost. After this all is uncertain and apocryphal. According to tradition, he preached in Phrygia, and died at Hierapolis.

Phil'ip the evangelist was one of the seven "deacons" appointed to superintend the daily distribution of food and alms among the disciples (Acts 6), and so to remove all suspicion of partiality. The persecution of which Saul was the leader must have stopped the "daily ministrations" of the Church. The teachers who had been most prominent were compelled to take flight, and Philip was among them. It is noticeable that the city of Samaria is the first scene of his activity. Acts 8. He is the precursor of St. Paul in his work, as Stephen had been in his teaching. The scene which brings Philip and Simon the sorcerer into contact with each other, Acts 8 : 9–13, in which the magician has to acknowledge a power over nature greater than his own, is interesting. This step is followed by another. On the road from Jerusalem to Gaza he meets the Ethiopian eunuch. Acts 8 : 26 ff. The history that follows is interesting as one of the few records in the New Testament of the process of individual conversion. A brief sentence tells us that Philip continued his work as a preacher at Azotus (Ashdod) and among the other cities that had formerly belonged to the Philistines, and, following the coast-line, came to Cæsarea. Then for a long period—nearly or quite twenty years—we lose sight of him. The last glimpse of him in the New Testament is in the account of St. Paul's journey to Jerusalem. It is to his house, as to one well known to them, that St. Paul and his companions turn for shelter. He has four daughters, who possess the gift of prophecy, and who apparently give themselves to the work of teaching instead of entering on the life of home. Acts 21 : 8, 9. He is visited by the prophets and elders of Jerusalem. One tradition places the scene of his death at Hierapolis in Phrygia. According to another, he died bishop of Tralles. The house in which he and his daughters had lived was pointed out to travelers in the time of Jerome.

Phil'ip Her'od I., II. [HEROD.]

Philip'pi (fĭ-lĭp'pī) (named from Philip of Macedonia), a city of Macedonia, about nine miles from the sea, so near Thrace it is often spoken of as Thracian and twelve miles distant from its port Neapolis, the modern *Kavalla*. The Philippi which St. Paul visited was a Roman colony founded by Augustus after the famous battle of Philippi, fought here between Antony and Octavius and Brutus and Cassius, B.C. 42. The remains which strew the ground near the small modern village of *Bereketli* are no doubt derived from that city. Philip, when he acquired possession of the site, found there a town named *Krenides*, perhaps from the

swampy character of the land south of the town. The plain in which it lies is of extraordinary fertility. The position, too, was on the main road from Rome to Asia, the *Via Egnatia*, which from Thessalonica to Constantinople followed the same course as the existing post-road. On St. Paul's visits to Philippi, see the following article. At Philippi the gospel was first preached in Europe. Lydia was the first convert. Here too Paul and Silas were imprisoned. Acts 16 : 23. The Philippians sent contributions to Paul to relieve his temporal wants.

Philippians (fĭ-lĭp'pĭanṣ), **Epistle to the,** was written by St. Paul from Rome in A.D. 62 or 63. St. Paul's connection with Philippi was of a peculiar character, which gave rise to the writing of this epistle. St. Paul entered its walls A.D. 52. Acts 16 : 12. There, at a greater distance from Jerusalem than any apostle had yet penetrated, the long-restrained energy of St. Paul was again employed in laying the foundation of a Christian church. Philippi was endeared to St. Paul not only by the hospitality of Lydia, the deep sympathy of the converts, and the remarkable miracle which set a seal on his preaching, but also by the successful exercise of his missionary activity after a long suspense, and by the happy consequences of his undaunted endurance of ignominies which remained in his memory, Philip. 1 : 30, after the long interval of eleven years. Leaving Timothy and Luke to watch over the infant church, Paul and Silas went to Thessalonica, 1 Thess. 2 : 2, whither they were followed by the alms of the Philippians. Philip. 4 : 16, and thence southward. After the lapse of five years, spent chiefly at Corinth and Ephesus, St. Paul passed through Macedonia, A.D. 57, on his way to Greece, and probably visited Philippi for the second time, and was there joined by Timothy. On returning from Greece, Acts 20 : 4, he again found a refuge among his faithful Philippians, where he spent some days at Easter, A.D. 57, with St. Luke, who accompanied him when he sailed from Neapolis. Once more, in his Roman captivity, A.D. 62, their care of him revived again. They sent Epaphroditus, bearing their alms for the apostle's support, and ready also to tender his personal service. Philip. 2 : 25. Strangely full of joy and thanksgiving amidst adversity, like the apostle's midnight hymn from the depth of his Philippian dungeon, this epistle went forth from his prison at Rome. "His letter," writes Farrar, "is like one of those magnificent pieces of music which, amid all its stormy fugues, and mighty discords, is dominated by some inner note of triumph which at last bursts forth into irresistible and glorious victory. It is new and marvellous, dictated by a worn and fettered Jew, of feeble frame, in afflicted circumstances, a victim of gross perjury, and bitter wrongs.

"It is a genuine and simple letter, the warm, spontaneous, loving effusion of a heart which could express itself with unreserved affection to a most kind and beloved church."

Philis'tia (fĭ-lĭs'tyȧ). The word thus translated (in Ps. 60:8; 87:4; 108:9) is in the original identical with that elsewhere rendered Palestine, which always means land of the Philistines. Philistia was the plain on the southwest coast of Palestine. It was 40 or 50 miles long on the coast of the Mediterranean from the desert of Shur to the plain of Sharon, and 10 miles wide at the northern end and 20 at the southern. This plain has been in all ages remarkable for the extreme richness of its soil. It was also adapted to the growth of military power; for while the plain itself permitted the use of war-chariots, which were the chief arm of offence, the occasional elevations which rise out of it offered secure sites for towns and strongholds. It was, moreover, a commercial country: from its position it must have been at all times the great thoroughfare between Phœnicia and Syria in the north and Egypt and Arabia in the south.

Philis'tines (fĭ-lĭs'tĭns) (perhaps *immigrants*). The origin of the Philistines is nowhere expressly stated in the Bible; but as the prophets describe them as "the Philistines from Caphtor," Amos 9:7, and "the remnant of the maritime district of Caphtor," Jer. 47:4, it is *prima facie* probable that they were the "Caphtorim which came out of Caphtor" who expelled the Avim from their territory and occupied it in their place, Deut. 2:23; and that these again were the Caphtorim mentioned in the Mosaic genealogical table among the descendants of Mizraim. Gen. 10:14. It is generally thought that Caphtor represents Crete, and that the Philistines mi-

grated from that island, either directly or through Egypt, into Palestine. [CAPHTOR.]

History.—The Philistines must have settled in the land of Canaan before the time of Abraham; for they are noticed in his day as a pastoral tribe in the neighborhood of Gerar. Gen. 21:32, 34; 26:1, 8. Between the times of Abraham and Joshua the Philistines had changed their quarters, and had advanced northward into the plain of Philistia. The Philistines had at an early period attained proficiency in the arts of peace. Their wealth was abundant, Judges 16:5, 18, and they appear in all respects to have been a prosperous people. Possessed of such elements of power, they had attained in the time of the judges an important position among eastern nations. About B.C. 1200 we find them engaged in successful war with the Sidonians. Justin xviii. 3. The territory of the Philistines, having been once occupied by the Canaanites, formed a portion of the promised land, and was assigned to the tribe of Judah. Josh. 15:2, 12, 45–47. No portion of it, however, was conquered in the lifetime of Joshua, Josh. 13:2, and even after his death no permanent conquest was effected, Judges 3:3, though we are informed that the three cities of Gaza, Ashkelon and Ekron were taken. Judges 1:18. The Philistines soon recovered these, and commenced an aggressive policy against the Israelites, by which they gained a complete ascendency over them. Individual heroes were raised up from time to time, such as Shamgar the son of Anath, Judges 3:31, and still more Samson, Judges 13–16; but neither of these men succeeded in permanently throwing off the yoke. They conquered the Israelites in the time of Eli, and captured the Ark. 1 Sam. 4:17. Samuel defeated them at Ebenezer (1 Sam. 7:7–14) and they "came no more into the borders of Israel" during the chief magistracy of Samuel. Nor were they after this to dispossess the Israelites of any of their territory. In the time of Saul they were very formidable. He defeated them at Geba, and Michmash (1 Sam. 13:1–23; 14:47, 52). After this the battles were very numerous. Goliath, their champion, was killed by the youthful David. When David's life was threatened by Saul he took refuge among the Philistines. The border warfare was continued. The scene of the next great conflict was far to the north, in the valley of Esdraelon. The battle on this occasion proved disastrous to the Israelites; Saul himself perished, and the Philistines penetrated across the Jordan and occupied the forsaken cities. 1 Sam. 31: 1-7. During the early part of David's reign he no doubt paid them tribute, as did Ishbosheth his rival. But on the union of the kingdom, he twice attacked them, and on each occasion with signal success, in the first case capturing their images, in the second recovered their prestige. The Philistines are often mentioned in the time of the Divided Kingdom, but their power was waning. Some paid tribute to Jehoshaphat, but they invaded Judah under his successor. They were conquered by Assyria, regained their independence and reduced again to tribute by Tiglathpileser in the reign of Ahaz of Judah. From the time of Hezekiah, the possession of Philistia apparently became the turning-point of the struggle between the two great empires of the East. The

PHILISTINES.
Representation of Philistines on an Egyptian monument about the date of the Exodus.

pursuing them "from Geba until thou come to Gazer." 2 Sam. 5: 17-25; 1 Chron. 14: 8-16. Henceforth the Israelites appear as the aggressors. About seven years after the defeat at Rephaim, David, who had now consolidated his power, attacked them on their own soil, and took Gath with its dependencies. The whole of Philistia was included in Solomon's empire, obtaining its independence on the separation at the time of Rehoboam. But they never Assyrians, under the general of Sargon, made an expedition against Egypt, and took Ashdod, as the key of that country. Isa. 20: 1, 4, 5. Under Sennacherib Philistia was again the scene of important operations. It seems probable that the Assyrians retained their hold on Ashdod until its capture, after a long siege, by Psammetichus. It was about this time that Philistia was traversed by a vast Scythian horde on their way to Egypt. The Egyptian ascendency was not as yet re-established, for we find the next king, Necho, compelled to besiege Gaza on his return from the battle of Megiddo. After the death of Necho the contest was renewed between the Egyptians and the Chaldeans under Nebuchadnezzar, and the result was specially disastrous to the Philistines. The "old hatred" that the Philistines bore to the Jews was exhibited in acts of hostility at the time of the Babylonish captivity, Ezek. 25: 15–17; but on the return this was somewhat abated, for some of the Jews married Philistian women, to the great scandal of their rulers. Neh. 13: 23, 24. From this time the history of Philistia is absorbed in the struggles of the neighboring kingdoms. The latest notices of the Philistines as a nation occur in 1 Macc. 3–5.

Institutions, religion, etc.—With regard to the institutions of the Philistines our information is very scanty. The five chief cities had, as early as the days of Joshua, constituted themselves into a confederacy, restricted however, in all probability, to matters of offence and defence. Each was under the government of a prince, Josh. 13: 3; Judges 3: 3, etc.; 1 Sam. 18: 30; 29: 6, and each possessed its own territory. The Philistines appear to have been deeply imbued with superstition: they carried their idols with them on their campaigns, 2 Sam. 5: 21, and proclaimed their victories in their presence. 1 Sam. 31: 9. The gods whom they chiefly worshipped were Dagon, Judges 16: 23; 1 Sam. 5: 3–5; 1 Chron. 10: 10; Ashtaroth, 1 Sam. 31: 10, and Baalzebub, 2 Kings 1: 2–6.

Philol′ogus (fĭ-lŏl′o-gŭs), a Christian at Rome to whom St. Paul sends his salutation. Rom. 16: 15.

Phin′ehas (fĭn′e-has). 1. Son of Eleazar and grandson of Aaron. Ex. 6: 25. He is memorable for having while quite a youth, by his zeal and energy at the critical moment of the licentious idolatry of Shittim, appeased the divine wrath, and put a stop to the plague which was destroying the nation. Num. 25: 7. (B.C. 1452.) For this he was rewarded by the special approbation of Jehovah, and by a promise that the priesthood should remain in his family forever. Num. 25: 10–13. He was appointed to accompany as priest the expedition by which the Midianites were destroyed, Num. 31: 6. Many years

later he also headed the party which was despatched from Shiloh to remonstrate against the altar which the transjordanic tribes were reported to have built near Jordan. Josh. 22: 13–32. In the partition of the country he received an allotment of his own—a hill on Mount Ephraim which bore his name. After Eleazar's death he became high priest—the third of the series. During his high priesthood came the civil war with Benjamin. Judges 20: 28. The verse which closes the book of Joshua is ascribed by tradition to Phinehas, as the description of the death of Moses at the end of Deuteronomy is to Joshua. The tomb of Phinehas, a place of great resort to both Jews and Samaritans, is shown at *Awertah,* four miles southeast of *Nablûs.*

2. Second son of Eli. 1 Sam. 1: 3; 2: 34; 4: 4, 11, 17, 19; 14: 3. Phinehas was killed with his brother by the Philistines when the ark was captured. [ELI.]

3. A Levite of Ezra's time, Ezra 8: 33.

Phle′gon (flē′gon) (*burning*), a Christian at Rome whom St. Paul salutes. Rom. 16: 14. (A.D. 57.) Pseudo-Hippolytus makes him one of the seventy disciples and bishop of Marathon.

Phœ′be (fē′bė) (*radiant*), the first and one of the most important of the Christian persons the detailed mention of whom fills nearly all the last chapter of the Epistle to the Romans. (A.D. 57.) What is said of her, Rom. 16: 1, 2, is worthy of special notice because of its bearing on the question of the deaconesses of the apostolic Church.

Phœni′ce, Phœnic′ia (fė-nĭsh′yà), a tract of country, of which Tyre and Sidon were the principal cities, to the north of Palestine, along the coast of the Mediterranean Sea; bounded by that sea on the west, and by the mountain range of Lebanon on the east. The name was not the one by which its native inhabitants called it, but was given to it by the Greeks. Its derivation is variously given, the most common of the older opinions being from the word for *palm tree.* The native name of Phœnicia was *Kenaan* (Canaan) or *Knâ,* signifying lowland, so named in contrast to the adjoining *Aram,* i. e. highland, the Hebrew name of Syria. The length of coast to which the name of Phœnicia was applied varied at different times. It is generally considered as extending from the pass called the

Ladder of Tyre, about 14 miles south of Tyre, to Arvad or Aradus on the north, a distance of 125 miles. Its breadth, between Lebanon and the sea, never exceeded 20 miles, and was generally much less. The whole of Phœnicia proper is well watered by various streams from the adjoining hills. The havens of Tyre and Sidon afforded water of sufficient depth for all the requirements of ancient navigation, and the neighboring range of the Lebanon, in its extensive forests, furnished what then seemed a nearly inexhaustible supply of timber for ship-building.

Language and race.—The Phœnicians spoke a branch of the Semitic language closely allied to Hebrew, Moabitish and others. Concerning the original race to which the Phœnicians belonged, nothing can be known with certainty, because they are found already established along the Mediterranean Sea at the earliest dawn of authentic history, and for centuries afterward there is no record of their origin. According to Herodotus, vii. 89, they said of themselves that they dwelt originally by the Erythræan Sea, that is the Indian Ocean. While this is not improbable neither the truth nor the falsehood of the tradition can now be proved. But there is one point respecting their race which can be proved to be in the highest degree probable, and which has peculiar interest as bearing on the Jews, viz., that the Phœnicians were of the same race as the Canaanites.

Commerce, etc.—Phœnicia was famous for its commerce and its colonies. The most ancient sailing expedition undertaken by an Egyptian king was manned and directed by Phœnicians. Since they were by far the most skilful navigators of the time they had almost a monopoly of such trade as required the use of ships. In regard to Phœnician trade, connected with the Israelites, it must be recollected that up to the time of David not one of the twelve tribes seems to have possessed a single harbor on the seacoast; it was impossible therefore that they could become a commercial people. But from the time that David had conquered Edom, an opening for trade was afforded to the Israelites. Solomon continued this trade with its king, obtained timber from its territory and employed its sailors and workmen. 2 Sam. 5 : 11; 1 Kings 5 : 9, 17, 18. The most famous of the Phœnician colonies

was Carthage on the northern coast of Africa, famous in Roman history. But other colonies, or trading posts were scattered over the islands and shores of the Mediterranean Sea.

The religion of the Phœnicians was a pantheistical personification of the forces of nature, and in its most philosophical shadowing forth of the supreme powers it may be said to have represented the male and female principles of production. In its popular form it was especially a worship of the sun, moon and five planets, or, as it might have been expressed according to ancient notions, of the seven planets—the most beautiful and perhaps the most natural form of idolatry ever presented to the human imagination. Their worship was a constant temptation for the Hebrews to Polytheism and idolatry.—1. Because undoubtedly the Phœnicians, as a great commercial people, were more generally intelligent, and as we should now say civilized, than the inland agricultural population of Palestine, and from that cause would naturally exercise a strong influence over them. 2. The worship of the Phœnicians was essentially demoralizing though in some ways attractive. Feasts were associated with religious rites. Sacred prostitution and the resulting licentiousness was common. On important occasions human sacrifices were offered.

The only other fact respecting the Phœnicians that need be mentioned here is that the invention of letters was universally asserted by the Greeks and Romans to have been communicated by the Phœnicians to the Greeks. For further details respecting the Phœnicians, see TYRE and ZIDON.

Phryg′ia (frĭj′ĭá). This word was rather ethnological than political, and denoted, in a vague manner, the western part of the central region of that peninsula. Accordingly, in two of the three places where it is used it is mentioned in a manner not intended to be precise. Acts 16 : 6; 18 : 23. By Phrygia we must understand an extensive district in Asia Minor, which contributed portions to several Roman provinces, and varying portions at different times. All over this district the Jews were probably numerous. The Phrygians were a very ancient people, and were supposed to be among the aborigines of Asia Minor. Several bishops from Phrygia were present at the Councils of

Nice, A.D. 325, and of Constantinople, A.D. 381, showing the prevalence of Christianity at that time.

Phu'rah (fū'rah) (*bough*), Gideon's servant, probably his armor-bearer, comp. 1 Sam. 14:1, who accompanied him in his midnight visit to the camp of the Midianites. Judges 7:10, 11.

Phut (fŭt), **Put,** the third name in the list of the sons of Ham, Gen. 10:6; 1 Chron. 1:8, elsewhere applied to an African country or people. The few mentions of Phut in the Bible clearly indicate a country or people of Africa, and, it must be added, probably not far from Egypt. Isa. 66:19; Jer. 46:9; Ezek. 27:10; 30:5; 38:5; Nah. 3:9. Some identify it with Libya, in the northern part of Africa, near the Mediterranean Sea; others argue strongly for "Punt" a name often found in Egyptian inscriptions. This comprised the whole African coast of the Red Sea, and was tributary to Egypt.

Phu'vah (fū'vah) (*mouth*), one of the sons of Issachar, Gen. 46:13, and founder of the family of the Punites.

Phygel'lus (fī'jĕl'lus) (*fugitive*). A man named with Hermogenes in 2 Tim. 1:15. [HERMOGENES.] R. V. Phygelus.

Phylactery. [FRONTLETS.]

Pi-be'seth (pī-bē'sĕth), a town of lower Egypt, mentioned in Ezek. 30:17, the same as Bubastis, so named from the goddess Bastet. It was situated on the west bank of the Pelusiac branch of the Nile. It was probably a city of great importance when Ezekiel foretold its doom. It is now called *Tell Basta,* and is entirely deserted. It lies close to the large town Zagazig, which is on the railway, about 45 miles northeast of modern Cairo.

Picture. In two of the three passages in which "picture" is used in the Authorized Version it denotes idolatrous representations, either independent images or more usually stones "portrayed," *i. e.* sculptured in low relief, or engraved and colored. Ezek. 23:14; Layard, *Nin. and Bab.* ii. 306, 308. Movable pictures, in the modern sense, were doubtless unknown to the Jews. The "pictures of silver" of Prov. 25:11 were probably baskets, as in the R. V.

Piece of gold. The rendering "pieces of gold," as in 2 Kings 5:5, is very doubtful; and "shekels of gold," as designating the value of the whole quantity, not individual pieces, is pref-

erable. Coined money was unknown in Palestine till the Persian period.

Piece of silver. I. In the Old Testament the word "pieces" is used in the Authorized Version in connection with money, when it denotes a certain amount of precious metal whether coined or uncoined. The word piece is used because from its vagueness it would answer where the value was unknown. Gen. 20:16; 37:28; 45:22; Judges 9:4; 16:5; 2 Kings 6:25; Hos. 3:2; Zech. 11:12, 13. In similar passages the word "shekels" occurs in the Hebrew. There are other passages in which the Authorized Version supplies the word "shekels" instead of "pieces," Deut. 22:19, 29; Judges 17:2, 3, 4, 10; 2 Sam. 18:11, 12, and of these the first two are translated "shekel" in the R. V. The shekel, be it remembered, was the common weight for money, and therefore most likely to be understood in an elliptical phrase. For values see the tables in the APPENDIX. II. In the New Testament two words are rendered by the phrase "piece of silver:" 1. *Drachma,* Luke 15:8, 9, Greek silver coin, equivalent, at the time of St. Luke, to the Roman denarius (16 cents). 2. *Silver* occurs only in the account of the betrayal of our Lord for "thirty pieces of silver." Matt. 26:15; 27:3, 5, 6, 9. Probably here shekels are intended.

Piety. This word occurs but once in the Authorized Version: "Let them learn first to show *piety* at home," better, "toward their own household" or family. 1 Tim. 5:4. It is used here probably in the sense of filial piety, dutifulness in the family, which is a familiar meaning of the Latin *pretas* and *pius* (cf. Pius Æneas of Vergil.)

Pigeon. [TURTLE-DOVE.]

Pi-hahi'roth (pī'ha-hī'roth), a place before or beside which the Israelites encamped, at the close of the third march from Rameses (the last place before they crossed the Red Sea), when they went out of Egypt. Ex. 14:2, 9; Num. 33:7, 8. It is an Egyptian word, perhaps signifying "the place where sedge grows."

Pi'late (pī'lat) (*armed with a spear*), **Pon'tius.** Pontius Pilate was the fifth Roman procurator of Judea, and under him our Lord worked, suffered and died, as we learn not only from Scripture, but from Tacitus (*Ann.* xv. 44). He was appointed A.D. 25–6, in the twelfth year of Tiberius. His arbitrary administration nearly drove the Jews to insurrection on several occasions. One of his first acts was to remove the headquarters of the army from Cæsarea to Jerusalem. The soldiers of course took with them their standards, bearing the image of the emperor, into the holy city. No previous governor had ventured on such an outrage. The people poured down in crowds to Cæsarea, where the procurator was then residing, and besought him to remove the images. After five days of discussion he gave the signal to some concealed soldiers to surround the petitioners and put them to death unless they ceased to trouble him; but this only strengthened their determination, and they declared themselves ready rather to submit to death than forego their resistance to an idolatrous innovation. Pilate then

COINS STRUCK BY PONTIUS PILATE.

yielded, and the standards were by his orders brought down to Cæsarea. His slaughter of certain Galileans, Luke 13: 1, led to some remarks from our Lord on the connection between sin and calamity. It must have occurred at some feast at Jerusalem, in the outer court of the temple. It was the custom for the procurators to reside at Jerusalem during the great feasts, and accordingly, at the time of our Lord's last Passover, Pilate was occupying his official residence in Herod's palace. The history of his condemnation of our Lord is familiar to all. We learn from Josephus that Pilate's anxiety to avoid giving offence to Cæsar did not save him from political disaster. The Samaritans were unquiet and rebellious; Pilate led his troops against them, and defeated them easily enough. The Samaritans complained to Vitellius, then president of Syria, and he sent Pilate to Rome to

answer their accusations before the emperor. When he reached it he found Tiberius dead and Caius (Caligula) on the throne, A.D. 37. Eusebius adds that soon afterward, "wearied with misfortunes," he killed himself. As to the scene of his death there are various traditions. One is that he was banished to Vienna Allobrogum (Vienne on the Rhone), where a singular monument— a pyramid on a quadrangular base, 52 feet high—is called Pontius Pilate's tomb. Another is that he sought to hide his sorrows on the mountain by the lake of Lucerne, now called Mount Pilatus; and there, after spending years in its recesses, in remorse and despair rather than penitence, plunged into the dismal lake which occupies its summit.

Pil′dash (pĭl′dăsh), one of the eight sons of Nahor, Abraham's brother, by his wife and niece, Milcah. Gen. 22: 22.

Pil′eha (pĭl′e-hà) (*ploughing*), the name of one of the chief of the people, probably a family, who signed the covenant with Nehemiah. Neh. 10: 24.

Pillar. The notion of a pillar is of a shaft or isolated pile, either supporting or not supporting a roof. But perhaps the earliest application of the pillar was the votive or monumental. This in early times consisted of nothing but a single stone or pile of stones. Gen. 28: 18; 31: 45, etc. The stone Ezel, 1 Sam. 20: 19, was probably a terminal stone or a waymark. The "place" set up by Saul, 1 Sam. 15: 12, is explained by St. Jerome to be a trophy. So also Jacob set up a pillar over Rachel's grave. Gen. 35: 20. The monolithic tombs and obelisks of Petra are instances of similar usage. Lastly, the figurative use of the term "pillar," in reference to the cloud and fire accompanying the Israelites on their march, or as in Cant. 3: 6 and Rev. 10: 1, is plainly derived from the notion of an isolated column not supporting a roof.

Pillar, Plain of the, or rather "oak of the pillar" (that being the real signification of the Hebrew word *elôn*), a tree which stood near Shechem, and at which the men of Shechem and the house of Millo assembled to crown Abimelech the son of Gideon. Judges 9: 6.

Pilled, Gen. 30: 37, 38; "peeled," Isa. 18: 2; Ezek. 29: 18. The verb "to pill" appears in old English as identical in meaning with "to peel, to strip."

ROWS OF PILLARS (MASSEBAS) CONNECTED WITH THE CANAANITE RELIGIOUS PRACTICES, E.G., DEUT. XII, 3. FROM GEZER.

Pil'tai (pĭl'tā) (*deliverances*), the representative of the priestly house of Moadiah or Maadiah, in the time of Joiakim the son of Jeshua. Neh. 12:17. (B.C. about 500.)

Pine tree. 1. Heb. *tidhâr*. Isa. 41: 19; 60:13. What tree is intended is not certain; but the rendering "pine" seems least probable of any. 2. *Shemen*, Neh. 8:15, is the wild olive, or perhaps the "oil tree," including any resinous tree.

Pinnacle (of the temple), Matt. 4: 5; Luke 4:9. The Greek word ought to be rendered not *a* pinnacle, but *the* pinnacle. The only part of the temple which answered to the modern sense of pinnacle was the golden spikes erected on the roof to prevent birds from settling there. But they were many. Perhaps the word means the battlement ordered by law to be added to every roof. According to Alford and others, it was the roof of Herod's royal portico of the temple, "which overhung the ravine of Kedron from a dizzy height," perhaps 600 feet.

Pi'non (pī'non) (*darkness*), one of the "dukes" of Edom,—that is, head

AN EASTERN PINE.

or founder of a tribe of that nation. Gen. 36: 41; 1 Chron. 1: 52.

Pipe (Heb. *châlil*). The Hebrew word so rendered is derived from a root signifying "to bore, perforate," and is represented with sufficient correctness by the English "pipe" or "flute," as in the margin of 1 Kings 1: 40. The pipe was the type of perforated wind instruments, as the harp was of stringed instruments. It was made of reed, bronze or copper. It is one of the simplest, and therefore probably one of the oldest, of musical instruments. It is associated with the tabret as an instrument of a peaceful and social character. The pipe and tabret were used at the banquets of the Hebrews, Isa. 5: 12, and accompanied the simpler religious services when the young prophets, returning from the high place, caught their inspiration from the harmony, 1 Sam. 10: 5; or the pilgrims, on their way to the great festivals of their ritual, beguiled the weariness of the march with psalms sung to the simple music of the pipe. Isa. 30: 29. The sound of the pipe was apparently a soft wailing note, which made it appropriate to be used in mourning and at funerals, Matt. 9: 23, and in the lament of the prophet over the destruction of Moab, Jer. 48: 36. It was even used in the temple choir, as appears from Ps. 87: 7. In later times the funeral and death-bed were never without the professional pipers or flute-players, Matt. 9: 23, a custom which still exists. In the social and festive life of the Egyptians the pipe played as prominent a part as among the Hebrews.

Pi'ram (pī'ram) (*like a wild ass; fleet*), the Amorite king of Jarmuth at the time of Joshua's conquest of Canaan. Josh. 10: 3. (B.C. 1450.)

Pir'athon (pĭr'a-thŏn) (*nakedness*), "in the land of Ephraim in the mount of the Amalekite," a place in Judges 12: 15. It is generally identified with *Ferata* which is about 6 miles south west of Nablus (Shechem) though other positions are proposed.

Pir'athonite (pĭr'a-thon-īte), a native of or dweller in Pirathon. Two such are named in the Bible:—1. Abdon ben-Hillel. Judges 12: 13, 15. 2. "Benaiah the Pirathonite, of the children of Ephraim." 1 Chron. 27: 14.

Pis'gah (pĭz'gah) (*division*), Num. 21: 20; 23: 14; Deut. 3: 27; 34: 1, a mountain range or district, the same as, or a part of, that called the mountains of

Abarim. Comp. Deut. 32: 49 with 34: 1. It lay on the east of Jordan, contiguous to the field of Moab, and immediately opposite Jericho. Its highest point or summit—its "head"—was Mount Nebo. [See NEBO.]

Pisid'ia (pi-sid'ĭ-à) was a district in Asia Minor north of Pamphylia, east of Lycia and Caria, south of Phrygia, and west of Lycaonia, etc. "Antioch of Pisidia" was an important city, especially in Christian annals. St. Paul passed through Pisidia twice, with Barnabas, on the first missionary journey, *i. e.*, both in going from Perga to Iconium, Acts 13: 13, 14, 51, and in returning. Acts 14: 21, 24, 25; comp. 2 Tim. 3: 11. It is probable also that he traversed the northern part of the district, with Silas and Timotheus, on the second missionary journey, Acts 16: 6; but the word Pisidia does not occur except in reference to the former journey.

Pi'son. [EDEN.]

Pit. [HELL.]

Pitch. The three Hebrew words so translated all represent the same object, viz., mineral pitch or asphalt in its different aspects. Asphalt is an opaque, inflammable substance, which bubbles up from subterranean fountains in a liquid state, and hardens by exposure to the air, but readily melts under the influence of heat. In the latter state it is very tenacious, and was used as a cement in lieu of mortar in Babylonia, Gen. 11: 3, as well as for coating the outside of vessels, Gen. 6: 14, and particularly for making the papyrus boats of the Egyptians water-tight. Ex. 2: 3. The Jews and Arabians got their supply in large quantities from the Dead Sea, which hence received its classical name of *Lacus Asphaltites*.

Pitcher. This word is used in the Authorized Version to denote the earthen water-jars or pitchers with one or two handles, used chiefly by women for carrying water, as in the story of Rebekah. Gen. 24: 15-20; but see Mark 14: 13; Luke 22: 10. This mode of carrying has been and still is customary both in the East and elsewhere. The vessels used for the purpose are generally borne on the head or the shoulder. The Bedouin women commonly use skin bottles. Such was the "bottle" carried by Hagar. Gen. 21: 14. The same word is used of the pitchers employed by Gideon's three hundred men. Judges 7: 16.

Pi'thom (pī'thom) (*city of the god Tum* [the setting sun]), one of the store-cities built by the Israelites for the first oppressor, the Pharaoh "which knew not Joseph," Ex. 1:11. It is at *Tell el-Maskhuta* on the south side of the sweet-water canal running from Cairo to Suez. This was the Egyptian *Pi-Tum*, and was fixed by explorations in 1883. It is the Patumus of Herodotus (ii. 159), near which Necho constructed a canal from the Nile to the Arabian Gulf.

Pi'thon (pī'thon), one of the four sons of Micah, the son of Mephibosheth. 1 Chron. 8:35; 9:41.

Plague, The. The bubonic plague, the disease particularly called in English "*the* plague" is a highly malignant form of typhus, accompanied by buboes (tumors). Like the cholera, it is most violent at the first outbreak, causing almost instant death. It is pretty clearly proven that it is carried from one person or place to another by rats and other animals, and whether strictly contagious or not certainly becomes epidemic unless strict precautions are taken. It has been from time immemorial the scourge of Bible lands, and is found for the most part where for one reason or another the sanitary conditions are not carefully attended to. Several Hebrew words are translated "pestilence" or "plague;" but not one of these words can be considered as designating by its signification the disease now called the plague. Whether the disease be mentioned must be judged from the sense of passages, not from the sense of words. The pestilence which came at Kibroth-Hattaavah may have been brought by the quails themselves from an infected region (Num. 11:33), though there is nothing to exactly determine its nature. Some plagues sent as judgments may have been either other sudden diseases, or even miraculous in their nature. Other pestilences, although sent as judgments, have the characteristics of modern epidemics, not being rapid beyond nature nor directed against individuals. Lev. 26:25; Deut. 28:21. In neither of these passages does it seem certain that the plague is specified. The notices in the prophets present the same difficulty. Hezekiah's disease has been thought to have been the plague, and its fatal nature, as well as the mention of a boil, makes this not improbable. On the other hand, there is no mention of a pestilence among his people at the time.

Plagues, The ten. The occasion on which the plagues were sent is described in Ex. 3–12. When Moses and Aaron came before Pharaoh, a miracle was required of them. Then Aaron's rod became a serpent. The Egyptian magicians called by the king produced what seemed to be the same wonder, not an uncommon one among eastern jugglers, the serpent being rendered rigid like a rod, and then released. Aaron's rod swallowed up the others. Ex. 7:9–12. It is interesting to note that the first time a wonder was produced by Moses without giving previous notice, the magicians "did so with their enchantments," but failed; a fact which strengthens us in the inference that the magicians succeeded merely by juggling. 1. *The plague of blood.* After this warning to Pharaoh, Aaron, at the word of Moses, waved his rod over the Nile, and the river was turned into blood, with all its canals and reservoirs, and every vessel of water drawn from them; the fish died, and the river stank. The Egyptians could not drink of it, and digged around it for water. This plague was doubly humiliating to the religion of the country, as the Nile was held sacred, as well as some kinds of its fish, not to speak of the crocodiles, which probably were destroyed. Ex. 7:16–25. Those who have endeavored to explain this plague by natural causes have referred to the changes of color to which the Nile is subject, the appearance of the Red Sea, and the so-called rain and dew of blood of the middle ages; the last two occasioned by small fungi of very rapid growth. However, its definite duration of the seven days, and its sudden disappearance show it to be plainly miraculous.

2. *The plague of frogs.*—When seven days had passed after the first plague, the river and all the open waters of Egypt brought forth countless frogs, which not only covered the land, but filled the houses, even in their driest parts and vessels, for the ovens and kneading-troughs are specified. Ex. 8:1–15. In upper Egypt at least the Egyptians worshipped the frog-headed goddess Heka. So this too may be considered a blow at their religion.

3. *The plague of lice.*—The dry land was now smitten by the rod, and its very dust seemed turned into minute

noxious insects, so thickly did they swarm on man and beast. The scrupulous cleanliness of the Egyptians would add intolerably to the bodily distress of this plague, by which also they again incurred religious defilement. As to the species of the vermin, there is a question. The rendering "lice" is an ancient one, but no species now known ever attack both man or beast, nor do they generate in the dust. Other authorities speak of them as stinging flies—"sand flies or fleas" (R. V. mar.). the larvæ of which are found in dried pools. The magicians, who had imitated by their enchantments the two previous miracles, were now foiled. They struck the ground, as Aaron did, and repeated their own incantations, but it was without effect. Being themselves attacked, they called them the "finger of God" (that is of their gods). Ex. 8 : 16–19.

4. *The plague of flies.*—After the river and the land, the air was smitten, being filled with winged insects, which swarmed in the houses and devoured the land, but Goshen was exempted from the plague. The word translated "swarms of flies" is rendered in the Septuagint by "dog-flies." Flies of all sorts are very common in Egypt, and this may have been an extraordinary number of a comparatively common insect. Some suppose it to be the great Egyptian beetle, the *Scarabæus sacer,* an object of worship by the Egyptians. Ex. 8 : 20–32.

5. *The plague of the murrain of beasts.*—Still coming closer and closer to the Egyptians, God sent a disease upon the cattle, which were not only their property but their deities. At the precise time of which Moses forewarned Pharaoh, the cattle of the Egyptians were smitten with a murrain and died, but not one of the cattle of the Israelites suffered. Ex. 9 : 1–7.

6. *The plague of boils.*—From the cattle the hand of God was extended to the persons of the Egyptians. Moses and Aaron were commanded to take ashes of the furnace, and to "sprinkle it toward the heaven in the sight of Pharaoh." It was to become "small dust" throughout Egypt, and "be a boil breaking forth [with] blains upon man and upon beast." Ex. 9 : 8–12. This accordingly came to pass. It was some inflammatory sore on the surface of the body, painful and disgusting.

7. *The plague of hail.*—The account of the seventh plague is preceded by a warning which Moses was commanded to deliver to Pharaoh, respecting the terrible nature of the plagues that were to ensue if he remained obstinate. Man and beast were smitten, and the herbs and every tree broken, save in the land of Goshen. The ruin caused by the hail was evidently far greater than that effected by any of the earlier plagues. Hail is now extremely rare, but not unknown, in Egypt, and it is interesting that the narrative seems to imply that it sometimes falls there. Ex. 9 : 13–34.

8. *The plague of locusts.*—The severity of this plague can be well understood by those who have been in Egypt in a part of the country where a flight of locusts has alighted. In this case the plague was greater than an ordinary visitation, since it extended over a far wider space, rather than because it was more intense; for it is impossible to imagine any more complete destruction than that always caused by a swarm of locusts. Ex. 10 : 1–20.

9. *The plague of darkness.*—"There was a thick darkness in all the land of Egypt three days;" while "all the children of Israel had light in their dwellings." It has been illustrated by reference to the samoom and the hot wind of the Khamseen. The former is a sand-storm which occurs in the desert, seldom lasting more than a quarter of an hour or twenty minutes, but for the time often causing the darkness of twilight, and affecting man and beast. The hot wind of the Khamseen usually blows for three days and nights, and carries so much sand with it that it produces the appearance of a yellow fog, against which artificial light is of little use, and it certainly is "darkness which may be felt." Three days is not an uncommon duration for this storm. Ex. 10 : 21–29.

10. *The death of the first-born.*—Before the tenth plague Moses went to warn Pharaoh:—"Thus saith the Lord, About midnight will I go out into the midst of Egypt; and all the first-born in the land of Egypt shall die, from the first-born of Pharaoh that sitteth upon his throne, even to the first-born of the maidservant that is behind the mill; and all the first-born of beasts." Ex. 11 : 4, 5. While there have been historical instances of the sudden breaking out of a pestilence, and the existence at the same time of a cattle disease,—and

the plague is often worst directly after the Khamseen, still this was clearly miraculous both in its severity, and the singling out of the first-born. The history of the ten plagues strictly ends with the death of the first-born. The gradual increase in severity of the plagues is perhaps the best key to their meaning. They seem to have been sent as warnings to the oppressor, to afford him a means of seeing God's will and an opportunity of repenting before Egypt was ruined. The lesson that Pharaoh's career teaches us seems to be that there are men whom the most signal judgments do not affect so as to cause any lasting repentance.

The following characteristics of the plagues may be specially noticed: (1) Their relation to natural phenomena. Each can be explained in some measure by natural causes. The miracle in each depends upon, (1) the fact of its coming when determined upon (2) usually its unexampled severity, and (3) its sudden disappearance at the command of God. All are marvellous, not for the most part as reversing, but as developing, forces inherent in nature, and directing them to a special end. (2) Their order. They are divided first into nine and one; the last one standing clearly apart from all the others. The nine are arranged in threes. In the first of each three the warning is given to Pharaoh in the morning. In the first and second of each three the plague is announced beforehand; in the third, not. At the third the magicians acknowledge the finger of God; at the sixth they cannot stand before Moses; and at the ninth Pharaoh refuses to see the face of Moses any more. The gradation of the severity of these strokes is no less obvious. In the first three no distinction is made among the inhabitants of the land; in the remaining seven a distinction is made between the Israelites, who are shielded from, and the Egyptians, who are exposed to, the stroke. (3) Their duration. It is probable that the plagues extended through a period of several months. The first plague occurred probably during the annual inundation of the Nile, hence about the middle of June (*Edersheim*) or August (Hastings' Bib. Dic.) The second, that of the frogs, in September, the time when Egypt often suffers in this way. The seventh (hail) came when the barley

was in ear, and before the wheat was grown, and hence in January or February; and the tenth came in the following March or April. (4) Their significance. Many, or nearly all, are directed against some Egyptian superstition. Jehovah is set over against the false gods and wrests from them their apparent dominion. He has power over nature, over disease, even over life and death. The victory was complete; upon all the gods of Egypt, Jehovah had executed judgment.

Plains. This one term does duty in the Authorized Version for no less than seven distinct Hebrew words. 1. *Abêl*. This word perhaps answers more nearly to our word " meadow " than any other. It occurs in the names of Abel-maim, Abel-meholah, Abel-shittim, and is rendered " plain " in Judges 11:33—" plain of vineyards." The R. V. gives it as a proper name " Abel-Cheramin " and R. V. mar. " the meadow of vineyards." 2. *Bîk'âh*. Fortunately we are able to identify the most remarkable of the *bîk'âhs* of the Bible, and thus to ascertain the force of the term, a broad plain between hills. The great plain or valley of Cœle-Syria, the " hollow land " of the Greeks, which separates the two ranges of Lebanon and Anti-Lebanon, is the most remarkable of them all. Out of Palestine we find denoted by the word *bîk'âh* the " plain of the land of Shinar," Gen. 11:2, the " plain of Mesopotamia," Ezek. 3:22, 23; 8:4; 37:1, 2, and the " plain in the province of Dura." Dan. 3:1. 3. *Ha-shefêlâh,* the technical designation of the depressed, flat or gently-undulating region west of the highlands of Judah. As to its western boundary there is a difference of opinion. It extended certainly to the Philistine frontier, but many include the Plain of the Philistines under the name. 4. *Elôn.* Our translators have uniformly rendered this word " plain;" but this is not the verdict of the majority or the most trustworthy of the ancient versions. They regard the word as meaning an " oak " or " grove of oaks," a rendering supported by nearly all the commentators and lexicographers of the present day. The passages in which the word occurs erroneously translated " plain " are as follows: Plain of Moreh, Gen. 12:6, Deut. 11:30; plain of Mamre, Gen. 13: 18; 14:13; 18:1; plain of Zaanaim

Judges 4:11; plain of the pillar, Judges 9:6; plain of Meonenim, Judges 9:37; plain of Tabor, 1 Sam. 10:3.

Ple'iades (plē'ya-dēz). The Hebrew word (*kîmâh*) so rendered occurs in Job 9:9; 38:31; Amos 5:8. In the last passage our Authorized Version has "the seven stars," although the Geneva version translates the word "Pleiades" as in the other cases. The Pleiades are a group of stars situated on the shoulder of the constellation Taurus. The rendering "sweet influences" of the Authorized Version, Job 38:31, is a relic of the lingering belief in the power which the stars exerted over human destiny. But some think the phrase arose from the fact that the Pleiades appear about the middle of April, and hence are associated with the return of spring, the season of *sweet influences*. The R. V. has "cluster of the Pleiades."

Plough. The ploughs of ancient Egypt consisted of a share—often pointed with iron or bronze—two han-

EASTERN PLOUGH.

dles, and a pole which was inserted into the base of the two handles. Ploughs in Palestine have usually but one handle, with a pole joined to it near the ground, and drawn by oxen, cows or camels.

Poch'ereth (pŏch'ĕrĕth). The children of Pochereth of Zebaim, R. V. "Pochereth-Hazzebaim" were among the children of Solomon's servants who returned with Zerubbabel. Ezra 2:57; Neh. 7:59.

Poetry, Hebrew. Nearly one third of the Old Testament is in poetry, and should be so printed in all our Bibles whichever version is used. For the form is a great aid in understanding and feeling the power of the spirit.

Nearly every kind of poetry is found in the Bible, and in its most perfect form and beauty of expression as well as in the supremest imagery, truth, and power.

The flights of Isaiah have never been surpassed. Job stands first in dramatic power. No modern hymns have equaled some of the Psalms.

The fact that the divine message is expressed in poetic form does not detract from its truth. On the contrary it is the most exact and powerful expression of certain truths.

The characteristics of Hebrew poetry are:—

1. Poetic imagery of exquisite form and surprising beauty, the richness and multitude of its metaphors, its exaltation of thought, its insight into the very inmost soul of things, its truth of life.

2. There is no use of rhyme in Hebrew poetry.

3. But there is rhythm expressed by time-beats or tones on which the emphasis falls, while the other syllables belonging to it, be they one or several, are passed over more lightly.

We notice this even in some of our hymns, particularly in the familiar hymn "Holy, Holy, Holy," and the way it has to be set to music in order to accommodate the irregularity of the number of syllables to a beat. "The number of syllables belonging to a single tone varies constantly, producing what would be designated, according to our canons of meter, a mingling of iambic, trochaic, dactylic and anapestic feet, but the rhythm is not often disturbed by this freedom."

4. The most distinctive characteristic of Hebrew poetry is parallelism or thought rhythm, in various forms.

(a) Where the same thought is repeated in other words in the second line.

(b) Where the thought is made more clear by contrast.

(c) Where the second line is a climax to the first.

(d) Where the thought of the first expression is made more clear by a familiar comparison.

"As in Greek, each strophe is answered rhythm for rhythm by its antistrophe, but, unlike the Greek, the Biblical antistrophe answers thought as well as rhythm."

Poetry in the Bible takes a great variety of forms.

Lyric Idyls, which treat not of war, nor heroic actions, but of homely domestic life.

Ballads interspersed with other forms.
Songs, like those in the early chapters of Luke.
Hymns, like the Psalms, which was really the Temple hymnal.
Dramatic poetry, like the book of Job.
Dramatic dialogue as in the Song of Songs.
Gnomic or didactic poetry expressed in epigrams, wise sayings, maxims, and aphorisms, as in Proverbs.
Rhapsodies is the name Professor Moulton gives to the poetic flights of Isaiah's prophecies,—dramatic, but such as no theater could compass; for their stage they need all space, and the time of their action extends to the end of all things. The speakers include God and the Celestial Hosts; Israel appears, Israel suffering or Israel repentant; Sinners in Zion, the Godly in Zion; the Saved and the Doomed, the East and the West answer one another.
The Refrain is used in Ps. 24, 46, 107, 118, 136.
Alphabetical Psalms, in which each verse, or series of verses, begins in Hebrew with the letters of the alphabet in succession; as Ps. 25, 34, 37, 119; and the book of Lamentations.

Pol'lux (pŏl'lux). [CASTOR AND POLLUX.]

Polygamy. [MARRIAGE.]

Pomegranate. The pomegranate tree, *Punica granatum,* derives its name from the Latin *pomum granatum,* "grained apple." The Romans gave it the name of *Punica,* as the tree was introduced from Carthage. It grows about 10–15 feet in height. The foliage is dark green, the flowers are crimson, the fruit, which is about the size of an orange, is red when ripe, which in Palestine is about the middle of October. It contains a quantity of juice. Mention is made in Cant. 8 : 2 of spiced wine of , the juice of the pomegranate. The hard rind is used in the manufacture of morocco leather, and together with the bark is sometimes used medicinally. The tree grows wild in northern Africa, northern Syria and perhaps in Gilead. It is still much cultivated in Palestine, and is found in many other countries. The pomegranate was early cultivated in Egypt; hence the complaint of the Israelites in the wilderness of Zin, Num. 20 : 5, this "is no place of figs, or of vines, or of pomegranates." Carved figures of the pomegranate adorned the tops of the pillars in Solomon's temple,

1 Kings 7 : 18, 20, etc.; and worked representations of this fruit, in blue, purple and scarlet, ornamented the hem of the robe of the ephod. Ex. 28 : 33, 34.

Pommels, only in 2 Chron. 4 : 12, 13. In 1 Kings 7 : 41, "bowls." The word signifies convex projections belonging to the capitals of pillars.

Pond. The ponds of Egypt, Ex. 7 : 19; 8 : 5, R. V. "Pools," were doubtless water left by the inundation of the Nile. Ponds for fish are mentioned in Isa. 19 : 10.

Pon'tius Pi'late (pŏn'shus). [PILATE.]

Pon'tus, a large district in the north of Asia Minor, extending along the coast of the Pontus Euxinus or Black Sea, from which the name was derived. It corresponds nearly to the modern Trebizond. It is three times mentioned in the New Testament—Acts 2 : 9; 18 : 2; 1 Pet. 1 : 1. All these passages agree in showing that there were many Jewish residents in the district. As to the annals of Pontus, the one brilliant passage of its history is the life of the great Mithridates. It became a Roman province in B.C. 63, when its ruler was finally conquered. Changes in organization and the boundaries of the province were made more than once. During B.C. 39 to A.D. 63 it was once more a kingdom, but at the latter date the whole region was made a Roman province, bearing the name of Pontus. It was conquered by the Turks in A.D. 1461, and is still under their dominion.

Pool. Pools, like the tanks of India, are in many parts of Palestine and Syria the only resource for water during the dry season, and the failure of them involves drought and calamity. Isa. 42 : 15. Of the various pools mentioned in Scripture, perhaps the most celebrated are the pools of Solomon near Bethlehem, from which he constructed aqueducts to supply Jerusalem with water. 2 Kings 20 : 20; Eccles. 2 : 6.

Poor. The general kindly spirit of the law toward the poor is sufficiently shown by such passages as Deut. 15 : 7, for the reason that (ver. 11) "the poor shall never cease out of the land." Among the special enactments in their favor the following must be mentioned : 1. The right of gleaning. Lev. 19 : 9, 10; Deut. 24 : 19, 21. 2. From the produce of the land in sabbatical years the poor and the stranger were to have their portion. Ex. 23 : 11; Lev. 25 : 6. 3. Re-en-

THE SO-CALLED POOLS OF SOLOMON, ABOVE BETHLEHEM.
Built for the water-supply of Jerusalem.

THE POOL OF MAMILLA, AT JERUSALEM.

try upon land in the jubilee year, with the limitation as to town homes. Lev. 25:25-30. 4. Prohibition of usury and of retention of pledges. Ex. 22:25-27; Lev. 25:35, 37, etc. 5. Permanent bondage forbidden, and manumission of Hebrew bondmen or bondwomen enjoined in the sabbatical and jubilee years. Lev. 25:39-42, 47-54; Deut. 15:12-15. 6. Portions from the tithes to be shared by the poor after the Levites. Deut. 14:29; 26:12, 13. 7. The poor to partake in entertainments at the feasts of Weeks and Tabernacles. Deut. 16:11, 14; see Neh. 8:10. 8. Daily payment of wages. Lev. 19:13. Principles similar to those laid down by Moses are inculcated in the New Testament, as Luke 3:11; 14:13; Acts 6:1; Gal. 2:10; James 2:15.

The "poor in spirit" are the humble, whether otherwise rich or poor. Matt. 5:3.

Poplar. This is the rendering of the Hebrew word *libneh,* which occurs in Gen. 30:37 and Hos. 4:13. Several authorities are in favor of the rendering of the Authorized Version, and think that "white poplar" (*Populus alba*) is the tree denoted; others understand the "storax tree" (*Styrax officinale,* Linn.). A principal argument for the latter is the Arabic name *lubna* which is still used for this tree. Both poplars and storax or styrax trees are common in Palestine, and either would suit the passages where the Hebrew term occurs. The *Styrax officinale* is a shrub from ten to twenty feet high, with ovate leaves, which are white underneath; the flowers are in racemes, and are white or cream-colored.

Por'atha (pŏr'a-thà), one of the ten sons of Haman slain by the Jews in Shushan the palace. Esther 9:8.

Porch. In the Old Testament: 1. *Misderon,* Judges 3:23 only. 2. *Ulam* or *Elam,* used in a number of references in 1 Kings, 1 Chron., 2 Chron., Ezekiel and Joel. It is used of the porch on the east of Solomon's temple, of two porches on his palace, and of two rooms near the gates. In the New Testament: 1. *Proaúlion,* a sort of covered passage, Mark 14:68. 2. *Pulón,* a doorway, probably with the same meaning as (1). Matt. 26:71. 3. *Stoa,* John 5:2, covered ways. "Solomon's porch" (*Stoa*) was a portico on the eastern side of the temple building.

Por'cius Fes'tus (pôr'cĭ-ŭs). [FESTUS.]

Porter. This word when used in the Authorized Version does not bear its modern signification of a carrier of burdens, but denotes in every case a gate-keeper, from the Latin *portarius,* the man who attended to the *porta* or gate.

Possession. [DEMONIACS.]

Post. 1. Probably, the door-case of a door, including the lintel and side posts. The posts of the doors of the temple were of olive wood. 1 Kings 6 33. 2. A courier or carrier of messages, used among other places in Job 9:25.

Pot. The term "pot" is applicable to so many sorts of vessels that it can scarcely be restricted to any one in particular. Some of the most common were (1) the *Sir* or boiling caldron. Ex. 16:3; 2 Kings 4:38; Eze. 11:3, 7; 24:6; Zech. 14:20, 21. (2) *Dud*, usually translated "basket," is translated "kettle" in 1 Sam. 2:14 and "caldron" in 2 Chron. 35:13. (3) *Parur*, 1 Sam. 2:14; Judges 6:19 and in R. V. of Num. 11:8, is used with several meanings. (4) The caldron of Job 41:20 is properly translated "rushes" in R. V. The "pots" set before the Rechabites, Jer. 35:5, were probably bulging jars or

STONE WATER-JARS.

bowls. The water-pots of Cana appear to have been large amphoræ, such as are in use at the present day in Syria. These were of stone or hard earthenware. The water-pot of the Samaritan woman may have been a leathern bucket, such as Bedouin women use.

Pot'iphar (pŏt'ĭ-far), an Egyptian name, also written Potipherah, signifies *belonging to the sun*. Potiphar, with whom the history of Joseph is connected, is described as "an officer of Pharaoh, the captain of the guard, an Egyptian." Gen. 39:1. In Gen. 37:36 the margins of both versions gives as a literal translation of the Hebrew "chief of the executioners." (B.C. 1728.) He appears to have been a wealthy man. Gen. 39:4–6. The view we have of Potiphar's household is exactly in accordance with the representations on the monuments. When Joseph was accused, his master contented himself with casting him into prison. Gen. 39:19, 20. After this we hear no more of Potiphar. [JOSEPH.]

Potiphe'rah, was priest or prince of On, and his daughter Asenath was given Joseph to wife by Pharaoh. Gen. 41: 45. 50: 46: 20.

Potsherd, also in Authorized Version "sherd," a broken piece of earthenware, Job 2:8. In Prov. 26:23, the same word is translated in the R. V. "an earthen vessel."

Pottage. [LENTILS.]

Potter's field, The, a piece of ground which, according to the statement of St. Matthew, Matt. 27:7, was

THE TRADITIONAL POTTER'S FIELD.

purchased by the priests with the thirty pieces of silver rejected by Judas, and converted into a burial-place for Jews not belonging to the city. [ACELDAMA.]

Pottery. The art of pottery is one of the most common and most ancient of all manufactures. It is abundantly evident, both that the Hebrews used earthenware vessels in the wilderness and that the potter's trade was afterward carried on in Palestine, although in the former vessels of skin and wood were more common because more suitable to a nomadic life. They had themselves been concerned in the potter's trade in Egypt, Ps. 81:6, and the wall-paintings minutely illustrate the Egyptian process. The clay, when dug, was trodden by men's feet so as to form a paste, Isa. 41:25. It was then placed by the potter on a horizontal wheel beside which he sat, and shaped with his hands. How early the wheel came into use in Palestine is not known.

but it seems likely that it was adopted from Egypt. Isa. 45:9; Jer. 18:3. The vessel was then smoothed and coated with a glaze, and finally burnt in a furnace. There was at Jerusalem a royal establishment of potters, 1 Chron. 4:23, from whose employment, and from the fragments cast away in the process, the Potter's Field perhaps received its name. Isa. 30:14.

Pound. 1. A weight, the translation of the Hebrew *Maneh*. A Maneh of gold was worth about $485 or $242 according to the standard in use. 1 Kings 10:17. A Maneh of silver was worth $32.30 or $16.15. Ezra 2:69; Neh. 7:71. In New Testament times it was used often to represent a sum of money. Luke 19:12–27. See *Mina*, Tables of WEIGHTS and MONEY in the Appendix.

2. The Roman libra or pound is intended in John 12:3; 19:39.

Præto'rium (præ-tō'rĭ-ŭm) (in the Revised Version often translated *palace*, Matt. 27:27; John 18:28, 33; 19:9), the headquarters of the Roman military governor, wherever he happened to be. In time of peace some one of the best buildings of the city which was the residence of the proconsul or prætor was selected for this purpose. Thus at Cæsarea that of Herod the Great was occupied by Felix, Acts 23:35, and at Jerusalem the new palace erected by the same prince was the residence of Pilate. After the Roman power was established in Judea, a Roman guard was always maintained in the Antonia. The meaning of the word in Philip. 1:13, translated in A. V. "palace" and in R. V. "prætorian guard," is variously explained. Some consider it the prætorian camp at Rome, erected by the emperor Tiberius, acting under the advice of Sejanus. It stood outside the walls, at some distance short of the fourth milestone. Others think it means that as St. Paul was at all times during his imprisonment in charge of the soldiers presumably of the Prætorian Guard (Acts 28:16, A. V.), the reference is to the spread of the gospel among these individuals.

Prayer "in religious usage is a devout petition to an object of worship, confined in Protestant usage to such petitions addressed to God; more generally any spiritual communion with God, including Confession, Petition, Adoration, Praise and Thanksgiving." (Century Dictionary.)

PRAYER AND A PERSONAL GOD. Prayer implies a personal God, who is our Father, in whose image we his children are created; and who governs, controls and guides all the forces of the universe material and spiritual. We cannot pray to a mere "bright Essence increate," or to a mere "Power that makes for righteousness." The fatherhood of God makes prayer a natural resource of his children.

PRAYER AND NATURAL LAW. The answer to prayer does not imply that our Father changes, or reverses, or suspends any law of nature God has made. He uses his laws just as his children do in their smaller sphere. When a doctor heals diseases that without him would end in death, when a child is caught in the machinery of a factory, and is rescued from it, when the lawn or the garden is dry and the owner produces a local shower by turning on water through his hose,—in no case do they break or reverse the laws of nature, but only use them. So our Heavenly Father, when he answers prayer for help in trouble, for rain in drought, for healing from sickness, for guidance in perplexities, does not need to change a single law in the least degree, but puts his own will into those laws and uses them. The scientific man can pray as naturally and hopefully as the simplest little child.

PRAYER AND THE HUMAN SOUL. Most prayers are answered by the influence of God's spirit upon the spirit of Man. The greatest needs of man are spiritual and moral. Even bodily healing to be truly blessed influences the spiritual life more than the bodily, as when Christ healed men when on earth. The earthly father's training of his child is still the best expression of God's dealings with his children.

PRAYER AND ITS ANSWER. *First.* The very act of praying brings us into communion with God, which is the best answer to prayer. The giving and receiving are the means of becoming acquainted with God. By them we realize that God is a person, with love and will and mind, to whom we can be drawn by a companionship closer than that of David and Jonathan, whose "hearts were knit together."

Second. But this answer cannot come, unless there be direct answers to prayer, gifts in response to the asking. Hence, there is a giving of the exact thing we ask for, in all cases where direct promises are made, or where it would be good for us to receive it. All acquaintance with another depends upon reciprocity.

Third. Many times the exact thing we ask for, in the form we ask for it, would be the worst thing for us, and what we really do *not* want. " We, ignorant of ourselves, beg often our own harms." We do not know enough to insist on just the things we desire in worldly matters.

Therefore, in such cases our heavenly Father gives us not merely a substitute for what we asked, but what we would have asked had we known all things pertaining to it as God knows them, what we really wanted, not what we thought we wanted.

"Delays are not denials," but only a waiting for the best time to come, for the fruits to ripen, for the soil to be prepared.

PUBLIC PRAYER. There are no directions as to prayer given in the Mosaic law: the duty is rather taken for granted, as an adjunct to sacrifice, than enforced or elaborated. It is hardly conceivable that, even from the beginning, public prayer did not follow every public sacrifice, or accompany it. Such a practice is alluded to in Luke 1:10 as common; and in one instance, at the offering of the first-fruits, it was ordained in a striking form. Deut. 26: 12–15. In later times it certainly grew into a regular service both in the temple and in the synagogue.

PRIVATE PRAYER. Besides this public prayer, it was the custom of all at Jerusalem to go up to the temple, at regular hours if possible, for private prayer, see Luke 18:10; Acts 3:1: and those who were absent were wont to " open their windows toward Jerusalem," and pray " toward " the place of God's presence. 1 Kings 8: 46–49; Ps. 5:7; 28:2; 138: 2; Dan. 6:10. The regular hours of prayer seem to have been three (see Ps. 55:17; Dan. 6:10) : " the evening," that is, the ninth hour, Acts 3:1; 10:3, the hour of the evening sacrifice, Dan. 9:21; the " morning," that is, the third hour, Acts 2:15, that of the morning sacrifice; and the sixth hour, or " noonday."

GRACE BEFORE MEAT, or giving thanks would seem to have been a common practice. See Matt. 15:36; Acts 27:35.

Jesus was accustomed to use this beautiful and helpful practice.

ATTITUDES IN PRAYER. The attitude has an effect upon the spirit, and those attitudes are best which are the natural or customary expression of the feeling and spirit of worship. (1) The posture of prayer among the Jews seems to have been most often standing, 1 Sam. 1:26; Matt. 6:5; Mark 11:25; Luke 18:11; unless (2) the prayer were offered with especial solemnity and humiliation, which was naturally expressed by kneeling, 1 Kings 8:54; comp. 2 Chron. 6:13; Ezra 9:5; Ps. 95:6; Dan. 6:10. (3) Prostration, that is kneeling with the face bent to the ground, Josh. 7:6; 1 Kings 18:42; Neh. 8:6. (4) In addition to these the hands were lifted (Ps. 63:4), or spread out with open upturned palms symbolical of the act of receiving. Ex. 9:29; Isa. 1:15.

FORMS OF PRAYER. The most important form of prayer is that given by our Lord, the spirit of which best expresses the spirit of true prayer. That it was a model and not an authoritative form is shown by the fact that recorded prayer in the New Testament is filled with its spirit, but not one takes its exact form. Its spirit is also interpreted by that of his prayer in Gethsemane and of the prayer recorded by St. John, John 17, the beginning of Christ's great work of intercession.

The only form of prayer given for perpetual use in the Old Testament is the one in Deut. 26:5–15, connected with the offering of tithes and first-fruits, and containing in simple form the important elements of prayer, acknowledgment of God's mercy, self-dedication and prayer for future blessing. To this may perhaps be added the threefold blessing of Num. 6:24–26, couched as it is in a precatory form, and the short prayer of Moses, Num. 10:35, 36, at the moving and resting of the cloud, the former of which was the germ of the 68th Psalm.

Presents. [GIFT.]

President (*sârĕcâ,* only used Dan. 6, the Chaldee equivalent for Hebrew *shôtêr*), a high officer in the Persian court, a *chief,* a *president,* used of the three highest ministers.

Priest. The English word is derived from the Greek *presbyter,* signifying an " elder " (Heb. *kôhên*). *Origin.—*The idea of a priesthood connects itself in all its forms, pure or corrupted, with the consciousness, more or less distinct, of sin. Men feel that they have broken a law. The power above them is holier than they are, and they dare not approach it. They crave for the intervention of some one of whom they can think as likely to be more acceptable than themselves. He must offer up their prayers, thanksgivings, sacrifices. He becomes their representative in "things pertaining unto God." He may become also (though this does not always follow) the representative of God to man. The functions of the priest and prophet may exist in the same person. No trace of a hereditary or caste priesthood meets us in the worship of the patriarchal age. Once and once only does the word *kôhên* meet us as belonging to a ritual earlier than the time of Abraham. Melchizedek is "the priest of the most high God." Gen. 14:18. In the worship of the patriarchs themselves, the chief of the family, as such, acted as the priest. The office descended with the birthright, and might apparently be transferred with it.

When established.—The priesthood was first established in the family of Aaron, and all the sons of Aaron were priests. They stood between the high priest on the one hand and the Levites on the other. [HIGH PRIEST; LEVITES.] The ceremony of their consecration is described in Ex. 29; Lev. 8.

Dress.—The dress which the priests wore during their ministrations consisted of linen drawers, with a close-fitting cassock, also of white linen. This came nearly to the feet, and was to be worn in its garment shape. Comp. John 19:23. The white cassock was gathered round the body with a girdle of needlework, in which, as in the more gorgeous belt of the high priest, blue, purple and scarlet were intermingled with white, and worked in the form of flowers. Ex. 28:39, 40; 39:2; Ezek. 44:17-19. Upon their heads they were to wear caps or bonnets in the form of a cup-shaped flower, also of fine linen. In all their acts of ministration they were to be barefooted.

Duties.—The chief duties of the priests were (1) to watch over the fire on the altar of burnt offering, and to keep it burning evermore both by day and night, Lev. 6:12; 2 Chron. 13:11; (2) to feed the golden lamp outside the vail with oil, Ex. 27:20, 21; Lev. 24:2; (3) to offer the morning and evening sacrifices, each accompanied with a meat offering and a drink offering, at the door of the tabernacle. Ex. 29:38-44. (4) They were also to teach the children of Israel the statutes of the Lord. Lev. 10:11; Deut. 33:10; 2 Chron. 15:3; Ezek. 44:23, 24. (5) During the journeys in the wilderness it belonged to them to cover the ark and all the vessels of the sanctuary with a purple or scarlet cloth before the Levites might approach them. Num. 4:5-15. As the people started on each day's march they were to blow "an alarm" with long silver trumpets. Num. 10:1-8. Other instruments of music might be used by the more highly-trained Levites and the schools of the prophets, but the trumpets belonged only to the priests.

Provision for support.—This consisted —1. Of one tenth of the tithes which the people paid to the Levites, *i. e.* one per cent. on the whole produce of the country. Num. 18:26-28. 2. Of the redemption money, for the first-born of man or beast. Num. 18:14-19. For the former the uniform rate of five shekels a head. 3. Of the redemption money paid in like manner for men or things specially dedicated to the Lord. Lev. 27. 4. Of the shew-bread, and certain parts of the flesh of the burnt offerings, peace offerings, trespass offerings, Lev. 6:26, 29; 7:6-10; 10:12-15; Num. 18:8-14. 5. Of an undefined amount of the first-fruits of corn, wine and oil. Ex. 23:19; Lev. 2:14; Deut. 26:1-10. 6. On their settlement in Canaan the priestly families had thirteen cities assigned them, with "suburbs" or pasture-grounds for their flocks. Josh. 21:13-19. 7. There was, after the exile, a further payment of a third, and later a half shekel for each Israelite for the support of the Temple. These provisions were obviously intended to secure the religion of Israel against the dangers of a caste of pauper priests, needy and dependent, and unable to bear their witness to the true faith. They were, on the other hand, as far as possible removed from the condition of a wealthy order. In fact, however, by all these means they had much property which was earning an income. In addition, in degenerate times they took pay for performing some of their duties.

Courses.—The priesthood was divided by David into four and twenty "courses" or orders, 1 Chron. 24:1–19; 2 Chron. 23:8; Luke 1:5, each of which was to serve in rotation for one week, while the further assignment of special services during the week was determined by lot. Luke 1:9. Each course appears to have commenced its work on the Sabbath, the outgoing priests taking the morning sacrifice, and leaving that of the evening to their successors. 2 Chron. 23:8.

Numbers.—If we may accept the numbers given by Jewish writers as at all trustworthy, the proportion of the priesthood to the population of Palestine, during the last century of their existence as an order, must have been far greater than that of the clergy has ever been in any Christian nation. But the teachers of all schools should be included with our clergy, if we would make the comparison fair. Their number is estimated as many thousands. It is, however, beyond a doubt that in many cases priests, Levites, and even Temple servants are included in any number reported. Priests alone are named in one authority of before 200 B.C. as 1500. This would naturally be increased before N. T. times. The reigns of the two kings David and Solomon were the culminating period of the glory of the Jewish priesthood. It will be interesting to bring together the few facts that indicate the position of the priests in the New Testament period of their history. The number scattered throughout Palestine was, as has been stated, very large. The priestly order, like the nation, was divided between contending sects. In the scenes of the last tragedy of Jewish history the order passes away without honor. The high priesthood is given to the lowest and vilest of the adherents of the frenzied Zealots. Other priests appear as deserting to the enemy. The destruction of Jerusalem deprived the order at one blow of all but an honorary distinction.

Prince, Princess. There are sixteen different Hebrew words translated "prince" in the Authorized Version. They nearly all have meanings corresponding exactly to our various uses of the English word. There are some which have a special signification such as—1. "Princes of provinces," 1 Kings 20:14, who were probably local governors or magistrates. 2. The "princes" mentioned in Dan. 6:1 (see Esther 1:1), who were the satraps or governors of provinces, as in R. V. The word *princess* is seldom used in the Bible, but the persons to which it alludes—"daughters of kings"—are frequently mentioned. Where it is used it apparently only is meant to call attention to the royal character.

Principality. In several passages of the New Testament the term "principalities and powers" appears to denote different orders of angels, good or bad. See Eph. 6:12.

Pris′ca (prĭs′kà) (*ancient*), 2 Tim. 4:19, or **Priscil′la** (a diminutive from *Prisca*), the wife of Aquila. [AQUILA.] To what has been said elsewhere under the head of AQUILA the following may be added: We find that the name of the wife is placed before that of the husband in Rom. 16:3; 2 Tim. 4:19; and (according to some of the best MSS.) in Acts 18:26. Hence we should be disposed to conclude that Priscilla was the more energetic character of the two. In fact we may say that Priscilla is the example of what the married woman may do for the general service of the Church, in conjunction with home duties, as Phœbe is the type of the unmarried servant of the Church, or deaconess.

Prison. [For imprisonment as a punishment, see PUNISHMENTS.] It is plain that in Egypt special places were used as prisons, and that they were under the custody of a military officer. Gen. 40:3; 42:17. During the wandering in the desert we read on two occasions of confinement "in ward"—Lev. 24:12; Num. 15:34; but as imprisonment was not directed by the law, so we hear of none till the time of the kings, when the prison appears as an appendage to the palace, or a special part of it. 1 Kings 22:27. Private houses were sometimes used as places of confinement. By the Romans the tower of Antonia was used as a prison at Jerusalem, Acts 23:10, and at Cæsarea the prætorium of Herod. The royal prisons in those days were doubtless managed after the Roman fashion, and chains, fetters and stocks were used as means of confinement. See Acts 16:24. One of the readiest places for confinement was a dry or partially dry wall or pit. Jer. 38:6–11.

Proch′orus (prŏk′o-rus) (*leader of the chorus*), one of the seven deacons, being the third on the list, and named next after Stephen and Philip. Acts 6: 5.

Proconsul (*for,* or *in place of, the consul*). At the division of the Roman provinces by Augustus, in the year B.C. 27, into senatorial and imperial, the emperor assigned to the senate such portions of territory as were peaceable and could be held without force of arms. Those which he retained were called *imperial,* and were governed by *legates* and *procurators.* [PROCURATOR.] Over the senatorial provinces the senate appointed by lot yearly an officer, who was called "proconsul," and who exercised purely civil functions. The provinces were in consequence called "proconsular."

Procurator. The Greek ἡγεμών, rendered "governor" in the Authorized Version, is applied in the New Testament to the officer who presided over the imperial province of Judea. It is used of Pontius Pilate, Matt. 27, of Felix, Acts 23, 24, and of Festus. Acts 26: 30. It is explained under PROCONSUL that after the battle of Actium, B.C. 27, the provinces of the Roman empire were divided by Augustus into two portions, giving some to the senate and reserving to himself the rest. The imperial provinces were administered by *legati.* No quæstor came into the emperor's provinces, but the property and revenues of the imperial treasury were administered by *procuratores,* who were distinctly the servants of the emperor and stood or fell by his pleasure. Sometimes a province was governed by a procurator with the functions of a legatus. This was especially the case with the smaller provinces and the outlying districts of a larger province; and such is the relation in which Judea stood to Syria. The headquarters of the procurator were at Cæsarea, Acts 23: 23, where he had a judgment seat, Acts 25: 6, in the audience chamber, Acts 25: 23, and was assisted by a council, Acts 25: 12, whom he consulted in cases of difficulty. He was attended by a cohort as body-guard, Matt. 27: 27, and apparently went up to Jerusalem at the time of the high festivals, and there resided at the palace of Herod, in which was the *prætorium* or "judgment hall." Matt. 27: 27; Mark 15: 16; comp. Acts 23: 35.

Prophet, Prophecy. The Hebrew word for prophet, *nābī,* means "one who announces or brings a message from God." Our word "prophet" has essentially the same meaning. one who speaks by divine inspiration as the interpreter or spokesman of God, whether it be a message of duty and warning, or a prediction of future events. The twofold meaning is due to the two senses of the preposition *pro* (in the Greek from which our word prophet is derived) "for" and "before;" so that a prophet is one who speaks *for* God, and one who tells *before* hand what is to take place.

THE NEED OF PROPHETS. There are two ways in which God reveals his will to his children. One is through his works; the other through his influence upon the spirit of man, probably upon the spirit of all men as they are able to receive it. But there are some persons who are able to receive much more than others, on account of their more susceptible psychological temperament, a more perfect moral character, a more sensitive conscience, a life nearer to God, a more spiritual nature, a more complete consecration to God and his will. To these God can reveal his will, and through them to their fellow men. These can become his prophets, whom he fills with his spirit, and whom he inspires to speak his word with authority.

THE PROPHETS WERE RAISED UP from the people, called of God for some particular purpose or need, as the Judges were raised up for special crises. They were not a class or a guild, inheriting the office. Prophecy was not an institution like the priesthood, and monarchy, but each one had a personal call to his work. This is true of most of the great men who have influenced the world's history.

THE WORK OF THE PROPHETS. The prophets were the moral and religious teachers of their nation, authoritative preachers of righteousness. Statesmen who guided the religious life which lay at the foundation of the nation's welfare, the counsellor of kings, revivalists and reformers who awakened the religious life of the people, forewarners of the certainty of the divine judgment on sin, proclaimers of the divine ideals, the golden age toward which the nation was to move.

"The prophet was not only the bearer, he was the embodiment of the idea of the theocracy. This idea, which is that of the communion of the living God with mankind, was realized in him, and through him in Israel. Though he could be distinguished from Israel, he was in truth Israel at its highest." (Hastings' Bible Dictionary.)

The prophets were also historians, using the earlier history of the nation as a light upon the path of the present, showing God's guiding hand, teaching Israel to avoid the rocks on which the nation was so often wrecked, and pointing clearly to the only conditions of success.

While the earlier prophets are reported and described, the later ones from the eighth century on wrote down their prophecies, as a perpetual means of instruction to all time.

THE METHODS OF THE PROPHETS. The prophets received their message in various ways: by visions, dreams, " thought-images," angels, and direct action of God upon the mind, inspiring them and revealing to them the needed truths. It is probable the mind of the prophet was not passive but intensely active during the revelation.

In giving the message to the people the prophets used almost every known method of impressing the truth: object lessons, dramatic actions, visible representations, visions, parables, history, preaching, warnings, the facts around them, the highest eloquence, the supremest poetry, predictions and miracles.

THE AUTHORITY OF THE PROPHETS over the people was derived from several sources:

1. Their own character as holy, self-denying, unselfish men.

2. Their message touched the conscience, which declared that the prophets were right.

3. Their message was in accordance with the results of the past history of the nation.

4. The assurance on the part of the prophets that they were messengers of God, and were speaking his truth, gave power to their words. They spoke with authority.

5. Miracles wrought by God through the prophets, confirmed the word not only of the prophets who wrought them, but of the whole school of prophets.

6. The fulfilment of their prophecies was a strong confirmation of the inspired messages. Only God could reveal the future as the prophets foretold it. There is not one of their prophecies which was not fulfilled or in the process of fulfilment. The glorious prophecies of the return and of the coming Messiah, were not completely fulfilled as many Jews expected, but the eras which included them did come, as the promised day comes with the first rays of the sun, although all the glories of the day do not stream upon us with the dawn. Conditional promises are accomplished when the conditions are fulfilled.

SCHOOLS OF THE PROPHETS. "Samuel planned and set up an institution, so to call it, that has made far more mark on the world than anything else that survives to us out of Israel or Greece or Rome. In his ripe and far-seeing years Samuel devised and founded and presided over a great prophetical school in his old age; an estate of learned and earnest-minded men, who were to watch over the religion and the morals of the people, in the prophetical spirit and in the prophetical name. And thus it came about that at Naioth in Ramah the first school of the prophets was set up."

"How far these companies and schools were ' organized,' may be largely a matter of inference; although a more or less permanent ' communal association ' of some kind seems clearly implied in the Scriptures, and has been brought into prominence by tradition. Their aim was evidently educational, and their function an important one in the development and direction of the political and religious life of the people." Professor Willis J. Beecher's *Prophets and the Promise.*

Prophets of the New Testament.—So far as their predictive powers are concerned, the Old Testament prophets find their New Testament counterpart in the writer of the Apocalypse; but in their general character, as specially illumined revealers of God's will, their counterpart will rather be found, first in the great Prophet of the Church and his forerunner, John the Baptist, and next in all those persons who were endowed with the extraordinary gifts of the Spirit in the apostolic age, the speakers with tongues and the interpreters of tongues, the prophets and the discerners of spirits, the teachers and workers of miracles. 1 Cor. 12: 10, 28. That predictive powers did occasionally exist in the New Testament prophets is proved by the case of Agabus, Acts 11: 28, but this was not their characteristic. The prophets of the New Testament were supernaturally-illuminated expounders and preachers.

Proselyte (*a visitor, a new comer*), the name given by the Jews to foreigners who adopted the Jewish religion. The dispersion of the Jews in foreign countries, which has been spoken of elsewhere [DISPERSION, THE], enabled them to make many converts to their faith. The converts who were thus attracted joined, with varying strictness, in the worship of the Jews. In Palestine itself, even Roman centurions learned to love the conquered nation, built synagogues for them, Luke 7 : 5, fasted and prayed, and gave alms after the pattern of the strictest Jews, Acts 10 : 2, 30, and became preachers of the new faith to the soldiers under them. Acts 10 : 7. Such men, drawn by what was best in Judaism, were naturally among the readiest receivers of the new truth which rose out of it, and became, in many cases, the nucleus of a Gentile Church. Proselytism had, however, its darker side. The Jews of Palestine were eager to spread their faith by the same weapons as those with which they had defended it. The Idumæans had the alternative offered them by John Hyrcanus of death, exile or circumcision. The Ituræans were converted in the same way by Aristobulus. Where force was not in their power, they obtained their ends by the most unscrupulous fraud. Those who were most active in proselytizing were precisely those from whose teaching all that was most true and living had departed. The vices of the Jew were engrafted on the vices of the heathen. A repulsive casuistry released the convert from obligations which he had before recognized, while in other things he was bound hand and foot to an unhealthy superstition. It was no wonder that he became "twofold more the child of hell," Matt. 23 : 15, than the Pharisees themselves. We find in the Talmud a distinction between proselytes of the gate and proselytes of righteousness. 1. The term *proselytes of the gate* was derived from the frequently-occurring description in the law, "the stranger that is within thy gates." Ex. 20 : 10, etc. Converts of this class were not bound by circumcision and the other special laws of the Mosaic code. It is doubtful, however, whether the distinction made in the Talmud ever really existed. 2. The *proselytes of righteousness,* known

also as proselytes of the covenant, were perfect Israelites. We learn from the Talmud that, in addition to circumcision, the bath of purification, decreed by the law (Lev. 15, Num. 19) and especially necessary in one coming from the defilement of heathenism, was also required to complete their admission to the faith. This is often spoken of as baptism, and certainly has the same symbolic meaning. The proselyte was placed in a tank or pool up to his neck in water. His teachers, who now acted as his sponsors, repeated the great commandments of the law. The baptism was followed, as long as the temple stood, by the offering or corban.

Proverbs, Book of, is "a Miscellany of Wisdom in five books," containing three hundred and seventy-five brief literary compositions wholly unconnected."

AUTHOR AND DATES. Two of these books are ascribed to Solomon and their date would be about B.C. 1000. Another book is said to be composed of Proverbs collected by men of Hezekiah, and would therefore be dated about 700 B.C. The rest are by unknown authors, some of them being placed as late as B.C. 200. The fifth book is made up of three appendices, the last of which, "The Praise of the Virtuous Woman," is an alphabetical acrostic.

CHARACTER OF THE BOOK. "The Biblical Book of Proverbs introduces itself as an Instruction Book primarily intended for the young, yet containing matter which may be of use to the mature as well.

ITS TOPIC. The book "treats of conduct in general, denouncing such evils as belong to a simple state of society," and portrays the varying aspects of life.

ITS METHOD is that of the gnome or brief practical maxims in poetic measure. Professor Moulton states the three characteristics of this method :

(1) "Antithesis is the very life blood of the proverb : Antithesis, in the form of adversative or other contrast, belongs to the vast majority of them."

(2) "Next in importance to antithesis, comparison is a mode of emphasis in proverbial sayings."

(3) "A third mode of treatment found in the Proverbs is the kind of comparison called Imagery."

THE LITERARY FORMS are (1) The Unit Proverb, consisting usually of a single couplet. (2) There are a few

Proverb clusters where several independent sayings are gathered about a common theme; (3) the Epigram. (4) Wisdom Sonnets.

Province. 1. In the Old Testament this word appears (a) in connection with the wars between Ahab and Ben-hadad. 1 Kings 20:14, 15, 19. The victory of the former is gained chiefly "by the young men of the princes of the provinces," *i. e.*, probably of the chiefs of tribes in the Gilead country. (b) More commonly the word is used of the divisions of the Chaldæan kingdom. Dan. 2:49; 3:1, 30, and the Persian kingdom. Ezra 2:1; Neh. 7:6; Esther 1:1, 22; 2:3, etc. 2. In the New Testament we are brought into contact with the administration of the provinces of the Roman empire. The classification of provinces supposed to need military control and therefore placed under the immediate government of the Cæsar, and those still belonging theoretically to the republic and administered by the senate, and of the latter again into proconsular and prætorian, is recognized, more or less distinctly, in the Gospels and the Acts. [PROCONSUL; PROCURATOR.] The στρατηγοί of Acts 16:22 ("magistrates," Authorized Version), on the other hand, were the *duumviri* or prætors of a Roman colony. The right of any Roman citizen to appeal from a provincial governor to the emperor meets us as asserted by St. Paul. Acts 25:11. In the council of Acts 25:12 we recognize the assessors who were appointed to take part in the judicial functions of the governor.

Psalms, Book of. This book was the Hebrew hymnal, *The Book of Praises,* the hymns being designed to be set to music and used in the worship of God in the Temple and especially in the synagogues after the exile. In the titles we have sometimes the names of the tune to which a psalm is to be sung, the instrument which is to accompany it, the choir to which it belongs, the voices which render it, as soprano or bass.

THE FIVE BOOKS. There are 150 Psalms divided into five books, ending with Psa. 41, 72, 89, 106, and 150, each of which closes with some form of the benediction,—"Amen and Amen," "Blessed be the Lord forevermore." As an old familiar hymn-book was named *Watts and Select,* so the Psalms may be called *David and Select.*

THE PSALTER WAS FORMED GRADUALLY, there being great eras of song arising from religious and political crises or deliverances which deeply impressed the national life. The remarkable development of the nation under David, the reformation under Hezekiah, the return from Exile, were eras of song. We can learn not a little concerning the formation of the Psalter by noting the development of modern hymnology. Every widespread revival of religion has been the inspirer of hymns. Great occasions produce great hymns. "Poets appear in clusters or constellations; for only in seasons of great peril, or signal and splendid triumph, are those deeper and stronger feelings called forth which are the soul of the truest and most perfect poetry."—Perowne.

The hymns thus produced are gathered into different collections. They are altered to meet new circumstances; long hymns have been divided into several short ones, as Bernard Cluny's "Jerusalem the Golden," and Whittier's "Our Master"; verses have been added to hymns by other authors, as to Newman's "Lead Kindly Light," and Smith's "My country 'tis of thee"; in other hymns stanzas have been omitted. Now all these things occur in the book of the Psalms, and help us to understand them. Psalms 14 and 53 are nearly the same. Psalm 70 is nearly the same as the latter part of Psalm 40. Psalm 108 is made up of the last portions of 57 and 60. Psalms 120–134 are a group by themselves in the fifth book of the Psalter.

THE DAVIDIC PSALMS. In the first book all the psalms except four are attributed to David. In the second book eighteen are ascribed to David. In this book the divine name is prevailingly Elohim, God, while in the first book the divine name is generally Jehovah. Two psalms in the second book (54 and 70) duplicate two in the first book (14 and 40:13–17) substituting the word God for Jehovah. One or more psalms in the remaining three books are ascribed to David. Now it is well understood that the titles, although very ancient, are not an authoritative part of the Psalms, any more than the titles at the top of the pages throughout our Authorized Version of the Bible are part of the Bible. It may be that the psalms entitled as his, are simply a part of a Davidic collection, by whomsoever written. At the same time later additions to psalms attributed to him, do not prove that he did not write the psalm. Perowne instances Psalm 51 attributed to David, "of which the last two verses were obviously added at the time of the return from the exile, the psalm itself having been written by David, as the title correctly informs us. Cheyne attributes very few psalms to David, but his arguments are often fallacious. It is probable that quite a large number were written by him.

INSCRIPTIONS. Many of the Psalms have inscriptions of various kinds. Some are called *Michtam*, "golden poem," or *Maschil*, "choice ode." The 4th is set to *Neginōth*, "stringed instruments." Psalms 6 and 12 are on *Sheminīth*, "the octave bass," for male voices. The 46th on *Alâmōth*, "after the manner of maidens," or a soprano song. Psalm 9 is set to the tune, "Death of the Son"; Psalm 22 to the tune, "Hind of the Morning"; Psalm 45 to the tune, "The Lilies"; Psalm 56 to the tune, "The Far-off Dove in Silent lands."

"To the chief Musician," that is for the leader of the Temple choir, either of the band or of the singers, occurs 55 times.

In Ps. 5 is *Nehiloth*, "to the flutes" or with flute accompaniment; in Ps. 8 and 84 *Upon Gittith*, probably means upon a Gathite instrument, or to a Gathite tune.

Selah, so frequently occurring, probably means an interlude, when the musical instruments played alone.

The Songs of Degrees are a group of fifteen Psalms, 120–134, each of which is entitled in the A. V., "A Song of Degrees," and in the R. V., "A Song of Ascents." Others translate, "Songs of the Upgoings," "Pilgrim Psalms," "The Traveler's Hymn Book."

"The Psalms," says Prof. M. R. Vincent, "are among the most charming portions of the Psalter, full of deep and tender feeling, simple and graceful in structure, so that a Spanish writer has said that this collection is to the rest of the Psalms what paradise was to the world at its first creation."

There are several explanations of the title of this booklet of Psalms, two of which are probably correct.

1. "The best modern scholars refer the word 'degrees' or 'ascents' to the successive stages of the pilgrimage which the Jews were accustomed to make thrice every year to the temple on Mount Zion. On such journeys it would be natural to beguile the tedium of the way, or to cheer the nightly encampment by the singing of familiar ballads, . . . and we may feel quite sure that we have here a brief collection of the popular songs which were used in this way."

2. Others think that they were the collection composed or selected for the return journey from Babylon up to Jerusalem, to be used by the two hundred singers who accompanied the caravan.

It is quite probable that both explanations are true. Such songs were doubtless sung by the people while going up to the great feasts, as is still the custom in the Orient. A book of such songs was gathered and added to from time to time, just as in our own day. New ones were composed for the return, as allusions in them to captivity may imply, though there were many captivities before the great exile. All of them at this time were made into the present little booklet of *Songs of the Goings Up*, which is incorporated into the latest of the five books of the Psalter.

Psaltery. This was a stringed instrument of music to accompany the voice. The Hebrew *nêbel* or *nebel* is so rendered in the Authorized Version in all passages where it occurs, except in Isa. 5 : 12; 14 : 11; 22 : 24, marg.; Amos 5 : 23; 6 : 5, where it is translated *viol*. The ancient viol was a six-stringed guitar. In the Prayer Book version of the Psalms the Hebrew word is rendered "lute." This instrument resembled the guitar, but was superior in tone, being larger, and having a convex back, somewhat like the vertical section of a gourd, or more nearly resembling that of a pear. These three instruments, the psaltery or sautry, the viol and the lute, are frequently associated in the old English poets, and were clearly instruments resembling each other, though still different. The Greek *psalterium* (ψαλτήριον), from which our word is derived, denotes an instrument played with the fingers instead of a plectrum or quill, the verb being used of twanging the bow-string. It is impossible to say positively with what instrument the *nebel* of the Hebrew exactly corresponded. From the fact that *nebel* in Hebrew also signifies a wine-bottle or skin, it has been conjectured that the term when applied to a musical instrument denotes a kind of bagpipe. The psalteries of David were made of cypress, 2 Sam. 6:5; those of Solomon of algum or almug trees. 2 Chron. 9: 11. Among the instruments of the band which played before Nebuchadnezzar's golden image on the plains of Dura, we again meet with the psaltery. Dan. 3:5, 10, 15, *pĕsantêrin.*

Ptolemæ'us (tŏl-e-mā'us), or **Ptol'-emy**, was the common name of the Greek dynasty of Egyptian kings. PTOLEMÆUS I. SOTER, the son of Lagus, a Macedonian of low rank, distinguished himself greatly during the campaigns of Alexander; at whose death he secured for himself the government of Egypt, where he proceeded at once to lay the foundations of a kingdom, B.C. 323. He abdicated in favor of his youngest son, Ptolemy II. Philadelphus, two years before his death, which took place in B.C. 283. Ptolemy Soter is generally held to be the "king of the south" in Dan. 11:5, one of those who should receive part of the empire of Alexander when it was "divided toward the four winds of heaven."

PTOLEMÆUS II. PHILADELPHUS, B.C. 285-247, the youngest son of Ptolemy I., was made king two years before his father's death, to confirm the irregular succession. The conflict between Egypt and Syria was renewed during his reign in consequence of the intrigue of his half-brother Magas. Ptolemy bestowed liberal encouragement on literature and science, founding the great library and museum at Alexandria, and gathered about him many men of learning, as the poet Theocritus, the geometer Euclid and the astronomer Aratus. This reign was a critical epoch for the development of Judaism, as it was for the intellectual history of the ancient world. The critical faculty was called forth in place of the creative, and learning in some sense supplied the place of original speculation. It was impossible that the Jew, who was now become as true a citizen of the world as the Greek, should remain passive in the conflict of opinions. It is enough now to observe the greatness of the consequences involved in the union of Greek language with Jewish thought. From this time the Jew was familiarized with the great types of western literature, and in some degree aimed at imitating them. A second time and in new fashion Egypt

disciplined a people of God. It first impressed upon a nation the firm unity of a family, and then in due time reconnected a matured people with the world from which it had been called out. He is thought to have been referred to in Dan. 11:6.

PTOLEMÆUS III. EUERGETES, B.C. 247-222, was the eldest son of Ptolemy Philadelphus and brother of Berenice the wife of Antiochus II. The repudiation and murder of his sister furnished him with an occasion for invading Syria, cir. B.C. 246. Dan. 11:7. He extended his conquests as far as Antioch, and then eastward to Babylon, but was recalled to Egypt by tidings of seditions which had broken out there. His success was brilliant and complete. He carried "captives into Egypt their gods [of the conquered nations], with their princes, and with their precious vessels of silver and of gold." Dan. 11:8. This capture of sacred trophies earned for the king the name *Euergetes*—"Benefactor." After his return to Egypt, cir. B.C. 243, he suffered a great part of the conquered provinces to fall again under the power of Seleucus.

PTOLEMÆUS IV. PHILOPATOR, B.C. 222-205. After the death of Ptolemy Euergetes the line of the Ptolemies rapidly degenerated. Ptolemy Philopator, his eldest son, who succeeded him, was to the last degree sensual, effeminate and debased. But externally his kingdom retained its power and splendor; and when circumstances forced him to action, Ptolemy himself showed ability not unworthy of his race. The description of the campaign of Raphia (B.C. 217) in the book of Daniel gives a vivid description of his character. Dan. 11: 10-12; cf. 3 Macc. 1: 1-3. After offering in the temple at Jerusalem sacrifices for the success then achieved, he attempted to enter the sanctuary. A sudden paralysis hindered his design; but when he returned to Alexandria he determined to inflict on the Alexandrine Jews the vengeance for his disappointment. He probably reduced their privileges, though the stories of their supernatural deliverance are not authentic. He was succeeded by his only child, Ptolemy V., who was at the time only four or five years old.

PTOLEMÆUS V. EPIPHANES, B.C. 205-181. The reign of Ptolemy Epiphanes was a critical epoch in the history of the Jews. The rivalry between the Syrian and Egyptian parties, which had for some time divided the people, came to an open rupture in the struggles which marked his minority. In the strong language of Daniel, "The robbers of the people exalted themselves to establish the vision." Dan. 11:14. The accession of Ptolemy and the confusion of a disputed regency furnished a favorable opportunity for foreign invasion. "Many stood up against the king of the south" under Antiochus the Great and Philip III. of Macedonia, who formed a league for the dismemberment of his kingdom. "So the king of the north [Antiochus] came, and cast up a mount, and took the most fenced city [Sidon], and the arms of the south did not withstand" [at Paneas, B.C. 198]. Dan. 11:14, 15. The Romans interfered, and in order to retain the provinces of Cœle-Syria, Phœnicia and Judea, Antiochus "gave him [Ptolemy] a young maiden" [his daughter Cleopatra as his betrothed wife]. Dan. 11:17. But in the end his policy only partially succeeded. After the marriage of Ptolemy and Cleopatra was consummated, B.C. 193, Cleopatra did "not stand on his side," but supported her husband in maintaining the alliance with Rome. The disputed provinces, however, remained in the possession of Antiochus; and Ptolemy was poisoned at the time when he was preparing an expedition to recover them from Seleucus, the unworthy successor of Antiochus.

PTOLEMÆUS VI. PHILOMETOR, B.C. 181–145. On the death of Ptolemy Epiphanes, his wife Cleopatra held the regency for her young son, Ptolemy Philometor, and preserved peace with Syria till she died, B.C. 173, when he took the government into his own hands, and an attempt was made to recover Syria. Comp. 2 Macc. 4:21. Antiochus Epiphanes seems to have made the claim a pretext for invading Egypt. The generals of Ptolemy were defeated near Pelusium, probably at the close of B.C. 171, 1 Macc. 1:16 ff.; and in the next year Antiochus, having secured the person of the young king, reduced almost the whole of Egypt. Comp. 2 Macc. 5:1. Meanwhile Ptolemy Euergetes II., the younger brother of Ptolemy Philometor, assumed the supreme power at Alexandria; and Antiochus, under the pretext of recovering the crown for Philometor, besieged Alexandria in B.C.

169. By this time, however, his selfish designs were apparent: the brothers were reconciled, and Antiochus was obliged to acquiesce for the time in the arrangement which they made. But while doing so he prepared for another invasion of Egypt, and was already approaching Alexandria when he was met by the Roman embassy led by C. Popillius Lænas, who, in the name of the Roman senate, insisted on his immediate retreat (B.C. 168), a command which the late victory at Pydna made it impossible to disobey. These campaigns, which are intimately connected with the visits of Antiochus to Jerusalem in B.C. 170, 168, are briefly described in Dan. 11:25–30. The whole of Syria was afterward subdued by Ptolemy, and he was crowned at Antioch king of Egypt and Asia. 1 Macc. 11:13. Alexander Balas, a rival claimant, attempted to secure the crown, but was defeated and afterward put to death by Ptolemy. But the latter did not long enjoy his success. He fell from his horse in the battle, and died within a few days. 1 Macc. 11:18. Ptolemy Philometor is the last king of Egypt of any importance, and his reign was marked also by the erection of the temple at Leontopolis.

PTOLEMÆUS VII., also called Euergetes, was at first co-ruler with his brother, and after the death of the latter reigned alone B.C. 146–117. He was of little importance, and was, practically at least, a subject of Rome. He is named in 1 Macc. 15:16 and perhaps in 1 Macc. 1:18.

Ptolema'is (tŏl-e-mā'is). [ACCHO.]

Pu'a (pū'à), properly Puvah. Phuvah the son of Issachar. Num. 26:23.

Pu'ah (pū'à). 1. The father of Tola, a man of the tribe of Issachar, and judge of Israel after Abimelech. Judges 10:1.

2. The son of Issachar, 1 Chron. 7:1, elsewhere called Phuvah and Pua.

3. (A different Hebrew word.) One of the two midwives to whom Pharaoh gave instructions to kill the Hebrew male children at their birth. Ex. 1:15.

Publican. The class designated by this word in the New Testament were employed as collectors of the Roman revenue. The Roman senate farmed the *vectigalia* (direct taxes) and the *portoria* (customs) to capitalists who undertook to pay a given sum into the treasury (*in publicum*), and so received the name of *publicani*. Contracts of this kind fell naturally into the hands of the *equites*, as the richest class of Romans. They appointed managers, under whom were the *portitores*, the actual custom-house officers, who examined each bale of goods, exported or imported, assessed its value more or less arbitrarily, wrote out the ticket, and enforced payment. The latter were commonly natives of the province in which they were stationed, as being brought daily into contact with all classes of the population. The name *publicani* was used popularly, and in the New Testament exclusively, of the *portitores*. The system was essentially a vicious one. The *portitores* were encouraged in the most vexatious or fraudulent exactions, and a remedy was all but impossible. They overcharged whenever they had an opportunity, Luke 3:13; they brought false charges of smuggling in the hope of extorting hush-money, Luke 19:8; they detained and opened letters on mere suspicion. It was the basest of all livelihoods. All this was enough to bring the class into ill favor everywhere. In Judea and Galilee there were special circumstances of aggravation. The employment brought out all the besetting vices of the Jewish character. The strong feeling of many Jews as to the absolute unlawfulness of paying tribute at all made matters worse. The scribes who discussed the question, Matt. 22:17, for the most part answered it in the negative. In addition to their other faults, accordingly, the publicans of the New Testament were regarded as traitors and apostates, defiled by their frequent intercourse with the heathen, willing tools of the oppressor. The class thus practically excommunicated furnished some of the earliest disciples both of the Baptist and of our Lord. Jesus was accused by the Pharisees of "eating with publicans and sinners," classing the two together and indicating by the accusation that such association proved that Jesus himself was evil. Matt. 9:11; Luke 15:2. It was doubtless Jesus' knowledge of the contempt in which they were held which made him contrast the two—the Pharisee and the publican—in their prayers. Luke 18:10. The position of Zacchæus as a "chief among the publicans," Luke 19:2, implies a gradation of some kind

among the persons thus employed by the Romans.

Pub'lius (pŭb'lĭ-ŭs), the chief man—probably the governor—of Melita, who courteously received St. Paul and his companions on the occasion of their being shipwrecked off that island, and lodged them for three days. Acts 28:7. (A.D. 59.)

Pu'dens (pū'denz) (*modest*), a Christian friend of Timothy at Rome. 2 Tim. 4:21. (A.D. 64.) According to legend he was the host of St. Peter and friend of St. Paul, and was martyred under Nero. It is interesting to note that in an inscription found in Rome, a man of the same name is said to have been a servant of Tiberius or Claudius. This may well be the same man. Martial, the Roman poet, gives the same three names together as does St. Paul—Pudens, Linus, and Claudia—referring to about the same time. In this case Claudia was the wife of Pudens. She is believed by scholars to have been of British origin.

Pu'hites (pū'hītes), **The**. According to 1 Chron. 2:53, the "Puhites" or "Puthites" belonged to the families of Kirjath-jearim, a town which is mentioned several times in the accounts of Jewish history.

Pul (pŭl), a country or nation mentioned in Isa. 66:19. It is spoken of with distant nations, and is supposed by some to represent the island Philæ in Egypt, and by others Libya. The majority of modern scholars, however, consider it to be a copyist's error for the name PUT.

Pul, an Assyrian king, and the first Assyrian monarch mentioned in Scripture. He made an expedition against Menahem, king of Israel, about B.C. 745. 2 Kings 15:19. *Pulu* was without doubt the original name of Tiglath-pileser III, but the Israelites knew him by this shortened form.

Pulse (*seeds*) usually means peas, beans and the seeds that grow in pods. In the Authorized Version it occurs only in Dan. 1:12, 16, as the translation of words the literal meaning of which is "seeds" of any kind. Probably the term denotes uncooked grain of any kind, as barley, wheat, millet, vetches, etc.

Punishments. The earliest theory of punishment current among mankind is doubtless the one of simple retaliation, "blood for blood." Viewed historically, the first case of punishment for crime mentioned in Scripture, next to the Fall itself, is that of Cain, the first murderer. That death was regarded as the fitting punishment for murder appears plain from the remark of Lamech. Gen. 4:24. In the postdiluvian code, if we may so call it, retribution by the hand of man, even in the case of an offending animal, for blood shed, is clearly laid down. Gen. 9:5, 6. Passing onward to Mosaic times, we find the sentence of capital punishment, in the case of murder, plainly laid down in the law. Ex. 21: 12, 14; Num. 35:19, 30, 31. The murderer was to be put to death, even if he should have taken refuge at God's altar or in a refuge city, and the same principle was to be carried out even in the case of an animal.

Offences punished with death.—I. The following offences also are mentioned in the law as liable to the punishment of death: 1. Striking, or even reviling, a parent. Ex. 21:15, 17. 2. Blasphemy, Lev. 24:14, 16, 23. 3. Sabbathbreaking. Ex. 31:14; 35:2; Num. 15: 32–36. 4. Witchcraft, and false pretension to prophecy. Ex. 22:18; Lev. 20: 27; Deut. 13:5; 18:20. 5. Adultery. Lev. 20:10; Deut. 22:22. 6. Unchastity. Lev. 21:9; Deut. 22:21, 23. 7. Rape. Deut. 22:25. 8. Incestuous and unnatural connections. Ex. 22:19; Lev. 20:11, 14, 16. 9. Man-stealing. Ex. 21:16; Deut. 24:7. 10. Idolatry, actual or virtual, in any shape. Lev. 20: 2; Deut. 13:6, 10, 15; 17:2–7; see Josh. 7 and 22:20 and Num. 25:8. 11. False witness in certain cases. Deut. 19:16, 19. 12. Incorrigibility joined to habitual drunkenness. Deut. 21:18–21. 13. Refusal to submit to the decrees of priest or judge. Deut. 17:12. Treason also was punished with death, but it does not appear until the time of the kings. II. But there is a large number of offences, some of them included in this list, which are named in the law as involving the penalty of "cutting off from the people." On the meaning of this expression some controversy has arisen. There are altogether thirty-six or thirty-seven cases in the Pentateuch in which this formula is used. By some it is thought to be merely excommunication; by others that with banishment or deprivation of civil rights. Still others consider that it is a sentence of death

to be executed in some cases without remission, but in others voidable—(1) by immediate atonement on the offender's part; (2) by direct interposition of the Almighty, *i. e.,* a sentence of death always "recorded," but not always executed.

Kinds of punishment.—Punishments are twofold, Capital and Secondary. I. *Capital.* 1. *Stoning* was the ordinary mode of execution. Ex. 17:4; Luke 20:6; John 10:31; Acts 14:5. In the case of idolatry, and it may be presumed in other cases also, the witnesses, of whom there were to be at least two, were required to cast the first stone. Deut. 13:9; Acts 7:58. 2. *Hanging* is mentioned as a distinct punishment. Num. 25:4; 2 Sam. 21:6, 9. 3. *Burning,* in pre-Mosaic times, was the punishment for unchastity. Gen. 38:24. Under the law it was ordered in the case of a priest's daughter. Lev. 21:9. Both hanging and burning were often done after death by some other method. 4. *Death by the sword* or *spear* is named in the law, Ex. 19:13; 32:27; Num. 25:7; and it occurs frequently in regal and post-Babylonian times. 1 Kings 2: 25, 34; 19:1; 2 Chron. 21:4, etc. 5. *Strangling* is said by the rabbins to have been regarded as the most common but least severe of the capital punishments, and to have been performed by immersing the convict in clay or mud, and there strangling him by a cloth twisted round the neck. 6. CRUCIFIXION is treated elsewhere. 7. *Drowning,* though not ordered under the law, was practised at Rome, and is said by St. Jerome to have been in use among the Jews. 8. *Sawing asunder* or crushing beneath iron instruments. 2 Sam. 12: 31, and perhaps Prov. 20:26; Heb. 11: 37. 9. *Pounding in a mortar* is alluded to in Prov. 27:22, but not as a legal punishment. Perhaps the expression is metaphorical with no actual ground in fact. *Precipitation,* attempted in the case of our Lord at Nazareth, and carried out in that of captives from the Edomites, and of St. James, who is said to have been cast from "the pinnacle" of the temple. Criminals executed by law were buried outside the city gates, and heaps of stones were flung upon their graves. Josh. 7:25, 26; 2 Sam. 18:17; Jer. 22:19. II. Of *secondary punishments* among the Jews the original principles were, 1. *Retaliation,* "eye for eye," etc. Ex. 21:24, 25. 2. *Compen-*

sation, identical (restitution) or analogous; payment for loss of time or of power. Ex. 21:18–36; Lev. 24:18–21; Deut. 19:21. *Slander* against a wife's honor was to be compensated to her parents by a fine of one hundred shekels, and the traducer himself to be punished with stripes. Deut. 22:18, 19. 3. *Stripes,* whose number was not to exceed forty, Deut. 25:3; whence the Jews took care not to exceed thirty-nine. 2 Cor. 11:24. 4. *Scourging* with thorns is mentioned Judges 8:16. The *stocks* are mentioned Jer. 20:2; *passing through fire,* 2 Sam. 12:31; *mutilation,* Judges 1:6; and see 2 Sam. 4:12; *plucking out hair,* Isa. 50:6; in later times, *imprisonment* and *confiscation* or *exile.* Ezra 7:26; Jer. 37:15; 38:6; Acts 4:3; 5:18; 12:4.

Pu'nites (pū'nītes), **The,** the descendants of Pua or Puvah, the son of Issachar. Num. 26:23.

Pu'non (pū'non) (*darkness*), one of the halting-places of the Israelite host during the last portion of the wandering. Num. 33:42, 43. By Eusebius and Jerome it is identified with Phæno, which contained the copper-mines so well known at that period, and was situated between Petra and Zoar.

Purification, in its legal and technical sense, is applied to the ritual observances whereby an Israelite was formally absolved from the taint of uncleanness. The essence of purification, in all cases, consisted in the use of water, whether by way of ablution or aspersion; but in the *majora delicta* of legal uncleanness, sacrifices of various kinds were added, and the ceremonies throughout bore an expiatory character. Ablution of the person and of the clothes was required in the cases mentioned in Lev. 15:18; 11:25, 40; 15:16, 17. In cases of childbirth the sacrifice was increased to a lamb of the first year, with a pigeon or turtle-dove. Lev. 12:6. The ceremonies of purification required in cases of contact with a corpse or a grave are detailed in Num. 19. The purification of the leper was a yet more formal proceeding, and indicated the highest pitch of uncleanness. The rites are described in Lev. 14:4–32. The necessity of purification was extended in the post-Babylonian period to a variety of unauthorized cases. Cups and pots and brazen vessels were washed as a matter of ritual observance. Mark 7:4. The washing of the hands before meals was conducted in a formal manner. Mark 7:3. What may have been the specific causes of uncleanness in those who came up to purify themselves before the Passover, John 11:55, or in those who had taken upon themselves the Nazirites' vow, Acts 21:24, 26, we are not informed. In conclusion it may be observed that the distinctive feature in the Mosaic rites of purification is their expiatory character. The idea of uncleanness was not peculiar to the Jew; but with all other nations simple ablution sufficed: no sacrifices were demanded. The Jew alone was taught by the use of expiatory offerings to discern to its fullest extent the connection between the outward sign and the inward fount of impurity.

Pu'rim (*lots*), the annual festival instituted to commemorate the preservation of the Jews in Persia from the massacre with which they were threatened through the machinations of Haman. Esther 9. It was probably called Purim by the Jews in irony. Their great enemy Haman appears to have been very superstitious, and apparently cast lots to ascertain a favorable day for carrying out his plans against the Jews. Esther 3:7. The festival lasted two days, and was regularly observed on the 14th and 15th of Adar. According to modern custom, as soon as the stars begin to appear on the 13th of the month as is ordinarily reckoned, but when by Jewish customary reckoning the 14th of the month has commenced, candles are lighted up in token of rejoicing, and the people assemble in the synagogue. After a short prayer and thanksgiving, the reading of the book of Esther commences. The book is written in a peculiar manner, on a roll called "the Roll" (*Megillah*). When the reader comes to the name of Haman, the congregation cry out, "May his name be blotted out," or, "Let the name of the wicked perish." When the Megillah is read through, the whole congregation exclaim, "Cursed be Haman; blessed be Mordecai; cursed be Zoresh (the wife of Haman); blessed be Esther; cursed be all idolaters; blessed be all Israelites, and blessed be Harbonah who hanged Haman." In the morning service in the synagogue, on the 14th, after the prayers, the passage is read from the law, Ex. 17:8–16, which relates the destruction of the Amalekites, the people of Agag, 1 Sam. 15:8, the supposed ancestor of Haman. Esther 3:1. The Megillah is then read again in the same manner. When the service in the synagogue is over, all give themselves up to merry-making.

Purse, a bag for money. The Hebrews, when on a journey, were provided with a bag, in which they carried their money, Gen. 42:35; Prov. 1:14; 7:20; Isa. 46:6, and, if they were merchants, also their weights. Deut. 25:13; Micah 6:11. This bag is described in the New Testament by the terms βαλάντιον (bag), Luke 10:4; 12:33; 22:35, 36, and γλωσσόκομον (originally the bag in which musicians carried the mouth-pieces of their instruments). John 12:6; 13:29. R. V. "box." The girdle also served as a purse. Matt. 10:9; Mark 6:8. Ladies wore ornamental purses. Isa. 3:24.

Put. 1 Chron. 1:8; Nah. 3:9. [PHUT.]

Pute'oli (pū-tē'o-lī) (*little wells*), the great landing-place of travelers to Italy from the Levant, and the harbor to which the Alexandrian corn-ships brought their cargoes. Acts 28:13. The celebrated bay which is now the Bay of Naples was then called "Sinus Puteolanus." The name Puteoli perhaps arose from the strong mineral springs whch are characteristic of the place. It was a favorite watering-place of the Romans, its hot springs being considered efficacious for the cure of various diseases. Here also ships usually discharged their passengers and cargoes, partly to avoid doubling the promontory of Circeium and partly because there was no commodious harbor nearer to Rome. Hence the ship in which Paul was conveyed from Melita landed the prisoners at this place, where the apostle stayed a week. Acts 28:13, 14. The associations of Puteoli with historical personages are very numerous. Scipio sailed from this place to Spain; Cicero had a villa in the neighborhood; here Nero planned the murder of his mother; Vespasian gave to this city peculiar privileges; and here Adrian was buried. In the fifth century it was ravaged by both Alaric and Genseric, and it never afterward recovered its former eminence. It is now a fourth-rate Italian town, still retaining the name of *Pozzuoli.* The remains of Puteoli are worthy of mention. Among them are the aqueduct, the reservoirs, portions (probably) of the baths, the great amphitheatre, and the building called the temple of Serapis. No Roman harbor has left as solid a memorial of itself as this one, at which St. Paul landed in Italy.

Pu'tiel (pū'tǐ-el). One of the daughters of Putiel was wife of Eleazar the son of Aaron, and mother of Phinehas. Ex. 6:25.

Pygarg occurs, Deut. 14:5, in the list of clean animals as the rendering of the Heb. *dishôn,* the name apparently of one species of antelope, though it is by no means easy to identify it.

Pyr'rhus (pir-rus), the father of Sopater of Berea. Acts 20:4, in Revised Version. (A.D. 57.)

Q

Quails. There can be no doubt that the Hebrew word in the Pentateuch, Ex. 16:13; Num. 11:31, 32, and in the 105th Psalm, denotes the common quail, *Coturnix dactylisonans.* The enormous quantity of quails taken by the Israelites has its parallel in modern times. Pliny states that they sometimes alight on vessels in the Mediterranean and sink them. Colonel Sykes states that 160,000 quails have been netted in one season on the island of Capri. The expression

THE QUAIL.

"as it were two cubits (high) upon the face of the earth," Num. 11:31, refers probably to the height at which the quails flew above the ground, in their exhausted condition from their long flight. As to the enormous quantities which the least-successful Israelite is said to have taken, viz., "ten homers" (*i. e.* eighty bushels) in the space of a night and two days, it may be that the "homers" here spoken of do not denote strictly the measure of that name, but simply "a heap." The Is-

raelites would have had little difficulty in capturing large quantities of these birds, as they are known to arrive at places sometimes so completely exhausted by their flight as to be readily taken, not in nets only, but by the hand. They "spread the quails round about the camp;" this was for the purpose of drying them. The Egyptians similarly prepared these birds. The expression "quails from the sea," Num. 11:31, is not intended to denote that the birds came from the sea as their starting-point, but it must be taken to show the direction from which they were coming. The quails were, at the time of the event narrated in the sacred writings, on their spring journey of migration northward. It is interesting to note the time specified: "it was at even" that they began to arrive; and they no doubt continued to come all the night. Many observers have recorded that the quail migrates by night.

Quar'tus (quar'tus) (*fourth*), a Christian of Corinth, Rom. 16:23, said to have been one of the seventy disciples, and afterward bishop of Berytus, (A.D. about 57.)

Quaternion, a group of four persons or things. In the N. T. it was a military term signifying a guard of four soldiers, two of whom were attached to the person of a prisoner, while the other two kept watch outside the door of his cell. Acts 12:4.

Queen. This title is properly applied to the queen-mother, since in an Oriental household it is not the wife but the mother of the master who exercises the highest authority. Strange as such an arrangement at first sight appears, it is one of the inevitable results of polygamy. An illustration of the queen-mother's influence is given in 1 Kings 2:19 ff. The term is applied to Maachah, 1 Kings 15:13; 2 Chron. 15:16, and to Jezebel, 2 Kings 10:13, and

543

to the mother of Jehoiachin or Jeconiah, Jer. 13:18; compare 2 Kings 24:12; Jer. 29:2.

Queen of heaven, Jer. 7:18; 45:17, 18, 19, 25, is the Phœnician goddess Ashtoreth or the Assyrian goddess Astarte, to whom the Hebrew women offered cakes in the streets of Jerusalem. These were both identified partly with the moon, and partly with the planet Venus.

Quicksands, The, more properly THE SYRTIS, Acts 27:17. The Syrtes were quicksands, large sand banks on the north coast of Africa, between the headlands of Tunis and Barca. The greater Syrtis, the easternmost, now called the Gulf of Sidra, was on the coast of Tripoli. The smaller, the western, now the Gulf of Cabes is on the coast of Tunis, or Carthage.

Quiver, a box made for the purpose of holding arrows. Gen. 27:3. There is nothing in the Bible to indicate either its form or material, or in what way it was carried. Other sources picture them slung over the back.

ASSYRIAN AND EGYPTIAN QUIVERS AND BOWS.

R

Ra'amah (rā'a-mah) (*quivering*), a son of Cush and father of the Cushite Sheba and Dedan. Gen. 10:7. The tribe of Raamah became afterward renowned as traders. Ezek. 27:22. The Septuagint identified the word with *Regma*, a city on the Persian Gulf.

Raami'ah (rā-a-mī'ah) (*trembling caused by Jehovah*), one of the chiefs who returned with Zerubbabel. Neh. 7: 7. In Ezra 2:2 he is called REELAIAH. (B.C. 536.)

Raam'ses (rà-ăm'sēz). Ex. 1:11. [RAMESES.]

Rab'bah (răb'bah), **Rab'bath** (*great*). 1. A very strong place east of the Jordan, and the chief city of the Ammonites. In five passages—Deut. 3:11; 2 Sam. 12:26; 17:27; Jer. 49:2; Ezek. 21:20—it is styled Rabbath (or Rabbah) of the Ammonites, or the children of Ammon; but elsewhere, Josh. 13:25; 2 Sam. 11:1; 12:27, 29; 1 Chron. 20: 1; Jer. 49:3, simply Rabbah. When first named it is mentioned as containing the bed or sarcophagus of the giant Og. Deut. 3:11. David sent Joab to besiege Rabbah, on account of the insult offered to his envoys. 2 Sam. 10: 1-6; 2 Sam. 11:1, 17, etc. Joab succeeded in capturing a portion of the place—the "city of waters," that is, the lower town, so called from its containing the perennial stream which rises in and still flows through it. The citadel still remained to be taken, but this was secured shortly after David's arrival. 2 Sam. 12:26-31. Long after, at the date of the invasion of Nebuchadnezzar, Jer. 49:2, 3, it had walls and palaces. It is named in such terms as imply that it was of equal importance with Jerusalem. Ezek. 21:20. From Ptolemy Philadelphus (B.C. 285-247) it received the name of Philadelphia. It was one of the cities of the Decapolis, and became the seat of a Christian bishop. Its ruins, which are considerable, are found at *Amman*, about 25 miles from the Jordan, at the north end of the Dead Sea.

It lies in a valley which the upper course of the *Wady Zerka*, identified with the Jabbok. The public buildings are said to be Roman, except the citadel, which is described as of large square stones put together without cement, and which is probably more ancient than the rest. 2. A city of Judah, named with Kirjath-jearim in Josh. 15:60 only. Some suggest its identification with *Rubba* about 14 miles southwest of Jerusalem.

Rab'bath-moab. [AR.]

Rab'bath of the Children of Ammon, and **Rabbath of the Ammonites.** [See RABBAH.]

Rabbi, a title of respect signifying *master, teacher,* given by the Jews to their doctors and teachers, and often addressed to our Lord, Matt. 23:7, 8; 26: 25, 49; Mark 9:5; 11:21; 14:45; John 1:38, 49; 3:2, 26; 4:31; 6:25; 9:2; 11:8. Another form of the title was Rabboni. John 20:16. The titles were used with different degrees of honor; the lowest being rab, *master;* second, rabbi, *my master;* and greatest of all, rabboni, *my lord, master.*

Rab'bith (rab'bith) (*multitude*), a town in the territory, perhaps on the boundary, of Issachar. Josh. 19:20 only. Perhaps the modern *Raba* on the south part of the range of Gilboa.

Rabbo'ni (răb-bō'nī). John 20:16. [RABBI.]

Rab'=mag (răb'măg), Jer. 39:3, 13, a title borne by a Babylonian official, apparently Nergal-sharezer, whether identical with the king called by the Greeks Neriglissar or not is a matter of doubt, but certainly possible. [NERGAL-SHAREZER]. The translation of his title is "the deeply wise prince" and probably means *chief of the magi;* at all events it was "an office of great power and dignity at the Babylonian court, and probably gave its possessor special facilities for gaining the throne."

Rab'saris (răb'sa-rĭs). The title of a high officer in the Assyrian court, perhaps the "chief of the eunuchs," or

35   545

chamberlains. It is used in the Bible with reference to three different persons. 1. An officer of the king of Assyria sent up with the Tartan and the Rabshakeh against Jerusalem in the time of Hezekiah. 2 Kings 18 : 17.

2. One of the princes of Nebuchadnezzar, who was present at the capture of Jerusalem, B.C. 586. Jer. 39 : 3. His name was probably Sarsechim.

3. The officer who ordered the release of Jeremiah, and permitted him to live in his own home. Jer. 39 : 13. His name was probably Nebushazban. Formerly (2) and (3) were thought to refer to one person—on the idea that Rabsaris was a proper name in itself. When considered as a title it is naturally inferred that the name preceding is the personal name. That is different in the two cases. The rendering in the R. V. gives color to this explanation.

Rab'shakeh (răb'sha-keh). The title of one of the three officers sent by Sennacherib to demand the surrender of Hezekiah. 2 Kings 18, 19; Isa. 36, 37. The A. V. wrongly renders it as the personal name. The original explanation "chief of the cupbearers" has always seemed a little doubtful, principally from the strangeness of employing such an officer on such a mission. The study of the cuneiform inscriptions discloses an officer *rab-saki*, "the chief of the heads" or chief captain-general, which is probably the title referred to.

Raca (rā'kà), a term of reproach and contempt meaning "empty" and hence "worthless." It is a much weaker word than the one translated "fool" which is a godless, moral reprobate. Matt. 5 : 22.

Race. [GAMES.]

Ra'chab (rā'kăb). Rahab the harlot. Matt. 1 : 5.

Ra'chal (rā'kăl) (*trade*), 1 Sam. 30 : 29, a town in the southern part of the tribe of Judah, one of the towns to which David sent presents out of the spoil of the Amalekites.

Ra'chel (rā'chel) (*ewe*, or *sheep*), the younger of the daughters of Laban, the wife of Jacob (B.C. 1753) and mother of Joseph and Benjamin. The incidents of her life may be found in Gen. 29–33, 35. The story of Jacob and Rachel has always had a peculiar interest. The beauty of Rachel, Jacob's deep love and long servitude for her, their marriage, and Rachel's death on giving birth to Benjamin, with Jacob's grief at her loss,

Gen. 48 : 7, makes a touching tale. Yet from what is related to us concerning her character there does not seem much to claim any high degree of admiration and esteem. She appears to have shared all the duplicity and falsehood of her family. See, for instance, Rachel's stealing her father's images, and the ready dexterity and presence of mind with which she concealed her theft. Gen. 31. "Rachel died and was buried on the way to Ephrath, which is Bethlehem." (B.C. 1729.) And Jacob set a pillar upon her grave; that is the pillar of Rachel's grave unto this day." Gen. 35 : 19, 20. The site of Rachel's tomb, "on the way to Bethlehem," "a little way to come to Ephrath," "in the border of Benjamin," has been shown at least since the 4th century A.D. It is about two miles south of Jerusalem and one mile north of Bethlehem. The present building is not ancient. Some feel that this does not answer all the references in the O. T., but no other site can be agreed upon.

Rad'dai (răd'da-ī) (*cutting under*), one of David's brothers, fifth son of Jesse. 1 Chron. 2 : 14.

Ra'gau (rā'gau), one of the ancestors of our Lord, son of Phalec. Luke 3 : 35. He is the same person with Reu, son of Peleg.

Ragu'el (ra-gū'el), or **Reu'el** (*friend of God*). Probably the same as Jethro. [JETHRO; HOBAB.] (B.C. 1530.) Num. 10 : 29.

Ra'hab (rā'hăb), or **Ra'chab** (*wide*), a celebrated woman of Jericho, who received the spies sent by Joshua to spy out the land, hid them in her house from the pursuit of her countrymen, was saved with all her family when the Israelites sacked the city, and probably was the same who later became the wife of Salmon and the ancestress of the Messiah. Josh. 2:1; Matt. 1:5. (B.C. 1450.) She was a "harlot," probably combining it with the more honorable occupation of weaving and dyeing. Her reception of the spies, the artifice by which she concealed them from the king, their escape, and the saving of Rahab and her family at the capture of the city, in accordance with their promise, are all told in the narrative of Josh. 2. The author of the Epistle to the Hebrews tells us that "by faith the harlot Rahab perished not with them that believed not, when she had received the spies with peace." Heb. 11 : 31; and St. James fortifies his doctrine of justification by works by asking, "Was not Rahab the harlot justified by works, when she had received the messengers, and had sent them out another way?" James 2:25. The chief objection to her identification with the Rahab of Matt. 1:5 (A. V. Rachab) is the short distance in time between Rahab who was an adult in 1450 B.C. and David, who was born about 1085 B.C. (both Ussher)— 365 years covered by the lives of Rahab after her marriage, Boaz, Obed, and of Jesse up to the birth of David. These are not irreconcilable 1. The time may be shorter than it is now reckoned. 2. There may have been some generations omitted in the record (but see Ruth 4:21, 22.)

Ra'hab (rā'hăb), a poetical name of Egypt, Ps. 89:10; Isa. 51:9, signifying "fierceness, insolence, pride." Rahab, as a name of Egypt, occurs once only without reference to the Exodus: this is in Ps. 87:4. In Isa. 30:7 the name is alluded to. In Job 9:13; 26:12, some interpreters understand a sea-monster, and in Isa. 51:9 it is parallel with dragon.

Ra'ham (rā'hăm) (*affection*). In the genealogy of the descendants of Caleb the son of Hezron, 1 Chron. 2:44, Raham is described as the son of Shema and father of Jorkoam.

Ra'hel (rā'hel), the original form in our Authorized Version in Jer. 31:15 of the now familiar Rachel.

Rain. In the Bible "early rain" signifies the rain of the autumn, Deut. 11:14, and "latter rain" the rain of spring. Prov. 16:15. For six months in the year, from May to October, no rain falls, the whole land becomes dry, parched and brown. The autumnal rains are eagerly looked for, to prepare the earth for the reception of the seed. These, the early rains, commence about the latter end of October, continuing through November and December. January and February are the coldest months, and snow falls, sometimes to the depth of a foot or more, at Jerusalem, but it does not lie long; it is very seldom seen along the coast and in the low plains. Rain continues to fall more or less during the month of March; it is very rare in April. Robinson observes that there are not, at the present day, "any particular periods of rain or succession of showers which might be regarded as distinct rainy sea-

sons. The whole period from October to March now constitutes only one continued season of rain, without any regularly-intervening term of prolonged fine weather. Unless, therefore, there has been some change in the climate, the early and the latter rains, for which the husbandman waited with longing, seem rather to have implied the first showers of autumn—which revived the parched and thirsty soil and prepared it for the seed—and the later showers of spring, which continued to refresh and forward both the ripening crops and the vernal products of the fields." James 5:7; Prov. 16:15.

Rainbow, the token of the covenant which God made with Noah when he came forth from the ark that the waters should no more become a flood to destroy all flesh. The right interpretation of Gen. 9:13 seems to be that God took the rainbow, which had hitherto been but a beautiful object shining in the heavens when the sun's rays fell on falling rain, and consecrated it as the sign of his love and the witness of his promise of protection. The rainbow is a symbol of God's faithfulness and mercy. In the "rainbow around the throne," Rev. 4:3, is seen the symbol of hope and the bright emblem of mercy and love, all the more true as a symbol because it is reflected from the storm itself.

Raisins. [VINE.]

Ra'kem (rā'kem) (*variegated*), a descendant of Machir the son of Manasseh. 1 Chron. 7:16.

Rak'kath (răk'kath) (*shore*), a fortified city in the tribe of Naphtali. Josh. 19:35. The Rabbis placed it on the western shore of the Sea of Galilee, not far from the warm baths of Tiberias.

Rak'kon (răk'kon), a place in the inheritance of Dan, not far from Joppa. Josh. 19:46.

Ram. [See BATTERING-RAM.]

Ram (*high, exalted*). 1. A son of Hezron and the father of Amminadab, born in Egypt after Jacob's migration there. Ruth 4:19. In Matt. 1:3, 4 and Luke 3:33 he is called ARAM in the Authorized Version, but RAM in the Revised Version of Matt. 1:3, 4, and ARNI in the Revised Version of Luke 3:33.

2. The first-born of Jerahmeel, and therefore nephew of the preceding, unless as some think the same man is in-

tended and there is a copyist's error. 1 Chron. 2:25, 27.

3. One of the kindred of Elihu. Job 32:2. Ewald identified this Ram with ARAM in Gen. 22:21, but Aram is not a descendant of Buz, but a nephew, and the name is not the same in the Hebrew.

Ra'ma (rā'ma), Matt. 2:18, referring to Jer. 31:15. It is the Greek form of Ramah.

Ra'mah (rā'mah) (*height*). This is the name of several places in the Holy Land. 1. One of the cities of the allotment of Benjamin. Josh. 18:25. Its site is at *er-Râm,* about five miles from Jerusalem, and near to Gibeah. Judges 4:5; 19:13; 1 Sam. 22:6. It was at this point that Jeremiah parted from the exiles who were on the way to Babylon. Jer. 40:1. Its people returned after the captivity. Ezra 2:26; Neh. 7:30.

2. The home of Elkanah, Samuel's father, 1 Sam. 1:19; 2:11, the birthplace of Samuel himself, his home and official residence, the site of his altar, ch. 7:17; 8:4; 15:34; 16:13; 19:18, and finally his burial-place. ch. 25:1; 28:3. It is also called *Ramathaimzophim.* All that is directly said as to its situation is that it was in Mount Ephraim, 1 Sam. 1:1, a district without defined boundaries. The position of Ramah is a much-disputed question. It is identified (a) with *Ramah* of Benjamin (1 above). (b) *Beit-Rima,* 12 miles northwest of Bethel. (c) *Ramallah,* 3 miles southwest of Bethel, which is less supported by tradition. Still other, but, according to Driver in Hastings' Bible Dictionary, less probable identifications are *Ramleh,* 12 miles southeast of Joppa, and *Neby Samwil,* a lofty eminence 4½ miles northwest of Jerusalem. The tradition as regards this last is a very late one.

3. One of the nineteen fortified places of Naphtali. Josh. 19:36. Dr. Robinson has discovered a *Rameh* northwest of the Sea of Galilee, about 8 miles east-southeast of Safed.

4. One of the landmarks on the boundary of Asher, Josh. 19:29, apparently between Tyre and Zidon. Robinson's identification with *Ramia,* 12 miles due east of the Ladder of Tyre, is generally favored.

5. By this name in 2 Kings 8:29 and

2 Chron. 22:6, only, is designated Ramoth-gilead.

6. A place mentioned in the catalogue of those reinhabited by the Benjamites after their return from the captivity. Neh. 11:33. Probably the same as 1.

Ramatha'im-zo'phim (rā'math-a'im-zō'fim) (*the two heights of the watchers*). [RAMAH, 2.]

Ra'mathite (rā'math-īte), **The.** Shimei the Ramathite, *i. e.* a native of Ramah, had charge of the royal vineyards of King David. 1 Chron. 27:27.

Ra'math-le'hi (rā'math-lē'hī) (*hill of the jawbone,* or *hill of Lehi*), the name bestowed by Samson on the scene of his slaughter of the thousand Philistines with the jawbone, Judges 15:17. Its location is uncertain, though several identifications are given.

Ra'math-miz'peh (rā'math-mǐz'peh) (*high place of the watch-tower*). [RAMOTH-GILEAD.]

Ra'math of the south, one of the towns at the extreme south limit of Simeon. Josh. 19:8. It is in all probability the same place as south Ramoth. 1 Sam. 30:27.

Rame'ses (rā-mē'sēz), or **Raam'ses** (*child of the sun*), a city of lower Egypt. Gen. 47:11; Ex. 12:37; Num. 33:3, 5. It was without doubt in the land of Goshen, which in Gen. 47:11 is also called "the land of Rameses." The city was one of the two store-cities built for the Pharaoh who first oppressed the children of Israel, the other being Pithom. Ex. 1:11. It was the starting place of the Israelites for the Exodus, and as their next stopping place was Succoth it could not be far from Pithom. It is probably between *Belbes* and *Tel-el-Maskhuta,* the latter of which is positively identified as PITHOM.

Rami'ah (rȧ-mī'ah), one who had taken "a strange wife." Ezra 10:25.

Ra'moth (*heights*). 1. A son of Bani who put away his foreign wife. Ezra 10:29. [JEREMOTH 6.]

2. A town of Issachar allotted to the Levites. 1 Chron. 6:73. [JARMUTH 2.]

3. [RAMOTH-GILEAD.]

4. A town in Simeon. Josh. 19:8; 1 Sam. 30:27.

Ra'moth-gil'ead (rā'moth-gǐl-e-ăd) (*heights of Gilead*), one of the great fastnesses on the east of Jordan, and the key to an important district. 1 Kings 4:13. It was the city of refuge for the tribe of Gad, Deut. 4:43; Josh. 20:8;

21:38, and the residence of one of Solomon's commissariat officers. 1 Kings 4:13. During the invasion related in 1 Kings 15:20, or some subsequent incursion, this important place had been seized by Ben-hadad I, king of Syria. The incidents of Ahab's expedition are well known. [AHAB.] Later it was taken by Israel, and held in spite of all the efforts of Hazael, who was now on the throne of Damascus, to regain it. 2 Kings 9:14. Henceforward Ramoth-gilead disappears from our view. Eusebius and Jerome specify the position of Ramoth as 15 miles from Philadelphia (*Ammân*), one however placing it east and the other west of that place. It may be Gerasa, the modern *Gerash*.

Ram's horns. [CORNET.]

Ra'pha (rā'fà) (*tall*). Son of Binea, among the descendants of Saul. 1 Chron. 8:37. Also called Rephaiah. 1 Chron. 9:43.

Ra'phael (rā'fa-el) (*God* [*El*] *has healed*). According to Jewish tradition, Raphael was one of the seven angels which stood round the throne of God—Michael, Uriel, Gabriel, Raphael, Izidkiel, Hanael and Kepharel.

Ra'phu (rā'fu), the father of Palti, the Benjamite spy. Num. 13:9.

Raven (*black*). The Hebrew *oreb* is applied to the several species of the crow family, a number of which are found in Palestine. The raven belongs to the family *Corvidæ,* of which there are numerous members in Palestine. It resembles the crow, but is larger; its black color is more iridescent, and it is gifted with greater sagacity. "There is something weird and shrewd in the expression of the raven's countenance, a union of cunning and malignity which may have contributed to give it among widely-severed nations a reputation for preternatural knowledge." One writer says that the smell of death is so grateful to them that when in passing over sheep a tainted smell is perceptible, they cry and croak vehemently. It may be that in passing over a human habitation, if a sickly or cadaverous smell arises, they would make it known by their cries, and so has arisen the idea that the croaking of a raven is the premonition of death. A raven was sent out by Noah from the ark. Gen. 8:7. This bird was not allowed as food by the Mosaic law. Lev. 11:15. Elijah was cared for by ravens. 1 Kings 17: 4, 6. They are expressly mentioned as

instances of God's protecting love and goodness. Job 38:41; Luke 12:24. The raven's carnivorous habits, and especially his readiness to attack the eye, are alluded to in Prov. 30:17. To the fact of the raven being a common bird in Palestine, and to its habit of flying

RAVEN.

restlessly about in constant search for food to satisfy its voracious appetite, may perhaps be traced the reason for its being selected by our Lord and the inspired writers as the especial object of God's providing care.

Razor. Besides other usages, the practice of shaving the head after the completion of a vow must have created among the Jews a necessity for the special trade of a barber. Lev. 14:8; Num. 6:9, 18; 8:7; Judges 13:5; Isa. 7:20; Ezek. 5:1; Acts 18:18. The razor in olden times probably did not differ from a knife, as the same word is used for both. Fifty years ago "a peculiarly shaped razor with a straight fixed handle was in use in Syria. Now European razors are universal."

Reai'a (rē-a-i'à), a Reubenite, son of Micah, and apparently prince of his tribe. 1 Chron. 5:5. The name is identical with

Reai'ah (*Jehovah has seen*). 1. A descendant of Shobal the son of Judah. 1 Chron. 4:2.

2. The children of Reaiah were a family of Nethinim who returned from

Babylon with Zerubbabel. Ezra 2:47; Neh. 7:50.

Re'ba (rē'bȧ) (*fourth*), one of the five kings of the Midianites slain by the children of Israel when Balaam fell. Num. 31:8; Josh. 13:21. (B.C. 1450.)

Rebec'ca. Rom. 9:10 only. [REBEKAH.]

Rebek'ah (rė-bĕk'kȧ) (*ensnarer*), daughter of Bethuel, Gen. 22:23, and sister of Laban, married to Isaac. She is first presented to us in Gen. 24, where the beautiful story of her marriage is related. (B.C. 1857.) For twenty years she was childless: then Esau and Jacob were born, the younger being the mother's companion and favorite. Gen. 25:19-28. Rebekah suggested the deceit that was practised by Jacob on his blind father. She directed and aided him in carrying it out, foresaw the probable consequence of Esau's anger, and prevented it by moving Isaac to send Jacob away to Padan-aram, Gen. 27, to her own kindred. Gen. 29:12. Rebekah's beauty became at one time a source of danger to her husband. Gen. 26:7. It has been conjectured that she died during Jacob's sojourn in Padan-aram.

Re'chab (rē'kăb) (*rider*). 1. One of the two "captains of bands" whom Ishbosheth took into his service, and who conspired to murder him. 2 Sam. 4:2. (B.C. 1048.)

2. The father of Malchiah, ruler of part of Beth-haccerem. Neh. 3:14. Perhaps the same as

3. The father or ancestor of Jehonadab. 2 Kings 10:15, 23; 1 Chron. 2:55; Jer. 35:6-19. It was from this Rechab that the tribe of the Rechabites derived their name. In 1 Chron. 2:55 the house of Rechab is identified with a section of the Kenites, a Midianitish tribe who came into Canaan with the Israelites, and retained their nomadic habits. The real founder of the tribe was Jehonadab. [JEHONADAB.] He and his people had all along been worshippers of Jehovah, circumcised, though not looked upon as belonging to Israel, and probably therefore not considering themselves bound by the Mosaic law and ritual. The worship of Baal was offensive to them. Jehonadab inaugurated a reformation and compelled a more rigid adherence than ever to the old Arab life. They were neither to drink wine, nor build houses, nor sow seed,

nor plant nor have any vineyard. All their days they were to dwell in tents. Jer. 35:6, 7. This was to be the condition of their retaining a distinct tribal existence. For two centuries and a half they adhered faithfully to this rule. The invasion of Judah by Nebuchadnezzar, in B.C. 607, drove the Rechabites from their tents to Jerusalem, where they stood proof against temptation, and were specially blessed. Jer. 35:2-19. Professed descendants of the sect still live as nomads in Mesopotamia and Arabia. The term had however in the time of the Apostles become merely a term for an ascetic. It is therefore probable that the claim of descent is unfounded.

Re'chabites (rē'kab-ītes). [RECHAB.]

Re'chah (rē'kah). Probably a place in Judah. 1 Chron. 4:12. Not mentioned elsewhere, and quite unknown.

Recorder, an officer of high rank in the Jewish state, exercising the functions, not simply of an annalist, but of chancellor or president of the privy council. In David's court the recorder appears among the high officers of his household. 2 Sam. 8:16; 20:24; 1 Chron. 18:15. In Solomon's he is coupled with the three secretaries. 1 Kings 4:3; comp. 2 Kings 18:18, 37; 2 Chron. 34:8.

Red Sea. 1. *Name.*—The sea known to us as the Red Sea was by the Israelites called "the sea," Ex. 14:2, 9, 16, 21, 28; 15:1, 4, 8, 10, 19; Josh. 24:6, 7, and many other passages, and specially "the sea of *sûph* or sedge," Ex. 10:19; 13:18; 15:4, 22; 23:31; Num. 14:25, etc. (In A. V., Red Sea.) Others call it *sea of reeds*, or of *weeds*. The color of the water is not red, but blue, or greenish-blue. There are many explanations of the origin of the name.

2. *Physical description.*—In extreme length the Red Sea stretches from the straits of *Bâb el-Mendeb* to the modern head of the Gulf of Suez, a distance of 1450 miles. Its greatest width may be stated at about 205 miles. At *Rás Mohammed,* on the north, the Red Sea is split by the granitic peninsula of Sinai into two gulfs; the westernmost, or Gulf of Suez, is now about 180 miles in length, with an average width of about 20, though it contracts to less than 10 miles; the easternmost, or Gulf of *el-'Akabeh,* is about 100 miles long, from the Straits of Tirán to the 'Akabeh, and 15 miles wide. The average depth of

the Red Sea is from 2500 to 3500 feet, though in places it is 1200 fathoms, about 7200 feet deep. Journeying southward from Suez, on our left is the peninsula of Sinai; on the right is the desert coast of Egypt, of limestone formation, like the greater part of the Nile valley in Egypt, the cliffs on the sea margin stretching landward in a great rocky plateau, while more inland a chain of volcanic mountains, beginning about lat. 28° 4' and running south, rear their lofty peaks at intervals above the limestone, generally about 15 miles distant.

3. *Ancient limits.*—The most important change in the Red Sea has been the drying up of its northern extremity. The land about the head of the gulf has risen and that near the Mediterranean become depressed. Geology has wellnigh proved that at one time the Mediterranean itself was not separated from the Red Sea. Indeed the head of the gulf has consequently retired gradually since the Christian era.

4. *Navigation.*—The sea, from its dangers and sterile shores, was, until the opening of the Suez Canal in 1869 rarely traversed by boats. The shores are chiefly barren rock and sand, and therefore very sparsely inhabited. Only two ports, Elath and Ezion-geber, are mentioned in the Bible. The earliest navigation of the Red Sea (passing by the pre-historical Phœnicians) is mentioned by Herodotus:—"Sesostris (Rameses II.) was the first who, passing the Arabian Gulf in a fleet of long vessels, reduced under his authority the inhabitants of the coast bordering the Erythræan Sea." Three centuries later, Solomon's navy was built "in Ezion-geber, which is beside Eloth, on the shore of the Red Sea (Yam Sûph), in the land of Edom." 1 Kings 9:26. The kingdom of Solomon extended as far as the Red Sea, upon which he possessed the harbors of Elath and Ezion-geber. [ELATH; EZION-GEBER.] It is possible that the sea has retired here as at Suez, and that Ezion-geber is now dry land. Jehoshaphat also "made ships of Tharshish to go to Ophir for gold; but they went not; for the ships were broken at Ezion-geber." 1 Kings 22:48. The scene of this wreck has been supposed to be *Edh-Dhahab,* but the identification rests principally on monkish legends. The Red Sea is now

since the opening of the Suez Canal the scene of a good trade, as a large number of vessels pass through it on their way to ports in the Far East.

5. *Passage of the Red Sea.*—The crisis of Exodus was the crossing of the Red Sea, the dividing line between slavery and freedom. There are two places where this crossing could have been made, and satisfy all the conditions recorded in Exodus.

The common view for many years has been that the crossing was over the shoals in the Northern part of the Gulf of Suez. Dr. Henry Clay Trumbull has advanced the most able arguments in his *Kadesh-barnea* in favor of this location. He says "The Israelites crossed near the town of Suez, on extensive shoals which run toward the southeast, in the direction of Ayun Musa (the Wells of Moses). The distance is about three miles at high tide. This is the most probable theory. Near here Napoleon, deceived by the tidal wave, attempted to cross in 1799, and nearly met the fate of Pharaoh." Niebuhr crossed at this part in 1762, on a dromedary, some Arabs, who were up to the knees in water, accompanying him on foot. The name of the Red Sea, in Hebrew, is *Yam Suph,* or the Sea of Weeds. The name may apply also to the lakes above, but is especially applicable to the northern part of the Red Sea; Dr. Trumbull's party halted near *Ayun Musa,* and two of them were tempted by the sight of the cool sea to walk down to its refreshing shores. But when they reached the sea it was not there, but there stretched before them a wide expanse of marine vegetation, sedge, and tall sea grasses, between the dry land and the blue waters beyond."

It is distinctly stated that the crossing was made possible by means of an east wind. A northeast wind would tend to drive the water off from the shoals. "M. de Lesseps mentioned to me the extraordinary effects of this kind which he had witnessed in such storms as occur only at intervals of fifteen or twenty years. He had seen the northern end of the sea in places blown almost dry, and again had seen the waters driven far over the land toward the Bitter Lakes."

The other probable view advocated by

many scholars, is that the Gulf of Suez at the time of the Exodus extended many miles northward to the Bitter Lakes. Professor George Frederick Wright who has lately examined this region states that "it is against all geological probabilities to assume that the land level at Suez was the same three thousand years ago that it is now. On the contrary, from the land movements which we know to be going on in that region, it is altogether probable that at the date of the Exodus the level was such that the Red Sea extended as far as Lake Timsah. The geologists who have visited the region seem to be unanimous in support of this general view. . . .

"Supposing now the children of Israel to have been encamped near the south end of the Bitter Lakes, with Pharaoh and his six hundred chariots in their rear, the situation would seem to be hopeless but for the divine intervention described in the sacred record. The strong east wind, however, which the Lord sent at this time would open the way of escape, and account for all the phenomena that are described; for this would press the water against the west side of the Red Sea, causing a resultant current to the south, and thus raise the water in the south end of the Red Sea and lower it at the north end. The extent of the effects produced by such a wind are amply illustrated in modern experience. For example, Lake Erie is 250 miles long, with its major axis lying nearly in the direction of the strongest winds. It is no unusual thing for a west wind to lower the water at Toledo seven feet below the average level, and at the same time to raise it seven feet above the level at Buffalo; while a change in the wind will exactly reverse the conditions, producing in a comparatively short time a difference of fourteen feet in the water levels at those two places. Similar phenomena are occasionally reported from Lake Menzales and the upper part of the Gulf of Suez.

"Supposing, therefore, the water to have been seven feet deep over the low land now separating Suez from the Bitter Lakes, the wind would easily open a passage several miles wide, across which the children of Israel could easily get in one night; while the returning current, on the cessation of the wind,

would be amply sufficient to overwhelm the tardy chariots of Pharaoh in their reckless pursuit. Nor is this at all derogatory to the miraculous character of the event" since it was God using his own laws by an act of his personal will.

Reed. Under this name may be noticed the following Hebrew words: 1. *Agmôn* occurs in Job 41:2, 20; Isa. 58:5, and metaphorically for the lowly in Isa. 9:14; 19:15. In Job 41:2 it is

PAPYRUS REED.

translated "rope" (A. V. "hook") and Job 41:20. R. V. "burning rushes." There is nothing either in the use of the term, nor in the etymology to give a clue to its signification. There can be no doubt that it denotes some aquatic reed-like plant, although there is no clue to the particular kind. 2. *Gôme,* translated "rush" and "bulrush" by the Authorized Version, R. V. "rush," "bulrushes" and "papyrus," Job 8:11; Ex. 2:3; Isa. 18:2. It was without doubt the celebrated paper-reed of the ancients which formerly was common in some parts of Egypt. The papyrus reed is not now found in Egypt; it grows, however, in Syria. The papyrus plant has an angular stem which grows from 10 to 15 feet high; its leaves are in tufts at the surface of the water; the flowers are in very small spikelets, which grow on the thread-like flowering branches which form a bushy crown to each stem. It was used for making paper, shoes, sails, ropes, mattresses, etc. The Greek name is βιβλos, from which came our word Bible—book—because books were made of the papyrus paper. This paper was always expensive among the Greeks. 3. *Kâneh,* a reed of any kind. 1 Kings 14:15; 2 Kings 18:21; Isa. 42:3, etc. *Kaneh-bosem,* translated "calamus," was a fragrant reed not grown in Palestine. It may be some scented grass of Europe or Asia. Caut. 4:14; Exod. 30:23; Jer. 6:20; Eze. 27:19.

The most notable reed in the Holy Land is the *Arundo donax,* which grows 8 to 20 feet high, and is thicker than a man's thumb. It has a jointed stalk like the bamboo, and is very abundant on the Nile, along the Dead Sea, Jordan and indeed almost any body of water. This was the reed used for measuring purposes. Ezek. 40:3, 5. This came to denote a fixed length of 6 cubits. 4. *Aroth* translated in A. V. of Isa. 19:7 as "paper reeds" is properly as in R. V. "meadows."

Reela'iah (rē-el-ā'yah) (*trembling caused by Jehovah*), one who went up with Zerubbabel. Ezra 2:2. In Neh. 7:7 he is called RAAMIAH. (B.C. 536.)

Refiner. The refiner's art was essential to the working of the precious metals. It consisted in the separation of the dross from the pure ore, which was effected by reducing the metal to a fluid state by the application of heat, and by the aid of solvents, such as alkali, Isa. 1:25, or lead, Jer. 6:29, which, amalgamating with the dross, permitted the extraction of the unadulterated metal. The instruments required by the refiner were a crucible or furnace and a bellows or blow-pipe. The workman sat at his work, Mal. 3:3: he was thus better enabled to watch the process, and let the metal run off at the proper moment.

Refuge, Cities of. [CITIES OF REFUGE.]

Re'gem (rē'gem) (*friend*), a son of Jahdai. 1 Chron. 2:47.

Re'gem=me'lech (rē'gem-mē'lek) (*friend of the king*). The names of Sherezer and Regem-melech occur in an obscure passage of Zechariah. ch. 7:2. They were sent on behalf of some of the captivity to make inquiries at the temple concerning fasting.

Rehabi'ah (rē-ha-bī'ah) (*Jehovah is wide*), the only son of Eliezer the son of Moses. 1 Chron. 23:17; 24:21.

Re'hob (rē'hŏb). 1. The father of Hadadezer king of Zobah, whom David smote at the Euphrates. 2 Sam. 8:3, 12.

2. A Levite or family of Levites who sealed the covenant with Nehemiah. Neh. 10:11.

3. The northern limit of the exploration of the spies. Num. 13:21. The site is not certainly identified. One suggestion is the ruins of *Hunin* in the valley of Huleh. Another, more probable, is Banias.

4, 5. Two of the towns allotted to Asher. Josh. 19:28, 30, unless both verses refer to the same town. Rehob was assigned to the Levites. Josh. 21:31. The situation of these towns is unknown.

Rehobo'am (rē'ho-bō'am), (*the people is enlarged*), son of Solomon by the Ammonite princess Naamah, 1 Kings 14:21, 31, and his successor. 1 Kings 11:43. Rehoboam selected Shechem as the place of his coronation (B.C. 937 as revised by the Assyrian records), probably as an act of concession to the Ephraimites. The people demanded a remission of the severe burdens imposed by Solomon, and Rehoboam, rejecting the advice of his father's counsellors, followed that of his young courtiers, and returned an insulting answer, which led to an open rebellion among the tribes, and he was compelled to fly to Jerusalem, Judah and Benjamin alone remaining true to him. Jeroboam was made king of the northern tribes. [JEROBOAM.] An expedition to reconquer Israel was forbidden by the prophet Shemaiah, 1 Kings 12:24; still during Rehoboam's lifetime peaceful relations between Israel and Judah were never restored. 2 Chron. 12:15; 1 Kings 14:30. In the fifth year of Rehoboam's reign the country was invaded by a host of Egyptians and other African nations under Shishak. Jerusalem itself was taken, and Rehoboam had to purchase an ignominious peace by delivering up all the treasures with which Solomon had adorned the temple and palace. The rest of Rehoboam's life was unmarked by any events of importance. He died B.C. 920, after a reign of 17 years, having ascended the throne at the age of 41. 1 Kings 14:21; 2 Chron. 12:13. He had 18 wives, 60 concubines, 28 sons and 60 daughters.

Reho'both (rē-hō'both) (*wide places*). 1. The third of the series of wells dug by Isaac, Gen. 26:22, in the Philistines' territory, identified as *er-Ruheibeh*, 16 miles south of Beersheba.

2. R. V. "Rehoboth-Ir," one of the four cities built by Asshur, or by Nimrod in Asshur, according as this difficult passage is translated. Gen. 10:11. Nothing certain is known of its position, but it was probably a suburb of Nineveh, a part of "Greater Nineveh."

3. The city of a certain Saul or Shaul, one of the early kings of the Edomites. Gen. 36:37; 1 Chron. 1:48. The affix "by the river" usually denotes the Euphrates, but some consider it as here having another signification and the site of the city is at all events unknown.

Re'hum (rē'hum) (*beloved*). 1. One who went up from Babylon with Zerubbabel. Ezra 2:2. (B.C. 536.)

2. "Rehum the chancellor." Ezra 4:8, 9, 17, 23. He was perhaps a kind of lieutenant-governor of the province under the king of Persia. (B.C. 535.)

3. A Levite of the family of Bani, who assisted in rebuilding the walls of Jerusalem. Neh. 3:17. (B.C. 445.)

4. One of the chief of the people, who signed the covenant with Nehemiah. Neh. 10:25.

5. A priestly family, or the head of a priestly house, who went up with Zerubbabel. Neh. 12:3. (B.C. 536.)

Re'i (rē'ī) (*friendly*), a person mentioned (in 1 Kings 1:8 only) as having remained firm to David's cause when Adonijah rebelled.

Reins (*i. e.* kidneys). In the ancient system of physiology the kidneys were believed to be the seat of desire and longing, which accounts for their often being coupled with the heart. Ps. 7:9; 26:2; Jer. 11:20; 17:10, etc.

Re'kem (*variegation*). 1. One of the five kings or chieftains of Midian slain by the Israelites. Num. 31:8.

2. One of the four sons of Hebron, father of Shammai. 1 Chron. 2:43, 44.

Re'kem (rē'kem), one of the towns of the allotment of Benjamin. Josh. 18:27. Its site is unknown.

Remali'ah (rĕm-alī'ah) (*Jehovah hath adorned*), the father of Pekah, captain of Pekahiah king of Israel, who slew his master and usurped his throne. 2 Kings 15:25-37; 16:1, 5; 2 Chron. 28:6; Isa. 7:1-9; 8:6.

Re'meth (rē'meth) (*height*), one of the towns of Issachar. Josh. 19:21. It is called Ramoth in 1 Chron. 6:73 and Jarmuth in Josh. 21:29.

Rem'mon (rĕm'mon) (*pomegranate*), R. V. "Rimmon," a town in the allotment of Simeon, Josh. 19:7; elsewhere accurately given in the Authorized Version as RIMMON.

Rem'mon-meth'o-ar (rĕm-mon-mĕth'o-är), a place which formed one of the landmarks of Zebulun. Josh. 19:13 only. Methoar does not really form a part of the name, but should be translated as in the Revised Version, "Rimmon which reaches to Neah." The identification with *Rumâneh* about 6 miles north of Nazareth has been generally accepted.

Rem'phan (rĕm'fan), R. V. "Rephan," Acts 7:43, and **Chi'un,** Amos 5:26, have been supposed to be names of an idol worshipped secretly by the Israelites in the wilderness. Much difficulty has been occasioned by this corresponding occurrence of two names so wholly different in sound. It is probably a corrupt transliteration of the name Chiun, or as more correctly pronounced *Kewan,* which corresponded probably to Saturn. The names of heathen deities were often distorted purposely by the Hebrews to show their contempt for them.

Re'phael (rē'fa-el) (*healed of God*), son of Shemaiah, the first-born of Obed-edom. 1 Chron. 26:7.

Re'phah (rē'fah), a son of Ephraim, and ancestor of Joshua. 1 Chron. 7:25.

Repha'iah (rĕf-ā'yah) (*Jehovah hath healed*). 1. The sons of Rephaiah appear among the descendants of Zerubbabel in 1 Chron. 3:21.

2. A Simeonite chieftain who made a successful expedition against the Amalekites of Mt. Seir. 1 Chron. 4:42.

3. Son of Tola the son of Issachar. 1 Chron. 7:2.

4. Son of Binea, and descendant of Saul. 1 Chron. 9:43.

5. The son of Hur, and ruler of a portion of Jerusalem. Neh. 3:9. (B.C. 445.)

Reph'aim (rĕf'a-im). [GIANTS.]

Reph'aim, The valley of, 2 Sam. 5:18, 22; 23:13; 1 Chron. 11:15; 14: 9; Isa. 17:5; also in Josh. 15:8 and 18:16, where it is translated in the Authorized Version "*the valley of the*

This agrees with Josephus and is the generally-accepted location of this valley. It is considered by some scholars, however, that the valley does not answer all the conditions. Some assert that there must have been at least two valleys by the name.

Rephan (rē'fan), the reading, in the Revised Version, for Remphan. Acts 7:43.

Reph'idim (rĕf'ĭ-dim). Ex. 17:1, 8; 19:2. This place lies in the march of the Israelites from Egypt to Sinai. Its

THE REPUTED VALE OF REPHIDIM.

giants," a spot which was the scene of some of David's most remarkable adventures. He twice encountered and defeated the Philistines there. 2 Sam. 5: 17–25; 23:13, etc. Since the latter part of the sixteenth century the name has been attached to the upland plain which stretches south of Jerusalem, and is crossed by the road to Bethlehem—the *el Bŭk'ah* of the modern Arabs. This valley begins near the valley of Hinnom, southwest of Jerusalem, extending toward Bethlehem. It is about a mile long, with hills on either side.

site is not certain, but it is perhaps *Wady Feiran,* a rather broad valley about 25 miles from *Jebel Musa* (Mount Sinai). Others place it in *Wady es Sheikh,* an eastern continuation of Feiran, and about 12 miles from Sinai. Here the Israelites fought their first battle and gained their first victory after leaving Egypt, the Amalekites having attacked them; here also the people murmured from thirst, and Moses brought water for them out of the rock. From this murmuring the place was called "Massah" and "Meribah."

Re'sen (rē'sen) (*bridle*), Gen. 10: 12, one of the cities built by Asshur, between Nineveh and Calah. Assyrian remains of some considerable extent are found near the modern village of *Sela-miyeh,* and it is perhaps the most probable conjecture that these represent Resen.

Re'sheph (rē'shef) (*flame*), a son of Ephraim. 1 Chron. 7: 25.

Re'u (rē'u) (*friend*), son of Peleg, in the line of Abraham's ancestors. Gen. 11: 18, 19, 20, 21; 1 Chron. 1: 25.

Reu'ben (ru'ben) (*behold a son*), Jacob's first-born child, Gen. 29: 32, the son of Leah. (B.C. 1752.) The notices of the patriarch Reuben give, on the whole, a favorable view of his disposition. To him and him alone the preservation of Joseph's life appears to have been due, and afterward he becomes responsible for Benjamin's safety. Gen. 37: 18–30; 42: 37. He was deprived of his birthright because of the crime of incest. Gen. 35: 22. He was said by his father in his dying blessing to be "unstable as water." At the time of the migration into Egypt, Reuben's sons were four. Gen. 46: 9; 1 Chron. 5: 3. The census at Mount Sinai, Num. 1: 20, 21; 2: 11, shows that at the exodus the men of the tribe above twenty years of age and fit for active warlike service numbered 46,500. The Reubenites maintained the ancient calling of their forefathers. Their cattle accompanied them in their flight from Egypt. Ex. 12: 38.

Territory of the tribe.—The portion of the promised land selected by Reuben was the northern part of the land of Moab, and had the special name of "the Mishor," with reference possibly to its evenness. Under its modern name of the *Belka* it is still esteemed beyond all others by the Arab sheep-masters. It was a fine pasture-land east of the Jordan, lying between the river Arnon on the south and Gilead on the north. The Reubenites aided their brethren to conquer the land west of the Jordan before they took entire possession of their own territory. The pile of stones or memorial altar which they erected on the bank of the Jordan, was erected in accordance with the unalterable habits of Bedouin tribes both before and since. This act was completely misunderstood, and was construed into an attempt to

set up a rival altar to that of the sacred tent. No judge, no prophet, no hero of the tribe of Reuben is handed down to us. They did not join in the contest against Sisera, and were reproached with the fact in Deborah's song. Judges 5: 15, 16. They engaged in border warfare for their own possessions, however, as they had a very exposed position. The last historical notice which we possess of them, records that they and the Gadites and the half-tribe of Manasseh were carried off by Pul and Tiglath-pileser. 1 Chron. 5: 26. Ezekiel assigns them a place among the restored tribes (48: 6, 7), and they are named in Revelation among the tribes that are sealed.

Reu'el (ru'el) (*friend of God*), one of the sons of Esau, by his wife Bashemath, sister of Ishmael. Gen. 36: 4, 10, 13, 17; 1 Chron. 1: 35, 37.

2. One of the names of Moses' father-in-law. Ex. 2: 18. (B.C. 1530.) [JETHRO.]

3. Father of Eliasaph, the leader of the tribe of Gad at the time of the census at Sinai. Num. 2: 14. (B.C. 1490.)

4. A Benjamite, ancestor of Elah. 1 Chron. 9: 8.

Reu'mah (ru'mah) (*elevated*), the concubine of Nahor, Abraham's brother. Gen. 22: 24.

Revelation, The Book of, the last book in the New Testament, and the fitting close of the Bible, since its last chapters present the consummation toward which the whole Biblical history is moving, the end and purpose of God's providential dealings with man, and of his redeeming love in Jesus Christ his Son.

THE AUTHOR. The arguments are very strongly in favor of the apostle John as the author, though others think it was written by another John called the Elder or Presbyter.

THE DATE OF WRITING was either A.D. 64–68 during the reign of Nero, or A.D. 90–96 in the reign of Domitian. Under both of these emperors the Christians suffered very severe persecutions. A short time ago most scholars favored the earlier date; but to-day there is a distinct tendency among scholars toward the later date under Domitian.

PLACE OF WRITING. The island of Patmos in the Ægean Sea 24 miles from the coast of Asia Minor, not far from Ephesus. The island is a rocky and barren island about 15 miles in circumference.

THEORIES CONCERNING THE REVELATION. Books innumerable have been written upon the Revelation, and there are many theories concerning the date, authorship, composition, sources, and interpretation of this book. It is impossible even to state them within the brief space at our disposal. We give only what after long study seems to us to be true and well-founded.

APOCALYPSE. The Greek name for this book is Apocalypse, of which Revelation, or the unveiling is a translation; for the book is the unveiling of the unseen spiritual world, and of the true vision of things to come, by means of symbols and metaphors that cannot be pictured. We can describe a man's character as to courage, love, spiritual insight, shrewdness, under the symbols of a lion, dove, eagle and fox, but we cannot put these symbols together as a picture of the man. Nearly every symbolic representation in Revelation is taken from other parts of the Bible, as Ezekiel, Daniel, the 24th chapter of Matthew. There are also a number of Jewish Apocalypses. From all these we understand the use of the Apocalyptic language; and only by so doing can we rightly interpret the book of Revelation. This use of language in no way affects the truth of the book.

THE CIRCUMSTANCES in which and for which the book was written.—The Book of Revelation was a message to the church in its darkest hours, when "the rulers of this darkness" combined to overwhelm it and sweep it from the face of the earth, "when it seemed trampled in irremediable defeat. It expressed the thoughts of men who had seen Peter crucified, and Paul beheaded. To understand it aright we must read it by the lurid light of the bale-fires of martyrdom. We must try to feel as Christians felt when they saw their brethren torn by the wild beasts of the amphitheater, or standing as living torches, each in his pitchy tunic, on one ghastly night in Rome; when the Devil, the Beast, and the False Prophet were holding foul orgies in the streets of the mystic Babylon, red with the blood of the martyrs of the Lord. It was written in the days of earthquakes, and

inundations, and volcanic outbursts, and horrible prodigies. Alike, Rome and Jerusalem had been deluged with massacre. The sun of human life seemed to be setting amid seas of blood."

At such an hour—perhaps the dimmest and most disastrous which ever fell upon an afflicted world—the Seer still prophesies triumphantly of the coming dawn. It is rather a pæan of exultation poured forth out of the midst of anguish, than a *"miserere* wrung from mighty grief." It is a book of war, but the war ends in triumph and peace. It is a book of thunder, but the rolling of the thunder dies away in liturgies and psalms.

The book gave hope and guidance to Christians then, and brings light and hope to all ages, because it describes the never-ending conflict of Christ with Antichrist of which the world's history is full, and all eternal principles are capable of infinite applications.—*Condensed from Farrar in Messages of the Books.* UNIVERSAL WORD FOR ALL AGES

The book was written for the times; but this does not mean that it had no visions beyond, or that its hopes were limited to the first age. On the contrary, it was the vision beginning near, but with an outlook down the ages to the final victory, that gave the most help, courage, and comfort to those times, just as the assured triumph of Christianity, and the ever-living Christ, inspire us with comfort and courage and hope in our darkest hours.

INTERPRETATIONS. The older interpretations of the book even down to last quarter of a century varied with modifications, between (a) The Historical or Continuous expositors, in whose opinion the Revelation is a progressive history of the fortunes of the Church from the first century to the end of time. (b) The Præterist expositors, who are of opinion that the Revelation has been almost or altogether fulfilled in the time which has passed since it was written; that it refers principally to the triumph of Christianity over Judaism and Paganism, signalized in the downfall of Jerusalem and of Rome.

Both of these are rejected by modern scholars, or greatly modified. (c) The modern view is that the book describes, in terms and by examples that belonged to the first century, the conflict of good with evil that rages through all times, or the principles and qualities, powers, moral forces that are working out the history of the world. The conflicts are repeated in every age—till the good shall reign triumphant.

THE MOVEMENT OF THE BOOK. In general we have in the first three chapters the Living Christ, the Leader and the Saviour; then in chapters 4 to 20 the long warfare of Christ and his people against evil; while chapters 21 and 22 describe the final triumph of the good in the Kingdom of God on earth and in heaven.

The most notable peculiarity of the book is the frequent change of scene from earth to heaven. The vision of the spiritual world, its powers and victories, revealed to those in persecution and trouble for their comfort, encouragement and hope.

In chapter I we see Jesus in his glory and power, our ever present Leader and King who had triumphed over death.

In chapters II and III, this Jesus gives encouragements and warnings to his people on earth, with the richest promises to all who overcome in the conflict to be described.

In chapters IV and V, the scene is transferred to heaven where there is a vision of the Almighty, Omnipresent God, in his glory and power, and the multitude of the redeemed from among those who were suffering martyrdom on earth.

In chapter VI, the scene is on earth and its persecutions, while in chapter VII the vision opens into heaven again, showing the triumph of those who were suffering for the sake of the Kingdom of God and its righteousness.

Thus we continue through chapter after chapter, as the seven seals are opened, the seven trumpets are announcing the coming of troubles, and the indignation of God against sin is poured from the seven vials (or rather bowls). The sins, the evils, the pains, the death represent pictures of what is still taking place in some parts of the world, and spiritually in all parts. Amid all this there are frequent visions of the real triumph of good, to give cheer and courage. Till at last evil is destroyed, and the Kingdom of God has come,

and the will of God is done on earth as it is in heaven.

Re'zeph (rē'zef) (*hearth-stone* [for cooking upon]), a place Sennacherib mentions, in his taunting message to Hezekiah, as having been destroyed by his predecessor. 2 Kings 19:12; Isa. 37:12. It is doubtless the town Rasappa which is often mentioned in the Assyrian records. It is now called *Rasafa* and is a few miles from the Euphrates towards Palmyra.

Rezi'a (rĕ-zī'à) (*delight*), an Asherite, of the sons of Ulla. 1 Chron. 7:39.

Re'zin (rē'zin) (*firm*). 1. King of Damascus. He was tributary to Assyria. In the time of Ahaz he joined with Pekah of Israel against Judah, about 735 B.C. Though unsuccessful in his siege of Jerusalem, 2 Kings 16:5; Isa. 7:1, he "recovered Elath to Syria." 2 Kings 16:6. Soon after this he was attacked, defeated and slain by Tiglathpileser II., king of Assyria, whose aid Ahaz had invoked, contrary to the advice of Isaiah. 2 Kings 16:9.

2. The founder of one of the families of the Nethinim. Ezra 2:48; Neh. 7:50.

Re'zon (rē'zon) (*prince*), son of Eliadah, a Syrian, who when David defeated Hadadezer king of Zobah, put himself at the head of a band of freebooters and set up a petty kingdom at Damascus. 1 Kings 11:23. He harassed the kingdom of Solomon during his whole reign.

Rhe'gium (rē'jĭ-ŭm) (*breach*), an Italian town situated on the western coast, just at the southern entrance of the Straits of Messina. The name oc-

CASTOR AND POLLUX.

curs in the account of St. Paul's voyage from Syracuse to Puteoli, after the shipwreck at Malta. Acts 28:13. By a curious coincidence, the figures on its coin are the very "twin brothers" which gave the name to St. Paul's ship.

It was originally a Greek colony; it was miserably destroyed by Dionysius of Syracuse. From Augustus it received advantages which combined with its geographical position in making it important throughout the duration of the Roman empire. The modern *Reggio* is the capital of Calabria, and a town of 43,000 inhabitants. Its distance across the straits from Messina is only about six miles.

Rhe′sa (rē′sȧ), son of Zorobabel in the genealogy of Christ. Luke 3 : 27.

Rho′da (rō′dȧ) (*rose*), the name of a maid who announced Peter's arrival at the door of Mary's house after his miraculous release from prison. Acts 12 : 13. (A.D. 44.)

Rhodes (*rosy*), a celebrated island in the Mediterranean Sea. It is triangular in form, about 43 miles long from north to south, and about 18 wide. It is noted now, as in ancient times, for its delightful climate and the fertility of its soil. The city of Rhodes, its capital, was famous for its huge brazen statue of Apollo, called the Colossus of Rhodes. It stood at the entrance of the harbor, and was so large that ships in full sail could pass between its legs. Rhodes is immediately opposite the high Carian and Lycian headlands at the southwest extremity of the peninsula of Asia Minor. Its position has had much

DIDRACHM OF RHODES.

to do with its history. Its real eminence began about 400 B.C. with the founding of the city of Rhodes, at the northeast extremity of the island, which still continues to be the capital. After Alexander's death it entered on a glorious period, its material prosperity being largely developed, and its institutions deserving and obtaining general esteem. We have notice of the Jewish residents in Rhodes in 1 Macc. 15 : 23. The Romans, after the defeat of Antiochus, assigned, during some time, to Rhodes certain districts on the mainland. Its Byzantine history is again eminent.

Under Constantine it was the metropolis of the " Province of the Islands." It was the last place where the Christians of the East held out against the advancing Saracens; and subsequently it was once more famous as the home and fortress of the Knights of St. John. It came under the control of Turkey, and was reduced to abject poverty. There are two cities—Rhodes the capital and Lindus—and forty or fifty villages with a total population of perhaps 30,000. It is now under the rule of Italy.

Ri′bai, or **Riba′i** (rī′bä-ī or rī-bā′ī) (*contentious*), the father of Ittai the Benjamite, of Gibeah. 2 Sam. 23 : 29; 1 Chron. 11 : 31.

Rib′lah (rib′lah) (*fertility*), one of the landmarks on the eastern boundary of the land of Israel, as specified by Moses. Num. 34 : 11. It seems hardly possible, without entirely disarranging the specification of the boundary, that the Riblah in question can be the same with the following, and no other has been found.

2. Riblah in the land of Hamath, a place on the great road between Palestine and Babylonia, at which the kings of Babylonia were accustomed to remain while directing the operations of their armies in Palestine and Phœnicia. Here Nebuchadnezzar waited while the sieges of Jerusalem and of Tyre were being conducted by his lieutenants. Jer. 39 : 5, 6; 52 : 9, 10, 26, 27; 2 Kings 25 : 6, 20, 21. In like manner Pharaoh-necho, after his victory over the Israelites under Josiah at Megiddo summoned Jehoahaz from Jerusalem to come before him at Riblah. 2 Kings 23 : 33. This Riblah still retains its ancient name, on the right (east) bank of the *el-Asy* (Orontes), upon the great road which connects *Baalbek* and *Hums,* about 35 miles northeast of the former place.

Riddle. In Biblical usage any dark saying of which the meaning must be thought out, is called a riddle. It is often used almost as a parallel to the word parable, so in Ps. 49 : 4 and 78 : 2, where the word is translated "dark saying." It is known that all ancient nations, and especially Orientals, were fond of riddles. The riddles which the queen of Sheba came to ask of Solomon, 1 Kings 10 : 1; 2 Chron. 9 : 1, were rather " hard questions " referring to profound inquiries. Solomon is said, however, to have been very fond of riddles. Riddles were generally proposed in verse, like the celebrated riddle of Samson. Judges 14:14–19. This, however, was not properly a riddle, since without possession of certain facts of which they were ignorant it was unguessable. After learning these facts through bribery it was easy to guess the riddle.

Rim'mon (rĭm'mon) (*pomegranate*), the name of several towns. 1. A city of Zebulun, 1 Chron. 6:77; Josh. 19:13, a Levitical city, the present *Rummaneh,* six miles north of Nazareth.

2. A town in the southern portion of Judah, Josh. 15:32, allotted to Simeon, Josh. 19:7; 1 Chron. 4:32. It is probably correctly identified with *Umm-er-Rumâmin* about 10 miles northeast of Beersheba.

3. Rimmon-parez (rĭm'mon-pā'rez) (*pomegranate of the breach*), the name of a march-station in the wilderness. Num. 33:19, 20. No place now known has been identified with it, although Ewald considers it the same as 2.

4. Rimmon the Rock, a cliff or inaccessible natural fastness, in which the six hundred Benjamites who escaped the slaughter of Gibeah took refuge. Judges 20:45, 47; 21:13. In the wild country which lies on the east of the central highlands of Benjamin the name is still found attached to a village perched on the summit of a conical chalky hill, visible in all directions, and commanding the whole country.

5. A Benjamite of Beeroth, the father of Rechab and Baanah, the murderers of Ish-bosheth. 2 Sam. 4:2, 5, 9.

Rim'mon, a deity worshipped by the Syrians of Damascus, where there was a temple or house of Rimmon. 2 Kings 5:18. It is the Hebraized form of *Ramman,* the name of a god of Assyria. He was one of the 12 chief gods, and presided over the storms, lightning and thunder. His representations are much like those of Jove with the thunder bolts. He was identical with the Syrian god *Hadad* who occupied as prominent a place among the Syrian deities. The compound Hadad-Rimmon is merely the union of the two names for the same deity, like that of *Adonis-Osiris* in Cyprus.

Ring. The earliest money was in the form of rings. Rings, on the finger, and in the ears and nose were much used in olden times. The most important use, however, was the *signet-ring,* which became the symbol of authority,

EGYPTIAN WEIGHING RINGS FOR MONEY. (See Money.)

in an age when few could sign their names. Gen. 41:42; Esth. 3:10. Rings were worn not only by men, but by women. Isa. 3:21. We may conclude from Ex. 28:11 that the rings contained

RINGS AND SIGNETS.

a stone engraven with a device or with the owner's name. The custom appears also to have prevailed among the Jews of the apostolic age. James 2:2. See SEAL.

Rin'nah (rĭn'nah) (*a shout*), one of the descendants of Judah. 1 Chron. 4: 20.

Ri'phath (rī'făth), the second son of Gomer. Gen. 10: 3. An ancient tradition identifies the name with the Riphæan mountains, which were supposed to form the northern boundary of the world. These may have been the Carpathian range in the northeast of Dacia.

Ris'sah (rĭs'sah) (*a ruin*), a march-station in the wilderness. Num. 33: 21, 22.

Rith'mah (rĭth'mah) (*broom*), a march-station in the wilderness, Num. 33: 18, 19, probably northeast of Hazeroth.

River. In the sense in which we employ the word, viz. for a perennial stream of considerable size, a river is a much rarer object in the East than in the West. With the exception of the Jordan and the Litany, the streams of the Holy Land are either entirely dried up in the summer months, and converted into hot lanes of glaring stones, or else reduced to very small streamlets, deeply sunk in a narrow bed, and concealed from view by a dense growth of shrubs. The perennial river is called *nahar* by the Hebrews. With the definite article, "*the* river," it usually signifies the Euphrates. Gen. 31: 21; Ex. 23: 31; Num. 24: 6; 2 Sam. 10: 16, etc. It is never applied to the fleeting fugitive torrents of Palestine. The term for these is *nachal,* for which our translators have used promiscuously, and sometimes, almost alternately, "valley," "brook" and "river." No one of these words expresses the thing intended; but the term "brook" is peculiarly unhappy. Many of the *wadys* of Palestine are deep, abrupt chasms or rents in the solid rock of the hills, and have a savage, gloomy aspect, far removed from that of an English brook. Unfortunately our language does not contain any single word which has both the meanings of the Hebrew *nachal* and its Arabic equivalent *wady,* which can be used at once for a dry valley and for the stream which occasionally flows through it.

River of Egypt. 1. The Nile. Gen. 15: 18. [NILE.]

2. A desert stream on the border of Egypt, still occasionally flowing in the valley called *Wâdy-el-'Arish.* The cen-

tre of the valley is occupied by the bed of this torrent, which only flows after rains, as is usual in the desert valleys. This stream is first mentioned as the point where the southern border of the promised land touched the Mediterranean, which formed its western border. Num. 34: 3–6. In the latter history we find Solomon's kingdom extending from the "entering in of Hamath unto the river of Egypt," 1 Kings 8: 65, and Egypt limited in the same manner where the loss of the eastern provinces is mentioned. 2 Kings 24: 7.

Riz'pah (rĭz'pah), concubine to King Saul, and mother of his two sons Armoni and Mephibosheth. The tragic story of the love and endurance with which she watched over the bodies of her two sons, who were killed by the Gibeonites, 2 Sam. 21: 8–11, has made Rizpah one of the most familiar objects in the whole Bible.

Road. This word occurs but once in the Authorized Version of the Bible, viz. in 1 Sam. 27: 10, where it is used in the sense of "raid" or "inroad." Where a travelled road is meant "path" or "way" is used, since the eastern roads are more like our paths.

Robbery. Robbery has ever been one of the principal employments of the nomad tribes of the East. From the time of Ishmael to the present day the Bedouin has been a "wild man," and a robber by trade. Gen. 16: 12. The Mosaic law on the subject of theft is contained in Ex. 22. There seems no reason to suppose that the law underwent any alteration in Solomon's time. Manstealing was punishable with death. Ex. 21: 16; Deut. 24: 7. Invasion of right in land was strictly forbidden. Deut. 27: 17; Isa. 5: 8; Micah 2: 2. There was a distinction made between common thieves or pilferers and robbers, or highwaymen, who in N. T. times were often rebels against the Roman power. The "two thieves" crucified with Jesus were doubtless "robbers," "brigands" "rebels."

Roe, Roebuck. The Hebrew words *yaalah* and *tsebi,* thus translated in the Authorized Version denote some species of antelope, probably the gazelle of Syria and Arabia. The gazelle was allowed as food, Deut. 12: 15, 22, etc.; it is mentioned as very fleet of foot, 2 Sam. 2: 18; 1 Chron. 12: 8; it was

36

hunted, Isa. 13:14; Prov. 6:5; it was celebrated for its loveliness. Cant. 2: 9, 17; 8:14. Another word *Yachmur*, translated in the A. V. fallow deer, is

THE WILD ROE.

translated "roebuck" in the R. V., probably correctly. Deut. 14:5; 1 Kings 4:23.

Ro'gelim (rō'gĕ-lĭm) (*place of fullers*), the residence of Barzillai the Gileadite, 2 Sam. 17:27; 19:31, probably in the north of Gilead.

Roh'gah (rōh'gah) (*clamor*), an Asherite, of the sons of Shamer. 1 Chron. 7:34.

Roll. A book in ancient times consisted of a single long strip of paper or parchment, which was usually kept rolled upon a stick, and was unrolled when a person wished to read it. The roll was usually written on one side only, and hence the particular notice of one that was "written within and without." Ezek. 2:10. The writing was arranged in columns.

Romam'ti-e'zer (rō-măm'tĭ-ē'zēr), one of the fourteen sons of Heman. 1 Chron. 25:4, 31.

Romans. 1. Inhabitants of Rome. 1 Macc. 8:1; Acts 2:10.

2. Representatives of the Roman Government. John 11:48; Acts 25:16.

3. The possessors of the right of Roman citizenship. Acts 16:21, 37, 38; 22:25-29. The right of Roman citizenship was given by birth from two Roman citizens legally married. It was acquired by purchase, or sometimes given either to individuals or districts as a reward for service, or as a political

measure. Its greatest value in New Testament times was the right of appeal to the Emperor, accompanied with the privilege of freedom from bonds, scourging or death save by a fair trial by the representatives of the people. The claim of Roman citizenship was always allowed, if made so as to reach the ears of the officer in charge, as it was an easy thing to establish, and any false claim to the right was punishable by death.

Romans, Epistle to the. 1. The *date* of this epistle is fixed at the time of the visit to Greece (Acts 20:3) during the winter and spring following the apostle's long residence at Ephesus, A.D. 58. On this visit he remained in Greece three months. 2. The *place of writing* was Corinth. 3. The *occasion* which prompted it, and the *circumstances* attending its writing, were as follows:—St. Paul had long purposed visiting Rome, and still retained this purpose, wishing also to extend his journey to Spain. Rom. 1:9-13; 15: 22-29. For the time, however, he was prevented from carrying out his design, as he was bound for Jerusalem with the alms of the Gentile Christians, and meanwhile he addressed this letter to the Romans, to supply the lack of his personal teaching. Phœbe, a deaconess of the neighboring church of Cenchreæ, was on the point of starting for Rome, ch. 16:1, 2, and probably conveyed the letter. The body of the epistle was written at the apostle's dictation by Tertius, ch. 16:22; but perhaps we may infer, from the abruptness of the final doxology, that it was added by the apostle himself. 4. The *origin of the Roman church* is involved in obscurity. If it had been founded by St. Peter, according to a later tradition, the absence of any allusion to him both in this epistle and in the letters written by St. Paul from Rome would admit of no explanation. It is equally clear that no other apostle was the founder. The statement in the Clementines that the first tidings of the gospel reached Rome during the lifetime of our Lord is evidently a fiction for the purposes of the romance. On the other hand, it is clear that the foundation of this church dates very far back. It may be that some of these Romans, "both Jews and proselytes," present on the day of Pentecost, Acts 2:

10, carried back the earliest tidings of the new doctrine; or the gospel may have first reached the imperial city through those who were scattered abroad to escape the persecution which followed on the death of Stephen. Acts 8 : 4; 11 : 19. At first we may suppose that the gospel was preached there in a confused and imperfect form, scarcely more than a phase of Judaism, as in the case of Apollos at Corinth, Acts 18 : 25, or the disciples at Ephesus. Acts 19 : 1–3. As time advanced and better-instructed teachers arrived, the clouds would gradually clear away, till at length the presence of the great apostle himself at Rome dispersed the mists of Judaism which still hung about the Roman church. 5. A question next arises as to the *composition of the Roman church* at the time when St. Paul wrote. It is more probable that St. Paul addressed a mixed church of Jews and Gentiles, the latter perhaps being the more numerous. Cicero tells us of a large Jewish community in Rome. Josephus tells us how 8000 Jews in Rome supported the complaints against Archelaus. The satires of Horace and Juvenal show that the Jews were far from popular in Rome, while no doubt their purer theism and higher morality attracted many adherents, and this was especially true of the early Christian church. All the literature of the early Roman church was written in the Greek tongue. 6. The heterogeneous composition of this church explains *the general character of the Epistle to the Romans.* In an assemblage so various we should expect to find, not the exclusive predominance of a single form of error, but the coincidence of different and opposing forms. It was therefore the business of the Christian teacher to reconcile the opposing difficulties and to hold out a meeting-point in the gospel. This is exactly what St. Paul does in the Epistle to the Romans. 7. In describing the *purport* of this epistle we may start from St. Paul's own words, which, standing at the beginning of the doctrinal portion, may be taken as giving a summary of the contents, ch. 1 : 16, 17. Accordingly the epistle has been described as comprising " the religious philosophy of the world's history." The atonement of Christ is the centre of religious history. The epistle, from its

general character, lends itself more readily to an *analysis* than is often the case with St. Paul's epistles. While this epistle contains the fullest and most systematic exposition of the apostle's *teaching,* it is at the same time a very striking expression of his *character.* Nowhere do his earnest and affectionate nature and his tact and delicacy in handling unwelcome topics appear more strongly than when he is dealing with the rejection of his fellow countrymen the Jews. 8. Internal evidence is so strongly in favor of the *genuineness* of the Epistle to the Romans that it has never been seriously questioned.

Rome. I. THE NATION. 1. *Its history.* —The nation called by the name of its metropolis and capital city, Rome, embraced very different amounts of territory at the various parts of its existence. Beginning as a city only, it gradually spread its conquests both by war and peace, till it was mistress of all the known world. It then gradually lost all it had gained till, politically, it was but a single city; though as the seat of the Supreme Head of the Catholic church, its influence always extended wherever the church had set its foot. As the capital of united Italy its political and religious importance have been existing side by side, in none too pleasant rivalry. The government of Rome originally a kingdom was from the beginning of history to 31 B.C. a republic. At that time Octavianus, grand nephew and adopted son of Julius Cæsar, assumed control as *Imperator,* under the surname of Augustus. From that time until its fall it was *the Roman Empire.*

Rome's first contact with Asia was in B.C. 192 when the war with Antiochus III., of Syria was begun, which ended by his defeat in the battle of Magnesia in 190 B.C. and a Roman protectorate over Syria. From that time Rome never lost hold of Asia. The first historic mention of Rome in the Bible is in 1 Macc. 1 : 10, about the year 161 B.C., when political relations of some sort were entered into with Judas Maccabæus. In the year 65 B.C., when Syria was made a Roman province by Pompey, the Jews were still governed by one of the Asmonæan princes. The next year Pompey himself marched an army into Judea and took Jerusalem. From this time the Jews were practically under the government of Rome. Finally, Antipater's son, Herod the Great, was made king by Antony's interest, B.C. 40, and confirmed in the kingdom by Augustus, B.C. 30. The Jews, however, were all this time tributaries of Rome, and their princes in reality were Roman procurators. On the banishment of Archelaus, A.D. 6, Judea became a mere appendage of the province of Syria, and was governed by a Roman procurator, who resided at Cæsarea. Such were the relations of the Jewish people to the Roman government at the time when the New Testament history begins.

2. *Its extent.*—Cicero's description of the Greek states and colonies as a "fringe on the skirts of barbarism" has been well applied to the Roman dominions before the conquests of Pompey and Cæsar. The Roman empire was still confined to a narrow strip encircling the Mediterranean Sea. Pompey added Asia Minor and Syria. Cæsar added Gaul. The generals of Augustus overran the northwest portion of Spain and the country between the Alps and the Danube. The boundaries of the empire were now the Atlantic on the west, the Euphrates on the east, the deserts of Africa, the cataracts of the Nile and the Arabian deserts on the south, the British Channel, the Rhine, the Danube and the Black Sea on the north. The only subsequent conquests of importance were those of Britain by Claudius and of Dacia by Trajan. The only independent powers of importance were the Parthians on the east and the Germans on the north. The population of the empire in the time of its greatest extent has been estimated at 120,000,000.

3. *The provinces.*—The usual fate of a country conquered by Rome was to become a subject province, governed directly from Rome by officers sent out for that purpose. Sometimes, however, petty sovereigns were left in possession of a nominal independence on the borders or within the natural limits of the province. Augustus divided the provinces into two classes—(1) Imperial; (2) Senatorial; retaining in his own hands, for obvious reasons, those provinces where the presence of a large military force was necessary, and committing the peaceful and unarmed

provinces to the senate. The New Testament writers invariably designate the governors of senatorial provinces by the correct title ἀνθύπατοι, proconsuls. Acts 13:7; 18:12; 19:38. A. V. "deputy." For the governor of an imperial province, properly styled "legatus Cæsaris," the word ἡγεμών (governor) is used in the New Testament. The provinces were heavily taxed for the benefit of Rome and her citizens. They are said to have been better governed under the empire than under the commonwealth, and those of the emperor better than those of the senate.

4. *The condition of the Roman empire at the time when Christianity appeared* has often been dwelt upon as affording obvious illustrations of St. Paul's expression that the "fullness of time had come." Gal. 4:4. The general peace within the limits of the empire, the formation of military roads, the suppression of piracy, the march of the legions, the voyages of the grain fleets, the general increase of traffic, the spread or the Latin language in the West as Greek had already spread in the East, the external unity of the empire, offered facilities hitherto unknown for the spread of a world-wide religion. The tendency, too, of a despotism like that of the Roman empire to reduce all its subjects to a dead level was a powerful instrument in breaking down the pride of privileged races and national religions, and familiarizing men with the truth that "God had made of one blood all nations on the face of the earth." Acts 17:24, 26. But still more striking than this outward preparation for the diffusion of the gospel was the appearance of a deep and wide-spread corruption, which seemed to defy any human remedy.

II. THE CITY.—The famous capital of the ancient world is situated on the Tiber at a distance of about 15 miles from its mouth. The "seven hills," Rev. 17:9, which formed the nucleus of the ancient city stand on the left bank. On the opposite side of the river rises the far higher side of the Janiculum. Here from very early times was a fortress with a suburb beneath it extending to the river. Modern Rome includes the site of the ancient city, and also on the right bank as well. The government quarter is in the northeastern portion, the modern part, where

THE ROMAN FORUM.

the great development of the city has been most marked since 1870 is in the north and east, and the papal quarter is on the right bank of the river. Rome is not mentioned in the Bible except in the books of Maccabees and in three books of the New Testament, viz., the Acts, the Epistle to the Romans and the Second Epistle to Timothy.

sar showed them some kindness; they were favored also by Augustus, and by Tiberius during the latter part of his reign. It is chiefly in connection with St. Paul's history that Rome comes before us in the Bible. In illustration of that history it may be useful to give some account of Rome in the time of Nero, the "Cæsar" to whom

THE COLISEUM AT ROME.

1. *Jewish inhabitants.*—The conquests of Pompey seem to have given rise to the first settlement of Jews at Rome, and many Jewish captives and immigrants were brought to Rome at that time. A special district was assigned to them, not on the site of the modern Ghetto, between the Capitol and the island of the Tiber, but across the Tiber in the quarter corresponding to the Trastevere of to-day. Many of these Jews were made freedmen. Julius Cæ-

St. Paul appealed, and in whose reign he suffered martyrdom.

2. *The city in Paul's time.*—The city at that time must be imagined as a large and irregular mass of buildings unprotected by an outer wall. It had long outgrown the old Servian wall; but the limits of the suburbs cannot be exactly defined. Neither the nature of the buildings nor the configuration of the ground was such as to give a striking appearance to the city viewed from

without. "Ancient Rome had neither cupola nor campanile," and the hills, never lofty or imposing, would present, when covered with the buildings and streets of a huge city, a confused appearance like the hills of modern London, to which they have sometimes been compared. The visit of St. Paul lies between two famous epochs in the history of the city, viz., its restoration by Augustus and its restoration by Nero. The boast of Augustus is well known, "that he found the city of brick, and left it of marble." Some parts of the city, especially the Forum and Campus Martius, must have presented a magnificent appearance, but many of the principal buildings which attract the attention of modern travellers in ancient Rome were not yet built. The streets were generally narrow and winding, flanked by densely-crowded lodging-houses (*insulæ*) of enormous height. Augustus found it necessary to limit their height to 70 feet. St. Paul's first visit to Rome took place before the Neronian conflagration; but even after the restoration of the city which followed upon that event, many of the old evils continued. The population of the city has been variously estimated. The numbers given for B.C. 15, vary from 1,300,000 to 2,265,000. At the beginning of the fourth century A.D., two authorities give the population as 1,200,000 and 1,470,000. In 1921 it was 664,571. At the beginning of the Christian era one-half of the population consisted, in all probability, of slaves. The larger part of the remainder consisted of pauper citizens supported in idleness by the miserable system of public gratuities. There appears to have been no middle class, and no free industrial population. Side by side with the wretched classes just mentioned was the comparatively small body of the wealthy nobility, of whose luxury and profligacy we learn so much from the heathen writers of the time. Such was the population which St. Paul would find at Rome at the time of his visit. We learn from the Acts of the Apostles that he was detained at Rome for "two whole years," "dwelling in his own hired house with a soldier that kept him," Acts 28 : 16, 30, to whom apparently, according to Roman custom, he was bound with a chain, Acts 28 : 20; Eph.

6 : 20; Philip. 1 : 13. Here he preached to all that came to him, no man forbidding him. Acts 28 : 30, 31. It is generally believed that on his "appeal to Cæsar" he was acquitted, and after some time spent in freedom, was a second time imprisoned at Rome. Five of his epistles, viz., those to the Colossians, Ephesians, Philippians, that to Philemon, and the Second Epistle to Timothy, were in all probability written from Rome, the latter shortly before his death, 2 Tim. 4 : 6, the others during his first imprisonment. It is universally believed that he suffered martyrdom at Rome.

3. *The localities in and about Rome* especially connected with the life of Paul are—(1) The Appian Way, by which he approached Rome. Acts 28 : 15. [APPII FORUM.] (2) His "own hired house" where he lived for two years. Acts 28 : 30. This may mean either the great camp of the Prætorian guards which Tiberius established outside the walls on the northeast of the city, or, a barrack attached to the imperial residence on the Palatine, or in any case in some place where he was brought in contact with those who formed a part of Nero's household. Phil. 1 : 13; 4 : 22. (3) The connection of other localities at Rome with St. Paul's name rests only on traditions of more or less probability. We may mention especially—(a) The Mamertine prison, or Tullianum, built by Ancus Martius near the Forum. It still exists beneath the church of St. Giuseppe dei Falegnami. It is said that St. Peter and St. Paul were fellow prisoners here for nine months. This is not the place to discuss the question whether St. Peter was ever at Rome. It may be sufficient to state that though there is no evidence of such a visit in the New Testament, unless Babylon in 1 Pet. 5 : 13 is a mystical name for Rome, yet early testimony and the universal belief of the early Church seem sufficient to establish the fact of his having suffered martyrdom there. [PETER.] The story, however, of the imprisonment in the Mamertine prison seems inconsistent with 2 Tim. 4 : 11. (b) The chapel on the Ostian road which marks the spot where the two apostles are said to have separated on their way to martyrdom. (c) The supposed scene of St.

Paul's martyrdom, viz., the church of St. Paolo alle tre fontane on the Ostian road. To these may be added—(d) The supposed scene of St. Peter's martyrdom, viz., the church of St. Pietro in Montorio, on the Janiculum. (e) The chapel Domine quo Vadis, on the Appian road, the scene of the beautiful legend of our Lord's appearance to St. Peter as he was escaping from martyrdom. (f) The places where the bodies of the two apostles, after having been deposited first in the catacombs, are supposed to have been finally buried—that of St. Paul by the Ostian road, that of St. Peter beneath the dome of the famous Basilica which bears his name. We may add, as sites unquestionably connected with the Roman Christians of the apostolic age—(g) The gardens of Nero in the Vatican, not far from the spot where St. Peter's now stands. Here Christians, wrapped in the skins of beasts, were torn to pieces by dogs, or, clothed in inflammable robes, were burnt to serve as torches during the midnight games. Others were crucified. (h) The Catacombs. These subterranean galleries, commonly from 8 to 10 feet in height and from 4 to 6 in width, and extending for miles, especially in the neighborhood of the old Appian and Nomentan Ways, were unquestionably used as places of refuge, of worship and of burial by the early Christians. The earliest dated inscription in the catacombs is A.D. 71. Discoveries proving and disproving many of the legends and traditions of early Rome are steadily being made in various parts of Rome, in the course of the systematic excavations being made under the direction of the Italian government. Ruins of churches dating back to the earliest period of Christianity, surely not long after the destruction of Pompeii have been found. It may be that other discoveries may be made which shall throw more light upon the history of the church at Rome and its connection with Paul and Peter. Nothing is known of the first founder of the Christian Church at Rome. Christianity may, perhaps, have been introduced into the city not long after the outpouring of the Holy Spirit on the day of Pentecost by the "strangers of Rome," who were then at Jerusalem. Acts 2:10. It is clear that there were many Christians at Rome before St. Paul visited the city. Rom. 1:8, 13, 15; 15:20. The names of twenty-four Christians at Rome are given in the salutations at the end of the Epistle to the Romans. Linus, who is mentioned 2 Tim. 4:21, and Clement, Philip. 4:3, are supposed to have succeeded St. Peter as bishops of Rome.

Roof. [HOUSE.]

Room. The references to "room" in Matt. 23:6; Mark 12:39; Luke 14:7, 8; 20:46, signify the highest place on the highest couch round the dinner or supper table—the "uppermost seat," as it is more accurately rendered in Luke 11:43, and R. V. substitutes in every case "place" or "seat," for this obsolete use of "room."

Rose occurs twice only, viz. in Cant. 2:1; Isa. 35:1. There is much difference of opinion as to what particular flower is here denoted; but it appears to

ROSE OF SHARON.

us most probable that the narcissus is intended. Chateaubriand mentions the narcissus as growing in the plain of Sharon. Roses are greatly prized in the East, more especially for the sake of the rose-water, which is in much request. There are seven species of wild roses in Syria.

Rosh (rŏsh) (*head*). In the genealogy of Gen. 46:21, Rosh is reckoned among the sons of Benjamin.

Rosh, Ezek. 38:2, 3; 39:1, probably a proper name, referring to the first of the three great Scythian tribes of which Magog was the head.

Rubies. Concerning the meaning of the Hebrew words translated "rubies" there is much difference of opinion. Job 28:18; see also Prov. 3:15; 8:11; 31:10. Some suppose "coral" to be intended; others "pearl," supposing that the original word signifies merely "bright in color," or "color of a reddish tinge." "Agate" in A. V. of Isa. 54:12; Eze. 27:16, is given as "rubies" by the R. V. The real ruby is a red sapphire, next in value to the diamond. The finest rubies are brought chiefly from Ceylon and Burmah.

Rue occurs only in Luke 11:42. The rue here spoken of is doubtless the common *Ruta graveolens,* a shrubby

RUE.

plant 2 to 4 feet high, of strong medicinal virtues. It is a native of the Mediterranean coasts. The Talmud enumerates rue amongst kitchen-herbs, and regards it as free of tithe, as being a plant not cultivated in gardens. In our Lord's time, however, rue was doubtless a garden plant, and therefore tithable.

Ru′fus (*red*) is mentioned in Mark 15:21 as a son of Simon the Cyrenian. Luke 23:26. (A.D. 30.) Again, in Rom. 16:13, the apostle Paul salutes a Rufus whom he designates as "elect in the Lord." This Rufus was perhaps identical with the one to whom Mark refers; but the name is so common that there is no proof of this.

Ruha′mah (*having obtained mercy*). Hos. 2:1. The name, if name it be, is symbolical, and is addressed to the daughters of the people, to denote that they were still the objects of love and tender compassion.

Ru′mah (rụ′mah) (*height*), mentioned once only—2 Kings 23:36. It has been conjectured to be the same place as Arumah, Judges 9:41, which was apparently near Shechem. There is another town of the name in Galilee.

Rush. [REED.]

Ruth, a Moabitish woman, the wife, first of Mahlon, secondly of Boaz, the ancestress of David and of Christ, and one of the four women who are named by St. Matthew in the genealogy of Christ. A severe famine in the land of Judah induced Elimelech, a native of Bethlehem-ephratah, to emigrate into the land of Moab, with his wife Naomi, and his two sons, Mahlon and Chilion. Ruth lived in the later period of the Judges, perhaps under Gideon or Eli during the 12th century B.C. After several years Naomi, now left a widow and childless, having heard that there was plenty again in Judah, resolved to return to Bethlehem, and her daughter-in-law Ruth returned with her. They arrived at Bethlehem just at the beginning of barley harvest, and Ruth, going out to glean, chanced to go into the field of Boaz, a wealthy man and a near kinsman of her father-in-law, Elimelech. Upon learning who the stranger was, Boaz treated her with the utmost kindness and respect, and sent her home laden with corn which she had gleaned. Encouraged by this incident, Naomi instructed Ruth to claim at the hand of Boaz that he should perform the part of her husband's near kinsman, by purchasing the inheritance of Elimelech and taking her to be his wife. With all due solemnity, Boaz took Ruth to be his wife, amidst the blessings and congratulations of their neighbors. Their son, Obed, was the father of Jesse, who was the father of David.

Ruth, Book of, "is the very ideal and type of the Idyl," describing the simple domestic life of Israel during the period, concerning which the book of Judges describes chiefly the wars and political changes. Instead of war, of national strife, of political struggle we have here great harvest festivals, transfers of land, emigration, marriage, farming life, and peaceful homes. To describe this idyllic life, to show the laws of marriage, and to give an account of David's ancestors are evidently its purpose; and the book was avowedly composed long after the time of the heroine. See Ruth 1:1; 4:7, 17. Its date and author are quite uncertain. The book of Ruth clearly forms part of the books of Samuel, supplying as it does the essential point of David's genealogy and early family history, and is no less clearly connected with the book of Judges by its opening verse and the epoch to which the whole book relates.

Rye (Heb. *cussemeth*) occurs in Ex. 9:32; Isa. 28:25; Ezek. 4:9. In all cases R. V. has "spelt" which is also found in the margin of the A. V. Spelt (*Triticum spelta*) is a sort of wild wheat not far different from common wheat. Spelt is not cultivated now in Syria and is unknown in its wild state. A better translation might be "Vetches."

S

Sabac'thani (sā-băk'tha-nī). See ELI.

Sab'aoth (săb'a-ŏth), **The Lord of,** occurs in Rom. 9 : 29; James 5 : 4, but is more familiar through its occurrence in the Sanctus of Te Deum—"Holy, holy, holy, Lord God of Sabaoth." Sabaoth is the Greek form of the Hebrew word for "hosts" in the sense of "armies," and is translated in the Authorized Version of the Old Testament by "Lord of hosts," "Lord God of hosts." There is a difference of opinion as to whether it means the leader of the armies of Israel, or of the armies of angels, or of the forces of nature. The first seems too narrow for all the references, while the last seems too vague.

Sabbath (*shabbâth*, "a day of rest.") The name is applied to divers great festivals, but principally and usually to the seventh day of the week, the strict observance of which is enforced not merely in the general Mosaic code, but in the Decalogue itself. The first scriptural notice of it, though it is not mentioned by name, is to be found in Gen. 2 : 3, at the close of the record of the six-days creation. There are not wanting indirect evidences of its observance by the patriarchs, as the intervals between Noah's sending forth the birds out of the ark, an act naturally associated with the weekly service, Gen. 8 : 7–12. It is in Ex. 16 : 23–29 in connection with the giving of the manna, that we find the first incontrovertible institution of the day, as one given to and to be kept by the children of Israel. Shortly afterward it was re-enacted in the Fourth Commandment. The beneficent character of the Fourth Commandment is very apparent in the version of it which we find in Deuteronomy. Deut. 5 : 12–15. Bondman and bondmaid, nay, even the beast of the field, is to have full right in it. "The stranger," too, is comprehended in the benefit. But the original proclamation of it in Exodus places it on a ground which, closely connected no doubt with these others, is yet higher and more comprehensive. Since God in his creative work rested on the seventh day, so man should rest and hallow the seventh day in God's honor. It is most important to remember that the Fourth Commandment is not limited to a mere enactment respecting one day, but prescribes the due distribution of a week, and enforces the six days' work as much as the seventh day's rest. A great snare has always been hidden in the word *work,* as if the commandment forbade occupation and imposed idleness. The terms in the commandment show plainly enough the sort of work which is contemplated—*servile work* and *business.* The prohibition of work is only subsidiary to the positive idea of joyful rest and *recreation,* in communion with Jehovah, who himself "rested and was refreshed." Ex. 31 : 17; comp. 23 : 12. When at the end of the 40 years of wandering Moses reviewed their history he assigned as a reason for the observance of the Sabbath, its serving as a memorial of Jehovah's deliverance of his people from bondage in Egypt. This is doubtless a *special motive* for the joy with which the Sabbath should be celebrated, and for the kindness which extended its blessings to the slave and the beast of burden as well as to the master: "that thy manservant and thy maidservant may rest *as well as thou."* Deut. 5 : 14. The Pentateuch presents us with but three applications of the general principle—Ex. 16 : 29; 35 : 3; Num. 15 : 32–36. The reference of Isaiah to the Sabbath gives us no details. The references in Jeremiah and Nehemiah show that carrying goods for sale, and buying such, were equally profanations of the day. A consideration of the spirit of the law and of Christ's comments on it will show that it is

571

work for worldly gain that was to be suspended; and hence the restrictive clause is prefaced with the positive command, "Six days *shalt thou* labor, and do all thy work;" for so only could the sabbatic rest be fairly earned. Hence, too, the stress constantly laid on permitting the servant and beast of burden to share the rest which selfishness would grudge to them. Thus the spirit of the Sabbath was joy, refreshment and mercy, arising from remembrance of God's goodness as the Creator and as the Deliverer from bondage. The Sabbath was a perpetual sign and covenant, and the holiness of the day is connected with the holiness of the people; "that ye may know that I am Jehovah that doth sanctify you." Ex. 31:12–17; Ezek. 20:12. *Joy* was the key-note of their service. Nehemiah commanded the people, on a day holy to Jehovah, "Mourn not, nor weep: eat the fat, and drink the sweet, and send portions to them for whom nothing is prepared." Neh. 8:9–12. The Sabbath is named as a day of special worship in the sanctuary. Lev. 19: 30; 26:2. It was proclaimed as a *holy convocation.* Lev. 23:3. In later times the worship of the sanctuary was enlivened by sacred music. Ps. 68:25–27; 150, etc. On this day the people were accustomed to consult their prophets, 2 Kings 4:23, and to give to their children that instruction in the truths recalled to memory by the day which is so repeatedly enjoined as the duty of parents; it was "the Sabbath of Jehovah" not only in the sanctuary, but "in all their dwellings." Lev. 23:3.

When we come to the New Testament we find the most marked stress laid on the Sabbath. In whatever ways the Jew might err respecting it, he had altogether ceased to neglect it. On the contrary, wherever he went its observance became the most visible badge of his nationality. Our Lord's mode of observing the Sabbath was one of the main features of his life, which his Pharisaic adversaries most eagerly watched and criticised. They had invented many prohibitions respecting the Sabbath of which we find nothing in the original institution. Some of these prohibitions were fantastic and arbitrary, in the number of those "heavy burdens and grievous to be borne"

which the latter expounders of the law "laid on men's shoulders." Comp. Matt. 12:1–13; John 5:10. That this perversion of the Sabbath had become very general in our Saviour's time is apparent both from the recorded objections to acts of his on that day and from his marked conduct on occasions to which those objections were sure to be urged. Matt. 12:1–15; Mark 3:2; Luke 6:1–5; 13:10–17; John 5:2–18; 7:23; 9:1–34. Christ's words do not remit the duty of keeping the Sabbath, but only deliver it from the false methods of keeping which prevented it from bestowing upon men the spiritual blessings it was ordained to confer. The almost total silence of the epistles in relation to keeping the Sabbath doubtless grew out of the fact that the early Christians kept the Sabbath, and that this period was one of change from the seventh to the first day of the week, and any definite rules would have been sure to be misunderstood. For many years both the first and the seventh days of the week were kept as Sabbaths; and gradually the first day of the week, the Lord's day, took the place among Christians of the seventh day, and they had the fullest warrant for the change. [LORD'S DAY.]

The Fourth Commandment of the Decalogue is just as binding now as it ever was, or as any other of the Ten Commandments. Those who argue that God has abolished this Sabbath, but has written the Sabbath law in our very natures, must have strange ideas of the wisdom of a God who abolishes a command he has made it necessary to keep. Christians in keeping the Lord's day keep the Fourth Commandment, as really as do those who keep what is called the seventh day. They keep every seventh day, only the counting starts from a different point. As to the method of keeping the Sabbath no rules are laid down; but no one can go far astray who holds to the principles laid down;—(1) *Rest.* Nothing is to be done in daily business, and no recreation taken which destroys the rest of others or takes from any the privileges of the Sabbath. (2) *Spiritual nurture.* One day in seven is to be set apart for the culture of the spiritual nature. These two principles of Sabbath-keeping will always go together. Only a religious Sabbath, which belongs to God, can be retained among men as a day of *rest*. If men can sport on the Sabbath, they will soon be made to work. Witness the large number of people who must minister to the sport of others. Also the fact that where the Sabbath is merely a day of pleasure the shops soon begin to stay open. Paris has been through this, and now is striving to do away with the work which has followed the pleasure which is still to be allowed. The only barrier that can keep the world out of the Sabbath, that can preserve it to the working people as a day of rest, is God's command to keep it sacred to him. When Sunday becomes merely a day of pleasure, it ceases to be a day of rest. So important is the Sabbath to man that no people can have the highest religious life, the truest freedom, the greatest prosperity, unless they be a Sabbath-keeping people, whose Sabbath is one of rest and of religion—(*a*) Because man needs the rest for his whole system. More is accomplished in six days than can be in seven days of work. The Sabbath was recognized as a weekly day of rest in Babylonia as early as 3800 B.C. (*b*) Because man needs it to care for his spiritual nature, for religion, and preparing for immortal life. (*c*) Because man needs it as a day for moral training and instruction; a day for teaching men about their duties, for looking at life from a moral standpoint. (*d*) It is of great value as a means of improving the mind. The study of the highest themes, the social discussion of them in the Sabbath-school, the instruction from the pulpit, the expression of religious truth in the prayer-meeting, give an ordinary person more mental training in the course of his life than all his school-days give. (*e*) So long as the best welfare of the individual and of the nation depends chiefly on their mental and moral state, so long will the Sabbath be one of God's choicest blessings to man, and the command contained within it a heavenly privilege and blessing.

Sabbath=day's journey. Acts 1:12. The law as regards travel on the Sabbath is found in Ex. 16:29. As some departure from a man's own place was unavoidable, it was thought necessary to determine the allowable amount, which was fixed at 2000 cubits or about 1000 yards, from the wall of the city. The permitted distance seems to have been grounded on the space to be kept between the ark and the people, Josh. 3: 4, in the wilderness, which tradition said was that between the ark and the tents. We find the same distance given as the circumference outside the walls of the Levitical cities to be counted as their suburbs. Num. 35:5. The *terminus a quo* was thus not a man's own house, but the wall of the city where he dwelt.

Sabbatical year. Each seventh year, by the Mosaic code, was to be kept holy. Ex. 23:10, 11; Lev. 25. The commandment is to sow and reap for six years, and to let the land rest on the seventh, "that the poor of thy people may eat; and what they leave the beasts of the field shall eat." It is added in Deut. 15 that the seventh year should also be one of release to debtors. Deut. 15: 1–11. Neither tillage nor cultivation of any sort was to be practised. The 50th year, as coming after the completion of seven sabbatical years, was held as a special year of Jubilee. [JUBILEE.] The constant neglect of this law from the very first was one of the national sins that were punished by the Babylonian captivity. Of the observance of the sabbatical year after the captivity we have a proof in 1 Macc. 6: 49.

Sabe'ans (sá-bē'ans). [SHEBA.]

Sab'tah (săb'tà) (*striking*), Gen. 10: 7, or **Sab'ta**, 1 Chron. 1:9, the third in order of the sons of Cush.

Sab'techa (săb'te-kà) or **Sab'techah** (*striking*), Gen. 10:7; 1 Chron. 1:9, the fifth in order of the sons of Cush.

Sa'car (sā'kär) (*wages*). 1. A Hararite, father of Ahiam. 1 Chron. **11:** 35. SHARAR in 2 Sam. 23:33.

2. The fourth son of Obed-edom. 1 Chron. 26:4.

Sackbut, Dan. 3:5, 7, 10, 15, the rendering in the Authorized Version of the Chaldee *sabbéca*. This is the Greek and Latin *sambuca*, and is probably a sort of harp. The real sackbut is a wind instrument like the trombone, which is not the instrument intended here. [MUSIC.]

Sackcloth, cloth used in making sacks or bags, a coarse fabric, of a dark color, made of goat's-hair, Isa. 50: 3; Rev. 6:12, and resembling the *cili-*

cium of the Romans. It was used also for making the rough garments used by mourners, which were in extreme cases worn next the skin. 1 Kings 21: 27; 2 Kings 6:30; Job 16:15; Isa. 32: 11.

Sacrifice. The universal prevalence of sacrifice shows it to have been primeval, and deeply rooted in the instincts of humanity. Whether it was first enjoined by an external command, or whether it was based on that sense of sin and lost communion with God which is stamped by his hand on the heart of man, is a historical question which cannot be determined. The first record of any sacrifice in the Scriptures shows it to be a well-established custom. Gen. 4:3, 4. In primitive nations there seems to have been both a feeling of dependence upon, and a feeling of fear of their gods. They were to them merely a superior order of human beings who could be gratified by gifts, offered as thank offerings and could be placated and their displeasure entirely averted by the sacrifice of burnt offerings. There was, then from the earliest times this broad distinction in offerings. 1. The first fruits of field or flock were offered as a sign of dependence upon the ruler of nature; offerings were made on every specially joyous occasion, or after any signal deliverance, or unusual blessing. 2. The burnt offering to placate an angry god in all times of distress; after any great disaster; or when about to do anything in which they felt the need of supernatural aid, —as when about to go to war.

There is a considerable difference of opinion as to how far the minutiæ of the sacrifices were fixed by Moses. The force of the arguments largely depends on the view taken of the Pentateuch, whether it is considered as one in time, or as composed of various documents extending over a long period of years. See PENTATEUCH, LEVITICUS, DEUTERONOMY. This point cannot be discussed here, and this article will be confined to the completed ritual, at whatever date it may have been definitely formulated.

The Mosaic ritual began with a covenant between God and His people. The sacrifices were then in accord with this idea. The *peace offerings* or *thank offerings,* etc., were acts of homage, in which the people acknowledged their Heavenly King; and signs of a happy relationship between them. The *burnt offerings,* the *sin offerings, guilt* or *trespass offerings,* etc., were an acknowledgment of wrong on the part of the people, showing a covenant broken, which could only be cemented by repentance, confession, and the symbolic offering of the life of the sinner as expiation.

Offerings were of two sorts,—animal and vegetable. The peace offering might consist of a bloodless sacrifice especially if it was a thank offering for some special occasion. But for the sin offering there must be the animal sacrifice, except for some special case of extreme poverty. These animal sacrifices were often accompanied by a meal or vegetable offering,—(which is called in the A. V. a meat offering). There was besides the *drink offering,* which was always made in connection with some other sacrifice. It was excluded from the sin and trespass offerings.

Sacrifices were of two sorts: public and private. The public sacrifices were at the expense of the nation, on behalf of the whole congregation. The regular sacrifices of the temple service were—1. *Burnt offerings.* (*a*) The daily burnt offerings; Ex. 29: 38–42; (*b*) the double burnt offerings on the Sabbath and new moons, Num. 28: 9–11; (*c*) the burnt offerings at the great festivals; Num. 28: 11–29: 39. 2. *Meal offerings.* (*a*) The daily meal offerings accompanying the daily burnt offerings, Ex. 29: 40, 41; (*b*) the shew bread, renewed every Sabbath, Lev. 24: 5, 9; (*c*) the special meal offerings at the Sabbath and the great festivals, Num. 28: 29; (*d*) the first-fruits, at the Passover, Lev. 23: 10–14, at Pentecost, Lev. 23: 17–20, the first-fruits of the dough and threshing-floor at the harvest time. Num. 15: 20, 21; Deut. 26: 1–11. 3. *Sin offerings.* (*a*) Sin offering each new moon, Num. 28: 15; (*b*) sin offerings at the Passover, Pentecost, Feast of Trumpets and Tabernacles, Num. 28: 22, 30; 29: 5, 16, 19, 22, 25, 28, 31, 34, 38; (*c*) the offering of the two goats for the people and of the bullock for the priest himself, on the Great Day of Atonement. Lev. 16. 4. *Incense.* (*a*) The morning and evening incense, Ex. 30: 7, 8; (*b*) the incense on the Great Day of Atonement. Lev. 16: 12. On behalf of the individual the sacrifices offered were: 1. The Passover, in which he was considered a member of the community, and took his individual part as such; and 2. Those on special occasions as in expiation of committed sin, after bodily accident or business misfortune, the healing from disease, or in fulfilment of a vow.

The especial interest in the Jewish sacrifices to the Christian of to-day arises from their consideration as types of the work Jesus Christ came to do in this world. References in the N. T. are many to Christ as our sacrifice, while the words "ransom," "redemption," "propitiation," "cleanse," "purify," "sanctify," are of frequent occurrence. The "Old Covenant" is referred to either explicitly, or by inference from the expression "New Covenant."

From the Epistle to the Hebrews we learn that the sin offering represented that covenant as broken by man, and as knit together again, by God's appointment, through the "shedding of blood." The shedding of the blood, the symbol of life, signified that the death of the offender was deserved for sin, but that the death of the victim was accepted for his death by the ordinance of God's mercy. Beyond all doubt the sin offering distinctly witnessed that sin existed in man, that the "wages of that sin was death," and that God had provided an atonement by the vicarious suffering of an appointed victim. The ceremonial and meaning of the burnt offering were very different. The idea of expiation seems not to have been absent from it, for the blood was sprinkled round about the altar of sacrifice; but the main idea is the offering of the whole victim to God, representing, as the laying of the hand on its head shows, the devotion of the sacrificer, body and soul, to him. Rom. 12: 1. The death of the victim was, so to speak, an incidental feature. The meal offerings, the peace or thank offering, the first-fruits, etc., were simply offerings to God of his own best gifts, as a sign of thankful homage, and as a means of maintaining his service and his servants. The characteristic ceremony in the peace offering was the eating of the flesh by the sacrificer. It betokened the enjoyment of communion with God. It is clear from this that the idea of sacrifice is a complex idea, in-

volving the propitiatory, the dedicatory and the eucharistic elements. Any one of these, taken by itself, would lead to error and superstition. All three probably were more or less implied in each sacrifice, each element predominating in its turn. The Epistle to the Hebrews contains the key of the whole sacrificial doctrine. The object of the epistle is to show the typical and probationary character of sacrifices, and to assert that in virtue of it alone they had a spiritual meaning. Our Lord is declared (see 1 Pet. 1: 20) "to have been foreordained" as a sacrifice "before the foundation of the world," or, as it is more strikingly expressed in Rev. 13: 8, "slain from the foundation of the world." The material sacrifices represented this great atonement as already made and accepted in God's foreknowledge; and to those who grasped the ideas of sin, pardon and self-dedication symbolized in them, they were means of entering into the blessings which the one true sacrifice alone procured. They could convey nothing in themselves; yet as types they might, if accepted by a true though necessarily imperfect faith, be means of conveying in some degree the blessings of the antitype. It is clear that the atonement, in the Epistle to the Hebrews, as in the New Testament generally, is viewed in a twofold light. On the one hand it is set forth distinctly as a vicarious sacrifice, which was rendered necessary by the sin of man, and in which the Lord "bare the sins of many." It is its essential characteristic that in it he stands absolutely alone, offering his sacrifice without any reference to the faith or the conversion of men. In it he stands out alone as the mediator between God and man; and his sacrifice is offered once for all, never to be imitated or repeated. Now, this view of the atonement is set forth in the epistle as typified by the sin offering. On the other hand the sacrifice of Christ is set forth to us as the completion of that perfect obedience to the will of the Father which is the natural duty of sinless man. The main idea of this view of the atonement is representative rather than vicarious. It is typified by the burnt offering. As without the sin offering of the cross this our burnt offering would be impossible, so also without the burnt offering the sin offering will to us be unavailing. With these views of our Lord's sacrifice on earth, as typified in the Levitical sacrifices on the outer altar, is also to be connected the offering of his intercession for us in heaven, which was represented by the incense. The typical sense of the meal offering or peace offering is less connected with the sacrifice of Christ himself than with those sacrifices of praise, thanksgiving, charity and devotion which we, as Christians, offer to God, and "with which he is well pleased," Heb. 13 : 15, 16, as with an "odor of sweet smell, a sacrifice acceptable to God." Philip. 4 : 18.

Sad'ducees, Matt. 3 : 7; 16 : 1, 6, 11, 12; 22 : 23, 34; Mark 12 : 18; Luke 20 : 27; Acts 4 : 1; 5 : 17; 23 : 6, 7, 8, a religious party or school among the Jews at the time of Christ. Except on one occasion, Matt. 16 : 1, 4, 6, Christ never assailed the Sadducees with the same bitter denunciations which he uttered against the Pharisees. The origin of their name is involved in great difficulties, but the most satisfactory conjecture is that the Sadducees or Zadokites were originally identical with the sons of Zadok, and constituted what may be termed a kind of sacerdotal aristocracy, this Zadok being the priest who declared in favor of Solomon when Abiathar took the part of Adonijah. 1 Kings 1 : 32–45. The higher priests belonged to this sect, which though always small was very wealthy and of great influence from their wealth and position. The leading difference between the Pharisees and Sadducees was that the latter maintained in opposition to the Pharisees, that the written law alone was obligatory on the nation, as of divine authority. They denied that the oral law upon which the Pharisees laid such stress was a revelation from God, though they agreed with them that many of its provisions were advisable. The distinctive doctrines of the Sadducees were (1) the denial of the resurrection, personal immortality and future retribution. (2) The denial of the existence of angels or spirits, Acts 23 : 8. (3) They upheld the freedom of the will to such an extent that they repudiated Divine Providence. Some of the early Christian writers attribute to the Sadducees the rejection of all the sacred Scriptures except the Penta-

teuch; a statement, however, that is now generally admitted to have been founded on a misconception of the truth, and it seems to have arisen from a confusion of the Sadducees with the Samaritans. Herod filled the ranks of the priesthood with his own creatures, and these naturally joined themselves to the Sadducees. During the Herodean dynasty, they possessed much political power, and much of the internal government of the country was committed to the Sanhedrim, in which they were very strong. The Pharisees however were the most numerous among the people, and, partly because of that, the most influential. When Jerusalem was taken by Titus, and the Jews found themselves destroyed as a nation the doctrines of the Sadducees naturally faded out of existence and disappeared from history. This was the more so that they had at all times been closely attached to the Temple, since they were largely priests. In addition, the spread of Christianity brought into prominence just those doctrines most opposed by the Sadducees, so that all Jews who resisted the new heresy, must rally round the standard of the oral law, and to assert that their holy legislator, Moses, had transmitted to his faithful people by word of mouth, although not in writing, the revelation of a future state of rewards and punishments.

Sa'doc (sa'dŏk) (*Greek form of Zadok, just*). 1. Zadok the ancestor of Ezra. Ezra 7 : 2.

2. A descendant of Zerubbabel in the genealogy of Jesus Christ. Matt. 1 : 14.

Saffron. Cant. 4 : 14. The word saffron is derived from the Arabic *zafran,* a word used for several plants. The saffron (*Crocus sativus*) is a kind of crocus of the iris family. It is used as a perfume, as a medicine, as a flavoring and as a yellow dye. Homer, Virgil and Milton refer to its beauty in the landscape. It abounds in Palestine. The dried stigmas and styles are dried and pulverized for use.

Sa'la, or **Sa'lah** (sā'là) (*sprout*), the son of Arphaxad, and father of Eber. Gen. 10 : 24; 11 : 12–15; Luke 3 : 35. R. V. "Shelah."

Sal'amis (săl'a-mĭs), a city at the east end of the island of Cyprus, and the first place visited by Paul and Barnabas, on the first missionary journey, after leaving the mainland at Seleucia. There was a large colony of Jews there, apparently, with several synagogues. Acts 13:5. Salamis was about 3 miles from the modern *Famagousta*. It was situated on the seashore at the eastern end of the great futile plain of Cyprus.

Sala'thiel (sà-lä'thĭ-el) (*I have asked God*). 1 Chron. 3:17. The Authorized Version has Salathiel in 1 Chron. 3:17, but everywhere else in the Old Testament Shealtiel, as in the R. V. here also.

Sal'cah (săl'kè), or **Sal'chah** (*a road*), R. V. "Salecah," a city named in the early records of Israel as the extreme limit of Bashan, Deut. 3:10; Josh. 13:11, and of the tribe of Gad. 1 Chron. 5:11. It is identical with the town of *Salkhad* 56 miles east of the Jordan, at the southern extremity of the Hauran range of mountains. It was an important place in Roman times. Some of the ancient houses still exist in the modern town.

Sa'lem (sä'lem) (*peace*). 1. The place of which Melchizedek was king. Gen. 14:18; Heb. 7:1, 2. No satisfactory identification of it is perhaps possible. Two main opinions have been current from the earliest ages of interpretation: (*a*) That of the Jewish commentators, who affirm that Salem is Jerusalem, on the ground that Jerusalem is so called in Ps. 76:2. Nearly all Jewish commentators hold this opinion, and also the majority of the best modern scholars. (*b*) Jerome, however, states that the Salem of Melchizedek was not Jerusalem, but a town eight Roman miles south of Scythopolis, and gives its then name as Salumias, and identifies it with Salim, near Aenon, where John baptized.

2. Ps. 76:2. It is agreed by all that Salem is here employed for Jerusalem.

Sa'lim (sä'lĭm), a place named John 3:23 to denote the situation of Ænon, the scene of St. John's last baptisms; Salim being the well-known town, and Ænon a place of fountains or other waters near it. It was on the west of the Jordan, but further than this its site has not yet been determined, though a number of identifications have been proposed. [SALEM.]

Sal'ma (săl'mà), or **Sal'mon** (*garment*), Ruth 4:20, 21; 1 Chron. 2:11, 51, 54; Matt. 1:4, 5; Luke 3:32, son of Nahshon, the prince of the children of Judah and father of Boaz, the husband of Ruth. Bethlehem-ephratah, which was Salmon's inheritance, was part of the territory of Caleb, the grandson of Ephratah; and this caused him to be reckoned among the sons of Caleb.

Sal'mon (*shady*). The form in Ps. 68:14 of Zalmon, the hill or "mount" not far from Shechem, on which Abimelech and his followers cut down the boughs with which they set the tower of Shechem on fire. Judges 9:48. Its exact position is not known.

Sal'mon (săl'mŏn), the father of Boaz. [SALMA.]

Salmo'ne (săl-mō'ne), the east point of the island of Crete. Acts 27:7. It is a bold promontory, and is visible for a long distance.

Salo'me (sà-lō'me) (*peaceful*). 1. The wife of Zebedee, Matt. 27:56; Mark 15:40, and thought by many to be the sister of Mary the mother of Jesus, to whom reference is made in John 19:25. The only events recorded of Salome are that she preferred a request on behalf of her two sons for seats of honor in the kingdom of heaven, Matt. 20:20, that she attended at the crucifixion of Jesus, Mark 15:40, and that she visited his sepulchre, Mark 16:1. She is mentioned by name on only the two latter occasions.

2. The daughter of Herodias by her first husband, Herod Philip. Matt. 14:6. She married in the first place Philip the tetrarch of Trachonitis, her paternal uncle, and secondly Aristobulus, the king of Chalcis.

Salt. Indispensable as salt is to ourselves, it was even more so to the Hebrews, being to them not only an appetizing condiment in the food both of man, Job 6:6, and beast, Isa. 30:24, see margin, and a valuable antidote to the effects of the heat of the climate on animal food, but also entering largely into the religious services of the Jews as an accompaniment to the various offerings presented on the altar. Lev. 2:13. They possessed an inexhaustible and ready supply of it on the southern shores of the Dead Sea. [SEA, THE SALT.] There is on its southwestern shore a cliff called Jebel Usdum, seven miles long and 30 to 60 feet high, which is composed almost entirely of salt. The salt-pits formed an important

37

source of revenue to the rulers of the country, and Antiochus conferred a valuable boon on Jerusalem by presenting the city with 375 bushels of salt for the temple service. As one of the most essential articles of diet, salt symbolized hospitality; as an antiseptic, durability, fidelity and purity. Hence the expression "covenant of salt," Lev. 2 : 13; Num. 18 : 19; 2 Chron. 13 : 5, as betokening an indissoluble alliance between friends; and again the expression "salted with the salt of the palace," Ezra 4 : 14; not necessarily meaning that they had "maintenance from the palace," as the Authorized Version has it, but that they were bound by sacred obligations of fidelity to the king. So in the present day, "to eat bread and salt together" is an expression for a league of mutual amity. It was probably with a view to keep this idea prominently before the minds of the Jews that the use of salt was enjoined on the Israelites in their offerings to God.

Salt, City of, the fifth of the six cities of Judah which lay in the "wilderness." Josh. 15 : 62. It is named with En-gedi, the site of which we know, so that it probably was situated on the western shore of the Dead Sea, between En-gedi and the salt mountain.

Salt Sea, or **Dead Sea.** [SEA, THE SALT.]

Salt, Valley of, a valley in which occurred two memorable victories of the Israelite arms: 1. That of David over the Edomites. 2 Sam. 8 : 13; 1 Chron. 18 : 12. 2. That of Amaziah. 2 Kings 14 : 7; 2 Chron. 25 : 11. It is perhaps the broad open plain which lies at the lower end of the Dead Sea, and intervenes between the lake itself and the range of heights which crosses the valley at six or eight miles to the south. A more probable identification perhaps is the plain extending from the southern end of the Dead Sea to the ascent of Akrabbim on the southern margin of the Ghor.

Sa′lu (sā′lū) (*elevated*), the father of Zimri the prince of the Simeonites, who was slain by Phinehas. Num. 25 : 14. Called also Salom. (B.C. 1452.)

Salutation. The customs of polite social intercourse in the East in both ancient and modern times required a formal word or act of salutation at both meeting and parting. The kiss on both cheeks, the kissing of the hand, and the actual prostration before another are still met with. These acts take much time, hence the injunction "salute no man by the way." 2 Kings 4 : 29; Luke 10 : 4. The words of salutation at meeting consisted in early times of various expressions of blessing, such as "God be gracious unto thee," Gen. 43 : 29; "The Lord be with you;" "The Lord bless thee." Ruth 2 : 4. Hence the term "bless" received the secondary sense of "salute." The salutation at parting consisted originally of a simple blessing, Gen. 24 : 60, but in later times the form "Go in peace," or rather "Farewell," 1 Sam. 1 : 17, was common.

MODES OF SALUTATION IN THE EAST.

In modern times the ordinary mode of address current in the East resembles the Hebrew *Es-selâm aleykum,* "Peace be on you," and the term "salaam," *peace,* has been introduced into our own language to describe the Oriental salutation. Letters in Palestine and Egypt all began with long formal greetings. Those in the Greco-Roman times were more direct and business-like, and the name of the writer usually stands first in it. It was also usually closed with a formal salutation. The Epistles of the New Testament usually follow these customs.

Sama′ria (să-mā′rĭ-à) (*watch mountain*). This city is situated 30 miles north of Jerusalem and about six miles to the northwest of Shechem, in a wide basin-shaped valley, six miles in diameter, encircled with high hills, almost on the edge of the great plain which

HILL OF SAMARIA (SEBASTIYEH) FROM THE SOUTH.

borders upon the Mediterranean. In the centre of this basin, which is on a lower level than the valley of Shechem, rises an oblong hill about 300 or 400 feet above the level of the valley, with steep yet accessible sides and a long flat top. This hill was chosen by Omri as the site of the capital of the kingdom of Israel. He "bought the hill of Samaria of Shemer for two talents of silver, and built on the hill, and occasions the siege was ineffectual. The possessor of Samaria was considered *de facto* king of Israel, 2 Kings 15 : 13, 14. In B.C. 722 Samaria was taken, after a siege of three years, by Shalmaneser king of Assyria, 2 Kings 18 : 9, 10, and the kingdom of the ten tribes was ended. Some years afterward the district of which Samaria was the centre was repeopled by Esarhaddon. Alexander the Great took the city,

PLAN OF SAMARIA, THE MODERN SEBASTIYEH.
(Harvard Expedition.)

called the name of the city which he built, after the name of the owner of the hill, Samaria." 1 Kings 16 : 23, 24. From the date of Omri's purchase, B.C. 881, Samaria retained its dignity as the capital of the ten tribes, and the name is given to the northern kingdom as well as to the city. Ahab built a temple to Baal there. 1 Kings 16 : 32, 33. It was twice besieged by the Syrians, in B.C. 859, 1 Kings 20 : 1, and in B.C. 849, 2 Kings 6 : 24–7 : 20; but on both killed a large portion of the inhabitants, and suffered the remainder to settle at Shechem. He replaced them by a colony of Syro-Macedonians, who occupied the city until the time of John Hyrcanus, who took it after a year's siege, and did his best to demolish it entirely. (B.C. 109.) It was rebuilt and greatly embellished by Herod the Great. He called it *Sebaste = Augusta*, after the name of his patron, Augustus Cæsar. The wall around it was 2½ miles

A GLIMPSE OF ANCIENT SAMARIA.

long, and in the centre of the city was a park 900 feet square, containing a magnificent temple dedicated to Cæsar. In the New Testament the city itself does not appear to be mentioned, but rather a portion of the district to which, even in older times, it had extended its name. Matt. 10 : 5 ; John 4 : 4, 5. At this day the city is represented by a small village retaining few vestiges of the past except its name, *Sebastiyeh,* an Arabic corruption of Sebaste. There are still the remains of two temples and of a quadrangle, perhaps a hippodrome. The ruins of the fine cathedral church of St. John, built between A.D. 1150 and 1180 over the reputed tomb of John the Baptist, is near the site of the East gate. St. Jerome, whose acquaintance with Palestine imparts a sort of probability to the tradition which prevailed so strongly in later days, asserts that Sebaste, which he invariably identifies with Samaria, was the place in which St. John the Baptist was imprisoned and suffered death. He also makes it the burial-place of the prophets Elisha and Obadiah.

Sama′ria, Country of. Samaria at first included all the tribes over which Jeroboam made himself king, whether east or west of the river Jordan. 1 Kings 13 : 32. But whatever extent the word might have acquired, it necessarily became contracted as the limits of the kingdom of Israel became contracted. [ISRAEL, KINGDOM OF.] The boundaries of Samaria in the time of Christ are very difficult to determine exactly. According to Josephus, whose description is not very intelligible, it was bounded on the north by Galilee, its northernmost village being Ginea, the modern *Jenin* on the southern edge of the plain of Esdraelon. It extended south to Acrabatta, *Akrabeh,* and other villages perhaps 6 or 7 miles south of Shechem. Its eastern boundary was the Jordan, and its western limit was Antipatris, as the coast belonged to Judah as far north as Ptolemais. It extended probably about 20 miles from north to south and 30 miles from east to west.

Samar′itans. Strictly speaking, a Samaritan would be an inhabitant of the *city* of Samaria; but the term was applied to all the people of the kingdom of Israel. After the captivity of Israel, B.C. 722, and in our Lord's time, the name was applied to a peculiar people whose origin was in this wise : At the final captivity of Israel by Shalmaneser, we may conclude that the cities of Samaria were not merely partially but wholly depopulated of their inhabitants in B.C. 722, and that they remained in this desolated state until, in the words of 2 Kings 17 : 24, "the king of Assyria brought men from Babylon, and from Cuthah, and from Ava, and from Hamath and from Sepharvaim, and placed them in the cities of Samaria instead of the children of Israel: and they possessed Samaria, and dwelt in the cities thereof." Thus the new Samaritans were Assyrians by birth or subjugation. These, called the "Cuthæans," were of course idolaters, and worshipped a strange medley of divinities. They were annoyed by beasts of prey, which had probably increased to a great extent before their entrance upon the land. On their explaining their miserable condition to the king of Assyria, he, believing that they had offended the god of the land, despatched one of the captive priests to teach them "how they should fear the Lord." The priest came accordingly, and henceforth, in the language of the sacred historian, they "feared the Lord, and served their graven images, both their children, and their children's children: as did their fathers, so do they unto this day." 2 Kings 17 : 41. A gap occurs in their history until Judah has returned from captivity. They then desire to be allowed to participate in the rebuilding of the temple at Jerusalem; but on being refused, become open enemies, frustrate the operations of the Jews through the reigns of two Persian kings, and are only effectually silenced in the reign of Darius Hystaspes, B.C. 519. The feud thus unhappily begun grew year by year more inveterate. Matters at length came to a climax. About B.C. 432, a certain Manasseh, a man of priestly lineage, married a daughter of Sanballat the Horonite, and was therefore expelled from Jerusalem by Nehemiah. He took refuge among the Samaritans, and a temple was built on Mt. Gerizim in which he and his family became the high priests. This temple lasted until the time of the Maccabees, when it was probably destroyed by John Hyrcanus. The animosity of the Samaritans became more intense than ever. They are said to have done everything in their power to annoy the Jews. Their own temple on Gerizim they considered to ple on it had fallen, wherever they were they directed their worship. To their copy of the law they arrogated an antiquity and authority greater than at-

THE SAMARITAN HIGH PRIEST.
This patriarch still officiates for a little remnant of less than two hundred of this ancient people.

be much superior to that at Jerusalem. There they sacrificed a Passover. Toward the mountain, even after the tem- tached to any copy in the possession of the Jews. The law (*i. e.* the five books of Moses) was their sole code; for they rejected every other book in the Jewish canon. The Jews, on the other hand, were not more conciliatory in their treatment of the Samaritans. Their attitude is given in the story of Jesus and the woman of Samaria, John 4. They now number only a few families, who for the most part live in *Nablus,* the ancient Shechem. The worship on Mt. Gerizim continues, and there is a priesthood, with a high priest. The Passover is still celebrated on Mt. Gerizim with all the ceremonies and regulations found in the law.

Samaritan Pentateuch, a recension of the commonly-received Hebrew text of the Mosaic law, in use among the Samaritans, and written in the ancient Hebrew or so-called Samaritan character. The origin of the Samaritan Pentateuch has given rise to much controversy, into which we cannot here enter. The two most usual opinions are—1. That it came into the hands of the Samaritans as an inheritance from the ten tribes whom they succeeded. 2. That it was introduced by Manasseh at the time of the foundation of the Samaritan sanctuary on Mount Gerizim. It differs in several important points from the Hebrew text. Among these may be mentioned: (1) Numerous comparatively minor changes, some due to haste on the part of the copyist, others made intentionally. For example the ages of the patriarchs are each changed, corresponding perhaps more nearly to the Septuagint, but differing radically even from that. (2) The most important change is in the Decalogue, which is there divided into nine commandments, a tenth being added, namely, a command to build a temple and offer sacrifices on Mt. Gerizim. By this they conceive of their sect as the only one obeying the law of God, which by this means was made a permanent obligation. (See cut p. 498.)

Sam=gar=ne'bo (săm'găr-nē'bó) (*be gracious, Nebo*), one of the princes or generals of the king of Babylon. Jer. 39 : 3.

Sam'lah (săm'lah) (*garment*), Gen. 36 : 36, 37; 1 Chron. 1 : 47, 48, one of the kings of Edom, successor to Hadad or Hadar.

Samos, a Greek island separated from Ionia by the narrow straits where the battle of Mycale was fought, B.C. 479.

St. Paul touched at Samos on his return from his third missionary journey. Acts 20 : 15.

Samothra'ce. In the Revised Version for Samothracia.

Samothra'cia (săm-o-thrā'shà), a mountainous island off the coast of Thrace. Mention is made of this island in the account of St. Paul's first voyage to Europe. Acts 16 : 11. Being very lofty and conspicuous, it is an excellent landmark for sailors, and must have been full in view, if the weather was clear, throughout that voyage from Troas to Neapolis.

Sam'son (săm'son), Judges 13–16. 1. The name Samson is derived from the Hebrew word for "sun," and means "sunny" or "sun-hero." He was born at Zorah in Dan, on the borders of Judah, 14 miles west of Jerusalem. His father's name was Manoah.

2. Even before his birth his mission was announced. He was to be one who should "begin to save Israel out of the hand of the Philistines," and to this end was to be consecrated to God. Judges 13. Only partially did Samson fulfil his ideal, but the presence of it influenced his whole life.

3. The consecration of Samson was through the Nazirite vow. [NAZARITE.] It is to be noted that, according to the record, Samson, with all his other failings, yet kept sacred the conditions of this vow. On the keeping of the vow his strength and prowess depended.

4. The first and most effective of the endowments of Samson for his mission was his great strength, which, in general, he used to deliver his nation from the power of the oppressor, although not always in the wisest way. While there may have been no others so strong as Samson, yet examples of great strength in lifting heavy weights and bending bars of iron, etc., take away all improbability from the story.

Samson's feats of strength were: (a) The slaying of a lion with his hands. (b) The slaying of thirty Philistines. (c) Another victory over the Philistines. (d) The breaking of the cords with which his own people bound him to deliver him to his enemies. (e) The slaying of a thousand Philistines with the jaw bone of an ass. (f) The carrying away of the gates of Gaza. (g) The breaking of the withes and ropes

Photo by Jan Wilga

RUINS OF SAMARIA.

and loom from Delilah. (h) The pulling down of the pillars of the Philistine temple.

5. A second special endowment of Samson was his sense of humor, his impulsive practical joking, puns, and riddles. These were an advantage to him even in his efforts to overcome the Philistine oppressors.

Note his riddle from the swarm of bees in a lion's carcass at his wedding feast; the setting on fire of the rich grain fields of the Philistines by three hundred foxes tied two and two by their tails with firebrands between; his manner of defending the secret of his strength from Delilah; and his compulsory sport for the Philistines, and the method of his final tragedy. "Nothing could disturb his radiant good humor."

Wit and humor are natural to some men and can be made efficient weapons for good. Some of the most effective blows for righteousness have been struck by humorous songs and caricatures, putting wickedness in comical situations, and turning the laugh against it.

His yielding to temptation led to the end of his career. He became infatuated with an attractive Philistine woman of Sorek, named Delilah, who, by many temptations and blandishments, learned from Samson the secret of his strength. The Philistines thus captured him at last, and put out his eyes, to render him harmless. Then they degraded him, putting him to work turning the great mill to grind their grain. Then they held a great festival in the temple of Dagon, to celebrate their victory over Samson. They brought forth the blind champion to make sport for them, and placed him between the two chief pillars which supported the roof that surrounded the court. Samson asked the lad who guided him to let him feel the pillars, to lean upon them. Then, with a fervent prayer that God would strengthen him only this once, to be avenged on the Philistines, he bore with all his might upon the two pillars; they yielded, and the house fell upon the lords and all the people. " So the dead which he slew at his death were more than they which he slew in his life." In Heb. 11:32 his name is enrolled among the worthies of the Jewish Church.

Sam'uel (săm'u-el) (*name of God*), was the son of Elkanah and Hannah, and was born at Ramathaim-zophim, among the hills of Ephraim. [RAMAH, No. 2.] (B.C. 1114.) Before his birth he was dedicated by his mother to the office of a Nazirite; and when a young child, 12 years old according to Josephus, he was placed in the temple, and "ministered unto the Lord before Eli." It was while here that he received his first prophetic call. 1 Sam. 3:1-18. He next appears, probably twenty years afterward, suddenly among the people, warning them against their idolatrous practices. 1 Sam. 7:3, 4. Then followed Samuel's first and, as far as we know, only military achievement, ch. 7: 5-12; but it was apparently this which raised him to the office of "judge." He visited, in the discharge of his duties as ruler, the three chief sanctuaries on the west of Jordan—Bethel, Gilgal and Mizpeh, ch. 7:16. His own residence was still his native city, Ramah, where he married, and two sons grew up to repeat under his eyes the same perversion of high office that he had himself witnessed in his childhood in the case of the two sons of Eli. In his old age he shared his power with them, 1 Sam. 8:1-4; but the people, dissatisfied, demanded a king, and Saul was finally anointed under God's direction, and Samuel surrendered to him his authority, 1 Sam. 12, though still remaining judge, ch. 7:15. The death of Samuel is described as taking place in the year of the close of David's wanderings.

He traveled through the whole land, appointed public meetings, and announced to the multitudes the lessons revealed to him by the spirit of God. Year after year he called together the elders of the people. At Ramah, his residence, frequent meetings of the tribes took place.

THE TIMES IN WHICH SAMUEL LIVED. It was toward the close of the period of the Judges, during which the people had been trained by rewards of obedience and the punishment of disobedience, by religious institutions and the love of God and righteousness in family life, and by the promises of God. During these centuries the people were under a government called the Theocracy,—that is, a condition where God only is king; and, while there were leaders and rulers, there was no political unity except that of the laws and religion of God. There was little compulsory virtue. This was a state of things where true religious and moral life was especially needful for success.

THE COUNTRY was but little larger than Wales and like it a land of mountains and hills, skirted through its whole length by the deep-lying Jordan valley on the east, and the harborless coast of the Mediterranean on the west.

THE TWELVE TRIBES were of one blood, one religion, one language, and one history; but there was little of the solidarity of a nation. The social unit was the tribe. Each tribe had its own political organization. They were loosely held together, and sometimes broke out into open war.

The people were an agricultural people untrained in the arts of war, lovers of home and of peace. Their chief wealth consisted in flocks, grain fields, and vineyards. Hence they were exposed to the raids of their warlike neighbors, as the Lowlanders of Scotland were to the forays of the Highlanders. The people lived in walled villages for safety, while their outlying fields, vineyards, and pasture lands were exposed.

Their enemies were warlike and on every side, always more or less hostile.

THE CRISIS. The chosen people were approaching a crisis "second in importance only to the Exodus," and there was needed a leader second only to Moses, a counsellor to whom all could turn for advice "amid the wreck of the ancient institutions and the rise and growth of the new."

SAMUEL AS JUDGE came into prominence with the great deliverance of the oppressed Israelites from the Philistine yoke recorded in 1 Samuel 7. The Israelites had gathered together at Mizpeh for a great religious service of repentance and confession of sin, and of a new consecration to the service of God. God showed his favor by a great thunderstorm in the face of the Philistine army, and with a mighty enthusiasm the people rushed into battle and gained a complete and lasting victory (v. 13). The place was marked by a stone, and was named Ebenezer, "The Stone of Help," on the very spot where twenty years before (1 Sam. 4:1; 7:2) the

Israelites had been defeated by the Philistines in the battle on account of which Judge Eli's new-born grandson was named Ichabod. "There is no glory," "for the glory is departed from Israel." (1 Sam. 4:21.)

SAMUEL AS PROPHET AND PRIEST is exemplified in his great reformation described in 1 Sam. 7:2-6, which was the moral and religious condition which made the Ebenezer victory wise and helpful.

"One great work that Samuel did was the establishment of THE SCHOOLS OF THE PROPHETS; schools for the training and education of young men, at Ramah, Bethel, Gilgal and Mizpeh.

SAMUEL THE HERO. When Saul became king, Samuel, formally and publicly, laid down his office of judge, just as Washington laid down his rank of commander-in-chief of our armies. And the twelfth chapter is called Samuel's farewell address, not because it was given near the close of his life, but because, like Washington's farewell address to the army, it marks the close of one phase of his public career. But as Washington afterwards entered public life as President, and was to the end of his days a man of weight and influence in the councils of the nation, so Samuel continued in public life as priest and prophet of God.

SAMUEL THE SPOTLESS STATESMAN. In this address Samuel called the people to witness and they testified to his generous, unselfish, patriotic, and holy life. His nobility was shown in yielding up his office, and aiding the people to obtain a king.

Samuel, Books of. 1. The two books of Samuel were originally one, and with the books of the Kings were regarded as furnishing a complete history of the two kingdoms of Israel and Judah. 1 Samuel is named in the title in our ordinary Bibles as "otherwise called, the First Book of the Kings"; the two books of Samuel and the two of Kings forming one volume of four books of the Kings.

2. These two books are named after Samuel, not because he was the author, but because he was the principal man of the transition period which they describe, from the rule of the Judges to the rule of Kings.

3. This transition period extended

over about one century, from the birth of Samuel (1146 or 1114 B.C.) to the accession of David to the throne (1055 or 1017 B.C.).

4. The author of the books is unknown; but it is generally agreed that they are *a compilation* from different sources, including the writings of Samuel (1 Sam. 10 : 25), the book of Nathan the prophet, and the book of Gad or Iddo the seer (1 Chron. 29 : 29; 2 Chron. 9 : 29), and the national anthology known as the book of Jasher (2 Sam. 1 : 18).

of modern events when we know that both accounts are true.

5. DATE. According to the *Cambridge Bible* the narrative was compiled as we have it soon after the division of the kingdom (975 or 937 B.C.). Hastings' *Bible Dictionary* (art. "Samuel") assigns one of the component narratives to the ninth century B.C. and the other to the eighth; while the final editor united them. The book of Samuel is one of the best specimens of Hebrew prose in the golden age of Hebrew literature.

SANBALLAT.

Portion of a Jewish Papyrus found at Assouan, Egypt (of date 408 B. C.), mentioning " Sanballat governor of Samaria," his sons.

The higher critics trace two great sources, written from different points of view, which the editor has contented himself, for the most part, with producing in a twofold form with little effort to harmonize the varying accounts. But the question arises whether in some cases the seemingly contradictory statements are accounts of the same event, and in other cases they are not descriptions of the same event from different points of view, such as are continually taking place in histories

In prose it holds the same place which Joel and the undisputed prophecies of Isaiah hold in poetical or prophetical language.

Sanbal′lat (săn-băl′lat) (*the moon god hath given life*). Neh. 2 : 10, 19; 13 : 28. He is called the "Horonite," which probably means a native of Beth-horon, though some explain it as of Horonaim. He held apparently some command in Samaria at the time Nehemiah was preparing to rebuild the walls of Jerusalem, B.C. 445, Neh. 4 : 2, and from the moment of Nehemiah's arrival in Judea he set himself to oppose every measure for the welfare of Jerusalem. His daughter married Manasseh, grand-

SANDALS.

son of the high priest, Eliashib. He was for that reason expelled from Jerusalem and became high priest of the Samaritans.

Sandals were ordinarily used by the Hebrews for protecting the feet. They consisted simply of soles attached to the feet by thongs. We have express notice of the thong (Authorized Version "shoe-latchet") in several passages, notably Gen. 14 : 23; Isa. 5 : 27; Mark 1 : 7. Sandals were made necessary by the burning heat of the ground as well as by the presence of stones and thorns, and were worn by all classes of society in Palestine, even by the very poor; and both the sandal and the thong or shoe-latchet were so cheap and common that they passed into a proverb for the most insignificant thing. Compare Gen. 14 : 23. Sandals were dispensed with in-doors, and therefore during meal-times the feet were uncovered. Luke 7 : 38; John 13 : 5, 6. It was a mark of reverence to cast off the shoes in approaching a place or person of eminent sanctity. Ex. 3 : 5; Josh. 5 : 15. It was also an indication of violent emotion, or of mourning, if a person appeared barefoot in public. 2 Sam. 15 : 30. To carry or to unloose a person's sandal was a menial office, betokening great inferiority on the part of the person performing it. Matt. 3 : 11.

San'hedrin (from the Greek συνέδριον, "a council-chamber"; commonly but incorrectly Sanhedrim), the supreme council of the Jewish people in the time of Christ and earlier. 1. The *origin* of this assembly is traced in the Mishna to the seventy elders whom Moses was directed, Num. 11 : 16, 17, to associate with him in the government of the Israelites; but this tribunal was probably temporary, and did not continue to exist after the Israelites had entered Palestine. In the lack of definite historical information as to the establishment of the Sanhedrin, it can only be said in general that the Greek etymology of the name seems to point to a period subsequent to the Macedonian supremacy in Palestine. From the few incidental notices in the New Testament, we gather that it consisted of chief priests, or the heads of the twenty-four classes into which the priests were divided, elders, men of age and experience, and scribes, lawyers, or those learned in the Jewish law. Matt. 26 : 57, 59; Mark 15 : 1; Luke 22 : 66; Acts 5 : 21. 2. The *number of members* is usually given as 71. The president of this body was styled *nasi,* and was chosen on account of his eminence in worth and wisdom. Often, if not generally, this pre-eminence was accorded to the high priest. The vice-president, called in the Talmud "father of the house of judgment," sat at the right hand of the president. Some writers speak of a second vice-president, but this is not sufficiently confirmed. While in session the Sanhedrin sat in the form of a half-circle. 3. The *place* in which the sessions of the Sanhedrin years before the destruction of Jerusalem, and consequently while the Saviour was teaching in Palestine, the sessions of the Sanhedrin were removed from the hall Gazith to a somewhat greater distance from the temple building, although still on Mount Moriah. After several other changes, its seat was finally established at Tiberias, where it became extinct A.D. 425. As a judicial body the Sanhedrin constituted a supreme court, to which belonged in the first instance the trial of false

THE SANHEDRIN IN COUNCIL. (From an old engraving.)

were ordinarily held was, according to the Talmud, a hall called Gazith, or Chamber of Hewn Stone, situated, according to Geo. Adam Smith's great work on *Jerusalem,* issued in 1908, "on the southern edge of the inner court of the Temple, but with a door into the outer court, so that a body consisting of laymen might have gathered in it." In special exigencies, however, it seems to have met in the residence of the high priest. Matt. 26:3. Forty prophets, of the high priest and other priests, and also of a tribe fallen into idolatry. As an administrative council, it determined other important matters. Their power over Jews was, subject to the Procurator's approval of their sentences of death, unlimited. Jesus was arraigned before this body as a false prophet, John 11:47, and Peter, John, Stephen and Paul as teachers of error and deceivers of the people. From Acts 9:2 it appears that the Sanhedrin exercised a degree of authority beyond the limits of Palestine. According to the Jerusalem Gemara the power of inflicting capital punishment was taken away from this tribunal forty years before the destruction of Jerusalem. With this agrees the answer of the Jews to Pilate. John 18 : 31. The Talmud also mentions a *lesser Sanhedrin* of twenty-three members in every city in Palestine in which were not less than 120 householders. Scholarship is divided on some questions concerning the organization of the Sanhedrin. The generally accepted view is that the Sanhedrin in Jerusalem was a single court, the supreme tribunal of the Jewish nation, both for religious and civil questions. But the *Jewish Encyclopedia,* and Dr. Adolph Büchler in *The Synedrion in Jerusalem* take the view that there were two great tribunals in the Holy City, with separate authorities, religious and civil.

Sansan′nah (*palm branch*), one of the towns in the south district of Judah, named in Josh. 15 : 31 only.

Saph (săf), one of the sons of the giant slain by Sibbechai the Hushathite. 2 Sam. 21 : 18. In 1 Chron. 20 : 4 he is called SIPPAI. (B.C. about 1050.)

Sa′phir (sā′fir) (*fair*), one of the villages addressed by the prophet Micah, Micah 1 : 11, is described by Eusebius and Jerome as "in the mountain district between Eleutheropolis and Ascalon," possibly represented by the village *es-Sawâfir,* 3 or 4 miles to the southeast of Ashdod.

Sapphi′ra (săf-fī′rà). [ANANIAS.]

Sapphire (Heb. *sappîr*), a precious stone, apparently of a bright-blue color, see Ex. 24 : 10; the second stone in the second row of the high priest's breastplate, Ex. 28 : 18; extremely precious, Job 28 : 16; it was one of the precious stones that ornamented the king of Tyre. Ezek. 28 : 13. It is uncertain whether the *sapphire* of the ancients was our gem of that name, a variety of corundum, or our *lapis lazuli* (*ultramarine*). But modern authorities seem to prefer the latter.

Sa′ra, Greek form of Sarah.

Sa′rah (sà′rah) (*princess*). 1. The wife and half-sister, Gen. 20 : 12, of Abraham, and mother of Isaac. Her name is first introduced in Gen. 11 : 29 as Sarai. The change of her name

from Sarai, *my princess* (i. e. Abraham's), to Sarah, *princess* (for all the race), was made at the same time that Abram's name was changed to Abraham,—on the establishment of the covenant of circumcision between him and God. Sarah's history is of course that of Abraham. [ABRAHAM.] She died at Hebron at the age of 127 years, **38** years before her husband, and was buried by him in the cave of Machpelah. (B.C. 1860.) She is referred to in the New Testament as a type of conjugal obedience in 1 Pet. 3 : 6, and as one of the types of faith in Heb. 11 : 11.

2. The daughter of Asher. Num. 26 : 46. R. V. Serah.

Sa′rai (sā′rā-i) (*my princess*), the original name of Sarah, the wife of Abraham.

Sa′raph (sā′răf) (*burning*), mentioned in 1 Chron. 4 : 22 among the descendants of Judah.

Sardine, Sardius (Heb. *ôdem*), the stone which occupied the first place in the first row of the high priest's breastplate. Ex. 28 : 17. The sard, which is probably the stone denoted by *ôdem,* is a superior variety of agate, sometimes called carnelian, and has long been a favorite stone for the engraver's art. Others argue that it means the red jasper.

Sar′dis, a city of Asia Minor, and capital of Lydia, situated about two miles to the south of the river Hermus, just below the range of Tmolus, on a spur of which its acropolis was built. It was 50 miles northeast of Smyrna. It was the ancient residence of the kings of Lydia, among them Crœsus, proverbial for his immense wealth. Cyrus is said to have taken $600,000,000 worth of treasure from the city when he captured it, about B.C. 549. Sardis was in very early times, both from the extremely fertile character of the neighboring region and from its convenient position, a commercial mart of importance. The art of dyeing wool is said to have been invented there. In the year 214 B.C. it was taken and sacked by the army of Antiochus the Great Afterward it passed under the dominion of the kings of Pergamos. Its productive soil must always have continued a source of wealth; but its importance as a central mart appears to have di minished from the time of the invasion of Asia by Alexander. The massive temple of Cybele still bears witness in its fragmentary remains to the wealth and architectural skill of the people that raised it. On the north side of the acropolis, overlooking the valley of the Hermus, is a theatre near 400 feet in diameter, attached to a stadium of about 1000. There are still considerable remains of the ancient city at *Sert-Kalessi*, now a tiny village, a station on the railway from Smyrna to Philadelphia. The only passages in which it is mentioned in the Bible are Rev. 1 : 11; 3 : 1–6.

Sar′dites, The, descendants of Sered the son of Zebulun. Num. 26 : 26.

Sar′dius. The same as **Sardine.** Ex. 28 : 17; 39 : 10; Ezek. 28 : 13; Rev. 21 : 20.

Sardonyx, a name compounded of *sard* and *onyx*, two precious stones, varieties of chalcedony or agate. The sardonyx is, as its name implies, a layer of sard upon one of onyx. It is not difficult to produce artificially. It is mentioned only in Rev. 21 : 20.

Sarep′ta (sȧ-rĕp′tȧ). [ZAREPHATH.]

Sar′gon (sär′gon) (*the strong one*), one of the greatest of the Assyrian kings, is mentioned by name but once in Scripture—Isa. 20 : 1. He was the successor of Shalmaneser IV, and was Sennacherib's father and his immediate predecessor. He reigned from B.C. 722 to 705, and seems to have been a usurper. He was undoubtedly a great and successful warrior. In his annals, which cover a space of fifteen years, from B.C. 722 to 706, he gives an account of his warlike expeditions against Babylonia and Susiana on the south, Media on the east, Armenia and Cappadocia toward the north, Syria, Palestine, Arabia and Egypt toward the west and southwest. It was after his accession that Samaria was taken. In B.C. 711 he sent his Tartan or commander-in-chief against Ashdod, which is the event which causes the mention of his name in Scripture. It is not as a warrior only that Sargon deserves special mention among the Assyrian kings. He was also the builder of useful works, and of one of the most magnificent of the Assyrian palaces.

Sa′rid (sä′rid) (*survivor*), a chief landmark of the territory of Zebulun. Josh. 19 : 10, 12. All that can with any certainty be gathered of its position is that it lay to the west of Chisloth-tabor.

Sa′ron (sā′ron), the district in which Lydda stood, Acts 9 : 35 only; the Sharon of the Old Testament. [SHARON.]

Sar′sechim (sär′sē-kĭm), one of the generals of Nebuchadnezzar's army at the taking of Jerusalem. Jer. 39 : 3. (B.C. 586.)

Sa′ruch (sā′ruk), Luke 3 : 35; Serug the son of Reu.

Sa′tan. The word itself, the Hebrew *sâtân,* is simply an " adversary," and is so used in 1 Sam. 29 : 4; 2 Sam. 19 : 22; 1 Kings 5 : 4; 11 : 14, 23, 25; Num. 22 : 22, 32; Ps. 109 : 6. This original sense is still found in our Lord's application of the name to St. Peter in Matt. 16 : 23. It is used as a proper name or title only four times in the Old Testament, viz. (with the article) in Job 1 : 6, 12; 2 : 1; Zech. 3 : 1, and (without the article) in 1 Chron. 21 : 1. It is with the scriptural revelation on the subject that we are here concerned; and it is clear, from this simple enumeration of passages, that it is to be sought in the New rather than in the Old Testament. I. *The personal existence* of a spirit of evil is clearly revealed in Scripture; but the revelation is made gradually, in accordance with the progressiveness of God's method. In the first entrance of evil into the world, the temptation is referred only to the serpent. In the book of Job we find for the first time a distinct mention of " Satan," the " adversary " of Job. But it is important to remark the emphatic stress laid on his subordinate position, on the absence of all but delegated power, of all terror and all grandeur in his character. It is especially remarkable that no power of spiritual influence, but only a power over outward circumstances, is attributed to him. The captivity brought the Israelites face to face with the great dualism of the Persian mythology, the conflict of Ormuzd with Ahriman, the co-ordinate spirit of evil; but it is confessed by all that the Satan of Scripture bears no resemblance to the Persian Ahriman. His subordination and inferiority are as strongly marked as ever. The New Testament brings plainly forward the power and the influence of Satan. From the beginning of the Gospel, when he appears as the personal tempter of our Lord, through all the Gospels, Epistles, and Apocalypse, it is asserted or implied, again and again, as a familiar and important truth. II. Of the *nature* and *original state* of Satan, little is revealed in Scripture. He is spoken of as a "spirit" in Eph. 2:2, as the prince or ruler of the "demons" in Matt. 12:24-26, and as having "angels" subject to him in Matt. 25:41; Rev. 12:7, 9. The whole description of his power implies spiritual nature and spiritual influence. We conclude therefore that he was of angelic nature, a rational and spiritual creature, superhuman in power, wisdom and energy; and not only so, but an archangel, one of the "princes" of heaven. We cannot, of course, conceive that anything essentially and originally evil was created by God. We can only conjecture, therefore, that Satan is a fallen angel, who once had a time of probation, but whose condemnation is now irrevocably fixed. The ideal of goodness is made up of the three great moral attributes of God—love, truth, and purity or holiness; combined with that spirit which is the natural temper of the finite and dependent creature, the spirit of faith. We find, accordingly, that the opposites of these qualities are dwelt upon as the characteristics of the devil. III. The *power of Satan* over the soul is represented as exercised either directly or by his instruments. His direct influence over the soul is simply that of a powerful and evil nature. Besides this direct influence, we learn from Scripture that Satan is the leader of a host of evil spirits or angels who share his evil work, and for whom the "everlasting fire is prepared." Matt. 25:41. Of their origin and fall we know no more than of his. But one passage—Matt. 12:24-26—identifies them distinctly with the "demons" (Authorized Version "devils") who had power to possess the souls of men. But the evil one is not merely the "prince of the demons;" he is called also the "prince of this world" in John 12:31; 14:30; 16:11, and even the "god of this world" in 2 Cor. 4:4; the two expressions being united in Eph. 6:12. The indirect action of Satan is best discerned by an examination of the title by which he is designated in Scripture. He is called emphatically *ho diábolos,* "the devil." The derivation of the word in itself implies only the endeavor to break the bonds between others and "set them at variance;" but common usage adds to this general sense the special idea of "setting at variance *by slander."* In the application of the title to Satan, both the general and special senses should be kept in view. His general object is to break the bonds of communion between God and man, and the bonds of truth and love which bind men to each other. The slander of God to man is best seen in the words of Gen. 3:4, 5. They attribute selfishness and jealousy to the Giver of all good. The slander of man to God is illustrated by the book of Job. Job 1:9-11; 2:4, 5. IV. *The method of satanic action* upon the heart itself. It may be summed up in two words— temptation and possession. On the subject of possession, see DEMONIACS.

V. Hastings' *Bible Dictionary* closes its article on Satan by a summary of which these are the concluding words: "The ultimate and fundamental truth of angelology and demonology has not been, and never can be destroyed by the march of modern science. . . . The assumption that other superhuman as well as subordinate agencies are at work, and that some of these are embodiments of evil influence, adds no fundamental difficulty to those which already exist. . . . Now it is a matter of historic notoriety that some personalities have lived in this world that might be called incarnations of evil influence. The supposition that other and superhuman personalities may also be foci of evil moral energy, and operate like ganglionic centres in a nervous system, presents no fundamental difficulty in addition to the difficulty already involved in the problem of evil. That Satan exists as a personal centre of evil influence, physical as well as moral (for the two are closely associated) is the undoubted teaching of the Bible. He is represented to us not as the absolute origin of evil, or the only source of it, but as its most potent superhuman representative."

Satyr, a sylvan deity or demigod of Greek mythology, represented as a monster, part man and part goat. Isa. 13:21; 34:14. The Hebrew word is

38

usually translated "he-goat." In the passages cited it probably refers to demons of woods and desert places. Comp. Lev. 17:7; 2 Chron. 11:15.

Saul (*desired*). 1. One of the early kings of Edom, and successor of Samlah. Gen. 36:37, 38; 1 Chron. 1:48. Properly here as in R. V. "Shaul."

2. The first king of Israel, the son of Kish, and of the tribe of Benjamin. (B.C. 1095-1055. Ussher.) He was remarkable for his strength and activity, 2 Sam. 1:23, and, like the Homeric heroes, of gigantic stature, taller by head and shoulders than the rest of the people, in personal appearance "every inch a king." His father, Kish, was a powerful and wealthy chief, though the family to which he belonged was of little importance. 1 Sam. 9:1, 21. His home was at Gibeah. A portion of his property consisted of a drove of asses. In search of these asses, gone astray on the mountains, he sent his son Saul. It was at this time that Saul met with Samuel at his home in Ramah, five miles north of Jerusalem, and was anointed by him to be king of Israel. Returning homeward, his call was confirmed by the incidents which, according to Samuel's prediction, awaited him. 1 Sam. 10:9, 10. What may be named the public call occurred at Mizpeh, when lots were cast to find the tribe and family which was to produce the king. When Saul, who had hidden himself, was found and stood forth as the chosen one, the majority of the people hailed him with enthusiasm. 1 Sam. 10:17-24. Returning to Gibeah, apparently to private life until all private jealousies should be overcome, he heard the threat issued by Nahash king of Ammon against Jabeshgilead. He speedily collected an army, and Jabesh was rescued. The effect was instantaneous on the people, and the monarchy was inaugurated anew at Gilgal. 1 Sam. 11:1-15. Although king of Israel, his rule was at first limited; but in the second year of his reign he began to organize an attempt to shake off the Philistine yoke, and an army was formed. Jonathan, the eldest son of the king, precipitated the struggle by an attack on the Philistine garrison of Geba. The whole nation was roused to resist the attack which must come from the infuriated Philis-

tines. In this crisis, Saul, who had expected Samuel to be present at Gilgal to offer the sacrifices before the army went into battle, became impatient at his delay and offered sacrifice himself. Samuel, arriving later, pronounced the first curse, on his impetuous zeal. 1 Sam. 13:5-14. An exploit of Jonathan and his armor-bearer gave an opening for a general battle which resulted in the defeat of the Philistines. It was in the heat of the pursuit that Saul made the rash vow which all but cost the life of his son. 1 Sam. 14:24, 44. The expulsion of the Philistines, although not entirely completed, ch. 14: 52, at once placed Saul in a position higher than that of any previous ruler of Israel, and he made war upon the neighboring tribes. In the war with Amalek, ch. 14:48; 15:1-9, he disobeyed the prophetical command of Samuel, which called down the second curse, and the first distinct intimation of the transference of the kingdom to a rival. The rest of Saul's life is one long tragedy. The frenzy which had given indications of itself before now at times took almost entire possession of him. In this crisis David was recommended to him. From this time forward their lives are blended together. [DAVID.] In Saul's better moments he never lost the strong affection which he had contracted for David. Occasionally, too, his prophetical gift returned, blended with his madness. 1 Sam. 19:24. But his acts of fierce, wild zeal increased. At last the end came. The Philistines, roused to action, invaded the country and encamped in the valley of Jezreel Saul went to meet them, and pitched on the slope of Gilboa. But he had lost his early courage, and forebodings of his fate seemed to trouble him. Feeling that Jehovah was against him he consulted one of the necromancers, the "Witch of Endor," who had escaped his persecution. At this distance of time it is impossible to determine the relative amount of fraud or of reality in the scene which follows, though the obvious meaning of the narrative itself tends to the hypothesis of some kind of apparition, ch. 28. On hearing the denunciation which the apparition conveyed, Saul fell the whole length of his gigantic stature on the ground, and remained motionless till the woman and his servants forced him to eat. The next day the battle came on. The Israelites were driven up the side of Gilboa. The three sons of Saul were slain. Saul was wounded. According to one account, he fell upon his own sword, 1 Sam. 31:4, and died. The body on being found by the Philistines was stripped and decapitated, and the headless trunk hung over the city walls of Bethshan, with those of his three sons, ch. 31:9, 10. The head was deposited (probably at Ashdod) in the temple of Dagon. 1 Chron. 10:10. The men of Jabesh-gilead, however, grateful for what he had done for them in the early part of his reign, marched by night to Bethshan, took his body from his enemies, and buried it on the site of his first victory. 1 Sam. 31:13.

3. The Jewish name of St. Paul.

Saw. Egyptian saws, so far as has yet been discovered, are single-handed. As is the case in modern Oriental saws, the teeth usually incline toward the handle, instead of away from it like ours. They have, in most cases, bronze blades, apparently attached to the handles by leathern thongs. We read of sawn stones used in the temple. 1 Kings 7:9. In 2 Sam. 12:31 and 1 Chron. 20:3, it seems to be stated that David used saws, etc., as instruments of torture. This does not seem consistent with David's character, and students have found that the change of a single letter in each case would give the sentence the meaning of setting the captives to hard labor with the saw, axe, harrow, etc.

Scapegoat. [ATONEMENT, DAY OF.]

Scarlet. [COLORS.]

Sceptre. This word originally meant a *rod* or *staff*. It was thence specifically applied to the shepherd's crook, Lev. 27:32; Micah 7:14, and to the wand or sceptre of a ruler. The allusions to it are all of a metaphorical character, and describe it simply as one of the insignia of supreme power. Gen. 49:10. We are consequently unable to describe the article from any biblical notice; we may infer that it was probably made of wood. The sceptre of the Persian monarch is described as "golden," *i. e.* probably of massive gold. Esther 4:11.

Sce'va (sē'và). A chief priest or member of one of the priestly families of the Jews. His seven sons were exorcists, and tried to exorcise demons in the name of Jesus, without success. Acts 19:14–16. (A.D. 54.)

Schools. In the early ages most of the instruction of young children was by the parents. After the captivity schools came more into use, and at the time of Christ were very abundant. The schools were in connection with the synagogues, which were found in every city and in almost every village of the land. Their idea of the value of schools may be gained from such sayings from the Talmud as "The world is preserved by the breath of the children in the schools;" "A town in which there are no schools must perish;" "Jerusalem was destroyed because the education of children was neglected." Josephus says, "Our principal care is to educate our children." The Talmud states that in Bechar there were 400 schools, having each 400 teachers, with 400 children each, and that there were 4000 pupils in the house of Rabban Simeon Ben-Gamaliel, but this is without doubt exaggerated. The pupils surrounded the teacher who sat slightly raised above his pupils, so that every one could see the teacher and hear his words. Benches were of later invention. The children read aloud to acquire fluency, and also to enable them to fix their studies permanently in the memory. The number of school-hours was limited, and during the heat of the summer was only four hours. The punishment employed was beating with a strap, never with a rod. The chief studies were their own language and literature, the chief school-book the Holy Scriptures, and there were special efforts to impress lessons of morality and chastity. In some schools they also studied mathematics, astronomy and the natural sciences. Beyond the schools for popular education there were higher schools or colleges scattered throughout the cities where the Jews abounded.

Schoolmaster. In Gal. 3:24, this word refers to the Roman slave who conducted the boys to the school and home again.

Scorpion (Heb. *'akrâb*), a well-known venomous insect of hot climates, shaped much like a lobster, and closely akin to the spider. It is usually not more than two or three inches long, but in tropical climates is sometimes six inches in length, and has been found as long as 12 inches. The wilderness of Sinai is especially alluded to as being inhabited by scorpions at the time of the exodus, and to this day these animals are common in the same district, as well as in some parts of Palestine. Scorpions are generally found in dry and in dark places, under stones and in ruins. They are carnivorous in their habits, and move along in a threatening attitude, with the tail elevated. The sting, which is situated at the end of

SCORPION.

the tail, has at its base a gland that secretes a poisonous fluid, which is discharged into the wound by two minute orifices at its extremity. In hot climates the sting often occasions much suffering, and sometimes alarming symptoms. The sting of the larger varieties is very apt to cause death; while that of even the smallest may do so if the throat is attacked. The "scorpions" of 1 Kings 12:11, 14; 2 Chron. 10:11, 14, have clearly no allusion whatever to the animal, but to some instrument of scourging—unless indeed the expression is a mere figure.

Scourging. There is a distinction in the word used between the *beating*,

SCOURGING.

with rods, and the *scourging*, with whips or scourges, made of cords or thongs of leather fastened to a handle. Usually there were three of these thongs in each scourge, and they were often reinforced with bits of metal which tore the skin and flesh. The principal places where the word is used is 1 Kings 12:11, 14; 2 Chron. 10:11, 14, where Rehoboam promises scourgings to his complaining people; and in the

FLAGELLUM OR SCOURGE.

New Testament in the accounts of the scourging of Christ, in the Gospels, and of Paul in 2 Cor. 11:24. The "scourge of small cords" used by Jesus when he drove the traffickers out of the Temple was merely the symbol of authority. John 2:15.

Scribes (Heb. *sôpherîm*). 1. A secretary, or government clerk. 2 Kings 12:10; Ezra 4:8. All clerks were called by this name in Old Testament times.

2. More specifically the scribes, or *Sopherim*, were those who copied, taught and explained the law. Ezra was one of the most noted of these scribes, and in his teaching the prototype of these of the New Testament times. There were few if any of these before the exile, as the Levites at that time performed all such duties as were needed.

In the earlier period after the exile the scribes belonged to the Levites; but gradually an independent class of laymen sprang up, and at last they were nearly all laymen. The written law, which was considered as binding by all the Jews, did not cover all the details of daily life, and some of its regulations were liable to be misunderstood by the less educated class of the people. The duty of the scribes, therefore, was (1) to add to the law the regulations for the minor details there omitted; (2) explanations of the law itself. These together formed the oral law. (3) The scribes were to teach the law to others, and later (4) make decisions, or practically be judges, under the law. Since it was understood that only the scribes fully understood the meaning of the law, their words grew to be honored above the law. It was greater crime to offend against them than against the law. The first step was taken toward annulling the commandments of God for the sake of their own traditions, Mark 7:13. The casuistry became at once subtle and prurient, evading the plainest duties, tampering with conscience, Matt. 15: 1-6; 23:16-23. We can therefore understand why they were constantly denounced by our Lord along with the Pharisees. The scribes repeated the traditions of the elders, it being considered a fault for a pupil to change even the expressions used by his teacher. But Jesus "spake as one having authority," "not as the scribes." Matt. 7:29. While they confined their teachings to the class of scholars, he "had compassion on the multitudes." Matt. 9:36. While they were to be found only in the council or in their schools, he journeyed through the cities and villages. Matt. 4:23; 9:35, etc. While they spoke of the kingdom of God vaguely, as a thing far off, he proclaimed that it had already come nigh to men. Matt. 4:17. In our Lord's time there were two chief parties, the disciples of Hillel and of Shammai. Nothing is known with certainty of the two leaders, though there are many traditions. The school of Hillel was distinguished for its mildness, and that of Shammai for its strictness in interpretation, but the differences in the two schools did not extend to any but trivial subjects. The special training for a scribe's office began, probably, about the age of thirteen. The boy who was destined by his parents to the calling of a scribe went to Jerusalem and applied for admission in the school of some famous rabbi. The requirements for the calling consisted principally of an accurate and prodigious memory, and patience enough to learn by heart the oral law. They also heard disputations on concrete cases, or disputed among themselves, their words being criticised by the teacher. The scholar with the best memory was considered the best scholar, since all, teacher as well as scholar, must adhere closely to the traditions of those before them. After a sufficient period of training, probably at the age of thirty the probationer was solemnly admitted to his office. At the time of Christ their influence was great. They had seats in the Sanhedrin; they comprised nearly all the teaching force of the country; and nearly all the judges came from their class. They leaned more to the side of the Pharisees than the Sadducees, though there is some indication that they were not all Pharisees. With the Pharisees they were denounced by Jesus for their hypocrisy, Matt. 23. In our Lord's time the passion for distinction was insatiable. The ascending scale of rab, rabbi, rabban, presented so many steps on the ladder of ambition. Other forms of worldliness were not far off. The salutations in the market-place, Matt. 23:7, the reverential kiss offered by the scholars to their master or by rabbis to each other, the greeting of Abba, father, Matt. 23:9, the long robes with the broad blue fringe, Matt. 23:5,—all these go to make up the picture of a scribe's life. Theoretically they were to take no pay for performing any of their regular duties. If they had no private fortune they must undertake secular work for support. But in fact there is no doubt that they received pay at least for teaching, in the later periods. With all the faults of the scribes, Jews and Christians alike owe them a debt of gratitude. After the fall of Jerusalem in A.D. 70, they set themselves diligently to work to reorganize Judaism. They worked quietly and peacefully, avoided extremes, and were successful in keeping what was left of the nation faithful to the faith of their fathers. The ordinances of the oral law were at last written down, and to them is due the preservation of all of the Hebrew scriptures which now exist.

Scrip. The Hebrew word thus translated appears in 1 Sam. 17:40 as a synonym for the bag in which the shepherds of Palestine carried their food or other necessaries. The scrip of the Galilean peasants was of leather, used especially to carry their food on a journey, and slung over their shoulders. Matt. 10:10; Mark 6:8; Luke 9:3; 22:35. The English word "scrip" is probably connected with *scrape, scrap,* and was used in like manner for articles of food.

Scripture. [SEE BIBLE.]

Scyth'ian occurs in Col. 3:11 as a generalized term for rude, ignorant, degraded. The name often included all the nomadic tribes, who dwelt mostly on the north of the Black and the Caspian Sea, stretching thence indefinitely into inner Asia, and were regarded by the ancients as standing extremely low in point of intelligence and civilization.

Scythop'olis. [BETH-SHEAN.]

Sea. The sea, *yâm,* is used in Scripture to denote—1. "The gathering of the waters," "the Ocean," as distinguished from dry land. Gen. 1:2, 10, etc. 2. Some portion of this, as the Mediterranean Sea, called the "hinder," the "western" and the "utmost" sea, Deut. 11:24; 34:2; Joel 2:20; "sea of the Philistines," Ex. 23:31; "the great sea," Num. 34:6, 7; Josh. 15:47; "the sea," Gen. 49:13; Ps. 80:11. Also frequently of the Red Sea. Ex. 15:4. [RED SEA.] 3. Inland lakes termed seas, as the Salt or Dead Sea. [See the special article.] 4. Any great collection of waters, as the river Nile, Isa. 19:5, and the Euphrates. Jer. 51:36.

Sea, Molten or **Brazen Sea.** In the place of the laver of the tabernacle, Solomon caused a laver to be cast for a similar purpose, which from its size was called a sea, as the Romans called large vessels "lakes" (*lacus*). It was made partly or wholly of the brass, or rather copper or bronze, which was captured by David from "Tibhath and Chun, cities of Hadarezer king of Zobah." 1 Kings 7:23-26; 1 Chron.

18:8. It is said to have been 15 feet in diameter and 7½ feet deep, and to have been capable of containing 2000, or, according to 2 Chron. 4:5, 3000 baths (18,000 to 27,000 gallons). The laver stood on twelve oxen, three toward each quarter of the heavens, and all looking outward. It was mutilated by Ahaz by being removed from its base of oxen and placed on a stone base, and was finally broken up by the Assyrians. 2 Kings 16:14, 17; 25:13.

Sea, The Salt, the usual and perhaps the most ancient name for the remarkable lake which to the western world is now generally known as the Dead Sea.

I. *Names.*—(1) The Salt Sea, Gen. 14:3; Deut. 3:17; (2) Sea of the Arabah or Plain, Deut. 3:17; Josh. 3:16; (3) The East Sea, Joel 2:20; (4) Sea of salt, and Sea of Sodom, in the Talmud; (5) The Asphaltic Lake, in Josephus; (6) The name "Dead Sea" appears to have been first used in Greek by Pausanias in the latter half of the second century of the Christian era. (7) The Arabic name is *Bahr Lût,* the "Sea of Lot."

II. *Description.*—The Dead Sea lies nearly north and south along a line corresponding to that of the Jordan valley, in the deep fissure which runs completely through Palestine, called in at least a part of its course the Ghor. It receives the waters of the Jordan, which amount to an average of six million tons of water every twenty-four hours. It also has a number of minor tributaries, which when fed by the melting snows of the mountains bring a vast quantity more. The sea has no outlet, yet such is the heat of the valley that even at the time of the greatest floods, the lake does not rise more than ten or fifteen feet. Viewed on the map, the lake is of an oblong form, of tolerably regular contour, interrupted only by a large and long peninsula which projects from the eastern shore near its southern end, and virtually divides the expanse of the water into two portions, connected by a long, narrow and somewhat devious passage. Its surface is from north to south about 47 English miles. Its greatest width is about 10 English miles. The depression of its surface, and the depth which it attains below that surface.

combined with the absence of any outlet, render it one of the most remarkable spots on the globe. The surface of the lake as ascertained by the officers of the Ordnance Survey is 1292 feet below the level of the Mediterranean at Jaffa. Its maximum depth, near the mouth of the Arnon, is 1278 feet. The water of the lake is not less remarkable than its other features. It is much saltier than the water of the ocean, the latter containing 6 pounds of salt to every 100 pounds of water, while in the former each 100 pounds contains from 20 to 28 pounds. In consequence of this, one bathing in the Dead Sea becomes almost ludicrously buoyant. Dr. Robinson "could never swim before, either in fresh or salt water," yet here he "could sit, stand, lie or swim without difficulty." (*B. R.* i. 506.) It has been long supposed that no life whatever existed in the lake, but while fish are very rare they do exist, and some lower forms of life are found in small numbers. The statements of ancient travelers and geographers to the effect that no living creature could exist on the shores of the lake, or bird fly across its surface, are amply disproved by later travelers. The springs on the margin of the lake harbor snipe, partridges, ducks, nightingales and other birds, as well as frogs; and hawks, doves and hares are found along the shore. The appearance of the lake does not fulfil the idea conveyed by its popular name. "The Dead Sea," says a recent traveler, "did not strike me with that sense of desolation and dreariness which I suppose it ought. I thought it a pretty, smiling lake—a nice ripple on its surface." The truth lies, as usual, somewhere between these two extremes. On the one hand, the lake certainly is not a gloomy, deadly, smoking gulf. In this respect it does not at all fulfil the promise of its name. At sunrise and sunset the scene must be astonishingly beautiful. But on the other hand, there is something in the prevalent sterility and the dry, burnt look of the shores, the overpowering heat, the occasional smell of sulphur, the dreary salt marsh at the southern end, and the fringe of dead driftwood round the margin, which must go far to excuse the title which so many ages have attached to the lake, and which

we may be sure it will never lose. The connection between this singular lake and the biblical history is very slight. In the topographical records of the Pentateuch and the book of Joshua it forms one among the landmarks of the boundaries of the whole country, as well as of the inferior divisions of Judah and Benjamin. Besides this the name occurs once or twice in the imagery of the prophets. In the New Testament there is not even an allusion to it. There is, however, one passage in which the "Salt Sea" is mentioned in a manner different from any of those already quoted, viz. as having been in the time of Abraham the vale of Siddim. Gen. 14:3. In consequence of this passage it has been believed that the present lake covered a district which in historic times had been permanently habitable dry land. But it must not be overlooked that the passage in question is the only one in the whole Bible to countenance the notion that the cities of the plain were submerged; a notion which does not date earlier than the Christian era. [SODOM; ZOAR.] The belief which prompted the idea of some modern writers that the Dead Sea was formed by the catastrophe which overthrew the "cities of the plain" is a mere assumption. It is not only unsupported by Scripture, but is directly in the teeth of the evidence of the ground itself. The destruction of Sodom and Gomorrah may have been by volcanic action, but it may be safely asserted that no traces of it have yet been discovered, and that, whatever it was, it can have had no connection with that far vaster and far more ancient event which opened the great valley of the Jordan and the Dead Sea, and at some subsequent time cut it off from communication with the Red Sea by forcing up between them the tract of the *Wady Arabah*. The researches of modern times have resulted in proving satisfactorily to those engaged that the Dead Sea exists in very nearly the same form and area as in the time of Abraham. Some slight decrease there may have been, however, as it is generally considered that in earlier times the Jordan had a larger flow of water.

Seah. [WEIGHTS AND MEASURES.]

Seal. The fact that reading and writing have always been in the East the possession of a small minority has attached great importance to the seal or signet. They are of very ancient use, by the Hebrews (Gen. 38:18, 25), Egyptians (Gen. 41:42) and by the Persians (Esth. 3:10; 8:2). They were of two sorts: (1) The small seal of precious. stone or metal engraved with the owner's device, and set in a ring,

SEAL WITH FRAME.

and (2) the larger cylinder of metal, stone or terra-cotta for sealing larger surfaces. The material used for the impression was often a lump of clay, attached to the document by strings. In other cases wax was used. In sealing a sepulchre or box, the fastening was covered with clay or wax, and the

SEAL AND SIGNETS.

impression from a seal of one in authority was stamped upon it, so that it could not be broken open without discovery. Job 14 : 17; 41 : 15; Dan. 6 : 17; Matt. 27 : 66; Rev. 5 : 1. Seals were used in the place of signatures; as a sign of authority; to secure a place or an article from intrusion. Many cylinder seals have been found in the re-

searches in Babylonia and elsewhere. They are in general much like the one pictured here.

Se'ba (sē'bà) (pl. *Sebaim;* in Authorized Version incorrectly rendered Sabeans) heads the list of the sons of Cush. Besides the mention of Seba in the lists of the sons of Cush, Gen. 10: 7; 1 Chron. 1:9, there are but three notices of the nation—Ps. 72:10; Isa. 43:3; 45:14. These passages seem to show that Seba was a nation of Africa, bordering on or included in Cush, and in Solomon's time independent and of political importance. It may perhaps be identified with the island of Meroë. Josephus says that Saba was the ancient name of the Ethiopian island and city of Meroë, but he writes Seba, in the notice of the Noachian settlements, Sabas. The island of Meroë lay between the Nile and its affluent the Atbara. Some consider that it is more nearly in the heart of Africa.

Se'bat (sē'băt) (*a rod*). [MONTH.]

Sec'acah (sĕk'a-kah), or **Seca'cah** (sĕk-ā'kah) (*enclosure*), one of the six cities of Judah which were situated in the *Midbar* ("wilderness"), that is, the tract bordering on the Dead Sea. Josh. 15:61. Its position is not known. Some identifications have been made, doubtfully, but are disputed.

Se'chu (sē'kū) (*the watch-tower*), a place mentioned once only—1 Sam. 19: 22—apparently as lying on the route between Saul's residence, Gibeah, and Ramah, that of Samuel. It was notorious for "the great well" (or rather cistern) which it contained. Several identifications have been proposed, but none are really satisfactory.

Secun'dus, a Thessalonian Christian who accompanied Paul to Europe. Acts 20:4. (A.D. 57.)

Seer. An old term for prophet.

Se'gub (sē'gŭb) (*elevated*). 1. The youngest son of Hiel the Bethelite, who rebuilt Jericho. 1 Kings 16:34.

2. Son of Hezron. 1 Chron. 2:21, 22.

Se'ir (sē'īr) (*hairy, shaggy*). 1. We have both "land of Seir," Gen. 32:3; 36:30, and "Mount Seir." Gen. 14:6 It is the original name of the mountain region extending along the east side of the Arabah, from the Dead Sea to the Elanitic Gulf. The Horites appear to have been the chief of the aboriginal inhabitants, Gen. 36:20; but it was ever afterward the possession of the Edomites, the descendants of Esau. The Mount Seir of the Bible extended much farther south than the modern province, as is shown by the words of Deut. 2:1–8.

2. Mount Seir, an entirely different place from the foregoing; one of the landmarks on the north boundary of the territory of Judah. Josh. 15:10 only. It lay westward of Kirjath-jearim, and between it and Beth-shemesh. It is commonly supposed to be the ridge upon which the modern village of *Saris* now stands.

Se'irath (sē'ĭ-răth) (R. V. "Seirah"), the place to which Ehud fled after his murder of Eglon. Judges 3:26, 27. It was in "Mount Ephraim," ver. 27, and apparently not far from Gilgal. Its locality was not known to even the earliest authorities, Eusebius and Jerome, and is not yet identified.

Se'la (sē'lå), or **Se'lah** (*the rock*), 2 Kings 14:7; Isa. 16:1; so rendered in the Authorized Version in Judges 1:36; 2 Chron. 25:12. Beyond any reasonable doubt the city later known as Petra, which is the Greek for "rock," or a translation of the Hebrew word. It was in the midst of Mount Seir, in the neighborhood of Mount Hor, and was the ancient capital of Edom. In the end of the fourth century B.C. it appears as the headquarters of the Nabatheans, who successfully resisted the attacks of Antigonus. This came to an end in A.D. 105, when Arabia Petræa became a province of Rome. The city Petra is one of the most remarkable of ancient cities, not only by its position shut in by mountain cliffs, and approached only by a narrow ravine, through which, and across the city's site, the river winds, but by reason of the ruins there, which are stupendous, works of art cut out of the solid rock. Recent discoveries reveal more and more of these wonders. See illustration under EDOM.

Se'lah (sē'lå). This word, which is found only in the poetical books of the Old Testament, occurs seventy-one times in the Psalms and three times in Habakkuk. It is very probably a musical or liturgical sign, but it is impossible to determine its meaning. There are at least six different opinions among authorities. The only thing known with certainty of it is that it has no grammatical or rhetorical connection with the passages in which it is found.

Se'la-Hammah'lekoth (sē'lå-hăm-mah'lĕ-kŏth) (*the cliff of escapes* or *of divisions*), a rock or cliff in the wilderness of Maon, southeast of Hebron, the scene of one of those remarkable escapes which are so frequent in the history of Saul's pursuit of David. 1 Sam. 23:28. The great gorge of *Wady Malaki* in this region would be a suitable position, where the two could be near enough to see each other easily, but be utterly unable to reach each other directly.

Se'led (*exultation*), one of the sons of Nadab, a descendant of Jerahmeel. 1 Chron. 2:30.

Seleu'cia (sē-lū'si-å) (named after its founder, Seleucus), near the mouth of the Orontes, was the seaport of Antioch. The distance between the two towns was about 16 miles. St. Paul, with Barnabas, sailed from Seleucia at the beginning of his first missionary circuit. Acts 13:4. This strong fortress and convenient seaport was constructed by the first Seleucus, and here he was buried. It retained its importance in Roman times, and in St. Paul's day it had the privileges of a free city. The remains are numerous.

Seleu'cus (sē-leū'kŭs), the name of five kings of the Greek dominion of Syria, who are hence called *Seleucidæ*. They ruled Syria from B.C. 312 to B.C. 65. Several allusions are made to them in Daniel 11, but only one—the fourth —is mentioned in the Apocrypha. This was "Seleucus Philopator," the son of Antiochus the Great, whom he succeeded B.C. 187. He was murdered B.C. 175.

Sem. SHEM the patriarch. Luke 3:36.

Semachi'ah (sĕm-a-kī'ah) (*Jehovah has sustained*), one of the sons of SHEMAIAH, 9. 1 Chron. 26:7.

Sem'ei (sĕm'e-ī) (the Greek form of Shimei). The father of Mattathias in the genealogy of Jesus Christ. Luke 3:26.

Sem'ein. In the Revised Version of Luke 3:26 for Semei.

Semit'ic Languages. [SHEMITIC LANGUAGES; HEBREW LANGUAGE.]

Sen'aah (sĕn'å-ah) (*thorny*). The

THE TAYLOR PRISM.

Face giving account of Sennacherib's campaign against Jerusalem.

"children (*i. e.* the inhabitants) of Senaah" are enumerated among the "people of Israel" who returned from the captivity with Zerubbabel. Ezra 2: 35; Neh. 7: 38. (B.C. 536.) The Magdal Senna of Eusebius and Jerome denotes a town seven miles north of Jericho.

Se'neh (sē'neh) (*thorn*), the name of one of the two isolated rocks between which ran the "passage of Michmash," 1 Sam. 14: 4. It was between these that Jonathan and his armorbearer passed when they surprised the Philistines at Michmash. Its name is retained in the *Wady Suweinit* on whose right bank the rock must have been.

Se'nir (sē'nir) (*coat of mail*), 1 Chron. 5: 23; Ezek. 27: 5, the Amorite name for Mount Hermon.

Sennach'erib (sĕn-năk'e-rĭb) (*the moon-god [Sin] has increased brothers*), was the son and successor of Sargon.

[SARGON.] Sennacherib mounted the throne B.C. 705. His efforts were directed to crushing the revolt of Babylonia, which he invaded with a large army. Merodach-baladan ventured on a battle, but was defeated and driven from the country. In B.C. 701, Sennacherib turned his arms toward the west, chastised Sidon, and, having probably concluded a convention with his chief enemy, fi-

SENNACHERIB ON HIS THRONE.

nally marched against Hezekiah, king of Judah. It was at this time that "Sennacherib came up against all the fenced cities of Judah, and took them." 2 Kings 18: 13. There is a slight question whether he made one or two campaigns against Judah, but the most of the authorities count it as only one. The Egyptians, coming to the aid of Hezekiah, were defeated and driven back, and swept through the country of Judah. While besieging Lachish he sent an insulting letter to Hezekiah at Jerusalem. In answer to Hezekiah's prayer an event occurred which relieved both Egypt and Judea from their danger. Either by the plague, or by some still more direct visitation from God the greater portion of his army was destroyed. The camp immediately broke up; the king fled. Sennacherib reached his capital in safety, and was not deterred by the terrible disaster which had befallen his arms from engaging in other wars, though he seems thenceforward to have carefully avoided Palestine. His account of the campaign in Palestine, on the Taylor Cylinder (HEZEKIAH) carefully avoids all mention of this catastrophe; as we should expect. Sennacherib was one of the most magnificent of the Assyrian kings. He seems to have been the first who fixed the seat of government permanently at Nineveh, which he carefully repaired and adorned with splendid buildings. His greatest work is the grand palace at Kouyunjik. He was assassinated in B.C. 681 by two of his sons, probably actuated by jealousy of their brother Esarhaddon, who however succeeded his father in the kingdom.

Senu'ah (sē-nū'ah), properly **Hassenuah** (with the definite article), a Benjamite. Neh. 11: 9.

Seo'rim (sē-ō'rĭm) (*barley*), the chief of the fourth of the twenty-four courses of priests. 1 Chron. 24: 8.

Se'phar (sē'far) (*a numbering*). A place which formed the limit of the territory of the sons of Joktan. Gen. 10: 30. It was without doubt in southern Arabia, and is commonly identified with *Zaphar*, a coast town in Hadramant.

Seph'arad (sĕf'a-răd), a name which occurs in Obad. 20 only. Its situation has always been a matter of uncertainty, though it is conjectured to have been the Shaparda of the Assyrian inscriptions, which was probably a district in the northern part of Asia Minor.

Sepharva'im (sĕf-ar-va'-ĭm) (*the two Sipparas*) is mentioned by Sennacherib in his letter to Hezekiah as a city whose king had been unable to resist the Assyrians. 2 Kings 19: 13; Isa. 37: 13, comp. 2 Kings 18: 34. It is identified with the famous town of Sippara, on the Euphrates above Babylon, which was near the border of Mesopotamia. The dual form indicates two divisions of the city—the equivalent of "twin-city." One part was the seat of the worship of the sun-god, and hence called "Sippara of Shemesh," *i. e.* "Sippara of the sun-god." The other part was the seat of the worship of Annuit the wife of the god of the sky, and hence was called "Sippara of Annuit."

Sep'tuagint (*the seventy*). The Septuagint or Greek version of the Old Testament appears at the present day in four principal editions:—1. Biblia Polyglotta Complutensis, A.D. 1514–1517. 2. The Aldine Edition, Venice, A.D. 1518. 3. The Roman Edition, edited under Pope Sixtus V., A.D. 1587. 4. "The Old Testament in Greek according to the Septuagint." Edited for the Syndics of the (Cambridge) University Press, by H. B. Swete, 1887–1899. The Jews of Alexandria had probably still less knowledge of Hebrew than their brethren in Palestine; their familiar language was Alexandrian Greek. They had settled in Alexandria in large numbers soon after the time of Alexander, and under the early Ptolemies. They would naturally follow the same practice as the Jews in Palestine; and hence would arise in time an entire Greek version. The commonly-received story respecting its origin is contained in an extant letter ascribed to Aristeas, who was an officer at the court of Ptolemy Philadelphus. This letter, which is addressed by Aristeas to his brother Philocrates, gives a glowing account of the origin of the Septuagint; of the embassy and presents sent by King Ptolemy to the high priest at Jerusalem, by the advice of Demetrius Phalereus, his librarian; the choosing of six interpreters from each of the twelve tribes, and their names; the copy of the law, in letters of gold; the feast prepared for the seventy-two, which continued for seven days; their lodging by the seashore; and the accomplishment of their work in seventy-two days, by conference and comparison. This is the story which probably gave to the version the title of the Septuagint, and which has been repeated in various forms by the Christian writers. But it is now generally admitted that the letter is spurious, and is probably the fabrication of an Alexandrian Jew shortly before the Christian era. Still there can be no doubt that there was a basis of fact for the fiction; on three points of the story there is no material difference of opinion, and they are confirmed by the study of the version itself:—1. The version was made at Alexandria. 2. It was begun in the time of the earlier Ptolemies, about 280 B.C. 3. The law (*i. e.* the Pentateuch) alone was translated at first. The Septuagint version was highly esteemed by the Hellenistic Jews before the coming of Christ. Because of the dispersion of the Jews through the world the Greek translation of their Scriptures was an important factor in preparing the way for Christ's coming. Its existence in a language which could be read throughout the world made even the Gentiles familiar with the beliefs of the Jews, and their wonderful history which would of course include the guiding Providence of God, and his promises of a Saviour to come, throughout the nations. Not less wide was the influence of the Septuagint in the spread of the gospel. For a long period the Septuagint was the Old Testament of the far larger part of the Christian Church. *Character of the Septuagint.*—The Septuagint is faithful in substance, but not minutely accurate in details. It has been clearly shown by students that the several books were translated by different persons, without any comprehensive revision to harmonize the several parts. Names and words are rendered differently in different books. Thus the character of the version varies much in the several books; those of the Pentateuch are the best. The poetical parts are, generally speaking, inferior to the historical, the original abounding with rarer words and expressions, but the Psalms are fairly well produced. The Version of Jeremiah differs considerably from the Hebrew manuscripts found to-day, while the translation of Isaiah is very poor. Ezekiel and the minor prophets (particularly Amos) seem to be better rendered. The close connection between the Old and the New Testament makes the study of the Septuagint most valuable, and indeed indispensable, to the theological student. It was manifestly the chief storehouse from which both Christ and his apostles drew their proofs and precepts.

Sepulchre. [BURIAL; TOMB.]

Se'rah (sē'rah), the daughter of Asher, Gen. 46:17; 1 Chron. 7:30, called in A. V. of Num. 26:46 SARAH.

Sera'iah (sĕr-ā'iah). 1. The king's scribe or secretary in the reign of David. 2 Sam. 8:17.

2. The high priest in the reign of Zedekiah, and ancestor of Ezra the Scribe. 2 Kings 25:18; 1 Chron. 6:14; Ezra 7:1; Jer. 52:24.

3. The son of Tanhumeth. 2 Kings 25:23; Jer. 40:8.

4. The son of Kenaz and brother of Othniel. 1 Chron. 4:13, 14.

5. Ancestor of Jehu, a Simeonite chieftain. 1 Chron. 4:35.

6. One of the twelve leaders who returned with Zerubbabel. Ezra 2:2. (B.C. 536.) Azariah in Neh. 7:7.

7. One of those sent to arrest Jeremiah and Baruch. Jer. 36:26.

8. A priest, or priestly family, who signed the covenant with Nehemiah. Neh. 10:2. Perhaps same as

9. A priest, the son of Hilkiah. Neh. 11:11.

10. The head of a priestly house which went up from Babylon with Zerubbabel. Neh. 12:1, 7.

11. The son of Neriah, and brother of Baruch. Jer. 51:59, 61. He went with Zedekiah to Babylon in the fourth year of his reign. (B.C. 594.) The R. V. calls him "the chief chamberlain," or (marg.) "quartermaster."

Seraphim (sĕr'a-fim) (*burning, glowing*), an order of celestial beings, whom Isaiah beheld in vision standing above Jehovah as he sat upon his throne. Isa. 6:2. They are described as having each of them three pairs of wings, with one of which they covered their faces (a token of humility); with the second they covered their feet (a token of respect); while with the third they flew. They seem to have borne a general resemblance to the human figure, ver. 2. Their occupation was twofold—to celebrate the praises of Jehovah's holiness and power, ver. 3, and to act as the medium of communication between heaven and earth, ver. 6.

Se'red (sē'red) (*fear*), the first-born of Zebulun. Gen. 46:14; Num. 26:26.

Ser'gius Pau'lus (sĕr'jĭ-ŭs paw'lus) was the proconsul of Cyprus when the apostle Paul visited that island with Barnabas on his first missionary tour. Acts 13:7, *seq.* (A.D. 47.) He is described as an intelligent man, truthseeking, eager for information from all sources within his reach. Though at first admitting to his society Elymas the magian, he afterward, on becoming acquainted with the claims of the gospel, yielded his mind to the evidence of its truth.

Serpent. The Hebrew word *nâchâsh* is the generic name of any serpent. It is used often in the Bible. Its shrewdness is mentioned in Gen. 3:1, and alluded to by our Lord in Matt. 10:16; the poisonous properties of some species are often mentioned, see Ps. 58:4; Prov. 23:32; the sharp tongue of the serpent is mentioned in Ps. 140:3;

SERPENT.
Denoting immortality.

Job 20:16; the habit serpents have of lying concealed in hedges and in holes of walls is alluded to in Eccles. 10:8; their dwelling in dry sandy places, in Deut. 8:15; their wonderful mode of progression did not escape the observation of the author of Prov. 30, who expressly mentions it as "one of the three things which were too wonderful for him," ver. 19. The art of taming and charming serpents is of great antiquity, and is alluded to in Ps. 58:5; Eccles. 10:11; Jer. 8:17, and doubtless intimated by St. James, James 3:7, who particularizes serpents among all other animals that "have been tamed by man." It was under the form of a serpent that the devil seduced Eve; hence in Scripture Satan is called "the old serpent," Rev. 12:9, and comp. 2

Cor. 11 : 3. The serpent all through the East became the emblem of the spirit of evil, and is so pictured even on the monuments of Egypt, although it had a double reputation, being also the emblem of Mercury and of the healing art. Some older commentators supposed that the serpent, prior to the Fall, moved along in an erect attitude, but this would necessitate a radical change in its anatomy, and it is probable that the mode of progression was not new. Probably after the Fall its grovelling on the earth was to be the memorial of its degradation, and of the loathing and disgust which it inspires in men. Serpents are said in Scripture to "eat dust," see Gen. 3 : 14;

THE VIPER.

Isa. 65 : 25; Micah 7 : 17; these animals, which for the most part take their food on the ground, do consequently swallow with it large portions of sand and dust. Much has been written on the question of the "fiery serpents" of Num. 21 : 6, 8, with which it is usual to erroneously identify the "fiery flying serpent" of Isa. 14 : 29 and 30 : 6. The latter probably has reference to a fabulous serpent found on the monuments in Egypt. The word "fiery" probably signifies "burning," in allusion to the sensation produced by the bite. The *Cerastes,* or the *Naia haje,* or any other venomous species frequenting Arabia, may denote the "serpent of the burning bite" which destroyed the children of Israel. The snake that fastened on St. Paul's hand when he was

at Melita, Acts 28 : 3, was perhaps the *Viper aspis,* though as no venomous snakes are now found in Malta, it is impossible to certainly identify it. [See also ADDER; ASP.]

Serpent, Brazen. When God punished the murmurs of the Israelites in the wilderness by sending among them serpents whose fiery bite was fatal, Moses, upon their repentance, was commanded to make a serpent of brass, whose polished surface shone like fire, and to set it up on the banner-pole in the midst of the people; and whoever was bitten by a serpent had but to look up at it and live. Num. 21 : 4–9. The comparison used by Christ, John 3 : 14, 15, adds a deep interest to this scene. To present the serpent form, as deprived of its power to hurt, impaled as the trophy of a conqueror, was to assert that evil, physical and spiritual, had been overcome, and thus help to strengthen the weak faith of the Israelites in a victory over both. Others look upon the uplifted serpent as a symbol of life and health, it having been so worshipped in Egypt. The two views have a point of contact, for the primary idea connected with the serpent is *wisdom.* Wisdom, apart from obedience to God, degenerates to cunning, and degrades and envenoms man's nature. Wisdom, yielding to the divine law, is the source of healing and restoring influences, and the serpent form thus became a symbol of deliverance and health; and the Israelites were taught that it would be so with them in proportion as they ceased to be sensual and rebellious. Preserved as a relic, whether on the spot of its first erection or elsewhere, the brazen serpent, called by the name of *Nehushtan,* became an object of idolatrous veneration, and the zeal of Hezekiah destroyed it with the other idols of his father. 2 Kings 18 : 4. [NEHUSHTAN.]

Se′rug (sē′rug) (*branch*), son of Reu and great-grandfather of Abraham. Gen. 11 : 20–23.

Servant. [SLAVE.]

Seth (sĕth) (*setting, slip*), Gen. 4 : 25; 5 : 3; 1 Chron. 1 : 1, the third son of Adam, and father of Enos. He was born after the murder of Abel.

Se′thur (sē′thur) (*hidden*), the Asherite spy, son of Michael. Num. 13 : 13. (B.C. 1490.)

Seven. Certain numbers in the sacred literature of the Hebrews seem to have possessed a distinct symbolical meaning. Of these the number seven seems to have been both the most common, and the most sacred in its symbolism. This use is not confined to the Hebrews, or even the Semites as a race, but is also found among the Aryans of Persia and even of Greece (Iliad xix., 243). Its sacredness dates back to remote antiquity. It may also have an idea of completeness. In Proverbs 9:1 we read of the seven pillars of Wisdom's house; in Judges 16:13, 19 of the seven locks of Samson's hair. God blessed the seventh day, and hallowed it. The 7th month was ushered in by the Feast of Trumpets, and signalized by the celebration of the Feast of Tabernacles and the Great Day of Atonement; 7 weeks was the interval between the Passover and the Pentecost; the 7th year the sabbatical year; and the year succeeding 7 × 7 years the Jubilee year. Seven days were appointed as the length of the feasts of Passover and Tabernacles; 7 days for the ceremonies of the consecration of priests, and so on; 7 victims to be offered on any special occasion, as in Balaam's sacrifice, Num. 23:1, and especially at the ratification of a treaty, the notion of seven being embodied in the very term signifying to swear, literally meaning to *do seven times*. Gen. 21:28.

Shaal'bim (shà-ăl'bim), or **Shaalab'bin** (*foxes*), a town in the allotment of Dan. Josh. 19:42; Judges 1:35; 1 Kings 4:9. By Eusebius and Jerome it is mentioned in the *Onomasticon* as a large village in the district of Sebaste (*i. e.* Samaria), and as then called Selaba. But this identification does not answer the conditions.

Shaal'bonite (shā-ăl'bō-nīte), **The.** Eliahba the Shaalbonite was one of David's thirty-seven heroes. 2 Sam. 23:32; 1 Chron. 11:33. He was a native of a place named Shaalbon, but where it was is unknown.

Sha'aph (shā'af). 1. The son of Jahdai. 1 Chron. 2:47.
2. The son of Caleb the brother of Jerahmeel, by his concubine Maachah. 1 Chron. 2:49.

Shaara'im (shā-a-rā'ĭm) (*two gates*). 1. A city in the territory allotted to Judah, Josh. 15:36; in Authorized Version incorrectly Sharaim. 1 Sam. 17:52.
2. Shaaraim, a town of Simeon, 1 Chron. 4:31. Called SHARUHEN in Josh. 19:6, and SHILHIM in Josh. 15:32.

Shaash'gaz (shà-ăsh'gaz) (*servant of the beautiful*), the eunuch in the palace of Xerxes who had the custody of the women in the second house. Esther 2:14.

Shab'bethai (shăb'be-thā) (*sabbatical*), a Levite in the time of Ezra. Ezra 10:15. It is apparently the same who with Jeshua and others instructed the people in the knowledge of the law. Neh. 8:7.

Shachi'a (shā-ki'a), a son of Shaharaim by his wife Hodesh. 1 Chron. 8:10.

Shad'dai (shăd'dā-ī), an ancient word, probably an epithet, rendered "Almighty" everywhere in the Authorized Version, is found in connection with *êl*, "God," El Shaddai being then rendered "God Almighty." By the name or in the character of El-Shaddai, God was known to the patriarchs, Gen. 17:1; 28:3; 43:14; 48:3; 49:25, before the name Jehovah, in its full significance, was revealed. Ex. 6:3. [GOD.]

Sha'drach (shā'drak) (*decree of the moon-god*). The name given in Babylon to Hananiah, one of the three faithful Hebrews whose story is told in Dan. 1–3. After their deliverance from the furnace, we hear no more of Shadrach, Meshach and Abednego, except in Heb. 11:33, 34; but there are repeated allusions to them in the later apocryphal books, and the martyrs of the Maccabæan period seem to have been much encouraged by their example.

Sha'ge (shā'gē) (*wandering*), father of Jonathan the Hararite, one of David's guard. 1 Chron. 11:34. [See SHAMMAH, 3.]

Shahara'im (shā-hărā'im) (*double dawn*), a Benjamite. 1 Chron. 8:8.

Shahaz'imah (shà-hăz'i-mah) (probably *lofty places*), one of the towns of the allotment of Issachar. Josh. 19:22 only.

Sha'lem (shā'lem) (*safe*). Gen. 33:18. Some consider this a proper name of a place. If so it must be *Salim*, 4 miles east of Shechem (*Nablus*).

THE BLACK OBELISK OF SHALMANESER.

But probably it is a common noun meaning, as in R. V., "in peace" or "in safety."

Sha'lim (shā'lim), **The land of** (*foxes*), a district through which Saul passed on his journey in quest of his father's asses. 1 Sam. 9:4 only. It probably was in Ephraim.

Shal'isha (shăl'i-shà), **The land of,** one of the districts traversed by Saul when in search of the asses of Kish. 1 Sam. 9:4 only. It was a district near Mount Ephraim. In it perhaps was situated the place called Baal-shalisha, 2 Kings 4:42, 15 miles north of Lydda.

Shal'lecheth (shăl'lĕ-kĕth) (*casting out*), **The gate,** one of the gates of the "house of Jehovah," which Solomon was to build. 1 Chron. 26:16. It was on the west side of the outer court, apparently at the head of the causeway which led up from the ravine later called the Tyropæan Valley. But there is so much uncertainty about the topography of the Temple in the time of Solomon that nothing definite can be decided.

Shal'lum (shăl'lum) (*retribution*). 1. The fifteenth king of Israel, son of Jabesh, conspired against Zachariah, killed him, and brought the dynasty of Jehu to a close, B.C. 741. Shallum, after reigning in Samaria for a month only, was in his turn dethroned and killed by Menahem. 2 Kings 15:10–14.

2. The husband of Huldah the prophetess, 2 Kings 22:14; 2 Chron. 34:22, in the reign of Josiah. (B.C. 630.)

3. A descendant of Sheshan. 1 Chron. 2:40, 41.

4. The fourth son of Josiah king of Judah, known in the books of Kings and Chronicles as Jehoahaz. 1 Chron. 3:15; Jer. 22:11. [JEHOAHAZ, 2.]

5. Son of Shaul the son of Simeon. 1 Chron. 4:25.

6. A high priest of the sons of Zadok. 1 Chron. 6:12, 13; Ezra 7:2.

7. A son of Naphtali. 1 Chron. 7:13. Also called SHILLEM.

8. The chief of a family of porters or gate-keepers of the east gate of the temple. 1 Chron. 9:17. Perhaps the same as

9. Son of Kore, a Korahite. 1 Chron. 9:19, 31.

10. Father of Jehizkiah, an Ephraimite. 2 Chron. 28:12.

11. One of the porters of the temple

who had married a foreign wife. Ezra 10:24.

12. One of the sons of Bani. Ezra 10:42.

13. The son of Halohesh and ruler of a district of Jerusalem. Neh. 3:12.

14. The uncle of Jeremiah, Jer. 32:7.

15. Father or ancestor of Maaseiah, Jer. 35:4; perhaps the same as 9.

Shal'lun (shăl'lun) (*spoliation*), the son of Colhozeh, and ruler of a district of Mizpah. Neh. 3:15.

Shal'mai (shăl'ma-i). The children of Shalmai were among the Nethinim who returned with Zerubbabel. Ezra 2:46; Neh. 7:48.

Shal'man (shăl'man), probably a contraction for Shalmaneser IV, king of Assyria. Hos. 10:14.

Shalmane'ser (shăl-ma-nē'sĕr) (*God Shulman is chief*). 1. The Assyrian king who fought with Jehu king of Israel was Shalmaneser II. He erected the obelisk which contains the name of Jehu (see pp. 280, 608). His name is not given in the Bible.

2. The Shalmaneser IV of the monuments. He led the forces of Assyria into Palestine, where Hoshea, the last king of Israel, had revolted against his authority. 2 Kings 17:3. Hoshea submitted and consented to pay tribute; but he soon after concluded an alliance with the king of Egypt, and withheld his tribute in consequence. In B.C. 723 Shalmaneser invaded Palestine for the second time, and, as Hoshea refused to submit, laid siege to Samaria. It is probable that Sargon succeeded Shalmaneser during the siege of Samaria, for it was in his reign that the city fell.

Sha'ma (shā'mà) (*hearing*), one of David's guard. 1 Chron. 11:44.

Shamari'ah (shăm-a-rī'ah) (*kept by Jehovah*), son of Rehoboam. 2 Chron. 11:19. Properly "Shemariah."

Sha'med (*destruction*), properly Shamer or Shemer; one of the sons of Elpaal the Benjamite. 1 Chron. 8:12.

Sha'mer. 1. A Merarite Levite. 1 Chron. 6:46.

2. Shomer, an Asherite. 1 Chron. 7:34.

Sham'gar (shăm'gär), son of Anath, judge of Israel. When Israel was in a most depressed condition, Shamgar was raised up to be a deliverer. With no arms in his hand but an ox-goad, Judges 3:31; comp. 1 Sam. 13:21, he made a

39

desperate assault upon the Philistines, and slew 600 of them.

Sham'huth (*desolation*), the fifth captain for the fifth month in David's arrangement of his army. 1 Chron. 27: 8. [SHAMMAH, 4.]

Sha'mir (shā'mir) (*a point* or *thorn*). 1. A town in the mountain district of Judah. Josh. 15:48 only. It is probably identified with *Somerah* about 13 miles southwest of Hebron.

2. A place in Mount Ephraim, the residence and burial-place of Tola the judge. Judges 10:1, 2. Perhaps *Samur*, half-way between Samaria and Jenin.

3. A Kohathite, son of Micah and grandson of Uzziel. 1 Chron. 24:24.

Sham'ma (shăm'mà) (*desolation*), one of the sons of Zophah, an Asherite. 1 Chron. 7:37.

Sham'mah (shăm'mah) (*desolation*). 1. The son of Reuel the son of Esau. Gen. 36:13, 17; 1 Chron. 1:37.

2. The third son of Jesse, and brother of David. 1 Sam. 16:9; 17:13. Called also Shimea, Shimeah and Shimei.

3. One of David's famous "Three." 2 Sam. 23:11–17. The name also appears as one of the "Thirty" preceded by the name "Jonathan" in 2 Sam. 23: 32, 33. In the parallel passage, 1 Chron. 11:34, it reads "Jonathan, the son of Shage the Hararite." It is generally considered by students that Shage here is a misreading for Shammah, and that in 2 Sam. the words "son of," have dropped out, making in that case Jonathan one of the Thirty, the son of the Shammah who was one of the Three.

4. The Harodite, one of David's mighties. 2 Sam. 23:25. He is called "SHAMMOTH the Harorite" in 1 Chron. 11:27, and "SHAMHUTH the Izrahite," 27:8.

Sham'mai (shăm'ma-i) (*desolate*). 1. The son of Onam. 1 Chron. 2:28, 32.

2. Son of Rekem. 1 Chron. 2:44, 45.

3. One of the descendants of Judah. 1 Chron. 4:17.

Sham'moth. [SHAMMAH, 4.]

Shammu'a (shăm-mŭ'à) (*fame*). 1. The Reubenite spy, son of Zaccur. Num. 13:4. (B.C. 1490.)

2. Son of David, by his wife Bath-sheba. 1 Chron. 3:5; 14:4.

3. A Levite, the father of Abda. Neh. 11:17. The same as SHEMAIAH, 6.

4. The representative of the priestly family of Bilgah or Bilgai, in the days of Joiakim. Neh. 12:18. (B.C. about 500.)

Shammu'ah, son of David, 2 Sam. 5:14; elsewhere called Shammua and Shimea.

Sham'sherai (shăm'she-rā) (*sun-like*), a Benjamite. 1 Chron. 8:26.

Sha'pham (shā'fam) (*bold*), a Gadite of Bashan. 1 Chron. 5:12.

Sha'phan (shā'fan) (*coney*), the scribe or secretary of King Josiah. 2 Kings 22:3, 14; 2 Chron. 34:8, 20. (B.C. 628.) He appears on an equality with the governor of the city and the royal recorder. 2 Kings 22:14; 2 Chron. 34:8, 9.

Sha'phat (shā'fat) (*judge*). 1. The Simeonite spy, son of Hori. Num. 13:5. (B.C. 1490.)

2. The father of the prophet Elisha. 1 Kings 19:16, 19; 2 Kings 3:11; 6:31.

3. One of the six sons of Shemaiah in the royal line of Judah. 1 Chron. 3:22.

4. One of the chiefs of the Gadites in Bashan. 1 Chron. 5:12.

5. The son of Adlai, who was over David's herds in the valleys. 1 Chron. 27:29.

Sha'pher (shā'fer), (*beauty*), **Mount**, Num. 33:23, the name of a desert station where the Israelites encamped during the wanderings in the wilderness. R. V. "Shepher."

Shar'ai (shăr'a-ī) (*free*), one of the sons of Bani. Ezra 10:40. (B.C. 457.)

Shara'im (shà-rā'im). [SHAARAIM.]

Sha'rar (shā'rar) (*strong*), the father of Ahiam the Hararite. 2 Sam. 23: 33. In 1 Chron. 11:35 he is called SACAR.

Share'zer (shà-rē'zer) (*protect the prince*). A son of Sennacherib, who, in conjunction with his brother Adrammelech, murdered his father. 2 Kings 19:37.

Shar'on (shâr'on) (*a plain*). 1. A district of the Holy Land occasionally referred to in the Bible, used with the article. 1 Chron. 27:29; Isa. 33:9; 35:2; 65:10. In Acts 9:35 called SARON. It is a part of the Maritime Plain between Joppa and Mount Carmel, and is a rich, well-watered district. It is about 55 miles long, and

9 or 10 broad, somewhat undulating, with oak groves and good pasturage. 2. Used without the article, 1 Chron. 5:16. Some district on the east of the Jordan, in the neighborhood of Gilead and Bashan. The name has not been met with in that direction.

Shar'onite, The (shär'on-īte) (*belonging to Sharon*). Shitrai, who had charge of the royal herds in the plain of Sharon, I Chron. 27:29, is the only Sharonite mentioned in the Bible.

Sharu'hen (shä-rụ'hen), a town named in Josh. 19:6 only, among those which were allotted within Judah to Simeon. Possibly it was the Canaanite fortress Sharuana, mentioned in the annals of Thotmes III, of Egypt. [SHAARAIM, 2.]

Sha'shai (*pale*), one of the sons of Bani in the time of Ezra. Ezra 10:40.

Sha'shak (shä'shäk) (*longing*), a Benjamite, one of the sons of Elpaal. 1 Chron. 8:14, 25.

Sha'ul (shä'ul) (*asked*). 1. The son of Simeon by a Canaanitish woman, Gen. 46:10; Ex. 6:15; Num. 26:13; 1 Chron. 4·24, and founder of the family of the Shaulites.

2. One of the kings of Edom. 1 Chron. 1:48, 49. In the Authorized Version of Gen. 36:37 he is less accurately called SAUL.

Sha'veh (shä'veh) (*plain*), **The valley of**, described Gen. 14:17 as "the king's dale," is mentioned again in 2 Sam. 18:18 as the site of a pillar set up by Absalom.

Sha'veh Kiriatha'im (shä'veh kĭr-ĭ-a-thä'im) (*plain of Kiriathaim*), mentioned Gen. 14:5 as the residence of the Emim at the time of Chedorlaomer's incursion. If the meaning usually given is correct it must have been near Kiriathaim, or *el-Kureiyat,* between Dibon and Medeba.

Shav'sha (shäv'shà), the royal secretary in the reign of David, 1 Chron. 18:16. He was very probably the same as SERAIAH in 2 Sam. 8:17 and SHEVA in 2 Sam. 20:25, and in 1 Kings 4:3, SHISHA. The original form of the name is unknown.

She'al (shē'al) (*asking*), one of the sons of Bani who had married a foreign wife. Ezra 10:29. (B.C. 457.)

Sheal'tiel (shē-ăl'tĭ-el) (*I asked God*), father of Zerubbabel. Ezra 3:

2, 8; 5:2; Neh. 12:1; Hag. 1:1, 12, 14; 2:2, 23.

Sheari'ah (shē'a-rī'ah) (*Jehovah hath esteemed*), one of the six sons of Azel, a descendant of Saul. 1 Chron. 8:38; 9:44.

Shearing=house, The, a place on the road between Jezreel and Samaria, at which Jehu, on his way to the latter, encountered forty-two members of the royal family of Judah, whom he slaughtered. 2 Kings 10:12, 14. It is possibly *Beit Kad*, 3 miles east of *Jenin* and 16 miles northeast of Samaria.

She'ar=ja'shub (shē'är-jä'shŭb) (lit. *a remnant shall return*), the symbolical name of the son of Isaiah the prophet. Isa. 7:3.

She'ba (shē'bà) (*an oath*). 1. The son of Bichri, a Benjamite, 2 Sam. 20:1–22, the last chief of the Absalom insurrection. The occasion seized by Sheba was the emulation between the northern and southern tribes on David's return. 2 Sam. 20:1, 2. Sheba traversed the whole of Palestine, apparently rousing the population, Joab following in full pursuit to the fortress Abel Beth-maachah, where Sheba was beheaded. 2 Sam. 20:3–22.

2. A Gadite of Gilead in Bashan. 1 Chron. 5:13, 16.

She'ba (*a man*). Probably more correctly Saba. The name of a race (Sabæans), several times mentioned in the Old Testament. Three pedigrees are given. 1. Sheba son of Raamah, son of Cush; Gen. 10:7. 2. Sheba son of Joktan, Gen. 10:28. 3. Sheba son of Jokshan, son of Keturah. Gen. 25:3. These are all considered by modern scholars as referring to a single race, related in some way to the various peoples mentioned in the pedigrees. Sheba was a country and people in southwestern Arabia, well-known since the middle of the 19th century through the discovery of many inscriptions in that region. They were a great commercial people (Isa. 60:6; Ezek. 27:22; Job 6:19) of Semitic origin and language. The Queen of Sheba, who visited Solomon (1 Kings 10), no doubt was a ruler among these people. The ruins *Meriaba* are the remains of Saba, a capital city.

She'ba, one of the towns of the allotment of Simeon, Josh. 19:2, possibly the same as Shema. Josh. 15:26.

She'bah or **Shibah** (*an oath*), the famous well which gave its name to the city of Beersheba. Gen. 26:33. [BEERSHEBA.]

She'bam (shē'bam) (R. V. "Sebam"), one of the towns in the pastoral district on the east of Jordan, assigned to the tribes of Reuben and Gad. Num. 32:3. It is probably the same as SHIBMAH, Num. 32:38, and SIBMAH, Josh. 13:19; Isa. 16:8, 9; Jer. 48:32.

Shebani'ah (shĕb-a-nī'ah) (*Jehovah hath dealt tenderly*). 1. A Levite in the time of Ezra. Neh. 9:4, 5. He sealed the covenant with Nehemiah. Neh. 10:10.

2. A priest or priestly family who sealed the covenant with Nehemiah. Neh. 10:4; 12:14. Called SHECHANIAH in Neh. 12:3.

3. Another Levite who sealed the covenant with Nehemiah. Neh. 10:12.

4. One of the priests appointed by David to blow with the trumpets before the ark of God. 1 Chron. 15:24.

Sheb'arim (shĕb'a-rĭm) (*the breaches*), a place named in Josh. 7:5 only, as one of the points in the flight from Ai.

She'bat. [MONTH.]

She'ber (shē'bēr) (*breaking*), son of Caleb ben Hezron by his concubine Maachah. 1 Chron. 2:48.

Sheb'na (shĕb'nà) (*tenderness*), a person of high position in Hezekiah's court, holding at one time the office of prefect of the palace, Isa. 22:15, but subsequently the subordinate office of secretary. Isa. 36:3; 2 Kings 19:2.

Sheb'uel (shĕb'u-el), or **Shebu'el** (*captive of God*). 1. A descendant of Moses, 1 Chron. 23:16; 26:24, called also SHUBAEL. 1 Chron. 24:20.

2. One of the fourteen sons of Heman the minstrel, 1 Chron. 25:4; called also SHUBAEL. 1 Chron. 25:20.

Shechani'ah (shĕk-a-nī'ah) (*Jehovah hath dwelt*). 1. The tenth in order of the priests who were appointed by lot in the reign of David. 1 Chron. 24:11.

2. A priest in the reign of Hezekiah. 2 Chron. 31:15. (B.C. 725.)

3. A descendant of Zerubbabel. 1 Chron. 3:21, 22.

4. Some descendants of Shechaniah returned with Ezra. Ezra 8:3. Probably this was the same as 3.

5. The sons of Shechaniah were another family who returned with Ezra.

Ezra 8:5. This may be a mistake for "of the sons of Zattu, Shechaniah the son of Jahaziel."

6. The son of Jehiel of the sons of Elam. Ezra 10:2.

7. The father of Shemaiah, 2. Neh. 3:29. Possibly the same as 3.

8. The son of Arah. Neh. 6:18.

9. The head of a priestly family who returned with Zerubbabel. Neh. 12:3. Also called SHEBANIAH.

She'chem (shē'kem) (*shoulder*). 1. An important city in central Palestine, in the valley between mounts Ebal and Gerizim, 32 miles north of Jerusalem and 5½ miles southeast of Samaria. Its present name, *Nablûs*, is a corruption of Neapolis, which succeeded the more ancient Shechem, and received its new name from Vespasian. On coins still extant ⁱᵗ is called Flavia Neapolis. The situation of the town is one of surpassing beauty. It lies in a sheltered valley, protected by Gerizim on the south and Ebal on the north. The feet of these mountains, where they rise from the town, are not more than five hundred yards apart. The site of the present city, which was also nearly or quite that of the Hebrew city, occurs exactly on the water-summit; and streams issuing from the numerous springs there flow down the opposite slopes of the valley, spreading verdure and fertility in every direction. Travellers vie with each other in the language which they employ to describe the scene that here bursts so suddenly upon them on arriving in spring or early summer at this paradise of the holy land. "The whole valley," says Dr. Robinson, "was filled with gardens of vegetables and orchards of all kinds of fruits, watered by fountains which burst forth in various parts and flow westward in refreshing streams. It came upon us suddenly like a scene of fairy enchantment. We saw nothing to compare with it in all Palestine." The allusions to Shechem in the Bible are numerous, and show how important the place was in Jewish history. Abraham, on his first migration to the land of promise, pitched his tent and built an altar under the oak (or terebinth) of Moreh at Shechem. "The Canaanite was then in the land;" and it is evident that the region, if not the city, was already in possession of the aboriginal race. See Gen. 12:6. At the time of Jacob's arrival here, after his sojourn in Mesopotamia, Gen. 33:18; 34, Shechem was a Hivite city, of which Hamor, the father of Shechem, was the headman. It was at this time that the patriarch purchased from that chieftain "the parcel of the field" which he subsequently bequeathed, as a special patrimony, to his son Joseph. Gen. 33: 19; Josh. 24:32; John 4:5. The field lay undoubtedly on the rich plain of the *Mukhna,* and its value was the greater on account of the well which Jacob had dug there, so as not to be dependent on his neighbors for a supply of water. In the distribution of the land after its conquest by the Hebrews, Shechem fell to the lot of Ephraim, Josh. 20:7, but was assigned to the Levites, and became a city of refuge. Josh. 21:20, 21. It acquired new importance as the scene of the renewed promulgation of the law, when its blessings were heard from Gerizim and its curses from Ebal, and the people bowed their heads and acknowledged Jehovah as their king and ruler. Deut. 27:11; Josh. 8:30–35. It was here Joshua assembled the people, shortly before his death, and delivered to them his last counsels. Josh. 24:1, 25. After the death of Gideon, Abimelech, his bastard son, induced the Shechemites to revolt from the Hebrew commonwealth and elect him as king. Judges 9. In revenge for his expulsion, after a reign of three years, Abimelech destroyed the city, and as an emblem of the fate to which he would consign it, sowed the ground with salt. Judges 9:34–45. It was soon restored, however, for we are told in 1 Kings 12 that all Israel assembled at Shechem, and Rehoboam, Solomon's successor, went thither to be inaugurated as king. Here, at this same place, the ten tribes renounced the house of David, and transferred their allegiance to Jeroboam, 1 Kings 12:16, under whom Shechem became for a time the capital of his kingdom. From the time of the origin of the Samaritans, the history of Shechem blends itself with that of this people and of their sacred mount, Gerizim. [SAMARIA.] Shechem has been thought to be the SYCHAR of John 4:5, near which the Saviour conversed with the Samaritan woman at Jacob's well, but modern scholars think them different places. The population of *Nablûs* is about 27,000, among whom are the remnant, fewer than 200, of the Samaritans, and a few Jews and Christians. The enmity between the Samaritans and Jews is as inveterate still as it was in the days of Christ. The Mohammedans, of course, make up the bulk of the population. The well of Jacob and the tomb of Joseph are still shown in the neighborhood of the town. The well of Jacob lies about a mile and a half east of the city, close to the lower road, and just beyond the hamlet of *Balâta.* The Christians sometimes call it *Bir es-Samariyeh*—"the well of the Samaritan woman." [JACOB'S WELL.] The tomb of Joseph lies about a quarter of a mile north of Jacob's well, exactly in the centre of the opening of the valley between Gerizim and Ebal. It resembles an ordinary grave of an eminent Moslem. There are in fact two small chapels shown as the original tomb of Joseph. There are Hebrew, Samaritan and Arabic inscriptions on the wall, but they are apparently modern, and have no importance. The tomb is in a very dilapidated condition.

2. The son of Hamor, the chieftain of the Hivite settlement of Shechem at the time of Jacob's arrival. Gen. 33:19; 34:2–26; Josh. 24:32; Judges 9:28.

3. A man of Manasseh, of the clan of Gilead. Num. 26:31.

4. A Gileadite, son of Shemida. 1 Chron. 7:19.

She'chemites (shē'kem-ītes), **The,** the family of Shechem son of Gilead. Num. 26:31; comp. Josh. 17:2.

Shechi'nah (shĕ-kī'nah) (*that which dwells*). This term is not found in the Bible. It was used by the later Jews, and borrowed by Christians from them, to express the visible majesty of the divine Presence, especially when resting or dwelling between the cherubim on the mercy-seat in the tabernacle and in the temple of Solomon, but not in the second temple. The use of the term is first found in the Targums, where it forms a frequent periphrasis for God, considered as *dwelling* among the children of Israel. The idea which the different accounts in Scripture convey is that of a most brilliant and glorious light, enveloped in a cloud, and usually concealed by the cloud, so that the cloud itself was for the most part alone visible; but on particular occasions the glory appeared. The allusions in the New Testament to the shechinah are not unfrequent: Luke 2: 9; John 1:14; Rom. 9:4; and we are distinctly taught to connect it with the incarnation and future coming of the Messiah as type with antitype.

Shed'eur (shĕd'ē-ûr), the father of Elizur, chief of the tribe of Reuben at the time of the exodus. Num. 1:5; 2:10; 7:30, 35; 10:18.

Sheep. Sheep were an important part of the possessions of the ancient

BROAD-TAILED SHEEP.

Hebrews and of eastern nations generally. The first mention of sheep occurs in Gen. 4:2. They were used in the sacrificial offerings, both the adult animal, Ex. 20:24, and the lamb. See

EASTERN SHEEPFOLD.

Ex. 29:38; Lev. 9:3; 12:6. Sheep and lambs formed an important article of food. 1 Sam. 25:18. The wool was used as clothing. Lev. 13:47. "Rams' skins dyed red" were used as a covering for the tabernacle. Ex. 25:5. Sheep and lambs were sometimes paid as tribute. 2 Kings 3:4. It is very striking to notice the immense numbers of sheep that were reared in Palestine in biblical times. The king of Moab paid an annual tribute of 100,000 lambs and 100,000 rams to the king of Israel, 2 Kings 3:4. Solomon sacrificed 120,-000 sheep at the dedication of the temple. 1 Kings 8:63. His household consumed 100 sheep a day. 1 Kings 4: 23. Sheep-shearing is alluded to in Gen. 31:19. Sheep-dogs were employed in biblical times. Job 30:1. Shepherds in Palestine and the East generally go before their flocks, which they induce to follow by calling to them, comp. John 10:4; Ps. 77:20; 80:1. The following quotation from Hartley's "Researches in Greece and the Levant," p. 321, is strikingly illustrative of the allusions in John 10:1-16: "Having had my attention directed last night to the words in John 10:3, I asked my man if it was usual in Greece to give names to the sheep. He informed me that it was, and that the sheep obeyed the shepherd when he called them by their names. This morning I had an opportunity of verifying the truth of this remark. Passing by a flock of sheep, I asked the shepherd the same question which I had put to the servant, and he gave me the same answer. I then bade him call one of his sheep. He did so, and it instantly left its pasturage and its companions a n d ran up to the hands of the shepherd with signs of pleasure a n d with a prompt obedience which I had never before observed in any other animal. It is also true i n this country that 'a stranger will they not follow, but will flee from him.' The shepherd told me that many of his sheep were still wild, that they had not yet learned their names, but that by teaching them they would all learn them." The common sheep of Syria and Palestine are the broad-tailed. As the sheep is an emblem of meekness, patience and submission, it is expressly mentioned as typifying these qualities in the person of our blessed Lord. Isa. 53:7; Acts 8:32, etc. The relation that exists between Christ, "the chief Shepherd," and his members is beautifully compared to that which in the East is so strikingly exhibited by the shepherds to their flocks. [SHEP-HERD.]

Sheep-gate, The, one of the gates of Jerusalem as rebuilt by Nehemiah. Neh. 3:1, 32; 12:39. It stood between the tower of Meah and the chamber of the corner, ch. 3:1, 32, or gate of the guard-house, ch. 12:39, Authorized Version, "prison-gate;" and was apparently near the northeast angle of the city wall.

Sheep=market, The. John 5:2. The word "market" is an interpolation of our translators. We ought probably to supply the word "gate."

Shehari'ah (shē-hȧ-rī'ah) (*dawning of Jehovah*), a Benjamite, son of Jehoram. 1 Chron. 8:26.

Shekel. [MONEY AND WEIGHTS.]

She'lah (shē'lah) (*a petition*). 1. The third son of Judah. Gen. 38:5, 11, 14, 26; 46:12; Num. 26:20; 1 Chron. 2:3; 4:21.

2. The proper form of the name of Salah. 1 Chron. 1:18, 24.

She'lanites (shē'lan-ites), **The,** the descendants of Shelah, 1. Num. 26:20.

Shelemi'ah (shel-e-mī'ah) (*Jehovah repays*). 1. One of the sons of Bani in the time of Ezra. Ezra 10:39. (B.C. 458.)

2. The father of Hananiah. Neh. 3:30.

3. A priest in the time of Nehemiah. Neh. 13:13.

4. The father of Jehucal, or Jucal, in the time of Zedekiah. Jer. 37:3.

5. The father of Irijah, the captain of the ward who arrested Jeremiah. Jer. 37:13.

6. The same as Meshelemiah and Shallum. 1 Chron. 26:14.

7. Another of the sons of Bani in the time of Ezra. Ezra 10:41.

8. Ancestor of Jehudi in the time of Jehoiakim. Jer. 36:14.

9. Son of Abdeel; one of those who received the orders of Jehoiakim to take Baruch and Jeremiah. Jer. 36:26. (B.C. 604.)

She'leph (shē'lef) (*extraction*), a son of Joktan, and the people descended

from him. The name is quite common in Yemen. Gen. 10:26; 1 Chron. 1:20.

She'lesh (shē'lesh) (*triad*), an Asherite, son of Helem. 1 Chron. 7:35.

Shel'omi (shĕl'o-mī) (*peaceful*), an Asherite, father of Ahihud. Num. 34:27. (B.C. before 1450.)

Shel'omith (shĕl'o-mĭth) (*peaceful*). 1. The daughter of Dibri, of the tribe of Dan, and mother of the Israelite who was put to death in the wilderness for blasphemy. Lev. 24:11.

2. The daughter of Zerubbabel. 1 Chron. 3:19.

3. Chief of the Izharites. 1 Chron. 23:18.

4. A descendant of Eliezer the son of Moses, in the reign of David. 1 Chron 26:25, 26, 28. R. V. "Shelomoth."

5. A Gershonite. 1 Chron. 23:9. R. V. "Shelomoth."

6. One whose sons returned from Babylon with Ezra. Ezra 8:10.

Shel'omoth (shĕl'o-moth), the same as Shelomith, 3. 1 Chron. 24:22.

Shelu'miel (shĕ-lū'mĭ-el) (*a friend is God*), the son of Zurishaddai, and prince of the tribe of Simeon at the time of the exodus. Num. 1:6; 2:12; 7:36, 41; 10:19. (B.C. 1491.)

Shem (*name*), probably the eldest son of Noah. Gen. 5:32. Apparently about 100 years old, married, and childless, at the time of the flood. After it, he, with his father, brothers, sisters-in-law and wife, received the blessing of God, Gen. 9:1, and entered into the covenant. He acted with filial respect to his father when the latter committed his great sin, and received the first blessing. Gen. 9:25-27. The portion of the earth occupied by the descendants of Shem, Gen. 10:21, 31, consists of a part of Asia Minor, Assyria, Arabia, etc. Modern scholars have given the name of Shemitic or Semitic to the languages spoken by his real or supposed descendants. [HEBREW.]

She'ma (shē'mà). 1. A Reubenite, ancestor of Bela. 1 Chron. 5:8. Same as SHEMAIAH, 4.

2. Son of Elpaal. 1 Chron. 8:13. Probably the same as SHIMHI. (B.C. after 1450.)

3. One of those who stood at Ezra's right hand when he read the law to the people. Neh. 8:4. (B.C. 458.)

4. A town in the south of Judah, perhaps SHEBA. Josh. 15 : 26.

Shem'aah (shĕm'ă-ah) (*the rumor*), a Benjamite of Gibeah, and father of Ahiezer and Joash. 1 Chron. 12 : 3.

Shemai'ah (shĕm-a-ī'ah) (*Jehovah has heard*). 1. A prophet in the reign of Rehoboam, who forbade him to make war against the revolted tribes, 1 Kings 12 : 22; 2 Chron. 11 : 2. (B.C. 934.) He wrote a chronicle containing the events of Rehoboam's reign. 2 Chron. 12 : 5, 15.

2. The son of Shechaniah, among the descendants of Zerubbabel. 1 Chron. 3 : 22; and perhaps Neh. 3 : 29.

3. A prince of the tribe of Simeon. 1 Chron. 4 : 37.

4. Son of Joel, a Reubenite. 1 Chron. 5 : 4. (Called SHEMA in verse 8.)

5. Son of Hasshub, a Merarite Levite. 1 Chron. 9 : 14; Neh. 11 : 15.

6. Father of Obadiah or Abda, a Levite. 1 Chron. 9 : 16. Called SHAMMUA in Neh. 11 : 17.

7. Son of Elizaphan, and chief of his house in the reign of David. 1 Chron. 15 : 8, 11. (B.C. 1042.) Possibly same as

8. A Levite, son of Nethaneel, and also a scribe in the time of David. 1 Chron. 24 : 6.

9. The eldest son of Obed-edom the Gittite. 1 Chron. 26 : 4, 6, 7.

10. A descendant of Jeduthun the singer, who lived in the reign of Hezekiah. 2 Chron. 29 : 14. Possibly the same as 6 or 23.

11. One of the sons of Adonikam who returned with Ezra. Ezra 8 : 13.

12. One of Ezra's messengers. Ezra 8 : 16.

13. A priest of the family of Harim, who put away his foreign wife at Ezra's bidding. Ezra 10 : 21. (B.C. 458.)

14. A layman of Israel, son of another Harim, who had also married a foreigner. Ezra 10 : 31. (B.C. 458.)

15. Son of Delaiah the son of Mehetabeel, a prophet in the time of Nehemiah. Neh. 6 : 10. (B.C. 446.)

16. The head of a priestly house who signed the covenant with Nehemiah. Neh. 10 : 8; 12 : 6, 18. (Perhaps two men.)

17. One of the princes of Judah at the time of the dedication of the wall of Jerusalem. Neh. 12 : 34.

18. A Levite of the lineage of Asaph. Neh. 12 : 35

19. One of the choir on the same occasion. Neh. 12 : 36. Perhaps the same as

20. A priest. Neh. 12 : 42.

21. A false prophet at Babylon in the time of Jeremiah, who prophesied a speedy return from captivity. Jer. 29 : 24–32.

22. A Levite in the reign of Jehoshaphat, among those commissioned to teach the law. 2 Chron. 17 : 8. (B.C. 867.)

23. A Levite in the reign of Hezekiah, 2 Chron. 31 : 15. (B.C. 726.) Possibly the same as 10.

24. A Levite in the reign of Josiah. 2 Chron. 35 : 9. (B.C. 628.)

25. The father of Urijah of Kirjath-jearim. Jer. 26 : 20.

26. The father of Delaiah. Jer. 36 : 12.

Shemari'ah (shĕm-a-rī'ah) (*Jehovah has kept*). 1. A Benjamite warrior who came to David at Ziklag. 1 Chron. 12 : 5. (B.C. 1057.)

2. One of the family of Harim, a layman of Israel who put away his foreign wife in the time of Ezra. Ezra 10 : 32. (B.C. 458.)

3. A son of Bani who did the same. Ezra 10 : 41.

Sheme'ber (shĕm-ē'ber), king of Zeboim, and ally of the king of Sodom when he was attacked by Chedorlaomer. Gen. 14 : 2. (B.C. 1913.)

She'mer (shē'mer) (*lees of wine*), the owner of the hill on which the city of Samaria was built. 1 Kings 16 : 24. (B.C. 881.) [SAMARIA.]

Shemi'da (shĕ-mī'dà) (*fame of wisdom*), a son of Gilead. Num. 26 : 32; Josh. 17 : 2.

Shemi'dah. Shemida the son of Gilead. 1 Chron. 7 : 19.

Shemida'ites (shĕ-mĭd-ā'ītes), The, the descendants of Shemida the son of Gilead. Num. 26 : 32.

Shem'inith (shem'ĭ-nĭth) (*eighth*), a musical term found in the titles of Ps. 6, and Ps. 12. Comp. 1 Chron. 15 : 21. It is variously explained as denoting the number of strings on the instrument used, the name of the key or pitch, or, in contrast with *alamoth*, soprano, "an octave below" or in the bass.

Shemir'amoth (shĕ-mĭr'a-mŏth) (*lofty name*). 1. A Levite in the choir of David. 1 Chron. 15 : 18, 20; 16 : 5.

2. A Levite in the reign of Jehoshaphat. 2 Chron. 17:8. (B.C. 867.)

Shemit'ic Languages (shē-mĭt'ic), the family of languages spoken by the descendants of Shem, chiefly the Hebrew, Chaldaic, Assyrian, Arabic, Phœnician and Aramaic or Syriac. The Jews in their earlier history spoke the Hebrew, but in Christ's time they spoke the Aramaic, sometimes called the Syro-chaldaic. They are perhaps more often called *Semitic* from the Greek form *Sem.*

Shemu'el (shē-mū'el) (*name of God*). 1. A commissioner appointed from the tribe of Simeon to aid in the division of the land of Canaan. Num. 34:20. (B.C. 1450.)

2. Samuel the prophet. 1 Chron. 6:33. R. V. "Samuel."

3. Son of Tola, and one of the chiefs of the tribe of Issachar. 1 Chron. 7:2.

Shen (shĕn) (*tooth*), a place mentioned only in 1 Sam. 7:12. Nothing is known of it.

Shena'zar (shĕn-ā'zar) (*splendid leader*), son of Jeconiah. 1 Chron. 3:18.

She'nir (shē'nir). [SENIR.]

Sheol. [See HELL.]

She'pham (shē'fam), a place on the eastern boundary of the promised land. Num. 34:10, 11.

Shephathi'ah. A Benjamite, father of Meshullam, 6. 1 Chron. 9:8. An incorrect form of SHEPHATIAH.

Shephati'ah (shĕf-a-tī'ah) (*Jehovah has judged*). 1. The fifth son of David. 2 Sam. 3:4; 1 Chron. 3:3.

2. The family of Shephatiah, 372 in number, returned with Zerubbabel. Ezra 2:4; Neh. 7:9; see also Ezra 8:8.

3. The family of another Shephatiah, who came up with Zerubbabel. They were classified with Solomon's servants. Ezra 2:57; Neh. 7:59.

4. A descendant of Judah, family of Perez. Neh. 11:4.

5. One of the princes of Judah who counselled Zedekiah to put Jeremiah to death on the ground that he was frightening the people by his prophecies. Jer. 38:1. (B.C. 589.)

6. One of the Benjamite warriors who joined David in his retreat at Ziklag. 1 Chron. 12:5. (B.C. 1057.)

7. Chief of the Simeonites in the reign of David. 1 Chron. 27:16.

8. Son of Jehoshaphat. 2 Chron. 21:2. (B.C. 845.)

Sheph'elah. A word variously rendered in the A. V. by "vale," "valley," "low country," "plain," etc., in R. V. uniformly "lowland," Jer. 17:26; 1 Chron. 27:28; Deut. 1:7; 2 Chron. 1:15; Jer. 32:44, etc. The term Shephelah, the translation of the Hebrew, is often used by modern scholars and commentators. It always refers to the region of low hills between the Philistine plain and the high central range of Palestine, in the southern part of Judah.

Shepherd. In a nomadic state of society every man, from the sheikh down to the slave, is more or less a shepherd. The progenitors of the Jews in the patriarchal age were nomads, and their history is rich in scenes of pastoral life. The occupation of tending the flocks was undertaken, not only by the sons of wealthy chiefs, Gen. 30:29 ff.; 37:12 ff., but even by their daughters. Gen. 29:6 ff.; Ex. 2:19. Later in the history, after the nation had settled in Palestine, and become less of a nomadic race, many of the wealthy owners employed shepherds at regular wages, or several less wealthy joined their flocks under the care of a single shepherd. The office of the eastern shepherd, as described in the Bible, was attended with much hardship, and even danger. He was exposed to the extremes of heat and cold, Gen. 31:40; his food was scanty, and such as he could find in a natural state; he had to encounter the attacks of wild beasts, occasionally of the larger species, such as lions, wolves, panthers and bears, 1 Sam. 17:34; Isa. 31:4; Jer. 5:6; Amos 3:12; nor was he free from the risk of robbers or predatory hordes. Gen. 31:39. He was responsible to the owner for the loss of any of the sheep (Gen. 31:39), unless he could prove that the loss was not due to his neglect (Ex. 22:10–13). The shepherd's equipment consisted of the following articles: a mantle, made probably of sheepskin with the fleece on, which he turned inside out in cold weather, as implied in the comparison in Jer. 43:12 (cf. Juv. xiv. 187); a scrip or wallet, containing a small amount of food, 1 Sam. 17:40; a sling, which is still the favorite weapon of the Bedouin shepherd, 1 Sam. 17:40; and lastly, a staff, which served the double purpose of a weapon against foes and a crook for the management of the flock. 1 Sam. 17:40; Ps. 23:4; Zech. 11:7. If the shepherd was at a distance from his home, he was provided with a light tent, Cant. 1:8; Jer. 35:7, the removal of which was easily effected. Isa. 38:12. There were in such places as were more commonly used as pastures, stone enclosures, or folds for the protection of the flocks by night. These often had the extra protection of a tower (Gen. 35:21; 2 Chron. 26:10; Micah 4:8). In other places the shepherd himself made a temporary fold with thorn branches, etc. The routine of the shepherd's duties appears to have been as follows: In the morning he led forth his flock from the fold, John 10:4, which he did by going before them and calling to them, as is still usual in the East; arrived at the pasturage, he watched the flock with the assistance of dogs, Job 30:1, and should any sheep stray, he had to search for it until he found it, Ezek. 34:12; Luke 15:4; he supplied them with water, either at a running stream or at troughs attached to wells, Gen. 29:7; 30:38; Ex. 2:16; Ps. 23:2; at evening he brought them back to the fold, and reckoned them to see that none were missing, by passing them "under the rod" as they entered the door of the enclosure, Lev. 27:32; Ezek. 20:37, checking each sheep, as it passed, by a motion of the hand, Jer. 33:13; and, finally, he watched the entrance of the fold throughout the night, acting as porter. John 10:3. The shepherd's office thus required great watchfulness, particularly by night, Luke 2:8; cf. Nah. 3:18. It also required tenderness toward the young and feeble, Isa. 40:11, particularly in driving them to and from the pasturage. Gen. 33:13. In large establishments there are various grades of shepherds, the highest being styled "rulers," Gen. 47:6, or "chief shepherds," 1 Pet. 5:4; in a royal household the title of *abbir*, "mighty," was bestowed on the person who held the post. 1 Sam. 21:7. [SHEEP.]

She'phi (shē'fī) (*smoothness*), son of Shobal, of the sons of Seir. 1 Chron. 1:40. Called also SHEPHO. Gen. 36:23.

She=pho (shē'fō). Gen. 36:23. [SHEPHI.]

Shephu'phan (shĕ-fū'făn) (*an adder*), a son or descendant of Bela the first-born of Benjamin. 1 Chron. 8:5. His name is also written SHEPHUPHAM (Authorized Version "Shupham"), Num. 26:39; SHUPPIM, 1 Chron. 7:12, 15; and MUPPIM. Gen. 46:21.

She'rah (shē'rah) (*kinswoman*), "daughter" of Ephraim, 1 Chron. 7:24, and foundress of the Beth-horons and of a town called Uzzen-sherah.

Sherebi'ah (shĕr-e-bi'ah), a Levite in the time of Ezra. Ezra 8:18, 24. (B.C. 458.) When Ezra read the law to the people, Sherebiah was among the Levites who assisted him. Neh. 8:7. He signed the covenant with Nehemiah. Neh. 10:12. Some say these were three different men.

She'resh (shē'rĕsh) (*root*), son of Machir the son of Manasseh by his wife Maachah. 1 Chron. 7:16.

Shere'zer (shĕ-rē'zer) (*protect the prince*), one of the people's messengers mentioned in Zech. 7:2.

She'shach (shē'shăk), is a term which occurs only in Jer. 25:26; 51:41, where it is evidently used as a synonym for Babylon. It was probably either an ancient cipher for Babylon, or a section of the city.

She'shai (shē'shā) (*whitish*), one of the three sons of Anak who dwelt in Hebron. Num. 13:22.

She'shan (shē'shăn), a descendant of Jerahmeel the son of Hezron. 1 Chron. 2:31, 34, 35.

Sheshbaz'zar (shesh-băz'zar). Most probably the Chaldæan or Persian name given to Zerubbabel in Ezra 1:8, 11; 5:14, 16, although some students distinguish between Zerubbabel the actual and Sheshbazzar the official founders of the temple, claiming that Zerubbabel succeeded Sheshbazzar. [ZERUBBABEL.]

Sheth (shĕth) (*compensation*). 1. The patriarch Seth. 1 Chron. 1:1.

2. In the Authorized Version of Num. 24:17, there is reason to regard it as an appellative, rather than as a proper name. Read instead of "the sons of Sheth," "the sons of tumult." Comp. Jer. 48:45.

She'thar (shē'thär), one of the seven princes of Persia and Media. Esther 1:14. (B.C. 483.)

She'thar=boz'nai (shē'thär-bŏz'na-ī), a Persian officer of rank in the reign of Darius Hystaspes. Ezra 5:3, 6; 6:6, 13.

She'va (shē'và) (*vanity*). 1. The scribe or royal secretary of David. 2 Sam. 20:25. He is called elsewhere SERAIAH, 2 Sam. 8:17; SHISHA, 1 Kings 4:3; and SHAVSHA. 1 Chron. 18:16.

2. Son of Caleb ben-Hezron by his concubine Maachah. 1 Chron. 2:49.

Shew=bread, Ex. 25:30; 35:13; 39:36, etc., literally "bread of the face" or "presence." Shew-bread was unleavened bread placed upon a table which stood in the sanctuary together with the seven-branched candlestick and the altar of incense. See Ex. 25:23–30 for description of this table. Every Sabbath twelve newly-baked loaves, representing the twelve tribes of Israel, were put on it in two piles, six in each, surmounted by a censer of incense, where they remained till the following Sabbath. Then they were replaced by twelve new ones, and were eaten by the priests in the holy place, out of which they might not be removed. It probably was for a standing expression of the people's gratitude for the bounties of Jehovah's providence, and the constant expression of man's dependence upon God. The old idea that "bread of the face" indicated that by eating of the bread, sight of God was obtained, is not upheld by either the true meaning of the word, or the history of the rite.

Shibboleth (shĭb'bo-lĕth), Judges 12:6. One difference between the local dialects of the Israelites east and west of the Jordan was in the pronunciation of the initial *sh*. The Ephraimites pronounced it as *s*. For this reason the Gileadites under Jephthah used it after a victory over the Ephraimites, to test those who wished to cross over the river. The pronunciation betrayed whether they were friends or enemies. In this way there fell 42,000 Ephraimites. There is no mystery in this particular word. Any word beginning with the sound *sh* would have answered equally well as a test. The word has come into use in the English language

with the meaning of test word, or pet phrase of a party or sect.

Shib'mah (shĭb'mah) (properly SIBMAH). [SHEBAM.]

Shi'cron (shī'krŏn) (*drunkenness*), one of the landmarks on the north boundary of Judah. Josh. 15:11 only. It lay between Ekron and Jabneel. Its site is unknown.

Shield. The ordinary shield consisted of a framework of wood covered with leather; it thus admitted of being burnt. Ezek. 39:9. It was frequently cased with metal, either brass or copper; its appearance in this case resembled gold when the sun shone on it. From this or because it was sometimes dyed, it had in battles often a red appearance. Nah. 2:3. It was anointed with oil before battle to make its surface slippery. Isa. 21:5. The shield was worn on the left arm, to which it was attached by a strap. Shields of state were covered with beaten gold. Shields were suspended about public buildings for ornamental purposes. 1 Kings 10:17. In the metaphorical language of the Bible the shield generally represents the protection of God: *e. g.* Ps. 3:3; 28:7; but in Ps. 47:9 it is applied to earthly rulers, and in Eph. 6:16 to faith. [ARMS.]

Shigga'ion (shĭg-gā'yon), Ps. 7, title, a musical term, the signification of which cannot be certainly known; perhaps a "wild, mournful ode."

Shi'hon (shī'hŏn) (*ruin*), a town of Issachar, named only in Josh. 19:19. Eusebius mentions it as then existing "near Mount Tabor," and its identification with *Ayun esh-Shain* is generally accepted.

Shi'hor (shī'hôr) **of Egypt.** [SIHOR.]

Shi'hor=lib'nath (shī'hôr-lĭb'nath) (*turbid* (stream) *of Libnath*), named only in Josh. 19:26 as one of the landmarks of the boundary of Asher. It is probably the *Nah es Zerka* near Carmel. According to Pliny it was the southern boundary of Phœnicia.

Shil'hi (shĭl'hī) (*armed*), the father of Azubah the mother of Jehoshaphat, 1 Kings 22:42; 2 Chron. 20:31.

Shil'him (shĭl'him) (*missiles*), one of the cities in the southern portion of the tribe of Judah. Josh. 15:32. [SHAARAIM, 2; SHARUHEN.]

Shil'lem (shĭl'lem) (*requital*), son

of Naphtali and an ancestor of the family of the Shillemites. Gen. 46:24; Num. 26:49. [SHALLUM, 7.]

Shil'lemites, The. [SHILLEM.]

Shilo'ah (shi-lō'ah), **The waters of,** a certain soft-flowing stream, Isa. 8:6, better known under the later name of Siloam—the only perennial spring of Jerusalem.

Shi'loh (shī'lō). In the Authorized Version of the Bible Shiloh is once used in a very difficult passage, in Gen. 49:10, "The sceptre shall not depart from Judah, nor a lawgiver from between his feet, until Shiloh come; and unto him shall the gathering of the people be." There are several explanations of the passage, none of which a r e really satisfactory. It has long been supposed to refer directly t o the Messiah, but there are several strong objections, one of the strongest being the absence o f a n y New Testament reference to the word. A n o t h e r possible rendering (R. V. marg.) is "Till he come to Shiloh." I n this case the allusion would be to the primacy of Judah in war, Judges 1:1, 2; 20:18; Num. 2:3; 10:14, which was t o continue until the promised land was conquered and the ark o f the covenant was solemnly deposited at Shiloh. B u t there are objections to this as well, one being that Judah never had a real connection with the town of Shiloh. A third rendering, that of the Septuagint is "Until that which is his shall come." This less definite reference to the Messianic hope may be the correct form. Still another rendering in ancient versions is "Till he come whose it is," a reading adopted by many of the Christian Fathers.

Shi'loh (*place of rest*), a city of Ephraim. In Judges 21:19 it is said that Shiloh is "on the north side of Bethel, on the east side of the highway that goeth up from Bethel to Shechem, and on the south of Lebonah." In agreement with this the traveler of our own day, going north from Jerusalem, passes *Beitin* the ancient Bethel, and

about 8 miles north of that place, turns aside to the right for about a mile, in order to visit *Seilûn*, the Arabic for Shiloh; and then passing through the narrow wady which brings him to the main road, leaves *el-Lebbân*, the Lebonah of Scripture, on the left, as he pursues "the highway" to *Nablûs*, the ancient Shechem. [SHECHEM.] Shiloh was one of the earliest and most sacred of the Hebrew sanctuaries. The ark of the covenant, which had been kept at Gilgal during the progress of the conquest, Josh. 18:1, *seq.*, was removed thence on the subjugation of the country, and kept at Shiloh from the last days of Joshua to the time of Samuel. Josh. 18:10; Judges 18:31; 1 Sam. 4:

THE SITE OF SHILOH.

3. It was here the Hebrew conqueror divided among the tribes the portion of the west Jordan region which had not been already allotted. Josh. 18:10; 19:51. In this distribution, or an earlier one, Shiloh fell within the limits of Ephraim. Josh. 16:1-10. The ungodly conduct of the sons of Eli occasioned the loss of the ark of the covenant, which had been carried into battle against the Philistines, and Shiloh from that time sank into insignificance. It stands forth in the Jewish history as a striking example of the divine indignation. Jer. 7:12.

Shilo'ni (shi-lō'nī). This word occurs in the Authorized Version only in Neh. 11:5, where it should be rendered—as it is in other cases—"the

Shilonite," that is, the descendant of Shelah the youngest son of Judah, as in 1 Chron. 9 : 5.

Shi'lonite, The, that is, the native or resident of Shiloh; a title ascribed only to Ahijah. 1 Kings 11 : 29; 12 : 15; 15 : 29; 2 Chron. 9 : 29; 10 : 15.

Shi'lonites, The, are mentioned among the descendants of Judah dwelling in Jerusalem at a date difficult to fix. 1 Chron. 9 : 5. They are doubtless the members of the house of Shelah, who in the Pentateuch are more accurately designated Shelanites.

Shil'shah (shĭl'shah) (*triad*), son of Zophah of the tribe of Asher. 1 Chron. 7 : 37.

Shim'ea (shĭm'e-à) (*fame*). 1. Son of David by Bath-sheba. 1 Chron. 3 : 5. (Same as SHAMMUA, 2.)

2. A Merarite Levite. 1 Chron. 6 : 30.

3. A Gershonite Levite, ancestor of Asaph the minstrel. 1 Chron. 6 : 39.

4. The brother of David, 1 Chron. 20 : 7, elsewhere called Shammah, Shimma and Shimeah.

Shim'eah. 1. Brother of David, and father of Jonathan. 2 Sam. 21 : 21; called also Shammah, Shimea, and Shimma.

2. A descendant of Jehiel, the father or founder of Gibeon. 1 Chron. 8 : 32.

Shim'eam (shĭm'e-am) (*fame*), a descendant of Jehiel, the founder or prince of Gibeon. 1 Chron. 9 : 38. Called SHIMEAH in 1 Chron. 8 : 32.

Shim'eath (shĭm'e-äth) (feminine of Shimeah), an Ammonitess, mother of Jozachar or Zabad, one of the murderers of King Joash. 2 Kings 12 : 21; 2 Chron. 24 : 26. (B.C. 796.)

Shim'ei (shĭm'e-ī) (*renowned*). 1. Son of Gershon the son of Levi, Num. 3 : 18; 1 Chron. 6 : 17; 23 : 7, 10; Zech. 12 : 13; called SHIMI in Ex. 6 : 17.

2. Shimei the son of Gera, a Benjamite of the house of Saul, who lived at Bahurim. (B.C. 1023.) When David and his suite were seen descending the long defile, on his flight from Absalom, 2 Sam. 16 : 5–13, the whole feeling of the clan of Benjamin burst forth without restraint in the person of Shimei. He ran along the ridge, cursing and throwing stones at the king and his companions. The next meeting was very different. The king was now returning from his successful campaign.

Just as he was crossing the Jordan, 2 Sam. 19 : 18, the first person to welcome him was Shimei, who threw himself at David's feet in abject penitence. But the king's suspicions were not set at rest by this submission; and on his death-bed he recalls the whole scene to the recollection of his son Solomon. Solomon gave Shimei notice that from henceforth he must consider himself confined to the walls of Jerusalem, on pain of death. 1 Kings 2 : 36, 37. For three years the engagement was kept. At the end of that time, for the purpose of capturing two slaves who had escaped to Gath, he went out on his ass, and made his journey successfully. 1 Kings 2 : 40. On his return the king took him at his word, and he was slain by Benaiah. 1 Kings 2 : 41–46.

3. One of the adherents of Solomon at the time of Adonijah's usurpation. 1 Kings 1 : 8. Perhaps same as

4. Solomon's commissariat officer in Benjamin. 1 Kings 4 : 18.

5. Son of Pedaiah, and brother of Zerubbabel. 1 Chron. 3 : 19. (B.C. 536.)

6. A Simeonite, who had sixteen sons and six daughters. 1 Chron. 4 : 26, 27.

7. A Reubenite descendant of Joel. 1 Chron. 5 : 4.

8. A Merarite Levite. 1 Chron. 6 : 29.

9. A Gershonite Levite, son of Jahath. 1 Chron. 6 : 42.

10. Son of Jeduthun, and chief of the tenth division of the singers. 1 Chron. 25 : 17.

11. The Ramathite who was over David's vineyards. 1 Chron. 27 : 27.

12. A Levite of the sons of Heman, who took part in the purification of the temple under Hezekiah. 2 Chron. 29 : 14. (B.C. 726.)

13. The brother of Cononiah the Levite, in the reign of Hezekiah. 2 Chron. 31 : 12, 13. Perhaps the same as the preceding.

14. A Levite in the time of Ezra who had married a foreign wife. Ezra 10 : 23.

15. One of the family of Hashum, who put away his foreign wife at Ezra's command. Ezra 10 : 33.

16. A son of Bani, who had also married a foreign wife, and put her away. Ezra 10 : 38. (B.C. 458.)

17. Son of Kish, a Benjamite, and ancestor of Mordecai. Esther 2 : 5.

Shim'eon (shĭm'e-on) (*hearing* (*prayer*)), a layman of Israel, of the family of Harim, who had married a foreign wife, and divorced her in the time of Ezra. Ezra 10:31. (B.C. 458.)

Shim'hi (shĭm'hī) (*renowned*), a Benjamite, apparently the same as Shema the son of Elpaal. 1 Chron. 8:21. R. V. "Shimei."

Shim'i (shĭm'ī)= SHIMEI, 1. Ex. 6:17.

Shim'ites, The, the descendants of Shimei the son of Gershon. Num. 3:21.

Shim'ma, the third son of Jesse, and brother of David. 1 Chron. 2:13. Same as SHIMEAH 1.

Shi'mon (shĭ'mon). The four son of Shimon are enumerated in an obscure genealogy of the tribe of Judah. 1 Chron. 4:20.

Shim'rath (shĭm'rath), a Benjamite, of the sons of Shimhi, 1 Chron. 8:21.

Shim'ri (shĭm'rī) (*vigilant*). 1. A Simeonite, son of Shemaiah. 1 Chron. 4:37.

2. The father of Jediael, one of David's guard. 1 Chron. 11:45.

3. A Kohathite Levite in the reign of Hezekiah. 2 Chron. 29:13. (B.C. 726.)

Shim'rith (shĭm'rith) (feminine of Shimri, *vigilant*), a Moabitess, mother of Jehozabad, one of the assassins of King Joash. 2 Chron. 24:26. In 2 Kings 12:21 she is called SHOMER. (B.C. 796.)

Shim'rom (shĭm'rŏm). 1 Chron. 7:1. [SHIMRON.]

Shim'ron (shĭm'rŏn) (*watch-height*). 1. A city of Zebulun. Josh. 11:1; 19:15.

2. The fourth son of Issachar according to the lists of Genesis, Gen. 46:13, and Numbers, Num. 26:24, and the head of the family of the Shimronites.

Shim'ronites, The. [SHIMRON.]

Shim'ron=me'ron (shim'rŏn-mē'rŏn) (*watch-height of Meron*). The king of Shimron-meron is mentioned as one of the thirty-one kings vanquished by Joshua. Josh. 12:20. It is probably identical with, and possibly the full name of the place elsewhere called SHIMRON, a city of Zebulun. Josh. 11:1; 19:15.

Shim'shai (shĭm'shā) (*sunny*), the scribe or secretary of Rehum, who was a kind of satrap of the conquered province of Judea and of the colony of Samaria, supported by the Persian court. Ezra 4:8, 9, 17, 23. He was apparently an Aramæan, for the letter which he wrote to Artaxerxes was in Syriac. Ezra 4:7.

Shi'nab (shī'năb), the king of Admah in the time of Abraham. Gen. 14:2. (B.C. 1913.)

Shi'nar (shī'när), the ancient name of the great alluvial tract through which the Tigris and Euphrates pass before reaching the sea—the tract known in later times as Babylonia. It was a plain country, where brick had to be used for stone and slime for mortar. Gen. 11:3. Among the cities were Babel (Babylon), Erech, Calneh or Calno and Accad. The Tell-el-Amarna inscriptions show that the same region was known by the name of *Shanhar* to the Semites of Mesopotamia.

Ship. While ships are mentioned in the Old Testament there are but few hints as to size or character. See Ezek. 27; Jonah 1; Dan. 11:30. For our knowledge of the merchant-ships of the ancients we are indebted to St. Luke in the narrative of St. Paul's voyage to Rome. Acts 27, 28. He accomplished this in three ships: first, the Adramyttian vessel which took him from Cæsarea to Myra, and which was probably a coasting-vessel of no great size, Acts 27:1–6; secondly, the large Alexandrian grain ship, in which he was wrecked on the coast of Malta, Acts 27:6–28:1; and thirdly, another large Alexandrian grain ship, in which he sailed from Malta by Syracuse and Rhegium to Puteoli. Acts 28:11–13. 1. *Size.* The narrative in Acts affords a good standard for estimating this. The ship in which St. Paul was wrecked had 276 persons on board, Acts 27:37, besides a cargo of wheat, Acts 27:10, 38; and all these passengers seem to have been taken on to Puteoli in another ship, Acts 28:11, which had its own crew and its own cargo. Now, in modern transport-ships, prepared for carrying troops, it is a common estimate to allow a ton and a half per man. On the whole, if we say that an ancient merchant-ship might range from 500 to 1000 tons, we are clearly within the mark. Lucian describes a vessel as 180 feet long and 45 in breadth. This was somewhere about 1200 or 1300 tons, and was so unusual that its size attracted

ROMAN GALLEY.

attention. "The exceptionally large war galley of Ptolemy Philopator measured 420 feet in length and 57 feet in breadth." (Davis' B.D.) 2. *Steering apparatus.*—Some commentators have fallen into strange perplexities from observing that in Acts 27:40 ("the fastenings of the rudders") St. Luke uses the plural. Ancient ships were in truth not steered at all by rudders fastened or hinged to the stern, but by means of two paddle-rudders, one on each quarter, acting in a rowlock or through a port-hole, as the vessel might be small or large. 3. *Build and orna-*

A PHŒNICIAN SHIP.
From an Egyptian Monument.

ments of the hull.—It is probable that there was no very marked difference between the bow and the stern. The "hold," Jonah 1:5, would present no special peculiarities. That personification of ships which seems to be instinctive led the ancients to paint or

perhaps to carve an eye on each side of the bow. An ornament of the ship which took Paul from Malta to Pozzuoli is more explicitly referred to. The "sign" of that ship, Acts 28:11, was Castor and Pollux; and the symbols of those heroes were doubtless painted or sculptured on each side of the bow, or carved as a figure-head. 4. *Under-girders.*—The imperfection of the build, and still more (see below, 6) the peculiarity of the rig, in ancient ships, resulted in a greater tendency than in our times to the starting of the planks, and consequently to leaking and foundering. Hence it was customary in case of necessity, to pass cables or chains, called "helps" or "undergirders" round the frame of the ship, at right angles to its length, and made tight. Acts 27:17. 5. *Anchors.*—Ancient anchors were similar in form to those which we use now, except that they were without flukes. The ship in which Paul was sailing had four anchors on board. The sailors on this occasion anchored by the stern. Acts 27:29. 6. *Masts, sails, ropes and yards.*—The rig of an ancient ship was more simple and clumsy than that employed in modern times. Its great feature was one large mast, with one large square sail fastened to a yard of great length. Hence the strain upon the hull, and the danger of starting the planks, were greater than under the present system, which distributes the mechanical pressure more evenly over the whole ship. Not that there were never more masts than one, or more sails than one on the same mast, in an ancient merchantman; but these were repetitions, so to speak, of the same general unit of rig. Another feature of the ancient, as of the modern, ship is the flag at the top of the mast. Isa. 30 : 17 (see margin). We must remember that the ancients had no compass, and very imperfect charts and instruments, if any at all. 7. *Rate of sailing.*—The rig which has been described is, like the rig of Chinese junks, peculiarly favorable to a quick run before the wind. Acts 16 : 11; 27 : 16. With such a wind an ancient ship could make fully seven knots an hour. It would, however, be a great mistake to suppose that ancient ships could not work to windward. But modern ships by their superior rig and build can do much better than those of olden times. 8. *Boats on the Sea of Galilee.*—In the narrative of the call of the disciples to be "fishers of men," Matt. 4 : 18–22; Mark 1 : 16–20; Luke 5 : 1–11, there is no special information concerning the characteristics of these. With the large population round the Lake of Tiberias, there must have been a vast number of both fishing-boats and pleasure-boats, and boat-building must have been an active trade on its shores. From accounts in other authors there seems to have been in Roman times a large number, ranging from the tiny pleasure or fishing boat, up to war galleys of a considerable size. There is no mention of boats on its waters in Old Testament times.

Shi′phi (shī′fĭ) (*abundant*), a Simeonite, father of Ziza. 1 Chron. 4 : 37.

Shiph′mite (shĭf′mīte) **The,** probably, though not certainly, the native of Shepham. 1 Chron. 27 : 27.

Shiph′rah (shĭf′rah) (*brightness*), Ex. 1 : 15, the name of one of the two midwives of the Hebrews who disobeyed the command of Pharaoh to kill the male children, vs. 15–21. (B.C. 1570.)

Shiph′tan (shĭf′tan) (*judicial*), father of Kemuel, a prince of the tribe of Ephraim. Num. 34 : 24.

Shi′sha (shī′shà), father of Elihoreph and Ahiah, the royal secretaries in the reign of Solomon. 1 Kings 4 : 3. He is apparently the same as Shavsha, who held the same position under David.

Shi′shak (shī′shak), king of Egypt, the Sheshonk I. of the monuments, first sovereign of the Bubastite twenty-second dynasty. His reign offers the first determined synchronism of Egyptian and Hebrew history. He must have been an able statesman, for he harbored the enemy of Solomon, Jeroboam (1 Kings 11 : 40) and yet avoided a rupture between the kingdoms. Either at the suggestion of Jeroboam, or shrewdly taking advantage of conditions in Palestine he invaded the country in the 5th year of Rehoboam. He exacted all the treasures of his city from Reho-

HEAD OF SHISHAK.
(*From temple of Karnak.*)

boam, and apparently made him tributary. 1 Kings 14 : 25, 26; 2 Chron. 12 : 2–9. Shishak has left a record of this expedition sculptured on the wall of the great temple of El-Karnak. It is a list of the countries, cities and tribes conquered or ruled by him, or tributary to him. It is not certain that Shishak's invasion was confined to the southern kingdom, though the passage in the Bible gives color to the belief.

Shittah tree, Shittim wood, is without doubt correctly referred to some species of *Acacia*, of which three or four kinds occur in the Bible lands. The wood of this tree—perhaps the *Acacia seyal* is more definitely signified —was extensively employed in the construction of the tabernacle. See Ex. 25, 26, 36, 37, 38. Even now common in Palestine, though it has been constantly used for lumber, and for making charcoal. Trees are found with trunks 2 feet in diameter. In olden times they very probably were sometimes three or four feet in diameter. The wood is close-grained and hard, of a fine yellow-brown color, and admirably adapted to cabinet work. The *A. seyal* is very common in some parts of the peninsula of Sinai. It yields the well-known substance called gum arabic, which is obtained by incisions in the bark, but it is impossible to say whether the ancient Jews were acquainted with its use. From the tangled thicket into which the stem of this tree expands, Stanley well remarks that hence is to be traced the use of the plural form of the Heb. noun *shittim*, the singular number occurring once only in the Bible. This acacia must not be confounded with the tree (*Robinia pseudo-acacia*) popularly known by this name in England, which is a North American plant, and belongs to a different genus and suborder. The true acacias belong to the order *Leguminosæ*, sub-order *Mimoseæ*.

Shit′tim (*the acacias*), the place of Israel's encampment between the con-

SHITTIM-WOOD. (*Acacia.*)

quest of the transjordanic highlands and the passage of the Jordan. Num. 25:1; 33:49; Josh. 2:1; 3:1; Micah

6:5. Its full name appears to be given in Num. 33:49 as Abel-Shittim, "the meadow, or moist place, of the acacias." It was "in the plains of Moab, on this side Jordan by Jericho," Num. 22:1; 26:3; 31:12; 33:48, 49; that is to say, it was in the Arabah or Jordan valley, opposite Jericho.

Shi′za (shī′zà) (*vehement love*), a Reubenite, father of Adina, 1 Chron. 11:42, one of David's warriors.

Sho′a (shō′à) (*rich*), a proper name which occurs only in Ezek. 23:23, in connection with Pekod and Koa. The three apparently designate districts of Assyria with which the southern kingdom of Judah had been intimately connected, and which were to be arrayed against it for punishment.

Sho′bab (shō′băb) (*restored*). 1. Son of David by Bath-sheba. 2 Sam. 5:14; 1 Chron. 3:5; 14:4.

2. Apparently the son of Caleb the son of Hezron by his wife Azubah. 1 Chron. 2:18.

Sho′bach (shō′băk) (*one who pours out*), the general of Hadadezer king of the Syrians of Zoba, who was defeated by David. 2 Sam. 10:15-18. In 1 Chron. 19:16, 18 he is called SHOPHACH.

Sho′bai (shō′ba-ĭ) (*one who leads captive*). The children of Shobai were a family of the door-keepers of the temple, who returned with Zerubbabel. Ezra 2:42; Neh. 7:45.

Sho′bal (shō′bal) (*flowing*). 1. A son of Seir the Horite, Gen. 36:20; 1 Chron. 1:38, and one of the "dukes" of the Horites. Gen. 36:29.

2. Son of Caleb the son of Hur, and founder or prince of Kirjath-jearim. 1 Chron. 2:50, 52; 4:1, 2.

Sho′bek (shō′bek) (*forsaker*), one of the heads of the people who sealed the covenant with Nehemiah. Neh. 10:24.

Sho′bi (shō′bī) (*one who takes captive*), son of Nahash of Rabbah of the children of Ammon. 2 Sam. 17:27. He was one of the first to meet David at Manhanaim on his flight from Absalom. (B.C. 1023.)

Sho′cho (shō′kō), 2 Chron. 28:18, one of the four varieties of the name Socoh.

Sho′choh, 1 Sam. 17:1, same as Socoh.

Sho′co, 2 Chron. 11:7, a variation in the Authorized Version of the name Socoh.

Shoe. [SANDAL.]

Sho'ham (shō'hăm) (*onyx*), a Merarite Levite, son of Jaaziah. 1 Chron. 24:27.

Sho'mer (shō'mēr) (*keeper*). 1. An Asherite, 1 Chron. 7:32; also called Shamer, ver. 34. R. V. "Shemer."

2. The mother of Jehozabad, who slew King Joash. 2 Kings 12:21. In the parallel passage in 2 Chron. 24:26 the name is converted into the feminine form Shimrith, who is further described as a Moabitess. [SHIMRITH.] (B.C. 796.)

Sho'phach (*one who pours out*), the general of Hadadezer. 1 Chron. 19:16, 18. [SHOBACH.]

Sho'phan (shō'fan), one of the fortified towns on the east of Jordan which were taken possession of and rebuilt by the tribe of Gad. Num. 32:35. [ATROTH.]

Shoshan'nim (shō-shan'nim) (*lilies*). "To the chief musician upon Shoshannim" is a musical direction to the leader of the temple choir which occurs in Pss. 45, 69, and most probably indicates the melody to which the psalms were to be sung. Shoshannim-eduth occurs in the same way in the title of Ps. 80. As the words now stand they signify "Lilies a testimony," and are probably a fragment of the beginning of an older psalm with which the choir were familiar.

Shu'ah (shū'ah). 1. Son of Abraham by Keturah. Gen. 25:2; 1 Chron. 1:32.

2. Properly Shuhah, brother of Chelub. 1 Chron. 4:11.

3. The father of Judah's wife, Gen. 38:2, 12; called also Shua.

Shu'al (shū'al) (*a jackal*), son of Zophah, an Asherite. 1 Chron. 7:36.

Shu'al, The land of, a district named in 1 Sam. 13:17 only. It is pretty certain from the passage that it lay north of Michmash, and not far from Ophrah, now *et-Taiyibeh.*

Shu'bael (shū'bā-ĕl). 1. Shebuel the son of Gershon. 1 Chron. 24:20.

2. Shebuel the son of Heman the minstrel. 1 Chron. 25:20.

Shu'ham (shū'ham) (*pitman*), son of Dan and ancestor of the Shuhamites. Num. 26:42.

Shu'hamites, The. [SHUHAM.]

Shu'hite (shū'hite) (*descendant of Shuah*). This ethnic appellative "Shuhite" is frequent in the book of Job,

but only as the epithet of one person, Bildad. The tribe may have been the *Suchu* of the inscriptions, on the west bank of the Euphrates south of Carchemish.

Shu'lamite (shū'lam-īte), **The,** one of the personages in the poem of Solomon's Song. 6:13. The name denotes a woman belonging to a place called Shulem, which is probably the same as Shunem. [SHUNEM.]

Shu'mathites (shū'math-ītes), **The,** one of the four families who sprang from Kirjath-jearim. 1 Chron. 2:53.

Shu'nammite, The, i. e. *the native of Shunem,* is applied to two persons: Abishag, the nurse of King David, 1 Kings 1:3, 15; 2:17, 21, 22, and the nameless hostess of Elisha. 2 Kings 4: 12, 25, 36.

Shu'nem (shū'nem) (*two resting-places*), one of the cities allotted to the tribe of Issachar. Josh. 19:18. It is mentioned on two occasions—1 Sam. 28:4; 2 Kings 4:8. It was besides the native place of Abishag. 1 Kings 1:3. It is mentioned by Eusebius as five miles south of Mount Tabor, and then known as Sulem. This agrees with the position of the present *Solam,* a village three miles north of Jezreel and five from Gilboa.

Shu'ni (shū'ni) (*calm, quiet*), son of Gad, and founder of the family of the Shunites. Gen. 46:16; Num. 26:15.

Shu'nites, The, the descendants of Shuni.

Shu'pham (shū'fam). [SHUPPIM.]

Shu'phamites, The, the descendants of Shupham or Shephupham, the Benjamite. Num. 26:39.

Shup'pim (shŭp'pim) (*serpents*). In the genealogy of Benjamin "Shuppim and Huppim, the children of Ir," are reckoned in 1 Chron. 7:12. Ir is the same as Iri the son of Bela the son of Benjamin, so that, if all the links are preserved, Shuppim was the great-grandson of Benjamin.

Shur (shūr) (*a wall*). Shur is first mentioned in the narrative of Hagar's flight from Sarah. Gen. 16:7. Abraham afterward "dwelled between Kadesh and Shur, and sojourned in Gerar." Gen. 20:1. The wilderness of Shur was entered by the Israelites after they had crossed the Red Sea. Ex. 15: 22, 23. It was also called the wilderness of Etham. Num. 33:8. It has not been identified, but probably was connected with the line of fortresses on the border of Egypt.

Shu'shan (shụ'shan), or **Su'sa** (a Persian name which to the Hebrews would suggest the *lily*.) It was originally the capital of the country called in Scripture Elam, and by the classical writers Susis or Susiana. Asshurbanipal captured it and later it became subject to the Babylonian kings. Cyrus is said to have made it one of his capitals, but its palace, according to inscriptions, was built by Darius Hystaspis. Daniel mentions Shushan (Dan. 8:2), and Nehemiah lived here. Neh. 1:1. It was captured by Alexander in B.C. 331, and again by Antigonus in B.C. 315. It was still defensible when the Saracens conquered Persia, but was then destroyed. Shushan was situated on the Ulai or Choaspes. It is identified with the modern *Sus* or *Shush,* and its ruins are about three miles in circumference. Here have been found the remains of the great palace built by Darius, the father of Xerxes, in which and the surrounding buildings took place the scenes recorded in the life of Esther. The great central hall was 343 feet long by 244 feet wide. The king's gate, says Schaff, where Mordecai sat, " was probably a hall 100 feet square, 150 feet from the northern portico. Between these two was probably the inner court, where Esther appeared before the king."

Shu'shan-e'duth (shụ'shan-ē'duth) *(the lily of testimony),* Ps. 60, is the singular form of " Shoshannim-eduth." Ps. 80. [SHOSHANNIM.]

Shu'thalhites (shụ'thal-ites), **The.** [SHUTHELAH.]

Shu'thelah (shụ'the-lah), head of an Ephraimite family, called after him Shuthalhites, Num. 26:35, and lineal ancestor of Joshua the son of Nun. 1 Chron. 7:20–27.

Si'a (sī'à). The "children of Sia" were a family of Nethinim who returned with Zerubbabel. Neh. 7:47. The name is written "Siaha" in Ezra 2:44.

Si'aha (sī'a-hà)= SIA. Ezra 2:44.

Sib'becai (sĭb'be-kā)= SIBBECHAI the Hushathite.

Sib'bechai *(entangling),* one of David's guard, and captain for the eighth month of 24,000 men of the king's army. 1 Chron. 11:29; 27:11. He belonged to one of the principal families of Judah, the Zarhites or descendants of Zerah, and is called "the Hushathite," probably from the place of his birth. Sibbechai's great exploit, which gave him a place among the mighty men of David's army, was his single combat with Saph or Sippai, the Philistine giant, in the battle at Gezer or Gob. 2 Sam. 21:18; 1 Chron. 20:4.

Sibboleth (sĭb'bo-lĕth), the Ephraimite pronunciation of the word Shibboleth. Judges 12:6. [SHIBBOLETH.]

Sib'mah (sĭb'mah). [SHEBAM.]

Sib'raim (sĭb'ra-ĭm), one of the landmarks on the northern boundary of the holy land as stated by Ezekiel. Ezek. 47:16. It has not been identified.

Si'chem (sī'kem). Gen. 12:6. [SHECHEM.]

Sic'yon (sĭk'yŏn), 1 Macc. 15:23, a celebrated Greek city in Peloponnesus, upon the Corinthian Gulf.

Sid'dim (sĭd'dim) *(plains),* **The vale of,** a place named only in one passage of Genesis—14:3, 8, 10. It was one of that class of valleys which the Hebrews designated by the word *emek.* This term appears to have been assigned to a broad, flattish tract, sometimes of considerable width, enclosed on each side by a definite range of hills. It was so far a suitable spot for the combat between the four and five kings, ver. 8; but it contained a multitude of bitumenpits sufficient materially to affect the issue of the battle. In this valley the kings of the five allied cities of Sodom, Gomorrah, Admah, Zeboim and Bela seem to have awaited the approach of the invaders. There is considerable doubt as to the meaning of "which is the Salt Sea." It cannot mean the identity of Siddim with the Dead Sea of to-day, as the most if not all of the latter is older than the time of Abraham. It may possibly be what is now the shallow southern end of the Dead Sea. [SEA, THE SALT.]

Si'don (sī'dŏn), the Greek form of the Phœnician name Zidon. [ZIDON.]

The city is usually spoken of at the present time by the Greek form, the old name being practically obsolete. A missionary school conducted in the city for many years by American missionaries, argues it of some importance.

Sido'nians, the Greek form of the word Zidonians. It occurs Deut. 3:9; Josh. 13:4, 6; Judges 3:3; 1 Kings 5:6. [ZIDON.]

Si'hon (sī'hŏn) *(a brush),* king of

the Amorites when Israel arrived on the borders of the promised land. Num. 21:21. (B.C. 1451.) Shortly before the time of Israel's arrival he had dispossessed the Moabites of a splendid territory, driving them south of the natural bulwark of the Arnon. Num. 21: 26–29. The Israelites asked permission to cross his territory. He refused, but the Israelites nevertheless entered it. He at once gathered his people together and attacked them. But the battle was his last. He and all his host were destroyed, and their district from Arnon to Jabbok became at once the possession of the conqueror.

Si'hor (si'hôr) (*dark*), accurately **Shi'hor**, once **The Shihor**, or **Shihor of Egypt**, when unqualified a name of the Nile. It is held to signify "the black" or "turbid." In Isa. 23:3; Jer. 2:18 the identity of Shihor with the Nile seems distinctly stated. The stream mentioned in Josh. 13:3; 1 Chron. 13:5 is probably that of the *Wády el' Arish.*

Si'las (si'las) (contracted form of Silvanus, (*sylvan*)), an eminent member of the early Christian Church, described under that name in the Acts, but as Silvanus in St. Paul's epistles. He first appears as one of the leaders of the church at Jerusalem, Acts 15:22, holding the office of an inspired teacher, 15:32. His name, derived from the Latin *silva,* "wood," betokens him a Hellenistic Jew, and he appears to have been a Roman citizen. Acts 16:37. He was appointed as a delegate to accompany Paul and Barnabas on their return to Antioch with the decree of the Council of Jerusalem. Acts 15:22, 32. Remaining in Antioch after the others had returned to Jerusalem (Acts 15:34) he was selected by St. Paul as the companion of his second missionary journey. Acts 15:40–17:10. At Berea he was left behind with Timothy while St. Paul proceeded to Athens, Acts 17:14, and we hear nothing more of his movements until he rejoined the apostle at Corinth. Acts 18:5. His presence at Corinth is several times noticed. 2 Cor. 1:19; 1 Thess. 1:1; 2 Thess. 1:1. Whether he was the Silvanus who conveyed St. Peter's first epistle to Asia Minor, 1 Pet. 5:12, is doubtful; the probabilities are in favor of the identity. A tradition of very slight au-

thority represents Silas to have become bishop of Corinth.

Silk. The only *undoubted* notice of silk in the Bible occurs in Rev. 18:12, where it is mentioned among the treasures of the typical Babylon. It is, however, in the highest degree probable that the texture was known to the Hebrews from the time that their commercial relations were extended by Solomon. The well-known classical name of the substance does not occur in the Hebrew language.

Sil'la (sĭl'là). "The house of Millo which goeth down to Silla" was the scene of the murder of King Joash. 2 Kings 12:20. What or where Silla was is entirely matter of conjecture.

Silo'ah (sĭ-lō'à), **The pool of,** properly "the pool of Shelah." Neh. 3:15. [SILOAM.]

Silo'am (sĭ-lō'am) (*sent*). *Shiloah,* Isa. 8:6; *Siloah,* R. V. "Shelah," Neh. 3:15; *Siloam,* John 9:7, 11. A pool at Jerusalem, "by the king's garden." Josephus states that it was at the extremity of the valley of the cheesemongers (or at the mouth of the Tyropæon Valley). There seems no doubt that the present *Birkit Silwan* occupies the site of the ancient pool. It is a mere suburban tank of no great size, and for many an age not particularly good or plentiful in its waters, though Josephus tells us that in his day they were both "sweet and abundant." A little way below the Jewish burying-ground, but on the opposite side of the valley, on where the Kedron turns slightly westward and widens itself considerably, is the fountain of the Virgin, near the beginning of that saddle-shaped projection of the temple hill supposed to be the Ophel of the Bible and the Ophlas of Josephus. At the back part of this fountain a subterraneous passage begins, through which the water flows, and through which a man may make his way, sometimes walking erect, sometimes stooping, sometimes kneeling, and sometimes crawling to Siloam. An inscription found in June, 1880, on the east side of the tunnel about 25 feet from its exit at Siloam records that it was excavated from both ends, the workmen meeting in the middle, and that it was 1200 cubits long. Conder measured it as 1706.8 feet. There is nothing in the

POOL OF SILOAM.

Photo by Jan Wilga

THE MODERN VILLAGE OF SILOAM.

inscription to oppose the view that it was made by Hezekiah. At a former time it had tributaries which sent their waters down from the city pools or temple wells to swell Siloam. It enters Siloam at the northwest angle; or rather enters a small rock-cut chamber which forms the *vestibule* of Siloam, about five or six feet broad. To this you descend by a few rude steps, under which the water pours itself into the main pool. This pool is oblong, about 58 feet long, 18 feet broad and 19 feet deep; but it is never filled, the water either passing directly through or being maintained at a depth of three or four feet. It is built on the site of the original pool which measured 75 feet by 71 feet. Surely after the Return, perhaps even as late as the time of Herod, a covered arcade ran around its four sides. This was its condition in the time of Christ. The present pool is a ruin, with no moss or ivy to make it romantic; its sides fallen in; its pillars broken; its stair a fragment; its walls giving way; the edge of every stone worn round or sharp by time; in some parts mere *débris*, though around its edges wild flowers, and among other plants the caper tree, grow luxuriantly. This pool, which we may call the *second,* seems anciently to have poured its waters into a *third* before it proceeded to water the royal gardens. This third is perhaps that which Josephus calls " Solomon's pool," and which Nehemiah calls the "king's pool." Neh. 2:14. The expression in Isa. 8:6, "waters of Shiloah that go softly," seems to point to the slender rivulet, flowing gently though once very profusely out of Siloam into the lower breadth of level where the king's gardens, or royal paradise, stood, and which is still the greenest spot about the holy city. Siloam is a sacred spot even to the Moslem; much more to the Jew. It was to Siloam that the Levite was sent with the golden pitcher on the "last and great day of the feast" of Tabernacles; it was from Siloam that he brought the water which was then poured over the sacrifice, in memory of the water from the rock of Rephidim; and it was to this Siloam water that the Lord pointed when he stood in the temple on that day and cried, "If any man thirst, let him come unto me and drink." The Lord sent the blind man to wash, not

in, as our version has it, but *at* (εἰς), the pool of Siloam; for it was the clay from his eyes that was to be washed off.

Siloam, Tower in. Luke 13:4. Of this we know nothing definitely beyond these words of the Lord. It was very likely one of the city towers on the Ophel ridge near Siloam.

Silva'nus (sĭl-vā'nus). [SILAS.]

Silver. In very early times silver was used for ornaments, Gen. 24:53, and for vessels of various kinds. Images for idolatrous worship were made of silver or overlaid with it, Ex. 20:23; Hos. 13:2; Hab. 2:19; Dan. 5:4, and the manufacture of silver shrines for Diana was a trade in Ephesus. Acts 19:24. But its chief use was as a medium of exchange, and throughout the Old Testament we find " silver " used for money, like the French *argent.* Silver was brought to Solomon from Arabia, 2 Chron. 9:14, and from Tarshish, 2 Chron. 9:21, which supplied the markets of Tyre. Ezek. 27:12. From Tarshish it came in the form of plates, Jer. 10:9, like those on which the sacred books of the Singhalese are written to this day. Spain appears to have been the chief source whence silver was obtained by the Romans. Possibly the hills of Palestine may have afforded some supply of this metal. Silver mixed with alloy is referred to in Jer. 6:30, and a finer kind, either purer in itself or more thoroughly purified, is mentioned in Prov. 8:19.

Silverlings, a word used once only in the Authorized Version, Isa. 7:23, as a translation of the Hebrew word elsewhere rendered " silver " or " shekel."

Sim'eon (sĭm'e-on) (*hearing*). 1. The second of Jacob's sons by Leah. His birth is recorded in Gen. 29:33. Besides the massacre of Shechem, Gen. 34:25, the only personal incident related of Simeon is the fact of his being selected by Joseph as the hostage for the appearance of Benjamin. Gen. 42:19, 24, 36; 43:23. The chief families of the tribe of Simeon are mentioned in the lists of Gen. 46:10. At the census of Sinai Simeon numbered 59,300 fighting men. Num. 1:23. When the second census was taken, at Shittim, the numbers had fallen to 22,-200, and it was the weakest of all the tribes. To Simeon was allotted a portion of land out of the territory of Judah, on its southern frontier, which contained eighteen or nineteen cities, with their villages, spread round the venerable well of Beersheba. Josh. 19 : 1-9; 1 Chron. 4 : 28-33. Of these places, with the help of Judah, the Simeonites possessed themselves, Judges 1 : 3, 17. What part the tribe took at the time of the division of the kingdom we are not told. It had practically been absorbed by Judah before that time. There are very few mentions of Simeon later. See 2 Chron. 15 : 9; 34 : 6.

The tribe was recognized by Ezekiel in his prophecies of the future Canaan. Ezek. 48 : 24, 25, 33. In the vision in Rev. 7 : 7, there were sealed 12,000 Simeonites.

2. A devout Jew, to whom it had been revealed by the Holy Spirit that he should live to see the Lord's Christ. He met Joseph and Mary with Jesus in the temple, took him in his arms, and gave thanks for what he saw and knew of Jesus. Luke 2 : 25-35.

3. An ancestor of Christ living before Zerubbabel. Luke 3 : 30.

Sim'eon Niger. Acts 13:1. [NIGER.]

Si'mon (contracted form of Simeon).

1. Son of Mattathias. [MACCABEES.]

2. Simon the brother of Jesus. The only undoubted notice of this Simon occurs in Matt. 13:55, Mark 6:3. He has been identified by some writers with Simon the Canaanite, and still more generally with Symeon who became bishop of Jerusalem after the death of James. The former of these opinions rests on no evidence whatever, nor is the latter without its difficulties.

3. Simon the Canaanite, one of the twelve apostles, Matt. 10:4; Mark 3: 18, otherwise described as Simon Ze- lotes, Luke 6:15; Acts 1:13. The lat- ter term, which is peculiar to Luke, is the Greek equivalent for the Chaldee term preserved by Matthew and Mark. [CANAANITE.] Each of these equally points out Simon as belonging to the faction of the Zealots, who were con- spicuous for their fierce advocacy of the Mosaic ritual.

4. Simon of Cyrene, a Hellenistic Jew, born at Cyrene, on the north coast of Africa. He was compelled to aid in carrying the cross when Jesus sank un- der the burden. Matt. 27:32; Mark 15:21; Luke 23:26; comp. John 19:17. Mark describes him as the father of Alexander and Rufus, perhaps because this was the Rufus known to the Roman

Christians, Rom. 16:13, for whom he more especially wrote.

5. Simon, a resident at Bethany, dis- tinguished as "the leper." It is not im- probable that he had been miraculously cured by Jesus. In his house Mary anointed Jesus preparatory to his death and burial. Matt. 26 : 6, etc.; Mark 14: 3, etc.; John 12 : 1, etc.

6. Simon Magus, a Samaritan living in the apostolic age, distinguished as a sorcerer or "magician," from his prac- tice of magical arts. Acts 8 : 9. The story in the New Testament is short. He so "amazed" the people of Sa- maria with his arts that he was pro- nounced to be "the power of God which is called great." Acts 8 : 10. He was apparently converted by Philip and received baptism at his hands, A.D. 36. Subsequently he witnessed the effect produced by the imposition of hands, as practised by the apostles Peter and John, and, being desirous of acquiring a similar power for himself, he offered a sum of money for it. His proposi- tion met with a severe denunciation from Peter, followed by a petition on the part of Simon, the tenor of which bespeaks terror, but not penitence. Acts 8 : 9-24. The memory of his peculiar guilt has been perpetuated in the word *simony*, as applied to all traffic in spir- itual offices. Ecclesiastical writings are full of traditions concerning this man, none of which seem to have any real ground. According to these he was born at Gitton, a village of Samaria, and probably educated in Alexandria. He became the pertinacious foe of the apostle Peter, whose movements he fol- lowed for the purpose of seeking en- counters, in which he was signally de- feated. He is said to have followed the apostle to Rome. His death is asso- ciated with this meeting. According to Hippolytus, the earliest authority on the subject, Simon was buried alive at his own request, in the confident assurance that he would rise on the third day.

7. Simon Peter. [PETER.]

8. Simon, a Pharisee, in whose house a penitent woman anointed the head and feet of Jesus. Luke 7 : 40.

9. Simon the tanner, a Christian con- vert living at Joppa, at whose house Peter lodged. Acts 9 : 43. The house was near the seaside, Acts 10 : 6, 32, for the convenience of the water. (A.D. 39.)

10. Simon the father of Judas Iscariot. John 6 : 71; 13 : 2, 26.

Sim'ri (sĭm'rī) (*vigilant*), properly Shimri, son of Hosah, a Merarite Levite in the reign of David. 1 Chron. 26 : 10.

Sin, a city of Egypt, mentioned only by Ezekiel. Ezek. 30 : 15, 16. The name is Hebrew, or at least Semitic, perhaps signifying *clay*. It is identified in the Vulgate with Pelusium, "the clayey or muddy" town. It is referred to as "Sin the stronghold of Egypt." This place was held by Egypt from that

their next encampment REPHIDIM. Num. 33 : 11, 12, where more camping places are given, places it between an encampment on the Red Sea after leaving Elim, and one at Dophkah, which together with Alush lay between this wilderness and Rephidim. It is generally considered as the wilderness west of the commonly received site of Mt. Sinai, on the shore of the Red Sea, or more exactly Gulf of Suez.

Sin offering. The sin offering among the Jews was the sacrifice in which the

THE REPUTED WILDERNESS OF SIN.

time until the period of the Romans. Herodotus relates that Sennacherib advanced against Pelusium, and that near Pelusium Cambyses defeated Psammenitus. In like manner the decisive battle in which Ochus defeated the last native king, Nectanebos, was fought near this city.

Sin, Wilderness of, a tract of the wilderness which the Israelites reached after leaving Elim.

The identification is uncertain. The reference in Ex. 16 : 1 puts it "between Elim and Sinai," Ex. 17 : 1 names

ideas of propitiation and of atonement for sin were most distinctly marked. The ceremonial of the sin offering is described in Lev. 4 and 6. The trespass offering is closely connected with the sin offering in Leviticus, but at the same time clearly distinguished from it, being in some cases offered with it as a distinct part of the same sacrifice; as, for example, in the cleansing of the leper. Lev. 14. The distinction of ceremonial clearly indicates a difference in the idea of the two sacrifices. The actual difference is, however, difficult to decide upon, and has given rise to much discussion. Apparently the sin offerings were—1. *Regular.* (*a*) For the whole people, at the New Moon, Passover, Pentecost, Feast of Trumpets and Feast of Tabernacles, Num. 28 : 15–29 : 38; besides the solemn offering of the two goats on the Great Day of Atonement. Lev. 16. (*b*) For the priests and Levites at their consecration, Ex. 29 : 10–14, 36; besides the yearly sin offering (a bullock) for the high priest on the Great Day of Atonement. Lev. 16. 2. *Special.* For any sin of "ignorance" and the like, recorded in Lev. 4 and 5. Josephus declares that the sin offering is presented by those " who fall into sin in ignorance," and the trespass offering by "one who has sinned and is conscious of his sin, but has no one to convict him thereof." Dr. Davis, in his Bible Dictionary gives h i s opinion as follows: " The sin offering was made for sins o f which t h e effect terminates primarily on the sinner; the trespass offering for sins of which the effects terminate primarily on another, and for which, in addition to the sacrifice, restitution was made. But sins committed deliberately and for which the penalty was death could not be expiated. Num. 15 : 30, 31."

Si′na, Mount, the Greek form of t h e well-known name Sinai. Acts 7 : 30, 38.

Si′nai (sī′nā-ī) (*pertaining to Sin* [the moon-god]). Nearly in the centre of the peninsula which stretches between the horns of the Red Sea lies a wedge of granite, grünstein and porphyry rocks rising to between 8000 and 9000 feet above the sea. Its shape resembles a scalene triangle. These mountains may be divided into two great masses—that of *Jebel Serbal* (6712 feet high), in the northwest above *Wady Feirán,* and the central group, roughly denoted by the general name of *Sinai.* This group rises abruptly from the *Wady es-Sheikh* at its north foot, first to the cliffs of the *Ras Sûfsâfeh,* behind which is the pinnacle of *Jebel Mûsa* (the Mount of

Moses), and farther back to the right of it the summit of *Jebel Katerin* (Mount St. Catherine).

1. *Names.*—These mountains are called Horeb, and sometimes Sinai. The distinction is one of usage, both names being applied to the same place by different persons.

2. *The mountain from which the law was given.*—Modern investigators are exceedingly uncertain as to the identity of Mt. Sinai, some being inclined to the belief that it was in Midian, east of the Gulf of Akaba, far from the traditional site. Others believe it Jebel Serbal, the principal objection to which

THE PEAK OF MT. SINAI.

is the lack of a suitable plain at its base for the encampment. The traditional site is the long range which rises from the plain *er-Rahah,* with the *Wady es-Sheikh* and *Wady es-Deir,* bordering it on the northeast. The plain of *er-Rahah* is about two miles long by half a mile broad, and is entirely suitable for a camping ground. Its size is such that the whole people of Israel, two million in number, would find ample accommodations for seeing and hearing. The peak overlooking this plain is *Ras es-Sûfsâfeh,* a precipitous cliff

THE PEAKS OF SINAI.

rising directly from the plain. If the law was proclaimed orally to the people from any of the peaks in this region this would certainly seem to answer the purpose perfectly. Dean Stanley says that "from the highest point of Ras Sûfsâfeh to its lower peak, a distance of about 60 feet, the page of a book distinctly but not loudly read was perfectly audible." *Jebel Musa,* at the southern end of the range is also a traditional site, but there is no such commodious plain at its foot. Some believe that the law was delivered to Moses on *Jebel Musa,* and proclaimed to the people from *Ras-es-Sûfsâfeh.* It has been thought for some time that the tradition naming *Jebel Musa* was much later than that naming *Jebel Serbal,* but a manuscript found in 1887 describes a pilgrimage which could only have had for its object the region of *Jebel Musa,* and the plain of *er-Rahah.*

Si′nim (sī′nim), a people noticed in Isa. 49:12, as living at the extremity of the known world. There are several theories as to their identity, but the most common is that it refers to China.

Si′nite (sī′nīte), a tribe of Canaanites, Gen. 10:17; 1 Chron. 1:15, whose position is to be sought for in the northern part of the Lebanon district.

Si′on (sī′on) (*elevated*), **Mount.** 1. One of the various names of Mount Hermon. Deut. 4:48 only.
2. The Greek form of the Hebrew name Zion, the famous mount of the temple. This form is always used in the Books of the Maccabees, and usually in the New Testament. Matt. 21:5; John 12:15; Heb. 12:22; Rev. 14:1. [JERUSALEM.] The modern form is ZION.

⟨ **Siph′moth** (sĭf′moth), one of the places in the south of Judah which David frequented during his freebooting life. 1 Sam. 30:28.

Sip′pai (*threshold*), Saph, one of the sons of Rephaim, or "the giants," slain by Sibbechai at Gezer. 1 Chron. 20:4. (B.C. about 1050.)

Si′rah (sī′rah), **The well of,** from which Abner was recalled by Joab to his death at Hebron. 2 Sam. 3:26 only. It was apparently on the northern road from Hebron. There is a spring and reservoir on the western side of the ancient northern road, about one mile out of Hebron, which is called *Ain Sarah,* which is probably the one.

Sir′ion (sĭr′i-ŏn) (*breastplate*), one of the various names of Mount Hermon, that by which it was known to the Zidonians. Deut. 3:9; Ps. 29:6.

Sis′amai (sĭs′ă-mā-ī), a descendant of Sheshan in the line of Jerahmeel. 1 Chron. 2:40.

Sis′era (sĭs′e-rà) (*battle array*). 1. Captain of the army of Jabin king of Canaan, who reigned in Hazor. He himself resided in Harosheth of the Gentiles. The particulars of the rout of Megiddo and of Sisera's flight and death are given under the heads of BARAK, DEBORAH, JAEL, KISHON. (B.C. 1229.)
2. After a long interval the name reappears in the lists of the Nethinim who returned from the captivity with Zerubbabel. Ezra 2:53; Neh. 7:55. It perhaps tells of Canaanite captives devoted to the lowest offices of the temple.

Sit′nah (sĭt′nah) (*enmity*), the second of the two wells dug by Isaac in the valley of Gerar, the possession of which the herdmen of the valley disputed with him. Gen. 26:21.

Sivan (sī′van). [MONTH.]

Slave. Slavery existed in remote antiquity. There is no record of its institution, and no indication of a period when it did not exist. It is recognized in the Mosaic code, apparently with a view to soften its hardships and give every one his rights. No Hebrew could become permanently the slave of another Hebrew, while the redemption of those in bondage to Gentiles was recognized as a duty. Slaves from the Gentiles were well treated among the Hebrews, and had certain recognized legal rights and could rise to responsible positions.

1. *Hebrew Slaves.*—Hebrews became slaves to others of their own race,—(1) because of debt, the debtor, and perhaps his children being held as slaves until the debt was "worked out." Ex. 22:3; 2 Kings 4:1; Neh. 5:5, 8; Amos 2:6; Matt. 18:25. (2) Thieves unable to make restitution on the scale prescribed by the law were treated as debtors. Ex. 22:1, 3. (3) On account of poverty men at times sold themselves or their children. Ex. 21:2, 7; Lev. 25:39, 47. A daughter of tender age was often sold as a maid-servant, with a view to her becoming the wife or the concubine of the purchaser or of his son. Ex. 21:7-11. This latter may in

some cases have been considered as dowry given to the parents of the bride. The price of the slave varied greatly according to circumstances, but was reckoned as averaging 30 shekels. Ex. 21 : 32. Joseph, at 17 years of age, was sold for 20 shekels. Gen. 37 : 28.

The legal status of a Hebrew slave among the Hebrews was quite different from that of a non-Hebrew slave. The condition of a Hebrew servant was by no means intolerable. His master was admonished to treat him, not "as a bond-servant, but as an hired servant and as a sojourner," and, again, "not to rule over him with rigor." Lev. 25 : 39, 40, 43. At the termination of his servitude the master was enjoined not to "let him go away empty," but to remunerate him liberally out of his flock, his floor and his wine-press. Deut. 15 : 13, 14. All the members of the Hebrew race, bond or free, were regarded as members of the commonwealth of Israel, and equal before God, having the same part in sacrifices and religious festivals (Ex. 12 : 44; Lev. 22 : 11; Deut. 12 : 12, 18; 16 : 11, 14), and enjoying the rest on the Sabbath day (Ex. 20 : 10; 23 : 12).

Still more valuable to the Hebrew slave was the legal right of manumission contained in the law. The debtor would of course be released when his debt was paid. But in the case of large debtors and heavy task masters that might take a long time. It was therefore a part of the Mosaic code that no Hebrew slave should be held longer than six years. In the seventh he was to "go out free." All purchases of slaves was based on this principle. At the year of Jubilee all slaves were set free, whatever their period of servitude. If a servant did not desire to avail himself of the opportunity of leaving his service, he was to signify his intention in a formal manner before the judges (or more exactly *at the place of judgment*), and then the master was to take him to the door-post, and to bore his ear through with an awl, Ex. 21 : 6, driving the awl into or "unto the door," as stated in Deut. 15 : 17, and thus fixing the servant to it. A servant who had submitted to this operation remained, according to the words of the law, a servant "forever." Ex. 21 : 6. Josephus and the Rabbinists however apply this regulation to the manumissions at the end of the seven years, and explain it as meaning only till the year of Jubilee. A Hebrew woman might enter into voluntary servitude on the score of poverty, and in this case she was entitled to her freedom after six years service, together with her usual gratuity at leaving, just as in the case of a man. Deut. 15 : 12, 13. The position of a maiden sold by her father was subject to the following regulations: (1) She could not "go out as the men-servants do," *i. e.* she could not leave at the termination of six years, or in the year of Jubilee, if her master was willing to fulfill the object for which he had purchased her. (2) Should he not wish to marry her, he should call upon her friends to procure her release by the repayment of the purchase money. (3) If he betrothed her to his son, he was bound to make such provision for her as he would for one of his own daughters. (4) If either he or his son, having married her, took a second wife, it should not be to the prejudice of the first. (5) If neither of the three first specified alternatives took place, the maid was entitled to immediate and gratuitous liberty. Ex. 21 : 7–11. If a master gave as wife to a Hebrew slave another slave, a non-Hebrew, neither she nor the children might leave with him when his term was ended, but became the absolute property of the master. Ex. 21 : 4, 5. The custom of reducing Hebrews to servitude appears to have fallen into disuse subsequent to the Babylonish captivity. Vast numbers of Hebrews were reduced to slavery as war-captives at different periods by the Phœnicians, Joel 3 : 6, the Philistines, Amos 1 : 6, the Syrians, 1 Macc. 3 : 41; 2 Macc. 8 : 11, the Egyptians, Joseph. *Ant.* xii. 2, § 3, and above all by the Romans. Joseph. *B. J.* vi 9, § 3.

II. *Non-Hebrew slaves.*—The majority of non-Hebrew slaves were war-captives, either of the Canaanites who had survived the general extermination of their race under Joshua or such as were conquered from the other surrounding nations Num. 31 : 26 ff. Besides these, many were obtained by purchase from foreign slave-dealers, Lev. 25 : 44, 45; and others may have been reduced to this state by either poverty or crime. The children of slaves remained slaves.

being the class described as "born in the house," Gen. 14 : 14; 17 : 12; Eccles. 2 : 7, and hence the number was likely to increase as time went on.

That the slave might be manumitted appears from Ex. 21 : 26, 27; Lev. 19 : 20.

The slave is described as the "possession" of his master, apparently with a special reference to the power which the latter had of disposing of him to his heirs, as he would any other article of personal property. Lev. 25 : 45, 46. But, on the other hand, provision was made for the protection of his person. Ex. 21 : 20; Lev. 24 : 17, 22. A minor personal injury, such as the loss of an eye or a tooth, was to be recompensed by giving the servant his liberty. Ex. 21 : 26, 27. The position of the slave in regard to religious privileges was favorable. Deut. 12 : 12, 18; 16 : 11, 14. The occupations of slaves were of a menial character, as implied in Lev. 25 : 39, consisting partly in the work of the house and partly in personal attendance on the master. It will be seen that the whole tendency of the Bible legislation was to mitigate slavery, making it little more than hired service. Christianity avoided a sudden reversal of these long-established usages, and enjoined on slaves obedience to the master (Eph. 6 : 5-8; 1 Pet. 2 : 18-21), even sending back a runaway slave (Philemon). But it inculcated principles which led by degrees to the abolition of slavery, beginning with the improved condition in the Roman empire.

Slime, translated *bitumen* in the Vulgate and in the R. V. margin. It is first spoken of as used for cement by the builders in the plain of Shinar or Babylonia. Gen. 11 : 3. The bitumen pits in the vale of Siddim are mentioned in the ancient fragment of Canaanitish history, Gen. 14 : 10; and the ark of papyrus in which Moses was placed was made impervious to water by a coating of bitumen and pitch. Ex. 2 : 3. Herodotus, i. 179, tells us of the bitumen found at Is, the modern *Hit*, a town of Babylonia, eight days' journey from Babylon. Bitumen, or asphalt, is "the product of the decomposition of vegetable and animal substances. It is usually found of a black or brownish-black color, externally not unlike coal, but it varies in consistency from a bright, pitchy condition, with a conchoidal fracture, to thick, viscid masses

of mineral tar."—*Encyc. Brit.* It is obtained in various places in Asia, and occasionally in a soft or liquid state on the surface of the Dead Sea.

Sling. [ARMS.]

Smith. [HANDICRAFT.]

Smyr′na (smĕr′nà) (*myrrh*), a city of Asia Minor, situated on the Ægean Sea, 40 miles north of Ephesus. Allusion is made to it in Rev. 2 : 8-11. It was founded by the successors of Alexander the Great, and was situated 3 miles from the city of the same name, which after a long series of wars with the Lydians had been finally taken and sacked by Alyattes. The ancient city was a colony of Aeolic Greeks, but was taken by the Ionians and transformed into an Ionian city. The message to the church at Smyrna was entirely laudatory, and they were exhorted to stand firm in the midst of persecution. Its bishop, Polycarp, suffered martyrdom in A.D. 169. Smyrna suffered much from earthquakes; in A.D. 178 or 180 it was destroyed by one, but was once rebuilt. In the time of Strabo the ruins of the old Smyrna still existed, and were partially inhabited, but the new city was one of the most beautiful in all Asia. The streets were laid out as near as might be at right angles. There was a large public library there, and also a handsome building surrounded with porticos which served as a museum. It was consecrated as a heroum to Homer, whom the Smyrnæans claimed as a countryman.

At the time of the World War Smyrna was still a large city of about 400,000 inhabitants, of which a larger proportion are Franks than in any other town in Turkey. It is the most important city of the region, and the railroad center. After the war the city was given to Greece for administration, though considered a part of Turkey. In the fighting in Asia Minor in 1922-23 the Greeks were driven out, and the city in great part burned. By the adjustment which followed it was given to Turkey.

Snail. 1. The Hebrew word *shabbelul* occurs only in Ps. 58 : 8, and is translated "snail" in all versions. It means, more literally, "moist, slimy one." It may denote one of the *Limacidae*, or shell-less variety, which are particularly noticeable for the slimy track they leave behind them, by which they seem to waste themselves away. To this, or to the fact that many of them are shrivelled up among the rocks in the long heat of the summer, the

SNAIL.

psalmist refers. 2. The Hebrew word *chômet* occurs only as the name of some unclean animal in Lev. 11:30. Perhaps some kind of lizard may be intended.

Snow. The historical books of the Bible contain only one notice of snow actually falling—2 Sam. 23:20; but the allusions in the poetical books are so numerous that there can be no doubt as to its being an ordinary occurrence in the winter months. Job 37:6; Ps. 147:16; 148:8. The snow lies deep in the ravines of the highest ridge of Lebanon until the summer is far advanced, and indeed never wholly disappears; the summit of Hermon also perpetually glistens with frozen snow. From these sources probably the Jews obtained their supplies of ice for the purpose of cooling their beverages in summer. Prov. 25:13. The liability to snow must of course vary considerably in a country of such varying altitude as Palestine. It never falls on the seaboard of Philistia, Sharon or Phœnicia, and seldom inland where the altitude is below 2000 feet. Around Jericho it never falls, and south of Hebron it is rare. In Jerusalem it often falls in December–March, but not every year, and the amount varies from a little over a foot to a few inches, though cases have been known of a fall of several feet. In Galilee it is more rare.

but sometimes falls occur, with a precipitation of several inches.

So. "So, king of Egypt," is once mentioned in the Bible—2 Kings 17:4. So has been variously identified as one of the kings of the 25th dynasty. There is an inscription found which speaks of a *Tartan* or commander-in-chief of Pharaoh who was sent against Sargon. His name, *Sibe,* is similar to the Hebrew *Seve,* a possible form of the word which appears as So.

Soap. The Hebrew term *bôrîth* is a general term for any substance of cleansing qualities. As, however, it appears in Jer. 2:22 in contradistinction to *nether,* which undoubtedly means "natron" or mineral alkali, it is fair to infer that *bôrîth* refers to vegetable alkali, or some kind of potash, which forms one of the usual ingredients in our soap. Numerous plants capable of yielding alkalies exist in Palestine and the surrounding countries; we may notice one named *hubeibeh* (the *Salsola kali* of botanists) found near

SALSOLA KALI.

the Dead Sea, the ashes of which are called *elkuli,* from their strong alkaline properties.

So'cho (sō'kō). 1 Chron. 4:18. One of the towns called Socoh, in Judah, which of the two cannot be certainly stated, although it seems probable it is 2.

So'choh (sō'kō), another form of the name Socoh, 1 Kings 4:10. Probably, though not certainly, Socoh, 1.

So'coh (sō'kȯ), the name of two towns in the tribe of Judah. 1. In the district of the Shephelah. Josh. 15:35; 1 Sam. 17:1; 2 Chron. 11:7; 28:18. In the time of Eusebius it bore the name of Soccoth, and lay between eight and nine Roman miles from Eleutheropolis, on the road to Jerusalem. It may be identified with *Shuweikeh*, on the edge of the valley of Elah, 13 miles west of Bethlehem. 2. Also a town of Judah, but in the mountain district. Josh. 15:48. It has been discovered about 10 miles southwest of Hebron; bearing, like the other Socoh, the name of *Shuweikeh*.

So'di (sō'dī), the father of Geddiel, the spy selected from the tribe of Zebulun. Num. 13:10.

Sod'om (sŏd'om) (*burning*), one of the most ancient cities of Syria. It is commonly mentioned in connection with Gomorrah, but also with Admah and Zeboim, and on one occasion— Gen. 14—with Bela or Zoar. Sodom was evidently the chief town in the settlement. The four are first named in the ethnological records of Gen. 10: 19 as belonging to the Canaanites. The position of Sodom is unknown, and probably can never be absolutely settled. There are three general opinions held. (1) That they were on the site now occupied by the Dead Sea. This is not a necessary inference from the Bible, though it was inferred therefrom. But still more conclusive as a proof is the absolute certainty from geological investigation that the Dead Sea was in existence for ages before Abraham. (2) These cities were in the Arabah, north or northwest of the Dead Sea. There are strong arguments for this position. (a) Abraham and Lot, standing on a height of land near Bethel, could see "all the plain of Jordan." Gen. 13:3, 10. It was one great oasis —"a garden of Jehovah," ver. 10. In the midst of the garden the four cities of Sodom, Gomorrah, Admah and Zeboim appear to have been situated. But it must be noted that "all the land" to be occupied by the Israelites is seen by Moses on Pisgah according to the statement in Deuteronomy, a fact which shows a possible exaggeration in the use of "all" here also. (b) Chedor-laomer, coming from the south fought at En-gedi before encountering the king of Sodom and his allies. (3)

They lay to the south of the Dead Sea as it then existed, either south or southwest of the present sea, or on a site now covered by the southern end of the Sea itself, which is there indubitably less ancient and more shallow than at its northern end. There are weighty arguments for this. (a) Asphalt, bitumen, is still found at the southern end. (b) Zoar, one of the five cities, the only one which escaped (Gen. 19:21) according to Josephus (War iv, 8, 4), was at the southern end, while other references to it in the Bible seem to point to this site. [ZOAR.] (c) If we must believe the cities to be covered by the lake the site at the southern end is the only possible one, since at its northern end it is from 600 to 1000 feet deep, and of far more ancient origin. (d) A fourth argument, is the existence of the salt mountain at the south of the lake, and its tendency to split off in columnar masses presenting a rude resemblance to the human form. But it is by no means certain that salt does not exist at other spots round the lake. (e) A fifth argument is drawn from the fact that Abraham saw the smoke of the burning cities from Hebron. It thus appears that on the situation of Sodom no satisfactory conclusion can at present be reached. Of the catastrophe which destroyed the city and the district of Sodom we can hardly hope ever to form a satisfactory conception. Some catastrophe there undoubtedly was; but what secondary agencies, besides fire, were employed in the accomplishment of the punishment cannot be safely determined in the almost total absence of exact scientific description of the natural features of the ground round the lake. We may suppose, however, that the actual agent in the ignition and destruction of the cities had been of the nature of a tremendous thunder-storm accompanied by a discharge of meteoric stones, and that these set on fire the bitumen with which the soil was saturated, and which was used in building the city. The miserable fate of Sodom and Gomorrah is held up as a warning in numerous passages of the Old and New Testaments. Mark 6:11; 2 Pet. 2:6; Jude 4–7.

Sod'oma (sŏd'ŏ-mȧ). Rom. 9:29. In this place alone the Authorized Version has followed the Greek and Vulgate form of the well-known name Sodom.

Sod'omites (sŏd'o-mites). This word does not denote the inhabitants of Sodom; but it is employed in the Authorized Version of the Old Testament for those who practiced as a religious rite the abominable and unnatural vice from which the inhabitants of Sodom and Gomorrah have derived their lasting infamy. 1 Kings 15 : 12.

Sol'omon (sol'ō-mŏn) (*peaceful*). I. *Early life.* Solomon was the son of David and Bathsheba. 2 Sam. 12:24; 1 Chron. 3:5. The former passage leads one to infer that he was the first son after their legal marriage; while the latter names him as the last of four. Some explain this by stating that he was named last as the most important.

His name, Solomon, means The Peaceful, one whose reign was foretold to be a reign of peace and quietness (1 Chron. 22:9). It may have also expressed the fact that David himself had found the peace of forgiveness. Nathan called him Jedidiah = "Beloved of Jehovah."

His parental inheritance was remarkably strong in several directions. His father David was in the maturity of his age, and his mother Bathsheba was the granddaughter of the wise Ahithophel, whose advice "was as if a man had inquired at the oracle of God."

"He inherited from his mother and the counsellor Ahithophel sagacity, quickness of judgment, judicial insight, and perhaps some measure of sensual weakness; from his father, thoughtfulness, literary tastes, the skill of ruling, and an interest in religion."

Of his personal appearance we have no direct description, as we have of the earlier kings. There are, however, materials for filling up the gap. Whatever higher mystic meaning may be latent in Ps. 45, or the Song of Songs, we are all but compelled to think of them as having had at least a historical starting-point. They tell of one who was, in the eyes of the men of his own time, "fairer than the children of men," the face "white and ruddy" as his father's, Cant. 5:10; 1 Sam. 17:42, bushy locks, dark as the raven's wing, yet not without a golden glow, the eyes soft as "the eyes of doves," the "countenance as Lebanon, excellent as the cedars," "the chiefest among ten thousand, the altogether lovely." Cant. 5:

9–16. Add to this all gifts of a noble, far-reaching intellect, large and ready sympathies, a playful and genial humor, the lips "full of grace," and the soul "anointed" as "with the oil of gladness," Ps. 45, and we may form some notion of what the king was like in that dawn of his golden prime.

He had a most excellent education, if we may judge by what he was in manhood. The common opinion is that he was placed under the care and training of Nathan; but there is no real proof of this, and there is no trace of prophetical influence over his later years. He showed however that he had been brought up in the religion and learning of the Jews. He developed a great taste for science and literature (1 Kings 4:32–34). He had the advantages of being the child of David's later years and of being under the influence of the subdued piety which characterized those years. His mother, too, doubtless joined with David in his penitential piety, for she had great influence over him to the last.

On the other hand, he was "born to the purple"; he was brought up in luxury and wealth, and knew nothing of the hardships which developed much of the character of his father. The influences of the court were often bad. He came in contact with other princes and he had to resist all the temptations of a beautiful and flattered youth.

II. *Accession to the throne.*—At some period, it is not known when, David had promised Bathsheba that Solomon should be his heir. In addition to the oath there were other reasons why Solomon seemed a fitting successor. On account of it he had probably received a different training from that given those who would not naturally ascend the throne. The older sons, born of heathen mothers in David's warrior days, were turbulent and of fierce passions. They would not be fitting heads for a nation chosen by God for his service. There is no difficulty in the fact that he was one of the younger children. The law of primogeniture did not hold among kings of that day, much being left to the choice of the father.

When David was old and feeble, Adonijah, Solomon's older brother, attempted to gain possession of the throne; but he was defeated through

Nathan and Bathsheba, and Solomon went down to Gihon and was proclaimed and anointed king. 1 Kings 1. A few months more and Solomon found himself, by his father's death, the sole occupant of the throne. The position to which he succeeded was unique. Never before, and never after, did the kingdom of Israel take its place among the great monarchies of the East. Large treasures, accumulated through many years, were at his disposal.

His first occupation was to make his seat secure, and to punish the heads of the conspiracy. Adonijah was pardoned, but later was put to death because he had asked for permission to marry Abishag, the young Shunammite for his wife, which was in Oriental ideas tantamount to another attempt upon the throne. Abiathar the high priest was degraded, and Joab was put to death. After he was strengthened in the kingdom he held a religious convocation at Gibeon, where during the night following he had the dream where he chose wisdom as the gift of God in preference to wealth or long life.

III. *Foreign policy.*—1. Egypt. The first act of the foreign policy of the new reign must have been to most Israelites a very startling one. He made affinity with Pharaoh, king of Egypt, by marrying his daughter. 1 Kings 3:1. The immediate results were probably favorable enough. The new queen brought with her as a dowry the frontier city of Gezer. Pharaoh's daughter always remained the principal personage at the court. From a worldly point of view this was a most valuable alliance, both commercially and politically. From Egypt he procured horses and chariots; his position made it possible for him to secure to himself a goodly share of profit in the commerce between Egypt and the nations of the Far East. From the religious point of view it paved the way for at least a tendency to idolatry, although all that can be absolutely proved is that he allowed his various wives perfect religious freedom, even going so far as to provide the altars for the idolatrous worship.

2. Tyre. The alliance with the Phœnician king rested on a somewhat different footing. It had been a part of David's policy from the beginning of his reign. Hiram had been "ever a lover of David." At once on hearing of Solomon's accession he sent ambassadors to salute him. A correspondence passed between the two kings, which ended in a treaty of commerce. The opening of Joppa as a port created a new coasting-trade, and the materials from Tyre were conveyed to that city on floats, and thence to Jerusalem. 2 Chron. 2:16. In return for these exports, the Phœnicians were only too glad to receive the grain and oil of Solomon's territory. The results of the alliance did not end here. Now, for the first time in the history of the Jews, they entered on a career as a commercial people. Still more important was the aid given by the Phœnicians in the building of the temple. His own subjects would apparently have been totally incapable of supplying the necessary skill for either the construction or the ornamentation of the numerous buildings from which much of his fame is derived. It was chiefly through Phœnicia that Hebrew art was derived.

3. The foregoing were the two most important alliances. There were many others, as in all probability most of his harem consisted of princesses or ladies of noble families sent to him to cement an alliance. The absence of any reference to Babylon and Assyria, and the fact that the Euphrates was recognized as the boundary of Solomon's kingdom, 2 Chron. 9:26, suggests the inference that the Mesopotamian monarchies were at this time comparatively feeble. Other neighboring nations were content to pay annual tribute in the form of gifts. 2 Chron. 9:28.

4. The survey of the influence exercised by Solomon on surrounding nations would be incomplete if we were to pass over that which was more directly personal—the fame of his glory and his wisdom. Wherever the ships of Tarshish went, they carried with them the report, losing nothing in its passage, of what their crews had seen and heard. The journey of the queen of Sheba, though from its circumstances the most conspicuous, did not stand alone. 5. Solomon was not a military ruler. His father had left him a wide kingdom, surrounded by neighbors who were nearly all subject or tributary. Only one military expedition seems to have been undertaken, that against Hamath in or-

der to secure the northeastern part of his dominions. Besides this he merely needed to see that his fortifications remained secure, and that the roads to his seaports were open and safe.

IV. *Internal history.*—The first prominent scene in Solomon's reign is one which presents his character in its noblest aspect. God in a vision having offered him the choice of good things he would have, he chose wisdom in preference to riches or honor or long life. The wisdom asked for was given in large measure, and took a varied range. The wide world of nature, animate and inanimate, the lives and characters of men, lay before him, and he took cognizance of all. But the highest wisdom was that wanted for the highest work, for governing and guiding, and the historian hastens to give an illustration of it. The pattern-instance is, in all its circumstances thoroughly oriental. 1 Kings 3:16–28.

His organization of the kingdom was complete. It seems to have, for the time, at least, entirely lost the tribal divisions, and all remains of patriarchal government. The monarchy was despotic. Officers were stationed in various parts of the land to apportion and secure the large amount necessary for the provisioning of the royal household. The army, also, was carefully organized though it had little beyond garrison duty to perform. In reference to the king's finances, the first impression of the facts given us is that of abounding plenty. Large quantities of the precious metals were imported from Ophir and Tarshish. 1 Kings 9:28. All the kings and princes of the subject provinces paid tribute in the form of gifts, in money and in kind, at "a [fixed] rate year by year." 1 Kings 10:25. Monopolies of trade contributed to the king's treasury. 1 Kings 10:28, 29. The total amount thus brought into the treasury in gold, exclusive of all payments in kind, amounted in one year to 666 talents. 1 Kings 10:14. It was hardly possible, however, that any financial system could bear the strain of the king's passion for magnificence. The cost of the temple was, it is true, provided for by David's savings and the offerings of the people; but even while that was building, yet more when it was finished, one structure followed on another with ruinous rapidity. All

the equipment of his court, the "apparel" of his servants, was on the same scale. A body-guard attended him, "threescore valiant men," tallest and handsomest of the sons of Israel. Forty thousand stalls of horses for his chariots, and twelve thousand horsemen, made up the measure of his magnificence. 1 Kings 4:26. As the treasury became empty, taxes multiplied and monopolies became more irksome.

He was a great builder and spent time and money in vast amounts in beautifying his capital. A description of the temple erected by Solomon is given elsewhere. [TEMPLE.] After seven years and a half the work was completed, and the day came to which all Israelites looked back as the culminating glory of their nation. In addition, and probably later in his reign, he built a palace for his queen, the daughter of Pharaoh (1 Kings 7:8); a palace for himself in building which thirteen years were spent (1 Kings 7:1); the house of the forest of Lebanon (1 Kings 7:2); Millo (1 Kings 9:24); aqueducts, cisterns, etc. He also built "store cities," and built or fortified other cities in various parts of his kingdom. (2 Chron. 8:4–6). We cannot ignore the fact that even now there were some darker shades in the picture. He reduced the "strangers" in the land, the remnant of the Canaanite races, to the state of helots, and made their life "bitter with all hard bondage." One hundred and fifty-three thousand, with wives and children in proportion, were torn from their homes and sent off to the quarries and the forests of Lebanon. 1 Kings 5:15; 2 Chron. 2:17, 18.

V. *His literary works.*—Little remains out of the songs, proverbs, treatises, of which the historian speaks. 1 Kings 4:32, 33. *Excerpta* only are given from the three thousand proverbs. Of the thousand and five songs we know absolutely nothing. Two psalms (72 and 127) are attributed to him by their titles. ECCLESIASTES and CANTICLES were formerly attributed to his pen; but modern scholarship has made it quite evident that though he is probably the hero in each case he is in neither case the author.

Solomon's Porch. [PALACE; TEMPLE.]

Solomon's servants, Children of. Ezra 2:55, 58; Neh. 7:57, 60. The persons thus named appear in the lists of the exiles who returned from the captivity. They were the descendants of the Canaanites who were reduced by Solomon to the helot state, and compelled to labor in the king's stone-quarries and in building his palaces and cities. 1 Kings 5:13, 14; 9:20, 21; 2 Chron. 8:7, 8. They appear to have formed a distinct order, inheriting probably the same functions and the same skill as their ancestors.

Solomon's Song. [CANTICLES.]

Solomon, Wisdom of. [WISDOM.]

Son. The term "son" is used in Scripture language to imply almost any kind of descent or succession, as a grandson is called a son. So *ben shânâh,* "son of a year," *i. e.* a year old; *ben kesheth,* "son of a bow," *i. e.* an arrow. The word *bar* (Aramaic for son) is often found in the New Testament in composition, as Bar-timæus.

Soothsayer. [DIVINATION.]

Sop. In eastern lands, where our table utensils are unknown, the meat, with the broth, is brought upon the table in a large dish, and is eaten usually by means of pieces of bread dipped into the common dish. The bread so dipped is called a "sop." It was such a piece of bread dipped in broth that Jesus gave to Judas, John 13:26; and again, in Matt. 26:23, it is said "he that dippeth his hand with me in the dish," *i. e.* to make a sop by dipping a piece of bread into the central dish.

Sop'ater (sŏp'a-tẽr), son of Pyrrhus of Berea, was one of the companions of St. Paul on his return from his third missionary journey. Acts 20:4. (A.D. 57.)

Soph'ereth (sŏf'e-rĕth) (*secretaryship*). "The children of Sophereth" were a family who returned from Babylon with Zerubbabel among the descendants of Solomon's servants. Ezra 2:55; Neh. 7:57.

Sorcerer. [DIVINATION.]

So'rek (sō'rek), **The valley of,** a wady in which lay the residence of Delilah. Judges 16:4. It is *Wady Surâr* which commencing about 13 miles west of Jerusalem near Beeroth (*Bireh*) runs in a generally northwestern direction. The name *Surik* is still borne by a ruin in the vicinity.

Sosip'ater (sṓ-sĭp'a-tẽr) (*saviour of his father*), kinsman or fellow tribesman of St. Paul, Rom. 16:21, is pos-

sibly the same person as Sopater of Berea. (A.D. 57.)

Sos'thenes (sŏs'the-nēṣ) (*of sound strength*), was a Jew at Corinth who was seized and beaten in the presence of Gallio. See Acts 18:12–17. The same or another Sosthenes is named in 1 Cor. 1:1. (A.D. 52.)

So'tai (sō'ta-ī) (*deviator*). The children of Sotai were a family of the descendants of Solomon's servants who returned with Zerubbabel. Ezra 2:55; Neh. 7:57.

South Ra'moth. [RAMATH OF THE SOUTH.]

Sow. [SWINE.]

Sower, Sowing. The operation of sowing with the hand is one of so simple a character as to need little description. The Egyptian paintings furnish many illustrations of the mode in which it was conducted. The sower held the vessel or basket containing the seed in his left hand, Ps. 126:6 (Authorized Version "precious") while with his right he scattered the seed broadcast. The "drawing out" of the seed is noticed, as the most characteristic action of the sower, in Amos 9:13. The sowing season began in October and continued to the end of February, wheat being put in before, and barley after, the beginning of January. The Mosaic law prohibited the sowing of mixed seed. Lev. 19:19; Deut. 22:9.

Spain. Rom. 15:24, 28. The designation in the Old Testament, TARSHISH, representing the *Tartessus* of the Greeks, probably prevailed until the fame of the Roman wars in that country reached the East, when it was superseded by its classical name. The mere intention of St. Paul to visit Spain whether he really did so or not, implies two interesting facts, viz., the establishment of a Christian community in that country, and that this was done by Hellenistic Jews resident there. The early introduction of Christianity into that country is attested by Irenæus and Tertullian.

Span. [WEIGHTS AND MEASURES.]

Sparrow (Heb. *tzippôr,* from a root signifying to "chirp" or "twitter," which appears to be a phonetic representation of the call-note of any passerine (sparrow-like) bird). This Hebrew word occurs upwards of forty times in the Old Testament. In all passages except two it is rendered by the Authorized Version indifferently "bird" or "fowl," and denotes any small bird, both of the sparrow-like species and such as the starling, chaffinch, greenfinch, linnet, goldfinch, corn-

SYRIAN SPARROW.

bunting, song-thrush, etc. Ps. 8 : 8. It may even denote a bird of prey such as the raven and the crow, which are passerine birds. Jer. 12 : 9; Ezek. 39 : 17. In Ps. 84 : 3 and Ps. 102 : 7 it

SPARROWS IN MARKET.

is rendered "sparrow." The Greek στρουθίον (Authorized Version "sparrow") occurs twice in the New Testa-

ment, Matt. 10 : 29; Luke 12 : 6, 7. The birds above mentioned are found in great numbers in Palestine, and are of very little value, selling for the merest trifle, and are thus strikingly used by our Saviour, Matt. 10 : 29, as an illustration of our Father's care for his children. Some consider that the blue thrush (*Petrocossyphus cynaneus*) is probably the bird to which the psalmist alludes in Ps. 102 : 7 as "the sparrow that sitteth alone upon the house-top." It is a solitary bird, eschewing the society of its own species, and rarely more than a pair are seen together. The English tree-sparrow (*Passer montanus*, Linn.) is also very common, and may be seen in numbers on Mount Olivet, and also about the sacred enclosure of the mosque of Omar. This is perhaps the exact species referred to in Ps. 84 : 3. Dr. Thompson, in speaking of the great numbers of the house-sparrows and field-sparrows in Palestine, says: "They are a tame, troublesome and impertinent generation, and nestle just where you do not want them. They stop up your stove- and water-pipes with their rubbish, build in the windows and under the beams of the roof, and would stuff your hat full of stubble in half a day if they found it hanging in a place that exactly suited them."

Spear. [ARMS.]

Spearmen. Acts 23 : 23. These were probably troops so lightly armed as to be able to keep pace on the march with mounted soldiers. By the Greek word used they are distinguished from the legionary soldiers and the cavalry, and in a late passage where the same Greek word is used, they are very clearly distinguished from the archers also.

Spice, Spices. 1. Heb. *bâsam, bôsem,* plural *besamin.* A generic name for the aromatic spices myrrh, cinnamon, cassia and calamus. They were vegetable substances possessing aromatic or pungent qualities. Southern Arabia was their great source. In Cant. 5 : 1, 13; 6 : 2 the word may refer more specifically to balsam or balm of Gilead; the tree which yields this substance is now generally admitted to be the *Balsamodenron opobalsamum.* [BALM.] 2. *Nĕcôth.* Gen. 37 : 25; 43 : 11. The most common explanation is that which refers the word to the Arabic *naka'at*, "the gum obtained from the tragacanth," but some deny that this is the true meaning of the Arabic. 3. *Sammîm*, a general term to denote those aromatic substances which were used in the preparation of the anointing oil, the incense offerings, etc. 4. The spices mentioned as being used by Nicodemus for the preparation of our Lord's body, John 19:39, 40, are "myrrh and aloes," by which latter word must be understood not the aloes of medicine, but the highly-scented wood of the *Aquilaria agallochum*.

Spider. The Hebrew word *'accâbîsh* in Job 8:14, Isa. 59:5 is correctly rendered "spider." But *sěmâmîth* is wrongly translated "spider" in Prov. 30:28; it refers probably to some kind of lizard. "There are many species of spider in Palestine: some which spin webs, like the common garden spider; some which dig subterranean cells and make doors in them, like the well-known trap-door spider of southern Europe; and some which have no web, but chase their prey upon the ground, like the hunting-and the wolf-spider."— *Wood's Bible Animals.*

Spikenard (Heb. *nêrd*) is mentioned twice in the Old Testament, viz. in Cant.

SPIKENARD.

1:12; 4:13, 14. The ointment with which our Lord was anointed as he sat at meat in Simon's house at Bethany consisted of this precious substance, the costliness of which may be inferred from the indignant surprise manifested by some

of the witnesses of the transaction. See Mark 14:3–5; John 12:3, 5. Spikenard, from which the ointment was made, was an aromatic herb of the valerian family (*Nardostachys jatamansi*). It was imported from an early age from Arabia, India and the Far East. It is now found on the slopes of the Himalayas. The costliness of Mary's offering (300 pence = $48) may best be seen from the fact that a penny (denarius, 15 to 17 cents) was in those days the day-wages of a common laborer. Matt: 20:2. In our day this would equal at least $300 and in places much more.

Spinning. The notices of spinning in the Bible are confined to Ex. 35:25, 26; Prov. 31:19; Matt. 6:28. The latter passage implies (according to the Authorized Version) the use of the same instruments which have been in vogue for hand-spinning down to the present day, viz. the distaff and spindle. The term rendered distaff however in Prov. 31:19, means the spindle itself, or the *whorl* of the spindle, a button of circular rim which was affixed to it, and gave steadiness to its circular motion. The "whorl" of the Syrian women was made of amber in the time of Pliny. The spindle was held perpendicularly in the one hand, while the other was employed in drawing out the thread. Spinning was the business of women among the Jews, though both men and women engaged in spinning among the Egyptians.

Sponge, a soft, porous marine substance. Sponges were for a long time supposed to be plants, but are now con-

SPONGE OF COMMERCE.

sidered by the best naturalists to belong to the animal kingdom. Sponge is mentioned only in the New Testament.

Matt. 27:48; Mark 15:36; John 19: 29. The commercial value of the sponge was known from very early times; and although there appears to be no notice of it in the Old Testament, yet it is probable that it was used by the ancient Hebrews, who could readily have obtained it from the Mediterranean, where it was principally found.

Spouse. [MARRIAGE.]

Sta'chys (stā'kĭs), a Christian at Rome, saluted by St. Paul in the Epistle to the Romans. Rom. 16:9. (A.D. 57.)

Stacte (stăk'tē) (Heb. *nâtâf*), the name of one of the sweet spices which composed the holy incense. See Ex. 30:34—the only passage of Scripture in which the word occurs. Some identify the *nâtâf* with the gum of the storax tree (*Styrax officinale*), but all that is positively known is that it sig-nifies an odorous distillation from some plant.

Standards. The Assyrian standards were emblematic of their religion, and were therefore the more valuable as instruments for leading and guiding men in the army. The forms were imitations of animals (1), emblems of deities (2), and symbols of power and wisdom (3). Many of them were crude, but others were highly artistic and of great cost. The Egyptian standards were designed in the same idea as those of the Romans, exhibiting some sacred emblem (5, 6, 8), or a god in the form of an animal (3, 4), a group of victory (7), or the king's name or his portrait as (1), of lower, and (2), of upper, Egypt, or an emblematic sign, as No. 9.

Star of the wise men. [MAGI.]

Stater. [MONEY.]

Steel. In all cases where the word "steel" occurs in the Authorized Version the true rendering of the Hebrew is "copper"; "bronze"; R. V. "brass." Whether the ancient Hebrews were acquainted with steel is not perfectly certain. It has been inferred from a passage in Jeremiah, 15:12, that the "iron from the north" there spoken of denoted a superior kind of metal, hardened in an unusual manner, like the steel obtained from the Chalybes of the Pontus, the ironsmiths of the ancient world. There is, however, a word in Hebrew, *paldâh*, which occurs only in Nah. 2:3, and is there rendered in the A. V. "torches," but which most probably denotes steel or hardened iron and is rendered "steel" in the R. V. It may refer to the flashing scythes of the Assyrian chariots. Steel appears to have been known to the Egyptians. The steel weapons in the tomb of Rameses III., says Wilkinson, are painted blue, the bronze red.

Steph'anas (stĕf'a-năs), a Christian convert of Corinth whose household Paul baptized as the "first-fruits of Achaia." 1 Cor. 1:16; 16:15.

Ste'phen (stē'ven), the first Christian martyr, was the chief of the seven (commonly called Deacons) appointed to rectify the complaints in the early Church of Jerusalem, made by the Hellenistic against the Hebrew Christians.

ASSYRIAN STANDARDS.

EGYPTIAN STANDARDS.

His name signifies "a crown," and he was the first of the Christians to receive the crown of martyrdom.

He was a Hellenist, that is one of the Greek speaking Jews who were dispersed throughout the empire.

Naturally his great work was in the synagogues of the foreign Jews, who were abundant in Jerusalem as their assembling places for Sabbath instruction and daily schools for their children indicate; just as in every great city here we find French and German and Swedish and other national churches and Jewish synagogues.

Stephen is thought by many to have

The source of his power was that he was filled with the Holy Spirit (Acts 6:5).

The fruits of his power were deeds of healing and love, wonderful miracles, "signs," which were God's indorsement of his teachings. It is almost impossible to *prove* that one's teachings are from God, except by deeds that only God can do—miracles of transformed character, or miracles of healing and help.

"A young man of such original genius and special grace that there was nothing he might not have attained to had he been allowed to live. His won-

SCENE OF STEPHEN'S DEATH.
The place where, according to tradition, Stephen was stoned.

been one of the Roman freedmen (the meaning of Libertines in Acts 6:9), a goldsmith from Rome, one of the community of Jews, "which had its origin in the thousands of Jewish captives taken to Rome by Pompey (B.C. 61), and afterward set at liberty and given the rights of Roman citizens."

He was a man of power, the power of faith and character aflame with the Holy Spirit. His eloquence was "logic on fire."

He was full of grace, and of graces, and the beauty of holiness. Grace and *power* do not always go together. Some things are beautiful, but not strong. Some things are strong and not beautiful.

derful openness of mind; his perfect freedom from all the prepossessions, prejudices, and superstitions of his day; his courage, his eloquence, his spotless character; with a certain sweet, and at the same time majestic manner, all combined to set Stephen in the very front rank both of service and of risk. He was already all but the foremost man of his day."—*Alexander Whyte, Bible Characters.* He shot far ahead of his six companions, and far above his particular office. First, he arrests attention by the "great wonders and miracles that he did." Then begins a series of disputations with the Hellenistic Jews of north Africa, Alexandria and Asia Minor. The subject of these disputations is not expressly mentioned; but from what follows it is obvious that he struck into a new vein of teaching, which evidently caused his martyrdom. He was arrested at the instigation of the Hellenistic Jews, and brought before the Sanhedrin. The witnesses contended that he had spoken blasphemous words against Moses, the Temple, and the religious customs of the Jews. His speech in his defence, and his execution by stoning outside the gates of Jerusalem, are related at length in Acts 7. In this speech he shows his knowledge of the political and religious history of his country. He speaks of the Law with the utmost respect. Some have asserted that Stephen must have opposed more strongly than others the ritual of the Jews, thus giving some ground for an accusation against him. But his speech shows no such tendency; his Christian companions would have been among the first to oppose such teaching; while all that would be necessary for a ground for accusation at that time would have been some attack on the "traditions of the elders," such as Jesus himself made. (Matt. 15.) It would seem that, just at the close of his argument, or before its close, Stephen saw a change in the aspect of his judges as if their patience was nearly exhausted. He broke off from his calm address, and turned suddenly upon them in an impassioned attack, which shows that he saw what was in store for him. As he spoke they showed by their faces that their hearts "were being sawn asunder," and they kept gnashing their set teeth against him; but still, though with difficulty, restraining themselves. He, in this last crisis of his fate, turned his face upward to the open sky, and as he gazed the vault of heaven seemed to him to part asunder; and the divine Glory appeared through the rending of the earthly veil—the divine Presence, seated on a throne, and on the right hand the human form of Jesus. Stephen spoke as if to himself, describing the glorious vision. As his judges heard the words, they would listen no longer. They broke into a loud yell; they clapped their hands to their ears; they flew as with one impulse upon him, and dragged him out of the city to the place of execution. Those who took the lead in the execution were

the persons who had taken upon themselves the responsibility of denouncing him. Deut. 17:7; comp. John 8:7. In this instance they were the witnesses who had reported or misreported the words of Stephen. They, according to the custom, stripped themselves; and placed their garments under the keeping of a young man from Tarsus, the future apostle of the Gentiles. [PAUL.] As the first volley of stones burst upon him, Stephen called upon the Master whose human form he had just seen in the heavens, and repeated almost the words with which he himself had given up his life on the cross, "O Lord Jesus, receive my spirit." Another crash of stones brought him on his knees. One loud, piercing cry, answering to the shriek or yell with which his enemies had flown upon him, escaped his dying lips. Again clinging to the spirit of his Master's words, he cried, "Lord, lay not this sin to their charge," and instantly sank upon the ground, and, in the touching language of the narrator, who then uses for the first time the words afterward applied to the departure of all Christians, but here the more remarkable from the bloody scenes in the midst of which death took place, *fell asleep.* His mangled body was buried by "devout men," probably Jews, who, while not followers of Christ, had known and respected Stephen; and felt the iniquity of their leaders in the illegal transaction. The importance of Stephen's career may be briefly summed up under three heads: 1. He was the first great Christian ecclesiastic, "the Archdeacon," as he is called in the eastern Church. 2. He is the first *martyr*—the protomartyr. To him the name "martyr" is first applied. Acts 22:20. 3. Through his death and the consequent scattering of the disciples the gospel was carried to the Gentiles. There is some question how far this was advocated in the teaching of Stephen himself.

Stocks. An instrument of punishment, consisting of two beams, the upper one being movable, with small openings between them, large enough for the ankles of the prisoner. The term "stocks" is applied in the Authorized Version to two different articles, one of which answers rather to our pillory, inasmuch as the body was placed in a bent position, by the confinement of the neck and arms as well as the legs, while the other answers to our "stocks," the feet alone being confined in it. The prophet Jeremiah was confined in the first sort, Jer. 20:2, which appears to have been a common mode of punishment in his day, Jer. 29:26, as the prisons contained a chamber for the special purpose, termed "the house of the pillory." 2 Chron. 16:10 (Authorized Version "prison-house"). The stocks, properly so called, are noticed in Job 13:27; 33:11; Acts 16:24. The term used in Prov. 7:22 (Authorized Version "stocks") more properly means fetters as in R. V.

Sto'ics (stō'ĭks). The Stoics and Epicureans, who are mentioned together in Acts 17:18, represent the two opposite schools of practical philosophy which survived the fall of higher speculation in Greece. The Stoic school was founded by Zeno of Citium in Cyprus, and derived its name from the painted "portico" (stoa) at Athens in which he taught. Zeno was followed by Cleanthes (*cir.* B.C. 260); Cleanthes by Chrysippus (B.C. 280-207), who was regarded as the intellectual founder of the Stoic system. "They regarded God and the world as power and its manifestation, matter being a passive ground in which dwells the divine energy. Their ethics were a protest against moral indifference, and to live in harmony with nature, conformably with reason and the demands of universal good, and in the utmost indifference to pleasure, pain and all external good or evil, was their fundamental maxim."— *American Cyclopædia.* The ethical system of the Stoics has been commonly supposed to have a close connection with Christian morality; but the morality of stoicism is essentially based on pride, that of Christianity on humility; the one upholds individual independence, the other absolute faith in another; the one looks for consolation in the issue of fate, the other in Providence; the one is limited by periods of cosmical ruin, the other is consummated in a personal resurrection. Acts 17:18. But in spite of the fundamental error of stoicism, which lies in a supreme egotism, the teaching of this school gave a wide currency to the noble doctrines of the fatherhood of God, the common bonds of mankind.

the sovereignty of the soul. Among their most prominent representatives were Zeno and Antipater of Tarsus, Epictetus, Seneca and Marcus Aurelius.

Stomacher. The Hebrew word so translated, Isa. 3:24, describes some article of female attire, the character of which is a mere matter of conjecture.

Stones. Besides the ordinary uses to which stones were applied, we may mention that large stones were set up to commemorate any remarkable event. Gen. 28:18; 35:14; 31:45; Josh. 4:9; 1 Sam. 7:12. Such stones were occasionally consecrated by anointing. Gen. 28:18. Heaps of stones were piled up on various occasions, as in token of a treaty, Gen. 31:45, 48, or over the grave of some notorious offender. Josh. 7:26; 8:29; 2 Sam. 18:17. The "white stone" noticed in Rev. 2:17 has been variously regarded. Some of the explanations are the pebble of acquittal used in the Greek courts; the lot cast in elections in Greece; the stone tablets written with the name of a person used in some method of casting lots; the stones in the high priest's breastplate; the tickets presented to the victors at the public games; the custom of writing on stones. Stones are used metaphorically to denote hardness or insensibility, 1 Sam. 25:37; Ezek. 11:19; 36:26, as well as firmness or strength. Gen. 49:24. The members of the Church are called "living stones," as contributing to rear that living temple in which Christ, himself "a living stone," is the chief or head of the corner. Eph. 2:20-22; 1 Pet. 2:4-8.

Stones, Precious. Precious stones are frequently alluded to in the Holy Scriptures; they were known and very highly valued in the earliest times. The art of engraving on precious stones was known from the very earliest times. Gen. 38:18. The twelve stones of the breastplate were engraved each one with the name of one of the tribes. Ex. 28:17-21. It is an undecided question whether the diamond was known to the early nations of antiquity. The Authorized Version gives it as the rendering of the Heb. *yahălôm,* but it is probable that the jasper or some form of onyx is intended. Precious stones are used in Scripture in a figurative sense, to signify value, beauty, durability, etc., in those objects with which they are compared. See Cant.

5:14; Isa. 54:11, 12; Lam. 4:7; Rev. 4:3; 21:11, 21.

Stoning. [PUNISHMENTS.]

Stork (Heb. *chasîdâh*), a large bird of passage of the heron family. The white stork (*Ciconia alba*, Linn.) is one of the largest and most conspicuous of land birds, standing nearly four feet high, the jet black of its wings and its bright-red beak and legs contrasting finely with the pure white of its plumage. Zech. 5:9. In the neighborhood of man it devours readily all kinds of offal and garbage. For this reason, doubtless, it is placed in the list of unclean birds by the Mosaic law.

THE STORK.

Lev. 11:19; Deut. 14:18. The range of the white stork extends over continental Europe, Africa and Asia as far at least as Burmah. The black stork (*Ciconia nigra*, Linn.), though less abundant in places, is scarcely less widely distributed but has a more easterly range than its congener. Both species are very numerous in Palestine. While the black stork is never found about buildings, but prefers marshy places in forests, and breeds on the tops of the loftiest trees, the white stork attaches itself to man, and for the service which it renders in the destruction of reptiles and the removal of offal has been repaid from the earliest times by protection and reverence. The derivation of *chasîdâh* (from *chesed,* "kindness") points to the paternal and filial attachment of which

the stork seems to have been a type among the Hebrews no less than the Greeks and Romans. It was believed that the young repaid the care of their parents by attaching themselves to them for life, and tending them in old age. That the parental attachment of the stork is very strong has been proved on many occasions. Few migratory birds are more punctual to the time of their reappearance than the white stork. The stork has no note, and the only sound it emits is that caused by the sudden snapping of its long mandibles.

Stranger. A "stranger," in the technical sense of the term, may be defined to be a person of foreign, *i. e.* non-Israelitish, extraction resident within the limits of the promised land. He was distinct from the proper "foreigner," inasmuch as the latter still belonged to another country, and would only visit Palestine as a traveller: he was still more distinct from the "nations," or non-Israelite peoples. The term may be compared with our expression "naturalized foreigner." The terms applied to the "stranger" have special reference to the fact of his *residing* in the land. The existence of such a class of persons among the Israelites is easily accounted for. The "mixed multitude" that accompanied them out of Egypt, Ex. 12:38, formed one element; the Canaanitish population, which was never wholly extirpated from their native soil, formed another and a still more important one; captives taken in war formed a third; fugitives, hired servants, merchants, etc., formed a fourth. With the exception of the Moabites and Ammonites, Deut. 23:3, all nations were admissible to the rights of citizenship under certain conditions. The stranger appears to have been eligible to all civil offices, that of king excepted. Deut. 17:15. In regard to religion, it was absolutely necessary that the stranger should not infringe any of the fundamental laws of the Israelitish state. If he were a bondman, he was obliged to submit to circumcision, Ex. 12:44; if he were independent, it was optional with him; but if he remained uncircumcised, he was prohibited from partaking of the Passover, Ex. 12:48, and could not be regarded as a full citizen. Liberty was also given to an uncircumcised stranger in regard to the use of prohibited food. Assuming, however, that the stranger was circumcised, no distinction existed in regard to legal rights between the stranger and the Israelite; the Israelite is enjoined to treat him as a brother. Lev. 19: 34; Deut. 10:19. The chief disability under which he labored was that if he became a bondman the laws regulating the release of slaves did not apply to him. Lev. 25:45, 46. It also appears that the "stranger" formed the class whence the hirelings were drawn; the terms being coupled together in Ex. 12:45; Lev. 22:10; 25:6, 40. The liberal spirit of the Mosaic regulations respecting strangers presents a strong contrast to the rigid exclusiveness of the Jews at the commencement of the Christian era. The growth of this spirit dates from the time of the Babylonish captivity.

Straw. Both wheat and barley straw were used by the ancient Hebrews chiefly as fodder for the horses, cattle and camels. Gen. 24:25; 1 Kings 4: 28; Isa. 11:7; 65:25. There is no intimation that straw was used for litter. It was employed by the Egyptians for making bricks, Ex. 5:7, 16, being chopped up and mixed with the clay to make them more compact and to prevent their cracking. [See BRICK.] The ancient Egyptians reaped their grain close to the ear, and afterward cut the straw close to the ground and laid it by. This was the straw that Pharaoh refused to give to the Israelites, who were therefore compelled to gather it and prepare it for themselves. The hardship consisted in allowing no extra time for this, but requiring the same number of bricks as when this portion of work was done for them. It resulted, however, in the use of a less suitable material than was usually provided, as the Hebrews had no time to search out and select the best for the purpose.

Stream of Egypt occurs once in the Old Testament—Isa. 27:12. [RIVER OF EGYPT.]

Street. The streets of a modern Oriental town present a great contrast to those with which we are familiar, being generally narrow, tortuous and gloomy, even in the best towns. Their character is mainly fixed by the climate and the style of architecture, the narrowness being due to the extreme heat,

and the gloominess to the circumstance of the windows looking for the most part into the inner court. The street called "Straight," in Damascus, Acts 9:11, was an exception to the rule of narrowness: it was a noble thoroughfare, one hundred feet wide, divided in the Roman age by colonnades into three avenues, the central one for foot passengers, the side passages for vehicles and horsemen going in different directions. The shops and warehouses were probably collected together into bazaars in ancient as in modern times. Jer. 37:21. That streets were generally unpaved may be inferred from the notices of the pavement laid by Herod the Great at Antioch, and by Herod Agrippa II, at Jerusalem. (Herodotus: Ant.) Hence pavement forms one of the peculiar features of the ideal Jerusalem. Rev. 21:21. Each street and bazaar in a modern town is locked up at night; the same custom appears to have prevailed in ancient times. Cant. 3:3.

Stripes. [PUNISHMENTS.]

Su'ah (sū'ah) (*sweepings*), son of Zophah, an Asherite. 1 Chron. 7:36.

Suc'coth (sŭk'koth) (*booths*). 1. An ancient town, first heard of in the account of the homeward journey of Jacob from Padan-aram. Gen. 33:17. The name is derived from the fact of Jacob's having there put up "booths" (*succôth*) for his cattle, as well as a house for himself. From the itinerary of Jacob's return it seems that Succoth lay between Peniel, near the ford of the torrent Jabbok, and Shechem. Comp. Gen. 32:30 and 33:18. In accordance with this is the mention of Succoth in the narrative of Gideon's pursuit of Zebah and Zalmunna. Judges 8:5-17. It would appear from this passage that it lay east of the Jordan, which is corroborated by the fact that it was allotted to the tribe of Gad. Josh. 13:27. Succoth is named once again after this—in 1 Kings 7:46; 2 Chron. 4:17—as marking the spot at which the brass foundries were placed for casting the metal work of the temple. *Tell Deir Alla,* one mile north of the Jabbok, and *Sakut* about 10 miles south of Beisan, west of the Jordan have been proposed, but neither answers the conditions.

2. The first camping-place of the Israelites when they left Egypt. Ex. 12:

37; 13:20; Num. 33:5, 6. This place was apparently reached at the close of the first day's march. Egyptologists consider it the equivalent of the Egyptian word *Thuku*, the name of the region of which Pithom was the capital.

Suc'coth-be'noth (sŭk'koth-bē'noth) occurs only in 2 Kings 17:30. It has generally been supposed that this term is pure Hebrew, and signifies the *tents of daughters;* which some explain as " the booths in which the daughters of the Babylonians prostituted themselves in honor of their idol," others as " small tabernacles in which were contained images of female deities." Many scholars believe that Succoth-benoth represents the Chaldæan goddess *Zarpanit,* the wife of Merodach, who was especially worshipped at Babylon.

Su'chathites (sū'kath-ītes), one of the families of scribes at Jabez. 1 Chron. 2:55.

Suk'kiim (sŭk'kĭ-ĭm) (*booth-dwellers*), a nation mentioned 2 Chron. 12:3 with the Lubim and Cushim as supplying part of the army which came with Shishak out of Egypt when he invaded Judah. The Sukkiim may correspond to some one of the shepherd or wandering races mentioned on the Egyptian monuments.

Sun. In the history of the creation the sun is described as the " greater light," in contradistinction to the moon, the " lesser light," in conjunction with which it was to serve " for signs, and for seasons, and for days, and for years," while its special office was " to rule the day." Gen. 1:14–16. The " signs " referred to were probably such extraordinary phenomena as eclipses, which were regarded as conveying premonitions of coming events. Jer. 10:2; Matt. 24:29 with Luke 21:25. The joint influence assigned to the sun and moon in deciding the " seasons," both for agricultural operations and for religious festivals, and also in regulating the length and subdivisions of the " years," correctly describes the combination of the lunar and solar year which prevailed at all events subsequent to the Mosaic period. Sunrise and sunset are the only defined points of time in the absence of artificial contrivances for telling the hour of the day. Between these two points the Jews recognized three periods, viz., when the sun became hot. about 9 ᴀ ᴍ.,

1 Sam. 11:9; Neh. 7:3; the double light, or noon, Gen. 43:16; 2 Sam. 4:5; and " the cool of the day," shortly before sunset. Gen. 3:8. The sun also served to fix the quarters of the hemisphere, east, west, north and south, which were represented respectively by the rising sun, the setting sun, Isa. 45:6; Ps. 50:1, the dark quarter, Gen. 13:14; Joel 2:20, and the brilliant quarter, Deut. 33:23; Job 37:17; Ezek. 40:24; or otherwise by their position relative to a person facing the rising sun—before, behind, on the left hand and on the right hand. Job 23:8, 9.

The worship of the sun, as the most prominent and powerful agent in the kingdom of nature, was widely diffused throughout the countries adjacent to Palestine. The Arabians appear to have paid direct worship to it without the intervention of any statue or symbol, Job 31:26, 27, and this simple style of worship was probably familiar to the ancestors of the Jews in Chaldæa and Mesopotamia. The Hebrews must have been well acquainted with the idolatrous worship of the sun during the captivity in Egypt, both from the contiguity of On, the chief seat of the worship of the sun, as implied in the name itself (On being the equivalent of the Hebrew Beth-shemesh, " house of the sun," Jer. 43:13), and also from the connection between Joseph and Potipherah (" he who belongs to Ra ") the priest of On. Gen. 41:45. After their removal to Canaan, the Hebrews came in contact with various forms of idolatry which originated in the worship of the sun; such as the Baal of the Phœnicians, the Molech or Milcom of the Ammonites, and the Hadad of the Syrians. The importance attached to the worship of the sun by the Jewish kings may be inferred from the fact that the horses sacred to the sun were stalled within the precincts of the temple. 2 Kings 23:11. In the metaphorical language of Scripture the sun is emblematic of the law of God, Ps. 19:5–7, of the cheering presence of God, Ps. 84:11, of the person of the Saviour, John 1:9; Mal. 4:2, and of the glory and purity of heavenly beings. Rev. 1:16; 10:1; 12:1.

Suretyship. In the entire absence of commerce the law laid down no rules on the subject of suretyship; but it is evident that in the time of Solomon commercial dealings had become so multiplied that suretyship in the commercial sense was common. Prov. 6: 1; 11:15; 17:18; 20:16; 22:26; 27: 13. But in older times the notion of one man becoming a surety for a service to be discharged by another was in full force. See Gen. 44:32. The surety of course became liable for his client's debts in case of his failure, in which lay the danger warned against.

Su'sa (sū'sà). [SHUSHAN.]

Su'sanchites (sụ'san-kītes) is found once only—in Ezra 4:9. It refers to the inhabitants of Susa, or Shushan, who were among the colonists settled by Osnappar, or Asshurbanipal, in Samaria.

Susan'na (su-zăn'nà) (*a lily*). 1. The heroine of the story of the Judgment of Daniel. The book which gives an account of her life is also called "The history of Susanna," and is one of the apocryphal books of the Bible.
2. One of the women who ministered to the Lord. Luke 8:3. (A.D. 28–30.)

Su'si (sū'sī), the father of Gaddi the Manassite spy. Num. 13:11.

Swallow (Heb. *dĕrôr* in Ps. 84:3, Prov. 26:2; Heb. *'âgûr* in Isa. 38:14, Jer. 8:7, which is translated in the R. V. "crane." [CRANE], and *Sus,* Isa.

SWALLOW.

38:14; Jer. 8:7. R. V., which in A. V. is translated "crane." The rendering of the Authorized Version for *dĕrôr* seems correct. The characters ascribed in the passages where the names occur are strictly applicable to the swallow, viz., its swiftness of flight, its nesting in the buildings of the temple, its mournful, garrulous note, and its regular migrations, shared indeed in common with several others. Many species of swallow occur in Palestine. All those common in England are found.

Swan (Heb. *tinshemeth*), thus rendered by the Authorized Version in Lev. 11:18; Deut. 14:16, where it occurs in the list of unclean birds. But either of the renderings "porphyrio" (purple water-hen) or "ibis" is more probable. Neither of these birds occurs elsewhere in the catalogue; both would be familiar to residents in Egypt, and the original seems to point to some water-fowl. The purple water-hen is allied to our corn-crake and water-hen, and is the largest and most beautiful of the family *Rallidæ*. It frequents marshes and the sedge by the banks of rivers in all the countries bordering on the Mediterranean, and is abundant in lower Egypt.

Swearing. [OATH.]

Sweat, Bloody. One of the physical phenomena attending our Lord's agony in the garden of Gethsemane is described by St. Luke, Luke 22:44: "His sweat was as it were great drops (lit. *clots*) of blood falling down to the ground." It used to be considered as a real exudation of blood, and examples quoted of similar cases in ancient and modern times, arising from violent mental emotion. None of the examples, however, are authenticated, and modern authorities generally prefer to consider it a simile "as it were" drops of blood.

Swine (Heb. *chăzîr*). The flesh of swine was forbidden as food by the Levitical law, Lev. 11:7; Deut. 14:8; the abhorrence which the Jews as a nation had of it may be inferred from Isa. 65:4 and 2 Macc. 6:18, 19. No other reason for the command to abstain from swine's flesh is given in the law of Moses beyond the general one which forbade any of the mammalia as food which did not literally fulfill the terms of the definition of a "clean animal," viz., that it was to be a cloven-footed ruminant. It is, however, probable that dietetical considerations may have influenced Moses in his prohibition of swine's flesh: it is generally believed that its use in hot countries is liable to induce cutaneous disorders; hence in a people liable to leprosy the necessity for the observance of a strict rule. Although the Jews did not breed swine during the greater period of their existence as a nation, there can be little doubt that the heathen nations of Palestine used the flesh as food. At the time of our Lord's ministry it would appear that the Jews occasionally violated the law of Moses with regard to swine's flesh. Whether "the herd of swine" into which the devils were allowed to enter, Matt. 8:32; Mark 5:13, were the property of the Jewish or

THE WILD BOAR.

of the Gentile (Greek) inhabitants of Gadara does not appear from the sacred narrative. The Greeks esteemed swine's flesh as food. The wild boar of the wood, Ps. 80:13, is the common *Sus scrofa*, which is frequently met with in the woody parts of Palestine, especially in Mount Tabor.

Sword. [ARMS.]

Sycamine tree is mentioned only in Luke 17:6. From the fact that Luke 17:6; 19:4 uses both names "Sycamine" and "Sycomore," we infer that he intended to distinguish between them, though the same *Hebrew* words are used for both. The sycamine is the mulberry tree (*Morus*). Both black and white mulberry trees are common in Syria and Palestine.

Sycamore, properly as in R. V. "Sycomore," not at all the same tree as the "Sycamore" of England and America. (Heb. *shikmâh*). Although it may be admitted that the *sycamine* is properly, and in Luke 17:6, the *mulberry,* and the *sycomore* the *fig-mulberry,* or sycomore-fig (*Ficus sycomorus*), yet the latter is the tree generally referred to in the Old Testament, and called by the Septuagint sycamine,

as 1 Kings 10:27; 1 Chron. 27:28; Ps. 78:47; Amos 7:14. The sycomore, or fig-mulberry, is in Egypt and Palestine a tree of great importance and very extensive use. It attains the size of a walnut tree, has wide-spreading branches, and affords a delightful shade. On this account it is frequently planted by the waysides. Its leaves are heart-shaped, downy on the under side, and fragrant. The fruit grows directly from the trunk itself on little sprigs, and in clusters like the grape. To make it eatable, each fruit, three or four days before gathering, must, it used to be said, be punctured with a sharp instrument or the finger-nail, this being, it was supposed, the original employment of the prophet Amos. Amos 7:14. But this is not done to-day, the fruit being plucked and eaten when ripe without preparation. So great was the value of these trees that David appointed for them in his kingdom a special overseer, as he did for the olives, 1 Chron. 27:28; and it is mentioned as one of the heaviest of Egypt's calamities that her sycomores were destroyed by hailstones. Ps. 78:47. Its value lay chiefly in its use as timber.

Sy'char (sī'kär), a place named only in John 4:5. Sychar was either a name applied to the town of Shechem or it was an independent place. The latter of these alternatives is now accepted by the majority of scholars, it being identified with *Askar* near Jacob's well.

Sy'chem (sī'kem), the Greek form of the word Shechem. It occurs in Acts 7:16 only. [SHECHEM.]

Sye'ne (sȳ-e'ne), properly Seveneh, a town of Egypt, on the frontier of Cush or Ethiopia, Ezek. 29:10, 30:6, represented by the modern *Assouan.*

Sym'eon (sȳm'e-ŏn). The Jewish form of the name SIMEON, used in the Revised Version.

Synagogue. 1. *History.*—The word *synagogue* (συναγωγή), which means a "congregation," is used in the New Testament to signify a recognized place of worship. A knowledge of the history and worship of the synagogues is of great importance, since they are the characteristic institution of the later phase of Judaism. The first clear mention of them is during the exile, in the abeyance of the temple-worship, but there are some reasons to think that they were in existence centuries earlier, though they doubtless received their full development on the return of the Jews from captivity. The whole history of Ezra presupposes the habit of solemn, probably of periodic, meetings. Ezra 8:15; Neh. 8:2; 9:1; Zech. 7:5. After the Maccabæan struggle for independence, we find almost every town or village had its one or more synagogues. Where the Jews were not in sufficient numbers to be able to erect and fill a

RUINS OF ANCIENT SYNAGOGUE
At Kefr Birim, in Galilee.

building, there was the *proseucha* (προσευχή), or place of prayer, sometimes open, sometimes covered in, commonly by a running stream or on the seashore, in which devout Jews and proselytes met to worship, and perhaps to read. Acts 16:13; Juven. *Sat.* iii. 296. It is hardly possible to overestimate the influence of the system thus developed. To it we may ascribe the tenacity with which, after the Maccabæan struggle, the Jews adhered to the religion of their fathers, and never again relapsed into idolatry.

2. *Structure.*—The size of a synagogue varied with the population. Its position was, however, determinate. It stood, if possible, on the highest ground, in or near the city to which it belonged. There is an early tradition that the worshipper must face Jerusalem, and that in consequence the synagogue was so constructed that the worshippers, as they entered and as they prayed, looked toward it. In Galilee, where several ruins have been found, the buildings ran north and south, with three doors in the entrance or south end. They were divided by rows of columns into three or five aisles, and some had a portico in front. The building was commonly erected at the cost of the district. Sometimes it was built by a rich Jew, or even, as in Luke 7:5, by a friendly proselyte. In the internal arrangement of the synagogue we trace an obvious analogy to the type of the tabernacle. At the upper end stood the chest which, like the older and more sacred ark, contained the Book of the Law. It gave to that end the name and character of a sanctuary. This part of the synagogue was naturally the place of honor. Here were the " chief seats," for which Pharisees and scribes strove so eagerly, Matt. 23:6, and to which the wealthy and honored worshipper was invited. James 2:2, 3. Here too, in front of the ark, still reproducing the type of the tabernacle, was, at least in some cases, the eight-branched lamp, lighted only on the greater festivals. Besides this there was one lamp kept burning perpetually. More toward the middle of the building was a raised platform, on which several persons could stand at once, and in the middle of this rose a pulpit, in which the reader stood to read the lesson or sat down to teach. In later times the congregation was divided, men on one side, women on the other, a low partition, five or six feet high, running between them. The arrangements of modern synagogues, for many centuries, have made the separation more complete by placing the women in low side-galleries, screened off by lattice-work.

3. *Officers.*—In smaller towns there was often but one rabbi. Where a fuller organization was possible, there was a college of elders, Luke 7:3, pre-

sided over by one who was "the chief of the synagogue," who had the responsibility of maintaining order, deciding on the order of public service, etc. Luke 8: 41, 49; 13: 14; Acts 18: 8, 17. The *chazzân* or "minister" of the synagogue, Luke 4: 20, had duties of a lower kind, resembling those of the Christian deacon or sub-deacon. He was to open the doors and to prepare the building for service. But he often was the one who read the Scriptures, and was either the schoolmaster of the synagogue school or his assistant. Besides these there were ten men attached to every synagogue, known as the *batlanim* (= *otiosi*). They were supposed to be men of leisure, not obliged to labor for their livelihood, able therefore to attend the week-day as well as the Sabbath services.

4. *Worship.*—It will be enough, in this place, to notice in what way the ritual, no less than the organization, was connected with the facts of the New Testament history, and with the life and order of the Christian Church. From the synagogue came the use of fixed forms of prayer. To that the first disciples had been accustomed from their youth. They had asked their Master to give them a distinctive one, and he had complied with their request, Luke 11: 1, as the Baptist had done before for his disciples, as every rabbi did for his. "Moses" was "read in the synagogues every Sabbath day," Acts 15: 21, the whole Pentateuch being read consecutively, so as to be completed, in one year. The writings of the prophets were read as second lessons in a corresponding order. They were followed by the *derash,* Acts 13: 15, the exposition, the sermon of the synagogue. The solemn days of the synagogue were the second, the fifth and the seventh, the last or Sabbath being the conclusion of the whole. The transfer of the sanctity of the Sabbath to the Lord's day involved a corresponding change in the order of the week, and the first, the fourth and the sixth became to the Christian society what the other days had been to the Jewish. From the synagogue, lastly, come many less conspicuous practices, which meet us in the liturgical life of the first three centuries: Ablution, entire or partial, before entering the place of meeting, John 13: 1-15; Heb. 10: 22;

standing, and not kneeling, as the attitude of prayer, Luke 18: 11; the arms stretched out; the face turned toward the east; the responsive amen of the congregation to the prayers and benedictions of the elders. 1 Cor. 14: 16.

5. *The Synagogue school.*—The synagogue was the place where the children received the first rudiments of such education as they had,—principally instruction in the law and other Scriptures. In the time of Jesus every synagogue probably had its school, and every boy began there his education.

6. *Judicial functions.*—The language of the New Testament shows that the officers of the synagogue exercised in certain cases a judicial power. It is not quite so easy, however, to define the nature of the tribunal and the precise limits of its jurisdiction. In two of the passages referred to—Matt. 10: 17; Mark 13: 9—they are carefully distinguished from the councils. It seems probable that the council was the larger tribunal of twenty-three, which sat in every city, and that under the term synagogue we are to understand a smaller court, probably that of the ten judges mentioned in the Talmud. Here also we trace the outline of a Christian institution. The Church, either by itself or by appointed delegates, was to act as a court of arbitration in all disputes among its members. The elders of the church were not, however, to descend to the trivial disputes of daily life. For the elders, as for those of the synagogue, were reserved the graver offences against religion and morals.

Synagogue, The Great. On the return of the Jews from Babylon, a great council was appointed, according to rabbinic tradition, to reorganize the religious life of the people. It consisted of 120 members, and these were known as the men of the Great Synagogue, the successors of the prophets, themselves, in their turn, succeeded by scribes prominent, individually, as teachers. Ezra was recognized as president. Their aim was to restore again the *crown,* or *glory,* of Israel. To this end they collected all the sacred writings of the former ages and their own, and so completed the canon of the Old Testament. They instituted the feast of Purim, organized the ritual of the synagogue, and gave their sanction to the *Shemôneh Esrêh,* the eighteen solemn benedictions in it. Much of this is evidently uncertain. The absence of any historical mention of such a body, not only in the Old Testament and the Apocrypha, but in Josephus, Philo, etc., has led some critics to reject the whole statement as a rabbinic invention. The narrative of Neh. 8:13 clearly implies the existence of a body of men acting as councillors under the presidency of Ezra; and these may have been an assembly of delegates from all provincial synagogues—a synod of the national Church.

Syn'tyche (sĭn'tĭ-kē) (*fortunate*), a female member of the church of Philippi whom Paul exhorts to become reconciled with another, EUODIAS. Philip. 4:2, 3. (A.D. 60.)

Syr'acuse (sĭr'a-kūse), the celebrated city on the eastern coast of Sicily. According to one authority, the city was the largest and richest that the Greeks possessed in any part of the world, being 22 miles in circumference. St. Paul arrived thither in an Alexandrian ship from Melita, on his voyage to Rome. Acts 28:12. The site of Syracuse rendered it a convenient place for the African grain ships to touch at, for the harbor was an excellent one, and the fountain Arethusa in the island furnished an unfailing supply of excellent water. The city is still called *Siracusa* but is much reduced in size and importance.

Syr'ia (sĭr'ĭ-à) is the term used throughout our version for the Hebrew *Aram,* as well as for the Greek Συρία. The word was first used by Herodotus. In Homer's list the name Ἀριμοι, Aramæans, is used. It is difficult to fix the limits of Syria, partly because of its loose use in Herodotus and Xenophon, who may have been misled by its likeness to *Assyria,* as Herodotus states them to have been of the same race (7:63). Syria as usually used by Strabo, Pliny and Ptolemy, indicates a country bounded by Amanus and Taurus on the north, by the Euphrates on the east, by the Arabian desert on the south and by the Mediterranean on the west. A more special use of the term "Syria," which still prevails, confined it to that part of the wider area which lies north of Palestine, and excluding Phœnicia. This tract is about 300 miles long from north to south, and from 50 to 150 miles broad. It contains an area of about 30,000 square miles.

General physical features.—The general character of the tract is mountainous, as the Hebrew name Aram (from a root signifying "height") sufficiently implies. The most fertile and valuable tract of Syria is the long valley intervening between Lebanon and Anti-Lebanon. Of the various mountain ranges of Syria, Lebanon possesses the greatest interest. It extends from the mouth of the Litany to *Arka,* a distance of nearly 100 miles. Anti-Libanus, as the name implies, stands over against Lebanon, running in the same direction, *i. e.* nearly north and south, and extending the same length. [LEBANON.] The principal rivers of Syria are the Litany and the Orontes. The Litany springs from a small lake situated in the middle of the Cœle-Syrian valley, about six miles to the southwest of Baalbek. It enters the sea about five miles north of Tyre. The source of the Orontes is but about 15 miles from that of the Litany. Its modern name is the *Nahr-el-Asi,* or "rebel stream," an appellation given to it on account of its violence and impetuosity in many parts of its course. The chief cities of Syria mentioned in the Bible are Damascus and Antioch.

History.—For the history during the earliest periods exclusively and in great measure for those of later periods we must rely on the accounts of neighboring peoples who conquered the country. The population was a mixture of Semites and "Hittites," with sometimes one predominating and sometimes the other. In the period before the settlement of the Israelites in Palestine, after the wilderness wandering the only Syrian town whose existence we find distinctly marked is Damascus, Gen. 14:15; 15:2, which appears to have been already a place of some importance. Next to Damascus must be placed Hamath. Num. 13:21; 34:8. Syria at this time, and for many centuries afterward, seems to have been broken up into a number of petty kingdoms, or more correctly, tribes. Some of these petty peoples came into contact with Israel in the days of Saul and later kings. 1 Sam. 14:47; 2 Sam. 8:3; 10:6, 16. [ZOBAH.] The kingdom of Solomon seems to have included a portion at least of the country Syria, north and

42

east of Palestine. 1 Kings 4:21. In Damascus, an independent kingdom was set up by Rezon, a native of Zobah. 1 Kings 11:23-25. The northern kingdom never seems to have had any control over the districts of Syria outside of Palestine. The two peoples waged war intermittently during the entire existence of the kingdom of Israel. During these periods Damascus and Hamath,—or Aram-Damascus and Aram-Zobah—were by far the strongest among the Syrian peoples. Syria was rarely free from the domination of some one of the "great powers" of the ancient world. It was tributary to Egypt, as we find in the Tel-el-Amarna letters; Babylonian and Assyrian records speak of conquests and tribute from one or all of its tribes. In B.C. 333 it submitted to Alexander without a struggle. Upon the death of Alexander, Syria became, for the first time, the head of a great kingdom. On the division of the provinces among his generals, B.C. 321, Seleucus Nicator received Mesopotamia and Syria. The city of Antioch was begun in B.C. 300, and, being finished in a few years, was made the capital of Seleucus' kingdom. The country grew rich with the wealth which now flowed into it on all sides.

Syria was added to the Roman empire by Pompey, B.C. 64, and was formed into a Roman province, under governors resident at Antioch. After the formal division of the provinces between Augustus and the senate, Syria, being from its exposed situation among the *provinciæ principis,* was ruled by legates, who were of consular rank (*consulares*) and bore severally the full title of "Legatus Augusti pro prætore." Judea occupied a peculiar position; a special procurator was therefore appointed to rule it, who was subordinate to the governor of Syria, but within his own province had the power of a legatus. On the fall of Jerusalem it was separated from Syria, and made a distinct province under an imperial legate. A little earlier, perhaps A.D. 42, Christianity had begun to spread into Syria, partly by means of those "scattered" at the time of Stephen's persecution, Acts 11:19, partly by the exertions of St. Paul. Gal. 1:21. The Syrian Church soon grew to be one of the most flourishing. Acts 13:1; 15:23, 35, 41, etc. Syria remained under Roman and Byzantine rule till A.D. 634, when it was overrun by the Mohammedans; after which it was for many years the scene of fierce contests, and was finally subjugated by the Turks, A.D. 1516, under whose rule it remained for about four hundred years, until the World War.

Sy′ro-phœni′cian (sī-ro-fē-nĭ′shĭ-ăn) occurs only in Mark 7:26. The word denoted either a Syrian resident in Phœnicia proper, or a Phœnician of Syria in distinction from one in the Carthaginian colony of Phœnicia. The former is the more likely explanation.

Syr′tis (sўr′tĭs), **The,** Acts 27:17; in the Revised Version in place of "quicksands" in the Authorized Version. It was the well-known *Syrtis Major,* the terror of all Mediterranean sailors. "It is a dangerous shallow on the coast of Africa, between Tripoli and Barca, southwest of the island of Crete." The other Syrtis, *Syrtis Minor,* was too far west to be feared by Paul's fellow voyagers. [QUICKSANDS.]

T

Ta'anach (tā'a-năk), an ancient Canaanitish city whose king is enumerated among the thirty-one kings conquered by Joshua. Josh. 12:21. It came into the half tribe of Manasseh, Josh. 17:11; 21:25; 1 Chron. 7:29, and was bestowed on the Kohathite Levites. Josh. 21:25. Taanach is almost always named in company with Megiddo, and they were evidently the chief towns of that fine rich district which forms the western portion of the great plain of Esdraelon. 1 Kings 4:12. It is still called *Ta'annuk*, and stands about four miles southeast of *Lejjûn* and 7 miles southwest of Jezreel.

Ta'anath=shi'loh (tā'a-năth-shī'lō) (*approach to Shiloh*), a place named once only—Josh. 16:6—as one of the landmarks of the boundary of Ephraim. It is the ruin *Tana* about 7 miles southeast of *Nablus*.

Tab'baoth (tăb'ba-oth) (*rings*). The children of Tabbaoth were a family of Nethinim who returned with Zerubbabel. Ezra 2:43; Neh. 7:46.

Tab'bath (tab'băth), a place mentioned only in Judges 7:22, in describing the flight of the Midianite host after Gideon's night attack. It was in the vicinity of Abel-Meholah, probably not far from the spot where the Samaritan hills approach the Jordan; but no trace of its site has been found.

Ta'beal (tā'be-al) (*God is good*). A man whose son went with the armies of Pekah, the king of Israel, and Rezin of Damascus, when they invaded Judah in the time of Ahaz. The son was to have been set up as puppet king of Jerusalem if the allies had succeeded in capturing the city. Isa. 7:6.

Ta'beel (tā'be-el) (*God is good*), an officer of the Persian government in Samaria in the reign of Artaxerxes. Ezra 4:7. His name appears to indicate that he was a Syrian.

Tab'erah (tăb'e-rah), the name of a place in the wilderness of Paran. Num.

11:3; Deut. 9:22. It has not been identified.

Tabering, an obsolete English word used in the Authorized Version of Nahum 2:7. The Hebrew word connects itself with *töph,* "a timbrel." The Authorized Version reproduces the original idea. The "tabour" or "tabor" was a musical instrument of the drum type, which with the pipe formed the band of a country village. To "tabour," accordingly, is to beat with loud strokes, as men beat upon such an instrument.

Tabernacle. The tabernacle was the *tent of Jehovah,* called by the same name as the tents of the people in the midst of which it stood. It was also called the *Sanctuary* and the *Tabernacle of the congregation,* A. V., better, the *Tent of meeting,* the dwelling place of God, where he manifests himself to his people. The first ordinances given to Moses, after the proclamation of the outline of the law from Sinai, related to the ordering of the tabernacle, its furniture and its service, as the type which was to be followed when the people came to their own home and "found a place" for the abode of God. During the forty days of Moses' first retirement with God in Sinai, an exact pattern of the whole was shown him, and all was made according to it. Ex. 25:9, 40; 26:30; 39:32, 42, 43; Num. 8:4; Acts 7:44; Heb. 8:5. The description of this plan is preceded by an account of the freewill offerings which the children of Israel were to be asked to make for its execution.

There are not a few difficulties in the way of obtaining an accurate idea of the form and construction of the tabernacle, from the descriptions given; as is usual in all attempts to realize a description. Even the form of so simple a thing as the golden candlestick it was impossible to copy in brass from the description given till the model was found in the triumphal arch of Titus at

659

TAB 660 **TAB**

Rome pictured among the treasures he brought from Jerusalem after its destruction.

Those who wish to enter upon this discussion can consult Hastings' *Bible Dictionary*, article, "Tabernacle."

THE COURT OF THE TABERNACLE, in which the tabernacle itself stood, was an oblong space, 100 cubits by 50 (*i. e.* 150 feet by 75), equal to two squares of 50 cubits each, having its longer axis east and west, with its front to the east. It was enclosed by a screen of pillars and linen curtains.

Pillars 5 cubits (7½ feet) high were placed in bronze sockets 5 cubits apart, twenty each on the north and south sides, and ten on the east and west.

On these pillars were hung long white curtains of fine-twined linen of a uniform height of 5 cubits; two of them were 100 cubits long; one 50 cubits for the west end; two were 15 cubits for the extremities of the east end, while the intervening 20 cubits were closed by six portieres of fine-twined linen, embroidered in gorgeous shades of purple on a white ground, for the entrance. The pillars were kept in position by cords fastened to bronze pins stuck in the ground.

We can understand this best by the accompanying diagram; similar to one given in Hastings' *Bible Dictionary*. This diagram will also show the situation and arrangement of the courts, the tabernacle and the furnishings for worship.

THE TABERNACLE ITSELF, or TENT OF MEETING.—This was a tent with wooden walls, 30 cubits (45 feet) long by 10 cubits (15 feet) wide; situated in the rear square of the court, with its front entrance on the middle dividing line between the two squares of the court.

The materials were—(*a*) Metals: gold, silver and brass. (*b*) Textile fabrics: blue, purple, scarlet and fine (white) linen, for the production of which Egypt was celebrated; also a fabric of goat's hair, the produce of their own flocks. (*c*) Skins: of the ram, dyed red, and of the badger. (*d*) Wood: the shittim wood, the timber of the wild acacia of the desert itself, the tree of the "burning bush." (*e*) Oil, spices and incense for anointing the priests and burning in the tabernacle. (*f*) Gems: onyx stones and the precious

stones for the breastplate of the high priest. The people gave jewels, and plates of gold and silver and brass, wood, skins, hair and linen; the women wove; the rulers offered precious stones, oil, spices and incense; and the artists soon had more than they needed. Ex. 25: 1-8; 35: 4-29; 36: 5-7.

The walls were made of boards 15 feet high and 27 inches wide; either solid boards, or, as Dr. Kennedy thinks, a framework of that width, set into

PLAN OF THE TABERNACLE.
Scale 1-32 inch to a cubit.
T—Tabernacle.
A—Brazen altar.
L—Laver in the court.
G—Golden candlestick.
S—Table of shewbread.
I—Golden altar of incense in Holy Place.
C, C—Curtains around the court.
E—Entrance to the court.
a—Ark in the Holy of Holies.

silver bases. These were held together by three series of rods, one at the top, one at the middle, and one near the base.

A Large Tent was placed over this Tent of Meeting, probably running over

TAB 661 TAB

a ridge-pole and held in place by strong cords, something like a huge A tent, as an additional protection against the weather.

Inside, the tent was adorned by a curtain of fine linen, blue and purple (crimson) and scarlet, woven with figures of cherubim. This curtain, according to Professor Strong, hung vertically upon the walls; others think it was an inner roof, and Colton considers it a special roof and wall covering for the Holy of Holies. "The veil," a curtain of the same material, hung from four pillars, divided the inner space into two apartments. The outer, toward the entrance, was the Holy Place, where a priest entered daily to serve the table, the altar of incense, and the candlestick. It was thirty feet long. The inner, toward the west, was the Most Holy Place, entered only by the high priest, and by him only once a year. It contained the ark, and was a cube, fifteen feet each way.

The Situation. When the tribes were encamped, the tabernacle was the central point of the encampment in a huge square; three tribes were on the north, three on the south, three east, and three west. Within this square was another occupied by the priests and Levites.

Within.—In the centre of the square court in front of the tent was the great brazen altar for burnt sacrifice. Moving toward the tent, we come to the great laver, 15 feet in front of its portiere entrance.

Entering the tent, we find the golden candlestick, the only source of light, for there were no windows, the table of shewbread, and the golden altar of incense.

In the Holy of Holies was only the ark of the testimony or witness containing the tables of the law.

THE RELIGIOUS MEANING.—At all times there is need of visible expressions and manifestations of the unseen spiritual things to help even the most educated, cultured, and holy men to realize the unseen God and character and life. So through nature we understand God and keep him in mind, as nearly all we know of the sun is revealed to us by the reflection of its rays on material particles in the air. So the institutions of religion are "the shadow of heavenly things" (Heb. 8:5). Still more were these institutions necessary in the early

education of man. So the great churches and cathedrals of the ages when few could read and write are filled with pictures and carvings of the Bible story.

Thus the tabernacle was the means of training the people who had just come out of Egypt in religious truth and religious life. There is no place for the tabernacle except under Moses at the very beginning of Jewish national history.

The tabernacle and its furnishings express the progress of man toward God, and the aids He has given them to come to him.

It may be easier to see the truth if we start where an Israelite must start, and where all must start in reaching the final goal of the Holy of Holies.

1. From without we enter the courts of the Lord where we come under the influence of religious teaching and companionship.

2. We first go to the great altar of sacrifice, a symbol of sacrifice for sin, and the forgiveness of God.

3. We next come to the laver, the symbol of the washing of regeneration, the cleansing from sin. "Wash me and I shall be whiter than snow," fitted to enter the Tabernacle itself.

4. The table of shewbread in the Holy Place teaches us that we need our daily spiritual bread in order to grow good and to be fitted for God's service as much as we need daily bread for our bodies. The healthy soul is full of hungers and thirsts, and every one of them needs the food that satisfies them. The soul that does not hunger is sickly, as is the body without appetite. Jesus Christ satisfies all these hungers.

5. Coming to the golden candlestick we see the symbol of the light of the world, the answer to the cry for more light; and that we too are to let our light shine in the dark world.

6. Next we draw near to the altar of incense which stood before the door of the Holy of Holies. The fragrance of incense, its preciousness, and its beautiful clouds rising to heaven make it a suitable symbol for prayer and thanksgiving, the means of communion with God.

7. After the experiences typified by these objects, one can meet God in the Holy of Holies. Here is the Mercy Seat of God's forgiving love. Here are

TAB 662 TAB

the cherubim, the perfect servants of God. Here are the commandments now written on the heart and life. Here is the shining presence of God himself.

HISTORY.—"The tabernacle, as the place in which Jehovah dwelt, was pitched in the centre of the camp, Num. 2:2, as the tent of a leader always is in the East; for Jehovah was the Captain of Israel. Josh. 5:14, 15. During the marches of Israel, the tabernacle was still in the centre. Num. 2. The tribes camped and marched around it in the order of a hollow square. In certain great emergencies it led the march. Josh. 3:11–16. Upon the tabernacle abode always the cloud, dark by day and fiery red by night, Ex. 40:38, giving the signal for the march, Ex. 40: 36, 37; Num. 9:17, and the halt. Num. 9:15–23. It was always the special meeting-place of Jehovah and his people. Num. 11:24, 25; 12:4; 14:10; 16: 19, 42; 20:6; 27:2; Deut. 31:14." During the conquest of Canaan the tabernacle, at first moved from place to place, Josh. 4:18; 8:30–35; 9:6; 10: 15, was finally located at Shiloh. Josh. 18:1; 22:9. Here it remained during the time of the judges, till it was captured by the Philistines, who carried off the sacred ark of the covenant. 1 Sam. 4:22. From this time forward the glory of the tabernacle was gone. When the ark was recovered, it was removed to Jerusalem, and placed in a new tabernacle, 2 Sam. 6:17; 1 Chron. 15:1; but the old structure still had its hold on the veneration of the community, and the old altar still received their offerings. 1 Chron. 16:39; 21:29. It was not till the temple was built, and a fitting house thus prepared for the Lord, that the ancient tabernacle was allowed to perish and be forgotten.

Tabernacles, The Feast of (Ex. 23: 16, "the feast of ingathering"), the third of the three great festivals of the Hebrews, which lasted from the 15th till the 22d of Tisri. 1. The following are the principal passages in the Pentateuch which refer to it: Ex. 23:16; Lev. 23: 34–36, 39–43; Num. 29:12–38; Deut. 16: 13–16; 31:10–13. In Neh. 8 there is an account of the observance of the feast by Ezra. 2. The time of the festival fell in the autumn, when the whole of the chief fruits of the ground, the corn, the wine and the oil, were gathered in. Ex. 23:16; Lev. 23:39; Deut. 16:13–

15. Its duration was strictly only seven days, Deut. 16:13; Ezek. 45:25; but it was followed by a day of holy convocation, distinguished by sacrifices of its own, which was sometimes spoken of as an eighth day. Lev. 23:36; Neh. 8:18. During the seven days the Israelites were commanded to dwell in booths or huts formed of the boughs of trees. The boughs were of the olive, palm, pine, myrtle and other trees with thick foliage. Neh. 8:15, 16. According to rabbinical tradition, each Israelite used to tie the branches into a bunch, to be carried in his hand, to which the name *lûlâb* was given. The burnt offerings of the Feast of Tabernacles were by far more numerous than those of any other festival. The eighth day was a day of holy convocation of peculiar solemnity. On the morning of this day the Hebrews left their huts and dismantled them, and took up their abode again in their houses. The main purposes of the Feast of Tabernacles are plainly set forth in Ex. 23:16 and Lev. 23:43. It was to be at once a thanksgiving for the harvest and a commemoration of the time when the Israelites dwelt in tents during their passage through the wilderness. In one of its meanings it stands in connection with the Passover, as the Feast of Abib, and with Pentecost, as the feast of harvest; in its other meaning, it is related to the Passover as the great yearly memorial of the deliverance from the destroyer and from the tyranny of Egypt.

The Feast of Tabernacles was somewhat like our thanksgiving season. It was the feast of ingathering, celebrating the harvest and rejoicing over the past deliverance of the nation. It was celebrated in booths, and everything about it was symbolical. *The feast* pointed to joy, gratitude, and hope. *Pouring out the water* symbolized the Holy Spirit's influences. *The temple illumination* typified the light of God. The *silver trumpets* marshaled the hosts of God and awakened from spiritual drowsiness. There are two particulars in the observance of the Feast of Tabernacles which appear to be referred to in the New Testament, but are not noticed in the Old. These were the ceremony of pouring out some water of the pool of Siloam and the display of some great lights in the court of the women. One

TAB 663 **TAB**

of the priests fetched some water in a golden ewer from the pool of Siloam, which he brought into the court through the water-gate. As he entered the trumpets sounded, and he ascended the slope of the altar. In the evening, both men and women assembled in the court of the women, expressly to hold a rejoicing for the drawing of the water of Siloam. At the same time there were set up in the court two lofty stands, each supporting four great lamps. These were lighted on each night of the festival. It appears to be generally admitted that the words of our Saviour, John 7 : 37, 38—" If any man thirst, let him come unto me and drink. He that believeth on me, as the Scripture hath said, out of his belly shall flow rivers of living water "— were suggested by the pouring out of the water of Siloam. Edersheim in *The Temple and its Services* thus describes this scene:

" Let us suppose ourselves in the number of worshippers who, on ' the last, the great day of the feast,' are leaving their ' booths ' at daybreak to take part in the service. The pilgrims are all in festive array. In his right hand each carries a branch consisting of a myrtle or willow branch tied together with a palm branch (Lev. 23 : 40). In his left hand he carries a bough of the so-called Paradise apple, a species of citron. Thus armed, the festive multitude would divide into three bands. One of these, to the sound of music, started in a procession from the temple. It followed a priest who bore a golden pitcher capable of holding three *log* (rather more than two pints). They proceeded to the fountain of Siloam, in the valley south of the temple. Here the priest filled from this fountain the golden pitcher, and brought it back into the court of the temple amid the shouts of the multitude and the sound of cymbals and trumpets. The rejoicing was so great that the rabbis used to say that he who had never been present at this ceremony, and at the other similar ceremonies by which this feast was distinguished, did not know what rejoicing meant. The return was so timed that they should arrive just as they were laying the pieces of the sacrifice on the great altar of burnt offering, towards the close of the ordinary morning sacrifice service. The water from the golden pitcher was poured upon the altar. Immediately the great ' Hallel,' consisting of Ps. 113–118, was chanted antiphonally, or, rather, with responses, to the accompaniment of the flute. At the close of this festive morning service there was a pause in the services while the priests prepared to offer the special sacrifices for the day. *At this moment there arose, so loud as to be heard throughout the temple, the voice of Jesus.* He interrupted not the services, for they had for the moment ceased; he interpreted, and he fulfilled them."

Tab′itha (tăb′ĭthá) (*gazelle*), also called Dorcas by St. Luke, a female disciple of Joppa, " full of good works," among which that of making clothes for the poor is specifically mentioned. While St. Peter was at the neighboring town of Lydda, Tabitha died; upon which the disciples at Joppa sent an urgent message to the apostle begging him to come to them without delay. Upon his arrival Peter found the deceased already prepared for burial, and laid out in an upper chamber, where she was surrounded by the recipients and the tokens of her charity. After the example of our Saviour in the house of Jairus, Matt. 9 : 25; Mark 5 : 40, " Peter put them all forth," prayed for the divine assistance, and then commanded Tabitha to arise. Comp. Mark 5 : 41; Luke 8 : 54. She opened her eyes and sat up, and then, assisted by the apostle, rose from her couch. This great miracle, as we are further told, produced an extraordinary effect in Joppa, and was the occasion of many conversions there. Acts 9 : 36–42. The name " Tabitha " is an Aramaic word, signifying a " female gazelle." St. Luke gives " Dorcas " as the Greek equivalent of the name.

Ta′bor (tā′bôr), or **Mount Ta′bor,** one of the most interesting and remarkable of the single mountains in Palestine. It rises abruptly from the northeastern arm of the plain of Esdraelon, to a height of 1843 feet above the sea, and stands entirely isolated, except on the west, where a narrow ridge connects it with the hills of Nazareth. It presents to the eye, as seen from a distance, a beautiful appearance, being symmetrical in its proportions, and rounded off like a hemisphere or the segment of a circle, yet varying

MOUNT TABOR.

Photo by Jan Wilga

somewhat as viewed from different directions. It is now called *Jebel-et-Tûr*. It lies about 5 or 6 miles east from Nazareth. "The slopes are steep and rocky, but the ascent can be made with ease—nearly everywhere on foot, and in more than one place on horse back." The top of Tabor consists of an irregular platform, embracing a circuit of half an hour's walk, and commanding wide views of the subjacent plain from end to end. Tabor is not mentioned in the New Testament, but makes a prominent figure in the Old. The book of Joshua, 19 : 22, mentions a Tabor, probably the mountain, as the boundary between Issachar and Zebulun. See ver. 12. Barak, at the command of Deborah, assembled his forces on Tabor, and descended thence, with "ten thousand men after him," into the plain, and conquered Sisera on the banks of the Kishon. Judges 4 : 6–15. Whether this is the Tabor at which the brothers of Gideon, each of whom "resembled the children of a king," were murdered by Zebah and Zalmunna is doubtful. Judges 8 : 18, 19. There are at present the ruins of a fortress round all the summit of Tabor. The Latin Christians have now an altar here, at which their priests from Nazareth perform an annual mass. The Greeks also have a chapel, where, on certain festivals, they assemble for the celebration of religious rites. The idea that our Saviour was transfigured on Tabor prevailed extensively among the early Christians, and still reappears often in popular religious works. It is impossible, however, to acquiesce in the correctness of this opinion. It can be proved from the Old Testament and from later history that a fortress or town existed on Tabor from very early times down to B.C. 53 or 50; and, as Josephus says that he strengthened the fortifications there about A.D. 60, it is morally certain that Tabor must have been inhabited during the intervening period, that is, in the days of Christ. Tabor, therefore, could not have been the Mount of Transfiguration [see HERMON]; for when it is said that Jesus took his disciples "up into a high mountain apart, and was transfigured before them," Matt. 17 : 1, 2, we must understand that he brought them to the summit of the mountain, where they were alone by themselves.

Ta'bor is mentioned in the lists of 1 Chron. 6 as a city of the Merarite Levites, in the tribe of Zebulun, ver. 77. The list of the towns of Zebulun, Josh. 19, contains the name of Chisloth-tabor, ver. 12. It is, therefore, possible, that Chisloth-tabor is abbreviated into Tabor by the chronicler.

Ta'bor, The plain of. This is an incorrect translation, and should be THE OAK OF TABOR. It is mentioned in 1 Sam. 10 : 3 only, as one of the points in the homeward journey of Saul after his anointing by Samuel.

Tabret. [TIMBREL.]

Tab'rimon (tăb'rĭ-mŏn) (properly Tabrimmon, i. e. *good is Rimmon*, the Syrian god), the father of Ben-hadad I., king of Syria in the reign of Asa. 1 Kings 15 : 18.

Tache. The word thus rendered occurs only in the description of the structure of the tabernacle and its fittings, Ex. 26 : 6, 11, 33 ; 35 : 11 ; 36 : 13 ; 39 : 33, and appears to indicate the small hooks or clasps by which a curtain is suspended to the rings from which it hangs, or connected vertically, as in the case of the veil of the Holy of Holies, with the loops of another curtain.

Tach'monite (tăk'mo-nīte), **The.** "The Tachmonite that sat in the seat," chief among David's captains, 2 Sam. 23 : 8, is in 1 Chron. 11 : 11 called "Jashobeam an Hachmonite," or, as the margin gives it, "son of Hachmoni." Kennicott has shown that the words translated "he that sat in the seat" are a corruption of Jashobeam, and that "the Tachmonite" is a corruption of the "son of Hachmoni," which was the family or local name of Jashobeam. Therefore he concludes "Jashobeam the Hachmonite" to have been the true reading.

Tad'mor (tăd'môr) (*city of palms*), called "Tadmor in the wilderness," is the same as the city known to the Greeks and Romans under the name of Palmyra. It lay between the Euphrates and Hamath, to the southeast of that city, in a fertile tract or oasis of the desert. Being situated at a convenient distance from both the Mediterranean Sea and the Persian Gulf, it had great advantages for caravan traffic. It was built by Solomon after his conquest of Hamath-zobah. 1 Kings 9 : 18 ; 2 Chron. 8 : 4. The city is nowhere else mentioned in the Bible. In the second century A.D. it seems to have been beautified by the emperor Hadrian. In the beginning of the third century—211-217 A.D.—it became a Roman colony under Caracalla. Subsequently, in the reign of Gallienus, the Roman senate invested Odenathus, a senator of Palmyra, with the regal dignity, on account of his services in defeating Sapor, king of Persia. On the assassination of Odenathus, his wife, Zenobia, seems to have conceived the design of erecting Palmyra into an independent monarchy; and in prosecution of this object, she for a while successfully resisted the Roman arms. She was at length defeated and taken captive by the emperor Aurelian, A.D. 273, who left a Roman garrison in Palmyra. This garrison was massacred in a revolt; and Aurelian punished the city by the execution not only of those who were taken in arms, but likewise of common peasants, of old men, women and children. From this blow Palmyra never recovered, though there are proofs of its having continued to be inhabited until the downfall of the Roman empire. The grandeur and magnificence of the ruins of Palmyra cannot be exceeded, and attest its former greatness. Among the most remarkable are the Tombs, the Temple of the Sun and the Street of Columns.

Ta′han (tā′hăn), a descendant of Ephraim. Num. 26:35. In 1 Chron. 7:25 he appears as the son of Telah.

Ta′hanites, The. Num. 26:35. [TAHAN.]

Ta′hath (tā′hăth). 1. A Kohathite Levite, ancestor of Samuel and Heman. 1 Chron. 6:24, 37.

2. Son of Bered, and great-grandson of Ephraim. 1 Chron. 7:20.

3. Grandson of the preceding. 1 Chron. 7:20.

Ta′hath (tā′hăth), the name of a desert station of the Israelites between Makheloth and Tarah. Num. 33:26. The site has not been identified.

Tah′panhes (tä-pan-hes), **Tehaph′= nehes, Tahap′anes** (tā′hap′a-nēz), a city of Egypt, mentioned in the time of the prophets Jeremiah and Ezekiel. The name is evidently Egyptian, and closely resembles that of the Egyptian queen Tahpenes. It was evidently a town of lower Egypt, near or on the eastern border. When Johanan and the other captains went into Egypt in

Jeremiah's time they established a colony here. Jer. 43:7; 44:1. It was an important town, being twice mentioned by the former prophet with Noph or Memphis. Jer. 2:16; 46:14. Its destruction by the Assyrians was prophesied by Jeremiah (43:8–13). No confirmation of this has been found in the monuments but the excavations give evidence of a violent destruction with conflagrations. It is doubtless the classic *Daphne,* a fortified city on the Pelusiac branch of the Nile (Herod. ii, 30, 107). The site is now a desolate mound on the edge of the desert, called *Defenneh.*

Tah′penes (täh′pĕ-nĕṣ), an Egyptian queen, was wife of the Pharaoh who received Hadad the Edomite, and who gave him her sister in marriage. 1 Kings 11:18–20.

Tah′rea (täh′rē-à) (*cunning*), son of Micah and grandson of Mephibosheth. 1 Chron. 9:41.

Tah′tim-hod′shi (täh′tim-hŏd′shī), **The land of,** one of the places visited by Joab during his census of the land of Israel. It occurs between Gilead and Dan-jaan. 2 Sam. 24:6. The word probably means *the Hittites towards Kadesh* and should not be considered a proper name.

Talent. [WEIGHTS AND MEASURES; MONEY.]

Tal′itha cu′mi (tăl′ĭ-thà kū′mī), two Aramaic words, Mark 5:41, signifying *damsel, arise.*

Tal′mai (tăl′mā) (*pertaining to furrows*). 1. One of the three sons of "the Anak" who were slain by the men of Judah. Num. 13:22; Josh. 15:14; Judges 1:10. (B.C. 1450.)

2. Son of Ammihud king of Geshur. 2 Sam. 3:3; 13:37; 1 Chron. 3:2. He was probably a petty chieftain, dependent on David.

Tal′mon (tăl′mon) (*oppressed*), the head of a family of door-keepers in the temple, "the porters for the camps of the sons of Levi." 1 Chron. 9:17; Neh. 11:19. Some of his descendants returned with Zerubbabel, Ezra 2:42; Neh. 7:45, and were employed in their hereditary office in the days of Nehemiah and Ezra. Neh. 12:25.

Ta′mah (tā′mah) (*laughter*). The children of Tamah or Thamah, Ezra 2:53, were among the Nethinim who returned with Zerubbabel. Neh. 7:55.

Ta′mar (tā′mar) (*palm tree*). 1. The wife successively of the two sons of Judah,—Er and Onan. Gen. 38: 6–30. Her importance in the sacred narrative depends on the great anxiety to keep up the lineage of Judah. It seemed as if the family were on the point of extinction. Er and Onan had successively perished suddenly. Judah's wife, Bathshuah, died; and there only remained a child, Shelah, whom Judah was unwilling to trust to the dangerous union, as it appeared, with Tamar, lest he should meet with the same fate as his brothers. Accordingly she resorted to the desperate expedient of entrapping the father himself into the union which he feared for his son. The fruits of this intercourse were twins, Pharez and Zarah, and through Pharez the sacred line was continued.

2. Daughter of David and Maachah the Geshurite princess, and thus full sister of Absalom. 2 Sam. 13 : 1–32; 1 Chron. 3 : 9. She and her brother were alike remarkable for their extraordinary beauty. This fatal beauty inspired a frantic passion in her half-brother Amnon, the oldest son of David. The intense hatred of Amnon succeeding to his brutal passion, and the indignation of Tamar at his barbarous insult, even surpassing her indignation at his shameful outrage, are pathetically and graphically told.

3. Daughter of Absalom, 2 Sam. 14 : 27. She was perhaps identical with Maachah, who became the wife of Rehoboam, although some consider her to have been the mother of Maachah. 1 Kings 15 : 2; 2 Chron. 11 : 20; 13 : 2.

4. A spot on the southeastern frontier of Judah, named in Ezek. 47 : 19; 48 : 28 only, evidently called from a palm tree. It must have been near the southern end of the Dead Sea, and is perhaps identical with the village *Thamara* mentioned by Eusebius and Jerome. It has not been identified.

Tamarisk. A tree of which there are nine species in Palestine, with durable wood and evergreen leaves. The word is not used in the Authorized Version, but the tree is most probably intended in Gen. 21 : 33; 1 Sam. 22 : 6; 31 : 13.

Tam'muz (tăm'mŭz) (*son of life*). Ezek. 8 : 14. He was originally the sun-god, primarily a god of Babylonia, slain by a wild boar while hunting, and mourned long and vainly by the goddess Istar. He is generally identified with Adonis, of Greek mythology, whose story is practically the same. According to Sayce, the Canaanites called him "Adonai" lord, from which when the myth reached Greece came the name Adonis. A festival in honor of Adonis was celebrated at Byblus in Phœnicia and in most of the Grecian cities, and even by the Jews when they degenerated into idolatry. It took place in July, and was accompanied by obscene rites.

Ta'nach (tä'năk), a slight variation of the name TAANACH. Josh. 21 : 25.

Tan'humeth (tăn'hu-měth) (*consolation*), the father of Seraiah in the time of Gedaliah. 2 Kings 25 : 23; Jer. 40 : 8.

Ta'phath (tä'fath) (*a drop*), the daughter of Solomon, who was married to Ben-Abinadab. 1 Kings 4 : 11.

Tap'puah (tăp'pu-ah) (*the apple-city*). 1. A city of Judah, in the district of the Shefelah or lowland. Josh. 15 : 34.

2. A place on the boundary of the "children of Joseph." Josh. 16 : 8; 17 : 8. Its full name was probably En-tappuah. Josh. 17 : 7. The city belonged to Ephraim but the land around it to Manasseh.

3. One of the sons of Hebron, of the tribe of Judah. 1 Chron. 2 : 43.

Ta'rah (tä'rah), a desert-station of the Israelites between Tahath and Mithcah. Num. 33 : 27. It is the same name as Terah.

Tar'alah (tär'a-lah) (*reeling*), one of the towns in the allotment of Benjamin. Josh. 18 : 27.

Tar'ea (tär'rē-à) the same as Tahreah, one of the sons of Micah. 1 Chron. 8 : 35.

Tares. There can be little doubt that the *zizania* of the parable, Matt. 13 : 25, 30, denotes the weed called "darnel" (*Lolium temulentum*). The darnel before it comes into ear is very similar in appearance to wheat; hence the command that the *zizania* should be left to the harvest, lest while men plucked up the tares "they should root up also the wheat with them." "It is customary to gather out of the grain fields, not only tares, but all the taller plants growing among the grain which can be easily pulled up without causing the person engaged to bend over in a way to endanger breaking the stalks of grain." "The allusion in the parable is in substantial accord with modern custom in the East which is to leave the cleaning of the fields until the grain is well advanced towards the harvest, and can be readily distinguished from all other plants." (G. E. Post in Hastings' *Bible Dictionary.*) The grains of the *L. temulentum,* if eaten by man and

TARES AND WHEAT

the herbivorous animals, produce convulsions, and even death, but are harmless to poultry.

Tar′gum. [See VERSIONS.]

Tar′pelites (tär′pel-ītes), **The,** a race of Assyrian colonists who were planted in the cities of Samaria after the captivity of the northern kingdom of Israel. Ezra 4:9. They have not been identified with any certainty.

Tar′shish (tär′shish). In the A. V. sometimes "Tharshish." 1. Probably Tartessus, a city and emporium of the Phœnicians in the south of Spain, represented as one of the sons of Javan. Gen. 10:4; 1 Kings 10:22; 1 Chron. 1:7; Ps. 48:7; Isa. 2:16; Jer. 10:9; Ezek. 27:12, 25; Jonah 1:3; 4:2. The identity of the two places is rendered highly probable by the following circumstances: 1st: There is a very close similarity of name between them, Tartessus being merely Tarshish in the Aramaic form. 2d. There seems to have been a special relation between Tarshish and Tyre, as there was at one time between Tartessus and the Phœ-

nicians. 3d. The articles which Tarshish is stated by the prophet Ezekiel, Ezek. 27:12, to have supplied to Tyre are precisely such as we know, through classical writers, to have been productions of the Spanish peninsula. In regard to tin, the trade of Tarshish in this metal is peculiarly significant, and, taken in conjunction with similarity of name and other circumstances already mentioned, is reasonably conclusive as to its identity with Tartessus. For even now the countries in Europe or on the shores of the Mediterranean Sea where tin is found are very few; and in reference to ancient times, it would be difficult to name any such countries except Iberia or Spain, Lusitania, which was somewhat less in extent than Portugal, and Cornwall in Great Britain. In the absence of positive proof, we may acquiesce in the statement of Strabo, that the river Bætis (now the Guadalquivir) was formerly called Tartessus, that the city Tartessus was situated between the two arms by which the river flowed into the sea, and that the adjoining country was called Tartessis.

2. From the book of Chronicles there would seem to have been a Tarshish accessible from the Red Sea, in addition to the Tarshish of the south of Spain. Thus, with regard to the ships of Tarshish, which Jehoshaphat caused to be constructed at Ezion-geber on the Elanitic Gulf of the Red Sea, 1 Kings 22:48, it is said in the Chronicles, 2 Chron. 20:36, that they were made to go to Tarshish; and in like manner the navy of ships, which Solomon had previously made in Ezion-geber, 1 Kings 9:26, is said in the Chronicles, 2 Chron. 9:21, to have gone to Tarshish with the servants of Hiram. It is not to be supposed that the author of these passages in the Chronicles contemplated a voyage to Tarshish in the south of Spain by going round what has since been called the Cape of Good Hope. The expression "ships of Tarshish" originally meant ships destined to go to Tarshish; and then probably came to signify large ships of a particular size and description, destined for long voyages, just as in English "East Indiaman" was a general name given to vessels, some of which were not intended to go to India at all. Hence we may infer that the

word Tarshish was also used to signify any distant place, and in this case would be applied to one in the Indian Ocean.

3. One of the seven highest princes of Persia. Esth. 1:14.

4. A Benjamite, son of Bilhan. A.V. THARSHISH. 1 Chron. 7:10.

Tar'sus (tär'sus), the chief town of Cilicia, "no mean city" in other respects, but illustrious to all time as the birthplace and early residence of the apostle Paul. Acts 9:11; 21:39; 22:3. Even in the flourishing period of Greek history it was a city of some considerable consequence. In the civil wars of Rome it took Cæsar's side, and on the occasion of a visit from him had its name changed to Juliopolis. Marc Antony made it a "free city"; a privilege which Augustus continued, and even increased. It was renowned as a place of education under the early Roman emperors. Strabo compares it in this respect to Athens and Alexandria. Tarsus also was a place of much commerce. It was situated in a wild and fertile plain on the banks of the Cydnus. The city is much decayed from its former greatness. Its population is about 25,000, of whom about half are Christians. No ruins of any importance remain.

Tar'tak, one of the gods of the Avite or Avvite colonists of Samaria. 2 Kings 17:31. According to rabbinical tradition, Tartak is said to have ʰeen worshipped under the form of an ass.

Tar'tan (tär'tan), which occurs only in 2 Kings 18:17 and Isa. 20:1, was long regarded as a proper name; but like Rabsaris and Rabshakeh, it is proved to be an official designation, and indicates the Assyrian commander-in-chief.

Tat'nai (tăt'na-ı̄) (*gift*), sat-rap of the province west of the Euphrates in the time of Darius Hystaspes. Ezra 5: 3, 6; 6:6, 13. (B.C. 520.) He opposed the rebuilding of the temple.

Taverns, The three. [THREE TAVERNS.]

Taxes. I. Under the judges, according to the theocratic government contemplated by the law, the only payments incumbent upon the people as of permanent obligation were for the support of the Tabernacle and the priesthood. These were maintained by the Tithes, the First-fruits, the Redemption-money of the first-born, and other offerings

as belonging to special occasions, and by the land which was permanently given for the use of the Levites.

II. The kingdom, with its centralized government and greater magnificence, involved, of course, a larger expenditure, and therefore a heavier taxation. The chief burdens appear to have been—(1) A tithe of the produce both of the soil and of live stock. 1 Sam. 8:15, 17; 1 Kings 4:7, 28. (2) Forced military service for a month every year. 1 Sam. 8:11, 12; 1 Kings 9:22; 1 Chron. 27:1. (3) Gifts to the king. 1 Sam. 10:27; 16:20; 17:18. (4) Import duties. 1 Kings 10:15. (5) The monopoly of certain branches of commerce. 1 Kings 9:28; 22:48; 10:28, 29. ₍6) The appropriation to the king's use of the early crop of hay. Amos 7:1. At times, too, in the history of both the kingdoms there were special burdens. A tribute of fifty shekels a head had to be paid by Menahem to the Assyrian king, 2 Kings 15:20, and under his successor Hoshea this assumed the form of an annual tribute. 2 Kings 17:4.

III. Under the Persian empire the taxes paid by the Jews were, in their broad outlines, the same in kind as those of other subject races. The financial system which gained for Darius Hystaspes the name of the "shopkeeper king" involved the payment by each satrap of a fixed sum as the tribute due from his province. In Judea, as in other provinces, the inhabitants had to provide in kind for the maintenance of the governor's household, besides a money payment of forty shekels a day. Neh. 5:14, 15. In Ezra 4:13, 20; 7:24, we get a formal enumeration of the three great branches of the revenue. The influence of Ezra secured for the whole ecclesiastical order, from the priests down to the Nethinim, an immunity from all three, Ezra 7:24; but the burden pressed heavily on the great body of the people. In addition to the taxes laid by the Persian rulers there was, after the Exile, a Temple tax voluntarily assumed by the people of half a shekel on each Israelite of 20 years or over. This later became a fixed tax, the collectors visited every town in Judea at a fixed time, and in foreign lands certain places were named where it should be paid.

IV. Under the Egyptian and Syrian kings the taxes paid by the Jews became yet heavier. The "farming" system of finance was adopted in its worst form. The taxes were put up to auction. The contract sum for those of Phœnicia, Judea and Samaria had been estimated at about 8000 talents. An unscrupulous adventurer would bid double that sum, and would then go down to the province, and by violence and cruelty, like that of Turkish or Hindoo collectors, squeeze out a large margin of profit for himself. V. The pressure of Roman taxation, if not absolutely heavier, was probably more galling, as being more thorough and systematic, more distinctively a mark of bondage. The capture of Jerusalem by Pompey was followed immediately by the imposition of a tribute, and within a short time the sum thus taken from the resources of the country amounted to 10,000 talents. When Judea became formally a Roman province, the whole financial system of the empire came as a natural consequence. The taxes were systematically farmed, and the publicans appeared as a new curse to the country. The *portoria* were levied at harbors, piers and the gates of cities. Matt. 9:9; Rom. 13: 7. In addition to this there was the poll-tax paid by every Jew, and looked upon, for that reason, as the special badge of servitude. United with this, as part of the same system, there was also, in all probability, a property tax of some kind. In addition to these general taxes, the inhabitants of Jerusalem were subject to a special house-duty about this period.

Taxing. The English word now conveys to us more distinctly the notion of a tax or tribute actually levied; but it appears to have been used in the sixteenth century for the registration or enrolment of the people for the purpose of a poll-tax. Two distinct registrations, or enrolments, are mentioned in the New Testament, both of them by St. Luke. The first is said to have been the result of an edict of the emperor Augustus, that "all the world (*i. e.* the Roman empire) should be taxed," Luke 2:1, and is connected by the evangelist with the name of Cyrenius or Quirinius. [CYRENIUS.] The second and more important, Acts 5:37, is distinctly associated, in point of time, with the revolt of Judas of Galilee.

Te'bah (tē'bah) (*slaughter*), eldest of the sons of Nahor, by his concubine Reumah. Gen. 22:24.

Tebali'ah (tĕb-a-lī'ah) (*Jehovah hath purified*), third son of Hosah of the children of Merari. 1 Chron. 26:11.

Te'beth (tē'beth). [MONTH.]

Tehin'nah (tĕ-hĭn'nah) (*supplication*), the father or founder of Ir-nahash, the city of Nahash, and son of Eshton. 1 Chron. 4:12.

Teil tree. [OAK.]

Teko'a (tē-kō'á), or **Teko'ah**. 1. A town in the tribe of Judah, 2 Chron. 11:6, on the range of hills which rise near Hebron and stretch eastward toward the Dead Sea. The "wise woman" whom Joab employed to effect a reconciliation between David and Absalom was obtained from this place. 2 Sam. 14:2. Here also Ira the son of Ikkesh, one of David's thirty, "the mighty men," was born, and was called on that account "the Tekoite." 2 Sam. 23:26. It was one of the places which Rehoboam fortified, at the beginning of his reign, as a defence against invasion from the south. 2 Chron. 11:6. Some of the people from Tekoa took part in building the walls of Jerusalem, after the return from the captivity. Neh. 3: 5, 27. In Jer. 6:1 the prophet exclaims, "Blow the trumpet in Tekoa, and set up a sign of fire in Beth-haccerem." But Tekoa is chiefly memorable as the birthplace of the prophet Amos. Amos 1:1. Tekoa is known still as *Tekŭ'a.* It lies on an elevated hill, which spreads itself out into an irregular plain of moderate extent. Various ruins exist, such as the walls of houses, cisterns, broken columns and heaps of building-stones.

2. A name occurring in the genealogies of Judah, 1 Chron. 2:24; 4:5, as the son of Ashur. There is little doubt that the town of Tekoa is meant.

Teko'ite (tē-kō'īte), **The.** Ira ben-Ikkesh, one of David's warriors, is thus designated. 2 Sam. 23:26; 1 Chron. 11:28; 27:9. The common people among the Tekoites displayed great activity in the repairs of the wall of Jerusalem under Nehemiah. Neh. 3:5, 27.

Tel-a'bib (tĕl-ā'bīb) (*cornhill*), a city of Babylonia, near the Chebar, one of the rivers or canals of that country. Some of the Jewish exiles were settled there. Its site is unknown. Ezek. 3 : 15.

Te'lah (tē'lah) (*fracture*), a descendant of Ephraim, and ancestor of Joshua. 1 Chron. 7 : 25.

Tel'aim (tĕl'a-ĭm) (*lambs*), the place at which Saul collected and numbered his forces before his attack on Amalek, 1 Sam. 15 : 4; may be identical with TELEM, which see.

Telas'sar (tē-lăs'sar) (*Assyrian hill*) is mentioned in 2 Kings 19 : 12 and in Isa. 37 : 12 as a city inhabited by "the children of Eden," which had been conquered and was held in the time of Sennacherib, by the Assyrians. It must have been in western Mesopotamia, in the neighborhood of Harran.

Te'lem (tē'lem) (*oppression*). 1. One of the cities in the extreme south of Judah, Josh. 15 : 24, probably the same as Telaim. The name *Dhallam* is found in connection with some Arabs living south of Moladah, *Tell Milh*—a position very suitable.

2. A porter or doorkeeper of the temple in the time of Ezra. Ezra 10 : 24. He was induced to put away his foreign wife.

Tel-har'sa, or **Tel-hare'sha** (tĕl-ha-rē'shà) (*hill of the wood*), one of the Babylonian towns or villages mentioned in Ezra 2 : 59; Neh. 7 : 61, along with Tel-melah and Cherub. Its site is unknown.

Tel-me'lah (tĕl-mē'lah). Another of the Babylonian towns mentioned as above.

Te'ma (tē'mà) (*south*), a son of Ishmael, Gen. 25 : 15; 1 Chron. 1 : 30; whence the tribe called after him, mentioned in Job 6 : 19; Jer. 25 : 23, and also the land occupied by this tribe. Isa. 21 : 13, 14. The name is identified with *Teima*, in N. Arabia, on an old route from the Gulf of Akaba to the Persian Gulf.

Te'man (tē'man) (*the south*). A son of Eliphaz, son of Esau by Adah. Gen. 36 : 11, 15, 42; 1 Chron. 1 : 36, 53.

2. A country, and probably a city named after the Edomite "duke" or from which the "duke" took his name. It is sometimes used as a synonym for Edom and is without doubt a district in Edom, but the references make it uncertain whether it is in the northern or southern part. Eze. 25 : 13; Am. 1 : 12; Jer. 49 : 20, 21. Eusebius speaks of it as 15 miles from Petra, but does not give the direction. No

trace of the city can be found, but it is thought to have been on the road between Elath and Bozrah.

Tem'ani (tĕm'a-nī). [TEMAN.]

Te'manite (tē'man-īte), an inhabitant of Teman. Job 2 : 11.

Tem'eni (tĕm'e-nī), son of Ashur the father of Tekoa, by his wife Naarah. 1 Chron. 4 : 6.

Temple. There is perhaps no building of the ancient world which has excited so much attention since the time of its destruction as the Temple which Solomon built at Jerusalem, and its successor as rebuilt by Herod. Its spoils were considered worthy of forming the principal illustration of one of the most beautiful of Roman triumphal arches, the Arch of Titus. Throughout the middle ages it influenced to a considerable degree the forms of Christian churches, and its peculiarities were the watchwords and rallying-points of all associations of builders.

PURPOSE OF THE TEMPLE. "The temple was the approach of a nation to their God. Israelites alone could enter its Inner Sanctuary." It was the symbol of God's presence among the people. It expressed by means of worship, and every available form of ceremony and symbolism, the presence and power and glory of God. It was the visible means of access to God. "Yet amid all the symbolism, God Himself was not adored in any material form. One could represent only His Presence or Dwelling. And this was double. God was both the Far and the Near, above all things, filling the Heavens, and yet abiding with His people. His Name dwelt there." He was transcendent, with His throne in Heaven, but the Temple was His earthly seat.

Thus the temple bound the nation together. It was the religious centre and capital. Its influence permeated the whole nation.

THE THREE TEMPLES. There were three temples in Jewish history,—(1) Solomon's for a little more than 400 years from about B.C. 1000 to 588, from Solomon to the Exile; (2) Zerubbabel's or the Temple of the Return, nearly 500 years, from its completion B.C. 515 to B.C. 20, when Herod began to build his temple or perhaps better, to transform the old into a new temple. (3) Herod's Temple, lasting only about 90

MOSQUE OF OMAR.
On Site of Jewish Temple Area.

years, from the time Herod began to build in B.C. 20, to its destruction by Titus, August, A.D. 70. The whole area, or platform with its various buildings was called the Temple.

THE SITE. All these temples were built upon the eastern hill of Jerusalem (see Art. JERUSALEM). The lower, southern part of this hill is now generally regarded by scholars as Mount Zion (or Sion). North of Zion was the temple platform, greatly enlarged by building immense walls around its southern and eastern sides. This plat-

walls formed a square of about 600 feet; but the sanctuary itself was comparatively small, inasmuch as it was intended only for the ministrations of the priests, the congregation of the people assembling in the courts. In this and all other essential points the temple followed the model of the tabernacle, from which it differed chiefly by having chambers built about the sanctuary for the abode of the priests and attendants and the keeping of treasures and stores. In all its dimensions, length, breadth and height on its ground

GROUND PLAN OF THE HOLY HOUSE OF SOLOMON'S TEMPLE.
P, Porch; H, Holy Place; H H, Holy of Holies; S, Stairway to Chambers; C C, Chambers; B, J, Pillars Boaz and Jachin.

form, nearly square, was gradually increased on its northern side. Solomon made it about 600 feet square, containing 12 acres. This area, according to Josephus, was nearly doubled when Herod built the third temple.

SOLOMON'S TEMPLE. In his later years David gathered a great amount of material for the temple to be builded by his son. The gold and silver alone accumulated by David were at the lowest reckoned to have amounted to 2450 million dollars, a sum which can be paralleled from secular history. The building occupied the site prepared for it by David, which had formerly been the threshing-floor of the Jebusite Ornan or Araunah, on Mount Moriah. The whole area enclosed by the outer

plan, the sanctuary itself was exactly double the size of the tabernacle.

The ground plan can best be understood by the accompanying diagram. Counting a cubit as eighteen inches, the main building was as follows:

Porch . . 30′ broad, 15′ deep, 180′ high.
Holy Place . 60′ long, 30′ wide, 30′ high.
Holy of Holies 30′ long, 30′ wide, 30′ high.
Chambers . 15′ wide on the two sides and rear.

The *Holy of Holies* was a cube. It was without light. It contained the Ark of the Covenant, and the Cherubim. It was entered only once a year and then by the high priest alone. The space over it, 15 feet high was probably occupied by upper chambers, gold lined, (1 Chron. 28:11; 2 Chron. 3:9.)

GROUND PLAN OF SOLOMON'S BUILDINGS.
After Geo. Adam Smith's "Jerusalem."

1. The Temple.
2. Court of the House of the Lord.
3. Greater or Outer Court.
4. King's house.
5. House of Pharaoh's Daughter.
6. "Other" or "Middle" Court.

7. Throne Hall.
8. Hall of Pillars.
9. House of the Forest of Lebanon.
P. Ascents to Palace and Temple.
W. Wall of present Temple platform.

In the *Holy Place* were ten golden candlesticks, ten tables of shewbread, and the altar of incense.

The front of *the Porch* was supported, after the manner of some Egyptian temples, by the two great brazen pillars, Jachin and Boaz, 18 cubits high, with capitals of 5 cubits more, adorned with lily-work and pomegranates. 1 Kings 7: 15–22.

Around three sides were *chambers for the priests* arranged in three stories. There were *two courts* (2 Chron. 33: 5). The outer court was surrounded by a wall partly of stone, partly of cedar; on the eastern border was a cloister or colonnade. This court was adorned with trees, and free to all the people. Within this quadrangle was a smaller court, the court of the priests, on the highest ridge of the hill, enclosing the temple, and the great brazen altar, and brazen sea, and the lavers.

In the inner court were the great brazen altar of sacrifice, fifteen feet high and thirty feet square, in sight of all the worshippers of the outer court, and the molten or brazen sea supported by twelve huge brazen oxen, each seven and one-half feet high.

The outer court was for the worshippers, who were intended to exercise the feelings suggested and symbolized by the ceremonies going on visibly in the court or unseen in the sanctuary, but well known as to their meaning.

The Temple was built of marble hewn into shape at the quarry, part of which was doubtless in the rock under the city. The whole interior was lined with woodwork of cedar and cypress, richly carved and overlaid with gold. Indeed, both within and without the building was conspicuous chiefly by the lavish use of the gold.

THE GROUP OF ROYAL BUILDINGS. We will understand better the temple built by Solomon if we see it in connection with the whole group of his royal buildings, covering the larger part of the eastern hill, thus including Zion as well as the Temple mount. The plan on page 674 is modified from Stade's. It is best described in George Adam Smith's new book *Jerusalem*, vol. 2, p. 58 f.

TEMPLE OF THE RETURN, built by governor Zerubbabel, with the aid of the prophets Zechariah and Haggai, and completed B.C. 515, twenty years after the first return from the captivity in Babylon. We see by the description in Ezra that this temple was about one-third larger than Solomon's. The dimensions are given in Ezra 6: 3, when quoting the decree of Cyrus, it is said, "Let the house be builded, the place where they offered sacrifices, and let the foundations thereof be strongly laid; the height thereof three-score cubits, and the breadth thereof three-score cubits, with three rows [rather stories] of great stones, and a row of new timber." While larger in size than Solomon's temple, it was greatly its inferior in architectural splendor, in ornamentation, and lavish display of gold and precious stones, and the beauty of its textile fabrics.

THE TEMPLE IN THE TIME OF CHRIST, called HEROD'S TEMPLE, because it was built by Herod the Great on the basis of the old temple.

This temple has by far the largest interest for Christians of to-day, because it is so closely associated with the life and teachings of our Lord, and with the apostles and the early church.

The sources of our knowledge concerning it, in addition to the New Testament, are (1) Josephus' *Antiquities*, xv, 11 and *Jewish Wars*, v, 5; (2) the tract *Middoth* of the *Mishna;* and (3) the holy site itself.

Among the most helpful books which sum up the conclusions of modern scholars are Professor George Adam Smith's *Jerusalem* and Professor Sanday's *Sacred Sites of the Gospels.*

This temple was begun by Herod in the winter of B.C. 20, 19. The house was completed in 18 months, being but a transformation of the old temple, the cloisters occupied 8 years more, but the work on the entire complex of courts and buildings dragged along slowly, even after the death of Herod, for nearly half a century (John 2: 20). This temple was destroyed by Titus, August, A.D. 70, having accomplished its purpose. A Mohammedan mosque now stands on its site.

GENERAL VIEW. To one standing upon the Mount of Olives the general plan of the Temple and its courts would be like that given in the accompanying plans. A large court surrounded by a high strong wall, making the whole one great fortification for defence.

Within the larger court toward the northwest was a smaller one of great strength and magnificence, 555 feet long from east to west, 230 feet wide, enclosed by a double wall of defence. This inner court was not level like the outer one, but consisted of several lesser courts each rising above the other by flights of stairs till that on which the temple building stood is 15 cubits higher than the level of the outer court of the Gentiles. The house towered 172 feet higher still. The whole was dominated by the tower of Antonia adjoin-

HEROD'S TEMPLE.

1. Thirteen trumpet-mouthed money boxes, on either side of the Court of the Women.
2. Shusan Gate, the still existing Golden Gate.
3. Gate with bridge across the Tyropean Valley to the street that led across the city to Jaffa Gate.
4. Gates to the commercial suburb.
5. Holy of Holies, containing the Ark of the Covenant.
6. Sanctuary, or Holy Place, containing candlestick, table and altar of incense.
7. The Porch.
8. The slaughter-house for sacrifices.
9. The Soreg or wall, shutting out all Gentiles.
10. Council of the Sanhedrim outside the wall. Hall Gazith, where the Sanhedrim sometimes met.
11. Beautiful Gate.

ing the northwest corner of the court of the Gentiles, a huge castle and barracks for the Roman soldier guard.

THE TEMPLE BUILDING stood upon the highest ground in the enclosure. The ground plan was in general the same as that of Solomon's temple, the interior being 60 [1] cubits (103 ft.) by 20 (35 ft.) wide, divided into (1) the *Holy of Holies,* a cube of 20 cubits each way entirely empty, with no openings for light, and (2) the *Holy Place,* 40 cubits long by 20 cubits wide, and 40 cubits high. Between them hung the great veil referred to in Matt. 27:51; Mark 15:38; Heb. 9:3.

In the Holy Place were the Altar of Incense, the Table of Shewbread, and seven-branched Candlestick. On both

propylæum, 11 cubits deep, 100 cubits high, but in width extending 15 cubits on either side, making its total frontage to be 100 cubits (172 feet). The vast entrance 122 feet high by 35 broad lay open without doors.

Thus there rises before us a building 172 feet high, 172 feet long, with a porch of 172 feet broad, "built of huge blocks of white stone with plates of gold upon the front, so that in the distance it appeared like a mountain covered with snow."

THE COURTS AROUND THE HOUSE were enclosed by a double wall which formed of the temple mount a strong inner fortification, a separate citadel which in A.D. 70 the Jews were able to hold for some time after Titus had pene-

THE TEMPLE OF HEROD—RESTORED BY FERGUSSON.

The covered Portico on the left is the Royal porch extending along the southern side of the Temple area. The colonnade running from left to right is Solomon's Porch extending across the eastern side of the area. The courts here are greatly condensed, but the true proportions can be seen on the ground plan of the whole area.

sides and the rear were three story buildings 40 cubits high containing chambers reached by winding stairs. Over it lay a second chamber of 40 cubits in height, which with the solid foundations 6 cubits high, the ceilings and roof made 100 cubits in all (172 feet).

THE PORCH was built as a great

trated the Court of the Gentiles. Around this series of courts at the foot of the terrace was a wall called the *Soreg,* 3 cubits high, surmounted by pillars on which were inscriptions forbidding all persons save those of the commonwealth of Israel to enter the enclosure. One of these inscriptions has been found. It reads in Greek,—

[1] Geo. Adam Smith counts a cubit as the sacred cubit, 20.67 inches.

HEROD'S TEMPLE.

CROSS SECTION SOUTH TO NORTH

COURT OF GENTILES

COURT OF GENTILES

TEMPLE

12 1

4   7 9 10 11

4 5 6 7 8

3

A cross-section of the Temple and its courts, showing elevations.

1. The Outer Wall of the Temple Area.
2. The Royal Porch which extended along the entire south side.
3. The Court of the Gentiles, where anyone could enter.
4. The wall or partition *Soreg*, beyond which no Gentile could pass on pain of death. This is referred to in Eph. 2:14.
5. The Chel or passageway, or terrace.
6. The flight of steps leading to the inner courts.
7. The gate house. There were ten of these gate houses around the court. It was probably these gates which are referred to in Acts 21:30.
8. The Court of the Men of Israel. The main portion of this court was on the east side. This is only a nar-

row passage. The court of the women was also on the east side between the Court of the Men of Israel and the Court of the Gentiles, but this did not extend at all around the south side of the Temple Building.

9. A second flight of steps.
10. The Court of the Priests.
11. The Temple Building proper.
12. The portico which ran entirely around the Temple Area just within the wall. On the south side it was more elaborate and called the Royal Porch (see 2). On the east side it was called Solomon's Porch. On this (the north side) and the west side it had no distinctive name.

"Let no Gentile enter inside of the barrier and the fence around the sanctuary. Any one trespassing will bring death upon himself as a penalty." Within this Soreg wall a flight of 14 steps led up to a narrow terrace, called the Chêl or Fortification, from which rose a high-towered and gated wall (25 cubits = 43 ft.), very thick like the walls of a fortress, with cloisters and chambers on the inside. These walls

HEROD'S TEMPLE.
Plan of the Holy House.

had 9 gates, 4 on the south, 4 on the north, and one on the east.

Within this double wall was the *Court of the Women,* that is the court into which all Jews, men and women, could enter, but women could not go beyond. The east gate leading from the Court of the Gentiles to the Court of the Women, was probably the gate Beautiful of Acts 3:2, 10. This gateway had magnificent doors of Corinthian brass seventy-five feet high, and adorned with plates of silver and gold. Compare the magnificent gates to the cathedrals of Europe, especially the splendid bronze doors of the Baptistery at Florence, which Michelangelo said were fit to be the gates of paradise.

The Court of the Women was "a large court 135 cubits square, and probably the finance and much other business of the temple was transacted within it." The vaults under the Court of Israel opened into it. Here were the Temple's Treasury and Exchange, and the 13 trumpet-shaped money boxes for offerings. Here we would see "a crowd of Levites in charge of the people's offerings, hucksters, money changers and worshippers on their way to the inner court. The Court of the Women had a gallery high enough to allow the women to view the services in the Court of the Priests. Into this gallery no men were admitted.

Fifteen steps led up from the Court of the Women to the *Court of Israel,* separated from one another by a wall. Beyond the Court of Israel, separated by a barrier, was the *Court of the Priests,* into which none but priests could enter.

In this court was the great *Altar of Sacrifices.* The base was 32 cubits square, and one cubit high. Above it the altar, 30 cubits square, rose 5 cubits high to a ledge one cubit broad on which were the horns of the altar; a little higher another ledge also a cubit broad, "the place for the feet of the priests"; and above this the hearth itself 24 cubits square. On the south a slope of masonry led to the ledge on which the officiating priests stood. This altar stood in front of the open porch of the sanctuary which was reached by a flight of 12 broad steps.

Such is the picture of this strong inner fortress, sanctuary within sanctuary, court within court, signifying a gradual progress toward God himself and his kingdom of righteousness.

THE COURT OF THE GENTILES was the great outer court surrounding the inner court just described. It was a vast stone stage, almost rectangular, held up above Ophel and the Kidron valley by a high and massive wall from 50 to 150 feet and more in height, according to the levels of the rock from which it rises. It was paved throughout. It was defended on all sides by the massive walls rising high above the platform. It was about 900 feet square. The Mishna defines it as a square of 500 cubits = 860 feet. The most magnificent part of the temple, in an architectural point of view, seems certainly to have been the porticos or cloisters which were added to the outer court when it was enlarged by Herod. The cloisters in the west, north and east sides were composed of double rows of Corinthian columns, 25 cubits or 43 feet in height, with flat roof, and resting against the outer wall of the tem-

THE HOLY STONE, THE PEAK OF MT. ZION.
Probably once the basis of the Temple Altar of burnt-offerings; now enclosed by the Mosque of Omar.

ple. The one on the east was called Solomon's Porch. These, however, were immeasurably surpassed in magnificence by the Royal Porch or Stoa Basilica, which overhung the southern wall. It consisted of 162 Corinthian columns in four rows. Each column was a monolith of white stone 25 cubits high. The columns were arranged as a nave and two aisles, that toward the temple being open, that toward the country closed by a wall. The breadth of the centre aisle was 45 feet; of the side aisles, 30 from centre to centre

30FT 45 FT. 30FT COURT OF THE GENTILES

CROSS-SECTION OF THE ROYAL PORCH, With its four rows of pillars and roof. Below are arched vaults or cellars.

of the pillars; their height 43 feet. Its section was thus something in excess of that of York Cathedral, while its total length was one stadium or 600 Greek feet, or 100 feet in excess of York or our largest Gothic cathedrals. The roof was ceiled with cedar, curiously carved and carefully polished. In these cloisters sat teachers with groups of disciples around them. "On the open pavement stand the booths of hucksters and money changers, and from the north sheep and bullocks are being driven toward the inner sanctuary."

GATES. The walls were pierced by at least 8 gates.

On the north one gate.

On the east toward the north the gate Shushan, now called "The Golden."

On the south at least two gates, low down in the wall, with passages leading under the Royal Porch to the Inner Temple.

On the west four gates, to the city.

The whole Temple Area was dominated by the *Tower of Antonia,* situated near the northwest angle of the temple area. Its basis was "a rock 50 cubits high and precipitous all around.

Around the edge ran a rampart 3 cubits high. The tower-like castle was 40 cubits high, while of the towers at the four corners three were 50 cubits high, and the fourth was 70 cubits so as to overlook the temple. This castle did not abut upon the temple cloisters, but between them was either a pair of bridges, as in Sanday's ground plan (facing p. 304), or an open space according to Professor G. A. Smith. Here was a Roman garrison.

THE TEACHING OF THE TEMPLE. The temple and all connected with it had a religious teaching for the people, most of whom could not read, but could understand symbols and visible expressions of great truths.

1. The temple taught the presence of God, and made it real. The arrangement of courts and rooms expressed the progress of the religious life, from the outer world into the court of general worship, then into the more sacred court, the Holy Place, the Holy of Holies.

2. We enter into the Court of the Gentiles through one of the gates which lead into it from the outer world. Men of every kind, from every race, could enter, and come within the influence of the true religion.

3. Entering the inner court is coming into the church and under its influences. It means a decision to begin the new Christian life.

4. We first come to the great altar of burnt offerings. It symbolized sacrifice for sin, some atoning power, expressing our need of forgiveness and God's willingness to forgive. It also expresses consecration to God, giving ourselves to him and to his service.

5. Next we come to the lavers for cleansing, symbolizing the "washing of regeneration," the cleansing of heart and life from sin, as does Christian Baptism.

6. Thus cleansed and forgiven we enter the Holy Place, expressing the holy and useful life of the people of God. Here we find the golden candlestick, signifying the light from heaven by which the Christian walks; the table of shewbread symbolizing the bread of life, and the altar of incense symbolizing the life of prayer.

7. We look through the hangings into the Holy of Holies, the presence of God himself, the perfected life of

heaven, toward which every true child of God is moving all his life, his ideal, his hope, his joy, his eternal home.

8. The people brought their offerings and sacrifices into the inner courts, for no religious service is perfect without the act of giving; and they returned with parts of the animals to join in family parties, or gatherings of friends to thanksgiving feasts all over the city.

9. The whole service was one of religious instruction and inspiration and the enthusiasm of numbers worshipping together.

Ten Commandments. The popular name in this, as in so many instances, is not that of the Hebrew. There we have the "TEN WORDS," Ex. 34:28; Deut. 4:13; 10:4; the "COVENANT," 1 Kings 8:21; 2 Chron. 5:10; 6:11, etc., or, very often as the solemn attestation of the divine will, the "TESTIMONY." Ex. 25:16, 21; 31:18, etc.

The Ten Commandments are a COVENANT OF LOVE, "a loving covenant of God with his people, and not arbitrary commandings of God to his subjects." They are "a loving covenant that binds two parties in mutual affection and fidelity," "having its statement of promises on the one hand, and responsibilities on the other." "A covenant among the Orientals is, and always has been, a sacred compact binding two parties in loving agreement."—*Henry Clay Trumbull.*

On the one hand, God agrees to be their God, giving his fatherly care and love and forgiveness and protection, while they, on their part, agree to keep his commandments and serve him alone. If they disobey, they forfeit all these blessings, as described in Deuteronomy 28-30. "Like her in the 'Knight's Dream of Raphael,' it carries in one hand the book of duty, 'This do, and thou shalt live'; but in the other the drawn sword, 'Do it not, and thou shalt perish.'"—*Farrar.*

THE TWO FORMS. (1) The original form contained in Ex. 20; and (2) a free citation of the words by Moses (Deut. 5:6-21) in his oration to Israel nearly forty years later. There are slight differences in expression, as would be natural in such a reference to them. Such changed forms are common in our reference to them and to the Beatitudes. They do not imply contradictions.

THE THREE-FOLD EXPRESSION OF THE LAW. God has spoken this law in three ways: (1) By his voice; (2) by writing them on the tablets of stone; and (3) he has written them on the very nature of man. It is necessary that they should be definitely expressed, because it would have taken ages for man to discover them by himself, and moreover, they needed the divine authority behind them to make them effective.

We are not to imagine that nothing of these commands was known before Moses. They were written on the hearts and consciences of men from the beginning. We see them in the early history.

THEY ARE A LAW FOR ALL MANKIND. The Jews said that this was the reason why the commandments were not delivered in Palestine, which belonged to Israel, but in the wilderness, which belongs to all the world. Heaven lives according to these commands. But they needed to be put in clear and memorable form, distinct, with God's whole nature and authority behind them. He impressed them on the Jews in such a way that they mark a decisive epoch not only in the history of the Jews, but of all mankind, "the greatest and most important event in universal history" up to the advent of Christ. "They are eternal, inexorable, irresistible!" They are germs or seeds from which the tree of the virtues grows and blossoms and bears fruit; unfolding their details through the ages according to their circumstances and needs. "There is not a sin but is aimed at and denounced in one or other of the ten! God looks over this awful 'world' of sin. He divides sins, just as we divide languages, into certain classes or sets. He takes ten great classes, or *nations,* or *languages,* or *tribes* of sins, and denounces them all," under the title of their head or chief. None of them have been repealed; for it would be absurd to repeal in words a law which is written in the very nature of man.

THE SUM of the ten commandments is Love to God and Love to Man.

THEIR CONNECTION WITH RELIGION. Love being the inspiration and the guide to the keeping of these commands, shows their intimate connection with religion. "Josephus said that in other systems virtue was made a part of religion, but in God's covenant with Israel religion was but a part of virtue. It would be truer to say that the two are inseparably united. In no other religion was it made so clear that the end of the law is to make men righteous. Because, if there be one thing which history has taught more clearly than another, it is that a nation cannot lose its religion without losing also its virtue and its integrity; and the fate of nation after nation, in epoch after epoch, has shown that ages of mental disbelief are ages also of moral iniquity."—*Farrar.*

THE TWO TABLES. Their division duty toward man. The fifth is a connecting link between the two tables, for the authority of parents heads the second table, as the earthly reflex of that authority of the Father of his people and of all men which heads the first, and as the first principle of the whole law of love to our neighbor; because we are all brethren, and the family is, for good and ill, the model of the state. 3. The division recognized by the old Jewish writers, Josephus and Philo, which places five commandments in each table. It has been maintained that the law of filial duty, being a close consequence of God's fatherly relation

CAMP OF BEDOUIN
in Galilee.

into *two tables* is not only expressly mentioned, but the stress laid upon the *two* leaves no doubt that the distinction was important, and that it answered to that summary of the law which was made both by Moses and by Christ into two precepts; so that the *first table* contained *Duties to God,* and the *second, Duties to our Neighbor.* There are three principal divisions of the two tables: 1. That of the Roman Catholic Church, making the first table contain three commandments, and the second the other seven. They unite the first and second, and divide the tenth into two. 2. The familiar division, referring the first four to our duty toward God and the six remaining to our to us, may be referred to the first table.

Tent. Among the leading characteristics of the nomad races, those two have always been numbered whose origin has been ascribed to Jabal the son of Lamech, Gen. 4: 20, viz., to be tent-dwellers and keepers of cattle. The same may be said of the forefathers of the Hebrew race; nor was it until the return into Canaan from Egypt that the Hebrews became inhabitants of cities. An Arab tent is called *beit,* " house;" its covering consists of black goat's hair cloth, Cant. 1: 5. This is sufficient to resist the heaviest rain. The tent-poles or columns are usually nine in number, placed in three groups; but many tents have only one pole.

others two or three. The tent is held in position by long cords fastened to the cloth, which are attached to short sticks or pins, which are driven into the ground with a mallet. Judges 4 : 21. Round the more exposed sides of the tent runs a piece of stuff removable at pleasure to admit air. The tent is divided into two apartments, separated by a carpet partition drawn across the middle of the tent and fastened to the three middle posts. When the pasture near an encampment is exhausted, the tents are taken down, packed on camels and removed. Gen. 26 : 17, 22, 25; Isa. 38 : 12. In choosing places for encampment, Arabs prefer the neighborhood of trees, for the sake of the shade and coolness which they afford. Gen. 18 : 4, 8. *Tent of the Congregation; Tent of Meeting.* [TABERNACLE.]

Te'rah (tĕ'rah), the father of Abram, Nahor and Haran, and through them the ancestor of the great families of the Israelites, Ishmaelites, Midianites, Moabites and Ammonites. Gen. 11 : 24–32. The account given of him in the Old Testament narrative is very brief. We learn from it simply that he was an idolater, Josh. 24 : 2, that he dwelt beyond the Euphrates in Ur of the Chaldees, Gen. 11 : 28, and that in the southwesterly migration, which from some unexplained cause he undertook in his old age, he went with his son Abram, his daughter-in-law Sarai, and his grandson Lot, "to go into the land of Canaan, and they came unto Haran, and dwelt there." Gen. 11 : 31. And finally, "the days of Terah were two hundred and five years; and Terah died in Haran." Gen. 11 : 32. (B.C. 1921.)

Teraphim (tĕr'a-fĭm). This word occurs only in the plural, and denotes images connected with magical rites. The derivation of the name is obscure. In one case—1 Sam. 19 : 13, 16—a single statue seems to be intended by the plural. The teraphim, translated "images" in the Authorized Version, carried away from Laban by Rachel were regarded by Laban as gods, and it would therefore appear that they were used by those who added corrupt practices to the patriarchal religion. Teraphim again are included among Micah's images. Judges 17 : 3–5; 18 : 17, 18, 20. Teraphim were consulted for oracular answers by the Israelites, Zech.

10 : 2; comp. Judges 18 : 5, 6; 1 Sam. 15 : 22, 23; 19 : 13, 16, LXX., and 2 Kings 23 : 24, and by the Babylonians in the case of Nebuchadnezzar. Ezek. 21 : 19–22.

Te'resh (tĕ'resh) (*strictness*), one of the two eunuchs whose plot to assassinate Ahasuerus was discovered by Mordecai. Esther 2 : 21; 6 : 2. He was hanged. (B.C. 479.)

Ter'tius (tĕr'shus) (*third*), probably a Roman, was the amanuensis of Paul in writing the Epistle to the Romans. Rom. 16 : 22. (A.D. 57.)

Tertul'lus (tĕr-tŭl'lus) (diminutive from *Tertius*), "a certain orator," Acts 24 : 1, who was retained by the high priest and Sanhedrin to accuse the apostle Paul at Cæsarea before the Roman procurator Antonius Felix. He evidently belonged to the class of professional orators. We may infer that Tertullus was of Roman, or at all events of Italian, origin. (A.D. 58.)

Tes'tament, New [NEW TESTAMENT; BIBLE.]

Tes'tament, Old. [OLD TESTAMENT; BIBLE.]

Tetrarch (tĕ'trärk), properly the sovereign or governor of the fourth part of a country. Matt. 14 : 1; Luke 3 : 1; 9 : 7; Acts 13 : 1. The title was, however, often applied to anyone who governed a Roman province, of whatever size. The title of king was sometimes used in courtesy to a tetrarch. Matt. 14 : 9; Mark 6 : 14, 22.

Thadde'us (thăd-dē'us), one of the twelve apostles. Matt. 10 : 3; Mark 3 : 18. From a comparison with the catalogue of St. Luke, Luke 6 : 16; Acts 1 : 13, it seems scarcely possible to doubt that the three names of Judas, Lebbeus and Thaddeus were borne by one and the same person. [See JUDAS OR JUDE.]

Tha'hash (thā'hăsh) (probably *porpoise*), son of Nahor by his concubine Reumah. Gen. 22 : 24.

Tha'mah (thā'mah) (*laughter*). "The children of Thamah" were a family of Nethinim who returned with Zerubbabel. Ezra 2 : 53.

Tha'mar (thā'mar). TAMAR, 1. Matt. 1 : 3.

Thammuz. [MONTHS.]

Thank offering, or Peace offering, the properly eucharistic offering among the Jews, in its theory indicated that the offerer was already reconciled to and in covenant with God. Its ceremonial is described in Lev. 3. The peace offerings, unlike other sacrifices, were not ordained to be offered in fixed and regular course. The only constantly recurring peace offering appears to have been that of the two firstling lambs at Pentecost. Lev. 23 : 19. The general principle of the peace offering seems to have been that it should be entirely spontaneous, offered as occasion should arise, from the feeling of the sacrificer himself. Lev. 19 : 5. On the first institution, Lev. 7 : 11–17, peace offerings are divided into "offerings of thanksgiving" and "vows or freewill offerings;" of which latter class the offering by a Nazirite on the completion of his vow is the most remarkable. Num. 6 : 14. We find accordingly peace offerings offered for the people on a great scale at periods of unusual solemnity or rejoicing. In two cases only —Judges 20 : 26; 2 Sam. 24 : 25—peace offerings are mentioned as offered with burnt offerings at a time of national sorrow and fasting.

Tha'ra (thā'rȧ). Terah the father of Abraham. Luke 3 : 34.

Thar'shish (thär'shĭsh). Probably Tartessus in Spain. [TARSHISH.] 2. A Benjamite, one of the family of Bilhan and the house of Jediael. 1 Chron. 7 : 10 only. R. V. Tarshish.

Theatre. For the explanation of the biblical allusions, two or three points only require notice. The Greek term, like the corresponding English term, denotes the *place* where dramatic performances are exhibited, and also the *scene* itself or *spectacle* which is witnessed there. It occurs in the first or local sense in Acts 19 : 29. The same Greek word in the other sense is translated "spectacle in 1 Cor. 4 : 9. Margin "theatre."

Thebes (Authorized Version No, the multitude of No, populous No, R. V. No, and No-Amon), a chief city of ancient Egypt, long the capital of the upper country, and the seat of the Diospolitan dynasties, that ruled over all Egypt at the era of its highest splendor. It was situated on both sides of the Nile, 400 or 500 miles from its mouth. [NO-AMON.] The origin of the city is lost in antiquity. Niebuhr is of opinion that Thebes was much older than Memphis, and that, "after the

centre of Egyptian life was transferred to lower Egypt, Memphis acquired its greatness through the ruin of Thebes." But both cities date from our earliest authentic knowledge of Egyptian history. The first allusion to Thebes in classical literature is the familiar passage of the Iliad (ix. 381–385) : "Egyptian Thebes, where are vast treasures laid up in the houses; where are a hundred gates, and from each two hundred men go forth with horses and chariots." In the first century before

THE COLOSSI AT THEBES.

Christ, Diodorus visited Thebes, and he devotes several sections of his general work to its history and appearance. Though he saw the city when it had sunk to quite secondary importance, he confirms the tradition of its early grandeur—its circuit of 140 stadia, the size of its public edifices, the magnificence of its temples, the number of its monuments, the dimensions of its private houses, some of them four or five stories high—all giving it an air of grandeur and beauty surpassing not only all other cities of Egypt, but of the world. It was conquered by Assyria, Babylonia and Persia, but still remained a city of importance. By the Roman prefect Cornelius Gallus it was totally destroyed in 30–29 B.C., for its part in a revolt in Upper Egypt. To Strabo (B.C. 24) Thebes was a city of ruins as it is to-day. *Monuments.*—The monuments of Thebes are the most reliable witnesses for the ancient splendor of the city. These are found in almost equal proportions upon both sides of the river. The plan of the city, as indicated by the principal monuments, was nearly quadrangular, measuring two miles from north to south and four from east to west. Its four great landmarks were, Karnak and Luxor upon the eastern or Arabian side, and *Qoornah* and *Medeenet Haboo* upon the western or Libyan side. There are indications that each of these temples may have been connected with those facing it upon two sides by grand *dromoi*, lined with sphinxes and other colossal figures. Upon the western bank there was almost a continuous line of temples and public edifices for a distance of two miles, from *Qoornah* to *Medeenet Haboo;* and Wilkinson conjectures that from a point near the latter, perhaps in the line of the colossi, the " Royal street" ran down to the river, which was crossed by a ferry terminating at Luxor, on the eastern side. Behind this long range of temples and palaces are the Libyan hills, which for a distance of five miles are excavated to the depth of several hundred feet for sepulchral chambers. Some of these, in the number and variety of their chambers, the finish of their sculptures, and the beauty and freshness of their frescoes, are among the most remarkable monuments of Egyptian grandeur and skill. The eastern side of the river is distinguished by the remains of Luxor and Karnak, the latter being of itself a city of temples. The approach to Karnak from the south is marked by a series of majestic gateways and towers, which were the appendages of later times to the original structure. The temple properly faces the river, *i. e.* toward the northwest. The courts and propylæa connected with this structure occupy a space nearly 1800 feet square, and the buildings represent almost every dynasty of Egypt. Ezekiel proclaims the destruction of Thebes by the arm of Babylon, Ezek. 30:14–16; and Jeremiah predicted the same overthrow. Jer. 46:25, 26. The city lies to-day a nest of Arab hovels amid crumbling columns and drifting sands.

The′bez (thē′bez) (*brightness*), a place memorable for the death of the brave Abimelech, Judges 9:50, was known to Eusebius and Jerome, in whose time it was situated " in the district of Neapolis," 13 Roman miles therefrom, on the road to Scythopolis. There it still is, its name—*Tubâs*—hardly changed.

Thela′sar (thė-lā′sar). [TELASSAR.]

Theoph′ilus (thė-ŏf′ĭ-lus) (*friend of God*), the person to whom St. Luke dedicated his Gospel and the Acts of the Apostles. Luke 1:3; Acts 1:1. From the honorable epithet applied to him in Luke 1:3, it has been argued with much probability that he was a person in high official position. All that can be conjectured with any degree of safety concerning him comes to this, that he was a Gentile of rank and consideration, who came under the influence of St. Luke or under that of St. Paul at Rome, and was converted to the Christian faith.

Thessalo′nians, Epistles to the. These Epistles are not only the earliest of Paul's extant writings, but the earliest in the New Testament.

THE FIRST EPISTLE to the Thessalonians was written by the apostle Paul at Corinth, A.D. 51 or 52, a few months after he had founded the church at Thessalonica, and soon after Silas and Timothy had joined Paul there, bringing news from Thessalonica.

THE SECOND EPISTLE followed after a short period, for Silas (Silvanus) and Timothy, were still with Paul (2 Thes. 1:1). Its purpose was to correct still further the misconceptions which led to the writing of the first epistle, and to give additional instruction and comfort. The general subject was the same in both.

The Epistle, says Farrar, "has the six features which occur in nearly all St. Paul's letters to churches, namely: (1) The greeting, (2) the thanksgiving, (3) a doctrinal section, (4) a practical section, (5) personal messages, (6) a final salutation."

HISTORICAL SITUATION. Three missionaries had come there from Philippi, two of them torn and bruised by a terrible flagellation at Philippi, emerging from the lowest dungeon of a prison, their whole aspect bespeaking " their poverty, their sufferings, their earthly insignificance." A famine, says Farrar, "was raging in the Roman empire, and the commonest necessaries of life had risen to six times their proper value." These poor persecuted wanderers supported themselves by weaving black goat's hair into tent cloth. Here they preached a few weeks, founded a church, and were driven away by persecution, before Paul had finished the work he had hoped to accomplish there. Paul longed to visit them again, and made three vain attempts to do so, from Berea, from Athens, from Corinth. He felt their need of training and of more knowledge of the truth, of comfort, of guidance. Instead, he sent Timothy there to strengthen them (1 Thes. 3:2). And finally, three or four months after he left them, he wrote them a letter. Timothy had just come back from Thessalonica, and had brought a report concerning the church, giving a favorable account in general. But two facts were made known by him. One was that they were suffering severe persecutions from both Jews and Gentiles; the other that they were discouraged and troubled by the death of some before the second coming of the Lord Jesus.

As a comfort and encouragement to the Thessalonians in their persecutions and troubles, Paul who himself had been driven from them by persecution, and knew by experience the truth of what he was saying, wrote them an Epistle whose keynote is hope and joy as seen through the darkness of affliction and calamity, stars shining through rifts in the clouds showing the heaven beyond. "Much affliction with joy of the Holy Ghost" (1 Thes. 1:6). This "was the sign of a new epoch in the history of human souls." This is reinforced by his emphasis on practical duties, for it is through these that men triumph over trouble, and are best prepared for the coming of the Lord. Paul assures the Thessalonians that the Lord is coming as he promised, but they had no need to fear that the living should be excluded from their share in the glories of that day. The Thessalonians were not mistaken as to the nearness of the coming which Christ had promised should be within a generation of his death, but they did not understand how he would come, and some failed to realize the true way of preparation for the coming.

Thessaloni'ca (thĕs-sa-lō-nī'ka). The original name of this city was Therma; and that part of the Macedonian shore on which it was situated retained through the Roman period the designation of the Thermaic Gulf. Cassander the son of Antipater rebuilt and enlarged Therma, and named it after his wife Thessalonica, the sister of Alexander the Great. The name ever since, under various slight modifications, has been continuous, and the city itself has never ceased to be eminent. Strabo in the first century speaks of Thessalonica as the most populous city in Macedonia. *Saloniki* is still the most important town of that part of Greece, with a population of over 170,000.

Visit of Paul.—St. Paul visited Thessalonica (with Silas and Timothy) during his second missionary journey, and introduced Christianity there. The first scene of the apostle's work at Thessalonica was the synagogue. Acts 17: 1–3. It is stated that the ministrations among the Jews continued for three weeks, ver. 2. Not that we are obliged to limit to this time the whole stay of the apostle at Thessalonica. A flourishing church was certainly formed there; and the epistles show that its elements were more Gentile than Jewish. [For persecution and further history see PAUL.] *Circumstances which led Paul to Thessalonica.*—Three circumstances must here be mentioned which illustrate in an important manner this visit and this journey as well as the two Epistles to the Thessalonians. 1. This was the chief station on the great Roman road called the *Via Egnatia,* which connected Rome with the whole region to the north of the Ægean Sea. 2. Placed as it was on this great road, and in connection with other important Roman ways, Thessalonica was an invaluable centre for the spread of the gospel. In fact it was nearly if not quite on a level with Corinth and Ephesus in its share of the commerce of the Levant. 3. The circumstance noted in Acts 17: 1, that here was the synagogue of the Jews in this part of Macedonia, had evidently much to do with the apostle's plans, and also doubtless with his success. Trade would inevitably bring Jews to Thessalonica; and it is remarkable that they have ever since had a prominent place in the annals of the city. *Later ecclesiastical history.*—During several centuries this city was the bulwark, not simply of the later Greek empire, but of Oriental Christendom, and was largely instrumental in the conversion of the Slavonians and Bulgarians. Thus it received the designation of "the orthodox city;" and its struggles are very prominent in the writings of the Byzantine historians.

Theu'das (thū'das) (*God-given*), the name of an insurgent mentioned in Gamaliel's speech before the Jewish council, Acts 5 : 35–39, at the time of the arraignment of the apostles. He appeared, according to Luke's account, at the head of about four hundred men. He was probably one of the insurrectionary chiefs or fanatics by whom the land was overrun in the last year of Herod's reign. Josephus speaks of a Theudas who played a similar part in the time of Claudius, about A.D. 44; but the Theudas mentioned by St. Luke must be a different person from the one spoken of by Josephus.

Thieves, The two. The men who under this name appear in the history of the crucifixion were robbers rather than thieves, belonging to the lawless bands by which Palestine was at that time and afterward infested. Against these brigands every Roman procurator had to wage continual war. It was necessary to use an armed police to encounter them. Luke 22 : 52. Of the previous history of the two who suffered on Golgotha we know nothing. They had been tried and condemned, and were waiting their execution before our Lord was accused. It is probable enough, as the death of Barabbas was clearly expected at the same time, that they had taken part in his insurrection. Some of these brigands were so from a mistaken sense of patriotism. The popular cry for Barabbas makes it at least possible that he was one of these, and if these were his followers they might be of the same class. Both caught at first the prevailing tone of scorn at the crucifixion, and reviled Jesus. One however, was at last touched with awe at the meekness and forgiving spirit of Jesus, and rebuking his fellow asked for acceptance by Jesus when he came into his kingdom.

Thim'nathah (thĭm'na-thah), a town in the allotment of Dan. Josh. 19 : 43 only. It is named between Elon and Ekron. [See TIMNAH.]

Thistle. [THORNS AND THISTLES.]

Thom'as (*a twin*), one of the apostles. According to Eusebius, his real name was Judas. This may have been a mere confusion with Thaddeus, who is mentioned in the extract, but it may also be that the name was his. Out of this name has grown the tradition that he had a twin-sister, Lysia, or that he was a twin-brother of our Lord, for which there is no ground. He is said to have been born at Antioch. In the catalogue of the apostles he is coupled with Matthew in Matt. 10 : 3 ; Mark 3 : 18 ; Luke 6 : 15, and with Philip in Acts 1 : 13. All that we know of him is derived from the Gospel of St. John ; and this amounts to three traits, which, however, so exactly agree together that, slight as they are, they place his character before us with a precision which belongs to no other of the twelve apostles except Peter, John and Judas Iscariot. This character is that of a man slow to believe, seeing all the difficulties of a case, subject to despondency, viewing things on the darker side, yet full of ardent love of his Master. The latter trait was shown in his speech when our Lord determined to face the dangers that awaited him in Judea on his journey to Bethany. Thomas said to his fellow disciples, "Let us also go, that we may die with him." John 11 : 16. His unbelief appeared in his question during the Last Supper : "Thomas saith unto him, Lord, we know not whither thou goest, and how can we know the way?" John 14 : 5. It was the prosaic, incredulous doubt as to moving a step in the unseen future, and yet an eager inquiry as to how this step was to be taken. The first-named trait was seen after the resurrection. He was absent from the first assembly when Jesus had appeared. The others told him what they had seen. He broke forth into an exclamation, the terms of which convey to us at once the vehemence of his doubt, and at the same time the vivid picture that his mind retained of his Master's form as he had last seen him lifeless on the cross. John 20 : 25. On the eighth day he was with them at their gathering, perhaps in expectation of a recurrence of the visit of the previous week ; and Jesus stood among them. He uttered the same salutation, "Peace be unto you;"

and then turning to Thomas, offered him the evidence he required. The effect on him was immediate. The conviction produced by the removal of his doubt became deeper and stronger than that of any of the other apostles. The words in which he expressed his belief contain a far higher assertion of his Master's divine nature than is contained in any other expression used by apostolic lips—" My Lord and my God." The answer of our Lord sums up the moral of the whole narrative: " Because thou hast seen me, thou hast believed: blessed are they that have not seen me, and yet have believed." John 20:29. In the New Testament we hear of Thomas only twice again, once on the Sea of Galilee with the seven disciples, where he is ranked next after Peter, John 21:2, and again in the assemblage of the apostles after the ascension. Acts 1:13. The earlier traditions, as believed in the fourth century, represent him as preaching in Parthia or Persia, and as finally buried at Edessa. The later traditions carry him farther east. His martyrdom, whether in Persia or India, is said to have been occasioned by a lance, and is commemorated by the Latin Church on December 21, by the Greek Church on October 6, and by the Indians on July 1.

Thorns and **Thistles.** There appear to be eighteen or twenty Hebrew words which point to different kinds of prickly

PALESTINE THORN.

or thorny shrubs. These words are variously rendered in the Authorized Version by "thorns," "briers," "thistles," etc. Palestine abounded in a great variety of such plants. Probably there is no country on earth where so many plants of this sort exist. As many as 200 different species of thorny plants are found there besides many
44

others which are " clothed with scabrous, strigose or stinging hairs, and another multitude with prickly fruits." One of the most striking sights in Palestine is the relish with which goats and camels eat these tough thorny plants. *Crown of thorns.*—The "crown of thorns," Matt. 27:29, which was put in derision upon our Lord's head before his crucifixion, is by some supposed to have been the *Rhamnus,* or *Spina Christi;* others think it the *Capparis spinosa.* [CROWN OF THORNS.]

Three Taverns, a station on the Appian Road, along which St. Paul traveled from Puteoli to Rome. Acts 28:15. The distances, reckoning southward from Rome, are given as follows in the *Antonine Itinerary:* "To Aricia, 16 miles; to Three Taverns, 17 miles; to Appii Forum, 10 miles;" and, comparing this with what is still observed along the line of road, it is generally inferred that "Three Taverns" was near the modern *Cisterna.* Just at this point a road came in from Antium on the coast. There is no doubt that "Three Taverns" was a frequent meeting-place of travelers.

Threshing. [AGRICULTURE.]

Threshold. Of the two words so rendered in the Authorized Version, one, *miphthân,* seems to be the special term for the threshold of the sanctuary proper. 1 Sam. 5:4; Zeph. 1:9; Ezek. 9:3; 10:4, 18; 46:2; 47:1.

Thresholds, The. This word, *Asuppê,* translated in the A. V. "the thresholds of the gates" is rendered in the R. V. "the storehouses of the gates." They were probably buildings for the storage of temple goods. Neh. 12:25.

Throne. The Hebrew word so translated applies to any elevated seat occupied by a person in authority, whether a high priest, 1 Sam. 1:9, a judge, Ps. 122:5, or a military chief. Jer. 1:15. The use of a chair in a country where the usual postures were squatting and reclining was at all times regarded as a symbol of dignity. 2 Kings 4:10; Prov. 9:14. In order to specify a throne in our sense of the term, it was necessary to add to the word the notion of royalty; hence the frequent occurrence of such expressions as "throne of the kingdom." Deut. 17:18; 1 Kings 1:46; 2 Chron. 7:18. The characteristic feature in the royal throne was its elevation: Solomon's throne was approached by six steps, 1 Kings 10:19; 2 Chron. 9:18; and Jehovah's throne is described as "high and lifted up." Isa. 6:1. The materials and workmanship of Solomon's throne were costly. It was made of wood inlaid with ivory and then covered with gold except where the ivory showed. It was furnished with arms or "stays." The steps were also lined with pairs of lions. As to the form of chair, we are

ASSYRIAN THRONE OR CHAIR OF STATE.

only informed in 1 Kings 10:19 that "the top was round behind." The king sat on his throne on state occasions. At such times he appeared in his royal robes. The throne was the symbol of supreme power and dignity. Gen. 41:40. Similarly, "to sit upon the throne" implied the exercise of regal power. Deut. 17:18; 1 Kings 16:11.

Thummim. [URIM AND THUMMIM.]

Thunder is hardly ever heard in Palestine from the middle of April to the middle of September; hence it was selected by Samuel as a striking expression of the divine displeasure toward the Israelites. 1 Sam. 12:17. Rain in harvest was deemed as extraordinary as snow in summer, Prov. 26:1, and Jerome states that he had never witnessed it in the latter part of June or July. *Comm.* on Amos 4:7. In the imaginative philosophy of the Hebrews, thunder was regarded as the voice of Jehovah. Job 37:2, 4, 5; 40:

9; Ps. 18:13; 29:3-9; Isa. 30:30, 31, who dwelt behind the thunder-cloud. Ps. 81:7. Thunder was, to the mind of the Jew, the symbol of divine power, Ps. 29:3, etc., and vengeance. 1 Sam. 2:10; 2 Sam. 22:14.

Thyati'ra (thī-a-tī'rà), an ancient city of Lydia, refounded by Seleucus Nicator, on the road from Pergamos to Sardis, and on the very confines of Mysia and Lydia, so as to be sometimes reckoned within the one and sometimes within the other. Dyeing apparently formed an important part of the industrial activity of Thyatira, as it did of that of Colossæ and Laodicea. It is first mentioned in connection with Lydia, "a seller of purple," Acts 16:14. One of the Seven Churches of Asia was established here. Rev. 2:18-29. The principal deity of the city was Apollo; but there was another superstition, of an extremely curious nature, which seems to have been brought thither by some of the corrupted Jews of the dispersed tribes. A fane stood outside the walls, dedicated to *Sambatha*—the name of the sibyl who is sometimes called Chaldæan, sometimes Jewish, sometimes Persian—in the midst of an enclosure designated "the Chaldæans' court." This seems to lend an illustration to the obscure passage in Rev. 2:20, 21. Now there is evidence to show that in Thyatira there was a great amalgamation of races. If the sibyl Sambatha was in reality a Jewess, lending her aid to the amalgamation of different religions, and not discountenanced by the authorities of the Judeo-Christian Church at Thyatira, both the censure and its qualification become easy of explanation. The present name of the city is *ak-Hissar* ("white castle"). It has a reputation for the manufacture of scarlet cloth. Its present population is about 12,000.

Thyine wood occurs in Rev. 18:12, where the margin has "sweet" (wood). There can be little doubt that the wood here spoken of is that of the *Thuya articulata,* Desfont., the *Callitris quadrivalvis* of present botanists. It is a cone-bearing tree and allied to the cypress. This tree was much prized by the ancient Greeks and Romans on account of the beauty of its wood for various ornamental purposes. It is dark brown, very hard and durable.

Tibe'rias (ti-bē'rĭ-às), a city in the time of Christ, on the Sea of Galilee; first mentioned in the New Testament, John 6:1, 23; 21:1, and then by Josephus, who states that it was built by Herod Antipas, and was named by him in honor of the emperor Tiberius. Tiberias was the capital of Galilee from the time of its origin until the reign of Herod Agrippa II., who changed the seat of power back again to Sepphoris, where it had been before the founding of the new city. Many of the inhabitants were Greeks and Romans, and foreign customs prevailed there to such an extent as to give offence to the stricter Jews. It is remarkable that the Gospels give us no intimation that the Saviour, who spent so much of his public life in Galilee, ever visited Tiberias. The place is only mentioned in the New Testament in John 6:23. *History.*—Tiberias has an interesting history apart from its strictly biblical associations. It bore a conspicuous part in the wars between the Jews and the Romans. The Sanhedrin, subsequent to the fall of Jerusalem, after a temporary sojourn at Jamnia and Sepphoris, became fixed there about the middle of the second century. Celebrated schools of Jewish learning flourished there through a succession of several centuries. The Mishna was compiled at this place by the great Rabbi Judah Hakkodesh, A.D. 190 or 220; and the Palestinian Talmud about 420 A.D. The city has been possessed successively by Romans, Persians, Arabs and Turks. *Present City.*—The ancient name has survived in that of the modern *Tŭbaryeh*, which occupies the original site. Near *Tŭbaryeh*, about a mile farther south along the shore, are the celebrated warm baths, which the Roman naturalists reckoned among the greatest known curiosities of the world. It was nearly destroyed in 1837 by an earthquake, by which 600 persons lost their lives. The population is now about 6000.

Tibe'rias (ti-bē'rĭ-às), **The Sea of.** John 21:1. [GALILEE, SEA OF.]

Tibe'rius (ti-bē'rĭ-ŭs) (in full, Tiberius Claudius Nero), the second Roman emperor, successor of Augustus, who began to reign A.D. 14 and reigned until A.D. 37. He was the son of Tiberius Claudius Nero and Livia, and hence a stepson of Augustus. He was born at Rome on the 16th of November, B.C. 42. He became emperor in his fifty-fifth year, after having distinguished himself as a commander in various

HEAD OF EMPEROR TIBERIUS.

wars, and having evinced talents of a high order as an orator and an administrator of civil affairs. He even gained the reputation of possessing the sterner virtues of the Roman character, and was regarded as entirely worthy of the imperial honors to which his

SILVER DENARIUS OF TIBERIUS.
(Penny, Matt. 18:28, etc., equals 16 cts.)

birth and supposed personal merits at length opened the way. Yet, on being raised to the supreme power, he suddenly became, or showed himself to be, a very different man. His subsequent life was one of inactivity, sloth and self-indulgence. He was despotic in his government, cruel and vindictive in his disposition. He died A.D. 37, at the age of 78, after a reign of twenty-three years. Our Saviour was put to death in the reign of Tiberius.

Tib′hath (tĭb′hath) (*extensive*), a city of Hadarezer, king of Zobah, 1 Chron. 18 : 8, which in 2 Sam. 8 : 8 is called Betah. Its exact position is unknown, but it was possibly on the eastern slopes of anti-Lebanon.

Tib′ni (tĭb′nĭ). After Zimri had burnt himself in his palace, there was a division in the northern kingdom, half of the people following Tibni the son of Ginath, and half following Omri. 1 Kings 16 : 21, 22. Omri was the choice of the army. Tibni was probably put forward by the people of Tirzah, which was then besieged by Omri and his host. The struggle between the contending factions lasted four years (comp. 1 Kings 16 : 15, 23), B.C. 889–885, when Tibni died.

Ti′dal (tĭ′dal), is mentioned only in Gen. 14 : 1, 9. (B.C. about 1913). In the A. V. he is called "king of nations." R. V. "king of Goiim." His name has recently been found by Mr. Pinches in a cuneiform tablet under the form of *Tudghula.* He is named as king of a people living in the mountains northeast of Babylonia, whose name is the Babylonian equivalent of the Heb. Goiim.

Tig′lath=pile′ser (tĭg-lăth-pī-lē′sĕr). (In 1 Chron. 5 : 26, and again in 2 Chron. 28 : 20, the name of this king is given as TILGATH-PILNESER, a corrupt form.) The Tiglath-pileser of the Old Testament is Tiglath-pileser III, whose original name, apparently, was Pulu. He first became known to the Israelites under the name of *Pul.* 2 Kings 15 : 19. He usurped the throne of Assyria about B.C. 745. Shortly after his accession he made a campaign against northern Syria, and Menehem of Israel among other neighboring kings, paid him tribute, B.C. 738. When Pekah of Israel and Rezin of Damascus made a league and attacked Ahaz of Judah the latter asked aid of the powerful Assyrian king. Tiglath-pileser then attacked Philistia, Phœnicia, Syria, and northern Israel, "took Ijon, and Abel-beth-maachah, and Janoah, and Kedesh, and Hazor, and Gilead, and Galilee, and all the land of Naphtali, and carried them captive to Assyria." 2 Kings 15 : 29. After the cap-

ture of Damascus and the death of Rezin, Tiglath-pileser held court at Damascus, and Ahaz was there, among other subject princes. 2 Kings 16 : 10. The revolt of Hoshea against Pekah in 729 B.C. was doubtless at Tiglath-pileser's instigation, or at least his connivance. After the fall of Damascus he returned to Nineveh. In 728 B.C. he occupied Babylon, and made himself king of that country, receiving the crown from the hands of Bel and becoming legitimate ruler of all western Asia. He built two palaces, one at Nineveh, and one at Calah, now *Nimrud.* He died B.C. 727, after a reign of 18 years, during which he raised the Assyrian empire to the highest point of power and glory. The records of his reign credit him with great executive and administrative ability, as well as military, and assign to him the first experiment in political centralization.

Ti′gris (tĭ′gris), is used by the LXX. as the Greek equivalent of the Hebrew *Hiddekel,* and occurs also in several of the apocryphal books, as in Tobit, ch. 6 : 1, Judith, ch. 1 : 6, and Ecclesiasticus, ch. 24 : 25. The Tigris, like the Euphrates, rises from two principal sources in the Armenian mountains, and flows into the Euphrates. Its length, is reckoned at 1146 miles. It receives, along its middle and lower course, no fewer than five important tributaries. These are the river of *Zakko* or eastern Tigris, the Great Zab (*Zab Ala*), the Lesser Zab (*Zab Asfal*), the *Adhem,* and the *Diyaleh.* We find but little mention of the Tigris in Scripture. It appears, indeed, under the name of Hiddekel, among the rivers of Eden, Gen. 2 : 14, and is there correctly described as "running eastward to Assyria;" but after this we hear no more of it, if we except one doubtful allusion in Nahum, ch. 2 : 6, until the captivity, when it becomes well known to the prophet Daniel. With him it is "the Great River." The Tigris, in its upper course, anciently ran through Armenia and Assyria.

Tik′vah (tĭk′vah) (*expectation*). 1. The father of Shallum the husband of the prophetess Huldah. 2 Kings 22 : 14.

2. The father of Jahaziah. Ezra 10 : 15.

Tik′vath (*expectation*), (in Revised

Version *Tokhath*), Tikvah the father of Shallum. 2 Chron. 34:22.

Til′gath=pilne′ser, a variation, and probably a corruption, of the name Tiglath-pileser. 1 Chron. 5:6, 26; 2 Chron. 28:20.

Ti′lon (ti′lon) (*gift*), one of the four sons of Shimon, whose family is reckoned in the genealogies of Judah. 1 Chron. 4:20.

Timæ′us (tī-mē′us), the father of the blind man, Bartimæus. Mark 10:46.

Timbrel, tabret (Heb. *tôph*). In old English tabor was used for any

TIMBREL.

drum. Tabouret and tabourine are diminutives of tabor, and denote the instrument now known as the tambourine. Tabret is a contraction of tabouret. The Hebrew *tôph* is undoubtedly the instrument described by travelers as the *duff* or *diff* of the Arabs. It was played principally by women, Ex. 15:20; Judges 11:34; 1 Sam. 18:6; Ps. 68:25, as an accompaniment to the song and dance. The *diff* of the Arabs is described by Russell as "a hoop (sometimes with pieces of brass fixed in it to make a jingling) over which a piece of parchment is stretched. It is beaten with the fingers, and is the true tympanum of the ancients." In Barbary it is called *tar.*

Tim′na (tĭm′nà), or **Tim′nah** (*restraint*). 1. A concubine of Eliphaz son of Esau, and mother of Amalek, Gen. 36:12; it may be presumed that she was the same as Timna sister of Lotan, mentioned in Gen. 36:22, and 1 Chron. 1:39.

2. A duke or phylarch of Edom in the last list in Gen. 36:40–43; 1 Chron. 1:51–54. Timnah was probably the name of a place or a district. [See the following article.]

Tim′nah (*portion*). 1. A place which formed one of the landmarks on the north boundary of the allotment of Judah. Josh. 15:10. It was later given to Dan, and was occupied by the Philistines both in the time of Samson and in that of Ahaz (2 Chron. 28:18). It is in the A. V. called Thimnathah in Josh. 19:43, and Timnath in Judges 14:1, 2, 5. The R. V. has Timnah in all places. The old name is retained almost unchanged and is now *Tibneh,* a village about 3 miles west of *Ain Shems* (Bethshemesh). The site is deserted, but there are ruins, vineyards and olive groves.

2. A town in the mountain district of Judah. Josh. 15:57. A distinct place from that just examined. It is now thought by most scholars to be Tibna, near Gibeah, and 8 miles west of Bethlehem. This is probably the same place which is inaccurately written Timnah in the Authorized Version, the scene of the adventure of Judah with his daughter-in-law Tamar. Gen. 38:12, 13, 14. There is nothing here to indicate its position.

3. TIMNA 2.

Tim′nath (tĭm-nath). [TIMNAH.]

Tim′nath=he′res (tĭm′nath-hē′rēz) (*portion of the sun*), the name under which the city and burial-place of Joshua is mentioned in Judges 2:9. [TIMNATH-SERAH.]

Tim′nath-se′rah (tĭm′nath-sē′rah) (*extra portion*), the name of the city which was presented to Joshua after the partition of the country, Josh. 19:50, and in "the border" of which he was buried. Josh. 24:30. It is specified as "in Mount Ephraim on the north side of Mount Gaash." In Judges 2:9 the name is TIMNATH-HERES, perhaps a copyist's error. Two sites are proposed for this place: (1) *Kefr Chares,* about 9 miles south of Shechem (*Nablûs*), which is according to existing Samaritan tradition the burial-place of both Joshua and Caleb. (2) *Tibneh,* the site approved by most moderns, by Josephus who calls it *Thamna,* and by Eusebius and Jerome. This is about 8½ miles south of the first site.

Tim′nite (tĭm′nīte), **The,** Samson's father-in-law, a native of Timnah. Judges 15:6.

Ti′mon (tī′mon), one of the seven, commonly called "deacons," chosen to look after the "daily ministration." Acts 6:1–6. He was probably a Hellenist.

Timo'theus (ti-mō'the-ŭs). The Greek name of Timothy. Acts 16 : 1; 17 : 14.

Tim'othy (*worshiper of God*). The well-known companion and assistant of St. Paul from the early part of his second missionary journey. The terms which the apostle applies to him, "my beloved son" (1 Cor. 4 : 17) and "my own son in the faith" (1 Tim. 1 : 2), seem to indicate that he had been the means of Timothy's conversion. Timothy was the son of one of those mixed marriages which, though condemned by stricter Jewish opinion, were yet not uncommon in the later periods of Jewish history. The father's name is unknown; he was a Greek, *i. e.* a Gentile, by descent. Acts 16 : 1, 3. The absence of any personal allusion to the father in the Acts or Epistles suggests the inference that he must have died or disappeared during his son's infancy. The care of the boy thus devolved upon his mother Eunice, a Jewess, and her mother Lois. 2 Tim. 1 : 5. Under their training his education was emphatically Jewish. "From a child" he learned to "know the Holy Scriptures" daily. The language of the Acts leaves it uncertain whether Lystra or Derbe was the residence of the devout family. The arrival of Paul and Barnabas in Lycaonia, A.D. 49, Acts 14 : 6, brought the message of glad tidings to Timothy and his mother, and they received it with "unfeigned faith." 2 Tim. 1 : 5. During the interval of seven years between the apostle's first and second journeys the boy grew up to manhood. Those who had the deepest insight into character, and spoke with a prophetic utterance, pointed to him, 1 Tim. 1 : 18; 4 : 14, as others had pointed before to Paul and Barnabas, Acts 13 : 2, as specially fit for the missionary work in which the apostle was engaged. Personal feeling led St. Paul to the same conclusion, Acts 16 : 3, and he was solemnly set apart to do the work and possibly to bear the title of evangelist. 1 Tim. 4 : 14; 2 Tim. 1 : 6; 4 : 5. A great obstacle, however, presented itself. Timothy, though reckoned as one of the seed of Abraham, had been allowed to grow up to the age of manhood without the sign of circumcision. With a special view to the feelings of the Jews, making no sacrifice of principle, the apostle, who had refused to permit the circumcision of Titus, "took and circumcised" Timothy. Acts 16 : 3. Henceforth Timothy was one of his most constant companions. They and Silvanus, and probably Luke also, journeyed to Philippi, Acts 16 : 12, and there the young evangelist was conspicuous at once for his filial devotion and his zeal. Philip. 2 : 22. His name does not appear in the account of St. Paul's work at Thessalonica, and it is possible that he remained some time at Philippi. He appears, however, at Berea, and remains there with Silas when Paul is obliged to leave, Acts 17 : 14, going afterward to join his master at Athens. 1 Thess. 3 : 2. From Athens he is sent back to Thessalonica, *ibid.,* as having special gifts for comforting and teaching. He returns from Thessalonica, not to Athens, but to Corinth, and his name appears united with St. Paul's in the opening words of both the letters written from that city to the Thessalonians. 1 Thess. 1 : 1; 2 Thess. 1 : 1. Of the next five years of his life we have no record. When we next meet with him, it is as being sent on in advance when the apostle was contemplating the long journey which was to include Macedonia, Achaia, Jerusalem and Rome. Acts 19 : 22. It is probable that he returned by the same route and met St. Paul according to a previous arrangement, 1 Cor. 16 : 11, and was thus with him when the Second Epistle was written to the church of Corinth. 2 Cor. 1 : 1. He returns with the apostle to that city, and joins in messages of greeting to the disciples whom he had known personally at Corinth, and who had since found their way to Rome. Rom. 16 : 21. He forms one of the company of friends who go with St. Paul to Philippi, and then sail by themselves, waiting for his arrival by a different ship. Acts 20 : 3–6. The absence of his name from Acts 27 leads to the conclusion that he did not share in the perilous voyage to Italy. He must have joined the apostle, however, apparently soon after his arrival at Rome, and was with him when the Epistles to the Philippians, to the Colossians and to Philemon were written. Philip. 1 : 1; 2 : 19; Col. 1 : 1; Phil. ver. 1. All the indications of this period point to incessant missionary activity.

From the two Epistles addressed to

Timothy we are able to put together a few notices as to his later life. It follows from 1 Tim. 1:3 that he and his master, after the release of the latter from his imprisonment, A.D. 63, revisited proconsular Asia; that the apostle then continued his journey to Macedonia, while the disciple remained, half reluctantly, even weeping at the separation, 2 Tim. 1:4, at Ephesus, to check, if possible, the outgrowth of heresy and licentiousness which had sprung up there. The position in which he found himself might well make him anxious. He had to rule presbyters most of whom were older than himself. 1 Tim. 4:12. Leaders of rival sects were there. The name of his beloved teacher was no longer honored as it had been. We cannot wonder that the apostle, knowing these trials, should be full of anxiety and fear for his disciple's steadfastness. In the Second Epistle to him, A.D. 66 or 67, this deep personal feeling utters itself yet more fully. The last recorded words of the apostle express the earnest hope, repeated yet more earnestly, that he might see him once again. 2 Tim. 4:9, 21. We may hazard the conjecture that he reached him in time, and that the last hours of the teacher were soothed by the presence of the disciple whom he loved so truly. Lock in Hastings' *Bible Dictionary* suggests that it may have been on this visit to Rome that Timothy was himself arrested on the occasion on which the writer of the Epistle to the Hebrews mentions his release (Heb. 13:23.) Beyond this all is apocryphal and uncertain. He continued, according to the old traditions, to act as bishop of Ephesus, and died a martyr's death under Domitian or Nerva. A somewhat startling theory as to the intervening period of his life has found favor with some. If he continued, according to the received tradition, to be bishop of Ephesus, then he, and no other, must have been the "angel" of the church of Ephesus to whom the message of Rev. 2:1-7 was addressed.

Timothy, First Epistle of Paul to.
The Epistles to Timothy and Titus are called the Pastoral Epistles, because they are principally devoted to directions about the work of the pastor of a church.

DATE, sometime in the interval between Paul's first and second imprisonments, A.D. 63-66.

PLACE OF WRITING. The absence of any local reference but that in 1 Tim. 1:3 suggests Macedonia or some neighboring district.

HISTORICAL SITUATION. Paul had recently been with Timothy, either at Ephesus, or in Macedonia, whither Timothy had come to see Paul. Comp. 1 Tim. 1:3 with Acts 20:17. Paul was so much impressed with the dangerous tendencies of certain false teachers at Ephesus that he urged Timothy to remain in that city, and some time after this, hearing that all was not prospering there, he wrote this letter to Timothy.

CHARACTER. The letter is a personal and not a theological one. The subjects are miscellaneous. Morality, Salvation and Truth are its keynotes. It contains many memorable sayings. The keynote is 3:16.

Timothy, second Epistle of Paul to.
DATE very late in Paul's life, during his last imprisonment. A.D. 66 or 67.

PLACE OF WRITING, a prison in Rome, probably its lower dungeon.

While some rationalistic critics argue that this Epistle was not written by Paul, the evidence in favor of its being authentic writing of Paul is very strong and convincing.

Like 1 Timothy this Epistle is a personal letter, full of affection for his beloved son in the Lord. According to Professor Walter Lock in Hastings' *Bible Dictionary,* its main interest is one of character, and two portraits emerge from it.

(1) The portrait of the Ideal Christian Minister. He is like Christ himself, and Isaiah's "Servant of the Lord," patient, gentle, hopeful, interceding; God's man, loyal, like a soldier, like an athlete, like a shepherd, a husbandman, a fisherman.

(2) The portrait of a Christian Minister with his work done, facing death. His eyes are turned mainly to the past or to the future. He has the assurance of hope, for while men may imprison the preacher, the word of God is unfettered. He provides for a succession of teachers. He sees the heavenly kingdom, eternal glory, the coming of the Lord, the triumph of his kingdom, the crown of righteousness.

"The Epistle is the letter of a good

shepherd who is laying down his life for the sheep."

Tin. Among the various metals found in the spoils of the Midianites, tin is enumerated. Num. 31:22. It was known to the Hebrew metal-workers as mixed with other metals. Isa. 1:25; Ezek. 22:18, 20. The markets of Tyre were supplied with it by the ships of Tarshish. Ezek. 27:12. It was used for plummets, Zech. 4:10, and was so plentiful as to furnish the writer of Ecclesiasticus, Ecclus. 47:18, with a figure by which to express the wealth of Solomon. Tin is not found in Palestine. Whence, then, did the ancient Hebrews obtain their supply? "Only three countries are known to contain any considerable quantity of it: Spain and Portugal, Cornwall and the adjacent parts of Devonshire, and the islands of Junk, Ceylon and Banca, in the Straits of Malacca." (Kenrick, "Phœnicia," p. 212.) There can be little doubt that the mines of Britain were the chief source of supply to the ancient world. [See TARSHISH.]

Tiph'sah (tif'sah) (*ford*). 1. A town mentioned in 1 Kings 4:24 as the limit of Solomon's empire toward the Euphrates. It was known to the Greeks and Romans under the name of Thapsacus, and was the point where it was usual to cross the Euphrates. Cyrus the younger, Darius and Alexander are all mentioned as crossing here at different times.

2. A place not far from Tirzah which was taken by Menahem after he had taken the throne from Shallum. 2 Kings 15:16. The site is uncertain.

Ti'ras (ti'ras) (*desire*), the youngest son of Japheth, Gen. 10:2, usually identified in ancient times with the Thracians, as presenting the closest verbal approximation to the name. It is now considered by most scholars that the conditions are best met by the *Tursenoi* or *Turusha*, a sea-faring people of Pelasgic origin mentioned in the Egyptian inscriptions and in Herodotus as living around the Ægean Sea.

Ti'rathites (ti'rath-ītes), **The,** one of the three families of scribes residing at Jabez, 1 Chron. 2:55, the others being the Shimeathites and Sucathites. The passage is hopelessly obscure.

Tire, an old English word for *headdress.* It was an ornamental headdress

worn on festive occasions, Ezek. 24:17, 23, and perhaps, as some suppose, also an ornament for the neck worn by both women, Isa. 3:18, and men.

Tir'hakah (tīr'ha-kah), or **Tirha'kah,** a king of Egypt, called king of Ethiopia (Cush), the opponent of Sennacherib. 2 Kings 19:9; Isa. 37:9. He may be identified with Tarkos or Tarakos, who was the third and last king of the twenty-fifth dynasty, which was of Ethiopians. His accession was probably about B.C. 691. Possibly Tirhakah ruled over Ethiopia before becoming king of Egypt.

Tir'hanah, son of Caleb ben-Hezron by his concubine Maachah. 1 Chron. 2:48.

Tir'ia (tīr'ĭ-à) (*fear*), son of Jehaleleel, of the tribe of Judah. 1 Chron. 4:16.

Tirshatha (tīr'sha-thà) (always written with the article), the title of the governor of Judea under the Persians, perhaps derived from a Persian root signifying *his reverence,* taken in its literal sense not in its ecclesiastical usage. It is added as a title after the name of Nehemiah, Neh. 8:9; 10:1, and occurs also in three other places. In the margin of the Authorized Version, Ezra 2:63; Neh. 7:65; 10:1, it is rendered "governor."

Tir'zah (tīr'zah) (*delight*), youngest of the five daughters of Zelophehad. Num. 26:33; 27:1; 36:11; Josh. 17:3. (B.C. 1450.)

Tir'zah, an ancient Canaanite city, whose king is enumerated among those overthrown in the conquest of the country. Josh. 12:24. It reappears as a royal city, the residence of Jeroboam I, and of his successors, 1 Kings 14:17, 18; and as the seat of the conspiracy of Menahem ben-Gaddi against the wretched Shallum. 2 Kings 15:16. Its reputation for beauty throughout the country must have been widespread. It is in this sense that it is spoken of in the Song of Solomon. Eusebius mentions it in connection with Menahem, and identifies it with a "village of Samaritans in Batanea." Its site has not yet been certainly identified.

Tish'bite (tĭsh'bīte), **The,** the well-known designation of Elijah. 1 Kings 17:1; 21:17, 28; 2 Kings 1:3, 8; 9:36. The name naturally points to a place called Tishbeh, or Tishbi as the residence of the prophet. No such place is mentioned elsewhere, and identification is almost impossible. Some identify it with Thisbe of Naphtali, but the Septuagint and Josephus both place it in Gilead.

Tis'ro or **Tish'ri.** [MONTHS.]

Tithe or **tenth,** the proportion of property devoted to religious uses from very early times. Instances of the use of tithes are found prior to the appointment of the Levitical tithes under the law. In biblical history the two prominent instances are—1. Abram presenting the tenth of all his property, or rather of the spoils of his victory, to Melchizedek. Gen. 14 : 20 ; Heb. 7 : 2, 6. 2. Jacob, after his vision at Luz, devoting a tenth of all his property to God in case he should return home in safety. Gen. 28 : 22. The first enactment of the law in respect of tithe is the declaration that the tenth of all produce, as well as of flocks and cattle, belongs to Jehovah, and must be offered to him; that the tithe was to be paid in kind, or, if redeemed, with an addition of one-fifth to its value. Lev. 27 : 30–33. This tenth is ordered to be assigned to the Levites as the reward of their service, and it is ordered further that they are themselves to dedicate to the Lord a tenth of these receipts, which is to be devoted to the maintenance of the priest. Num. 18 : 21–28. This legislation is modified or extended in the book of Deuteronomy. Commands are given to the people—1. To bring their tithes, together with their votive and other offerings and first-fruits, to the chosen centre of worship, there to be eaten in festive celebration in company with their children, their servants and the Levites. Deut. 12 : 5–18. 2. All the produce of the soil was to be tithed every year, and these tithes, with the firstlings of the flock and herd, were to be eaten at the central sanctuary. 3. But in case of distance, permission is given to convert the produce into money, which is to be taken to the appointed place, and there laid out in the purchase of food for a festal celebration, in which the Levite is, by special command, to be included. Deut. 14 : 22–27. 4. Then follows the direction that at the end of three years all the tithe of that year is to be gathered and laid up "within the gates," and that a festival is to be held, of which the stranger, the fatherless and the widow, together with the Levite, are to partake. Deut. 14 : 28, 29. 5. Lastly, it is ordered that after taking the tithe in each third year, "which is the year of tithing," an exculpatory declaration is to be made by every Israelite that he has done his best to fulfill the divine command. Deut. 26 : 12–14. These tithes in early times took the place of our modern taxes, as well as of gifts for the support of religious institutions.

Ti'tus (ti'tus). Our materials for the biography of this companion of St. Paul must be drawn entirely from the notices of him in the Second Epistle to the Corinthians, the Galatians, and to Titus himself, combined with the Second Epistle to Timothy. He is not mentioned in the Acts at all, but is frequently referred to in Paul's Epistles. He was born of Gentile parents, and was doubtless a much younger man, than Paul whose companion he was, and through whom Titus was converted. Tit. 1 : 4. From Gal. 2 : 1–3, compared with Acts 15 : 2, we learn that Titus was one of the delegation from Antioch who accompanied Paul and Barnabas to the council at Jerusalem which was to decide the question of the necessity of circumcision to the Gentile Christians, and their relation to the Jewish Christians. Titus is very emphatically spoken of as a Greek, that is, a Gentile, by which it is most probably meant that both his parents were Gentiles. It is certain that Titus had not been already circumcised and that it was not now required of him. (Gal. 2 : 3.) Paul's circumcision of Timothy (Acts 16 : 3), was because Timothy, as the personal attendant of Paul and Silas, would come more in contact with the Jewish Christians than would Titus. Later Titus was sent on a mission to Corinth. This had reference to the immoralities rebuked in the First Epistle, and to the collection for the poor Christians of Judea. 2 Cor. 8 : 6. Titus joined Paul in Macedonia (2 Cor. 7 : 6, 7). Paul sent him back from Macedonia to Corinth, in company with two other trustworthy Christians, bearing the Second Epistle, and with an earnest request, *ibid.* 8 : 6, 17, that he would see to the completion of the collection, ch. 8 : 6.

In the interval between Paul's first

and second imprisonment at Rome, he and Titus were together in Crete. Titus 1 : 5. We see Titus remaining in the island when St. Paul left it, and receiving there a letter written to him by the apostle. He is to complete what St. Paul had been obliged to leave unfinished, ch. 1 : 5, and he is to organize the church throughout the island by appointing presbyters in every city. It seems probable that this disciple had been with St. Paul in Rome during his final imprisonment; but this cannot be asserted confidently. The traditional connection of Titus with Crete is much more specific and constant, though here again we cannot be certain of the facts. He is said to have been permanent bishop in the island, and to have died there at an advanced age. The modern capital, *Candia,* appears to claim the honor of being his burial-place. In the fragment by the lawyer Zenas, Titus is called bishop of Gortyna. Lastly, the name of Titus was the watchword of the Cretans when they were invaded by the Venetians.

Titus, Epistle to. There are no specialties in this Epistle which require any very elaborate treatment distinct from the other Pastoral Letters of St. Paul. It was written about the same time and under similar circumstances with 1 Timothy, in the autumn of 64, in the interval between Paul's two Roman imprisonments. Paul and Titus had worked together in Crete, and Paul had left Titus there to organize and train the church, which false teachers had entered. It is thought that Paul took advantage of the fact that Zenas and Apollos (3 : 13), were starting on a journey which would take them past Crete, to send a letter to Titus. Like the Epistles to Timothy, this was essentially a private letter from a man of 'arge experience and of great authority and influence to a young pastor who, though able and consecrated, needed and would highly value the advice of a man like Paul. "The leading thought of the epistle is the importance of good works in all those representing or professing Christianity," as a proof of the honesty of the profession.

Ti'tus Jus'tus. The form given in the Revised Version, of the proselyte Justus, at whose house in Corinth Paul preached when driven from the synagogue.

Ti'zite (tī'zīte), **The,** the designation of Joha, one of the heroes of David's army. 1 Chron. 11 : 45. It occurs nowhere else, and nothing is known of the place or family which it denotes.

To'ah (tō'ah) (*lowly*), a Kohathite Levite, ancestor of Samuel and Heman. 1 Chron. 6 : 34. Also called Nahath.

Tob (tŏb) (*good*), **The land of,** a place in which Jephthah took refuge when expelled from home by his brethren, Judges 11 : 3, and where he remained, at the head of a band of freebooters, till he was brought back by the sheikhs of Gilead, ver. 5. The narrative implies that the land of Tob was not far distant from Gilead; at the same time, from the nature of the case, it must have lain out toward the eastern deserts. It is undoubtedly mentioned again in 2 Sam. 10 : 6, 8, as Ishtob, *i. e. man of Tob,* meaning, according to a common Hebrew idiom, the *men of Tob.* No identification of the ancient district with any modern one has yet been adopted.

Tob-adoni'jah (tŏb-ăd-o-nī'jah) (*Good is the Lord Jehovah*), one of the Levites sent by Jehoshaphat through the cities of Judah to teach the law to the people. 2 Chron. 17 : 8. (B.C. 868.)

Tobi'ah (tŏ-bī'ah) (*Jehovah is good*). 1. "The children of Tobiah" were a family who returned with Zerubbabel, but were unable to prove their connection with Israel. Ezra 2 : 60; Neh. 7 : 62.

2. "Tobiah the slave, the Ammonite," played a conspicuous part in the rancorous opposition made by Sanballat the Moabite and his adherents to the rebuilding of Jerusalem. Neh. 6. Tobiah, though a slave, Neh. 2 : 10, 19— unless this is a title of opprobrium—and an Ammonite, found means to ally himself with a priestly family, and his son Johanan married the daughter of Meshullam the son of Berechiah. Neh. 6 : 18. He himself was the son-in-law of Shechaniah the son of Arah, Neh. 6 : 18, and these family relations created for him a strong family faction among the Jews.

Tobi'jah (tŏ-bī'jah) (*Jehovah is good*). 1. One of the Levites sent by Jehoshaphat to teach the law in the cities of Judah. 2 Chron. 17 : 8. (B.C. 868.)

2. One of the captivity in the time of Zechariah, in whose presence the prophet was commanded to take crowns of silver and gold and put them on the head of Joshua the high priest. Zech. 6:10, 14.

To'bit, Book of, a book of the Apocrypha, which still exists at present in Greek, Latin, Syriac and Hebrew texts, but probably written originally in Greek. The scene of the book is placed in Assyria, whither Tobit, a Jew, had been carried as a captive by Shalmaneser. It is represented as completed shortly after the fall of Nineveh (B.C. 606), Tob. 14:15, and written, in the main, some time before. Tob. 12:20. But the whole tone of the narrative bespeaks a later age; and above all, the doctrine of good and evil spirits is elaborated in a form which belongs to a period considerably posterior to the Babylonian captivity. Asmodeus iii. 8; vi. 14; viii. 3; Raphael xii. 15. It cannot be regarded as a true history. It is a didactic narrative; and its point lies in the moral lessons which it conveys, and not in the incidents. In modern times the moral excellence of the book has been rated highly, except in the heat of controversy. Nowhere else is there preserved so complete and beautiful a picture of the domestic life of the Jews after the return. Almost every family relation is touched upon with natural grace and affection. A doctrinal feature of the book is the firm belief in a glorious restoration of the Jewish people. Tob. 14:5; 13:9–18. But the restoration contemplated is national, and not the work of a universal Saviour. In all there is not the slightest trace of the belief in a personal Messiah.

To'chen (tō'ken) (*task*), a place mentioned in 1 Chron. 4:32 only, among the towns of Simeon.

Togar'mah (to-gär'mah), a son of Gomer, of the family of Japheth, and brother of Ashkenaz and Riphath. Gen. 10:3. His descendants became a people engaged in agriculture, breeding horses and mules to be sold in Tyre. Ezek. 27:14. They were also a military people, well skilled in the use of arms. Togarmah was probably the ancient name of Armenia.

To'hu (tō'hu), an ancestor of Samuel the prophet, perhaps the same as Toah. 1 Sam. 1:1; comp. 1 Chron. 6:34.

To'i (tō'ī) (*erring*), king of Hamath on the Orontes, who, after the defeat of his powerful enemy the Syrian king Hadadezer by the army of David, sent his son Joram or Hadoram to congratulate the victor and do him homage with presents of gold and silver and brass. 2 Sam. 8:9, 10.

To'la (tō'lä). 1. The first-born of Issachar, and ancestor of the Tolaites. Gen. 46:13; Num. 26:23; 1 Chron. 7:1, 2.

2. Judge of Israel after Abimelech. Judges 10:1, 2. He is described as "the son of Puah the son of Dodo, a man of Issachar." Tola judged Israel for twenty-three years at Shamir in Mount Ephraim, where he died and was buried. (B.C. 1179–1156.)

To'lad (tō'lăd), one of the towns of Simeon, 1 Chron. 4:29, elsewhere called El-tolad.

To'laites (tō'lä-ītes), **The,** descendants of Tola the son of Issachar. Num. 26:23.

Tomb. Burial in eastern countries follows speedily upon death; within twenty-four hours if possible. This was therefore the case with the Jews when resident in Palestine, in Bible times. It was due (1) to the rapid decomposition of the dead body in hot countries, and (2) to prevent the defilement coming from contact with a corpse (Num. 19:11–14). The preparations were not very elaborate. The body was swathed with linen cloths in which were spices. In the case of Ananias (Acts 5:6) his outer garments formed the winding sheet. The burning of the dead, practiced by some peoples, was a rare exception among the Jews, and only used in cases of emergency, such as the burning of the bodies of Saul and his sons by the men of Jabesh-Gilead (1 Sam. 31:11, 12) and even here the bones received honorable burial later. (2 Sam. 21:12–14). Neither was the body embalmed as in Egypt. It was a great indignity for the body to remain unburied, and the Jews had something of the idea of other nations, that the spirit in such a case was doomed to wander, homeless, and might bring misfortune to his family. Coffins were unknown among the early Israelites, and are unused by the Jews of the East to-day. The only coffin named in the Bible is that in which Joseph's embalmed remains were taken from Egypt for burial in Canaan.

The graves of the dead were variously made. Sometimes they were merely dug in the earth as is usual with us, and as the eastern Jews do to-day. Sometimes natural caves or grottoes were utilized as burial-places. Often tombs or sepulchres were provided before death, for one's self or one's fam-

served as places of refuge on many occasions. (Judges 6:2; 1 Sam. 13:6; Mark 5:2, 3).

The simplest form of a rock-hewn tomb is that where a single grave is sunk into the surface of the rock, or into the face of a cliff, and covered by a slab of stone, fitted and fastened into place. These stones are in some cases ornamented, but the majority are

THE GARDEN TOMB.

"Now in the place . . . there was a garden; and in the garden a new sepulchre"—John 19:41—"which was hewn out of a rock."—Mark 15:46. This tomb is on the west side of Calvary, near the Damascus Gate. It is the property of the English and is enclosed by a wall.

ily—and either hewed out in the solid rock, or built up of masonry,—the former being by far the most common. Into this family grave no stranger's body was admitted; it became holy ground, and a permanent possession. Of this sort was the tomb of Joseph of Arimathea, in which the body of Jesus was laid; a tomb hollowed in the rock and unused as yet, "his own new tomb." The cliffs near Jerusalem are full of these sepulchres, which

plain, and whitewashed, in order to distinguish them from the surrounding rock.

The most common form, however, is that in which a number of graves are grouped together in or round a common chamber. These are of several degrees of elaboration. (1) A natural cavern in the softer limestone has been enlarged, by having the graves dug around it, each fitted with its individual slab of stone to cover it. (2) A single artificially formed cave with graves around three of its sides—either leading out from it, or as shelves in the chamber itself. (3) A more elaborate form, where a single entrance leads into a number of chambers, each in form like (2). There is usually a vestibule also, from which one passes to an ante-chamber which may be with or without tombs, out of which open the chambers of the sepulchre proper. The door

to the outside chamber when the cavern was an artificial one, was quite small and was closed by a great stone which was sometimes circular, and ran in grooves in the rock. This arrangement explains several references in the New Testament. Thus in John 11:39, Jesus says "Take away the stone," and (ver. 41) "they took away the stone," without difficulty, apparently, probably rolling it aside. And in ch. 20:1 the same expression is used, "the stone is taken away." In this case the stone is considered too heavy for the women to roll away, but they apparently expect to find some man there to aid them. There is still in existence a good example,—that known as the "tomb of the kings"—which is closed by a stone rolled across its entrance. The earlier the tomb the simpler its construction, and the smaller the amount of ornamentation. Nearly all the famous tombs bearing traditional names assigning them to ancient dates are of recent origin, probably the greater part of them of the Byzantine period.

Tombs of the patriarchs.—One of the most striking events in the life of Abraham is the purchase of the field of Ephron the Hittite at Hebron, in which was the cave of Machpelah, in order that he might therein bury Sarah his wife, and that it might be a sepulchre for himself and his children. There he and his immediate descendants were laid 3700 years ago, and there they are believed to rest now, under the great mosque of Hebron; but no one in modern times has seen their remains, or been allowed to enter into the cave where they rest.

Tomb of the kings.—Of the twenty-two kings of Judah who reigned at Jerusalem from 1048 to 590 B.C., eleven, or exactly one-half, were buried in the "city of David." Of all these it is merely said that they were buried in "the sepulchres of their fathers" or "of the kings" in the city of David except of two—Asa and Hezekiah. Two more of these kings—Jehoram and Joash—were buried also in the city of David, "but not in the sepulchres of the kings." From Neh. 3:16, it would seem that some kings had their tombs close under the temple walls, so near that they might be said to be within the temple. This is possible, since some were certainly buried in their own gardens (2 Kings 21:18, 26), and the palaces of the kings stood practically within the same enclosure as the original temple. Burial places in general were outside of the walls of the city, the kings alone being accorded burial within them. The burial places of the kings of Judah cannot now be identified. The fine monument to the north of Jerusalem, commonly known as the Tombs of the Kings, and now known to the natives as *Kubur es-Salatin* (Tombs of the Sultans) has been identified as the tomb of Helena, queen of Adiabene. Its construction proves it to have been built near the Christian era. For a long time it was thought that not a vestige of the tomb existed, the real tomb having been otherwise identified. It was said that "she with her brother was buried in the pyramids which she had ordered to be constructed at a distance of three stadia from Jerusalem." Joseph. *Ant.* xx. 4, § 3. This is confirmed by Pausanias, viii. 16. The tomb was situated outside the third wall, near a gate between the tower Psephinus and the Royal Caverns. *B. J.* v. 22 and v. 4, § 2.

Monuments over graves.—In the Grecian period monuments erected over graves became common, and probably the larger portion of those now recognized on the east side of the Kidron valley belong to this period, or to the still later period after the subjugation of the country to Rome. There are around Jerusalem, in the valleys of Hinnom and Jehoshaphat and on the plateau to the north, a number of remarkable rock-cut sepulchres, with more or less architectural decoration, sufficient to enable us to ascertain that they are all of nearly the same age, and to assert with very tolerable confidence that the epoch to which they belong must be between the introduction of Roman influence and the destruction of the city by Titus, A.D. 70.

ROCK-HEWN TOMBS AT PETRA, IN EDOM.

In the village of Siloam there is a monolithic cell of singularly Egyptian aspect, which De Saulcy assumed to be chapel of Solomon's Egyptian wife. It is now usually assigned to the Herodian age, as are also "Absalom's Pillar," perhaps the tomb of Alexander Jannaeus, and the tomb of Zechariah, and the tomb of St. James. The last named is probably the earliest, and may date to the first century, B.C. The people still cling to their ancient cemeteries in the valley of Jehoshaphat with a tenacity singularly characteristic of the East. [BURIAL.]

Tongues, Gift of. One of the symbolic signs which followed the descent of the Holy Spirit upon the disciples on the day of Pentecost was the gift of speaking with tongues. As in the case of the other signs, like the wind and the flame, so the power of speaking with tongues made real to the people the invisible power of the Holy Spirit, and expressed one of the effects of the gift upon the world, the ability and the impulse to bear the good news of the Gospel to all the world.

THE NATURE OF THE GIFT OF TONGUES. In order to understand this it is necessary (1) to compare the various references to this phenomenon, especially the record here with the chapter in which Paul gives directions concerning it (1 Cor. 14); (2) to imagine or have experience of what would take place under such circumstances; (3) to study psychologically and historically similar phenomena.

Of all the many books referring to this event, Dr. Walker's *The Gift of Tongues* seems to me to come nearest the truth. The following summary agrees with his book.

1. The phenomena described by Paul and by Luke are essentially the same, and differ much less than appears on the surface. Dr. Arthur Wright in his *New Testament Problems* says, "I have read through the section in question (1 Cor. 12:1–14:33) with all the care that I could command, and have been forced to the conclusion that though some of Paul's illustrations undoubtedly favor the theory of incoherent noises, yet his application of them does not do so, and, on the whole, foreign languages are undoubtedly implied." (See under "9" below.)

2. The miracle, if we call it so, that is, the direct action of God upon the disciples, in sending upon them his Holy Spirit, produced a new, high, ecstatic, overpowering religious experience, hitherto unknown to them, something akin to Paul's experience recorded in 2 Cor. 12:1–4.

3. That this was a good, sane experience is shown by its results—the utterance of praises to God, and a new character. The experience inspired and developed all that was best in their natures, love, joy, peace, and all the fruits of the Spirit.

4. This experience was a part of the process which was transforming Galilean fishermen into world-wide apostles.

5. It was natural, and well within modern psychological facts, that this experience should so affect body and mind as to produce unusual manifestations.

6. In the words of Dean Alford: "I believe the event to have been a sudden and powerful inspiration of the Holy Spirit, by which the disciples uttered not of their minds, but as mouthpieces of the Spirit, the praises of God in various languages, hitherto, and possibly at the time itself, unknown to them."

7. It was not a permanent endowment with the power to speak foreign languages; for there are no signs of the use of such a power in the whole story of Paul's missionary labors, but the contrary, and there was really little need of such an endowment since Greek was understood in nearly all lands.

8. It is not implied that each one spoke in several languages, but that one or another spoke in them all.

9. This would account for the incoherent sounds of which Paul speaks; for to all those who did not understand the particular language spoken, the sounds would be unintelligible, "barbarian" voices "without signification."

CONFIRMATORY FACTS. It is probable that the languages spoken were those lying in the sub-conscious memory, awakened by the powerful influence upon the disciples. The development of the study of the mind and its sub-conscious activity, within the last few years, favors this explanation.

Coleridge tells a story of a young

woman in Germany who could neither read nor write, but who, during a fever, was heard talking Greek, Latin, and Hebrew. Whole sheets were written down, and found to consist of intelligible sentences, but disconnected. The mystery was unveiled by the discovery that in her childhood she lived with a Protestant pastor, a great Hebrew scholar, who was accustomed to read aloud books in these languages; many of the passages she uttered were identified as those in his books.

A revival in Wales some years ago brought out similar instances. The Yorkshire *Post* of that period says:

"Young Welshmen and Welshwomen who know little or no Welsh, and who certainly cannot carry on a sustained conversation in their parents' tongue, and who are supposed to have derived little or no benefit from the Welsh services, now, under the influence of the revival, voluntarily take part in public prayer—but the language employed is almost invariably not the familiar English, but the unknown, or supposed to be unknown, Welsh Biblical phrases, and the peculiar idiomatic expressions connected with a Welsh prayer, which they never used before."

Mr. William T. Ellis, a newspaper man from Philadelphia, wrote regarding a visit to Kedgaon, India, where Pandita Ramabai had a well-known school for girls: "I have stumbled upon an extraordinary religious manifestation. . . . I shall simply narrate, soberly and consecutively, what I have seen and heard concerning this 'baptism with fire,' and pouring out of 'the gift of tongues,' whereby ignorant Hindu girls speak in Sanskrit, Hebrew, Greek, English, and other languages as yet unidentified.

"In other parts of India, dramatic in the extreme have been the confessions of sin, and restitution therefor, and the reconciliations between enemies.

"Everywhere there is an agreement that the lives of the people have been markedly altered for the better."

Topaz, one of the gems used in the high priest's breastplate, Ex. 28:17; 39: 10; Ezek. 28:13; one of the foundations also of the New Jerusalem, in St. John's description of the city. Rev. 21:20. The topaz of the ancient Greeks and Romans is usually considered to be our chrysolite, while their chrysolite is our topaz. Chrysolite is a silicate of magnesia and iron; it is so soft as to lose its polish unless carefully used. It varies in color from a pale-green to a bottle-green.

To'phel (tō'fel) (*mortar*), Deut. 1: 1, has been identified with *Tŭfileh* on a wady of the same name running north of Bozra toward the southeast corner of the Dead Sea, but several reasons make it a very doubtful identification.

To'phet (tō'fet), (once **To'pheth),** was in the "valley of the son of Hinnom," Jer. 7:31, which is "by the entry of the east gate." Jer. 19:2. The discussion of the position of Hinnom is given elsewhere. [HINNOM.] The name Tophet occurs only in the Old Testament. 2 Kings 23:10; Isa. 30:33; Jer. 7:31, 32; 19:6, 11, 12, 13, 14. The New does not refer to it, nor the Apocrypha. Tophet has been variously translated. The derivation is quite uncertain. The two principal opinions are, —"place of abhorrence" and "place of burning." Other "fanciful explanations are given, but they have no true foundation." Probably it was defiled by idols and polluted by the sacrifices of Baal and the fires of Molech. Then it became the place of abomination, the very gate or pit of hell. The pious kings defiled it and threw down its altars and high places, pouring into it all the filth of the city, till it became the "abhorrence" of Jerusalem.

Tor'mah (tôr'mah) occurs only in the margin of Judges 9:31. By a few commentators it has been conjectured that the word was originally the same with ARUMAH in ver. 41, but the R. V. translates it "craftily."

Tortoise (Heb. *tsâb*). The *tsâb* occurs only in the Authorized Version in Lev. 11:29, as the name of some unclean animal. The Hebrew word may be identified with the kindred Arabic *dhab,* "a large kind of lizard," and is translated in the R. V. "great lizard."

To'u (tō'u), or **To'i,** king of Hamath. 1 Chron. 18:9, 10.

Tower. Watch-towers or fortified posts in frontier or exposed situations are mentioned in Scripture, as the tower of Edar, etc., Gen. 35:21; Isa. 21:5, 8, 11; Micah 4:8, etc.; garrisons in Syria. 2 Sam. 8:6. Besides these military structures, we read in Scripture of towers built in vineyards as an almost necessary appendage to them. Isa. 5 : 2; Matt. 21 : 33; Mark 12 : 1. Such towers are still in use in Pales-

WATCH-TOWER.

tine in vineyards, especially near Hebron, and are used as lodges for the keepers of the vineyards.

Town clerk, the title ascribed in our version to the magistrate at Ephesus who appeased the mob in the theatre at the time of the tumult excited by Demetrius and his fellow craftsmen. Acts 19 : 35. The original service of this class of men was to record the laws and decrees of the state, and to read them in public.

Trachoni'tis (trăk-o-nī'tis) (*a rugged region*), Luke 3 : 1, is in all probability the Greek equivalent for the Aramaic Argob, the modern *el-Lejah*. It was in the time of Christ, with Iturea, the tetrarchy of Philip the brother of Herod the tetrarch of Galilee. It lay behind Damascus. [ARGOB.]

Trance. (1) In the only passage— Num. 24 : 4, 16—in which this word occurs in the English of the Old Testament there is, as the italics show, no corresponding word in Hebrew. It is omitted entirely in the R. V. In the New Testament we meet the word three times—Acts 10 : 10; 11 : 5; 22 : 17. The ἔκστασις (*i. e.* trance) is the state in which a man has passed out of the usual order of his life, beyond the usual limits of consciousness and volition, being rapt in visions of distant or future things. The causes of this state are to be traced commonly to strong religious impressions. Whatever explanation may be given of it, it is true of many, if
45

not of most, of those who have left the stamp of their own character on the religious history of mankind, that they have been liable to pass at times into this abnormal state. The union of intense feeling, strong volition, long-continued thought (the conditions of all wide and lasting influence), aided in many cases by the withdrawal from the lower life of the support which is needed to maintain a healthy equilibrium, appears to have been more than the "earthen vessel" will bear. The words which speak of "an ecstasy of adoration" are often literally true. As in other things, so also here, the phenomena are common to higher and lower, to true and false, systems. We may not point to trances and ecstasies as proofs of a true⸝revelation, but still less may we think of them as at all inconsistent with it. Thus, though we have not the word, we have the thing in the "deep sleep," the "horror of great darkness," that fell on Abraham. Gen. 15 : 12. Balaam, as if overcome by the constraining power of a Spirit mightier than his own, "sees the vision of God, *falling*, but with opened eyes." Num. 24 : 4. Saul, in like manner, when the wild chant of the prophets stirred the old depths of feeling, himself also "prophesied" and "fell down"—most, if not all, of his kingly clothing being thrown off in the ecstasy of the moment—"all that day and all that night." 1 Sam. 19 : 24. Something there was in Jeremiah that made men say of him that he was as one that "is mad and maketh himself a prophet." Jer. 29 : 26. In Ezekiel the phenomena appear in more wonderful and awful forms. Ezek. 3 : 15. As other elements and forms of the prophetic work were revived in "the apostles and prophets" of the New Testament, so also was this. Though different in form, it belongs to the same class of phenomena as the gift of tongues, and is connected with "visions and revelations of the Lord." In some cases, indeed, it is the chosen channel for such revelations. Acts 10 : 11; 22 : 17-21. Wisely for the most part did the apostle draw a veil over these more mysterious experiences. 2 Cor. 12 : 1-4.

Transfiguration, The. The event in the earthly life of Christ in which he was visibly glorified in the presence of the three disciples who at all times stood nearest to him. Matt. 17:1–13; Mark 9:2–13; Luke 9:28–36. *Place.*—Though tradition locates the transfiguration on Mount Tabor, there is little to confirm this view, and modern critics favor Mount Hermon, the highest mountain-top in Gaulanitis, or one of the spurs of the Anti-Lebanus. *Time.*—The transfiguration probably took place at night, because it could then be seen to better advantage than in daylight, and Jesus usually went to mountains to spend there the night in prayer. Matt. 14:23, 24; Luke 6:12; 21:37. The apostles are described as *having kept themselves awake* through the act of transfiguration. Luke 9:32 (R. V. Marg.). *The Narratives.*—The three Synoptic Gospels are singularly alike in the details of the story; it was six days after the events just narrated; on a high mountain apart; in the presence of the chosen three,—Peter, James and John; the supernatural light, the two heavenly visitants,—Moses the lawgiver, and Elijah the chief of the prophets; their conference with Jesus; the suggestion of Peter; the overshadowing cloud and the Divine voice; the joyful awe of the disciples; the return to ordinary conditions; and the charge of silence. St. Luke, Luke 9:31, adds the subject of their communing: "They spake of his decease which he should accomplish at Jerusalem." The silence of John is easily explained by the purpose of its writing. The transfiguration itself or, as the Germans call it, the *glorification,* consisted in a visible manifestation of the inner glory of Christ's person, accompanied by an audible voice from heaven. It was the revelation and anticipation of his future state of glory, which was concealed under the veil of his humanity in the state of humiliation. The cloud which overshadowed the witnesses was bright or light-like, luminous, of the same kind as the cloud at the ascension. *Significance of the Transfiguration.*—This event marked a distinct crisis in the ministry of Christ. 1. Those who see in his life a gradual realization of the depth and the details of his mission regard this as the supreme moment of "self-discovery," and of "self-dedication." "In that high hour Christ knew himself." 2. It confirmed the faith of the three favorite

disciples, and prepared them for the great trial which was approaching, by showing them the real nature and glory and power of Jesus. They were, through their daily communication with him, growing to realize that he was something more than human; they had reached the stage where they could acknowledge him as the Messiah; this event precipitated the crisis. 3. It certainly transformed his ministry. He spent more time in private converse or in the semi-privacy of the Temple courts; he calls attention more strongly to the spirit which animates him, and to the Father; he seeks more strongly to convince his disciples both of his Messiahship, and of the necessity for his suffering and death. 4. Much has been made, especially in former times, of the especial significance of the appearance of the two heavenly visitants, representatives of the Law and the Prophets, as Christ himself was of the Gospel; and also of the fact that these two are the only ones, since the formation of the chosen nation, who were accorded a supernatural passing out of life. This is important and certainly should be well considered. There has, however, according to some scholars, been an undue stress, leading to the inmost heart of Spiritualism. We must not lose sight of the earthly Jesus in seeking for the Divine Christ.

Treasure-cities. The kings of Judah had keepers of their treasures both in city and country, 1 Chron. 27:25, and the places where these magazines were laid up were called treasure-cities, and the buildings treasure-houses. Pharaoh compelled the Hebrews to build him treasure-cities. Ex. 1:11. [Pithom.]

Treasury, Mark 12:41; Luke 21:1, a name given by the rabbins to thirteen chests in the temple, called trumpets from their shape. They stood in the court of the women. It would seem probable that this court was sometimes itself called "the treasury" because it contained these repositories.

Trespass offering. [Sin offering.]

Tribute. The chief biblical facts connected with the payment of tribute have been already given under Taxes. The tribute (money) mentioned in Matt. 17:24, 25 was the half shekel (worth about 32 cents) applied to defray the general expenses of the temple. After the destruction of the temple this was sequestrated by Vespasian and his successors and transferred to the temple of the Capitoline Jupiter. This "tribute" of Matt. 17:24 must not be confounded with the tribute paid to the Roman emperor. Matt. 22:17. The temple rate, though resting on an ancient precedent—Ex. 30:13—was, as above, a fixed annual tribute of comparatively late origin.

Tribute money. [TAXES; TRIBUTE.]

Tro'as (trō'ăs), the city from which St. Paul first sailed, in consequence of a divine intimation, to carry the gospel from Asia to Europe. Acts 16:8, 11. It is mentioned on other occasions. Acts 20:5, 6; 2 Cor. 2:12, 13; 2 Tim. 4:13. Its full name was Alexandria Troas (Liv. xxxv. 42), and sometimes it was called simply Alexandria, sometimes simply Troas. It was first built by Antigonus, under the name of Antigonia Troas, and peopled with the inhabitants of some neighboring cities. Afterward it was embellished by Lysimachus, and named Alexandria Troas. Its situation was on the coast of Mysia, opposite the southeast extremity of the island of Tenedos. Under the Romans it was one of the most important towns of the province of Asia. In the time of St. Paul it was a *colonia* with the *Jus Italicum.* The modern name is *Eski-Stamboul,* with considerable ruins. We can still trace the harbor in a basin about 400 feet long and 200 broad.

Trogyl'lium (trŏ-jĭl'lĭ-ŭm) is the rocky extremity of the ridge of Mycale, exactly opposite Samos. Acts 20: 15. A little to the east of the extreme point there is an anchorage, which is still called *St. Paul's Port.* [SAMOS.]

Troph'imus (trŏf'ĭ-mŭs) (*nutritious*). Both Trophimus and Tychicus accompanied Paul from Macedonia as far as Asia, but Tychicus seems to have remained there, while Trophimus proceeded with the apostle to Jerusalem. (A.D. 57.) There he was the innocent cause of the tumult in which St. Paul was apprehended. Acts 21:27–29. From this passage we learn two new facts, viz., that Trophimus was a Gentile, and that he was a native of Ephesus. Trophimus was probably one of the two brethren who, with Titus, conveyed the second Epistle to the Corinthians. 2 Cor. 8:16–24. [TYCHICUS.]

Trumpet. [CORNET.]

Trumpets, Feast of, Num. 29:1; Lev. 23:24, the feast of the new moon, which fell on the first of Tisri. It differed from the ordinary festivals of the new moon in several important particulars. It was a day of solemn rest from ordinary labor, and a holy convocation was held. Instead of the mere

ANCIENT TRUMPETS.

blowing of the trumpets of the temple at the time of the offering of the sacrifices, it was "a day of blowing of trumpets." The sacrifices for the first day of the month (Num. 28:11–15) were doubled on the first day of the seventh month except for one young bullock (Num. 29:1–6). It has been conjectured that Ps. 81, one of the songs of Asaph, was composed expressly for the Feast of Trumpets. The psalm is used in the service for the day by the modern Jews. Various meanings have been assigned to the Feast of Trumpets; but there seems to be no sufficient reason to call in question the common opinion of Jews and Christians, that it was the festival of the New Year's day of the civil year, the first of Tisri, the month which commenced the sabbatical year and the year of jubilee.

Tryphe'na (trī-fē'nà) and **Trypho'-sa** (trī-fō'sà) (*delicate*), two Christian women at Rome, enumerated in the conclusion of St. Paul's letter. Rom.

16:12. (A.D. 57.) They may have been sisters, but it is more likely that they were fellow deaconesses. We know nothing more of these two sister workers of the apostolic time, although the name Tryphena is found in the "Acts of Paul and Thekla," as that of a wealthy lady. There is historical authority for her existence. She was a descendant of Mark Antony, and relative of the emperor Claudius.

Trypho′sa. [TRYPHENA.]

Tu′bal (tụ′bal) is reckoned with Javan and Meshech among the sons of Japheth. Gen. 10:2; 1 Chron. 1:5. The three are again associated in the enumeration of the sources of the wealth of Tyre. Ezek. 27:13. Tubal and Javan, Isa. 66:19, Meshech and Tubal, Ezek. 32:26; 38:2, 3; 39:1, are nations of the north. Ezek. 38:15; 39:2. They are the *Tibareni* of Herodotus and lived in the mountainous districts southeast of the Black Sea. In the Assyrian inscriptions the name appears as *Tabal* or *Tubla.*

Tu′bal=cain (tụ′bal-kān), the son of Lamech the Cainite by his wife Zillah. Gen. 4:22. He was the forger of cutting instruments of copper and iron.

Turtle, Turtle=dove (Heb. *tôr*). The name is phonetic, evidently derived from the plaintive cooing of the bird. It is one of the smaller members of the group of birds which ornithologists usually call *pigeons.* The turtle-dove occurs first in Scripture in Gen. 15:9. In the Levitical law a pair of turtle-doves or of young pigeons is constantly prescribed as a substitute for those who were too poor to provide a lamb or a kid. The offering of two young pigeons must have been one easily within the reach of the poorest. The admission of a pair of turtle-doves was perhaps a yet further concession to extreme poverty, for they were extremely numerous, and their young might easily be found and captured by those who did not possess pigeons. There are three species of turtle-dove common in Palestine; the *turtur auritus,* or true turtle-dove, about 12 inches long; the *turtur risorius,* or collared turtle-dove, a larger species, 13 inches long; and the *turtur senegalensis,* the palm or Egyptian turtle-dove, the smallest, about 10 inches long. It is not improbable that the palm-dove may

in some measure have supplied the sacrifice in the wilderness, for it is found in amazing numbers wherever the palm tree occurs, whether wild or cultivated. From its habit of pairing for life, and its fidelity to its mate, the turtle-dove was a symbol of purity and an appropriate offering. The regular migration of the turtle-dove and its return in the spring are alluded to in Jer. 8:7 and Cant. 2:11, 12. It is from its plaintive note doubtless that David in Ps. 74:19, pouring forth his lament to God, compares himself to a turtle-dove.

Twin Brothers. This term is used in the Revised Version of Acts 28:11 for CASTOR AND POLLUX, which see.

Tych′icus (tĭk′ĭ-kŭs) (*fateful*), a companion of St. Paul on some of his journeys, and a native of Asia. Acts 20:4. (Compare 21:29.) (A.D. 57–66.) There is much probability in the conjecture that Tychicus and Trophimus were the two brethren who were associated with Titus, 2 Cor. 8:16–24, in conducting the business of the collection for the poor Christians in Judea.

Tyran′nus (ti-răn′nus) (*sovereign*), the name of a man in whose school or place of audience Paul taught the gospel for two years, during his sojourn at Ephesus. See Acts 19:9. (A.D. 52, 53.) The presumption is that Tyrannus himself was a Greek, and a public teacher of philosophy or rhetoric, and his school was a seat of culture. Paul may have alternated sessions with Tyrannus, and thus gained a hearing among the more intellectual people of the city. "The school of Tyrannus alone had never been a great moral or perhaps even intellectual force in Ephesus. But the school of Tyrannus with Paul to teach in it exerted a tremendous influence in all that region."

Tyre (*a rock*), a celebrated commercial city of Phœnicia, on the coast of the Mediterranean Sea. Its Hebrew name, *Tzôr,* signifies a rock; which well agrees with the site of *Sûr,* the modern town, on a rocky peninsula, formerly an island. There is no doubt that, previous to the siege of the city by Alexander the Great, Tyre was situated on an island; but, according to the tradition of the inhabitants, there was a city on the mainland before there was a city on the island; Herodotus states that he was informed by the

Tyrian priests that it had been founded 2300 years before his visit, or 2750 B.C. The city on the mainland received the name of Palætyrus, or Old Tyre. *Notices in the Bible.*—In the Bible Tyre is named for the first time in the book of Joshua 19 : 29, where it is adverted to as a fortified city (in the Authorized Version "the strong city"), in reference to the boundaries of the cious metals and workmen, and gave him sailors for the voyage to Ophir and India, while on the other hand Solomon gave Hiram supplies of corn and oil, ceded to him some cities, and permitted him to make use of some havens on the Red Sea. 1 Kings 9 : 11–14, 26–28; 10 : 22. These friendly relations survived for a time the disastrous secession of the ten tribes, and

VIEW OF TYRE.

tribe of Asher. But the first passages in the Hebrew historical writings, or in ancient history generally, which afford glimpses of the actual condition of Tyre are in the book of Samuel, 2 Sam. 5 : 11. Hiram king of Tyre sent cedar wood and workmen to David, for building him a palace; and subsequently (in the book of Kings) aided in the same way the building of Solomon's temple. It is evident that under Solomon there was a close alliance between the Hebrews and the Tyrians. Hiram supplied Solomon with cedar wood, pre-

a century later Ahab married a daughter of Ethbaal king of the Zidonians, 1 Kings 16 : 31, who, according to Menander, was Ithobal king of Tyre. When mercantile cupidity induced the Tyrians and the neighboring Phœnicians to buy Hebrew captives from their enemies, and to sell them as slaves to the Greeks and Edomites, there commenced denunciations, and at first threats of retaliation. Joel 3 : 4–8; Amos 1 : 9, 10. When Shalmaneser, king of Assyria, had taken the city of Samaria, had conquered the kingdom of Israel, and carried its inhabitants into captivity, he laid siege to Tyre, which, however, successfully resisted his arms. It is in reference to this siege that the prophecy against Tyre in Isaiah, ch. 23, was uttered. After the siege of Tyre by Shalmaneser, Tyre remained a powerful state, with its own kings, Jer. 25:22; 27:3; Ezek. 28:2-12; remarkable for its wealth, with territory on the mainland, and protected by strong fortifications. Ezek. 26:4, 6, 8, 10, 12; 27:11; 28:5; Zech. 9:3. Our knowledge of its condition thenceforward until the siege by Nebuchadnezzar depends entirely on various notices of it by the Hebrew prophets; but some of these notices are singularly full, and especially the twenty-seventh chapter of Ezekiel furnishes us, on some points, with details such as have scarcely come down to us respecting any one city of antiquity excepting Rome and Athens. *Siege by Nebuchadnezzar.*—In the midst of great prosperity and wealth, which was the natural result of extensive trade, Ezek. 28:4, Nebuchadnezzar, at the head of an army of the Chaldees, invaded Judea and captured Jerusalem. As Tyre was so near to Jerusalem, and as the conquerors were a fierce and formidable race, Hab. 1:6, it would naturally be supposed that this event would have excited alarm and terror amongst the Tyrians. Instead of this, we may infer from Ezekiel's statement, Ezek. 26:2, that their predominant feeling was one of exultation. It explained by the fact that the Tyrians had become gradually the sworn enemies of Israel. The reformations in Judah, and the denunciations of the prophets may have had considerable to do with this change. After the famous battle of Carchemish in 605 B.C., Nebuchadnezzar laid siege to Tyre. That siege lasted thirteen years, and it is still a disputed point whether Tyre was actually taken by Nebuchadnezzar on this occasion. However this may be, it is probable that, on some terms or other, Tyre submitted to the Chaldees. The rule of Nebuchadnezzar over Tyre, though real, may have been light, and in the nature of an alliance. *Attack by the Persians; Capture by Alexander.*—During the Persian domination the Tyrians were subject in name to the Persian king,

and may have given him tribute. With the rest of Phœnicia they had submitted to the Persians without striking a blow. Toward the close of the following century, B.C. 332, Tyre was assailed for the third time by a great conqueror. At that time Tyre was situated on an island nearly half a mile from the mainland; it was completely surrounded by prodigious walls, the loftiest portion of which on the side fronting the mainland reached a height of not less than 150 feet; and notwithstanding the persevering efforts of Alexander, he could not have succeeded in his attempt if the harbor of Tyre to the north had not been blockaded by the Cyprians and that to the south by the Phœnicians, thus affording an opportunity to Alexander for uniting the island to the mainland by an enormous artificial mole. The materials for this he obtained from the remains of old Tyre, scraping the very dust from her rocks into the sea, as prophesied by Ezekiel (Ezek. 26:3, 4, 12, 21) more than 250 years before. The immediate results of the capture by Alexander were most disastrous to Tyre, as its brave defenders were put to death; and in accordance with the barbarous policy of ancient times, 30,-000 of its inhabitants, including slaves, free females and free children, were sold as slaves. Within 18 years, however, Tyre was rebuilt, and resettled, and strong enough to offer strong resistance to Antigonus. It gradually recovered its prosperity through the immigration of fresh settlers, though its trade is said to have suffered by the vicinity and rivalry of Alexandria. Under the Macedonian successors of Alexander it shared the fortunes of the Seleucidæ. Under the Romans, at first it enjoyed a kind of freedom. Strabo gives an account of it in the time of Augustus, and speaks of the great wealth which it derived from the dyes of the celebrated Tyrian purple, which, as is well known, were extracted from shell-fish found on the coast, belonging to a species of the genus *Murex. Tyre in the time of Christ and since.*—When visited by Christ, Matt. 15:21; Mark 7:24, Tyre was perhaps more populous than Jerusalem, and if so it was undoubtedly the largest city which the Saviour is known to have visited. At the time of the crusades it was still a flourishing city, when it surrendered to the Christians on the 27th of June, 1124. It continued more than a century and a half in the hands of Christians, but was deserted by its inhabitants in A.D. 1291, upon the conquest of Acre (Ptolemais) by the sultan of Egypt and Damascus. This was the turning-point in the history of Tyre, which has never recovered from the blow. Its present condition is a fulfilment of Ezekiel's prophecy, Ezek. 26:5. It is considered too insignificant to be a port of call for the local steamers which call at Acre and Sidon.

The ruins of its ancient grandeur can be seen through the clear water of the harbor, but the town of to-day is small and of no account.

Ty′rus (tī′rus). This form is employed in the Authorized Version of the books of Jeremiah, Ezekiel, Hosea (Joel has "Tyre"), Amos and Zechariah, as follows: Jer. 25:22; 27:3; 47:4; Ezek. 26:2, 3, 4, 7, 15; 27:2, 3, 8, 32; 28:2, 12; 29:18; Hos. 9:13; Amos 1:9, 10; Zech. 9:2, 3.

U

U'cal (ụ'kal) (*I am strong*). According to the received text of Prov. 30: 1, Ithiel and Ucal must be regarded as proper names; and if so, they must be the names of disciples or sons of Agur the son of Jakeh, an unknown sage among the Hebrews. But there is great obscurity about the passage. A slight change in the text would give the rendering of the R. V. margin: "I have wearied myself and am consumed."

U'el (ū'el) (*will of God*), one of the family of Bani, who during the captivity had married a foreign wife. Ezra 10: 34. (B.C. 458.)

Uk'naz (ŭk'năz). In the margin of 1 Chron. 4: 15 the words "even Kenaz" in the text are rendered "Uknaz," as the proper name.

U'lai (ū'la-i), is mentioned by Daniel, Dan. 8: 2, 16, as a river near to Susa, where he saw his vision of the ram and the he-goat. It has been generally identified with the Eulæus of the Greek and Roman geographers, a large stream in the immediate neighborhood of that city. The Eulæus has been by many identified with the modern *Kerkha,* and by others with the modern *Karun,* both near Susa. The fact is probably that what are now the upper Kerkha and the lower Karun were formerly a single stream.

U'lam (ū'lam) (*front*). 1. A descendant of Gilead, the grandson of Manasseh and father of Bedan. 1 Chron. 7. 17.

2. The first-born of Eshek, a descendant of the house of Saul. 1 Chron. 8: 39, 40.

Ul'la (ŭl'là) (*yoke*), an Asherite, head of a family in his tribe. 1 Chron. 7: 39.

Um'mah (ŭm'mah) (*union*), one of the cities of the allotment of Asher. Josh. 19: 30 only. By some it is identified with *'Alma,* in the highlands on the coast, about five miles east-northeast of *Ras en-Nakhûra.* Others think it a slip for Acco.

Unclean meats. These were things strangled, or dead of themselves or through beasts or birds of prey; whatever beast did not both part the hoof and chew the cud; and certain other smaller animals rated as "creeping things;" certain classes of birds mentioned in Lev. 11 and Deut. 14, twenty or twenty-one in all; whatever in the waters had not both fins and scales; whatever winged insect had not besides four legs the two hindlegs for leaping; besides things offered in sacrifice to idols; and all blood or whatever contained it (save perhaps the blood of fish, as would appear from that only of beast and bird being forbidden, Lev. 7: 26), and therefore flesh cut from the live animal; as also all fat, at any rate that disposed in masses among the intestines, and probably wherever discernible and separable among the flesh. Lev. 3: 14–17; 7: 23. The eating of blood was prohibited even to "the stranger that sojourneth among you." Lev. 17: 10, 12–14. As regards blood, the prohibition indeed dates from the declaration to Noah against "flesh with the life thereof, which is the blood thereof," in Gen. 9: 4, which was perhaps regarded by Moses as still binding upon all Noah's descendants. It is noteworthy that the practical effect of the rule laid down is to exclude all the *carnivora* among quadrupeds, and so far as we can interpret the nomenclature, the *raptores* among birds. They were probably excluded as being not averse to human carcasses, and in most eastern countries acting as the servitors of the battle-field and the gibbet. Among fish those which were allowed contain unquestionably the most wholesome varieties, save that they exclude the oyster. Practically the law left among the allowed meats an ample variety. All na-

712

tions of antiquity made a difference between animals which were suitable for food or sacrifice, and those which were not. The distinction was based on proved unsuitableness or unwholesomeness for food, and at times upon a certain abhorrence for some animals,—in some cases the animals which were worshipped. This is true to-day with the Mohammedans, and with the people of India and countries with a similar worship. The distinction so common among ancient nations was adopted in the Mosaic code, some animals being added out of consideration to the special religion of the Israelites. There is also a sanitary aspect to the case. Swine are said to be peculiarly liable to disease in their own bodies. This probably means that they are more easily led than other creatures to the foul feeding which produces it. As regards the animals allowed for food, comparing them with those forbidden, there can be no doubt on which side the balance of wholesomeness lies. Yet there is some doubt whether this idea was in the minds of the people at any time.

Uncleanness. The distinctive idea attached to ceremonial uncleanness among the Hebrews was that it cut a person off for the time from social privileges, and left his citizenship among God's people for the while in abeyance. Not only were the Israelites to be "separated from other people," but they were to be "holy *unto God*," Lev. 20: 24, 26; "a kingdom of priests, and a holy nation." The importance to physical well-being of the injunctions which required frequent ablution, under whatever special pretexts, can be but feebly appreciated in our cooler and damper climate. Uncleanness, as referred to man, may be arranged in three degrees: 1. That which defiled merely "until even," and was removed by bathing and washing the clothes at the end of it; such were all contacts with dead animals. 2. That graver sort which defiled for seven days, and was removed by the use of the "water of separation;" such were all defilements connected with the human corpse. 3. Uncleanness from the morbid puerperal or menstrual state, lasting as long as that morbid state lasted; and in the case of leprosy lasting often for life. As the human person was itself the seat of a covenant token, so male and female had each their ceremonial obligations in proportion to their sexual differences. There is an emphatic reminder of human weakness in the fact of birth and death—man's passage alike into and out of his mortal state—being marked with a stated pollution. The corpse bequeathed a defilement of seven days to all who handled it, to the "tent" or chamber of death, and to sundry things within it. Nay, contact with one slain in the field of battle, or with even a human bone or grave, was no less effectual to pollute than that with a corpse dead by the course of nature. Num. 19: 11–18. This shows that the source of pollution lay in the mere fact of death. The duration of defilement caused by the birth of a female infant being double that due to a male, extending respectively to eighty and forty days in all, Lev. 12: 2–5, may perhaps represent the woman's heavier share in the first sin and first curse. Gen. 3: 16; 1 Tim. 2: 14. Among causes of defilement should be noticed the fact that the ashes of the red heifer, burnt whole, which were mixed with water, and became the standing resource for purifying uncleanness in the second degree, themselves became a source of defilement to all who were *clean*, even as of purification to the unclean, and so the water. Somewhat similarly the scapegoat, who bore away the sins of the people, defiled him who led him into the wilderness, and the bringing forth and burning the sacrifice on the Great Day of Atonement had a similar power. This lightest form of uncleanness was expiated by bathing the body and washing the clothes. Besides the water of purification made as aforesaid, men and women, in their "issues," were, after seven days, reckoned from the cessation of the disorder, to bring two turtledoves or young pigeons to be killed by the priests. All these kinds of uncleanness disqualified for holy functions; as the layman so affected might not approach the congregation and the sanctuary, so any priest who incurred defilement abstain from holy things. Lev. 22: 2–8. The religion of the Persians shows a singularly close correspondence with the Levitical code.

Undergirding. Acts 27: 17. [Ship.]

Unicorn, the rendering of the Authorized Version of the Hebrew *rēêm,* a word which occurs seven times in **the,**

Old Testament as the name of some large wild animal. The *rĕêm* of the Hebrew Bible, however, has nothing at all to do with the one-horned animal of the Greek and Roman writers, as is evident from Deut. 33:17, where, in the blessing of Joseph, it is said, "His glory is like the firstling of his bullock, and his horns are like the horns of *a unicorn;*" not, as the text of the Authorized Version renders it, "the horns of *unicorns.*" The two horns of the *rĕêm* are "the ten thousands of Ephraim and the thousands of Manasseh." This text puts a one-horned animal entirely out of the question. Considering that the

THE WILD OX (Unicorn).

rĕêm is spoken of as a two-horned animal of great strength and ferocity, that it was evidently well known and often seen by the Jews, that it is mentioned as an animal fit for sacrificial purposes, and that it is frequently associated with bulls and oxen, we think there can be no doubt that some species of wild ox is intended. The allusion in Ps. 92:10, "But thou shalt lift up, as a *rĕêym,* my horn," seems to point to the mode in which the *Bovidæ* use their horns, lowering the head and then tossing it up. It is probable that it was the gigantic *Bos primigenius,* or aurochs, now extinct, but of which Cæsar says, "These uri are scarcely less than elephants in size, but in their nature, color and form are bulls. Great is their strength and great their speed; they spare neither man nor beast when once they have caught sight of them."—*Bell. Gall.* vi. 28.

Un'ni (ŭn'nī) (*depressed*). 1. One of the Levite musicians in the time of David. 1 Chron. 15:18, 20. (B.C. 1042.)

2. A second Levite (unless the family of the foregoing be intended) concerned in the sacred office after the return from Babylon. Neh. 12:9. R. V. "Unno." (B.C. 535.)

U'phaz (ū'făz). Jer. 10:9; Dan. 10:5. [OPHIR.]

Ur (ûr). 1. The land of Haran's nativity, Gen. 11:28, the place from which Terah and Abraham started "to go into the land of Canaan." Gen. 11:31. It is called in Genesis "Ur of the Chaldæans," while in the Acts St. Stephen places it, by implication, in Mesopotamia, ch. 7:2, 4. These are all the indications which Scripture furnishes as to its locality. It has been identified by the most ancient traditions with the city of Orfah in the highlands of Mesopotamia. In later ages this was called Edessa, and was celebrated as the capital of Abgarus or Acbarus, who was said to have received the letter and portrait of our Saviour. A second tradition, which appears in the Talmud, finds Ur in Warka, 120 miles southeast from Babylon and four east of the Euphrates. This, however, was the Erech of Holy Scripture, and does not answer the conditions. This place bears the name of *Huruk* in the native inscriptions, and was in the countries known to the Jews as the land of the Chaldæans. A third tradition is the received opinion of modern scholars generally. This fixes Ur in the extreme south of Chaldæa, at *Mugheir,* not very far above—and probably in the time of Abraham actually upon—the head of the Persian Gulf. Among the ruins which are now seen at the spot are the remains of one of the great temples, of a model similar to that of Babel, dedicated to the moon, to whom the city was sacred.

2. Father of one of David's guard. 1 Chron. 11:35. AHASBAI in 2 Sam. 23:34.

Ur'bane (ûr'bāne or ûr-bā'nē) (*of the city; polite*) the Greek form of the Latin Urbanus, as it is given in the Revised Version. He was a Christian disciple who is in the long list of those whom St. Paul salutes in writing to Rome. Rom. 16:9. (A.D. 57.)

U'ri (ū'rī) (*fiery*). 1. The father of Bezaleel, one of the architects of the tabernacle. Ex. 31:2; 35:30; 38:22; 1 Chron. 2:20; 2 Chron. 1:5. He was of the tribe of Judah, and grandson of Caleb ben-Hezron.

2. The father of Geber, Solomon's commissariat officer in Gilead. 1 Kings 4 : 19.

3. One of the gatekeepers of the temple in the time of Ezra. Ezra 10 : 24. (B.C. 458.)

Uri'ah (ū-rī'ah) (*light of Jehovah*). 1. A Hittite and one of David's thirty "mighty men." 2 Sam. 11. 1 Chron. 11 : 41; 2 Sam. 23 : 39. His name, however, and his manner of speech, 2 Sam. 11 : 11, indicate that he had adopted the Jewish religion. He was the husband of Bath-sheba [BATH-SHEBA]. He followed Joab to the war with Ammon, but was sent back to Jerusalem, at an order from the king on the pretext of asking news of the war—really in the hope that his return to his wife might cov r the shame of his own crime. The king met with an unexpected obstacle in the austere, soldier-like spirit which guided all Uriah's conduct, and which gives us a high notion of the character and discipline of David's officers. On the morning of the third day David sent him back to the camp with a letter containing the command to Joab to cause his destruction in the battle. The device of Joab was to observe the part of the wall of Rabbath-ammon where the greatest force of the besieged was congregated, and thither, as a kind of forlorn hope, to send Uriah. A sally took place. Uriah and the officers with him advanced as far as the gate of the city, and were there shot down by the archers on the wall. Just as Joab had forewarned the messenger, the king broke into a furious passion on hearing of the loss. The messenger, as instructed by Joab, calmly continued, and ended the story with the words, "Thy servant also, Uriah the Hittite, is dead." In a moment David's anger is appeased. It is one of the touching parts of the story that Uriah falls unconscious of his wife's dishonor.

2. High priest in the reign of Ahaz. Isa. 8 : 2; 2 Kings 16 : 10–16. He is probably the same as Urijah the priest, who built the altar for Ahaz. 2 Kings 16 : 10. (B.C. about 731.)

3. A priest of the family of Hakkoz, the head of the seventh course of priests. Ezra 8 : 33; Neh. 3 : 4, 21. URIJAH 2.

4. A priest who stood by Ezra while he addressed the people. Neh. 8 : 4. URIJAH 3.

Uri'as (ū-rī'as). 1. Urian, the husband of Bath-sheba. Matt. 1 : 6.

U'ri-el. 1. A Kohathite Levite, son of Tahath. 1 Chron. 6 : 24. Very likely the same as

2. Chief of the Kohathites in the reign of David. 1 Chron. 15 : 5, 11. (B.C. 1042.)

3. Uriel of Gibeah was the father of Maachah or Michaiah, the favorite wife of Rehoboam and mother of Abijah. 2 Chron. 13 : 2. [MAACHAH 3 and TAMAR 3.]

Uri'jah (ū-rī'jah) (*light of Jehovah*). 1. Urijah the priest in the reign of Ahaz, 2 Kings 16 : 10, probably the same as URIAH, 2.

2. A priest of the family of Koz or Hakkoz, the same as URIAH, 3.

3. One of the priests who stood at Ezra's right hand when he read the law to the people. Neh. 8 : 4. (B.C. 458.)

4. The son of Shemaiah of Kirjath-earim. He prophesied in the days of Jehoiakim, B.C. 608, agreeing with Jeremiah that the kingdom of Judah was about to be destroyed, and the king sought to put him to death; but he escaped, and fled into Egypt. His retreat was soon discovered; Elnathan and his men brought him out of Egypt, and Jehoiakim slew him with the sword and cast his body forth among the graves of the common people. Jer. 26 : 20–23.

U'rim and Thum'mim (*lights and perfections*). When the Jewish exiles were met on their return from Babylon by a question which they had no data for answering, they agreed to postpone the settlement of the difficulty till there should rise up "a priest with Urim and Thummim." Ezra 2 : 63; Neh. 7 : 65. The inquiry what those Urim and Thummim themselves were seems likely to wait as long for a final and satisfying answer. On every side we meet with confessions of ignorance. The mysterious words meet us for the first time, as if they needed no explanation, in the description of the high priest's apparel. Over the ephod there is to be a "breastplate of judgment" of gold, scarlet, purple and fine linen, folded square and doubled, a "span" in length and width. In it are to be set four rows of precious stones, each stone with the name of a tribe of Israel engraved on it, that Aaron "may bear them on his heart." Then comes a further order. Inside the breastplate, **are**

to be placed "the Urim and the Thummim," and they too are to be on Aaron's heart when he goes in before the Lord. Ex. 28:30. Not a word describes them. They are mentioned as things already familiar both to Moses and the people, connected naturally with the functions of the high priest as mediating between Jehovah and his people. The command is fulfilled. Lev. 8:8. They pass from Aaron to Eleazar with the sacred ephod and other *pontificalia*. Num. 20:28. When Joshua is solemnly appointed to succeed the great hero-lawgiver, he is bidden to stand before Eleazar, the priest, "who shall ask counsel for him after the judgment of Urim," and this counsel is to determine the movements of the host of Israel. Num. 27:21. In the blessings of Moses they appear as the crowning glory of the tribe of Levi: "thy Thummim and thy Urim are with thy Holy One." Deut. 33:8, 9. In what way the Urim and Thummim were consulted is quite uncertain. Josephus and the rabbins supposed that the stones gave out the oracular answer by preternatural illumination; others believe them to be small articles used as in casting lots; but it seems to be far simpler and more in agreement with the different accounts of inquiries made by Urim and Thummim, 1 Sam. 14:3, 18, 19; 23:4, 9, 11, 12; 28:6; Judges 20: 28; 2 Sam. 5:23, etc., to suppose that the answer was given simply by the word of the Lord to the high priest, comp. John 11:51, when clothed with the ephod and the breastplate, he had inquired of the Lord. Such a view agrees with the true notion of the breastplate.

Usury. The word usury has come in modern English to mean excessive interest upon money loaned, either formally illegal or at least oppressive. In the Scriptures, however, the word did not bear this sense, but meant simply interest of any kind upon money. The Jews were forbidden by the law of Moses to take interest from their brethren, but were permitted to take it from foreigners. The prohibition grew out of the agricultural status of the people, in which ordinary business loans were not needed, and such loans as were required should be made only as to friends and brothers in need. The practice of mortgaging land, sometimes at exorbitant interest, grew up among the Jews during the captivity, in direct

violation of the law. Lev. 25:36, 37; Ezek. 18:8, 13, 17.

U′tha-i (u′tha-ī) (*helpful*). 1. The son of Ammihud, of the children of Pharez the son of Judah. 1 Chron. 9:4. 2. One of the sons of Bigvai, who returned in the second caravan with Ezra. Ezra 8:14. (B.C. 459.)

Uz (ŭz) (*wooded*). 1. A son of Aram, Gen. 10:23; 1 Chron. 1:17, and consequently a grandson of Shem. 2. A son of Nahor by Milcah. Gen. 22:21; Authorized Version, Huz. 3. A son of Dishan, and grandson of Seir. Gen. 36:28. 4. The country in which Job lived. Job 1:1. As far as we can gather, "the land of Uz" lay either east or southeast of Palestine, Job 1:3; adjacent to the Sabæans and the Chaldæans, Job 1: 15, 17, consequently north of the southern Arabians and west of the Euphrates; and, lastly, adjacent to the Edomites of Mount Seir, who at one period occupied Uz, probably as conquerors, Lam. 4:21. According to tradition the home of Job was in the Hauran.

U′zai (ū′za-ī), the father of Palal, who assisted Nehemiah in rebuilding the city wall. Neh. 3:25.

U′zal (ū′zal) (*wandering*), a son of Joktan, Gen. 10:27; 1 Chron. 1:21, whose descendants formed the inhabitants of *San'à*, the capital city of the Yemen (a district of Arabia), which was originally *Azál*. From its position in the centre of the best portion of that kingdom, it must always have been an important city. San'à is situated about 150 miles from Aden and 100 miles from the coast of the Red Sea. It is one of the most imposing cities of Arabia.

Uz′za (ŭz′za) (*strength*). 1. A Benjamite of the sons of Ehud. 1 Chron. 8:7. 2. Elsewhere called UZZAH. 1 Chron. 13:7, 9, 10, 11. [UZZAH.] 3. The children of Uzza were a family of Nethinim who returned with Zerubbabel. Ezra 2:49; Neh. 7:51. 4. Properly Uzzah. As the text now stands, Uzzah is a descendant of Merari, 1 Chron. 6:29; but there appears to be a gap in the verse.

Uz′za, The garden of, the spot in which Manasseh king of Judah and his son Amon were buried. 2 Kings 21:

18, 26. It was the garden attached to Manasseh's palace, ver. 18. The fact of its mention shows that it was not where the usual sepulchres of the kings were. No clue, however, is afforded to its position.

Uz'zah (*strength*), one of the sons of Abinadab, in whose house at Kirjath-jearim the ark rested for twenty years. Uzzah probably was the second and Ahio the third. They both accompanied its removal when David first undertook to carry it to Jerusalem. (B.C. 1042.) Ahio apparently went before the new cart, 1 Chron. 13 : 7, on which it was placed, and Uzzah walked by the side. "At the threshing-floor of Nachon," 2 Sam. 6 : 6, or Chidon, 1 Chron. 13 : 9, the oxen stumbled, perhaps slipping over the smooth rock. Uzzah caught the ark to prevent its falling. The profanation was punished by .his instant death, to the great grief of David, who named the place Perez-uzzah (*the breaking-forth on Uzzah*). But Uzzah's fate was not merely the penalty of his own rashness. The improper mode of transporting the ark, which ought to have been borne on the shoulders of the Levites, was the primary cause of his unholy deed; and David distinctly recognized it as a punishment on the people in general, "because we sought him not after the due order."

Uz'zen-she'rah (ŭz'zen-shē'rah) (*portion of Sherah*), a town founded or rebuilt by Sherah, an Ephraimite woman, the daughter either of Ephraim himself or of Beriah. It is named only in 1 Chron. 7 : 24, in connection with the two Beth-horons.

Uz'zi (ŭz'zĭ) (*my strength*). 1. Son of Bukki, and father of Zerahiah, in the line of the high priests. 1 Chron. 6 : 5, 51; Ezra 7 : 4. Though Uzzi was the lineal ancestor of Zadok, it does not appear that he was ever high priest.

2. Son of Tola the son of Issachar. 1 Chron. 7 : 2, 3.

3. Son of Bela, of the tribe of Benjamin. 1 Chron. 7 : 7.

4. Another, or the same, from whom descended some Benjamite houses, which were settled at Jerusalem after the captivity. 1 Chron. 9 : 8.

5. A Levite, son of Bani, and overseer of the Levites dwelling at Jerusalem, in the time of Nehemiah. Neh. 11 : 22.

6. A priest, chief of the father's house of Jedaiah, in the time of Joiakim the high priest. Neh. 12 : 19. (B.C. about 500.)

7. One of the priests who assisted Ezra in the dedication of the wall of Jerusalem. Neh. 12 : 42. Perhaps the same as the preceding. (B.C. 446.)

Uzzi'a (ūz-zī'ah) (*strength of Jehovah*), one of David's guard, and apparently a native of Ashtaroth beyond Jordan. 1 Chron. 11 : 44.

Uzzi'ah (ūz-zī'ah) (*strength of Jehovah*). 1. King of Judah B.C. 767–736. He was probably regent during his father's lifetime (2 Kings 14 : 22), perhaps in 589 B.C. In some passages his name appears in the lengthened form Azariah. After the murder of Amaziah, he was chosen by the people to succeed him. His reign which is given as 52 years, probably includes both his reign as regent, 21 years, and his independent reign, 31 years. The 16 years given as his age at his accession is very likely the age when he began his rule as regent. For the greater part of his reign he lived in the fear of God, and showed himself a wise, active and pious ruler. He never deserted the worship of the true God, and was much influenced by Zechariah, a prophet who is mentioned only in connection with him. 2 Chron. 26 : 5. So the southern kingdom was raised to a condition of prosperity which it had not known since the death of Solomon. The end of Uzziah was less prosperous than his beginning. Elated with his splendid career, he determined to burn incense on the altar of God, but was opposed by the high priest Azariah and eighty others. See Ex. 30 : 7, 8; Num. 16 : 40; 18 : 7. The king was enraged at their resistance, and, as he pressed forward with his censer, was suddenly smitten with leprosy. This lawless attempt to burn incense was the only exception to the excellence of his administration. 2 Chron. 27 : 2. Uzziah was buried "with his fathers," yet apparently not actually in the royal sepulchres. 2 Chron. 26 : 23. During his reign a great earthquake occurred. Amos 1 : 1; Zech. 14 : 5.

2. A Kohathite Levite, and ancestor of Samuel. 1 Chron. 6 : 24.

3. A priest of the sons of Harim, who

had taken a foreign wife in the days of Ezra. Ezra 10:21. (B.C. 458.)

4. Father of Athaiah or Uthai. Neh. 11:4.

5. Father of Jehonathan, one of David's overseers. 1 Chron. 27:25.

Uz'ziel (ŭz'zĭ-el) (*my strength is God*). 1. Fourth son of Kohath, father of Mishael, Elzaphan or Elizaphan and Zithri, and uncle to Aaron. Ex. 6:18, 22; Lev. 10:4.

2. A Simeonite captain, son of Ishi, in the days of Hezekiah. 1 Chron. 4:42.

3. Head of a Benjamite house, of the sons of Bela. 1 Chron. 7:7.

4. A musician, of the sons of Heman, in David's reign. 1 Chron. 25:4.

5. A Levite, of the sons of Jeduthun, in the days of Hezekiah. 2 Chron. 29:14, 18. (B.C. 726.)

6. Son of Harhaiah, a goldsmith in the days of Nehemiah, who took part in repairing the wall. Neh. 3:8. (B.C. 446.)

Uzzi'elites, The, the descendants of Uzziel, and one of the four great families of the Kohathites. Num. 3:27; 1 Chron. 26:23.

V

Vajez'atha (vă-jĕz'a-thà) (*strong as the wind(?)*), one of the ten sons of Haman whom the Jews slew in Shushan. Esther 9:9. (B.C. 473.)

Vale, Valley. It is hardly necessary to state that these words signify a hollow sweep of ground between two more or less parallel ridges of high land. The structure of the greater part of the Holy Land does not lend itself to the formation of valleys in our sense of the word. The abrupt transitions of its crowded rocky hills preclude the existence of any extended sweep of valley. Vale or valley is employed in the Authorized Version to render five distinct Hebrew words. 1. *'Êmek*. This appears to approach more nearly to the general sense of the English word than any other. It is connected with several places. 2. *Gaï* or *gê*. Of this there is fortunately one example which can be identified with certainty—the deep hollow which compasses the southwest and south of Jerusalem. This identification establishes the *gê* as a deep and abrupt ravine, with steep sides and narrow bottom. 3. *Nachal*. This word answers to the Arabic *wady*, and expresses, as no single English word can, the bed of a stream often wide and shelving, and like a "valley" in character, which in the rainy season may be nearly filled by a foaming torrent, though for the greater part of the year dry. 4. *Bik'âh*. This term appears to mean rather a plain than a valley, though so far resembling it as to be enclosed by mountains. It is rendered by "valley" in Deut. 34:3; Josh. 11:8, 17; 12:7; 2 Chron. 35:22; Zech. 12:11. 5. *Has-Shĕfêlâh*. The district to which the name *has-Shĕfêlâh* is applied in the Bible has no resemblance whatever to a valley, but is a broad, swelling tract of land, but is a broad, swelling tract of many hundred miles in area, which sweeps gently down from the mountains of Judah to the Mediterranean. It is rendered "the vale" in Deut. 1:7; Josh. 10:40; 1 Kings 10:27; 2 Chron. 1:15; Jer. 33:13; and "the valley" or "the valleys" in Josh. 9:1; 11:2, 16; 12:8; 15:33; Judges 1:9; Jer. 32:44.

Vani'ah (vă-nī'ah) (perhaps *distress*), one of the sons of Bani. Ezra 10:36. (B.C. 458.)

Vash'ni (văsh'nī) (*strong*), the firstborn of Samuel as the text now stands, 1 Chron. 6:28; but in 1 Sam. 8:2 the name of his first-born is Joel. Most probably in the Chronicles the name of Joel has dropped out, and Vashni is a corruption of "and (the) second."

Vash'ti (văsh'tī) (Pers. *best*), the "queen" of Ahasuerus, who, for refusing to show herself to the king's guests at the royal banquet, when sent for by the king, was repudiated and deposed. Esther 1. (B.C. 483.) Many attempts have been made to identify her with historical personages; but it is far more probable that she was only one of the inferior wives, dignified with the title of queen, whose name has utterly disappeared from history.

Ve'adar. [MONTHS.]

Veil. With regard to the use of the veil, it is important to observe that it was by no means so general in ancient as in modern times. Much of the scrupulousness in respect of the use of the veil dates from the promulgation of the Koran, which forbade women appearing unveiled except in the presence of their nearest relatives. In ancient times the veil was adopted only in exceptional cases, either as an article of ornamental dress, Cant. 4:1, 3; 6:7 (R. V.), or by betrothed maidens in the presence of their future husbands, especially at the time of the wedding, Gen. 24:65; or, lastly, by women of loose character for purposes of concealment. Gen. 38:

14. Among the Jews of the New Testament age it appears to have been customary for the women to cover their heads (not necessarily their faces) when engaged in public worship.

Veil of the tabernacle and temple. [TABERNACLE; TEMPLE.]

Versions, Ancient, of the Old and New Testaments. In treating of the ancient versions that have come down to us, in whole or in part, they will be described in the alphabetical order of the languages.

ÆTHIOPIC VERSION.—Christianity was introduced into Æthiopia in the fourth century, through the labors of Frumentius and Ædesius of Tyre, who had been made slaves and sent to the king. The Æthiopic version which we possess is in the ancient dialect of Axum; hence some have ascribed it to the age of the earliest missionaries, but it is probably of a later date. In 1548–9 the Æthiopic New Testament was also printed at Rome, edited by three Abyssinians.

ARABIC VERSIONS.—1. *Arabic versions of the Old Testament* were made from the Hebrew (tenth century), from the Syriac and from the LXX. 2. *Arabic versions of the New Testament.* There are four versions. The first, the Roman, of the Gospels only, was printed in 1590–1.

ARMENIAN VERSION.—In the year 431, Joseph and Eznak returned from the Council of Ephesus, bringing with them a Greek copy of the Scriptures. From this a version in Armenian was made by Isaac, the Armenian patriarch, and Miesrob. The first printed edition of the Old and New Testaments in Armenian appeared at Amsterdam in 1666, under the care of a person commonly termed Oscan or Uscan, and described as being an Armenian bishop.

CHALDEE VERSIONS.—*Targum*, a Chaldee word of uncertain origin, is the general term for the Chaldee, or more accurately Aramaic, versions of the Old Testament. 1. The Targums were originally oral, and the earliest Targum, which is that of Onkelos on the Pentateuch, began to be committed to writing about the second century of the Christian era; though it did not assume its **present** shape till the end of the third **or the** beginning of the fourth century.

So far, however, from superseding the oral Targum at once, it was, on the contrary, strictly forbidden to read it in public. Its language is Chaldee, closely approaching in purity of idiom to that of Ezra and Daniel. It follows a sober and clear though not a slavish exegesis, and keeps as closely and minutely to the text as is at all consistent with its purpose, viz. to be chiefly and above all *a version for the people.* Its explanations of difficult and obscure passages bear ample witness to the competence of those who gave it its final shape. It avoids, as far as circumstances would allow, the legendary character with which all the later Targums entwine the biblical word. 2. *Targum on the prophets,*—viz. Joshua, Judges, Samuel, Kings, Isaiah, Jeremiah, Ezekiel and the twelve minor prophets,—called TARGUM OF JONATHAN BEN-UZZIEL. We shall probably not be far wrong in placing this Targum some time, although not long, after Onkelos, or about the middle of the fourth century. 3 and 4. *Targum of Jonathan ben-Uzziel and Jerushalmi-Targum on the Pentateuch.*—Onkelos and Jonathan on the Pentateuch and prophets, whatever be their exact date, place, authorship and editorship, are the oldest of existing Targums, and belong, in their present shape, to Babylon and the Babylonian academies flourishing between the third and fourth centuries A.D.

EGYPTIAN VERSIONS.—Of these there are three,—the *Memphitic,* of lower Egypt, the *Coptic,* of upper Egypt, and the *Thebaic,* with some fragments of another. The Thebaic was the earliest, and belongs to the third century.

GOTHIC VERSION.—In the year 318 the Gothic bishop and translator of Scripture, Ulphilas, was born. He succeeded Theophilus as bishop of the Goths in 348; through him it is said that the Goths in general adopted Arianism. The great work of Ulphilas was his version of the Scriptures. As an ancient monument of the Gothic language the version of Ulphilas possesses great interest; as a version the use of which was once extended widely through Europe, it is a monument of the Christianization of the Goths; and as a version *known* to have been made in the fourth century, and transmitted to us in ancient MSS., it has its value in textual criticism.

GREEK VERSIONS OF THE OLD TESTAMENT.—1. *Septuagint.*—[See SEPTUAGINT.] 2. *Aquila.*—It is a remarkable fact that in the second century there were three versions executed of the Old Testament Scriptures into Greek. The first of these was made by Aquila, a native of Sinope in Pontus, who had become a proselyte to Judaism. It was made during the reign of Hadrian, A.D. 117–138. 3. *Theodotion.*—The second version of which we have information as executed in the second century is that of Theodotion. He is stated to have been an Ephesian, and he seems to be most generally described as an Ebionite. 4. *Symmachus* is stated by Eusebius and Jerome to have been an Ebionite; Epiphanius and others, however, style him a Samaritan. It may be that as a Samaritan he made this version for some of that people who employed Greek, and who had learned to receive more than the Pentateuch.

LATIN VERSIONS.—[VULGATE.]

SAMARITAN VERSIONS.—[SAMARITAN PENTATEUCH.]

SLAVONIC VERSION.—In A.D. 862 there was a desire expressed or an inquiry made for Christian teachers in Moravia, and in the following year the labors of missionaries began among the Moravians. These missionaries were Cyrillus and Methodius, two brothers from Thessalonica. To Cyrillus is ascribed the invention of the Slavonian alphabet and the commencement of the translation of the Scriptures. He appears to have died at Rome in 868, while Methodius continued for many years to be the bishop of the Slavonians. He is stated to have continued his brother's translation.

SYRIAC VERSIONS.—1. *Of the Old Testament.* (*a*) From the Hebrew. In the early times of Syrian Christianity there was executed a version of the Old Testament from the original Hebrew, the use of which must have been as widely extended as was the Christian profession among that people. It is highly improbable that any part of the Syriac version is older than the advent of our Lord. The Old Syriac has the peculiar value of being the first version from the Hebrew original made for

Christian use. The first printed edition of this version was that which appeared in the Paris Polyglot of Le Jay in 1645. (*b*) The Syriac version from the Hexaplar Greek text. The only Syriac version of the Old Testament up to the sixth century was apparently the Peshito. The version by Paul of Tela, a Monophysite, was made in the beginning of the seventh century; for its basis he used the Hexaplar Greek text—that is, the LXX., with the corrections of Origen, the asterisks, obeli, etc., and with the references to the other Greek versions. In fact, it is from this Syriac version that we obtain our most accurate acquaintance with the results of the critical labors of Origen. It is from a MS. in the Ambrosian Library at Milan that we possess accurate means of knowing this Syriac version. 2. *The Syriac New Testament Versions.* (*a*) The Peshito Syriac New Testament. It may stand as an admitted fact that a version of the New Testament in Syriac existed in the second century. (*b*) The Curetonian Syriac Gospels. Among the MSS. brought from the Nitrian monasteries in 1842, Dr. Cureton noticed a copy of the Gospels, differing greatly from the common text; and this is the form of text to which the name of Curetonian Syriac has been rightly applied. Every criterion which proves the common Peshito not to exhibit a text of extreme antiquity equally proves the early origin of this.

Versions, English. 1. WYCLIF. With Wyclif began a new era of Bible translation. Before his time the translations were fragmentary, and for the most part paraphrases. The New Testament was translated by Wyclif himself, the whole being completed by 1380. The Old Testament was undertaken by Nicholas de Hereford, but was interrupted, and ends abruptly (following so far the order of the Vulgate) in the middle of Baruch. The version was based entirely upon the Vulgate. Wyclif himself seems to have supplied the last books, so that by the middle of 1382 the whole Bible was in the hands of the people. The following characteristics may be noticed as distinguishing this version: (1) The general homeliness of its style. (2) The substitution, in many cases, of English equivalents for quasi-technical words. (3) The extreme literalness with which in some instances, even at the cost of being unintelligible, the Vulgate text is followed, as in 2 Cor. 1:17-19.

2. TYNDAL.—The work of Wyclif stands by itself. Whatever power it exercised in preparing the way for the Reformation of the sixteenth century, it had no perceptible influence on later translations. With Tyndal we enter on a continuous succession. He is the patriarch, in no remote ancestry, of the Authorized Version. More than Cranmer or Ridley he is the true hero of the English Reformation. His work began soon after the invention of printing. "Ere many years," he said at the age of thirty-six (A.D. 1520), he would cause "a boy that driveth the plough" to know more of Scripture than the great body of the clergy then knew. He prepared himself for the work by long years of labor in Greek and Hebrew. First the Gospels of St. Matthew and St. Mark were published tentatively. In 1525 the whole of the New Testament was printed in quarto at Cologne, and in small octavo at Worms. In England it was received with denunciations. Tunstall, bishop of London, preaching at Paul's Cross, asserted that there were at least two thousand errors in it, and ordered all copies of it to be bought up and burnt. An act of Parliament (35 Hen. VIII. cap. 1) forbade the use of all copies of Tyndal's "false translation." The treatment which it received from professed friends was hardly less annoying. In the meantime the work went on. Editions were printed one after another. The last appeared in 1535, just before his death. To Tyndal belongs the honor of having given the first example of a translation based on true principles, and the excellence of later versions has been almost in exact proportion as they followed his. While some of his renderings are uncouth and others incorrect, yet the exquisite grace and simplicity which have endeared the Authorized Version to men of the most opposite tempers and contrasted opinions is due mainly to his clear-sighted truthfulness.

3. COVERDALE.—A complete translation of the Bible, different from Tyndal's, bearing the name of Miles Coverdale, printed probably at Zurich, appeared in 1535. The undertaking itself, and the choice of Coverdale as the translator, were probably due to Cromwell. He was content to make the translation at second hand "out of the Douche (Luther's German Version) and the Latine." Fresh editions of his Bible were published, keeping their ground in spite of rivals, in 1537, 1539, 1550, 1553. He was called in at a still later period to assist in the Geneva Version.

4. MATTHEW.—In the year 1537, a large folio Bible appeared as edited and dedicated to the king by Thomas Matthew. No one of that name appears at all prominently in the religious history of Henry VIII., and this suggests the inference that the name was adopted to conceal the real translator. The tradition which connects this Matthew with John Rogers, the proto-martyr of the Marian persecution, is all but undisputed. Matthew's Bible reproduces Tyndal's work, in the New Testament entirely, in the Old Testament as far as 2 Chron., the rest being taken with occasional modifications from Coverdale. A copy was ordered, by royal proclamation, to be set up in every church, the cost being divided between the clergy and the parishioners. This was, therefore, the first Authorized Version.

5. TAVERNER (1539).—The boldness of the pseudo-Matthew had frightened the ecclesiastical world from its propriety. Coverdale's version was, however, too inaccurate to keep its ground. It was necessary to find another editor, and the printers applied to Richard Taverner. But little is known of his life. The fact that, though a layman, he had been chosen as one of the canons of the Cardinal's College at Oxford indicates a reputation for scholarship, and this is confirmed by the character of his translation. In most respects this may be described as an expurgated edition of Matthew's. So far as we know Taverner's Bible was only once reprinted.

6. CRANMER.—In the same year as Taverner's, and coming from the same press, appeared an English Bible, in a more stately folio, with a preface containing the initials T. C., which implied the archbishop's sanction. Its first edition was called *The Great Bible*, from its size. In a new edition (1540) Cranmer added a long preface, from which

it was henceforth called Cranmer's Bible. Cranmer's version presented, as might be expected, many points of interest. The prologue gave a more complete ideal of what a translation ought to be than had as yet been seen. Words not in the original were to be printed in a different type. It was reprinted again and again, and was the Authorized Version of the English Church till 1568—the interval of Mary's reign excepted. From it, accordingly, were taken most, if not all, the portions of Scripture in the Prayer-books of 1549 and 1552. The Psalms as a whole, the quotations from Scripture in the Homilies, the sentences in the Communion Services, and some phrases elsewhere, still preserve the remembrance of it.

7. GENEVA.—The exiles who fled to Geneva in the reign of Mary entered on the work of translation with more vigor than ever. The Genevan refugees—among them Whittingham, Goodman, Pullain, Sampson and Coverdale himself—labored "for two years or more, day and night." Their translation of the New Testament was "diligently revised by the most approved Greek examples." The New Testament, translated by Whittingham, was printed in 1557, and the whole Bible in 1560. Whatever may have been its faults, the Geneva Bible, commonly called the Breeches Bible from its rendering of Gen. 3:7, was unquestionably, for sixty years, the most popular of all versions. Not less than eighty editions, some of the whole Bible, were printed between 1558 and 1611. It kept its ground for some time even against the Authorized Version, and gave way, as it were, slowly and under protest. It was the version specially adopted by the great Puritan party through the whole reign of Elizabeth and far into that of James. As might be expected, it was based on Tyndal's version. It presents, in a calendar prefixed to the Bible, something like a declaration of war against the established order of the Church's lessons commemorating Scripture facts and the deaths of the great reformers, but ignoring saints' days altogether. It was the first English Bible which entirely omitted the Apocrypha. The notes were characteristically Swiss, not only in their theology, but in their politics.

8. THE BISHOPS' BIBLE.—The facts just stated will account for the wish of Archbishop Parker to bring out another version, which might establish its claims against that of Geneva. Great preparations were made. Eight bishops, together with some deans and professors, brought out the fruit of their labors in a magnificent folio (1568 and 1572). It was avowedly based on Cranmer's; but of all the English versions it had probably the least success. It did not command the respect of scholars, and its size and cost were far from meeting the wants of the people.

9. RHEIMS AND DOUAY.—The successive changes in the Protestant versions of the Scriptures were, as might be expected, matter of triumph to the controversialists of the Latin Church. Some saw in it an argument against any translation of Scripture into the spoken language of the people. Others pointed derisively to the want of unity which these changes displayed. There were some, however, who took the line which Sir T. More and Gardiner had taken under Henry VIII. They did not object to the principle of an English translation. They only charged all the versions hitherto made with being false, corrupt, heretical. To this there was the ready retort that they had done nothing; that their bishops in the reign of Henry had promised, but had not performed. It was felt to be necessary that they should take some steps which might enable them to turn the edge of this reproach. The English Catholic refugees who were settled at Rheims undertook a new English version. The New Testament was published at Rheims in 1582, and professed to be based on "the authentic text of the Vulgate." Notes were added, as strongly dogmatic as those of the Geneva Bible, and often keenly controversial. The work of translation was completed somewhat later by the publication of the Old Testament at Douay in 1609.

10. AUTHORIZED VERSION.—The position of the English Church in relation to the versions in use at the commencement of the reign of James was hardly satisfactory. The Bishops' Bible was sanctioned by authority. That of Geneva had the strongest hold on the affections of the people. Scholars, Hebrew scholars in particular, found grave fault with both. Among the demands of the Puritan representatives at the Hampton Court Conference in 1604 was one for a

new, or at least a revised, translation. The work of organizing and superintending the arrangements for a new translation was one specially congenial to James, and accordingly in 1606 the task was commenced. It was intrusted to 47 scholars. The Bishops' Bible was to be followed, and as little altered as the original would permit. The old ecclesiastical words to be kept. The division of the chapters to be altered either not at all or as little as possible. No marginal notes to be affixed but only for the explanation of Hebrew and Greek words. For three years the work went on, the separate companies comparing notes as directed. When the work drew toward its completion, it was necessary to place it under the care of a select few. Two from each of the three groups were accordingly selected, and the six met in London to superintend the publication. The final correction, and the task of writing the arguments of the several books, was given to Bilson, bishop of Winchester, and Dr. Miles Smith, the latter of whom also wrote the dedication and preface. The version thus published did not at once supersede the versions already in possession. The fact that five editions were published in three years shows that there was a good demand. But the Bishops' Bible probably remained in many churches, and the popularity of the Geneva Version is shown by not less than thirteen reprints, in whole or in part, between 1611 and 1617. It is not easy to ascertain the impression which the Authorized Version made at the time of its appearance.

No marginal notes were permitted, except certain explanations of Hebrew and Greek words. A new set of headings of chapters and columns was prepared, and the dates (mostly from Ussher) with which we are familiar, were first inserted in 1701. The Revisers of the Revision of 1881 say in their preface: "We have had to study this great Version carefully and minutely, line by line; and the longer we have been engaged upon it the more we have learned to admire its simplicity, its dignity, its power, its happy turns of expression, its general accuracy, and, we must not fail to add, the music of its cadences, and the felicities of its rhythm."

The Revised Version.—Various revisions of the A. V. have been attempted,

for the knowledge of the Greek text has been greatly enlarged, words have changed their meaning, translations were imperfect, and inaccurate. So that after 300 years, it was time for an authoritative revision by the best scholarship of England and America. "Revision had its origin in action taken by the Convocation of the Province of Canterbury in February, 1870, and it has been conducted throughout on the plan laid down in Resolutions of both Houses of the Province, and, more particularly, in accordance with Principles and Rules drawn up by a special Committee of Convocation in the following May. Two Companies, the one for the revision of the Authorized Version of the Old Testament, and the other for the revision of the same Version of the New Testament, were formed in the manner specified in the Resolutions, and the work was commenced on the twenty-second day of June, 1870. Shortly afterwards, steps were taken, under a resolution passed by both Houses of Convocation, for inviting the co-operation of American scholars; and eventually two Committees were formed in America, for the purpose of acting with the two English Companies, on the basis of the Principles and Rules drawn up by the Committee of Convocation." A set of eight rules was prepared for these committees. They were to make as few changes as possible consistent with faithfulness. They aimed to render a work that had reached this high standard of excellence still more excellent, to increase its fidelity without destroying its character. The Revision of the New Testament occupied ten and a half years. The First Revision took about six years. This was submitted to the American company, and then two and a half years more were occupied with the Second Version; the rest of the time was occupied in consultations and emendations. The New Testament was issued in 1881, the Old Testament in 1885. One of the chief difficulties in the way of its general acceptance is the method of paragraphing simply by subjects, putting even dialogues in solid form; thus making the book far more difficult to read, either alone or with others, and less attractive to the common people.

The American Revision.—The American committee in making the Revision gave their English brethren the decisive vote in disputed questions. But they preserved a list of their preferences, which they hoped might be approved by scholars and finally adopted. They kept at work on the revising, and especially during the last four years before their Revision was published in 1901. For the most part this Revision is the same as the English Revision; but they had the advantage of all the criticisms of the Revision by scholars on both sides of the water, for making many minor improvements, besides those they had originally preferred. For example, they substitute "Jehovah" for "LORD" in caps; "Sheol" for "hell" and "the grave" in the Old Testament; "justice" for "judgment," etc. In a number of cases, intelligible English idioms have been substituted for obscure and archaic phraseology. The paragraphing has been improved, but is still far from the ideal, and far less helpful to ordinary readers than even the old verse forms. On the whole it is probably the most perfect Revision yet made. The number of readings wherein the text used for the Revised New Testament differed from that used in the King James' edition is about 6,000, and it is this more accurate Greek text that gives the chief basis for its superior claims. The American differs from the English in only about twenty-five instances.

Village. This word, in addition to its ordinary sense, is often used, especially in the enumeration of towns in Josh. 13, 15, 19, to imply unwalled suburbs outside the walled towns. Arab villages, as found in Arabia, are often mere collections of stone huts, "long, low, rude hovels, roofed only with the stalks of palm leaves," or covered for a time with tent-cloths, which are removed when the tribe change their quarters. Others are more solidly built, as are most of the modern villages of Palestine, though in some the dwellings are mere mud-huts.

Vine, the well-known valuable plant (*Vitis vinifera*) very frequently referred to in the Old and New Testaments, and cultivated from the earliest times. The first mention of this plant occurs in Gen. 9:20, 21. That it was abundantly cultivated in Egypt is evident from the frequent representations on the monuments, as well as from the scriptural allusions. Gen. 40:9–11; Ps. 78:47. The vines of Palestine were celebrated both for luxuriant growth and for the immense clusters of grapes which they produced, which were sometimes carried on a staff between two men, as in the case of the spies, Num. 13:23, and as has been done in some instances in modern times. Special mention is made in the Bible of the vines of Eshcol, Num. 13:24; 32:9, of Sibmah, Heshbon and Elealeh, Isa. 16:8, 9, 10; Jer. 48:32, and of Engedi. Cant. 1:14. From the abundance and excellence of the vines, it may readily be understood how frequently this plant is the subject of metaphor in the Holy Scriptures. To dwell under the vine and fig tree is an emblem

VINE.

of domestic happiness and peace, 1 Kings 4:25; Ps. 128:3; Micah 4:4; the rebellious people of Israel are compared to "wild grapes," "an empty vine," "the degenerate plant of a strange vine," etc. Isa. 5:2, 4; Jer. 2:21; Hos. 10:1. It is a vine which our Lord selects to show the spiritual union which subsists between himself and his members. John 15:1–6. The ancient Hebrews probably allowed the vine to go trailing on the ground or upon supports. This latter mode of cultivation appears to be alluded to by Ezekiel. Ezek. 19:11, 12. The vintage, which formerly was a season of general festivity, began in September. The towns were deserted; the people lived among the vineyards in the lodges and tents. Comp. Judges 9:27; Isa. 16:10; Jer. 25:30. The grapes were gathered with shouts of joy by the "grape gatherers," Jer. 25:30, and put into baskets. See

Jer. 6:9. They were then carried on the head and shoulders, or slung upon a yoke, to the "wine-press." Those intended for eating were perhaps put into flat open baskets of wickerwork, as was the custom in Egypt. In Palestine, at present, the finest grapes, says Dr. Robinson, are dried as raisins, and the juice of the remainder, after having been trodden and pressed, "is boiled down to a sirup, which, under the name of *dibs*, is much used by all classes, wherever vineyards are found, as a condiment with their food." The vineyard, which

GATHERING GRAPES.

was generally on a hill, Isa. 5:1; Jer. 31:5; Amos 9:13, was surrounded by a wall or hedge in order to keep out the wild boars, Ps. 80:13, jackals and foxes. Num. 22:24; Neh. 4:3; Cant. 2:15; Ezek. 13:4, 5; Matt. 21:33. Within the vineyard was one or more towers of stone in which the vine-dressers lived. Isa. 1:8; 5:2; Matt. 21:33. The vat, which was dug, Matt. 21:33, or hewn out of the rocky soil, and the press, were part of the vineyard furniture. Isa. 5:2.

Vine of Sodom occurs only in Deut. 32:32. It is generally supposed that this passage alludes to the celebrated apples of Sodom, of which Josephus speaks, "which indeed resemble edible fruit in color, but, on being plucked by the hand, are dissolved into smoke and ashes." Some consider it the *'ushar* fruit, the *Asclepias (Calotropis) procera* of botanists, which "resembles externally a large smooth apple or orange, hanging in clusters of three or four together, and when ripe is of a yellow color. It is now fair and delicious to the eye and soft to the touch; but, on being pressed or struck, it explodes with a puff, like a bladder or puff-ball, leaving in the hand only the shreds of

the thin rind and a few fibres. It is indeed filled chiefly with air, which gives it the round form." But this grows on a shrub, not a vine. Others think of the Colocynth, which is bitter and powdery inside, and grows on a vine. But most commentators now consider the expression figurative, no real fruit being intended.

Vinegar. The Hebrew word translated "vinegar" was applied to a beverage consisting generally of wine or strong drink turned sour, but sometimes artificially made by an admixture of barley and wine, and thus liable to fermentation. It was acid even to a proverb, Prov. 10:26, and by itself formed an unpleasant draught, Ps. 69:21, but was used by laborers. Ruth 2:14. Similar was the *acetum* of the Romans—a thin, sour wine, consumed by soldiers. It was often diluted with water and then called *posca*. This was probably the beverage of which the Saviour partook in his dying moments. Matt. 27:48; Mark 15:36; John 19:29, 30.

Vineyards, Plain of the. R. V. Abel-Cheramim. This place, mentioned only in Judges 11:33, lay east of the Jordan, on the Moab plateau.

Viol. [PSALTERY.]

Viper. [SERPENT.]

Voph'si (vŏf'sī), father of Nahbi, the Naphtalite spy. Num. 13:14.

Vows. A vow is a solemn promise made to God to perform or to abstain from performing a certain thing. The earliest mention of a vow is that of Jacob. Gen. 28:18–22; 31:13. The law therefore did not introduce, but regulated the practice of, vows. Three sorts are mentioned: 1, vows of devotion; 2, vows of abstinence; 3, vows of destruction. 1. By vows of devotion, any person or possession might be devoted or set aside for the sanctuary, save such as were already set apart for sacred uses, such as the first-born of either man or beast. Lev. 27:26. Anything thus set apart might be redeemed at one-fifth above its assessed value excepting animals fit for sacrifice, which were not to be redeemed or changed. Lev. 27:9, 10, 33. Persons devoted to God might be redeemed at a valuation according to age and sex, on the scale given in Lev. 27:1–7; 2 Kings 12:4. If not redeemed he became a servant of the sanctuary. 1 Sam. 1:11, 24, 28.

Usually, however, he was redeemed, as the number of the Levites made the service of others unnecessary. Among general regulations affecting vows, the following may be mentioned: (1) Vows were entirely voluntary, but once made were regarded as compulsory. Num. 30:2; Deut. 23:21; Eccles. 5:4. (2) If persons in a dependent condition made vows, as an unmarried daughter living in her father's house, or a wife, the vow, if her father, or her husband, heard and disallowed it, was void; but if they heard without disallowance, it was to remain good. Num. 30:3–16. (3) Votive offerings arising from the produce of any impure traffic were wholly forbidden. Deut. 23:18. 2. For vows of abstinence, see CORBAN. 3. For vows of extermination, see ANATHEMA, and Ezra 10:8; Micah 4:13.

Vul'gate, The, the Latin version of the Bible. The influence which it exercised upon western Christianity is scarcely less than that of the LXX. upon the Greek churches. Both the Greek and the Latin Vulgate have been long neglected; yet the Vulgate should have a very deep interest for all the western churches. For many centuries it was the only Bible generally used; and, directly or indirectly, it is the real parent of all the vernacular versions of western Europe. The Gothic version of Ulphilas alone is independent of it. The name is equivalent to *Vulgata editio* (the *current* text of Holy Scripture). This translation was made by Jerome—Eusebius Hieronymus—w h o was born about 340 A.D. at Stridon in Dalmatia, and died at Bethlehem in 420 A.D. This great scholar probably alone for 1500 years possessed the qualifications necessary for producing an original version o f t h e Scriptures for the use of the Latin churches. Going to Rome, h e w a s requested by Pope Damasus, A.D. 383, to make a revision of the old Latin version o f t h e New Testament, whose history is lost in obscurity. In middle life Jerome began the study of the Hebrew, and made a new version of the Old Testament from the original Hebrew, which was completed A.D. 404. The critical labors of Jerome were received with a loud outcry of reproach. He was accused of disturbing the repose of the Church and shaking the founda-

tions of faith. But clamor based upon ignorance soon dies away; and the New translation gradually came into use equally with the Old, and at length supplanted it. The vast power which the Vulgate has had in determining the theological terms of western Christendom can hardly be overrated. By far the greater part of the current doctrinal terminology is based on the Vulgate. *Predestination, justification, supererogation* (supererogo), *sanctification, salvation, mediation, regeneration, revelation, visitation* (met.), *propitiation,* first appear in the Old Vulgate. *Grace, redemption, election, reconciliation, satisfaction, inspiration, scripture,* were devoted there to a new and holy use. *Sacrament* and *communion* are from the same source; and though *baptism* is Greek, it comes to us from the Latin. It would be easy to extend the list by the addition of *orders, penance, congregation, priest;* but it can be seen from the forms already brought forward that the Vulgate has left its mark both upon our language and upon our thoughts. It was the version which alone they knew who handed down to the reformers the rich stores of mediæval wisdom; the version with which the greatest of the reformers were most familiar, and from which they had drawn their earliest knowledge of divine truth.

Vulture. The rendering in the Au-

THE VULTURE.

thorized Version of the Hebrew *dââh, dayyâh,* and also in Job 28:7 of *ayyâh.* There seems no doubt that the Authorized Version translation is incorrect, and that the original words refer to some of the smaller species of raptorial birds. In the R. V. the first two are translated "kite," and the third "falcon." [KITE.] But the Hebrew words *nesher*, invariably rendered "eagle" in the Authorized Version and *racham*, rendered "gier eagle" are doubtless two varieties of the true vulture. [EAGLE.]

See Job 28 : 7; Lev. 11 : 14; Deut. 14 : 13; Isa. 34 : 17.

W

Wages. The earliest mention of wages is of a recompense, not in money, but in kind, to Jacob from Laban. Gen. 29: 15, 20; 30: 28; 31: 7, 8, 41. In Egypt money payments by way of wages were in use, but the terms cannot now be ascertained. Ex. 2: 9. The only mention of the rate of wages in Scripture is found in the parable of the householder and the vineyard, Matt. 20: 2, where the laborer's wages are set at one denarius per day, 16 cents. The usual pay of a soldier in the later days of the Roman republic was ten *asses,* or about 10 cents a day. Tac. *Ann.* i. 17; Polyb. vi. 39. In earlier times it is probable that the rate was lower; but it is likely that laborers, and also soldiers, were supplied with provisions. The law was very strict in requiring daily payment of wages. Lev. 19: 13; Deut. 24: 14, 15. The employer who refused to give his laborers sufficient victuals is censured, Job 24: 11, and the iniquity of withholding wages is denounced. Jer. 22: 13; Mal. 3: 5; James 5: 4.

Wagon. The Oriental wagon is a vehicle composed of two or three planks with two solid circular blocks of wood, from two to five feet in diameter for wheels. For the conveyance of passengers, mattresses or clothes are laid in the bottom, and the vehicle is drawn by buffaloes or oxen. [CART and CHARIOT.]

Walls. Only a few points need be noticed. 1. The practice common in Palestine of carrying foundations down to the solid rock, as in the case of the temple, with structures intended to be permanent. Luke 6: 48. 2. A feature of some parts of Solomon's buildings, as described by Josephus, corresponds remarkably to the method adopted at Nineveh of incrusting or veneering a wall of brick or stone with slabs of a more costly material, as marble or alabaster. 3. Another use of walls in Palestine is to support mountain roads or terraces formed on the sides of hills

FORTRESS.
Representation of a Syrian fortress on a monument of Sennacherib.

for purposes of cultivation. 4. The "path of the vineyards," Num. 22: 24, is a pathway through vineyards, with walls on each side.

Wandering in the Wilderness. [WILDERNESS OF THE WANDERING.]

War. The most important topic in connection with war is the formation of

THE CATAPULT,
A machine for throwing heavy darts.

729

the army which is destined to carry it on. [ARMY.] Formal proclamations of war were not necessarily interchanged between the belligerents. Before entering the enemy's district spies were sent to ascertain the character of the country and the preparations of its inhabit-

THE CROW.

ants for resistance. Num. 13:17; Josh. 2:1; Judges 7:10; 1 Sam. 26:4. The combat assumed the form of a number of hand-to-hand contests; hence the high value attached to fleetness of foot and strength of arm. 2 Sam. 1:23; 2:18; 1 Chron. 12:8. At the same time various strategic devices were practiced,

BATTERING-RAM AND TOWER.

such as the ambuscade, Josh. 8:2, 12; Judges 20:36, surprise, Judges 7:16, or circumvention. 2 Sam. 5:23. Another mode of settling the dispute was by the selection of champions, 1 Sam. 17; 2

Sam. 2:14, who were spurred on to exertion by the offer of high reward. 1 Sam. 17:25; 18:25; 2 Sam. 18:11; 1 Chron. 11:6. The contest having been decided, the conquerors were recalled from the pursuit by the sound of a trumpet. 2 Sam. 2:28; 18:16; 20:22. The siege of a town or fortress was conducted in the following manner: A line of circumvallation was drawn round the place, Ezek. 4:2; Micah 5:1, constructed out of the trees found in the neighborhood, Deut. 20:20, together with earth and any other materials at hand. This line not only cut off the besieged from the surrounding country, but also served as a base of operations for the besiegers. The next step was to throw out from this line one or more mounds or "banks" in the direction of the city, 2 Sam. 20:15; 2 Kings 19:32; Isa. 37:33, which were gradually increased in height until they were about half as high as the city wall. On this mound or bank towers were erected, 2 Kings 25:1; Jer. 52:4; Ezek. 4:2; 17:17; 21:22; 26:8, whence the slingers and archers might attack with effect. *Catapults* were prepared for hurling large darts and stones; and the *crow*, a long spar, with iron claws at one end and ropes at the other, to pull down stones or men from the top of the wall. *Battering-rams*, Ezek. 4:2; 21:22, were brought up to the walls by means of the bank, and scaling-ladders might also be placed on it. The treatment of the conquered was extremely severe in ancient times. The bodies of the soldiers killed in action were plundered, 1 Sam. 31:8; 2 Chron. 20:25; the survivors were either killed in some savage manner, Judges 9:45; 2 Sam. 12:31; 2 Chron. 25:12, mutilated, Judges 1:6; 1 Sam. 11:2, or carried into captivity. Num. 31:26.

Washing the hands and feet. As knives and forks were not used in the East, in Scripture times, in eating, it was necessary that the hand, which was thrust into the common dish, should be scrupulously clean; and again, as sandals were ineffectual against the dust and heat of the climate, washing the feet on entering a house was an act both of respect to the company and of refreshment to the traveler. The former of these usages was transformed by the Pharisees of the New Testament age into a matter of ritual observance, Mark 7:3, and special rules were laid down as to the time and manner of its performance. Washing the feet did not rise to the dignity of a

EASTERN WASHING-VESSELS.

ritual observance except in connection with the services of the sanctuary. Ex. 30:19, 21. It held a high place, however, among the rites of hospitality. As soon as a guest presented himself at the tent door, it was usual to offer the necessary materials for washing the feet. Gen. 18:4; 19:2; 24:32; 43:24; Judges 19:21. It was a yet more com-

WASHING THE HANDS.

plimentary act, betokening equally humility and affection, if the host himself performed the office for his guest. 1 Sam. 25:41; Luke 7:38, 44; John 13:5–14; 1 Tim. 5:10. Such a token of hospitality is still occasionally exhibited in the East.

Watches of night. The Jews, like the Greeks and Romans, divided the night into military watches instead of hours, each watch representing the period for which sentinels or pickets remained on duty. The proper Jewish reckoning recognized only three such watches, entitled the first or "beginning of the watches," Lam. 2:19, the middle watch, Judges 7:19, and the morning watch. Ex. 14:24; 1 Sam. 11:11. These would last respectively from sunset to midnight; from midnight to cock crow, perhaps 2 A.M.; and from cock crow to sunrise. After the establishment of the Roman supremacy, the number of watches was increased to four, which were described either according to their numerical order, as in the case of the "fourth watch," Matt. 14:25, or by the terms "even," "midnight," "cock-crowing" and "morning." Mark 13:35. These terminated respectively at 9 P.M., midnight, 3 A.M. and 6 A.M.

Water of jealousy. Num. 5:11–31. The ritual prescribed consisted in the husband's bringing before the priest the woman suspected of infidelity, and the essential part of it is unquestionably the oath, to which the "water" was subsidiary, symbolical and ministerial. With her he was to bring an offering of barley meal. As she stood holding the offering, so the priest stood holding an earthen vessel of holy water mixed with the dust from the floor of the sanctuary, and, declaring her free from all evil consequences if innocent, solemnly devoted her in the name of Jehovah to be "a curse and an oath among her people" if guilty. He then "wrote these curses in a book, and blotted them out with the bitter water," and having thrown the handful of meal on the altar, "caused the woman to drink" the potion thus drugged, she moreover answering to the words of his imprecation, "Amen, amen." Josephus adds, if the suspicion was unfounded, she obtained conception; if true, she died infamously. This was the origin of the ordeals of the Middle Ages. But the ancient rite was entirely different from most trials of this kind, for the bitter water the woman must drink was harmless in itself, and only by a direct act of God could it injure her if guilty; while in most heathen trials the suspected party must take poison, or suffer that which only a miracle would save them from if they were innocent.

Water of separation. [PURIFICATION.]

Wave offering. This rite, together with that of "heaving" or "raising" the offering, was an inseparable accompaniment of peace offerings. In such the right thigh or shoulder, considered the choicest part of the victim, was to be "heaved," and became the share of the officiating priest: the breast was to be "waved," and belonged originally to Aaron and his sons. Hence later to the priests also. The remainder of the peace offering was eaten by the worshiper. The same rite was observed in the case of the offering of the sheaf of first ripe grain on the second day of the Passover; of the two lambs and two loaves of new grain at Pentecost; of the guilt offering of the leper; and of the meal offering of jealousy. The scriptural notices of these rites are to be found in Ex. 29:24–28; Lev. 7:30, 34; 8:27; 9:21; 10:14, 15; 14:12, 21; 23:10, 15, 20; Num. 5:25; 6:20; 18:11, 18, 26–29, etc. By Jewish tradition the first part of the motion signified the presentation of the offering to God, while the movement back again signified his acceptance and gift of the offering to the priest.

Weapons. [ARMS.]

Weasel (*chôled*) occurs only in Lev. 11:29, in the list of unclean animals; it is either a weasel or a mole, authorities not being sure which. The corresponding word in Arabic and Syriac means a mole; but that fact is not at all conclusive. It may mean several animals of the weasel family. Both the weasels and moles are common in Palestine.

Weaving. The art of weaving appears to be coeval with the first dawning of civilization. We find it practiced with great skill by the Egyptians at a very early period. The "vestures of fine linen" such as Joseph wore, Gen. 41:42, were the product of Egyptian looms. The Israelites were probably acquainted with the process before their sojourn in Egypt; but it was undoubtedly there that they attained the profi-

ANCIENT ROMAN LOOM.

ciency which enabled them to execute the hangings of the tabernacle, Ex. 35:35; 1 Chron. 4:21, and other artistic textures. The Egyptian loom was either horizontal or upright, and the weaver stood or squatted at his work. The common loom of the country to-day is upright, and very simple. The textures produced by the Jewish weavers were very various. The coarser kinds, such as tent-cloth, sack-cloth and the "hairy garments" of the poor, were made of goat's or camel's hair. Ex. 26:7. Matt. 3:4. Wool was extensively used for ordinary clothing, Lev. 13:47; Prov. 27:26; 31:13; Ezek. 27:18; while for finer work flax was used, varying in quality, and producing the different textures described in the Bible as "linen" and "fine linen." The mixture of wool and flax in cloth intended for a garment was interdicted. Lev. 19:19; Deut. 22:11.

Wedding. [MARRIAGE.]

Week. There can be no doubt about the great antiquity of measuring time by a period of seven days. Gen. 8:10; 29:27. The Babylonians and Assyrians knew the seven-day week, and according to both the Hebrew and the Babylonian account it was in vogue before the time of the flood. The Jews named no day but the seventh, calling that the Sabbath. [SABBATH.] The week and the naming of the individual days was of late introduction into Roman usage. The Greeks used the ten day division of the month, as did the Egyptians in early times. There is no certainty as to when the seven day period was established in Egypt, but it was, according to Dio Cassius, borrowed by Rome from Egypt not long before the second century A.D.

Weeks, Feast of. [PENTECOST.]

Weights and Measures. There is a considerable variety of statements in regard to the values of the various weights and measures as expressed in modern terms. In this article they are in accord with the tables in the Appendix, which were prepared after careful comparison of all the eminent authorities on the subject.

The tables of the weights and measures, with their equivalents in modern values will be found in the APPENDIX.

A. WEIGHTS. The unit of weight was the SHEKEL (*i. e. weight*) called sometimes the *holy shekel* or the *shekel of the sanctuary.* This weight was about 224 grains heavy standard, or 112 grains light standard. It was subdivided into the *beka* (*i. e. half*), or *half shekel,* weighing 112 grains or 56 grains; the *rebah* (*i. e. quarter*), of 56 grains or 28 grains; and the *gerah* (*i. e. grain*) of 11.2 grains or 5.6 grains. The higher weights were the *libra,* Greek *litra,* the "pound" of John 12 : 3, equivalent to 20 shekels or about 11½ ounces Avoirdupois; the *Maneh,* Greek *Mina,* the "pound" of Matthew, equivalent to 50 shekels or 2 pounds Troy, or 1 pound 8 oz. Avoir., by the heavy standard, and half that by the light standard; and the *silver Talent* (*i. e. circle*), 3000 shekels, by heavy standard, 117 lbs. Troy, or 96½ Avoir.

The Gold Talent was a different weight, estimated from the gold shekel. It weighed 131 lbs. Troy, or 108 Avoir. by heavy standard, and half that by the light standard.

B.   MEASURES.—I. MEASURES OF LENGTH. In the Hebrew, as in every other system, measures of length are of two classes; the smaller measures of length; and measures for land and distance. The two are connected by having one unit, the *cubit.* 1. The smaller measures of length were all originally derived from the measurements of certain parts of the human body, in every case however parts of the hand and forearm, while in Roman measurements the foot was in use.

The unit was the *cubit,* originally the length of the human arm from the tip of the middle finger to the elbow. The ordinary equivalent for this is 18 inches, though in early times it was more, at one time even about 25 inches. The legal cubit of the Talmudists was about 22 inches. There are a great variety of these standards, as might naturally be expected.

The smaller measures were: the *digit,* or finger-breadth, $\frac{1}{24}$ of a cubit or about ¾ inch; Jer. 52 : 21; the *palm* or handbreadth, of four digits, or about 3 inches, Ex. 25 : 25; 1 Kings 7 : 26; 2 Chron. 4 : 5; and the *span,* the full reach between the tips of the thumb and little finger, equal to ½ cubit, or nearly 9 inches, Ex. 28 : 16; 1 Sam. 17 : 4; Ezek. 43 : 13. A larger measure was the *reed* of 6 cubits or about 8⅔ feet. (These equivalents are given on the basis of the common estimate of the cubit of 18

inches.) *Ezekiel's reed,* was a longer measure, of about 10 feet in length, Eze. 40 : 5–8; 42 : 16–19. 2. Of measures of distance the smallest was the *cubit,* of about 18 inches, the same as before. The Roman foot was practically the same as ours, but does not come into the Hebrew measures. The *pace,* of nearly 5 feet, 2 Sam. 6 : 13; the *furlong,* about $\frac{1}{10}$ of an English mile, Luke 24 : 13; John 6 : 19; 11 : 18; Rev. 14 : 20; 21 : 16; the mile (the Roman mile), 1000 paces, about $\frac{9}{10}$ of an English mile, Matt. 5 : 41; and the *Sabbath Day's Journey,* which was the same distance; were the longer measures of distance. [See SABBATH DAY'S JOURNEY.] The *furlong* and *mile* are not mentioned in the Old Testament. The *fathom* used in sounding by the Alexandrian mariners in St. Paul's voyage, is the Greek ὀργυια, *i. e.* the *full stretch* of the two arms from tip to tip of the middle finger, which is about equal to the height, and in a man of full stature is six feet. For estimating *area,* and especially *land,* there is no evidence that the Jews used any special system of *square measures,* but they were content to express by the *cubit* the *length* and *breadth* of the surface to be measured, Num. 35 : 4, 5; Ezek. 40 : 27, or by the *reed.* Ezek. 41 : 8; 42 : 16–19; Rev. 21 : 16.

II. MEASURES OF CAPACITY.—1. The measures of capacity for *liquids* were: The *log,* Lev. 14 : 10, etc., the name originally signifying *basin.* This was about one pint. The *cab,* about 2 quarts; the *hin,* frequently noticed in the Bible. Ex. 29 : 40; 30 : 24; Num. 15 : 4, 7, 9; Ezek. 4 : 11, etc., about 6 quarts; and the *bath,* the name meaning "measured," about 9 gallons, the unit of liquid measure, 1 Kings 7 : 26, 38; 2 Chron. 2 : 10; Ezra 7 : 22; Isa. 5 : 10; and the largest of the liquid measures, the *homer,* or *cor,* equivalent to 86 gallons. 2. In dry measure the *log* and *cab* were also used, as are our pints and quarts for both liquid and dry measure. The *omer,* mentioned only in Ex. 16 : 16–36, was nearly 7 pints. The word implies a *heap,* and secondarily a *sheaf.* The *sĕâh,* or "measure," this being the etymological meaning of the term, and appropriately applied to it, inasmuch as it was the ordinary measure for household purposes, was nearly 1½ pecks. Gen. 18 : 6; 1 Sam. 25 : 18; 2 Kings 7 : 1, 16. The Greek equivalent occurs in

Matt. 13:33; Luke 13:21. The *ephah,* the unit of dry measure, equivalent to 1 bushel, 3 quarts, is of frequent recurrence in the Bible. Ex. 16:36; Lev. 5:11; 6: 20; Num. 5:15; 28:5; Judges 6: 19; Ruth 2:17; 1 Sam. 1:24; 17: 17; Ezek. 45:11, 13; 46:5, 7, 11, 14. The *homer,* meaning *heap.* Lev. 27:16; Num. 11:32; Isa. 5: 10; Ezek. 45:13. It is elsewhere termed *cor,* from the circular vessel in which it was measured. 1 Kings 4:22; 5:11; 2 Chron. 2:10; 27:5; Ezra 7:22; Ezek. 45:14. The Greek equivalent occurs in Luke 16:7. It held about 11 bushels. In the New Testament we have notices of the following foreign measures; the *metrêtês,* John 2:6, Authorized Version "firkin," for liquids. This was the same as the *bath,* about 9 gallons; the *choinix,* Rev. 6:6, Authorized Version "measure," for dry goods, about one quart; the *modius,* applied to describe any vessel of moderate dimensions, Matt. 5:15; Mark 4:21; Luke 11:33, Authorized Version "bushel," though properly meaning a Roman measure, amounting to about a peck.

Well. Wells in Palestine are usually excavated from the solid limestone rock, sometimes with steps to descend into them. Gen. 24:16. The brims are furnished with a curb or low wall of stone,

ANCIENT WELL IN PALESTINE.

bearing marks of high antiquity in the furrows worn by the ropes used in drawing water. It was on a curb of this sort that our Lord sat when he conversed with the woman of Samaria, John 4:6. It had a stone cover, such as the woman placed on the mouth of the well at Bahurim, 2 Sam. 17:19, where the Authorized Version weakens the sense by using the article *a.* The usual methods for raising water are the following: 1. The rope and bucket, or water-skin. Gen. 24:14–20; John 4: 11. 2. The *sakiyeh,* or Persian wheel. This consists of a vertical wheel furnished with a set of buckets or earthen jars attached to a cord passing over the wheel, which descend empty and return full as the wheel revolves. 3. A method very common in both ancient and modern Egypt is the *shadoof,* a simple contrivance consisting of a lever moving on a pivot, which is loaded at one end with a lump of clay or some other weight, and has at the other a bowl or bucket. Wells are usually furnished with troughs of wood or stone, into which the water is emptied for the use of persons or animals coming to the wells. Unless machinery is used, which is commonly worked by men, women are usually the water-carriers.

Whale. As to the signific...nification of the Hebrew

MODERN SHADOOF.

terms *tan* and *tannîn,* variously rendered in the Authorized Version by "dragon," "whale," "serpent," "sea-monster," see DRAGON. It remains for us in this article to consider the transaction recorded in the book of Jonah, of that prophet having been swallowed up by some "great fish" which in Matt. 12:40 is called *cētos* (κῆτος), rendered in our version by "whale." In the first place, it is necessary to observe that the Greek word *cētos,* used by St. Matthew, is not restricted in its meaning to "a whale," or any *Cetacean;* like the Latin *cete* or *cetus,* it may denote any sea-monster, either "a whale," or "a shark," or "a seal," or "a tunny of enormous size." Two or three species of whale are found in the Mediterranean Sea, among them the sperm whale, which has a gullet sufficiently large to admit the body of a man. But it is more probable that it was one of the other marine monsters, perhaps a shark, which have been known indubitably to have swallowed men and even larger animals whole.

Wheat, the well-known valuable cereal, cultivated from the earliest times, is first mentioned in Gen. 30:14, in the account of Jacob's sojourn with

EGYPTIAN WHEAT.

Laban in Mesopotamia. Egypt in ancient times was celebrated for the growth of its wheat; the best quality was all bearded; and the same varieties existed in ancient as in modern times. Babylonia was also noted for the excellence of its wheat and other cereals. Syria and Palestine produced wheat of fine quality and in large quantities. Ps. 81:16; 147:14, etc. There appear to be two or three kinds of wheat at present grown in Palestine. In the parable of the sower our Lord alludes to grains of wheat which in good ground produce a hundred-fold. Matt. 13:8. The common *Triticum vulgare* will sometimes produce one hundred grains in the ear. Wheat is reaped toward the end of April, in May, and in June, according to the differences of soil and position; it was sown either broadcast and then ploughed in or trampled in by cattle, Isa. 32:20, or in rows, Isa. 28:25, which was considered the best method. The wheat was put into the ground in the winter, and some time after the barley; in the Egyptian plague of hail, consequently, the barley suffered, but the wheat had not appeared, and so escaped injury.

Widow. Under the Mosaic dispensation no legal provision was made for the maintenance of widows. They were left dependent partly on the affection of relations, more especially of the eldest son, whose birthright, or extra share of the property, imposed such a duty upon him, and partly on the privileges accorded to other distressed classes, such as a participation in the triennial third tithe, Deut. 14:29; 26:12, in harvest, Deut. 24:19-21, and in religious feasts. Deut. 16:11, 14. With regard to the remarriage of widows, the only restriction imposed by the Mosaic law had reference to the contingency of one being left childless, in which case the brother of the deceased husband had a right to marry the widow. Deut. 25:5, 6; Matt. 22:23-30. In the apostolic Church the widows were sustained at the public expense, the relief being daily administered in kind, under the superintendence of officers appointed for this special purpose. Acts 6:1-6. Particular directions are given by St. Paul as to the class of persons entitled to such public maintenance. 1 Tim. 5:3-16. Out of the body of such widows a certain number were to be enrolled, the qualifications for such enrolment being that they were not under sixty years of age; that they had been "the wife of one man," probably meaning *but once married;* and that they had led useful and charitable lives. vs. 9, 10. We are not disposed to identify the widows of the Bible either with the deaconesses or with the πρεσβύτιδες of the early Church. The order of widows existed as a separate institution, contemporaneously with these offices, apparently for the same eleemosynary purpose for which it was originally instituted. It was abolished by the Synod of Laodicea A.D. 364.

Wife. [MARRIAGE.]

Wilderness of the Wandering. The region in which the Israelites spent nearly 38 years of their existence after they had left Egypt, and spent a year before Mount Sinai. They went as far as Kadesh, on the southernmost border of Palestine, from which place spies were sent up into the promised land. These returned with such a report of the inhabitants and their walled cities that the people were discouraged, and began to murmur and rebel. For their sin they were compelled to remain 38 years longer in the wilderness, because it showed that they were not yet prepared and trained to conquer and to hold their promised possessions. The wilderness of the wandering was the great central limestone plateau of the Sinaitic peninsula. It was bordered on the east by the valley of the Arabah, which runs from the Dead Sea to the head of the eastern branch of the Red Sea. On the south and southwest were the granite mountains of Sinai, and on the north the Mediterranean Sea and the mountainous region south of Judea. It is called the *Desert of Paran,* and *Badiet et-Tih,* which means "Desert of the Wandering." The children of Israel were not probably marching as a nation from place to place in this wilderness during these 38 years, but they probably had headquarters at Kadesh-barnea; and from that centre spread themselves over the surrounding region "as do the Bedouin Arabs of the present day, in a half-savage, homeless state, moving about from place to place, and pitching their tents wherever they could find pasture for their flocks and herds." Testimony of travelers assures us that there would be no difficulty in finding forage for their cattle. "Mr. Fronton and Mr. Sicard took the same route from Egypt toward Canaan that the Israelites took, and they give this as their testimony: 'With respect to forage, they would be at no loss. The ground is covered with tamarisk, broom,

clover, and saint foin, of which latter especially camels are passionately fond, besides almost every variety of odoriferous plant and herb proper for pasturage.

"'The whole sides of the valley through which the children of Israel marched are still tufted with brushwood, which doubtless afforded food for their beasts. Lastly, the herbage underneath these trees and shrubs is completely covered with snails of a prodigious size and of the best sort, and, however uninviting such a repast might appear to us, they are here esteemed a great delicacy.' These mollusks of the land would aid in sustaining the people."

Mrs. Lewis, who made the notable discoveries of ancient manuscripts in the convent on Mount Sinai, says on her return from her fourth visit there: "No doubt there was more vegetation in the peninsula in ancient times than there is now; but even at the present day there are more flocks of sheep and goats about than the sandy, stony character of the country would lead one to suppose." Toward the close of the forty years from Egypt they again assembled at Kadesh, and, once more under the leadership of the Shechinah, they marched down the Arabah on their way to the promised land.

Willows are mentioned in Lev. 23: 40; Job 40: 22; Ps. 137: 2; Isa. 44: 4 With respect to the tree upon which the captive Israelites hung their harps, there can be no doubt that the weeping willow, *Salix babylonica,* is intended. This tree grows abundantly on the banks of the Euphrates, in other parts of Asia as in Palestine. The Hebrew word translated willows is generic, and includes several species of the large family of *Salices,* which is well represented in Palestine and the Bible lands.

Willows, The brook of the, a wady mentioned by Isaiah, Isa. 15: 7, in his dirge over Moab. It is situated on the southern boundary of Moab, and is probably what is now called *Wady-el-Aksa.*

Wills. Under a system of close inheritance like that of the Jews, the scope for bequest in respect of land was limited by the right of redemption and general re-entry in the jubilee year; but the law does not forbid bequests by will of such limited interest in land as was consistent with those rights. The case of houses in walled towns was different, and there can be no doubt that they must, in fact, have frequently been bequeathed by will. Lev. 25 : 30. Two instances are recorded in the Old Testament under the law of testamentary disposition, (1) effected in the case of Ahithophel, 2 Sam. 17 : 23, (2) recommended in the case of Hezekiah. 2 Kings 20 : 1; Isa. 38 : 1. [HEIR.]

Wimple, an old English word for hood or veil, used in the Authorized Version of Isa. 3 : 22. The same Hebrew word is translated "veil" in the A. V. Ruth 3 : 15, but it signifies rather a mantle, as translated in R. V.

Window. The window of an Oriental house consists generally of an aperture closed in with lattice-work. Judges 5 : 28; Prov. 7 : 6, Authorized Version "casement;" Eccles. 12 : 3, Authorized Version "window;" Cant. 2 : 9; Hos. 13 : 3, Authorized Version "chimney." Glass has been introduced into Egypt in modern times as a protection against the cold of winter, but lattice-work is still the usual, and with the poor the only, contrivance for closing the window. The windows generally look into the inner court of the house, but in every house one or more look into the street. In Egypt these outer windows generally project over the doorway. [HOUSE.]

Wine. The manufacture of wine is carried back in the Bible to the age of Noah, Gen. 9 : 20, 21, who is said to have planted a vineyard, and manufactured and drunk the wine. The natural history and culture of the vine are described under a separate head. [VINE.] Other words translated usually "strong drink" mean wine made from grain, dates and other fruits. Beverages from these were very common in the East, and in Egypt. But the use of the word "wine" is confined to that made of the grape, which is sometimes spoken of as "the vine," or "the fruit of the vine." One exception in the A. V. seems to be Cant. 8 : 2, where mention is made of the "spiced wine of the juice of my pomegranate." The R. V., however, places a comma after "spiced wine," which alters the sense. In Palestine the main vintage takes place in September, and is celebrated with great rejoicings. The ripe fruit was gathered in baskets, Jer. 6 : 9, as represented in Egyptian paintings, and was carried to

the wine-press. It was then placed in the upper one of the two vats or receptacles of which the wine-press was formed, and was subjected to the process of "treading," which has prevailed in all ages in Oriental and south-European countries. Neh. 13 : 15; Job 24 : 11; Isa. 16 : 10; Jer. 25 : 30; 48 : 33; Amos 9 : 13; Rev. 19 : 15. A certain amount of juice exuded from the ripe fruit from its own pressure before the treading commenced. This appears to have been kept separate from the rest of the juice, and to have

EGYPTIAN WINE-PRESS.

formed the "sweet wine" noticed in Acts 2 : 13. [See below.] The "treading" was effected by one or more men, according to the size of the vat. They encouraged one another by shouts. Isa. 16 : 9, 10; Jer. 25 : 30; 48 : 33. Their legs and garments were dyed red with the juice. Gen. 49 : 11; Isa. 63 : 2, 3. The expressed juice escaped by an aperture into the lower vat, or was at once collected in vessels. A hand-press was occasionally used in Egypt, but we have no notice of such an instrument in the Bible. As to the subsequent treatment of the wine we have but little information. Sometimes it was preserved in its unfermented state and drunk as "must," but more generally it was bottled off after fermentation. It was first stored in large ox-skins, some being known to-day large enough to hold 60 gallons. When the deposit of dregs or lees had taken place the clear wine was poured into new vessels (Jer. 48 : 11). This is the "well-refined wine" of Isa. 25 : 6. Drinking the lees was used allegorically

47

in the sense of the bitter punishment consequent upon sin. (Ps. 75:8.) To wine is attributed the "darkly-flashing eye," Gen. 49:12, Authorized Version "red;" the unbridled tongue, Prov. 20: 1; Isa. 28:7; the excitement of the spirit, Prov. 31:6; Isa. 5:11; Zech. 9: 15; 10:7; the enchained affections of its votaries, Hos. 4:11; the perverted judgment, Prov. 31:5; Isa. 28:7; the in-

EGYPTIANS EXPRESSING THE JUICE OF THE GRAPE.

decent exposure, Hab. 2:15, 16; and the sickness resulting from the *heat* (*chemâh,* Authorized Version "bottles") of wine, Hos. 7:5. The allusions to the effects of *tîrôsh* are confined to a single passage, but this a most decisive one, viz. Hos. 4:11, "Whoredom and wine (*yayin*) and new wine (*tîrôsh*) take away the heart," where *tîrôsh* appears as the climax of engrossing influences, in immediate connection with *yayin*. It has been disputed whether the Hebrew wine was fermented; but the impression produced on the mind by a general review of the above notices is that the Hebrew words indicating wine refer to fermented, intoxicating wine. The notices of fermentation are not very decisive. A certain amount of fermentation is implied in the distension of the leather bottles when new wine was placed in them, and which was liable to burst old bottles. The mingling that we read of in conjunction with wine may have been designed either to increase or to diminish the strength of the wine, according as spices or water formed the ingredient that was added. The notices chiefly favor the former view; for mingled liquor was prepared for high festivals, Prov. 9:2, 5, and occasions of excess. Prov. 23:30; Isa. 5:22. At the same time strength was not the sole object sought; the wine "mingled with myrrh," given to Jesus, was designed to

deaden pain, Mark 15:23. In the New Testament the character of the "sweet wine," noticed in Acts 2:13, calls for some little remark. It could not be *new* wine in the proper sense of the term, inasmuch as about eight months must have elapsed between the vintage and the feast of Pentecost. This would effectually prevent its being any form of unfermented drink. Besides, the word used certainly signifies a n intoxicating drink,—a s the apostles a r e accused o f being under its power by those w h o must have known of its character. It was probably t h e must, or drip from the untrodden grapes, which after fermenting w a s certainly intoxicating. There can be little doubt that the wines of Palestine varied in quality, and were named after the localities in which they were made. The only wines of which we have special notice belonged to Syria; these were the wine of Helbon, Ezek. 27:18, and the wine of Lebanon, famed for its aroma, Hos. 14:7. With regard to the uses of wine in private life there is little to remark. It was produced on occasions of ordinary hospitality, Gen. 14:18, and at festivals, such as marriages. John 2:3. Under the Mosaic law wine formed the usual drink offering that accompanied the daily sacrifice, Ex. 29:40, the presentation of the first-fruits, Lev. 23:13, and other offerings. Num. 15:5. Tithe was to be paid of wine, as of other products. The priest was also to receive first-fruits of wine, as of other articles. Deut. 18:4; comp. Ex. 22:29. The use of wine at the paschal feast was not enjoined by the law, but had become an established custom, at all events in the post-Babylonian period. The wine was mixed with warm water on these occasions. Hence in the early Christian Church it was usual to mix the sacramental wine with water. No unfermented wine is now known in Palestine, and there is no evidence of its use at any time. The fermentation of wine was not at all considered a similar substance to the leaven of bread, and was not at any time prohibited to the Jews. Most probably the simple wines of antiquity were incomparably less deadly than the stupefying and ardent beverages of our western nations. It is certain that to-day the light grape-wines of Palestine and southern Europe produce no such effects as the grain-made beverages of northern Europe and America, nor even of wines in those climates.

A great attempt has been made to prove the wine drunk at the Lord's Supper unfermented, by and for the sake of the temperance workers of our day and nation. Such attempts are apt to do more harm than good, among those familiar with eastern customs today, or the history of those nations. But "the apostle Paul has stated the case for total abstinence in Rom. 14 in a way that does not need the treacherous aid of doubtful exegesis for its support." (Hastings' *Bible Dictionary*.)

Wine=press. From the scanty notices contained in the Bible we gather that the wine-presses of the Jews consisted of two receptacles or vats placed at different elevations, in the upper one of which the grapes were trodden, while the lower one received the expressed juice. The two vats are mentioned together only in Joel 3:13: "The press is full: the vats overflow"—the upper vat being full of fruit, the lower one overflowing with the must. [WINE.] The two vats were usually hewn out of the solid rock. Isa. 5:2, margin; Matt. 21:33. Ancient wine-presses, so constructed, are still to be seen in Palestine.

Winnowing. [AGRICULTURE.]

Wisdom of Jesus, Son of Sirach. [ECCLESIASTICUS.]

Wisdom, The, of Solomon, a book of the Apocrypha, may be divided into three parts, the first, chs. 1–5, describing the conflict which the Divine Wisdom has constantly to carry on with the godless wisdom of this world, and the victory to which she leads those who surrender themselves to her. The second part, chs. 6–9, sets forth the great advantages of Wisdom, and describes Solomon's experience in his search for it. The third part, chs. 10–19, gives the wonders wrought by wisdom in the history of Israel. *Doctrinal character.*— The theological teaching of the book offers, in many respects, the nearest approach to the language and doctrines of Greek philosophy that is found in any Jewish writing up to the time of Philo. There is much in the views which it gives of the world, of man and of the divine nature which springs rather from the combination or conflict of Hebrew and Greek thought than from the independent development of Hebrew thought alone. Yet the author's zeal for the Jewish religion is undoubted. He is not hampered by it, nor does he seek, like Philo, to make it acceptable by "allegorizing explanations." His aim is, apparently, to provide a sure hold for the professors of the Jewish faith, surrounded on all sides by Greek philosophy, and disturbed by internal dissensions and by apostasy. In connection with the Old Testament Scriptures, the book, as a whole, may be regarded as carrying on one step farther the great problem of life contained in Ecclesiastes and Job. *Date.*— From internal evidence it seems most reasonable to believe that the work was composed in Greek at Alexandria some time before the time of Philo, or perhaps between B.C. 100 and 50, possibly between B.C. 120 and 80. The author was without doubt an Egyptian Jew, with a Greek education, but a true observer of the Law. There are Hebraisms, but not such as would prove a Hebrew original. It seems impossible to study this book dispassionately and not feel that it forms one of the last links in the chain of providential connection between the Old and New Covenants. It would not be easy to find elsewhere any pre-Christian view of religion equally wide, sustained and definite.

Wise men. [MAGI.]

Witch, Witchcrafts. [DIVINATION; MAGIC.]

Witness. Among people with whom writing is not common, the evidence of a transaction is given by some tangible memorial or significant ceremony. Abraham gave seven ewe-lambs to Abimelech as an evidence of his property in the well of Beersheba. Jacob raised a heap of stones, "the heap of witness," as a boundary-mark between himself and Laban. Gen. 21:30; 31:47, 52. The tribes of Reuben and Gad raised an "altar" as a witness to the covenant between themselves and the rest of the nation. Joshua set up a stone as an evidence of the allegiance promised by Israel to God. Josh. 22:10, 26, 34; 24:26, 27. But written evidence was by no means unknown to the Jews. Divorce was to be proved by a written document. Deut. 24:1, 3. In civil contracts, at least in later times, documentary evidence was required and carefully preserved. Isa. 8:16; Jer. 32:10–16. On the whole the law was very careful to provide and enforce evidence for all its infractions and all transactions bearing on them. Among special provisions with respect to evidence are the following: 1. Two witnesses at least are required to establish any capital charge. Num. 35:30; Deut. 17:6; John 8:17; 2 Cor. 13:1; comp. 1 Tim. 5:19. 2. In the case of the suspected wife, evidence besides the husband's was desired. Num. 5:13. 3. The witness who withheld the truth was censured. Lev. 5:1. 4. False witness was punished with the penalty due to the offence which it sought to establish. Deut. 19:16, 19. 5. Slanderous reports and officious witness are discouraged. Ex. 20:16; 23:1; Lev. 19:16, 18, etc. 6. The witnesses were the first executioners. Deut. 13:9; 17:7; Acts 7:58. 7. In case of an animal left in charge and torn by wild beasts, the keeper was to bring the carcass in proof of the fact and disproof of his own criminality. Ex. 22:13. 8. According to Josephus, women and slaves were not admitted to bear testimony. While there is no evidence of this in the Bible, it seems reasonable from the fact that in capital cases the witnesses were required to take part in the execution. In the New Testament the original notion of a witness is exhibited in the special form of one who attests his belief in the gospel by personal suffering. Hence it is that the use of the ecclesiastical term "martyr," the Greek word for "witness," has arisen.

Wizard. [DIVINATION; MAGIC.]

Wolf. There can be little doubt that the wolf of Palestine is the common *Canis lupus,* and that this is the animal so frequently mentioned in the Bible. The wolf is a fierce animal of the same species as the dog, which it resembles. The common color is gray with a tinting of fawn, and the hair is long and black. The Syrian wolf is of lighter color than the wolf of Europe. It is the dread of the shepherds of Palestine. Wolves were doubtless far more common in biblical times than they are now, though they are occasionally seen by modern travelers. The following

are the scriptural allusions to the wolf: Its ferocity is mentioned in Gen. 49:27; Ezek. 22:27; Hab. 1:8; Matt. 7:15; its nocturnal habits, in Jer. 5:6; Zeph. 3:3; Hab. 1:8; its attacking sheep and lambs, Matt. 10:16; Luke 10:3; John 10:12. Isaiah, Isa. 11:6; 65:25, foretells the peaceful reign of the Messiah under the metaphor of a wolf dwelling with a lamb; cruel persecutors are compared with wolves. Matt. 10:16; Acts 20:29.

Women. The position of women in the Hebrew commonwealth contrasts favorably with that which in the present day is assigned to them generally in eastern countries. The most salient point of contrast in the usages of ancient as compared with modern Oriental society was the large amount of liberty enjoyed by women. Instead of being immured in a harem, or appearing in public with the face covered, the wives

OUTER GARMENTS OF WOMEN
As used by Mohammedans of recent times.

and maidens of ancient times mingled freely and openly with the other sex in the duties and amenities of ordinary life. Rebekah travelled on a camel with her face unveiled, until she came into the presence of her affianced. Gen. 24:64, 65. Jacob saluted Rachel with a kiss in the presence of the shepherds. Gen. 29:11. Women played no inconsiderable part in public celebrations. Ex. 15:20, 21; Judges 11:34. The odes of Deborah, Judges 5, and of Hannah, 1 Sam. 2:1, etc., exhibit a degree of intellectual cultivation which is in itself a proof of the position of the sex in that period. Women also occasionally held public office, particularly that of prophetess or inspired teacher. Ex. 15 : 20; Judges 4 : 4; 2 Kings 22 : 14; Neh. 6 : 14; Luke 2 : 36. The management of household affairs devolved mainly on the women. The value of a virtuous and active housewife forms a frequent topic in the book of Proverbs. ch. 11 : 16; 12 : 4; 14 : 1; 31 : 10; etc. Her influence was of course proportionably great.

Wood. [FOREST.]

Wool was an article of the highest value among the Jews, as the staple material for the manufacture of clothing. Lev. 13 : 47; Deut. 22 : 11; Job 31 : 20; Prov. 31 : 13; Ezek. 34 : 3; Hosea 2 : 5. The importance of wool is incidentally shown by the notice that Mesha's tribute was paid in a certain number of rams "with the wool." 2 Kings 3 : 4. The wool of Damascus was highly prized in the mart of Tyre. Ezek. 27 : 18.

Worm, the representative in the Authorized Version of several Hebrew words. *Sâs,* which occurs in Isa. 51 : 8, probably denotes some particular species of moth, whose larva is injurious to wool. *Rimmâh,* Ex. 16 : 24, points evidently to various kinds of maggots and the larvæ of insects which feed on putrefying animal or vegetable matter, rather than to earthworms. *Tôlê'âh* is applied in Deut. 28 : 39 to some kinds of larvæ destructive to the vines, and in Ex. 16 : 20; Isa. 66 : 24 of a maggot similar to the *rimmâh.* Man is figuratively spoken of as this sort of maggot, in Job 25 : 6; Isa. 41 : 14; and as that denoted by *rimmâh* in Job 25 : 6 also. (The two Hebrew words in this verse are different.) In Job 19 : 26; 21 : 26; 24 : 20, there is an allusion to worms (insect larvæ) feeding on the dead bodies of the buried. There is the same allusion in Isa. 66 : 24, which words are applied by our Lord, Mark 9 : 44, 46, 48, metaphorically to the torments of the guilty in the world of departed spirits. The valley of Hinnom, near Jerusalem, where the filth of the city was cast, was alive with worms. The death of Herod Agrippa I. was caused by worms. Acts 12 : 23.

Wormwood. A generic term for the species Artemisia, of which five species are found in Palestine. The word occurs frequently in the Bible, and generally in a metaphorical sense. In Jer. 9 : 15; 23 : 15; Lam. 3 : 15, 19, wormwood is symbolical of bitter calamity and sorrow; unrighteous judges are said to "turn judgment to wormwood." Amos

WORMWOOD.

5 : 7. The Orientals typified sorrows, cruelties and calamities of any kind by plants of a poisonous or bitter nature.

Worshiper, a translation of the Greek word *neocoros,* used once only, Acts 19 : 35; in the margin and Revised Version, "temple-keeper." The *neocoros* was originally an attendant in a temple, probably intrusted with its charge. The term *neocoros* became thus applied to cities or communities which undertook the worship of particular emperors even during their lives. The first occurrence of the term in connection with Ephesus is on coins of the age of Nero, A.D. 54–68.

Wrestling. [GAMES.]

Writing. There is no account in the Bible of the origin of writing. That the Egyptians in the time of Joseph were acquainted with writing of a certain kind there is evidence to prove, but there is nothing to show that up to this period the knowledge extended to the Hebrew family. At the same time there is no evidence against it, and this coupled with the fact that nearly all nations, Egyptians and Babylonians as early as the 40th century before Christ, were familiar with it, may well be considered a proof of its existence. Writing is first distinctly mentioned in Ex. 17 : 14, and the connection clearly implies that it was not then employed for the first time, but was so familiar as to be used for historic records. It is not absolutely necessary to infer from this that the art of writing was an accomplishment possessed by every Hebrew citizen. If we examine the instances in which writing is mentioned in connection with individuals, we shall find that in all cases the writers were men of superior position. In Isa. 29: 11, 12 there is clearly a distinction drawn between the man who was able to read and the man who was not, and it seems a natural inference that

PAPYRUS.

A packet of papyrus documents, written by a Jewish colony at Assouan, fifth century B.C.

the accomplishments of reading and writing were not widely spread among the people, when we find that they are universally attributed to those of high rank or education—kings, priests, prophets and professional scribes. Still, later in the history of Israel, when schools were common, it is reasonable to suppose that all, or at least the large proportion of the people could write. (See Luke 1: 63; 16: 6, 7.) The Tel-el-Amarna tablets discovered in 1887 contain correspondence between the Egyptian governors of Palestine, and the king or his ministers. Moses must have been instructed in writing as well as in other learning.

ALPHABET.—The invention of the alphabet is generally credited to the Phœnicians, who as the daring seamen

and adventurous colonizers of the ancient world, certainly brought their alphabet to the use of other nations. It was the universal belief, or perhaps better, tradition, among ancient writers that the Phœnicians originally brought it from Egypt. This seemed so reasonable, from the known influence of Egyptian civilization upon other nations, that when once the hieroglyphic writings had been deciphered, repeated attempts were made to trace the growth of the alphabet therefrom. It proved even more difficult than was expected, but was at last effected by Emanuel de Rougé, a French Egyptologist, who traced it to the Hieratic script of the early Empire, much older than the writing of the monuments; a form so ancient as to have become almost unused at the time of the Exodus. From this came what is known as the "Semitic Alphabets," among which is the Phœnician. Through them, as has been stated, a form of the alphabet extended to the western nations.

The early history of the Hebrew alphabet must be reconstructed from the more modern discoveries of inscriptions. The Moabite Stone, erected about 850 B.C., is written in a dialect scarcely differing from the ancient Hebrew, and in the ancient Hebrew characters. The Siloam inscription assigned to B.C. 700 or 650 is written in characters considerably modified. These seem to have been in use through the times of the Maccabees, as the inscriptions on their coins are in these characters. They are still to be found in the sacred script of the few surviving Samaritans. In this one example is to be found the only remnant of the ancient Phœnician alphabet.

These and other recent discoveries show that the square Hebrew character is of comparatively modern date, though doubtless used for literary purposes long before the time of Christ. The book from which he read at the Synagogue service (Luke 4: 17) was no doubt in this square character. Still this is not the character of the earliest extant Hebrew writing, though its direct ancestor. It was probably about the first or second century after Christ that the square character assumed its present form; though in a question involved in so much uncertainty it is impossible to pronounce with great positiveness. The names of the several letters of the Hebrew language have long been familiar to English readers from their having been used to mark the divisions of the 119th Psalm. The R. V. gives in addition the modern form of the Hebrew letter. It will be seen that they are 22 in number. The vowels are mere points, dots, and the fact that they were not commonly used in more

with little authority. In Ancient Hebrew, also, as in Ancient Latin and Ancient Greek, no divisions were made between the words. The same is the case with the Phœnician inscriptions. The various readings in the LXX. show that, at the time this version was made, in the Hebrew MSS. which the translators used the words were written in a continuous series. The modern syn-

AN ANCIENT BOUND BOOK.

ancient times is the reason for the uncertainty as to the reading in some places in the Hebrew Scriptures. It is as it would be in English were the vowels omitted—GRT might mean GiRT, GRiT, GReaT, GRaTe, eGReT, etc. The points were inserted in the 7th century, A.D., and merely represent the traditional pronunciation, and hence

agogue rolls and the MSS. of the Samaritan Pentateuch have no vowelpoints, but the words are divided, and the Samaritan in this respect differs but little from the Hebrew. WRITING MATERIALS, ETC.—The oldest documents which contain the writing of a Semitic race are probably the bricks of *clay* in Nineveh and Babylon, on which are impressed the cuneiform Syrian inscriptions. There is, however, no evidence that they were ever used by the Hebrews, although the Tel-el-Amarna tablets, written by Egyptian governors in Palestine were of this sort. *Stone* was in use in all parts of the world for inscriptions intended to be permanent. (Ex. 31 : 18 ; Josh. 8 : 30–32 ; cf. Job 19 : 24.) *Wood* was largely used in some countries, and is doubtless spoken of in Isa. 30 : 8 and Hab. 2 : 2. Other substances as wax, bark, linen, and lead were used in ancient times, but there is no evidence of their being used by the Hebrews. Very probably the most common material which the Hebrews used for writing was dressed skin in some form or other. We know that the dressing of skins was practiced by the Hebrews, Ex. 25 : 5 ; Lev. 13 : 48, and they may have acquired the knowledge of the art from the Egyptians, among whom it had attained great perfection, the leather-cutters constituting one of the principal subdivisions of the third caste. Perhaps the Hebrews may have borrowed, among their other acquirements, the use of papyrus from the Egyptians, but of this we have no positive evidence. In the Bible the only allusions to the use of papyrus are in 2 John 12, where *chartes* (Authorized Version " paper ") occurs, which refers especially to papyrus paper, and 3 Macc. 4 : 20, where *charteria* is found in the same sense. Herodotus, after telling us that the Ionians learned the art of writing from the Phœnicians, adds that they called their books skins, because they made use of sheep-skins and goat-skins when short of paper. Parchment was used for the MSS. of the Pentateuch in the time of Josephus, and the *membranæ* of 2 Tim. 4 : 13 were skins of parchment. It was one of the provisions in the Talmud that the law should be written on the skins of clean animals, tame or wild, or even of clean birds. The skins when written upon were formed into rolls (*mêgillôth*). Ps. 40 : 7 ; comp. Isa. 34 : 4 ; Jer. 36 : 14 ; Ezek. 2 : 9 ; Zech. 5 : 1. They were rolled upon one or two sticks and fastened with a thread, the ends of which were sealed. Isa. 29 : 11 ; Dan. 12 : 4 ; Rev. 5 : 1, etc. The rolls were generally written on one side only, except in Ezek. 2 : 10 ; Rev. 5 : 1. They were divided into columns (Authorized Version " leaves," Jer. 36 : 23) ; the upper margin was to be not less than three fingers broad, the lower not less than four ; and a space of two fingers breadth was to be left between

WRITING TABLETS.

every two columns. But besides skins, which were used for the more permanent kinds of writing, tablets of wood covered with wax, Luke 1 : 63, served for the ordinary purposes of life. Several of these were fastened together and formed volumes. They were written upon with a pointed style, sometimes of iron. Ps. 45 : 1 ; Jer. 8 : 8 ; 17 : 1. For harder materials a graver, Ex. 32 : 4 ; Isa. 8 : 1, was employed. For parchment or skins a reed was used. 3 John 13 ; comp. Jer. 36 : 23. The ink, Jer. 36 : 18, literally "black," like the Greek μέλαν, 2 Cor. 3 : 3 ; 2 John 12 ; 3 John 13, was of lampblack dissolved in gall-juice. It was carried in an inkstand, which was suspended at the girdle, Ezek. 9 : 2, 3, as is done at the present day in the East. The modern "inkhorn" is of metal, and consists of a small receptacle for the very thick ink used, joined to a long, tube-like holder for the reed pens. This long portion is thrust into the girdle. To professional scribes there are allusions in Ezra 7 : 6 ; Ps. 45 : 1.

Y

Yarn. The word translated "fine linen" in the A. V. of Prov. 7:16 is in the R. V. rendered "yarn." The fine thread or yarn of Egypt was most probably linen. The words "linen yarn" also occur in the A. V. in an extremely obscure passage in 1 Kings 10:28; 2 Chron. 1:16. The Hebrew Received Text is questionable. The R. V. translates the words "drove."

Year, the highest ordinary division of time. Two years were known to, and apparently used by, the Hebrews. 1. A year of 360 days appears to have been in use in Noah's time. 2. The year commonly in use among the Hebrews was essentially solar, for the offering of productions of the earth, first-fruits, harvest produce and ingathered fruits, was fixed to certain days of the year, two of which were in the periods of great feasts, the third itself a feast reckoned from one of the former days. But it is certain that the months were lunar, each commencing with a new moon. The year would naturally then have only 354.37 days. There must therefore have been some method of adjustment. Although no mention of it is made in the Bible, and its existence cannot be proved, it is most probable that it was in the same way which the Babylonians used to adjust the year in use there,—the addition of a thirteenth month whenever the twelfth ended too long before the equinox for the offering of the first-fruits to be made at the time fixed. This seems pretty certainly the case after the Babylonian Exile. The Jews had two commencements of the year, whence it is commonly but inaccurately said that they had two years, the sacred year and the civil. We prefer to speak of the sacred and civil reckonings. The sacred reckoning was that instituted at the Exodus, according to which the first month was Abib; by the civil reckoning the first month was the seventh. The interval between the two commencements was thus exactly half a year. The year was divided into—1. *Seasons.* Two seasons are mentioned in the Bible, "summer" and "winter." The former properly means the time of cutting fruits, the latter that of gathering fruits; they are therefore originally rather summer and autumn than summer and winter. But that they signify ordinarily the two grand divisions of the year, the warm and cold seasons, is evident from their use for the whole year in the expression "summer and winter." Ps. 74:17; Zech. 14:8. 2. *Months.* [MONTH.] 3. *Weeks.* [WEEK.]

Year, Sabbatical. [SABBATICAL YEAR.]

Year of Jubilee. [JUBILEE, YEAR OF.]

Yoke. 1. A well-known implement of husbandry, frequently used metaphorically for *subjection, e. g.* 1 Kings 12:4, 9–11; Isa. 9:4; Jer. 5:5; hence an "iron yoke" represents an unusually galling bondage. Deut. 28:48; Jer. 28:13. 2. A pair of oxen, so termed as being yoked together. 1 Sam. 11:7; 1 Kings 19:19, 21. 3. The term is also applied to a certain amount of land, 1 Sam. 14:14, equivalent to that which a couple of oxen could plough in a day, Isa. 5:10 (Authorized Version "acre"), corresponding to the Latin *jugum.* In the N. T. the word is usually used in the figurative sense of subjection, or the burden imposed as the mark of subjection. Matt. 11:29; 23:4.

Z

Zaana'im (zā-a-nā'im) (*removings*), probably a sacred tree—mentioned as marking the spot near which Heber the Kenite was encamped when Sisera took refuge in his tent. Judges 4 : 11. Its situation is quite uncertain. By Josh. 19 : 33 it was a frontier town of Naphtali, and it is said to have been "near Kadesh." Several sites are proposed. Couder considers it to have probably been on the table-land west of the Sea of Galilee. ZAANANIM.

Za'anan (zā'a-năn). [ZENAN.]

Zaanan'nim (zā-a-năn'nĭm). The form used in Joshua for ZAANAIM. It is used in the Revised Version in both places.

Za'avan (zā'a-văn), or **Za'van** (*unquiet*), a Horite chief, son of Ezer the son of Seir. Gen. 36 : 27; 1 Chron. 1 : 42.

Za'bad (zā'băd) (*gift*). 1. Son of Nathan, son of Attai, son of Ahlai, Sheshan's daughter. 1 Chron. 2 : 31–37. He is thought by some to be identical with the "Zabad son of Ahlai" of 1 Chron. 11 : 41, one of David's mighty men. None of his deeds have been recorded.

2. An Ephraimite, if the text of 1 Chron. 7 : 21 is correct.

3. Son of Shimeath, an Ammonitess; an assassin who, with Jehozabad, slew King Joash, according to 2 Chron. 24 : 26 (B.C. 796); but in 2 Kings 12 : 21 his name is written, probably more correctly, JOZACHAR.

4. A layman of Israel, of the sons of Zattu, who put away his foreign wife at Ezra's command. Ezra 10 : 27. (B.C. 458.)

5. One of the descendants of Hashum, who had married a foreign wife after the captivity. Ezra 10 : 33. (B.C. 458.)

6. One of the sons of Nebo, whose name is mentioned under the same circumstances as the two preceding. Ezra 10 : 43.

Zab'bai (zăb'bā) (*humming*). 1.

One of the descendants of Bebai, who had married a foreign wife in the days of Ezra. Ezra 10 : 28. (B.C. 458.)

2. Father of Baruch, who assisted Nehemiah in rebuilding the city wall. Neh. 3 : 20. Perhaps the same as 1.

Zab'bud (zab'bud) (*given*), one of the sons of Bigvai, who returned in the second caravan with Ezra. Ezra 8 : 14. (B.C. 458.)

Zab'di (zăb'dĭ) (*gift of* [Jehovah]). 1. Son of Zerah the son of Judah, and ancestor of Achan. Josh. 7 : 1, 17, 18. Elsewhere called ZIMRI.

2. A Benjamite, of the sons of Shimhi. 1 Chron. 8 : 19.

3. David's officer over the produce of the vineyards for the wine-cellars. 1 Chron. 27 : 27.

4. Son of Asaph the minstrel, Neh. 11 : 17; called ZACCUR in Neh. 12 : 35 and ZICHRI in 1 Chron. 9 : 15.

Zab'diel (zăb'dĭ-ĕl) (*gift of God*). 1. Father of Jashobeam, the chief of David's guard. 1 Chron. 27 : 2.

2. A priest, son of the great men, or, as the margin gives it, "Haggedolim." Neh. 11 : 14.

Za'bud (zā'bud) (*given*), son of Nathan, 1 Kings 4 : 5, is described as a priest (Authorized Version "principal officer"), and as holding at the court of Solomon the confidential post of "king's friend," which had been occupied by Hushai the Archite during the reign of David. 2 Sam. 15 : 37; 16 : 16; 1 Chron. 27 : 33.

Zab'ulon (zăb'u-lŏn), the Greek form of the name Zebulun. Matt. 4 : 13, 15; Rev. 7 : 8.

Zac'cai (zăk'ka-ī) (*pure*). The sons of Zaccai, to the number of 760, returned with Zerubbabel. Ezra 2 : 9; Neh. 7 : 14.

Zacchæ'us (zăk-kē'us) (*pure*), a tax-collector near Jericho, who, being short in stature, climbed up into a sycomore tree in order to obtain a sight of Jesus as he passed through that place. Luke 19:1-10. Zacchæus was a Jew, as may be inferred from his name and from the fact that the Saviour speaks of him expressly as "a son of Abraham." The term which designates his office—"the chief among the publicans"—is unusual, but describes him, no doubt, as the superintendent of customs or tribute in the district of Jericho, where he lived. The office must have been a lucrative one in such a region, and it is not strange that Zacchæus is mentioned by the evangelists as a rich man. The Saviour spent the night probably in the house of Zacchæus, and the next day pursued his journey. He was in the caravan from Galilee which was going to Jerusalem to keep the Passover.

Zac′chur (zak′kur), a Simeonite, of the family of Mishma. 1 Chron. 4:26. R. V. "Zaccur."

Zac′cur (*mindful*). 1. Father of Shammua, the Reubenite spy. Num. 13:4.

2. A Merarite Levite, son of Jaaziah. 1 Chron. 24:27.

3. Son of Asaph the singer. 1 Chron. 25:2, 10; Neh. 12:35. [ZABDI, 4.]

4. The son of Imri, who assisted Nehemiah in rebuilding the city wall. Neh. 3:2. (B.C. 446.)

5. A Levite, or family of Levites, who signed the covenant with Nehemiah. Neh. 10:12.

6. A Levite whose son or descendant Hanan was one of the treasurers over the treasuries appointed by Nehemiah. Neh. 13:13.

Zachari′ah (zăk-a-rī′ah) (*remembered by Jehovah*), or properly **Zechariah.** 1. Son of Jeroboam II., fourteenth king of Israel, and the last of the house of Jehu. There is a difficulty about the date of his reign. Most chronologers assume an interregnum of eleven years between Jeroboam's death and Zachariah's accession. The latter event took place B.C. 741. His reign lasted only six months. He was killed in a conspiracy of which Shallum was the head, and by which the prophecy in 2 Kings 10:30 was fulfilled. 2 Kings 14:29; 15:8-12.

2. The father of Abi or Abijah, Hezekiah's mother. 2 Kings 18:2.

Zachari′as (zăk-a-rī′as) (Greek form of *Zachariah*). 1. Father of John the Baptist. Luke 1:5, etc. He was a priest of the course of Abia, the eighth of the twenty-four courses who minis-

tered at the temple in turn. He lived in the hill country of Judea. His wife's name was Elisabeth. John was born to them in their old age, and the promise of this son was communicated to Zacharias by an angel while he was offering incense and praying in the temple.

2. Son of Barachias, who, our Lord says, was slain by the Jews between the altar and the temple. Matt. 23:35; Luke 11:51. There has been much dispute who this Zacharias was. Many of the Greek fathers have maintained that the father of John the Baptist is the person to whom our Lord alludes; but there can be little or no doubt that the allusion is to Zechariah, the son of Jehoiada, who lived during the reign of Joash king of Israel. 2 Chron. 24:20, 21. He may have been called "the son" of Barachias from his grandfather; or the words may have slipped from a note in the margin to the text. He is mentioned as being the martyr last recorded in the Hebrew Scriptures (as Abel was the first),—2d Chronicles being the last book in their canon.

Za′cher (zā′kĕr) (*memorial*), one of the sons of Jehiel, the father or founder of Gibeon, by his wife Maachah. 1 Chron. 8:31. [ZECHARIAH, 3.]

Za′dok (zā′dŏk) (*just*). 1. Son of Ahitub, and one of the two chief priests in the time of David, Abiathar being the other. There is some confusion in the different accounts of his descent, causing a considerable difference of opinion among commentators. It is generally supposed, however that Zadok was of the house of Eleazar the son of Aaron, 1 Chron. 24:3. He was, according to Josephus the "young man mighty of valor" who joined David at Hebron after Saul's death, 1 Chron. 12:28. When Absalom revolted, and David fled from Jerusalem, Zadok and all the Levites bearing the ark accompanied him. When Absalom was dead, Zadok and Abiathar were the persons who persuaded the elders of Judah to invite David to return. 2 Sam. 19:11. When Adonijah, in David's old age, set up for king, and had persuaded Joab, and Abiathar the priest, to join his party, Zadok was unmoved, and was employed by David to anoint Solomon to be king in his room. 1 Kings 1:34. For this fidelity he was rewarded by Solomon, who "thrust out Abiathar from being priest unto the Lord," and "put in

Zadok the priest" in his room. 1 Kings 2:27, 35. From this time, however, we hear little of him. Zadok and Abiathar were of nearly equal dignity. 2 Sam. 15:35, 36; 19:11. The duties of the office were divided.

2. According to the genealogy of the high priests in 1 Chron. 6:12, there was a second Zadok, son of a second Ahitub, son of Amariah, about the time of King Ahaziah. It is probable that no such person as this second Zadok ever existed, but that the insertion of the two names is a copyist's error.

3. Father of Jerushah, the wife of King Uzziah and mother of King Jotham. 2 Kings 15:33; 2 Chron. 27:1.

4. Son of Baana, and

5. Son of Immer, persons who repaired portions of the wall in Nehemiah's time. Neh. 3:4, 29.

6. In 1 Chron. 9:11 and Neh. 11:11 mention is made, in a genealogy, of Zadok, the son of Meraioth, the son of Ahitub; but it can hardly be doubtful that Meraioth is inserted by the error of a copyist, and that Zadok the son of Ahitub is meant.

Za'ham (zā'hăm) (*loathing*), son of Rehoboam by Abihail the daughter of Eliab. 2 Chron. 11:19.

Za'ir (zā'ĭr) (*small*), a place named, in 2 Kings 8:21 only, in the account of Joram's expedition against the Edomites. It has been conjectured that Zair is identical with Zoar.

Za'laph (zā'laf) (*fracture*), father of Hanun, who assisted in rebuilding the city wall. Neh. 3:30.

Zal'mon (zăl'mŏn) (*shady*), an Ahohite, one of David's guard. 2 Sam. 23:28. Also called ILAI.

Zal'mon, Mount, a wooded eminence in the immediate neighborhood of Shechem. Judges 9:48.

Zalmo'nah (zăl-mō'nah) (*shady*), a desert-station of the Israelites, Num. 33:41. Its site is not known.

Zalmun'na (zăl-mŭn'nà). [ZEBAH.]

Zamzum'mim (zăm-zŭm'mim), Deut. 2:20 only, the Ammonite name for the people who by others were called Rephaim. They are described as having originally been a powerful and numerous nation of giants. From a slight similarity between the two names, and from the mention of the Emim in connection with each, it is conjectured that the Zamzummim are identical with the Zuzim.

Zano'ah (zà-nō'ah) (*foul water*). 1. A town of Judah in the Shefelah or plain, Josh. 15:34; Neh. 3:13; 11:30; generally identified with Zânû'a.

2. A town of Judah in the highland district, Josh. 15:56, possibly identical with Zanúta, about 12 miles south of Hebron.

3. In the genealogical lists of the tribe of Judah in 1 Chron., Jekuthiel is said to have been the father of Zanoah, ch. 4:18. As Zanoah is the name of a town of Judah, this mention of Bithiah probably points to some colonization of the place by Egyptians or by Israelites directly from Egypt. It is variously identified with 1 and 2.

Zaph'nath=paane'ah (zăf'nath-pā'a-nĕ'ah), a name given by Pharaoh to Joseph. Gen. 41:45. The rabbins interpreted Zaphnath-paaneah as Hebrew, in the sense *revealer of a secret*. But the name was distinctly Egyptian. In 1886 it was explained by comparison with other Egyptian names as meaning "Said God, he liveth," and later investigations seem to have established it.

Za'phon (zā'fon) (*north*), a place mentioned in the enumeration of the allotment of the tribe of Gad. Josh. 13:27. It was in the Jordan valley east of the river, and most probably is the Amatho of the Talmud, or the modern Amateh, a little north of the Jabbok.

Za'ra (zā'rah), the son of Judah. Matt. 1:3. [ZERAH, 2.]

Za'rah (zā'rah), the son of Judah. Gen. 38:30; 46:12. [ZERAH, 2.]

Za'reah (zā're-ah), the same as Zorah and Zoreah. Neh. 11:29. [ZORAH.]

Za'reathites, The, the inhabitants of Zareah or Zorah. 1 Chron. 2:53.

Za'red (zā'red), **The valley of.** [ZERED.]

Zar'ephath (zăr'e-făth) (*smelting place*), the residence of the prophet Elijah during the latter part of the drought. 1 Kings 17:9, 10. It was about 8 miles south of Zidon. It is represented by the modern village of Sûrafend. Of the old town considerable indications remain. One group of foundations is on a headland called Ain el Kanatarah; but the chief remains are south of this, and extend for a mile or more, with many fragments of columns, slabs and other architectural features. In the Authorized Version in the New Testament Zarephath appears under the Greek form of SAREPTA, but in the R.

V. the ancient name is restored. Luke 4 : 26.

Zar'etan (zăr'e-tăn). Josh. 3 : 16, also given **Zar'tanah**, 1 Kings 4 : 12, and **Zar'than**, 1 Kings 7 : 46. R. V. "Zar'ethan" in all places. A village "beneath Jezreel," near the towns of Bethshean and Adam. The bronze castings for the temple were made between Succoth and Zarethan. In the parallel passage, 2 Chron. 4 : 17, it is called Zeredatha. R. V. Zeredah. The place cannot be precisely located. All that is known being in the Jordan valley not far from *el-Damieh*, the city of Adam, named in Josh. 3 : 16. Apparently also ZERERATH, R. V. Zererah, of Judges 7 : 22 is the same place.

Za'reth-sha'har (zā'reth-shā'har) (*splendor of the dawn*), a place mentioned only in Josh. 13 : 19, in the catalogue of the towns allotted to Reuben.

Zar'hites (zär'hītes), **The**, a branch of the tribe of Judah, descended from Zerah the son of Judah. Num. 26 : 13, 20; Josh. 7 : 17; 1 Chron. 27 : 11, 13. R. V. "Zerahites."

Zar'tanah. 1 Kings 4 : 12. [ZARE-TAN.]

Zar'than. 1 Kings 7 : 46. [ZARE-TAN.]

Zat'tu (zăt'tu). The sons of Zattu were a family of laymen of Israel who returned with Zerubbabel. Ezra 2 : 8; Neh. 7 : 13.

Za'van (zā'van). 1 Chron. 1 : 42. [ZAAVAN.]

Za'za (zā'zȧ), one of the sons of Jonathan, a descendant of Jerahmeel. 1 Chron. 2 : 33.

Zebadi'ah (zĕb-a-dī'ah). 1. A Benjamite of the sons of Beriah. 1 Chron. 8 : 15.

2. A Benjamite of the sons of Elpaal. 1 Chron. 8 : 17.

3. One of the sons of Jeroham of Gedor, who joined David at Ziklag. 1 Chron. 12 : 7.

4. Son of Asahel, the brother of Joab. 1 Chron. 27 : 7.

5. Son of Michael, of the sons of Shephatiah. Ezra 8 : 8.

6. A priest of the sons of Immer, who had married a foreign wife after the return from Babylon. Ezra 10 : 20.

7. Third son of Meshelemiah the Korhite. 1 Chron. 26 : 2.

8. A Levite in the reign of Jehoshaphat. 2 Chron. 17 : 8.

9. The son of Ishmael and prince of the house of Judah in the reign of Jehoshaphat. 2 Chron. 19 : 11.

Ze'bah (zē'bah) (*victim*) and **Zalmun'na** (*deprived of protection*), the two "kings" of Midian who commanded the great invasion of Palestine and who finally fell by the hand of Gideon himself. Judges 8 : 5–21; Ps. 83 : 11. While Oreb and Zeeb, two of the inferior leaders of the incursion, had been slain, with a vast number of their people, by the Ephraimites, at the central fords of the Jordan, the two kings had succeeded in making their escape by a passage farther to the north (probably the ford near Bethshean), and thence by the *Wady Yabîs*, through Gilead, to Karkor, high up on the Hauran. Here they were reposing with 15,000 men, a mere remnant of their huge horde, when Gideon overtook them. The people fled in dismay, and Gideon captured the two kings and brought them to his native village, Ophrah, where he slew them because they had killed his brothers.

Zeba'im (zė-bā'im), mentioned in the catalogue of the families of "Solomon's slaves" who returned from the captivity with Zerubbabel. Ezra 2 : 57; Neh. 7 : 59. The R. V. connects it with the previous name "Pochereth," making the true name "Pochereth-hazzebaim." [POCHERETH.]

Zeb'edee (zĕb'e-dē) (Greek form of "Zebadiah," *gift of Jehovah*), a fisherman of Galilee, the father of the apostles James the Great and John, Matt. 4 : 21, and the husband of Salome. Matt. 27 : 56; Mark 15 : 40. He probably lived either at Bethsaida or in its immediate neighborhood. It has been inferred from the mention of his "hired servants," Mark 1 : 20, and from the acquaintance between the apostle John and Annas the high priest, John 18 : 15, that the family of Zebedee were in easy circumstances, comp. John 19 : 27, although not above manual labor. Matt. 4 : 21. He appears only twice in the Gospel narrative, namely, in Matt. 4 : 21, 22; Mark 1 : 19, 20, where he is seen in his boat with his two sons mending their nets.

Zebi'na (ze-bī'nȧ) (*acquired*), one of the sons of Nebo who had taken foreign wives after the return from Babylon. Ezra 10 : 43.

Zebo'im (zė-bō'im). 1. One of the cities of the "plain" or circle of Jordan destroyed with Sodom. It is mentioned in Gen. 10:19; 14:2, 8; Deut. 29:23; Hos. 11:8. For the general site of these cities see Sodom. In Gen. 14: 2, 8, the name is given more correctly in the Authorized Version Zeboiim.

2. The valley of Zeboim, a ravine or gorge, apparently east of Michmash, mentioned only in 1 Sam. 13:18, in describing the route taken by a band of Philistines. The wilderness is no doubt the district of uncultivated mountain tops and sides which lies between the central district of Benjamin and the Jordan valley. In that very district there is a wild gorge bearing the name of *Shuk ed-Dubba'*, "ravine of the hyena," the exact equivalent of *Ge hattsebo'im.*

Zebu'dah (ze-bū'dah) (*bestowed*), wife of Josiah and mother of King Jehoiakim. 2 Kings 23:36. R. V. "Zebidah."

Ze'bul (zē'bul) (*habitation*), chief man (Authorized Version "ruler") of the city of Shechem at the time of the contest between Abimelech and the native Canaanites. He showed unswerving fidelity to Abimelech. Judges 9 : 28, 30, 36, 38, 41. (B.C. 1179.)

Zeb'ulonite, a member of the tribe of Zebulun. Judges 12 : 11, 12. Applied only to Elon, the one judge produced by the tribe. R. V. "Zebulunite."

Zeb'ulun (zĕb'u-lŭn) (*a habitation*), the tenth of the sons of Jacob, according to the order in which their births are enumerated; the sixth and last of Leah. Gen. 30:20; 35:23; 46:14; 1 Chron. 2:1. His birth is mentioned in Gen. 30:19, 20. Of the individual Zebulun nothing is recorded. The list of Gen. 46 ascribes to him three sons, founders of the chief families of the tribe (comp. Num. 26:26) at the time of the migration to Egypt. The tribe is not recorded to have taken part, for evil or good, in any of the events of the wandering or the conquest. In the Blessing of Jacob, Gen. 49:13, Zebulun is spoken of as being a haven of ships, and having its border on Zidon. Josephus supports this by stating that it extended from the Sea of Gennesaret to the Mediterranean. But by its description of the boundaries in Josh. 19, we learn that it was bounded on the east by Naphtali along the entire shore of the Sea of Galilee, and on the west was separated from the Mediterranean by Asher, and somewhat by Manasseh.

The boundaries are uncertain, and a small portion may once have touched the sea. Another explanation is that being *near* the sea it had easy access to its ports. Remote from the centre of government, Zebulun remains throughout the history, with one exception, in the obscurity which envelops the whole of the northern tribes. That exception, however, is a remarkable one. The conduct of the tribe during the struggle with Sisera, when they fought with desperate valor side by side with their brethren of Naphtali, was such as to draw down the special praise of Deborah, who singles them out from all the other tribes. Judges 5 : 18.

Zeb'ulunites (zĕb'u-lŭn-ites), **The,** the members of the tribe of Zebulun. Num. 26:27 only, in A. V.

Zechari'ah (zĕk-a-rī'ah). 1. The eleventh in order of the twelve minor prophets. He is called in his prophecy the son of Berechiah and the grandson of Iddo, whereas in the book of Ezra, ch. 5:1; 6:14, he is said to have been the son of Iddo. It is natural to suppose, as the prophet himself mentions his father's name, whereas the book of Ezra mentions only Iddo, that Berechiah had died early, and that there was now no intervening link between the grandfather and the grandson. Zechariah, like Jeremiah and Ezekiel before him, was priest as well as prophet. He seems to have entered upon his office while yet young, Zech. 2:4, and must have been born in Babylon, whence he returned with the first caravan of exiles under Zerubbabel and Jeshua in B.C. 536. The younger prophet acted in concert with the more aged Haggai. Both prophets had the same great object before them; both directed all their energies to the building of the second temple. To their influence we find the rebuilding of the temple in a great measure ascribed. If the later Jewish accounts may be trusted, Zechariah, as well as Haggai, was a member of the Great Synagogue. His mature life extended from B.C. 520 to 479. In what may be called the peculiarities of his prophecy, he approaches more nearly to Ezekiel and Daniel, than to the other prophets. Like them he delights in visions; like them he uses symbols and allegories rather than the bold figures and metaphors which lend so much force and beauty to the writings of the earlier prophets. Generally speaking, Zechariah's style is pure, and remarkably free from Chaldaisms.

2. Son of Meshelemiah or Shelemiah, a Korhite, and keeper of the north gate of the tabernacle of the congregation. 1 Chron. 9:21; 26:2.

3. One of the sons of Jehiel. 1 Chron. 9:37. [ZACHER.]

4. A Levite of the second order in the temple band as arranged by David, appointed to play with psalteries. 1 Chron. 15:18, 20. (B.C. 1042.)

5. One of the princes of Judah in the reign of Jehoshaphat. 2 Chron. 17:7, (B.C. 868.)

6. Son of the high priest Jehoiada, in the reign of Joash king of Judah, 2 Chron. 24:20, and therefore the king's cousin. After the death of Jehoiada, Zechariah probably succeeded to his office, and in attempting to check the reaction in favor of idolatry which immediately followed, he fell a victim to a conspiracy formed against him by the king, and was stoned in the court of the temple. He is probably the same as the "Zacharias son of Barachias" who was slain between the temple and the altar. Matt. 23:35. [ZACHARIAS, 2.]

7. A Kohathite Levite in the reign of Josiah. 2 Chron. 34:12. (B.C. 628.)

8. The leader of the sons of Pharosh who returned with Ezra. Ezra 8:3. (B.C. 458.)

9. Son of Bebai. Ezra 8:11.

10. One of the chiefs of the people whom Ezra summoned in council at the river Ahava. Ezra 8:16. He or another of the same name stood at Ezra's left hand when he expounded the law to the people. Neh. 8:4. (B.C. 450.)

11. One of the family of Elam who had married a foreign wife after the captivity. Ezra 10:26. (B.C. 458.)

12. Ancestor of Athaiah or Uthai. Neh. 11:4.

13. A Shilonite, descendant of Shelah. Neh. 11:5.

14. A priest, son of Pashur. Neh. 11:12.

15. The representative of the priestly family of Iddo in the days of Joiakim the son of Jeshua. Neh. 12:16. (B.C. about 500.) Probably the same as Zechariah the prophet, the son of Iddo.

16. An Asaphite, son of Jonathan, who blew with the trumpets at the dedication of the city wall by Ezra and Nehemiah. Neh. 12:35. (B.C. 446.)

17. A priest who also took part in the dedication of the wall. Neh 12:41.

18. A chief of the Reubenites at the time of the captivity by Tiglath-pileser. 1 Chron. 5:7. (B.C. 740.)

19. One of the priests who accompanied the ark from the house of Obededom. 1 Chron. 15:24. (B.C. 1042.)

20. Son of Isshiah or Jesiah, a Kohathite Levite descended from Uzziel. 1 Chron. 24:25. (B.C. 1042.)

21. Fourth son of Hosah, of the children of Merari. 1 Chron. 26:11.

22. A Manassite, father of Iddo. 1 Chron. 27:21.

23. The father of Jahaziel. 2 Chron. 20:14.

24. One of the sons of Jehoshaphat. 2 Chron. 21:2.

25. A prophet in the reign of Uzziah, who had "understanding in the vision of God," and exercised a powerful influence for good upon the king. Nothing more is known of him. 2 Chron. 26:5. (B.C. 760.)

26. The father of Abijah or Abi, Hezekiah's mother. 2 Chron. 29:1. [ZECHARIAH, 29.]

27. One of the family of Asaph in the reign of Hezekiah. 2 Chron. 29:13. (B.C. 725.)

28. One of the rulers of the temple in the reign of Josiah. 2 Chron. 35:8. (B.C. 628.)

29. The son of Jeberechiah, who was taken by the prophet Isaiah as one of the "faithful witnesses to record," when he wrote concerning Maher-shalal-hash-baz. Isa. 8:2. He may have been the Levite of the same name who in the reign of Hezekiah assisted in the purification of the temple. 2 Chron. 29:13. Another conjecture is that he is the same as Zechariah the father of Abijah, the queen of Ahaz.

Zechariah, The book of. The book of Zechariah, in its existing form, consists of two principal parts, viz. chs. 1–8 and chs. 9–14. The first of these divisions is allowed by all critics to be the genuine work of Zechariah the son of Iddo. The remainder of the book is regarded by many critics as prophecies of one or more prophets, whose writings have been joined to those of Zechariah. The first suggestion of this came from Joseph Mede in 1653, who argues that chs. 9 to 11 were written by Jeremiah, because Matthew in quoting Zech. 11:13, refers it to Jeremiah. (Matt. 27:9.)

The argument for different authors is not unanswerable, but the question is too abstruse to be discussed in a popular dictionary like this, and the decision is unimportant.

The genuine prophecies of Zechariah, chs. 1–8, are remarkable instances of the prophetic method.

Historical Circumstances.—Sixteen years before this a large company of Jews had returned from their captivity in Babylon (536 B.C.), and began to re-build the temple. But opposition, poverty, enemies, delayed the work for years. But now (B.C. 520), the people had just been awakened from their lethargy, and had begun anew to build the temple, amid the ruins of the old. They were few. Most of them were poor. They were discouraged. Their enemies were persistent and cruel. They were trying to bring the whole power of the empire against these few people and their feeble enterprise. Drought and mildew had ruined their crops. Even God seemed to be against them.

The aged Haggai had aroused enthusiasm and the work on the temple had begun. It had been going on but a few weeks when the younger prophet Zechariah came to his aid. His first brief address was spoken in November, 520, after the second prophecy of Haggai, who followed with two more messages from God. Then Zechariah came again upon the scene, three months after his first prophecy, in January or February, 519, when one memorable night God sent to Zechariah a series of eight visions—living pictures—object-lessons —which the prophet rehearsed to the people the next morning. Two years later as the work was progressing he brought another message from the Lord. The Jews, we are told, "prospered through the prophesying" (Ezra 6:14); and in about four years the temple was finished.

Each vision was an answer to a doubt or a discouragement.

I. *The Doubt* was lest God had forgotten the world and left it to wild disorder.

The First Vision showed God's messengers coming to him from all parts of the world.

II. *The Doubt* that the poor, weak Jews could build their temple and remain the people of God against the mighty armies and organizations which were opposed to them.

The Second Vision was of 4 great horns symbolizing their enemies, while 4 spectral forms representing the moral forces of God were silently filing these horns toward their destruction.

III. *The Third Vision*—by a measuring line such as was used for laying out the streets and walls of a city, and by an angel bidding the measurer to stop because no line was long enough to express the extent of the city of God,—removed the Discouragement arising from the smallness of the city and the weakness of the people. And in like manner the remaining five visions brought courage and hope, to a discouraged people, so that within four years the Temple was completed.

Four phrases in Zechariah should be engraved in letters of gold upon the memory:

"Not by might, nor by power, but by my spirit saith the Lord."

"A brand plucked out of the fire."

"Who hath despised the day of small things?"

"And the streets of the city [the new Jerusalem] shall be full of boys and girls playing in the streets thereof."

Ze′dad (zē′dăd) (*mountain side*), one of the landmarks on the north border of the land of Israel, as promised by Moses, Num. 34:8, and as restored by Ezekiel. Ezek. 47:15. A place named *Sŭdŭd* or *Sadad* exists to the east of the northern extremity of the chain of Anti-Lebanon, about fifty miles east-northeast of *Baalbec*. This is believed by many to be identical with Zedad.

Zedeki′ah (zĕd-e-kī′ah) (*justice of Jehovah*). 1. The last king of Judah and Jerusalem. He was the son of Josiah by his wife Hamutal, and therefore own brother to Jehoahaz. 2 Kings 24:18; comp. 23:31. His original name was Mattaniah, which was changed to Zedekiah by Nebuchadnezzar when he carried off his nephew Jehoiachin to Babylon, and left him on the throne of Jerusalem. Zedekiah was but twenty-one years old when he was thus placed in charge of an impoverished kingdom, B.C. 597. His history is contained in a short sketch of the events of his reign given in 2 Kings 24:17–25:7, and with some trifling variations, in Jer. 39:1– 7; 52:1–11, together with the still shorter summary in 2 Chron. 36:10, etc.;

and also in Jer. 21, 24, 27, 28, 29, 32, 34, 37, 38, and Ezek. 17: 11-21. From these it is evident that Zedekiah was a man not so much bad at heart as weak in will. It is evident from Jer. 27 and 28 that the earlier portion of Zedekiah's reign was marked by an agitation throughout the whole of Syria against the Babylonian yoke. Jerusalem seems to have taken the lead, since in the fourth year of Zedekiah's reign we find ambassadors from all the neighboring kingdoms—Tyre, Sidon, Edom and Moab—at his court to consult as to the steps to be taken. Jer. 27:2. Before the end of this year he made a personal visit to Babylon. He was at this time distinctly loyal. Jer. 51:59. The first act of rebellion of which any record survives was the formation of an alliance with Egypt, of itself equivalent to a declaration of enmity with Babylon, in the 8th year of his reign. As a natural consequence it brought on Jerusalem an immediate invasion of the Chaldæans. The fullest account of the siege of Jerusalem in the Bible is given by Jeremiah. Josephus (x. 7, § 3) relates it more fully. Judea was ravaged, and the whole country reduced, except Jerusalem and two strong places in the western plain, Lachish and Azekah, which still held out. Jer. 34:7. Called away for a time by an attack from Pharaoh and the Egyptians, on the tenth day of the tenth month of Zedekiah's ninth year (B.C. 589), the actual siege of Jerusalem began. Jer. 52:4. From this time forward the siege progressed slowly but surely to its consummation. The city was indeed reduced to the last extremity. The bread had for long been consumed, Jer. 38:9, and all the terrible expedients had been tried to which the wretched inhabitants of a besieged town are forced to resort in such cases. At last, after sixteen dreadful months, the catastrophe arrived. It was on the ninth day of the fourth month, about the middle of July, at midnight, as Josephus with careful minuteness informs us, that the breach in those strong and venerable walls was effected. The moon, nine days old, had gone down. The wretched remnants of the army quitted the city in the dead of night; and as the Chaldæan army entered the city at one end, the king and his wives fled from it by the opposite gate. They took the road

toward the Jordan. As soon as the dawn of day permitted it, swift pursuit was made. The king's party were overtaken near Jericho and carried to Nebuchadnezzar, who was then at Riblah, at the upper end of the valley of Lebanon. Nebuchadnezzar, with a refinement of barbarity characteristic of those cruel times, ordered the sons of Zedekiah to be killed before him, and lastly his own eyes to be thrust out. He was then loaded with brazen fetters, and at a later period taken to Babylon, where he died.

2. Son of Chenaanah, a false prophet at the court of Ahab, head, or, if not head, virtual leader, of the college. (B.C. 855.) He appears but once, viz. as spokesman when the prophets are consulted by Ahab on the result of his proposed expedition to Ramoth-gilead. 1 Kings 22; 2 Chron. 18. Zedekiah had prepared himself for the interview with a pair of iron horns, with which he illustrated the manner in which Ahab should drive the Syrians before him. When Micaiah the prophet of the Lord appeared and had delivered his prophecy, Zedekiah sprang forward and struck him a blow on the face, accompanying it by a taunting sneer.

3. The son of Maaseiah, a false prophet in Babylon. Jer. 29:21, 22. He was denounced in the letter of Jeremiah for having, with Ahab the son of Kolaiah, buoyed up the people with false hopes of restoration from Babylon, and for profane and flagitious conduct. Their names were to become a by-word, and their terrible fate a warning.

4. The son of Hananiah, one of the princes of Judah in the time of Jeremiah. Jer. 36:12. (B.C. 605.)

Zeeb (zē'eb) (*wolf*), one of the two "princes" of Midian in the great invasion of Israel. (B.C. about 1180.) He is always named with Oreb. Judges 7: 25; 8:3; Ps. 83:11. Zeeb and Oreb were not slain at the first rout of the Arabs, but at a later stage of the struggle, probably in crossing the Jordan at a ford farther down the river. Zeeb, the wolf, was brought to bay in a wine-press which in later times bore his name —the "wine-press of Zeeb." [OREB.]

Ze'lah (zē'lah) (*a rib*), a city in the allotment of Benjamin, Josh. 18:28, contained the family tomb of Kish, the father of Saul. 2 Sam. 21:14.

48

Ze'lek (zē'lĕk) (*fissure*), an Ammonite, one of David's guard. 2 Sam. 23: 37; 1 Chron. 11: 39.

Zelo'phehad (zė-lō'fe-hăd), son of Hepher, son of Gilead, son of Machir, son of Manasseh. Josh. 17: 3. He was apparently the second son of Hepher. 1 Chron. 7: 15. Zelophehad came out of Egypt with Moses, but died in the wilderness, as did the whole of that generation. Num. 14: 35; 27: 3. On his death without male heirs, his five daughters, just after the second numbering in the wilderness, came before Moses and Eleazar to claim the inheritance of their father in the tribe of Manasseh. The claim was admitted by divine direction. Num. 26: 33; 27: 1–11.

Zelo'tes (zė-lō'tēz), the epithet given to the apostle Simon to distinguish him from Simon Peter. Luke 6: 15. R. V. " Simon which was called the Zealot." [CANAANITE; SIMON, 5.]

Zel'zah (zĕl'zah) (*shadow*), a place named once only, 1 Sam. 10: 2, as on the boundary of Benjamin, close to Rachel's sepulchre, five miles southwest of Jerusalem.

Zemara'im (zĕm-a-rā'im) (*two cuttings*), a town in the allotment of Benjamin, Josh. 18: 22. It is generally identified with *es-Sumra* about 5½ miles northwest of Jericho.

Zemara'im, Mount. A mountain mentioned in 2 Chron. 13: 4 only, as "in Mount Ephraim," that is to say, within the general district of the highlands of that great tribe. It was probably near the city of the same name.

Zem'arite (zĕm'a-rīte), **The,** one of the Hamite tribes who are represented in the genealogical tables as " sons of Canaan." Gen. 10: 18; 1 Chron. 1: 16. Nothing is certainly known of this ancient tribe. The old interpreters place them at Emessa, the modern *Hums.* Modern scholars think it connected with the *Tsumur* of the *Tel-el-Amarna* tablets, if not identical with it.

Zemi'ra (zė-mī'ra) (*a song*), one of the sons of Becher the son of Benjamin. 1 Chron. 7: 8.

Ze'nan (zē'nan) (*pointed*), a town in the allotment of Judah, situated in the district of the Shefelah. Josh. 15: 37. It is probably identical with ZAANAN. Micah 1: 11.

Ze'nas (zē'nas), a believer who is mentioned in Titus 3: 13 in connection with Apollos. He is further described

as " the lawyer." It is impossible to determine whether Zenas was a Roman jurisconsult or a Jewish doctor, but the latter seems more probable.

Zephani'ah (zĕf-a-nī'ah) (*Jehovah has hidden*). 1. The ninth in order of the twelve minor prophets. His pedigree is traced to his fourth ancestor, Hezekiah, Zeph. 1: 1, supposed to be the celebrated king of that name. The chief characteristics of this book are the unity and harmony of the composition, the grace, energy and dignity of its style, and the rapid and effective alternations of threats and promises. The general tone of the last portion is Messianic, but without any specific reference to the person of our Lord. The date of the book is given in the inscription—viz. the reign of Josiah, from 639 to 608 B.C. It is most probable, moreover, that the prophecy was delivered before the 18th year of Josiah.

2. The son of Maaseiah, Jer. 21: 1, and *sagan* or second priest in the reign of Zedekiah. (B.C. 588.) He was probably a ruler of the temple, whose office it was, among others, to punish pretenders to the gift of prophecy. Jer. 29: 29. On the capture of Jerusalem he was taken and slain at Riblah. Jer. 52: 24, 27; 2 Kings 25: 18, 21.

3. Father of Josiah, Zech. 6: 10, who lived in the time of Zechariah. [JOSIAH 2.]

4. A Levite of the family of Kohath and house of Izhar. 1 Chron. 6: 36–38.

Ze'phath (zē'fath) (*watch-tower*), the earlier name, Judges 1: 17, of a Canaanite town, which after its capture and destruction was called by the Israelites Hormah. [HORMAH.]

Zeph'athah (zĕf'a-thah) (*watchtower*), **The valley of,** the spot in which Asa joined battle with Zerah the Ethiopian. 2 Chron. 14: 10 only.

Ze'phi (zē'fī). 1 Chron. 1: 36. [ZEPHO.]

Ze'pho (zē'fō) (*watch*), son of Eliphaz, son of Esau, Gen. 36: 11, and one of the " dukes " or phylarchs of the Edomites, ver. 15. In 1 Chron. 1: 36 he is called ZEPHI.

Ze'phon (zē'fon) (*watching*), the son of Gad, Num. 26: 15, and ancestor of the family of the Zephonites. Called ZIPHION in Gen. 46: 16. (B.C. 1706.)

Zer (zĕr) (*flint*), a fortified town in the allotment of Naphtali, Josh. 19: 35 only. Its site is quite uncertain.

Ze'rah (zē'rah) (*rising*(of the sun)).
1. A son of Reuel, son of Esau, Gen. 36:
13; 1 Chron. 1:37, and one of the
"dukes" of the Edomites. Gen. 36:17.
2. Less properly, Zarah, twin son, with
his elder brother Pharez, of Judah and
Tamar. Gen. 38:30; 1 Chron. 2:4;
Matt. 1:3. His descendants were called
Zarhites, Ezrahites and Izrahites. Num.
26:20; 1 Kings 4:31; 1 Chron. 27:8, 11.
3. Son of Simeon, 1 Chron. 4:24,
called ZOHAR in Gen. 46:10.
4. A Gershonite Levite, son of Iddo
or Adaiah. 1 Chron. 6:21, 41.
5. The Ethiopian or Cushite, an invader of Judah, defeated by Asa about
B.C. 902. [ASA.] Zerah is probably the
Hebrew name of Usorken I., second king
of the Egyptian twenty-second dynasty;
or Usorken II., his second successor.
In the fourteenth year of Asa, Zerah
the Ethiopian, with a mighty army (a
million according to the account), invaded his kingdom, and advanced unop-
posed in the field as far as the valley
of Zephathah at Mareshah. The Egyptian monuments enable us to picture the
general disposition of Zerah's army.
The chariots formed the first corps in
a single or double line; behind them,
massed in phalanxes, were heavy-armed
troops; probably on the flanks stood
archers and horsemen in lighter forma-
tions. After a prayer by Asa, his army
attacked the Egyptians and defeated
them. The chariots, broken by the
charge and with horses made unman-
ageable by flights of arrows, must have
been forced back upon the cumbrous
host behind. So complete was the overthrow that the Hebrews could capture
and spoil the cities around Gerah, which
must have been in alliance with Zerah.
The defeat of the Egyptian army is
without parallel in the history of the
Jews. On no other occasion did an
Israelite army meet an army of one of
the great powers and defeat it.
Zerahi'ah (zĕr-a-hī'à) (*Jehovah has
risen*). 1. A priest, son of Uzzi and
ancestor of Ezra the scribe. 1 Chron.
6:6, 51; Ezra 7:4.
2. Father of Elihoenai of the sons of
Pahath-moab, whose descendants returned from the captivity with Ezra.
Ezra 8:4.
Ze'red (zē'red) (*exuberant growth*),
Deut. 2:13, 14, or **Za'red** (zā'red),
Num. 21:12, a brook or torrent-valley
(*nachal*) crossed by the Israelites at

the farthest limit of their wilderness
wandering. It was probably either the
Sail Saideh which enters the Arnon
from the southeast, or the upper course
of the *Wady Kerak*. Dr. Robinson suggests its identity with the *Wady el-Ahsy;*
but this is the southern boundary of
Moab, while the station just preceding
was east of Moab.
Zer'eda (zĕr'e-dà) (*coolness*), the
native place of Jeroboam. 1 Kings 11:
26. Zereda or Zeredah is probably identical with Zeredathah and Zarthan or
Zartanah or Zaretan in the valley of
the Jordan. [ZARETAN.]
Zered'athah. [ZARETAN.]
Zer'erath (zĕr'e-răth). [ZARETAN.]
Ze'resh (zē'resh) (*gold*), the wife of
Haman the Agagite. Esther 5:10, 14;
6:13. (B.C. 474.)
Ze'reth (zē'reth) (*splendor*), son of
Ashur, the founder of Tekoa, by his
wife Helah. 1 Chron. 4:7.
Ze'ri (zē'rī), one of the sons of Jeduthun in the reign of David. 1 Chron.
25:3. [IZRI.]
Ze'ror (zē'rôr) (*a bundle*), a Benjamite, ancestor of Kish the father of
Saul. 1 Sam. 9:1.
Zeru'ah (zĕ-rụ'ah) (*smitten, leprous*),
the mother of Jeroboam the son of Nebat. 1 Kings 11:26.
Zerub'babel (zĕ-rŭb'ba-bĕl) (*born at
Babel,* i. e. *Babylon*). One who played
an important part at the time of the return from the Babylonish captivity in
the first year of Cyrus; usually considered the head of the tribe of Judah at
the period. When Cyrus, after the conquest of Babylon, adopted the wise
policy of allowing the Jews to return to
Jerusalem, he appointed him as Persian
governor. "Sheshbazzar, the prince of
Judah" (Ezra 1:8), that is the legal
heir to the throne of David. The general opinion has been that Sheshbazzar
was the Babylonian name of Zerubbabel,
and therefore that he was appointed by
Cyrus governor of Judah. Late authorities are regarding the two as different, Sheshbazzar being the uncle, perhaps, of Zerubbabel. It seems generally acknowledged by these scholars,
however, that Zerubbabel went from
Babylon to Jerusalem with the body of
exiles under "Sheshbazzar;" that he
was the prime mover, in connection with
the high priest Jeshua, in the rebuilding
of the temple; and that at some time
previous to the accession of Darius Hy-

staspis he was actual governor of the land (Hag. 1:14). It does not seem fully proved that the two names cannot refer to the same man, as in the similar cases of Shadrach, Meshach, Abednego and Belteshazzar (Daniel). However this point is decided, it seems agreed by all that on arriving at Jerusalem, Zerubbabel's great work, which he set about immediately, was the rebuilding of the temple. In the second month of the second year of the return, the foundation was laid with all the pomp which could be commanded. The efforts of the Samaritans were successful in putting a stop to the work during the seven remaining years of the reign of Cyrus and through the eight years of Cambyses and Smerdis. Nor does Zerubbabel appear quite blameless for this long delay. The difficulties in the way of building the temple were not such as need have stopped the work for such a long time; and during this long suspension of sixteen years Zerubbabel and the rest of the people had been busy in building costly houses for themselves. But in the second year of Darius (B.C. 520), largely owing to the stimulus supplied by the prophets Haggai and Zechariah, the work was begun in earnest. After much opposition [see NEHEMIAH] and many hindrances and delays, the temple was at length finished, in the sixth year of Darius, and was dedicated with much pomp and rejoicing. [TEMPLE.] No mention is made of Zerubbabel at the dedication of the temple, and the rest of his life is lost in obscurity. A Jewish tradition relates that he returned to Babylon, and died there. His apocryphal history is told in 1 Esdr. 3–7. The exact parentage of Zerubbabel is a little obscure, from his being always called the son of Shealtiel, Ezra 3:2, 8; 5:2, etc.; Hag. 1:1, 12, 14, etc., and appearing as such in the genealogies of Christ, Matt. 1:12; Luke 3:27; whereas in 1 Chron. 3:19 he is represented as the son of Pedaiah, Shealtiel or Salathiel's brother, and consequently as Salathiel's nephew. Either there is an error in transcription in 1 Chron. 3:19, or else he was the true son of Pedaiah but the legal heir of Shealtiel, who had died childless. In either case he was the grandson of Jehoiachin the captive king of Judah (Jeconiah, 1 Chron. 3:17), the legal successor and heir of his royal estate, and the lineal descendant of David.

In the New Testament the name appears in the Greek form of Zorobabel.

Zerui′ah (zĕr-u-ī′ah) (*divided*), the mother of the three leading heroes of David's army—Abishai, Joab and Asahel—known as the "sons of Zeruiah." Of Zeruiah's husband there is no mention in the Bible. 1 Sam. 26:6.

Ze′tham (zē′tham) (*olive*), the son of Laadan, a Gershonite Levite. 1 Chron. 23:8.

Ze′than (zē′than) (*olive*), a Benjamite of the sons of Bilhan. 1 Chron. 7:10.

Ze′thar (zē′thär) (*conqueror*), one of the seven eunuchs of Ahasuerus. Esther 1:10. (B.C. 483.)

Zi′a (zī′ā) (*motion*), one of the Gadites who dwelt in Bashan. 1 Chron. 5:13.

Zi′ba (zī′ba), a servant of Saul whom David made steward of Saul's son Mephibosheth. 2 Sam. 9:2–12; 16:1–4; 19:17, 29. [MEPHIBOSHETH.]

Zib′eon (zĭb′e-on) (*dyed*), father of Anah, whose daughter Aholibamah was Esau's wife. Gen. 36:2. Although called a Hivite, he is probably the same as Zibeon the son of Seir the Horite. vs. 20, 24, 29; 1 Chron. 1:38, 40.

Zib′ia (zĭb′ĭa) (*gazelle*), a Benjamite, apparently the son of Shaharaim by his wife Hodesh. 1 Chron. 8:9.

Zib′iah (zĭb′ĭ-a) (*gazelle*), a native of Beersheba, and mother of King Joash. 2 Kings 12:1; 2 Chron. 24:1.

Zich′ri (zĭk′rī) (*memorable*). 1. Son of Izhar of the family of Kohath. Ex. 6:21. (B.C. 1491.)

2. A Benjamite of the sons of Shimhi. 1 Chron. 8:19.

3. A Benjamite of the sons of Shashak. 1 Chron. 8:23.

4. A Benjamite of the sons of Jeroham. 1 Chron. 8:27.

5. Son of Asaph, elsewhere called ZABDI and ZACCUR. 1 Chron. 9:15.

6. A descendant of Eliezer the son of Moses. 1 Chron. 26:25.

7. The father of Eliezer, the chief of the Reubenites in the reign of David. 1 Chron. 27:16.

8. One of the tribe of Judah, father of Amasiah, a captain in the army of Jehoshaphat. 2 Chron. 17:16. Possibly the same as

9. Father of Elishaphat, one of the conspirators with Jehoiada. 2 Chron. 23:1. (B.C. before 842.)

10. An Ephraimite hero in the invad-

ing army of Pekah the son of Remaliah. 2 Chron. 28: 7. (B.C. 734.)

11. Father or ancestor of JOEL, 13. Neh. 11: 9.

12. A priest of the family of Abijah, in the days of Joiakim the son of Jeshua. Neh. 12: 17. (B.C. about 500.)

Zid′dim (zĭd′dim) (*sides*), a fortified town in the allotment of Naphtali. Josh. 19: 35. It is perhaps *Hattin*, about 5½ miles northwest of Tiberias, and less than a mile from the celebrated Horns of Hattin.

Zidki′jah (zĭd-kī′jah) (*righteousness of Jehovah*), a priest or family of priests who signed the covenant with Nehemiah. Neh. 10: 1. R. V. "Zedekiah."

Zi′don (zī′dŏn), or **Si′don**, Gen. 10: 15, 19; Josh. 11: 8; 19: 28; Judges 1: 31; 18: 28; Isa. 23: 2, 4, 12; Jer. 25: 22; 27: 3; Ezek. 28: 21, 22; Joel 3: 4; Zech. 9: 2; Matt. 11: 21, 22; 15: 21; Mark 3: 8; 7: 24, 31; Luke 6: 17; 10: 13, 14, an ancient and wealthy city of Phœnicia, on the eastern coast of the Mediterranean Sea, about twenty English miles to the north of Tyre. Its Hebrew name, *Tsîdôn*, signifies *fishing* or *fishery*. Its modern name is *Saida*. It is situated in the narrow plain between the Lebanon and the sea. From a biblical point of view this city is inferior in interest to its neighbor Tyre; though in early times Sidon was the more influential of the two cities. Homer uses Zidon and Zidonian as synonymous with Phœnicia and Phœnician, but never mentions Tyre. In the Bible also the name seems often to have been used for the Phœnicians as a whole. Except for short spaces of time during the building and restoration of the temple (1 Chron. 22: 4; Ezra 3: 7), the Zidonians and Israelites seem to have been enemies. Their border was assigned to Asher (Josh. 19: 28), but they were always unconquered, and were among the Canaanite nations left "to prove Israel." Judges 3: 3. They were always a source of temptation and danger to the Israelites, Josh. 13: 6; Judges 1: 31; 3: 3; 10: 6, and became at some times their active oppressors, Judges 10: 12. From the time of Solomon to the invasion of Nebuchadnezzar Zidon is not often directly mentioned in the Bible, and it appears to have been subordinate to Tyre. Ahab married the daughter of Ethbaal, king of the Zidonians (1 Kings 16: 31); a marriage denounced as a sin surpassing that of Jero-

boam. The political history of Zidon is closely connected with that of Tyre and other Phœnician cities, although the rivalry among them was so strong that only occasionally were they allies. It was tributary to Assyria from the time of Asshurbanipal; revolted in the reign of Shalmanezer IV.; and was entirely subjugated by Sennacherib. When Babylon became supreme, Zidon united in an alliance with a large number of the surrounding peoples for better protection against both Babylon and Egypt. It was however not successful, for they were in 605 B.C. overrun and laid waste by the Babylonians. Revolting in 598 B.C., Nebuchadnezzar invaded and conquered Phœnicia, humbling Tyre. Upon this Zidon became the chief of the Phœnician cities. Jeremiah and Ezekiel predict the same judgment upon Zidon because of its attitude towards the people of God (Jer. 25: 22; 27: 3, 6; Ezek. 28: 21, 22); and Joel holds them up to abhorrence as having made merchandise of captured Israelites, and of the sacred vessels of the temple. Joel 3: 4–6. During the Persian domination Zidon seems to have attained its highest point of prosperity; and it is recorded that, toward the close of that period, it far excelled all other Phœnician cities in wealth and importance. Its prosperity was suddenly cut short by an unsuccessful revolt against Persia, which ended in the destruction of the town, B.C. 351. Forty thousand persons are said to have perished in the flames. Zidon, however, gradually recovered from the blow, and became again a flourishing town. Zidonians came to hear Christ (Mark 3: 8) and Tyre and Zidon are favorably compared with the unbelieving cities of Galilee (Matt. 11: 21, 22). It is the most northern city mentioned in Christ's journeys, and one miracle, that of the Syrophœnician woman, is recorded as being performed in its vicinity. The town *Saida* still shows signs of its former wealth, and its houses are better constructed and more solid than those of Tyre, many of them being built of stone; but it is a poor, miserable place, without trade or manufactures worthy of the name. The city that once divided with Tyre the empire of the seas is now almost without a vessel. Silk and fruit are its staple products. Its population is estimated at 12,000, most of whom are Moslems, and the rest

VIEW OF SIDON.

Catholics, Maronites and Protestants. There is a flourishing Protestant mission here.

Zif (zĭf). 1 Kings 6:1. [MONTH.]

Zi'ha (zī'hà) (*parched*). 1. The children of Ziha were a family of Nethinim who returned with Zerubbabel. Ezra 2:43; Neh. 7:46.

2. Overseer of the Nethinim in Ophel. Neh. 11:21. Probably identical with the preceding.

Zik'lag (zĭk'lăg), a place which possesses a special interest from its having been the residence and the private property of David. It is first mentioned in the catalogue of the towns of Judah in Josh. 15:31, and was allotted to Simeon. Josh. 19:5. We next encounter it in the possession of the Philistines, 1 Sam. 27:6, when it was, at David's request, bestowed upon him by Achish king of Gath. He resided there for a year and four months. 1 Sam. 27:6, 7; 30:14, 26; 1 Chron. 12:1, 20. It was there he received the news of Saul's death. 2 Sam. 1:1; 4:10. He then relinquished it for Hebron. 2 Sam. 2:1. Ziklag is finally mentioned as being reinhabited by the people of Judah after their return from the captivity. Neh. 11:28. The situation of the town is difficult to determine, the most probable identification yet made being *Zuheilika,* about 11 miles southeast of Gaza.

Zil'lah (zĭl'lah) (*a shadow*). [LAMECH.]

Zil'pah (zĭl'pah) (*dropping*), a Syrian given by Laban to his daughter Leah as an attendant, Gen. 29:24, and by Leah to Jacob as a concubine. She was the mother of Gad and Asher. Gen. 30:9–13; 35:26; 37:2; 46:18. (B.C. 1753.)

Zil'thai (zĭl'thā-ī) (*shady*). 1. A Benjamite, of the sons of Shimhi. 1 Chron. 8:20.

2. One of the captains of thousands of Manasseh who deserted to David at Ziklag. 1 Chron. 12:20. (B.C. 1055.)

Zim'mah (zĭm'mah) (*counsel*). A Gershonite Levite, son of Shimei, and descendant of Jahath. 1 Chron. 6:20, 42. Most probably the father or ancestor of Joah, a Gershonite in the reign of Hezekiah. 2 Chron. 29:12.

Zim'ran (zĭm'ran), the eldest son of Keturah. Gen. 25:2; 1 Chron. 1:32. His descendants are not mentioned, nor is any hint given that he was the founder of a tribe. Some have seen the name in *Zabram,* a town west of Mecca, on the Red Sea.

Zim'ri (zĭm'rī). 1. The son of Salu, a Simeonite chieftain, slain by Phinehas with the Midianitish princess Cozbi. Num. 25:14, 15. (B.C. 1450.)

2. Fifth sovereign of the separate kingdom of Israel, of which he occupied the throne for the brief period of seven days, B.C. 889. Originally in command of half the chariots in the royal army, he gained the crown by the murder of King Elah, son of Baasha. But the army made their general, Omri, king, who marched against Tirzah, where Zimri was. Zimri retreated into the innermost part of the late king's palace, set it on fire, and perished in the ruins. 1 Kings 16:9–20.

3. One of the five sons of Zerah the son of Judah. 1 Chron. 2:6. Called ZABDI in Josh. 7:1.

4. A Benjamite, descendant of Saul. 1 Chron. 8:36; 9:42.

5. An obscure name, mentioned Jer. 25:25 in probable connection with Dedan, Tema, Buz, Arabia, the "mingled people." Nothing further is known respecting Zimri, but the name may possibly be the same as, or derived from, ZIMRAN.

Zin (zĭn), the name given to a portion of the desert tract between the Dead Sea, *Ghôr,* and *Arabah* on the east, and the general plateau of the *Tih* which stretches westward. It was directly adjacent to the wilderness of Paran, since Kadesh is named in each. The country in question consists of two or three successive terraces of mountain converging to an acute angle at the Dead Sea's southern verge, toward which also they slope. Idumea was conterminous with Judah; since Kadesh was also a city in the border of Edom. [See KADESH. Num. 13:21; 20:1; 27:14; 33:36; 34:3; Josh. 15:1.]

Zi'na (zī'nà) (*abundance*); Zizah, the second son of Shimei the Gershonite. 1 Chron. 23:10, comp. 11.

Zi'on (zī'ŏn). [JERUSALEM.]

Zi'or (zī'or) (*smallness*), a town in the mountain district of Judah. Josh. 15:54. It belongs to the same group with Hebron, and is probably to be identified with *Sair,* about 6 miles northeast of that town.

Ziph (zĭf), the name of two towns in Judah. 1. In the south, named between Ithnan and Telem. Josh. 15:24

It does not appear again in the history, nor has any trace of it been met with.
2. In the hill-country of Judah. Josh. 15 : 55. The place is immortalized by its connection with David. 1 Sam. 23 : 14, 15, 24; 26 : 2. These passages show that at that time it had near it a wilderness (*i. e.* a waste pasture-ground) and a wood. The latter has disappeared, but the former remains. The name of *Zif* is found about 4 miles south of Hebron, attached to a rounded hill of some 100 feet in height, which is called *Tell Zif.*
3. Son of Jehaleleel. 1 Chron. 4 : 16.

Zi'phah (zī'fåh) (*feminine of Ziph*), another son of Jehaleleel. 1 Chron. 4 : 16.

Ziph'im (zĭf'ĭm), **The,** the inhabitants of ZIPH, 2. In this form the name is found in the Authorized Version only in the title of Ps. 54. In the R. V. here, and in both versions in the narrative it occurs in the more usual form of ZIPHITES. 1 Sam. 23 : 19; 26 : 1.

Ziph'ion (zĭf'ĭ-on), son of Gad, Gen. 46 : 16; elsewhere called Zephon.

Ziph'ron (zĭf'rŏn) (*fragrance*), a point in the north boundary of the promised land as specified by Moses. Num. 34 : 9.

Zip'por (zĭp'por) (*sparrow*), father of Balak king of Moab. Num. 22 : 2, 4, 10, 16; 23 : 18; Josh. 24 : 9; Judges 11 : 25. Whether he was the "former king of Moab" alluded to in Num. 21 : 26 we are not told.

Zip'porah or **Zippo'rah** (zĭp-pō'rah), daughter of Reuel or Jethro, the priest of Midian, wife of Moses and mother of his two sons Gershom and Eliezer. Ex. 2 : 21; 4 : 25; 18 : 2, comp. 6. (B.C. 1530.) The only incident recorded in her life is that of the circumcision of Gershom. Ex. 4 : 24–26.

Zith'ri (zĭth'rī), properly Sithri; one of the sons of Uzziel the son of Kohath. Ex. 6 : 22. In Ex. 6 : 21 some modern editions have Zithri. It should be Zichri, as in original edition of 1611.

Ziz (*brightness*), **The cliff of,** the pass by which the horde of Moabites, Ammonites and Mehunim made their way up from the shores of the Dead Sea to the wilderness of Judah near Tekoa. 2 Chron. 20 : 16 only; comp. 20. It was very probably the pass of *Ain Jidy*—the very same route which is taken by the Arabs in their marauding expeditions at the present day.

Zi'za (zī'zà) (*plenty*). 1. Son of Shiphi, a chief of the Simeonites in the reign of Hezekiah. 1 Chron. 4 : 37. (B.C. about 725.)
2. Son of Rehoboam by Maachah the daughter or granddaughter of Absalom. 2 Chron. 11 : 20.

Zi'zah, a Gershonite Levite, second son of Shimei, 1 Chron. 23 : 11; miscopied ZINA in ver. 10.

Zo'an (zō'an) (*place of departure*), an ancient city of lower Egypt, called Tanis by the Greeks. It stood on the eastern bank of the Tanitic branch of the Nile. Its name indicates a place of departure from a country, and hence it has been identified with Avaris (Tanis, the modern *San*), the capital of the earliest kings of the 12th dynasty. It is said in Num. 13 : 22 to have been built seven years after Hebron, and existed before the time of Abraham. According to Manetho, it was taken by the Shepherd kings in their invasion of Egypt, and by them rebuilt, and garrisoned with 240,000 men. This city is mentioned in connection with the plagues in Ps. 78 : 12, 43. Egyptologists differ very much in the interpretation of the monumental evidence. Many think that Rameses II. raised Zoan again to importance, refortified and enlarged it, also founding a new temple city. This new town was named *Pi Ramessu,* the city of Rameses. If these statements are true, it was the place of meeting between Moses and Pharaoh and Moses wrought his wonders on the field of Zoan, a rich plain extending thirty miles toward the east. It was still an important city in the time of Isaiah. Isa. 19 : 11, 13; 30 : 4; Ezek. 30 : 14. It is now an insignificant collection of fishermen's huts and still retains the name of *San.* But there are wide ruins which have been explored by the Palestine Exploration Fund which prove it a once flourishing city, a colossal statue of Rameses II. has been found, and there are remains of temples and other costly buildings and obelisks.

Zo'ar (zō'ar) (*smallness*), one of the most ancient cities of the land of Canaan. Its original name was BELA. Gen. 14 : 2, 8. It was in intimate connection with the cities of the "plain of Jordan"—Sodom, Gomorrah, Admah and Zeboiim. See also Gen. 13 : 10, but not 10 : 19. In the general destruction of the cities of the plain, Zoar was spared to afford shelter to Lot. Gen.

19:22, 23, 30. It is mentioned in the account of the death of Moses as one of the landmarks which bounded his view from Pisgah, Deut. 34:3, and it appears to have been known in the time both of Isaiah, Isa. 15:5, and Jeremiah. Jer. 48:34. These are all the notices of Zoar contained in the Bible. It was situated in the same district with the four cities already mentioned, viz. in the "plain" or "circle" of the Jordan, and the narrative of Gen. 19 evidently implies that it was very near to Sodom. vs. 15, 23, 27. The definite position of Sodom is, and probably will always be, a mystery; but indications seem to point to the southern end of the Dead Sea. [SODOM.] All the *post-biblical* references to Zoar place it indubitably at the southern end of the Dead Sea, and it seems unlikely that the Zoar of Josephus was on a different site from the biblical Zoar. There are also biblical *data* which also seem to support this view. It is closely connected with Moab.

Zo'ba, or **Zo'bah** (zō'bah), the name of a portion of Syria which formed a separate kingdom in the time of the Jewish monarchs Saul, David and Solomon. It probably was eastward of Cœle-Syria, and extended thence northeast and east toward, if not even to, the Euphrates. We first hear of Zobah in the time of Saul, when we find it mentioned as a separate country, governed apparently by a number of kings who owned no common head or chief. 1 Sam. 14:47. Some forty years later than this we find Zobah under a single ruler, Hadadezer son of Rehob. He had wars with Toi king of Hamath, 2 Sam. 8:10, and held various petty Syrian princes as vassals under his yoke. 2 Sam. 10:19. David, 2 Sam. 8:3, attacked Hadadezer in the early part of his reign, defeated his army, and took from him a thousand chariots, seven hundred (seven thousand, 1 Chron. 18:4) horsemen and 20,000 footmen. Hadadezer's allies, the Syrians of Damascus, were defeated in a great battle. The wealth of Zobah is very apparent in the narrative of this campaign. A man of Zobah, Rezon son of Eliadah, made himself master of Damascus, where he proved a fierce adversary to Israel all through the reign of Solomon. 1 Kings 11:23-25. Solomon also was, it would seem, engaged in a war with Zobah itself. 2 Chron. 8:3. This is

the last that we hear of Zobah in Scripture. The name, however, is found at a later date in the inscriptions of Assyria, where the kingdom of Zobah seems to intervene between Hamath and Damascus.

Zobe'bah (zō-bē'bah) (*gentle movement*), son of Coz, of the tribe of Judah. 1 Chron. 4:8.

Zo'har (zō'här) (*light*). 1. Father of Ephron the Hittite. Gen. 23:8; 25:9.

2. One of the sons of Simeon, Gen. 46:10; Ex. 6:15; called ZERAH in 1 Chron. 4:24.

3. The name of a Judahite family called *Jezoar* in the A. V. and "Izhar" in the R. V. 1 Chron. 4:7.

Zo'heleth (zō'he-leth) (*serpent*), **The stone.** This was "by En-rogel," 1 Kings 1:9; and therefore, if En-rogel be the modern *Um-ed-Deraj*, this stone, "where Adonijah slew sheep and oxen," was in all likelihood not far from the well of the Virgin.

Zo'heth (zō'heth), son of Ishi of the tribe of Judah. 1 Chron. 4:20.

Zo'phah (zō'fah) (*a cruse*), son of Helem or Hotham the son of Heber, an Asherite. 1 Chron. 7:35, 36.

Zo'phai (zō'fā), a Kohathite Levite, son of Elkanah and ancestor of Samuel. 1 Chron. 6:26. In ver. 35 he is called ZUPH.

Zo'phar (zō'far) (*chirper*), one of the three friends of Job. Job 2:11; 11:1; 20:1; 42:9.

Zo'phim (zō'fim) (*watchers*), **The field of,** a spot on or near the top of Pisgah, from which Balaam had his second view of the encampment of Israel. Num. 23:14. The position of the field of Zophim is not defined. Possibly it is not a proper name.

Zo'rah (zō'rah) (*hornet*), a town in the allotment of the tribe of Dan. Josh. 19:41. It is previously mentioned, ch. 15:33, in the catalogue of Judah, among the places in the district of the Shefelah (Authorized Version "Zoreah"). It was the residence of Manoah and the native place of Samson, Judges 13:2, and he was buried near the town. Judges 16:31. It is mentioned among the places fortified by Rehoboam. 2 Chron. 11:10. It is identical with the modern village of *Sŭr'ah*, on the north side of the Valley of Sorek, about 2 miles southwest of Eshtaol.

Zo'rathites (zō'rä-thītes), **The,** *i. e.*

the people of Zorah, mentioned in 1 Chron. 4:2 as descended from Shobal.

Zo'reah (zō're-ah). Josh. 15:33. [ZORAH.]

Zo'rites (zō'rītes), **The**, are named in the genealogies of Judah, 1 Chron. 2:54, apparently among the descendants of Salma and near connections of Joab. Some explain them as the same as the ZORATHITES.

Zorob'abel (zȯ-rŏb'a-bĕl). Matt. 1:12, 13; Luke 3:27. [ZERUBBABEL.]

Zu'ar (zū'ar) (*littleness*), father of Nethaneel, the chief of the tribe of Issachar at the time of the Exodus. Num. 1:8; 2:5; 7:18, 23; 10:15.

Zuph (zŭf) (*honeycomb*), **The land of**, a district at which Saul and his servant arrived after passing through the possessions of Shalisha, of Shalim and of the Benjamites. It apparently lay to the south of the land of Benjamin. 1 Sam. 9:4–6. It evidently contained the city in which they encountered Samuel, ver. 6, and that again was certainly not far from the "tomb of Rachel."

Zuph (zŭf), a Kohathite Levite, ancestor of Elkanah and Samuel. 1 Sam.

1:1; 1 Chron. 6:35. In 1 Chron. 6:26 he is called ZOPHAI.

Zur (zûr) (*a rock*). **1.** Father of Cozbi, Num. 25:15, and one of the five princes of Midian who were slain by the Israelites when Balaam fell. Num. 31:8. (B.C. 1451.)

2. Son of Jehiel, the founder of Gibeon. 1 Chron. 8:30; 9:36.

Zu'riel (zū'rĭ-el) (*my rock is God*), son of Abihail, and chief of the Merarite Levites at the time of the Exodus. Num. 3:35.

Zurishad'dai (zū-rĭ-shăd'da-ī) (*my rock is the Almighty*), father of Shelumiel, the chief of the tribe of Simeon at the time of the Exodus. Num. 1:6; 2:12; 7:36, 41; 10:19.

Zu'zim (zŭ'zim), **The**, an ancient people who, lying in the path of Chedorlaomer and his allies, were attacked and overthrown by them. Gen. 14:5. The Zuzim perhaps inhabited the country of the Ammonites, originally settled by the Zamzummim, who are known to have been exterminated and succeeded in their land by the Ammonites. [ZAMZUMMIM.]

APPENDIX.

APPENDIX.

APPENDIX.

TABLE OF CONTENTS.

APPENDIX.

THE CHRONOLOGY OF THE BIBLE.

There is the greatest possible uncertainty with regard to all of the early dates of the world's history, and it is impossible to determine the truth. The extremes are, in fact, from a reckoning by the Jews of the date of the Creation as 3760 B. C. to the generalization of some scientific schools that it may be millions of years in the past.

The dates found in the margins of our Bibles are at most points admirably accurate. They were reduced to system by Archbishop Ussher in 1650 A. D. and first added to the English Bible by Bishop Lloyd, in the great edition of 1701. "Its greatest fault is its attempt to reduce the history to millennial periods. Ussher believed that the earth was created just 4000 years before the birth of Jesus, and that Solomon's Temple was dedicated just 1000 years before the birth of Jesus, and he pulls some parts of the Chronology awry, to make it fit this theory. He regards the Biblical numbers for the times before Abraham as chronological, which, I think, is a mistake. * * * There are some matters of detail in which he lacked information that is now accessible."—*Prof. Willis K. Beecher,* in "Dated Events of the Old Testament."

The dates of Archbishop Ussher for this period are convenient for keeping the succession of events, but are not authoritative, as is agreed even by the most conservative scholars. They are only one of several possible arrangements. Opinions of chronologers as to the "era of Creation" vary indeed by many centuries.

The probabilities from geological facts, and the inferences from Egyptian and Babylonian civilization, place the date of the beginning of the human race hundreds, perhaps thousands, of years earlier. In fact, the question of date is very uncertain, and is insoluble at present.

See Article on "Chronology," page 118.

We have taken for the three principal authorities for our tables, Ussher, Beecher, and Hastings' *Bible Dictionary*, adding others from time to time.

Prof. John D. Davis, in his *Dictionary of the Bible* (Presbyterian), suggests that the names in the list of patriarchs in Genesis 5 may be understood as individuals, and their families spoken of collectively, and the longevity is the period during which the family had leadership, as Israel denotes the patriarch and his descendants. Thus the list would run thus: (1) Adam. Year 1. The family of Seth originated when Adam was 130 years old. Adam and his direct line were at the head of affairs 930 years when they were superseded by (2) Seth and his family, A. M. 930, who were at the head of affairs for 912 years; and so on through the list. Thus "the years from the Creation of Adam to the Flood would be 8225." But this may be greatly modified at different points.

Beecher has a similar idea of the reckoning of this period

I. CREATION OF MAN TO THE FLOOD.

Events in Scripture History.	Places.	Dates.		Other Historical Events.
		Ussher.		
THE CREATION. "In the Beginning."	....	4004	Various dates varying from **3760** to 5872 in regular chronology, besides those estimating much more.	First king of Egypt *before* 4500 B. C.
Adam and Eve created.............	Eden......	4004	....	First king of Babylon *before* 4500 B. C.
The Fall.......................	"	4004	5411	
Birth of Cain..................	Armenia (?).	....	....	First fixed date in history 4241.
Birth of Abel..................	"	....	....	
Murder of Abel.................	"	....	....	
Birth of Seth..................	"	3875	....	Sargon I, Babylon, 3800(?) [or 3400(?) or 2800(?)].
Death of Adam..................	"	3874	5181	
Translation of Enoch...........	"	3074	4481	Menes, beginning of dynasties, Egypt, 3400 or 3000.
Birth of Noah..................	"	3017	3914	
THE FLOOD......................	"	2948	3755	Chinese empire *before* 2270.
		2348	3155	Tyre built 2267.

II. FROM THE FLOOD TO THE EXODUS.

Events in Scripture History.	Places.	Dates.			Other Historical Events.
		Ussher.	Beecher.		
The Flood..................	Babylonia....	2348	....	....	Seventh ruler of China died 2257.
The confusion of tongues......	Babylonia....	2247	....	....	Hammurabi (Amraphel) and his code, contemporary with Abraham.
Death of Noah...............	Arabia.......	1998	....	....	
Birth of Abram at Ur........	Chaldea......	1996	(2003)	....	
First emigration, to Haran in ..	Mesopotamia .	1926	....	....	
The Call of Abram. Second migration to...............	Canaan	1921	1928	2250	Nineveh built 2218(?). Zoroaster 2115(?).
Abram in Egypt.............	Egypt........	1920	1927(?)		Celts in Europe about 2000.
Abram and Lot separate......	Canaan......	1918	1924		Hyksos in Egypt in time of Abraham, probably.
Lot's capture and escape......	Sodom.......	1913	1921		Dates vary from 2100–1675.
The Covenant with Abraham..	Hebron......	1912	1920		
Birth of Ishmael.............	"	1910	1917		
Renewal of Covenant. Change of Abram's name to Abraham	"	1897	1904		Sesostris I, Egypt, 1980–1935(?).
Destruction of Sodom.........	Sodom.......	1897	1904		
Birth of Isaac..............	Moab.......	1896	1903		
Ishmael sent away...........		1892	1901(?)		
Covenant with Abimelech....		1891	1900(?)		
Moab and Ammon born.......		1897	1899(?)		
Ishmael marries an Egyptian ..		....	1895(?)		
Sacrifice of Isaac.............	Moriah......	1871	1879		
Death of Sarah.............	Hebron......	1860	1866		
Abraham marries Keturah....		....	1865(?)		
Marriage of Isaac and Rebekah.	Lahai-roi....	1857	1864		Expulsion of Hyksos from Egypt about 1860(?).
Birth of Jacob and Esau......	Beersheba....	1837	1844		Others say 1820,
Death of Abraham...........	"	1822	1828(?)		Others say their rule began 1675.
Esau sells his birthright.......	Lahai-roi....	1804	1827(?)		They were expelled before the time of Joseph.
Isaac forbidden to enter Egypt goes to...................	Gerar........	1804	1826(?)		
Esau marries Hittite wives....		1796	1805		Thutmose III, Egypt, 1753 or 1501(?).
Jacob obtains birthright blessing	Beersheba..	1760	1784(?)		Rameses II, 1567–1500 or 1292–1225.
Jacob goes to Padan-aram....		1760	1784(?)		
Esau's Ishmaelite marriages...		1760	1783(?)		[The date of the Exodus depends both on which of these kings is considered the "Pharaoh of the Oppression," and their dates. Rameses II is usually considered that Pharaoh, with the later date. Beecher reconciles the history, giving Rameses the earlier date, but still making him the "Pharaoh of the Oppression."]
Death of Ishmael...........		1773	1781(?)		
Jacob marries Leah and Rachel.	Padan-aram ..	1753	1776(?)		
Birth of Jacob's children (except Benjamin)...............	" ..	1752–1739	1775–1752		
Jacob returns to Canaan......		1739	1747		
Jacob's name changed to Israel	Peniel........	1739	1747		
Birth of Benjamin and death of Rachel................	Bethlehem....	1729	1747		
Joseph sold into Egypt from...	Dothan.......	1718	1736		
Joseph put in prison.........	Egypt........	1718	1725		
Death of Isaac..............	Hebron......	1716	1724		
Joseph exalted..............	Egypt........	1716	1723		Cecrops founds Athens, 1556(?).
Jacob and his family move to Goshen....................	"	1706	1715		Corinth founded 1520(?).
Death of Jacob.............	"	1689	1698		Sparta founded 1516.
Death of Joseph............	"	1635	1643		Amenhotep II of Egypt, perhaps the Pharaoh of the Exodus(?).
Beginning of oppression of Israel	"	1573	1599(?)		
Birth of Moses.............	Arabia......	1571	1578		
Exile of Moses begins.........	"	1531	1539		Merneptah, perhaps the Pharaoh of Exodus.
Call of Moses. Burning bush..	"	1492	1499		Tel-el-Amarana letters, 1500–1450 (?).
Plagues of Egypt............	Egypt........	1492–1	1499–8	Various dates, from 1500 to 1200 B. C....	
The Exodus. In April......		1491	1498		

APPENDIX.

III. FROM THE EXODUS TO THE CONQUEST.
(For a discussion of the date of the Exodus, see article "Exodus.")

EVENTS IN SCRIPTURE HISTORY.	PLACES.	DATES.		
		Ussher.	Beecher.	
THE EXODUS in April		1491	1498	Varying dates.
The giving of the manna	Arabia	1491	1498	
The giving of the law	Mt. Sinai	1491	1498	
The golden calf	"	1491	1498	
The Tabernacle set up [March or April(?)]	"	1490	1497	
The ceremonial law given	"	1490	1497	
Wandering for 40 years in Desert of	Paran	1491–1451	1498–1459	
New start for Canaan from	Kadesh	1452	1459	
Death of Aaron on	Mt. Hor	1452	1459	
Brazen serpent	The Arabah	1452	1459	
Balaam's blessing	Moab	1452	1459	
Death of Moses	Nebo-Pisgah	1451	1459	
Passing over Jordan opposite	Jericho	1451	1458	
The Fall of Jericho	"	1451	1458	
Defeat at Ai	Near Jericho	1451	1458	
Law read from Ebal and Gerizim	Shechem	1451	1458	
Conquest of Canaan		1451–1443	1458–1449	
Cities of Refuge appointed		1444	1453	Josephus puts
Joshua renews the covenant	Shechem	1427	1451(?)	death of Joshua
Death of Joshua	Timnath-serah	1427	1450(?)	in 1434.

IV. THE PERIOD OF THE JUDGES.
(For an explanation of varying dates, see article "Judges." This table follows Beecher.)

EVENTS IN SCRIPTURE HISTORY.	PLACES.	DATES.		OTHER EVENTS.
		Ussher.	Beecher.	
Death of Joshua	Timnath-serah	1427	1450(?)	1406, Minos, Crete(?)
Oppression of Cushan-rishathaim, 8 years		1402–1394	1441–1434	1326, Isthmian games.
OTHNIEL, deliverer and judge	Near Hebron	1394–1354	till 1419	
Capture of Leshem—renamed Dan	No. Palestine	1406	1416(?)	
Oppression by Eglon of Moab, 18 years		1354–1336	1397–1380	
EHUD, of Benjamin deliverer	Near Jericho	1336	1380	
Oppression by Jabin of Canaan, 20 years	Northern tribes	1316–1296	1370–1351	
Oppression by Philistines (3 years)	Southern tribes		1353–1351	
DEBORAH of Ephraim delivers from Jabin	No. Palestine	1296	1351	
BARAK of Naphtali delivers from Jabin	"	1296	1351	
SHAMGAR of Judah delivers from Philistines	So. Palestine	1296	1351	Sidon's greatest power, 1300.
Oppression by Midianites, 7 years		1256–1249	1329–1323	1263, Argonauts(?)
GIDEON, deliverer and judge	So. Galilee	1249–1209	1323–1299	1263, Pythian games.
Ruth during this period(?)	Moab and Bethlehem	1322		1235, Theseus(?)
ABIMELECH, "Captain of Israel," 3 years	Shechem	1209–1206	1298–1296	Trojan war, 1193–1183.
TOLA, judge 23 years	Mt. Ephraim	1206–1183	1295–1273	
Oppression by Philistines begins			1283	
JAIR, judge 22 years	Gilead	1183–1161	1272–1251	
SAMSON, judge	So. West. Israel	1116–1096	1250–1231	
Oppression by Ammonites, 18 years	Eastern Israel	1161–1143	1230–1213	1152, Alba Longa.
JEPHTHAH, judge 6 years	Gilead, E. Israel	1143–1137	1212–1207	
IBZAN, judge 7 years	Bethlehem, E. Israel	1137–1130	1206–1200	
ELON, judge 10 years	Zebulun	1130–1120	1199–1190	
ABDON, judge 8 years	Ephraim	1120–1112	1189–1182	
Oppression by Philistines again			1182	
Ruth in this period(?)				
ELI, high priest, acts as judge	Western Israel	1154–1114	1182–1142	
Boaz marries Ruth at this time(?)	Bethlehem	1312	1173(?)	
Birth of Samuel	Ramah		1171(?)	
Bad conduct of Eli's sons	Shiloh		1168	
Call of Samuel		1141	1160(?)	
Ark captured by Philistines	Aphek	1141	1142	
Death of Eli	Shiloh	1141	1142	
Samuel, "influential citizen," not judge	Ramah		1141–1122	Dorian Migration, 1104(?)
SAMUEL, judge of Israel	"	1120–1095	1121–1103	Tiglath-Pileser I.
He was "judge," but not "chief magistrate" for the rest of his life, till	"	1060	1065(?)	Assyria, 1115–1105. Tyre first rank, 1100. Standard Chinese Dictionary, 1100.

49

V. THE UNITED KINGDOM.

EVENTS IN SCRIPTURE HISTORY.	PLACES.	DATES.				OTHER EVENTS.
		Ussher.	Beecher.	Standard B. D.	Jewish Cyclopedia	
Israel asks for a king.........	....	1095	1103(?)			Chow dynasty in China brings us to historic ground, 1123–255.
SAUL chosen and made king...	Gilgal..........	1095	1102			
Saul's victory over Ammon....	....	1095	1102			
Birth of David..............	Bethlehem......	1085	1092			
Saul's final rejection and break with Samuel..............	....	1079	1078(?)			
Private anointing of David....	Bethlehem......	1065	1077(?)			
David becomes Saul's minstrel	....	1063	1074(?)			
David and Goliath...........	Ephes-dammim..	1063	1073(?)			
David's marriage to Michal....	....	1062	1071(?)			
David's outlaw life, 7 years.....	....	1062–1055	1068–1063			
David spares Saul's life (skirt)	Engedi..........	1060	1066(?)			
Death of Samuel..............	Ramah....	1060	1065(?)			
David and Nabal.............	Carmel..........	1059	1065(?)			
The spear and the cruse incident	....	1058	1065(?)			
David among the Philistines...	Ziklag..........	1057	1064			
Death of Saul and Jonathan....	Gilboa..........	1056	1063			
DAVID becomes king in Judah..	Hebron.........	1056	1063	1010		Hiram, King of Tyre, contemporary of David and Solomon.
War between David and Ish-bosheth...................	....	1056–1048	1063–1056			
David king over all Israel.....	....	1048	1055	1003	1047	
Jerusalem becomes capital.						
Period of war.................	....	1048–1042	1055–1043			
Ark brought to Jerusalem......	....	1042	1042(?)			
The great promise to David....	Jerusalem......	1042	1041(?)			Homer thought by some to be contemporary with David.
Birth of Solomon.............	"	1033	1041(?)			
Preparation for building the temple...................	"	1023	1023			
Absalom's rebellion...........	....					
Solomon anointed and proclaimed..................	Jerusalem......	1015	1022			
Death of David...............	"	1015	1022			
SOLOMON becomes real king....	Jerusalem......	1015	1022	971	1017	Homer, 1000(?) Zoroaster, 1000(?)
Temple foundations laid......	"	1012	1019	967		
Temple dedicated.............	"	1004	1011	960		
Visit of Queen of Sheba to Solomon....................	"	995	995(?)			Shishak in Egypt.
Jeroboam flees to Shishak in Egypt....................	....	980	986(?)			
Death of Solomon............	Jerusalem......	975	983	931		

VI. THE DIVIDED KINGDOMS OF JUDAH AND ISRAEL.

JUDAH. Kings and Events.	Years of Reign.	Ussher.	Beecher.	Hastings B.D.	Jewish Cyclop.	Assyr. Eponym.	Years of Reign.	ISRAEL. Kings and Events.	CONTEMPORARY HISTORY.
REHOBOAM, 17 years.........	1	975	982	939	978	931	1	JEROBOAM I, 22 years.	Shishak monument.
Influx of Levites, etc., from Israel			980	936		930		Semi-idolatry established.	
Rehoboam forsakes Jehovah	3		978	934	960	927		Exodus of religious people to Judah.	
Invasion by Shishak.	5	957	965	922	958	914	3	Prophets: *Ahijah* and *Shemaiah.*	
ABIJAH, 3 years.........	17	955	962	919	956	911	5		
		954	961	918	955	910	18		
ASA, 41 years.........	1	953	960	917		909	20		
Land at rest 10 years			949				22		
Invasion by Zerah the Ethiopian...	3	941	948		932	898	1	NADAB, parts of 2 years.	
Great revival and reformation	14	941	947	894		897	2	BAASHA, 24 years.	
War with Israel.....	15		937	893	931		1	Civil war with Judah.	Moabite stone naming Omri
	16						12	ELAH. Parts of 2 years.	
	26	930				886	13	ZIMRI, 7 days.	
Decline.	27	929	936	882	920	885	14	OMRI, 12 years. Great enlargement of kingdom.	
	38	918	925	878	917	874	24		Shalmaneser II, Assyria.
JEHOSHAPHAT, 25 years.........	41	917	921	862	900	870	1	AHAB, 22 years. Marries Jezebel.	
Wide extended revival.			905	861	899	854	12	Idolatry introduced. *Elijah.*	Battle of Karkar, 854, Assyr.
Outward prosperity.	6	854	904	857	895	853		Religious persecution.	
Decline through alliance with Jezebel.	7	853	900	854	892	849	21	AHAZIAH. Co-regnant, 2 years.	
JEHORAM. Co-regnant, 4 years	1	893	897	850	888	846	22	JEHORAM, 12 years. *Elisha.*	
Alone, 4 years.........	4		893	849	887		2		
AHAZIAH. Part of one year...	5	885	893	843	881	842	5	Mesha of Moab revolts.	Black Obelisk, with name of Jehu.
ATHALIAH, 6 years.........	1	884	892		859	841	8		907 (?) Homer, Hesiod.
Murder of seed-royal.	2		886				12	JEHU, 28 years. Zealous reformer.	884 (?) Lycurgus.
Baal worship.								Destroys house of Ahab.	878 (?) } Carthage founded.
Temple desecrated.								Tributary to Assyria.	858 (?)
JOASH, 40 years.........	6	878	864	821	842	835	1	JEHOAHAZ, 17 years.	Sheshonk III, Egypt.
Temple and its worship restored	23	856	850	807		813	7		820 (?) Lycurgus, Sparta.
Zechariah, son of Jehoiada.	37	842	847			799	28	*Jehoash,* Co-regnant, 3 years. Hazael's expedition.	814 Macedonia founded.
AMAZIAH.........	40	840	846	803	840	795	1	JEHOASH, sole ruler 16 years,	
Defeat of Edom.	1	840					15		
							17		

VI. THE DIVIDED KINGDOMS OF JUDAH AND ISRAEL. (Continued.)

JUDAH. Kings and Events.	Years of Reign.	Usher.	Beecher.	Hastings B.D.	Jewish Cyclop.	Assyr. Eponym.	Years of Reign.	ISRAEL. Kings and Events.	CONTEMPORARY HISTORY.
Conquest by Jehoash of Israel. Nominal ruler under suzerainty of Israel......	14 15		833 832				15	Victories over Damascus.	814 (?) Carthage founded.
Death of Amaziah......... INTERREGNUM for 11 years....	1 11 1	825	818	804	825	782	16 15	Conquest of Judah. JEROBOAM II, 41 years.	797. Damascus taken by Assyrians.
UZZIAH, 52 years.... Also called Azariah. Amos.	15 16	811	806	801	811	767	27	Suzerain of all peoples from Mediterranean to Euphrates. Jonah(?) Amos(?) Hosea(?)	Blank in Assyrian history. Confusion in Egyptian.
Succeeds Jeroboam as suzerain of region.... Isaiah. Leprosy of Uzziah (?).... Jotham regent 23 years....	38 39 40 1	773 772 772	791 769 768 767	763 763 762	773 773 772 772	741 741 741	4 1 22 1	Death of Jeroboam. INTERREGNUM, 22 years. ZECHARIAH, 6 months. SHALLUM, 1 month. MENAHEM, 10 years. Hosea(?)	First Olympiad, 776 B. C. The Jewish Cyclopedia gives 2 reigns of Jeroboam II, 825-799 and 788-773: Israel being under Syria 799 to 788. Rome founded 753. Draco.
Eclipse of sun by which Assyrian dates are determined. June 15, 763 B.C........	44	761 759	763 758 755	763 752 750	761 759 758	738 737 736	5 10	PEKAHIAH, 2 years. PEKAH, 20 years.	Expedition of Pul or Tiglath-pileser of Assyria, captures Damascus and Samaria. 733(?)
JOTHAM sole king 16 years....	49 52	742	754 740 739 738	749		735	1 2 16 17 18	Invasion of Judah.	The Jewish Cycl. gives 2 reigns for Pekah, 759-744, and 735-730. Time between Israel under Menahem II, under Assyria.
Invasion by Israel and Rezin of Damascus........ AHAZ, 16 years........	1	742	736	741	742 734	734	20	Deportation by Tiglath-pileser. Death of Pekah. Hoshea, governor.	
Tributary to Assyria.......... Micah.	23 1 15 16						1	HOSHEA, king 9 years.	Taylor Cylinder.
HEZEKIAH, 29 years.... Great Passover........	1 2 4	730 726	726 723 722 720	730 727 722 721	730 727 Jan. 721	734 722	4 5 7 9	First siege and capture of Samaria. { Final FALL OF SAMARIA. { End of Kingdom of Israel.	Year in Rome begun with January, 713. Sargon I, Assyria, 722. Sennacherib, Assyria, 705.
First invasion of Sennacherib, Hezekiah's sickness. Second invasion of Sennacherib MANASSEH, 55 years....	6 14 23 29	697	710 701 694	698	698			First Mikado in Japan, 660-585	Esarhaddon, Assyria, 681.

Event	Yr.			Authorities are practically agreed on these dates.
Death of Isaiah(?)	1	679	....	
Manasseh carried to Babylon(?)	16	648	....	
Manasseh's return and reformation	47			
Nahum.	48	647	....	
Amon, 2 years	55	642	642	642
Josiah, 31 years	1	640	640	640
Zephaniah				
Josiah begins reforms	12	639	....	
Jeremiah begins prophesying	13	638	....	
Josiah's great reformation } Reformation passover	17	627 626 622	....	
Jehoahaz, 3 months	31	608	600	
Jehoiakim, 11 years	1	607	609	609
First captivity begins. First deportation	1	605	606	
Habakkuk. Second deportation	3 / 10	598	598	
Jehoiachin, 3 months	11	597	598	
The great deportation				
Zedekiah, 11 years	1	597	588	
Ezekiel. Siege of Jerusalem	1 / 9	588		
Destruction of Jerusalem and the Temple	11	586	586	
Beginning of great captivity	11	586	586	

Contemporary history:

Second Messenian war, 685–668.
Byzantium founded, 659.
Scythian invasion.
Draco's legislation, 624 [621?]
"Buddha," India, 623–543.
Public beginning, July, 594.
Phenicians circumnavigate Africa, 604.
Solon's legislation, 594.
Seven wise men in Greece, 593.
Pythian games begin, 588.

Median Empire independent, 640.
Expedition of Pharaoh Necho, 608.
Destruction of Nineveh, 606.
Nebuchadnezzar, 604.
Carchemish, 603.
Daniel in exile, 605.
Expounds King's dream, 603.

APPENDIX.

VII. THE CAPTIVITY AND RETURN.

JEWISH EVENTS.	Ussher.	Beecher.	Hastings	CONTEMPORARY HISTORY.
First captivity	606	605	......	
Final captivity	586	586	586	
The golden idol	580	......	......	Nebuchadnezzar besieges Tyre, 585.
Last of Ezekiel's prophecies	571	......	......	Æsop.
Jehoiachin released	......	561	......	Evil Merodach, Babylon, 562.
				Temple of Diana, Ephesus, 552.
				Public library at Athens, 544.
Belshazzar's feast	538	539	......	Babylon taken by Cyrus, 539.
Daniel in den of lions	538	538	......	First year of Cyrus, 538.
The decree for the return	536	538	538	Pythagoras, 540–510.
End of first reckoning of 70 years				
First return. 50,000 under ZERUBBABEL	......	538	538–7	Pisistratus, Athens, 560–527.
Foundation of Temple laid	......	537–6	536	Nabonidus, Babylon, 556.
Haggai. Long delay	......	......	......	Darius in Babylon, 521.
Zechariah. Building of Temple resumed	......	520	520	
TEMPLE DEDICATED	516	516	516	Beginning of Roman republic, 510.
End of second reckoning of 70 years				Marathon, 490.
No knowledge of events until	......	......	......	Xerxes (Ahasuerus), 489.
Feast of Ahasuerus (Xerxes)	......	483	......	Invasion of Greece, 480.
Esther becomes queen	......	479	......	Herodotus, Socrates.
Haman's plot	......	474	......	Xenophon, Plato.
Second return under EZRA	......	458	458	First decemvirate, Rome, 451.
Return under NEHEMIAH	......	......	......	Pericles, Athens, 444.
Wall of Jerusalem rebuilt	......	444	445	Parthenon, Athens, 443–438.
Malachi. Reforms	......	......	......	First Peloponnesian war, 431.
Death of Nehemiah. After	......	391	......	Xenophon's retreat, 401.

NOTE.—It will perhaps be easier to understand the double reckoning of the 70 years' captivity by the following diagram showing how it is reckoned as beginning at different points, and closing at equi-different points.

First captivity, 606–605.   70 years.   First return, 536.

Final captivity, 586.   70 years.   Temple completed, 516.
Destruction of Temple.

VIII. PERIOD BETWEEN THE TESTAMENTS.

B. C.	JEWISH HISTORY.	CONTEMPORARY HISTORY.	B. C.	JEWISH HISTORY.	CONTEMPORARY HISTORY.
350	Jaddua, High Priest	Egypt a Persian Province.	149	....	Third Punic War: Rome.
359	....	Philip II of Macedon.	146	....	Greece a Roman Province.
336	....	Darius Codomannus, king of Persia.	141	Deliverance of Judea complete.	
		Alexander the Great.	109	Pharisees and Sadducees first mentioned.	
332	Alexander visits Jerusalem.	Alexandria in Egypt founded.	107	Aristobulus "king."	
331	Jews settle in Alexandria.	Battle of Arbela.	63	Pompey captures Jerusalem.	Judea annexed to Rome. Conspiracy of Catiline.
330	Onias I, High Priest.	End of Persian Empire.	58	Herod in Palestine.	Cæsar in Gaul.
320	Ptolemy takes Jerusalem.	Ptolemy I, Soter.	54	Crassus plunders Temple.	
312	Seleucidæ in Syria.	Seleucus I, Nicator.	48	....	Battle of Pharsalia.
301	Palestine under Egypt	Battle of Ipsus.	47	Antipater procurator. Herod governor of Galilee.	Cæsar dictator at Rome.
284	Septuagint.				
264	....	First Punic War: Rome.	44	....	Cæsar assassinated.
261	....	Manetho, in Egypt.	40	Herod king of Judea.	
219	Beginning of War of Antiochus and Ptolemy.	Second Punic War: Rome.	37	Herod takes Jerusalem.	
198	Antiochus the Great master of Palestine		31	Earthquake in Judea.	BATTLE OF ACTIUM. Egypt a Roman Province.
170	Tyranny of Antiochus Epiphanes.		30	....	Temple of Janus closed.
			29	....	Augustus made Emperor.
167	Revolt of Maccabees.		27	....	
166	Judas Maccabeus.		19	Herod begins rebuilding the Temple.	
165	Rededication of Temple.		4	Herod dies at Jericho	

APPENDIX.

IX. THE NEW TESTAMENT PERIOD.

(For fuller details see Harmony of the Life of Christ, and Chronology of Acts.)

	CHRISTIAN HISTORY.	CONTEMPORARY HISTORY.
Dec. B. C. 5	Birth of Christ.	Death of Herod the Great.
A. D. 30	Crucifixion.	Augustus Cæsar, 30 B. C. to 19th August A. D. 14.
		Tiberius emp. 14 A. D.–16th March A. D. 37.
" 30	Pentecost.	Pont.us Pilate, 26 A. D.–early A. D. 36.
" 36	Conversion of Pau .	Caligula emp. 16th March 37–24th January 41.
" 44	Death of Herod.	Herod Agrippa I made king, A. D. 37.
" 47	1st Missionary Journey.	Claudius emp. 24 January 41–13th October 54.
" 49	Council at Jerusalem.	
" 49	2d Missionary Journey.	
" 52	3d Missionary Journey.	Nero emp. 13th October 54–9th June 68.
" 60	Paul at Rome.	
" 62	Close of the Acts.	Burning of Rome 19th July 64.
" 66	Martyrdom of Paul.	Outbreak of Jewish War, 66.
		Galba, Otho, and Vitellius, emps. 9th June, 68–20th December 69.
" 70	Destruction of Jerusalem.	Vespasian emp. 1st July 69.

DATE OF THE BIRTH OF CHRIST.

Many people are greatly perplexed by the statement that Jesus was born four years before the time from which we count his birth; or, as we generally express it, "four years before Christ, *i. e.*, December 25, B.C. 5. The reason is simple. No one began to reckon dates generally from the birth of Christ till centuries had passed. The general method was from the founding of Rome (A.U.C.) and not till after Rome ceased to be the mistress of the world would people begin to think seriously of a change. Finally, in A.D. 526, a monk, Dionysius Exiguus, made the calculations, but made an error of four years. He placed the birth of Christ in the year of Rome 754. But Herod the Great, who slew the innocents of Bethlehem, died in April of the year of Rome 750; so that Jesus must have been born several months before. The date, December 25th, is generally accepted, but we cannot be sure of that. It is quite certain, however, that Jesus must have been born at the very end of B.C. 5, which is practically four years before our era (one week from December 25, B.C. 5, would be January 1, B.C. 4). Since it is manifestly impossible to rectify the dates in all books and records throughout the world, we simply apply the true dates to the life of Christ, and say he was five years old at the close of A.D. I.
The following table may aid in making the matter clear.

Year of Rome (*Anno Urbis Conditæ* = A.U.C.)	749	750	751	752	753	754	755	756
Year of Our Lord (*Anno Domini* = A.D.)..	B.C. 5	B.C. 4	B.C. 3	B.C. 2	B.C. 1	A.D. 1	A.D. 2	A.D. 3
Age of Jesus.........................	birth	1st year	2d year	3d year	4th year	5th year	6th year	7th year

HARMONY OF THE LIFE OF CHRIST.

John the Baptist	Period	Outline	Events	Place	Date	Matt.	Mark.	Luke.	John.
		INTRODUCTION.	Pre-existence						1:1-14
			Genealogies			1:1-17		3:23-28	
B.C. 5. *Childhood and Youth*	PREPARATIONS.	CHILDHOOD. B.C. 4 to A.D. 26 AND YOUTH.	Birth of John the Baptist foretold	Jerusalem	Sept., B.C. 6			1:5-23	
			Annunciation to Mary	Nazareth	Mar., B.C. 5			1:26-38	
			Birth of John the Baptist	Judea	June, B.C. 5			1:57-80	
			Birth of Jesus	Bethlehem	Dec. 25, B.C. 5	1:18-25		2: 1-20	
			Presentation in the Temple at	Jerusalem	Feb. 2, B.C. 4			2:22-39	
			Visit of the Magi	Bethlehem	Early Feb., B.C. 4	2: 1-12			
			Flight into Egypt		Feb., B.C. 4	2:13-23			
			Childhood and youth	Nazareth	B.C. 2-A.D. 26	2:23		2:39, 40 51, 52 2:41-50	
			First passover he attended	Jerusalem	April, A.D. 8			2: 1-18	
A.D. 27. Summer.		PREPARATIONS. A.D. 26-27.	Ministry of John the Baptist	Wilderness of Judea	Summer, A.D. 26 to Mar. A.D. 28	3: 1-12	1: 1-8	3: 1-18	1:19-28
			Baptism of Jesus	Jordan	Jan. A.D. 27	3:13-17	1: 9-11	3:21-23	1:29-34
			Temptation of Jesus	Wilderness of Judea	Jan–Feb, A.D. 27	4: 1-11	1:12, 13	4: 1-13	
PUBLIC MINISTRY OF JOHN	JUDEAN MINISTRY. (About one year.) Feb. ... Dec.	FIRST YEAR OF JESUS' MINISTRY A.D. 27.	First disciples won	Bethabara	A.D. 27. February				1:35-51
			First miracle: Wedding at Cana	Cana	"				2: 1-12
			First cleansing of the Temple	Jerusalem	April 11-17				2:13-25
			First recorded discourse: Nicodemus	Judea	"				3: 1-21
			First ministry in Judea	Judea	Summer and Autumn				3:22-36
			First converts in Samaria: Jacob's Well	Sychar	December				4: 1-42
			Healing of the nobleman's son	Capernaum					4:43-54
	April A.D. 28.	YEAR OF BEGINNINGS.	Passover		A.D. 28. March or April				5: 1
Imprisoned, March A.D. 28.			Imprisonment of John the Baptist	Macherus	March	14: 3-5	6:17-18	3:19-20	
			Beginning of Great Galilean Ministry	Galilee	April	4:12	1:14, 15	4:14, 15	
			[First (?) rejection at Nazareth]	Nazareth	April			4:16-30	
			Takes up residence at Capernaum	Capernaum		4:13-17		4:31	
		SECOND YEAR.	Calls first disciples to follow him	Capernaum	April, May	4:18-22	1:16-20	5: 1-11	
			Cure of demoniac in Synagogue	Capernaum			1:21-28	4:31-37	
			Many miracles of healing	Capernaum and Galilee	April and May	4:23-25; 8:14-17	1:29-39	4:38-44	
			Cure of a leper	Galilee	May	8: 2-4	1 40-45	5:12-16	
			Healing a paralytic	Capernaum	May, June	9: 2-8	2: 1-12	5:17-26	
			Call of Matthew: His feast	Capernaum		9: 9-17	2:13-22	5:27-39	
			Healing at Pool of Bethesda	Jerusalem					5: 2-47
			Discourse on the Sabbath: Man with withered hand	Capernaum	Midsummer	12: 1-14	2:23-3:6	6: 1-11	
			Appointing of the twelve Apostles	Horns of Hattin		10: 2-4	3:13-19	6:12-19	

Period	Event	Place	Time	Matt.	Mark	Luke	John
A.D. 28.	The Sermon on the Mount.	Horns of Hattin	Midsummer	Chaps. 5-7		6:20-49	
	Healing of the Centurion's servant.	Capernaum	"	8: 5-13		7: 1-10	
	Raising of the widow's son.	Nain	"			7:11-17	
	John the Baptist sends messengers to Jesus	Galilee	"	11: 2-19		7:18-35	
	Warnings and Invitations			11:20-30			
	(Perhaps at beginning of Perean Ministry.)						
Years of Fundamental Principles.	Anointing of Jesus by the penitent woman	Galilee	Autumn			7:36-50	
	Another tour of Galilee.					8: 1-3	
	Blind and dumb demoniac.	Capernaum	"	12:22-45		11:14-36	
	Visit of his mother and brethren.	"	"	12:46-50		8:19-21	
	Eight parables by the seaside.		"	13: 1-53		8: 4-18	
	Stilling of the tempest.	Sea of Galilee	"	8:18-27		8:22-25	
	Restoration of the demoniac.	Gergesa	"	8:28-34		8:26-39	
	Jairus' daughter raised: Woman cured	Capernaum	"	9:18-26		8:40-56	
	Cure of two blind and one dumb.	"	"	9:27-34			
Third Year.	Second (?) rejection at Nazareth.	Nazareth.	Winter.	13:53-58	6: 1-6	(4:16-30)	
	The twelve sent out to preach.	Galilee.	"	9:35-11:1	6: 6-13	9: 1-6	
	Death of John the Baptist.	Macherus	March.	14: 1-12	6:14-29	9: 7-9	
	Feeding of the 5,000.	Bethsaida	April.	14:13-21	6:30-46	9:10-17	6: 1-15
	Jesus walks on the water.	Sea of Galilee	"	14:22-33	6:47-52		6:16-21
	Heals many sick.	Gennesaret.	"	14:34, 35	6:53-56		
	Discourse on the Bread of Life.	Capernaum	"				6:22-71
A.D. 29.	Eating with unwashed hands.	"	A.D. 29. Winter.	15: 1-20	7: 1-23		
	Heals daughter of Syrophenician woman.	Region of Tyre and Sidon	Summer.	15:21-28	7:24-30		
	Miracles of healing in Decapolis.	Decapolis.	"	15:29-31	7:31-37		
	Feeding the 4,000.	Capernaum and Sea of Galilee	"	15:32-39	8: 1-10		
	Demand for a sign from heaven, and the warning.	Bethsaida.	"	16: 1-12	8:11-21		
	Blind man healed.	Near Cæsarea-Philippi.	"		8:22-26		
	Peter's great confession of faith.		"	16:13-20	8:27-30		
Year of Development.	Jesus for the first time foretells his death and resurrection.		"	16:21-28	8:31-9:1	9:18-21	
	The Transfiguration.		"	17: 1-13	9: 2-13	9:22-27	
	Healing of the demoniac boy.		"	17:14-21	9:14-29	9:28-36	
	Jesus again foretells his death.	Galilee.	"	17:22, 23	9:30-32	9:37-43	
	Jesus and the children.	Capernaum.	"	18: 1-14	9:33-50	9:43-45	
	Discourse and parable on forgiving: "The Unmerciful Servant".	"	"	18:15-35		9:46-50	
Great Deeds amid Great Opposition.	At the Feast of Tabernacles.	Jerusalem.	Autumn, Oct. 11-18.				7:1-10:21
	Discourses and discussion.	"	"				7:10-36
	The water of life.	"	"				7:37-39
	Is not this the Christ?	"	"				7:40-43
	Officers sent to arrest him.	"	"				7:44-53
	(The adulteress.)	"	"				8: 1-11
	Discourse on light and freedom.	"	"				8:12-59
	Healing of man born blind.	"	"				9: 1-39
	The Good Shepherd.	"	"				10: 1-21
	Returns to Galilee.		Autumn.				
	Final departure from Galilee.		Nov.-Dec.	19:1	10:1	9:51	

The Great Galilean Ministry (one year and nine months).

Martyred. Mar., A.D. 29

HARMONY OF THE LIFE OF CHRIST—Continued.

JOHN THE BAPTIST	PERIOD	OUTLINE	EVENTS	PLACE	DATE	MATT.	MARK.	LUKE.	JOHN.
	Dec. A.D. 29.		Repulse by the Samaritans	Samaria	Nov.-Dec.			9:51-62	
			The mission of the Seventy	Perea	"			10:1-24	
			Parable of the Good Samaritan	"	"			10:25-37	
			Discourse on prayer	"	"			11:1-13	
			Answers attacks of Pharisees	"	"			11:14-54	
	PEREAN MINISTRY (four or five months).		Discourses on great moral truths; The Rich Fool; the Watchful Servant, etc.	"	"			12:1-59	
			Discourses: Galileans slain by Pilate; healing on Sabbath; Parables of mustard seed and leaven; the strait gate; lament over Jerusalem	"	"			13:1-35	
			Jesus the guest of Mary and Martha	Bethany				10:38-42	
			Feast of Dedication. Discourses	Jerusalem	Dec. 20-27				10:22-39
		A.D. 30.	Jesus retires beyond Jordan	Perea	January				10:40-42
			Dines with a Pharisee	"	"			14:1-14	
			Parable of the Great Supper	"	"			14:15-24	
			Counting the cost of discipleship	"	"			14:25-35	
			Parables of lost sheep and lost coin	"	"			15:1-10	
		THREE MONTHS.	Parable of prodigal son	"	"			15:11-32	
			Parable of the unjust steward	"	"			16:1-13	
			Parable of the rich man and Lazarus	"	"			16:14-31	
			Teachings on forgiveness	"	"			17:1-10	
			Raising of Lazarus	Bethany	February				11:1-46
			Retreat to Ephraim	Ephraim	Feb., March				11:47-57
			The healing of the ten lepers	Borders of Samaria	March			17:11-19	
			On the coming of the kingdom	Perea	"			17:20-37	
		CULMINATION OF MIRACLES AND TEACHING.	Parable of the importunate widow	"	"			18:1-8	
			Parable of the Pharisee and publican	"	"			18:9-14	
			Discourse about divorce	"	"	19:2-12	10:2-12		
			Christ blesses little children	"	"	19:13-15	10:13-16	18:15-17	
			The rich young man	"	"	19:16-30	10:17-31	18:18-30	
			The laborers in the vineyard	"	"	20:1-16			
	March, A.D. 30.		Jesus again predicts his death	"	"	20:17-19	10:32-34	18:31-34	
			Ambitious request of James and John	"	"	20:20-28	10:35-45		
			Healing two blind men (one being Bartimeus)	Jericho	"	20:29-34	10:46-52	18:35-43	
			Visit to Zaccheus the publican	"	"			19:1-10	
			Parable of the pounds (Minæ)	"	"			19:11-28	
	Friday, Mar. 31.		Jesus arrives at Bethany	Bethany	Friday, March 31				12:1
			Anointing by Mary	Bethany	Sat., April 1	26:6-13	14:3-9		12:2-11
			Triumphal Entry. Visit to Temple. Return to Bethany	Jerusalem	Sun., April 2	21:1-11	11:1-11	19:29-44	12:12-19

Jerusalem and Vicinity. — **THE LAST WEEK.**

Section	Event	Place	Time	Matt.	Mark	Luke	John
	Cursing of barren fig tree	Mt. of Olives	Mon, April 3	21:18,19	11:12-14	......	......
	Cleansing of the Temple and return to Bethany	Jerusalem	Mon, April 3	21:12-17	11:15-19	19:45-48	12:37,38
LAST DAY OF PUBLIC TEACHING.	The fig tree withered. Lesson on faith	Mt. of Olives	Tues, April 4	21:20-22	11:20-26	......	......
	Christ's authority challenged	Temple at Jerusalem	"	21:23-27	11:27-33	20: 1-8	......
	Three parables of warning:						
	The two sons			21:28-32	......	......	......
	The wicked husbandmen			21:33-46	12: 1-12	20: 9-19	......
	Marriage of king's son			22: 1-14	......	......	......
	Three questions by Jewish rulers:						
	Tribute to Cæsar			22:15-22	12:13-17	20:20-26	......
	About the resurrection			22:23-33	12:18-27	20:27-40	......
	The great commandment			22:34-40	12:28-34	......	......
	Christ's unanswerable question: "What think ye of Christ?"			22:41-46	12:35-37	20:41-44	......
	Woes against Scribes and Pharisees			23: 1-36	12:38-40	20:45-47	......
	Lamentation over Jerusalem			23:37-39	......	......	......
	The widow's two mites	Jerusalem		......	12:41-44	21: 1-4	......
	Greeks seeking Jesus	Jerusalem		......	......	......	12:20-50
	Prophecy of the destruction of Jerusalem and the end of the world	Mt. of Olives		24: 1-51	13: 1-37	21: 5-36	......
	Parable of the ten virgins	"		25: 1-13	......	......	......
	Parable of the talents	"		25:14-30	......	......	......
	The last judgment	"		25:31-46	......	......	......
	Conspiracy between rulers and Judas	Jerusalem		26: 1-5, 14-16	14: 1,2, 10-11	22: 1-6	......
THE LAST DAY WITH THE DISCIPLES. A.D. 30.	Jesus in retirement	Bethany	Wed, April 5	......	......	......	......
	Preparation for the Passover	Jerusalem	Thurs, April 6	26:17-19	14:12-16	22: 7-13	......
	Arrival at the upper room	"	"	26:20	14:17	22:14	......
	Strife for precedence	"	"	......	......	22:24-30	......
	Jesus washes the disciples' feet	"	"	......	......	......	13: 1-20
	The last supper	"	"	......	......	22:15-18	......
	Jesus declares the betrayer. Judas goes out	"	"	26:21-25	14:18-21	22:21-23	13:21-35
	Institution of the Lord's Supper	"	"	26:26-30	14:22-25	22:19-20	(1 Cor. 11: 23-25)
	Jesus foretells the fall of Peter	"	"	26:30-35	14:26-31	22:31-38	13:36-38
	Christ's farewell discourses	"	"	......	......	......	Chaps. 14-16
	Prayer of Jesus for the disciples	"	"	......	......	......	17: 1-26
	Jesus goes forth. Peter's confidence	"	"	......	......	22:39	18: 1-3
	The agony in the Garden of Gethsemane	Mt. of Olives	"	26:36-46	14:32-42	22:40-46	......
	Betrayal by Judas	"	"	26:47,48	14:43-45	22:47,48	18: 4-9
	The arrest	"	Midnigh.	26:50-56	14:46-52	22:49-53	18:10-12
THE JEWISH TRIAL.	The trial before the Jewish authorities:	Jerusalem	Friday, April 7 1-5 A. M.				
	Annas and then Caiaphas	"	"	......	......	22:54,55	18:13-15
	Before Caiaphas	"	"	26:57,58	14:53,54	......	18:19-24
	Before the Sanhedrin			26:59-66	14:55-64	......	......

HARMONY OF THE LIFE OF CHRIST—Continued.

PERIOD	OUTLINE	EVENTS	PLACE	DATE	MATT.	MARK.	LUKE.	JOHN.
THE LAST WEEK.	THE JEWISH TRIAL.	Denials by Peter.	Jerusalem	(A.D. 30, Friday, April 7.) 1-3 A. M.	26:69-75	14:66-72	22:56-62	18:15-18, 25-27
		Mockery by enemies.	"	"	26:67, 68	14:65	22:63-65	
		Legal meeting of Sanhedrin; Jesus condemned for blasphemy.	"	5-6 A. M.	27:1, 2	15:1	22:66-71; 23:1 (Acts 1:18, 19)	
		Death of Judas.	"		27:3-10			
	THE ROMAN TRIAL.	Jesus before Pilate.	"	"	27:11-14	15:2-5	23:2-5	18:28-38
		Jesus sent to Herod.	"	"			23:6-12	
		Pilate seeks to release Jesus; people demand Barabbas.	"	"	27:15-23	15:6-14	23:13-23	18:38-40
		Jesus condemned, scourged and mocked by soldiers. "Ecce Homo." Other attempts by Pilate to release Jesus.	"	"	27:26-30	15:15-19	23:24, 25	19:1-3
		Jesus led away to be crucified.	"	9 A. M.	27:24, 25 27:31-34, 38	15:20, 23, 25, 27, 28	23:26-32	19:4-16 19:16-18
	THE CRUCIFIXION.	The superscription.	"		27:37	15:26	23:38	19:19-22
		First word from the cross: "Father, forgive them," etc.	"				23:33, 34	
		Soldiers cast lots for garments.	"		27:35, 36	15:24	23:34	19:23, 24
		Jews mock at Jesus on the cross.	"		27:39-44	15:29-32	23:35-37	
		Second word from the cross: to the penitent thief.	"				23:39-43	
		Third word: "Woman, behold thy son."	"	12 M.				19:25-27
		Darkness covers the land.	"		27:45	15:33	23:44, 45	
		Fourth word: cry of distress to God	"		27:46, 47	15:34, 35		19:28, 29
		Fifth word: "I thirst"	"		27:48, 49	15:36		19:30
Friday, Apr. 7.		Sixth word: "It is finished"	"					19:30
		Seventh word: "Into thy hands," etc.	"	3 P. M.	27:50-56	15:37-41	23:46 23:45-49	19:31-37
		Jesus dies. Veil rent. Earthquake.	"					
		Jesus is pierced in the side.	"					
		The burial.	"	3-6 P. M.	27:57-61	15:42-47	23:50-56	19:38-42
DAYS.		The watch at the tomb.	"	Sat., April 8.	27:62-66			
	THE RESURRECTION.	The morning of the resurrection.	"	Sunday, April 9.	28:2-4	16:1-4	24:1, 2	20:1
		Women come to tomb.	"	"	28:1			20:2
		Mary Magdalene calls Peter and John.	"	"				20:3-10
		The women at the tomb.	"	"	28:5-8	16:5-8	24:3-8	
		Peter and John at the tomb.	"	"			24:12	20:3-10
		Jesus appears to Mary Magdalene.	"	"		16:9-11		20:11-18
		Jesus appears to the women.	"	"	28:9, 10		24:9-11	
		The guards report to the priests.	"	"	28:11-15			
		The walk to Emmaus.	"	"		16:12, 13	24:13-35	
		Jesus appears to Peter.	Jerusalem	"	(1Cor.15:5)		24:34	

	Event	Place	Date				
RESURRECTION				(1Cor.15:5)	16:14	24:36-48	20:19-23
THE GREAT FORTY DAYS.	Jesus appears to the Apostles except Thomas	Jerusalem	Sunday, April 9	(1Cor.15:5)	16:14	24:36-48	20:19-23
	Jesus appears to all the Apostles, including Thomas	Jerusalem	Sunday, April 16				20:24-29
	Jesus appears to seven in Galilee	Sea of Galilee	April				21: 1-23
	Appears to over 500 at once	"	April, May	28:16-20	16:15-18	(1Cor.15:6)	
	Jesus appears to James					(1Cor.15:7)	Acts 1:1-18
	Jesus appears to the Apostles	Jerusalem				24:49	Acts 1.9-12
THE ASCENSION	The Ascension	Bethany	Thurs., May 18		16:19	24:50-53	20:30, 31; 21:24, 25
	The conclusions of Mark and John				16:20		21:24, 25
PROOFS OF CONTINUED LIFE.	Holy Spirit given at Pentecost	Jerusalem	Sunday, May 28			Acts 2:1-11	
	Jesus appears to Paul	Damascus	A.D. 36			(Acts 22:6-16)	
	Jesus appears to John	Patmos	A.D. 68 or 96				(Rev. 1:9-20)

APPENDIX.

CHART OF THE LIFE OF JESUS CHRIST.

Life of Jesus

ANCESTRY. On one side God himself. On the other every phase of character, every human tendency represented in his genealogy.

PREPARATIONS FOR HIS COMING.

1. Universal peace.
2. One empire.
3. One language generally known.
4. The Jews with the Scriptures in all lands.
5. A general awakening.

Birth of Jesus about December, B.C.5.

CHILDHOOD AND YOUTH.

1. Home training.
2. Bible study.
3. Schooling.
4. Different languages.
5. Travel to Jerusalem.
6. Great religious meetings.
7. Village life.
8. Work at a trade.
9. Knowledge of his country's history and hopes.
10. A perfect and beautiful character.

PREPARATIONS FOR HIS MINISTRY.

1. John the Baptist.
2. Baptism.
3. The Holy Spirit.
4. The Voice from God.
5. Temptation.

JOHN'S MINISTRY OF PREPARATION began six months before Jesus began to preach, continued through the first year and three months into the second year.

First Year.—Year of Beginnings.

1. First disciples.
2. First miracle.
3. First reform.
4. First discourse.
5. First tour.
6. First Samaritan disciple.
7. Healing of the nobleman's son.

Second Year.—Year of Principles.

A. Imprisonment of John the Baptist, March.

1. The pool of Bethesda.
2. Organization. Choosing apostles.
3. Sermon on the Mount.
4. Miracles proving his authority and illustrating his work.
5. Forgiveness of sins.
6. Seeking the lost.
7. Life from the dead.
8. The light of the world.
9. Warnings and invitations.
10. Parables.

The year in which Jesus laid down and worked out many of the fundamental principles and truths of his kingdom.

Third Year.—Year of Development.

B. The Death of John the Baptist in March.

1. Feeding the five thousand.
2. Miracles: The dropsical man, the ten lepers, blind Bartimeus.
3. The transfiguration.
4. At the Feast of Tabernacles.
5. Discourses in the Temple.
6. Healing of one born blind.
7. The good shepherd.
8. Parables: The great supper, the lost sheep, the lost coin, the prodigal son, the unjust steward, the rich man and Lazarus, the pounds.

Last Three Months.

Raising of Lazarus.
Miracles.
Parables.
Instructions.
Children.
Zaccheus.

Last Week.

Triumphal entry.
Cleansing the Temple.
Last great day of public teaching.
Instructions of his disciples.
The Lord's Supper.
The trial. The crucifixion. The burial.

Resurrection Days.

Forty days. Eleven appearances, between April 9 and May 18, A.D. 30.
The Ascension, Thursday, May 18, from Mount of Olives.

The Ever-Living Saviour.

Return through the Holy Spirit. A Saviour in heaven. Ever abiding with his people. Coming again in his kingdom, a universal king; the world redeemed.

Chart labels: John — Birth — Jesus — Birth — Divine origin — Human ancestry — Childhood of Jesus — youth — childhood — AD 26 summer — First AD 27 Year — JUDEA — Year of — Ministry of John — Beginnings — Second Year — GALILEE — Year of — A.D. 28 — Principles — Third Year — GALILEE — Increasing opposition — Year of — A.D. 29 — Development — Perean Ministry, 4 to 5 months — Perea — Last Three Months — Jan. Feb. March. AD 30 — Last Week — Sat. Apr.1 — Sun. Apr.2 — Mon. Apr.3 — Tue. Apr.4 — Wed. Apr.5 — Thur. Apr.6 — Fri. Apr.7 — Sat. Apr.8 — Anointed at Bethany — Triumphal Entry — Cleansing Temple — Great Day of Teaching — Rest at Bethany — Passover Lord's Supper — Trial Crucifixion Burial — In the Tomb — The Crucifixion — April 9. Resurrection Days May 18 — 40 days — 11 Appearances — Ascension — The Ever-living Saviour

782

APPENDIX.

THE APOSTLES AND THEIR HISTORY.

	NAME.	SURNAME.	PARENTS.	HOME.	BUSINESS.	WRITINGS.	WORK.	DEATH.
1	SIMON.	Peter } Cephas } = *Rock.*	Jonah.	*Early life:* Bethsaida. *Later:* Capernaum.	Fisherman.	1 Peter. 2 Peter. (Mark?).	A missionary among the Jews, as far as Babylon, 1 Pet. 5:13. Probably=Rome.	*Trad.:* Crucified head downward, at Rome.
2	ANDREW.		Jonah.	*Early life:* Bethsaida. *Later:* Capernaum.	Fisherman.		*Tradition:* Preached in Scythia, Greece and Asia Minor.	*Trad.:* Crucified on St. Andrew's cross (×).
3	JAMES the greater or elder.	Boanerges, or *Sons of Thunder.*	Zebedee and Salome.	Bethsaida and afterward in Jerusalem.	Fisherman.		Preached in Jerusalem and Judea.	Beheaded by Herod, A.D. 44, at Jerusalem.
4	JOHN, the beloved disciple.				Fisherman.	Gospel. 3 Epistles. Revelation.	Labored among the churches of Asia Minor, especially Ephesus.	Banished to Patmos, A.D. 95. Recalled. Died a natural death. *Trad.*
5	JAMES the less or younger.		Alpheus or Cleophas and Mary.	Galilee.		(Epistle of James(?)	Preached in Palestine and Egypt. Bishop of Jerusalem(?)	*Trad.:* Crucified in Egypt; or thrown from a pinnacle.
6	JUDE.	Same as Thaddeus and Lebbeus.		Galilee.		Epistle of	Preached in Assyria and Persia. *Trad.*	Martyred in Persia. *Trad.*
7	PHILIP.			Bethsaida.			Preached in Phrygia.	Died martyr at Hierapolis in Phrygia. *Trad.*
8	BARTHOLOMEW.	Nathaniel.		Cana of Galilee.				Flayed to death. *Trad.*
9	MATTHEW.	Levi.	Alpheus.	Capernaum.	Tax-collector.	Gospel.		*Trad.:* Died a martyr in Ethiopia.
10	THOMAS.	Didymus.		Galilee.			Claimed by the Syrian Christians as the founder of their church; perhaps also in Persia and India.	*Trad.:* Shot by arrows while at prayer.
11	SIMON.	The Cananean, or *Zelotes.*		Galilee.				*Trad.:* Crucified.
12	JUDAS.	Iscariot.		Kerioth of Judea.				Suicide.

APPENDIX.

CHRONOLOGY OF THE ACTS.
DATES ACCORDING TO RECENT SCHEMES.

Date, A.D.	Acts.	Events.	Place.	Hastings B.D.	Ramsay.	Harnack.	Lightfoot.	Encycl. Biblica.	Lewin.	Contemporary History.
30. April, May.	1: 1-3	Resurrection days	Galilee							Tiberius, emperor, 14-37 A.D.
30. May 18	1: 4-12	Commission to Apostles and Ascension	Bethany							Pontius Pilate, Procurator, 26-36. PAUL enters public life, A.D. 29, aged 30.
30	1:13, 14	Waiting for the promise of the Father	Jerusalem, in an upper room	29-30	30	29 or 30	30	30	30	
	1:15-26	Election of Matthias to take the place of Judas	"							
	2: 1-13	Pentecost; the Gift of Tongues	Jerusalem	29-30	30	29 or 30	30	30		Seneca. 4 B.C.-65 A.D. Essays and Tragedies.
	2:14-36	Peter's address	"							
	2:37-41	The first converts: 3000	"							
	2:42-47	The early church.	Temple courts							
	3: 1-10	The lame man healed.	"	29-30	30	29 or 30	30	30		Gamaliel. 30-40 A.D.
	3:11-26	Second address by Peter								
	4: 1-22	The first persecution: Peter and John imprisoned.	Jerusalem							
	4:23-37	A fresh baptism of the Spirit.	"							
	5: 1-11	Ananias and Sapphira.	"							Philo Judaeus. 20 B.C.—after 40 A.D.
	5:12-16	Spread of Gospel in Jerusalem.	"							
	5:17-42	Second persecution: Sanhedrin.	"							
	6: 1-7	Appointment of deacons.	"							
30 to 34	6: 8-15	Preaching of Stephen.	"						35	
35	7: 1-60	Martyrdom of Stephen.	"						36	Deposition of Pontius Pilate. 36. Sent to Rome for trial. Vitellius takes his place as governor.
35-36	8: 1-4	General persecution.		36	33	30	34	31-35		
36	8: 5-25	Philip the Evangelist in	Samaria						37	PAUL, aged 37. Death of Tiberius, 16 March, 37. Accession of Caligula
	8:26-40	Philip and the Ethiopian.	Road to Gaza	36	33	30	34	31-35	38	Release of Herod Agrippa I. Banishment of Antipas, 39. Caligula orders his statue to be set up at Jerusalem.
	9: 1-22 (Gal. 1:17)	Conversion of Saul of Tarsus. Saul in Arabia.	Near Damascus							
38	9:23-27	St. Paul persecuted; escapes	Damascus	38	35, 36	33				
	9:28-29	St. Paul preaches in Jerusalem.	Jerusalem							
38-40	9:30	St. Paul goes to Cilicia.	Tarsus, etc.							
	9:31-35	St. Peter cures Aeneas.	Lydda							
	9:36-42	Dorcas restored to life.	Joppa						40	
41	10: 1-48	Cornelius the Centurion converted.	Caesarea							Claudius Emperor, Jan. 24, 41, to Oct. 13, 54. Seneca in exile, 41-49.
	11: 1-18	The question of admitting the Gentiles.	Jerusalem							
38-41	11:19-21	First Gentile church.	Antioch						42	
41	11:22,23	Herod Agrippa I, King of Judea.	Antioch						41	Romans in Britain, 43.
42,43	11:25,26	Barnabas at Antioch.								
42,43	12: 1, 2	Paul called from Tarsus to	Jerusalem							
44. Spring	12: 3-18	Martyrdom of St. James. Imprisonment and deliverance of St. Peter	"							
44. Early Summer	12:19-23	Death of Herod Agrippa I	Caesarea	44	44	44	44	44	44	Death of Herod Agrippa I, 44.

Date	Ref.	Event	Place							Date	Historical events
44-46	11:27-30	Famine. Relief sent to Jerusalem by Barnabas and Saul		46	45,46	45			45	45	London founded, 47.
46	12:24, 25	Return of Saul and Barnabas with John Mark to	Antioch								Expulsion of Jews from Rome, 48(?)
March 47 to 49	13: 1-14:28	First Missionary Journey, Saul and Barnabas		47-49	47-50	48-51	48		48 or 49		
	13: 1-3	Ordained as Missionaries	Antioch								
49	13: 4-52	In Cyprus and Antioch of Pisidia	Asia Minor								
49	14: 1-20	In Iconium, Lystra, Derbe	Asia Minor								
	14:21-25	Revisiting the churches	"								
	14:26-28	Report to home church	Antioch								
50	15: 1-35	Council at Jerusalem	" in Syria	49	50	51	51			49	Caractacus defeated in Britain
50-52	15:40; 18:22	Second Missionary Journey, St. Paul and Silas	Jerusalem	49-52	50-53						
	16: 1-5	Revisiting the churches	Asia Minor and Greece								
50-52	16: 6-11	St. Paul enters Europe	Asia Minor								
50-52	16:12-40	St. Paul at Philippi; Lydia; conversion of jailer	Macedonia								
	17: 1-14	St. Paul in Thessalonica and Berea	Philippi								
	17:15-34	St. Paul at Athens	Macedonia								
51-52	18: 1-18	St. Paul at Corinth. Crispus	Greece								
		1 and 2 Thessalonians									
51-52	18:18-22	Returns home via Ephesus and Cæsarea to		late in 50	late in 51	late in 52	late in 52	47-49			
52	18:22	Brief visit to Jerusalem	Antioch	52	53	54		53		52	Gallio pro-consul at Corinth.
	18:22, 23	St. Paul in Antioch	Jerusalem / Syria								
53-57	18:23-21:16	Third Missionary Journey	Asia Minor and Greece	52-56	53-57					53	Felix, procurator, 52-59
53	18:24-28	Apollos at Ephesus	Asia Minor							58	
53-56	19: 1-11	St. Paul nearly three years at	Ephesus		56					54-58	Nero, emperor, 54-68.
	19:12-20	Sceva the Exorcist	"		Dec.Jan. Feb.57					54-57	Birth of Tacitus, 55.
	19:21-41	Riot at Ephesus. Diana	"								
57	20: 1-5	St. Paul revisits Macedonia	Macedonia	55		53	57			57	St. Peter at Corinth, 55 or 56
		2 Corinthians		55		53	58			58	
57	20: 6-12	St. Paul three months at Corinth	Greece								
		Romans									
	20:13-16	St. Paul at Troas. Eutychus	Troas								
	20:17-38	Sails to Miletus									
	21: 1-16	Address to Ephesian elders at	Miletus	56	57	54		54			
	21:17-20	Journey by Tyre and Cæsarea to	Jerusalem								
	21:21-40	St. Paul's reception by church	"								
	22:1-23:11	St. Paul's arrest in Temple	"								
	23:12-22	St. Paul a prisoner in Castle of Antonia									
	23:23-35	The conspiracy against Paul's life									
57	24: 1-22	St. Paul sent secretly to	Cæsarea							58	
	24:23-27	St. Paul's trial before Felix	"								
59	25: 1-12	St. Paul in prison two years at	"							59	Festus, procurator, 59-63.
	25:13-26:32	St. Paul accused to Festus. He appeals to Cæsar. St. Paul before Festus and Agrippa	"							60	St. Luke's Gospel probably written.

CHRONOLOGY OF THE ACTS.—*Continued.*

DATES ACCORDING TO RECENT SCHEMES.

Date, A.D.	Acts	Events	Place	Hastings B.D.	Ramsay	Harnack	Light-foot	Encycl. Biblica	Lewin	Contemporary History.
Sept. 59 / 60	27: 1-44 / 28: 1-10 / 28:11-29	St. Paul's voyage and shipwreck.. / St. Paul on the Island of Malta.... / St. Paul at Rome: Conference with the Jews....	Mediterranean / "							Nero murders Agrippina.
61, 62	28:30, 31	Paul a prisoner in his own hired house at.	Rome	59	60	57	61	57 or 61	61	Rebellion of Boadicea in Britain. Boadicea defeated by Suetonius about 62.
		Philippians	"							
		Colossians	"							
		Philemon	"							
		Ephesians	"	61	62	59	63	59 or 63	62	
		Close of the history in the *Acts*								
62-68 / 63		*Probable composition of Acts....* / First trial. Release....	"	61	62				63	Great earthquake at Pompeii.
		Hebrews (?)								
		Goes to Asia by way of Macedonia.								
		Sails with Titus to Crete and returns to Ephesus....								
		Leaving Timothy goes by Philippi to Corinth.							64	Great Fire of Rome, ascribed by Nero to the Christians, July 19, 64
		1 Timothy.								
		Titus.								
		Journey to Spain (?).								
		Winters at Nicopolis.								
		Journey to Dalmatia(?) and through Macedonia to Troas....								
65 / 66		Martyrdom of St. Peter. / Second arrest. Sent to Rome.		64, 65	65, 67				65	
66		Trial before Emperor....		64, 65	66, 67	64	67	July or Aug. 64	66	Jewish war begins. Massacre by Florus at Jerusalem. Repulse of Cestius Gallus.
		2 Timothy. / Martyrdom of St. Paul....	Rome							
Aug. 70		Destruction of Jerusalem....		70	70	70	70	70	70	

* What follows in this column is based chiefly on tradition. There are great differences of opinion among authorities as to dates and even facts.

NOTE.—The dates in the left-hand column are very nearly in accord with those of Mr. C. H. Turner in Dr. Hastings' *Dictionary of the Bible,* and not far from the average of the leading authorities. Dates are also given from a number of leading scholars to show the variation of opinions, usually with narrow limits, and that we must be "consistent with what Harnack describes as relative rather than absolute chronology." The dates of secular events are derived originally from Tacitus, Josephus, and Eusebius. These do not in all cases agree, although there are considerations, such as the different times of beginning the year, which may bring them closer together. But the dates are abundantly accurate for all practical purposes.

APPENDIX.

MEASURES.
I. Measures of Capacity (Liquid).

						Earlier.				Later.				Approximate.		
					Litres.	Gallons.	Quarts.	Pints.	Litres.	Gallons.	Quarts.	Pints.	Gallons.	Quarts.	Pints
Log =				Roman *sextarius*	.51			.90	.56			.99		½	1
4				*Cab*	2.05		1	1.6	2.24		1	1.96		2	
12	3			*Hin*	6.12	1	1	.8	6.75	1	1	1.8	1½	6	
72	18	6		*Bath*=Ephah	36.92	8	0	1	40.5	8	3	1.28	9	36	
720	180	60	10	*Homer* or Cor.	369.2	81	4	0	405.	89	0	.8	90		

"Measure" (Ps. 80:5; Isa. 40:12) = ⅓ Bath = 1 Seah of Dry Measure.
"Measure" (Luke 16:6) = Bath = about 9 gals.
"Firkin" (John 2:6) = Gk. *Mĕtrētēs'* = Bath = about 9 gals.
"Pot" (Mk. 7:4) = Rom. *Sextarius* = about one pint.

These tables are in accordance with the equivalents as given in Hastings' *Bible Dictionary*. The standards varied so at different times it is impossible to determine with absolute exactness. The numbers in the "approximate equivalents" columns are near enough for all practical purposes to-day

The relations of these measures to one another are correct, but there is a double uncertainty as to the exact modern equivalents; for the capacity of the Hebrew measures cannot be accurately determined, and there is no uniformity as to the exact capacity of the English and American measures. There are, for instance, four different quarts in use named in the *Century Dictionary*.

The Bath was the Unit of Liquid Measurement, as was its equivalent, the Ephah of Dry Measure, Gk. *Mĕtrētēs'*. According to Josephus it contained 72 Attic Sextarii = .96 pint × 72 = 8 gallons, 5.12 pints, or one bushel and five pints Dry Measure. According to Colonel Conder, LL.D., in the Quarterly Statement of the Palestine Exploration Fund for April, 1902, the Bath occupied a cube of the small cubit, 13.33 inches; or the cube of 36 barleycorns = 12 inches.

A Litre, the Unit of Capacity in the Metric System, is the volume of one kilogram of water = one cubic decimetre = 0.88 of an imperial quart, or 1.056 United States quarts.

II. Measures of Capacity (Dry).

						Earlier.					Later.					Approximate.			
					Litres.	Bushels.	Pecks.	Quarts.	Pints.	Litres.	Bushels.	Pecks.	Quarts.	Pints.	Bushels.	Pecks.	Quarts.	Pints.
Log.				Roman *Sextarius*	.51				.90	.56				.99				1
4				*Cab*	2.05			1	1.6	2.25			1	1.96		2		
7.2	1.8			*Omer*	3.7			3	.5	4.05			3	1.13				7
24	6	3½		*Seah*	12.3		1	2	1.6	13.5		1	3	1.76	1½			
72	18	10	3	*Ephah*	36.92	1	0	0	1	40.5	1	0	3	1.28	1			
720	180	100	30	10 *Homer* or Cor.	369.2	10	0	5	0	405.	11	0	4	.8	11			

"Measure" (Rev. 6:6) = Gk. *Choinix* = nearly one quart (.96).
"Measure" (1 Kin. 4:22; 2 Chr. 2:10) = homer.
"Bushel" (Mat. 5:15) = Rom. *Modius* = nearly a peck (.96).
The Ephah was the Unit of Dry Measure as the Bath was of Liquid.
According to the careful calculations of Lieut.-Gen. Sir Charles Warren, an Ephah or Bath contained **2333.3** cubic inches. A Log contained 32.4 cubic inches, or a cube each of whose sides = 3.185 inches.
The foregoing tables will explain many texts in the Bible. Take for instance Isa. 5:10, "For 10 acres of vineyard shall yield one bath (nearly 9 gallons; or 3¼ quarts to an acre), and a homer of seed (10 or 11 bushels) shall yield but an Ephah" (1 bush. 3 qts.) or about ¹/₁₀ as much as the seed sown.

APPENDIX.

III. Measures of Length (Smaller).

				Roman and Attic Standard.			Talmudic Standard.		
				Metres.	Feet.	Inches.	Metres.	Feet.	Inches.
Digit=Finger breadth				0.0185	0	0.728	.023	0	0.91
4	*Palm*=Hand breadth			0.074	0	2.912	.092	0	3.64
12	3	*Span*		0.222	0	8.737	.277	0	10.93
24	6	2	Cubit=The Unit of Measure	0.444	1	5.48	.555	1	9.85
144	36	12	6	*Reed*	2.664	8	8.87	3.330	10	11.10
168	42	14	7	*Ezekiel's Reed*	3.108	10	2.3	3.885	12	8.95

The tables of measures of length and surface are in accord with those in Harper's *Classical Dictionary* and the Oxford Cyclopedic concordance. The unit of measurement was the *Cubit* which was originally the length of the human arm from the elbow to the tip of the middle finger. But standards vary, although the relations of the measures to one another are always as given. The cubit is given, approximately, as *a foot and a half*, and is now generally reckoned as 18 inches, except where especial exactness is required. The length of the foot varied in different periods and countries. See Harper's *Classical Dictionary*, article "Cubitus," and the tables in the Appendix.

The cubit in very early times is said to have been 25.19 inches; and after the Exile the legal cubit of the Talmudists was 21.85 inches. Col. Conder makes the cubit of 6 palms to be 16 inches, but gives five different lengths for the cubit according to the number of barleycorns of which three=one inch (but this varies).

According to Lieut.-Gen. Sir Charles Warren, K.C.B., F.R.S., the length of the cubit regulated everything connected with weights and measures, and even the weight of the gold, silver, and copper coinage. The building cubit of Egypt was 20.6 British inches, or 7 palms, while the common cubit was 6 palms, or 7.75 inches. "With this length Goliath at 6 cubits one span would have measured 9 feet 7.3 inches. The bedstead of Og (9 by 4 cubits) would have measured 13 feet 3.75 inches by 5 feet 11 inches."

The *metre* is 39.37 English inches.

The *Fathom* of Acts 27:28 is a Greek and Roman measure, of approximately 6 feet.

IV. Measures of Length (Land and Distance).

									English Standard.			
									Metres.	Miles.	Feet.	Inches.
Foot =Rom. Pes...									0.296	......	......	11.65
1½	"	=	1 Cubit=nearly 18 inches.....................................						0.444	......	1	5.48
5	"	=	3⅓	"	=	1 *Pace*, Passus....................................			1.48	......	4	10.27
600	"	=	400	"	=	120	"	= *Furlong*, stadium.......................	177.6	0.110	582	8.40
5000	"	=	3333⅓	"	=	1000	"	= 8 " = Mile, Mille Passuum........	1480	0.92	4856	......
5000	"	=	3333⅓	"	=	1000	"	= 8 " = A Sabbath day's journey......	1480	0.92	4856	......

Encyclopedia Biblica names a "pace" of 2 cubits, or about 3 feet.

A modern pace is either military=2½ ft. or geometric=5 ft.

A furlong is often spoken of roughly as 600 ft.

The relations of the measures to one another are correct, but the standards vary slightly. The Roman Stadium, or furlong, being 185 metres, the Attic 177, the Olympic 192.

The Roman mile was a little more than nine-tenths of an English mile.

A metre, 39.37 English inches. The English foot is .3048 of a metre.

APPENDIX.

			ENGLISH STANDARD.			
			Sq. ft.	Acres.	Sq. rods	Sq. ft.
Pes Quadratus. Roman square foot......			0.9425	....	....	0.9425
14,400	*Actus Quadratus.* "Furrow," 120 ft. long, squared............ Heb. Määnäh, 1 Sam. 14:14.		13,571	5/16	49	231.7
28,800	2	*Jugerum* = Roman acre............ Heb. Sĕmêd, "yoke," Isa. 5: 10.	27,143	5/8	99	190

The *Actus* was the basis of the whole system of Roman land measurement. It was 120 Roman feet long and 4 wide.
The *Actus Quadratus*, or actus squared, was a square 120 feet each way.
The *Jugerum*, "yoke" was the common measure of land. It was the area which a yoke of oxen could plow in one day, and measured 120 x 240 feet.

WEIGHTS.

							ORDINARY HEAVY WEIGHT.			LIGHT WEIGHT.		
							Grains.	Pounds.	Oz.	Grains.	Pounds.	Oz.
Gerah, "grain" = 1/20 shekel......							11.2			·5.6		
5	*Rebah*, "quarter" = ¼ shekel						56			28		
10	2	*Bekah*, "half" = ½ shekel					112			56		
20	4	2	SHEKEL				224.5		½	112		¼
400	80	40	20	*Libra*, Gk. *Litra*, the Pound of John 12:3......			5,050		Avoir. 11.356			
1000	200	100	50	2½	*Mina*, Pound of Mat. (silver); Maneh		11,225	Troy 2 Avoir. 1	0 8	5,612	Troy 1 Avoir. 0	0 12
60,000	12,000	6,000	3,000		60	*Talent* (silver); Kikkar, "circle"	673,500	Troy 117 Avoir. 96⅓		336,750	Troy 58 Avoir. 48	5+ 0
						Talent (gold)	758,000	Troy 131 Avoir. 108		379,000	Troy 65 Avoir. 54	5+ 0

The above table is in accord with the article by A. R. S. Kennedy, D.D., in Hastings' *Bible Dictionary*, and with the weights given in the Tables of Money.

But there was a great variation in those times as there is now in different countries and at different times in the same country.

Dr. Kennedy makes the shekel = 224.5. Harper's *Classical Dictionary* makes it 240, and the Mina and Talent are increased accordingly.

The *Encyclopedia Biblica* gives a large Babylonian shekel = 336.6.

The Mina (pound) Heavy Weight Troy = 2 lbs.
    "   "   "   " Avoir. = 1⅔ lbs.
    "   " Light Weight Troy = 1 lb.
    "   "   "   " Avoir. = ¾ lb.
    " Silver Roman   "   " = 1⁵/₇ lbs.
    "   " Babylonian   "   " = 2½ lbs.
    The Shekel is the unit of weight.
    The Pound Avoir. = 7,000 grains.
    The Pound Troy = 5,760 grains.
Pound in John 12.3; 19.39 = the Litra = Roman Libra = 5,050 grains = 11 ounces, 237½ grains. Pound in Luke 19: 13, etc. = the Mina.

APPENDIX.

MONEY TABLES.
I. Money of the Old Testament.

GOLD AND SILVER VALUES.	HEAVY OR COMMON STANDARD						LIGHT STANDARD					
	Weight in Grains Troy	£	s.	d.	$	cts.	Weight in Grains Troy	£	s.	d.	$	cts.
Shekel (silver) = 4 drachmas or denarii	224½	......	2	9 nearly	......	64.6	112¼	1	4½ nearly	..	......	32½
15 *Shekel* (gold)............	252⅔	2	1	0	9	69	126⅓	1	0	6	4	85
50 ...... *Mina* (silver)	11,225	6	16	8	32	30	5,612½	3	8	4	16	15
...... 50 .. *Mina* (gold)	12,630	102	10	0	484	75	6,315	51	5	0	242	38
3,000 ...... 60 .. *Talent* (silver)	673,500 =96½ lbs. Avoir.	410	0	0	1,940 nearly	00	336,750	205	0	0	970 nearly	00
...... 3,000 .. 60 .. *Talent* (gold)..	758,000 =108 lbs. Avoir.	6,150	0	0	29,085	0	379,000	3,075	0	0	14,542	50
Dram, A. V. *"Daric,"* R. V. (Ezra 8:27; Neh. 7:22) a gold Persian coin	130	1	1	1	5	60						

The *shekel* was the unit of value in common use.
The value of the silver shekel varied at different times. The best specimens now extant weigh from 218 to 220 grains. Hastings reckons it as weighing 224½ grains, as above. Harper's *Classical Dictionary* makes it 240 grains.
The reason for the different weights of the silver and gold shekels and their multiples lay in the fact that the ratio of silver to gold was 13.3 to 1, a very inconvenient ratio. Therefore the weight of the gold shekel was increased so that its value equalled 15 silver shekels.
There are no coins mentioned in the Bible before the Exile, and only one, the gold daric, in the O. T. There were, however, ingots or bars of gold and silver of definite weight for convenience of trade.
These tables are taken from the *Oxford Cyclopedic Concordance*, for which the present editor computed them from a careful comparison of Hastings' *Bible Dictionary* and Harper's *Classical Dictionary*.
One pound avoirdupois contains 7,000 grains. One pound troy contains 5,760 grains.

APPENDIX.

II. MONEY OF THE NEW TESTAMENT.

(From Augustus to Nero.)

A. COPPER OR BRASS COINS.					Weight in grains, Harper's Classical Dictionary	Weight in grains, Hastings' Bible Dictionary	£	s.	d.	$	cts.
Mite (Greek *Lepton*). Matt. 12:2; Lu. 21:2; 12:59...........						(Hastings calls it ⅛ farthing.)			¼ farth.		⅛
2	*Farthing* (Greek *Kodiantes*) the Roman Quadrans. Mt. 5:16; Mk. 12:42					(Hastings calls it ⅜ farthing)			½ farth.		¼
8	4	*Farthing,* Assarion=As. Matt. 10:29; Lu. 12:6 ..			4				½ d.		1
32	16	4	*Sestertius* (Roman)						2		4
128	64	16	4	*Denarius* (Roman) see "silver coins"..							

B. SILVER COINS AND VALUES.											
Denarius (Roman), the silver penny=ordinary day's wage. *Drachma* (Greek). Matt. 29:19; Lu. 15:8; 20:24; Acts 19:19.					60	56			8½		16
2	*Didrachma,* "Tribute money." Matt. 22:19........ } *Half Shekel.* Matt. 17:24......................... }				120	112¼		1	4½		32¼
4	2	*Shekel* (Jewish)= Stater (Roman). Matt. 17:27 .... } Tetradrachm (Greek) .... } Argurion, "piece of silver." Matt. 26:15 . }			240	224½		2	9		64.6
100	50	25	*Mina* (=Maneh) "Pound." Lu. 19:13-25..		6,000	5,612	3	8	4	16	15
6,000	3,000	1,500	60	Talent. Matt. 25	360,000	333,750	205	0	0	970	00
25	*Aureus,* the gold coin in Palestine in the time of Augustus=nearly ¼ mina. Matt. 10:9....................				126	120.3	1	0	0	5 nearly	00

The *Denarius* was the standard coin of Roman, as the *Shekel* was of Jewish, currency. The coin was about the size of an English half-crown, and a little larger than a half dollar.

Since in all our coins there is an appreciable amount of alloy, the calculations of the equivalents in English money are based upon the price at which the Royal Mint buys pure gold (in 1902) viz.: £3, 17s. 10½d.. per oz. of 480 grains.

The equivalents in dollars and cents are based upon the amount of pure silver in the standard dollar of 416 grs.=371½ grs. Silver and gold are estimated at the proportion of 16 to 1.

The variations in the values are very perplexing. No one standard was maintained in any country during different periods; and standards varied greatly at the same period in different countries. The tables therefore are approximate, or average. But with all due allowances for variations of value of both the ancient and modern coins, it is exact enough for all practical purposes.

These tables of money values will explain many parables and incidents in the Bible where money is mentioned. For example we can understand why Naaman (2 Kings 5:23) considered two servants necessary for carrying two talents of silver and a few garments,—the talents weighed 50–100 pounds each, according to the standard used. The "30 pieces of silver" received by Judas as the reward of his treachery amounted to $24, or, according to the value of money at that time, the wage of a common laborer for about six months. The poor widow commended by Christ gave only ⅛ of a cent—but it was all she had. The man who was given but one talent, in the parable, received at the lowest calculation nearly $1,000, or an amount it would have taken a laboring man twenty years to earn.

APPENDIX.

III. COMPARATIVE TABLE OF VALUES.
(SILVER TO GOLD=16 TO 1.)

From Col. C. R. Conder, LL.D., in *Palestine Exploration Fund*, April, 1902, showing the variations in values. (The values in dollars and cents are computed from the values in English money by using the *approximate* equivalents of £1=$5; 1s.=24 cents; 1d.=2 cents. **Exact** equivalent January 15, 1912=£1=$4.87½).

	Hebrew £ s. d.	Hebrew $	Babylonian £ s. d.	Babylonian $	Phoenician £ s. d.	Phoenician $	Persian £ s. d.	Persian $	Attic £ s. d.	Attic $	Roman £ s. d.	Roman $
Quarter Shekel	0-0-10	.20	0-0-8½	.17	0-0-7½	.15	0-0-8	.16	0-0-8½	.17	0-0-6¼	.12½
Half Shekel	0-1-8	.40	0-1-5½	.35	0-1-3	.30	0-1-4	.32	0-1-5½	.35		
Three-quarter Shekel	0-2-6	.60	0-2-1½	.51	0-1-10½	.45	0-2-0	.48	0-2-1½	.51		
Shekel	0-3-4	.80	0-2-10	.68	0-2-6	.60	0-2-8	.64	0-2-10	.68		
Maneh silver, light standard	4-3-4	20.80	4-3-4	20.80	5-0-0	25.00	4-0-0	20.00	3-8-6	17.04	3-2-6	15.60
" " heavy	8-6-8	41.60	8-6-8	41.60			8-0-0	40.00				
Talent " ligut	250-0-0	1250.	250-0-0	1250.	500-0-0	2500.	247-10-0	1137½	436-12-8	2183.		
" " heavy	500-0-0	2500.	500-0-0	2500.			495-0-0	2375.				
Maneh, gold, light	66-13-4	333.20	66-13-4	333.20	80-0-0	400.	64-0-0	320.	55-1-0	275.24	41-13-4	208.20
" " heavy	133-6-8	666.40	133-6-8	666.40	160-0-0	800.	128-0-0	640.		550.48		416.40
Talent " light	4000-0-0	20,000.	4000-0-0	20,000.	8000-0-0	40,000.	3840-0-0	19,200.	3333¼-0-0	16,670		
" " heavy	8000-0-0	40,000.	8000-0-0	40,000.			7680-0-0	38,400.				
Gold unit	1-0-10	5.20	1-0-10	5.20			1-1-0	5.24	0-18-0	4.32	1-1-0	5.24

MONTHS: JEWISH CALENDAR.

Year Sacred	Civil	Month	Festivals	English Month (Nearly)	Corresponding Dates 1925-26	1931-32	1935-36	Seasons and Productions	
I	7	NISAN OR ABIB. 30 days. Exod. 12:2.	1. New Moon. 14. The Passover (Ex. 1=1.15; 13:3-10 (John 12:3). 15-21. Festival of Unleavened Bread. *[16. First-fruits of Barley harvest presented (Lev. 23:10-12)].	April	March 26 / April 8 / April 9-15	March 19 / April 1 / April 2-8	April 4 / April 17 / April 18-24	Fall of the latter or Spring rains (Deut. 11:14). Floods (Josh. 3:15). Barley ripe at Jericho.	
II	8	IYAR OR ZIF. 29 days. (Iyar=later name.) 1 Kings 6:1.	1. New Moon. 14. Second Passover, for those who could not keep the first (Num. 9:10, 11).	May	April 25 / May 8	April 18 / May 1	May 4 / May 17	Wheat partly in the ear. Barley harvest general (Ruth 1:22).	HARVEST
III	9	SIVAN. 30 days. Esth. 8:9.	1. New Moon. 6. Pentecost or Feast of Weeks. *[First-fruits of wheat harvest (Lev. 23:17, 20), and First-fruits of all the ground (Ex. 23:19; Deut. 26:2-10)].	June	May 24 / May 29	May 17 / May 22	June 2 / June 7	Wheat ripens. Wheat harvest. Summer begins.	
IV	10	THAMMUZ. 29 days. Zech. 8:19.	1. New Moon. 17. Fast. Taking of Jerusalem.	July	June 23 / July 9	June 16 / July 2	July 2 / July 18	No rain from April to Sept. (1 Sam. 12:17). Heat increases.	HOT SEASON

		Month	Festivals and events	Modern month	July 22 / July 30	July 15 / July 23	July 31 / Aug. 8	Season	
V	11	Ab. 30 days. Ezra 7:9.	1. New Moon...........	August	July 22 July 30	July 15 July 23	July 31 Aug. 8	HOT SEASON	The streams dry up. Heat intense. Vintage (Lev. 26:5).
			9. Fast. Destruction of Temple......						
VI	12	Elul. 29 days. Neh. 6:15.	1. New Moon....	September	Aug. 21	Aug. 14	Aug. 30		Heat still intense. (2 Kings 4:18-20). Grape harvest general. (Num. 13:23).
VII	1	Tishri or Ethanim. 30 days. 1 Kings 8:2. 2 Chron. 5:3.	1. New Year. Day of Blowing of Trumpet. Day of Judgment and Memorial. (Num. 29:1).	October	Sept. 19 Sept. 28	Sept. 12 Sept. 21	Sept. 28 Oct. 7	SEED TIME	Former or early rains begin (Joel 2:23). Plowing and sowing begin.
			10. Day of Atonement (Lev. 16).						
			15-21. Feast of Tabernacles (Lev. 23:34) *First-fruits of wine and oil (Deut. 16:13)].		Oct. 3-9	Sept. 26-Oct. 2	Oct. 12-18		
			22. Shemini Atzeret. Feast of Solemn Assembly.		Oct. 10	Oct. 3	Oct. 19		
VIII	2	Marchesvan or Bul. 29 days. Neh. 1:1.	1. New Moon....	November	Oct. 19	Oct. 12	Oct. 28		Rain continues. Wheat and barley sown. Vintage in N. Palestine.
IX	3	Kislev. 30 days. Neh. 1:1. (Chislev.)	1. New Moon.	December	Nov. 18	Nov. 11	Nov. 27	WINTER	Winter begins. Snow on the mountains.
			25. Chanukah, or Feast of Dedication begins (1 Macc. 4:52-59, John 10:22, 29).		Dec. 12-19	Dec. 5-12	Dec. 21-28		
X	4	Tebeth. 29 days. Esth. 2:16.	1. New Moon.	January	Dec. 18	Dec. 11	Dec. 27		Coldest month. Hail, snow (Josh. 10:11).
			10. Fast. Siege of Jerusalem.		Dec. 27	Dec. 20	Jan. 5, 1936		
XI	5	Shebat. 30 days. Zech. 1:7.	1. New Moon.	February	Jan. 16, 1926	Jan. 9, 1932	Jan. 25	COLD SEASON	Weather gradually becomes warmer.
XII	6	Adar. 29 days. Esth. 3:7; 9:27.	1. New Moon.	March	Feb. 15	Feb. 8	Feb. 24		Thunder and hail frequent. Almond tree blossoms.
			13. Fast of Esther.		Feb. 27	....	Mar. 7		
			14-15. Feast of Purim.		Feb. 28-Mar. 1	....	Mar. 8-9		
XIII Leap Year		Veadar.	1. New Moon.	March-April		Mar. 9			(Intercalary month.)
			13. Fast of Esther.			Mar. 21			
			14-15. Feast of Purim.			Mar. 22-23			

* These festivals are no longer observed.

NOTE.—The Jewish day begins the evening previous, at sunset.

NOTE.—This calendar has been adapted to the three years 1925–26, 1931–32, 1935–36, in order to show the variations of the months from the corresponding ones given in the column of modern months. The years are representative ones, and show well the range of dates.

NOTE.—The Jewish year being strictly lunar, contains but 354 days, or 12 lunations of the moon. But in a cycle of nineteen years an intercalary month, Veadar, is seven times introduced, to render the average length of the year nearly correct. "It was added whenever on the 16th of Nisan the barley was not yet ripe. But two inter-calary years were not allowed in succession."

APPENDIX.

ANIMALS OF THE BIBLE.

I.—MAMMALIA.

For descriptions and references see under each name. Palestine has always had a large variety of animals, owing to the great diversity in its climate, from Alpine cold to almost torrid heat. Only the more interesting of those named in the Bible are here given. Those starred are not named in the *Canonical* books, but we know the animal existed in Bible lands.

Antelope (Pygarg).
Antelope (Wild ox).
Ape.
Ass, Domestic.
Ass, Wild.
Badger (Dolphin?). (R. V. "Seal.")
Bat.
Bear (now rare).
Behemoth (Hippopotamus?).
Boar.
Bull, Domestic.
Bull, Wild.
Camel.
*Cat.
Cattle.
‡Chamois (Wild goat or Wild sheep).
Coney.
Deer—various kinds.
Dog.

*Dolphin (Badger).
Dragon (R. V. "Jackal").
Dromedary (More correctly the word means "young camel").
*Elephant(?).
Fallow deer (R. V. "Roe-buck").
Ferret (R. V. "Gecko," a lizard).
Fox (Jackal, though the true fox is found).
Gazelle.
Goat.
Goat, Wild.
Greyhound (war horse?).
Hare.
Hart, hind (now rare).
*Hippopotamus (Behemoth).
Horse.
*Hyena (probably referred to where translation is "doleful creatures").

Jackal (Dragon and Fox).
Leopard (now rare).
Lion (now extinct).
Mole-rat (Chameleon).
Mouse.
Mule.
Ox.
Ox. Wild (now extinct).
*Porcupine (Bittern in A. V.).
Pygarg (Antelope) (now rare).
Ram.
*Rhinoceros.
Roe-buck (Gazelle).
Sheep.
Swine.
Unicorn (Wild bull) (now extinct).
Weasel (or Pole-cat).
Wolf.

II.—BIRDS.

There are about 350 kinds of birds found in Palestine. The following are among the most interesting. For descriptions see under each name. Those marked with a star are not named in Scripture. The most of these listed in Leviticus and Deuteronomy are of classes rather than individuals,—"the hawk after its kind."

*Bee-eater.
Bittern (R. V. "Porcupine").
*Blackbird.
*Blackcap.
*Bulbul.
*Chat.
Cormorant.
*Corn-bunting.
Crane.
*Crow (Raven).
Cuckoo (R.V. "Sea-mew").
Dove.
*Ducks.
*Dunlin.
Eagle.
Falcon.
Gier Eagle (R.V. "Vulture").
Glede.
*Goldfinch.
*Grakle.
Great Owl (R. V. "Arrowsnake").
*Grouse (Sand-grouse).
*Harrier.
Hawk.

Hens and Cock.
Heron (R.V. "Ibis").
Hoopoe.
Horned Owl (R. V.).
*Ibis (A. V. "Heron").
*Jay.
Kestrel (Hawk).
*Kingfisher.
Kite (A. V. "Glede;" R. V. "Falcon")
Lapwing (Hoopoe).
*Lark.
Little Owl.
*Magpie.
Night-hawk.
*Nightingale.
*Nightjar (Night-hawk).
*Nuthatch.
Osprey.
Ossifrage (R. V. "Gier Eagle").
Ostrich.
Owl.
Partridge.
Peacock.

Pelican.
Pigeon (Turtledove).
*Plover.
Quail.
Raven.
*Redstart.
*Robin.
*Sand-grouse.
*Sandpiper.
Screech Owl (R.V. "Night-monster").
*Shrike.
Sparrow.
*Starling.
Stork.
*Sunbird.
Swallow.
Swift (Swallow).
*Thrush.
*Tit, great.
Turtledove.
Vulture.
*Wagtail.
*Water-rail.

III.—FISH AND WATER ANIMALS.

(a) Fish.

No fish are named specifically in the Bible. A few of the more common found in the inland waters are given below. Tristram mentions 43 species.

Bream.
Carp.
Perch.
Dogfish.
Barbel.

Minnow.
Sheath-fish (unedible).
Skates (unedible).
Lampreys (unedible).
Sharks (unedible).

Eels (unedible).

Those marked "unedible" were prohibited by the laws of Israel, and are not now eaten by the Arabs.

(b) Water Animals.

For descriptions of those named in the Bible see under each name.

Jonah's "Great fish" (Shark?).
Tobit's fish = Sheath-fish(?).
Onycha

Pearls (the producer not named).
Purple = the murex.
Corals.

Sponge.
Whale (crocodile?). (R. V "Sea-monster.")

APPENDIX.

IV.—Reptiles and Amphibia.

Names starred not found in Authorized Version, but the beast is probably meant.

Adder (sometimes generic).
Asp.
Chameleon (A. V. "Mole").
Chameleon = monitor lizard(?).
Cockatrice.
*Crocodile (A. V. "tortoise").
*Crocodile (A. V. "Leviathan").

Dragon = any monster.
Frog.
*Gecko (A. V. "Ferret").
Leviathan = Crocodile.
Lizard.
Serpent (generic term).

*Toad.
Tortoise.
Viper.
Arrowsnake (R. V.) (A. V. "Great owl").
Basilisk.

V.—Insects and Other Smaller Animals.

Ant.
Bee.
Beetle (R. V. Cricket) = locust(?).
Canker-worm = locust.
Caterpillar = locust.
*Cochineal—from which comes "crimson" or "scarlet."
Flea.

Fly (many varieties).
Gnat.
Grasshopper = locust.
Hornet.
Horse-leech.
Lice.
Locust—several varieties.
*Mosquito.

Moth.
Palmer-worm = locust.
Scorpion.
Snail.
Spider.
Wasp.
Worm.

BOTANY OF THE BIBLE.

Owing to the great variety of climate—from Alpine cold to torrid heat—we find the plants of all zones in Palestine. Those mentioned in the Bible are noted below. Those names prefixed by an asterisk (*) are not found in the A. V., but the plants are supposed to be indicated by the original text. For descriptions see under each name.

Algum or Almug tree.
Almond tree.
Aloes or Lign-Aloes.
Anise (Dill).
Apple.
Ash.
Balm or Balsam.
Balsam.
Barley.
Bay tree.
Bdellium (?).
Bean.
Box tree.
Bramble, brier (generic term).
Bulrush (generic term).
Bush (Burning).
Calamus.
Camphire (Henna).
Cane.
*Caper-berry (R. V. of Eccl. 12 : 5; A. V. "desire").
Cassia.
Cedar.
Chestnut tree.
Cinnamon.
*Citron (see Apple).
Cockle.
Coriander.
Corn (= grain).
*Cotton.
Cucumber.
Cummin.
Cypress.
*Dill (Anise).
Dove's dung.
Ebony.
Elm.
Fig tree.

Fir.
Fitches.
Flag (generic term).
Flax.
Frankincense.
Galbanum.
Gall.
Garlic.
Gopherwood.
Gourd.
Gourd, Wild.
Grass (generic).
Hay (generic term).
Hazel (Almond).
Heath.
Hemlock.
Herbs, Bitter (generic).
Husks (Carob).
Hyssop.
Juniper.
*Ladanum (A. V. "Myrrh").
Leeks.
Lentils.
Lily (generic).
Mallow (Salt wort).
Mandrake.
Manna-tree.
Melons (generic).
Millet.
Mint.
Mulberry.
Mustard.
Myrrh.
Myrtle.
Nard (Spikenard).
Nettles (generic).
Nuts.

Oak (generic).
Oil tree (generic).
Olive.
Onions.
Palm tree.
Pannag.
Pine tree.
Pomegranate.
Poplar.
Pulse (generic).
Reed (generic).
Rose of Sharon (Narcissus).
Rue.
Rush.
Rye.
Saffron.
Shittah tree.
Shittim wood.
Sodom, Vine of.
Spelt.
Spicery.
Spikenard.
Stacte.
*Styrax.
Sycamine.
Sycomore.
Tares.
Teil tree.
Terebinth.
Thistle.
Thistle, Thorn (generic).
Thyine wood.
Vine.
Weeds (Seaweed).
Wheat.
Willow (generic).
Wormwood.

MINERAL SUBSTANCES OF THE BIBLE.

For description see under each name.

Bitumen, A. V. "slime."
Clay, for house - building; "mud houses."

Clay, for brick-making.
Nitre, carbonate of soda.
"Red earth."

Salt.
Sand.
Sulphur.

METALS OF THE BIBLE.

Copper, brass (better *bronze*).
Gold.

Iron and steel.
Lead.

Silver.
Tin.

APPENDIX.

PRECIOUS STONES OF THE BIBLE.

Adamant (= corundum?).
Agate.
Amber (probably the yellow amber).
Amethyst.
Beryl (A. V. onyx).
Carbuncle = garnet(?).
Chalcedony.
Chrysolite = topaz (?).
Chrysoprase.
Diamond.

Emerald.
Jacinth or Hyacinth.
Jasper.
Ligure.
Onyx.
Sapphire.
Sardine or Sardius.
Sardonyx.
Topaz = Chrysolite(?).

LAKES AND SEAS OF SCRIPTURE.

Sea of Galilee; also known as
 Sea of Chinnereth.
 Sea of Chinneroth.
 Lake of Gennesaret.
 Lake of Tiberias.
"Great Sea" = the Mediterranean.

"Salt Sea" = Dead Sea. Also known as
 Sea of the Arabah.
 Sea of the Plain.
 "East Sea."
 "The Sea."

MOUNTAINS OF SCRIPTURE.

Abarim.	Gerizim.	Hor (another).	Nebo.
Ararat.	Gilboa.	Horeb.	Olivet.
Bashan.	Gilead.	Lebanon.	Seir.
Carmel.	Hermon.	Moab, Mts. of.	Sinai.
Ebal.	Hor.	Moriah.	Tabor.
			Zion or Sion.

RIVERS AND BROOKS OF SCRIPTURE.

Abana, River.
Arnon, River.
Chebar, River (canal).
Cherith, Brook.
Egypt, River of (R. V. Brook of).
Egypt, Stream of (Nile).
Euphrates, River.
Gihon, River.
Hiddekel, River.

Jabbok, River.
Jordan, River.
Kanah, River (R. V. Brook).
Kidron, Brook.
Kishon, River.
Pharpar, River.
Pison, River.
Zared, Brook.

BREASTPLATE OF THE HIGH PRIEST.

(Set in gold) R. V. Ex. 28: 17–20. The names are taken from the text and margin of the R. V. of Exodus. The figures show the order of the stones as given in Exodus.

3 Emerald.	2 Topaz.	1 Ruby, or Sardius.
6 Sardonyx. (Diamond, A. V.)	5 Sapphire.	4 Carbuncle.
9 Amethyst.	8 Agate.	7 Amber, or Jacinth.
12 Jasper.	11 Beryl.	10 Chalcedony, or Chrysolite.

JEWISH SECTS AND PARTIES.

The following is a list of the main distinctions in Biblical times:—

 1. Pharisees ⎫
 2. Sadducees ⎬ Distinctions chiefly religious.
 3. Essenes ⎭
 4. Herodians ⎫
 5. Zealots ⎬ Distinctions chiefly political.
 6. Galilæans ⎪
 7. Assassins ⎭

Subordinate terms connected with the above.

8. Scribes.	12. Publicans.
9. Lawyers.	13. Samaritans.
10. Nazirites.	14. Sanhedrin.
11. Proselytes.	15. Synagogue.

See under each title.

RECKONING OF DAY AND NIGHT. WATCHES.

The *Natural* Day was from sunrise to sunset.
The *Natural* Night was from sunset to sunrise.
The *Civil* Day was from sunset one evening to sunset the next; for "the Evening and the Morning were the first day."

NIGHT (*Ancient*).

First Watch (Lam. 2: 19) till midnight.
Middle Watch (Jud. 7: 19) till 3 A. M.
Morning Watch (Ex. 14: 24) till 6 A. M.

DAY (*Ancient*).

Morning till about 10 A. M.
Heat of day till about 2 P. M.
Cool of day till about 6 P. M.

NIGHT (*New Testament*).

First Watch, *evening* = 6 to 9 P. M.
Second Watch, *midnight* = 9 to 12 P. M.
Third Watch, *cock-crow* = 12 to 3 A. M.
Fourth Watch, *morning* = 3 to 6 A. M.

DAY (*New Testament*).

Third hour = 9 A. M.
Sixth hour = 12 midday.
Ninth hour = 3 P. M.
Twelfth hour = 6 P. M.

APPENDIX.

STATISTICS OF THE BIBLE.

	OLD TESTAMENT.	NEW TESTAMENT.	WHOLE BIBLE.
Number of books	39	27	66
Number of chapters	929	260	1,189
Number of verses	23,214	7,959	31,173
Number of words	592,439	181,253	773,692
Number of letters	2,728,100	838,380	3,566,480
Middle book	Proverbs.	2 Thessalonians.	Micah and Nahum.
Middle chapter	Job 29.	Romans 13 and 14.	Psalm 117.
Middle verse	2 Chronicles 20: 17.	Acts 17: 17.	Psalm 118: 8.
Least book	Obadiah.	3 John.	3 John.
Least verse	1 Chronicles 1: 1.	John 11: 35.	John 11: 35.

These facts were ascertained by a gentleman in 1718; also by an English gentleman, at Amsterdam, in 1772; and the investigation is said to have taken each gentleman three years.

MIRACLES IN THE OLD TESTAMENT.

There is much difference of opinion as to what constitutes a miracle, in the sense of making it suitable for classification in such a list as this. Numbers of these events are not necessarily miracles; e. g. the plagues of Egypt; but the concurrence of so many, with the fact of their coming at the exact moment when most needed, shows it must have been by the hand of God, even though he used his own laws in carrying out his designs.

MIRACLES.	REFERENCES.
Aaron's rod turned into a serpent	Exod. 7 : 10-12.
The ten plagues of Egypt:	
1. Water turned into blood	Exod. 7 : 20-25.
2. Frogs	" 8 : 5-14.
3. Lice	" 8 : 16-18.
4. Flies	" 8 : 20-24.
5. Murrain	" 9 : 3-6.
6. Boils and blains	" 9 : 8-11.
7. Thunder and hail	" 9 : 22-26.
8. Locusts	" 10 : 12-19.
9. Darkness	" 10 : 21-23.
10. Death of the first born	" 12 : 29-30.
Parting of the waters of the Red Sea	" 14 : 21-31.
The curing of the waters of Marah	" 15 : 23-25.
Feeding with manna	" 16 : 14-35
Water from the rock at Rephidim	" 17 : 5-7.
Death of Nadab and Abihu	Lev. 10 : 1-2.
Burning of the Congregation at Taberah	Num. 11 : 1-3.
Death of Korah, Dathan and Abiram	" 16 : 31-35.
Budding of Aaron's rod at Kadesh	" 17: 8.
Water from the rock at Meribah	" 20 : 7-11.
The brazen serpent	" 21 : 8-9.
The stoppage of the Jordan stream	Josh. 3 : 14-17.
Staying of sun and moon under Joshua(?)	" 10 : 12-14.
Smiting of Philistines and fall of Dagon	1 Sam. 5 : 3-12.
Death of Uzzah when he touched the ark	2 Sam. 6 : 7.
Withering of Jeroboam's hand, and destruction of altar at Bethel	1 Kings 13 : 4-6.
The staying of the cruse of oil and meal at Zarephath (Elijah)	1 Kings 17 : 14-16.
The raising of the widow's son at Zarephath (Elijah)	" 17 : 17-24.
The burning of the sacrifice at Mt. Carmel (Elijah)	" 18 : 30-38.
Burning of the captains and their companies (Elijah)	2 Kings 1 : 10-12.
Dividing of the waters of Jordan (Elijah)	" 2 : 7-8.
Dividing of the waters of Jordan (Elisha)	" 2 :14.
Cure of the waters of Jericho (Elisha)	" 2 : 21-22.
"Tearing" of the mocking lads at Bethel (Elisha)	" 2 : 24.
Supply of water to the allied armies in Moab (Elisha)	" 3 : 16-20.
Increase of the widow's oil (Elisha)	" 4 : 2-7.
Raising of the Shunammite's son (Elisha)	" 4 : 32-37.
Healing the deadly pottage (Elisha)	" 4 : 38-41.
Feeding one hundred men with twenty loaves (Elisha)	" 4 : 42-44.
Cure of Naaman's leprosy and its transfer to Gehazi (Elisha)	" 5 : 10-14,27.
Making an iron axe swim (Elisha)	" 6 : 5-7.
Smiting the Syrian army (Elisha)	" 6 : 18-20.
Resurrection of a dead man by touching bones of Elisha	" 13 : 21.
Destruction of Sennacherib's army	" 19 : 35.
Return of the sun by the dial of Ahaz	" 20 : 9-11.
Smiting of Uzziah with leprosy	2 Chr 26 : 16-21.
Deliverance of the three children from the fiery furnace	Dan. 3 : 19-27.
Deliverance of Daniel from the lions	" 6 : 16-23.
Deliverance of Jonah from the sea monster	Jon. 2 : 1-10.

APPENDIX.

MIRACLES OF OUR LORD.

MIRACLES.	MAT.	MARK.	LUKE.	JOHN.
I. *Narrated in one Gospel only.*				
Two blind men healed.....................	9:27			
A dumb demoniac healed....................	9:32			
Stater in the mouth of the fish.............	17:24			
The deaf and dumb man healed.............		7:31		
A blind man healed.........................		8:22		
When Christ passed unseen through the multitude			4:30	
Draught of fishes...........................			5:1	
Raising the widow's son....................			7:11	
Healing the crooked woman.................			13:11	
Healing the man with the dropsy...........			14:1	
Healing the ten lepers......................			17:11	
Healing the ear of Malchus, servant of the high priest.....			22:50	
Turning water into wine....................				2:1
Healing the nobleman's son (of fever)......				4:46
Healing the impotent man at Bethesda.....				5:1
Healing the man born blind................				9:1
Raising of Lazarus.........................				11:43
Draught of fishes...........................				21:1
II. *Narrated in two Gospels.*				
Demoniac in synagogue cured...............		1:23	4:33	
Healing centurion's servant (of palsy)......	8:5		7:1	
The blind and dumb demoniac..............	12:22		11:14	
Healing the daughter of the Syrophenician.	15:21	7:24		
Feeding the four thousand..................	15:32	8:1		
Cursing the fig tree.........................	21:18	11:12		
III. *Narrated in three Gospels.*				
Healing the leper...........................	8:2	1:40	5:12	
Healing Peter's mother-in-law...............	8:14	1:30	4:38	
Stilling the storm..........................	8:26	4:37	8:22	
The legion of devils entering swine.........	8:28	5:1	8:27	
Healing the man sick of the palsy..........	9:2	2:3	5:18	
Healing woman with issue of blood.........	9:20	5:25	8:43	
Raising of Jairus' daughter.................	9:23	5:38	8:49	
Healing the man with a withered hand......	12:10	3:1	6:6	
Walking on the sea.........................	14:25	6:48		6:19
Curing demoniac child......................	17:14	9:17	9:38	
Curing blind Bartimæus (two blind men, Mat. 20.)...........	20:30	10:46	18:35	
IV. *Narrated in four Gospels.*				
Feeding the five thousand...................	14:19	6:35	9:12	6:5

MIRACLES IN THE EARLY CHURCH.

MIRACLES.	REFERENCES.
Gift of tongues at Pentecost...................................	Acts 2 : 1–14
Healing of the lame man at the Temple gate by Peter and John..................	" 3 : 1–11
Death of Ananias and Sapphira at word of Peter..........................	" 5 : 1–11
Numerous acts of healing at Jerusalem by all the Apostles....................	" 5 : 12–16
Opening of the prison doors to the Apostles.............................	" 5 : 17–25
Cases of healing in Samaria by Philip the Deacon........................	" 8 : 6, 7, 13
Cure of Æneas at Lydda by Peter..................................	" 9 : 32–35
Raising of Dorcas at Joppa by Peter................................	" 9 : 36–41
Deliverance of Peter from prison at Jerusalem.........................	" 12 : 5–17
Blindness of Elymas, at Cyprus, at word of Paul.......................	" 13 : 9–11
Healing of impotent man at Lystra by Paul...........................	" 14 : 8–12
Cure of possessed girl at Philippi by Paul............................	" 16 : 16–18
Numerous miracles of healing by Paul...............................	" 19 : 11, 12
Raising of Eutychus at Troas by Paul...............................	" 20 : 7–12
Cure of Publius and others at Malta by Paul..........................	" 28 : 7–10

APPENDIX.

PARABLES.

PARABLES IN THE OLD TESTAMENT.

PARABLES.	BY WHOM SPOKEN.	REFERENCES.
The ewe lamb....................	Nathan to David...................	2 Sam. 12 : 1-4.
Two brethren and avengers.........	Widow of Tekoah....................	2 Sam. 14 : 1-11.
Escaped captive...................	Man of the sons of the prophets to Ahab......	1 Kings 20 : 35-40.
Vineyard and grapes...............	Isaiah to Judah and Jerusalem.................	Isa. 5 : 1-7.
Eagles and vine...................	Ezekiel to Israel...................	Ezek. 17 : 3-10.
Lions' whelps....................	Ezekiel to Israel...................	Ezek. 19 : 2-9.
The boiling pot...................	Ezekiel to Israel...................	Ezek. 24 : 3-14.
PARABOLIC FABLES.		
Trees choosing a king.............	Jotham to Shechemites..................	Judges 9 : 7-15.
Micaiah's vision................		1 Kings 22 : 19-23.
Thistle and cedar.................	Jehoash to Amaziah...................	2 Kings 14 : 9; 2 Chron. 25:18.

PARABLES OF OUR LORD.

PARABLES.	MATT.	MARK.	LUKE.	LEADING LESSONS.
I. *Recorded in one Gospel.*				
The tares.............................	13:24			Good and evil in life and judgment.
The hid treasure......................	13:44			Value of the gospel.
The goodly pearl......................	13:45			The seeker finding salvation..
The draw-net..........................	13:47			Visible Church a mixed body.
The unmerciful servant................	18:23			Duty of forgiveness.
The labourers in the vineyard.........	20:1			Precedence in service gives no claim to priority in reward.
The two sons..........................	21:28			Insincerity and repentance.
The marriage of the king's son........	22:2			Necessity of robe of righteousness.
The ten virgins.......................	25:1			Watchful preparation and careless security.
The talents...........................	25:14			Use of advantages.
The sheep and goats...................	25:31			Love the test of life.
The seed growing secretly.............		4:26		The law of growth in religion.
The householder......................		13:34		Watchfulness.
The two debtors.......................			7:41	Gratitude for pardon.
The good Samaritan....................			10:30	Active benevolence.
The importunate friend................			11:5	Perseverance in prayer.
The rich fool.........................			12:16	Worldly-mindedness.
Servants watching....................			12:35	Expectancy of the Second Coming.
The wise steward......................			12:42	Conscientiousness in trust.
The barren fig tree...................			13:6	Unprofitableness under grace.
The great supper.....................			14:16	Universality of the Divine call.
Tower; king going to war.............			14:28	Prudence and self-denial.
The piece of money...................			15:8	Joy over penitence.
The prodigal son.....................			15:11	Fatherly love to returning sinner.
The unjust steward...................			16:1	Faithfulness to trust.
The rich man and Lazarus.............			16:19	Hopeless future of the unfaithful.
Unprofitable servants................			17:7	God's claim on all our service.
The unjust judge.....................			18:2	Advantage of persevering prayer.
The Pharisee and publican............			18:10	Self-righteousness and humility.
The pounds...........................			19:12	Diligence rewarded, sloth punished.
II. *Recorded in two Gospels.*				
House on rock, and on the sand........	7:24		6:47	Consistent and false profession.
The leaven...........................	13:33		13:20	Pervading influence of religion.
The lost sheep.......................	18:12		15:4	Joy over penitent.
III. *Recorded in three Gospels.*				
Candle under a bushel................	5:15	4:21	8:16; 11:33	Dissemination of truth.
New cloth on old garment.............	9:16	2:21	5:36	New doctrine on old prejudices.
New wine in old bottles..............	9:17	2:22	5:37	New spirit in unregenerate heart.
The sower............................	13:3	4:3	8:5	Hearers divided into classes.
The mustard-seed.....................	13:31	4:30	13:18	Spread of the gospel.
The wicked husbandmen................	21:33	12:1	20:9	Rejection of Christ by the Jews.
The fig tree and all the trees.......	24:32	13:28	21:29	Indications of Second Advent.

MAP 1

PHYSICAL MAP OF THE HOLY LAND

Copyright by C. S. HAMMOND & CO., N. Y.

Scale of Miles

0 5 10 20 30 40

Perennial Rivers Seasonal Rivers and Streams

Elevations in feet.

Modern Arabic names are underlined.

ALTITUDES IN FEET

5000
3000
2000
1000
500
Sea — Level
600 — -500
-1000

Mediterranean Sea
(The Great Sea)

The coast of the Holy Land is very regular with no natural harbors.

The Jordan Valley is the northern end of the Great Rift Valley which extends over 3000 miles to Lake Nyasa in southern Africa.

The Dead Sea shore is the earth's lowest point of land — 1292 feet below sea level. The maximum depth of the Dead Sea is 1300 feet below the level of the shore.

The annual rainfall of the Holy Land varies from under 5 inches in the Negeb to over 40 inches in the mountains of Lebanon.

PHOENICIA
MOUNT LEBANON
Sidon
Damascus
Tyre
Dan
UPPER GALILEE
Lake Hule
(L. Semechonitis)
BASHAN
Accho
Sea of Galilee
(Chinnereth)
LOWER GALILEE
Nazareth Mt. Tabor 1929
1732 Plain of Esdraelon or Jezreel
Hill of Moreh
Dor
Mt. 1630
Caesarea
Beth-shan
Plain of Sharon
SAMARIA
Samaria Mt. Ebal 3084
Shechem
Mt. Gerizim 2890
GILEAD
Jabbok R.
Jebel Yosha 3852
EPHRAIM
Joppa
AMMON
Tell Asur 3333
Rabbath-ammon
Jericho
Jerusalem Mt. of Olives 2680
Bethlehem
Plain of Moab
Mt. Nebo 2631
Plain of Philistia
Shephelah
Hebron
Wilderness of Judah
Gaza
Arnon R. (W. el Mojib)
MOAB
Raphia
Beer-sheba
Kir-moab
IDUMAEA
DESERT
Negeb
Ascent of Akrabim
Wilderness of Zin
EDOM
Jebel Helal 2936
Kadesh-barnea
Arabah
El Ghor

34° A B C 36°
33°
32°
31°

Longitude 35° East of Greenwich

MAP 2

THE NATIONS ACCORDING
TO GENESIS 10

Copyright by C.S. HAMMOND & CO., N.Y.

Scale of Miles

0 100 200 400 600

GOMER Descendants of Japheth OFHIR Descendants of Shem
LUBIM Descendants of Ham

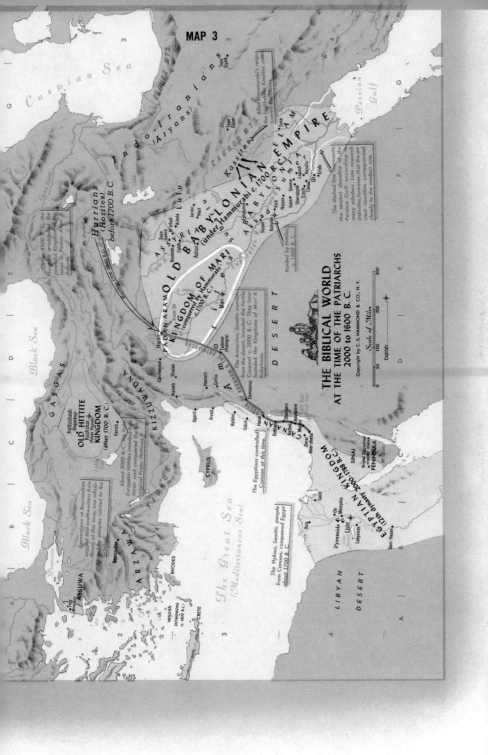

MAP 3

THE BIBLICAL WORLD
AT THE TIME OF THE PATRIARCHS
2000 to 1600 B.C.

Copyright by C. S. HAMMOND & CO., N.Y.

Scale of Miles
0   50   100   200   300

Capitals: ★

MAP 4

CANAAN BEFORE THE CONQUEST

Copyright by C. S. HAMMOND & CO., N. Y.

Scale of Miles

0 5 10 20 30 40

Perennial Rivers
Seasonal Rivers & Streams
Capitals..............

Phoenicians from the cities of Sidon and Tyre traded throughout the Mediterranean.

Canaan at this time was an Egyptian province organized on a city-state system. The local kings were only required to pay tribute and to furnish labor for Egyptian royal projects.

The 13th and 12th century kingdoms of Bashan, Ammon, Moab and Edom displaced the Rephaim, Zuzim, Emim and Horites respectively.

The destroyed cities of Sodom and Gomorrah are believed to be beneath the shallow waters of the Dead Sea which now cover the Vale of Siddim (shaded portion).

The Great Sea

(Mediterranean Sea)

HITTITE EMPIRE
Ubi
Damascus

BASHAN
(KINGDOM OF OG)

MOUNT LEBANON

Sidonians
Phoenicians

Sidon
Zarephath
Tyre
Kanah
Misrephoth-maim
Achzib
Accho
Achshaph
Kedesh
Hazor
Merom
Chinnereth
Madon
Shimron
Jokneam
Dor
Megiddo
Taanach
Ibleam
Dothan
Sochoh
Tirzah
Shechem
Jacob's Well
Aphek
Tappuah
Joppa
Ono
Lod
Gezer
Bethel
Ai
Ekron
Chephirah
Gibeon
Beeroth
Jericho
Gilgal
Kirjath-jearim
Ashdod
Beth-shemesh
Jerusalem (Jebus, Salem)
Makkedah
Libnah
Jarmuth
Ashkelon
Gath
Adullam
Bethlehem
Gaza (Azzah)
Eglon
Lachish
Kirjath-arba (Hebron)
Mamre
Raphia
Kirjath-sepher (Debir)
Hazeon-tamar (En-gedi)
Sharuhen
Gerar
Beer-sheba
Arad
Hormah
Rehoboth
Kadesh-barnea (En-mishpat)

Mt. Carmel
Mt. Tabor
Mt. Eb.
Mt. Gerizim
Sea of Chinnereth
Yarmuk R.
Karnaim
Ashtaroth
Edrei
Ham
Ramoth-gilead
Beth-shan
Pella
Jabesh-gilead
Mahanaim
Succoth
Penuel (Peniel)
Adam
Jazer
Rabbath-ammon
Heshbon
Mt. Nebo (Pisgah)
Medeba
Jahaz
Kiriathaim
Dibon
Aroer
Laish (Dan)

Canaanites
Hivites
Plain of Sharon
Jebusites
Hittites
Kenites
Amalekites
Amorites
KINGDOM OF SIHON
AMMON
MOAB
EDOM
MT. SEIR

Jordan River
Jabbok R.
Plains of Moab
Salt Sea (Dead Sea)
Arnon R.
Gerar R.
Besor R.
Ar
Kir-moab (Kir-haresheth)
Zoar
Bozrah
Oboth
Punon

Wilderness of Zin
Ascent of Akrabbim
Arabah
River of Egypt

MAP 5

THE ROUTE OF THE EXODUS AND
THE CONQUEST OF CANAAN

Copyright by C. S. HAMMOND & CO., N. Y.

Scale of Miles

0   20   40   60   80   100

Perennial Rivers ....
Seasonal Rivers & Streams ....
Capitals ....
Israelite Expansion & Settlement

Trade Routes ....
Route of the Exodus ....
Israelite Campaigns in Canaan

Joshua defeated the allied kings of northern Canaan at the Battle by the Waters of Merom.

Egypt exercised loose control over Canaan at this time.

After the fall of Jericho Joshua conquered central and southern Canaan.

Egyptian forts near the coast barred the direct route to Canaan to the Israelites.

Possible sites of the crossing of the Red Sea (The Sea of Reeds).

Israelites wandered in the wilderness for a generation. Exact route unknown.

Israel's enemy, the Amalekites, wandered as nomads between Canaan and Mt. Sinai.

In the land of Goshen the Israelites dwelt in bondage.

Traditional site where Moses received the Ten Commandments.

The Great Sea
(Mediterranean Sea)

Nile Delta

GOSHEN

Rameses or Zoan (Tanis)
Baal-zephon
Sin (Pelusium)
L. Balluh
Pi-beseth (Bubastis)
Pithom
Succoth
Etham
Bitter Lakes

On (Heliopolis)

Memphis

Pyramids

Nile River

Heracleopolis

Lycopolis

E G Y P T (M I Z R A I M)

Wilderness of Etham

Wilderness of Shur

River of Egypt

Jebel Hellal

Wilderness of Paran

Marah

Elim

Wilderness of Sin

Dophkah

Alush

Rephidim
Jebel Serbal
Mt. Sinai ? Mt. Horeb

Kibroth-hattaavah
Taberah
Hazeroth

SINAI PENINSULA

Gulf of Suez

Gulf of Aqaba

Kadesh-barnea

Beer-sheba

Hormah ?
Unsuccessful invasion

Gaza (Azzah)
Ashkelon
Ashdod
Gath
Eglon
Lachish
Debir
Libnah
Makkedah
Gezer
Joppa
Aphek
Gibeon Ai
Jericho
Jerusalem (Jebus)
Jarmuth
Hebron
Salt (Dead) Sea

Shiloh
Shechem
Mt. Gerizim
Mt. Ebal

Megiddo
Dor
Taanach?
Beth-shan

Mt. Carmel

Accho
Shimron
Madon

Tyre
Kedesh
Merom
Hazor
Misrephoth-maim

Sidon

LEBANON

HITTITE EMPIRE
Ubi
Damascus
Mt. Hermon

Laish (Dan)

BASHAN
(OG)
Ashtaroth

Edrei

Gilead

Jabbok

Jazer
Rabbath-ammon
Heshbon
Mt. Nebo (Pisgah)
Medeba
Jahaz
Dibon

AMMON

MOAB
Kir-moab

Ar

Zered

Zoar
Ije-abarim
Oboth

Punon

Bozrah

EDOM

Arabah

MT. SEIR

Mt. Hor ? (Jebel Harun)

Ezion-geber
Elath

LAND OF MIDIAN

DESERT

Red Sea

MAP 6

CANAAN AS DIVIDED
AMONG THE TWELVE TRIBES
c. 1200-1020 B.C.
Copyright by C. S. HAMMOND & CO., N. Y.

Scale of Miles

0 5 10   20   30   40

Perennial Rivers   Seasonal Rivers & Streams

Part of the tribe of Dan,
unable to secure its inheritance,
migrated north and captured
Laish, renaming it Dan.

Although all of Bashan was
assigned to the half tribe of
Manasseh, it is doubtful that
settlement reached beyond the
Yarmuk Valley.

The Israelites were unable
to capture the fortified towns
of the plains during the early
period of settlement.

During the period of
Judges, invading Ammon-
ites, Moabites and Midianites were repulsed by the
Israelites.

The Israelites were
under constant attack
from Philistine invaders
who occupied the coastal
area at about this time.

The cities assigned to
Simeon were also a part
of the inheritance of Judah.
Simeon as a tribe was later
absorbed by Judah.

The priestly tribe of Levi
did not receive a definite
territory but instead was
allotted 48 cities distributed
over the tribal areas.

The Great Sea

(Mediterranean Sea)

Sidon
Zarephath
Tyre
Kanah
Hammon
Misrephoth-maim
Achzib
Abdon
Beth-emek
Accho
Achshaph
Cabul
Aphek
Ramah
Hannathon
Rimmon
Shimron
Gath-hepher
Harosheth
Jokneam
Dor
Megiddo
Taanach
Ibleam
Dothan
Bezek
Tirzah
Theboz
Mt. Ebal
Pirathon
Janohah
Aphek
Tappuah
Gath-rimmon
Joppa (Japho)
Bene-berak
Ono
Lod
Beth-horon
Gezer
Gibbethon
Kiriath-jearim
Eltekeh
Zorah
Chesalon
Timnah
Makkedah
Azekah
Libnah
Gath
Mareshah
Keilah
Eglon
Lachish
Debir
Gerar
Ziklag
Anab
Madmannah
Jattir
Beer-sheba
Moladah
Beth-palet
Aroer
Rehoboth
Raphia
Sharuhen

Abel-beth-maachah
Laish or Leshem (Dan)
Kedesh
En-hazor
Iron
Hazor
Chinnereth
Madon
Hammath
Chesulloth
Sarid
Shunen
Jezreel
Harod
Beth-shan
Abel-meholah
Shechem
Taanath-shiloh
Shiloh
Ataroth
Naarath
Bethel
Ai
Mizpeh
Gibeon
Geba
Jericho
Gilgal
Beth-hoglah
Adam
Jerusalem (Jebus)
Bethlehem
Etam
Tekoa
Beth-zur
Hebron
Ziph
Carmel
Maon
En-gedi
Arad
Hormah

DAN
Bashan
MANASSEH
Karnaim
Geshur
Ashtaroth
Golan
Argob
Edrei
Ramoth-gilead
Havoth-jair
Camon
Pella
Jabesh-gilead
Mahanaim
Zaphon
Succoth
Penuel
Mizpeh
Jazer
Betonim
Jogbehah
Rabbath-ammon
Beth-nimrah
Abel-shittim
Mephaath
Heshbon
Beth-jeshimoth
Mt. Nebo
Baal-meon
Elealeh
Medeba
Jahaz
Zareth-shahar
Ataroth
Kiriathaim
Dibon
Aroer
Ar
Kir-moab (Kir-haresheth)

Damascus

MT. HERMON
MOUNT LEBANON
Sidonians (Phoenicians)

MT. CARMEL
MT. GILBOA
Sea of Chinnereth
Plain of Sharon
Plain of Jezreel
Mt. Gerizim

Gilead
AMMON
REUBEN
MOAB
EDOM

ZEBULUN
ISSACHAR
MANASSEH
EPHRAIM
BENJAMIN
JUDAH
Caleb
SIMEON
Kenites
Philistines
Cherethites

ASHER
NAPHTALI

Salt Sea (Dead Sea)

Wilderness of Zin
Ascent of Akrabbim

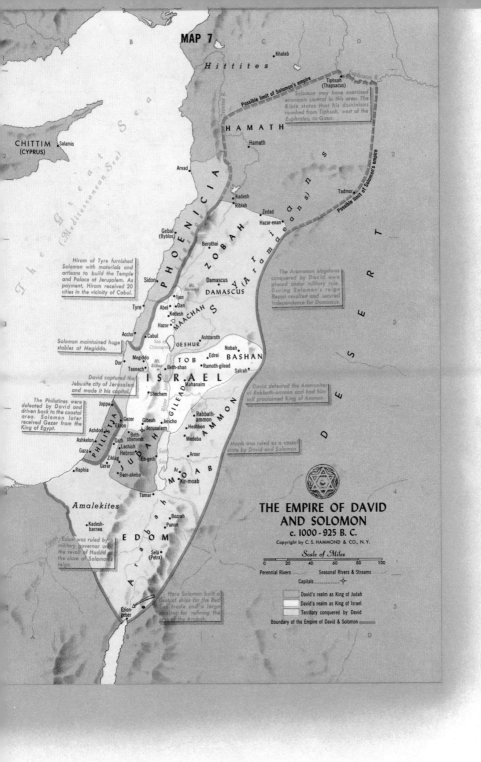

MAP 7

Hittites

• Khalab

Possible limit of Solomon's empire

• Tiphsah
(Thapsacus)

Euphrates R.

Solomon may have exercised economic control in this area. The Bible states that his dominions reached from Tiphsah, west of the Euphrates, to Gaza.

H A M A T H

• Hamath

CHITTIM
(CYPRUS)

• Salamis

• Arvad

Possible limit of Solomon's empire

• Tadmor

The Great Sea (Mediterranean Sea)

P H O E N I C I A

• Kadesh
• Riblah

Z O B A H

Berothai •

• Zedad

• Hazar-enan

S Y R I A (A r a m a e a n s)

Gebal •
(Byblos)

Hiram of Tyre furnished Solomon with materials and artisans to build the Temple and Palace at Jerusalem. As payment, Hiram received 20 cities in the vicinity of Cabul.

Sidon •

Damascus •

DAMASCUS

The Aramean kingdoms conquered by David were placed under military rule. During Solomon's reign Rezon revolted and secured independence for Damascus.

Tyre •
• Ijon
• Abel • Dan
• Kadesh

Mt. Hermon

M A A C H A H

Hazor •

Accho •

• Cabul

GESHUR

• Ashtaroth

Solomon maintained huge stables at Megiddo.

Sea of Chinnereth

Nobah •

Dor •

Megiddo •
• Taanach

Mt. Gilboa

• Beth-shan

T O B
• Edrei

B A S H A N

Ramoth-gilead •

Salcah •

I S R A E L

G I L E A D

David captured the Jebusite city of Jerusalem and made it his capital.

• Shechem

Mahanaim •

D E S E R T

Joppa •

The Philistines were defeated by David and driven back to the coastal area. Solomon later received Gezer from the King of Egypt.

Gezer •

Ekron •
• Gibeah
• Jericho

A M M O N

David defeated the Ammonites at Rabbath-ammon and had himself proclaimed King of Ammon.

Ashdod •
• Beth-shemesh

P H I L I S T I A

Gath •
• Jerusalem

• Rabbath-ammon

Ashkelon •
• Lachish
• Hebron

J U D A H

• Heshbon

Gaza •
Ziklag •

• En-gedi

• Medeba

M O A B

Gerar •
• Beer-sheba

• Aroer

Moab was ruled as a vassal state by David and Solomon.

Raphia •

Amalekites

• Tamar

• Ar

• Kir-moab

THE EMPIRE OF DAVID AND SOLOMON

c. 1000 - 925 B. C.

Copyright by C. S. HAMMOND & CO., N.Y.

Scale of Miles

• Kadesh-barnea

• Bozrah

• Punon

E D O M

Edom was ruled by a military governor until the revolt of Hadad at the close of Solomon's reign.

• Sela
(Petra)

| 0 | 20 | 40 | 60 | 80 | 100 |

Perennial Rivers   Seasonal Rivers & Streams

Capitals ....

☐ David's realm as King of Judah
☐ David's realm as King of Israel
☐ Territory conquered by David
▬ Boundary of the Empire of David & Solomon

Here Solomon built a fleet of ships for the Red Sea trade and a large smelter for refining the ores of the Arabah.

• Ezion-geber

MAP 8

THE KINGDOMS OF ISRAEL AND JUDAH
c. 925-842 B. C.

Copyright by C. S. HAMMOND & CO., N. Y.

Scale of Miles

0   5   10   20   30   40

Perennial Rivers ....
Seasonal Rivers & Streams ....
Capitals ....
Egyptian & Syrian Attacks ....

Elijah took refuge in Zarephath and brought back to life the widow's son.

In the reign of Baasha the cities of northern Israel were raided by the King of Damascus in league with Asa, King of Judah.

Aram waged almost constant war against Israel. The Syrians were held in check by Ahab until his death in battle at Ramoth-gilead.

Elijah challenged the prophets of Baal at Mt. Carmel.

The introduction of Phoenician cults following the marriage of Ahab with Jezebel caused violent reactions in Israel that eventually wiped out the house of Omri.

Samaria, fortress capital of Israel was built by Omri c. 870 B.C.

Moab was ruled as a vassal kingdom during the Omri dynasty. The Dibon stele commemorates the victory of Mesha, King of Moab, over Israel and the return of Moabite independence.

Shishak (Sheshonk), Egyptian Pharaoh, raided the divided kingdoms, plundering Jerusalem c. 925 B. C.

During the reign of Jehosaphat Judah regained control over Edom.

The Great Sea
(Mediterranean Sea)

Sidon
Zarephath
Tyre
Ijon
Abel-beth-maachah
Dan
Kedesh
Hazor
Accho
Cabul
Chinnereth
Karnaim
Ashtaroth
Hammath
Aphek
Edrei
Dor
Plain of Jezreel
Megiddo
Shunem
Jezreel
Taanach
Beth-shan
Dothan
Ibleam
Havoth-jair
Ramoth-gilead
Jabesh-gilead
Mahanaim
Tishbe
Sochoh
Abel-meholah
Samaria
Tirzah
Shechem
Janohah
Penuel
Aphek
Shiloh
Joppa
Jeshanah
Lod
Zemaraim
Beth-horon
Bethel
Mizpeh
Jericho
Gilgal
Ramah
Geba
Jabneel
Gezer
Aijalon
Rabbath-ammon
Ekron
Gibbethon
Zorah
Jerusalem
Elealeh
Ashdod
Timnah
Beth-shemesh
Heshbon
Azekah
Shoco
Bethlehem
Medeba
Ashkelon
Libnah
Etam
Baal-meon
Jahaz
Adullam
Tekoa
Mareshah
Gath
Beth-zur
Ataroth
Lachish
Hebron
Dibon
Debir
Adoraim
Aroer
Gaza
Ziph
En-gedi
Gerar
Ziklag
Ar
Raphia
Beer-sheba
Kir-moab
(Kir-haraseth)
Valley of Salt

Damascus
Abana R.
MOUNT LEBANON
MT. HERMON
PHOENICIA
ARAM
MT. CARMEL
Kishon R.
Mt. Tabor
Sea of Chinnereth
GESHUR
Yarmuk
Bashan
River Jordan
GILEAD
Jabbok
AMMON
Mt. Ebal
Mt. Gerizim
Cherith R.
Mt. Nebo
MOAB
Salt or Dead Sea
Arnon R.
ISRAEL
Plain of Sharon
JUDAH
Wilderness of Judah
PHILISTIA
EDOM

Syrians

MAP 9

THE ASSYRIAN EMPIRE
824 to 625 B.C.

Copyright by C.S. Hammond & Co., N.Y.

Scale of Miles

0 50 100   200   300

Capitals ■

Assyrian Empire – 824 B.C.   Assyrian Empire – 671 B.C.

MAP 10

JUDAH AFTER THE FALL OF ISRAEL
c. 700 B.C.

Copyright by C. S. HAMMOND & CO., N. Y.

Scale of Miles

0 5 10   20   30

Perennial Rivers ....
Seasonal Rivers & Streams ———
Capitals .... ✛

The Great Sea

(Mediterranean Sea)

With the conquest of Samaria in 721 B.C. by Sargon II, the Kingdom of Israel came to an end.

In 701 B.C. Sennacherib captured 46 cities of Judah as he pushed down toward the Egyptians, defeating them at Eltekeh.

In 701 B.C. Jerusalem was besieged, though not taken, by Sennacherib.

Sennacherib conquered Phoenicia, with the exception of Tyre, in 701 B.C.

After Samaria fell, Sargon II exiled most of the influential people. The Ten Tribes were moved to various parts of Mesopotamia and disappeared forever from the pages of history.

Ammon, Moab and Edom fell to the Assyrian Esarhaddon in 690 B.C., but they were never held long enough to be organized as regular provinces of the empire.

Here Sargon II defeated the Egyptian army in 720 B.C.

Judah was never a province of Assyria. Throughout Assyrian domination, it preserved a nominal independence under its own king, though paying tribute regularly and homage when it was required.

Damascus

Sidon
Zarephath

Tyre

PHOENICIA

MOUNT-LEBANON

MT-HERMON

DAMASCUS

Ijon   Dan
Abel-beth-maachah

Kedesh   QARNINI

Achzib
Accho   Hazor

Ramah   GALILEE   Karnaim

B a s h a n

Ashtaroth

Jotbah   Chinnereth   Aphek

Sea of Galilee

Gath-hepher   Hammath   HAURAN

Plain of   Mt Tabor   Edrei
MEGIDDO   Jezreel
Jokneam   Shunem

Dor   Megiddo   Jezreel   Ramoth-gilead

Taanach

Dothan   Beth-shan
Pella

S A M A R I A   Mahanaim

Samaria   GILEAD

Mt Ebal
Shechem
Gerizim

Aphek   Shiloh   AMMON

Joppa   Rabbath-ammon

Lod

Jabneh   Bethel   Ai   Michmash   Jericho   Elealeh
(Jabneel)   Ekron   Mizpeh   Geba   Gilgal
Gederoth   Gibbethon   Gibeon   Ramah   Anathoth   Heshbon
Eltekeh   Ajalon   Gibeah   Nob   Mt Nebo   Medeba
Ashdod   Beth-shemesh   Jerusalem
Saphir   Timnah   Jahaz
Libnah   Adullam
Ashkelon   Gath   Moresheth-gath   Tekoa   Dibon
Mareshah
Gaza   Lachish   Hebron   En-gedi   Aroer
Adoraim
Debir   M O A B
Dumah
Gerar   Ar
Raphia
Beer-sheba   Kir-moab
(Kir-haresheth)
Zoar

J U D A H

E D O M

EGYPTIAN KINGDOM

PHILISTIA

Plain of Sharon

DU·RU

Mt CARMEL

Jordan River

Salt Sea (Dead Sea)

Leontes R.

Yarmuk R.

Jabbok R.

Arnon R.

MAP 11

GREAT EMPIRES OF THE
SIXTH CENTURY B.C.

Copyright by C. S. HAMMOND & CO., N.Y.

Scale of Miles

100   200   300   400   500

Capitals

Limits of the Persian Empire c. 500 B.C.

Persian Royal Road.

Red Sea–Nile Canal Built by Darius I

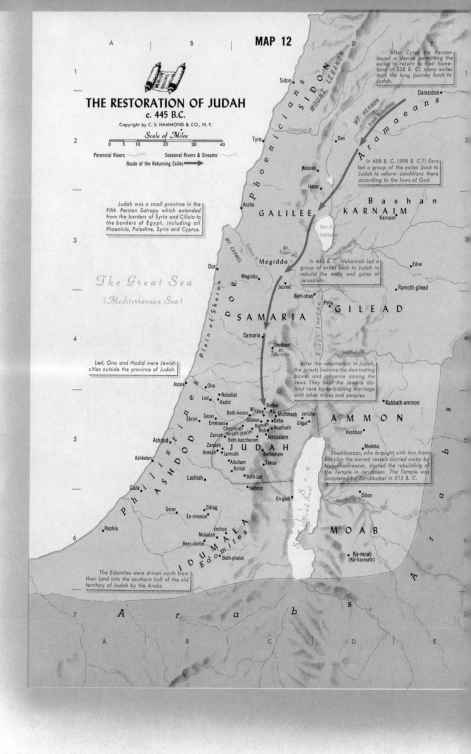

MAP 12

THE RESTORATION OF JUDAH
c. 445 B.C.

Copyright by C. S. HAMMOND & CO., N. Y.

Scale of Miles

0 5 10 20 30 40

Perennial Rivers — Seasonal Rivers & Streams

Route of the Returning Exiles ➤

After Cyrus the Persian issued a decree permitting the exiles to return to their homeland in 538 B. C., many exiles took the long journey back to Judah.

In 458 B. C. (398 B. C.?) Ezra led a group of the exiles back to Judah to reform conditions there according to the laws of God.

Judah was a small province in the Fifth Persian Satrapy which extended from the borders of Syria and Cilicia to the borders of Egypt, including all Phoenicia, Palestine, Syria and Cyprus.

In 445 B. C. Nehemiah led a group of exiles back to Judah to rebuild the walls and gates of Jerusalem.

Lod, Ono and Hadid were Jewish cities outside the province of Judah.

After the reformation in Judah, the priests became the dominating power and influence among the Jews. They kept the Jews a distinct race by forbidding marriage with other tribes and peoples.

Sheshbazzar, who brought with him from Babylon the sacred vessels carried away by Nebuchadnezzar, started the rebuilding of the Temple in Jerusalem. The Temple was completed by Zerubbabel in 515 B. C.

The Edomites were driven north from their land into the southern half of the old territory of Judah by the Arabs.

The Great Sea
(Mediterranean Sea)

Sidon
Damascus
Tyre
Dan
Kedesh
Hazor
Accho
GALILEE
BASHAN
KARNAIM
Karnaim
Megiddo
Megiddo
Dor
Jezreel
Beth-shan
Pella
Edrei
Ramoth-gilead
SAMARIA
GILEAD
Samaria
Shechem
Joppa
Ono
Neballat
Lod
Hadid
Mizpeh
Bethel
Ai
Michmash
Jericho
Rabbath-ammon
Beth-horon
Gibeon
Geba
Gilgal
AMMON
Ekron
Gezer
Emmaus
Chephirah
Ramah
Nob
Anathoth
Heshbon
Zareah
Kirjath-jearim
Jerusalem
Medeba
Ashdod
Zanoah
Beth-haccherem
JUDAH
Azekah
Jarmuth
Bethlehem
Ashkelon
Adullam
Keilah
Tekoa
Lachish
Beth-zur
Gaza
Hebron
En-gedi
Dibon
Gerar
Ziklag
En-rimmon
Raphia
Jeshua
Moladah
IDUMAEA
Edomites
Beer-sheba
Kir-moab
(Kir-hareseth)
Beth-phelet
MOAB
Phoenicians
SIDON
MOUNT LEBANON
MT. HERMON
From Babylonia
Arameans
Leontes R.
Kishon R.
Mt. Tabor
Sea of Galilee
Yarmuk R.
River Jordan
Jabbok R.
Arnon R.
Salt Sea (Dead Sea)
Philistia
ASHDOD
Plain of Sharon
DOR
MT. CARMEL
A r a b s
A r a b i a

A B C D E
1
2
3
4
5
6
7

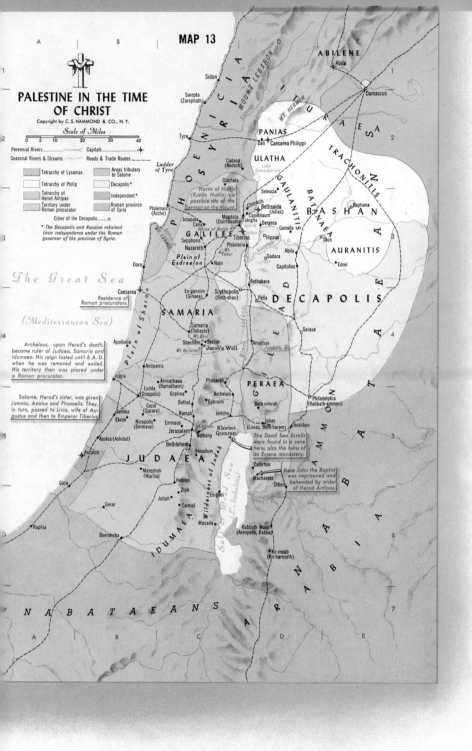

MAP 13

PALESTINE IN THE TIME OF CHRIST

Copyright by C. S. HAMMOND & CO., N. Y.

Scale of Miles

0   5   10   20   30   40

Perennial Rivers ....   Capitals ....

Seasonal Rivers & Streams ....   Roads & Trade Routes _____

Tetrarchy of Lysanias   Areas tributary to Salome

Tetrarchy of Philip   Decapolis *

Tetrarchy of Herod Antipas   Independent *

Territory under Roman procurator   Roman province of Syria

Cities of the Decapolis.........□

* The Decapolis and Ascalon retained their independence under the Roman governor of the province of Syria.

Archelaus, upon Herod's death, became ruler of Judaea, Samaria and Idumaea. His reign lasted until 6 A.D. when he was removed and exiled. His territory then was placed under a Roman procurator.

Salome, Herod's sister, was given Jamnia, Azotus and Phasaelis. They, in turn, passed to Livia, wife of Augustus and then to Emperor Tiberius.

The Dead Sea Scrolls were found in a cave here; also the ruins of an Essene monastery.

Here John the Baptist was imprisoned and beheaded by order of Herod Antipas.

ABILENE
• Abila
Sidon
• Damascus
Sarepta (Zarephath)
MOUNT LEBANON
PHOENICIA
MT. HERMON
ITURAEA
Tyre
PANIAS
Dan • Caesarea Philippi
Cadasa (Kedesh)
ULATHA
Lake Semechonitis
TRACHONITIS
Ladder of Tyre
Gischala
BATANAEA
GAULANITIS
Horns of Hattin (Kurûn Hattin) is a possible site of the Sermon on the Mount.
Seleucia
Chorazin
BASHAN
Raphana
Ptolemais (Accho)
Jotapata
Cana
Magdala (Dalmanutha)
Tabgha
Bethsaida (Julias)
Dion
GALILEE
Sepphoris
Tiberias
Gergesa
AURANITIS
Nazareth
Mt. Tabor
Philoteria
Hippos
Gamala
Plain of Esdraelon
Nain
Abila
• Edrei
Dora
Gadara
Capitolias
Bethabara
Caesarea
Residence of Roman procurators.
En-gannim (Ginaea)
Scythopolis (Beth-shan)
Pella
DECAPOLIS
The Great Sea
(Mediterranean Sea)
SAMARIA
Samaria (Sebaste)
Mt. Ebal
Shechem
Mt. Gerizim
Jacob's Well
Sychar
Amathus
Gerasa
Plain of Sharon
GILEAD
Apollonia
Joppa
Antipatris
Arimathaea (Ramathaim)
Phasaelis
PERAEA
Lydda (Diospolis)
Gophna
Archelais
Philadelphia (Rabbath-ammon)
Gezer (Gazara)
Bethel
• Ephraim
Beth-nimrah
Jamnia
Ramah
Jericho
Ekron
Nicopolis (Emmaus)
Emmaus
Mt. of Olives
Julias (Livias, Beth-haram)
Heshbon
Azotus (Ashdod)
Jerusalem
Bethany
Khirbet Qumran
Bethlehem
Herodium
Ascalon
Callirhoe
Macherus
Dibon
JUDAEA
Mareshah (Marisa)
Hebron
Gaza
Ziph
Wilderness of Judah
En-gedi
Dead Sea (L. Asphaltitis)
Gerar
Juttah
Carmel
Masada
• Raphia
Beersheba
IDUMAEA
Rabbath Moab (Areopolis, Rabba)
Kir-moab (Kir-haresheth)
N A B A T A E A N S
A R A B I A
MOAB
AMMON
River Jordan
PHOENICIA

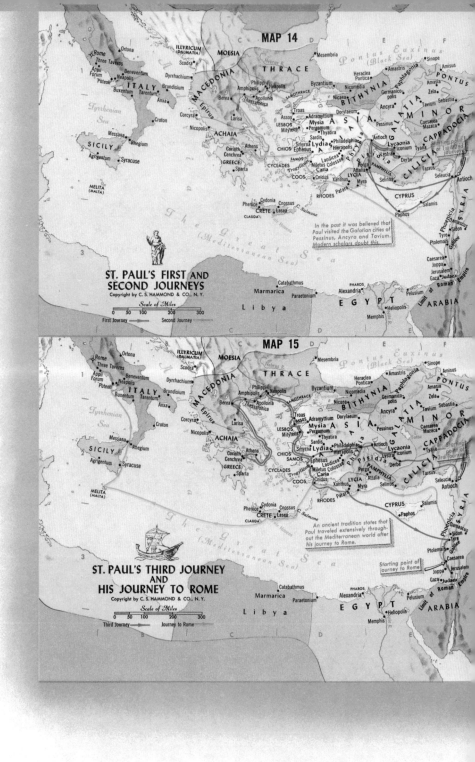

MAP 14

ST. PAUL'S FIRST AND
SECOND JOURNEYS
Copyright by C. S. HAMMOND & CO., N. Y.

Scale of Miles
0   50   100   200   300
First Journey   Second Journey

In the past it was believed that
Paul visited the Galatian cities of
Pessinus, Ancyra and Tavium.
Modern scholars doubt this.

MAP 15

ST. PAUL'S THIRD JOURNEY
AND
HIS JOURNEY TO ROME
Copyright by C. S. HAMMOND & CO., N. Y.

Scale of Miles
0   50   100   300
Third Journey   Journey to Rome

An ancient tradition states that
Paul traveled extensively throughout the Mediterranean world after
his journey to Rome.

Starting point of
journey to Rome

MAP 18

THE HOLY LAND TODAY
Copyright by C. S. HAMMOND & CO., N.Y.
Scale of Miles
0   10   20   30   40   50

Perennial Rivers
Capitals
Armistice Demarcation
    Lines
Railroads
Seasonal Rivers & Streams
International Boundaries
Demilitarized Zone
    Boundaries
Ancient Sites

Mediterranean
Sea

LEBANON

SYRIA

SYRIAN DESERT

ISRAEL

NEGEV

EGYPT

SINAI
PENINSULA

JORDAN

THE INHERITANCE OF THE TWELVE TRIBES
Scale of Miles